Two year olds of 2016

32ND EDITION

Two year olds of 2016

32ND EDITION

STEVE TAPLIN

Foreword by Charlie Hills

Raceform

FRONT COVER: Frankie Dettori and Shalaa win the Group 1 Middle Park Stakes at Newmarket in 2015. Copyright © Racing Post / Edward Whitaker.

BACK COVER: Steve Taplin (left) and Charlie Hills (right)

Published in 2016 by Raceform
27 Kingfisher Court, Hambridge Road, Newbury, Berkshire, RG14 5SJ

Copyright © Steve Taplin 2016

The right of Steve Taplin to be identified as the author of this work has been asserted by him in accordance with the Copyright, Designs and Patents Act 1988.

All rights reserved. No part of this publication may be reproduced, stored in a retrieval system, or transmitted in any form or by any means, electronic, mechanical, photocopying, recording, or otherwise, without the prior written permission of the publishers.

A catalogue record for this book is available from the British Library.

ISBN: 978-1-910498-67-5

Designed by Fiona Pike

Printed in Great Britain by CPI Group (UK) Ltd, Croydon, CR0 4YY

Contents

Foreword by Charlie Hills	7
Introduction	9
Fifty to Follow	11
Ten to Follow in Ireland	15
Star Two-Year-Olds	16
The Bloodstock Experts Mark Your Card	17
The Frankel File	28
Trainers' Bargain Buys	32
Two-Year-Olds of 2016	35
Sires Reference	341
Sires Index	358
Racing Trends	364
Horse Index	370
Dams Index	383

Foreword

I feel privileged to have been asked to write the foreword for Steve Taplin's excellent publication on juveniles, which is must-read material for anyone with an interest in Flat racing.

The beauty of training two-year-olds is they allow you to dream one of them might be the next superstar we are all looking for and Steve's book helps guide the reader to which fairy tales could come true.

I remember a bullish assessment of Canford Cliffs from Richard Hannon a few years ago, while I was pleased to give Just The Judge a favourable mention when I was interviewed in 2012; it would be great if some of my two-year-olds this term turned out to be anywhere near as good as she was.

Whether a two-year-old is an early type or backend prospect with Classic aspirations for the following season, these pages cover all the angles and are an essential tool for punters and racing professionals.

It is difficult at this time of year for trainers to accurately predict how each horse will develop and progress, but Steve's in-depth analysis makes it much easier to understand certain results, even if the Coventry winner pops up at 100-1!

I really enjoy the interviews with the trainers as it is always useful to know the strength of the opposition, particularly when it comes to unraced horses and deciding where to run mine; we all want winners so it's helpful to have an idea what we're up against.

It is not just trainers Steve speaks to, but a good number of bloodstock agents and stud managers whose views are often illuminating and worth following, especially for horses they have purchased.

Each year it impresses me how open trainers are with Steve, which demonstrates the level of trust he has built up within the industry. Steve's love for the sport shines through on every page, but that passion is punctuated with well-researched information and perceptive pointers.

The easy-to-follow style and layout means it is one of the most-thumbed publications on my bookshelf and it is unlikely I am alone in that.

Charlie Hills. April 2016.

Introduction

Here we go again! The 32nd edition of "Two-Year-Olds" puts the spotlight on the best two-year-old racehorses in training in England and Ireland.

Lambourn trainer Charlie Hills, son of retired legendary trainer Barry, was happy to endorse this year's book by writing the foreword. I've been a welcome visitor to the Hills' yard for many years and it's always one of the highlights of my few days in Lambourn each spring.

After six months of pedigree research, when the spring arrives I set off interviewing as many trainers as possible in less than a month. As I write there looks like being just short of 70 trainer interviews in the book this year. There's never a problem filling the book with nice horses and very often it's a case of "which ones do I leave out"? New trainers to the book this year are Lambourn's Owen Burrows, Richard Hughes and Joseph Tuite and the Newmarket trio of Giles Bravery, Dave Morris and George Scott.

My racing partnership (The Living Legend Racing Partnership) continues to get winners and 2015 was no exception. Both our horses, the Mick Channon trained Chilworth Icon and Breslin, won and we're hoping to continue the good run with two new horses in training this year with Andrew Balding. The four-year-old maiden filly Cape Spirit and the two-year-old colt Stag Party will fly the flag for us. To have horses in training at Kingsclere's wonderful Park House Stables, which of course is steeped in racing history, is a real privilege for me. I love visiting Kingsclere, but I recall that my first visit began inauspiciously. About twenty years ago I was driving there on the A34 when one of my tyres suffered a blowout, which meant I arrived over half an hour late and got a ticking off from trainer Ian Balding. He must have been very understanding because I've been back every year since!

Some of you will recall my story in last year's Introduction about the two-year-old nominated by William Haggas as his Bargain Buy. He actually named the horse Bargain Buy there and then on the telephone to his owner and to Weatherbys. Well almost twelve months to the day, the colt won on his debut as a three-year-old at Lingfield. I was so busy visiting trainers in Newmarket that day I would have missed it if William hadn't kindly nudged me to say he was running!

It's always a bit of a treat when a trainer takes me onto the gallops in his 4x4 to watch a few of his two-year-olds working. Next time though I'll be wise to Tom Dascombe's trick of telling you to bring your hot coffee along with you, just so he can pelt along and laugh as you spill it all over your jeans!

The recordings of my trainer interviews usually go without a hiccup, but there was one incident this year, when Sir Mark Prescott rang me to ask if I was free to do the interview on the phone there and then. I wasn't going to say no, so the recording went ahead, we shared a joke or two, I thanked him and said goodbye. I immediately pressed the play button on the recorder but the only voice I could hear was my own! Mortified, I rang him back to apologise and to ask him to do it all again. Can you imagine? I needn't have worried though – he was very understanding and charming about it, but then as quick as a flash he said "that's two interviews I've done this year, which means I get next year off!"

This season is of special significance to two-year-old fans because the brilliant racehorse Frankel has his first crop of runners. I've added a small section dedicated to his two-year-olds that appear in this book, just as a sort of quick reference to Frankel fans (which means just about all of us I'd say).

Regular readers will be aware that each year the book has a number of "horses to follow" lists, such as the 'Fifty To Follow' and the 'Bloodstock Experts Mark Your Card'. They are always useful for those who want to follow a select number of horses. The "Bloodstock

Experts" always do well and last year was no exception with 41 individual winners of 64 races including the top-class colt Shalaa. The big priced winners amongst the "Trainers' Bargain Buys" no doubt make it a particular favourite section for lots of punters. Peter Chapple-Hyam was clever enough to nominate Marcel last year and he duly won the Group 1 Racing Post Trophy at 33-1.

As usual, the two-year-olds in the book are listed under their trainers and my aim is to choose those horses most likely to be winners. You'll notice a 'star rating' for each of the two-year-olds, so take note in particular of those with three stars or more. There are no star ratings for those two-year-olds without any comments from the trainer. I think to give them a rating based on the pedigree alone is too speculative.

The following is a rough guide to my description of the ability of family members mentioned in the pedigree assessment of every two-year-old, based upon professional ratings. Please note that these descriptions are standard throughout the book in the vast majority of cases, but there are instances where I rely upon my own judgement of each horse's rating.

Below 60 = moderate
60 – 69 = modest
70 – 79 = fair
80 – 89 = quite useful
90 – 99 = fairly useful
100 – 107 = useful
108 – 112 = very useful
113 – 117 = smart
118 – 122 = very smart
123 – 127 = high-class
128 – 134 = top-class
135 and above = outstanding

To make it easier to find a specific horse the book is comprehensively indexed. So you'll find an index of the horses, their dams and their sires.

The book is divided into the following sections:

Fifty To Follow.

Ten to Follow in Ireland.

Star Two-Year-Olds. This system gives an instant appraisal of the regard in which a horse is held. Those horses awarded the maximum of five stars are listed here.

The Bloodstock Experts Mark Your Card. Bloodstock agents and stud managers suggest potentially smart two-year-olds bought or raised by them.

Bargain Buys. A list of relatively cheaply bought two-year-olds the trainers feel will turn out to be good deals.

The Frankel File. A quick reference to the two-year-olds from Frankel's first crop with comments in the book.

Two-Year-Olds of 2016. The main section of the book, with each two-year-old listed under the trainer. Trainers' comments (when given) are in italics after the pedigree assessments. Readers should bear in mind that all the trainers' comments come from my interviews which took part from late March to mid-April.

Stallion Reference, detailing the racing and stud careers of sires with two-year-old representatives in the book.

Stallion Index.

Racing Trends. An analysis of some juvenile events that regularly highlight the stars of the future. It includes a list of three-year-olds to follow this season.

Index of Two-Year-Olds.

Index of Dams.

Inevitably there are some unnamed horses in the book, but please access my website www.stevetaplin.co.uk throughout the season for updates on those horses named after the book was published.

Researched and compiled by
Steve Taplin BA (Hons).

Fifty to Follow

AL HAMDANY (IRE)
b.c. Kodiac – Easy Times (Nayef). *"He's quite forward and is actually ready to step up now. An early type and a nice mover that shows ability, he should be running from late April onwards and he's definitely capable of winning a maiden. We like him".* Marco Botti.

ALROOM (IRE)
b.c. Kodiac – Beverley Macca (Piccolo). *"I like him and he'll be one of the early ones. Very uncomplicated and solid, he'll run in mid-May and we'll try and turn him into an Ascot horse. He'll do well this year and he's a straightforward colt with a good mind".* William Haggas.

ANNA MEDICI
b.f. Sir Percy – Florentia (Medicean). *"A lot of the family win at two including the dam's first two foals...if her record is anything to go by this filly should show something this year".* Sir Mark Prescott.

ASAAS (USA)
ch.c. Distorted Humor – Affectionately (Galileo). *"From the family of Invincible Spirit and Kodiac, he's a precocious horse and I see him as a May/June starter. Very natural and very easy on the eye, I like him and you should definitely put him in the book".* Roger Varian.

BALGAIR
ch.g. Foxwedge – Glencal (Compton Place). *"A very nice type who was a lovely yearling at the sales and now he's a good, strong, tough sort who knows his job. One to look forward to in the summer, he's probably a six/seven furlong 2-y-o".* Jonathan Portman.

BEE CASE
br.f. Showcasing – Binabee (Galileo). *"She looks really quick, will probably stay six furlongs in time and is still strengthening up. She could be a Royal Ascot type of filly when you consider that she's well-bred, by a good stallion, shows lots of speed and has a lovely attitude. In late April she'll be ready to rock n roll".* Hugo Palmer.

BISMARCK THE FLYER (IRE)
b.c. Requinto – Livia's Wake (Galileo). *"Very sharp, he'll be one of our first runners and he seems to have plenty of ability. He goes really well and he's a proper 2-y-o with the scope to continue throughout the season".* Richard Hannon.

CLASSICAL TIMES
b.f. Lawman – Sunday Times (Holy Roman Emperor). *"She's lovely, the first foal of Sunday Times and she's her spitting image...she's coming together well and is quite strong now. I see her being out by July time, she's really nice and could be anything, so I like her very much. Seven furlongs should be right for her".* Peter Chapple-Hyam.

COASTAL CYCLONE
b.c. Canford Cliffs – Seasonal Cross (Cape Cross). *"I like this colt and his half-brother Storm Rock did well for us last year. I think this colt is more precocious than Storm Rock, so I hope he can give us some sport, starting off in the first half of the season, over six/seven furlongs".* Harry Dunlop.

COVERHAM (IRE)
b.c. Bated Breath – Mark Too (Mark Of Esteem). *"He's very nice, I'm very pleased with him, he's working and should be out by the end of April or early May. Very well put together and pretty laid back, he's doing everything we've asked so far and I think he'll get seven furlongs later on".* James Bethell.

CUTTIN' EDGE (IRE)
b.c. Rip Van Winkle – How's She Cuttin' (Shinko Forest). *"If he was by a more successful sire he'd have cost three times his purchase price. I like him, he moves well and at this present time I couldn't say anything but nice things about him. He's developing, has a good page and will make a 2-y-o".* Willie Muir.

DARING GUEST
b.c. Fast Company – Balm (Oasis Dream). *"A gorgeous horse. He'll be out by the end of April and I wouldn't be surprised if he was an*

Ascot 2-y-o. He could win over five furlongs, but he'll be better over six and he's a nice type". George Margarson.

DARK DESTROYER (IRE)
b.c. Helmet – Oeuvre D'art (Marju). "He's absolutely gorgeous. A strong, very good-moving horse that'll want six furlongs. Marju is a good sire of broodmares and we like this horse a lot". Joseph Tuite.

DRAGSTONE ROCK
ch.c. Dragon Pulse – Rock Exhibition (Rock Of Gibraltar). "A very nice horse, he's a good-looking individual and already at this early stage of his career he looks promising. I trained the dam's first two winners so I'm hoping this one will continue the family tradition". David Elsworth.

EMMAUS (IRE)
b.c. Invincible Spirit – Prima Luce (Galileo). "He's a cracking horse, very easy on the eye and a good mover. There's a lot to like about him. He'll make a 2-y-o by July I should think and he should be one to look out for". Roger Varian.

ESSENTIAL
b.c. Pivotal – Something Blue (Petong). "He's a lovely horse and probably my nicest 2-y-o at this stage. He's got a solid pedigree, he's very correct and has a really good attitude. I'm going to give him an opportunity to be a Royal Ascot horse...he's very nice and has a lot of quality". George Scott.

FAIR HEAD (IRE)
b.f. Iffraaj – Dawaama (Dansili). "A fast filly, she's strong and very powerful. Probably a 2-y-o for May or June, she goes well and we're happy with her so far". Ed Dunlop.

HARBOUR MASTER
b.c. Harbour Watch – Roodeye (Inchinor). "I trained his half-sister Prize Exhibit who finished fourth in the Breeders' Cup Juvenile... the early signs are very good for this horse. I like him, he's a beautiful mover and showing the signs of looking quite smart already". Jamie Osborne.

HATHIQ (IRE)
b.c. Exceed And Excel – Madany (Acclamation).

"He's a lovely colt and in the last three weeks he's really changed. He's doing everything right at the minute, he's a lovely horse, a good size and well put-together...He looks mature enough to push on with soon and being by Exceed And Excel he should be sharp. A lovely model". Owen Burrows.

HEAVEN'S ROCK (IRE)
b.c. Requinto – Rockfleet Castle (Rock Of Gibraltar). "A strong, box of a horse...He'll be out in May or June and from what I've seen of him if we've got one 2-y-o that might be the type for something like the Molecomb, he could be the one...I love him". Tom Dascombe.

HIGH EXCITEMENT (USA)
b.f. Blame – Excelente (Exceed And Excel). "A real nice filly and maybe one for Royal Ascot. Very good-looking and well-made, she's done well lately and has a great temperament. Could be anything". Charlie Hills.

INGLEBY MACKENZIE
b.c. Sixties Icon – Natalie Jay (Ballacashtal). "He's a very nice colt, he'll want six/seven furlongs and he does everything nice. He has all the attributes the sire gives them – attitude, size and a touch of quality". Mick Channon.

JUANITO CHICO (IRE)
br.c. Pour Moi – Miss Kittyhawk (Hawk Wing). "We like him a lot, he's a very nice horse. He's finding life very easy at the moment, would be as nice as we've got and may have enough toe to start over six furlongs before stepping up to seven. He's not over-big, just a well-proportioned horse and with scope". William Jarvis.

JUS PIRES (USA)
br.c. Scat Daddy – Liza Lu (Menifee). "A big, strong imposing horse, he's one for late summer/autumn over seven furlongs. I like what I see and he's got the size, strength and scope to be a good horse in time. He's a horse I really like and if I have a proper one amongst my 2-y-o's he could be the one". Jeremy Noseda.

KODIAC PEARL
b.f. Kodiac – Valmirez (Smart Strike). "She has plenty of pace and she's in full work

at the moment so she'll probably make her debut in May. A typical Kodiac, she's got a fair bit of boot and she wants to race…she'll have a future". Robert Cowell.

LIGHTNING NORTH
b.f. Mayson – Purple Tiger (Rainbow Quest). "The dam has produced plenty of useful five furlong 2-y-o's and this filly is very much in the same mould. So we'd expect her to win two-year-old races over five furlongs". James Tate.

LITTLE MISS LUCKY (IRE)
b.f. Clodovil – Lucky Leigh (Piccolo). "A proper sharp-looking 2-y-o type, she does what it says on the tin'. A very strong pocket-rocket for five furlongs, she has quite a good 2-y-o sprinting pedigree". James Given.

MAORI BOB (IRE)
b.c. Big Bad Bob – Tekhania (Dalakhani). "This colt did his first bit of easy work this morning and I think he'll come to hand quite quickly. The dam has bred two 2-y-o winners and this is a nice horse who will be a 2-y-o over six/seven furlongs". Michael Bell.

MILIUM (USA)
gr.f. First Defence – Magnifica (Mizzen Mast). "A neat filly, we're just starting to kick on with her a bit now, she's nice, sharp and ready to go. Should win at two". Amanda Perrett.

MUMS THE WORD
b.f. Mayson – Tell Mum (Marju). "A beautiful filly, she's very sharp and racy. Could be a Queen Mary filly and I really like her". Richard Hannon.

NAYYAR
ch.c. Exceed And Excel – Miss Queen (Miswaki). "A good-looking little colt, he's the right size for a 2-y-o and he's going to grow much more. I don't think he's a five furlong horse, but he's got a good skin on him at the minute and he looks a smart little horse. I like him a lot". Charlie Hills.

OCCURRENCE
b.f. Frankel – Arrive (Kahyasi). "A beautiful filly with a very nice pedigree to back it up,

we all like her and she seems to have a nice temperament. I trained the dam and there's plenty of stamina in the pedigree, so this could be a mile and a half filly. But she's attractive and probably looks more like Frankel than some of the others I've seen". Roger Charlton.

ODE TO GLORY
b.f. Poet's Voice – Blue Lyric (Refuse To Bend). "A lovely looking filly, she's strong, a bit feisty but goes very nicely and she's one we're looking forward to. There's speed on the dam's side and I guess this filly will want six furlongs to a mile. Not a big filly, but well-made and she looks the part". Rae Guest.

PETER STUYVESANT (IRE)
b.g. Elusive City – Dream For Life (Oasis Dream). "A good-looking horse, he travels well… I should imagine he'll be racing in May or June because he's all there and we like him. Six furlongs should be his trip and the way he's going I'd be disappointed if he's not a nice horse". Denis Coakley.

POET'S PRINCESS
ch.f. Poet's Voice – Palace Affair (Pursuit Of Love). "A sharp filly, I could run her now but she has a nice pedigree and I don't want to knock her about early on. If everything goes alright she'll be out in May. She looks well-bought and quite neat". Hughie Morrison.

RAINBOW MIST (IRE)
b.c. Lilbourne Lad – Misty Night (Galileo). "He goes very well and is one to watch out for…he's got the pace to win over five or six furlongs but he'll probably get seven later on. He's very nice and we like him". Ann Duffield.

RETRIBUTION
b.c. Iffraaj – The Giving Tree (Rock Of Gibraltar). "A lovely horse and the nicest one I bought on spec last year. He's very well-made, has a great attitude and he's a big, strong colt. He'll make a 2-y-o, starting off at six furlongs". David Lanigan.

SILVERLIGHT
b.c. Dubawi – Arizona Jewel (Dansili). "A colt that moves well, he's very likeable and is probably a seven furlong type 2-y-o, but we might run him over six in mid-season.

He's strong and has a good attitude". John Gosden.

SIMMY'S TEMPLE
b.f. Royal Applause – Samasana (Redback). "She ran well on her debut in the Brocklesby and we'll probably look out for a fillies' novice for her in late April. Small and racy-looking, she obviously wants five furlongs now but looks as if she might get six later". Keith Dalgleish.

SPIRITOUS (USA)
b.c. Invincible Spirit – Andina (Singspiel). "This is a neat, 'together' 2-y-o type and I'd hope to be running him in May. He has the speed for six furlongs and he's working particularly well". John Gosden.

SUN ANGEL
b.f. Sir Prancealot – Fuerta Ventura (Desert Sun). "She looks nice, quite mature and level. One that'll be ready for us to carry on with quite soon, she's a good size and a good mover that seems to enjoy her work". Henry Candy.

SUPER JULIUS
ch.c. Bated Breath – Paradise Isle (Bahamian Bounty). "He's very nice. He's from a small family so he's not big but he's got plenty about him and has plenty of pace. I like him very much and he might be racing in April". Eve Johnson Houghton.

SUPER TALENT (IRE)
b.c. Helmet – Eastern Joy (Dubai Destination). "One of my favourites at the moment, this is a big, strong, imposing type with good bone and plenty of top line on him. A real good-moving sort, I like him a lot and he has a lot of class about him. We'll take our time with him". Saeed bin Suroor.

THE NAZCA LINES (IRE)
ch.c. Fast Company – Princess Banu (Oasis Dream). "He shows us a lot of speed at home, he's a good mover...he'll be out sooner rather than later and we like him quite a lot, the dam was as tough as nails and he looks very similar. He's very straightforward and just about ready to go". John Quinn.

TORCELLO
ch.c. Born To Sea – Islandagore (Indian Ridge). "He's a lovely horse and we're really pleased with him. Really athletic, we loved him as a yearling and he was probably our number one pick from Book Two at Tattersalls. By an exciting first-season sire in Born To Sea, he goes nicely but we won't be rushing him". Andrew Balding.

TROPICAL ROCK
b.f. Fastnet Rock – Tropical Treat (Bahamian Bounty). "This is a lovely filly, I'd be confident she'd make a 2-y-o at around six furlongs and she may even be quick enough for five considering her mother was a listed winner over that trip. So she's a nice filly and we like her very much". Ralph Beckett.

ULTIMATE AVENUE
b.c. Excelebration – Dance Avenue (Sadler's Wells). "He's one of our most exciting 2-y-o's. Big, but very athletic and light on his feet, he's done plenty and done it all extremely well. He's just filling his frame now and should be a 2-y-o for mid-summer, probably starting in a seven furlong maiden". Ed Walker.

UNIT OF ASSESSMENT (IRE)
b.c. Dragon Pulse – Before The Storm (Sadler's Wells). "I like him, he's a nice colt and probably wants a bit of cut in the ground looking at the pedigree. He'll have the speed for six furlongs and will probably end up a miler I would have thought. Coming along nicely, he's a really well-made, strong-looking colt. Should be ready around June time". William Knight.

UNNAMED
b.f. Galileo – Daneleta (Danehill). "A very nice filly and she's fairly precocious for a Galileo. She could be out in July, she's a nice type, not very big but well put together". Luca Cumani.

UNNAMED
b.c. Galileo – Walklikeanegyptian (Danehill). "A real athlete, it's a good family and one I know well. He's a much better looking horse than his brother The Corsican, he has a good attitude and wants to please. I'm very pleased with him". David Simcock.

Ten to Follow in Ireland

CAPE SUNSHINE (IRE)
b.f. Cape Blanco – Shermeen (Desert Style). *"A good-moving filly and a half-sister to a Phoenix Stakes winner, she probably won't take as long to come to hand as you might expect for a Cape Blanco. She'll set off at six furlongs I should think and end up a seven furlongs/mile filly at the back-end of the season".* Tommy Stack.

CASCAVELLE (IRE)
gr.c. Shamardal – Majestic Silver (Linamix). *"He's very much a quality colt. Very likeable, we'll see him running in July/August and I like him. He's quite similar to his 3-y-o half-brother True Solitaire although he has more strength than him".* Dermot Weld.

HEAD MONITOR
b.c. Archipenko – Almiranta (Galileo). *"A lovely, big Archipenko colt, he has a lot of quality about him, goes nicely and he was an early foal. So despite his size he could be out as early as May".* Jessie Harrington.

JACK FLASH (IRE)
gr.c. Dark Angel – Lexi The Princess (Holy Roman Emperor). *"He's our most precocious 2-y-o colt. He's ready to run, he's maturing all the time and you'll see him from May onwards. My type of horse".* Ger Lyons.

MORITZBURG
ch.c. Dutch Art – Providencia (Oasis Dream). *"He's certainly one of the most forward colts we have, he's a beautiful horse with a good action and he goes well. A smart colt with a good temperament, he could start off at six furlongs because he has pace".* Michael Halford.

PRESIDENTIAL (IRE)
b.c. Invincible Spirit – Poetical (Croco Rouge). *"A half-brother to Dragon Pulse, he's a very nice horse, I like him and he'll be a 2-y-o over six/seven furlongs in mid-season. Not a big horse, but he has quality, so he's typical of the sire".* Kevin Prendergast.

PSYCHEDELIC FUNK (IRE)
ch.c. Choisir – Parabola (Galileo). *"He already has a race entry and he's typical of what I would call smart – he could be anything. I love the fella and he's very precocious. He could win wherever he goes and he was a bargain for what he cost".* Ger Lyons.

REHANA (IRE)
b.f. Dark Angel – Rayka (Selkirk). *"She's a lovely mover, clean-winded and with a good attitude. It looks like she'll make a 2-y-o around June time over six furlongs because she's been showing pace in her work. We like her".* Michael Halford.

RENAMED ME KING (IRE)
b.c. Kodiac – Unicamp (Royal Academy). *"He's a sharp-looking colt who is showing a fair bit and he should be able to run in early May although he wants good, fast ground – not soft. He seems to know his job and he's going nicely at the moment. He'll run well when he runs".* John Oxx.

TILLY TROTTER (IRE)
b.f. Kodiac – Inourthoughts (Desert Style). *"Already a winner at Dundalk over five furlongs, she's a sharp, very attractive filly. The plan now is to head for the listed six furlong race at Naas about three weeks before Royal Ascot. A very good-looking, precocious filly".* Dermot Weld.

Star Two-Year-Olds

The stars placed along the side of each two-year-old in the main section of the book give the reader an instant appraisal of the regard in which they are held. The highest rating a horse can attain is five stars.

Bear in mind that some of the "Five Star" horses will be at their peak as three-year-olds, so you should definitely keep an eye on them next year as well.

The five-star two-year-olds of 2016 are listed below for quick reference.

SECRET SOUL	Ralph Beckett
SHIMMERING LIGHT	Michael Bell
SUPER TALENT	Saeed bin Suroor
DUTCH QUALITY	Marco Botti
FAIR EVA	Roger Charlton
RED LABEL	Luca Cumani
GLOBAL APPLAUSE	Ed Dunlop
SWISS STORM	David Elsworth
JEWEL HOUSE	John Gosden
b.c. Frankel – Dar Re Mi (Singspiel).	John Gosden
DIAGNOSTIC	William Haggas
WUROOD	William Haggas
MUQAATIL	Richard Hannon
SAWLAAT	Richard Hannon
MUSAWAAT	Charlie Hills
KUIPER BELT	David Lanigan
OKOOL	Owen Burrows
TZAVO	Hugo Palmer
ZOFFANIST	Amanda Perrett
FIRST DANCE	James Tate
WATCHMAN	Roger Varian

The Bloodstock Experts Mark Your Card

Each year the number of winners from this section increases. Last year the Experts tipped no less than 53 winners of 73 races – by far the best total yet! They included the dual Group 1 winner Shalaa who was selected by two different experts. Make sure you take careful note of these selections!

The experts who selected two individual winners apiece last year were Alistair Donald, Peter Doyle, Ed Harper, Richard Knight and Kirsten Rausing.

With three winners apiece were Ross Doyle (whose picks included the Group 3 and listed winner Great Page), Angus Gold, Luke Lillingston (including the listed winner Argentero), Amanda Skiffington and Paul Thorman (including the Group 3 winner La Rioja).

David Redvers managed to pick four winners from six and they included the Group 3 winner La Rioja. Chris Richardson also had four winners and he only had four picks. A gold star goes to both these experts!

Charlie Gordon-Watson gave me seven selections and I'm pleased to say that five of them won notably the top-class 2-y-o colt and dual Group 1 winner Shalaa.

Harry Herbert's selections were split between the Highclere and Al Shaqab teams. The former included four winners from six selections with the best of them being Foundation (Group 2 Royal Lodge Stakes). The eight selections under the Al Shaqab banner included six winners, notably the aforementioned Shalaa. A total of ten winners from fourteen. Very impressive!

As their percentage of winners to selections were exactly the same and they both picked Shalaa, the top tipster award for 2015 is shared between Charlie Gordon-Watson and Harry Herbert.

Let's hope all the experts this year have been inspired to pick a similarly successful group of two-year-olds.

Remember, most of the two-year-olds selected here can be found in the main section of the book listed under their trainers and highlighted by the symbol ♠

MALCOLM BASTARD

MAGIC PASS
ch.c. Raven's Pass – Magic America. He was late coming in to be broken (January), but he's a neat colt that travels very well and could be a nice horse. In training with Andrew Balding.

MEYRICK
b.c. Helmet – Esteemed Lady. A really nice colt with size, scope and strength, he needs a bit of time but he's got pace and a good temperament. Could be a really nice sort come August time. William Haggas.

NIGHT LAW
b.f. Lawman – Night Carnation. A neat, well-balanced, forward-going filly that shows a nice amount of pace for this time of the year. Andrew Balding.

UNNAMED
ch.f. Nathaniel – Clizia. A very good-looking, strong bodied filly, she travels nicely on the bridle and could be a very nice horse come the autumn. Trainer unknown at the time of going to press.

The following two-year-olds are all still with me (early April) but are bound for John Gosden's Clarehaven Stables.

COME SOFTLY
b.f. Dansili – Teeky. This is a very nice filly. She's strong and has a good action.

OXFORD THINKING (IRE)
b.c. Holy Roman Emperor – Larceny. A colt with size, scope and strength, he travels really well on the bridle and I think he might be a nice colt around August time.

PETERPORT
b.c. Nathaniel – Spinning Queen. A big, strong colt with a nice action. He travels very well on the bridle and you'd hope he'd be a very nice back-end 2-y-o.

UTMOST (USA)
c. Giant's Causeway – Fugitive Angel. He only came in to me to be broken in early February but he canters really well and in time we think he's going to be a really nice colt.

UNNAMED
b.c. Dansili – Giants Play. A big, strong colt, he has a little bit of knee action but goes extremely well for a horse of his type at this time of the year.

UNNAMED
b.f. Fastnet Rock – Rose Blossom. A strong, quality filly, she ticks all the boxes. Will want time being by Fastnet Rock, but she's very highly thought of.

UNNAMED
b.f. Sea The Stars – Royale Danehill. A very strong filly that travels really well on the bridle. She should win as a back-end 2-y-o and I'd expect her to be a very good 3-y-o.

Heading For The Breeze-Up Sales.

UNNAMED
ch.c. More Than Ready – Alina (USA). He shows tons of pace, he's medium-sized with a seriously good temperament and I would hope he'd be a very good mid-season 2-y-o.

UNNAMED
b.c. Harlan's Holiday – Glowing. A quality horse that moves extremely well, he'll want seven furlongs but he's very highly thought of. n.b. This colt was led out unsold at 70,000 Gns at the Craven Breeze Up Sale.

UNNAMED
ch.c. Frankel – Noahs Ark. A good-looking colt, slightly unfurnished at the moment but showing plenty of pace. He has a very nice action and should be a decent back-end 2-y-o and better still next year. n.b. Bought for 100,000 Gns by Mr John Dance at the Craven Breeze Up Sale.

MATT COLEMAN

BUZZ
gr.c. Motivator – Tiysha. A colt who only cost €13,000 as a yearling at the Arqana October Yearling Sale, but about whom trainer Hughie Morrison is giving us very positive vibes.

LITTLE MISS LUCKY (IRE)
b.f. Clodovil – Lucky Leigh. A full-sister to black type 2-y-o Something Lucky, she's a precocious filly who trainer James Given likes.

MAGICAL DREAMER (IRE)
b.f. Acclamation – Double Fantasy. A sharp filly who is well regarded by trainer James Fanshawe.

UNNAMED
ch.c. Harbour Watch – Dress Code. A strong, precocious type who only cost 11,000 Gns, he's a half-brother to classy 2-y-o's Dress To Impress and Lucky General. Showing speed on the gallops for Harry Dunlop.

ALISTAIR DONALD

DARK HERO
b.c. Kodiac – Mistress Marina. €125,000 Goffs Orby. He's not very big, but he's looking very sharp, loving his work and should be out early. Charlie Hills.

GLORIOUS FOREVER
ch.c. Archipenko – Here To Eternity. 110,000 Gns Tattersalls October Book 2. The own brother to listed winner Time Warp, he's a very similar scopey horse that's bred for his 3-y-o career but does everything easily, so he can also make a mid-season 2-y-o like his brother. Ed Walker.

HURRICANE RUSH
b.c. Helmet – Without Precedent. 60,000 Gns Tattersalls October Book 2. The sire has started with a bang and this is a strong colt that we've always loved. Bred for 6f to 1m, he has a great attitude and should be ready mid-summer. Charlie Hills.

ULTIMATE AVENUE
b.c. Excelebration – Dance Avenue. €340,000 Goffs Orby. I think he was the most expensive one by his sire, a gorgeous strapping colt that oozes class, he's a big horse that will be better at 3 yrs but could be ready by the middle of the summer. Ed Walker.

PETER DOYLE

CHAPARRACHIK
b.c. High Chaparral – Chocolat Chaud. This fellow was well forward as a yearling and is a strong colt and a great mover. Amanda Perrett.

GIANT TREASURE
b.c. Shamardal – Ballybacka Lady. A great sort for a new and hopefully lucky partnership. If all goes well he could be top-class. Richard Hannon.

HARLEQUIN STORM
b.c. Clodovil – Convidada. Built like a real 2-y-o type with a good attitude. Hopefully will not keep us waiting too long. Dean Ivory.

INFERAD
b.f. Lonhro – Aquarius Star. A lovely colt with a great outlook and should make into a late two year old and hopefully a good three year old. Richard Hannon.

ROSS DOYLE

BISMARCK THE FLYER
b.c. Requinto – Livia's Wake. Purchased for £36,000 Doncaster Premier Sale. He was a very strong yearling with a decent walk and being a first foal he looked like he would be an early type. Requinto was a fast horse and this fella's dam is by Galileo so it could be a nice mix to provide a decent horse. Richard Hannon.

GIOVANNI ACUTO
gr.c. Redoute's Choice – Alla Speranza.

Purchased for €140,000 at Goffs Orby Sale. He is a very strong, good looking and great walking first foal out of a black type mare and his father is very capable of getting a top class horse. The minute was saw him we hoped we would be able to buy him and hopefully he goes on to be a nice horse for the middle of the season. Richard Hannon.

MUMS THE WORD
b.f. Mayson – Tell Mum. Purchased for 52,000 Gns at Tattersalls Part 2 Sale. She is a very racy filly from a fast family with the looks to go with it. Mayson was a top class sprinter and her dam was a fast filly in her own right with Richard Hannon, so fingers crossed she will have speed to burn. Could be an early enough sort. Richard Hannon.

TOMILY
b.c. Canford Cliffs – Cake. Recommended the mating, therefore a homebred. He is a very nice physical, medium size, good strength and a great mover. The mating did not take too much time to come up with as we purchased Canford Cliffs as a yearling and we also purchased the dam Cake as a yearling and both were trained by Richard Hannon. He looks like he will be able to hold his own fairly early in the season, his mother was a very fast two year old and we are big believers in his father making it as a stallion. Richard Hannon.

WILL EDMEADES

HIMSELF
b.c. High Chaparral – Self Centred. Homebred by Bunny Roberts and raised at Fair Winter Farm, this is the first foal of a two-year-old winner, whose second dam is Myself – hence the name. Always a lovely colt, he has a low boredom threshold and managed to fracture a splint in June last year, which had to be plated. A January foal with a good degree of precocity, he should make a summer two year old for Richard Hannon.

LIMELITE
b.f. Dark Angel – Light It Up. A three-parts sister to a useful two year old Dangerous Moonlite, who achieved a rating of 96 for Richard Hannon Snr. She was bought at Tattersalls October Book 2 and impressed more with each inspection. She is very correct

with a charming disposition and does all that is asked of her with the minimum of fuss. Richard Hannon.

OCEANUS
b.c. Born To Sea – Alkhawarah. From the immediate family of Shalaa and Dragon Pulse and by a first season horse whose progeny impressed, this colt was bought at DBS for Thurloe Thoroughbreds. My catalogue comments were 'good sort, two year old, correct, outlook', which summed him up in a nutshell. He is with Ed Dunlop and apparently shaping up well.

SHOZITA
b.f. Showcasing – Azita. Another purchase for Thurloe, this flashy individual came from Tattersalls October Book 1. The trainer was very keen on her at the sale. She has a nice page, albeit not a precocious one, and hopefully her sire will bring her forward at two – probably later in the season. Ralph Beckett.

UNNAMED
ch.f. Pivotal – Best Terms. A Barnett bred from the family of Time Charter, this is the first foal of the champion two year old filly in England in 2011 who won the Queen Mary and the Lowther. Mother was notably small and, although this filly is not over big, she is strong with a great step to her. Her new owner has sent her to William Haggas, who is pleased with her progress.

ALEX ELLIOTT

AMERICAN PATROL (IRE)
ch.c. Rio De La Plata – Gutter Press. Bought from Tattersalls October Book 2 for 105,000 Gns. A beautiful mover who has been showing up well. Owned by The Gredley family and in training with Michael Bell.

BUSH HOUSE
b.c. Canford Cliffs – Magena. £150,000 from Doncaster Premier. A hold up after the sale has meant he is a little off the pace at the moment, but being a May foal he has plenty of time to catch up and he should make up into a smart sort. Owned by The Gredley family, this colt is in training with Hugo Palmer.

MISTRESS QUICKLY (IRE)
b.f. Mastercraftsman – In My Life. Bought 110,000 Gns from Tattersalls October Book 2. A filly for later in the year and bred to be better with time. Keep an eye out for her at the back-end of the season. Owned by Mr and Mrs M Slade and in training with Ralph Beckett.

PLEASELETMEWIN (IRE)
b.c. Power – Jacaranda Ridge. Bought from the Doncaster Silver sale for £36,000. This colt is one of the reasons I've picked Power as leading first season sire (by winners). He's done extremely well since he was purchased and there's a good word for him. Owned by Mr Richard Roberts and in training with Ralph Beckett.

UNNAMED
b.c. Hat Trick – Desert Sky. A half-brother to the first horse I bought as an agent named No Jet Lag, who went on to win a Grade 2 in America before running well in the Breeders' Cup Mile. This is a fast, early horse who has been showing up well. Robert Cowell.

TOM GOFF

GALLIGREY
b.f. Sir Percy – Crystal Gal. This is a filly that was purchased for Andrew Black's Chasemore Farm in Surrey for 170,000gns at Tattersalls from Julia Scott's Glebe Stud in Newmarket. She is a lovely filly. Her dam is by Galileo and was Group 3 placed from the family of Classic Park. I saw her very early in the proceedings at the sale and thought she was a magnificently active individual. Fingers crossed she might be quite sharp. Lucy Wadham.

THE AMBER FORT (USA)
b.c. Elusive Quality – Unreachable. This was a lovely and fairly sharp colt that was purchased for $100,000 at Keeneland September last year from Padraig Campion's Blandford Stud, USA. A proper two-year-old type, he has since grown a bit which was probably no bad thing. I saw him the other day, he's got a lot of class and his third dam is Razyana, dam of the great Danehill. We've been lucky with the sire before so let's hope the lightning can arrive for us another time! John Gosden.

UNNAMED
b.f. Fastnet Rock – Great Hope. A lovely, real quality filly purchased with John Gosden for 50,000gns at Tattersalls from Croom House Stud, Ireland. It's very early days obviously as she hails from the family of Soldier of Fortune. But I really loved her and she has loads of class. I would like to think that she has an engine in there but she won't be that early. John Gosden.

UNNAMED
b.f. Quality Road – Kinda Wonderful. A high-quality filly by the sire of Group 1 winner Hootenanny. She has settled in well and they like her although she might need a bit of time. She always had plenty of presence and realised $120,000 at Keeneland September. Although she was foaled in Kentucky, she looks like a European type and I'm very hopeful. George Baker.

CHARLIE GORDON-WATSON

Last year I gave you seven selections of which five won (including Shalaa!) and two were placed. This year I am not so convinced or confident. As with last year I am giving you quite a cross section of horses and have put in two colts by Invincible Spirit in the hope that there is another Shalaa amongst them! There is not an obvious early season horse but more mid-season from the July meeting onwards.

GLOBAL APPLAUSE
b.c. Mayson – Crown. He appears to have come forward very much on his own even though he is a big, strong horse. Seems to have natural ability and will be out in the next few weeks. Ed Dunlop.

UNNAMED
b.c. Dark Angel – And Again. This colt is nicely forward and I imagine he could run in a nice maiden in the next few weeks, maybe at the Guineas meeting. Charlie Fellowes.

UNNAMED
b.c. Invincible Spirit – Alshakr. Has a very similar pedigree and profile to Shalaa in that he is from a Shadwell family, is owned by Al Shaqab and trained by John Gosden. I wouldn't think he'd be as forward as Shalaa but hopefully he'll develop into a very good type. He was also he was in the same block of boxes at Tattersalls, so let's hope lightning can strike twice! John Gosden.

UNNAMED
b.f. Dubawi – Brigitta. I first saw this filly in early June and always had her on my radar. We were pleasantly surprised by what she cost. A very neat, strong filly. John Gosden

UNNAMED
b.c. Zoffany – Glympse. This horse could be deceptive and maybe earlier than you might expect. I very much like Zoffany and particularly this one. Luca Cumani

UNNAMED
ch.f. Zebedee – Hawattef. She looked an early type as a yearling and looks now exactly as you would expect her to, although she has the scope and the pedigree to do more than that, being a half-sister to Kodi Bear. Michael Bell

UNNAMED
c. Invincible Spirit – Precocious Star. Bred to be fast, he certainly looked fast as a yearling and he has a pedigree to be fast. It was particularly encouraging that the master trainer Mr Fabre selected him to train. Andre Fabre

UNNAMED
c. Acclamation – Tribune. Once again it was a nice surprise that this horse was selected by Mr Fabre. For an Acclamation he probably has more size and scope than most of them. I really like the stallion and would buy ten a year if I could, but Richard Hannon seems to get most of them! Andre Fabre

ED HARPER

COPING STONE
b.f. Bahamian Bounty – Brick Tops. 34,000 Gns from Tattersalls Book 3. The nicest yearling we sold in Book 3, she's very classy and plenty of good judges were trying to steal her at the sales. David Brown.

UNNAMED
ch.c. Harbour Watch – Dress Code. 11,000 Gns. Tattersalls Book 2. He is a very powerful colt from a mare that has bred plenty of good performers. However, he loosened his front

shoe on the day of his sale and was slightly lame when sold, so the buyers backed off which is why he was so cheap. Harry Dunlop.

UNNAMED
b.f. Makfi – Pearl Spirit. 22,000 Gns from Tattersalls Book 2. A ball of muscle, she doesn't have a nice athletic walk but that wouldn't put me off as it is a trait of the Dubawi sire line. She is out of a half-sister to Fleeting Spirit and looked like an early 2-y-o type, short and round. Simon Crisford.

TREVOR HARRIS

MUSHAIREB
b.c. Invincible Spirit – Hidden Brief. A homebred colt, he was sold to Al Shaqab for 105,000 Gns. He's an athletic mover with good scope and is closely related to the exciting Harzand. Perhaps one for the latter part of the season. Richard Fahey.

SWISS STORM
b.c. Frankel – Swiss Lake. Another homebred, this colt is a half-brother to some very useful sprinters including the stallion Swiss Spirit. Swiss Storm is doing very well and is a great mover with an excellent attitude. Early vibes are exciting and we very much look forward to seeing him out mid-season. David Elsworth.

UNNAMED
b.c. Invincible Spirit – Dark Promise. A quality colt, this homebred was sold at Tattersalls October Book 1 to John Ferguson for 575,000 Gns. Out of the listed winning Shamardal mare Dark Promise (a half-sister to Oaks winner Love Divine), he is closely related to multiple Group 1 winners Dan Excel and Sixties Icon. Charlie Appleby

UNNAMED
b.f. Exceed And Excel – Lady Hawkfield. This filly was purchased at Tattersalls October Book 1 for 180,000 Gns. A very racy and athletic filly, she is closely related to Minding being out of a half-sister to Lillie Langtry. She looks like she'll come to hand readily. John Gosden.

HARRY HERBERT

Here are my selections from the Highclere and Al Shaqab two-year-olds.

HIGHCLERE

CONTENTMENT
b.f. Cacique – Cartimandua. This stunning daughter of Cacique really looks the part and has a faultless action. I suspect she could be a mid-season starter and she is a filly we are really looking forward to this season. William Haggas.

CONTRAST
ch.c. Dutch Art – Israar. A flashy but very racy son of Dutch Art who moves like a dream. He has certainly caught the eye of his trainer and could be a May starter. Richard Hannon

FABRIC
b.f. Acclamation – Decorative. This is a really strong, precocious daughter of Acclamation out of a mare that we raced at Highclere. She is finding it all very easy and provided she continues to remain sound and well, this is a filly who could be running before Royal Ascot. Richard Hannon.

PRECISION
b.c. Galileo – Pearl Earrine. A son of Galileo who has improved significantly since we bought him as yearling last August in Deauville. Being bred as he is I am sure that Sir Michael will take his time, but I was delighted with his physical progress when I saw him in Newmarket and he could well make his mark late summer. Sir Michael Stoute.

AL SHAQAB

HATHFA
gr.f. Dark Angel – Nepali Princess. This is a very strong, precocious daughter of Dark Angel who has thrived since arriving in Richard Hughes' Weathercock House Stables. She is very forward going and could easily be ready to roll before Royal Ascot. Richard Hughes.

MAZYOUN
b.c. Mayson – Hypnotize. This is a very well grown, powerful individual and Hugo Palmer reports him to be finding it all very easy. He

really is a significant individual who looks as though he is a three-year-old already. He could well make up into a May starter. Hugo Palmer.

ZAHIYA
b.f. Invincible Spirit – Dalasyla. This is a stunning filly who honestly could be anything. Looking at her recently she has done well physically and I suspect that she could be ready to run in July. She is an absolute beauty! Hugo Palmer.

UNNAMED
b.c. Frankel – Dar Re Mi. This is an absolute belter of a colt who boasts an impeccable pedigree. He won't be early but hopefully he will be making his mark in the second half of the season. John Gosden.

UNNAMED
b.c. Zoffany – Glympse. This is a very strong and imposing son of Zoffany who is pleasing his trainer and who to my eyes looks as though he will be an exciting mid-season prospect. Luca Cumani.

RICHARD KNIGHT

BREAKING FREE
ch.c. Kyllachy – Hill Welcome. A colt from Doncaster from a family I know well. He looks likely to be sharp and early. John Quinn.

GEORGE REME
ch.c. Power – My Sweet Georgia. I was keen to purchase a Power yearling having missed out on the sire himself by a whisker and this was a lovely colt from Doncaster. John Quinn.

UNIT OF ASSESSMENT
b.c. Dragon Pulse – Before The Storm. Another one from Doncaster and by the first season sire Dragon Pulse. William Knight.

UNNAMED
b.c. Footstepsinthesand – All Night Dancer. Purchased from Goffs Sportsman sale and by a sire I like a lot, he was very racy and had lots of quality. William Knight.

UNNAMED
ch.c. Mayson – Viola Da Braccio. A foal I purchased with loads of size, scope and quality – he won't be early but he could be good. Goes to the breeze up sales.
n.b. This colt was led out unsold at 20,000 Gns at the Tattersalls Craven Breeze Up.

UNNAMED
b.f. Exceed And Excel – Photo Flash. Another foal I purchased who looks sharp and has a smart pedigree behind her. I'd hope she will be winning early. Goes to the breeze up sales.
n.b. This colt was sold for 100,000 Gns to David Redvers at the Tattersalls Craven Breeze Up.

DAVID MCGREAVY

CAPPANANTY CON
gr.c. Zebedee – Fairmont. A really likeable colt, bought as a foal for 21,000 Gns, then resold as a yearling. He has continued to please his trainer and appears to have plenty of ability. Dean Ivory.

UNNAMED
b.f. Danehill Dancer – Blanche Dubawi (Dubawi). One of the last produce by the sire, a real quality filly who looks the part. The dam was very talented for Noel Quinlan and this filly should enhance the family. Giles Bravery.

UNNAMED
ch.f. Fast Company – Olindera. A very promising filly by a very good sire who gets speedy types. She should pay her way during the summer. Desmond Donovan.

JOHNNY MCKEEVER

AWAIT THE STORM
ch.c. Fast Company – Stormchaser. A £38,000 Doncaster Premier purchase, bought for Richard Foden for whom I have been very lucky. A very fast looking, sharp, early sort whom we expect to see out early on. He could be a Royal Ascot type. Brian Meehan.

UNNAMED
b.f. Acclamation – Dutch Diamond. Bought at Goffs Orby for €52,000. A smart, racy 2-y-o type bought for Mrs Zorka Wentworth and will be trained by Karl Burke in Middleham.

UNNAMED
b.f. So You Think – Germaine. Bought for €90,000 at Goffs Orby. A gorgeous filly who will take a little time, she was bought for Steve Parkin of Clipper Logistics for whom I have been so lucky in the past. Karl Burke.

KIRSTEN RAUSING

ALABASTER
gr.c. Archipenko – Alvarita. Sold for 100,000 Gns at Tattersalls October Sales Book Two from Staffordstown to Sir Mark Prescott. A fourth-generation Lanwades-bred, he follows his dam and granddam being trained by the Master of Heath House Stables. He is a half-brother to 5 winners including the Group 3 winner Alla Speranza, his dam was a listed winner and his granddam world champion 3-y-o filly Alborada. A late foal, he is still quite forward and may yet be seen out by July/August. Sir Mark Prescott.

ENSIGN
b.c. Invincible Spirit – Alta Moda. Sold for 190,000 Gns Tattersalls October Sales Book Two from Staffordstown to M.V. Magnier. A fourth-generation Lanwades-bred, this colt is a half-brother to the useful winners Groor and Ghurair. He is a grandson of dual Champion Stakes winner Alborada. A lovely colt and a good mover, he always looked a class act at home, as a foal and yearling. A.P. O'Brien, Ireland

GIOVANNI ACUTO
gr.c. Redoute's Choice – Alla Speranza. Sold at Goffs Orby by Staffordstown to Peter and Ross Doyle for €140,000. A fifth-generation Lanwades-bred, this colt is the first foal out of a Group 3 winning grand-daughter of dual Champion Stakes winner Alborada. His sire has produced numerous top 2-y-o's in Australasia, his dam won at two and his first three dams are all Black Type winners. Could be seen out by mid-summer. Richard Hannon

GLORIOUS FOREVER
ch.c. Archipenko – Here To Eternity. Sold for 110,000 Gns at Tattersalls October Sales Book Two from Staffordstown to Blandford Bloodstock. A third-generation Lanwades-bred, he is an own brother to 2015 2-y-o Time Warp who won four consecutive races including a listed in France (trained by Sir Mark Prescott). This colt, the second foal of his dam, much resembles his brother but may be a little bigger. He was a lovely, strong yearling and seems much liked by his new connections. Ed Walker.

HEAD MONITOR
b.c. Archipenko – Almiranta. Sold for 115,000 Gns at Tattersalls December Yearling Sales from Staffordstown to the BBA Ireland. A fourth-generation Lanwades-bred, this colt is a half-brother to the very good Group-winning French 2-y-o Alea Iacta and the promising now 3-y-o Alyssa. His granddam is a listed winner and his third dam was world champion 3-y-o filly Alborada. An exceptional yearling, he could be seen out towards the second half of the season this year. Mrs J. Harrington, Ireland

BRUCE RAYMOND

EXPRESS LADY
b.f. Helmet – Star Express. A home bred filly, she's strong, powerful and very racy. Hugo Palmer.

NIBRAS BOUNTY (IRE)
ch.c. Bahamian Bounty – Oh Sedulous. Cost 52,000 Gns from Tattersalls Book 2. A nice colt, he's strong, racy and has some quality. Richard Hannon.

SEAFRONT
b.f. Foxwedge – Lomapamar. 18,000 Gns from Tattersalls Book 3. He looks fast and goes that way too. James Tate.

UNNAMED
b.f. Sepoy – Samdaniya. 100,000 Gns purchase from Tattersalls October Book 2. A mature and racy filly. John Gosden

UNNAMED
b.c. Rio De La Plata – Silver Miss. Bought for 26,000 Gns at Tattersalls December sale. He's a strong, athletic colt. James Tate.

DAVID REDVERS

ACT OF VALOUR
b.c. Harbour Watch – B Berry Brandy. 75,000 Gns Tattersalls October Book 2. An immensely impressive individual who seems to take one stride to everything else's two and has a super temperament like his Dad. Looks a mid-summer two year old and I would be very hopeful he will be seen in some of the better races towards the back end. Trained by M O'Callaghan.

BRUTAL
b.c. Pivotal – Loreto. £250,000 Doncaster Premier Sale. A proper horse with a serious action, pedigree and price tag to match. Apparently, Brutal means something quite different on the other side of the Irish Sea so I will have to live with that! Ger Lyons.

PEACE TERMS
b.f. Teofilo – Intapeace. 70,000 Gns Tattersalls October Book 2. A beautifully balanced filly by one of my favourite stallions (with one of my favourite trainers who is just as good with a colt as he is with a filly and hates being pigeonholed). Ralph Beckett.

SOUTH SEAS
ch.c. Lope De Vega – Let It Be Me. 145,000Gns Tattersalls October Book 1. Typical of his super young sire he is a bit plain and workmanlike looking, but when he moves it all works beautifully and he's just the sort of horse I love. Andrew Balding.

VELVETEEN
b.f. Exceed And Excel – Ermine And Velvet. 50,000 Gns Tattersalls October Book 1. Looks an early season, forward going type. We can dream of Ascot and our trainer is very good with these speedy fillies. Ger Lyons.

CHRIS RICHARDSON

CIRCULATE
b.f. Dutch Art – Royal Whisper. From the family of Acclamation, she was bought at the Doncaster Bloodstock Sale for £68,000 and is a small, neat, well balanced filly who, all being well, in the hands of her trainer William Haggas should prove a sharp 2-y-o like her sire.

PANOVA
b.f. Invincible Spirit – Safina. A stakes-placed daughter of Russian Rhythm. Safina is the dam of Marenko, who last year was second in the Group 2 May Hill Stakes and the Group 3 Prix du Calvados. With Sir Michael Stoute, Panova looks a sharp sort in the making.

SPIN DOCTOR
ch.f. Mayson – Doctor's Glory. A half-sister to five Stakes winners including the Group 3 Princess Elizabeth Stakes winner Clinical, the Group 3 Horris Hill Stakes winner Cupid's Glory and the dual listed stakes winner Courting, to name but three. A May foal, but a sharp-looking filly with Richard Fahey who trained her sire Mayson to Group 1 success.

ED SACKVILLE

TAI HANG DRAGON
b.f. Tamayuz – Give A Whistle. A very well bred filly who looks strong and speedy. Richard Hannon.

WEDDING BREAKFAST
ch.f. Casamento – Fair Countenance. A balanced, attractive filly who I thought was very good value. She'll take a bit of time but looks a nice prospect. Hugo Palmer.

ROBIN SHARP

CHOUMICHA
b.f. Paco Boy – Galicuix. A beautiful filly, we sold her at Doncaster Premier and she was the joint-top priced ever at that sale. I believe the trainer is delighted with her. Hugo Palmer.

OMEROS
ch.c. Poet's Voice – Caribbean Pearl. Bought by Amanda Skiffington for 50,000 Gns from Tattersalls October Book 1. He's a beautiful, well-balanced colt. Looks a racehorse. Hugo Palmer.

POET'S QUEST
b.f. Poet's Voice – Quest For Freedom. A lovely filly, she was in Book 1 of the Tattersalls October Sales but was unsold at 38,000 Gns. We couldn't understand why she didn't sell. She's big, strong and mature. Dean Ivory.

UNNAMED
b.f. Acclamation – Choral. Sold to Richard Brown of Blandford Bloodstock for 60,000 Gns. She looked every inch a fast, early two-year-old. David Simcock.

UNNAMED
ch.f. Raven's Pass – Pivotal Lady. We sold her for 38,000 Gns from Book 1 of the October Sales. She's very nice, straightforward and sure to be a racehorse. Marco Botti.

AMANDA SKIFFINGTON

CURVE BALL (IRE)
b.c. Requinto – Royal Esteem. A lovely, sharp-looking 2-y-o colt who the trainer says I must include. He's forward and going well. Richard Hughes.

ESCOBAR
b.c. Famous Name – Saying Grace. Not an early 2-y-o but a really lovely colt, who is a great mover. Looking at him you would have to think he will be worth waiting for. Hugo Palmer.

LEWINSKY (IRE)
b.f. Famous Name – Happy Flight. A very attractive filly, who does everything right and moves well. She reminded Hugo and I strongly of the first horse I bought for him, called Making Eyes, who was a stakes winner – let's hope she will be too. Hugo Palmer.

MOJITO (IRE)
b.c. Requinto – Narva. Another beautiful, big colt who should be exciting in the second half of the season. Time will tell, but he certainly looks the part. William Haggas.

OMEROS
ch.c. Poet's Voice – Caribbean Pearl. A colt who reminds me strongly of Galileo Gold. To look at, he is strikingly similar, so fingers crossed! Hugo Palmer.

HYPERFOCUS (IRE)
b.br.c. Intense Focus – Jouel. An attractive colt who I am told has a great attitude. Everyone concerned with him seems to be very high on him. Hugo Palmer.

PETER STANLEY

ENDLESS CHARM
ch.f. Dubawi – Whazzis (Desert Prince). A truly stunning foal, she always looked very sharp and she's a beautiful mover. Charlie Appleby.

EXQUISITE RUBY
b.f. Exceed And Excel – Ruby Rocket. A sharp, precocious type who had a set back early on but should get going by mid-summer. Charlie Hills.

SCOONES
ch.c. Sepoy – Hannda. A classy colt who will need a bit of time but should be a quality back end 2-y-o. J Fanshawe.

UNNAMED
b.f. Galileo – A Z Warrior. A classy filly with huge quality and a tremendous walk. Aidan O'Brien.

LARRY STRATTON

FEEL THE VIBES
b.c. Medicean – Apple Dumpling. She's the second foal of a half-sister to seven winners from a branch of the wonderful Hardiemma family which I've had a bit of success with. Encouragingly, the trainer who initially had his half-brother came back and bought this one. Richard Hannon.

UNNAMED
b.c. Poet's Voice – China. Bred in partnership. From a great winner-producing source in Pantycoed Stud and out of a mare who is six for six with her runners. Neither his sire nor dam (a half-sister to One Way Street) are obvious sources of early sorts, so he is one for the second half of the season. Philip Hide.

UNNAMED
ch.c. Arcano – On Her Way. The second foal of a good winning mare, bred in partnership by Whatton Manor Stud, Adam Driver and me. By a sire who fell from favour very quickly, and not an early-looking type, but very athletic and in the hands of someone who knows a runner when he sees one and will do a bloody good job of getting the best out of it. Charlie McBride.

THE BLOODSTOCK EXPERTS MARK YOUR CARD

UNNAMED
b.f. Pastoral Pursuits – Royal Arruhan. Bred by Louise Parry and me, out of a non-winner who has bred just one little winner in Italy from three runners, but from a great speed family – Averti, Reesh, Pastoral Player, et al – and a speedy little sort herself who might surprise by outrunning both her immediate family and her yearling price tag. Scott Dixon.

PAUL & SARA THORMAN

BARROCHE
b.f. Kodiac – Dark Arts. We both loved this filly and she has all the ingredients needed to be a proper 2-y-o. A hugely successful sire, a speedy dam line, a grand temperament, a backside with real power and an excellent trainer. Clive Cox.

QUEEN OF TIME
b.f. Harbour Watch – Black Belt Shopper. Having tipped La Rioja from this yard last year and my tipping didn't stop her, I'm going for another of Mr Candy's. A very nice filly, very elegant, we might not see her too quickly but I'm a fan of the sire so hope she can be decent. Henry Candy.

THE DALEY EXPRESS (IRE)
b.c. Elzaam – Seraphina. The trainer has had a fairly quiet season or two, but he can train a 2-y-o alright. This was a gorgeous colt, with great balance and movement. He was a May foal though, so we might not see him for a bit. Ed McMahon.

TURPIN'S TREASURE
b.f. Dick Turpin – Poyle Caitlin. We sold her as a foal and really liked her, Tim Easterby bought her as a yearling and he has often bought inexpensive, rather unfashionably bred fillies that are very quick. He has a great eye and if she's any good the Super Sprint could be a possible, the dam Poyle Caitlin has bred fast horses already. Tim Easterby.

CHARLIE & TRACY VIGORS

SANTA ANABAA (IRE)
b.f. Exceed And Excel – Santa Agata. Tattersalls October Sale Book 1. A lovely filly whose price rose from 45,000 Guineas as a foal to 330,000 Guineas as a yearling. She was always very strong and mature and is out of a mare who was Stakes placed at two. John Oxx.

WAR OF SUCCESSION
b.c. Casamento – Rohlindi. Bought from Tattersalls October Sale Book 2 for 85,000 Gns. A strong, imposing homebred colt from the first crop of Casamento. He is probably one for the second half of the season from a family full of good two year olds. Andrew Balding.

UNNAMED
gr.f. Dark Angel – Mahaazen. Bought from Doncaster Premier for £52,000. A very athletic and racy filly who always struck us as a precocious type. Roger Varian.

UNNAMED
b.c. Kodiac – Cool Cousin. Goes to Goffs UK Breeze Up Sale. He's been working exceptionally well leading up to the Breeze Ups and looks a very fast and precocious type by the leading sire of two year olds, Kodiac.

The Frankel File

A champion at two, three and four years of age, he's now the first-season sire everyone wants to follow. Here's a list of the Frankel two-year-olds I've discussed with the trainers this spring. One theme that did come up time and time again is that many of his first crop sons and daughters don't necessarily resemble him. Rather they seem to share more similarities with the dam. Nevertheless as one leading trainer said to me *"He had the best book of mares ever. He just can't fail"*.

ALWAATHEQ (IRE)
ch.c. Frankel – Tariysha (Daylami). *"You won't see much of him this season, he's big and backward and if we get one run into him at the back-end I'll be happy. He was a late foal and he was quite late coming in, but he's a lovely model, he has a good action on him and he floats along. He's changing all the time so, fingers crossed, he could be very nice"*. Owen Burrows.

AURORA GOLD
b.f. Frankel – Midsummer (Kingmambo). *"A smallish filly, I don't dislike her at all but the dam won over a trip so it's much more of a three-year-old pedigree. For this season she's a seven furlong/mile prospect for August onwards"*. John Gosden.

BINT BATAL
b.f. Frankel – Platonic (Zafonic). *"Bred to be a better 3-y-o with her pedigree but she's a beautiful-moving filly. She's doing well, but is very much one for later on over seven furlongs and a mile"*. Ed Dunlop.

CAPTOR
b.c. Frankel – Hasten (IRE) (Montjeu). *"A lovely horse, he's very natural, has a lot of size and scope and has done everything asked of him. Out of the three Frankel's I've got he's probably the nicest one and I think he could be a very progressive horse. It's a lovely family, he's slightly unfurnished and not the finished article yet, but he shows up nicely and does everything very naturally"*. David Simcock.

COMMANDER
b.c. Frankel – Model Queen (Kingmambo). *"A lovely colt, he ticks all the boxes and is beautiful to look at – he cost a fair bit so he ought to be. He's a very good mover with a good mind, won't be early but he's a nice type of horse"*. Roger Varian.

CRACKSMAN
b.c. Frankel – Rhadegunda (Pivotal). *"I trained the mother and she was a tough, staying type that won a listed in France. This colt is a lot like her and I see him as an autumn 2-y-o. He has good attitude and he moves well"*. John Gosden.

CUNCO (IRE)
b.c. Frankel – Chrysanthemum (Danehill Dancer). *"From the Book One catalogue at Tattersalls where he didn't sell, he's a small, neat, strong colt and shows natural speed. He'll be quite early and I'll probably start him at five furlongs"*. John Gosden.

ELYAASAAT
b.c. Frankel – Lahudood (Singspiel). *"By a champion out of a Breeders' Cup winner. This horse has yet to arrive, but I saw him out in Dubai in March and he's a beautiful colt with a great step to him and weighs around 560 kilos. He has every chance of being a star and whilst I can't envisage him being anything but a back-end two-year-old, he could be a very exciting three-year-old"*. William Haggas.

EUROPIUM
b.f. Frankel – Revered (Oasis Dream). *"A nice, strong filly but she's very much one for the second part of the year, probably in September or October over seven furlongs. More of a three-year-old type"*. Dermot Weld.

FAIR EVA
ch.f. Frankel – African Rose (Observatory). *"A very nice filly out of a good mare, she has a good action and is forward-going. Hopefully she'll be one of our earlier runners, quite possibly in May. She looks 'together' and she's*

a very good mover with a fast ground action. Looks exciting at the moment". Roger Charlton.

KHATTAR
b.c. Frankel – Danceabout (Shareef Dancer).
"He's got a real air about him this lad. At the sale he really filled the bridle – he's got a purposeful, workmanlike attitude. He's getting stronger and stronger, moves like Frankel when he canters and gallops but actually looks like his damsire Shareef Dancer. A lovely colt – I love all three of my Frankels. One for seven furlongs and a mile later on, he doesn't look like he wants rushing but he's doing it all himself quite naturally". Hugo Palmer.

LIGHTENING FAST
b.c. Frankel – Lightening Pearl (Marju).
"He's the star of the show – our Group One horse. He's lovely and the image of his mother, she was introduced in June and he'll probably come out around the same time. Like the other Frankel I have he can't do enough for you – always trying to please and impress you. If he keeps progressing like that he'll be very nice". Ger Lyons.

MAJORIS (IRE)
b.c. Frankel – Drops (Kingmambo).
"I've got three Frankels and I think this one is the most forward. He's the smallest of them, the mare wasn't a great deal but it's a lovely family and I would imagine this would be one of Frankel's first runners. I'm hoping he'll start in a Newbury maiden in early June and then go for the Chesham Stakes. I'm very happy with him, he's a nice colt and all of my Frankels are beautiful movers and they have active minds, but not silly or quirky". Hugo Palmer.

NOTHING BUT DREAMS
b.f. Frankel – Danedream (Lomitas).
"It's very nice for us to have a filly by Frankel and whose dam won the Arc. She's on the small side, but I believe the dam was the same and she was a cheap yearling so maybe she was an ugly duckling that turned into a swan. Physically this filly is improving all the time but she needs more time still. It's too early to judge her really and she's probably one for the back-end of the season". Roger Varian.

OCCURRENCE
b.f. Frankel – Arrive (Kahyasi).
"A beautiful filly with a very nice pedigree to back it up, we all like her and she seems to have a nice temperament. I trained the dam and there's plenty of stamina in the pedigree, so this could be a mile and a half filly. But she's attractive and probably looks more like Frankel than some of the others I've seen". Roger Charlton.

OMNEEYA
b.f. Frankel – Amanee (Pivotal).
"A very sweet filly, she comes from a good family and I like her but we're just taking our time with her. She's gone out for a break now for a few weeks, she was a late foal and I don't think she'll be ready until mid-summer at the earliest. There's plenty to like about her, she has a great attitude and she's a nice mover". Marco Botti.

SEIRIOS
b.c. Frankel – Drifting (Sadler's Wells).
"We had his half-brother who was very backward. This fellow is a smarter type of horse, a little bit more natural and a bit more forward. He got a sore shin just as we were about to step him up but he moves well. We don't know enough about him yet but he's certainly a second half of the season 2-y-o". David Simcock.

SEVEN HEAVENS
b.c. Frankel – Heaven Sent (Pivotal).
"A nice type of colt with a quick action, business-like and with a good engine. He's likeable but has a late foaling date and I see him being on the racecourse around June/July". John Gosden.

SOLO SAXOPHONE (IRE)
b.c. Frankel – Society Hostess (Seeking The Gold). "A late summer/autumn type 2-y-o, he's a nice medium-sized colt with good conformation. He's straightforward, immature at this time, but he'll make up into a nice horse". Dermot Weld.

SPECIAL OPS
b.c. Frankel – Diary (Green Desert).
"A gorgeous colt, I have two Frankels and although they're completely different types they both have great attitudes to the job – they try to please you every time they go to

the gallops. This colt is not as precocious as he thinks he is, but he'll still be out from June onwards over seven furlongs. He's starting to thrive and if he continues to improve the way he is doing he could be anything". Ger Lyons.

SWISS STORM
b.c. Frankel – Swiss Lake (Indian Ridge).
"He had a little setback which is fine now but it just set us back by about a month. In the bigger picture it won't affect him at all but I was hoping to get to Royal Ascot with him. This is a lovely, big horse and he looks like his half-brother Swiss Spirit. He'll be our star two-year-old I think – you've only got to watch him move. An exciting colt". David Elsworth.

THE GRAND VISIR
b.c. Frankel – Piping (Montjeu).
"A lovely mover and a nice, back-end of the season type horse. If he shows speed he'll start over seven furlongs. He could be a quality horse next year, he has a nice pedigree, was a bit weak behind but he's done well and he moves well". William Haggas.

TZAVO
b.c. Frankel – Hazel Lavery (Excellent Art).
"Of the three Frankels I have this is the only one that looks like him and as such, he's very impressive to look at. He's very immature but furnishing and maturing all the time. He's been in, done well, had a break and he's back in pre-training now. He moves really well and his pedigree makes you dream he may be the heir to his Dad. He's hard to fault".
Hugo Palmer.

WATCHMAN
b.c. Frankel – Zomaradah (Deploy).
"He's a lovely horse and he does look a bit like Frankel to me. He has a very impressive action, a good mind and he's just a nice horse. His starting point on the track would be in July at the earliest". Roger Varian.

YARAKI
b.f. Frankel – Superstar Leo (College Chapel).
"She's the closest one we've had to her mother and she's lovely. Very strong, very well-made, she should be a 2-y-o. We're a bit biased in favour of Superstar Leo because she's been such a star to us, but this is a strong, quality filly with a big backside and she should be a summer 2-y-o". William Haggas.

ZEFFERINO
ch.c. Frankel – Turama (Pivotal).
"A strong, rather idle horse and it's hard to know what to make of him, he's so laid-back at the moment but I guess he's just mentally immature. He looks more like Pivotal than Frankel and from what I can gather most Frankel 2-y-o's tend to take after the mare rather than him". Roger Charlton.

UNNAMED
b.f. Frankel – Beyond Desire (Invincible Spirit).
"A small filly, but maybe that's because she was a first foal. She hasn't come into training yet". William Haggas.

UNNAMED
b.c. Frankel – Dar Re Mi (Singspiel).
"A lovely horse with scope, he has great presence about him and he moves well. A really nice type of horse for seven furlongs around July time. He looks good". John Gosden.

UNNAMED
b.c. Frankel – Dorcas Lane (Norse Dancer).
"A deep, strong, very good-moving colt. The dam didn't win until January as a 3-y-o when she won at 50-1 first time out, but he looks like he'll come together before that. A quite forward-looking, strong 2-y-o that I'd hope to get out in June or July". Roger Charlton.

UNNAMED
b.f. Frankel – Dynaforce (Dynaformer).
"She's very nice but she's not a precocious filly at all. She's unlike what you'd expect from a Frankel because she's quite leggy, tall and a little bit narrow, so she needs to develop a long time before she even sees a racecourse. That's probably coming from the female line. Hopefully she'll debut in the autumn". Luca Cumani.

UNNAMED
ch.f. Frankel – Finsceal Beo (Mr Greeley).
"What a privilege it is to get a horse like this. She's obviously an attractive filly with a classy look to her, she's a nice mover and has a lovely attitude. Unfortunately she met with a setback in February so she's been out of training for a bit, but when she was here we liked everything about her, which I suppose is natural. She has a good attitude and a lovely action and could be anything. The dam has bred a stakes

winner, so she can do it. If all goes well I'd say she's more likely to be a Guineas type than Oaks - I just hope she's good. She'll probably start her career at seven furlongs". William Haggas. (The most expensive Frankel offspring to be sold at auction to date, S.T.)

UNNAMED
b.f. Frankel – First (Highest Honor). *"She's on the small side and needs to develop plenty, so there's a long way to go with her"*. David Simcock.

UNNAMED
b.c. Frankel – Icon Project (Empire Maker). *"A nice natured horse that moves well but he's immature. He definitely needs time and needs to just strengthen up a bit. He may change a lot but at the moment you'd think he'd be running once or twice in the autumn, no more than that. The mare took time to come to hand and she did well in America on dirt"*. Roger Charlton.

UNNAMED
ch.f. Frankel – Kirinda (Tiger Hill). *"I'd say she could be a late summer 2-y-o and I like the look of her – she doesn't look weak"*. William Haggas.

UNNAMED
b.c. Frankel – Latin Love (Danehill Dancer). *"A nice horse as you'd expect being by Frankel, but we haven't done much with him yet so he'll take a bit of time. He's actually done well in the last few weeks, physically he's getting stronger but we'll just keep him ticking over until later in the year. I like him and he's a bit of a character but he's still a bit weak at the moment. Hopefully he'll find some speed once he matures"*. Richard Hannon.

UNNAMED
b.f. Frankel – Marie De Medici (Medicean). *"A very stocky, strong filly with a good top line on her. She's a good mover but just a bit headstrong – she likes to do her own thing, so maybe that's the Frankel in her. A real nice filly"*. Saeed bin Suroor.

UNNAMED
b.c. Frankel – Marine Bleue (Desert Prince). *"I haven't seen him yet, but it's a later developing family and I should think he'll be the same. For example, his year-older half-sister by Makfi will start her career shortly in a 3-y-o maiden. I have four Frankel's and they're all different shapes and sizes"*. David Simcock.

UNNAMED
b.c. Frankel – Reaching (Dansili). *"He's a stunning racehorse except for being on the small side – if he was two inches taller he'd almost be the perfect specimen. A really attractive colt that does everything nicely and moves very well, he's got a bit of character, was quite weak but is now strengthening up well and should be ready for when the seven furlong maidens start. It's a brilliant family, so he's bred to be very good but whether his size will let him down only time will tell"*. Ed Walker.

UNNAMED
b.c. Frankel – Sand Vixen (Dubawi). *"A nice type and a good, strong-topped colt. Showing good speed, he's not the biggest but he looks a nice horse. Our two Frankels are similar types"*. Saeed bin Suroor.

Trainers' Bargain Buys

It's always interesting to find out the trainers' picks from those purchases bought with a relatively modest sum. Each spring I put the following to each trainer "Name one of your two-year-olds, bought at the yearling sales for 30,000 Guineas or less, you think will prove to be a bargain?" The horses listed below are their recommendations.

In 2015 we got 16 winners of 24 races in this section, which was just a touch better than 2014 (16 of 21). Those with the most handsome starting prices were Marcel (an inspired pick by Peter Chapple-Hyam because of course he won the Group 1 Racing Post Trophy at 33-1), Banksea (also 33-1), Cara's Muse, Pinch A Kiss (both 25-1), Bukle (20-1), Dark Defender, Threebagsue (both 14-1) and Four's Company (12-1). Handsome prices indeed!

Eve Johnson Houghton is the boss here with six winners in the last six years (Orientalist, Bling King, Vestibule, Drive On, British Embassy and Cara's Muse). Other trainers to note are Tom Dascombe with an excellent five winners from six and James Given (four winners from the last five).

Horse	Price	Trainer
WIND IN THE TREES (FR)	€26,000	George Baker
MAKKADANDDANG	25,000 Gns	Andrew Balding
WHAT A BOY	£11,000	Ralph Beckett
FIRE BRIGADE	£26,000	Michael Bell
COVERHAM (IRE)	20,000 Gns	James Bethell
BORNTOSIN (IRE)	€12,000	Marco Botti
b.c. Equiano – Haiti Dancer	7,500 Gns	Giles Bravery
MAGGI MAY	23,000 Gns	David Brown
ANGEL DOWN	£26,000	Henry Candy
ZIG ZAG GIRL	800 Gns	Mick Channon
POKER ALICE	22,000 Gns	Peter Chapple-Hyam
ORANGE GIN	€7,500	Roger Charlton
PETER STUYVESANT (IRE)	20,000 Gns	Denis Coakley
FIERY SPICE	11,000 Gns	Robert Cowell
PARTY NIGHTS	12,000 Gns	Luca Cumani
CLEM FANDANGO	€11,000	Keith Dalgleish
FIERY CHARACTER (IRE)	€18,000	Tom Dascombe
RAINBOW MIST (IRE)	£12,000	Ann Duffield
MAGDALENE FOX	27,000 Gns	Ed Dunlop
ch.c. Harbour Watch – Dress Code	11,000 Gns	Harry Dunlop
b.f. Cape Blanco – Carini	12,000 Gns	David Elsworth
VOTE	8,000 Gns	James Eustace
SCUDDING (USA)	20,000 Gns	Charlie Fellowes
MIGHTASWELLSMILE	6,000 Gns	James Given
ch.f. Kyllachy – Solfilia	10,000 Gns	Rae Guest
BIOLOGIST	20,000 Gns	William Haggas
VINCY (IRE)	€20,000	Michael Halford
LUDUAMF (IRE)	18,000 Gns	Richard Hannon
LADY BEWARE	€22,000	Jessie Harrington
b.c. Harbour Watch – Al Hawa	18,000 Gns	Richard Hughes
GIRL SQUAD (IRE)	7,000 Gns	William Jarvis
DIABLE D'OR (IRE)	€16,000	Eve Johnson Houghton
ch.c. Thewayyouare – Ask Annie	€24,000Y.	William Knight
FLOODED	4,000 Gns	Daniel Kubler

GETGO	20,000 Gns	David Lanigan
KING ELECTRIC (IRE)	€25,000	Ger Lyons
DARING GUEST	25,000 Gns	George Margarson
SIR PLATO	£6,000	Rod Millman
SHEILA'S LAD	4,000 Gns	Stan Moore
BERNARDO O'REILLY	£10,000	Dave Morris
TEMPLE CHURCH (IRE)	27,000 Gns	Hughie Morrison
MOONLIGHT SILVER	20,000 Gns	Willie Muir
b.c. Sixties Icon – Rose Cheval	6,500 Gns	Jamie Osborne
COPPER KNIGHT	£30,000	Hugo Palmer
GARNETTA	20,000 Gns	Amanda Perrett
BALGAIR	12,000 Gns	Jonathan Portman
RISE AGAIN (IRE)	€9,000	Kevin Prendergast
br.g. Zebedee – Journey's End	15,000 Gns	John Quinn
STAY SHARP	£20,000	George Scott
MISS SUGARS	10,000 Gns	David Simcock
SEAFRONT	18,000 Gns	James Tate
DONTFORGETTOCALL	€11,000	Joseph Tuite
GOLDEN SLAM	£15,000	Roger Varian
TONAHUTU (IRE)	£16,000	Ed Vaughan
ch.c. Tagula – Fashion Guide	€28,000	Ed Walker
UPENDED	17,000 Gns	Chris Wall

Two-Year-Olds of 2016

CHARLIE APPLEBY
(GODOLPHIN)

1. ENDLESS CHARM ★★★♠
ch.f. Dubawi – Whazzis (Desert Prince). February 9. Sixth foal. Sister to the fairly useful 2015 2-y-o 6f and 7f winner Culturati and half-sister to the French 2-y-o 1m winner and 3-y-o listed-placed Whim (by Nayef), the fairly useful dual 10f winner Valiant (by Galileo), the fair 7f winner Feng Shui (by Iffraaj) and the fair 9f winner Of Course Darling (by Dalakhani). The dam won the Group 3 1m Premio Sergio Cumani and is a half-sister to 5 winners including Whazzat (Chesham Stakes). The second dam, Wosaita (by Generous), a fair 12.3f placed maiden, is a half-sister to 10 winners including the Group 1 10.5f Prix de Diane winner Rafha (dam of the Haydock Sprint Cup winner Invincible Spirit) and the Group 3 12f Blandford Stakes winner Chiang Mai (dam of the Group 1 Pretty Polly Stakes winner Chinese White). *"A typical Dubawi filly from the family of Invincible Spirit, the dam has bred two 2-y-o winners from five previous foals including this filly's full-brother Culturati who opened his account last September".*

2. FIRST NATION ★★★
b.c. Dubawi – Moyesii (Diesis). April 11. Half-brother to the 2-y-o Group 1 winner Gran Criterium winner Kirklees (by Jade Robbery), to the Group 1 St Leger winner Mastery (by Sulamani), the very useful 1m to 14f winner Famous Kid, the fair 2-y-o dual 7f winner Oscan (both by Street Cry) and the fair 1m (at 2 yrs) to 11f winner Auden (by Librettist). The dam, a 9.5f winner in France, is a half-sister to 3 winners including the French Group 3 winner Bowman. The second dam, Cherokee Rose (by Dancing Brave), won the Group 1 Haydock Park Sprint Cup and the Group 1 Prix Maurice de Gheest and is a half-sister to 4 winners. *"He's from a predominantly staying family but he's related to the Sprint Cup winner Cherokee Rose and is showing natural pace, so he may be out early".*

3. NEVER A WORD (USA) ★★★
b.br.c. Lonhro – Janetstickettocats (Storm Cat). March 3. Half-brother to the US 2-y-o Grade 3 8.5f winner Lucky Player (by Lookin At Lucky). The dam was placed third once over 6f in the USA from five starts. The second dam, Ticket To Houston (by Houston), won two stakes events in the USA at 2 yrs. *"An impressive, dark brown colt by a champion stallion in Australia".*

4. ROMANTIC VIEW ★★★
b.f. Shamardal – Mondalay (Monsun). March 9. Second foal. Sister to Sabato, placed fourth twice over 6f at 2 yrs in 2015. The dam is a half-sister to 6 winners including the sire Manduro, a triple Group 1 winner from 1m to 10f (including the Prince Of Wales's Stakes) and the German listed 11f winner and Group 2 placed Mandela. The second dam, Mandellicht (by Be My Guest), a winner and listed-placed in Germany, is a half-sister to 6 winners. *"A strong, well grown filly by a leading stallion in Shamardal".*

5. SECRET STRATEGY (IRE) ★★★
b.c. Kodiac – Shall We Tell (Intikhab). March 5. Sixth foal. €100,000foal. Goffs November foals. R O'Gorman. Half-brother to the modest 2-y-o 1m and 10f winner Paddy's Saltantes (by Redback). The dam is an unraced half-sister to 6 winners including Group 1 Prix de Diane winner and 1,000 Guineas second Confidential Lady. The second dam, Confidante (by Dayjur), a fairly useful 3-y-o dual 7f winner, is a half-sister to 7 winners including the Group/Grade 3 winners White Crown and Drilling For Oil. *"A nice, forward going type that should be out early".*

6. UNNAMED ★★
gr.c. Dubawi – Claba Di San Jore (Barathea). April 23. Tenth foal. Brother to the unplaced 2015 2-y-o La Mortola and half-brother to 6 winners including the Italian Group 1 10f winner Crackerjack King (by Shamardal), the Italian Group 1 12f winners Jakkalberry (by Storming Home) and Awelmarduk (by Almutawakel) and the Italian listed 10f and

listed 12f winner and Group 2 Prix Niel third Kidnapping (by Intikhab). The dam, a minor Italian 3-y-o winner, is a half-sister to 9 winners. The second dam, Claw (by Law Society), a listed-placed Italian winner of 7 races, is a half-sister to 5 winners. *"A big, scopey colt who will be lovely in time".*

7. UNNAMED ★★★
b.c. Dubawi – Goathemala (Black Sam Bellamy). April 8. Fourth foal. 725,000Y. Tattersalls October Book 2. John Ferguson. Half-brother to the German listed 7f winner Goiania (by Oasis Dream). The dam, a German Group 3 11f winner, is a sister to a German listed winner and a half-sister to another. The second dam, Global World (by Big Shuffle), a 2-y-o winner and listed-placed in Germany, is a full or half-sister to 10 winners including the German Group winners Global Dream and Global Thrill. *"This colt is very typical of his sire, with plenty of class".*

8. UNNAMED ★★★
b.c. Sepoy – Miss Brown To You (Fasliyev). March 25. Fifth foal. 160,000Y. Tattersalls October Book 1. John Ferguson. Half-brother to the Group 2 Goodwood Cup and Group 2 Princess Of Wales's Stakes winner Big Orange (by Duke Of Marmalade) and to the modest 9f winner Empowermentofwomen (by Manduro). The dam, a fair 1m winner, is a half-sister to 7 winners including the dual Group 3 5f winner Almaty and the very useful triple 1m and Hong Kong Group 1 winner Race. The second dam, Almaaseh (by Dancing Brave), placed once over 6f at 3 yrs, is a half-sister to 8 winners including the 2,000 Guineas and Champion Stakes winner Haafhd. *"A well grown, muscular colt who loves his work".*

9. UNNAMED ★★★
b.c. Cape Cross – Sahraah (Kingmambo). March 17. Second foal. The dam is an unraced half-sister to several winners including the Group 3 Prix Gladiateur winner Ley Hunter and the US Grade 2 placed Gabriel's Hill. The second dam, Lailani (by Unfuwain), winner of the Group 1 Irish Oaks, the Group 1 Nassau Stakes and two US Grade 1 events, is a half-sister to several winners including the listed 12f winner Copper Carnival. *"A neat colt with a great attitude".*

10. UNNAMED ★★★
ch.c. Raven's Pass – Sayyedati Storm (Storm Cat). April 12. Third foal. 220,000Y. Tattersalls October Book 1. John Ferguson. Half-brother to the very useful Group 3 12f Cumberland Lodge winner Star Storm (by Sea The Stars). The dam is an unplaced half-sister to 5 winners including the smart 2-y-o Group 2 7f Champagne Stakes winner Almushahar. The second dam, Sayyedati (by Shadeed), won the Group 1 7f Moyglare Stud Stakes and the Group 1 6f Cheveley Park Stakes at 2 yrs, the 1,000 Guineas and Prix Jacques le Marois at 3 yrs and the Sussex Stakes at 5 yrs. She is a full or half-sister to 8 winners including the multiple Group 1 winner Golden Snake. *"A lovely big colt who is coming to hand nicely".*

GEORGE BAKER

11. ALTIKO TOMMY ★★★
b.c. Kodiac – Altishaan (Darshaan). April 28. Seventh foal. 32,500Y. Tattersalls October Book 2. Blandford Bloodstock. Half-brother to the fair 2-y-o 6f winner Easily Averted (by Averti) and to a minor winner in Germany by Montjeu. The dam is an unraced half-sister to 6 minor winners. The second dam, Altiyna (by Troy), a winner and third in the Group 2 Park Hill Stakes, is a half-sister to 8 winners included the disqualified Oaks winner Aliysa. (Paul Bowden). *"He's quite a punchy, feisty sort and he should be an early 2-y-o. I'll be taking him for a racecourse gallop at Kempton and then hopefully run him in mid-April over five furlongs. I won't push him and if we end up starting over six furlongs it won't be the end of the world. At the moment it's looking like instant action for him, he's done everything very easily, he's very uncomplicated and I like him".*

12. INFANTA ISABELLA ★★★
b.f. Lope De Vega – Shemissa (Fairy King). May 7. Eleventh foal. 50,000Y. Tattersalls October Book 1. George Baker. Half-sister to 6 winners including the US listed stakes winner and Group 1 Prix Jean-Luc Lagardere third Shediak (by Selkirk) and the fairly useful Irish 1m winner Shehira (by Sendawar). The dam is an unraced half-sister to 6 winners including the French dual Group 3 winner Shemima. The second dam, Shemaka (by Nishapour), won the Group 1 Prix de Diane and is a half-sister

to 5 winners. (Chriselliam Partnership). *"My wife, Candida, went to Stratford Place Stud to look at this filly and when the owner Chris Wright sent her to the sales we bought her – only for Chris to buy her back off us because he thought she'd have made more! She won't run until July at the earliest, she has lovely conformation but she's big and solid and is just hacking away for now. My gut feeling is that she's going to be a lovely, long-striding 3-y-o next year".*

13. TALLULAH ROSE ★★★★
b.f. Exceed And Excel – Blinking (Marju). April 8. Fifth foal. 80,000Y. Tattersalls October Book 2. Blandford Bloodstock. Half-sister to the quite useful listed-placed 12f winner Twitch (by Azamour) and to the fair 10f winner Maracuja (by Medicean). The dam is an unraced sister to Viva Pataca, a winner of 18 races and nearly £6 million in prize money here and in Hong Kong from 6f (at 2 yrs) to 12f and a half-sister to 3 winners including the US Grade 1 winner Laughing. The second dam, Comic (Be My Chief), a quite useful 10f and 11.5f winner, is a half-sister to 4 winners including the 2-y-o Group 3 Solario Stakes winner Brave Act. (Mr & Mrs Bailey and Partners). *"She's a lovely, early sort. I took her to Kempton for a piece of work last week where Steve Drowne rode her and he was very pleased with her. She looks an early type, we love the sire and she wasn't cheap but I hope she was good value. She could be running in early April, all being well. A very straightforward filly with plenty of speed".*

14. WIND IN THE TREES (FR) ★★
b.f. Sunday Break – Swift Winged (Motivator). April 29. First foal. €26,000Y. Osarus September. Stroud/Coleman. The dam is an unplaced half-sister to several winners including the useful triple listed 15f winner Swift Wing. The second dam, Swift Spring (by Bluebird), was a moderate 7f winner. (Allez France). *"A nice, precocious filly, despite being a late April foal she's showing all the signs to say that she'll be out sooner rather than later. She's a 2-y-o type and she'll take her racing, so I can see her starting off here in April and then racing in France".* **TRAINERS' BARGAIN BUY**

15. UNNAMED ★★★
gr.f. Dark Angel – First Lady (Indian Ridge). February 15. Third foal. £70,000Y. Doncaster Premier. Hillen & Baker. Half-sister to the fair 2-y-o 6f winner State Of The Union (by Approve). The dam is an unraced half-sister to 9 winners including the Group 3 5f Premio Omenoni winner Kathy College. The second dam, Katy Guest (by Be My Guest), won at 2 and 3 yrs in Italy and is a half-sister to 4 winners. (Earl Of Brecknock & Partners). *"We managed to buy her at Doncaster just before Godolphin did a deal with Yeomanstown Stud to buy into Dark Angel. Hopefully we slipped under the radar a bit because they may well be supporting him at the sales even more than they may have done previously. Dark Angel is a sire that gets horses that are very tough, hardy and dependable, and he's been very lucky for us. We're not in a rush with this filly but she's coming to hand pretty well and I would suggest she'd be starting off at six furlongs in May."*

16. UNNAMED ★★★
b.f. Dark Angel – Jasmine Flower (Kyllachy). March 10. Third foal. 95,000Y. Tattersalls October Book 2. Amanda Skiffington. The dam is an unraced sister to the listed-placed winner Nasri and a half-sister to 4 winners including the Group 2 third Ellmau. The second dam, Triple Sharp (by Selkirk), a quite useful 10f and hurdles winner, is a half-sister to 6 winners including the Group 2 Prix Eugene Adam winner Triple Threat and to the unraced dam of the top-class miler Canford Cliffs. (Delancey Real Estate Asset Management Ltd). *"She's pretty classy, as you'd hope considering her price because for us she was expensive. She's very straightforward and like most of the Dark Angel's you know you could ride her at the poll tax rioters and she wouldn't flinch! We'll take her for an away day at a racecourse before we get going. Ours are never over-cooked on debut and I'm hoping she'll be lovely 3-y-o next year. Nevertheless she's given me no reason to stop with her".*

17. UNNAMED ★★★ ♠
b.f. Quality Road – Kinda Wonderful (Silver Train). April 22. Second foal. $120,000Y. Keeneland September. Blandford Bloodstock.

The dam, unplaced in two starts, is a half-sister to the US winners Graded stakes placed Magical Illusion, Lily O'Gold and Shah Jehan. The second dam, Voodoo Lily (by Baldski), won the Grade 3 Colombia Stakes in the USA. *"I was let loose in Kentucky to buy this filly. She'll definitely need time because she's a lovely, big, stocky type. She looks like she'd take plenty of graft but we're not doing that at the moment because she needs to grow into herself. I would imagine that she'd be a July/August 2-y-o and I like her a lot but I'm not going to rush her".*

18. UNNAMED ★★
b.c. Miesque's Son – Lisselan Firefly (Monashee Mountain). March 9. Fourth foal. €46,000Y. Osarus September. Half-brother to the useful French 5f (at 2 yrs) and US 6.5f winner and Group 3 5f Prix de Bois second To My Valentine (by Dyhim Diamond). (Allez France). *"I bought three yearlings to form a cross channel syndicate and this is one of them. Hopefully we can exploit the French premiums by running here once and then going to France to try and win in the provinces. I'd hope to run this colt in late April and he shows plenty of toe".*

19. UNNAMED ★★
b.c. Kyllachy – Ragazza Mio (Generous). April 30. Fifth foal. 62,000Y. Tattersalls October Book 2. Charlie Gordon-Watson. Half-brother to the French winner and Group 3 Prix Minerve third Gosh (by Peintre Celebre) and a minor French winner by Zamindar. The dam, a dual winner in France and listed-placed twice, is a half-sister to the Group 3 10.5f Prix Penelope winner and Group 1 Prix Saint-Alary third Perfect Hedge, which is a half-sister to 7 winners including the Group 1 Australian winner He's Your Man. The second dam, Via Saleria (by Arazi), won once at 4 yrs and is a half-sister to 12 winners including Poliglote (Group 1 Criterium de Saint-Cloud). *"We're in no rush with him because he's still growing and developing and is a bit 'up behind', so he needs to strengthen in front and he's just cantering away every day for now. I'm hoping he'll be a better 3-y-o and his pedigree certainly suggests he will be. At the earliest I would suggest he might be out in late May over six furlongs".*

20. UNNAMED ★★★
b.c. Elusive Quality – Sovereign Crisis (Congrats). January 25. First foal. $75,000Y. Keeneland September. Not sold. The dam, a minor dual winner at 3 yrs in the USA, is a half-sister to the US Grade 3 winner and Grade 2 placed Elusive Lady. The second dam, Song Of Royalty (by Unbridled's Song), is an unraced half-sister to 4 minor winners. *"I love Elusive Quality's but they can have a certain feistiness about them and he certainly does. He's not in any way nasty, he just needs to have the feistiness channelled in the right direction. He's definitely got something about him and he's coming along nicely. I would hope to see him racing in May".*

ANDREW BALDING

21. ANCIENT FOE ★★
b.c. Shamardal – Pearl Dance (Nureyev). March 2. Brother the fairly useful dual 1m winner Born In Bombay and half-brother to the Group 3 9f Prix Chloe winner Sparkling Beam (by Nayef), the very useful 9f winner and Group 1 Prix Marcel Boussac third Rainbow Springs and the useful 2-y-o dual 7f winner Ridge Dance (both by Selkirk). The dam, a useful 2-y-o 6f winner and third in the Group 1 Moyglare Stud Stakes, is a half-sister to the German listed winner and Group 1 German Derby fourth Ocean Sea and the US winner and Grade 3 third Dixie Splash. The second dam, Ocean Jewel (by Alleged), is an unraced half-sister to 6 minor winners. (George Strawbridge). *"He's had a setback and won't be with me for a bit, but we had the full brother Born In Bombay. This colt will be a back-end of the season type 2-y-o. I'm very happy with my two-year-olds this year, I think they're as nice a bunch as we've had for a good while and more forward than usual as well".*

22. APPRECIATING ★★★
b.f. New Approach – Star Value (Danehill Dancer). April 15. First foal. The dam is an unraced three-parts sister to the French listed 10f winner Shemala and a half-sister to 5 winners including the French Group 3 10f and Group 3 15f winner Shemima. The second dam, Shemaka (by Nishapour), was a smart filly and winner of the Group 1 10.5f Prix de Diane, the Group 3 10f Prix de la Nonette and

the Group 3 9f Prix de Conde. (The Queen). "She's not the biggest but she's very athletic and goes nicely. She's a bit backward in her coat at the moment, but I'd expect her to be a mid-summer 2-y-o. A nice, athletic, easy moving filly".

23. ATKINSON GRIMSHAW ★★
ch.c. Rio De La Plata – Cosabawn (Barathea). April 14. Ninth foal. 40,000Y. Tattersalls December. Andrew Balding. Half-brother to the quite useful 2-y-o 1m winner Barawin (by Hawk Wing) and to the fair 7f winner Strandhill (by Footstepsinthesand). The dam is an unplaced half-sister to 7 winners. The second dam, Riyda (by Be My Guest), a listed winner, is a half-sister to 5 winners including the Group 3 Royal Whip Stakes winner Rayseka. (D E Brownlow). "Quite a tall, rangy type who's done a lot of growing since the sale and needs to furnish a bit more".

24. AWARE ★★★★
b.br.f. Street Cry – Satulagi (Officer). May 1. Fifth foal. Half-sister to the quite useful 1m (at 2 yrs) to 11f winner Teolagi (by Teofilo) and to the modest 6f and 7f winner of 4 races at 2 and 3 yrs One More Roman (by Holy Roman Emperor). The dam, a useful listed 7f winner at 2 yrs, is a half-sister to 8 winners including the Grade 3 Iroquois Stakes winner Motor City. The second dam, Shawgatny (by Danzig Connection), won over 9f in Ireland and is a sister to the dual Group 3 winner Star Of Gdansk. (Mrs F Hay). "I like her, she's done bits and pieces upsides and goes very nicely. Very feminine and beautiful, she's a seven furlong type 2-y-o to watch out for.

25. BERKSHIRE BOY (IRE) ★★★
b.c. Elzaam – Circuit City (Exit To Nowhere). April 23. Seventh foal. 50,000Y. Tattersalls October Book 2. Andrew Balding. Half-brother to the French 2-y-o 7.5f and subsequent Hong Kong winner Flash Ram (by Langfuhr) and to 2 minor 3-y-o winners in France and the USA by Rossini and Tale Of The Cat. The dam, a minor French 3-y-o winner, is a half-sister to 5 winners including the listed Prix Finlande winner and French 1,000 Guineas second Karmifira and the listed 1m Prix Coronation winner Kart Star. The second dam, Karmiska (by Bikala), won the Group 3 10f Prix de la Nonette and is a full or half-sister to 6 winners. (Berkshire Parts & Panels). "I'm very happy with him. He's done a fair bit now and he wouldn't be far off a run. We'll probably start him off at five furlongs although he'll definitely want six. He's coming along really nicely".

26. BOHEMIAN FLAME ★★★★
b.c. Zoffany – Red Japonica (Daylami). April 3. Sixth foal. €45,000Y. Goffs Orby. Kern/Lillingston. Brother to the 2015 Irish 6f placed 2-y-o Camellia Japonica and half-brother to the fair 6f and 7f winner of 5 races Kinglami (by Kingsalsa) and a minor winner abroad by Sadler's Wells. The dam is an unraced half-sister to 5 winners including the Group 1 Fillies' Mile and dual Group 2 10f Blandford Stakes winner Red Bloom and the listed winner Red Gala. The second dam, Red Camellia (by Polar Falcon), winner of the Group 3 7f Prestige Stakes, was third in the French 1,000 Guineas and is a half-sister to 4 winners. (Kennet Valley Thoroughbreds II). "He looks a natural 2-y-o, the sire did well last year and this is a good, fine, strong horse. I think he was exceptionally well-bought, he's a lovely type and I'm very pleased with him. Hopefully he'll be out in May".

27. CHARTBUSTER ★★★
gr.c. Mastercraftsman – Gift Dancer (Imperial Dancer). March 13. Second foal. 40,000Y. Tattersalls October Book 2. Axom. Half-brother to Sixties Groove (by Sixties Icon), unplaced on his only start at 2 yrs in 2015. The dam is an unraced half-sister to 6 winners including the Group 1 Irish 1,000 Guineas and US Grade 1 winner Samitar and the 2-y-o Group 3 Albany Stakes winner Nijoom Dubai. The second dam, Aileen's Gift (by Rainbow Quest), is an unraced half-sister to 5 winners including the dam of the Group 2 Gimcrack Stakes winner Shameel. (Owners Group 015). "He's very untypical of most Mastercraftsman's in that he's quite close coupled, stocky and strong. A 2-y-o type that's just starting to step up a gear now, he should be fairly active this summer".

28. CONTANGO ★★
ch.c. Casamento – Call Later (Gone West). April 20. Fifth foal. 50,000Y. Tattersalls December. Kern/Lillingston. Half-brother to the listed 2-y-o 7f winner Be Ready (by New

Approach), to the modest triple 10f winner Ana Shababiya (by Teofilo) and the modest 5f to 13f winner of 7 races from 3 to 7 yrs Trending (by Dark Angel). The dam is an unraced half-sister to 6 winners including the multiple US Grade 1 winner Ventura. The second dam, Estala (by Be My Guest), won over 1m at 2 yrs in France and was listed-placed and is a half-sister to 4 stakes winners. (Kennet Valley Thoroughbreds XII). *"A nice, scopey, good-looking horse, he'll take time and we wouldn't want to hurry him"*.

29. COUNT OCTAVE ★★★
b.c. Frankel – Honorine (Mark Of Esteem). April 22. Closely related to the Group 1 12f Irish Derby and US Grade 1 Secretariat Stakes winner Treasure Beach (by Galileo) and half-brother to the fairly useful listed 11.5f winner Honor Bound (by Authorized), the fairly useful 12f winner Elidor (by Cape Cross) and the fair 10f winner Timeless (by New Approach). The dam, a quite useful 1m and 10f winner, is a half-sister to the Group 2 Hardwicke Stakes and Group 3 Earl Of Sefton Stakes winner and triple Group 1 placed Indian Creek. The second dam, Blue Water (by Bering), a French listed 12f winner, was Group 3 placed and is a half-sister to 3 winners. (Qatar Racing Ltd). *"He hasn't come in yet, but he's a fine, big, rangy type of horse that's going to take a bit of time"*.

30. DROCHAID ★★★★
ch.c. Mastercraftsman – Avon Lady (Avonbridge). February 13. Second foal. 40,000Y. Tattersalls October Book 1. Andrew Balding. Half-brother to King Of Naples (by Excellent Art), unplaced in one start at 2 yrs in 2015. The dam, a quite useful 7f to 8.5f winner of 4 races, is a half-sister to one winner. The second dam, Delightful Rhythm (by Diesis), is an unraced half-sister to 3 winners. (Mick & Janice Mariscotti). *"A very nice horse, he's out of an Avonbridge mare so there's a bit of speed in the family. I just like the way he goes and I'd say he'd have enough speed for six furlongs which you wouldn't necessarily expect from a Mastercraftsman. A really nice horse, he'll start at six furlongs and will certainly stay seven in time"*.

31. EASTERN ★★
b.f. Shamardal – Thought Is Free (Cadeaux Genereux). April 4. Fifth foal. Half-sister to the fairly useful dual 1m winner, German Group 2 1m second and listed 10.5f third Merry Me (by Invincible Spirit). The dam, a fairly useful 6f listed-placed 2-y-o, is a half-sister to 6 winners including the Group 3 third Day Of Conquest and the dam of the Group 1 winner Hearts Of Fire. The second dam, Dayville (by Dayjur), a quite useful triple 6f winner, is a half-sister to 4 winners including the Grade 1 Yellow Ribbon Handicap winner Spanish Fern. (Mrs F H Hay). *"We have the half-sister Merry Me who is decent and Group-placed. This is a fine, big filly that'll take a bit of time but I'd hope to get a run or two into her this year"*.

32. FAIR COP ★★★★
b.f. Exceed And Excel – Speed Cop (Cadeaux Genereux). April 13. Fourth foal. Half-sister to the useful 6f (including at 2 yrs) and 5f winner of 5 races Desert Law, to the fair 6f winner Desert Command (both by Oasis Dream) and the fairly useful 2-y-o 6f winner Top Cop (by Acclamation). The dam, a useful 2-y-o listed 5.2f winner and third in the Group 2 Flying Childers Stakes, is a sister to the fairly useful triple 5f winner Siren's Gift and a half-sister to 2 winners. The second dam, Blue Siren (by Bluebird), a very useful winner of 3 races from 5f to 7f and disqualified in the Group 1 5f Nunthorpe Stakes, is a half-sister to several winners. (J C Smith). *"A lovely filly from a good family, she looks every inch a 2-y-o and she should make up into a decent one. Probably one for six furlongs in June and she's got a fair bit of size and scope to her"*.

33. FARLEIGH MAC ★★★★
ch.c. Equiano – Le Badie (Spectrum). March 6. Third foal. 48,000Y. Tattersalls October Book 2. Not sold. Half-brother to the fairly useful 8.5f (at 2 yrs) to 12f winner Montaly (by Yeats) and to the fair 1m winner Farlety (by Royal Applause). The dam, a listed-placed winner of 3 races from 2 to 4 yrs in Italy, is a half-sister to 5 winners including the 2-y-o listed winner Lady Angharad (herself dam of the Group 3 and Canadian Grade 2 winner Barefoot Lady). The second dam, Lavezzola (by Salmon Leap), a winner of 3 races and listed-placed in Italy, is a half-sister to 4 winners. (Farleigh Racing).

"We had Montaly out of the mare and he was a very decent stayer by Yeats. I also had the Royal Applause half-sister and she won as well, but this is the best individual we've had out of the mare. He goes very nicely, looks a proper 2-y-o type and I have fairly high hopes for him".

34. GALACTIC PRINCE ★★★
ch.c. Dubawi – Opera Gal (Galileo). January 23. First foal. The dam, a very useful listed 10f and listed 12f winner, is a half-sister to two winners. The second dam, Opera Glass (by Barathea), a quite useful 8.5f winner, is a sister to the very smart 2-y-o Group 3 7f Solario Stakes winner and Group 1 Dewhurst Stakes third Opera Cape and a half-sister to the high-class stayer Grey Shot and the smart sprint winner of 4 races Night Shot. (J C Smith). "The dam was a good filly we had here, she was just a smashing horse and I was very keen to get her offspring. This is a first foal and he's not the biggest but he's a real, grand type. He looks like a typical Dubawi to me and I should think he'll want ten furlongs in time, but we'll be looking to start him at seven furlongs in mid-summer".

35. HIDDEN STEPS ★★★
b.f. Footstepsinthesand – Hidden Valley (Haafhd). March 19. First foal. The dam, a fair 2m winner, is a half-sister to numerous winners including the very smart Group 2 1m Oettingen-Rennen and Group 3 8.5f Diomed Stakes winner Passing Glance, the smart Group 3 7f Prix de Palais-Royal and European Free Handicap winner Hidden Meadow and the smart listed winners Scorned and Kingsclere. The second dam, Spurned (by Robellino), a fairly useful 2-y-o 7f winner, later stayed 10f. (Kingsclere Racing Club). "Definitely worth a mention, she looks nice on the gallops and is a nicely-made filly that should want six furlongs. I really like the way she goes".

36. HIGH COMMANDER ★★★★
b.c. Teofilo – Pellinore (Giant's Causeway). April 30. Fourth foal. 160,000Y. Tattersalls October Book 1. David Redvers. Half-brother to the fair 2-y-o 7f winner Rock Kristal (by Fastnet Rock). The dam, a modest fourth over 10f from 3 starts, is a sister to the 2,000 Guineas winner Footstepsinthesand and a half-sister to 3 winners including the Group 1 Phoenix Stakes winner Pedro The Great and the dam of the dual Group 1 winner Power and the Group 2 winner Thakafaat. The second dam, Glatisant (by Rainbow Quest), winner of the Group 3 7f Prestige Stakes, is a half-sister to 8 winners and to the placed dam of the very smart 2-y-o Superstar Leo. (Qatar Racing Ltd). "A lovely horse that goes nicely, I'm really pleased with him and he's just a smashing horse that reminds me of a Galileo we had for Qatar Racing called Rocky Rider. He was a useful horse and a similar type, slightly smaller and more of a 2-y-o version that what a Galileo or Teofilo can be. He'll be alright this year".

37. HIGHLAND PASS ★★
b.br.f. Passing Glance – Lady Brora (Dashing Blade). April 6. Fourth foal. Half-sister to the fair 2015 8.5f fourth placed 2-y-o Brorocco (by Shirocco) and to the high-class 2-y-o Group 1 1m Racing Post Trophy and Group 2 1m Royal Lodge Stakes winner Elm Park (by Phoenix Reach). The dam, a fair 1m winner, is a half-sister to 2 winners. The second dam, Tweed Mill (by Selkirk), a quite useful 3-y-o 8.5f winner, is a half-sister to 5 winners. (Kingsclere Racing Club). "A half-sister to Elm Park, she's a nice, athletic filly and seems to be pretty straightforward. One to start off in a seven furlong maiden around July time".

38. HORSEPLAY ★★★
b.f. Cape Cross – Mischief Making (Lemon Drop Kid). March 26. Fourth foal. Sister to the fairly useful 10f (at 2 yrs), 11f and hurdles winner Devilment (by Cape Cross) and half-sister to the quite useful 8.5f to 12f winner More Mischief (by Azamour). The dam, a winner of 4 races from 9f to 13f including a listed event and second in the Group 3 Sagaro Stakes, is a half-sister to 3 winners including the dual listed 7f winner That Is The Spirit. The second dam, Fraulein (by Acatenango), won over 7f and 1m at 2 yrs, the Grade 1 10f E P Taylor Stakes and a listed 1m event at Ascot and is a half-sister to 6 winners. (Cliveden Stud). "She was late in but she hasn't put a foot wrong and she's a lovely natured filly. Goes nicely and she'll probably be one for seven furlongs in mid-summer".

39. IMPACT POINT (JPN) ★★★★
b.c. Deep Impact – Rumba Boogie (Rainbow Quest). April 26. The dam is a half-sister to minor winners in the USA by Gulch and Deputy Minister. The second dam, Key Flyer (by Nijinsky), won the listed 8.5f Palisades Stakes on turf in the USA and is a sister to the Grade 2 Matchmaker Stakes winner Key Dancer and a half-sister to the dam of the champion Japanese 3-y-o's Dance Partner and Dance In The Dark. (Qatar Racing Ltd). *"He's had a little setback but we wouldn't be expecting to see him out before September anyway. He's a fine, athletic horse and it's a great privilege to have a Deep Impact to train. There are only a handful of Deep Impact two-year-olds in training in Europe so it'll be fascinating to see how they go as because the sire has done fantastically well and is the Galileo of Japan."*

40. INTIMATE ART ★★★
ch.c. Dutch Art – Intimacy (Teofilo). February 6. First foal. €90,000Y. Goffs Orby. Peter & Ross Doyle. The dam is an unraced half-sister to 5 winners including the Grade 1 10f E P Taylor Stakes and Group 2 10f Prix Jean Romanet winner Folk Opera. The second dam, Skiphall (by Halling), placed 5 times at 3 yrs in France, stayed 10.5f and is a half-sister to 7 winners including the 2-y-o listed winner Innocent Air and the French and US listed winner and US Grade 1 placed Skipping. (Thurloe Thoroughbreds XXXIV). *"He's had slightly open knees so we've had to take a bit of a rain check with him, but he's a good-bodied type that should be out in mid-summer".*

41. INVESTIGATION ★★★
gr.c. Rip Van Winkle – Syann (Daylami). February 10. Second foal. €30,000Y. Goffs Orby. Andrew Balding. The dam, a fairly useful Irish listed-placed 9f winner, is a half-sister to 7 winners. The second dam, Hedera (by Woodman), a quite useful 2-y-o 7f winner, is a half-sister to 6 winners. (Martin & Valerie Slade). *"A lovely, big, rangy horse with a big stride on him. I'm really pleased with him, he goes nicely upsides which is nice to see early on with a horse that's going to stay middle-distances. He'll take time but he goes alright".*

42. ISOMER ★★★★
ch.c. Cape Blanco – Nimue (Speightstown). February 1. Second foal. $52,000Y. Keeneland January. Not sold. The dam, a quite useful dual 7f winner at 3 and 4 yrs, is a half-sister to the US Grade 2 Peter Pan Stakes winner Go Rockin' Robin. The second dam, Flag Support (by Personal Flag), was unraced. (Mrs F H Hay). *"A smashing horse, he goes really nicely, is a good-looking type and has already shown decent ability. He should be ready for when the six furlong races start".*

43. KINGSTON TASMANIA ★★★
b.c. Kheleyf – Derartu (Last Tycoon). April 16. Half-brother to the fair dual 7f winner Kingston Acacia (by King Of Roses). The dam won over 7f and 1m in Australia. (Mr Richard Haines). *"He goes well and we had the half-sister who was a handy seven furlong filly. This colt goes nicely and I think he'll be fine for six furlongs in early June. The owner's father owned and bred the famous Australian horse Kingston Town, so he tends to name his horses after him".*

44. KNOW THE TRUTH
b.f. Lawman – Snow Key (Cozzene). March 24. Fifth foal. Half-sister to the fair 12f to 14.5f winner Paris Snow (by Montjeu). The dam, a French listed 9f winner of 4 races, was third in the Group 3 7f Prix de la Porte Maillot and is a half-sister to 8 winners including the US dual Grade 2 winner Powder Bowl. The second dam, Snowbowl (by Northjet), a US stakes-placed winner of 4 races, is a half-sister to 7 winners including Group 1 Prix de l'Abbaye winner Silver Fling. (George Strawbridge).

45. LEONTES ★★★
ch.c. Paco Boy – Robema (Cadeaux Genereux). March 8. Fifth foal. 33,000Y. Tattersalls December. Andrew Balding. Half-brother to the fairly useful 2-y-o 1m winner Atlantic Sun (by Roderic O'Connor). The dam, a quite useful 7m and 1m winner of 3 races, is a sister to the listed-placed winner Granted (the dam of two listed winners) and a half-sister to 4 winners including the US Grade 1 placed winner Lucky Chappy. The second dam, Germane (by Distant Relative), a useful winner of the Group 3 7f Rockfel Stakes and placed in two listed events, is a half-sister to 9 winners

including the very useful German dual listed Fabriano. (D E Brownlow). *"He looked a very sharp, early type but he's had a little setback. Hopefully that won't hold him back too long because he has a lot of speed and looks a proper 2-y-o sprinting type".*

46. LOOK MY WAY ★★
b.c. Pour Moi – Casual Glance (Sinndar). February 6. Fifth foal. Half-brother to Northern Outlook (by Selkirk), placed fourth over 1m from two starts at 2 yrs. The dam, a fairly useful 12f winner, is a half-sister to numerous winners including the very smart Group 2 1m Oettingen-Rennen and Group 3 8.5f Diomed Stakes winner Passing Glance, the smart Group 3 7f Prix de Palais-Royal and European Free Handicap winner Hidden Meadow, the smart listed 11f winner Scorned and the useful 6f (at 2 yrs) and listed 1m winner Kingsclere. The second dam, Spurned (by Robellino), a fairly useful 2-y-o 7f winner, later stayed 10f. (Kingsclere Racing Club). *"A nice type, he'll be out later in the summer and he goes nicely. It's a family we've had here for years and this is the best we've had out of the mare".*

47. MAGIC PASS ★★ ♠
ch.c. Raven's Pass – Magic America (High Yield). March 11. Fifth foal. Half-brother to the French dual 5f winner at 2 and 3 yrs and Group 3 second Sara Lucille (by Dansili). The dam, a 2-y-o Group 3 7f Prix Miesque winner and second in the Group 1 6f Prix Morny, is a half-sister to the US Grade 3 placed Psychic Income. The second dam, Shoofha (by Bluebird), is an unplaced sister to the Group 3 and US Grade 3 winner Delilah and a half-sister to 4 winners. (George Strawbridge). *See the comment on this colt in the Bloodstock Expert's section.*

48. MAKKADANDDANG ★★★
ch.c. Mastercraftsman – Penny Cross (Efisio). April 12. Seventh living foal. 25,000Y. Tattersalls October Book 2. Andrew Balding. Half-brother to the very useful 2-y-o 7f winner and Group 3 1m Autumn Stakes second Prompter (by Motivator), to the fairly useful 6f winner and multiple listed-placed Penny Drops (by Motivator) and the fair 10f to 14f and jumps winner Quinsman (by Singspiel). The dam, a useful 7f to 8.5f winner of 3 races, was listed placed twice and is a half-sister to 7 winners including the Group 2 Celebration Mile winner Priors Lodge. The second dam, Addaya (by Persian Bold), ran once unplaced and is a half-sister to 8 winners abroad. (Mr P Fox). *"I like the way he's going. We gelded him early because he was a bit cheeky but it seems to have done him good. He's done a couple of bits upsides and I would have thought he'd be one for seven furlongs around late June".*
TRAINERS' BARGAIN BUY

49. MANOLITO DE MADRID (GER) ★★★
b.c. Soldier Hollow – Molly Maxima (Big Shuffle). March 25. €52,000Y. Baden Baden. Richard Venn. Half-brother to the German listed 1m winner and Group 2 third Molly Le Clou (by Doyen). The dam is a German 1m placed sister to 4 winners including the German Group 3 1m winners Molly Art and Molly Max out of Molly Dancer (by Shareef Dancer). (Mr N M Watts). *"A colt we bought him in Germany, he's not the biggest but he has a very good way of going. Very neat and athletic, he certainly shows a bit of ability already. He'll have enough speed for seven furlongs in mid-summer and should stay further next year".*

50. MAX ZORIN (IRE) ★★★★
b.c. Cape Cross – My (King's Best). May 8. Sixth living foal. 37,000Y. Tattersalls October Book 2. Not sold. Half-brother to the quite useful 11f winner Keeping (by Teofilo). The dam is an unplaced half-sister to 4 winners including the very smart dual Group 3 12f winner Laaheb. The second dam, Maskunah (by Sadler's Wells), is an unraced half-sister to 6 winners including the high-class middle-distance horses and multiple Group 1 winners Warrsan and Luso, the Nell Gwyn Stakes winner Cloud Castle and the Group 2 Gallinule Stakes winner Needle Gun. (Chelsea Thoroughbreds). *"He goes nicely and he's done quite a bit of upsides work. I would have thought he'd want to start at six furlongs and he'll be getting a mile later on this year. Looks to have some ability".*

51. MEYANDI ★★★★
ch.c. Mount Nelson – Susi Wong (Selkirk). March 29. Tenth foal. 35,000Y. Tattersalls

October Book 2. Andrew Balding. Half-brother to 6 winners including the Group 3 St Simon Stakes and Group 3 13f Ormonde Stakes winner Buccellati (by Soviet Star), the Italian listed 2-y-o winner and Group 3 6f second Golden Stud (by In The Wings) and the Scandinavian listed winner La Petite Chinoise (by Dr Fong). The dam, a listed-placed 3-y-o winner in Germany, is a half-sister to 4 winners. The second dam, Stay That Way (by Be My Guest), is an unraced full or half-sister to 8 winners including the Coronation Stakes winner Chalon (dam of the dual Group 1 winner Creator). (Mick & Janice Mariscotti). *"He's a lovely horse and I'm so glad we bought him because I'm lucky enough to have trained his half-brother Buccellati. This is a very different type and has more scope to him – a little bit rangier as a physical model. He's done well since he came in and goes really nicely. I'm a fan of the sire but they don't tend to come early, so I'd expect this colt to be a July type 2-y-o".*

52. MUCHO APPLAUSE (IRE) ★★★
b.c. Acclamation – Pediment (Desert Prince). April 24. Fifth foal. €100,000Y. Goffs Orby. Andrew Balding. Half-brother to Impediment (by Pivotal), unplaced in two starts at 2 yrs in 2015 and to a minor 3-y-o winner in Italy by High Chaparral. The dam, a quite useful 11f winner, is a half-sister to 7 winners including the listed winners Portal and Ice Palace and the dam of the dual Group 2 winner Spacious. The second dam, White Palace (by Shirley Heights), a quite useful 3-y-o 8.2f winner, is a half-sister to one winner. (Transatlantic Racing). *"A big Acclamation colt, he's solid and with a fantastic temperament. He's done a couple of bits of work, goes nicely and although he's a bit backward in his coat at the moment I would have thought he'd be racing any time from mid-May onwards".*

53. NATIVE PROSPECT ★★★
ch.c. Bated Breath – Jakarta Jade (Royal Abjar). April 12. Seventh foal. 27,000Y. Tattersalls October Book 2. Andrew Balding. Half-brother to 4 winners including the fairly useful Irish 1m winner and Group 3 12f Noblesse Stakes third Jakarta Jazz (by Marju) and two minor 3-y-o winners in France by Dutch Art and Marju. The dam, a useful 9f (at 2 yrs), 1m and 12f winner, was listed-placed and is a half-sister to 6 winners including the dual Group 3 winner Dubai Prince. The second dam, Desert Frolic (by Persian Bold), a fairly useful 11f to 13f winner, is a half-sister to 6 winners including the Champion Stakes and dual US Grade 1 winner Storming Home. (Mick & Janice Mariscotti). *"A lovely horse with a great, big, long stride on him. He's done really well in the last month. I like the way he goes, he's the only Bated Breath I've got and it certainly wouldn't put me off buying another".*

54. NAVAL WARFARE (IRE) ★★★
b.c. Born To Sea – Three Days In May (Cadeaux Genereux). May 14. Sixth living foal. €105,000Y. Goffs Orby. David Redvers. Half-brother to the Group 2 Hungerford Stakes and Group 3 Diomed Stakes winner Gregorian, to the useful listed-placed 8.5f winner Manderley and the fairly useful 2-y-o 6f winner Kalam Daleel (all by Clodovil). The dam, a fair 3-y-o 6f winner, is a half-sister to 8 winners including the very useful Group 1 Cheveley Park Stakes second Crazee Mental - herself dam of the multiple Group 2 winner Premio Loco. The second dam, Corn Futures (by Nomination), a fair 2-y-o 6f winner, is a half-sister to 7 winners. (Qatar Racing Ltd). *"He was a late foal and he'll take a bit of time, but he has a good attitude and will be more of a late summer/early autumn project".*

55. NIGHT LAW ★★★ ♠
b.f. Lawman – Night Carnation (Sleeping Indian). March 14. First foal. The dam, a very useful winner of 5 races including the Group 3 5f Sandown Sprint Stakes, is a half-sister to 2 winners including the useful 1m winner Yeaman's Hall. The second dam, Rimba (by Dayjur), a fair 7f placed maiden, is closely related to the very useful 7f and 7.3f winner Rainald. (George Strawbridge). See Malcolm Bastard's comment on this filly in the Bloodstock Expert's section.

56. OPERA QUEEN ★★
b.f. Nathaniel – Opera Glass (Barathea). April 2. Half-sister to the very useful listed 10f and listed 12f winner Opera Gal (by Galileo), to the fair 12f winner Opera Lad (by Teofilo) and the modest 14f winner Opera Buff (by Oratorio). The dam, a quite useful 8.5f winner, is a sister

to the very smart 2-y-o Group 3 7f Solario Stakes winner and Group 1 Dewhurst Stakes third Opera Cape and a half-sister to the high-class stayer Grey Shot and the smart sprint winner of 4 races Night Shot. The second dam, Optaria (by Song), was a quite useful 2-y-o 5f winner. (J C Smith). *"A lovely, rangy type of filly, it's a pleasure to have her because we know the family well. One for the back-end of the season".*

57. ORSINO ★★

b.c. Galileo – Birmanie (Aldebaran). April 19. Fourth foal. 75,000Y. Tattersalls December. Andrew Balding. Closely related to the French 2-y-o dual 1m winner Aldar (by New Approach) and to a minor winner in France by Montjeu. The dam was placed at 3 yrs in France and is a half-sister to 3 winners including the multiple US Grade 1 winner English Channel and the US Grade 2 placed Sedgefield, and to the dam of the Group 2 Rockfel Stakes winner Lucida. The second dam, Belva (by Theatrical), is an unraced sister to the US Grade 1 winner Pharma and to the multiple US Grade 2 winner Hap and a half-sister to 5 winners. (D E Brownlow). *"A big Galileo, he was very weak and unfurnished when we bought him but he's done very well. He has a lovely way of going and although we won't be pressurising him to be a 2-y-o I'd be disappointed if he didn't have a couple of runs this year".*

58. PERFECT ANGEL (IRE) ★★

br.f. Dark Angel – The Hermitage (Kheleyf). March 13. Third foal. 17,000Y. Tattersalls October Book 2. Andrew Balding. Sister to the 2015 5f placed 2-y-o Lone Angel (from two starts) and to the fair 6f winner Where's Sue. The dam, a quite useful listed-placed 2-y-o 5f winner, is a half-sister to 9 winners including the listed winners and Group 1 placed Crown Of Light and Alboostan. The second dam, Russian Countess (by Nureyev), a useful French 2-y-o 1m winner, was listed-placed twice and is a half-sister to 5 winners. (Mildmay Racing & D H Caslon). *"She hasn't come in due to some temperament issues which I think they've now ironed out. I loved her as a yearling and thought she was a smashing type, so as long as we can channel her energies in the right direction you'd hope* she'd come good, especially as the sire can do little wrong".

59. POET'S VANITY ★★

b.f. Poet's Voice – Vanity (Thatching). February 10. Tenth foal. 200,000Y. Tattersalls October Book 1. Blandford Bloodstock. Half-sister to 5 winners including the Group 3 6f Ballyogan Stakes and dual listed winner and Group 1 second Lesson In Humility (by Mujadil), to the useful listed 1m winner Boastful (by Clodovil) and the quite useful 2-y-o 6f winner Sensasse (by Imperial Ballet). The dam, a fair 5f and 6f placed maiden, is a half-sister to 6 winners including the listed winner Ffestiniog (herself the dam of 3 stakes winners). The second dam, Penny Fan (by Nomination), placed once over 5f, is closely related to Rivers Rhapsody (listed 5f Scarbrough Stakes) and a half-sister to Regal Scintilla (Group 3 5f Prix d'Arenburg). (Mrs M E Wates). *"A fine, big, filly, she's just going through an awkward growing stage and she'll be a longer term project. I'd love her to be good because the Wates have been very loyal owners to us".*

60. SOUTH SEAS (IRE) ★★★★ ♠

ch.c. Lope De Vega – Let It Be Me (Mizzen Mast). March 19. First foal. 145,000Y. Tattersalls October Book 1. David Redvers. The dam is an unplaced half-sister to the listed Chesham Stakes winner and Singapore Group 1 second Zaidan. The second dam, Element Of Truth (by Atticus), a fairly useful 1m winner, was listed-placed and is a half-sister to 5 winners including the multiple Group 3 winner Ramooz and the Group 1 Fillies Mile third My Hansel. (Qatar Racing Ltd). *"The first Lope De Vega I've had, he's a grand horse, very straightforward and a lovely mover. He's done a few bits upsides and shows ability so he could be anything".*

61. STAG PARTY (IRE) ★★★

b.c. Thewayyouare – Betrothed (Oratorio). April 2. Second foal. €20,000Y. Tattersalls Ireland September. Andrew Balding. The dam, a quite useful Irish 1m winner, is a half-sister to 4 minor winners. The second dam, Ring The Relatives (by Bering), a fair 7f and 10f placed 3-y-o (from two starts), is a half-sister to the Irish listed winner and French Group 2 placed Just Special and to the listed winner

Blue Gold. (Living Legend Racing Partnership). *"He's done well physically since he came in but is just lacking a bit in mental maturity. I'm sure that'll come the more we do with him and I would have thought he'd be ready by June over seven furlongs".*

62. TORCELLO ★★★★
ch.c. Born To Sea – Islandagore (Indian Ridge). April 21. Tenth foal. 40,000Y. Tattersalls October Book 2. Andrew Balding. Half-brother to the fair 2015 2-y-o 7.5f winner Fool To Cry (by Fast Company), to the fairly useful 7f (at 2 yrs) to 10f winner of 5 races Island Sunset (by Trans Island), the listed-placed 6f (at 2 yrs) and 7f winner of 6 races Alice's Dancer, the 2-y-o 6f winner Iron Range, the Irish 2-y-o 7f winner Tintean (all by Clodovil) - all three quite useful, and the fair 2-y-o winners Right Ted and Toby's Dream (both by Mujadil). The dam, a listed-placed 7f winner, is a half-sister to the 2-y-o listed 6f winner Lady Of Kildare. The second dam, Dancing Sunset (by Red Sunset), winner of the Group 3 10f Royal Whip Stakes, is a full or half-sister to 5 winners. (Mick & Janice Mariscotti). *"He's a lovely horse and we're really pleased with him. Really athletic, we loved him as a yearling and he was probably our number one pick from Book Two at Tattersalls. By an exciting first-season sire in Born To Sea, he goes nicely but we won't be rushing him".*

63. WAR OF SUCCESSION ★★★★ ♠
b.c. Casamento – Rohlindi (Red Ransom). January 31. First foal. 85,000Y. Tattersalls October Book 2. David Redvers. The dam, a modest 5.5f placed maiden, is a half-sister to 8 winners including the useful 5f (at 2 yrs) and listed 7f winner Kalindi (herself the dam of 3 stakes winners), the useful 6f and 7f winners Mahmoom and Tayseer. The second dam, Rohita (by Waajib), a fairly useful 2-y-o 5f and 6f winner, was third in the Group 3 6f Cherry Hinton Stakes and is a half-sister to 5 winners. (Qatar Racing Ltd). *"He goes very well, he's done bits upsides and he's a solid, handsome horse who seems very unfussed by it all. I would think he'd be starting at six furlongs and we'll take it from there".*

64. WINE LIST ★★★★
ch.c. Champs Elysees – Masandra (Desert Prince). April 28. Fifth foal. 50,000Y. Tattersalls October Book 2. Andrew Balding. Half-brother to the fairly useful 10f to 12f winner Elbereth (by Mount Nelson) and to the modest 12f winner Masaadr (by Manduro). The dam is an unplaced half-sister to 2 winners. The second dam, Masawa (by Alzao), an Irish 3-y-o 1m winner, is a half-sister to the very useful Group 2 10f Gallinule Stakes winner Massyar, to the French 1m to 10f and subsequent Grade 3 1m Arcadia Stakes winner Madjaristan and the high-class broodmare Masskana (dam of the Group 1 winners Dank, Eagle Mountain and Sulk). (Another Bottle Register). *"A lovely horse with a good way of going but he's one for later on. I train his half-sister Elbereth who is quite useful. Champs Elysees is a decent stallion and it wouldn't surprise you if he got a really good horse or two and hopefully this colt will be one of them. I like the way he goes and he's a really nice horse".*

65. UNNAMED ★★★★
b.c. Mount Nelson – Carsulae (Marju). March 9. Second foal. 80,000Y. Tattersalls October Book 2. Rabbah Bloodstock. Half-brother to Strada Di Carsoli (by Showcasing), placed fourth over 7f in Ireland on his only start at 2 yrs in 2015. The dam is an unraced half-sister to 8 winners including the listed Cecil Frail Stakes winner Blhadawa. The second dam, Trois Heures Apres (by Soviet Star), is an unraced half-sister to 4 winners including the listed 10f winner and Oaks third Mezzogiorno (herself dam of the Group 2 Blandford Stakes winner Monturani). (Sheikh J D Al Maktoum). *"A smashing horse that goes very nicely. He's one of those middle-distance types who shows a bit of speed now, so he's one that I'd rate. A nice horse".*

66. UNNAMED ★★★
br.f. Kyllachy – Life Rely (Maria's Mon). April 2. Fifth foal. 100,000Y. Tattersalls October Book 2. Rabbah Bloodstock. Half-sister to the French winner of 8 races, including twice over 5.5f at 2 yrs, Wild Horse (by Kheleyf), to the fair 7f winner Saratoga Slew (by Footstepsinthesand) and the minor Italian winner of 6 races Alta Definizione (by Hawk Wing). The dam is an unraced half-sister to 3 winners including

the Group 1 Italian Oaks winner and Group 1 Moyglare Stud Stakes third Menhoubah. The second dam, Private Seductress (by Private Account), a US stakes-placed winner of 3 races, is a half-sister to 4 winners. (Sheikh J D Al Maktoum). *"She's a nice filly that's done a few bits and pieces upsides and I'm pretty happy with her. She's a good physical specimen and hopefully she'll be alright".*

67. UNNAMED ★★★
b.c. Lilbourne Lad – Make Amends (Indian Ridge). January 17. First living foal. 25,000Y. Rabbah Bloodstock. The dam, a modest winner of 6 races from 7f to 10f, is a half-sister to 3 winners. The second dam, Chill Seeking (by Theatrical), a fairly useful 10f winner, is a half-sister to 5 winners. (Sheikh J D Al Maktoum). *"A really good-looking type, we're just beginning to do a bit more with him. I'm pleased with the way he's going and he's a very handsome horse so hopefully be alright".*

68. UNNAMED ★★
b.f. Camacho – Passata (Polar Falcon). May 18. Ninth foal. 50,000Y. Tattersalls December. Rabbah Bloodstock. Half-sister to 6 winners including the champion German 2-y-o and Group 2 Criterium de Maisons-Laffitte winner Pomellato the French listed-placed Pom Pom Pom (both by Big Shuffle) and the Group 3 14f Italian St Leger winner Parivash (by Singspiel). The dam won once at 3 yrs in Germany and is a half-sister to 7 winners. The second dam, Premier Amour (by Salmon Leap), a German Group 3 11f winner and third in the Group 1 French Oaks, is a half-sister to 9 winners. (Sheikh J D Al Maktoum). *"She's a stocky, strong-looking filly that goes nicely and has a good attitude. She'll make a 2-y-o later on but she was a late foal so we'll be mindful of that".*

DAVID BARRON

69. BING BANG BANK (IRE)
br.c. Big Bad Bob – Causeway Charm (Giant's Causeway). April 4. Fifth foal. 55,000Y. Tattersalls October Book 2. KIR & Sackville/Donald. Brother to the fair 2015 2-y-o 1m winner D'Niro and half-brother to the fairly useful 2-y-o 6f and 7f winner and Group 3 Musidora Stakes second Lily Rules (by Aussie Rules). The dam is an unplaced half-sister to 6 winners including the German dual listed winner Chan Chan. The second dam, Candy Charm (by Capote), is an unraced half-sister to 7 winners. (Kangyu International Racing (HK) Ltd).

70. DIRCHILL (IRE)
b.c. Power – Bawaakeer (Kingmambo). March 21. Second foal. €48,000Y. Goffs Sportsmans. Harrowgate Bloodstock. The dam is an unraced half-sister to the French winner and dual Group 3 third Ipswich. The second dam, Imperial Beauty (by Imperial Ballet), winner of the Group 1 5f Prix de l'Abbaye and second in the Group 1 6f Cheveley Park Stakes, is a full or half-sister to 6 winners. (Elliot Brothers, Peacock & Partner).

71. GLORIOUS POLITICS
b.c. Delegator – Pelican Key (Mujadil). March 21. Fifth foal. 45,000Y. Tattersalls October Book 2. KIR & Sackville/Donald. Half-brother to the fairly useful 6f and 7f winner Shared Equity (by Elnadim), to the fair 2-y-o 6f winner Jumeirah Moon (by Kheleyf) and the moderate 6f winner Plum Bay (by Nayef). The dam, a quite useful 2-y-o 5f winner, is a half-sister to 2 winners including the dam of the Group 2 Superlative Stakes winner Birchwood. The second dam, Guana Bay (by Cadeaux Genereux), is an unraced sister to one winner and a half-sister to 5 winners including the Group 2 winners Prince Sabo and Millyant. (Kangyu International Racing (HK) Ltd).

72. HOTFILL
b.c. Showcasing – Reel Cool (Reel Buddy). March 11. Fifth foal. £46,000Y. Doncaster Premier. Harrowgate Bloodstock. Half-brother to the moderate 8.5f winner Ice Maiden (by Major Cadeaux). The dam is an unplaced half-sister to 5 winners including the useful 10f listed winner Maid Of Camelot. The second dam, Waterfowl Creek (by Be My Guest), a quite useful 3-y-o dual 1m winner, is a sister to the Group 1 Coronation Stakes third Guest Artiste, closely related to the Group 2 Child Stakes winner Inchmurrin (herself dam of the very smart colt Inchinor) and a half-sister to 6 winners including the 2-y-o Group 2 6f Mill Reef Stakes winner Welney. (Elliot Brothers, Peacock & Partner).

73. LIQUID (IRE)
ch.c. Zoffany – Playful Promises (Elnadim). April 13. Fourth foal. £40,000Y. Doncaster Silver. Harrowgate Bloodstock. The dam is an unplaced half-sister to one winner. The second dam, Playful (by Piccolo), a fairly useful 2-y-o dual 5f winner, was listed-placed and is a half-sister to 5 winners. (Mr R Hull).

74. WICK POWELL
b.c. Sakhee's Secret – London Welsh (Cape Cross). January 31. First foal. €32,000Y. Tattersalls Ireland September. Harrowgate Bloodstock. The dam ran once unplaced and is a half-sister to 3 minor winners. The second dam, Croeso Cariad (by Most Welcome), a very useful 2-y-o 5f and 7f Italian listed winner, was second in the Group 2 1m Falmouth Stakes and is a half-sister to 6 winners including the Irish listed winner and multiple Group 1 placed Mona Lisa. (Dr N J Barron).

75. UNNAMED
b.c. Compton Place – Beautiful Lady (Peintre Celebre). March 6. Fourth foal. £28,000Y. Tattersalls October Book 3. Harrowgate Bloodstock. Half-brother to the fair 2015 2-y-o 7f winner Outback Blue (by Aussie Reigns) and to the minor US 3-y-o winner Practising (by Rail Link). The dam, a winner, is a half-sister to 3 winners including the useful 1m (at 2 yrs) and 9f winner and Group 3 Dee Stakes second Putra Sas. The second dam, Puteri Wentworth (by Sadler's Wells), a quite useful 12f to 2m 4f winner, is a half-sister to 4 winners including the very smart dual listed 5f winner Watching. (Dr N J Barron).

76. UNNAMED
b.f. Bahamian Bounty – Hulcote Rose (Rock Of Gibraltar). April 18. Second foal. 22,000Y. Tattersalls October Book 3. Harrowgate Bloodstock. Half-sister to the quite useful 2016 3-y-o dual 7f winner Bear Faced (by Intikhab). The dam, a fair 6f (at 2 yrs) to 8.5f winner of 5 races, is a half-sister to 2 minor winners. The second dam, Siksikawa (by Mark Of Esteem), ran once unplaced and is a half-sister to 7 winners including the Group/Graded stakes winners Labeeb, Fanmore and Alrassaam. (Mr M J Rozenbroek).

77. UNNAMED
b.c. Equiano – Marine Girl (Shamardal). March 2. First foal. £28,000Y. Doncaster Silver. Harrowgate Bloodstock. The dam, a fair 8.5f winner, is a half-sister to 5 winners including the listed 12f winner and Group 2 12f Ribblesdale Stakes third Marani. The second dam, Aquamarine (by Shardari), won the listed Cheshire Oaks and is a half-sister to the St Leger winner Toulon. (All About York II & Partner).

78. UNNAMED
b.c. Kyllachy – Responsive (Dutch Art). February 11. First foal. £33,000Y. Doncaster Premier. Harrowgate Bloodstock. The dam, a quite useful 2-y-o 6f winner, is a half-sister to 6 winners. The second dam, Xtrasensory (by Royal Applause), a fairly useful 2-y-o 6f winner, is a half-sister to 7 winners. (Mr M J Rozenbroek).

RALPH BECKETT

79. ABOUTTIMEYOUTOLDME ★★★
ch.c. Mastercraftsman – Mary Boleyn (King's Best). April 24. Third foal. 42,000Y. Tattersalls October Book 2. A C Elliott. Half-brother to the quite useful 2015 2-y-o 7f winner Marylebone (by Shamardal) and to the fair 1m winner Clotilde (by Dubawi). The dam, a French listed 9f winner, is a half-sister to 4 winners including the fairly useful 6f winner of 5 races Kaldoun Kingdom. The second dam, Bint Kaldoun (by Kaldoun), a quite useful 7f (at 2 yrs) to 12f placed maiden, is a sister to the German listed sprint winner Shy Lady (herself dam of the St James's Palace Stakes winner Zafeen) and a half-sister to 6 winners. (Black, Morecombe, Roberts & Anderson).
"The pedigree has taken an upturn since I bought him because the dam has bred two winners. He's a nice horse that's going to need time as his pedigree suggests, but we like him. He'll want seven furlongs to a mile from late July onwards I should think".

80. ALBIZZIA ★★
b.f. Archipenko – Altitude (Green Desert). April 21. Fourth foal. 90,000Y. Tattersalls October Book 2. Not sold. McKeever Bloodstock. Half-sister to the fair 1m winner Alegra (by Galileo). The dam, a fair 12f winner, is a half-sister to 8 winners including the Group 1

winners Alborada and Albanova. The second dam, Alouette (by Darshaan), a useful 1m (at 2 yrs) and listed 12f winner, is a sister to the listed winner Arrikala and a half-sister to the Nassau Stakes and Sun Chariot Stakes winner Last Second (dam of the French 2,000 Guineas winner Aussie Rules), the Doncaster Cup winner Alleluia (dam of the Prix Royal-Oak winner Allegretto) and the placed dam of the Group 1 winners Quarter Moon and Yesterday. (Miss K Rausing). *"A lovely, straightforward filly, she's training well and although it'll be a while before we step her up, we like her. One for seven furlongs plus later in the year".*

81. AMABILIS ★★★
b.f. Champs Elysees – Pure Joy (Zamindar). April 6. Half-sister to the quite useful 2-y-o dual 5f winner Escalating (by Three Valleys). The dam, a French 2-y-o listed 5f placed maiden, is a half-sister to 5 winners including the Group 1 Prix Jean Prat winner Mutual Trust. The second dam, Posteritas (by Lear Fan), a fairly useful listed 10f winner, is a half-sister to 7 winners. (Khalid Abdulla). *"A lovely filly, she'll improve as the year goes on. The dam bred a quick horse in Escalating but I'm conscious that Champs Elysees will add a bit more stamina".*

82. AUREANA ★★★
b.f. Kyllachy – Going For Gold (Barathea). April 19. Third foal. 9,500Y. Tattersalls October Book 3. Not sold. Half-sister to the quite useful 2015 2-y-o 1m winner Chicadoro (by Paco Boy). The dam, a fair 12f winner, is a half-sister to 4 winners. The second dam, Flash Of Gold (by Darshaan), a fair 12f placed maiden, is a half-sister to 5 winners including the smart Group 2 12f Ribblesdale Stakes and Group 2 13.3f Geoffrey Freer Stakes winner Phantom Gold. (James Ortega). *"She's a bit more forward than her half-sister Chicadoro who took a while to come to hand, although she did win as a 2-y-o. This is an athletic, good-moving filly and although she's a mid-April foal I can see her coming to hand by June time".*

83. BEACH BREAK ★★★
b.c. Cacique – Wemyss Bay (Sadler's Wells). February 25. Fourth foal. The dam is an unraced sister to the 1m (at 2 yrs) and Group 1 10f Grand Prix de Paris winner Beat Hollow and a half-sister to 3 winners including the US Grade 3 winner Yaralino. The second dam, Wemyss Bight (by Dancing Brave), a very smart filly, won 5 races including the Group 1 12f Irish Oaks and the Group 2 12f Prix de Malleret. (Khalid Abdulla). *"He's not a big horse, he's quite close-coupled and I think he'll come to hand over seven furlongs and a mile later in the year. He'll be a nice horse".*

84. BUTTERFLY LILY ★★★
gr.f. Lawman – Bruxcalina (Linamix). February 16. Third foal. 40,000Y. Tattersalls October Book 2. Not sold. Half-sister to the fairly useful 1m and 10f winner Librisa Breeze (by Mount Nelson). The dam, a winner over 10f in France and listed-placed over 11f, is a half-sister to 6 winners including the Group 3 Prix La Force winner and French Derby third Baraan. The second dam, Brusca (by Grindstone), won 3 minor races at 3 and 4 yrs in the USA and is a half-sister to 6 winners including the US dual Grade 3 winner and Grade 1 placed Somali Lemonade. (Newsells Park Stud). *"She was a filly I liked very much at the sales, so I was delighted when they sent her to us. Obviously with Lawman and Linamix there it's a real fillies' pedigree, so I'm hoping she'll turn into a nice filly but it will be later in the year over seven furlongs and a mile".*

85. CHARITY ★★
b.br.f. Azamour – Feis Ceoil (Key Of Luck). March 31. Second foal. Half-sister to the modest 2015 6f placed 2-y-o Atrayu (by Jeremy). The dam, a fair 7f winner, is a half-sister to 7 winners including the French Group winners Stretarez and Street Shaana. The second dam, Street Opera (by Sadler's Wells), a minor Irish 14f winner, is a half-sister to 10 winners including the Group winners Grape Tree Road, Red Route and Windsor Castle. (R Allcock). *"She's not a big filly, she hasn't been here long but she's settled in nicely and we like her. She'll want ten furlongs next year and we'll be training her with that in mind".*

86. DANDY ROLL ★★★★
b.c. Dandy Man – Soranna (Compton Place). April 10. Fourth foal. €60,000Y. Tattersalls Ireland September. Kern/Lillingston. The dam, a fair Irish 6f (at 2 yrs) and 1m winner, is a half-

sister to 7 minor winners. The second dam, White-Wash (by Final Straw), a quite useful 1m and 10f winner, is a half-sister to 3 winners. (Kennet Valley Thoroughbreds III). *"A strong little fella, he'll be racing by late April or early May. He's a strong, forward going type with a good attitude"*.

87. DR JULIUS NO ★★★
b.c. Dick Turpin – Royal Assent (Royal Applause). January 15. Third foal. £30,000Y. Doncaster Premier. A C Elliott. Half-brother to the moderate 2015 7.5f fourth placed 2-y-o Outback Princess (by Aussie Rules) and to the fair 2-y-o 8.5f winner Royal Altitude (by Zamindar). The dam, placed fourth over 1m at 3 yrs on her only start, is a sister to the useful 6f (at 2 yrs) and 1m winner Royal Warrant and a half-sister to 7 winners including the useful Banknote, a listed 1m winner of 7 races from 7f to 1m. The second dam, Brand (by Shareef Dancer), is an unraced half-sister to 6 winners. (Chelsea Thoroughbreds). *"A forward-going sort of horse and a January foal, we'll be looking to get on with him for his syndicate owners. He'll be racing sooner rather than later"*.

88. FEARSOME ★★
b.c. Makfi – Lixian (Linamix). March 13. Seventh living foal. €70,000Y. Arqana Deauville August. David Redvers. Half-brother to the French dual 3-y-o winner and listed-placed Bit By Bit (by Rail Link) and to the modest 1m winner Tomintoul Star (by Dansili). The dam, placed at 2 and 3 yrs in France, is a half-sister to 2 winners. The second dam, New Abbey (by Sadler's Wells), a useful 11.6f and 12f winner, was second in the Group 3 12f Princess Royal Stakes and is a half-sister to the Irish Oaks winner Wemyss Bight. (Qatar Racing Ltd). *"Quite a lengthy sort of colt with a big stride, he won't come to hand for a while and he'll get a mile no problem but we like him"*.

89. FOR THE ROSES ★★★
b.f. Nathaniel – Ivory Rose (Green Desert). February 11. First foal. €175,000Y. Arqana Deauville August. David Redvers. The dam, placed twice at 3 yrs in France, is a half-sister to one winner. The second dam, Bal De La Rose (Cadeaux Genereux), won 4 races at 2 and 3 yrs in France including a Group 3 event in Lyon and is a half-sister to the French 2,000 Guineas and French Derby winner Lope De Vega. (Qatar Racing Ltd). *"Not a big filly, but she's strong. She'll take some time but I can see her doing well in the second half of the year over seven furlongs and a mile"*.

90. HARAKA (IRE) ★★
b.f. Fastnet Rock – Luna Wells (Sadler's Wells). April 17. Eleventh foal. 50,000Y. Tattersalls October Book 1. Not sold. Half-sister to 7 winners including the smart 2-y-o 6f and UAE Group 3 winner and Group 2 7f Challenge Stakes second Cat Junior, the listed-placed 2-y-o 6f winner The Wild Swan (both by Storm Cat) and the French 2-y-o 7f winners Racingisdreaming (by Fusaichi Pegasus) and Tierra Luna (by Giant's Causeway). The dam won the Group 1 10f Prix Saint-Alary, the Group 3 10f Prix de la Nonette and the Group 3 9.3f Prix Vanteaux and is a half-sister to the French 2,000 Guineas winner Linamix, the Group 2 Grand Prix d'Evry winner Long Mick and the smart broodmare Luna Blue. The second dam, Lunadix (by Breton), won over 6f and 1m. (Andy Smith and Friends). *"The dam is quite old now but this filly is strong enough and I wouldn't say she's backward, but she's one for seven furlongs or a mile later in the year*.

91. HERE AND NOW ★★★
b.c. Dansili – Look Here (Hernando). April 18. Third foal. Half-brother to the fair 2016 3-y-o 10.5f winner Hereawi (by Dubawi). The dam, a 7f (at 2 yrs) and Group 1 Epsom Oaks winner, is a half-sister to numerous winners. The second dam, Last Look (by Rainbow Quest), is an unraced half-sister to two minor winners. (J H Richmond-Watson). *"His sister Hereawi won last week so that cheered us all up because it's a family close to all of us. This colt is a really lovely horse and he's got a bit more scope than either of the dam's first two foals. We've got a bit to look forward to over seven furlongs and a mile in the autumn"*.

92. INCONCEIVABLE (IRE) ★★★
b.f. Galileo – Mohican Princess (Shirley Heights). January 28. Eleventh foal. 400,000Y. Tattersalls October Book 1. China Horse Club. Sister to 3 winners including the listed 12f and listed 2m winner Eye Of The Storm and

the fairly useful triple 12f winner Livia Galilei and half-sister to 5 winners including the Group 3 6f Sirenia Stakes and Group 3 1m Joel Stakes winner Satchem (by Inchinor) and the useful 2-y-o 6f winner and Group 2 7f second Oui Say Oui (by Royal Applause). The dam, fourth over 10f, is a half-sister to 5 winners. The second dam, Mohican Girl (by Dancing Brave), a dual listed 10f winner, is a half-sister to the Yorkshire Oaks winners Untold and Sally Brown. (China Horse Club). *"It's a staying pedigree and we'll train her with that in mind, but she's not a big filly and there's plenty of strength about her, so I hope she'll appear in the second half of the year. Looks a nice filly".*

93. MANNERS MAKETH MAN (IRE) ★★★
b.c. Lope De Vega – Dabawiyah (Intikhab). February 18. Fifth foal. €50,000Y. Goffs Orby. A C Elliott. Half-brother to the modest 2-y-o 7f winner Absolutely Right (by Teofilo). The dam, placed once over 10f, is a half-sister to 7 winners including the Group 3 12f Gordon Stakes winner Rabah and the useful 2-y-o 6f winner and Group 1 Cheveley Park Stakes third Najiya. The second dam, The Perfect Life (by Try My Best), won the Group 3 5f Prix du Bois, was second in the Group 2 Prix Robert Papin and is a sister to Last Tycoon (Breeders' Cup Mile, King's Stand Stakes and William Hill Sprint Championship) and a half-sister to the dams of the Group 1 winners Immortal Verse, Sense Of Style and Valentine Waltz. (R Roberts). *"A great big horse with a plain head which I think is the sire's influence. He has a lovely way about him, he's a good walker and I bought him on spec but it didn't take me long to sell him because he's a nice horse. Seven furlongs later in the year will suit him".*

94. MISTRESS QUICKLY (IRE) ★★★ ♠
b.f. Mastercraftsman – In My Life (Rainbow Quest). February 13. Fifth foal. 110,000Y. Tattersalls October Book 2. A C Elliott. Half-sister to the very useful 9f winner and listed-placed Fighter Boy (by Rock Of Gibraltar), to the fairly useful 7f (at 2 yrs) and 12f winner and Group 2 Park Hill Stakes third Alta Lilea, the fair 11.5f winner Time Of My Life (both by Galileo) and the fair 11f to 13f winner Jeu De Vivre (by Montjeu). The dam, placed once at 3 yrs in Japan, is a sister to the 2-y-o Group 1 10f Criterium de Saint-Cloud winner Special Quest and a half-sister to 9 winners including the 2-y-o Group 2 7f Criterium de Maisons-Laffitte winner Moiava. The second dam, Mona Stella (by Nureyev), won the Group 2 9.2f Prix de l'Opera and is closely related to the French 1,000 Guineas and Prix Vermeille winner Dancing Maid. (Mrs M E Slade). *"A big, scopey filly like a lot by her sire but she has a good way of going. She'll want seven furlongs or a mile later in the year".*

95. MUNRO ★★★★
b.c. Kyllachy – Meddle (Diktat). March 21. Sixth foal. 35,000Y. Tattersalls October Book 3. Charlie Gordon-Watson. Brother to the fair 2-y-o dual 6f winner Anastazia and half-brother to the fair 6f (at 2 yrs) to 1m winner of 7 races Darnathean (by Librettist), the modest 9.5f and 11.5f winner Little Jazz (by Doyen) and the moderate 9f and 10f winner Entrapping (by Tiger Hill). The dam is an unplaced half-sister to 4 winners including the Group 3 6.3f Anglesey Stakes winner Pan Jammer. The second dam, Ingerence (by Akarad), was placed three times in France and is a half-sister to 6 winners including the Group 3 10.5f Prix Penelope winner La Monalisa. (Emma Capon & Mrs Simon March). *"A good-looking horse, I should imagine he stood out at the Book 3 sales because he's got a bit about him. Plenty of size, he's a strong horse and I would hope he'll be appearing over six furlongs in the middle of the year. I like him".*

96. NOBLE BALLAD ★★★
b.c. Royal Applause – Melody Maker (Diktat). May 3. Half-brother to the fair 2015 2-y-o 6f winner, on her only start, Nassuvian Pearl (by Bahamian Bounty), to the quite useful 7f (including at 2 yrs) and 1m winner of 7 races Haaf A Sixpence (by Haafhd) and the fair 7f (at 2 yrs) and 1m winners Hard To Handel (by Stimulation) and Starlight Serenade (by Three Valleys). The dam, unplaced in two starts, is a half-sister to several minor winners. The second dam, First Musical (by First Trump), a fairly useful winner of 4 races from 5f to 6f at 2 yrs and second in the listed Firth Of Clyde Stakes, is a half-sister to 5 winners. (Melody Racing). *"From a family we know well, I've trained every one out of the mare and they've all done well. He's a strong little horse but he's*

a late foal and we're going to look after him for a bit. Although everything out of the mare wins at two it's always in the second half of the year. This colt is going to be a six furlong 2-y-o".

97. PEACE TERMS ★★★★ ♠
b.f. Teofilo – Intapeace (Intikhab). March 7. Second foal. 70,000Y. Tattersalls October Book 2. David Redvers. Half-sister to the quite useful 2015 2-y-o 7f winner Gift Wrap (by Raven's Pass). The dam, fairly useful listed-placed Irish 6f (at 2 yrs) and 7f winner, is a sister to the smart Group 3 winning sprinter and 2-y-o Group 2 placed Hoh Mike and a half-sister to 6 winners. The second dam, Magical Peace (by Magical Wonder), a quite useful Irish 6f winner, is a half-sister to one winner. (Qatar Racing Ltd). *"A lovely filly, it's a fast pedigree on the dam's side but she's just grown of late and we're just holding on to her. She has her own opinions but I believe that's typical of the family and we like her. Six/seven furlongs will suit her a bit later on".*

98. PIAFFE (USA) ★★
b.f. Successful Appeal – Palisade (Gone West). May 10. Half-sister to the Hong Kong Grade 1 1m winner Giant Treasure, to the US Grade 3 7f and Grade 3 1m winner and Grade 1 Santa Monica Handicap second Jibboom (both by Mizzen Mast), the useful 7f and 1m winner (including at 2 yrs) Self Evident (by Known Fact), the quite useful 12f winner Action Front (by Aptitude) and a jumps winner by With Approval. The dam, a quite useful 2-y-o 7f winner, is a half-sister to the useful 3-y-o 1m winner Emplane and to the useful 2-y-o 1m winner Boatman. The second dam, Peplum (by Nijinsky), a useful winner of the listed Cheshire Oaks, is a half-sister to the top class filly Al Bahathri, winner of the 1,000 Guineas and the Coronation Stakes. (Khalid Abdulla). *"A nice filly, but she was a late foal so she's going to need a bit of time. She's got a bit of size and scope and we'll find out in the fullness of time where we are with her".* The sire does well with his 2-y-o winners in the USA and his best winners to date include the US Grade 1 9f turf winner Her Emmynency, the US 2-y-o Grade 1 7f winners Appealing Zophie and J.P's Gusto, and the multiple Graded stakes winner Successful Dan.

99. PLEASELETMEWIN (IRE) ★★★ ♠
b.c. Power – Jacaranda Ridge (Indian Ridge). April 4. Fifth foal. £36,000Y. Doncaster Silver. A C Elliott. Half-brother to the quite useful 2-y-o dual 6f winner Silver Ridge (by Verglas) and to a minor winner in Qatar by Intikhab. The dam, a quite useful 7f winner, is a half-sister to 4 winners including the very smart Group 1 12f Gran Premio del Jockey Club and listed 10f winner Rainbow Peak and the smart 7f (at 2 yrs) and 1m listed winner Celtic Heroine. The second dam, Celtic Fling (by Lion Cavern), a fair 3-y-o 8.3f winner, is a half-sister to the champion 2-y-o Celtic Swing, winner of the French Derby and the Racing Post Trophy. (R Roberts). *"A lovely horse, I trained his half-brother Silver Ridge who did well for us. This is a nicer colt, he has more size and scope and I can see him making a 2-y-o".*

100. POWER SURGE (IRE) ★★★
ch.g. Power – Silver Skates (Slip Anchor). May 6. Seventh foal. €50,000Y. Goffs Orby. A C Elliott. Half-brother to 3 winners including the fairly useful 2-y-o 7.5f winner and Group 3 Chester Vase second Icon Dream (by Sadler's Wells), the quite useful 10.5f winner Jessie Jane (by Dylan Thomas) and the fair triple 7f winner Striker Torres (by Danehill Dancer) and to the unraced daughter of the Group 1 Phoenix Stakes winner La Collina. The dam is a placed half-sister to 8 winners including the Group 2 Derrinstown Derby Trial winner Fracas. The second dam, Klarifi (by Habitat), a listed 7f winner, is a full or half-sister to 7 winners including the dam of the Irish Oaks winner Wemyss Bight. (The Outlaws). *"We had to geld him to stop him misbehaving. His pedigree suggests he'll need a bit of time but he goes well, he moves well and just has to fill his frame".*

101. REALLY SUPER ★★★
b.f. Cacique – Sensationally (Montjeu). April 18. Third foal. Half-sister to the modest 2015 2-y-o 1m winner Senza Una Donna (by Sir Percy) and to the fairly useful 1m winner of 4 races at 2 and 3 yrs Greatest Journey (by Raven's Pass). The dam, a fair 9f winner, is a half-sister to the US Grade 2 winner Sun Boat. The second dam, One So Wonderful (by Nashwan), won the Group 1 Juddmonte International and is a half-sister to 8 winners

including the Group 2 Dante Stakes winner Alnasr Alwasheek. (Helena Springfield Ltd). *"I trained the dam and this filly has more strength than she had. The dam was quite narrow whereas this filly has a bit more substance to her. I can see her turning into a nice 3-y-o, so I would imagine that this year she'll have one or two runs at the back-end".*

102. REIGN ON ★★★★
ch.c. Equiano – Queens Jubilee (Cayman Kai). March 8. Eighth foal. £32,000Y. Doncaster Premier. A C Elliott. Half-brother to 5 winners including the fair 2015 2-y-o 6f winner Prince Hellvelyn (by Hellvelyn), the fairly useful 6f (at 2 yrs) to 8.5f winner of 5 races Yourartisonfire, the fair dual 5f winner (including at 2 yrs) Almond Branches (both by Dutch Art), the quite useful 5f and 6f winner at 2 to 4 yrs Rural Celebration (by Pastoral Pursuits) and the fair 7f and 1m winner Fibs And Flannel (by Tobougg). The dam, a modest 2-y-o 6f winner, is a half-sister to two listed winners. The second dam, Miss Mercy (by Law Society), was a modest 2-y-o 6f winner. (What Asham Partnership). *"We'll be pressing on with him and he'll be running in April or at the latest in May. A strong little horse, he'll be a five/six furlong 2-y-o for sure".*

103. RISTRETTO (USA) ★★★★
br.f. Medaglia D'Oro – Visit (Oasis Dream). April 14. The dam, winner of the Group 3 6f Princess Margaret Stakes and the Group 3 7f Oak Tree Stakes, was placed in several Group/Grade 1 events here and in the USA and is a half-sister to the very smart Group 1 10f Pretty Polly Stakes winner Promising Lead. The second dam, Arrive (by Kahyasi), a very useful 10f (at 2 yrs) and listed 13.8f winner, is a half-sister to the 2-y-o 5f winner (stayed 1m) Hasili (herself dam of the top-class performers Banks Hill, Heat Haze, Cacique, Intercontinental, Champs Elysees and Dansili). (Khalid Abdulla). *"A very nice filly, she's not very big but I believe the dam wasn't either. I'm hopeful she'll make a 2-y-o around six furlongs in mid-summer and she'll probably get further as well".*

104. SECRET SOUL ★★★★★
b.f. Street Cry – Shastye (Danehill). February 17. Seventh foal. 800,000Y. Tattersalls October Book 1. Charlie Gordon-Watson. Half-sister

to the Group 2 10.5f Middleton Stakes and dual listed winner and Group 1 Oaks second Secret Gesture, to the smart 7f winner Sir Isaac Newton (both by Galileo) and a winner in Australia by Medicean. The dam, a useful listed-placed 12f and 13f winner, is a half-sister to 8 winners including Sagamix (Prix de l'Arc de Triomphe), Sagacity (Group 1 Criterium de Saint-Cloud) and the Group 2 Prix de Malleret winner Sage Et Jolie (dam of the Group 1 winner Sageburg). The second dam, Saganeca (by Sagace), won the Group 3 12.5f Prix de Royallieu and was second in the Group 1 Gran Premio di Milano. (Newsells Park Stud). *"Obviously an expensive filly and the sister to a good filly as we know. There's a lot more substance to her than Secret Gesture who was very light-framed. This filly has a lot more strength about her. She'll make a 2-y-o in the second half of the season over seven furlongs and a mile and I like her very much".*

105. SHOZITA ★★★★♠
b.f. Showcasing – Azita (Tiger Hill). April 27. First foal. 85,000Y. Tattersalls October Book 1. Will Edmeades. The dam is an unraced half-sister to the very smart Group 3 Huxley Stakes winner of 6 races at around 10f Danadana. The second dam, Zeeba (by Barathea), a fair 12f winner, is a sister to the useful listed 14f winner Lost Soldier Three and a half-sister to 7 winners. (Thurloe Thoroughbreds XXXVIII). *"With Showcasing as the sire you'd think we'd be cracking on, but she's a May foal and she's grown plenty of late. So we're giving her a bit of time. She's a filly I like a lot, she's got a bit about her and she'll make a 2-y-o in the second half of the season, over six furlongs I hope".*

106. SINGING SANDS ★★★
b.f. Harbour Watch – Elektra Marino (Mount Nelson). March 29. First foal. €40,000Y. Tattersalls Ireland September. David Redvers. The dam is an unraced half-sister to 6 winners including the dual Group 1 King's Stand Stakes winner and sire Equiano and the useful listed 7f winner Evita Peron. The second dam, Entente Cordiale (by Ela-Mana-Mou), placed third once over 12f from 3 starts, is a half-sister to 4 winners. (Qatar Racing Ltd). *"She was quite plain but she's grown on me of late. There's a bit of size to her, she's tall, a good-moving filly with a bit of scope and I think*

she'll make a 2-y-o at some point. So we'll be getting on with her before long".

107. SOUND BAR ★★★★
b.c. Oasis Dream – Milford Sound (Baratheon). February 13. Half-brother to the 2015 2-y-o 1m winner from two starts Carntop, to the 10.5f (in France) and hurdles winner Quebec (both by Dansili) and the quite useful 9.5f winner Mitre Peak (by Shamardal). The dam, a fair French 1m winner, is a half-sister to 7 winners including the Prix de l'Arc de Triomphe and Grand Prix de Paris winner Rail Link, the French Group 2 12f and dual Group 3 10f winner Crossharbour and the smart French 1m and 10f performer Chelsea Manor. The second dam, Docklands (by Theatrical), a French 1m and 10f performer, is a half-sister to the smart performer at up to 9f Wharf. (Khalid Abdulla). *"A half-brother to Carntop who we have here and we like, this horse is a bit more forward looking, but I'm conscious that the dam is a sister to Rail Link and that they get better with time. So I would imagine that he'll be a seven furlong/mile horse later in the year. He's a lovely horse".*

108. SPEED FREAK ★★★★
b.f. Fastnet Rock – The Thrill Is Gone (Bahamian Bounty). February 16. First foal. £55,000Y. Doncaster Premier. David Redvers. The dam, a fairly useful 2-y-o 5f winner, was listed-placed three times and is a half-sister to 8 winners including the very useful 2-y-o dual Group 3 5f winner Bungleinthejungle, the listed winners Muarrab and Waveband and the Group-placed Group Therapy and Classic Encounter. The second dam, Licence To Thrill (Wolfhound), a quite useful dual 5f winner, is a half-sister to 4 winners including the useful 2-y-o 5f winner Master Of Passion. (Qatar Racing Ltd). *"The dam was very quick and this filly looks like she may be too. She's forward, not a big filly but well-developed and strong. We'll be cracking on with her shortly".*

109. SUBATOMIC ★★★
gr.f. Makfi – Miss Universe (Warning). April 8. Eleventh living foal. 110,000Y. Tattersalls October Book 1. David Redvers. Half-brother to 8 winners including the dual listed 1m winner Donativum, the useful 2-y-o 7f winner Tasdeed (both by Cadeaux Genereux), the 2-y-o 8.6f and subsequent US Grade 2 winner Worldly (by Selkirk), the Italian listed 1m winner Nice Danon (by Sakhee), the fairly useful 8.3f, 10f and hurdles winner Day To Remember (by Daylami) and the quite useful listed placed 2-y-o 1m winner Comeback Queen (by Nayef). The dam, a useful 2-y-o 6f winner and third in the Group 3 Solario Stakes, is a half-sister to 5 winners. The second dam, Reine d'Beaute (by Caerleon), a fairly useful 1m and 9f winner, is a half-sister to 8 winners. (Qatar Racing Ltd). *"Not a big filly but a strong one, she's a 'butty' sort and I hope she won't take that long. The Makfi's are hardy, workmanlike sorts and she's in that mould. A mid-season type for seven furlongs".*

110. SYNDICATE ★★★
b.f. Dansili – Indication (Sadler's Wells). March 14. Sister to the very useful listed 9f winner and Group 2 placed Stipulate. The dam, a fair 9.5f winner, is a half-sister to 4 winners including the Group 3 7f Supreme Stakes winner Stronghold and the listed winner Take The Hint. The second dam, Insinuate (by Mr Prospector), a useful listed 1m winner, is a half-sister to numerous winners including the useful 6f and 7f winner and listed-placed Imroz. (Khalid Abdulla). *"A full sister to Stipulate, she's a lovely filly who will want some time and no doubt seven furlongs to a mile later in the year. She's got a good way of going, is very straightforward and has a lovely action".*

111. TROPICAL ROCK ★★★★
b.f. Fastnet Rock – Tropical Treat (Bahamian Bounty). April 11. Half-sister to the 2016 dual 6f placed 3-y-o Steam Ahead (by Dream Ahead). The dam, a useful 2-y-o 5f and 3-y-o listed 5f winner, was second in the Group 3 6f Summer Stakes and is a half-sister to 2 winners. The second dam, Notjustaprettyface (by Red Ransom), a fairly useful 2-y-o 5f winner, was listed-placed twice and fourth in the Group 2 Lowther Stakes and is a half-sister to a winner in the UAE. (J C Smith). *"I think I'm right in saying that the dam was the first winner I trained for Jeff Smith. This is a lovely filly, I'd be confident she'd make a 2-y-o at around six furlongs and she may even be quick enough for five considering her mother was a listed winner over that trip. So she's a nice filly and we like her very much".*

112. WARM WORDS ★★★
b.f. Poet's Voice – Limber Up (Dansili). January 22. Second foal. 55,000Y. Tattersalls October Book 2. A C Elliott. Half-sister to the quite useful 2015 2-y-o 6f winner Rasheeq (by Vale Of York). The dam is an unraced half-sister to 5 winners including the listed 1m and listed 10f winner and Group 1 Nassau Stakes third Moneycantbuymelove. The second dam, Sabreon (by Caerleon), a quite useful 10.2f winner, is a half-sister to 7 winners including the French 2,000 Guineas and US Grade 1 winner Landseer and the listed winner and Group 1 placed Ikhtyar. (Warm Words Partnership). *"Poet's Voice didn't have many 2-y-o winners last year but the dam bred a fast 2-y-o by Vale Of York, so I'm hoping this filly will make a 2-y-o. She was bought with that in mind, she looks a 2-y-o type and we'll be cracking on with her shortly. A January foal, she'll be a six furlong type and will get seven later in the year".*

113. WHAT A BOY ★★★
b.c. Paco Boy – Kurtanella (Pastoral Pursuits). April 13. Third foal. £11,000 2-y-o. Tattersalls Ireland Ascot February. Not sold. Brother to the fair 2015 2-y-o 5f winner Another Boy. The dam, a quite useful 2-y-o 5f and 6f winner, is a half-sister to one winner. The second dam, Aconite (by Primo Dominie), is an unplaced half-sister to 7 winners including the Group-placed 2-y-o's Lake Pleasant and Power Lake. (Mrs P Snow & Partners). *"His brother Another Boy won for us early on last year and this is a nicer horse with a bit more size and scope. He should be ready to run in May and six furlongs will be his game, certainly initially. He should win as a 2-y-o".* **TRAINERS' BARGAIN BUY**

114. UNNAMED ★★★
ch.f. Lope De Vega – Fairnilee (Selkirk). April 26. Sixth foal. €60,000Y. Goffs Orby. Not sold. Half-sister to the quite useful 7f (including at 2 yrs) and 1m winner George Cinq (by Pastoral Pursuits) and to the moderate 14f winner Sweet Fernando (by Hernando). The dam, a modest 6f winner, is a half-sister to 2 winners. The second dam, Fantastic Belle (by Night Shift), a quite useful 6f winner, is a sister to the Canadian Grade 2 winner Moon Solitaire and a half-sister to 9 winners including the Group 3 10f Gordon Richards Stakes winner Germano. (Clipper Logistics). *"A lovely filly. A lot by this sire can be big and plain but she isn't. I wouldn't say she was particularly forward but she's lovely and we'll see her out around July or August time".*

115. UNNAMED ★★★★
b.f. Galileo – Louvain (Sinndar). April 25. Half-sister to the Grade 1 Breeders' Cup Juvenile Fillies' Turf and Group 1 French 1,000 Guineas winner Flotilla (by Mizzen Mast), to the fairly useful 10f winner of 3 races Marshgate Lane (by Medaglia D'Oro) and a minor French 3-y-o winner by Maria's Mon. The dam won at 2 yrs in France and 6 races in the USA including the Grade 3 Miesque Stakes and is a half-sister to 6 winners including the listed winner Laajooj. The second dam, Flanders (by Common Grounds), a very useful sprint winner of 6 races including the listed Scarbrough Stakes, was second in the Group 2 King's Stand Stakes and is a half-sister to 7 winners. (Sheikh Mohammed bin Khalifa Al Thani). *"Not a big filly, but she's sweet and a sister to a decent 2-y-o in Flotilla. I hope she'll make a decent 2-y-o herself in the second half of the year over seven furlongs plus. She's very nice and has a good way of going".*

116. UNNAMED ★★★★
b.f. Oasis Dream – Magic Tree (Timber Country). April 16. Half-sister to the Group 1 Eclipse Stakes, Group 2 York Stakes and Group 3 Brigadier Gerard Stakes winner Mukhadram (by Shamardal), to the useful 7f and 9.5f winner and Group 3 Musidora Stakes third Woodland Aria (by Singspiel) and the quite useful 12f to 2m winner Entihaa (by Tiger Hill). The dam ran once unplaced and is a half-sister to the Group 1 winner Gran Criterium winner Kirklees and the St Leger winner Mastery. The second dam, Moyesii (by Diesis), won once and is a half-sister to 3 winners including the French Group 3 winner Bowman. (Alvediston Stud & Manor Farm). *"A lovely filly with a very good pedigree, she's strong and you'd say that she's certain to make a 2-y-o at some point. There's enough size and plenty of strength about her. We like her".*

117. UNNAMED ★★★
b.f. Fastnet Rock – Maryinsky (Sadler's Wells). January 26. Closely related to the Group 1

Pretty Polly Stakes, Irish Oaks, Nassau Stakes and Yorkshire Oaks winner Peeping Fawn (by Danehill) and half-sister to the 2-y-o Group 1 Criterium International winner Thewayyouare (by Kingmambo). The dam, a 2-y-o 7f winner and second in the Group 1 Fillies Mile, is a half-sister to Better Than Honour (Grade 2 9f Demoiselle Stakes), Turnberry Isle (Group 2 1m Beresford Stakes) and Smolensk (Group 2 1m Prix d'Astarte). The second dam, Blush With Pride (by Blushing Groom), won the Grade 1 9f Kentucky Oaks and the Grade 1 8.5f Santa Susana Stakes and is a half-sister to several smart winners and to the dam of El Gran Senor and Try My Best. (Sheikh Mohammed bin Khalifa Al Thani). *"A big, backward filly but with a big stride on her, she carries plenty of condition and she's got a lot of filling out to do yet. We'll see her at the back-end I think and she'll want a mile".*

118. UNNAMED ★★★★
b.f. Dark Angel – Red Intrigue (Selkirk). January 24. Second foal. 180,000Y. Tattersalls October Book 1. Shawn Dugan. Half-sister to the useful 2015 2-y-o 5f winner listed Dragon Stakes winner Riflescope (by Raven's Pass). The dam, a fair 10f winner, is a half-sister to 4 winners including the smart Irish dual Group 3 7f winner Redstone Dancer and the useful listed 7f winner Red Liason. The second dam, Red Affair (by Generous), an Irish listed 10f winner, is a half-sister to 6 winners. (Qatar Racing Ltd & China Horse Club). *"She had a problem earlier this month but up to that she was going well. I think she'll make a 2-y-o, probably over six furlongs, and hopefully she'll come to hand in mid-summer. There's plenty of size and strength about her".*

119. UNNAMED ★★
b.f. Lawman – Smart Step (Montjeu). February 28. First foal. 190,000Y. Tattersalls October Book 2. BLM Bloodstock. The dam, a modest 1m to 10f winner, is a half-sister to 4 winners including the listed-placed This Is The Day and Vanity Rules. The second dam, Miss Pinkerton (by Danehill), a useful 6f (at 2 yrs) and listed 1m winner, is a half-sister to 5 winners including the smart 7f (at 2 yrs) and 10f winner and Group 2 placed Grand Central. (Sheikh Mohammed bin Khalifa Al Thani). *"It's a late developing pedigree and she's a backward filly. But I loved her at the sales and it's a real fillies' pedigree. She'll probably only have the odd run at the back-end, she's not a big filly, but she has a good action and we like her".*

120. UNNAMED ★★★
ch.f. New Approach – Wake Me Up (Rock Of Gibraltar). February 24. Second foal. €100,000foal. Goffs November foals. Justin Casse. The dam is an unplaced half-sister to the Group 1 National Stakes, Dewhurst Stakes, 2,000 Guineas and St James's Palace Stakes winner Dawn Approach. The second dam, Hymn Of The Dawn (by Phone Trick), placed fourth once at 2 yrs, is a half-sister to 3 winners including the Grade 1 third Galantas. (Andrew Rosen). *"A lovely filly, she's not very big and she has some developing to do. She's cantering away but she won't be doing much more for a while and she's one for the second half of the year".*

121. UNNAMED ★★★
b.c. High Chaparral – Witch Of Fife (Lear Fan). March 15. Twelfth living foal. €43,000Y. Goffs Orby. James McHale. Closely related to the very useful 2-y-o Group 3 7f Silver Flash Stakes winner Cabaret (by Galileo) and half-brother to 4 winners including the 2-y-o Group 3 7f Solario Stakes winner Drumfire (by Danehill Dancer), the useful Group 2 6f Gimcrack Stakes second and Hong Kong stakes winner Ho Choi (by Pivotal) and the quite useful dual 1m winner Loreto (by Holy Roman Emperor). The dam, a fairly useful listed-placed 2-y-o 6f and 7f winner, is a half-sister to 6 winners. The second dam, Fife (by Lomond), a fairly useful listed-placed 1m winner, is a half-sister to the dam of the Group/Grade 1 winners Frenchpark and Pearly Shells. *"For a High Chaparral he's quite forward so he could come to hand earlyish. We'll be getting on with him before long but he'll need seven furlongs for sure".*

MICHAEL BELL

122. ABACUS ★★★
b.c. Sixties Icon – Friendlier (Zafonic). March 29. Ninth foal. Half-sister to the fairly useful 2-y-o 1m winner and 3-y-o listed 10f placed Madame Defarge (by Motivator), to the fairly useful 7f (at 2 yrs) and 1m winner Foolin

Myself (by Montjeu), the fairly useful 7f (at 2 yrs) and 1m winner Unex El Greco, the quite useful 2-y-o 7f and subsequent US Grade 3 9f winner Gender Agenda (both by Holy Roman Emperor) and the fair 2-y-o 1m and subsequent UAE 7f winner Comradeship (by Dubawi). The dam is an unraced half-sister to User Friendly, winner of the Oaks, the St Leger, the Irish Oaks and the Yorkshire Oaks. The second dam, Rostova (by Blakeney), a fairly useful winner from 12f to 14f, is a half-sister to 7 winners. (WJ & TCO Gredley). *"A promising horse with bags of scope, the mare's got a good record and he looks capable of winning races. He's a very good mover by a sire who does remarkably well with his 2-y-o's considering he was a stayer. He'll be on the track in the second half of the season".*

123. ABBU RAHY ★★
b.c. Mayson – Abandon (Rahy). April 8. Fifth foal. 35,000Y. Tattersalls October Book 2. A C Elliott. Half-brother to the fair 7f winner After The Sunset and to the minor winner of 6 races abroad Relinquish (both by Pivotal). The dam, a quite useful 10f to 12f winner of 4 races, is a half-sister to 5 winners including the smart 1m to 14f and subsequent Australian dual Group 1 winner Tawqeet. The second dam, Caerless (by Caerleon), a fair 11.7f winner, is a half-sister to the Group 3 1m Prix de la Grotte winner Baya and to the Italian Group 2 winner Narrative. (Jaber Abdullah). *"He's quite heavy at the moment so we haven't done a lot with him and he's a bit behind some of the others. A strong, well-made horse, he's been on the back burner and hasn't been in a position to show me anything yet".*

124. AIR MINISTRY (IRE) ★★
b.c. High Chaparral – Hadarama (Sinndar). April 4. Fourth foal. 55,000Y. Tattersalls October Book 2. R Frisby. Brother to the 14f and 2m winner The Cashel Man and to the 12f and 14f winner Thunder Pass – both quite useful. The dam, a quite useful Irish 12f winner, is a half-sister to 5 winners including the Irish Group 3 7.5f Concorde Stakes winner Hamairi, the listed 6f winner Hanabad and the dam of the Group 1 winner Seal Of Approval. The second dam, Handaza (by Be My Guest), a 1m winner at 3 yrs in Ireland, is a half-sister to 6 winners. (WJ & TCO Gredley). *"A very athletic colt, but given his pedigree we won't be in a rush. Very stoutly bred, he's going to take time but he's a very good mover".*

125. AMERICAN PATROL (IRE) ★★★ ♠
ch.c. Rio De La Plata – Gutter Press (Raise A Grand). March 15. Fifth foal. 105,000Y. Tattersalls October Book 2. W J Gredley. Half-brother to the moderate triple 7f winner Jackie Love (by Tobougg). The dam ran twice unplaced and is a half-sister to 5 winners including the Group 2 5f Prix du Gros-Chene and triple Group 3 5f winner Tax Free and the Group 3 5f Prix de Saint-Georges and multiple listed winner Inxile. The second dam, Grandel (by Owington), is an unraced half-sister to 3 minor winners. (WJ & TCO Gredley). *"He hasn't got a lot of pedigree other than the fact that the second dam has done well. Despite that and the fact his sire is a relatively inexpensive stallion we pushed the boat out to buy him. He's a very attractive horse and a fine, big, strong, easy mover with a very good head carriage".*

126. CHEVAL BLANCHE ★★★★
gr.f. Stay Thirsty – Primrose Hill (Giant's Causeway). January 25. Third foal. 65,000Y. Tattersalls October Book 1. R Frisby. Half-sister to the French and US winner and dual French Group 3 10.5f placed Hug And A Kiss (by Thewayyouare) and the minor US 2-y-o winner Belsize Park (by Munnings). The dam, placed twice at 2 yrs in the USA, is a sister to the minor US stakes winner Bow Bells and a half-sister to a US Grade 3 placed winner. The second dam, Marylebone (by Unbridled's Song), won the US Grade 1 Matron Stakes and is a half-sister to 6 winners. (The Hon. Mrs J M Corbett & Mr C Wright). *"I like this filly a lot. I don't know much about the sire except that he stands in America and is a son of Bernardini who was pretty talented. The dam's first two foals have won and this looks like another one for sure. This is a nice filly, I really like her. She's strong, deep-girthed, well-made, with a good head and outlook. Very good-looking".* The sire, Stay Thirsty (by Bernardini), was Grade 1 placed in the USA at 2 yrs and later won the Travers Stakes and the Cigar Mile (both Grade 1). His first 2-y-o's appear this year and his stallion fee is $10,000.

127. COMPRISE ★★★
b.c. Pivotal – Constitute (Common Grounds). March 6. Tenth foal. 45,000Y. Tattersalls October Book 2. John & Jake Warren. Brother to the fairly useful 6f and 7f winner and listed-placed Enrol and to the minor Italian winner of 13 races Appoint and closely related to the fairly useful listed-placed dual 6f winner at 2 and 3 yrs Enact and the fair 2-y-o 6f and subsequent German winner Assembly (both by Kyllachy). The dam, a quite useful 1m winner, is a half-sister to 7 winners including the listed winner and Group 3 second Battle Chant. The second dam, Appointed One (by Danzig), a Grade 3 placed US stakes winner, is a sister to the Group 2 1m Lockinge Stakes winner Emperor Jones and a half-sister to the Group 1 William Hill Futurity Stakes winner Bakharoff. (Royal Ascot Racing Club). *"A strong, good-moving horse, he looks like making a 2-y-o from mid-summer onwards. A fine, easy-moving colt".*

128. DANCING ELEGANCE ★★★
ch.f. Nathaniel – Parisian Elegance (Zilzal). February 27. Eighth foal. 31,000Y. Tattersalls October Book 1. R Frisby. Half-sister to 6 winners including the useful 7f winner (at 2 yrs) and listed 6f placed March On Beetroot (by Cape Cross), the fairly useful triple 1m winner Cosmopolitan (by Cadeaux Genereux), the fair 6f (at 2 yrs) and 7f winner Broughtons Charm (by Invincible Spirit) and the fair French dual 6f winner Rappel (by Royal Applause). The dam, a fairly useful dual 5f winner at 2 yrs and third in the Group 3 Princess Margaret Stakes, is a half-sister to 7 winners including the triple Group 3 winning sprinter Majestic Missile. The second dam, Tshusick (by Dancing Brave), a quite useful 7f winner at 3 yrs, is a half-sister to 3 winners. (Chippenham Lodge Stud). *"Out of a speedy mare who has a good breeding record, this filly looks as if she'll be quite early. She looks quite sharp".*

129. DREAM MACHINE ★★
ch.c. Dream Ahead – Last Cry (Peintre Celebre). April 2. Fifth foal. 60,000Y. Tattersalls October Book 2. A C Elliott. Half-brother to the fair 10f, 2m and hurdles winner Master Fong (by Dr Fong), to the modest 8.5f to 11f winner Madeira Girl (by Bachelor Duke) and a hurdles winner by Jeremy. The dam, a 3-y-o 1m winner and listed-placed in France, is a half-sister to 6 winners. The second dam, Last Dream (by Alzao), won once at 3 yrs and is a half-sister to 6 winners including the French Group 1 winners Fijar Tango and Lost World. (Mr J Barnett & Mr Timmy Hyde). *"He's a fine, big, scopey horse and one for the second half of the year. A good mover with plenty of scope, he'll want seven furlongs to start with".*

130. ELEMENTARY ★★★
b.c. Exceed And Excel – Humdrum (Dr Fong). February 25. Second foal. Half-brother to the quite useful 2015 2-y-o 6f winner Husbandry (by Paco Boy). The dam, a fairly useful 7f and 1m winner of 4 races (including at 2 yrs), is a half-sister to 6 winners including the useful listed 6f winner of 4 races Musical Comedy. The second dam, Spinning Top (by Alzao), a useful 10f winner, is a half-sister to numerous winners including the fairly useful 3-y-o 7f and subsequent US dual 9f winner Daytime. (The Queen). *"He'll be quite an early bird, he's very athletic and looks like a 2-y-o. I'd say we'll be starting him at six furlongs and build up from there. In my mind's eye I see him as a specialist miler in time".*

131. FIRE BRIGADE ★★★★
b.c. Firebreak – Island Rhapsody (Bahamian Bounty). February 23. Second foal. 26,000Y. Doncaster Premier. Richard Frisby. Half-brother to the promising 2015 placed 2-y-o Cockney Island (by Cockney Rebel). The dam, a fair 6f winner, is a half-sister to 7 winners. The second dam, Lovely Lyca (by Night Shift), a fair 1m and 11.8f winner, is a sister to the listed 1m winner Barboukh (herself dam of the Group 3 10f Prix Exbury winner Barbola) and a half-sister to 6 winners. (Fish, Fox & Ware). *"I like this horse a lot. The sire isn't a fashionable stallion but he's had a few good ones and he was a good racehorse, winning the Brocklesby and only just getting beat in the Coventry. This colt is a strong, well-made 2-y-o type for five/six furlongs and I really like him".* **TRAINERS' BARGAIN BUY**

132. GLASSALT ★★★
b.f. Medaglia D'Oro – Abergeldie (Street Cry). February 1. First foal. The dam, a fair 1m winner, is a half-sister to the fairly useful 6f (including at 2 yrs) and 5f winner of 7 races

and listed-placed Cheviot. The second dam, Camlet (by Green Desert), a fairly useful dual 6f (including at 2 yrs), is a half-sister to the Group 1 Fillies Mile and Irish 1,000 Guineas winner Gossamer, to the Breeders' Cup Mile, Irish 2,000 Guineas and Queen Anne Stakes winner Barathea and the triple Group 3 1m winner Zabar. (The Queen). *"She hasn't done a lot yet but she's a very good mover and is one for the second half of the season. She's got a bit of size and scope and is an attractive filly"*.

133. JE SUIS CHARLIE ★★★★
b.c. High Chaparral – Fin (Groom Dancer). March 12. Fifth foal. 21,000Y. Tattersalls October Book 2. A C Elliott. Brother to the minor French 12f winner Seasons In The Sun and half-brother to the quite useful 10f winner Haalan (by Sir Percy) and the quite useful Irish 12f and hurdles winner Fatcatinthehat (by Authorized). The dam won 4 races in France and the USA including a listed stakes and is a half-sister to 5 winners including the listed winner Bonne Etoile. The second dam, Bonne Ile (by Ile de Bourbon), won 7 races here and in the USA including the Grade 1 Yellow Ribbon Invitational Handicap and is a sister to the Group 3 winner Ile de Nisky and a half-sister to the Group 3 winner Hi Lass. *"This is a nice, good-looking colt that was relatively inexpensive. It's a nice pedigree, he looks well-bought and he could be a classy horse. High Chaparral who basically is the poor man's Galileo – he's the next best if you're like me and can't afford Galileo's out of stakes-winning mares. I've been lucky with High Chaparral and I like this colt"*.

134. JIVE TALKING ★★★
ch.f. Zoffany – Inis Boffin (Danehill Dancer). March 26. Fourth foal. €45,000Y. Goffs Orby. BBA (Ire). Half-sister to the 2015 Irish 7f placed 2-y-o Qatari Hunter (by Footstepsinthesand). The dam, a fair 9f winner, is a half-sister to 4 winners. The second dam, Windmill (by Ezzoud), a fair 13.8f winner, is a half-sister to 8 winners including the Group 2 12f Ribblesdale Stakes winner Gull Nook (herself dam of the top-class colt Pentire), the Group 3 12f Princess Royal Stakes winner Banket and the Group 3 Ormonde Stakes winner Mr Pintips. (Mrs B V Sangster). *"She looks relatively sharp and I should think she'll be racing by June time. The sire had a great first season last year and this filly looks like a 2-y-o"*.

135. KSCHESSINSKA ★★
b.f. Sir Percy – Les Hurlants (Barathea). March 31. Tenth foal. 32,000Y. Tattersalls October Book 3. W J Gredley. Half-sister to the useful 2-y-o 7f and 1m winner and Group 3 1m Prix de Chenes third Happy Crusader (by Cape Cross), to the quite useful 1m (including at 2 yrs) and 9f winner of 6 races here and in USA Roar Of Applause (by Royal Applause), the quite useful 12f and 14f winner Bute Hall (by Halling) and the quite useful 9f (at 2 yrs) and 12f winner Spear (by Almutawakel). The dam, a minor French 12f winner, is a half-sister to 4 minor winners. The second dam, Howlin' (by Alleged), won once in France and is a half-sister to 4 winners. (WJ & TCO Gredley). *"This filly has improved a lot physically since she was bought. She's one for the second half of the season and is a nice, middle-distance filly in the making"*.

136. MAORI BOB (IRE) ★★★★
b.c. Big Bad Bob – Tekhania (Dalakhani). April 15. Fourth foal. €62,000Y. Goffs Orby. R Frisby. Half-brother to the fair 6f (at 2 yrs) and 5f winner Luis Vaz de Torres (by Tagula) and to the modest 2-y-o 5f winner Hello Beautiful (by Captain Rio). The dam is an unraced half-sister to 3 winners including the Hong Kong Group 2 winner Wade Giles. The second dam, Tekindia (by Indian Ridge), a minor French 3-y-o winner, is a half-sister to 6 winners. (Messrs' P & C Phillipps, Mr T Redman). *"I'm a fan of the sire, this colt did his first bit of easy work this morning and I think he'll come to hand quite quickly. The dam has bred two 2-y-o winners and this is a nice horse who will be a 2-y-o over six/seven furlongs"*.

137. MERLIN ★★★
b.f. Oasis Dream – Momentary (Nayef). February 1. First foal. The dam, a fairly useful listed 10f winner, is a half-sister to one winner. The second dam, Fleeting Memory (by Danehill), a quite useful 10.2f winner, is a half-sister to a hurdles winner. (The Queen). *"He's pretty forward, he'll have the boot for six furlongs and he's a very powerful horse. His mother was kind to us because she was a stakes winner but this colt is all Oasis Dream I think. He'll make a relatively early 2-y-o"*.

138. MISS FAY ★★★
br.f. Sayif – Lough Mewin (Woodman).
February 12. Fourth foal. €80,000Y. Goffs Orby.
R Frisby. Half-sister to the US Grade 3 10f
Santa Barbara Handicap winner of 7 races and
Grade 1 Matriarch Stakes second Queen Of
The Sand (by Footstepsinthesand) and to the
quite useful 10f and 11f winner and listed-
placed Rydan (by Intense Focus). The dam is
an unraced half-sister to the listed winner and
Group 2 Richmond Stakes third Bodyguard
and to the listed winner White Gulch. The
second dam, White Wisteria (by Ahonoora), is
an unraced half-sister to 6 winners including
the dam of the Irish 2,000 Guineas winner
Bachelor Duke. (Saleh Al Homaizi & Imad Al
Sagar). *"The dam has bred two good ones so
far, this is an early foal and looks like being
a 2-y-o for sure. She's created a favourable
impression".*

139. PEACE TELEGRAM ★★★
b.c. Henrythenavigator – Princess Danah
(Danehill). March 15. Sixth foal. The dam, a
modest 9f winner, is a half-sister to 10 winners
including the very useful dual 1m winner
Kismah. The second dam, Thaidah (Vice
Regent), a 5f (at 2 yrs) and listed 7f winner, is
a half-sister to the champion US 2-y-o Devil's
Bag and to the top-class filly Glorious Song
(the dam of Singspiel and Rahy). (Saleh Al
Homaizi & Imad Al Sagar). *"The dam has been
disappointing so far, so she needs a winner.
This chap looks alright though and he looks
capable of winning as a 2-y-o".*

140. PRINCE MONOLULU ★★
ch.c. Kyllachy – Corrine (Spectrum). January
28. Sixth foal. 90,000Y. Tattersalls October
Book 2. A C Elliott. Half-brother to the fairly
useful Irish 1m (at 2 yrs) and 14f winner Liszt
(by Galileo), to the fair 7f winner Al Emirati
(by Tamayuz) and the moderate 10f winner
Goodwood Moonlight (by Azamour). The
dam won four races including a listed event
in Norway and is a half-sister to 7 winners.
The second dam, La Luna (by Lyphard), a
winner over 9f at 3 yrs in France, is a sister to
the Group 3 Prix Daphnis and Group 3 Prix
Thomas Bryon winner Bellypha and a half-
sister to 6 winners including the Prix Eugene
Adam winner Bellman. (WJ & TCO Gredley).
*"The dam stayed very well and it's been a job
to get this colt fit because he carries plenty of
condition, but he's willing. He's a bit behind
the others and I see him coming to himself in
the second half of the season".*

141. RAY'S THE MONEY ★★★
b.c. Dragon Pulse – Riymaisa (Traditionally).
March 25. Fifth foal. 33,000Y. Tattersalls
October Book 2. A C Elliott. Half-brother to
the quite useful 2015 2-y-o dual 6f winner
and listed-placed Unilit (by Approve) and
to a 2-y-o winner in Sweden by Majestic
Missile. The dam, placed at 3 yrs in France, is
a half-sister to 5 winners including the listed
10f Pretty Polly Stakes winner Riyalma. The
second dam, Riyafa (by Kahyasi), was a listed
12f winner at Ascot. *"He looks like being quite
early, he goes well and he's a good mover
who's been pleasing us at home. It's the first
season for Dragon Pulse 2-y-o's, but he was
a good racehorse and he's had a couple of
runners already, so they seem to be coming
to hand".*

142. RONALD R (IRE) ★★★★
ch.c. Nathaniel – Amazon Beauty (Wolfhound).
February 1. Fifth living foal. 130,000Y.
Tattersalls October Book 2. Bill Gredley.
Half-sister to the fair 6f winner Miss Brazil (by
Exceed And Excel). The dam won twice at 2
and 3 yrs in France, was third in the Group 3
Prix de Seine-et-Oise and is a half-sister to 3
winners including the US stakes winner and
Group 1 Prix Saint-Alary second Asti. The
second dam, Astorg (by Lear Fan), won the
listed 1m Prix de la Calonne and is a half-sister
to 8 winners including the Group 3 winners
Android and Article Rare. (WJ & TCO Gredley).
*"A nice horse and the Nathaniels I've got have
made a good impression on me. This colt
goes well, he did his first bit of easy work this
morning and I'm hoping he'll come to hand
relatively quick. The dam was speedy, it's a
nice pedigree, he has an early foaling date and
he's going to be a 2-y-o. We like him".*

143. SEASIDE DREAMER ★★★
b.c. Pivotal – Striving (Danehill Dancer). March
10. Fifth foal. 72,000Y. Tattersalls October
Book 1. R Frisby. Closely related to the quite
useful 2-y-o 6f winner Showpiece (by Kyllachy)
and half-brother to the fair 6f (including at
2 yrs) and 7f winner Best Endeavour and the

minor winner of 8 races abroad Streamer (both by Medicean). The dam, a modest 1m and 10f placed maiden, is a sister to the listed 1m winner Pirateer and a half-sister to 6 winners including Wannabe Grand (Group 1 6f Cheveley Park Stakes). The second dam, Wannabe (by Shirley Heights), a quite useful 1m and 10f winner, is a half-sister to the Group 1 Cheveley Park Stakes second Tanami. (Mr Michael Lowe). *"He's a nice horse but he hasn't been asked to do anything serious yet because Pivotal doesn't get many early birds, so I'm not rushing him. It's a very fast family on the dam's side and she's bred three winners already. So it's a good pedigree, he has a good temperament and we like him".*

144. SHE ★★
ch.f. Dubawi – First City (Diktat). April 8. First foal. 75,000Y. Tattersalls December. Unex. The dam, a smart 6f (at 2 yrs) and UAE Group 2 1m winner, was third in the Group 1 Falmouth Stakes and is a half-sister to one winner. The second dam, City Maiden (by Carson City), is an unraced half-sister to the French listed winner and Group 3 placed Vernoy. (WJ & TCO Gredley). *"She's turned out back at the stud because she's small and she needs to grow and fill her frame".*

145. SHIMMERING LIGHT ★★★★★
ch.f. Dubawi – Summertime Legacy (Darshaan). May 9. Tenth foal. Half-sister to 7 winners including the 2-y-o Group 1 10f Criterium de Saint-Cloud winner Mandaean (by Manduro), the Group 1 10f Prix Saint-Alary winner Wavering (by Refuse To Bend), the 2-y-o 7f winner and Group 1 Fillies' Mile third Winters Moon (by New Approach), the 2-y-o 1m winner Golden Heritage (by Halling) and the quite useful 6f (at 2 yrs) to 10f winner of 4 races Mister Green (by Green Desert). The dam, winner of the 2-y-o Group 3 1m Prix des Reservoirs and third in the Group 1 Prix Saint-Alary, is a half-sister to 4 winners. The second dam, Zawaahy (by El Gran Senor), a fairly useful 1m winner and placed at up to 11.5f, is closely related to the Derby winner Golden Fleece. (The Queen). *"This could be a very nice filly. Very athletic, she's a half-sister to two Group 1 winners and although she was a May foal she looks quite precocious. She's quite 'busy' and the type you have to be careful* not to do too much with too soon. If she fulfils her potential she'll be an extremely valuable broodmare for the royal paddocks".

146. STICKS MCKENZIE ★★
b.c. Sepoy – Bended Knee (Refuse To Bend). March 16. Fourth foal. 65,000Y. Tattersalls October Book 2. Stetchworth & Middle Park Studs. The dam, a fair 7f winner, is a half-sister to 5 winners including the very useful listed 7f winner Flambeau. The second dam, Flavian (by Catrail), a fairly useful 6f (at 2 yrs) and 7f winner, is a half-sister to 7 winners. (WJ & TCO Gredley). *"He's just beginning to get it together so we haven't done a lot with him yet but he could be alright and he looks capable of winning. Sticks McKenzie was a pianist who used to entertain people in the bars in London"*

147. THREE DUCHESSES ★★★
b.f. Dutch Art – Three Ducks (Diktat). April 26. Third foal. Half-sister to Langham (by Royal Applause), second over 6f on her only start at 2 yrs in 2015 and to the fair triple 7f winner at 2 and 3 yrs Three Gracez (by Kyllachy). The dam, a fair dual 1m winner at 2 and 3 yrs, is a half-sister to 7 winners including the French listed 7f winner Thames and the fairly useful triple 1m winner (including at 2 yrs) Three Wrens. The second dam, Three Terns (by Arctic Tern), won over 9f in France and is a half-sister to 3 winners including the Group 3 1m Prix des Reservoirs winner Three Angels. (The Hon. Major James Broughton). *"She's quite sharp and she'll be one of our earlier fillies for sure. She's a little natural and quite feisty".*

148. WAR OFFICE (IRE) ★★
b.c. Dutch Art – Slieve Mish (Cape Cross). January 27. Third foal. 110,000Y. Tattersalls October Book 1. W J Gredley. The dam, a fairly useful 3-y-o 7f and 1m winner, is a half-sister to 5 winners including the Irish 2-y-o 7f winner and dual Group 3 placed Chivalrous. The second dam, Aspiration (by Sadler's Wells), a 10f winner in Ireland, is a sister to the Group 1 1m Gran Criterium winner Sholokhov and a half-sister to the listed winners Zavaleta, Napper Tandy and Affianced (herself dam of the Irish Derby winner Soldier Of Fortune). (WJ & TCO Gredley). *"He's gone back to the stud for a break because he needs time but hopefully he'll be a back-end 2-y-o. He's all*

Cape Cross rather than Dutch Art, so he isn't precocious".

149. WINSTON C (IRE) ★★★★
b.c. Rip Van Winkle – Pitrizza (Machiavellian). March 11. Eleventh foal. 55,000Y. Tattersalls October Book 2. W J Gredley. Half-brother to 6 winners including the useful Irish 2-y-o 6f winner and Group 3 Tyros Stakes third Vilasol, the 2-y-o listed 7.5f winner Snow Watch (both by Verglas), the quite useful 1m to 12f winner of 14 races The Lock Master (by Key Of Luck) and the fair 6f and 7f winner of 4 races Perfect Treasure (by Night Shift). The dam, a minor French 12f winner, is a half-sister to 4 other minor winners. The second dam, Unopposed (by Sadler's Wells), is an unraced half-sister to 11 winners including the dam of the dual Group 2 winner and sire Titus Livius. (WJ & TCO Gredley). *"A very good-moving son of Rip Van Winkle. He goes pretty well, the mare has bred a stakes winner and we like him. He'll be a 2-y-o alright and I think he'll be more forward than his pedigree suggests".*

150. UNNAMED ★★
b.f. Elusive Quality – Badalona (Cape Cross). April 16. Fourth foal. Half-sister to the quite useful 1m (at 2 yrs) and 10f winner Banditry (by Iffraaj). The dam, a quite useful 2-y-o 1m winner, is a sister to one winner and a half-sister to numerous winners including the very useful 2-y-o 6f winner and Group 1 Cheveley Park Stakes third Badminton, the useful 2-y-o 7f winner and Group 3 7f Vintage Stakes third Fox and the useful 6f and 7f winner and Group 3 Nell Gwyn Stakes second Cala. The second dam, Badawi (by Diesis), was a useful 1m and 9f winner of 4 races. (Sheikh Marwan Al Maktoum). *"A relatively weak filly, we're just giving her time but she's correct and just not ready for us to press Go yet. She could be alright but she's backward at the moment".*

151. UNNAMED ★★★
ch.f. Raven's Pass – Dancing Abbie (Theatrical). March 19. Second foal. Half-sister to the quite useful dual 12f and hurdles winner Galizzi (by Dansili). The dam, a 9f winner here and a listed 9f winner in Norway, was third in the Group 2 11f Italian Oaks. The second dam, Sicy d'Alsace (by Sicyos), won the Grade 1 9f Del Mar Oaks. (Sheikh Marwan Al Maktoum). *"A good mover,*

she has rather immature knees at the moment but she's a quality filly and the dam was very tough. She could be quite nice and has a lovely deep-girth but her knees need to mature properly before we press on".

152. UNNAMED ★★★
br.c. Arcano – Folle Blanche (Elusive Quality). March 3. Second foal. €38,000Y. Goffs Orby. A C Elliott. Half-brother to Roman Magic (by Holy Roman Emperor), unplaced in two starts at 2 yrs in 2015. The dam, placed twice at 2 and 3 yrs in France, is a half-sister to 4 winners including the dam of the champion Japanese 2-y-o filly Shonan Adela. The second dam, Always Loyal (by Zilzal), won 3 races including the French 1,000 Guineas and the Group 3 1m Prix de la Grotte and is a half-sister to the top-class sprinter Anabaa, the Group 3 Prix d'Arenburg winner Key Of Luck and the listed winner Country Belle (dam of the Group 2 Gimcrack Stakes winner Country Reel). (Fish, Fox & Ware). *"A fine, big horse, we're just taking our time with him but he has a good pedigree, he moves well and he'll be a nice horse in the second half of the year".*

153. UNNAMED ★★★
b.g. Sir Prancealot – Hapipi (Bertolini). March 21. Third foal. £26,000Y. Doncaster Premier. A C Elliott. Half-brother to the fair 2-y-o 5f and 7f winner Danot (by Zebedee). The dam is an unraced sister to the smart Group 3 6f Duke Of York Stakes and listed 6f and 7f winner of 8 races Prime Defender. The second dam, Arian Da (by Superlative), a fair 2-y-o 5f winner, is a full or half-sister to 7 winners. (Fish, Fox & Ware). *"I had to geld to make him focus on his day job, but he's turned the corner now and we're just stepping him up. He looks quite sharp".*

154. UNNAMED ★★★ ♠
ch.f. Zebedee – Hawattef (Mujtahid). February 15. Eleventh foal. 280,000Y. Tattersalls October Book 2. Charlie Gordon-Watson. Half-sister to 7 winners including the listed 7f (at 2 yrs) and Group 2 Celebration Mile winner and Group 1 Dewhurst Stakes second Kodi Bear (by Kodiac), the fair 11f and 12f winner Ralphy Lad (by Iffraaj), the moderate 7f winner Princess Cammie (by Camacho) and 3 winners in Italy (two of them at 2 yrs) by Danetime,

Fath and Chevalier. The dam is an unraced half-sister to 2 minor winners. The second dam, Madary (by Green Desert), won twice at 3 yrs and is a half-sister to 6 winners and to the unraced Dievotchka (the dam of four Group winners). (Lady Bamford). *"A filly from a pretty good family, she was a very attractive yearling and hence the high price tag because if you're an owner-breeder trying to get into good families you have to dig deep. She looks sharp and I'd say she'd have the boot for six furlongs for sure".*

155. UNNAMED ★★★
b.f. Poet's Voice – Juniper Girl (Revoque). April 8. Fourth foal. 40,000Y. Tattersalls October Book 1. Not sold. Half-sister to the fair 2-y-o 10f winner Kifaaya (by Intikhab) and to the fair 10f (at 2 yrs), 13f and hurdles winner Forced Family Fun (by Refuse To Bend). The dam, a useful 7f (at 2 yrs), 12f and 2m winner, is a half-sister to the Group 2 Italian 1,000 Guineas winner Golden Nepi. The second dam, Shajara (by Kendor), is a placed half-sister to 4 winners. (Mr M B Hawtin). *"I trained the dam and the half-brother Forced Family Fun. This filly has her mother's genes alright, she's nice, she'll be a 2-y-o and is very much one for the second half of the season. The sire's record needs to improve but he's by Dubawi so he's got time on his side".*

156. UNNAMED ★★★
b.c. Raven's Pass – Rainbow Desert (Dynaformer). January 29. Third foal. 70,000Y. Tattersalls October Book 1. A C Elliott. The dam, a quite useful 1m winner, is a half-sister to 7 winners including the US Grade 1 Del Mar Oaks winner Dublino. The second dam, Tuscoga (by Theatrical), was unplaced in 2 starts and is a sister to the Grade 1 Matriarch Stakes winner Duda and a half-sister to 5 winners. (Saleh Al Homaizi & Imad Al Sagar). *"I like this horse, he's a very good mover and although I haven't had that many for the Rabbah Bloodstock owners over the years I think this is the best I've had. He moves very well, he's very powerful and straightforward and he was an early foal. I can see him coming to hand fairly early and he'll do himself justice as a 2-y-o".*

JAMES BETHELL

157. CONISTONE ★★★
ch.f. Poet's Voice – Protectress (Hector Protector). February 19. Ninth foal. 22,000Y. Tattersalls October Book 1. J Bethell. Half-sister to the quite useful multiple all-weather winner from 9f to 14f Stand Guard (by Danehill), to the fair dual 12f winner Omnipresent and the fair 1m winner Wafeira (by Dansili). The dam, a useful 2-y-o listed 7f winner, is a half-sister to 4 winners including the useful 12f to 14f winner and listed-placed Market Forces (by Lomitas). The second dam, Quota (Rainbow Quest), a useful 10f winner, is a sister to 4 winners including the Group 1 1m Racing Post Trophy winner and St Leger second Armige. (Clarendon Thoroughbred Racing). *"A nice, well-balanced filly, hopefully she'll be out before the end of April. She goes nicely and I'm very pleased with her. She seems to know her job well, she's not very big and I'll be starting her off at five furlongs because she shows a bit of speed and she's quite nicely 'together'".*

158. COVERHAM (IRE) ★★★★
b.c. Bated Breath – Mark Too (Mark Of Esteem). April 1. Third foal. 20,000Y. Tattersalls October Book 2. J Bethell & J Delahooke. Half-brother to the modest 13f winner The Compeller (by Lawman). The dam is an unraced half-sister to the Group 3 6f Greenlands Stakes winner Tiger Royal and to the dam of the 2-y-o listed winner and Group 2 placed Sir Xaar. The second dam, Lady Redford (by Bold Lad), ran once unplaced and is a half-sister to 5 winners. (Clarendon Thoroughbred Racing). *"He's very nice, I'm very pleased with him, he's working and should be out by the end of April or early May. Very well put together and pretty laid back, he's doing everything we've asked so far and I think he'll get seven furlongs later on".*
TRAINERS' BARGAIN BUY

159. FLAWLESSLY ★★★
b.f. Exceed And Excel – Privalova (Alhaarth). January 23. Third foal. €80,000Y. Goffs Orby. Salcey Forest Stud. The dam, third in the listed Prix Yacowlef and a minor 3-y-o winner in Canada, is a half-sister to 2 winners including the dual Group 2 Prix Daniel Wildenstein winner Special Kaldoun. The second dam, Special Lady (by Kaldoun), was placed at 2

yrs in France and is a half-sister to 5 minor winners. (Mr J Dance). *"She's quite sharp and I would hope she'd be out by late April or early May. She's not very big and looks to go nicely".*

160. HAWORTH ★★★
b.c. Showcasing – Some Diva (Dr Fong). February 6. Sixth foal. 30,000Y. Tattersalls October Book 2. J Bethell / J Delahooke. Half-brother to the 2-y-o 1m winner Shannon Spree (by Royal Applause), to the 10f and 11.5f winner Spin Cast (by Marju), the 14f, 2m and hurdles winner Scrafton (by Leporello) and the 6f and 7f winner of 7 races Black Truffle (by Kyllachy) – all modest. The dam, a modest 9f winner, is a half-sister to the Group 1 Middle Park Stakes winner Primo Valentino and the Group 2 6f Cherry Hinton Stakes winner Dora Carrington. The second dam, Dorothea Brooke (by Dancing Brave), won over 9f and is a half-sister to 6 winners. (Clarendon Thoroughbred Racing). *"I trained his half-brother Scrafton who was basically a two miler, but this colt has definitely got more speed than he had! He's quite nice and I would have thought he'd be out by mid-May, probably over six furlongs, he's medium sized and pretty well put-together".*

161. JESSINAMILLION ★★
b.c. Mine – Miss Apricot (Indian Ridge). May 5. Half-brother to the modest 2015 2-y-o 5f winner Fruit Salad, to the modest 8.5f winner Charlcot (both by Monsieur Bond), the quite useful 5f and 6f winner of 5 races Apricot Sky (by Pastoral Pursuits) and the winner Princess Peaches (by Notnowcato). (David Kilburn). *"This colt is named after our daughter, who we sadly lost. The stallion was a horse I trained to win three Bunbury Cups, The Hunt Cup and the Victoria Cup, and the mare was the only thoroughbred he covered so it'll be interesting to see how this colt goes on! He's turning out to be a nice horse and the dam's had four winners out of four runners, so we should hopefully have some fun with him".*

162. PLAGE DEPAMPELONNE ★★★
gr.f. Redoute's Choice – Arabescatta (Monsun). March 27. Second foal. 45,000Y. Tattersalls October Book 2. C de Moubray. The dam, a minor French 3-y-o winner of 4 races, is a half-sister to 2 winners including the Group 2 Irish Derby Trial winner, Irish Derby second and St Leger second Midas Touch. The second dam, Approach (by Darshaan), a 7.5f (at 2 yrs) and listed 10f winner, was second in a US Grade 2 9.5f event and in the Group 3 May Hill Stakes and is a full or half-sister to 8 winners including the French 2,000 Guineas and US Grade 1 winner Aussie Rules. (Chris Wright). *"She's only been here a couple of weeks, she's well put together and a nice mover. A likeable, well-made filly with a good action, she'll be one for the middle of the season hopefully".*

163. PORTLEDGE (IRE) ★★★
b.c. Acclamation – Off Chance (Olden Times). April 18. First living foal. 60,000Y. Tattersalls October Book 2. J Bethell / J Delahooke. The dam, a useful winner of 5 races from 1m to 10f including a listed stakes, was placed in another five listed events. The second dam, La Notte (by Factual), a quite useful 2-y-o 6f winner, is a sister to a Scandinavian listed winner and a half-sister to 6 winners. (Mr T Buckingham). *"He's a very nice colt, probably a bit backward for an Acclamation, but I think the family are that way. This fellow will be a mid-summer 2-y-o and he's a really nice colt".*

164. SPIRIT OF ROME (IRE) ★★
ch.f. Mastercraftsman – Zagreb Flyer (Old Vic). April 16. Thirteenth foal. 25,000Y. Tattersalls October Book 1. James Bethell. Closely related to the Group 3 7f C L Weld Park Stakes winner and US Grade 3 second Venturi, to the French listed winner and Group 1 Criterium de Saint-Cloud third Feels All Right and the modest 12f winner Danehill Flyer (all by Danehill Dancer) and half-sister to one winner. The dam is an unraced half-sister to 8 winners including the listed winner and Group 1 Italian Oaks second Flying Girl. The second dam, Flying Clipper (by Tepukei), ran once unplaced and is a half-sister to the 2,000 Guineas winner To-Agori-Mou. (Mr J Lund). *"Very backward at the moment, she's one for much later on. Quite tall, rangy and leggy".*

SAEED BIN SUROOR
(GODOLPHIN)

Many thanks to Saeed's assistant Tony Howarth for kindly chatting about the Godolphin two-year-olds with me.

165. ABOVE NORMAL ★★★
b.c. Street Cry – Saoirse Abu (Mr Greeley). February 12. Half-brother to the fairly useful 1m (at 2 yrs) to 12f and hurdles winner Ennistown (by Authorized). The dam, winner of the Group 1 Moyglare Stud Stakes and Group 1 Phoenix Stakes at 2 yrs, was third in the 1,000 Guineas. The second dam, Out Too Late (by Future Storm), is an unraced half-sister to the dam of the Oaks and Irish Derby winner Balanchine. *"A big, scopey, athletic colt, he's a nice stamp of a horse and wouldn't want to be rushed. A good-moving, rangy type and very correct, he's one for the middle to back-end of the season".*

166. DUBAI HERO (FR) ★★★
b.c. Dark Angel – Bugie D'Amore (Rail Link). February 25. First foal. 100,000Y. Tattersalls October Book 2. John Ferguson. The dam won the Group 3 1m Premio Dormello at 2 yrs and is a half-sister to 4 winners. The second dam, Asmita (by Efisio), an Italian listed winner of 7 races at 3 and 4 yrs, was a half-sister to 3 minor winners. *"Quite a big, robust type, he's not as small as some of the other Dark Angels, but very strong with a good shoulder and plenty of bone. He's showing plenty of speed, but because of his size we're reining him in at the moment. He does everything easily and we like to think he'll be running around July time".*

167. DUBAI ONE (IRE) ★★★★
ch.f. Exceed And Excel – Dresden Doll (Elusive Quality). March 27. Sister to the quite useful 6f winner Role Player and half-sister to the 2015 2-y-o 1m winner, on his only start, Prize Money (by Authorized). The dam, a fair 2-y-o 5f winner, is a half-sister to 9 winners including the Irish 1,000 Guineas, Coronation Stakes and Nassau Stakes winner Crimplene, the Group 3 12.3f Chester Vase winner Dutch Gold and the 10f winner Group 2 12f Lancashire Oaks second Loyal Spirit. The second dam, Crimson Conquest (by Diesis), a quite useful 2-y-o 6f winner, is a half-sister to the US stakes winner Sword Blade. *"Probably the most precocious 2-y-o we have at the moment. She's showing lots of natural speed, is quite athletic-looking and although she hasn't been the most straightforward she does everything with so much ease. We may possibly run her at the Craven meeting but she won't be rushed and she's got a bit of scope as well. She's a filly we like".*

168. ENNJAAZ (IRE) ★★★
b.c. Poet's Voice – Hall Hee ((Invincible Spirit). April 4. Fourth foal. Closely related to the fair 2-y-o 1m winner Here Now (by Dubawi) and half-brother to the fair 2-y-o 7f winner Sherinn (by Refuse To Bend). The dam, a quite useful dual 1m winner, is a full or half-sister to several winners including the listed 14f March Stakes winner Jadalee and the useful dual 7f winner Alexander Duchess. The second dam, Lionne (by Darshaan), is an unraced half-sister to 5 winners including the Derby and Dewhurst Stakes winner Sir Percy. *"A big, imposing type, he's quite tall, has a nice top line on him and is a good-moving horse for the middle to the end of the season. Has a bit of quality about him".*

169. FALCON'S VIEW ★★★
b.c. Dubawi – New Morning (Sadler's Wells). March 27. Half-brother to the 9.5f to 12f winner of 4 races Winterlude, to the 2-y-o 7f winner Mighty Ambition (both by Street Cry) and the 8.5f and 12f winner Sadeek's Song (by Kingmambo) – all fairly useful. The dam, a very useful listed 10f winner, is a sister to 6 winners including the high-class Grade 1 Breeders' Cup Filly & Mare Turf, Group 1 1m Nassau Stakes and Group 1 Yorkshire Oaks winner Islington, the very smart 10f performer Greek Dance and the smart stayer Election Day. The second dam, Hellenic (by Darshaan), won the Yorkshire Oaks and was second in the St Leger and is a half-sister to numerous winners including the Group 2 Lanson Champagne Vintage Stakes second Golden Wave. *"Quite a tall, leggy, good-moving individual, he's cantering daily. A nice horse that won't be early but hopefully he should be out by mid-season. I like him".*

170. KANANEE (USA) ★★★
b.c. Exceed And Excel – Zoowraa (Azamour).

March 18. Second foal. The dam, a useful 2-y-o listed 7f winner, is a half-sister to 3 winners including the useful 6f to 1m UAE winner of 5 races Almaram. The second dam, Beraysim (by Lion Cavern), a very useful winner of the listed 7f Oak Tree Stakes, is a half-sister to the useful 2-y-o 7f winner Velour. *"A nice, medium-sized individual, he's strong and very mature looking. In full work, he's doing everything easily and we'd hope to be running him in April".*

171. MIGYAAS (USA) ★★★
b.c. Lonhro – Nasmatt (Danehill). February 6. Half-brother to the useful 2-y-o 1m and subsequent UAE listed 10f winner Emmrooz (by Red Ransom), to the quite useful UAE 6f and 7f winner of 4 races Latkhaf (by Pivotal) and the fair 1m winners Jaahiez (by More Than Ready) and Towbaat (by Halling). The dam, a fairly useful listed-placed 2-y-o 6f winner, is closely related to the Group 2 6f Lowther Stakes and Group 3 5f Queen Mary Stakes winner Bint Allayl and to the Group 3 7f Jersey Stakes winner Kheleyf. The second dam, Society Lady (by Mr Prospector), a fair 6f and 7f placed 2-y-o, is a full or half-sister to numerous winners including the useful French 2-y-o 5.5f winner Kentucky Slew. (Sheikh Ahmed Al Maktoum). *"Quite a big, imposing type, he's a very nice mover and stands over a lot of ground. He's in full work but hasn't done anything serious yet. A nice horse".*

172. NAAEEBB (USA) ★★★
b.br.c. Lonhro – My Dubai (Dubai Millennium). February 28. Half-brother to the quite useful 6f to 1m winner Mishaal (by Kheleyf), to the quite useful dual 7f winner Mizwaaj (by Invincible Spirit) and the fair 7f and 9f winner Naddwah (by Pivotal). The dam, placed over 7f on her only start, is a half-sister to 7 winners including the very smart triple Group 2 7f winner Iffraaj, the useful dual 2-y-o Group 3 7f Prix du Calvados winner Kareymah and the useful dual 1m winner Jathaabeh. The second dam, Pastorale (by Nureyev), a fairly useful 3-y-o 7f winner, ran only twice more including in a walk-over. *"A small but strong colt, he's a precocious, speedy type. Showing good speed at present, with a bit of luck he should be early and I like the look of him".*

173. REACH HIGH ★★★
ch.c. Distorted Humor – Silent Moment (Giant's Causeway). March 21. First foal. The dam, a quite useful 10f and 11f winner, is a half-sister to the US multiple Grade 1 winner from 7f to 10f Congaree and to the US stakes winner and Grade 1 placed Sangaree. The second dam, Mari's Sheba (by Mari's Book), was third in the Grade 1 Santa Anita Oaks. *"A nice, precocious type, he's done a few strong canters and hopefully he'll be running towards the end of April. A good-moving sort with a good top line, he's quite a big 2-y-o but shows lots of speed. I like him, he's a nice horse".*

174. REALLY SPECIAL ★★★
b.f. Shamardal – Rumh (Monsun). February 24. First foal. The dam, a useful listed 10f winner of 4 races, is out of the German Group 3 1m winner Royal Dubai (by Dashing Blade), herself a half-sister to the Grade 1 Beverly D Stakes winner Royal Highness. *"Quite leggy and a little bit weak at the moment, she stands over a lot of ground and is a good-moving filly with a nice attitude. One for the middle of the season onwards, she's one that we quite like".*

175. RECORD NUMBER (USA) ★★★
b.br.c. War Front – Bauble Queen (Arch). April 7. First foal. $900,000Y. Keeneland September. John Ferguson. The dam, a US Grade 2 winner and placed two more Graded stakes, is a half-sister to 4 winners including the minor US stakes winner Leamington. The second dam, Muneefa (by Storm Cat), a fair 6f winner, is a half-sister to 4 winners including the Group 3 Rose Of Lancaster Stakes winner Fahal. *"A nice, big, imposing sort. He's quite tall in stature and hasn't done much due to a couple of small problems but he's cantering daily now. Very forward-going, he has a good stride on him and he'd be one for the middle part of the season I should imagine".*

176. SILVER LINE (IRE) ★★★
gr.c. Dark Angel – Admire The View (Dubawi). March 8. Third foal. 150,000Y. Tattersalls October Book 2. John Ferguson. Half-brother to the fair 2015 multiple 6f placed 2-y-o Little Swift (by Kodiac). The dam, a quite useful 7f (including at 2 yrs) and 1m winner, is a half-sister to 2 winners. The second dam, Miss Honorine (by Highest Honor), a winner of 4

races at 3 and 4 yrs in Ireland including three listed events from 1m to 10f, was Group 3 placed twice and is a half-sister to 8 winners. *"Showing lots of precocity and speed, I would imagine he'll be running in May. Not the biggest, he looks precocious but he's a good-moving sort and we should be able to crack on with him".*

177. SUPER TALENT (IRE) ★★★★★
b.c. Helmet – Eastern Joy (Dubai Destination). March 24. Half-brother to the 2015 2-y-o Group 3 7f Oh So Sharp Stakes winner First Victory (by Teofilo), to the 2-y-o Group 3 1m May Hill Stakes winner and Group 1 Fillies' Mile third Ihtimal (by Shamardal) and the very useful listed-placed triple 1m winner at 2 and 3 yrs Always Smile (by Cap Cross). The dam, placed fourth over 11f in France, is a half-sister to 6 winners including the Group 1 10.5f Prix de Diane winner West Wind and the very useful listed 12f winner Redbridge. The second dam, Red Slippers (by Nureyev), a Group 2 10f Sun Chariot Stakes winner, is a sister to the Derby third Romanov and closely related to the Oaks and Irish Derby winner Balanchine. *"One of my favourites at the moment, this is a big, strong, imposing type with good bone and plenty of top line on him. A real good-moving sort, I like him a lot and he has a lot of class about him. We'll take our time with him".*

178. TOP SCORE ★★★
b.c. Hard Spun – Windsor County (Elusive Quality). February 25. First foal. The dam is an unraced sister to the Breeders' Cup Classic and Queen Elizabeth II Stakes winner Raven's Pass and to the US stakes winner and Grade 2 placed Gigawatt. The second dam, Ascutney (by Lord At War), won the US Grade 3 Miesque Stakes and is a sister to the US stakes winner Words Of War (herself dam of the Grade 1 Del Mar Oaks winner No Matter What and the US Grade 2 winner E Dubai) and a half-sister to 8 winners. *"Not the biggest, but he's showing good speed at the moment. He's done a couple of pieces of work and he's very honest, has a good attitude and with luck we should see him out in May".*

179. UNNAMED ★★★
b.f. Distorted Humor – Achieving (Bernardini). February 22. Second foal. $550,000Y.

Keeneland September. John Ferguson. The dam, a minor 3-y-o winner in Canada, is a half-sister to the US Grade 1 winner Streaming. The second dam, Teeming (by Storm Cat), a minor Canadian 4-y-o winner, is a half-sister to the US Grade 1 winners Jazil and Rags To Riches. *"She's a bit on the weak side, but there's a lot of class about her and she's doing everything very easily. We'll give her a bit more time, she's quite athletic and a nice filly".*

180. UNNAMED ★★★
ch.c. Street Cry – Aryaamm (Galileo). March 20. Seventh foal. Brother to the 2-y-o Group 2 7f Champagne Stakes winner Saamidh and half-brother to the useful listed-placed 12f winner Talmada and the fairly useful 7f and 1m (both at 2 yrs) and 1m winner Yarroom (both by Cape Cross). The dam, a quite useful 10f winner, is a half-sister to the French 6f (at 2 yrs) and 7.5f winner and Group 2 1m third Mathematician. The second dam, Zibilene (by Rainbow Quest), a useful listed-placed 12f winner, is a half-sister to the Breeders' Cup Mile, Irish 2,000 Guineas and Queen Anne Stakes winner Barathea and the Fillies Mile and Irish 1,000 Guineas winner Gossamer. *"A good-topped individual, he's doing everything well. We wouldn't be in a rush with him, he'll have a bit of stamina and we won't be thinking about him until the middle of the season, but he's nice".*

181. UNNAMED ★★★
b.f. Shamardal – Catchline (Bertolini). February 24. Third foal. 260,000Y. Tattersalls October Book 1. John Ferguson. Sister to the Media Book, unplaced in one start at 2 yrs in 2015 and half-sister to the useful dual 1m winner Emirates Skycargo (by Iffraaj). The dam is an unraced half-sister to 4 winners including the very smart Group 1 1m Premio Vittoria di Capua winner Ancient World and to the Grade 1 12f CCA Oaks winner Jilbab. The second dam, Headline (by Machiavellian), is an unraced half-sister to the Grade 1 1m Del Mar Futurity winner and smart sire Saratoga Six and to the Group 1 1m William Hill Futurity winner Dunbeath. *"A lovely looking filly, she has good bone and is a good-moving type. She does everything easily but we won't rush her and she looks to have a bit of class about her. Everything she does, she does well, she*

has a good mind on her and hopefully we'll get her going from June onwards".

182. UNNAMED ★★★
b.f. Invincible Spirit – Dubai Smile (Pivotal). March 6. Second foal. The dam, a minor French 3-y-o 1m winner, is a half-sister to one winner. The second dam, Hi Dubai (by Rahy), won the listed Pretty Polly Stakes and is a sister to Fantastic Light, a winner of six Group/Grade 1 events including the Breeders' Cup Turf, the Prince of Wales's Stakes and the Irish Champion Stakes. *"A real good-looking filly, she's very sensible and straightforward. A nice mover that's doing everything we ask, she's stocky and strong, won't be rushed but has a bit of class about her I think".*

183. UNNAMED ★★★
ch.f. Dubawi – Express Way (ARG) (Ahmad). March 4. Half-sister to the Group 1 7f Prix Jean-Luc Lagardere and Italian dual Group 1 winner Rio De La Plata, to the quite useful 2-y-o 7f winner Ihsas (both by Rahy), the Argentine Grade 1 winner El Expresivo (by Candy Stripes), the fairly useful 1m winner Expressly (by Street Cry) and the fair 10f and 12f winner Arabian Beauty (by Shamardal). The dam, placed in Argentina, is a half-sister to 2 minor winners out of the unraced Escaline (by Hawk). *"Not the biggest but quite robust and she has good bone and a good attitude. One for June/July I should imagine and with a bit of luck she'll be a nice horse. There's plenty of top line on her".*

184. UNNAMED ★★★
b.c. Dubawi – Gonbarda (Lando). February 27. Sixth foal. Half-brother to the high-class Group 1 1m Lockinge Stakes and Group 1 10f Champion Stakes winner Farhh, to the very smart Group 3 10f winner and Group 1 Champion Stakes fourth Racing History, the very useful 1m winner of 4 races and Group 3 third Basem and the fairly useful 2-y-o 1m winner Welcome Gift (all by Pivotal). The dam, a German dual Group 1 12f winner, is a full or half-sister to numerous winners including Gonfilia, winner of the Group 3 8.5f Princess Elizabeth Stakes and four listed events. The second dam, Gonfalon (by Slip Anchor), is a half-sister to several winners. *"A nice horse. Not as tall as his half-brothers Farhh and Racing History, but quite close-coupled and a strong looking type. He's very forward-going and a good mover".*

185. UNNAMED ★★★
br.c. Dream Ahead – Lake Moon (Tiger Hill). March 23. Second foal. €360,000Y. Goffs Orby. John Ferguson. Half-brother to the French 7.5f (at 2 yrs) and listed 9f winner Meteoric (by Lope De Vega). The dam, a minor French 3-y-o winner, is a half-sister to 9 winners including the Group 3 Gordon Stakes winner Cap O'Rushes and the Group 3 Joel Stakes winner Splendid Era. The second dam, Valley Of Gold (by Shirley Heights), a smart winner of the Italian Oaks, is a half-sister to 4 winners including the 2-y-o Group 3 7f Vintage Stakes winner Dublin and the French Group 2 placed Dream Play. *"A very big colt, we won't be in too much of him because of his size but he's a good mover, covers a lot of ground and has a big stride on him. He has good bone and he's a nice horse for later on".*

186. UNNAMED ★★★
b.c. Distorted Humor – Love Theway Youare (Arch). April 17. First foal. $200,000Y. Keeneland September. John Ferguson. The dam won the Grade 1 Vanity Handicap and was second in the Grade 1 Santa Margarita Invitational and is a half-sister to a US stakes-placed winner. The second dam, Diversa (by Tabasco Cat), a US stakes winner of 4 races and Grade 3 placed, is a half-sister to 7 winners. *"A little bit on the weak side because he's quite a big horse and has to grow into himself, but he looks a nice type. He has a good action, a good length of stride and is very forward-going. We wouldn't be in a rush with him but we like him and you'd think he'd be a nice type for the middle to back-end".*

187. UNNAMED ★★★
b.f. Frankel – Marie De Medici (Medicean). March 22. Second foal. Half-sister to Local Time (by Invincible Spirit), a useful 2-y-o Group 3 7f Oh Sharp Stakes winner here and subsequently a Group 3 winner in the UAE (9.5f) and Turkey (1m). The dam, a useful 7f (at 2 yrs) and listed 10f winner, was second in the Group 3 1m Prix des Reservoirs and is a half-sister to the Group 1 12f Grand Prix de Paris winner Erupt. The second dam, Mare

Nostrum (by Caerleon), won the Group 3 Prix Vanteaux and was placed in the Prix Vermeille and Prix Saint-Alary and is a half-sister to 7 winners including the US Grade 1 winner Aube Indienne. *"A very stocky, strong filly with a good top line on her. She's a good mover but just a bit headstrong – she likes to do her own thing, so maybe that's the Frankel in her. A real nice filly".*

188. UNNAMED ★★★
ch.f. Distorted Humor – Michita (Dynaformer). March 2. Sister to Great Order, placed fourth over 7f on his only start at 2 yrs in 2015 and to the minor US dual 1m winner Gavroche and half-sister to the quite useful 1m and 9.5f winner Thatchmaster (by Street Cry). The dam, winner of the Group 2 12f Ribblesdale Stakes and the listed 10f Height Of Fashion Stakes winner, was third in the Yorkshire Oaks and the Prix Vermeille (both Group 1) and is a sister to one winner and a half-sister to the US 6f to 1m winner and Grade 3 placed Thunder Mission. The second dam, Thunder Kitten (by Storm Cat), a US 6.5f to 8.5f winner (including a Grade 3), is a half-sister to the Japanese Group 1 1m winner Nobo True. *"She's very leggy, very scopey and a little bit on the weak side still, but she's a good-moving, forward-going type that stands over a lot of ground. One for the middle to back-end and she has a bit of class about her".*

189. UNNAMED ★★★
ch.c. Shamardal – Next Holy (Holy Roman Emperor). March 1. First foal. €140,000Y. Arqana Deauville August. John Ferguson. The dam, a listed-placed winner in Germany at 3 and 4 yrs, is a half-sister to 7 winners including the German Group 1 winners Next Desert and Next Gina. The second dam, Night Petticoat (by Petoski), won the Group 2 German Oaks and is a half-sister to 8 winners. *"Quite a nice horse, he's a good-looking chestnut who is very forward-going. He has a good stride on him, a nice action and a good top. He won't be rushed but he'll be a nice type".*

190. UNNAMED ★★★
ch.c. Dubawi – Portmanteau (Barathea). May 3. Fifth foal. Brother to the 2015 1m fourth placed 2-y-o, from two starts, Tautology and to the Group 1 10f Premio Roma and UAE dual Group 1 winner Hunter's Light and half-brother to the French listed-placed 9.5f and 12f winner Linda Radlett (by Manduro). The dam, a quite useful dual 10f winner, is a half-sister to numerous winners including the smart Group 3 10f Sandown Classic Trial winner Courteous and the useful listed 12f winner Scriptwriter. The second dam, Dayanata (by Shirley Heights), is an unraced sister to the French Derby winner and sire Darshaan and a half-sister to the Prix Vermeille winner Darara and the Prix de Royallieu winner Dalara. *"This is a nice horse, he's in full work and going well. A medium-sized, strong, good-shouldered colt and a good mover, he has a very good attitude. Doing everything well at the moment, he should be a summer horse and we'll crack on with him I think".*

191. UNNAMED ★★★
b.c. Frankel – Sand Vixen (Dubawi). March 8. The dam, a 2-y-o Group 2 5f Flying Childers Stakes and listed St Hugh's Stakes winner, is a half-sister to 4 winners including the smart listed 6f winner and Group 3 Greenham Stakes third So Will I. The second dam, Fur Will Fly (by Petong), was placed once over 6f at 3 yrs and is a half-sister to 4 winners. *"A nice type and a good, strong-topped colt. Showing good speed, he's not the biggest but he looks a nice horse. Our two Frankels are similar types".*

192. UNNAMED ★★★
ch.c. Sea The Stars – Something Mon (Maria's Mon). February 18. Ninth foal. 230,000foal. Tattersalls December. John Ferguson. Half-brother to 6 winners including the useful 2-y-o Group 3 7f Oh So Sharp Stakes winner Raymi Coya (by Van Nistelrooy), the US stakes-placed winner Olympia Fields (by Alydeed), the fairly useful 11.5f winner Hikari and the quite useful 12f winner Theturnofthesun (both by Galileo). The dam is an unraced half-sister to 5 winners including the champion German 2-y-o and Group 2 winner Somethingdifferent. The second dam, Try Something New (by Hail The Pirates), won the Grade 1 Spinster Stakes in the USA and is a half-sister to 5 winners. *"A nice, strong-topped, good-moving horse. He's very willing and for a horse that will get a trip he's showing precocity and likes to go forward. We wouldn't be in a hurry with him but we like him".*

193. UNNAMED ★★★
b.f. Cape Cross – Waitress (Kingmambo).
March 5. The dam, listed-placed over 7f in France, is a half-sister to 4 winners including the French 1m winner and Group 3 Prix de la Grotte second Woven Lace. The second dam, Do The Honours (by Highest Honor), a French 5.5f (at 2 yrs) and Group 3 6f Prix de Meautry winner, is a half-sister to 8 winners including Seba (Chesham Stakes). *"A smallish, good-boned and good-moving individual, she's in full work and is showing a bit of speed already. We won't be in a rush with her but she's very forward going".*

194. UNNAMED ★★★
b.c. Lemon Drop Kid – Winner (Horse Chestnut). March 27. Seventh foal. $320,000Y. Keeneland September. John Ferguson. Half-brother to 3 winners including the US Grade 3 winner Ocho Ocho Ocho (by Street Sense) and the US winner and Grade 2 placed Private Ensign (by A P Indy). The dam, a minor 3-y-o winner, is a half-sister to the US Grade 3 winner Animal Spirits. The second dam, Pennant Champion (by Mr Prospector), a minor US 3-y-o and 4-y-o winner, is a sister to the Grade 1 winners Miner's Mark and Traditionally. *"Not the most robust but very athletic and forward-going. Very willing and one for the middle of the season I should imagine".*

JIM BOLGER

195. BEAN FEASA
b.f. Dubawi – Speirbhean (Danehill). April 6. Eighth foal. Half-sister to the champion 2-y-o colt and Group 1 Dewhurst Stakes and Group 1 National Stakes winner Teofilo, to the fairly useful Irish 10f winner Senora Galilei and the quite useful 7f winner Teo's Sister (all by Galileo). The dam, an Irish listed 1m winner, is a half-sister to numerous winners including the Irish listed 9f winner Graduated. The second dam, Saviour (by Majestic Light), won 3 races at 2 and 3 yrs and is a half-sister to 5 winners including the triple US Grade 1 winner Judge Angelucci and the US Grade 1 winners Peace and War. (Godolphin).

196. COMEDIENNE
ch.f. Archipenko – Claiomh Solais (Galileo). March 4. Second foal. Half-sister to the quite useful 2015 6f and 7f placed 2-y-o Clear Cut (by Acclamation). The dam, a very useful Irish 1m winner and dual Group 3 placed, is a sister to the smart 2-y-o dual Group 3 6f winner and 1,000 Guineas second Cuis Ghaire, to the Group 3 9f winner Scintillula and the Irish 2-y-o 7f winner and Group 1 Coronation Stakes second Gile Na Greine. The second dam, Scribonia (by Danehill), is an unraced half-sister to 6 winners including the 2-y-o listed 6f winner and dual Group 1 placed Luminata. (Miss K Rausing).

197. CONSTANT COMMENT (IRE)
b.f. Fastnet Rock – Livia Galilei (Galileo). January 21. First foal. 75,000Y. Tattersalls October Book 2. BBA (Ire). The dam, a fairly useful triple 12f winner, is a sister to the listed 12f and listed 2m winner Eye Of The Storm and a half-sister to 5 winners including the dual Group 3 winner Satchem. The second dam, Mohican Princess (by Shirley Heights), was fourth over 10f on her only start and is a half-sister to 5 winners. (Mrs June Judd).

198. CONTESSA CONFESSA (IRE)
b.f. Lope De Vega – Pardoven (Clodovil). January 20. First foal. 100,000Y. Tattersalls October Book 2. BBA (Ire). The dam is an unraced half-sister to 10 winners including the very useful 6f (at 2 yrs) to 10f winner and Group 3 placed Firebet, the useful 10f winner Dancing Phantom and the UAE winner and Group 3 placed Seeking The Prize. The second dam, Dancing Prize (by Sadler's Wells), a useful maiden and third in the listed Lingfield Oaks Trial, is a sister to 3 winners including the Group 1 Fillies Mile second and good broodmare Dance To The Top and a half-sister to 5 winners including the dual listed winner and Australian Group 1 second Polar Bear. (Mrs June Judd).

199. DAWN OF A NEW ERA (IRE)
b.f. New Approach – Hymn Of The Dawn (Phone Trick). May 28. Ninth foal. €480,000Y. Goffs Orby. BBA (Ire). Sister to the Group 1 National Stakes, Dewhurst Stakes, 2,000 Guineas and St James's Palace Stakes winner Dawn Approach and to the 2015 2-y-o Group 2 7f Futurity Stakes winner and Group 1 National Stakes second Herald The Dawn

and half-sister to the fair 5f (at 2 yrs) to 7f winner Comadoir (by Medicis). The dam, placed fourth once at 2 yrs, is a half-sister to 3 winners including the Grade 1 third Galantas. The second dam, Colonial Debut (by Pleasant Colony), was placed in the USA and is a half-sister to 6 winners. (Mrs June Judd).

200. EIRIAMACH NA CASCA
b.f. Intense Focus – Night Visit (Sinndar). April 7. Seventh foal. €240,000foal. Goffs November foals. Mick Flanagan. Half-sister to the Irish Derby winner Trading Leather, to the fairly useful 11f and 12f winner Wexford Town (both by Teofilo) and the fair 7f winner Gleadhradh (by Chevalier). The dam is an unraced half-sister to 4 minor winners. The second dam, Moonlight Sail (by Irish River), a French 2-y-o 7f winner, is a sister to the Champion Stakes, 1,000 Guineas and Prix de l'Opera winner Hatoof and to the US Grade 1 1m winner Irish Prize and a half-sister to the dual 10f listed winner Insijaam and the 12f listed winner Fasateen. (Mrs J S Bolger).

201. GOLDEN HANDCUFFS (IRE)
ch.f. New Approach – Tiffilia (Macho Uno). February 13. First foal. €45,000foal. Goffs November. Sean Dowling. The dam, a fair Irish 2-y-o 7f winner, is a half-sister to 2 minor winners. The second dam, Tiffed (Seattle Slew), is an unraced half-sister to 3 minor winners. (Godolphin).

202. GOLDRUSH (IRE)
b.f. Frankel – Alexander Goldrun (Gold Away). March 1. Third foal. €1,700,000Y. Goffs Orby. China Horse Club. The dam, a top-class and multiple Group 1 winner of £1.9 million (Nassau Stakes, Pretty Polly Stakes, Prix de l'Opera etc), is a half-sister to 5 winners including the Group 3 Prix de la Jonchere winner and Group 1 placed Medicis. The second dam, Renashaan (by Darshaan), a listed winner in France, was third in the Group 3 9f Prix Vanteaux and is a half-sister to 4 minor winners. (China Horse Club).

203. IN SOMNO (IRE)
ch.f. Dream Ahead – Maoineach (Congaree). March 2. Third foal. Half-sister to the fairly useful 7f winner Aerialist (by Sea The Stars). The dam won the Group 3 6f Round Tower Stakes (at 2 yrs) and the Group 3 7f Leopardstown 1,000 Guineas Trial and is a half-sister to 2 winners including the US listed winner and Group 2 placed Tiz Now Tiz Then. The second dam, Trepidation (by Seeking The Gold), is an unraced half-sister to 3 winners. (Mrs J S Bolger).

204. MODERN APPROACH (IRE)
b.f. New Approach – Janey Muddles (Lawman). March 3. First foal. The dam, a useful Irish 2-y-o 6f winner, is a half-sister to the fair 6f (at 2 yrs) to 8.5f winner My Single Malt. The second dam, Slip Dance (by Celtic Swing), a dual sprint listed winner, was second in the Group 3 7f Sweet Solera Stakes and is a half-sister to 8 winners including the Group 3 winner Air Chief Marshal and the dual listed winner Misu Bond. (Mrs June Judd).

205. QUEEN OF THE RING (IRE)
b.f. Teofilo – Aiseiri (Rock Of Gibraltar). May 17. Second foal. €48,000Y. Goffs Orby. Not sold. The dam ran twice unplaced and is a half-sister to the Group 2 Irish Derby Trial winner Light Heavy and to the dam of the Group 1 Dewhurst Stakes winner Parish Hall. The second dam, Siamsa (by Quest For Fame), a fair Irish 9f and 11f winner, is a half-sister to 4 winners. (Mrs J S Bolger).

206. RINGSIDE SUPPORT (IRE)
b.c. Teofilo – Halla Siamsa (Montjeu). May 5. Brother to the fairly useful 2015 2-y-o listed-placed 9f winner Siamsaiocht, to the very smart 2-y-o Group 1 7f Dewhurst Stakes winner Parish Hall and the useful 2-y-o 1m winner and Group 2 Futurity Stakes third Hall Of Fame. The dam, a quite useful Irish 10f winner, is a half-sister to the Group 2 Irish Derby Trial winner Light Heavy. The second dam, Siamsa (by Quest For Fame), a fair Irish 9f and 11f winner, is a half-sister to 4 winners. (Godolphin).

207. TEO'S MUSIC (IRE)
b.f. Intense Focus – Teo's Sister (Galileo). April 13. Firs foal. The dam, a quite useful Irish 7f winner, is a sister to 2 winners including the champion 2-y-o colt and Group 1 Dewhurst Stakes and Group 1 National Stakes winner Teofilo. The second dam, Speirbhean (by Danehill), an Irish listed 1m winner, is a half-

sister to numerous winners including the Irish listed 9f winner Graduated. (Mrs J S Bolger).

208. TRADFEST (IRE)
b.f. High Chaparral – Take Flight (Pivotal). January 26. Second foal. 190,000Y. Tattersalls October Book 2. BBA (Ire). Half-sister to the 2015 2-y-o Group 3 6f Round Tower Stakes winner and Group 2 Criterium de Maisons-Laffitte third Smash Williams (by Fracas). The dam, a fair 2-y-o 5f winner, is a half-sister to 6 winners including the Irish 1,000 Guineas winner Saoire. The second dam, Polish Descent (by Danehill), is an unraced half-sister to 4 winners. (Mrs J S Bolger).

209. UNNAMED
b.br.c. Lonhro – Danelagh (Danehill). January 30. Half-brother to the Group 1 12f Dubai Sheema Classic and multiple Hong Kong Group 1 winner Vengeance Of Rain, to the Australian Group 1 10f winner Dizelle (both by Zabeel), the quite useful 11f and 12f winner Queen Of Denmark (by Kingmambo) and the fair 2-y-o 7f winner Intiba (by Street Cry). The dam won the Group 1 6f Blue Diamond Stakes at 2 yrs in Australia. (Godolphin).

MARCO BOTTI
210. AL HAMDANY (IRE) ★★★★
b.c. Kodiac – Easy Times (Nayef). February 17. First foal. 42,000Y. Tattersalls October Book 2. HE Sultan Aldeen MS Al-Khalifa. The dam is an unraced half-sister to 4 winners. The second dam, Easy To Love (by Diesis), a quite useful 4-y-o 11.5f winner, is a sister to the Oaks winner Love Divine (herself dam of the St Leger winner Sixties Icon) and a half-sister to 5 winners including the listed winners Dark Promise and Floreeda. (Sheikh A Z A M Al Khalifa). *"He's quite forward and is actually ready to step up now. An early type and a nice mover that shows ability, he should be running from late April onwards and he's definitely capable of winning a maiden. We like him".*

211. AMNA ★★★
b.f. Sayif – Island Dreams (Giant's Causeway). February 2. Third foal. Half-sister to the quite useful 2015 2-y-o 8.5f winner Mr Khalid (by Pour Moi) and to the quite useful 2-y-o 1m winner Who'sthedude (by Duke Of Marmalade). The dam, placed fourth over 10f on her only start, is a half-sister to 3 winners including the Group 2 Betfred Mile winner and Group 1 Champion Stakes second Rob Roy. The second dam, Camanoe (by Gone West), ran unplaced twice and is a half-sister to 8 winners including the US Grade 1 winner Super Staff. (Saleh Al Homaizi & Imad Al Sagar). *"A nice filly and a half-sister to a promising colt we have called Mr Khalid. Quite a few Sayif 2-y-o's look like they may be early types but in this filly's case she's quite leggy and still a bit unfurnished. So we've allowed her a bit more time, but there's plenty to like about her. She's a good mover with a good temperament and is one for seven furlongs in the middle of summer".*

212. BAHAMAS (IRE) ★★
b.c. Rip Van Winkle – Gwyllion (Red Ransom). April 12. Fifth foal. £60,000Y. Doncaster Premier. Jamie Lloyd/Marco Botti. Half-brother to the Swedish winner of 5 races at 2 and 3 yrs Tom Hagen (by Kheleyf), to the fair 7.5f winner Montefalcon (by Footstepsinthesand) and the fair 12f and 13f winner Bayan Kasirga (by Aussie Rules). The dam, placed fourth once over 7f at 2 yrs, is a half-sister to 5 winners including the Grade 2 Canadian Stakes and Group 3 Nell Gwyn Stakes winner Barefoot Lady. The second dam, Lady Angharad (by Tenby), a winner of 5 races from 6f to 10f including the 2-y-o listed Woodcote Stakes, is a half-sister to 5 minor winners. *"A nice sort and a good-looking colt, he'll take a little time but he's straightforward and we like him but he's one for the autumn I should think".*

213. BASHEER ★★★
b.c. Dubawi – Reem (Galileo). March 7. Second foal. Half-brother to the unraced Rasmee (by Fastnet Rock). The dam, a UAE listed 7f winner, was third in two Group 3 events there and is out of the Australian 6.8f winner Al Afreet (by Danehill). (Sheikh Mohammed bin Khalifa Al Maktoum). *"He's different to the other Dubawi 2-y-o we have because he's a little bit smaller and more precocious. He moves well, he's very laid back and he's going nicely. We haven't done much with him yet but he's definitely a nice colt and he'll make a 2-y-o".*

214. BOBBIO (IRE) ★★★
ch.c. Choisir – Balladiene (Noverre). February 17. First foal. €50,000Y. Tattersalls Ireland September. Jamie Lloyd / Marco Botti. The dam, a fair 7f and 1m winner of 5 races including at 2 yrs, is a half-sister to one winner. The second dam, Kinnego (by Sri Pekan), is an unplaced half-sister to 5 winners including the Group 2 Pretty Polly Stakes winner Lady Upstage. (Promenade Bloodstock Ltd). *"When we bought him he was on the small side but he's done really well over the winter and developed into a nice 2-y-o. He's lovely, has a great temperament and definitely shows speed for the small amount he's done so far. One for July over six furlongs I should think".*

215. BORNTOSIN (IRE) ★★★
b.c. Born To Sea – Mrs Beeton (Dansili). May 1. Third foal. €12,000Y. Goffs Orby. Jamie Lloyd/Marco Botti. Half-brother to the quite useful 2015 2-y-o 6f and 7f winner Four's Company (by Fast Company). The dam, a fair 1m winner, is a half-sister to the very smart multiple Group 3 10f winner Stotsfold. The second dam, Eliza Acton (by Shirley Heights), a fair 2-y-o 1m winner, is a half-sister to 4 winners including listed 10f Winter Derby and subsequent US Grade 3 winner Supreme Sound and to the unraced Why So Silent (dam of the Group 3 winner Leporello and the listed winners Calypso Grant and Poppy Carew). (G Manfredini). *"A nice colt, he wasn't an expensive yearling but I like him a lot. We're not putting too much pressure on him. He's out of a Dansili mare and at the moment he looks like a bargain. Quite good-looking, he moves well and has a great temperament".*
TRAINERS' BARGAIN BUY

216. CASSINA DI NOTTE (IRE) ★★★
ch.c. Casamento – Nightswimmer (Noverre). April 10. Third foal. 58,000Y. Tattersalls October Book 2. SC Rencati. Half-brother to the fairly useful 7f and 1m winner (including at 2 yrs) Mutarakez (by Fast Company) and to the fair 5f winner of 6 races Bashiba (by Iffraaj). The dam is an unplaced half-sister to 4 winners including the 2-y-o listed 5f winner and Group 3 placed Waterways. The second dam, Buckle (by Common Grounds), a fair dual 1m winner at 3 yrs, subsequently won in France and is a half-sister to 8 winners.

(Scuderia Rencati SRL). *"A very good-looking horse, he's done enough to say he has ability and I'm sure he'll be above average. He started to grow and go 'up behind' so at some point we'll back off him and give him more time. We'll bring him back and he should make a 2-y-o by July or August. We like him and he's a straightforward colt with no issues and he has ability".*

217. CLENMISTRA (IRE) ★★★★
ch.f. Poet's Voice – Expedience (With Approval). March 30. Sixth foal. £50,000Y. Doncaster Premier. Tony Nerses. Half-sister to the minor Italian 2-y-o winner Azamourday (by Azamour) and a 4-y-o winner in Qatar by Bahamian Bounty. The dam, a fair 1m winner, is a half-sister to 8 winners including the 2-y-o Group 3 Autumn Stakes winner and Group 1 Racing Post Trophy second Fantastic View. The second dam, Promptly (by Lead On Time), a quite useful 6f winner here, also won a minor 1m stakes in the USA and is a half-sister to 7 winners. (Saleh Al Homaizi & Imad Al Sagar). *"She's very straightforward, a good size and I like her a lot. Mentally she's actually quite forward but being by Poet's Voice I suppose she'll need some time and probably seven furlongs".*

218. DRIVER'S GIRL (USA) ★★★
b.br.f. Candy Ride – Sharbat (Dynaformer). February 3. Fourth foal. $40,000. Keeneland September. The dam, a US stakes-placed winner of 3 races at 3 and 4 yrs, is a half-sister to 4 winners including the Group 3 Prix Minerve winner and Group 1 Prix Vermeille second Pomology. The second dam, Sharp Apple (by Diesis), a US stakes winner of 4 races at 4 yrs, is a half-sister to 4 winners. (Gute Freunde Partnership). *"She's quite forward and ready to go. We're aiming to run her in late April and she definitely shows ability".*

219. DUTCH QUALITY ★★★★★
b.c. Dutch Art – Miss Quality (Elusive Quality). February 23. Third foal. 280,000Y. Tattersalls October Book 2. Tony Nerses. Half-brother to Vivre Pour Vivre (by Pour Moi), unplaced in two starts at 2 yrs in 2015 and to the minor French 2-y-o winner Thuit (by Duke Of Marmalade). The dam, placed twice at 3 yrs in France, is a half-sister to 5 winners including

the stakes winner Desert Gold (dam of the Group 1 Fillies' Mile winner White Moonshine). The second dam, Desert Stormette (by Storm Cat), a minor US 4-y-o winner, is a sister to the Grade 1 Breeders' Cup Sprint winner Desert Stormer and a half-sister to 7 winners. (Saleh Al Homaizi & Imad Al Sagar). *"He's quite forward and he'll be stepped up into fast work now. He looks like he'll be ready by the beginning of May and he definitely has ability. I'd be disappointed if he didn't show something this year. He's quite correct and I can see why he was expensive because he's a good-looking horse. I'll nominate him as my five star 2-y-o!"*

220. MABROOK ★★★★
b.c. Dubawi – Mahbooba (Galileo). February 14. First foal. The dam won 7 races including the South African 2-y-o Grade 1 7f Golden Slipper and a Group 2 9f event in the UAE. The second dam, Sogha (by Red Ransom), is a half-sister to the French dual Group 3 and dual listed winner Slew The Red. (Sheikh Mohammed bin Khalifa Al Maktoum). *"A very good-looking horse, he's quite robust and looks a typical Dubawi. We're not going to put any pressure on him now because he's going to want seven furlongs plus from mid-summer. A really nice horse that could be anything, he carries himself nicely in the canter and is quite athletic. I think he'll make a 2-y-o for sure".*

221. MAGICAL FOREST (IRE) ★★★★
b.f. Casamento – Hurry Home Hydee (Came Home). April 29. Third foal. £22,000Y. Doncaster Premier. Jamie Lloyd/Marco Botti. The dam is an unraced half-sister to 4 winners. The second dam, Ra Hydee (by Rahy), a minor US 3-y-o winner, is a half-sister to 7 winners including two US stakes winners. (Mr J Allison). *"She's quite forward. When we started with her she seemed a bit buzzy and I thought we'd have to be patient, but actually she's coming to hand nicely. We're trying to get her ready for the beginning of May and I think she has the speed to start over five furlongs but she'll get further for sure".*

222. MANDARIN (GER) ★★★
b.c. Lope De Vega – Margarita (GER) (Lomitas). March 31. Third foal. 55,000Y. Tattersalls October Book 1. Jamie Lloyd. The dam, a listed-placed winner in Germany, is a sister to the Group 1 Italian Oaks winner Meridiana and a half-sister to 7 winners Including the Group 2 German Oaks winner Monami. The second dam, Monbijou (by Dashing Blade), a German listed-placed winner, is a half-sister to 6 winners. (Sheikh Mohammed bin Khalifa Al Maktoum). *"I like this horse a lot because when we bought him he was really raw at the sales and didn't walk very well. But he's shaped up into a nice 2-y-o, he's quite big and I don't think he's going to be precocious, but he's a nice mover. One for the second part of the season".*

223. MISS NOURIYA ★★★★
b.f. Galileo – Nouriya (Danehill Dancer). February 6. Second foal. Half-sister to the 2015 2-y-o 7f winner, on her only start, Aljazzi (by Shamardal). The dam, a very useful dual listed 10f winner, is a half-sister to 4 winners including the fairly useful 2-y-o 7f winner and triple listed 10f placed Lady Nouf. The second dam, Majestic Sakeena (by King's Best), is an unraced half-sister to the German listed sprint winner Shy Lady (dam of the St James's Palace Stakes winner Zafeen) and to the French listed winner Sweet Story. (Saleh Al Homaizi & Imad Al Sagar). *"She's a half-sister to a nice 3-y-o we have, Aljazzi. We like her a lot, she's got plenty of quality, is quite immature at this stage but her sister was the same. In my opinion she probably has more scope than Aljazzi. I think she'll be ready for the second half of the season and there's plenty to like about her".*

224. MOOLAZIM ★★
b.c. Tamayuz – Empire Rose (ARG) (Sunray Spirit). March 28. Second foal. Half-brother to the fairly useful 2015 2-y-o 1m winner and 3-y-o UAE Group 3 second Lazzam (by Archipenko). The dam, a fairly useful 7.5f winner in South Africa, is a half-sister to the Argentine dual Group 2 1m winner Empire Aztec. (Sheikh Mohammed bin Khalifa Al Maktoum). *"He had a little setback and he's still quite unfurnished. He'll take a bit of time to be back in full work, but I hope he recovers 100% because we like him and he could be a nice horse".*

225. OMNEEYA ★★★
b.f. Frankel – Amanee (Pivotal).
May 16. First foal. The dam, a South African Grade 2 1m winner, is a half-sister to 2 winners. The second dam, Moon Is Up (by Woodman), a listed 1m winner and Group 3 placed in France, is closely related to the French 2,000 Guineas, the St James's Palace Stakes and Prix du Moulin winner Kingmambo and the smart Group 3 6f winner Miesque's Son and a half-sister to the high-class triple Group 1 winner East of the Moon. (Sheikh Mohammed bin Khalifa Al Maktoum). *"A very sweet filly, she comes from a good family and I like her but we're just taking our time with her. She's gone out for a break now for a few weeks, she was a late foal and I don't think she'll be ready until mid-summer at the earliest. There's plenty to like about her, she has a great attitude and she's a nice mover".*

226. PIRATE LOOK (IRE) ★★
b.c. Canford Cliffs – Gerika (Galileo). April 8. 65,000Y. SGA September (Italy). Not sold. The dam, a 10f winner in Italy, is a half-sister to 6 winners including the Italian triple listed 1m winner Donoma and the Italian dual listed 10f winner Right Connection. The second dam, Green Tern (by Miswaki Tern), won once at 2 yrs in Italy and is a full or half-sister to 8 winners including the Group 3 Italian St Leger winner Green Senor. (La Tesa SPA). *"The breeder sent him quite late, so he's just been cantering and we haven't done much with him. He had a testicle removed as well, so all-in-all he's weak at the moment and being by Canford Cliffs out of a Galileo mare we won't see him out until the back-end of the season".*

227. SAYIF EL BARRI ★★★
b.c. Sayif – Missy O'Gwaun (King's Best). April 7. Second foal. The dam, a fair Irish 12f winner, is a sister to the Japanese Grade 3 2m winner Cosmo Meadow and to the fairly useful 2-y-o 7f winner Angelonmyshoulder and a half-sister to the 7f (at 2 yrs) and Group 3 10f Blue Wind Stakes winner Beauty O'Gwaun. The second dam, Angel Of The Gwaun (by Sadler's Wells), is an unraced sister to 3 winners including the Derby third Let The Lion Roar and a half-sister to the St Leger winner Millenary and the Group 3 Princess Royal Stakes winner Head In The Clouds. (Saleh Al Homaizi & Imad Al Sagar). *"This is quite a forward colt, he's a bit cheeky and I hope he settles down when we start fast work. Nothing nasty, but a bit of a handful. He should be an early type, definitely has ability and he's quite a nice colt. I have three Sayif's and the two colts look like precocious 2-y-o's, whereas we're giving the filly a bit more time because we know the family".*

228. SHIFT CROSS ★★★
br.f. Cape Cross – Rose Shift (Night Shift). February 10. Half-sister to the Italian 2-y-o listed 7.5f winner and Group 1 1m Gran Criterium second Rosa Eglanteria (by Nayef), to the Italian listed placed (over 9f and 12f) Fantastic Shift (by Fantastic Light) and the Italian 2-y-o listed 7.5f winner Ransom Shift (by Red Ransom). The dam, a 7.5f (at 2 yrs) and listed 1m winner of 10 races in Italy, is a half-sister to the US Grade 2 9f and Grade 2 10f winner Whilly. The second dam, Santa Rosa (by Lahib), placed over 7f at 2 yrs, is a half-sister to the Group 2 7f Challenge Stakes winner Decorated Hero. (Scuderia Blueberry SRL). *"A really good-looking filly with a great temperament, we like her a lot and she moves beautifully but she'll need time. No doubt she'll want seven furlongs plus from September onwards. We're happy with her but she's just doing routine canters".*

229. SOUNDS OF APRIL (IRE) ★★
b.f. Exceed And Excel – Wickwing (In The Wings). April 8. Closely related to the Italian winner of 3 races and dual Group 3 10f placed Delicatezza (by Danehill Dancer) and to the quite useful dual Group 1 winner Winter Serenade (by Fastnet Rock) and half-sister to the fair 10f winner Speed Boogie (by Oasis Dream). The dam, an Italian Group 3 10f winner, is a half-sister to 3 winners here and abroad. The second dam, Chetwynd (Exit To Nowhere), is an unraced half-sister to 5 winners including the dam of the dual Group 1 winner Roderic O'Connor. (La Tesa SPA). *"She's quite nice, the family all want a mile and a quarter but she's by Exceed And Excel and looks a more compact filly than the half-sister I trained Winter Serenade. So this is definitely an earlier type but whether she'll need seven furlongs*

I'm not sure, because she doesn't look like a sprinter. She's still on the weak side and still growing, so we'll give her some time".

230. SPECIALE DI GIORNO (IRE) ★★★
b.f. High Chaparral – Special Assignment (Lemon Drop Kid). April 11. Second foal. €30,000Y. Goffs Orby. Jamie Lloyd/Marco Botti. The dam is an unraced half-sister to 8 winners including the US triple Grade 2 winner Quest Star. The second dam, Tinaca (by Manila), is an unplaced half-sister to 5 winners including the dual US Grade 2 winner Mariah's Storm (the dam of Giant's Causeway). (Scuderia Rencati SRL). "I like her, she's a very smart filly and for a High Chaparral she's going nicely at this stage. I didn't expect her to show any speed yet but actually she's coming to hand nicely. We don't want her ready until the seven furlong races from the end of June onwards, so we're being careful not to do too much yet, but she's showing ability. She was quite small as a yearling but she's grown and she's going to be medium-sized".

231. UNNAMED ★★★ ♠
ch.f. Raven's Pass – Pivotal Lady (Pivotal). May 3. Second living foal. 38,000Y. Tattersalls October Book 1. Jamie Lloyd. Half-sister to the fair 7f winner Zwan Awal by Dubawi). The dam is an unraced half-sister to 5 winners including the smart Group 3 7f Solario Stakes (at 2 yrs) and Group 1 Prix Jean Prat winner Best Of The Bests and the smart 6f (at 2 yrs) and 9f winner and Group 2 Dante Stakes third Dunhill Star. The second dam, Sueboog (by Darshaan), a very useful winner of the Group 3 7.3f Fred Darling Stakes, was third in the Musidora Stakes and the Nassau Stakes and is a half-sister to 8 winners. "She was a May foal and we felt she just needed some time so she's just gone out for a break. She's done well and has definitely shown ability for what we've done so far. She seems like a nice filly".

GILES BRAVERY

232. PATCHING ★★★
b.f. Foxwedge – Crinolette (Sadler's Wells). April 5. Fourteenth foal. 60,000Y. Tattersalls October Book 1. Not sold. Half-sister to the useful 2-y-o 6f winner and Group 2 6f Richmond Stakes third Cedarberg (by Cape Cross), to the fairly useful 5f to 1m winner of 5 races from 2 to 5 yrs Cravat (by Dubai Destination) and the fair dual 7f winner Materialism (by Librettist). The dam, unplaced over 8.2f on her only start, is a half-sister to the very smart dual Group 3 7f winner and sire Desert Style. The second dam, Organza (by High Top), a useful 10f winner, is a half-sister to the Group 1 Prix de la Foret winner Brocade – herself the dam of Barathea and Gossamer. "This is a nice filly that's well put together and there's plenty of white about her. A good mover that covers a lot of ground, she's very strong and very good at what she does, in fact she's just relentless and it's hard to get to the bottom of her – so we don't try!"

233. UNNAMED ★★★ ♠
b.f. Danehill Dancer – Blanche Dubawi (Dubawi). February 12. First foal. 90,000Y. Tattersalls December. Not sold. The dam, a fairly useful listed 6f winner, is a half-sister to one winner. The second dam, Dixie Belle (by Diktat), a Group 3 5f and listed 6f winner, is a half-sister to one winner. "The last Danehill Dancer yearling to go through a ring, she'll run in May over six furlongs and she's very good. The family tend to be big, so I'm hoping she won't grow much more but we'll have to see. The grandam won her maiden in May and this filly might be ready to race then too".

234. UNNAMED ★★★
b.c. Equiano – Haiti Dancer (Josr Algarhoud). April 17. Sixth foal. 7,500Y. Tattersalls October Book 3. Not sold. Half-brother to a winner in Germany by Kheleyf. The dam, a modest 2-y-o 7f winner, is a half-sister to 9 winners including the listed-placed winner and useful broodmare Park Charger. The second dam, Haitienne (by Green Dancer), won once at 3 yrs in France and is a half-sister to 7 winners. "The sire seems to have improved his record over the past year. This colt is very light on his feet but the family tend to take a bit of time. He's forward going though and we might get him out in late May or June if he doesn't start to grow". **TRAINERS' BARGAIN BUY**

235. UNNAMED ★★
b.f. Teofilo – Musical Bar (Barathea). April 5. Fourth foal. Half-sister to the quite useful 2-y-o 6f winner Chord Chart (by Acclamation). The dam, a fairly useful 7f winner and second

in a listed event over 1m (both her starts), is a half-sister to 4 winners including the Prix Marcel Boussac, 1,000 Guineas and Irish 1,000 Guineas winner Finsceal Beo and the Group 2 German 2,000 Guineas winner Frozen Power. The second dam, Musical Treat (by Royal Academy), a useful 7f winner and listed-placed twice, won at 4 yrs in Canada and the USA and is a half-sister to 6 winners. *"This is the third one we've had out of the mare but the other two have been disappointing. The filly we had last year didn't stop growing but she's coming back in soon. I can't tell you much about this filly yet, except she won't be out before September. We're just taking our time with her for now"*.

236. UNNAMED ★★
b.f. Intikhab – Solace (Langfuhr). April 12. First foal. 6,000Y. Tattersalls Book 3. Not sold. The dam, a modest 9.5f (at 2 yrs) and 8.5f winner, is a half-sister to two winners. The second dam, Songerie (by Hernando), won the Group 3 1m Prix des Reservoirs at 2 yrs, was third in the Group 2 Park Hill Stakes and is a sister to the fairly useful 2-y-o 7.2f and German listed winner and Group 1 Italian Oaks third Souvenance and a half-sister to 8 winners including the useful listed winners Soft Morning and Sourire. *"We like her a lot and we've been lucky with the sire. We bought this filly as a foal and retained her at the yearling sales. I see her as a seven furlong filly so we won't be rushing her. She's a nice, big, scopey filly and I just hope her temperament stays intact with her being by Intikhab"*.

DAVID BROWN
237. COPING STONE ★★★ ♠
b.f. Bahamian Bounty – Brick Tops (Danehill Dancer). February 11. First foal. 34,000Y. Tattersalls October Book 3. John Fretwell. The dam, a fair 2-y-o 6f winner, is a half-sister to 3 minor winners. The second dam, Rag Top (by Barathea), a useful 2-y-o Group 3 7f C L Weld Park Stakes and listed 6f Swordlestown Stud Sprint Stakes winner, is a half-sister to 9 winners. (J C Fretwell). *"She's a nice filly that's doing everything right and I can see her wanting six furlongs this year. She was an early foal and the dam won as a 2-y-o so hopefully she'll be OK"*.

238. EQUITY ★★★
ch.c. Equiano – Trinny (Rainbow Quest). April 7. Seventh foal. 20,000Y. Tattersalls October Book 2. D H Brown. Half-brother to the quite useful 2015 2-y-o dual 5f winner Birdcage (by Showcasing), to the quite useful 6f and 7f winner You're The Boss (by Royal Applause) and the modest 6f and 7f winner of 5 races Orwellian (by Bahamian Bounty). The dam is an unraced half-sister to 2 winners. The second dam, Mall Queen (by Sheikh Albadou), won the listed Prix Yacowlef and is a half-sister to 8 winners including the listed winner Munnaya (dam of the US Grade 1 winner Alpha). (Just For Girls Partnership). *"A very nice, very strong horse that's showing us plenty. He'll be a five/six furlong 2-y-o and I can see him being out around mid-May"*.

239. HARBOUR SIREN ★★★
b.f. Harbour Watch – Dee Dee Girl (Primo Dominie). April 7. Fifth foal. £34,000Y. Doncaster Silver. David Redvers. Half-sister to the useful 2-y-o 6f and 7f winner Magic Casement (by Proclamation), to the fairly useful dual 5.5f winner at 2 and 3 yrs Handsome Dude (by Showcasing) and the quite useful 5f winner of 11 races, including at 2 yrs, Noodles Blue Boy (by Makbul). The dam, a moderate 2-y-o 7f winner, is a half-sister to 3 minor winners here and abroad. The second dam, Chapel Lawn (by Generous), is an unraced half-sister to 3 winners. (Qatar Racing Ltd). *"A lovely, big filly. She'll set off in the second half of the season over seven furlongs"*.

240. LOOTING ★★★
b.c. Bahamian Bounty – Alice Alleyne (Oasis Dream). March 13. Third foal. 45,000Y. Tattersalls December. John Fretwell. Half-brother to the quite useful 2015 Irish 7f placed 2-y-o Araqeel (by Dutch Art). The dam, a quite useful 7f (at 2 yrs) and 6f winner, is a half-sister to 2 winners including the Irish listed winner and Group 2 third Avenue Gabriel. The second dam, Vas Y Carla (by Gone West), a quite useful 7f placed 2-y-o, is a half-sister to 5 winners including the Group 2 Great Voltigeur Stakes third Avalon. (J C Fretwell). *"A six/seven furlong filly for mid-season. She's a strong 2-y-o and a lovely specimen"*.

241. MAGGI MAY (IRE) ★★★
b.f. Kodiac – Virevolle (Kahyasi). April 17. Seventh foal. 23,000Y. Tattersalls December. D H Brown. Half-sister to four minor winners in Europe by Alhaarth, Key Of Luck, Sleeping Indian and Tagula. The dam is an unraced half-sister to 10 winners including the French listed winner Valley Quest and the Group 3 1m Prix des Reservoirs third Valdara (herself the dam of 3 stakes winners). The second dam, Valverda (by Irish River), a minor 3-y-o winner in France, is a half-sister to the Group 3 winners Verria and Voreas. (Mr D H Brown & Mr Clive Watson). *"She looks very sharp, she'll start over five furlongs but will get six in time. I think she was well-bought and she's a nice-looking filly".* **TRAINERS' BARGAIN BUY**

242. ONE TOO MANY (IRE) ★★★
gr.f. Zebedee – Speckled Hen (Titus Livius). April 14. Fifth foal. 30,000Y. Tattersalls December. John Fretwell. Half-sister to the fair 2015 2-y-o 5f and 6f winner Rockfield Last (by Frozen Power), to the useful 7f to 9f winner Third Time Lucky (by Clodovil) and the French 2-y-o 6f winner Baba O'Riley (by Whipper). The dam, placed fourth once from 8 starts, is a half-sister to 2 winners. The second dam, Colouring (by Catrail), a fair Irish 1m winner, is a half-sister to 3 winners. (J C Fretwell). *"A sharp filly, she'll be out early doors over five furlongs and she's a nice prospect".*

243. ON SHOW (IRE) ★★★
b.c. Iffraaj – Effige (Oratorio). March 20. First foal. £46,000Y. Doncaster Premier. John Fretwell. The dam won 4 minor races in Italy and is a half-sister to 4 winners including the smart 2009 6f Goffs Million Sprint winner Lucky General. The second dam, Dress Code (by Barathea), a quite useful 2-y-o 5f winner, is a sister to the useful 2-y-o Group 3 7f C L Weld Park Stakes winner Rag Top and a half-sister to 9 winners. (J C Fretwell). *"He's very forward, so he's not long away from his first run. A very strong, sharp colt".*

244. QUANTUM FIELD (USA) ★★★
b.f. Distorted Humor – Bootery (Storm Boot). February 16. Half-sister to Neck 'N Neck (by Flower Alley), a US Grade 2 8.5f and triple Grade 3 winner from 1m to 12f. (Qatar Racing Ltd). *"She'll start her career in mid-April.*

She'll get six furlongs later and probably even further but she shows enough speed to start at five. A very strong filly and a fine specimen".

245. RAPID RISE (IRE) ★★★
b.c. Fast Company – French Doll (Titus Livius). February 25. Second foal. £34,000Y. Doncaster Premier. John Fretwell. Brother to the unplaced 2015 2-y-o Emballer. The dam is an unplaced half-sister to 6 winners including the listed Free Handicap winner Kamakiri. The second dam, Alpine Flair (by Tirol), is an unraced half-sister to 2 listed winners in the France and Italy. (J C Fretwell). *"Similar to the Iffraaj 2-y-o we have in that he'll be out early in the season. Probably the strongest colt we have, he's well-advanced".*

246. STEVIE BROWN ★★
b.c. Bushranger – Oriental Romance (Elusive City). April 15. First foal. 2,500foal. Tattersalls December. Not sold. The dam, unplaced on her only start, is a half-sister to 6 winners here and in Italy including the fairly useful 2-y-o dual 6f winner Murbeh. The second dam, My Funny Valentine (by Mukaddamah), won 7 races at 2 to 4 yrs in Italy including two listed events and is a half-sister to 3 minor winners. (Brown, Bolland, Goforth & Watson). *"A very strong, nicely put-together colt that's progressing well. One for six furlongs and above, we named him after my son who sadly passed away last year, so he has to be good".*

247. TRADING PUNCHES (IRE) ★★
b.c. Elzaam – Kiralik (Efisio). March 19. Eighth foal. 35,000Y. Tattersalls December. John Fretwell. Half-brother to the fair 9f winner Adlington (by Dansili) and to the modest 7f and 1m winner Nouvelli Dancer (by Lilbourne Lad). The dam, an Italian listed winner of 3 races and third in the Group 2 Italian 1,000 Guineas, is a full or half-sister to 5 winners including the 2-y-o Group 3 6f Princess Margaret Stakes and subsequent US 3-y-o Grade 2 8.5f winner and Grade 1 9f third River Belle (the dam of two stakes winners). The second dam, Dixie Favor (by Dixieland Band), was a quite useful Irish 6f (at 2 yrs) to 1m winner. (J C Fretwell). *"He's a mid-to-late season prospect. Very big and strong, at the moment I'd say he'd want seven furlongs, but you never know he may sharpen up".*

248. WEDDING DRESS ★★★
b.f. Tamayuz – Dream Day (Oasis Dream). March 9. Fifth foal. £36,000Y. Doncaster Premier. John Fretwell. Half-brother to the French 2-y-o 9.5f winner and listed-placed Delhi (by High Chaparral) and to the quite useful 5f winner Dark Side Dream (by Equiano). The dam, a fairly useful 2-y-o 6f winner and second in the Group 3 Nell Gwyn Stakes, is a sister to one winner and a half-sister to 4 winners including the useful Group 3 Supreme Stakes third Sabbeeh. The second dam, Capistrano Day (by Diesis), a smart listed 7f winner, was third in the Group 3 Fred Darling Stakes, fourth in the 1,000 Guineas and is a full or half-sister to 5 winners. (J C Fretwell). *"A nice, sharp filly, she'll be racing in May. The dam won as a 2-y-o and this filly should be speedier than the 2-y-o winner she had in France by High Chaparral".*

249. YORKSHIRE ROVER ★★★
b.c. Doncaster Rover – Mother Jones (Sleeping Indian). April 6. First foal. The dam, a fair 5f to 6f winner of 5 races at 3 and 4 yrs, is a sister to the fairly useful sprint winner of 5f races Sleepy Sioux and a half-sister to one winner. The second dam, Bella Chica (by Bigstone), a fairly useful 2-y-o winner of 3 races from 5f to 6f, is a half-sister to two winners. (Mr Browns Boys). *"I trained both the sire and the dam. I have three by the sire and this one will be the first to run. He's sharp and the dam was the same, so we'll be getting him out when we get some decent ground".*

250. UNNAMED ★★★
b.f. Royal Applause – Dubai Bounty (Dubai Destination). April 11. Second foal. £52,000Y. Doncaster Premier. David Brown. Half-sister to the 2015 2-y-o Group 3 5f Molecomb Stakes winner Kachy (by Kyllachy). The dam, a fair 8.5f (at 2 yrs) to 12.5f winner, is a half-sister to one winner. The second dam, Mary Read (by Bahamian Bounty), a useful 2-y-o dual 5f winner, was second in the Group 3 Molecomb Stakes and is a full or half-sister to 7 winners. (Mrs F Denniff). *"She looks to have lots of ability. I see her as being a six/seven furlong 2-y-o".*

OWEN BURROWS

251. AKHLAAQ ★★★
b.c. New Approach – Misheer (Oasis Dream). April 10. Third foal. 400,000Y. Tattersalls October Book 1. Shadwell Estate Co. Half-brother to the useful listed 6f winner of 4 races Mistrusting (by Shamardal). The dam, a winner of 3 races including the Group 2 6f Cherry Hinton Stakes and second in the Group 1 Cheveley Park Stakes, is a full or half-sister to 3 winners. The second dam, All For Laura (by Cadeaux Genereux), a fairly useful 2-y-o 5f winner, is a full or half-sister to 5 winners. (Hamdan Al Maktoum). *"He's very nice, just cantering away at the minute, he's not over big and we're pleased with what we've seen so far. He ought to make a 2-y-o, going off his size and pedigree".*

252. ALFAWARIS ★★
b.c. Frankel – Kareemah (Peintre Celebre). April 15. Fourth foal. Half-brother to the 2015 7f placed 2-y-o (on his only start) Ehtiraas (by Oasis Dream) and to the fair 12f winner Saraha (by Dansili). The dam, a French listed 10f winner, is a half-sister to 4 winners including the French listed 9f and subsequent US Grade 1 10f and Grade 1 11f winner Lahudood. The second dam, Rahayeb (by Arazi), a fair 12.3f winner, is a full or half-sister to 4 winners. (Hamdan Al Maktoum). *"He's not arrived here from Derrinstown Stud yet. I don't think he's expected to arrive until the end of April at the earliest".*

253. ALWAATHEQ (IRE) ★★
ch.c. Frankel – Tariysha (Daylami). May 16. Sixth foal. 700,000Y. Tattersalls October Book 1. Shadwell Estate Co. Half-brother to the 2-y-o Group 1 6f Prix Morny and Group 2 6f July Stakes winner Arcano (by Oasis Dream) and to the quite useful 9f winner El Muqbil (by Medicean). The dam is an unraced half-sister to 3 winners and to the dam of the Group 1 Prix de l'Abbaye winner Gilt Edge Girl and the Group 2 Flying Childers Stakes winner Godfrey Street. The second dam, The second dam, Tarwiya (by Dominion), won the Group 3 7f C L Weld Park Stakes, was third in the Irish 1,000 Guineas and is a half-sister to 5 winners including the Group 3 Norfolk Stakes winner Blue Dakota. (Hamdan Al Maktoum). *"You won't see much of him this season, he's big*

and backward and if we get one run into him at the back-end I'll be happy. He was a late foal and he was quite late coming in, but he's a lovely model, he has a good action on him and he floats along. He's changing all the time so, fingers crossed, he could be very nice".

254. ALWAFAAH (IRE) ★★★
b.f. Invincible Spirit – Ghandoorah (Forestry). May 12. Second foal. Sister to the quite useful 2015 7f placed 2-y-o Fawaareq. The dam is an unraced half-sister to 7 winners including the 1,000 Guineas and Coronation Stakes winner Ghanaati and the Group 3 12f Cumberland Lodge Stakes winner and Group 1 Champions Stakes second Mawatheeq. The second dam, Sarayir (by Mr Prospector), a listed 1m winner, is closely related to the top-class Champion Stakes winner Nayef and a half-sister to the 2,000 Guineas, Eclipse, Derby and King George winner Nashwan. (Hamdan Al Maktoum). "She's a typical 2-y-o filly at this time of the year in that she's really changed in the last few weeks. A good-actioned filly, she looks quite sharp, she's very athletic and I'd like to think she'll make a mid-summer 2-y-o".

255. ARZAAK (IRE) ★★★
br.c. Casamento – Dixieland Kiss (Dixie Union). March 3. Second foal. 110,000foal. Tattersalls December. Shadwell Estate Co. Half-brother to the 2015 2-y-o Group 2 6f Lowther Stakes and Group 3 6f Princess Margaret Stakes winner Besharah (by Kodiac). The dam is an unraced half-sister to 3 winners including the US stakes winner and triple Grade 3 placed Kiss Mine. The second dam, Kiss The Devil (by Kris S), a US Grade 3 winner of 6 races from 3 to 5 yrs, is a half-sister to 4 winners. (Hamdan Al Maktoum). "He's a neat colt and looks as if he should be racing sooner rather than later. He's improved a lot in the last few weeks and his coat is developing nicely. Hopefully he'll be racing in May".

256. AZALY (IRE) ★★★
ch.c. Sepoy – Azzoom (Cadeaux Genereux). March 23. Second foal. 110,000Y. Tattersalls October Book 2. Shadwell Estate Co. The dam, a 7f placed 2-y-o, is a half-sister to 5 winners including the very useful 6f (at 2 yrs) and listed 7f winner Levera. The second dam, Prancing (by Prince Sabo), a useful 2-y-o 5f winner, stayed 1m and is a full or half-sister to 4 winners including the Group 1 6f Middle Park Stakes winner First Trump. (Hamdan Al Maktoum). "When we bought him he looked like he'd be early but in the last month he's done nothing but grow and lengthen. So he doesn't look quite so early now and we're in limbo with him at the moment, just going steady away".

257. HATHIQ (IRE) ★★★★
b.c. Exceed And Excel – Madany (Acclamation). April 7. Second foal. Half-brother to the very smart 2015 2-y-o 7f winner and Group 1 Dewhurst Stakes second Massaat (by Teofilo). The dam, a fairly useful 2-y-o dual 6f winner, is a half-sister to 6 winners including the 2-y-o Group 3 Prix du Bois winner and Group 2 Prix Robert Papin third Dolled Up and the 2-y-o listed Prix Zeddaan and subsequent US stakes winner Zeiting. The second dam, Belle De Cadix (by Law Society), The dam, a minor 13f winner at 3 yrs in Ireland, is a half-sister to 5 winners here and abroad. (Hamdan Al Maktoum). "He's a lovely colt and in the last three weeks he's really changed. He's doing everything right at the minute, he's a lovely horse, a good size and well put-together, although he's a little bit smaller than his 3-y-o half-brother Massaat. He looks mature enough to push on with soon and being by Exceed And Excel he should be sharp. A lovely model".

258. JAAZEM (IRE) ★★
b.c. Dark Angel – Miss Indigo (Indian Ridge). April 30. Tenth foal. €360,000Y. Goffs Orby. Shadwell Estate Co. Brother to the useful 2-y-o Group 3 6f July Stakes winner Alhebayeb and to the fairly useful 2-y-o 7f winner Azmaam and half-brother to the useful listed 5f winner and Group 3 third Humidor (by Camacho) and four modest sprint winners by Camacho, Distant Music (2) and Desert Style. The dam is a placed half-sister to 8 winners including the useful listed 10f Pretty Polly Stakes winner Musetta. The second dam, Monaiya (by Shareef Dancer), a French 7.5f and 1m winner, is a full or half-sister to 9 winners including the Canadian Grade 2 winner Vanderlin. (Hamdan Al Maktoum). "He's just had a slight problem so he's only trotting at the minute so we'll have to be patient with him. He's a nice model

though and hopefully he'll start cantering again soon".

259. JAZAALAH (USA) ★★
b.f. Hard Spun – Teeba (Seeking The Gold). April 20. Sister to the Irish 1m and UAE listed 7f winner of 7 races and Group 2 1m second Ghaamer and half-sister to the fairly useful dual 12f winner Kalaatah (by Dynaformer) and the minor US 6.5f winner Ekhlaas (by Bernardini). The dam, a fairly useful 1m winner, was listed placed twice and is closely related to 2 winners including the smart 7f (at 2 yrs) and 10f listed winner Imtiyaz and a half-sister to 5 winners including Bint Shadayid, winner of the Group 3 7f Prestige Stakes and placed in the 1,000 Guineas and the Fillies Mile. The second dam, Shadayid (by Shadeed), won the 1,000 Guineas and the Prix Marcel Boussac and was Group 1 placed a further five times. (Hamdan Al Maktoum). *"She's just arrived from Dubai. She's a big, scopey, active filly and perhaps one for seven furlongs this year. She's got a bit of quality about her but other that I haven't seen enough of her to comment".*

260. MAFAAHEEM (IRE) ★★
b.c. Shamardal – Hammiya (Darshaan). March 16. Half-sister to the useful 7f winner Masaalek (by Green Desert), to the German listed 10f winner Shaqira (by Redoute's Choice) and the fairly useful 7f (at 2 yrs) and 1m winner and listed second Adhwaa (by Oasis Dream). The dam, a useful listed Cheshire Oaks winner, is a half-sister to 3 winners including the useful 2-y-o 1m winner Achill Bay. The second dam, Albacora (by Fairy King), winner of the listed 1m Prix Herod, is closely related to the Prix de Saint-Georges winner and French 1,000 Guineas second Pont-Aven (dam of the Gimcrack Stakes winner Josr Algharoud and the dual Group winner Saint Marine). (Hamdan Al Maktoum). *"Another one just in from Dubai. He's a big, scopey colt but looks as if he's going to want a bit of time".*

261. MUHAJJAL ★★★★
b.c. Cape Cross – Muqantara (First Samurai). January 25. First foal. 180,000Y. Tattersalls October Book 2. Shadwell Estate Co. The dam ran once unplaced and is a half-sister to 3 winners including the Group 2 Debutante Stakes winner and dual Group 1 placed Laughing Lashes. The second dam, Adventure (by Unbridled's Song), won 2 minor races in the USA at 3 yrs and is a half-sister to 7 winners including the Group 1 Racing Post Trophy winner Palace Episode. (Hamdan Al Maktoum). *"A very good-actioned horse, he just needs to strengthen a little bit, so he looks as if he'll want a bit of time. If I remember rightly the dam was trained by Sir Michael Stoute and was quite well thought of, but she had a problem and was only raced once. This is her first foal, I like him and I think he's a very nice colt with a good mind on him".*

262. NAJASHEE (IRE) ★★★★
gr.c. Invincible Spirit – Tonnara (Linamix). March 22. Seventh foal. €700,000Y. Arqana Deauville August. Shadwell France. Closely related to the Group 1 St James's Palace Stakes winner Most Improved (by Lawman) and half-brother to the Group 1 Criterium International winner Ectot (by Hurricane Run) and the minor French 11f winner Merville (by Montjeu). The dam, unplaced in two starts, is a half-sister to 7 winners including the Group 3 Prix de Flore winner Albisola. The second dam, Mahalia (by Danehill), won the listed Prix Imprudence and is a half-sister to 7 winners including the French Group 3 winner Muroto and the good broodmare Zivania (the dam of 5 stakes winners). (Hamdan Al Maktoum). *"Big and scopey, he's a lovely stamp of a horse and there isn't anything not to like about him, but he'll need plenty of time. He's a good mover, certainly has a bit of quality and he's one of Sheikh Hamdan's favourites. He's cantering away and looks as if he'll be a seven furlong 2-y-o".*

263. OKOOL (FR) ★★★★★
b.c. Cape Cross – Seschat (Sinndar). January 30. Third foal. €320,000Y. Arqana Deauville August. Shadwell France. The dam, placed four times at 3 yrs in France and Germany, is a half-sister to 9 winners including the multiple Group 1 placed Salutino. The second dam, Saderlina (by Sadler's Wells), a 3-y-o winner in France and listed-placed twice, is a sister to the listed winner Swalina and a half-sister to 7 winners including Caerlina (Group 1 Prix de Diane). (Hamdan Al Maktoum). *"A beautiful colt. He's a big, scopey horse, very nice and*

moves well. He's one for the middle to back-end of the season and he's lovely. He's going to stay well, so we might not see him until much later on, but I like him a lot".

264. TALAAYEB ★★★★
b.f. Dansili – Rumoush (Rahy). February 27. Third foal. Half-sister to the useful 2015 2-y-o 7f winner and Group 2 Royal Lodge Stakes third Muntazah (by Dubawi). The dam, a very useful 1m (at 2 yrs) and listed 9f winner, was third in the Oaks and is a half-sister to numerous winners including the 1,000 Guineas and Coronation Stakes winner Ghanaati and the Group 3 12f Cumberland Lodge Stakes winner and Group 1 Champion Stakes second Mawatheeq. The second dam, Sarayir (by Mr Prospector), winner of a listed 1m event, is closely related to the Champion Stakes winner Nayef and a half-sister to Nashwan and Unfuwain. (Hamdan Al Maktoum). *"She's a half-sister to Muntazah who did well last year, but she's a smaller model than him which isn't a bad thing because he's massive. She's another one who's turned herself inside out over the past few weeks. She's a lovely, quality filly, moves well and she should be a mid-season 2-y-o".*

265. TAWAAFEEJ (IRE) ★★★★
gr.c. Zebedee – Absolutely Cool (Indian Ridge). April 19. Seventh foal. £140,000Y. Doncaster Premier. Shadwell Estate Co. Half-brother to four winners including the Group 2 Railway Stakes and Group 2 Prix Robert Papin winner Kool Kompany, the hurdles winner Prussian Eagle (both by Jeremy) and the French winner of 8 races including 10f placed Ridge City (by Elusive City). The dam, an Irish 1m placed maiden, is a half-sister to 3 minor winners. The second dam, Absolute Glee (by Kenmare), a 1m (at 2 yrs) and 10f winner, was third in the Group 3 C L Weld Park Stakes and is a half-sister to 4 winners including the US listed winner Step With Style. (Hamdan Al Maktoum). *"One of the most forward of my 2-y-o's, he looks 'all there' and in a couple of weeks we can start going a stride quicker. A good stamp of a horse, he moves nicely and could well be a six furlong 2-y-o".*

266. TEQANY (IRE) ★★★★
gr.c. Dark Angel – Capulet Monteque (Camacho). March 1. Second foal. 380,000Y. Tattersalls October Book 1. Shadwell Estate Co. Brother to the useful 2015 2-y-o 6f winner and listed-placed Juliette Fair. The dam, a quite useful 5f and 6f placed maiden in Ireland, won at 3 yrs in Qatar and is a half-sister to 8 winners including the listed Scarborough Stakes winner and Group 2 King's Stand Stakes second Flanders and to the dam of the dual Group 1 winning sprinter Lethal Force. The second dam, Family at War (by Explodent), a fair 2-y-o 5f winner, is a half-sister to 4 minor winners in the USA. (Hamdan Al Maktoum). *"A lovely horse and probably the biggest, scopiest Dark Angel I've ever had anything to do with. He needs to strengthen now and fill out but he should be pretty sharp. I'd like to see him changing in the next month or so and make a mid-season 2-y-o".*

267. THAMMIN ★★★
b.c. Dark Angel – Gimme Some Lovin (Desert Style). January 30. First foal. £170,000Y. Doncaster Premier. Shadwell Estate Co. The dam, a modest 6f winner here, later won 13 races in Greece and is a half-sister to 8 winners including the dual 2-y-o Group 3 winner Bungle Inthejungle. The second dam, Licence To Thrill (by Wolfhound), a quite useful dual 5f winner, is a half-sister to 4 winners including the useful listed-placed 2-y-o 5f winner Master Of Passion. *"He's cantering now after a small setback and he just needs to get some weight off. He'll be one to press on with in the next few weeks because he looks pretty forward. Looking at him I'd say six furlongs should be right for him".*

HENRY CANDY

268. ANGEL DOWN ★★★★
b.c. Kyllachy – Falling Angel (Kylian). March 22. Second foal. £26,000Y. Doncaster Premier. Henry Candy. The dam, a fair 7f winner, is a half-sister to 6 minor winners here and abroad. The second dam, Belle Ile (by Diesis), a modest 1m winner, is a sister to the listed winner Bonne Etoile and a half-sister to 4 winners. (Thurloe Thoroughbreds XX). *"He's developed really well and he's a big, strong horse now. He moves well and the way he looks now he'd be one of the more forward*

ones, so he could be running in May. There's a fair bit of stamina on the dam's side so we'll wait for the six furlong races with him". **TRAINERS' BARGAIN BUY**

269. CANFORD TOR (IRE) ★★★
b.c. Canford Cliffs – Igreja (Southern Halo). May 13. Thirteenth foal. €30,000Y. Goffs Sportsmans. Henry Candy. Half-brother to 4 winners here and abroad including the quite useful 9.5f winner Blue Train (by Sadler's Wells). The dam, winner of the Group 1 Cape Fillies' Guineas in South Africa, is a half-sister to 6 winners including the Grade 1 winner in South America Taimazov. The second dam, Heiress (by Greinton), is an unraced half-sister to 3 US stakes winners. (Simon Broke & Partners). *"He was a very late foal but he looks a sharp sort and a six furlong type 2-y-o. He was tiny when I bought him and he's growing a lot at the moment. Moves nicely, but he won't be able to do much until mid-summer".*

270. COBALTY ISLE (IRE) ★★★
b.c. Kodiac – Shamarlane (Shamardal). April 15. First foal. €48,000Y. Goffs Sportsmans. Henry Candy. The dam, a modest 7f and 9f winner, is a half-sister to 4 winners. The second dam, Robin Lane (by Tenby), a quite useful listed-placed 9f to 12f winner of 6 races, is a half-sister to 4 winners. (Geoff Buck & Henry Candy). *"He looks very strong, he's a good mover and just needs to grow but he's doing that now. I can see him making a 2-y-o by the summertime and he looks nice".*

271. DECRUZ ★★★
b.f. Dark Angel – Yazmin (Green Desert). March 21. Ninth foal. €28,000Y. Goffs Sportsmans. Henry Candy. Half-sister to the fairly useful 2-y-o 6f and subsequent US winner Yasinisi (by Kalinisi), to the modest 12f and 13f winner Ardmaddy (by Generous), the Italian winner of 9 races from 2 to 5 yrs Ibiscus (by Zafonic) and two minor winners abroad by Barathea and Diktat. The dam, a fairly useful 2-y-o 6f winner, is a half-sister to 2 winners. The second dam, All My Heart (by Sharpen Up), is an unraced half-sister to 7 winners. (Potensis Bloodstock Ltd). *"She goes well, she's a good mover and looks 'together', so she should be racing by June time and she looks nice. The sire's yearlings are becoming hard to buy".*

272. EULA VARNER ★★★
b.f. Showcasing – Tremelo Pointe (Trempolino). April 3. Fourth foal. 75,000Y. Tattersalls October Book 3. H Candy. Half-sister to Aldair, placed fourth over 1m from two stars at 2 yrs in 2015 and to the minor Italian 2-y-o and French 3-y-o 1m winner Mefite (both by Pastoral Pursuits). The dam, a modest 1m winner, is a half-sister to 5 winners including the listed City Of York Stakes winner and Group 1 1m Queen Anne Stakes third Dream Eater and the Group 3 12f St Simon Stakes third Dreamspeed. The second dam, Kapria (by Simon Du Desert), a French 11f winner of 3 races, was third in the Group 3 Prix Penelope and is a half-sister to 4 winners. (Andrew Whitlock Racing). *"Very big and very strong, she's a bit heavy and has immature knees at the moment so I'll just have to go a bit carefully. Despite all that she's a terrific mover and she'll be a nice filly when she's matured a bit. One for the mid-summer onwards".*

273. GREY THOU ART (IRE) ★★★
gr.f. Canford Cliffs – Roystonea (Polish Precedent). March 16. Eighth foal. Half-sister to the smart 2015 2-y-o Group 2 1m Royal Lodge Stakes winner Foundation (by Zoffany), to the fairly useful 2-y-o 7f winner Misterioso (by Iffraaj), the fairly useful 7f (at 2 yrs) to 8.5f winner Vastonea (by Verglas), the quite useful Irish 2-y-o 7f winner Take A Chance (by Hawk Wing) and a minor 2-y-o winner abroad by Xaar. The dam, a listed-placed winner of 2 races over 7f and 1m in France, is a half-sister to 4 winners including the French listed winners Bermuda Grass and Bermuda Rye. The second dam, Alleluia Tree (by Royal Academy), a French 2-y-o winner, is a half-sister to 7 winners and to the unraced dam of the triple Group 1 winner Scorpion. (Sir Edmund Loder). *"She came in very late and has done very little so far, but she looks tough and sharp. She'll be a 2-y-o or nothing and is one for early summer I should think".*

274. GUIDING STAR ★★★★
b.f. Iffraaj – Still I'm A Star (Lawman). January 20. First foal. €110,000Y. Arqana Deauville August. David Redvers. The dam, a dual 10f placed maiden, is a half-sister to 10 winners including the very useful Group 3 1m Desmond Stakes winner Swift Gulliver

and the useful 2-y-o 6f and subsequent dual US stakes winner Abderian. The second dam, Aminata (by Glenstal), a useful winner of the Group 3 5f Curragh Stakes and the listed 6f Smurfit Italia Stakes, is a half-sister to 4 winners. (Qatar Racing Ltd). *"Not very big but very strong, she has a lovely character, likes eating and sleeping and she's a good mover. She shouldn't take long and may be one of our nicer 2-y-o's".*

275. HAMELIN POOL ★★★
b.c. High Chaparral – Presbyterian Nun (Daylami). March 3. Half-brother to Denham Sound (by Champs Elysees), placed third over 1m on both her starts at 2 yrs in 2015. The dam, a fairly useful 2-y-o 7f winner, was listed-placed and is a half-sister to 5 winners including the Group 3 7f Minstrel Stakes winner Jedburgh. The second dam, Conspiracy (by Rudimentary), a useful 2-y-o listed 5f winner, is a half-sister to 7 winners including the Group 2 10f Sun Chariot Stakes winner Ristna and the dual listed winner Gayane. (The Earl Cadogan). *"He'll take time but he's a good-looking horse and has a bit of class about him. I could see him making his debut over seven furlongs in the autumn".*

276. JAKASTAR (IRE) ★★
ch.f. Zebedee – Sportsticketing (Spectrum). April 27. Seventh foal. €28,000Y. Goffs Sportsmans. Henry Candy. Half-sister to the quite useful 5f to 7f winner of 4 races Paz Soprana (by Namid), to the fair 1m winner Blues Music (by Indian Ridge), the multiple hurdles winner Sporting Boy (by Barathea) and a minor winner in Italy by Kheleyf. The dam, a fair Irish 12f winner, is a half-sister to 5 minor winners. The second dam, Ridaya (by Last Tycoon), an Irish 1m and 9f winner, was listed placed and is a half-sister to 6 winners. (Potensis Bloodstock Ltd). *"She was very small and sharp when I bought her but she's grown a heck of a lot. A good mover, she looks OK and is probably a six/seven furlong 2-y-o".*

277. KING OF NEPAL ★★★
b.c. Sepoy – Empress Anna (Imperial Ballet). January 31. Seventh foal. 38,000Y. Tattersalls October Book 2. Henry Candy. Half-brother to 6 winners including the quite useful 7f (at 2 yrs) to 8.5f winner Lady Marl (by Duke Of Marmalade),the fair 10f winner Rockfast (by Fastnet Rock), the fair 7f winner Poker Hospital (by Rock Of Gibraltar) and the fair 7f winner Greenflash (by Green Desert). The dam, a minor winner at 3 yrs in the USA, is a half-sister to 5 winners including the Irish listed winner and Group 3 placed Clean Cut. The second dam, Cutlers Corner (by Sharpen Up), a very useful winner of the 5f Rous Stakes, is a half-sister to 6 winners. (First Of Many). *"He's a big horse, a super mover and an early foal. The knees look mature and he should be racing by June/July time, starting at six furlongs".*

278. QUEEN OF TIME ★★★★ ♠
b.f. Harbour Watch – Black Belt Shopper (Desert Prince). April 7. Tenth foal. 26,000Y. Tattersalls October Book 3. H Candy. Half-sister to 7 winners including the 2015 2-y-o 6f winner from two starts Bounce (by Bahamian Bounty), the quite useful triple 7f winner Star Asset (by Dutch Art), the quite useful 2-y-o 7f winner Cheque Book (by Araafa), the modest 6f winner Exit Strategy (by Cadeaux Genereux) the Japanese winner of 8 races from 3 to 7 yrs Leo Parade and the fair 12f winner Black Label (both by Medicean). The dam, a quite useful 2-y-o 6f winner, was listed-placed and is a half-sister to one winner. The second dam, Koumiss (by Unfuwain), a French maiden that stayed 10f, is a half-sister to 8 winners including the listed Queen's Vase winner Arden. (First Of Many). *"Like lot of Harbour Watch 2-y-o's from what I can gather she's grown a fair bit. So she's quite tall now but she's a very good mover and covers a huge amount of ground. She looks like a nice filly and we've got her half-sister Bounce who we like. This filly should be out around May/June time probably over six furlongs – she wouldn't be a five furlong 2-y-o that's for sure".*

279. REBECCA ROCKS ★★★★
b.f. Exceed And Excel – Rebecca Rolfe (Pivotal). January 25. Second foal. Half-sister to the modest 2015 5f placed 2-y-o Rosie Royce (by Acclamation). The dam, a French listed 5f winner and Group 3 5f second, is a half-sister to 2 winners. The second dam, Matoaka (by A P Indy), a fairly useful 7f winner, is a half-sister to 2 winners including the 2-y-o listed 1m winner and 3-y-o Group 3 placed Battle

Chant. (Hunscote Stud). *"She's got an early birthday and has mature knees but she's just 'up behind' at the moment so just needs a bit more time. She's a good mover and I think she should be OK to race around May/June time. She looks nice".*

280. SUN ANGEL ★★★★
b.f. Sir Prancaelot – Fuerta Ventura (Desert Sun). April 2. Fifth foal. 100,000Y. Tattersalls October Book 1. David Redvers. Half-sister to the unplaced 2015 2-y-o Thrilled (by Kodiac), to the useful listed-placed 6f and 7f winner of 4 races at 2 and 3 yrs The Gold Cheongsam (by Red Clubs) and the fair 6f winner Hope And Faith (by Zebedee). The dam, a useful listed-placed Irish 1m to 9.5f winner of 3 races, and is a half-sister to 3 winners including the useful 2-y-o listed 6f winner and Group 2 6f Mill Reef Stakes second Sir Xaar. The second dam, Cradle Brief (by Brief Truce), is an unraced half-sister to the Group 3 6f Greenlands Stakes winner Tiger Royal. (Qatar Racing Ltd). *"She looks nice, quite mature and level. One that'll be ready for us to carry on with quite soon, she's a good size and a good mover that seems to enjoy her work".*

281. WILLWAMS ★★
b.c. Duke Of Marmalade – Aweebounce (Dubawi). March 14. Second foal. The dam is an unraced half-sister to 3 winners including the Swedish Group 3 winner Hurricane Red. The second dam, Bounce (by Trempolino), won two minor races at 3 yrs in France and is a half-sister to 3 winners including the 2-y-o Group 1 second Simplex. (Potensis Bloodstock Ltd). *"He's going to take a bit of time but he's a good, strong sort and a good mover. One to start at seven furlongs in the autumn I should think".*

MICK CHANNON

282. AMELIA DREAN ★★★
ch.f. Kyllachy – Lady Scarlett (Woodman). February 16. Ninth foal. Half-sister to 7 winners including the Group 3 7f Prix du Palais Royal winner Rossa Corsa (by Footstepsinthesand), the quite useful 2-y-o 1m winner Whistleinthewind (by Oratorio), the quite useful 5f and 6f winner of 7 races and listed-placed Sunrise Safari (by Mozart) and the quite useful 10f winner Val O'Hara (by Ad Valorem). The dam is an unraced half-sister to 5 winners including the Hong Kong listed winner and Irish Derby third Desert Fox and the US Grade 3 winners Poolesta and Home Of The Free. The second dam, Radiant (by Foolish Pleasure), won once at 3 yrs and is a half-sister to the triple Grade 1 winner Gold And Ivory. *"She's a little bit behind some of the others but I think she'll come quick. You wouldn't want to leave her out of the book because she's a 2-y-o alright and she's a nice filly. Not the biggest, but she looks to have an engine and she's a nice filly to deal with".*

283. BILLY'S BOOTS ★★
ch.c. Winker Watson – Solmorin (Fraam). March 31. Half-brother to the modest 2015 2-y-o Shine Likeadiamond (by Atlantic Sport), placed ten times over 5f, to the fairly useful dual 5f winner (including at 2 yrs) Lucky Leigh, the modest 6f (including at 2 yrs) and 5f winner of 7 races Saxonette (both by Piccolo), the modest 6f (at 2 yrs) and 5f winner Majestic Rose (by Imperial Dancer) and the modest dual 1m winner (including at 2 yrs) Alfredtheordinary (by Hunting Lion). The dam is an unplaced half-sister to 2 winners. (M R Channon). *"He looks sharp and he'll certainly be running shortly. I'm not saying he's a star but he's just a nice horse and most of the family wins. He's a sharp 2-y-o and we'll get on and run him. For a Winker Watson he's got quite good 'timber'".*

284. CARAVELA (IRE) ★★
b.f. Henrythenavigator – Stella Point (Pivotal). March 23. First foal. The dam, a fairly useful 10f winner, is a sister to the quite useful dual 1m winner Call To Reason and a half-sister to 3 winners including the quite useful Irish 1m and 11f winner and listed-placed Cilium. The second dam, Venturi (by Danehill Dancer), winner of the Group 3 7f C L Weld Park Stakes, was second in two US Grade 3 events and is a sister to the French listed winner and Group 1 Criterium de Saint-Cloud third Feels All Right. (Jon & Julia Aisbitt). *"A filly for later on, she's one for the back-end over a mile. She'll make up into a nice filly, I trained the mother and his filly is a better specimen than she was".*

285. CHICAGO STAR ★★★
b.c. Exceed And Excel – Librettista (Elusive Quality). May 12. Third foal. 60,000foal. Tattersalls December. Gill Richardson. Half-brother to the fairly useful 10f and 12f winner of 4 races Frenzified (by Yeats). The dam, a fair dual 10f winner, is a half-sister to the Australian Group 3 placed Metastasio. The second dam, Libretto (by Singspiel), is an unraced half-sister to the Grade 2 E P Taylor Stakes winner Truly A Dream and to the French Group 2 2m winner Wareed. (Jon & Julia Aisbitt). *"One of the sharper ones, she'll be ready to rock n roll from late April onwards and five furlongs won't be a problem. She's an Exceed An Excel and you have to keep the lid on them for a while. I'm very happy with her"*.

286. DEVILLISH GUEST (IRE) ★★★★
gr.c. Dark Angel – Leceile (Forest Camp). April 20. Second foal. 180,000Y. Tattersalls October Book 2. Gill Richardson. The dam, a quite useful listed-placed triple 10f winner, is a half-sister to 2 winners. The second dam, Summerwood (by Boston Harbor), a minor US 3-y-o winner, is a half-sister to 7 winners including the Group 1 Dewhurst Stakes third and US Grade 3 winner Firm Pledge. (John Guest Racing). *"Very nice indeed. One of the star picks, he's a very big unit but very natural as well and he does everything easily. If he was smaller we'd be cracking on with him but as it is he's a quality colt, a very good-looking horse and he has a fair bit of ability too"*.

287. DEWAN (IRE) ★★★
b.c. Elzaam – So Blissful (Cape Cross). April 20. Fourth foal. £32,000Y. Doncaster Premier. Gill Richardson. Half-brother to the modest 6f and 7f winner Medicean Bliss (by Medicean). The dam, a fair 3-y-o 7f winner, is a half-sister to 3 minor winners. The second dam, Royal Devotion (by Sadler's Wells), an Irish listed 12f winner, is a closely related to the 2-y-o listed 6f Silver Flash Stakes winner April Starlight and to the dual listed winner Thady Quill and a half-sister to the US Grade 3 8.5f winner Humble Eight. (Nick & Olga Dhandsa/John & Zoe Webster). *"A nice colt for later on. He's a nice, big strong colt and he's just taking his time coming to hand, so he won't be early"*.

288. ESTRELLADA ★★★
b.f. Oasis Dream – Gallic Star (Galileo). March 5. Second foal. Half-sister to the unraced 2015 2-y-o Star Blaze (by Shamardal). The dam, a fairly useful 2-y-o 6f and listed 1m winner, was third in the Group 2 Ribblesdale Stakes and is a half-sister to one winner. The second dam, Oman Sea (by Rahy), a quite useful 2-y-o 6f winner, is a sister to the Group 3 Criterion Stakes winner Racer Forever. (Jon & Julia Aisbitt). *"She a nice filly but being out of a Galileo mare she won't be out until the second half of the season. The dam won over six furlongs and not many Galileo's do that"*.

289. FATHER MCKENZIE ★★★
b.c. Sixties Icon – Queen Of Narnia (Hunting Lion). January 28. Sixth foal. Brother to the fair 2-y-o 6f winner The Sixties and to the modest 2-y-o 6f winner Sakuramachi. The dam, a modest 2-y-o 5f winner, is a half-sister to the useful 5f (at 2 yrs) to 1m winner Dayglow Dancer out of the unraced Fading (by Pharly). (M R Channon). *"He's a very nice colt, he does everything good and just needs a bit of time. A very good-looking horse, around May time you could see a different horse altogether"*.

290. HARLEQUIN ROSE (IRE) ★★★
ch.f. Dutch Art – Miss Chaussini (Rossini). February 21. Sixth foal. 50,000Y. Tattersalls October Book 2. Gil Richardson. Half-sister to the 2016 3-y-o 1m winner Telegram (by Dream Ahead), to the fairly useful dual 7f (at 2 yrs) to 10f winner Strictly Silver (by Dalakhani), the fairly useful 2-y-o 5f winner Muir Lodge (by Exceed And Excel), the fair 7f (at 2 yrs) to 10f winner Coincidentally (by Acclamation) and the fair 6f winner Chaussini (by Dubawi). The dam, a fair Irish 3-y-o 7f winner, is a half-sister to 9 winners. The second dam, Chaussons Roses (by Lyphard), is an unraced sister to the French dual Group 3 winner Tenue De Soiree and a half-sister to the triple Group 1 winner Baiser Vole and the dual Group 2 winner Squill. (Harlequin Direct Ltd). *"More of a six furlong filly than five, she's got a bit of size about her and she's good-looking. Everything's nice about her, so she'll be fine around May or June time"*.

291. INGLEBY MACKENZIE ★★★★
b.c. Sixties Icon – Natalie Jay (Ballacashtal). May 4. Half-brother to the fairly useful 6f (at 2 yrs) and 10f winner and Group 3 7f Prix du Calvados third Fork Handles (by Doyen), to the modest dual 11f and hurdles winner Hoar Frost (by Fraam) and the poor 8.5f winner Think (by Sulamani). The dam, a fair winner of 5 races from 6f to 1m, is a half-sister to 3 winners including the listed Sceptre Stakes winner You Know The Rules. The second dam, Falls Of Lora (by Scottish Rifle), won 6 races from 6f to 14f and from 2 to 4 yrs and is a half-sister to 10 winners. (M R Channon). *"Out of a good old mare of ours, he's a very nice colt, he'll want six/seven furlongs and he does everything nice. He has all the attributes the sire gives them – attitude, size and a touch of quality. He's named after the Hampshire cricket captain of the early Sixties".*

292. JULIE IN THE CROWN ★★★★
b.f. Harbour Watch – Jules (Danehill). March 4. Ninth foal. 16,000Y. Doncaster Premier. Not sold. Half-sister to 6 winners including the fair 2016 3-y-o 7f winner Trodero (by Mastercraftsman), the useful 6f and 7f winner of 7 races from 2 to 5 yrs Golden Desert (by Desert Prince), the quite useful dual 7f winner (including at 2 yrs) Romantic Wish (by Hawk Wing), the quite useful triple 1m winner Stosur (by Mount Nelson), the modest 1m to 14f winner of 8 races The Blue Dog (by High Chaparral). The dam, a fair 7f winner, is a half-sister to 10 winners including the dam of the Australian Group 1 winner Prowl. The second dam, Before Dawn (by Raise A Cup), a champion US 2-y-o filly, won two Grade 1 events. (Mr M Stewkesbury). *"She's very nice, sharp and certainly a 2-y-o. She'll be running in May and then we'll see where we go with her. A well put together filly, she's one to look out for because she looks an athlete and joined the top group quickly. It's too early to say it, but you do wonder if Ascot might be on the agenda".*

293. KIRUNA PEAK (IRE) ★★
ch.f. Arcano – Kirunavaara (Galileo). April 14. Fourth foal. 14,000Y. Tattersalls December. Gill Richardson. Half-sister to Delavand (by Tamayuz), unplaced on his debut at 3 yrs in 2016, to the fairly useful listed-placed dual 7f winner at 2 and 3 yrs Bartel (by Aussie Rules) and the minor German 3-y-o winner Kelida Dancer (by Clodovil). The dam, placed at 2 and 3 yrs in Germany, is a half-sister to 3 winners there. The second dam, Kimbajar (by Royal Abjar), won three listed races from 7f to 1m at 3 and 4 yrs in Germany and is a half-sister to 4 winners including the 1,000 Guineas and Oaks winner Kazzia (herself dam of the UAE Group 1 winner Eastern Anthem). (M R Channon). *"Needs time. We'll see her later in the season over seven furlongs or a mile and I can't see her being ready much before then".*

294. KOEMAN ★★★★
b.c. Dutch Art – Angelic Note (Excellent Art). February 22. First foal. 60,000Y. Tattersalls October Book 2. Gill Richardson. The dam is an unplaced half-sister to the Group 2 Lowther Stakes winner Infamous Angel. The second dam, Evangeline (by Sadler's Wells), is an unraced half-sister to 4 winners including the listed winner Sgt Pepper. (Taplin & Bunney Partnership). *"He's one for the second half of the season, but he's a nice colt by a good stallion. Should be worth waiting for".*

295. MYLADYJANE (IRE) ★★★
gr.f. Mastercraftsman – Candlehill Girl (Shamardal). April 18. First foal. €100,000Y. Goffs Orby. Gill Richardson. The dam, a fair Irish 5f and 6f placed maiden, is a half-sister to 5 winners including the dual listed-placed Valentina Girl. The second dam, Karamiyna (by Shernazar), a French listed 10.8f winner, is a sister to the Group 1 10.5f Prix Ganay, Group 2 10f Nassau Stakes, Group 2 10f Sun Chariot Stakes and Group 1 10f German winner Kartajana and a half-sister to the Australian Group 1 winner Karasi. (Nick & Olga Dhandsa/John & Zoe Webster). *"She'll be a six/seven furlong filly but she's be a nice filly later on. Mastercraftsman 2-y-o's do need a bit of time".*

296. PATTIE ★★★
ch.f. Sixties Icon – Excellent Day (Invincible Spirit). March 8. Second foal. Sister to Harrison, a quite useful 2015 2-y-o 9f winner from two starts. The dam, a fair 5f (at 2 yrs) and 7f winner, is a half-sister to 2 winners including Dalkey Girl, a quite useful 2-y-o 5f winner here and listed placed over 12f at 4 yrs

in Scandinavia. The second dam, Tosca (by Be My Guest), is an unraced half-sister to 8 minor winners here and abroad. (M R Channon). *"Very nice, she's a full-sister to Harrison. I haven't done a lot with her because she had a little setback but she'll be my dark horse for later in the year. She's cantering away but you won't see her until the seven furlong and mile races".*

297. PAVELA (IRE) ★★★
b.f. Approve – Passage To India (Indian Ridge). March 31. Fourth foal. £21,000Y. Doncaster Premier. Gill Richardson. Sister to the quite useful dual 5f winner at 2 and 3 yrs Appleberry. The dam, placed four times at 2 and 3 yrs, is a sister to the Italian triple Group 3 winner Rosendhal and a half-sister to 3 winners. The second dam, Kathy College (by College Chapel), won 8 races including the Group 3 5f Premio Omenoni and is a half-sister to 9 winners. (Insignia Racing Ltd). *"A nice, big filly and one I think could be alright. She's strong and six furlongs would probably be her best trip. Hopefully she'll start off around May time".*

298. PERFECT IN PINK ★★★
ch.f. Raven's Pass – Fashion Rocks (Rock Of Gibraltar). April 27. Fourth foal. 100,000Y. Tattersalls October Book 1. Gill Richardson. Half-sister to the fair 2015 5f and 6f placed 2-y-o Justice Rock (by Acclamation). The dam, a useful 2-y-o listed 6f winner, is a half-sister to 4 winners. The second dam, La Gandilie (by Highest Honor), a dual 2-y-o winner in France including a listed event, was third in the Group 3 Prix Chloe and is a half-sister to 4 winners including the Italian listed winner Totostar. (G D P Materna). *"A nice filly but she'll need six/seven furlongs. A strong, good-looking filly".*

299. RAFFLE KING (IRE) ★★★★
b.c. Kodiac – Tap The Dot (Sharp Humor). March 19. First foal. 48,000Y. Tattersalls October Book 2. Gill Richardson. The dam is an unraced half-sister to two winners. The second dam, Tip The Scale (by Valiant Nature), a minor US stakes winner, is a half-sister to 11 winners including the US Grade 2 winner Eleusis. (Taplin & Bunney Partnership). *"He looks a 2-y-o alright, we won't be hanging around with him and he'll certainly be racing by May I would have thought, as long as everything goes alright. He's a lovely, strong colt and everything's spot on about him".*

300. SAYESSE ★★★
b.c. Sayif – Pesse (Eagle Eyed). February 19. Fifth living foal. 5,500Y. Tattersalls October Book 3. Gill Richardson. Half-brother to the modest 2015 6f and 7f placed 2-y-o Invigorate (by Stimulation) and to the minor Italian winner of 5 races at 2 and 3 yrs Super Aurora (by Refuse To Bend). The dam, a minor Italian winner of 7 races including at 2 yrs, is a half-sister to 8 winners including the 2-y-o Group 1 1m Racing Post Trophy winner Kingsbarns and the US Grade 3 winner Sweeter Still. The second dam, Beltisaal (by Belmez), placed 5 times at 3 yrs in France, is a half-sister to 5 winners including the listed winner and Group 2 placed Kafhar. (Lord Ilsley Racing). *"By the first season sire Sayif, he'll do plenty of racing throughout the year. He's done everything right and he'll start off at five furlongs but be better over six. He looks tough, wants to get on with it and looks a nice type".*

301. SHAWAMI (IRE) ★★★★
b.f. Acclamation – Valeur (Rock Of Gibraltar). March 8. Second foal. The dam, placed once over 1m from two starts, is a half-sister to numerous winners including the Group 1 6f Haydock Park Sprint Cup winner and good sire Invincible Spirit, the Group 3 12f Princess Royal Stakes winner Acts Of Grace and the dual Group 3 winner Sadian. The second dam, Rafha (by Kris), a very smart winner over 6f (at 2 yrs) and the Group 1 10.5f Prix de Diane, the Group 3 Lingfield Oaks Trial and the Group 3 May Hill Stakes, is a half-sister to 9 winners including the Group 2 Blandford Stakes winner Chiang Mai (herself dam of the Group 1 Pretty Polly Stakes winner Chinese White). (Prince A A Faisal). *"She's not very big but she's sharp and we're trying to keep her under wraps but I can see her coming to hand by May time. I'm very pleased with her and none of the family are big but they're all pretty good. One to keep an eye on in the early part of the season".*

302. STRINGYBARK CREEK ★★★
b.c. Bushranger – Money Note (Librettist). February 14. Second foal. 4,000Y. Tattersalls October Book 3. Gill Richardson. Half-brother

to the fair 2015 multiple placed 2-y-o and 2016 3-y-o 6f winner Kyllukey (by Kyllachy). The dam is an unplaced half-sister to 6 winners including the very smart Group 1 1m Gran Criterium winner and 2,000 Guineas second Lend A Hand. The second dam, Janaat (by Kris), a fair 12f winner, is a sister to the French 3-y-o listed 10.5f winner Trefoil and a half-sister to 11 winners including the smart middle-distance winners Maysoon, Richard of York, Third Watch and Three Tails (the dam of 3 Group winners). (M R Channon). *"He'll be racing in April and I couldn't say he's small because he's grown. He's a nice colt alright".* This colt won at the second time of asking, at Kempton in early April.

303. WHITELEY (IRE) ★★★★
b.f. Dark Angel – Carallia (Common Grounds). February 19. Sixth foal. 45,000Y. Tattersalls October Book 2. Gill Richardson. Sister to the useful listed 6f winner of 4 races and Group 3 Hackwood Stakes third Divine and to the fairly useful 5f (at 2 yrs) to 7f winner of 7 races Alejandro and half-sister to the fairly useful Irish 2-y-o 7f winner Carazam (by Azamour) and the French 2-y-o 1m winner Maitres Des Airs (by Hawk Wing). The dam, a listed-placed Irish 6f winner, is a half-sister to 7 winners including the Group 1 Prix de la Foret winner Caradak. The second dam, Caraiyma (by Shahrastani), won over 9f in Ireland and is a sister to the Irish dual Group 3 winner Cajarian and a half-sister to 6 winners. (Peter Taplin & Susan Bunney). *"A very nice filly and a sister to Divine, she'll be one to look out for over six furlongs from May onwards".*

304. ZIG ZAG GIRL ★★★
b.f. Sixties Icon – Mistic Magic (Orpen). April 5. Second foal. 800Y. Doncaster November. Not sold. Sister to the fair dual 7f winner at 2 and 3 yrs Caltra Colleen. The dam, a fairly useful 2-y-o 7f winner, is a half-sister to 2 winners. The second dam, Mistic Sun (by Dashing Blade), won 3 races at 2 and 5 yrs in Germany and the USA, was listed-placed and is a half-sister to 6 winners. (M R Channon). *"I think she's a better filly than her sister Caltra Colleen. She's showing all the right signs and she'll be ready to go in April. A nice filly that'll probably be better over six furlongs than five".*
TRAINERS' BARGAIN BUY

305. UNNAMED ★★★★
b.f. Fast Company – Amazing Win (Marju). April 30. Second foal. £20,000Y. Doncaster Silver. Gill Richardson. The dam, a modest 5.5f and 6f winner of 4 races at 4 yrs, is a half-sister to one minor winner. The second dam, Aqaba (by Lake Coniston), a modest 6f placed 2-y-o, is a half-sister to 4 winners including Alcazar (Group 1 Prix Royal-Oak) and Lady Of Chad (Group 1 Prix Marcel Boussac). *"She's lovely, shows plenty of speed and will come to hand quickly. She'll be running in May for sure. The mother was tough and probably better than she actually achieved but she kept on having wee problems but she was always willing. You'd have to hope you get a straighter run with this filly".*

306. UNNAMED ★★★
b.c. Foxwedge – And I (Inchinor). April 16. Fourth foal. 32,000Y. Tattersalls December. Gill Richardson. Half-brother to the minor Italian winner of 3 races at 3 and 4 yrs Nil By Mouth (by Cockney Rebel). The dam, a fair 6f placed maiden, is a sister to the smart listed 6f winner and Group 3 Greenham Stakes third So Will I and a half-sister to 4 winners including the 2-y-o Group 2 5f Flying Childers Stakes and listed St Hugh's Stakes winner Sand Vixen. The second dam, Fur Will Fly (by Petong), was placed once over 6f at 3 yrs and is a half-sister to 4 winners. *"He's a big colt and I haven't done as much with him because he was bought later and he's a bit behind the others. But I think he's very nice and he's doing everything right".*

307. UNNAMED ★★
ch.c. Harbour Watch – April (Rock Of Gibraltar). March 20. Fourth foal. 30,000Y. Tattersalls October Book 2. Gill Richardson. Half-brother to the modest 6f winner Ealain Aibrean (by Excellent Art) and to the modest 2-y-o 7f winner Liffey View (by Arcano). The dam, a fair Irish 5f winner, is a half-sister to 5 winners including the US Grade 3 winner Starstruck. The second dam, Agnetha (by Big Shuffle), a smart winner of the listed Silver Flash Stakes (at 2 yrs) and the Group 3 5f King George Stakes, is a sister to the smart German Group 2 sprint winner Areion and to the Irish listed winner Anna Frid and a half-sister to 5 winners. *"He threw a splint which has held us*

up a bit, so I can't tell you a lot about him but he's strong. One for the middle of the season I'd say".

308. UNNAMED ★★
ch.f. Sixties Icon – Five Bells (Rock Of Gibraltar). April 27. Fourth foal. Sister to the modest 7f (at 2 yrs) to 10f winner of 3 races Chilworth Bells and half-sister to the moderate 2-y-o 6f seller winner Ding Ding (by Winker Watson). The dam was unplaced on both her starts. The second dam, Gold Mist (by Darshaan), a quite useful 10f and 14f winner, is a full or half-sister to 3 winners. (Norman Court Stud I). *"Quite a nice filly, she goes well and although I don't think she's a star she'll certainly win and we'll be getting on with her".*

309. UNNAMED ★★★
b.f. Clodovil – Nadinska (Doyen). April 19. Third foal. Half-sister to the fair triple 7f winner (including at 2 yrs) Wink Oliver (by Winker Watson). The dam, a modest 6f winner, is a half-sister to 5 winners including the Group 2 1m Prix de Sandringham winner Laugh Out Loud and the useful 6f (at 2 yrs), 10f and listed 12f winner Suzi's Decision. The second dam, Funny Girl (by Darshaan), was placed from 7f to 9f. (Norman Court Stud). *"A little bit backward but very nice, she's a good-looking filly and has a bit of size. A strong 2-y-o for the middle of the season, she's just playing catch up for now but you don't want to leave her out".*

310. UNNAMED ★★
b.f. Born To Sea – Puerto Oro (Entrepreneur). February 8. Seventh foal. £20,000Y. Doncaster Premier. Gill Richardson. Half-sister to the German and Polish 6f and 7f winner of 5 races at 2 and 3 yrs and dual Group 3 placed Exciting Life (by Titus Livius) and to a winner in Macau by Thousand Words. The dam, a modest Irish 6f (at 2 yrs) and 7f placed maiden, is a half-sister to the Group 3 Prix de Cabourg winner Hunan. The second dam, Foolish Fun (by Fools Holme), was placed at 2 yrs and is a half-sister to 5 winners. *"She's threw a splint so she's a bit behind at present, but she'll be alright and she'll make a 2-y-o in the second half of the season. A nice filly".*

311. UNNAMED ★★★
b.c. Tagula – Sharadja (Doyoun). April 18. €30,000Y. Goffs HIT November. Bobby O'Ryan. Half-brother to the fairly useful 6f winner of 5 races Parisian Pyramid (by Verglas), to the quite useful 2-y-o 5f winner Jerrazzi (by Kodiac), the fair 7f to 10f winner of 10 races She's Our Lass (by Orpen) and the fair 7f and 10f winner King Of Rhythm (by Imperial Ballet). The dam is an unraced half-sister to 2 winners. The second dam, Sharadiya (by Akarad), was fairly useful 9.6f winner. *"A nice horse, he'll need six or seven furlongs to be at his best this year. He's not taking the eye just yet, not because of lack of ability, but he was a late April foal and he's not quite as precocious as some of the others".*

312. UNNAMED ★★
b.c. Kyllachy – Sonny Sunshine (Royal Applause). March 27. Third foal. 60,000Y. Tattersalls October Book 2. Gill Richardson. The dam is an unraced half-sister to 4 winners including the multiple Group 1 winning sprinter Sole Power. The second dam, Demerger (by Distant View), is an unraced half-sister to 5 winners. (Malih L Al Basti). *"He's taking a bit of time because he's a bit babyish. I thought he'd be sharper than he's turned out but nevertheless he's a nice colt".*

313. UNNAMED ★★★
b.c. New Approach – Sweet Lilly (Tobougg). April 17. Fourth foal. 60,000Y. Tattersalls October Book 1. Not sold. Half-brother to the quite useful 2015 2-y-o 7.5f winner Zaina Rizeena (by Shamardal), to the German 7.5f (at 2 yrs) and 1m winner Rosy Blush (by Youmzain) and the fair 1m winner Lilly Junior (by Cape Cross). The dam, a smart triple listed winner and second in the Group 3 Musidora Stakes, is a half-sister to 3 winners. The second dam, Maristax (by Reprimand), a fair 2-y-o 7f winner, is closely related to the useful 2-y-o listed 5f winner Four-Legged-Friend and a half-sister to 6 winners including the dual US Grade 3 winner Superstrike and the dam of the Group 1 winning sprinters Goodricke and Pastoral Pursuits. *"He's a good-looking horse and looks a 2-y-o but he's quite backward because he came in late. A big, strong horse, you won't see him until July".*

PETER CHAPPLE-HYAM

314. AWARE (GER) ★★★★
b.c. Lawman – Amorama (Sri Pekan). February 26. Sixth foal. €45,000Y. Arqana Deauville October. Private Sale. Half-brother to 4 winners including the Group 2 Prix Hocquart winner and Group 1 Grand Prix de Paris second Ampere (by Galileo) and the minor French middle-distance winners Amoa (by Ghostzapper) and Amorine (by Montjeu). The dam, a US Grade 1 John C Mabee Handicap and Grade 1 Del Mar Oaks winner, is a half-sister to 5 winners including the Japanese Group 2 placed Uncoiled and the French listed 1m winner Table Ronde and to the unraced dam of the Group 1 Prix Jean Romanet winner Odeliz. The second dam, Tanzania (by Alzao), was a minor Irish 12f and 13f winner. (Mrs Fitri Hay). *"A very nice horse. He's going to want plenty of time but he does everything really good. I see him as one for August or September over seven furlongs and he's very similar to Marcel (also a son of Lawman) but not as strong. He'll get there, he has a good pedigree and I like him".*

315. BELLA ALISSA ★★
b.f. Dutch Art – Crazy Too (Invincible Spirit). February 25. First foal. The dam, placed three times over 5f at 2 and 3 yrs, is a modest half-sister to 2 winners. The second dam, Reform Act (by Lemon Drop Kid), a 1m (at 2 yrs), 10f and listed 12f winner in Ireland and third in the Grade 2 Long Island Handicap in the USA, is a half-sister to 4 winners including the US winner and dual Grade 1 placed Soul Search. (Saleh Al Homaizi & Imad Al Sagar). *"A small filly, she was an early foal so I have to start moving her along now to find out how early she is. She's perfectly sweet and well put together, but because of her size she needs to be out sooner rather than later. All being well she should be out in May, probably over six furlongs and we'll see how we go.*

316. CHARLIE RASCAL (FR) ★★★
b.c. Myboycharlie – Rascafria (Johannesburg). May 4. Second foal. €9,000Y. Arqana Deauville October. Private Sale. The dam ran once unplaced and is a half-sister to 3 winners including the US Grade 2 second Literacy. The second dam, Tuviah (by Eastern Echo), was placed in the USA and is a half-sister to the Group 3 Park Stakes winner Duck Row. (Paul Hancock). *"He goes really well for a big horse, he'll be better over seven furlongs, does everything right and I like him a lot. He could be more than useful and I think he's another bargain buy. His owner Paul Hancock is so lucky this colt is bound to be a winner".* This colt was named 'No Pain No Gain' at the sales, but at the time of going to press the owner intends to change it.

317. CLASSICAL TIMES ★★★★
b.f. Lawman – Sunday Times (Holy Roman Emperor). February 10. First foal. The dam, a smart Group 3 7f Sceptre Stakes winner and Group 1 6f Cheveley Park Stakes second, is a half-sister to the fairly useful 6f listed-placed 2-y-o and 6f 3-y-o winner Question Times. The second dam, Forever Times (by So Factual), a fairly useful 5f (at 2 yrs) to 7f winner, is half-sister to 7 winners including Welsh Emperor (Group 2 7f Hungerford Stakes) and the listed 5f winner Majestic Times. (Mr A Belshaw). *"She's lovely, the first foal of Sunday Times and she's her spitting image. I thought she'd want plenty of time but she's coming together well and is quite strong now. I see her being out by July time, she's really nice and could be anything, so I like her very much. Seven furlongs should be right for her".*

318. HOTCAKE ★★
ch.f. Archipenko – Heat Of The Night (Lear Fan). May 6. Sixth foal. Half-sister to the modest 2015 dual 1m placed 2-y-o Hot To The Touch (by Aussie Rules), to the fair 2-y-o 5f winner Long Lost Love (by Langfuhr) and the modest 7f winner Here To Eternity (by Stormy Atlantic). The dam, a dual 9f winner here, subsequently won a listed 1m event in Germany and is a half-sister to the Irish 7f and Grade 2 hurdles winner Convincing. The second dam, Hot Thong (by Jarraar), was a Brazilian Grade 3 7f winner and a half-sister to 4 winners. (Miss K Rausing). *"She's going to want plenty of time, being by Archipenko. She's just cantering now and I've been taking my time with the fillies anyway. She'd be one for August time over seven furlongs or a mile".*

319. MISS PATIENCE ★★★
b.f. Excelebration – Connote (Oasis Dream). January 30. First foal. 38,000Y. Tattersalls October Book 2. Stephen Hillen. The dam is an unraced half-sister to 6 winners including the Group 1 July Cup and Group 1 Prix de l'Abbaye winner Continent. The second dam, Krisia (by Kris), won over 12f and is a half-sister to 6 winners including the French listed 10.5f and 12f winner Short Pause and the dam of the Group 1 Grand Prix de Paris winner Zambezi Sun. (Mrs Fitri Hay). *"She was showing a lot in February/early March and then went through a very weak phase, so I left her alone. It's not a bad pedigree at all and she was well-bought I think. Six furlongs in May should be her starting point with a view to seeing how we stand. I like her a lot".*

320. POKER ALICE ★★★★
b.f. Holy Roman Emperor – Grain Only (Machiavellian). April 21. Seventh foal. 22,000Y. Tattersalls October Book 3. Blandford Bloodstock. Half-sister to the Australian Group 3 12f winner of 7 races Caravan Rolls On, to the quite useful 8.5f (at 2 yrs) to 14f winner of 4 races and listed-placed Gabrial's Star (both by Hernando), the quite useful 2-y-o 7f winner Noble Metal (by With Approval) and the modest 7.5f (at 2 yrs) and 1m winner Multi Grain (by Sir Percy). The dam is an unraced half-sister to 4 minor winners. The second dam, All Grain (by Polish Precedent), a useful 12.6f winner and third in the Group 3 Lancashire Oaks, is a sister to the Irish Oaks and Yorkshire Oaks winner Pure Grain and a half-sister to 7 winners. *"I've had half the family and every time I see one for sale I have to buy it because one day I will get it right with this family! She'll be a six furlong filly in May/June, does everything easy and isn't far off a piece of work. I like her a lot, and although she's out of a Machiavellian mare and all the family have stayed, she's got plenty of speed. Six furlongs should be perfect for her".*
TRAINERS' BARGAIN BUY

321. READER'S CHOICE ★★★
b.c. Redoute's Choice – Forever Times (So Factual). March 21. Seventh foal. 20,000Y. Tattersalls October Book 1. Not sold. Closely related to the fair 2015 6f placed 2-y-o Udontdodou (by Fastnet Rock) and to the smart Group 3 Sceptre Stakes winner and Group 1 6f Cheveley Park Stakes second Sunday Times (by Holy Roman Emperor) and half-brother to the fairly useful 2-y-o listed 6f placed and 3-y-o 6f winner Question Times (by Shamardal) and the fair 1m winner Russian Reward (by Iffraaj). The dam, a fairly useful 5f (at 2 yrs) to 7f winner, is half-sister to 8 winners including Welsh Emperor (Group 2 Hungerford Stakes) and the listed 5f winner Majestic Times. The second dam, Simply Times (by Dodge), is an unplaced half-sister to 5 winners. (Mr A Belshaw). *"He goes along really nicely, he's done a couple of canters upsides and does it really nice. He'll be OK over six furlongs to start with but will probably want further. The sire was a good horse but not as a 2-y-o, but this colt doesn't look like that and it's a 2-y-o family on the dam's side. So all being well he should make a 2-y-o alright".*

322. REDICEAN ★★★★
b.c. Medicean – Red Halo (Galileo). March 14. First foal. 34,000Y. Tattersalls October Book 2. Troy Steve. The dam, placed fourth once over 1m at 2 yrs from two starts, is a half-sister to 2 minor winners. The second dam, St Roch (by Danehill), is an unraced sister to the US Grade 1 winner Luas Line and a half-sister to 5 winners including the Group 2 Bosphorus Cup winner Lost In The Moment. (High Rollers). *"He's a nice horse, goes really well and he's just done his first bit of work. I like him a lot, he'll be better over six furlongs but I might start him in a Newbury maiden over five. He's very sharp and yet he's huge – like a tank already. So he could be a very good horse or I've got it totally wrong - which is possible!"*

323. SAYIF DANCING ★★★
b.c. Sayif – Keep Dancing (Distant Music). April 22. Second foal. Half-brother to the useful 2015 2-y-o 7f and 1m winner Special Season (by Lope De Vega). The dam, a modest 6f winner, is a sister to one winner and a half-sister to 5 winners including the 2-y-o Group 2 July Stakes winner Alhebayeb and the listed 5f winner Humidor. The second dam, Miss Indigo (by Indian Ridge), is a placed half-sister to 8 winners including the useful listed 10f Pretty Polly Stakes winner Musetta. (Saleh Al Homaizi & Imad Al Sagar). *"I like this horse but when I found out I was getting a*

Sayif I didn't know whether to be happy or sad because Sayif was a nightmare to train. But this colt is totally different, a bit of a late foal but he's doing everything right. He moves well, goes well, looks sharp and six furlongs in May or June should suit. He might surprise a few people, including me!"

324. WARDY (IRE) ★★
b.c. Dandy Man – Why Now (Dansili). April 18. Seventh foal. 50,000Y. Tattersalls October Book 2. Stephen Hillen. Half-brother to the fair 2015 2-y-o 5f winner Rosealee (by Zebedee), the quite useful 5f and 6f winner of 5 races (including at 2 yrs) Here Now And Why, the fair 2-y-o winner Woodland Mill, (both by Pastoral Pursuits), the quite useful 2-y-o 6f winner What About You (by Statue Of Liberty) and the fair 5f to 1m winner Al Freej (by Iffraaj). The dam, a fair 5f and 6f winner, is a half-sister to 4 winners. The second dam, Questionable (by Rainbow Quest), is an unraced sister to the Group 3 15f Prix Berteux winner Ecologist and a half-sister to 7 winners including the St James's Palace Stakes second Greensmith. (Mrs Fitri Hay). *"I thought he was quite sharp and was moving him along a bit, but I think I've sent him weak. He does everything alright, there are no problems whatsoever, but he's not going to be out until mid-summer. He'll be a sharp horse, he has to be, but he just lives on his nerves a bit at the moment".*

325. UNNAMED ★★
b.f. Kheleyf – Kalinova (Red Ransom). March 26. Fifth foal. 24,000Y. Tattersalls October Book 2. Brian Grassick Bloodstock. Half-sister to the quite useful 2-y-o 6f and subsequent Saratoga winner Stars Above Me (by Exceed And Excel). The dam is an unraced half-sister to 5 winners including the Group 1 Fillies Mile, Falmouth Stakes, Sussex Stakes and Matron Stakes winner Soviet Song, the useful 5f (at 2 yrs) and triple 6f winner Baralinka and the dam of the Group 1 Prix Jean Romanet winner Ribbons. The second dam, Kalinka (by Soviet Star), a quite useful 2-y-o 7f winner, is a half-sister to 2 winners. (Mrs Clodagh McStay). *"She's not the biggest, but I like her and she's starting to do some fast work now because it's time to find out what she's capable of. She has a good temperament for a Kheleyf (they can be a bit funny) and does everything right, but how good she is I don't know. She'll be better over six furlongs than five and when you wind up some of these Kheleyf's they get sharp. I don't mind her at all".*

326. UNNAMED ★★
ch.f. Casamento – Lady Caprice (Kyllachy). March 16. Second foal. 8,000Y. Tattersalls October Book 3. Not sold. Half-sister to the unplaced 2015 2-y-o Was Asleep (by Lord Shanakill). The dam, a modest triple 5f winner at 2 and 3 yrs, is a half-sister to 2 other minor winners. The second dam, Lady Betambeau (by Grand Lodge), is an unplaced sister to the listed Atalanta Stakes winner Lady Bear. (Tony Elliott). *"She's quite nice, she's grown a lot and will want plenty of time but I see her as a seven furlong filly. I'll start her at six around June or July time, she's not a bad filly and has a good attitude".*

327. UNNAMED ★★★
b.c. Teofilo – Nyarhini (Fantastic Light). February 20. Fifth foal. 58,000Y. Tattersalls October Book 1. A Elliott. Half-brother to the fairly useful 7f (at 2 yrs) and listed 1m winner Token Of Love (by Cape Cross), to the fairy useful 5f (at 2 yrs) and 7f winner Dashing David (by Lemon Drop Kid) and the fair 1m winner Sigurwani (by Arch). The dam, a fairly useful 6f winner (at 2 yrs), was listed-placed over 1m and 10f and is a half-sister to 9 winners including the Group 1 Coronation Stakes winner Rebecca Sharp, the Group 3 Lingfield Derby Trial winner Mystic Knight and the listed Cheshire Oaks winner Hidden Hope. The second dam, Nuryana (by Nureyev), a useful winner of the listed 1m Grand Metropolitan Stakes, is a half-sister to 5 winners. (Tony Elliott). *"A nice horse but he'll want plenty of time so we'll just have to take it easy with him for now. He's a great mover and has a great attitude, I'm a big fan of the sire and I like this colt a lot, but he's one for the back-end of the season over seven furlongs or a mile. How good he'll be I don't know yet".*

328. UNNAMED ★★
b.f. Authorized – Sagina (Shernazar). April 30. Ninth foal. 1,000Y. Tattersalls October Book 3. A C Elliott. Half-sister to a winner in Spain by Medicean and a hurdles winner by Tobougg. The dam, placed twice at 3 and 4

yrs in France, is a sister to the US listed stakes winner Capracotta and a half-sister to 7 winners including the listed winner Salim Toto. The second dam, Villasanta (by Corvaro), is a placed half-sister to 8 winners including four stakes winners in France. *"She has a staying pedigree so she'll obviously want plenty of time. Owned by some good friends of mine, she's nice but probably won't be out until September over a mile. She was very cheap but they can't lose money and I think they'll only make money on her. She's alright this filly".*

ROGER CHARLTON

329. ABATEMENT ★★
b.c. Bated Breath – Iwunder (King's Best). May 14. Sixth foal. 115,000Y. Tattersalls October Book 2. John & Jake Warren. Half-brother to the quite useful 1m winner No Wunder (by Rock Of Gibraltar), to the fair 10f and hurdles winner Lady Chloe (by Noverre) and the minor Italian winner of 5 races Kheywunder (by Kheleyf). The dam, a modest 1m placed maiden, is a half-sister to 4 winners including the Irish listed winner Molly-O. The second dam, Sweetest Thing (by Prince Rupert), won over 7f and 10f in Ireland and is a half-sister to 3 winners including the listed City Of York Stakes winner Reported. (Highclere Thoroughbred Racing). *"The Bated Breath foals and yearlings were popular at the sales and this is a well-grown, good-moving, attractive colt. The dam hasn't bred a 2-y-o winner yet and he was a late foal but I would hope he'd be running by June or July. He's bred to need seven furlongs I'd say".*

330. BLAZED (IRE) ★★★
gr.c. Dark Angel – Sudden Blaze (Soviet Star). April 20. Third foal. 125,000Y. Tattersalls October Book 2. Charlie Gordon-Watson. The dam is an unraced sister to the US Grade 3 11f winner and Grade 1 placed Rosinka and a half-sister to 6 winners including the US Grade 1 winner King's Drama. The second dam, Last Drama (by Last Tycoon), won and was listed placed twice over 10f in France and is a sister to the listed winner and smart broodmare Tycoon's Drama. (HRH Sultan Ahmad Shah). *"A fairly late foal, he's from a fast family and should be a mid-season 2-y-o. Physically he's done well since the sales and of course the sire is very successful with his 2-y-o's".*

331. CARACAS ★★
b.c. Cacique – Bourbonella (Rainbow Quest). March 6. Ninth foal. Half-brother to the high-class Group 1 1m Prix du Moulin, Group 2 Summer Mile and Group 3 7f Jersey Stakes winner Aqlaam, to the fair 7f and 1m winner Araqella (both by Oasis Dream), the fairly useful 1m and UAE listed winner Nine Realms (by Green Desert) and the fair 12f to 15f winner Curacao (by Sakhee). The dam is an unraced half-sister to 9 winners including the high-class and multiple winning stayer Persian Punch and the Group 3 7f Solario Stakes winner Island Magic. The second dam, Rum Cay (by Our Native), a fair 14.6f winner, is a half-sister to 3 winners including the listed winner of 10 races Gymcrak Premiere. (David Hearson). *"A very strong, neat colt, we haven't done a lot with him yet so it's hard to know where we're at with him".*

332. CASIMIRO (IRE) ★★★★
ch.c. Casamento – Glyndebourne (Rahy). February 22. Third foal. 75,000Y. Tattersalls October Book 2. Amanda Skiffington. The dam is an unplaced half-sister to 2 winners including the listed winner and Group 2 third Portrayal. The second dam, True Glory (by In The Wings), a quite useful 11f winner, is a half-sister to 7 winners including the very smart Grade 2 10f E P Taylor Stakes winner Truly A Dream and the French dual Group 2 winner Wareed. (Hearson & Inglett). *"A very strong, powerful colt that looks like Casamento and/ or Shamardal with a slightly plain head. He looks like he ought to be a 2-y-o and we like him. We haven't done much with him yet but he looks the part physically".*

333. COMRADE CONRAD (IRE) ★★
b.c. Canford Cliffs – View (Galileo). April 12. Second foal. €78,000Y. Tattersalls Ireland September. Amanda Skiffington. Brother to the unplaced 2015 2-y-o Northern Beau. The dam ran twice unplaced and is a half-sister to one winner. The second dam, Trading Places (by Dansili), is an unraced half-sister to 11 winners including the Group 3 6f July Stakes winner Wharf, the top-class broodmare Docklands (dam of the Arc winner Rail Link) and the dam of the French 2-y-o Group 1 winner Linda's Lad. (Michael Pescod). *"There's a lot of stamina in his pedigree including the*

damsire Galileo. He's grown and done well since the sales and I guess he's going to be one for the second half of the season over seven furlongs and a mile".

334. DAGONET (IRE) ★★★
b.c. Sir Prancealot – Dubai Diamond (Octagonal). April 18. Ninth foal. 37,000Y. Tattersalls December. Amanda Skiffington. Half-brother to the 2-y-o listed 5f second Hexagonal (by One Cool Cat) and to 4 winners including the fair 10f and 12f winner of 4 races Bavarian Nordic (by Barathea), the modest 8.5f to 9.5f winner Smart Violetta (by Smart Strike) and a minor Italian 2-y-o winner by Amadeus Wolf. The dam, a French 7f placed maiden, is a half-sister to 9 winners including the Grade 1 Atto Mile winner Riviera. The second dam, Manureva (by Nureyev), a French listed 1m winner, is a half-sister to 8 winners including Macoumba (Prix Marcel Boussac) and Septieme Ciel (Prix de la Foret). (Michael Pescod). *"A relatively early type from the first crop of the sire. He's a good-moving horse and has quite a speedy pedigree".*

335. DISCOVERED (IRE) ★★★
ch.c. Bated Breath – Sandglass (Zafonic). March 25. Seventh foal. 160,000Y. Tattersalls October Book 1. Charlie Gordon-Watson. Half-brother to the minor Italian winner of 2 races at 3 and 4 yrs Time Signal (by Champs Elysees). The dam, a fairly useful 10f winner, is a half-sister to 6 winners including the Group 1 Falmouth Stakes winner Timepiece, the Group 1 10f Criterium de Saint-Cloud winner Passage Of Time and the Group 2 10f King Edward VII Stakes winner Father Time. The second dam, Clepsydra (Sadler's Wells), a quite useful 12f winner, is a half-sister to 6 winners including the listed 10.5f winner Double Crossed (dam of the dual Champion Stakes winner Twice Over). (HRH Sultan Ahmad Shah). *"An attractive colt from a Juddmonte family, his relations haven't been early and we don't know much about Bated Breath yet, but he looks strong and together. Seems a nice horse".*

336. DISTANT (USA) ★★★
b.br.f. First Defence – Ventoux (Galileo). March 13. First foal. The dam won in France over 12f and is a half-sister to 2 winners including the Group 1 Cheveley Park Stakes, 1,000 Guineas and French 1,000 Guineas winner Special Duty. The second dam, Quest To Peak (by Distant View), ran once unplaced and is a sister to Sightseek, winner of seven Grade 1 events in the USA from 7f to 9f and a half-sister to the US dual Grade 1 winner Tates Creek. (Khalid Abdulla). *"A lovely, very attractive, rangy filly that's likely to be a back-end 2-y-o and make a nice 3-y-o. Her dam won over twelve furlongs, but she's a half-sister to a champion 2-y-o filly in Special Duty. It's a good family and she's attractive".*

337. ESPRIT DE CORPS ★★★★
b.c. Sepoy – Corps De Ballet (Fasliyev). February 21. Seventh foal. 80,000Y. Tattersalls October Book 2. Mrs A Skiffington. Half-brother to the 2-y-o 6f and subsequent Hong Kong winner Georges Lane (by Diamond Green), to the quite useful 5f and 6f winner of 13 races (including at 2 yrs) Dark Lane (by Namid), the quite useful triple 7f winner Dance Company (by Aussie Rules), the fair 6f winner of 4 races at 2 and 3 yrs Gold Waltz (by Acclamation) and the fair 7f winner Compton Park (by Compton Place). The dam, a fairly useful 5f (at 2 yrs) and 6f winner, is a half-sister to 7 winners including the prolific Hong Kong winner of 8 races and £750,000 Quick Action. The second dam, Dwell (by Habitat), was a fairly useful listed-placed 1m winner. (Hearson & Inglett). *"From the first crop of Sepoy who hasn't started off particularly well in Australia but he had some nice yearlings. This is a very solid, good-looking colt and a half-brother to five winners that were mainly six furlong horses. He's a February foal so you'd hope to see him running from June onwards. We like what we see so far".*

338. EYNHALLOW ★★★
b.c. Nathaniel – Ronaldsay (Kirkwall). February 27. Fifth foal. £160,000Y. Doncaster Premier. Howson & Houldsworth. Half-brother to the 6f (at 2 yrs) and Group 3 7f Jersey Stakes winner and dual Group 1 placed Gale Force Ten (by Oasis Dream) and to the fair 1m (at 2 yrs) and 10f winner Offshore (by Iffraaj). The dam, a listed 11f winner of 4 races, is a half-sister to 5 winners including the dam of the US dual Grade 3 winner Pickle. The second dam, Crackling (by Electric), a modest 9f and 12f

winner, is a half-sister to 4 winners including Bianca Nera (Group 1 7f Moyglare Stud Stakes) and the dam of the Group 1 Fillies' Mile winner Simply Perfect. (Mr R J McCreery & Partners). *"He came in here very late, I like him and he's a good-looking horse. He moves nicely, won't be early but what we've seen of him we like"*.

339. FAIR EVA ★★★★★
ch.f. Frankel – African Rose (Observatory). April 12. Fourth foal. Half-sister to the fairly useful dual 1m winner Hakka (by Dansili). The dam, winner of the Group 1 6f Sprint Cup and a listed 7f event in France, is a sister to the 2-y-o Group 3 1m Prix d'Aumale winner Helleborine and a half-sister to one winner. The second dam, New Orchid (by Quest For Fame), a useful 10f winner and third in the Group 3 Lancashire Oaks, is a half-sister to 3 winners including the champion 2-y-o and Group 1 7f Dewhurst Stakes winner Distant Music. (Khalid Abdulla). *"A very nice filly out of a good mare, she has a good action and is forward-going. Hopefully she'll be one of our earlier runners, quite possibly in May. She looks 'together' and she's a very good mover with a fast ground action. Looks exciting at the moment"*.

340. FIREGATE (USA) ★★
b.f. First Defence – Media Fire (Bernardini). First living foal. The dam ran twice unplaced and is a half-sister to the Group 1 1m Prix du Moulin and Group 1 10.5f Prix de Diane winner Nebraska Tornado, to the Group 2 10f Prix Eugene Adam winner Burning Sun and the US Grade 3 winner Mirabilis. The second dam, Media Nox (by Lycius), a useful 2-y-o winner of the Group 3 5f Prix du Bois, is a half-sister to the very useful Bonash, a winner of 4 races in France from 1m to 12f including the Prix d'Aumale, the Prix Vanteaux and the Prix de Malleret. (Khalid Abdulla). *"She's going to need time. She's a rangy, scopey filly and one for the autumn and next year"*.

341. ORANGE GIN (IRE) ★★★
b.c. Bushranger – Gin Twist (Invincible Spirit). February 2. First foal. €7,500foal. Goffs November. Kern/Lillingston. The dam, a fair 5f (including at 2 yrs) and 6f winner of four races, is a half-sister to 2 winners. The second dam, Winding (by Irish River), is an unplaced half-sister to 4 winners including the Group 3 placed Silver Desert out of the Group 1 Prix de l'Abbaye winner Silver Fling. (A Bengough). *"He was an early foal and the dam won four races from 22 starts, so she was obviously tough and she was a winning 2-y-o in May. He hasn't been here long but he looks like a colt we could start off in May and from a category of value he looks like he wasn't expensive"*.
TRAINERS' BARGAIN BUY

342. HANDFUL (IRE) ★★★
b.f. Dark Angel – Delia Eria (Zamindar). January 9. First foal. The dam, a minor French 10f winner, is out of the 10f and 11f seller winner Flow Beau (by Mtoto). (Trevor Stewart). *"A deep, strong filly and being by Dark Angel you'd hope she'd make a 2-y-o from May onwards. She moves well and looks OK"*.

343. KAZAWI ★★★
ch.c. Dubawi – Kazeem (Darshaan). April 9. Tenth foal. 485,000Y. Tattersalls October Book 1. Not sold. Brother to the Group 1 Tattersalls Gold Cup, Prince Of Wales's Stakes and Eclipse Stakes winner of 10 races Al Kazeem and half-brother to the fair 7f winner Azeema (by Averti) and the fair 1m and jumps winner Park Lane (by Royal Applause). The dam is an unplaced sister to the winner and subsequent US dual Grade 2 third Treasurer and a half-sister to 5 minor winners. The second dam, Kanz (by The Minstrel), won the Group 3 Princess Elizabeth Stakes, was second in the Group 1 Yorkshire Oaks and is a half-sister to 9 winners including the dams of the Group 1 winners Glint Of Gold, Diamond Shoal and I Want To Be. (D J Deer). *"He holds a special place here at Beckhampton, being a full brother to Al Kazeem. If anything, this colt is a bigger and rangier horse and he couldn't be anything other than an autumn type 2-y-o. He hasn't been here long, he behaves nicely and he's here because he didn't make his reserve at the sale, which we're pleased about"*.

344. LEAPT ★★
b.c. Nathaniel – Liel (Pivotal). January 12. Third foal. Half-brother to Leap (by Pounced), placed fourth over 6f on her only start at 2 yrs in 2015. The dam, a modest 7f fourth-placed maiden, is a half-sister to 5 winners. The

second dam, Magical Romance (by Barathea), a 2-y-o Group 1 6f Cheveley Park Stakes winner, is a sister to the fairly useful 2-y-o 7f winner and subsequent Canadian Grade 3 placed Saree and closely related to the Oaks, Irish Oaks and Yorkshire Oaks winner Alexandrova and the smart listed 2-y-o 1m winner Masterofthehorse. (Lady Rothschild). *"An attractive, nice-moving colt that hasn't been with me for long but he looks fine".*

345. MAGELLAN ★★
b.c. Sea The Stars – Hector's Girl (Hector Protector). February 9. 62,000foal. Tattersalls December. Troy Steve. Half-brother to the Group 3 10f Rose Of Lancaster Stakes and dual listed 10f winner Class Is Class (by Montjeu), to the quite useful 10f winners Ascot Lime (by Pivotal) and Always The Lady (by Halling), the fair dual 6f winner Jubilant Queen (by Kyllachy) and the modest 1m winner Lysander The Greek (by Exceed And Excel). The dam, a useful 2-y-o 6f winner, was third in the Group 3 7f Nell Gwyn Stakes. The second dam, Present Imperfect (by Cadeaux Genereux), a modest 5f placed 3-y-o, is a half-sister to numerous winners including the high-class sprinter College Chapel. (Mrs D Swinburn). *"A huge horse, he stands 17 hands, but he's light on his feet and moves well. Looks exciting considering his size but I can't imagine him running until the back-end and he'll get better as he gets older. A nice horse".*

346. MATHS PRIZE ★★
b.c. Royal Applause – Hypoteneuse (Sadler's Wells). February 3. Third foal. Half-brother to the fairly useful 7f and 1m winner of 3 races Pythagorean (by Oasis Dream). The dam, a fair 12f winner, is a sister to 4 winners including the Oaks second Flight Of Fancy and the dual listed 7f winner Golden Stream and a half-sister to 4 winners. The second dam, Phantom Gold (by Machiavellian), a very useful winner from 1m (at 2 yrs) to 12f including the Group 2 Ribblesdale Stakes and the Group 3 St Simon Stakes, is a sister to the listed 10f winner Fictitious and a half-sister to the 1m winner and dual listed-placed Tempting Prospect. (The Queen). *"There's a lot of stamina in his pedigree, so although he's by Royal Applause he's probably one for the middle of the year over seven furlongs and a mile".*

347. MISS ANTICIPATION ★★★
b.f. Bated Breath – Dusting (Acclamation). April 3. First foal. €50,000Y. Tattersalls Ireland September. Chris Humber / Amanda Skiffington. The dam is an unraced half-sister to 4 minor winners. The second dam, Housekeeper (by Common Grounds), a fairly useful 7f (at 2 yrs), 1m and subsequent US winner, is a half-sister to 4 winners including the very smart Group 1 10f Premio Presidente della Repubblica winner Polar Prince. (Humber & Inglitt). *"Looks together and she ought to be a May/June 2-y-o. Moves well".*

348. NATAVIA ★★★★
ch.f. Nathaniel – Our Queen Of Kings (Arazi). March 24. Twelfth foal. 600,000Y. Tattersalls October Book 1. Juddmonte Farms. Half-sister to 7 winners including the Group 1 Sun Chariot Stakes winner Spinning Queen (by Spinning World), the useful 10f and 12f winner and 2-y-o 7f listed-placed Shannon Springs (by Darshaan), the fairly useful dual 7f winner Amber Queen (by Cadeaux Genereux), the quite useful 5f (at 2 yrs) to 10f and hurdles winner Changing The Guard (by King's Best) and the quite useful 7f (at 2 yrs) to 9f winner King Of The Danes (by Dansili). The dam is an unraced half-sister to 7 winners including the Grade 1 9f Hollywood Derby winner Labeeb, and the Group/Grade 2 winners Fanmore and Alrassam. The second dam, Lady Blackfoot (Prince Tenderfoot), was a very useful Irish listed winning sprinter. *"She's very nice. An attractive, nice-natured, strong filly that won't be early. It's a pedigree to treat with respect and she's probably an autumn 2-y-o".*

349. NUNCIO ★★★
b.c. Authorized – Sweet Pilgrim (Talkin Man). February 12. Third foal. Half-brother to the modest 2016 2-y-o 7f seller winner Sixties Pilgrim (by Sixties Icon). The dam, a modest 6f winner, is a half-sister to 4 winners. The second dam, Faraway Moon (by Distant Relative), was a modest 6f to 1m placed half-sister to 4 winners. (Mrs Sandy Hames). *"You wouldn't expect an Authorized to be early but if you look at him you'd say he will be. He looks strong, powerful and neat, so maybe the speed is from the female side of the pedigree".*

350. OCCURRENCE ★★★★
b.f. Frankel – Arrive (Kahyasi). March 5. Half-sister to the very smart Group 3 6f Princess Margaret Stakes and Group 3 7f Oak Tree Stakes winner Visit, to the quite useful 2-y-o 7f winner Revered, the fairly useful 12f to 13.5f winner Pressure Point (all by Oasis Dream) and the very smart Group 1 10f Pretty Polly Stakes winner Promising Lead (by Danehill). The dam, a very useful 10f (at 2 yrs) and listed 13.8f winner, is a half-sister to the 2-y-o 5f winner Hasili (dam of the top-class performers Banks Hill, Heat Haze, Cacique, Intercontinental, Champs Elysees and Dansili). The second dam, Kerali (by High Line), a quite useful 7f winner, is a half-sister to Bold Fact (Group 3 6f July Stakes) and So Factual (Group 1 Nunthorpe Stakes). (Khalid Abdulla). *"A beautiful filly with a very nice pedigree to back it up, we all like her and she seems to have a nice temperament. I trained the dam and there's plenty of stamina in the pedigree, so this could be a mile and a half filly. But she's attractive and probably looks more like Frankel than some of the others I've seen".*

351. PRINCESS DE LUNE (IRE) ★★★
gr.f. Shamardal – Princess Serena (Unbridled's Song). March 9. Seventh foal. 300,000Y. Tattersalls October Book 1. Not sold. Sister to the Australian dual Group 2 winner Puissance de Lune and to the quite useful 7f winner Majesty and half-sister to the quite useful 2-y-o 7f winner Serena's Storm (by Statue Of Liberty and herself dam of the dual Group 1 winner Rizeena), the fairly useful dual 7f winner Invincible Fresh (by Footstepsinthesand) and the fair 7f winner of 4 races (including at 2 yrs) Serene Oasis (by Oratorio). The dam, a minor US 4-y-o winner, is a half-sister to 5 winners including the US Grade 2 winner Doubles Partner. The second dam, Serena's Sister (Rahy), is an unplaced sister to the outstanding US winner of eleven Grade 1 events and smart broodmare Serena's Song. (Round Hill Stud). *"Not here yet, but I believe she's a promising filly and she has a nice pedigree".*

352. SAND SHOE ★★★
b.f. Footstepsinthesand – Dolma (Marchand de Sable). February 19. Half-sister to the smart Group 3 9f and triple listed 1m winner of 8 races Thistle Bird (by Selkirk), to the fairly useful 7f (at 2 yrs) and 1m winner McCreery (by Big Bad Bob), the quite useful 7f to 10f and Grade 2 winning hurdler Old Guard (by Notnowcato) and the quite useful 2-y-o 5f winner Don Marco (by Choisir). The dam won 6 races over 6f and 7f (including at 2 yrs), notably three listed events at 3 yrs. The second dam, Young Manila (by Manila), was listed-placed over 10f and is a half-sister to Fabulous Hostess, a winner of three Group 3 events from 11f to 13f. (Lady Rothschild). *"From a family I know quite well, they all have their quirks but this filly is a good mover and I hope we can produce another nice filly for her owner breeder. They all improve considerably with age".*

353. SFUMATO ★★★★
br.c. Bated Breath – Modern Look (Zamindar). February 5. Third foal. Half-brother to the fair 1m winner Eye Contact (by Dansili). The dam, winner of the 2-y-o Group 2 1m winner Prix de Sandringham, is closely related to 2 winners by Zafonic including the listed 6f winner Arabesque and a half-sister to 4 winners including the Australian triple Group 1 winner Foreteller. The second dam, Prophecy (by Warning), winner of the Group 1 6f Cheveley Park Stakes, was second in the Group 3 7f Nell Gwyn Stakes. (Khalid Abdulla). *"A very nice horse out of a good mare who was a good 2-y-o herself. This is a very attractive colt, he's bred to be a horse with some speed and hopefully he'll be racing by mid-summer. We like him".*

354. SILENT ECHO ★★★
b.c. Oasis Dream – Quiet (Observatory). February 20. Third foal. The dam, a quite useful 2-y-o 8.5f winner, is a half-sister to 6 winners including the listed 10.5f winner Double Crossed (dam of the multiple Group 1 winner Twice Over) and to Clepsydra (the dam of four stakes winners including the Group 1 winners Timepiece and Passage Of Time). The second dam, Quandary (by Blushing Groom), a useful listed winner of 3 races from 9f to 10f, is a half-sister to 8 winners including All At Sea (Group 1 Prix du Moulin). (Khalid Abdulla). *"A nice horse by Oasis Dream and out of a very good family that includes Twice Over. The dam won at Leicester in the autumn of her 2-y-o*

days and this colt looks like making a 2-y-o as well, as you'd hope being by Oasis Dream".

355. SOLAR CROSS ★★★
b.c. Sea The Stars – Nantyglo (Mark Of Esteem). April 10. Seventh foal. 75,000Y. Tattersalls October Book 1. Amanda Skiffington. Half-brother to the modest dual 9f winner Valley Tiger (by Tiger Hill). The dam, a useful 6f (at 2 yrs) and listed 1m winner, was third in the Group 2 6f Mill Reef Stakes and is a half-sister to 5 winners. The second dam, Bright Halo (by Bigstone), a minor French 9f winner, is a half-sister to 9 winners including the Group 1 Irish Oaks winner Moonstone, the Breeders' Cup second L'Ancresse and the Group 1 10f Prix Saint-Alary winner Cerulean Sky (herself dam of the Group 2 Doncaster Cup winner Honolulu). (De Zoete, Inglett, Mercer, Smartt). *"A rangy horse as you'd expect by Sea The Stars, the dam was a 2-y-o winner and has a slightly disappointing breeding record to date but this seems to be a nice horse. He's tough, not that backward and hopefully he'll be racing by the middle of the year".*

356. SOLAR SHOWER ★★★
b.c. Oasis Dream – Solar Pursuit (Galileo). March 6. Second foal. Half-brother to the 2015 2-y-o 7f winner from two starts Paling (by Zamindar). The dam is an unraced half-sister to 8 winners including Meteor Storm (Grade 1 10f Manhattan Handicap, Polish Summer (Group 2 12.5f Grand Prix de Deauville), the listed 10f winner Morning Eclipse and the French Group 3 2m winner Host Nation. The second dam, Hunt The Sun (by Rainbow Quest), is an unraced sister to the high-class Rothmans International, Prix Royal-Oak and Prix Kergorlay winner Raintrap and to the very smart Criterium de Saint-Cloud and Prix du Conseil de Paris winner Sunshack. (Khalid Abdulla). *"Very strong, powerful and good-looking, he's a promising horse out of a very successful middle-distance family. One for the autumn".*

357. STONE THE CROWS ★★
b.c. Cape Cross – Stars In Your Eyes (Galileo). March 19. Second foal. Half-brother to the fair 2015 2-y-o 7f winner Banksea (by Lawman). The dam, a fair 12f winner, is a half-sister to 5 winners including the listed 1m winner New Mexican and the Group 2 Dante Stakes third Co-ordinated Cut. The second dam, Apache Star (by Arazi), a fairly useful 7f (at 2 yrs) to 9f winner, was listed placed twice at up to 11.4f and is a half-sister to 6 winners including the US stakes winner and Grade 3 placed Duke Of Green. (A E Oppenheimer). *"He's only just arrived so I don't know anything about him yet, but he's an attractive, big, rangy colt. I imagine he could only be an autumn 2-y-o over a mile".*

358. TIME CHASER ★★★
b.f. Dubawi – Passage Of Time (Dansili). March 12. Sister to the very smart Group 2 1m Joel Stakes and Group 3 10f Tercentenary Stakes winner Time Test and half-sister to the useful 11f and 12f winner Retirement Plan (by Monsun). The dam, winner of the Group 1 10f Criterium de Saint-Cloud (at 2 yrs) and the Group 3 10.3f Musidora Stakes, is a sister to the Group 2 12f King Edward VI Stakes winner Father Time and a half-sister to the Group 1 Falmouth Stakes winner Timepiece. The second dam, Clepsydra (by Sadler's Wells), a quite useful 12f winner, is a half-sister to numerous winners including the useful listed 10.5f winner Double Crossed. (Khalid Abdulla). *"Not here yet but I believe she's very nice. The reports are good".*

359. ZEFFERINO ★★
ch.c. Frankel – Turama (Pivotal). February 3. First foal. The dam, unplaced on her only start, is a half-sister to 6 winners including the Group 1 1m Sun Chariot Stakes winner Spinning Queen and the listed-placed 10f and 12f winner Shannon Springs. The second dam, Our Queen Of Kings (by Arazi), is an unraced half-sister to 7 winners including the Grade 1 9f Hollywood Derby winner Labeeb and the Group/Grade 2 winners Alrassaam and Fanmore. (Saleh Al Homaizi & Imad Al Sagar). *"A strong, rather idle horse and it's hard to know what to make of him, he's so laid-back at the moment but I guess he's just mentally immature. He looks more like Pivotal than Frankel and from what I can gather most Frankel 2-y-o's tend to take after the mare than from him".*

360. UNNAMED ★★★
b.f. Poet's Voice – Acquifer (Oasis Dream). March 19. Third foal. 58,000Y. Tattersalls October Book 2. Axom. Half-sister to the quite useful 2-y-o dual 7f winner Arethusa (by Rip Van Winkle). The dam, a fair dual 6f placed maiden at 2 and 3 yrs, is a half-sister to 6 winners including the Italian Group 3 winner Guest Connections, the listed winner Lady Of the Lake and the smart broodmare Llia (dam of the Group 1 Irish St Leger winner Sans Frontieres). The second dam, Llyn Gwynant (by Persian Bold), won the Group 3 1m Desmond Stakes and the Group 3 1m Matron Stakes and is a half-sister to 2 winners. (Axom). *"The sire is a big horse and I guess his progeny need time, but this filly is out of an Oasis Dream mare and she looks quite forward, well-made and strong. You'd hope that she'd be running by June or July".*

361. UNNAMED ★★★
ch.c. Bated Breath – Condition (Deploy). January 31. Seventh foal. 230,000Y. Tattersalls October Book 1. Charlie Gordon-Watson/ Al Shaqab Racing. Closely related to the French 10f winner and listed-placed Homepage (by Dansili) and half-brother to the French listed 1m winner Dreamt (by Oasis Dream). The dam, a listed-placed 11f winner, is a half-sister to 3 winners including the French listed and US stakes winner Night Chapter. The second dam, Context (by Zafonic), placed five times in France at around 1m, is a half-sister to 4 winners including the US Grade 2 winner Bon Point. (Al Shaqab Racing). *"A backward horse from a family I know well. He's a nice looking colt and he moves well, but I think he's very much one for the second half of the year unlike some by this sire who might come a bit earlier".*

362. UNNAMED ★★★★
b.c. Frankel – Dorcas Lane (Norse Dancer). March 8. First foal. 160,000Y. Tattersalls October Book 1. Not sold. The dam, winner of the listed Pretty Polly Stakes and third in the Group 2 Ribblesdale Stakes and Group 2 Lancashire Oaks, is a half-sister to 7 winners. The second dam, Waqood (by Riverman), a fair middle-distance placed 3-y-o, is a full or half-sister to 5 winners including Harayir, a winner of six races from 6f to 1m including the 1,000 Guineas, the Celebration Mile, the Challenge Stakes and the Lowther Stakes. (Bjorn Nielson). *"A deep, strong, very good-moving colt. The dam didn't win until January as a 3-y-o when she won at 50-1 first time out, but he looks like he'll come together before that. A quite forward-looking, strong 2-y-o that I'd hope to get out in June or July".*

363. UNNAMED ★★★
b.c. Frankel – Icon Project (Empire Maker). April 17. Third foal. The dam, winner of the Grade 1 Personal Ensign Stakes and the Grade 3 New York Stakes, is a half-sister to 6 winners including the US Grade 2 winner Lasting Approval. The second dam, La Gueriere (by Lord At War), a US Grade 1 Queen Elizabeth II Challenge Cup Stakes winner, is a sister to a stakes winner and a half-sister to 11 winners including the US Grade 1 winner Al Mamoon. (Andrew Rosen). *"A nice natured horse that moves well but he's immature. He definitely needs time and needs to just strengthen up a bit. He may change a lot but at the moment you'd think he'd be running once or twice in the autumn, no more than that. The mare took time to come to hand and she did well in America on dirt".*

DENIS COAKLEY

364. HENRIQUA ★★★
b.f. Henrythenavigator – Child Bride (USA) (Coronado's Quest). February 16. Ninth foal. 12,000Y. Tattersalls October Book 2. D Coakley. Half-sister to the modest 2015 2-y-o 10f winner Jassur (by Canford Cliffs), to the US Grade 2 12f and 14f winner Juniper Pass (by Lemon Drop Kid) and 3 minor winners in the USA and Argentina by Out Of Place, Holy Bull and Theatrical. The dam is an unraced half-sister to 6 winners including the dam of the US Grade 2 winner Postponed and to the dam of the Group 1 Racing Post Trophy winner Crowded House. The second dam, Chapel Of Dreams (by Northern Dancer), won two Grade 2 stakes in the USA and is a half-sister to Storm Cat. (West Ilsley Racing). *"She's just gone a bit light so I may have to take my time with her, but she travels well. I'd be hoping for June time and six furlongs with her".*

365. KEEPER'S CHOICE (IRE) ★★★
ch.f. Intikhab – Crossing (Cape Cross).
April 9. Fourth foal. 14,000Y. Tattersalls
October Book 2. D Coakley. Half-sister to the
fair 8.5f winner Saltwater Creek (by Marju).
The dam, a fairly useful 1m to 10f and
bumpers winner in Ireland, was listed-placed
three times and is a half-sister to 3 winners.
The second dam, Piney River (by Pharly), was
placed over 6f and 7f and is a half-sister to
8 winners including the smart dual Group 3
Monaassib. (Keeper's 12). *"She's nice, has a
good stride on her and she does things quite
well at the moment. She's quite big and quite
leggy so to look at her you'd say she'd take a
bit of time, but the way she rides and works at
the minute she might be out sooner, maybe
May or June".*

366. PETER STUYVESANT (IRE) ★★★★
b.g. Elusive City – Dream For Life (Oasis
Dream). April 11. Third foal. 20,000Y. Tattersalls
October Book 3. Denis Coakley. The dam
won two minor races in France at 3 and 4 yrs
and is a half-sister to 7 winners including the
Group 1 Gran Criterium winner Night Style
and the listed Prix d'Automne winner Maid
Of Dawkins. The second dam, Style For Life
(by Law Society), won 2 races in France over
middle-distances, was listed-placed and is
a half-sister to 8 winners including the Irish
Derby winner Grey Swallow. (Chris van Hoorn
Racing). *"A good-looking horse, he travels well
and hopefully he'll prove good value. I should
imagine he'll be racing in May or June because
he's all there and we like him. Six furlongs
should be his trip and the way he's going
I'd be disappointed if he's not a nice horse".*
TRAINERS' BARGAIN BUY

367. POWER HOME (IRE) ★★★
b.f. Power – Ascendancy (Sadler's Wells). April
10. Tenth foal. 10,000Y. Tattersalls October
Book 3. Denis Coakley. Half-sister to the
fairly useful 10f and 12f winner of 4 races
Nicholascopernicus, to the fairly useful 12f,
14f and hurdles winner Ascendant (both by
Medicean), the quite useful 12f and jumps
winner Tawaagg (by Kyllachy) and the fair
8.5f to 12f winner Emulating (by Duke Of
Marmalade). The dam is an unraced full
or half-sister to 8 winners including the
Australian Group 1 second Polar Bear and the

Group 1 Fillies' Mile second Dance To The Top
(dam of the Group 2 winner Bankable). The
second dam, Aim For The Top (by Irish River),
won the Group 3 7f Premio Chiusura and is
a half-sister to the Gimcrack Stakes winner
Splendent. (Count Calypso Racing). *"A good-
moving filly, she's strong but has just gone
slightly leggy so she might take a little bit of
time, but she's nice and we like her. Probably
one for the second half of the season, starting
at six and then moving up to seven furlongs".*

368. SHEILA'S ROCK (IRE) ★★★★
b.f. Fastnet Rock – Crystal Curling (Peintre
Celebre). April 26. Sixth foal. 17,000Y.
Tattersalls December. Denis Coakley. Closely
related to the fair 1m winner Sparkling Crystal
(by Danehill Dancer) and to a minor winner
abroad by Oratorio. The dam, a fairly useful
2-y-o 7f winner, is a half-sister to 5 winners
including the dam of the Group 3 Minstrel
Stakes winner Three Rocks. The second dam,
State Crystal (by High Estate), won the Group
3 12f Lancashire Oaks and was placed in the
Yorkshire Oaks and the Prix Vermeille. She is a
half-sister to 6 winners including the Group 1
Fillies' Mile winner Crystal Music, the Group 3
winners Dubai Success and Solar Crystal and
the Irish Derby third Tchaikovsky. (R J Styles).
*"A lovely filly, she's nice and strong and she'll
probably be one of my first 2-y-o runners.
She's going nicely, does things easily and
travels well. I like her, there's nothing wrong
with her at all and she was just a bit fat at the
sales. She was good value I think".*

ROBERT COWELL

369. ALWAYS AMAZING ★★★★
ch.c. Kyllachy – Amazed (Clantime). March
12. Tenth foal. 65,000Y. Tattersalls October
Book 2. Rabbah Bloodstock. Half-brother to
the useful 2-y-o listed 6f and 3-y-o listed 5f
winner Dazed And Amazed (by Averti) and
to the quite useful sprint winners Mayhab
(by Cadeaux Genereux), Quite A Thing (by
Dutch Art), Nawaaff (by Compton Place) and
Stunned (by Shamardal). The dam, a modest
5f placed 3-y-o, is a sister to the Group 3 Prix
du Petit Couvert winner Bishops Court and
a half-sister to 5 winners including the listed
winning sprinter Astonished. The second dam,
Indigo (by Primo Dominie), a quite useful
2-y-o 5f winner, is a half-sister to 5 winners.

(A Al Mansoori). *"He's a nice horse, he's ready to run and is one of the more forward types in the yard. I'd say he's above average, a maiden should come his way and then hopefully he'll step up to the next level. A useful looking horse with a fast pedigree".*

370. BENTAYGA GIRL ★★★
b.f. Dubawi – Coyote (Indian Ridge). April 17. Twelfth foal. 200,000Y. Tattersalls October Book 1. Cool Silk Partnership. Half-sister to the useful listed 12f winner and Group 3 Prix Gontaut-Biron third Eradicate (by Montjeu), to the Group 3 Park Express Stakes winner and Irish 1,000 Guineas third Oh Goodness Me (by Galileo), the fairly useful listed placed 2-y-o 1m winner Colima (by Authorized) and the quite useful 10f to 14f and hurdles winner Huff And Puff (by Azamour). The dam was a fairly useful listed-placed 1m winner. The second dam, Caramba (by Belmez), won the Group 2 1m Falmouth Stakes and the Group 2 10f Nassau Stakes and is a half-sister to 7 winners including Lemon Souffle (Moyglare Stud Stakes). (Cool Silk Partnership). *"She's was just an average size when we bought her but she's blossomed considerably since. Just cantering at the moment, she hasn't done any work but by the way she looks she'll may be speedier than initially anticipated. She's bulking up, looks a nice type and she has a good pedigree."*

371. ELLIPTICAL ★★★
ch.f. Foxwedge – Gyroscope (Spinning World). February 26. Fifth foal. The dam, a quite useful 1m and 10f winner, is a half-sister to the high-class Group 3 7f Supreme Stakes and Group 3 7f Criterion Stakes winner Arakan. The second dam, Far Across (by Common Grounds), is an unraced half-sister to 5 winners including the Group/Grade 3 winners Donkey Engine and Petit Poucet. (Cheveley Park Stud). *"She had a little injury about a month ago but she'd shown promise before that and she's back in work now. She has an engine and I see her making a 2-y-o by mid-season, probably over six furlongs".*

372. FIERY SPICE (IRE) ★★★
ch.c. Dream Ahead – High Spice (Songandaprayer). April 10. Third foal. 11,000Y. Tattersalls October Book 3. AB Racing. Brother to the modest 2016 5f and 6f placed 3-y-o Spice Mill and half-brother to the modest 4-y-o dual 5f winner More Spice (by Exceed And Excel). The dam, a quite useful triple 5f winner at 2 and 3 yrs, is a half-sister to 3 minor winners in the USA. The second dam, Erin Moor (by Holy Bull), a US 2-y-o 7f and 1m winner, was Grade 3 placed and is a half-sister to 6 winners including the US Grade 3 winner Willa On The Move. *"He looks a nice individual, I quite like him and he'll be out in mid-season. A good sort, we've trained both the dam's first two foals and as a physical specimen this is the best of the three".*
TRAINERS' BARGAIN BUY

373. KODIAC PEARL ★★★★
b.f. Kodiac – Valmirez (Smart Strike). April 29. First foal. £42,000Y. Doncaster Premier. Cool Silk Partnership, Stroud & Coleman. The dam is an unraced half-sister to the US stakes winner and Grade 1 third Maybelline. The second dam, Greathearted (by Giant's Causeway), is an unraced half-sister to 8 winners including the US Grade 3 winner and high-class sire Elusive Quality. (Cool Silk Partnership). *"She has plenty of pace and she's in full work at the moment so she'll probably make her debut in May. A typical Kodiac, she's got a fair bit of boot and she wants to race, so as long as we can keep the lid on her she'll have a future".*

374. PRINCESS HOLLY ★★★
b.f. Compton Place – Khyber Knight (Night Shift). March 30. Sixth foal. £32,000Y. Doncaster Premier. A C Elliott. Half-sister to the Italian winner of 11 races and 1m listed-placed Red Roof (by Statue Of Liberty), to the fair 5f placed Westhoughton (by Equiano) – subsequently a 1m winner in the UAE and the modest 2-y-o 7f winner Autopilot (by Kyllachy). The dam, a moderate 1m and 10f placed maiden, is a half-sister to 7 winners. The second dam, Peshawar (by Persian Bold), is an unraced half-sister to 7 winners including the German 1,000 Guineas winner Princess Nana. (Khalifa Dasmal & Partner). *"She's quite speedy, ready to run and looks like she'll start in April or early May. A likeable type that should win a maiden within her first few starts, then we'll have to see if she can progress. She's not particularly big but she's bulky".*

375. SOMEWHERE SECRET ★★★
ch.c. Sakhee's Secret – Lark In The Park (Grand Lodge). March 29. Sixth foal. Brother to the fairly useful dual 7f (at 2 yrs), 5f and 6f winner Secretinthepark and half-brother to the quite useful 1m and 10.5f winner of 8 races Dolphin Rock (by Mark Of Esteem) and the modest triple 5f winner at 2 and 3 yrs Passionada (by Avonbridge). The dam, a moderate 1m winner at 3 yrs, is a half-sister to several winners including the quite useful 1m to 12f winner of 8 races Invasian. The second dam, Jarrayan (by Machiavellian), is an unplaced half-sister to several winners including the 2-y-o listed 6f Silver Flash Stakes winner Desert Sky. (Mia Racing). *"A full-brother to a nice horse we have called Secretinthepark. He's very similar to him in that he's very tall and leggy, but he does show speed already and he's in my second batch of 2-y-o's coming through. For a big horse he covers the ground and I'd say he'll be out in mid-season. He'll keep developing and be a better 3-y-o, but he does look like he's got something about him".*

376. VISIONARY (IRE) ★★★★
b.c. Dream Ahead – Avodale (Lawman). January 27. First foal. 20,000Y. Tattersalls October Book 3. R Cowell. The dam, placed at 2 and 3 yrs in France, is a half-sister to one minor winner. The second dam, Aldovea (by Nashwan), a minor French 3-y-o winner, is a half-sister to 8 winners including the French listed winner and Group 2 second Bashaayeash. (K A Dasmal). *"Quite a biggish, well-built and powerful colt, he's ready to run. He looks a sprinting type, I'd say a maiden should come his way quite easily and he could well progress into something better".*

377. WAISHBOOSHBASH ★★
ch.f. Kheleyf – Crystal Moments (Haafhd). April 15. Fourth foal. The dam, a quite useful 5f, 6f (both at 2 yrs) and 7f winner, is a half-sister to 3 minor winners. The second dam, Celestial Choir (by Celestial Storm), a quite useful 7f to 12f winner of 9 races on the flat, also won 7 races over jumps and is a half-sister to 5 winners. (Mohammed Jaber). *"She's going to need a bit of time because she's quite tall and lengthy. Probably one for the back-end, I haven't done anything with her yet and she's just cantering".*

378. UNNAMED ★★★
b.c. Invincible Spirit – Areyaam (Elusive Quality). May 15. Fifth foal. Half-brother to the quite useful 2015 2-y-o 5f winner Southern Belle (by Aqlaam), to the useful 2-y-o 7f and listed 1m winner Go Angellica, the fair 7f winner Arabian Music (both by Kheleyf) and the quite useful 2-y-o dual 6f winner My Lucky Liz (by Exceed And Excel). The dam, a fair maiden, was placed three times over 1m and is a half-sister to 2 winners. The second dam, Yanaseeni (by Trempolino), is an unplaced sister to the German-trained middle-distance dual Group 1 winner Germany (by Trempolino) and to 4 minor winners in the USA. (A Jaber). *"He's a bit weak at the moment and will come into his own in the second half of the season, so he's just going steady for now. The dam has bred three 2-y-o winners already, but this colt was a late foal".*

379. UNNAMED ★★★★
b.c. Kodiac – Cakestown Lady (Petorius). April 2. Fifth foal. 55,000Y. Tattersalls October Book 2. Rabbah Bloodstock. Brother to the fairly useful Irish 7f winner of 5 races from 2 to 6 yrs Seanie and half-brother to the moderate Irish 7f winner Loveisthedrug (by No Excuse Needed) and a minor winner abroad by Bushranger. The dam, a fairly useful 7f winner, is a half-sister to 2 winners. The second dam, Sally Gone (by Last Tycoon), is an unraced half-sister to 3 winners. (A Al Mansoori). *"Quite a speedy individual, he looks like a typical 2-y-o type, short-coupled and stocky. He'll be fast, he's done a fair bit of work and has a bit of a sore shin at the moment so I'm giving him a bit of time, but essentially he's one to look forward to. He looks like he'll have an engine".*

380. UNNAMED ★★★ ♠
b.c. Hat Trick – Desert Sky (Green Desert). March 18. Seventh foal. 32,000Y. Tattersalls October Book 2. A C Elliott. Half-brother to the fair 2015 multiple 6f placed 2-y-o Munira Eyes (by Cape Blanco) and to 3 winners including the US Grade 2 1m winner No Jet Lag (by Johar) and to the French 2-y-o dual 6f winner and Group 3 6f Prix de Cabourg third Optari (by Diesis). The dam, a 2-y-o listed 6f Silver Flash Stakes winner, is a sister to the 6f winner and UAE listed placed Moonis and

a half-sister to 2 winners. The second dam, Badrah (by Private Account), is a 1m placed half-sister to 5 winners including the dual Group 3 winner Husyan. (M Al Shafar). *"He looked quite a forward individual a month ago and then typical 2-y-o problems have come his way. He's on the easy list but I quite like him and he's shown us a fair bit of zip. A lengthy horse that'll get further in time, but he's got speed".*

381. UNNAMED ★★★
ch.c. Helmet – Lady Gorgeous (Compton Place). February 26. First foal. The dam, a fairly useful 2-y-o 6f winner, was listed-placed over 7f at 3 yrs and is a half-sister to 3 winners including the French Group 3 placed Kartica. The second dam, Cayman Sunset (by Night Shift), a useful 7f and listed 9f winner, is a sister to the useful dual Irish 7f winner (including at 2 yrs) and Group 3 Beresford Stakes third Tarfaa and a half-sister to 4 winners. (Jaber Abdullah). *"Quite a nice-looking horse, he needs a bit of time despite being an early foal. He's got some developing to do and he'll be one for later in the season, but he looks like he'll turn into a very nice horse in time".*

382. UNNAMED ★★
gr.f. Dark Angel – Mickleberry (Desert Style). April 15. First foal. 34,000Y. Tattersalls October Book 2. A C Elliott. The dam, a moderate 5f winner, is a half-sister to 6 winners including the Group 2 July Stakes winner Alhebayeb. The second dam, Miss Indigo (by Indian Ridge), is a placed half-sister to 8 winners including the useful listed 10f Pretty Polly Stakes winner Musetta. (Jaber Abdullah). *"She's just started work, she's quite tall and leggy. She'll develop into a nice individual in time but she does need that time".*

383. UNNAMED ★★★★
b.c. Equiano – Morning After (Emperor Jones). February 18. Sixth foal. 32,000Y. Tattersalls October Book 3. Rabbah Bloodstock. Half-brother to the quite useful 7f winner Elizona (by Pastoral Pursuits) and to the modest 1m winner Dazzled (by Starcraft). The dam, a fair 2-y-o 5.5f winner, is a half-sister to 5 winners. The second dam, Oneftheditch (by With Approval), a modest 1m to 10f winner of 5 races, is a half-sister to 6 winners. (M Al Shafar). *"Quite a stocky little individual, he has a lovely temperament and knows his job. He's got a tiny issue at the moment which will take a few weeks to sort out, but he'll make a 2-y-o and he'll be out in a couple of months. He shows a lot of speed".*

384. UNNAMED ★★★
ch.f. Mayson – Resistance Heroine (Dr Fong). March 21. Fifth foal. 32,000Y. Tattersalls October Book 2. A C Elliott. Half-sister to the fairly useful 5f (at 2 yrs) and 6f winner and listed-placed Nosedive (by Observatory) and to the modest 2-y-o 6f winner Iwilsayzizonlyonce (by Kyllachy). The dam is a placed half-sister to 7 winners including the Group 3 winners Violette and Silca's Gift. The second dam, Odette (by Pursuit Of Love), a fair 3-y-o 5f and 5.7f winner, is a half-sister to 4 winners. (Jaber Abdullah). *"A stocky individual, she's still a bit 'up behind' and I think she'll be 16 hands when she's finished growing. So I'm not in a rush with her, but she's a nice, flashy looking filly and one for the middle of the season onwards".*

SIMON CRISFORD

385. ETIKAAL
ch.c. Sepoy – Hezmah (Oasis Dream). March 6. First foal. The dam, a fairly useful listed-placed 7f (at 2 yrs) and 6f winner, is a half-sister to 3 winners including the useful listed 6f winner of 3 races (including at 2 yrs), Aeolus. The second dam, Bright Moll (by Mind Games), a fairly useful 2-y-o 5f and 6f winner, is a half-sister to 4 winners including the Group 2 Mill Reef Stakes second Doctor Brown.

386. RAAWY
b.c. Dutch Art – Age Of Chivalry (Invincible Spirit). March 11. Fifth foal. £190,000Y. Doncaster Premier. Shadwell Estate Co. Half-brother to the fairly useful 2015 2-y-o 6f winner Age Of Empire (by Royal Applause) and to the moderate 2-y-o 7f winner Oxslip (by Three Valleys). The dam won twice over 5f (at 2 yrs) and the Group 3 6f Ballyogan Stakes and is a sister to 2 winners and a half-sister to Sebastian Flyte (a winner here and in the USA where he was Grade 1 placed). The second dam, Aravonian (by Night Shift), won once over 1m at 3 yrs.

387. RED ENSIGN (IRE)
b.c. Dark Angel – Rayon Rouge (Manduro). January 25. First foal. 250,000Y. Tattersalls October Book 2. Crisford Racing. The dam is an unplaced half-sister to the Irish listed-placed winner Reglisse. The second dam, Regalline (by Green Desert), a fair Irish 1m winner, is a half-sister to 5 winners including the Irish Group 3 2,000 Guineas Trial winner Recharge.

388. SWEET SUE
ch.f. Nathaniel – Fleur de Lis (Nayef). March 7. Fourth foal. Half-sister to the fair 2015 7f and 1m placed 2-y-o Ronnie Baird (by Poet's Voice). The dam ran once unplaced and is a half-sister to 6 winners including the useful Irish dual 12f and smart hurdles winner Song Of The Sword. The second dam, Melodist (by The Minstrel), won over 1m (at 2 yrs), the Irish Oaks (in a dead-heat with Diminuendo) and the Italian Oaks. She is a half-sister to 5 winners including the high-class US filly Love Sign (a winner of three Grade 1 events) and the dual US Grade 2 winner Fatih.

389. YAMARHABA MALAYEEN (IRE)
ch.c. Rip Van Winkle – Obama Rule (Danehill Dancer). January 15. Second foal. 48,000Y. Tattersalls October Book 2. Crisford Racing. The dam, winner of the Group 3 9f Dance Design Stakes, is a sister to the Group 3 Princess Margaret Stakes winner Osaila and a half-sister to 2 minor winners. The second dam, Mennetou (by Entrepreneur), is an unraced half-sister to 5 winners including the 'Arc winner Carnegie.

390. UNNAMED
ch.c. Exchange Rate – Blessings Count (Pulpit). March 23. Sixth foal. $140,000Y. Keeneland September. Margaret O'Toole. Half-brother to 2 winners including the US stakes-placed Minds Eyes (by Macho Uno). The dam was unplaced in two starts and is a half-sister to 7 winners including the stakes winners and Grade 2 placed Winning Season and Laguna Seca. The second dam, Topicount (by Private Account), was a Grade 2 and Grade 3 winner of 9 races in the USA.

391. UNNAMED
b.c. Invincible Spirit – Bryanstown (Galileo).

May 21. Second foal. 88,000foal. Tattersalls December. Abbey Farm. Half-brother to the fair 2015 1m placed La Celebs Ville (Sea The Stars). The dam, placed fourth over 9f at 4 yrs on her only start, is a half-sister to 4 minor winners. The second dam, Stiletta (by Dancing Brave), is an unraced sister to the Epsom and Irish Derby winner Commander In Chief and a half-sister to the champion 2-y-o and miler Warning, the US Grade 1 winner Yashmak, the Irish Derby second Deploy and the Great Voltigeur Stakes winner Dushyantor.

392. UNNAMED
b.f. Invincible Spirit – Counterclaim (Pivotal). April 26. Fifth foal. 80,000Y. Tattersalls October Book 1. Sackville/Donald. Half-sister to the 2015 2-y-o 7f and 8.5f winner Good Trip (by Dansili), to the quite useful dual 1m winner Power Game (by Shamardal) and the fair 6f winner Mukhabarat (by Exceed And Excel). The dam, a French 11f winner and second in the Group 2 Italian Oaks, is a half-sister to 5 minor winners. The second dam, Dusty Answer (by Zafonic), a quite useful 2-y-o 7f winner, was listed placed over 1m and is a half-sister to 5 winners including the listed 1m and subsequent US Grade 2 winner Spotlight and the dam of the Group 1 winner and sire Zoffany.

393. UNNAMED
b.c. Poet's Voice – Indian Love Bird (Efisio). March 25. Seventh living foal. Half-brother to the Group 2 6f Duke Of York Stakes and Group 3 1m Craven Stakes winner and triple Group 1 placed Delegator (by Dansili) and to the useful 7f (including at 2 yrs) and 1m winner of 4 races Correspondent (by Exceed And Excel). The dam is an unraced sister to the smart Group 1 7f Prix de la Foret winner Tomba and the French Derby winner Holding Court. The second dam, Indian Love Song (by Be My Guest), a modest middle-distance placed maiden, is a full or half-sister to 4 winners.

394. UNNAMED
b.c. More Than Ready – Limonar (Street Cry). March 27. Second foal. 220,000 2-y-o. Tattersalls Craven Breeze Up. Shadwell Estate Co. The dam, a French listed 1m winner at 3 yrs, is a half-sister to 5 winners including the

US Grade 1 Shoemaker Mile Stakes winner Talco. The second dam, Trylko (by Diesis), second over 6f at 2 yrs on her only start, is a half-sister to 6 winners including the Irish 2,000 Guineas winner Bachelor Duke.

395. UNNAMED
b.c. Equiano – Majoune (Take Risks). April 15. Eleventh foal. £78,000 2-y-o. Tattersalls Ireland Ascot Breeze Up. Dermot Cantillon. Half-brother to the useful 7f (at 2 yrs) and German Group 3 11f winner Majoune's Song, to the fair 1m and 10f winner Aryal (both by Singspiel), the fairly useful 10.2f to 14f winner and German listed-placed Maria's Magic and the fair 12f winner Magic Moth (both by Mtoto). The dam won 4 races including the Group 3 11f Prix Corrida and is a half-sister to 10 winners including the Group 3 1m Prix des Reservoirs winner and Group 1 10.5f Prix de Diane second Mousse Glacee. The second dam, Madame Est Sortie (by Longleat), won the Group 3 10.5f Prix Penelope and is a half-sister to 5 winners.

396. UNNAMED
gr.c. Cape Cross – Middle Persia (Dalakhani). April 7. Fourth foal. 90,000Y. Tattersalls October Book 1. Crisford Racing. Half-brother to the listed 11.5f Derby Trial winner Kilimanjaro (by High Chaparral). The dam, a fair Irish 1m winner, is a half-sister to 6 winners including Nayarra (Group 1 1m Gran Criterium) and Wonderfully (Group 3 Silver Flash Stakes). The second dam, Massara (by Danehill), a listed 6f winner and second in the Group 2 Prix Robert Papin at 2 yrs, is a sister to the smart sire Kodiac, closely related to the Group 1 6f Haydock Park Sprint Cup winner Invincible Spirit and a half-sister to 8 winners including the Group 3 winners Acts Of Grace and Sadian.

397. UNNAMED
b.f. Kyllachy – Represent (Exceed And Excel). January 31. First foal. 210,000 2-y-o. Tattersalls Craven Breeze Up. Crisford Racing. The dam, a fair 6f and 7f winner, is a half-sister to 11 winners including the Group 2 Bosphorus Cup winner Connecticut, the smart 1m winner and listed-placed Castleton and the German listed winner and Group 3 placed Fleurie Domaine. The second dam, Craigmill (by Slip Anchor), a fair 2-y-o 7f winner, is a half-sister to 6 winners including the Group 3 Park Hill Stakes winner Coigach and the Park Hill Stakes second and smart broodmare Applecross.

398. UNNAMED
b.c. Canford Cliffs – Shannon Spree (Royal Applause). February 22. First foal. 45,000Y. Tattersalls October Book 2. Stroud/Coleman. The dam, a fair 2-y-o 1m winner, is a half-sister to 3 minor winners. The second dam, Some Diva (by Dr Fong), a modest 9f winner, is a half-sister to 3 winners including the Group 1 Middle Park Stakes winner Primo Valentino and the Group 2 6f Cherry Hinton Stakes winner and Group 1 6f Phoenix Stakes third Dora Carrington.

LUCA CUMANI

399. BUCKEYE ★★★
b.c. Shamardal – Tenderly (Danehill). March 24. Sixth living foal. €140,000Y. Baden Baden. Brookdale Farm. Half-brother to the US Grade 3 7f winner Ten Meropa (by Johannesburg) and four minor winners in France, the USA, Japan and Germany by Monsun, Vindication, Johar and Unbridled's Song. The dam, placed second over 1m, is a half-sister to 10 winners including the Group 1 Champion Stakes, Grand Prix de Saint-Cloud and Hong Kong Cup winner Pride and the dam of the 1,000 Guineas and Group 2 Rockfel Stakes winner Speciosa. The second dam, Specificity (by Alleged), winner of the listed 12.2f George Stubbs Stakes, is a half-sister to the 10 winners including the St Leger and Irish St Leger winner Touching Wood. (Mr J S Kelly). *"He's shown me a bit of speed and I think he's going to be alright. He won't be very precocious but he should be a seven furlongs/one mile colt for August or September".*

400. CHIEF CRAFTSMAN ★★★
b.c. Mastercraftsman – Eurolink Raindance (Alzao). February 2. Seventh foal. 125,000Y. Tattersalls October Book 2. Charlie Gordon-Watson. Half-brother to the fairly useful 7f winner House (by Elusive Quality), to the quite useful 8.5f (at 2 yrs) and 14.5f winner Maastricht (by Tiger Hill) and the fair 1m winner of 5 races Toymaker (by Starcraft). The dam, a useful 2-y-o 6f and 7f and subsequent US Grade 3 winner, is a half-sister to 4 winners

including the Group 3 10f winner Mango Mischief. The second dam, Eurolink Mischief (by Be My Chief), a quite useful 12f winner, is a half-sister to 3 winners including the useful middle-distance colt and listed winner Duke Of Eurolink. (Mr J D Cotton). *"A very nice, big horse, he's goes well but the sire doesn't necessarily get them too speedy. One for the mid-summer onwards".*

401. CROSSING PATHS (IRE) ★★★
b.f. Cape Cross – Rebelline (Robellino). April 14. Tenth foal. 420,000Y. Tattersalls October Book 1. Not sold. Hadden Bloodstock. Sister to the smart Group 3 Irish 2,000 Guineas Trial winner and Group 1 10.5f Tattersalls Rogers Cup second Recharge and half-sister to 5 winners including the useful 7f (at 2 yrs) and listed 9.5f winner I'm Yours and the quite useful Irish 2-y-o 6f winner Redoubtable (both by Invincible Spirit). The dam won the Group 1 10.5f Tattersalls Gold Cup and the Group 2 Pretty Polly Stakes and is a sister to the Group 2 Blandford Stakes winner Quws and a half-sister to 5 winners. The second dam, Fleeting Rainbow (by Rainbow Quest), placed over 10f, is a half-sister to 3 winners. (Merry Fox Stud II Ltd). *"A well-bred filly that's done very well physically. She'll be a mid-season type, seems to be going OK and I'm pleased with her".*

402. DUBARA ★★★★
b.f. Dubawi – Kibara (Sadler's Wells). May 1. Seventh foal. Half-sister to the fairly useful 1m (at 2 yrs) to 12f winner of 3 races Kikonga (by Danehill Dancer), to the quite useful 10f and 12f winner Kinshasa (by Pivotal) and the quite useful 11f and 12f winner of 3 races Kiwayu (by Medicean). The dam, a fair 11f winner, is a sister to 5 winners including the St Leger and Great Voltigeur Stakes winner Milan and half-sister to 3 winners including the Group 2 Great Voltigeur Stakes third Go For Gold. The second dam, Kithanga (by Darshaan), was a smart winner of 3 races including the Group 3 12f St Simon Stakes and the listed 12f Galtres Stakes. (Fittocks Stud). *"A bit on the small side, but this branch of the family can be that way. She goes well, I'm happy with her, Dubawi's are not necessarily precocious horses but she could be alright for six or seven furlongs in July. Promising".*

403. GLORIOUS ROCKET ★★★
b.c. Bated Breath – Up And About (Barathea). February 13. Twelfth foal. 35,000Y. Tattersalls October Book 2. Sackville/Donald. Half-brother to 7 winners including the fairly useful listed-placed 6f to 10f of 6 races from 2 to 4 yrs Take It To The Max (by Bahamian Bounty), the fairly useful 2-y-o 1m winner Tamarillo (by Daylami and herself dam of the Group 3 Oak Tree Stakes winner Summer Fete), the fairly useful 6f (at 2 yrs) and 7f winner of 4 races and listed-placed Wake Up Call (by Noverre), the fairly useful dual 7f winner Kyllachy Rise (by Kyllachy) and the quite useful 7f (at 2 yrs) and 10f winner All About Time (by Azamour). The dam, a fair 14.8f winner, is a half-sister to 9 winners including the Group 1 placed Musicanna. The second dam, Upend (by Main Reef), won the Group 3 St Simon Stakes and is a half-sister to 6 winners. (Kangyu International Racing (HK) Ltd). *"He's nice, I like him but he's big and I haven't been able to do much with him yet. A likeable horse that'll come in his own time".*

404. GOD GIVEN ★★★★
b.f. Nathaniel – Ever Rigg (Dubai Destination). March 26. Fourth foal. Half-sister to the Group 1 King George VI and Queen Elizabeth Stakes, Group 2 12f Great Voltigeur Stakes and Group 2 12f Prix Foy winner Postponed (by Dubawi). The dam, a fair 12f winner, is a half-sister 5 winners including the fairly useful listed-placed Bite Of The Cherry and the listed-placed Pietra Dura (dam of the US Grade 3 winner and Grade 1 second Turning Top). The second dam, Bianca Nera (by Salse), winner of the Group 1 7f Moyglare Stud Stakes and the Group 2 6f Lowther Stakes, is half-sister to 4 winners including the Group 1 Moyglare Stud Stakes second Hotelgenie Dot Com (dam of the dual Group 1 winner Simply Perfect). (St Albans Bloodstock). *"She's lovely, a half-sister to Postponed, she's very good-looking and moves very well. The sire's not likely to get many precocious types, but she should be able to start off in mid-summer over seven furlongs. I like her".*

405. GREAT COURT ★★★
gr.f. Mastercraftsman – Neat Shilling (Bob Back). April 11. Tenth foal. 32,000Y. Tattersalls December. Charlie Gordon-Watson. Half-sister

to the listed winner and UAE Group 2 placed Kalahari Gold (by Trans Island), to the quite useful 7f (at 2 yrs) to 10f and hurdles winner Mr Jack Daniells, the fair 9.8f winner Nickels And Dimes (by Teofilo), the fair 6f (at 2 yrs) to 1m winner of 5 races Tidy (both by Mujadil) and the moderate 5f winner Staceymac (by Elnadim). The dam is an unraced sister to the Irish 7f (at 2 yrs) and 10f winner and Group 3 placed Fill The Bill and a half-sister to 6 winners including the US Grade 3 winner Riddlesdown. The second dam, Neat Dish (by Stalwart), won once over 6f at 2 yrs in Ireland, was second in the Group 3 Railway Stakes and is a half-sister to 9 winners including the US Grade 1 placed Western Winter. (Mr J Shack & Mr G Barnard). *"I think she's OK, she's a great mover and physically she's a very nice filly. A likable type and one for the mid-summer over seven furlongs".*

406. LIGHTABLE ★★★
b.f. Shamardal – Luminance (Danehill Dancer). March 5. Second foal. The dam is an unraced half-sister to 4 winners including the fairly useful 2-y-o 7f winner and Group 3 Irish 1,000 Guineas Trial second Devotion. The second dam, Bright Bank (by Sadler's Wells), is an unraced half-sister to 8 winners including the very useful listed 6f and 7f winner and dual Group 1 placed My Branch (herself the dam of the Group 1 Sprint Cup winner Tante Rose). (Fittocks Stud). *"She could be a six furlong filly come July time because she's strong, well-built and muscled. There's nothing wrong with her".*

407. MARKETEER ★★★
b.f. Oasis Dream – Barter (Daylami). April 11. Fourth foal. 240,000Y. Tattersalls October Book 1. Not sold. Half-sister to the fairly useful 2015 listed-placed 2-y-o 1m winner Haggle (by Pivotal), to the quite useful 1m winner Bermondsey (by Galileo) and the fair 10f winner Petticoat Lane (by High Chaparral). The dam is an unplaced half-sister to 11 winners including the very useful listed 12f winner and good broodmare Puce and the dam of the Group 1 winners Alexandrova and Magical Romance. The second dam, Souk (by Ahonoora), a fairly useful 7f winner, was listed placed over 1m and is a half-sister to 3 winners. (Emma Capon & Fittocks Stud). *"She's done very well physically but it's not a precocious family. She's one for the autumn, so let's hope she does at least as well as her half-sister Haggle did last year".*

408. PARISIAN CHIC (IRE) ★★★
b.f. Kodiac – Divine Design (Barathea). April 30. Fourth foal. 78,000Y. Tattersalls October Book 2. Charlie Gordon-Watson. Half-sister to the very useful 2-y-o 5f and 6f winner and listed-placed Angelic Lord (by Dark Angel). The dam is an unplaced half-sister to the useful 2-y-o listed 5f winner and Group 1 Nunthorpe Stakes third Piccadilly Filly. The second dam, Tortue (by Turtle Island), a quite useful Irish 1m and 9f winner, is a half-sister to 5 winners including Tiraaz (Group 1 Prix Royal-Oak). (Bedford House Fillies' Syndicate). *"In theory she should be much earlier than most of mine, but she's quite small and growing at the moment so it depends how quickly she finished her growing process. She could be one to see out in July over six furlongs".*

409. PARTY NIGHTS ★★★
b.f. Lawman – Funseeker (Halling). April 11. Third living foal. 12,000Y. Tattersalls October Book 2. Charlie Gordon-Watson. Half-sister to a minor winner abroad by King's Best. The dam, a modest 7f and 1m placed 2-y-o, is a sister to the Group 1 Grand Prix de Paris winner Cavalryman and a half-sister to 5 winners. The second dam, Silversword (by Highest Honor), a winner at 3 yrs in France and Group 3 placed, is a full or half-sister to 6 winners. *"A good-looking filly and I really don't know why she only cost 12,000 Gns. She goes well, isn't a speedster, but all being well she'll be out in August".* **TRAINERS' BARGAIN BUY**

410. PINCHECK (IRE) ★★★
b.c. Invincible Spirit – Arty Crafty (Arch). March 7. Fourth foal. €370,000Y. Goffs Orby. Anglia Bloodstock. Closely related to the quite useful 2-y-o 7f winner Enraptured (by Oasis Dream). The dam, a modest 10f and 12f winner of 4 races, is a sister to the US Grade 1 11f winner Prince Arch and a half-sister to the Group 1 National Stakes winner Kingsfort. The second dam, Princess Kris (by Kris), a quite useful 3-y-o 1m winner, is half-sister to 8 winners including the Group 3 May Hill Stakes winner Intimate Guest and to the placed dam of the US Grade 1 winner Luas Line. (Mr J S Kelly).

"He's strange because he's a lovely horse but for an Invincible Spirit he's amazingly big – probably one of the biggest we have in the yard. He goes well but he'll have to be given some time to get stronger. Probably an autumn 2-y-o".

411. PRESENCE PROCESS ★★
b.c. Dansili – Loulwa (Montjeu). March 29. Half-brother to the useful listed winner of 5 races over 5f and 6f and Group 2 third Justineo (by Oasis Dream), to the fair 7f winner Bella Lulu (by Iffraaj) and the modest 6f winner Elhaam (by Shamardal). The dam, a fairly useful 11f and listed 13f winner, is a half-sister to 5 winners including the Group 2 6f Mill Reef Stakes winner and Group 1 placed Galeota and the fairly useful 2-y-o 5f Weatherbys Supersprint winner Lady Livius. The second dam, Refined (by Statoblest), a fairly useful dual 5f winner, is a half-sister to 6 winners including the very smart Group 3 7f Criterion Stakes winner Pipe Major. (Saleh Al Homaizi & Imad Al Sagar). *"A difficult horse to judge. He's very small but the dam was a middle-distance filly, so it's difficult to know which way he's going to go. Time will tell"*.

412. RED LABEL ★★★★★
b.c. Dubawi – Born Something (Caerleon). April 13. Eighth foal. 375,000Y. Tattersalls October Book 1. Jamie McCalmont. Half-brother to the UAE listed-placed winner Tarbawi (by Anabaa) and to the quite useful 7f (at 2 yrs) and 1m winner Best Example (by King's Best). The dam, a winner of 4 races in France and the USA and third in the Group 3 Prix de la Grotte, is a sister to the Group 3 Prix Cleopatre winner Gold Round and a half-sister to 10 winners including the outstanding multiple Group 1 winner Goldikova and the Group 1 Prix Vermeille winner Galikova. The second dam, Born Gold (by Blushing Groom), won over 8.3f and is a sister to the Group 1 1m Prix Marcel Boussac and Group 1 1m Coronation Stakes winner Gold Splash. (Mr J S Kelly). *"I like him a lot and he's probably my favourite at the moment. It's easy to be swayed by the fact he's by Dubawi but he does go very well and he's a good-looking horse. Very likeable, he should definitely win as a 2-y-o and we'll start him off around July time over seven furlongs".*

413. RICKRACK (IRE) ★★
b.f. Teofilo – Arazena (Woodman). January 28. Ninth foal. 260,000Y. Tattersalls October Book 1. Jamie McCalmont. Closely related to the 2-y-o 9f winner and listed-placed Obligation (by Galileo) and half-sister to 5 winners including the French 2-y-o 1m winner, Group 3 second and Hong Kong Group 1 Champions Mile second Arasin, the moderate 6f (at 2 yrs) and 5f winner Milady Eileen (both by Footstepsinthesand) and the useful 2-y-o dual 7f winner and listed-placed City Of Troy (by Grand Lodge). The dam, a French 11f winner, is a half-sister to 5 winners including the dam of the US Grade 2 Clark Handicap winner Quest. The second dam, Mysterious Star (by Nijinsky), was unraced. (Mr J S Kelly). *"A big filly and a staying type for the autumn, she's likeable and has an early foaling date but she has a staying pedigree".*

414. SO SLEEK ★★★
b.f. Lawman – So Silk (Rainbow Quest). April 28. Sixth foal. 450,000Y. Tattersalls October Book 1. Lordship Stud & Kern/Lillingston. Half-sister to the smart Group 2 14.5f Park Hill Stakes winner and Group 1 British Champions Fillies/Mare Stakes second Silk Sari (by Dalakhani), to the US winner and listed-placed Fashion Fund and the quite useful 2-y-o 1m winner Dreamlike (both by Oasis Dream). The dam is an unraced half-sister to 5 winners including the 2-y-o Group 1 Racing Post Trophy winner Ibn Khaldun. The second dam, Gossamer (by Sadler's Wells), won the Group 1 Fillies' Mile and the Group 1 Irish 1,000 Guineas and is a sister to the Breeders' Cup Mile and Irish 2,000 Guineas winner Barathea and a half-sister to 6 winners. (Lordship Stud). *"It's a family that takes time, so I would say she's one for the autumn. She's a big filly and very good-looking, in fact she's probably as attractive a filly as the mare has had".*

415. SPINNAKA (IRE) ★★★
b.f. Invincible Spirit – Spinning Well (Pivotal). April 7. Fourth foal. 160,000Y. Tattersalls October Book 1. Fittocks Stud. Half-sister to the fair 2015 Irish 7f placed Laws Of Spin (by Lawman) and to the 2-y-o fair 2-y-o 1m winner Tanqeya (by Intense Focus). The dam, a fair 12f winner at 4 yrs, is a half-sister to 4 winners including the Australian Group 1

winner Opinion and the Irish/German Group 3 winners Anam Allta and Fox Hunt. The second dam, Kiltubber (by Sadler's Wells), an Italian listed 12f winner, is a half-sister to 3 winners. (Fittocks Stud & Mr A Bengough). *"One of the more precocious ones, she seems to be doing well, she's attractive and could be a six furlong filly in June/July".*

416. SPUN GOLD ★★★
ch.c. Exceed And Excel – Victoire Celebre (Stravinsky). April 27. Fourth foal. Half-brother to the useful 10f to 12f winner here and Australian listed 9.5f winner Arab Dawn (by Dalakhani), to the quite useful 1m and 10f winner Laurence (by Dubawi) and the quite useful 6f and 7f winner Lionheart (by Zamindar). The dam ran twice unplaced and is a half-sister to the Group 2 Prix du Muguet winner Vetheuil, the Group 3 Prix de l'Opera winner Verveine (dam of the Grade 1 winners Vallee Enchantee and Volga) and the dams of the Group 1 winners Maid's Causeway and Vespone. The second dam, Venise (by Nureyev), is an unraced three-parts sister to the Mill Reef Stakes and Richmond Stakes winner Vacarme and a half-sister to the Prix Jacques le Marois winner Vin de France. (Fittocks Stud & Mr A Bengough). *"A nice horse, he's quite big but he could be relatively early. He comes from a mile and a half family, but the sire can put a lot of precocity and speed into a 2-y-o. So six or seven furlongs would be his starting point".*

417. UNNAMED ★★★
gr.c. Dream Ahead – America Nova (Verglas). April 27. Fifth foal. 82,000Y. Tattersalls October Book 1. Charlie Gordon-Watson. Half-brother to the 2-y-o 6f and 7f and subsequent Australian Group 2 6f and Group 3 7.5f winner Sir Patrick Moore and to the Group 3 Prix des Reservoirs winner Stellar Path (both by Astronomer Royal). The dam, a French 2-y-o listed 1m winner, is a half-sister to 4 winners including the French listed winner Cat Nova. The second dam, Las Americas (by Linamix), won 5 minor races in France from 3 to 5 yrs and is a half-sister to 2 winners. (Buxted Partnership). *"A nice, good-looking horse and he could be one for June or July. It's difficult to be precise as to what trip he'll want, but maybe he'll get away with six furlongs to start with before stepping him up".*

418. UNNAMED ★★★
b.f. Raven's Pass – Aneedah (Invincible Spirit). February 10. Second foal. 370,000Y. Tattersalls October Book 2. Tony Nerses. The dam, a fairly useful 2-y-o 1m winner, was listed-placed and is a half-sister to 2 winners including the dual Group 2 winning sprinter Muthmir and the 2-y-o Group 3 7f C L Weld Park Stakes winner My Titania. The second dam, Fairy Of The Night (by Danehill), an Irish 7f listed and 9.5f winner, is a sister to one winner and a half-sister to 3 winners including the US Grade 3 12f and Irish listed 11f winner Dress Rehearsal. (Saleh Al Homaizi & Imad Al Sagar). *"She's probably one of the most precocious of the fillies. She's small, butty and strong, seems to be going well".*

419. UNNAMED ★★★
gr.f. Galileo – Bewitched (Dansili). January 19. Second foal. 360,000Y. Tattersalls October Book 1. NAS. The dam, a smart winner of 8 races from 5f to 7f including the Ballycorus Stakes, the Bengough Stakes and the Renaissance Stakes twice (all Group 3 events) and is a half-sister to 4 minor winners. The second dam, Abbatiale (by Kaldoun), won the Group 3 Prix Penelope, was second in the Group 1 Prix de Diane and is a half-sister to the French listed winner and Group 2 placed Aubergade. (Al Shaqab Racing). *"She's a gorgeous filly but despite the fact she was an early foal shell want seven furlongs from the middle of the season onwards. She's lovely".*

420. UNNAMED ★★★
b.c. Zoffany – Chocolate Mauk (Cozzene). April 9. Seventh foal. 58,000Y. Tattersalls October Book 2. Charlie Gordon-Watson. Half-brother to 2 minor winners in the USA by Posse and Purge. The dam is an unplaced half-sister to 8 winners including the US stakes winners Total Bull and Seattle Pattern and the dam of the US Grade 1 winner Archarcharch. The second dam, Pattern Step (by Nureyev), won the Grade 1 Hollywood Oaks and is a half-sister to the Grade 2 winner Motley. (Dahab Racing). *"A good-looking horse and definitely one to consider as a 2-y-o, he goes well and is one to start off in mid-season".*

421. UNNAMED ★★★★
b.f. Galileo – Daneleta (Danehill). January 29. Ninth foal. €300,000Y. Goffs Orby. F Barberini. Half-sister to 5 winners including the 2-y-o Group 1 7f Dewhurst Stakes winner Intense Focus (by A P Indy), the fairly useful 6f (at 2 yrs) and 1m winner Jalaa, the fairly useful dual 10f winner Dane Street (both by Street Cry) and the quite useful 9.5f winner Spin Point (by Pivotal). The dam, a 2-y-o 7f winner and third in the Group 3 Railway Stakes, is a sister to the Group 3 12f Noblesse Stakes winner Danelissima and a half-sister to 7 winners. The second dam, Zavaleta (by Kahyasi), a dual listed 7f winner, is a half-sister to 9 winners including Sholokov (2-y-o Group 1 1m Gran Criterium). (Clipper Logistics). *"A very nice filly and she's fairly precocious for a Galileo. She could be out in July, she's a nice type, not very big but well put together".*

422. UNNAMED ★★
b.f. Frankel – Dynaforce (Dynaformer). March 1. Third foal. 450,000Y. Tattersalls October Book 1. Charlie Gordon-Watson / Al Shaqab Racing. Half-sister to the minor US 3-y-o winner Lady Dyna (by Tapit). The dam won 5 races including the Grade 1 Flower Bowl Invitational and the Grade 1 Beverly D Stakes and is a half-sister to 11 winners including the US dual Grade 1 winner Cetewayo and the US Grade 2 winner Bowman Mill. The second dam, Aletta Maria (by Diesis), won 3 races in the USA at 3 and 4 yrs and is a sister to the Group 3 Lancashire Oaks winner Pharian and a half-sister to the Group 2 winner Raah Algharb. (Al Shaqab Racing). *"She's very nice but she's not a precocious filly at all. She's unlike what you'd expect from a Frankel because quite leggy, tall and a little bit narrow, so she needs to develop a long time before she even sees a racecourse. That's probably coming from the female line. Hopefully she'll debut in the autumn".*

423. UNNAMED ★★★★ ♠♠
b.c. Zoffany – Glympse (Spectrum). April 21. Seventh foal. 200,000Y. Tattersalls October Book 1. Charlie Gordon-Watson / Al Shaqab Racing. Half-brother to the fairly useful 2-y-o 7f and hurdles winner Whipper's Boy (by Whipper), to the fair 5f winner Supercharged (by Iffraaj) and the fair Irish 2-y-o 7f winner Westering Home (by Mull Of Kintyre). The dam, placed fourth once over 9f in Ireland, is a half-sister to 4 winners and to the dams of six stakes winners. The second dam, Seasonal Pickup (by The Minstrel), won four listed races in Ireland and is a half-sister to the dam of the Irish Derby winner Grey Swallow. (Al Shaqab Racing). *"A very nice colt, he's big but very strong with it and potentially he could be a July 2-y-o for seven furlongs plus".*

424. UNNAMED ★★★
b.c. Rock Of Gibraltar – Muluk (Rainbow Quest). April 25. Fifth foal. 68,000Y. Tattersalls October Book 2. Charlie Gordon-Watson. Half-brother to the quite useful 7f (at 2 yrs) and 1m winner Intiwin (by Intikhab) and to the fair 8.5f and 10f winner Daisy Boy (by Cape Cross). The dam, a fairly useful Irish 1m winner, is a half-sister to 5 minor winners. The second dam, Messina (by Sadler's Wells), is a placed half-sister to 9 winners including Enthused (Group 2 6f Lowther Stakes and Group 3 6f Princess Margaret Stakes). *"A very good-looking horse, I like him and he could be a July type 2-y-o for seven furlongs. A likeable horse".*

425. UNNAMED ★★
b.f. Fastnet Rock – Victoire Finale (Peintre Celebre). May 6. Seventh foal. Half-sister to the useful 1m, 9f (both at 2 yrs) and listed 10f winner and Group 1 Epsom and Irish Oaks third Volume (by Mount Nelson), to the useful dual 1m winner (including at 2 yrs) Validus and the fairly useful dual 1m winner Velox (both by Zamindar). The dam, a useful French 1m winner, was fourth in a listed event and is a half-sister to numerous winners including the French Group 2 winner Vertical Speed. The second dam, Victoire Bleue (by Legend Of France), won the Group 1 Prix du Cadran. (Stuart Stuckey). *"I like this filly and it's a family that's done well for us. It's a staying family so she'll take a bit of time, but she goes well and we like her".*

KEITH DALGLEISH

426. CLEM FANDANGO ★★★★
b.f. Elzaam – Question (Coronado's Quest). March 14. Fifth foal. €11,000Y. Arqana Deauville August. F Barberini. Half-sister to the French 6.5f winner Happy Sun Percy (by Sir Percy). The dam is an unplaced half-sister

to several winners including the useful 7f and 1m winner Commander Cave (by Tale Of The Cat). The second dam, Royal Shyness (by Royal Academy), a useful 2-y-o 6f winner, was third in the Group 1 6f Cheveley Park Stakes and subsequently won a listed stakes race in the USA and is a half-sister to 8 winners. (Middleham Park Racing LXXV). *"She's a nice, medium-sized filly, her attitude is fantastic and she switches off and picks up just when you need her to. She'll be making her debut in April"*. **TRAINERS' BARGAIN BUY**

427. CLIFF BAY (IRE) ★★
b.c. Elzaam – Lost Highway (Danehill Dancer). March 31. First foal. €20,000Y. Goffs Orby. B O'Ryan/K Dalgleish. The dam, a moderate 9.5f and 12f placed maiden, is a half-sister to 4 winners including the Group 3 Gordon Stakes winner Rebel Soldier. The second dam, En Garde (by Irish River), a quite useful 2-y-o 5.7f winner, is a half-sister to 7 winners including the top-class Group 1 1m Queen Elizabeth II Stakes and Group 1 9.3f Prix d'Ispahan winner Observatory and the Group 2 Prix de Malleret winner High Praise. *"He's a big, babyish colt so I won't be in a hurry with him. Probably one for late summer but there is something about him I like"*.

428. HOLLYWOOD HARRY (IRE) ★★
ch.c. Dandy Man – Alifandango (Alzao). April 19. £20,000Y. Doncaster Premier. Bobby O'Ryan/K Dalgleish. Half-brother to the modest 6f winner Miss Poppets (by Polar Falcon) and the moderate Irish 14f and 2m winner Seismic (by Papal Bull). The dam, a fair 1m winner, is a half-sister to several winners including the useful listed 10f winner Ocean Air. The second dam, Fandangerina (by Grey Dawn II), a stakes-placed winner in the USA, is a half-sister to 8 winners. *"A small, compact, chunky 2-y-o type. He's ready for an entry now so I'll start him at five furlongs and I wouldn't be surprised if he was getting six in the summer"*.

429. KODI DA CAPO (IRE) ★★★
b.f. Kodiac – Red Trance (Soviet Star). April 7. Eighth foal. £26,000Y. Doncaster Premier. Tom Malone. Half-sister to the 2015 Italian 2-y-o winner Desilva (by Zebedee), to the modest 5.5f (at 2 yrs) and 6f winner Red Hearts (by Red Clubs, the modest 12f and hurdles winner Hypnotic Gaze (by Chevalier) and the moderate 2-y-o 1m winner Magic Empress (by Baltic King). The dam, a fair 2-y-o 5f winner, is a half-sister to 7 winners including the Group 3 Prix Miesque third Arabian Spell. The second dam, Truly Bewitched (by Affirmed), a quite useful 2-y-o 6f winner, is a half-sister to 9 winners including the US Grade 2 winner Chinese Dragon. (Equus I). *"She's small and sharp, certainly a 2-y-o and typical of the sire in that she's hardy. She's due for a run now"*. This filly made her debut at Wolverhampton where she ran a promising third.

430. LOMU ★★
b.c. Dandy Man – Miss Me (Marju). March 28. Sixth foal. £14,000Y. Doncaster Premier. Not sold. The dam won twice over 1m and was listed-placed over 9f in France. The second dam, Sandskip (by Sanglamore), is an unraced half-sister to 7 winners including two listed winners and the dams of the Group 1 winners Proportional and Folk Opera. (S J Macdonald). *"A big, good-looking colt with a great attitude, he's one of those that could either be on the track in May or I'll have to give him more time. I'll start him off at five furlongs, but I wouldn't be surprised if he was going seven by the back-end of the season"*.

431. OUR LOIS (IRE) ★★
b.f. Bushranger – Atishoo (Revoque). April 10. Seventh foal. €10,000Y. Tattersalls Ireland September. Tom Malone / Keith Dalgleish. Half-sister to 4 winners including the fair 2015 2-y-o 6f winner Saturn Lace, the fair 2-y-o 5f winner Kodatish (both by Kodiac) and the fairly useful 6f, 7f (both at 2 yrs) and 10f winner and listed-placed Sonoran Sands (by Footstepsinthesand). The dam, a modest Irish 1m placed maiden, is a half-sister to 4 winners including the listed winner and Group 2 Pretty Polly Stakes second Snippets. The second dam, Sniffle (by Shernazar), is an unplaced half-sister to the US Grade 1 winner Frenchpark and the Prix Vermeille winner Pearly Shells. (Equus Syndicate). *"She's tall, leggy and not that precocious, so I would think she needs at least a couple of months longer before she'll be ready to run"*.

432. SCARPACH ★★
b.c. Pastoral Pursuits – Bijan (Mukaddamah). April 26. Ninth foal. £20,000Y. Doncaster Silver. Bobby O'Ryan /K Dalgleish. Half-brother to the fair 6f winner of 9 races (including at 2 yrs) Gung Ho Jack (by Moss Vale), to the modest 6f (at 2 yrs) and 5f winner Ramblin Bob (by Piccolo), the moderate 5f winner Cliffords Reprieve (by Kheleyf) and a winner abroad by Sleeping Indian. The dam, a modest 5f (at 2 yrs) and 6f winner, is a half-sister to 6 winners including the Group 3 Ballyogan Stakes winner Yomalo. The second dam, Alkariyh (by Alydar), a fairly useful 2-y-o 6f winner, is a half-sister to 5 winners. (Mr A G MacLennan). *"A nice-sized, good-looking colt, he could probably do with filling out a bit but his attitude is good. He hasn't really got the hang of what's meant to happen yet, but he was quite a late foal and just needs to mature mentally a bit. I'd hope to see him make his debut in the summer".*

433. SIMMY'S TEMPLE ★★★★
b.f. Royal Applause – Samasana (Redback). February 16. First foal. £12,000Y. Doncaster Premier. Bobby O'Ryan/Keith Dalgleish. The dam, a modest 7f and 1m winner of 3 races, is a half-sister to 3 other minor winners. The second dam, Singitta (by Singspiel), is an unplaced half-sister to 3 winners including the dam of the Group 3 July Stakes winner Nevisian Lad. (Middleham Park Racing LX). *"She ran well on her debut in the Brocklesby and we'll probably look out for a fillies' novice for her in late April. Small and racy-looking, she obviously wants five furlongs now but looks as if she might get six later".*

434. SOMNAMBULIST ★★★
b.c. Rip Van Winkle – Sister Moonshine (Averti). February 14. February 14. 21,000Y. Tattersalls October Book 2. Tom Malone. The dam, a modest 6f placed maiden, is a half-sister to 8 winners including the 2-y-o Group 1 6f Cheveley Park Stakes winner and Group 2 Cherry Hinton Stakes second Donna Blini (herself dam of the Japanese dual Group 1 winner Gentildonna) and the US Grade 3 winner Magical. The second dam, Cal Norma's Lady (by Lyphard's Special), a quite useful 2-y-o 6f and 7f winner, is a half-sister to one winner. (Mr J S Morrison & Partner). *"I like him, he's a big, rangy colt. He's the type of*

2-y-o that's going well at this stage although he shouldn't be, going off his size and his sire. You could be tempted to push buttons, but we'll be in no hurry with him and we'll just keep ticking away for now. I would say he'd run around August time and just going off his looks he maybe should have cost a lot more than he did".

435. UNNAMED ★★★
b.c. Elusive Quality – Ebony Street (Street Cry). February 13. First foal. €50,000Y. Goffs Orby. B O'Ryan / K Dalgleish. The dam is an unplaced half-sister to one winner. The second dam, Menhoubah (by Dixieland Band), won the Group 1 Italian Oaks, was third in the 2-y-o Group 1 Moyglare Stud Stakes and is a half-sister to 2 winners. (Weldspec Glasgow Ltd). *"A handy-sized, racy colt that was rushing things a bit too much early on, but he's slowed down now and getting on with things. He's ready for an entry now".*

436. UNNAMED ★★★
ch.c. Intikhab – Fantastic Opinion (Fantastic Light). March 23. Third foal. £55,000Y. Doncaster Premier. Bobby O'Ryan & K Dalgleish. Half-brother to the fair 2015 Irish 6f placed 2-y-o Touch Of Frost (by Silver Frost). The dam is an unplaced half-sister to 7 winners. The second dam, Golden Opinion (by Slew O'Gold), won the Group 1 Coronation Stakes and the Group 3 Prix du Rond Point, was second in the July Cup and third in the French 1,000 Guineas and is a half-sister to 7 winners. (Weldspec Glasgow Ltd). *"He's a nice big colt with a good attitude and he moves well. I won't be in a rush with him and he hasn't done anything serious yet. One for the autumn I should think".*

437. UNNAMED ★★
bl.c. Kheleyf – Impulsive Decision (Nomination). April 2. Eleventh foal. 8,000Y. Tattersalls October Book 3. Bobby O'Ryan / Keith Dalgleish. Half-brother to 8 winners including the fairly useful 2-y-o 6f winner and listed-placed Cammies Future, the quite useful 6f to 1m winner of 5 races Santefisio (both by Efisio), the quite useful 6f winner of 3 races Fabreze, the modest 10f winner Elbow Beach (both by Choisir) and the fair 7f and 1m winner of 5 races (including at 2

yrs) Ermine Grey (by Wolfhound). The dam, a modest 6f (at 2 yrs) and 1m winner, is a half-sister to 5 winners. The second dam, Siva (by Bellypha), won 3 races in France from 1m to 11f and is a half-sister to 5 winners including the French Group 3 winner Sealy. (Weldspec Glasgow Ltd). *"He's kind of leggy at this stage, he's doing fine but I'm in no hurry with him. I've had a couple of the family before and generally they take a bit of time. For what he cost I think he was well-bought"*.

438. UNNAMED ★★★
ch.f. Bahamian Bounty – Moynsha Lady (Namid). February 22. Third foal. 15,000Y. Doncaster Premier. Middleham Park Racing (private sale). Half-sister to the 2016 3-y-o Southwell 1m winner Hutton (by Lawman). The dam is an unraced half-sister to 8 winners including the 2-y-o 6f and subsequent US stakes winner and Group 2 6f Coventry Stakes third Luck Money and the 2-y-o Group 3 7f Prix du Calvados winner Charlotte O'Fraise. The second dam, Dundel (by Machiavellian), a quite useful 7f winner, is a half-sister to 6 winners including the Group 3 6f winner Seltitude. *"She's sharp, smallish, racy-looking and tries hard. She's ready to run so I can see her making her debut in April over five furlongs and I think she'll go six later on"*.

439. UNNAMED ★★★
b.c. Harbour Watch – Spring Fashion (Galileo). April 19. Fourth foal. €80,000Y. Goffs Sportsmans. Bobby O'Ryan / K Dalgleish. Half-brother to the modest 12f winner Major Mac (by Shirocco). The dam, a moderate 9.5f fourth-placed maiden, is a half-sister to 4 minor winners. The second dam, Darina (by Danehill), an Irish 3-y-o winner of 4 races including a listed 10f event, was second in the Group 3 1m Matron Stakes and is a half-sister to 4 winners. (Weldspec Glasgow Ltd). *"A good-sized colt, I haven't pushed any buttons with him at all but his attitude is good. I like him, he moves well and he's forward-going. We'll start asking him a bit more in a month's time"*.

TOM DASCOMBE

440. ARC ROYAL ★★★
ch.c. Arcano – Royal Blush (Royal Applause). March 11. Second foal. £37,000Y. Doncaster Premier. Sackville/Donald. Half-brother to the quite useful dual 6f winner (including at 2 yrs in 2015) A Momentofmadness (by Elnadim). The dam, a fair 2-y-o 6f winner, is a half-sister to 8 winners including the fairly useful listed 1m Masaka Stakes winner Jazz Jam. The second dam, Applaud (by Band), winner of the Group 3 6f Cherry Hinton Stakes, is a full or half-sister to 6 winners. (Satchell Moran Solicitors). *"Arcano's aren't that popular so they can be relatively inexpensive and we did have had quite a nice one last year. This colt has just done his first piece of work, he's a nice, strong colt and he'll be out shortly. He's decent, he'll win a maiden and I'd say he'll be suited by six furlongs"*.

441. BIG TIME BABY (IRE) ★★★
b.c. Dandy Man – Royal Majestic (Tobougg). March 17. Second foal. £45,000Y. Doncaster Premier. Sackville/Donald. The dam, a fair 7f and 1m winner at 2 yrs, is a half-sister to 3 minor winners. The second dam, Golden Symbol (by Wolfhound), is an unplaced half-sister to 4 minor winners. (The Jones' & Owen Promotions). *"I've fallen into the trap before of saying "this Dandy Man is great" but in my experience they have a habit of letting you down. This colt is lovely to look at, does everything easily and we think he's nice so I hope he's not like the others we've had. He moves well and looks like a five furlong sprinter that'll get six. I'm going to treat him carefully, as if he's a filly, and we'll see if that works"*.

442. BLACKBELLE (IRE) ★★★★
br.f. New Approach – Wadaat (Diktat). March 26. Fourth foal. 45,000Y. Tattersalls October Book 1. Sackville/Donald. Sister to the fair 2015 2-y-o 7f winner Al Khafji. The dam, a useful 1m winner and second in the Group 2 Italian Oaks, is a half-sister to 7 winners including the Italian Group 3 placed Mrs Snow. The second dam, Shining Vale (by Twilight Agenda), is an unraced half-sister to the German and Italian Group 2 winner Walzerkoenigin (herself dam of the Group 1 German Derby winner Wiener Walzer). (L A Bellman). *"A sweet filly, she's a bit backward and we won't be in a rush with her. She's a nice type but I haven't done a lot with her yet and she'll be one for the second half of the

season, probably over seven furlongs to start with. The last time I spent a similar amount on a yearling from Book 1 was for Crowley's Law who ended up Grade 1 placed at Keeneland".

443. CHEERFILLY (IRE) ★★★
br.f. Excelebration – Classic Remark (Dr Fong). April 10. Fifth foal. €70,000Y. Goffs Orby. Sackville/Donald. Half-sister to the fair 1m and 10f winner Close At Hand (by Exceed And Excel) and to a 2-y-o winner in Spain by Authorized. The dam, a listed 10f winner, is a half-sister to 5 winners including the listed Lingfield Oaks Trial and subsequent US Grade 3 winner and Group 1 Nassau Stakes second Cassydora. The second dam, Claxon (by Caerleon), a very useful 1m (at 2 yrs) and Group 2 10f Premio Lydia Tesio winner, is a half-sister to 3 winners including the dual Group 2 placed Bulwark. (L A Bellman). *"She's by Excelebration – a sire we're quite excited about. A beautiful black filly, she's quite sweet and has a great attitude but she's tall and rangy, so she wants a bit of time. One for mid-summer onwards, of the horses we've got there are a few that might turn out to have quality – and she could be one of them".*

444. CONQUERESS (IRE) ★★★
ch.f. Dandy Man – Sesmen (Inchinor). April 15. Sixth foal. €30,000Y. Tattersalls Ireland September. Sackville/Donald. Half-sister to the promising 2015 2-y-o 1m winner Chastushka (by Poet's Voice), to the quite useful 1m winner Batrana (by Cape Cross) and the minor Italian winner of 4 races at 3 and 4 yrs Fifun (by Pivotal). The dam won 4 races at 2 and 3 yrs including the 2-y-o Group 3 7f Prestige Stakes. The second dam, Poetry In Motion (by Ballad Rock), a modest 5f winner at 4 yrs, is a half-sister to 5 winners including the German Group 3 winner and US Grade 2 placed Neshad. (Deva Racing Dandy Man Partnership). *"A nice filly, she looked a bit small when we bought her but she's grown and grown. She was really sick in the winter and I had to leave her alone, but it's done her a world of good. Not only is she a lot bigger but she's come into her coat now and is ready to be trained. I haven't worked her but I think she'll have plenty of speed when we do ask her".*

445. DECADENT TIMES ★★★
b.c. Art Connoisseur – Be Special (Sri Pekan). April 29. Sixth foal. €8,500Y. Tattersalls Ireland September. Bob Baggs. Half-brother to 2 minor winners in Italy by Stuck and Ivan Denisovich. The dam, a minor Italian winner of 2 races at 2 and 3 yrs, is a half-sister to 7 winners including the Italian listed winner and useful broodmare Salsa Sound. The second dam, Stua (by Caerleon), an Italian winner of 5minor races, is a half-sister to the Group 2 Sandown Mile winner Penny Drops. (The Roaring Twenties). *"Pretty narrow and very forward, he's done nothing wrong, he's very professional and was a cheap horse by a sire that nobody rates. He's run twice and was placed both times, but he's sure to win".* This colt was beaten into second at Beverley next time out.

446. EARTHA KITT ★★
b.f. Pivotal – Ceiling Kitty (Red Clubs). February 5. First foal. The dam won 3 races including the Group 2 5f Queen Mary Stakes and the listed Marygate Stakes and is a half-sister to the fair 2-y-o triple 5f winner Van Go Go. The second dam, Baldovina (by Tale Of The Cat), is a placed half-sister to the Japanese dual Group 3 winner One Carat. The second dam, Baldwina (by Pistolet Bleu), won the Group 3 Prix Penelope and is a half-sister to 5 winners. (Chasemore Farm). *"The dam was our Queen Mary winner and unfortunately she died giving birth to a colt foal. So this is her only filly and as such she's very important to both Chasemore Farm and to me. She's not actually in the yard yet but she'll be here in a few days. She's surprisingly tall and doesn't look anything like her mother. Other than that I can't tell you anything about her except to say that we'll be doing our best to ensure she has the best chance of being a racehorse".*

447. EXCITING TIMES ★★★
ch.c. Tamayuz – Catwalk (Pivotal). February 7. First foal. €60,000Y. Goffs Orby. Sackville/Donald. The dam, a quite useful 6f winner, is a half-sister to 6 winners including the 2-y-o Group 2 5f Flying Childers Stakes winner Sir Prancealot (by Tamayuz) and the French listed 10f winner of 10 races Nice Applause. The second dam, Mona 'Em (by Catrail), a listed sprint winner, is a half-sister

to 4 winners. (Mr D R Passant). *"He's an interesting horse because the more work I give him the fatter he gets – which clearly shouldn't be the case! It's difficult to know whether he's going to be early or late, but he's close-coupled, has a reasonably pedigree and I think the sire is under-rated. We're still learning about this colt, but it's interesting to see that he's quite closely related to Sir Prancealot".*

448. FIERY CHARACTER (IRE) ★★★★
br.f. Dragon Pulse – Intricate Dance (Aptitude). April 2. Fifth foal. €18,000Y. Goffs Sportsmans. Sackville/Donald. Half-sister to Daydream (by Dream Ahead), a modest second over 1m at 3 yrs in 2016 and to two minor winners abroad by Le Vie Dei Colori (at 2 yrs in Poland) and Excellent Art. The dam ran twice unplaced and is a half-sister to 3 winners including the very useful listed 7f (at 2 yrs) and listed 1m winner Short Dance and to the placed dam of the Group 2 and triple Group 3 winner Lolly For Dolly. The second dam, Clog Dance (by Pursuit Of Love), a useful maiden, was second in the Group 3 7f Rockfel Stakes and the listed 10f Pretty Polly Stakes and is a half-sister to 6 winners including the smart 14f Ebor Handicap winner Tuning. (The Roaring Twenties). *"We have a few Dragon Pulse 2-y-o's and going by them I think he's going to be a good sire. This is our nicest early season 2-y-o filly, she goes well, has a great attitude, is straightforward and has size and scope. She's taken everything I've thrown at her and she comes back for more. We like her and she'll get further than five furlongs but we won't be hanging around".* This filly won first time out at Newmarket at 33-1. **TRAINERS' BARGAIN BUY**

449. FOUR DRAGONS ★★★
ch.f. Dragon Pulse – Mysterious Girl (Teofilo). February 18. First foal. £30,000Y. Doncaster Premier. Sackville/Donald. The dam is an unraced half-sister to one winner. The second dam, Mazaaya (by Cozzene), a quite useful 7f (at 2 yrs) and 10f winner, is a sister to the useful 10f winner and dual listed-placed Cozy Maria (herself dam of the Group 2 Flying Childers winner and sire Zebedee) and a half-sister to 8 winners in the North America and Argentina. (O'Halloran, Owen, Satchell, Willcock). *"Very sharp, she's owned by four very enthusiastic ladies and as you can see they named her after themselves! She's due to run at Ripon in mid-April, she's not very big but she's all there and we like the sire. Very light on her feet, she's quite nice and we like her".*

450. FULL INTENTION ★★★
b.c. Showcasing – My Delirium (Haafhd). April 16. Second foal. £54,000Y. Doncaster Premier. Sackville/Donald. Brother to the very useful 2015 2-y-o Group 3 5f Cornwallis Stakes and listed 5f winner Quiet Reflection. The dam, a quite useful 2-y-o 6f winner, is a half-sister to one winner. The second dam, Clare Hills (by Orpen), won the 2-y-o listed 5f Hilary Needler Trophy and is a half-sister to 3 winners. (Mr J Dance). *"A nice colt that was due to run in the Brocklesby but unfortunately we had to pull him out. We'll find another race for him and he'll be winning shortly. He's quite nice, he's by a good sire and since we bought him his full sister has won a Group 3, so if we had to buy him again we'd have to pay more than we did. He looks like a proper 2-y-o, he's very athletic looking, five furlongs is fine for him to start with and he'll get six at least".* This colt was slightly unlucky to be beaten on his debut at Windsor on soft ground in mid-April.

451. HAZY MANOR (IRE) ★★★
b.f. Tagula – Hazarama (Kahyasi). April 23. Twelfth foal. €32,000Y. Goffs Sportsmans. Sackville/Donald. Sister to the useful 2015 2-y-o 7f winner Humphrey Bogart and to the quite useful 6f (at 2 yrs), 10f and hurdles winner Domino Dancer and half-sister to 3 winners including the fair 10f winner Devote Myself (by Kodiac). The dam won over 13f and is a half-sister to 6 winners including the Group 3 winners Hazariya and Hazarista. The second dam, Hazaradjat (by Darshaan), won twice at 2 and 3 yrs and is a full or half-sister to 10 winners including Hittite Glory (Flying Childers and Middle Park Stakes). (Excel Racing & Partners). *"I'll probably start her off at six furlongs in the middle of May and she's a nice-looking filly, light and leggy but surprisingly sharp considering that. I think this filly will do well for the owners, she'll get seven furlongs and I think she'll improve as the season goes on".*

452. HEAVEN'S ROCK (IRE) ★★★★
b.c. Requinto – Rockfleet Castle (Rock Of Gibraltar). March 24. Third foal. £40,000Y. Doncaster Premier. Sackville/Donald. The dam, a moderate Irish 9f placed maiden, is a half-sister to 2 minor winners here and one in Japan. The second dam, Chelsea (by Miswaki), a minor French 4-y-o winner, is a half-sister to 7 winners including the US Grade 1 winner Super Staff and the French/US triple Group 2 winner Public Purse. (Tom Cleverley & Stephen Mound). *"I rode this colt all winter and I loved him. In January and February he was my favourite two-year-old, he's a strong, box of a horse, but for some reason he hasn't quite gone the way I wanted him to. That's probably because he's just not physically ready and I think he'll come good given a bit more time. He'll be out in May or June and from what I've seen of him if we've got one 2-y-o that might be the type for something like the Molecomb, he could be the one. From the little I've seen of this colt I love him".*

453. IMDANCINWITHURWIFE (IRE) ★★★
b.f. Sir Prancealot – Bishop's Lake (Lake Coniston). February 16. Sixth foal. 32,000Y. Tattersalls October Book 1. Sackville/Donald. Half-sister to the Group 3 Blue Wind Stakes winner Euphrasia (by Windsor Knot), to the fairly useful listed-placed 2-y-o 5f winner Langavat (by Bushranger), the modest 6f (at 2 yrs) to 9f winner Lakeman (by Tillerman) and the modest 1m winner Strike A Deal (by Chineur). The dam, a quite useful listed-placed dual 2-y-o 6f winner, is a half-sister to 8 winners including the Group placed 2-y-o's Sir Reginald and Henrik. The second dam, Clincher Club (by Polish Patriot), a fair 5f (at 2 yrs) and 7.5f winner, is a half-sister to 9 winners. (Hong Kong Crew). *"We've got a few by this sire, they're all very fast and this filly had a run in France in a 900m race but didn't get home in the soft ground. She'll want tight tracks like Wolverhampton where she can save energy. She's very small but she has a decent pedigree and it would be nice to get a win out of her early on".* This filly won at Wolverhampton on the 9th April.

454. KACHESS ★★★
b.f. Kyllachy – Fibou (Seeking The Gold). April 19. Seventh foal. £40,000Y. Doncaster Premier. Sackville/Donald. Closely related to the modest 2-y-o 6f winner Finoon and to the UAE 6f and 7f winner Faulkner (both by Pivotal) and half-sister to two winners abroad by Oasis Dream and Cape Cross. The dam ran once unplaced and is a half-sister to 4 winners. The second dam, Lilium (by Nashwan), a listed 7f (at 2 yrs) and listed 12f winner, was third in the Group 3 Princess Royal Stakes and is a half-sister to 6 winners including the 2-y-o Group 1 6f Middle Park Stakes winner Lujain. (Mr D J Lowe). *"A nice type, she's a good shape and the dam's had four winners from four runners. She'll start over six furlongs, hasn't worked yet but she's got a bit of quality about her and we won't be in a rush".*

455. KATMANDOO (USA) ★★★
b.c. Kitten's Joy – Granny Franny (Grand Slam). January 30. Fifth foal. 230,000Y. Tattersalls October Book 1. Sackville/Donald. Brother to the US Grade 1 Queen Elizabeth II Challenge Cup winner Kitten's Dumplings, to the US listed stakes winner Granny Mc's Kitten and the US winner and Grade 3 placed Granny's Kitten. The dam won 3 minor races at 3 and 4 yrs in the USA. The second dam, Franziska (by Sadler's Wells), placed fourth oneover 9f, is a half-sister to 5 winners including the Group 3 Curragh Stakes winner Aminata. (Burns, Smyth, Studholme). *"A lovely colt by Kitten's Joy, he's hopefully a horse we'll have here for a couple of years. We'll let him develop and give him a bit of time, but physically he's done enormously well. I doubt we'll see him out before mid-summer and we'll give him a couple of runs this season before hopefully having a proper 3-y-o".*

456. LEGATO (IRE) ★★★
ch.c. Power – Lisa Gherardini (Barathea). April 19. Second foal. €40,000Y. Tattersalls Ireland September. Sackville/Donald. Half-brother to the quite useful 2015 Irish dual 6f placed 2-y-o Aspar (by Holy Roman Emperor). The dam is an unplaced half-sister to 3 winners including the Group 2 Coventry Stakes third Rakaan. The second dam, Petite Spectre (by Spectrum), a fair 2-y-o 6f winner, is a half-sister to 9 winners including the useful 2-y-o Group 3 7f C L Weld Park Stakes winner Rag Top. (Alan & Sue Cronshaw). *"A huge horse, to me he was the standout at the*

sale. Despite his size he was the one I wanted because you have to have a variety of horses, he's going to have plenty of time and is just doing one canter at the moment. He's got a huge stride on him and if he's got any ability he's going to be decent. He's very laid back with a lovely attitude".

457. LUCATA ★★★
b.c. Sir Prancealot – Toy Show (Danehill). April 5. Ninth foal. £10,000Y. Doncaster Premier. Dave Thompson. Half-brother to the fairly useful 2-y-o 5f winner Cleveland Street (by Windsor Knot), to the quite useful 1m to 10f winner of 5 races Wing Play (by Hawk Wing), the fair 1m (at 2 yrs) to 2m and hurdles winner Knight's Parade (by Dark Angel) and the minor Italian winner Capo Malfatano (by Hurricane Run). The dam, a quite useful triple 10f winner (including at 2 yrs), is a half-sister to 6 minor winners. The second dam, March Hare (by Groom Dancer), a modest middle-distance placed maiden, is a half-sister to 7 winners including the smart 1m and 10f listed winner Inglenook. (The Roaring Twenties). *"He's had a run already and did nothing wrong, but he's very small and will be running again soon. I think he'll need to win pretty soon due to his size".*

458. NANCY HART ★★★
b.f. Sepoy – Lucky Token (Key Of Luck). April 24. Fifth foal. 34,000Y. Tattersalls December. Not sold. Half-sister to the unplaced 2015 2-y-o Polymnia (by Poet's Voice) and to a winner in Hong Kong at 4 yrs by Exceed And Excel. The dam, a fair 9f winner, is a half-sister to 9 winners including the multiple Group 1 winner Sky Lantern (1,000 Guineas, Coronation Stakes etc,), the 2-y-o Group 3 6f Round Tower Stakes winner Arctic and the Group 3 2m Queens Vase winner Shanty Star. The second dam, Shawanni (by Shareef Dancer), a useful 2-y-o 7f winner, is a half-sister to the Group 3 winners Blatant and Songlark. (Mr D Ward). *"A gorgeous looking filly, she came in late and it was a bit of a shock to her system at first. We introduced her to the string slowly and having looked small initially she's now looks much bigger. She's strong, powerful and has a lovely back-end to her. She looks like she'll be fast but we've only cantered her so far. I guess being by Sepoy she'll want fast ground, she's very light on her feet and on looks she'd be one of the nicest fillies we've got. We like Sepoy and have a couple of his two-year-olds".*

459. PLAYFUL TRICKSTER ★★★
br.f. Intikhab – Anyaas (Green Desert). February 23. Ninth foal. €14,000Y. Tattersalls Ireland September. John Long. Half-sister to the fair 2-y-o 7f winner Pearl Dealer (by Marju) and the moderate Irish 7f winner Non Tiscordadime (by Haafhd), the minor Qatar 3-y-o winner Golden Zephyr (by Tamayuz) and a minor winner in Australia by Nayef. The dam, a 1m winner at 3 yrs in the UAE, is a half-sister to one winner. The second dam, Anwaar (by Machiavellian), an Irish 2-y-o 1m winner, is a half-sister to 2 winners. (The Roaring Twenties). *"She was second on her debut at Kempton in late March. A big filly, we were pleased with her debut and she can only improve for that. I'd like to think she'll be winning her maiden shortly and we picked her up reasonably cheaply".*

460. RED SHANGHAI (IRE) ★★★
ch.f. Tamayuz – Rouge Noir (Saint Ballado). April 10. Ninth foal. €12,000Y. Tattersalls Ireland September. Michael Flynn. Half-sister to the promising 2015 6f placed 2-y-o Mutarajjil (by Acclamation) and to 5 winners including the useful 2-y-o listed 5f winner of 13 races here and in Scandinavia Light The Fire (by Invincible Spirit), to the useful 2-y-o 7f winner and listed-placed Cadley Road (by Elusive City), the fair 2-y-o 7f winner Joohaina (by New Approach) and the Italian winner of 7 races from 2 to 4 yrs Crazy Duck (by Kheleyf). The dam, a minor winner at 3 yrs in the USA, is a half-sister to 6 winners in Japan. The second dam, Ardana (by Danehill), won the Group 3 Premio Bagutta and is a half-sister to 5 winners. (Manor House Racing Club). *"A small, angular, narrow 2-y-o, she's racy and she'll be racing in April. A genuine, game little filly, she's bred to be a 2-y-o and she looks like one that'll run a lot, She's light-framed, so touch wood there's a chance she'll stay injury free and I think she'll run plenty of times and win a couple".*

461. SHADOW WING (IRE) ★★★
ch.f. Sakhee's Secret – Go Maggie Go (Kheleyf). March 12. Second foal. €31,000Y. Tattersalls Ireland September. Salcey Forest. Half-sister to the Italian 2-y-o listed 5f winner Terre Brune (by Dutch Art). The dam, a modest triple 5f winner, is a half-sister to 8 winners. The second dam, Born To Glamour (by Ajdal), a winner over 6f in Ireland at 2 yrs, is a half-sister to 9 winners including the French listed winner North Haneena. (Mr J Dance). *"I was a bit dubious about her early doors but she doesn't half give it some effort. She's a bit long in the back and has a huge head, so she's not the prettiest but to be fair to her she has a go. She'll win, I don't expect her to be a Fillies' Mile prospect but I'd be surprised if she didn't win a race or two as the season developed. Five furlongs will be fine for her and I'm pleasantly surprised with her progress".*

462. SIDEWINDER ★★
b.c. Majestic Missile – Ron's Secret (Efisio). April 23. Thirteenth foal. €34,000Y. Tattersalls Ireland September. Sackville/Donald. Brother to the quite useful 2015 2-y-o 6f winner Market Choice and half-brother to 6 winners including the Group 3 Grand Prix de Vichy winner Agent Secret (by Pyrus), the French middle-distance and hurdles winner Imperial Secret (by Imperial Ballet) and the French middle-distance winner Acteur Secret (by Captain Rio). The dam, a fair 1m and 9f winner of 3 races, is a half-sister to 6 winners. The second dam, Primrose Bank (by Charlottown), a 3-y-o winner, is a half-sister to 6 winners. (The Sidewinder Partnership). *"He's the kind of animal that should go on any ground from five to seven furlongs and give his local owners a lot of fun around Chester. He looks genuine, tough and honest, he's reasonably light-framed and quite tall. I think he'd the kind of horse we might have here for a few years and just enjoy running him locally".*

463. STAR OF RORY (IRE) ★★★★
b.c. Born To Sea – Dame Alicia (Sadler's Wells). February 25. Eighth foal. 80,000Y. Tattersalls October Book 1. Sackville/Donald. Half-brother to 5 winners including the quite useful 8.5f winner Principle Equation (by Oasis Dream), the fair 2-y-o 6f winner Flip Flop (by Footstepsinthesand) and the fair Irish 12f winner Lady Alicia (by Hawk Wing). The dam won over 9f and is a half-sister to the Irish Group 2 1m and US Grade 2 9f winner Century City and the US stakes winner Hidden Cat. The second dam, Alywow (by Alysheba), a champion filly in Canada, won the Grade 3 8.5f Nijana Stakes, was second in two US Grade 1 events and is a half-sister to 6 winners. (Mr D R Passant & Hefin Williams). *"The most expensive yearling I bought last year. He's on the back burner a bit, cantering daily but not being pushed. I would expect him to want further than five or six furlongs so there's no point in getting him ready early on. He'll probably be out in June and it would be lovely to think he'll make a decent 3-y-o as well".*

464. WAKENED (IRE) ★★
b.f. Rip Van Winkle – Goldamour (Fasliyev). February 25. Second foal. €58,000Y. Goffs Orby. Sackville/Donald. Half-sister to the fair 2015 3-y-o 6f winner Big Amigo (by Bahamian Bounty). The dam, placed at 3 yrs in France, is a half-sister to 3 minor winners. The second dam, Glamadour (by Sanglamore), a winner over 11.5f in France, is a half-sister to 11 winners including the outstanding multiple Group 1 winner Goldikova and the Group 1 Prix Vermeille winner Galikova. (L Rutherford & M Wilmshurst). *"We bought her on the strength of the dam's 3-y-o Big Amigo who we have here. He works like a Group horse but actually is only rated 75. This filly is very sweet but we haven't done much with her because she's not an early type".*

465. UNNAMED ★★★★
ch.c. Bahamian Bounty – Aliante (Sir Percy). February 5. First foal. £70,000Y. Doncaster Premier. Sackville/Donald. The dam, a modest 12f winner, is a half-sister to 7 winners including the South African Group 3 winner Kingston Mines. The second dam, Alexandrine (by Nashwan), a fair 10f to 13f winner of 4 races, is a half-sister to the Nassau Stakes and Sun Chariot Stakes winner Last Second (dam of the French 2,000 Guineas winner Aussie Rules), the Doncaster Cup winner Alleluia (dam of the Prix Royal-Oak winner Allegretto) and the dams of the Group 1 winners Alborada, Albanova, Yesterday and Quarter Moon. (Manor House Stables). *"A nice colt bought at*

Doncaster, I like the sire and this is a gorgeous specimen, really pleasing to look at and very confident in his own ability. He really fancies himself, he's always posing, has only worked once so far but we like the look of him".

466. UNNAMED ★★★
ch.c. Showcasing – Douro (Manduro). February 4. First foal. 32,000Y. Tattersalls October Book 2. Sackville/Donald. The dam is an unraced half-sister to 2 minor winners. The second dam, Tamso (by Seeking The Gold), is an unraced half-sister to 4 stakes winners including the French 1,000 Guineas winner Matiara. (Manor House Stables). *"He's had a setback but he's fine now and will be out later in the summer. A typical 2-y-o sprinter, he's strong, not over-big and very bullish"*.

467. UNNAMED ★★★
b.c. Exceed And Excel – Glory Power (Medicean). March 5. First foal. €100,000Y. Arqana Deauville August. Sackville Donald. The dam, a listed-placed winner of 3 races in France at 3 and 4 yrs, is a half-sister to 2 winners. The second dam, Sandbox (by Grand Lodge), a listed-placed winner in France, is a half-sister to 6 winners including the Group 3 Prix de Psyche winner Serisia. *"He looks like a proper 2-y-o and I'd like to think he could be one for something like the July Stakes later on. He won't be ready for Ascot and we're just nursing him a little bit. He's very stocky but not as strong as he looks. When he comes good he should be worth looking out for"*.

468. UNNAMED ★★★
b.c. Sepoy – Max One Two Three (Princely Heir). March 4. Third foal. The dam, a 2-y-o listed 6f Rockingham Stakes winner, is a sister to one winner and a half-sister to another. The second dam, Dakota Sioux (by College Chapel), a fairly useful 7f and 1m winner of 8 races from 3 to 5 yrs, is a half-sister to 5 winners including a listed winner in Italy and Hong Kong. (Laurence Bellman & Chasemore Farm). *"The dam was my first ever black type winner and unfortunately she died and there's nothing left of the family but this colt. He's enormous, so although we got him going we're giving him a bit of a break now. He'll come good and he'll be a nice horse for later in the season"*.

469. UNNAMED ★★★
b.c. Excelebration – Nigh (Galileo). January 9. First foal. €100,000Y. Arqana Deauville August. Sackville/Donald. The dam is an unraced half-sister to 4 winners including the Group 1 Golden Jubilee Stakes and Group 1 Nunthorpe Stakes winner Kingsgate Native. The second dam, Native Force (by Indian Ridge), a quite useful 1m winner, is a half-sister to 2 winners. (Trowbridge, O'Halloran, Lowe, Jones). *"He's a particularly lovely individual. Tall, rangy, good-bodied and with plenty of size about him. Plain bay in colour with no white at all on him, I loved him at the sales. We don't know if the sire is going to be a success or not yet, but as an individual I really like this colt. Not an early type, but hopefully he'll be a fast colt for the second half of the season"*.

470. UNNAMED ★★★
b.c. Dream Ahead – Valandraud (College Chapel). May 7. Half-brother to the quite useful 2-y-o 5f and subsequent Hong Kong listed-placed winner Final Answer (by Kyllachy), to the fair 5f winner of 5 races Electric Qatar, the fair 2-y-o 5f winner Polar Vortex (both by Pastoral Pursuits) and the minor winner of 8 races in Italy from 2 to 5 yrs Rio Ther (by Bertolini). The dam is an unraced half-sister to 3 winners. The second dam, Guana Bay (by Cadeaux Genereux), is an unraced sister to one winner and a half-sister to 5 winners including the Group 2 winners Prince Sabo and Millyant. (Chasemore Farm & Owen Promotions). *"I remember doing your 2-y-o's book a few years ago and I gave you Electric Qatar as the best one, but as it turned out although he had plenty of ability he had no guts. This is a half-brother to that horse. He's a bit long and unfurnished, he's a May foal and we're going slowly with him. He should be fast on pedigree but he won't be early, so we'll just have to see how it goes"*.

ANN DUFFIELD

471. BAJAN SPICE ★★★
b.f. Pastoral Pursuits – Centenerola (Century City). March 25. Third foal. £35,000Y. Doncaster Premier. Ann Duffield. Sister to the fair 5f (at 2 yrs) and 6f winner of 3 races Scentpastparadise. The dam, a fair 7f winner, is a half-sister to 4 winners including the Canadian Grade 2 and Group 3 Nell Gwyn

Stakes winner Barefoot Lady. The second dam, Lady Angharad (by Tenby), a winner of 5 races from 6f to 10f including the 2-y-o listed Woodcote Stakes, is a half-sister to 5 minor winners here and in Italy. (David Barker). *"A big, backward filly, we think she's got ability and she has a great big stride on her. She's growing so we're not doing much with her yet, but we really like her. She's bigger and classier than her full sister Scentpastparadise who we also trained".*

472. BENIDICTION (IRE) ★★★
ch.f. Zebedee – Elizabelle (Westerner). April 19. Third foal. €36,000Y. Tattersalls Ireland September. Salcey Forest Stud. Sister to the fairly useful 2-y-o 6f, 7f and 1m winner Power Play and half-sister to the quite useful 2015 2-y-o 6f and 9f winner Southdown Lad (by Lilbourne Lad). The dam, a modest 7f placed 2-y-o, is a half-sister to 2 winners including the smart 2-y-o Group 2 7f Vintage Stakes winner Orizaba. The second dam, Jus'chillin' (by Efisio), was placed twice over 6f at 2 yrs and is a half-sister to 11 winners including Bay Empress (Group 3 Brownstown Stakes). (Mr J Dance). *"A tough, game filly, she's not very big and she'll be starting her career in April. It's a good 2-y-o pedigree".*

473. CALAMERO ★★
b.f. Camacho – Hel's Angel (Pyrus). February 26. Second foal. 7,000Y. Doncaster November. Not sold. Half-sister to the modest 2015 2-y-o 10f winner Heaven Scent (by Phoenix Reach). The dam, a fair 1m and 12f winner of 5 races, is a half-sister to 3 winners. The second dam, Any Dream (by Shernazar), an Irish 4-y-o 1m 5f winner, is a half-sister to the Group 3 7f Concorde Stakes winner Tarry Flynn. (Mrs Helen Baines). *"We had the mare Hel's Angel who won five races for us and her first foal won last year. This is a very tall, backward filly that won't be seen until late summer onwards".*

474. DAVINCI DAWN ★★★
b.f. Poet's Voice – Bonnie Brae (Mujahid). February 20. First foal. £92,000Y. Doncaster Premier. Ann Duffield. The dam, a useful 6f and 7f winner of 5 races, is a half-sister to 4 winners. The second dam, Skara Brae (by Inchinor), is an unraced half-sister to 5 minor winners. (David Barker, Ian & Nancy Farrington). *"The first foal of a Bunbury Cup winner, she was an early foal but she's a little bit behind where I thought she'd be. She could probably run towards the end of May though and she could be an exciting prospect".*

475. DUBAI KNIGHTS (IRE) ★★
b.c. Sir Prancealot – Dubai Princess (Dubai Destination). April 1. Fifth foal. £22,000Y. Doncaster Premier. Ann Duffield. Half-brother to the quite useful 5f and 6f winner Taquka (by Kodiac), to the modest 5f winner of 10 races Windforpower (by Red Clubs) and the modest dual 5f winner Zebs Lad (by Zebedee). The dam, a fairly useful listed-placed 5f and 6f winner at 2 and 3 yrs, is a half-sister to 3 winners including the dual listed 5f winner and good broodmare Swiss Lake. The second dam, Blue Iris (by Petong), a winner of 5 races over 5f and 6f including the Weatherbys Super Sprint and the Redcar Two-Year-Old Trophy, is a half-sister to 10 winners. *"He's not far off starting his career, but I'd expect him to get seven furlongs later on".*

476. HOT NATURED (IRE) ★★★★
b.f. Canford Cliffs – Teddy Bears Picnic (Oasis Dream). April 29. Fifth foal. £65,000Y. Doncaster Premier. Salcey Forest Stud & John Dance. Half-sister to the fairly useful 2-y-o 6f and 7f winner and Group 3 Somerville Tattersall Stakes third Nezar (by Mastercraftsman) and to a minor winner abroad by Hurricane Run. The dam is an unraced half-sister to 3 winners. The second dam, Jackie's Opera (by Indian Ridge), is an unraced half-sister to 5 winners including the dual French listed winner Arabian King. (Mr J Dance). *"A nice, well-bred filly, she wants a bit of time but she's a lovely, scopey filly. I like her – she's classy".*

477. INDIGO BEAT ★★★
b.f. Tamayuz – Silver Kestrel (Silver Hawk). March 27. Seventh foal. £27,000Y. Doncaster Premier. Ann Duffield. Half-sister to the 2-y-o Group 3 6f Albany Stakes winner and Group 2 Cherry Hinton Stakes second Habaayib and to the fair dual 5f winner (including at 2 yrs) Golden Flower (both by Royal Applause). The dam, a minor winner of 2 races at 3 and 4 yrs in the USA, is a half-sister to 5 winners. The

second dam, Salty Perfume (by Salt Lake), won the Grade 2 Adirondack Stakes in the USA and is a half-sister to 6 winners including the German Group 2 winner Green Perfume. (Mr J Dance). *"A nicely-bred filly, she won't be as good as her half-sister Habaayib but she looks capable and we like her. One to start in May over five/six furlongs I should think".*

478. LADOFASH ★★★
b.c. Canford Cliffs – Curras Spirit (Invincible Spirit). February 5. Second foal. £36,000Y. Doncaster Premier. Ann Duffield. The dam is an unraced half-sister to 3 winners including the Group 3 2m Sagaro Stakes winner Shipmaster. The second dam, Cover Look (by Fort Wood), won two Group 2 events and was Group 1 placed in South Africa and is a half-sister to 7 winners. (Mr J Dance). *"A classy, lovely-looking horse and a good mover. I could see him being out in May and I like him".*

479. LAST PARADISE ★★★
b.f. Caradak – Exotic Beauty (Barathea). April 20. €16,000Y. Osarus September. Salcey Forest Stud. The dam, a quite useful 2-y-o 5f and 6f winner, is a half-sister to 2 winners including the 2-y-o listed 5f winner Janina. The second dam, Lady Dominatrix (by Danehill Dancer), won 4 races including a Group 3 5f event, was second in the Group 2 Flying Five and is a half-sister to 3 winners. (Mr J Dance). *"She came from France and was the last one to be broken in. She was very small but she's really grown and we like her, she's tough and the dam won the Ripon Hornblower".*

480. MIMIC'S MEMORY ★★
b.f. Sayif – Blue Crest (Verglas). February 3. Second foal. £8,000Y. Doncaster Silver. C & D Bloodstock. Half-sister to the fair 2015 2-y-o 6f winner My Amigo (by Stimulation). The dam, a minor dual winner at 3 yrs in France, is a half-sister to 4 winners. The second dam, Ideale Dancing (by Shining Steel), a minor winner at 2 and 3 yrs in France, is a half-sister to 3 winners. (ICM Racing). *"My Amigo's half-sister by a new stallion, Sayif, she's a big, backward filly that definitely needs time. She'll be ready in mid-to-late summer, she's a good mover and a horse with the potential to go beyond her 2-y-o career".*

481. MISS BATES ★★★
b.f. Holy Roman Emperor – Jane Austen (Galileo). April 19. Fifth foal. 28,000Y. Tattersalls October Book 2. Not sold. Half-sister to the quite useful 2015 2-y-o 7f winner Mansfield (by Exceed And Excel) and to the 4-y-o 11f debut winner Queen's Novel (by King's Best). The dam, a useful Irish listed 12f winner, is a sister to the listed-placed winner Acapulco and a half-sister to 3 winners. The second dam, Harasava (by Darshaan), is an unraced half-sister to 5 winners. (The Duchess of Sutherland). *"She's been working better than she's entitled to, given that she wasn't an early foal and she's out of a Galileo mare. So we're pleased with her and I can see us her starting off in May over six furlongs".*

482. PANTHER IN PINK (IRE) ★★★
gr.f. Zebedee – Annus Iucundus (Desert King). April 21. Eighth foal. £30,000Y. Doncaster Premier. Ann Duffield. Half-sister to the quite useful 2015 2-y-o 5f winner King's Mimic, to the modest 6f and 7f winner Lady Ranger (both by Bushranger), the quite useful 2-y-o dual 5f winner and listed placed Jack Who's He (by Red Clubs) and a minor winner at 4 yrs in the USA by Verglas. The dam, a modest 13f and 17f winner, is a half-sister to 4 winners including the Group 2 Duke Of York Stakes winner The Kiddykid. The second dam, Mezzanine (by Sadler's Wells), is an unraced half-sister to 3 minor winners. (Mr P Bamford, Ms Jenny Bianco, Brian & Malcolm Plows). *"Her half-brother Kings Mimic won over five furlongs for us last year and we thought he was exceptionally good but sadly he broke a leg. It's a family very capable of getting winners, this filly is going really well, I'm very pleased with her and five furlongs will be her trip".*

483. PEACH PAVLOVA (IRE) ★★
b.f. Elzaam – Zvezda (Nureyev). April 6. £9,000Y. Doncaster Premier. Not sold. Half-sister to the fairly useful 2-y-o Group 3 7f C L Weld Park Stakes placed maiden Silk Dress and to a hurdles winner by Arafaa. The dam is an unplaced full or half-sister to 5 winners including Zentsov Street, a 7f (at 2 yrs) and subsequent US stakes winner and third in the Group 1 Dewhurst Stakes and the Grade 1 Hollywood Derby. The second dam, Storm

Fear (by Coastal), is a maiden half-sister to the dam of Bakharoff and Emperor Jones. (E & R Stott). *"A little bit backward at the minute so she'll want time, but she's a lovely mover, well-balanced and genuine. A nice filly that likes her work, we like her".*

484. RAINBOW MIST (IRE) ★★★★
b.c. Lilbourne Lad – Misty Night (Galileo). April 9. Second foal. £12,000Y. Doncaster Premier. C Buckingham. Brother to the 2016 3-y-o 7f debut winner Misty Lord. The dam is an unraced half-sister to 3 winners including the useful 7f and 1m winner and listed-placed Greyfriarschorista. The second dam, Misty Heights (by Fasliyev), an Irish listed 9f winner, was Group 3 placed twice and is a half-sister to 10 winners including the Group 3 winner Madeira Mist, herself the dam of Joshua Tree (winner of the Grade 1 Canadian International three times). (Craig Buckingham). *"He goes very well and is one to watch out for. Not far off a run, he's got the pace to win over five or six furlongs but he'll probably get seven later on. He's very nice and we like him".*
TRAINERS' BARGAIN BUY

485. ROYAL BLUE CARAVEL (IRE) ★★★
b.f. Henrythenavigator – Holly Blue (Bluebird). January 16. Eleventh foal. €68,000Y. Goffs Orby. Not sold. Half-sister to 6 winners including the Irish 2-y-o and subsequent South African triple Group 2 winner Gibraltar Blue, to the quite useful 10f and 11f winner Pilgrims Rest (both by Rock Of Gibraltar), the Irish 5f (at 2 yrs) and listed 6f winner Scream Blue Murder (by Oratorio). The dam, a useful listed 1m winner, is a half-sister to 6 minor winners. The second dam, Nettle (by Kris), a useful listed 7f winner, is a half-sister to 5 winners. (ICM Racing). *"She had an injury which has set her back a bit, but she's very nice and we'll try and win a maiden with her. Then if she's good enough we'll try and get her some black-type to strengthen her pedigree even further".*

486. SUGAR BEACH ★★★★
b.f. Canford Cliffs – Aktia (Danehill Dancer). February 10. 50,000Y. Arqana Deauville August. Horse France. The dam, a quite useful 9f to 12f winner of 3 races, is a half-sister to numerous winners including the useful 2-y-o 6f listed winner Fashion Rocks. The second dam, La Gandilie (by Highest Honor), a dual 2-y-o winner in France including a listed event, was third in the Group 3 Prix Chloe and is a half-sister to 4 winners including the Italian listed winner Totostar and also to the placed dams of the French Group 3 winners Linda Regina and Star Of Akkar. (Mrs Sue Bianco & Ms Jenny Bianco). *"A very nice filly, she's classy and has a lovely temperament. She's growing, doing very well and we like her very much. One for the second half of the season, I think she's got the pace for six furlongs but she'll get seven".*

487. TWIZZEL ★★★★
b.f. Equiano – Greensand (Green Desert). March 10. Tenth living foal. €50,000Y. Tattersalls Ireland September. Salcey Forest Stud. Half-sister to the fair 9f to 11f winner Fongs Gazelle (by Dr Fong) and to the modest 7f (at 2 yrs) and dual 6f winner Song Of Praise (by Compton Place). The dam, a fairly useful 2-y-o 6f winner, is a half-sister to 5 winners including the US Grade 2 9f Honeymoon Handicap winner and Grade 1 placed Country Garden. The second dam, Totham (by Shernazar), a quite useful 12f winner, is a half-sister to 6 winners. (Mr J Dance). *"She's ready to run any time because she's done all the prep work and is a capable filly for five and six furlongs".*

488. UNCLE CHARLIE ★★★
b.c. Vale Of York – Velvet Kiss (Danehill Dancer). April 8. Third foal. £8,000Y. Doncaster Silver. Ann Duffield. Half-brother to the quite useful 2015 2-y-o 7f winner Zealous (by Intense Focus) and to the fair Irish dual 10.5f winner Witty Repartee (by Iffraaj). The dam, a minor winner at 3 yrs in Italy, is a half-sister to 4 winners. The second dam Chiara Gioffry (by Great Commotion), won 6 minor races at 2 to 5 yrs in Italy is a half-sister to 10 winners. (Mrs A McCubbin). *"He's a lovely colt with the pace to win over six furlongs although he'll get seven later on. He's still growing and I really like him".*

489. UNNAMED ★★★
b.c. Intense Focus – Breedj (Acclamation). March 15. Second foal. €20,000Y. Tattersalls Ireland September. Ann Duffield. The dam,

a listed 5f placed 2-y-o, is a half-sister to 3 minor winners. The second dam, Kildare Lady (by Indian Ridge), is an unraced half-sister to 7 winners including the very useful 2-y-o listed 6f winner and Group 3 7f Lanson Champagne Vintage Stakes third Shaard. (Mrs Ann Starkie). *"A very nice, genuine and tough colt. He goes well, he'll be a five/six furlong type but he may get further later on".*

490. UNNAMED ★★★★
b.f. Equiano – Quixada (Konigstiger). March 25. Third foal. The dam, a minor winner at 3 yrs in Germany is a half-sister to 3 winners including the Group 1 Premio Presidente Della Repubblica winner Querari and the German Group 3 winner Quasillo. The second dam, Quetana (by Acatenango), a German listed-placed winner of 3 races at 3 and 4 yrs, is a half-sister to 7 winners including Quilanga (Group 3 Prix de Psyche). *"A very classy filly and she'll be racing from mid-summer onwards. A lovely-moving, beautifully-balanced filly, we haven't worked her yet but we really like what we see so far".*

ED DUNLOP

491. AL EMARATALYOUM (IRE) ★★★
ch.c. Lope De Vega – Heart Of Ice (Montjeu). April 30. Fourth foal. 85,000Y. Tattersalls October Book 1. Charlie Gordon-Watson. The dam, a minor French 2-y-o 9f winner, is a half-sister to 9 winners including the French listed winner and subsequent Grade 1 Hollywood Derby second Fast And Furious and the US Grade 2 12f winner Herboriste. The second dam, Helvellyn (by Gone West), a quite useful 8.3f winner, is a half-sister to 6 winners. (M Alharbi). *"A neat, attractive colt, I would think being by Lope De Vega he'll be a seven furlong 2-y-o and he goes OK".*

492. ALLIGATOR ★★★
ch.c. Sepoy – See You Later (Emarati). February 24. Tenth living foal. 31,000Y. Tattersalls October Book 2. Stroud/Coleman & Ed Dunlop. Half-brother to 6 winners including the very useful 5f and listed 6f Cammidge Trophy winner of 6 races from 2 to 4 yrs Aahayson (by Noverre), the useful 5f and 6f winner of 6 races (including a UAE Group 3) Take Ten (by Bahamian Bounty), the fairly 2-y-o 5f winner and listed-placed Betimes (by New Approach) and the fairly useful 6f and 7f winner of 8 races Thebes (by Cadeaux Genereux). The dam, a dual 5f winner and listed-placed 3 times, is a half-sister to the 2-y-o Group 3 Horris Hill Stakes winner Peak To Creek and the dual listed winner Ripples Maid. The second dam, Rivers Rhapsody (by Dominion), a listed 5f winner, is a half-sister to the Group 3 5f winner Regal Scintilla. (Ciao For Now Syndicate). *"A strong, powerful, six furlong horse, he's a bit lazy but he goes OK. One for June/July time".*

493. AL NAFOORAH ★★★
b.f. Bated Breath – Cat O' Nine Tails (Motivator). January 17. First foal. €90,000Y. Arqana Deauville August. Charlie Gordon-Watson. The dam, a fair 12f and 14f winner of 4 races, is a half-sister to 5 winners including the dual Group 3 winner Purr Along. The second dam, Purring (by Mountain Cat), a quite useful 7f winner, is a half-sister to the Group 2 1m Falmouth Stakes and Group 3 1m Prix de Sandringham winner Ronda (herself dam of a US dual Group 3 winner) and to the smart 1m (at 2 yrs) and listed 2m winner Silver Gilt. (M Alharbi). *"A nice, scopey filly that shows some speed, but she's got stamina on the dam's side. She goes nicely and we like her, probably the type to make a 2-y-o from mid-season onwards".*

494. BINT BATAL ★★★
b.f. Frankel – Platonic (Zafonic). February 15. Eighth living foal. €1,150,000Y. Arqana Deauville August. Charlie Gordon-Watson. Half-sister to 4 winners including the Group 3 Prix du Lutece winner (Pacifique (by Montjeu) and the French listed 11f winner Prudenzia (by Dansili and herself dam of the Irish Oaks winner Chicquita). The dam, a minor winner at 4 yrs in France, is a half-sister to 5 winners including the Group 2 12f Lancashire Oaks winner Pongee. The second dam, Puce (by Darshaan), a listed 12f winner, was Group 3 placed and is a half-sister to 10 winners including the dam of the Group 1 winners Alexandrova and Magical Romance. (Mr A S Al Naboodah). *"Bred to be a better 3-y-o with her pedigree but she's a beautiful-moving filly. She's doing well, but very much one for later on over seven furlongs and a mile".*

495. BOOSHBASH (IRE) ★★★
gr.f. Dark Angel – Surrey Storm (Montjeu).
March 15. First foal. 43,000Y. Tattersalls
October Book 2. Charlie Gordon-Watson.
The dam, a minor French 3-y-o winner, is a
half-sister to 2 winners including the French
listed winner Andry Brusselles. The second
dam, Dont Dili Dali (by Dansili), a very useful
7f (at 2 yrs) and listed 1m Masaka Stakes
winner, was third in the Group 3 Dahlia Stakes
and is a half-sister to 5 winners. (M Alharbi).
*"She moves nicely and we're happy with her
so far, but there is stamina in the pedigree and
she's more of a seven furlong 2-y-o from late
summer onwards. Goes well".*

496. CONDENSED ★★★
b.f. Dansili – Cut Short (Diesis). January 19.
Seventh foal. Half-sister to the useful 2-y-o
listed 6f winner Brevity (by Street Cry), to
the 2-y-o 1m winner and US Grade 1 third
Concise (by Lemon Drop Kid), the fairly useful
Irish 10.5f and 12.5f winner Fog Of War (by
Azamour), the quite useful 9f winner Fluctuate
(by Exchange Rate) and the fair 5f winner
Special Quality (by Elusive Quality). The dam,
a quite useful 1m (here) and US winner, is
a sister to the dual Group 2 2-y-o winner
Daggers Drawn. The second dam, Sun And
Shade (by Ajdal), a useful 2-y-o 6f winner
here and a stakes-placed winner in the USA,
is a half-sister to the dual Group 2 winner
Madame Dubois (dam of the Group 1 winners
Indian Haven and Count Dubois). (Cliveden
Stud). *"A strong, neat, powerful filly, she hasn't
been with me very long but the mother was
decent and fast. She looks one for mid-season
and goes well up Warren Hill".*

497. FAIR HEAD (IRE) ★★★★
b.f. Iffraaj – Dawaama (Dansili). February 17.
Second foal. £32,000Y. Doncaster Premier.
Stroud/Coleman. Ed Dunlop. The dam is an
unraced half-sister to 5 winners including
the Group 2 1m Prix de Sandringham winner
Baqah. The second dam, Filfilah (by Cadeaux
Genereux), a useful 6f and 7f winner, is a
full or half-sister to 6 winners including the
Canadian Grade 2 winner Muntej. (J L Stitt, J
G Stitt & Sir A Page-Wood). *"A fast filly, she's
strong and very powerful. Probably a 2-y-o for
May or June, she goes well and we're happy
with her so far".*

498. GLOBAL APPLAUSE ★★★★★ ♠
b.c. Mayson – Crown (Royal Applause).
February 11. Third foal. 78,000Y. Tattersalls
October Book 1. Charlie Gordon-Watson.
Half-brother to High Ranking (by Paco Boy),
unplaced in two starts at 2 yrs in 2015. The
dam, a quite useful dual 5f (at 2 yrs) and 6f
winner, is a half-sister to the 2-y-o winner and
Group 2 Rockfel Stakes second Cochabamba.
The second dam, Bolivia (by Distant View), is
an unraced half-sister to 11 winners including
the listed winners Bequeath, Bal Harbour and
Binary. (Dr J Hon). *"He's a fast, five furlong colt
and should be racing in April. Tall, scopey and
goes nicely. My five-star pick for this year".*

499. INSTIGATION ★★★
b.f. Bated Breath – Rainbow's Edge (Rainbow
Quest). April 25. 38,000foal. Tattersalls
December. Charlie Gordon-Watson. Closely
related to the fair 12f, 2m and hurdles winner
Discovery Bay (by Dansili) and half-sister to
the very useful 2-y-o 6f (at 2 yrs) and listed
10f winner Peacock (by Paco Boy) and the
quite useful 10f to 2m winner of 4 races Purple
Spectrum (by Verglas). The dam, a fair 12f
winner, is a half-sister to 3 winners including
the 2-y-o listed 7f winner Free Agent. The
second dam, Film Script (by Unfuwain), was
a useful 10f and 12f listed winner. (Mr W P
Wyatt). *"I have three by Bated Breath and I
think they're all mid-season types. She's fast-
looking, still a little bit backward in her coat
and hasn't done any fast work yet".*

500. KHITAAMY (IRE) ★★★
b.c. Approve – Halliwell House (Selkirk).
April 25. 50,000Y. Tattersalls October Book
2. Shadwell Estate Co. Half-brother to the
quite useful triple 6f winner Inciting Incident
(by Camacho) and to the fair dual 5f winner
(including at 2 yrs) Dusty Storm (by Kyllachy).
The dam ran once unplaced and is a half-sister
to 6 winners including the Group 2 Italian
Oaks second Counterclaim. The second dam,
Dusty Answer (by Zafonic), a quite useful
2-y-o 7f winner, was listed placed over 1m
and is a half-sister to 5 winners including the
listed 1m and subsequent US Grade 2 winner
Spotlight and the dam of the Group 1 Phoenix
Stakes winner and sire Zoffany. (Hamdan Al
Maktoum). *"A strong, powerful looking colt
and a six furlong 2-y-o for mid to late May".*

501. KOHINOOR DIAMOND ★★
b.f. Excelebration – Gems Of Araby (Zafonic). May 12. Fifth foal. €35,000Y. Goffs Orby. Stroud/Coleman/Dunlop. Half-sister to the fairly useful 2-y-o 1m winner Il Boro (by Oratorio). The dam, a fair 10f placed maiden, is a half-sister to 7 winners including the Group 1 Falmouth Stakes winner Timepiece, the Group 1 10f Criterium de Saint-Cloud winner Passage Of Time and the Group 2 King Edward VII Stakes winner Father Time. The second dam, Clepsydra (by Sadler's Wells), a quite useful 12f winner, is a half-sister to 6 winners including the useful listed 10.5f winner Double Crossed (herself dam of the multiple Group 1 winner Twice Over). (Bluehills Racing Ltd). *"A big, tall, immature filly, she won't see the racecourse until later in the season".*

502. MAGDALENE FOX ★★★★
ch.c. Foxwedge – Malelane (Prince Sabo). April 24. Fifth living foal. 27,000Y. Tattersalls October Book 2. McKeever Bloodstock. Half-brother to the fair 2015 2-y-o 7f winner Novinophobia (by Showcasing), to the quite useful 5f and 6f winner of 6 races from 2 to 5 yrs Secret Missile (by Sakhee's Secret), the modest 5f and 6f winner of 4 races Compton Prince (by Compton Place) and the moderate 5f to 7f winner of 7 races Novalist (by Avonbridge). The dam, a poor 5f placed maiden, is a half-sister to 6 winners including the Group 3 Prix du Petit Couvert winner Bishops Court and the listed winning sprinter Astonished. The second dam, Indigo (by Primo Dominie), a quite useful 2-y-o 5f winner, is a half-sister to 5 winners. *"I like him, he's a nice colt and is still a little bit 'up behind' so he'll grow. He shows some speed and looks like a six furlong horse for mid-season".* **TRAINERS' BARGAIN BUY**

503. MAKMAN (IRE) ★★★
b.c. Kodiac – Sheila Blige (Zamindar). March 24. Ninth foal. 130,000Y. Tattersalls October Book 2. Shadwell Estate Co. Brother to Kodachrome, placed fourth once over 6f at 2 yrs in 2015 and half-brother to Lady Lily (by Desert Sun), a quite useful 2-y-o 5f and 6f winner of 4 races here and a listed-placed winner of 6 races in Scandinavia, to the Italian 2-y-o winner World All Fruit (by Refuse To Bend) and the fair Irish 9f winner Apt (by Danetime). The dam, a quite useful 2-y-o 5f winner, is a half-sister to 6 winners including the very useful 1m (at 2 yrs) to 12f winner and Group 3 third Naked Welcome. The second dam, Stripanoora (by Ahonoora), was placed once at 3 yrs and stayed 1m and is a full or half-sister to 5 minor winners. (Hamdan Al Maktoum). *"He's an attractive, scopey horse, goes OK and he's already had a run at Kempton where he finished third".*

504. MOAMAR ★★★
ch.c. Sepoy – Palitana (Giant's Causeway). February 25. First foal. 300,000Y. Tattersalls October Book 1. John & Jake Warren. The dam, placed once over 1m at 2 yrs from two starts, is a sister to the 2,000 Guineas winner Footstepsinthesand and a half-sister to 4 winners including the Group 1 Phoenix Stakes winner Pedro The Great and the dam of the Group 1 National Stakes winner Power. The second dam, Glatisant (by Rainbow Quest), winner of the Group 3 7f Prestige Stakes, is a half-sister to 8 winners. (Mr A S Al Naboodah). *"A good-looking colt, he's just about to do some fast work and he'll be out in mid-season over six furlongs. I think he was the most expensive yearling by Sepoy".*

505. MUDALLEL (IRE) ★★★★
b.c. Invincible Spirit – Lixirova (Sickly). March 23. Second foal. 380,000Y. Tattersalls October Book 1. Blandford Bloodstock. The dam won 3 races in France at 2 yrs including the Group 3 7f Prix Miesque and is a half-sister to 2 winners. The second dam, Linorova (by Trempolino), is an unraced half-sister to 5 winners. (Mr A S Al Naboodah). *"An attractive, scopey horse, he's one for six/seven furlongs in mid-season. A good-looking colt".*

506. MULZIM ★★
b.c. Exceed And Excel – Samaah (Cape Cross). February 5. First foal. The dam is an unraced half-sister to 4 winners including the Group 1 Golden Jubilee Stakes and Group 1 Nunthorpe Stakes winner Kingsgate Native. The second dam, Native Force (by Indian Ridge), a quite useful 1m winner, is a half-sister to 2 winners. (Hamdan Al Maktoum). *"A big, backward horse, he's a nice colt and shouldn't be discounted, but he won't be seen out until later on".*

507. MUSHAREEFA (IRE) ★★
b.f. Makfi – Winesong (Giant's Causeway). February 2. Sixth foal. €90,000Y. Arqana Deauville August. Charlie Gordon-Watson. Closely related to the Group 2 Princess Of Wales's Stakes and Group 2 Jockey Club Stakes winner Universal and to the fair Irish 9f and 10.5f winner Windward Passage (both by Dubawi) and half-sister to the fair Irish 12f winner Madam Mo (by Motivator). The dam, placed third over 10f, is a half-sister to 6 winners including the 2-y-o Group 1 6f Cheveley Park Stakes winner Seazun. The second dam, Sunset Café (by Red Sunset), a minor Irish 12f winner, is a sister to the Group 3 Prix Foy winner Beeshi and a half-sister to 8 winners. (M Alharbi). *"A big, scopey filly that goes nicely but she's probably a seven furlong type for the autumn".*

508. OCEANUS ★★★★ ♠
b.c. Born To Sea – Alkhawarah (Intidab). Second foal. £65,000Y. Doncaster Premier. Will Edmeades. The dam, a modest 7.5f placed maiden, is a half-sister to numerous winners including the smart 2-y-o Group 1 6f Middle Park Stakes winner Hayil and the US Grade 2 second Tamhid. The second dam, Futuh (by Diesis), a fairly useful 2-y-o 6f winner, is a half-sister to 7 winners including the Canadian stakes winner Rose Park (dam of the dual US Grade 1 winner Wild Rush). (Thurloe Thoroughbreds XXXVII). *"An interesting pedigree as he's from the same family as last year's good 2-y-o Shalaa – they have the same second dam. We don't know about the sire Born To Sea yet, but this colt has done some fast work and goes OK. Probably one to start in a six furlong maiden, he's a neat, good-moving horse".*

509. RIPPER STREET (IRE) ★★★
b.c. Big Bad Bob – Caster Sugar (Cozzene). February 22. Third foal. 43,000Y. Tattersalls October Book 2. Ed Dunlop. Half-brother to the quite useful 2015 2-y-o 7f winner Barleysugar (by Kyllachy) and to the fairly useful 2-y-o 7f and 1m winner Mukhayyam (by Dark Angel). The dam, a fair 1m to 11f winner of 4 races, is a half-sister to 3 minor winners here and abroad. The second dam, Only Royale (by Caerleon), won 9 races including the Group 1 Yorkshire Oaks (twice)

and the Group 2 Jockey Club Stakes and is a half-sister to 5 winners. (The MHSL Racing Partnership). *"A six/seven furlong 2-y-o for mid-season, he's neat, attractive and goes OK".*

510. SANAM ★★★
b.c. Oasis Dream – Seta (Pivotal). April 30. Second foal. 420,000Y. Tattersalls October Book 1. Blandford Bloodstock. Brother to the quite useful 2015 2-y-o 6f winner Seastrom. The dam, a very useful triple listed winner over 7f and 1m, was third in the Group 2 May Hill Stakes and is a half-sister to 7 winners including the Group 2 Prix de Pomone winner Armure and the listed winners Gravitas, Berlin Berlin and Affirmative Action. The second dam, Bombazine (by Generous), a useful 10f winner, is a half-sister to 7 winners including the Group 1 winners Barathea and Gossamer (herself dam of the Group 1 winner Ibn Khaldun). (Mr A S Al Naboodah). *"A beautiful horse but he was quite a late foal, he's backward and needs time. One for later in the season over six/seven furlongs".*

511. SPARKLE ★★★★
b.f. Oasis Dream – Gemstone (Galileo). February 27. Second foal. 190,000Y. Tattersalls October Book 1. John & Jake Warren. Half-sister to the fair 2015 2-y-o 6.5f winner Bedrock (by Fastnet Rock). The dam, a useful 2-y-o listed 1m Silken Glider Stakes winner, was second in the Group 3 Park Express Stakes and is a half-sister to 3 minor winners. The second dam, Kincob (by Kingmambo), a modest 1m placed 3-y-o, is a half-sister to 6 winners including the Irish 2,000 Guineas winner Bachelor Duke. (Old Road Securities plc). *"One for the middle-to-end of the season although the pedigree suggests a little bit later, she's a strong, powerful filly".*

512. SUKOOT (IRE) ★★
ch.c. Sir Prancealot – Yandina (Danehill). March 26. Sixth foal. £60,000Y. Doncaster Premier. Shadwell Estate Co. Half-brother to the unplaced 2015 Irish 2-y-o Bearwood (by Canford Cliffs). The dam, a quite useful dual 7f winner, is out of the unraced Lughz (by Housebuster), herself an unraced half-sister to 5 winners including Alshakr (Group 2 Falmouth Stakes). (Hamdan Al Maktoum).

"A big, tall, good-looking horse but more of a late-season type".

513. THE LACEMAKER ★★★
b.f. Dutch Art – Sospel (Kendor). January 27. Fourteenth foal. 90,000Y. Tattersalls October Book 1. Blandford Bloodstock. Half-sister to 10 winners including the Group 3 6f Premio Tudini winner Charming Woman (by Invincible Spirit), the Italian listed winner Men's Magazine (by Dr Devious) and the Italian listed-placed winner Vanity Woman (by Nayef). The dam, a minor German 2-y-o winner, is a half-sister to 3 other minor winners. The second dam, Scene Galante (by Sicyos), won 3 minor races at 4 yrs in France and is a half-sister to 6 winners including the German dual Group 3 winner Ladoni. (Mrs G A Rupert). *"A nice filly for seven furlongs later in the year".*

514. ZAMJAR ★★★
b.c. Exceed And Excel – Cloud's End (Dubawi). April 26. Second foal. 110,000Y. Tattersalls October Book 1. Charlie Gordon-Watson. Half-brother to the modest 2015 5f placed 2-y-o Chandresh (by Holy Roman Emperor). The dam, a quite useful 6f (at 2 yrs) and 7f winner, is a half-sister to 6 winners including the champion 2-y-o filly and Group 1 6f Cheveley Park Stakes winner Airwave (herself the dam of three stakes winners) and the Group 1 5f Nunthorpe Stakes winner Jwala. The second dam, Kangra Valley (by Indian Ridge), a moderate 2-y-o 5f winner, is a half-sister to 7 minor winners. (Mr A S Al Naboodah). *"A nice colt. He's attractive, racy, goes OK and is probably a six/seven furlong 2-y-o".*

515. UNNAMED ★★★
b.c. Holy Roman Emperor – Annalina (Cozzene). April 6. Seventh foal. 32,000Y. Tattersalls October Book 2. Ed Dunlop / Charlie Gordon-Watson. Half-brother to the fairly useful 2-y-o 6f winner Dr No (by Aussie Rules), to the quite useful 12f winners Hepworth (by Singspiel) and Sagamore (by Azamour), the quite useful 10f and 11.5f winner Portrait (by Peintre Celebre) and the Japanese winner and Group 3 placed Kyoei Basara (by Aussie Rules). The dam is an unraced half-sister to 6 winners including the US Grade 2 Long Island Handicap winner Olaya. The second dam, Solaia (by Miswaki), won the listed Cheshire Oaks and was second in the Group 3 Lancashire Oaks and is a half-sister to 3 winners. *"An attractive, scopey, seven furlong horse for later in the year".*

516. UNNAMED ★★★★
b.f. War Front – Gilt (Bernardini). April 16. Second foal. $425,000Y. Keeneland September. Blandford Bloodstock. The dam is an unplaced half-sister to 8 winners including the Grade 2 Tom Fool Handicap winner Exchange Rate and the Group 3 Rose Of Lancaster Stakes winner Sabre d'Argent. The second dam, Sterling Pound (by Seeking The Gold), won the Grade 3 Honey Bee Handicap and is a half-sister to 4 minor winners. (Mr A S Al Naboodah). *"A nice, attractive filly, she's racy and the type for six/seven furlongs in mid-season. Should be one to follow".*

517. UNNAMED ★★
b.c. The Factor – Jive Talk (Kingmambo). April 7. Eighth foal. €80,000Y. Goffs Orby. Charlie Gordon-Watson / G Bolton. Half-brother to the quite useful 7f (at 2 yrs), 1m and subsequent US stakes-placed winner Mr Irons (by Mr Greeley). The dam is an unraced half-sister to 4 winners including the US Grade 2 Buena Vista Handicap and dual Group 3 winner Dance Parade and the US Grade 3 winner Ocean Queen. The second dam, River Jig (by Irish River), a useful 2-y-o 9f winner here, later won over 12f in Italy and is a half-sister to 6 winners. (Mr G B Bolton). *"A big, backward horse that needs some time. He goes well but he's not ready yet".* The sire won over 6f at 2 yrs and was a top-class 7f performer at 3 yrs on dirt/AW, winning two Grade 1 stakes in the USA. His first crop of runners appear this year.

518. UNNAMED ★★★
ch.c. Lope De Vega – Pietra Dura (Cadeaux Genereux). March 6. Tenth foal. 160,000Y. Tattersalls October Book 1. Charlie Gordon-Watson. Half-brother to the 2015 2-y-o 7f debut winner Amanaat (by Exceed And Excel), to the quite useful 7f, 1m and subsequent US Grade 3 10f winner and Grade 1 second Turning Top (by Pivotal), to the quite useful 2-y-o 6f winner Curly Wee (by Excellent Art) and the 9f winner (on his only start) Hollander

NUNNERY STUD

MUHAARAR
Oasis Dream - Tahrir

MUKHADRAM
Shamardal - Magic Tree

NAYEF
Gulch - Height Of Fashion

Discover more about the Shadwell Stallions at www.shadwellstud.co.uk
Or call Richard Lancaster, Johnnie Peter-Hoblyn or Rachael Gowland on
+44(0)1842 755913
Email us at: nominations@shadwellstud.co.uk

SHADWELL
STANDING FOR SUCCESS

THE YEAR OF THE DRAGON

Dragon Pulse
Fee: €5,000 1st October terms

- Highest ever rated 2YO by Gr.1 sire Kyllachy whose own Champion sire Pivotal is currently responsible for Champion European 2nd Season Sire Siyouni
- Speedy juvenile, won Futurity Stakes (Gr.2), 2nd National Stakes (Gr.1)
- Out of Poetical (LR 2YO), immediate family of Shalaa (by Invincible Spirit)
- First yearlings sold for €144,000, €120,000, €110,000, €107,000, €104,000, €87,000
- First runners 2016

"Probably one of the nicest colts we have at Everleigh. We're really happy with our Dragon Pulse's and this colt has a good engine and finds everything fairly easy at the moment. We're chuffed with him. A very nice horse".

Richard Hannon on his Dragon Pulse colt ex Taalluf (bred by Mr. G. Johnston King).

IRISH NATIONAL STUD
www.irishnationalstud.ie

John Osborne, Gary Swift, Sinead Hyland or Helen Boyce
Tel: +353 (0)45 521251 Gary +353 (0)86 6031979

The SpeedForce

*Cheveley Park Stud has some **strikingly fast stallions**...*

↯ DUTCH ART
Sire of **Group 1** winning sprinters **GARSWOOD** and **SLADE POWER**.

↯ GARSWOOD
Group 1 winning sprinter by **DUTCH ART** from a speedy family.
First crop foals in 2016

↯ KYLLACHY
Sire of **Group 1** winning sprinters **TWILIGHT SON** and **SOLE POWER**.

↯ LETHAL FORCE
Champion sprinter by **DARK ANGEL** who broke the 6f course record at Newmarket.
First crop yearlings in 2016

↯ MAYSON
Group 1 July Cup winner and **INVINCIBLE SPIRIT**'s top rated sprinter.
First crop 2yos in 2016

↯ MEDICEAN
Sire of **10 individual Group 1** winners, including leading sire **DUTCH ART**.

↯ PIVOTAL
Sire of **26** individual **Group 1** winners and **125 Group/Stakes** winners to date.

Cheveley Park Stud
Duchess Drive, Newmarket, Suffolk CB8 9DD
Tel: (01638) 730316 · Fax: (01638) 730868 · enquiries@cheveleypark.co.uk · www.cheveleypark.co.uk

SMARTER.
EASIER.
FASTER.

YOUR NEW & IMPROVED MOBILE BETTING EXPERIENCE

"SLICK AND EASY"

THE SUN

EASIER NAVIGATION.
Find your race, horse and markets faster

RACING POST FORM.
Integrated within the racecard

NEW LIVE RACING FEATURE.
Live races streamed direct from the racecard

IMPROVED RESULTS SERVICE.
Fast results summary and detailed Racing Post evaluation of each race and horse

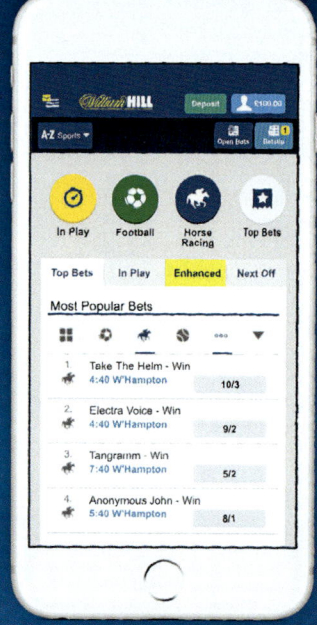

William HILL

WHEN THE FUN STOPS STOP™

gambleaware.co.uk

Image for illustration purpose only. William Hill rules apply. Over 18s only.
FOR ADVICE & INFORMATION VISIT WWW.GAMBLEAWARE.ORG.UK. NATIONAL GAMBLING HELPLINE 0808 8020 133.

(by Fasliyev). The dam, a listed-placed 2-y-o 7f winner, is a half-sister to 4 winners including the dam of the Group 1 King George VI winner Postponed. The second dam, Bianca Nera (by Salse), won the Group 1 7f Moyglare Stud Stakes and the Group 2 6f Lowther Stakes and is a half-sister to 4 winners. (Mr A S Al Naboodah). *"Backward, he needs time but he's a nice colt for seven furlongs this season. He'll probably be a ten furlong horse next year".*

519. UNNAMED ★★★★
b.br.c. Distorted Humor – Spare Change (Bernardini). January 30. First foal. $250,000Y. Keeneland September. Blandford Bloodstock. The dam, a minor winner at 2 yrs in the USA, is a half-sister to 4 winners including the dam of the US Grade 3 winner and triple Grade 1 placed Feathered. The second dam, Finder's Fee (by Storm Cat), won the Grade 1 Acorn Stakes and the Grade 1 Matron Stakes and is a half-sister to 8 winners. (Mr A S Al Naboodah). *"A strong, powerful, neat colt. Racy and tough, he'll start in a six furlong maiden and he goes OK".*

HARRY DUNLOP

520. ASSANILKA (FR) ★★★★
b.f. Diamond Green – Regal Step (Royal Applause). March 16. Fourth foal. €35,000Y. Osarus September. Stroud/Coleman. Half-sister to the French listed-placed 7.5f and 1m winner Djoko (by Air Chief Marshal). The dam, a quite useful 2-y-o 5f winner, is a half-sister to 6 winners. The second dam, Two Step (by Mujtahid), a modest 5f and 7f winner at 4 and 5 yrs, is a half-sister to 3 winners. (The Three Musketeers). *"She's going to be one for July time over six/seven furlongs, I like her and she'll be running in France for us. She's quite big and needs to mature a bit more, but she's worth looking out for".*

521. ATLANTIC BEAUTY ★★★
ch.f. Archipenko – Medaille D'Or (With Approval). February 2. Second foal. €33,000Y. Tattersalls Ireland September. Stroud/Coleman & Harry Dunlop. Half-sister to the fair 2015 7f placed 2-y-o California Lad (by Aussie Rules). The dam, a fair 9.5f and 10f winner, is a half-sister to 10 winners. The second dam, Crockadore (by Nijinsky), won 7 races in Ireland and the USA including the Grade 2 12f Orchid Handicap and the Grade 3 11f Sheepshead Bay Handicap (both on turf). She is closely related to the Group 3 Flying Five winner Flowing and a half-sister to 9 winners. (Daniel McAuliffe & Anoj Don). *"A sister to a 3-y-o we have called California Lad who we like. The sire's done very well and this filly seems to have some speed. I should think she'll be one for seven furlongs come mid-season. I'm pleased with her".*

522. COASTAL CYCLONE ★★★★
b.c. Canford Cliffs – Seasonal Cross (Cape Cross). March 12. Third foal. Half-brother to the quite useful 1m (at 2 yrs) and 8.5f winner Storm Rock (by Rock Of Gibraltar). The dam, a fair 1m winner of 4 races, is a half-sister to 5 winners including the very useful 6f to 12f winner of 4 races (including the listed Galtres Stakes) Brushing. The second dam, Seasonal Blossom (by Fairy King), is an unplaced half-sister to 7 winners including the US Grade 2 winner Wait Till Monday and the Irish Group 3 winner Token Gesture (dam of the Grade 1 winner Relaxed Gesture). (Malcolm Aldis & Susan Abbott Racing). *"I like this colt and his half-brother Storm Rock did well for us last year. I think this colt is more precocious than Storm Rock, so I hope he can give us some sport, starting off in the first half of the season, over six/seven furlongs".*

523. LIMELIGHT LADY ★★★
b.f. Sakhee's Secret – Green Room (FR). March 19. Half-sister to the quite useful 11.5f winner L'Ingenue (by New Approach) and to the modest 2m winner Duke's Den (by Duke Of Marmalade). The dam, a useful Italian listed 12f winner of 4 races, was placed in two other listed events here and is a half-sister to 4 winners. The second dam, Scarlet Plume (by Warning), won 2 races including the Group 3 1m Premio Dormello and is a half-sister to 4 winners out of the Oaks winner Circus Plume. (Windsor House Stables Partnership/Carolyn & Nigel Elwes). *"She's showing some speed – I think Sakhee's Secret is obviously bringing that into play. I like what she's doing at the moment and, fingers crossed, she could be running around May time. She's quite rangy and my father trained the dam who was more of a 3-y-o really. This filly is still quite weak but she's going the right way".*

524. NETLEY ABBEY ★★★
b.c. Myboycharlie – Ana Style (Anabaa Blue). February 13. First foal. €32,000Y. Arqana Deauville August V2. Private sale. The dam won 3 minor races in France at 2 and 3 yrs and is a half-sister to 6 winners including Chinandega (Group 3 Prix des Reservoirs). The second dam, European Style (by Ezzoud), was unraced. (Woodley, Bromfield, Cross, Whitaker). *"I like him, he's showing some speed and the sire has been doing well just recently. This is a big, strong colt that should be ready around June time and he'll be heading over to France to do most of his racing there for us".*

525. ROCK ON DANDY ★★★
gr.c. Rajsaman – Minnie's Mystery (Highest Honor). April 27. Seventh foal. €43,000Y. Arqana Deauville October. Stroud/Coleman & H Dunlop. Half-brother to 3 winners including the quite useful 6f to 1m winner of 6 races Dream Walker (by Gold Away) and the moderate 10f and 12f winner Roy Rocket (by Layman). The dam, an 8.5f to 12f winner of 5 races in Jersey, is a half-sister to one winner and to the dam of the Group 2 Celebration Mile winner Kodi Bear. The second dam, Madary (by Green Desert), won twice at 3 yrs and is a half-sister to 6 winners and to the unraced Dievotchka (the dam of four Group winners). (Daniel MacAuliffe & Anoj Don). *"Rajsaman is an interesting new sire in France. This colt is doing some faster work now and I like him. He's probably a six furlong horse, but I might start him at five at the end of April all being well. He's a strong colt, not too big but with a good depth to him and he looks precocious enough".*

526. WINNING BID ★★
b.c. Captain Gerrard – Best Bidder (Mr Greeley). April 16. Fourth foal. 9,500Y. Doncaster November. Stroud/Coleman & H Dunlop. Half-brother to the fair 2-y-o 6f winner Multiplier (by Multiplex). The dam is an unplaced half-sister to one minor winner in the USA. The second dam, Party Stripes (by Candy Stripes), is an unplaced half-sister to 5 winners. (Mr Khalifa Dasmal). *"He's doing some faster work and hopefully he'll be on the track in April, although I think he'll be better over six furlongs than five".*

527. UNNAMED ★★★ ♠♠
ch.c. Harbour Watch – Dress Code (Barathea). March 19. Eighth living foal. 11,000Y. Tattersalls October Book 2. Stroud/Coleman & Harry Dunlop. Half-brother to 5 winners including the smart 6f Goffs Million Sprint winner Lucky General (by Hawk Wing), the quite useful Irish 2-y-o 7f winner Slaney Rock (by Rock Of Gibraltar) and the fair listed-placed dual 5f winner (including at 2 yrs) Dress To Impress (by Fasliyev). The dam, a quite useful 2-y-o 5f winner, is a sister to the useful 2-y-o Group 3 7f C L Weld Park Stakes winner Rag Top and a half-sister to 8 winners. The second dam, Petite Epaulette (by Night Shift), a fair 5f winner at 2 yrs, is a half-sister to 3 winners including the Group 1 1m Gran Criterium second Line Dancer. (Mrs Susan Roy). *"I like him, he didn't cost a great deal but he's a big, strong horse. There's some speed in the family, but nevertheless he's going to take a bit more time and he's one we should see out in mid-season".* **TRAINERS' BARGAIN BUY**

TIM EASTERBY

528. BREAKWATER BAY (IRE)
b.c. Lilbourne Lad – Aqualina (King's Theatre). April 22. Sixth foal. £22,000Y. Doncaster Premier. Half-brother to the quite useful dual 1m winner Mister Ross (by Medicean). The dam, a 7f (at 2 yrs) and 1m winner in Ireland, was second in the Group 3 Irish 1,000 Guineas Trial and is a half-sister to 7 winners including the Group 3 Anglesey Stakes winner and Group 1 National Stakes second Malvernico. The second dam, Malvern Beauty (by Shirley Heights), a useful 10.5f winner, is a half-sister to 2 winners. (Reality Partnerships III).

529. COMPUTABLE
ch.c. Compton Place – Kummel Excess (Exceed And Excel). January 20. Second foal. £75,000Y. Doncaster Premier. Tim Easterby. Half-brother to the fairly useful 2-y-o 5f winner Excessable (by Sakhee's Secret). The dam, a modest 5f (at 2 yrs) and 6f winner, is a half-sister to 4 minor winners here and abroad. The second dam, Ipanema Beach (by Lion Cavern), a modest 1m and 8.5f winner, is a half-sister to 3 winners. (Mr B Guerin, Mrs E J Wills & Habton Farms).

530. DREAMORCHID
br.f. Dream Ahead – Dark Orchid (Shamardal). February 16. First foal. £25,000Y. Doncaster Premier. Tim Easterby. The dam, a moderate 7f placed maiden, is a half-sister to 7 winners including the listed winner Gardening Leave. The second dam, Misty Waters (by Caerleon), is an unraced half-sister to the Group 1 Falmouth Stakes winner Music Show. (Mrs J P Connew).

531. HUGGING THE RAILS (IRE)
b.c. Royal Applause – Aqraan (In The Wings). February 4. Fourth foal. £34,000Y. Doncaster Premier. Tim Easterby. The dam, a fairly useful Irish 7f and 10f winner, is a half-sister to 9 winners including the useful triple 6f (including at 2 yrs) and subsequent UAE listed 5f winner Taqseem. The second dam, Elshamms (by Zafonic), a fairly useful 2-y-o 7f winner and third in the Group 3 Prestige Stakes, is a half-sister to 10 winners. (CDM Developments, North West).

532. KICK KING KATIE (IRE)
br.f. Showcasing – Provence (Averti). March 17. Fifth foal. €37,000Y. Tattersalls Ireland September. Tim Easterby. Half-sister to the modest 1m winner Glorious Dancer (by Royal Applause). The dam was a fair 7f winner at 3 yrs. The second dam, Prowse (by King Of Kings), is a placed half-sister to 7 winners including Chelsey Flower (Grade 1 Flower Bowl Invitational). (Ontoawinner SDH Project Services Ltd).

533. MY CHERRY BLOSSOM
b.f. Kyllachy – Echo River (Irish River). February 21. Eighth foal. £25,000Y. Doncaster Premier. Tim Easterby. Half-brother to 4 winners including the quite useful 2-y-o 6f and smart hurdles winner Marsh Warbler (by Baratheo), the fair 7f (including at 2 yrs) to 12f and hurdles winner of 9 races (including at 2 yrs) Ravi River and the modest 1m and hurdles winner My Manekineko (by Authorized). The dam, a useful 2-y-o 6f and listed 7f winner, is a half-sister to 5 winners. The second dam, Monaassabaat (by Zilzal), a 6f (at 2 yrs) and listed 10f Virginia Stakes winner, is a half-sister to 8 winners including Bitooh (Group 2 Criterium de Maisons-Laffitte). (Mrs J E Pallister).

534. SHEPPARD'S GIFT
b.f. Dick Turpin – Sheppard's Watch (Night Shift). April 12. Eighth foal. £26,000Y. Doncaster Premier. Tim Easterby. Half-sister to the modest 2015 2-y-o 7f winner Big Sky, to the minor French 4-y-o winner Satwa Star (by King's Best) and a hurdles winner by Dansili. The dam, a very useful 6f (at 2 yrs), Group 3 7.5f Concorde Stakes and dual listed winner, is a full or half-sister to 2 winners. The second dam, Sheppard's Cross (by Soviet Star), a quite useful triple 7f winner, is a half-sister to 5 winners. (Habton Farms).

535. SUITED
b.f. Paco Boy – Birthday Suit (Daylami). March 27. Seventh foal. 22,000Y. Doncaster Premier. Tim Easterby. Half-sister to the quite useful triple 6f winner Bimbo (by Iffraaj), to the fair 12f and 14f winner Excelsior Academy (by Montjeu) and a winner in Qatar by Tiger Hill. The dam, a useful 2-y-o dual 5f winner and third in the Group 2 Cherry Hinton Stakes, is a half-sister to 10 winners including the Irish 1,000 Guineas winner Classic Park and the US Grade 2 winner Rumpipumpy. The second dam, Wanton (by Kris), a useful 2-y-o 5f winner and third in the Group 2 Flying Childers Stakes, is a half-sister to 8 winners including the listed 5f winner and good broodmare Easy Option. (Ontoawinner 10 & Partner).

536. TURPIN'S TREASURE ♠
b.f. Dick Turpin – Poyle Caitlin (Bachir). March 24. £18,000Y. Doncaster November. Tim Easterby. Half-sister to the quite useful 2-y-o 5f and 6f winner of 3 races Puddle Duck (by Pastoral Pursuits), to the fair 7f winner Poyle Jessica (by Royal Applause) and the fair 7f (at 2yrs) and 10f winner Marhaba Malayeen (by Dutch Art). The dam, a modest 1m fourth placed maiden, is a half-sister to 4 winners including the Group 2 Lowther Stakes winner Jemima. The second dam, Poyle Fizz (by Damister), is an unraced full or half-sister to 4 winners.

537. UNNAMED
gr.f. Zoffany – Gleaming Silver (Dalakhani). March 31. Third foal. €31,000Y. Goffs Orby. Half-sister to Rasasee (by Rip Van Winkle), placed third over 9.5f on his only start at

2 yrs in 2015 and to the modest 3-y-o 1m winner from two starts Silversmith (by Mastercraftsman). The dam, a fair Irish 3-y-o 1m winner, is a half-sister to 2 winners including the useful 2-y-o listed 9f winner Tiz The Shot. The second dam, Green Lassy (by Green Tune), won over 13f and 14f at 4 yrs in Ireland and is a half-sister to 5 winners including the French dual Group 2 winner (over 15f and 2m) Cut Quartz. (Miss B C Duxbury).

DAVID ELSWORTH

538. DASH OF SPICE ★★★
br.c. Teofilo – Dashiba (Dashing Blade). April 18. Brother to the fairly useful 1m (at 2 yrs) and 12f winner Dashing Star and half-brother to the dual Group 2 Lancashire Oaks winner of 7 races Barshiba (by Barathea), the useful 2-y-o listed 1m winner Doctor Dash, the fair 2-y-o 1m winner Dashing Doc (both by Dr Fong), and the modest dual 10f winner Westhaven (by Alhaarth). The dam, a useful 9f and 10f winner, is a half-sister to several winners including the fairly useful 10f and 12f winner Smart Blade. The second dam, Alsiba (by Northfields), a modest winner of one race at 4 yrs, was a staying half-sister to several winners and to the dam of the Irish St Leger winner Oscar Schindler. (J C Smith). *"A home-bred of Jeff Smith's, he's related to lots of good middle-distance horses and as his pedigree suggests he'll be like that too. One for the back-end of the season and for next year, but he's a nice, big, scopey colt that looks like his half-brother Dashing Star".*

539. DRAGSTONE ROCK ★★★★
ch.c. Dragon Pulse – Rock Exhibition (Rock Of Gibraltar). March 30. Half-brother to the very useful listed winner of 6 races over 5f and 6f and Group 1 Middle Park Stakes third Justice Day (by Acclamation) and to the quite useful dual 1m winner Yorkshire Dales (by Vale Of York). The dam, a fair Irish 1m winner, is a half-sister to 4 winners. The second dam, Finity (by Diesis), a useful 2-y-o 7f winner, was third in the Group 3 7f C L Weld Park Stakes and is a half-sister to 4 winners including Cavalryman (Group 1 Grand Prix de Paris). *"A very nice horse, he's a good-looking individual and already at this early stage of his career he looks promising. I trained the dam's first two winners so I'm hoping this one will continue the family tradition".*

540. IVOR'S FANCY ★★★
ch.f. Zebedee – Fantasy Princess (Johannesburg). April 4. Third foal. €8,000Y. Tattersalls Ireland September. David Elsworth. The dam, a fair 2-y-o 7f winner, is a half-sister to 8 winners in the USA and Mexico. The second dam, Fantasy (by Cadeaux Genereux), placed second over 7f from 2 starts at 2 yrs, is a half-sister to 9 winners including the listed winner and Group 2 second Smirk. (Ivor Perry/D Elsworth). *"A precocious 2-y-o, the owner likes to have a bit of fun with cheap, early types and this filly fits the bill".*

541. IVOR'S MAGIC ★★★
ch.f. Zebedee – Rinneen (Bien Bien). April 26. Sixth foal. €13,000Y. Tattersalls Ireland September. David Elsworth. Half-sister to the fair 6f (at 2 yrs) to 8.5f winner The Blue Banana and to the fair dual 12f winner Diaktoros (both by Red Clubs). The dam, a modest 6f (at 2 yrs) and 12f placed maiden, is a half-sister to 6 winners including the dual listed 6f winner Lady Links (herself dam of the dual listed winner Selinka). The second dam, Sparky's Song (by Electric), a moderate 10.2f and 12f winner, is a half-sister to the very smart Group 1 6.5f winner Bold Edge and to the listed winner and Group 3 5f Temple Stakes second Brave Edge. (Ivor Perry/D Elsworth). *"An early type, she's precocious and looks like a winner".*

542. LADY LOUISE ★★★
b.f. Intikhab – Lady Gabrielle (Dansili). May 5. First foal. The dam, a fair dual 10f winner, is a half-sister to 2 minor winners. The second dam, Zither (by Zafonic), a fairly useful 6f (at 2 yrs) and 7f winner, is a half-sister to 3 winners including the useful 2-y-o listed 6f winner Dowager and the useful 1m (at 2 yrs) and 10f winner Dower House. (Luke Lillingston, Julian Nettlefold & David Elsworth). *"We trained the mare as a 3-y-o and this is her first foal. She's a nice, big, quality filly who will probably be in my second batch of runners. She was a May foal but she's well-grown and we'll give her all the time she needs. A good-moving filly with an excellent temperament".*

543. MITIGATE ★★★
b.f. Lawman – Marika (Marju). February 23. Tenth foal. 90,000Y. Tattersalls October Book 1. Suzanne Roberts. Half-sister to 5 winners including the French dual listed 6f winner of 6 races Sabratah (by Oasis Dream), the quite useful 7f (including at 2 yrs) and 1m winner Folly Lodge (by Grand Lodge) and the quite useful 10f winner Raw Impulse (by Makfi). The dam, a useful 6f listed and 1m winner, is a half-sister to 8 winners including the Group 3 Fred Darling Stakes winner Sueboog (dam of the Group 1 winner Best Of The Bests). The second dam, Nordica (by Northfields), a useful 6f and 1m winner, is a half-sister to 2 winners. (GB Partnership). *"A half-sister to a good filly in Sabratah, the owner is overdue some success on this side of the Channel and we think this might be the one to do it. She looks the business, but like her sister she'll probably show her best form as a 3-y-o".*

544. PRIZE DIVA ★★★
b.f. Motivator – Premier Prize (Selkirk). March 1. Eighth foal. Sister to the 1m (at 2 yrs), Group 2 12.5f Grand Prix de Deauville and Group 3 10f Prix Gontaut-Biron winner Cocktail Queen and half-sister to the quite useful dual 1m winner at 2 and 3 yrs Gold Prince (by Nayef) and the fair 7f and 1m winner Hidden Fire (by Alhaarth). The dam, a useful 7f (at 2 yrs) and listed 10f winner, was third in the Group 2 Sandown Mile and is a half-sister to 7 winners including the Group 2 15f Prix Kergorlay winner Gold Medallist. The second dam, Spot Prize (by Seattle Dancer), a useful filly, won over 5f at 2 yrs and was fourth in the Oaks. (J C Smith). *"She's a full-sister to Cocktail Queen who we trained and like her this filly will be a much better 3-y-o. A big, fine individual, she'll be a quality filly in time. Both Cocktail Queen and the dam won as 2-y-o's, so hopefully this filly will emulate them".*

545. SATIN RIBBON ★★★
ch.f. Shamardal – Seattle Ribbon (Seattle Dancer). February 13. Half-sister to 9 winners including the smart listed 10f winner and Group 2 Dante Stakes third Snoqualmie Boy, the very useful listed 1m (at 2 yrs) and listed 10f winner Snoqualmie Girl (both by Montjeu), the fairly useful 2-y-o 7f winner Seattle Drive (by Motivator), the quite useful 1m and 10f winner Snoqualmie Star (by Galileo), the quite useful 2-y-o 6f winner Robocop and the fair 10f winner Seattle Storm. The dam, placed over 9f and 10f at 3 yrs, is a sister to the 2-y-o Group 1 1m winner Seattle Dancer. The second dam, Golden Rhyme (by Dom Racine), was a quite useful 7f winner. (J C Smith). *"This filly is a 3-y-o type but I'm hopeful she'll run to a good level at the back-end of this season. I haven't asked her any questions yet".*

546. SNOW SQUAW ★★★★
ch.f. Excelebration – Snoqualmie Girl (Montjeu). March 4. The dam, a very useful listed 1m (at 2 yrs) and listed 10f winner, is a sister to the smart listed 10f winner and Group 2 Dante Stakes third Snoqualmie Boy and a half-sister to 6 winners including the fairly useful 2-y-o 7f winner Seattle Drive. The second dam, Seattle Ribbon (Seattle Dancer), placed over 9f and 10f at 3 yrs, is a sister to the 2-y-o Group 1 1m winner Seattle Dancer. (J C Smith). *"A very attractive filly, we like her a lot and she looks like a 2-y-o type. A speedy looking filly who is giving us good signals".*

547. SWISS STORM ★★★★★ ♠
b.c. Frankel – Swiss Lake (Indian Ridge). March 6. Ninth foal. 235,000Y. Tattersalls October Book 1. Suzanne Roberts. Half-brother to 7 winners including the Group 3 6f Prix de Meautry and Group 3 5f Prix de Petit Couvert winner Swiss Diva (by Pivotal), the very useful 6f (at 2 yrs) and Group 3 5f winner Swiss Spirit (by Invincible Spirit), the useful triple listed 6f winner Swiss Dream (by Oasis Dream) and the smart 2-y-o 5f winner and triple Group 2 placed Swiss Franc (by Mr Greeley). The dam, a dual listed 5f winner (including at 2 yrs), and second in the Group 2 Flying Childers Stakes, is a half-sister to 4 winners. The second dam, Blue Iris (by Petong), was a useful listed-placed winner of 5 races over 5f and 6f. (Lordship Stud & D Elsworth). *"He had a little setback which is fine now but it just set us back by about a month. In the bigger picture it won't affect him at all but I was hoping to get to Royal Ascot with him. This is a lovely, big horse and he looks like his half-brother Swiss Spirit. He'll be our star two-year-old I think – you've only got to watch him move. An exciting colt".*

548. TISBUTADREAM ★★★★
ch.f. Dream Ahead – Choose Me (Choisir). March 26. Third foal. €100,000Y. Goffs Orby. Suzanne Roberts. Half-sister to the 2015 2-y-o debut 1m winner Persuasive (by Dark Angel) and to the fairly useful 6f and 7f winner Amazour (by Azamour). The dam, a very useful 6f (at 2 yrs) to 10f winner of 4 races including a listed 7f event in Ireland, was third in the Group 2 Blandford Stakes and is a half-sister to 5 minor winners. The second dam, Hecuba (by Hector Protector), a fairly useful 10f winner, is a half-sister to 7 winners including the German Group 2 winner Bad Bertrich Again and the Group 3 Scottish Classic winner Prolix. *"The mare's only had two previous foals and they've both won. She's owned in partnership with Sean Coughlan and if there was any doubt about this filly being any good that would quash it because he's the luckiest man in the world! Rather an attractive, flashy filly, we have high expectations of her and she's likely to be a precocious 2-y-o".*

549. TRADE ROUTE (IRE) ★★
gr.c. Mastercraftsman – Shanghai Visit (Peintre Celebre). April 18. Seventh foal. Half-brother to the fair Irish 5f winner Shanghai Beauty (by Jeremy) and to a minor winner abroad by Red Clubs. The dam is an unplaced half-sister to 3 winners including the 2-y-o Group 1 Middle Park Stakes and Group 1 Prix Morny winner and sire Bahamian Bounty. The second dam, Clarentia (by Ballad Rock), a very useful winner of 5 races at up to 6f, was third in the Group 3 Cornwallis Stakes. *"A quality looking colt who we hope will show his best form at the end of this season and next year".*

550. UNNAMED ★★★
b.f. Fastnet Rock – Ardbrae Lady (Overbury). April 10. Seventh foal. 70,000Y. Tattersalls October Book 1. Suzanne Roberts. Closely related to the quite useful listed-placed 7f winner Jammy Guest (by Duke Of Marmalade) and half-sister to the useful Irish listed-placed 7f (at 2 yrs) and 11f winner Jackaroo and to the minor Japanese 2-y-o and 3-y-o winner Red Shanks (both by Galileo). The dam, a useful winner of the Group 3 1m Park Express Stakes and second in the Irish 1,000 Guineas, is a half-sister to 7 winners including the listed winners Radio Gaga and Obe Gold. The second dam, Gagajulu (by Al Hareb), won 5 races over 5f at 2 yrs and is a half-sister to 4 winners. *"A nice little filly that looks precocious despite being by Fastnet Rock. It's early days but we like her a lot".*

551. UNNAMED ★★★
b.f. Cape Blanco – Carini (Vettori). February 16. Sixth foal. 12,000Y. Tattersalls October Book 2. D Elsworth. Half-sister to the minor US stakes-placed winner of 6 races from 2 to 4 yrs Forgotten People (by Van Nistelrooy), to the minor French 2-y-o winner Araneide (by Aragorn) and a winner abroad by Lion Heart. The dam, a fairly useful 2-y-o 7f and 1m winner and third in the listed Lupe Stakes, subsequently won in the USA and is a half-sister to 4 winners. The second dam, Secret Waters (by Pharly), a fairy useful 12f to 14f winner, was listed-placed twice and is a half-sister to 9 winners including the Group 3 Solario Stakes winner and very smart broodmare Shining Water. *"She's from a family fairly close to my heart, I think she was very well-bought and I expect her to be a nice 2-y-o later on".* **TRAINERS' BARGAIN BUY**

552. UNNAMED ★★
b.c. Pour Moi – Chatline (One Cool Cat). February 2. Third foal. 150,000Y. Tattersalls October Book 2. Hillen/Tabor. The dam, a quite useful Irish 3-y-o 6f winner, is a half-sister to 5 winners including the smart listed 6f winner and Group 3 second Mugharreb. The second dam, Marling (by Lomond), a high-class winner of the Cheveley Park Stakes, the Irish 1,000 Guineas, the Coronation Stakes and the Sussex Stakes is a half-sister to 7 winners including the Irish 2,000 Guineas and Prix de l'Abbaye second Caerwent. (Mrs Doreen Tabor). *"A colt from a very good family that goes back to the champion sprinter Marwell. A most attractive colt, we haven't yet decided how early he'll be but he'll progress as the season goes on and be a better 3-y-o".*

553. UNNAMED ★★
b.f. Pour Moi – Haretha (Alhaarth). April 6. Third living foal. €34,000Y. Goffs Orby. S A Roberts. Half-sister to the fair 7f to 8.5f winner Malekat Jamal (by Dutch Art). The dam is an unraced half-sister to 5 winners including the

Group 1 10f Nassau Stakes and Group 10.4f Musidora Stakes winner Zahrat Dubai. The second dam, Walesiana (by Star Appeal), won the German 1,000 Guineas and is a half-sister to 8 winners. *"I think she'll end up a middle-distance filly but she's nice and she'll be running as a 2-y-o in the second half of the season"*.

554. UNNAMED ★★★

ch.f. Bahamian Bounty – Paradise Place (Compton Place). February 15. First foal. 20,000Y. Tattersalls December. Suzanne Roberts. The dam, a modest 6f winner, is a sister to the 2-y-o 6f and subsequent US Grade 2 winner Passified and a half-sister to 5 winners including the fairly useful 6f winner of 3 races (including at 2 yrs) Zomerlust. The second dam, Passiflora (by Night Shift), a fair 2-y-o 6f winner, is a half-sister to the Group 2 6f Cork And Orrery Stakes winner Harmonic Way. *"She's an attractive filly who could well make up into a nice 2-y-o"*.

JAMES EUSTACE

555. ENVOY ★★★

gr.c. Delegator – La Gessa (Largesse). March 26. Fifth foal. £17,000Y. Doncaster Premier. Not sold. Half-brother to the fairly useful 2015 2-y-o 5f and 6f winner Poet's Prize (by Compton Place), to the quite useful 5f, 6f (both at 2 yrs) to 1m winner Tommy's Secret (by Sakhee's Secret), the ill-fated Irish 2-y-o 7f winner Case Statement (by Showcasing) and the modest 7f (at 2 yrs) to 9f winner of 5 races Wordismybond (by Monsieur Bond). The dam, a moderate 10f and 13f winner at 3 and 4 yrs, is a half-sister to one winner. The second dam, En Grisaille (by Mystiko), a moderate 6f (at 2 yrs) and 10f winner, is a half-sister to 5 winners including the multiple listed winner Angus Newz. (H R Moszkowicz). *"A horse with a lot of size and scope, but despite that he's already shown us that he's nice. I wouldn't think of running him yet because of his size, but it's interesting to note that his 2-y-o half-brother last year, Poet's Prize, won the Tattersalls Book 3 bonus race and I believe that as a yearling he didn't necessarily look like he'd be a 2-y-o type, but he clearly was. I like this colt and he's well worth putting in the book because he's a nice horse, full stop"*.

556. FLAME OUT ★★★★

b.f. Excelebration – Hidden Fire (Alhaarth). April 3. Second foal. Half-sister to the quite useful 2016 3-y-o 7f and listed 1m winner Sea Of Flames (by Aqlaam). The dam, a fair 7f and 1m winner, is a half-sister to 2 winners including the 1m (at 2 yrs) and Group 2 12.5 Grand Prix de Deauville winner Cocktail Queen. The second dam, Premier Prize (by Selkirk), a useful 7f (at 2 yrs) and listed 10f winner, was third in the Group 2 Sandown Mile and is a half-sister to 7 winners including the Group 2 15f Prix Kergorlay winner Gold Medalist. (J C Smith). *"A nice filly, she's a half-sister to Sea Of Flames who has recently won four races including a listed for David Elsworth. The dam has since died, so this filly is the last of her foals. She's done nothing wrong at all, but having said that she's done very little so far, but since day one she's looked a filly with a bit of quality"*.

557. MUSIC SEEKER ★★

b.c. Henrythenavigator – Danehill Music (Danehill Dancer). February 14. Fourth foal. 30,000foal. Tattersalls December. Hursley Bloodstock. Half-brother to the very useful 1m to 10f winner and listed-placed Seussical (by Galileo). The dam, winner of the Group 3 1m Park Express Stakes and the listed 1m Celebration Stakes, is a half-sister to 8 minor winners. The second dam, Tuesday Morning (by Sadler's Wells), is an unraced half-sister to one winner in Germany. (J C Smith). *"He was bought as a foal and he's a nice, big horse with plenty of bone. A nice type, he seems to have a good attitude but won't be ready until much later in the season. You'd be forgiven for thinking he'd be starting over seven furlongs, but he's done so little it would be unfair to guess at this stage"*.

558. PENNY GREEN ★★★

b.f. Halling – Penelewey (Groom Dancer). March 6. Eighth foal. Half-sister to Pennerley (by Aqlaam), unplaced in one start at 2 yrs in 2015, to the useful 1m (at 2 yrs) and 10f winner Jedediah (by Hernando) and the modest 7f and 8.5f winner of 3 races Marksbury (by Mark Of Esteem). The dam, a useful 6f and 7f winner of 3 races, is a half-sister to 7 winners here and abroad. The second dam, Peryllys (by Warning), is a placed half-sister to 6 winners. (Major M G Wyatt). "She's coming along nicely and despite being by Halling she's just started fast work. I've had a few of the family and none of them have been early, but this filly just is. She's pretty level, medium-sized and I do like her. I'm very pleased with her and I think she's the nicest model I've had out of the mare".

559. VOTE ★★★
b.f. Aqlaam – Bidding Time (Rock Of Gibraltar). February 27. Fifth foal. 8,000Y. Tattersalls October Book 3. James Eustace. Half-sister to Bond Trader (by Monsieur Bond), placed third on her debut over 7f at 3 yrs in 2016 and to the minor Italian winner of 4 races from 3 to 5 yrs Paolina Bella (by Sakhee's Secret). The dam ran twice unplaced and is a half-sister to 5 winners including the listed-placed Pietra Dura (herself dam of the US Grade 3 winner Turning Top) and the dam of the Group 1 King George VI winner Postponed. The second dam, Bianca Nera (by Salse), won the Group 1 Moyglare Stud Stakes and the Group 2 Lowther Stakes and is a half-sister to 4 winners including the dam of the Group 1 Fillies' Mile and Falmouth Stakes winner Simply Perfect. (Rushby, Hagen, McCreery & Eustace). "Medium-sized and pretty level, rather like another of my two-year-old fillies, Penny Green, she's done well physically since she was broken-in and has just started fast work. A nice filly from a nice family". **TRAINERS BARGAIN BUY**

560. WILD SHOT ★★
br.c. So You Think – Highland Shot (Selkirk). April 3. Half-brother to the fair 2015 8.5f placed 2-y-o Shadow Spirit (by Makfi), to the smart German Group 2 1m, Group 3 9f Darley Stakes and listed 1m Pomfret Stakes winner of 6 races Highland Knight (by Night Shift), the fair dual 1m winner Great Shot (by Marju) and a hurdles winner by Dr Fong. The dam, a fairly useful 7f to 9f winner, is a half-sister to 8 winners including the very smart 2-y-o Group 3 7f Solario Stakes winner and Group 1 Dewhurst Stakes third Opera Cape, the high-class stayer Grey Shot and the smart sprint winner of 4 races Night Shot. The second dam, Optaria (by Song), a quite useful 2-y-o 5f winner, is out of the unplaced Electo (by Julio Mariner). (J C Smith). "I have the 3-y-o half-sister Shadow Spirit who isn't a big filly.

This colt, despite being by So You Think who is a big stallion, is also on the small side. As an individual he does look like a 2-y-o and if he is we'll go with it until he tells us otherwise".

561. UNNAMED ★★
b.f. High Chaparral – Rainbow Queen (FR) (Spectrum). February 26. Eighth foal. Half-sister to Folly Bergere (by Champs Elysees), placed third over 7f at Newmarket on her only start at 2 yrs in 2015, to the quite useful dual 7f winner Sir Isaac (by Key Of Luck) and the quite useful 10f and 12f of 3 races winner Quixote (by Singspiel). The dam won 4 races from 6f to 1m at 3 and 4 yrs in Belgium and France and is a half-sister to 4 winners including the Group 3 Prix Miesque winner Stella Blue (herself dam of the triple listed winner Sirius Prospect). The second dam, Libanoor (by Highest Honor), won 4 races at 3 yrs in France and is a sister to the French triple Group 3 winner Take Risks and to three listed-placed winners. (Mr & Mrs R Scott). "A backward filly, she came in late and is only just ridden away, but she's improved immensely physically. Quite an attractive filly, she's going to be a staying type next year and beyond".

RICHARD FAHEY

562. ABIENTO
b.c. Requinto – Nose One's Way (Revoque). April 2. Sixth foal. 40,000Y. Tattersalls October Book 2. Aidan O'Ryan / R Fahey. Half-brother to the quite useful 2015 2-y-o 5f winner Gin In The Inn (by Alfred Nobel), to the fairly useful 5f (at 2 yrs) and 6f winner Grandad's World (by Kodiac), the Irish 4-y-o 1m winner Kavaco (by Choisir) and to a minor winner in Italy by Oratorio. The dam, a winner over hurdles, is a half-sister to 5 winners including the 2-y-o Group 3 Sirenia Stakes winner and Group 1 Cheveley Park Stakes second Dhanyata. The second dam, Preponderance (by Cyrano de Bergerac), a quite useful 2-y-o dual 5f winner, is a half-sister to 6 winners.

563. ATTEQ
b.c. Invincible Spirit – Wallis (King's Best). April 30. Second foal. 310,000Y. Tattersalls October Book 1. John & Jake Warren for Al Shaqab Racing. The dam, a quite useful 6f and 1m winner here, subsequently won and was stakes-placed in the USA. She is a half-sister

to 5 winners including the Grade 1 Northern Dancer Turf and dual Grade 2 Sky Classic winner Forte Dei Marmi (by Selkirk) and the very useful 12f and listed 14f winner Savarain. The second dam, Frangy (by Sadler's Wells), a fair dual 12f winner, is a full or half-sister to 8 winners including the German 1m to 9.5f winner of 7 races and listed-placed Flying Heights.

564. BUCCANEER'S COVE (IRE)
b.c. Footstepsinthesand – Primissima (Second Set). April 6. Sixth foal. €90,000Y. Goffs Orby. Norman Steel. Half-brother to the quite useful 2-y-o dual 6f winner Primitorio, to the fair 7f to 10f winner Size (both by Oratorio) and the useful 2-y-o 5f and subsequent US listed winner and Group 3 6f Albany Stakes third Premier Steps (by Footstepsinthesand) and the fair dual 1m winner Marmalad (by Duke Of Marmalade). The dam won at 3 yrs in Germany and is a half-sister to 5 winners there. The second dam, Princess Taufan (by Taufan), won the listed National Stakes, was third in the Group 2 Lowther Stakes and is a half-sister to the dam of the Group 3 winner Gracefully.

565. CANALETTO (IRE)
b.c. Galileo – Francesca D'Gorgio (Proud Citizen). March 19. Half-brother to the useful 6f (at 2 yrs) and listed 1m winner Amazonas (by Cape Cross). The dam, a fairly useful 2-y-o 6f winner, was listed placed at 3 yrs and is a half-sister to the US 2-y-o winner and Grade 1 9f second Blonde Fog. The second dam, Betty's Solutions (by Eltish), a minor US dual 3-y-o 6f to 1m winner, is a half-sister to the dam of the US Grade 1 winner My Trusty Cat.

566. CARSON CITY
ch.c. Excelebration – Humhum (Medicean). February 22. First foal. £35,000Y. Doncaster Premier. Willie Browne. The dam, placed twice in France at 2 and 3 yrs, is a half-sister to 3 minor winners. The second dam, Danehill Dreamer (by Danehill), is an unraced half-sister to 8 winners including the Group 1 winners Compton Admiral and Summoner.

567. CHAMPION HARBOUR
b.c. Harbour Watch – Drastic Measure (Pivotal). February 19. Fifth foal. 45,000Y. Tattersalls October Book 1. Aidan O'Ryan/

R Fahey. Half-brother to the modest 7f (at 2 yrs) to 10f winner Sutton Sid (by Dutch Art). The dam, a modest 5f placed 2-y-o, is a half-sister to 3 winners including the dam of the US listed winner and Grade 3 placed Driving Snow. The second dam, Danse Classique (by Night Shift), an Irish listed-placed 7f winner, is a half-sister to 5 winners including the high-class Irish Oaks, Yorkshire Oaks and Prix de l'Opera winner Petrushka.

568. CHEERFUL CHARACTER (IRE)
b.f. Tagula – Eucharist (Acclamation). February 25. Second foal. €30,000Y. Tattersalls Ireland September. Aidan O'Ryan / R Fahey. The dam, a fairly useful 2-y-o 5f to 7f winner of 4 races, was third in the Group 3 Fred Darling Stakes. The second dam, Satin Rose (by Lujain), a moderate 12f winner, is a half-sister to 4 other minor winners.

569. CLEF
b.f. Dutch Art – Humouresque (Pivotal). April 9. Seventh foal. Sister to the fair 10f winner Lyric Piece and half-sister to the fairly useful listed-placed 10f and 11f winner Piano, to the fair 11f winner Holberg Suite (both by Azamour) and the fair Irish 7f and 1m winner Solid Air (by Linamix). The dam, a smart Group 3 10.5f Prix Penelope winner, is a sister to 2 winners including the Group 2 placed Mighty and a half-sister to the very smart sprinter and multiple Group 3 winner Danehurst. The second dam, Miswaki Belle (by Miswaki), second over 7f on her only start, is a half-sister to 8 winners including the smart Group 3 6f Cherry Hinton Stakes winner and 1,000 Guineas third Dazzle. (Cheveley Park Stud).

570. COOL CLIMATE (IRE)
b.c. Bated Breath – Spanish Sun (El Prado). May 9. Seventh living foal. €45,000Y. Goffs Sportsmans. Not sold. Half-brother to the promising 2016 3-y-o 1m fillies' maiden winner Swiss Range (by Zamindar), to the fair 7f winner Solar Verde and the 11f winner (on her only start) Cordoba (both by Oasis Dream). The dam, a 7f (at 2 yrs) and Group 2 12f Ribblesdale Stakes winner, is a sister to the Group 1 12f Grand Prix de Saint-Cloud winner Spanish Moon. The second dam, Shining Bright (by Rainbow Quest), a French 10f winner, is a half-sister to the Group 2 12f

Grand Prix de Chantilly winner Daring Miss and the Group 3 12f Prix de Royaumont winner Apogee.

571. CULLINGWORTH (IRE)
b.c. Kodiac – Think (Marchand De Sable). April 27. Seventh foal. 36,000Y. Tattersalls October Book 2. Aidan O'Ryan / R Fahey. Brother to the moderate Burning Love, placed fourth once over 6f at 2 yrs in 2015 and half-brother to the fair 9f (at 2 yrs) to 12.5f winner of 5 races Card High (by Red Clubs) and the modest 4-y-o 1m winner Filosofo (by Teofilo). The dam, a French 2-y-o 6f winner, was third in the Group 3 Prix du Bois and is a half-sister to 8 minor winners. The second dam, Montagne Bleue (by Legend Of France), is a placed half-sister to 5 winners.

572. ELDORADO CREEK
b.c. High Chaparral – Trail Of Tears (Exceed And Excel). February 10. First foal. 60,000Y. Tattersalls October Book 2. Charlie Gordon-Watson. The dam, a modest 2-y-o 5f to 7f placed maiden, is a half-sister to 4 winners including the Group 3 winner and French 2,000 Guineas third Bowman and the dam of the Group 1 winners Kirklees and Mastery. The second dam, Cherokee Rose (by Dancing Brave), won the Group 1 Haydock Park Sprint Cup and the Group 1 Prix Maurice de Gheest and is a half-sister to 4 winners.

573. EL NINO SEA
b.c. Sea The Stars – Mayano Sophia (Rock Of Gibraltar). February 12. Fifth foal. 36,000Y. Tattersalls October Book 2. Not sold. Half-brother to a winner in Japan by Manduro. The dam, a dual 7f winner in France at 2 and 3 yrs, was listed-placed and is a half-sister to 4 winners including the listed Woodcote Stakes winner High Award. The second dam, Tarascon (by Tirol), winner of the Group 1 7f Moyglare Stud Stakes and the Group 1 Irish 1,000 Guineas, is a half-sister to the Group 2 Prix Guillaume d'Ornano winner Mister Monet and to the very useful 5f winner and Moyglare Stud Stakes and Cheveley Park Stakes placed Mala Mala.

574. FORSTER SQUARE (IRE)
b.c. Dandy Man – Massuci (Montjeu). March 2. Fourth foal. 35,000Y. Tattersalls December.

Aidan O'Ryan / R Fahey. The dam, a fair Irish 13f winner, is a half-sister to 3 winners. The second dam, Darina (by Danehill), an Irish 3-y-o winner of 4 races including a listed 10f event, was second in the Group 3 1m Matron Stakes and is a half-sister to 4 winners.

575. GEEGO
ch.c. Compton Place – Valediction (Fantastic Light). April 18. First foal. £30,000Y. Doncaster Premier. R Fahey. The dam, a minor winner at 3 yrs in Italy, is a half-sister to 2 winners including the US Grade 2 and Grade 3 placed Lamentation. The second dam, Dark Veil (by Gulch), a minor Irish 10f winner, is a half-sister to 5 winners including the UAE dual Group 3 6f winner of 7 races Conroy.

576. GOLCONDA KING (IRE)
gr.c. Dark Angel – Vanity's Girl (Compton Place). April 1. First foal. 200,000Y. Tattersalls October Book 1. Aidan O'Ryan/R Fahey. The dam, a moderate 7f placed 3-y-o, is a half-sister to 5 winners including the Group 3 6f Ballyogan Stakes and dual listed winner and Group 1 second Lesson In Humility, and the useful listed 1m winner Boastful. The second dam, Vanity (by Thatching), a fair 5f and 6f placed maiden, is a half-sister to 6 winners including the listed winner Ffestiniog (herself the dam of 3 stakes winners).

577. GOLCONDA PRINCE (IRE)
b.c. Arcano – Mujarah (Marju). April 12. Second foal. 85,000Y. Tattersalls October Book 2. Aidan O'Ryan / R Fahey. Half-brother to the smart 2015 2-y-o Group 2 6f Mill Reef Stakes winner and Group 2 Gimcrack Stakes second Ribchester (by Iffraaj). The dam is an unplaced half-sister to 6 winners including the Group 3 14f Curragh Cup winner Tactic. The second dam, Tanaghum (by Darshaan), a useful listed-placed 10f winner, is a half-sister to 8 winners including the smart Group 2 10f Premio Lydia Tesio winner Najah.

578. IN FIRST PLACE
b.c. Bated Breath – Carved Emerald (Pivotal). April 14. Third foal. 30,000Y. Tattersalls October Book 2. Aidan O'Ryan / R Fahey. The dam, a quite useful 7f winner, is a half-sister to 7 winners including the listed 6f winner and Group 3 Princess Margaret Stakes second Vital

Statistics. The second dam, Emerald Peace (by Green Desert), a useful listed 5f winner of 4 races and second in the Group 2 5f Flying Childers Stakes, is a half-sister to 9 winners.

579. KING'S ADVICE
ch.c. Frankel – Queen's Logic (Grand Lodge). April 23. Half-brother to 6 winners including the Group 2 6f Lowther Stakes, Group 3 6f Princess Margaret Stakes (both at 2 yrs) and Group 2 6f Diadem Stakes winner Lady Of The Desert (by Rahy), the fairly useful dual 10f winner Prince Of Stars (by Sea The Stars), the 2-y-o 1m and subsequent UAE 6f winner Go On Be A Tiger (by Machiavellian), the 6f winner Dunes Queen (by Elusive Quality) and the 11f winner Abu Nayef (by Nayef) – the last three all quite useful. The dam, a champion 2-y-o filly and winner of the Group 1 6f Cheveley Park Stakes and the Group 2 6f Lowther Stakes, is a half-sister to the top-class multiple Group 1 winner Dylan Thomas. The second dam, Lagrion (by Diesis), was placed 5 times in Ireland and stayed 12f and is a full or half-sister to 3 winners.

580. KOCOLLADA
b.f. Kodiac – Collada (Desert Prince). April 30. Seventh foal. 60,000Y. Tattersalls October Book 2. Rabbah Bloodstock. Sister to the quite useful dual 6f winner Have A Great Day and half-sister to the fairly useful 7f (at 2 yrs) to 10.5f winner and dual Group 3 placed Cai Shen, the fair 10f winner Dynamic Duo (both by Iffraaj) and a winner in Greece by Celtic Swing. The dam is an unplaced half-sister to 3 winners including the 2-y-o Group 3 7f Horris Hill Stakes winner and French 2,000 Guineas second Clearing. The second dam, Bright Spells (by Alleged), a French 12f winner, is a sister to 3 winners including the Group 2 German winner Non Partisan and a half-sister to 7 winners including the dam of the Grade/Group 1 winners Raintrap and Sunshack.

581. LADY IN QUESTION (IRE)
b.f. Elzaam – Black Meyeden (Black Minnaloushe). April 13. Third foal. €35,000Y. Tattersalls Ireland September. Aidan O'Ryan / R Fahey. The dam ran twice unplaced and is a half-sister to 6 winners including the Group 3 placed Hasanat. The second dam, Eye Witness (by Don't Forget Me), is a placed sister to

the listed winner and useful broodmare Well Beyond.

582. LIQUID GOLD (IRE)
b.f. Nathaniel – Northern Mischief (Yankee Victor). March 24. Seventh foal. €95,000foal. Goffs November foals. Norman Steel. Half-sister to a minor 3-y-o winner in the USA by Ghostzapper. The dam won two races in the USA, was third in the Grade 1 Hollywood Starlet Stakes and is a half-sister to 5 winners including the US champion older mare and triple Grade 1 winner Gourmet Girl. The second dam, Rhondaling (by Welsh Pageant), won twice at 2 yrs and was third in the Group 3 C L Weld Park Stakes and is a half-sister to 3 minor winners.

583. LOVING CLARETS (IRE)
b.f. Mayson – Flying Clarets (Titus Livius). April 27. Half-sister to the fair 2015 2-y-o 6f winner Flowing Clarets (by Pastoral Pursuits) and to the modest dual 6f winner at 2 and 3 yrs Flighty Clarets (by Bahamian Bounty). The dam, a useful 1m (at 2 yrs) to 11f winner, was third in the Group 3 Middleton Stakes, is a half-sister to 4 winners including the fairly useful listed-placed Borders Belle. The second dam, Sheryl Lynn (by Miller's Mate), won 2 races at 3 and 4 yrs in Germany and is a half-sister to 3 winners.

584. MEGAN LILY (IRE)
b.f. Dragon Pulse – Nebraas (Green Desert). May 15. Ninth foal. €40,000Y. Goffs Orby. Nick Bradley/Jason Kelly. Half-sister to 6 winners including the fairly useful listed 6f (at 2 yrs) and 10f winner and Group 3 third Seehorn, the quite useful 8.5f winner Aimhirgin Lass (both by Pivotal), the Group 3 7.5f Concorde Stakes and Group 3 Irish 1,000 Guineas Trial winner Yellow Rosebud (by Jeremy) and the quite useful 6f and 7f winner of 10 races My Kingdom (by King's Best). The dam is an unraced half-sister to 6 winners including the Group 1 Golden Jubilee Stakes winner Malhub. The second dam, Arjuzah (by Ahonoora), won the listed 7f Sceptre Stakes.

585. MUSHAIREB ♠
b.c. Invincible Spirit – Hidden Brief (Barathea). March 13. Third foal. 105,000Y. Tattersalls October Book 1. Al Shaqab Racing. The dam, a

fairly useful listed-placed 10f winner, is a sister to the Group 3 winner and Group 1 Irish Oaks third Hazarista and a half-sister to 5 winners including the Group 3 winner Hazariya. The second dam, Hazaradjat (by Darshaan), a 7f (at 2 yrs) and 10f winner in Ireland, is a full or half-sister to 10 winners including the Flying Childers and Middle Park Stakes winner Hittite Glory.

586. PRIVATE MATTER
b.c. Mayson – Privacy Order (Azamour). February 8. First foal. The dam is an unplaced half-sister to the French 10f winner and Group 2 Prix Greffulhe second Untold Secret. The second dam, Confidential Lady (by Singspiel), winner of the Group 3 7f Prix du Calvados (at 2 yrs) and the Group 1 10.5f Prix de Diane, is a half-sister to 5 winners. (Cheveley Park Stud).

587. PUNTE LINKE (IRE)
gr.f. Dark Angel – Eroica (Highest Honor). March 17. Eighth foal. 65,000Y. Tattersalls December. Highfield Farm. Half-sister to 5 winners including the 2-y-o Group 3 1m Premio Dormello (by Elusive City), the Italian 2-y-o listed 7.5f winner Saent (by Strategic Prince) and the quite useful listed-placed 8.5f (at 2 yrs) to 12f winner of 6 races Tepmokea (by Noverre). The dam, a German listed-placed 2-y-o winner, is a half-sister to 3 winners. The second dam, Eirehill (by Danehill), won two races at 3 and 4 yrs in Germany and is a half-sister to 10 winners including German and Italian Group 1 winner Elle Danzig.

588. QUEEN KINDLY
ch.f. Frankel – Lady Of The Desert (Rahy). January 14. First foal. The dam, a Group 2 6f Lowther Stakes, Group 3 6f Princess Margaret Stakes (both at 2 yrs) and Group 2 6f Diadem Stakes winner, is a half-sister to 5 winners including the fairly useful dual 10f winner Prince Of Stars. The second dam, Queen's Logic (by Grand Lodge), a champion 2-y-o filly and winner of the Group 1 6f Cheveley Park Stakes and the Group 2 6f Lowther Stakes, is a half-sister to the top-class multiple Group 1 winner Dylan Thomas.

589. RASHFORD'S DOUBLE (IRE)
b.c. Zoffany – Ardent Lady (Alhaarth). April 11. Eighth living foal. €60,000Y. Goffs Orby. A O'Ryan / Middleham Park. Half-brother to the modest 2015 6f to 1m placed 2-y-o Livella Fella (by Strategic Prince), to the fairly useful Irish 1m winner and listed placed Gatamalata (by Spartacus), the Italian winner and 7.5f listed placed Denusa (by Aussie Rules), the fair 2-y-o 6f and 8.5f winner Daniella de Bruijn (by Orpen) and the fair 2-y-o 5f winner First Choice (by Choisir). The dam, a fair 9.5f winner, is a half-sister to 6 winners. The second dam, Arvika (by Baillamont), a minor French 3-y-o winner, is a half-sister to 5 winners.

590. REINSTORM
b.c. Canford Cliffs – Bridle Belle (Dansili). February 20. First foal. The dam, a quite useful 7f (at 2 yrs) to 12f winner of 5 races, is a half-sister to the useful 7f (at 2 yrs) and listed 1m UAE 1,000 Guineas winner Siyaadah and the 2-y-o 1m and subsequent US Grade 3 winner Strathnaver. The second dam, River Belle (by Lahib), won the Group 3 6f Princess Margaret Stakes and the US Grade 2 8.5f Mrs Revere Stakes, was Grade 1 placed and is a half-sister to 5 winners including the Group 2 Italian 1,000 Guineas third Kiralik.

591. ROSEBRIDE
b.f. Mayson – Wedding Party (Groom Dancer). March 24. Half-sister to the very useful 7f winner and triple listed-placed Party Doctor (by Dr Fong), to the German listed-placed Dream Wedding (by Medicean), the fair 5f to 7f winner First Knight (by Kyllachy) and the modest 2-y-o 5f winner Wedlock (by Pivotal). The dam, a quite useful 6f and 7f winner, was listed-placed and is a half-sister to 4 winners including the Group 2 May Hill Stakes winner Pollenator. The second dam, Ceanothus (by Bluebird), was placed over 7f and 12f and is a half-sister to 4 winners including the US Grade 2 12f Orchid Handicap and Grade 3 8.5f Suwannee River Handicap winner Golden Pond.

592. RUBIESNPEARLS
b.f. Kyllachy – Piece Of Cake (Exceed And Excel). February 1. First foal. €75,000Y. Goffs Orby. Norman Steel. The dam, a modest 6f placed maiden, is a half-sister to 6 winners including the useful 2-y-o 6f winner and Group 2 May Hill Stakes second High Heel

Sneakers. The second dam, Sundae Girl (by Green Dancer), a fair 2-y-o 6f winner, is a half-sister to 6 winners including the Peruvian champion Faaz.

593. SENATOR
ch.c. Frankel – Red Bloom (Selkirk). April 7. Half-brother to the fairly useful 10f to 12f winner of 5 races Vasily (by Sadler's Wells) and to the fair 9.5f winner Sea The Bloom (by Sea The Stars). The dam, winner of the Group 1 Fillies' Mile and Group 2 10f Blandford Stakes (twice), is a full or half-sister to 4 winners including the listed winner Red Gala. The second dam, Red Camellia (by Polar Falcon), winner of the Group 3 7f Prestige Stakes, was third in the French 1,000 Guineas and is a half-sister to 4 winners. (Cheveley Park Stud).

594. SPIN DOCTOR ♠
ch.f. Mayson – Doctor's Glory (Elmaamul). May 10. Half-sister to numerous winners including the very useful Group 3 9f and triple listed 1m winner Clinical (by Motivator), the smart Group 3 7f Horris Hill Stakes winner of 7 races Cupid's Glory, the fairly useful 7f (at 2 yrs) and listed 1m and 10f winner Courting, the fairly useful listed 6f winner of 5 races Prescription (by Pivotal), the fair 2-y-o dual 5f winner Bridal Path (by Groom Dancer) and the Scandinavian listed winner Magnificence (by Sadler's Wells). The dam, a fairly useful 5.2f (at 2 yrs) and 6f winner, is a half-sister to 6 winners including the useful On Call, a listed winner of 7 races at up to 2m. The second dam, Doctor Bid (by Spectacular Bid), is an unraced half-sister to the Group 3 Prix Thomas Bryon winner Glory Forever.

595. STARLIGHT ROMANCE (IRE)
b.f. Excelebration – Takizada (Sendawar). February 3. Second foal. €110,000Y. Goffs Orby. Norman Steel. The dam, placed from 1m to 10.5f, is a half-sister to 7 winners including the US dual Grade 2 and Group 3 12f Meld Stakes winner Takarian, the listed 12f Galtres Stakes winner and dual Group 2 third Tanoura, the Group 2 Royal Whip Stakes Takali and the Group 3 Minstrel Stakes winner Takar. The second dam, Takarouna (by Green Dancer), won the Group 2 12f Pretty Polly Stakes and is a sister to the smart Group 2 Dante Stakes winner Torjoun and a half-sister to 4 winners.

596. SHOW ME THE MUSIC
b.f. Dubawi – Music Show (Noverre). April 14. First foal. The dam won 5 races including the Group 1 Falmouth Stakes and the Group 2 Rockfel Stakes and is a half-sister to the useful winner and triple listed-placed Fantasia Girl. The second dam, Dreamboat (by Mr Prospector), a fair 7f winner, is a sister to the French listed-placed winner Sweetheart and a half-sister to 5 winners including the listed 7f Prix Imprudence winner and Group 2 placed Stunning.

597. SIX STRINGS
b.c. Requinto – Island Music (Mujahid). April 6. Third foal. €50,000Y. Goffs Orby. A O'Ryan / R Fahey. Half-brother to the modest 2-y-o dual 6f winner Chetan (by Alfred Nobel). The dam, a far 7f winner, is a half-sister to one winner. The second dam, Ischia (by Lion Cavern), a modest 7.5f placed maiden, is a half-sister to 7 winners.

598. SOBRIETY
ch.c. Dutch Art – Purity (Pivotal). March 27. Fourth foal. Half-brother to the fair 2015 2-y-o 7f winner Notary (by Lawman). The dam is an unraced half-sister to the Group 1 Lockinge Stakes winner Virtual and a half-sister to 6 winners including the Group 2 Coventry Stakes winner Iceman. The second dam, Virtuous (by Exit To Nowhere), a fairly useful 2-y-o 1m winner, was third in the listed 11.5f Oaks Trial and is a half-sister to 3 winners. (Cheveley Park Stud).

599. SPRINGWOOD
ch.c. Zebedee – Nasharaat (Green Desert). March 22. Fourth foal. £26,000Y. Doncaster Premier. RF Racing Ltd. Half-brother to the quite useful Irish 6f and 7f winner Trinity Force (by Iffraaj) and to modest 1m winner Wolf Spirit (by Amadeus Wolf). The dam, a minor Irish 7f winner, is a half-sister to 5 winners including the listed second Qalahari. The second dam, Daqtora (by Dr Devious), a minor Irish 11f winner, is a half-sister to 7 winners including the 2-y-o Group 1 1m National Stakes winner Mus-If and the winner of three listed events Jammaal.

600. STARLITE SIENNA (IRE)
b.f. Elusive Pimpernel – Devious Diva (Dr Devious). February 23. Sixth foal. €34,000Y.

Tattersalls Ireland September. F Barberini / N Bradley. Half-sister to the Group 3 7f Sceptre Stakes and listed 1m winner Realtra (by Dark Angel). The dam, a minor 7f winner in Ireland at 2 yrs, is a half-sister to 8 winners. The second dam, Dawn Chorus (by Mukaddamah), is an unraced half-sister to 6 winners.

601. VATICAN HILL (IRE)
b.c. Canford Cliffs – Empress Ella (Holy Roman Emperor). March 22. Second foal. £35,000Y. Doncaster Premier. Robin O'Ryan. The dam is an unplaced half-sister to 2 winners. The second dam, Bella Bella (by Sri Pekan), a quite useful dual 7f winner, is a half-sister to 5 winners including the German listed winner and Group 3 third Silk Petal (herself dam of the listed winner Star Tulip) and the dam of the Group 2 winners Tashawak and Fairy Queen.

602. VAULTED
b.f. Kyllachy – Palatial (Green Desert). March 20. Tenth foal. Half-sister to 6 winners including the Group 2 1m May Hill Stakes (at 2 yrs) and Group 2 1m Windsor Forest Stakes winner and 1,000 Guineas second Spacious (by Nayef), to the Canadian Grade 2 7f winner Dimension (by Medicean), the useful 7f (at 2 yrs) and 1m winner Artimino (by Medicean), the fair 11.5f winner Ye Hade Ye Dalil (by Raven's Pass), the fair 6f winner Spice Run (by Zafonic). The dam, a useful 7f winner of 4 races at 2 and 3 yrs, is a half-sister to 7 winners including the listed 10f winners Portal and Ice Palace. The second dam, White Palace (by Shirley Heights), was a quite useful 3-y-o 8.2f winner. (Cheveley Park Stud).

603. VENTURA JAZZ
br.f. Dandy Man – Aljafliyah (Halling). April 30. Eighth foal. £45,000Y. Doncaster Premier. Middleham Park Racing. Half-sister to the fairly useful dual 6f (at 2 yrs), 2m and hurdles winner Waltz Darling (by Iffraaj), to the fairly useful 2-y-o 5f and 6f winner The Only Boss and the fairly useful dual 6f winner Championship (both by Exceed And Excel). The dam is an unplaced half-sister to 5 winners including the US stakes winner and Grade 2 placed Sohgol. The second dam, Arruhan (by Mujtahid), a quite useful 5f (at 2 yrs) and 7f winner, is a half-sister to 5 winners including the smart listed 7f winner Royal Storm.

CHARLIE FELLOWES

604. BEAUCHAMP OPAL ★★
b.f. Pastoral Pursuits – Orange Sunset (Roanoke). April 18. Half-sister to the quite useful dual 1m winner French Art (by Peintre Celebre) and to the fair 1m to 12f winner of 5 races Ssafa (by Motivator). The dam won 5 races including listed events in Ireland (over 12f) and the USA and was third in the Grade 2 La Prevoyante Handicap. She is a half-sister to 3 winners out of the unplaced Classical Flair (by Riverman), herself a half-sister to 6 winners. (Erik Penser). *"A small, strong filly, she came in very late but I'd expect her to catch up pretty quickly. She looks like a 2-y-o through and through, we'll see her on the track in June I should imagine and she's doing well".*

605. CRYPTONITE (IRE) ★★★
br.c. Dark Angel – Bowness (Efisio). April 26. Fifth foal. €120,000Y. Goffs Orby. Charlie Gordon-Watson. Closely related to the fair 2-y-o 6f winner Luna Mission (by Acclamation). The dam, a quite useful 5f and 6f winner, was third in the listed 5f Land O'Burns Stakes and is a half-sister to 3 winners including the Group 2 5f King's Stand Stakes and Group 3 5f Cornwallis Stakes Dominica. The second dam, Dominio (by Dominion), a 2-y-o listed 5f winner, was second in the Group 2 5f Temple Stakes and is a half-sister to 6 winners including the very smart Group 1 5f Nunthorpe Stakes winner Ya Malak. (Mr C Bacon). *"A strong, bullock of a horse. The ease with which he's doing his exercise is almost fooling me into thinking he's early and I don't think he is. A good-looking colt, I'm pleased with him but not rushing him. A lovely, big, strong, black horse".*

606. CRYSTAL STANZA ★★
b.g. Poet's Voice – Clear Impression (Danehill). February 28. Sixth foal. 12,000Y. Tattersalls October Book 2. Charlie Fellowes / Charlie Gordon-Watson. Half-brother to the fair 6f winner of 6 races Pettochside (by Refuse To Bend) and to two minor winners abroad by Dubawi and Dubai Destination. The dam, a fairly useful 3-y-o 6f winner, was listed-placed three times and is a half-sister to 2 winners. The second dam, Shining Hour (by Red Ransom), won the Group 3 5f Queen Mary Stakes and is a full or half-sister to 7 winners.

"A small, strong horse with a mind of his own, I gelded him and I think that will help him a huge amount. I would expect him to be out in the first half of the season".

607. GENTLE WHISPER ★★★
b.f. Lawman – Speak Softly To Me (Ogygian). April 18. Fourteenth foal. 42,000Y. Tattersalls December. Charlie Gordon-Watson. Half-sister to the minor US stakes winner and Grade 3 placed High Maintenance (by Danehill), to the fairly useful Irish 7f winner and listed-placed Charlotte Bronte, the quite useful 2-y-o 7f winner Snow Mountain (both by Danehill Dancer) and the fair 11f, 12f and hurdles winner Contra Mundum (by Giant's Causeway). The dam is an unraced half-sister to 8 winners including the dam of the Group 1 winners Green Tune and Pas de Reponse. The second dam, Ocean's Answer (by Northern Answer), a stakes winner in Canada, is a half-sister to Storm Bird. (Mrs E Capon). *"She's a small, compact little filly, really good-looking and she'll be a 2-y-o. She's cantering away and I'd be hopeful that she'd be out around May/June time".*

608. HIGH ON LOVE ★★★
br.f. Requinto – Cant Hurry Love (Desert Prince). March 20. Fifth foal. €42,000Y. Tattersalls Ireland September. Charlie Gordon-Watson. Half-sister to the fair 9f winner Intent (by Jeremy) and to the modest 2-y-o 6f winner Reflected Love (by Mujadil). The dam is an unraced half-sister to 3 winners including the Irish listed winner and Group 2 placed Mister Tee. The second dam, Clipper (by Salse), a useful 1m winner (at 2 yrs) and listed placed over 10f, is a half-sister to 5 winners including the dam of the Oaks winner Talent. (Equine Enthusiasts). *"A lovely filly, she's the most forward of my 2-y-o's and I've backed off her now after one piece of work. She could well be out by the end of April, I'm delighted with her so far and she's just a good-looking, forward filly. As a yearling I think she was the best walker of the sales season – she just has this fantastic walk on her and she's the same when cantering".*

609. JUPITER ASCENDING ★★
b.c. Excelebration – Habita (Montjeu). February 3. First foal. 80,000Y. Tattersalls October Book 1. Charlie Gordon-Watson. The dam is an unraced half-sister to 6 winners including the Singapore Gold Cup and Gran Premio del Jockey Club winner Kutub, the Irish 2-y-o listed 9f winner On The Nile and the Irish listed 1m winner In The Limelight. The second dam, Minnie Habit (Habitat), an Irish 4-y-o 9f winner, is closely related to the 5f Curragh Stakes and 6f Railway Stakes winner Bermuda Classic (herself dam of the Coronation Stakes winner Shake The Yoke and the Phoenix Sprint Stakes winner Tropical) and a half-sister to 6 winners. (Mr C Bacon). *"A really attractive, scopey colt. He's very good-looking and couldn't be doing any better at the moment, but he's one for the back-end of the season and next year".*

610. SCUDDING (USA) ★★★
b.f. Mizzen Mast – Pearl In The Sand (Footstepsinthesand). March 23. First foal. 20,000Y. Tattersalls December. Not sold. The dam, a fairly useful Irish maiden, was placed three times at 2 yrs including in a listed 6f event at the Curragh and is a sister to one winner and a half-sister to the useful 2-y-o dual 5f winner and Group 2 5f Norfolk Stakes second Reckless Reward (by Choisir). The second dam, Champagne Toni (by Second Empire), ran unplaced twice and is a half-sister to 9 winners including the smart Group 3 6f Prix de Meautry winner Andreyev. (W McAlpin). *"She's as tough as old boots and she'll be one of our earliest fillies. She was late coming in but she caught up and I could work her now if I wanted her to, but I'm just holding on to her. She'll be out by late April I should think, she has a lovely attitude and always wants to be at the head of the pack".*
TRAINERS' BARGAIN BUY

611. SENTINEL ★★★
b.c. Sepoy – Baralinka (Barathea). March 15. Half-brother to the fairly useful 2-y-o listed 5f winner of 3 races Marlinka, to the fair 1m winner State Fair (both by Marju), the quite useful 5f and 6f winner of 6 races Searchlight (by Kyllachy) and the fair 2-y-o dual 1m winner Finbar (by Nayef). The dam, a useful 5f (at 2 yrs) and triple 6f winner, is a half-sister to the Group 1 Fillies Mile, Falmouth Stakes, Sussex Stakes and Matron Stakes winner Soviet Song (by Marju). The second dam,

Kalinka (by Soviet Star), a quite useful 7f winner, is a half-sister to 2 winners. (Elite Racing Club). *"He's exactly what you'd expect him to look like. He's by a sprinter and out of a very good sprinting family of Elite Racing's – and he's a sprinter too. A small, compact, strong colt and he's going to be a 2-y-o. He'll be racing by mid-season".*

612. ZAIN STAR (IRE) ★★★★
b.c. Shamardal – Astrologie (Polish Precedent). February 12. Third foal. 115,000Y. Tattersalls December. Charlie Gordon-Watson. Half-brother to the quite useful dual 10f winner Barreesh (by Giant's Causeway) and to the French 10.5f winner San Sicario (by Smart Strike). The dam, a French listed 11f and 12f winner, was Grade 3 placed in the USA and is a half-sister to 4 winners including the Group 2 10f Prix Greffulhe winner Quest For Honor. The second dam, Quest For Ladies (by Rainbow Quest), a US listed stakes winner, is a half-sister to 4 winners including the dam of the French Derby winner Blue Canari. (Mr A Al Banwan). *"A big, strong colt I bought in December, he has a lovely, laid-back attitude and does everything well. Because he came in late he's a bit behind a few of them but he's cantering and he's not backward. A July/August type hopefully".*

613. UNNAMED ★★★★ ♠
b.c. Dark Angel – And Again (In The Wings). March 19. Fourth foal. 180,000Y. Tattersalls October Book 1. Charlie Gordon-Watson. Half-brother to Rehearse (by Big Bad Bob), last of four over 7f on his only start at 2 yrs in 2015 and to the minor French 4-y-o winner of 3 races Dylanelle (by Dylan Thomas). The dam, a quite useful 10f and 12f winner, is a half-sister to 5 winners including the Group 1 9f Prix Jean Prat winner Olden Times and the useful listed 6f winner and Group 1 Cheveley Park Stakes third Festoso. The second dam, Garah (by Ajdal), a very useful winner of 4 races over 6f, was third in the Group 2 Temple Stakes and is a half-sister to 6 winners. *"Probably the most forward of my colts, he finds everything easy and although he's not very big he has a beautiful action. He really covers the ground for a small horse and I hope he'll be ready to race in May".*

614. UNNAMED ★★★
b.c. Mayson – Danceatdusk (Desert Prince). May 20. Half-brother to the fair 2015 2-y-o 6f winner Red Artist (by Archipenko), to the quite useful 2-y-o 7f winner Ninita (by Storming Home), the fair 2-y-o 5f winner Speed The Plough (by Kyllachy) and the modest 6f winner Ooi Long (by Echo Of Light). The dam is an unraced half-sister to 8 winners including the smart 1m (at 2 yrs) and listed 10f winner Island Sound and the smart 1m winner and Group 3 1m Joel Stakes third Fair Trade. The second dam, Ballet (by Sharrood), a moderate 5f and 6f placed maiden, is a half-sister to 10 winners including the May Hill Stakes winner Satinette. *"He's a funny little horse because he came in very late after having had a few temperament issues early on, but after being broken in he's incredibly straightforward. Cantering away now, he's quite slight and not a big, powerful colt. The mare has done well, with four winners from four foals, and this colt has all the attributes to continue that run. Straightforward, athletic, enjoys his work and looks like he'll make a nice 2-y-o".*

615. UNNAMED ★★★★
b.c. Invincible Spirit – Doula (Gone West). February 21. Eleventh foal. 250,000Y. Tattersalls October Book 1. Charlie Gordon-Watson. Brother the 2-y-o 7f winner (on his only start here) Better Announce and half-brother to 4 winners including the listed-placed dual 7f (at 2 yrs) to 10f winner Humungous (by Giant's Causeway), the useful Irish 11f winner and dual Group 3 placed Amazing Beauty (by Galileo) and the minor US winner of 3 races Dixie King (by Dixie Union). The dam, a minor US 3-y-o turf winner, is a half-sister to the US Grade 2 winner Cat Chat (dam of the US Grade 2 winner In Lingerie) and to the dam of the US Grade 1 winner Dixie Chatter. The second dam, Phone Chatter (by Phone Trick), was a dual US Grade 1 winner. *"If there's a top-class horse in this bunch he's probably the one. He's a beautiful, scopey individual that just exudes quality. He won't be early and will probably start off in a maiden in the autumn. He's doing everything right, doing plenty of cantering and I really like him".*

616. UNNAMED ★★
b.c. Vale Of York – Dubai Pearl (Refuse To Bend). April 16. Second foal. 21,000Y. Tattersalls October Book 3. Not sold. Half-brother to the unplaced 2015 2-y-o Alzebarh (by Poet's Voice). The dam is an unraced half-sister to one minor winner. The second dam, Caribbean Pearl (by Silver Hawk), a fair 10f and 12f winner, is a half-sister to the Group 3 7f Criterion Stakes winner Racer Forever. (M Obaida). *"Physically he's not the most impressive horse in the world, but he has a fantastic attitude and temperament. He enjoys his work and he's improving, filling out and strengthening all the time. Not the biggest or the strongest, but if his attitude is anything to go by he'll do alright".*

617. UNNAMED ★★★
b.f. Lawman – Ellbeedee (Dalakhani). March 12. Second foal. Half-sister to the quite useful 2015 2-y-o listed-placed 6f winner Bournemouth Belle (by Canford Cliffs). The dam, a fair 10f winner, is a half-sister to 6 winners including the French 2-y-o 1m winner and subsequent US Grade 2 San Clemente Handicap and Grade 2 San Gorgonio Handicap winner Uncharted Haven. The second dam, Tochar Ban (by Assert), a quite useful 10f winner, is a half-sister to 6 winners including the listed Italian winner Isticanna (herself dam of the Group 2 Royal Whip Stakes winner Chancellor). (Saleh Al Homaizi & Imad Al Sagar). *"She's nice. She's a madam but she's doing really well. She was fooling me into thinking she's earlier than she actually is, but that's a good sign because you want them to be doing it easier than they should be. She'll be one for mid-season and I really like the way she's finding everything so far".*

618. UNNAMED ★★
b.c. Holy Roman Emperor – Flambeau (Oasis Dream). February 26. First foal. 200,000Y. Tattersalls October Book 2. Charlie Gordon-Watson. The dam, a very useful listed 7f winner and second in the Group 3 Chartwell Stakes, is a half-sister to 5 winners. The second dam, Flavian (by Catrail), a fairly useful 6f (at 2 yrs) and 7f winner, is a half-sister to 7 winners. *"A beautiful horse, he's a big, strong colt but I'm not sure if he'll run in this country because he has a Hong Kong owner. At best, he may just have the odd run at the back-end. He cost 200 Grand and looking at him you can see why".*

619. UNNAMED ★★
b.c. Mawatheeq – Tasheyaat (Sakhee). April 18. Second foal. €12,000Y. Tattersalls Ireland September. Charlie Gordon-Watson. Half-brother to Samaawy (by Alhaarth), unplaced in one start at 2 yrs in 2015. The dam, a quite useful 10f winner, is a half-sister to 5 winners including the useful listed 6f winner Judhoor and the fairly useful 7f and 1m winner. The second dam, Almurooj (by Zafonic), a moderate 5f and 6f placed maiden, is a half-sister to 7 winners, notably the 2,000 Guineas and Champion Stakes winner Haafhd. (Mr S bin Khalifa Al Kuwari). *"He's the one that's improved the most since they came in from the yearling sales. He was a frame of a horse and a bit plain, but he's a lovely, strong colt now. He's one for the second half of the year and is turning into a really good-looking horse".*

JAMES GIVEN

620. ALFONSO MANANA ★★
ch.c. Dutch Art – Chance For Romance (Entrepreneur). April 16. Seventh foal. £17,000Y. Doncaster November. Not sold. Half-brother to the quite useful triple 5f winner Noble Asset (by Compton Place), to the fair 6f (including at 2 yrs) and 5f winner of 7 races Kylladdie (by Kyllachy) and a winner in Germany and Italy by Cadeaux Genereux). The dam, a fair 2-y-o 5.5f winner, is a half-sister to 12 winners including the 2-y-o Group 3 5f Queen Mary Stakes winners Romantic Myth and Romantic Liason. The second dam, My First Romance (Danehill), ran twice unplaced and is a half-sister to 6 minor winners here and abroad. (Mrs S Oliver). *"He's going to take a bit of time, but he certainly gives the feeling that he's physically developing into what looks like a proper sprinter. So he's a slowly maturing type but I think Dutch Art's can be that way. Not a big colt, but he's developing a powerful body".*

621. DUSKY MAID (IRE) ★★★
b.f. Dark Angel – Dream Scape (Oasis Dream). February 21. First foal. £62,000Y. Doncaster Premier. A & E Bloodstock. The dam, a fair

3-y-o 9f winner, is out of the fair 2-y-o 9f winner Whatizzit (by Galileo), herself a half-sister to 5 winners including the useful 7f (at 2 yrs), listed 1m and Italian Group 3 1m winner Whazzis and the listed Chesham Stakes winner Whazzat. (Cool Silk Partnership). *"A strong filly that's taking a little bit of time to come to hand. She's a mid-summer type 2-y-o and just pulling herself now, although she's done plenty of conditioning work and just needs to get fitter. Despite the fact she's by Dark Angel there is some stamina in the pedigree but I should imagine she'll start off at six furlongs".*

622. JURASSIC ★★
b.f. Rock Of Gibraltar – Confusion (Anabaa). January 26. First foal. The dam, a minor French 3-y-o winner, is a half-sister to 3 other minor winners. The second dam, Red Stella (by Nureyev), a French listed 12f winner, is a half-sister to Special Quest (Group 1 Criterium de Saint-Cloud) and Moiava (Group 2 Criterium de Maisons-Laffitte). (Fishdance & Tony Hirschfeld). *"A home-bred, she's a good-topped, strong type and coming to hand steadily. Probably one for the mid-summer over six/seven furlongs – we don't know enough about her yet to really say, but I would guess that's where we'll be at".*

623. LITTLE MISS LUCKY (IRE) ★★★ ♠
b.f. Clodovil – Lucky Leigh (Piccolo). February 6. Third foal. 19,000Y. Tattersalls October Book 3. Stroud/Coleman & J Given. Sister to the French listed-placed 2-y-o 5f to 6.5f winner of 3 races Something Lucky. The dam, a fairly useful dual 5f winner (including at 2 yrs), was fourth in the Group 2 Queen Mary Stakes and is a full or half-sister to three modest 2-y-o winners. The second dam, Solmorin (by Fraam), is an unplaced half-sister to 2 minor winners. (P Foster & Friends). *"A proper sharp-looking 2-y-o type, she 'does what it says on the tin'. A very strong pocket-rocket for five furlongs, she has quite a good 2-y-o sprinting pedigree".*

624. MIA TIA ★★★
ch.f. Equiano – Tia Mia (Dr Fong). February 28. Fourth foal. £20,000Y. Doncaster Premier. Cool Silk Partnership, Stroud & Coleman. Half-sister to two winners in Sweden by Mount Nelson. The dam, a fairly useful listed-placed 2-y-o 5f winner, is a half-sister to 4 winners. The second dam, Giusina Mia (by Diesis), won once over 10f in Italy and is a half-sister to 4 winners. (Cool Silk Partnership). *"We trained the dam to win first time out and then she was listed-placed at York. This filly is a slightly bigger version at this time of their lives than her mother, she's done quite a lot of conditioning work but won't be out any time soon. Mid-summer onwards will be her time and I would think she'll be a sharp type like her mother".*

625. MIGHTASWELLSMILE ★★★
b.f. Elnadim – Intishaar (Dubai Millennium). February 6. Seventh foal. 6,000Y. Tattersalls October Book 3. Tim Bostwick. Half-sister to the quite useful 10f winner Tabjeel (by Sakhee), to the fair 2-y-o 6f winner Bairam (by Haafhd) and the fair 7f and 8.5f winner Zaaneh (by Aqlaam). The dam is an unraced half-sister to 2 winners. The second dam, Bint Shadayid (by Nashwan), a very useful winner of the Group 3 7f Prestige Stakes, was placed in the 1,000 Guineas and the Fillies Mile and is a half-sister to 7 winners including the smart listed 10f winner Imtiyaz. (Mr Tim Bostwick). *"A very sharp filly with a sweet nature, she's quick and gallops very well. She was bought with a view to racing her early and trying to sell her on. To look at her you'd think she'd improve as the months go on, but she's doing well now".* **TRAINERS' BARGAIN BUY**

626. PAQUITA BAILARINA ★★
ch.f. Paco Boy – Prima Ballerina (Pivotal). February 16. Fourth foal. 3,500Y. Doncaster November. James Given. Half-sister to the fair 5f winner of 5 races from 2 to 6 yrs Boxing Shadows (by Camacho) and to the fair 7f and 1m winner Playtothewhistle (by Sakhee's Secret). The dam is an unplaced half-sister to 2 winners including the German triple Group 3 placed Keep Cool. The second dam, Kirov (by Darshaan), a quite useful 1m winner, is a half-sister to 6 winners including the UAE Group 2 winner and Group 1 placed Bankable and the Group 3 10f winner Cheshire. (R C Spore). *"Quite a sweet filly, she's going to take a bit of time but her dam has already bred two winners rated 70+. There's a fair amount of stamina in the family and Paco Boy doesn't seem to have injected too much precocity. She'll be one for the mid to late summer as*

she's grown an awful lot and needs to fill her frame now".

627. SAVANNAH SLEW ★★★★
b.f. Kheleyf – Saratoga Slew (Footstepsinthesand). March 31. First foal. The dam, a fair 7f winner, is a half-sister to 3 winners including the French winner of 8 races (including twice at 2 yrs over 6f) Wild Horse (by Kheleyf). The second dam, Life Rely (by Maria's Mon), is an unraced half-sister to 3 winners including the Group 1 Italian Oaks winner and Group 1 Moyglare Stud Stakes third Menhoubah. (Dachel Stud). *"A home-bred, she has entries already and should be racing in April. She's going very well, she's really sharp and is a big, shiny, healthy-looking filly. Well-muscled and quite masculine, we like her quite a bit, but we have to keep on the right side of her a bit – maybe that's the Kheleyf influence coming out. Quick to learn and speedy".*

628. STARBOARD WATCH ★★★
bl.f. Harbour Watch – Makhsusah (Darshaan). February 3. Eighth foal. Tattersalls October Book 3. Half-sister to the useful 2-y-o 6f and 7f and subsequent US stakes winner Market Day (by Tobougg), to the quite useful 2-y-o 1m, 9f and subsequent winner Wild Rose (by Doyen), the quite useful 9.5f and 10f winner Arabian Heights (by Araafa), the modest 6f winner Motivated Choice (by Compton Place) and a minor winner at 4 yrs in France by Lomitas. The dam is an unraced half-sister to 9 winners here and abroad. The second dam, Zephyrine (by Highest Honor), is an unraced half-sister to 3 winners including Mutamam (Grade 1 Canadian International). (McGoldrick Racing). *"She's a nice filly, quite big and although she only came in late she's catching up pleasingly. She'll make a 2-y-o before mid-season I should think".*

629. STREET JAZZ ★★★
b.f. Acclamation – Wake Up Call (Noverre). January 28. First foal. £75,000Y. Doncaster Premier. Cool Silk Partnership, Stroud & Coleman. The dam, a fairly useful 6f and 7f winner of 4 races at 3 and 4 yrs, was listed-placed and is a half-sister to 6 winners and to the dams of the Group/Graded stakes winner Summer Fete and Up In Time. The second

dam, Up And About (by Barathea), a fair 14.8f winner, is a half-sister to 8 winners including the listed winner and Group 1 placed Musicanna. (Cool Silk Partnership). *"Similar to my 2-y-o filly Dusky Maid in that she's taking a bit of time to come to hand and they're both at a similar stage. They're both nice, sharp-looking 2-y-o's that haven't quite come to hand yet but are in the process of doing so".*

630. TAWNY PORT ★★★
ch.c. Arcano – Tawaasul (Haafhd). February 3. First foal. 15,000foal. Tattersalls December. Not sold. The dam, a fair 1m winner, is a half-sister to 2 winners. The second dam, Muwakleh (by Machiavellian), winner of the UAE 1,000 Guineas and second in the Newmarket 1,000 Guineas, is a sister to the Dubai World Cup and Prix Jean Prat winner Almutawakel and to the useful 10f winner Elmustanser and a half-sister to the smart 10f winner Inaaq. (Lovely Bubbly Racing). *"He's the absolute opposite of what you might expect a first foal to be. He's very strong, looks like a 3-y-o already and he's working now so he could well be racing in late April. He's a good moving colt with a really nice temperament and although we'll be starting him at five furlongs he could well stay further than that in time".*

631. TRUE ROMANCE (IRE) ★★
gr.c. Mastercraftsman – Full Of Love (Hawk Wing). May 12. The dam, a quite useful dual 1m winner, is a half-sister to one winner. The second dam, Charmingly (by King Of Kings), is an unplaced half-sister to 7 winners including the Group 3 third Charlock. (Suzanne & Nigel Williams). *"A well-proportioned, balanced colt, he was a late foal and is just taking a bit of time. The expectation is that he'll make a seven furlong 2-y-o later on".*

632. WARM OASIS ★★★
gr.c. Oasis Dream – Warling (Montjeu). January 29. Second foal. 200,000Y. Tattersalls October Book 1. Cool Silk Partnership. Brother to the fairly useful 2015 2-y-o 7f winner Hayadh. The dam, a fairly useful 11f winner, is closely related to the French 2-y-o 10f winner of 3 races and Group 3 Prix Exbury second War Is War and a half-sister to 3 winners. The second dam, Walkamia (by Linamix), won the Group 3 10.5f Prix Fille de l'Air and is a sister

to 2 winners including the Group 2 11f Prix Noailles winner Walk On Mix and a half-sister to 8 winners. (Cool Silk Partnership). *"I'm told that his full-brother who won in June on his debut last year is quite a compact, Oasis Dream type, but this colt is much more like the damsire Montjeu and he won't be winning so early. A big horse, he's rangy but he is a good mover. We won't be seeing him until the back-end over seven furlongs or a mile".*

633. YES YOU ★★
ch.f. Choisir – Mexican Milly (Noverre). April 20. Second foal. Half-sister to the fair 6f to 1m placed maiden Arms Around Me (by Lope De Vega). The dam, a modest dual 6f placed 2-y-o, is a half-sister to a winner in Italy out of the moderate 1m placed maiden Forest Bride (by Woodman). (Suzanne & Nigel Williams). *"A small, compact, sharp 2-y-o type that's come to hand quickly, she knows her job and she's sensible and speedy. She'll be racing in mid-April".*

634. UNNAMED ★★★
b.f. Bated Breath – Cesseras (Cape Cross). February 13. Second foal. 6,000Y. Tattersalls October Book 3. Stroud/Coleman & James Given. The dam, a minor French 3-y-o winner, is a sister to the smart 6f, 7f (both at 2 yrs) and Group 3 9f Darley Stakes winner and Group 1 1m Racing Post Trophy second Charlie Farnsbarns and a half-sister to 2 minor winners. The second dam, Lafleur (by Grand Lodge), is an unplaced half-sister to 10 winners including the listed winners and Group 1 placed Crown Of Light and Alboostan. *"I bought three yearlings in the autumn with a view to getting them out early, hopefully seeing them run well and finding an owner for them. This filly is one of them and she's a smallish, compact, strong 2-y-o type that's coming along nicely".*

JOHN GOSDEN

635. ALMUKALA (IRE) ★★
b.c. Invincible Spirit – Vedela (Selkirk). February 7. Third foal. Half-brother to the 2015 French 7f placed 2-y-o Sea Of Knowledge (by Sea The Stars). The dam is an unraced half-sister to 3 winners including Vadamar (Group 2 Grand Prix de Deauville) and the French listed winner Vedouma. The second dam, Vadawina (by Unfuwain), won the Group 1 Prix Saint-Alary winner and is a half-sister to 6 winners including the French Group 3 winners Vadapolina and Vazira. *"A neat colt, but on the dam's side he's not bred to be precocious so I think he's more of a mid-season 2-y-o".*

636. ASKING PRICE (USA) ★★
b.f. First Defence – Price Tag (Dansili). March 27. The dam, a French 2-y-o 7f and subsequent US Grade 1 1m Matriarch Stakes winner, is a sister to the very useful 7f (at 2 yrs) and 10f winner Labarinto and half-sister to 3 winners. The second dam, Tarocchi (by Affirmed), a minor French 10.5f winner, is a half-sister to numerous winners including Privity (Group 2 12f Prix de Malleret) and Zindari (Group 3 9f Prix Saint Roman). (Khalid Abdulla). *"A mid-season type 2-y-o, promising at this stage but it's early days yet".*

637. AURORA GOLD ★★
b.f. Frankel – Midsummer (Kingmambo). April 19. Ninth foal. Half-sister to the high-class racemare Midday, a winner of six Group 1 races (Breeders' Cup Filly & Mare Turf, Prix Vermeille, Yorkshire Oaks and Nassau Stakes (three times)), to the fairly useful 10f winner Shoal, the fair 10f winner Popular (all by Oasis Dream), the smart 1m (at 2 yrs) and Group 3 7f winner and Group 1 Nassau Stakes third Hot Snap (by Pivotal) and the useful listed-placed 10f and 12f winner Midsummer Sun (by Monsun). The dam, a quite useful listed-placed 11f winner, is a half-sister to the Oaks and Fillies Mile winner Reams of Verse and the Eclipse Stakes and Phoenix Champion Stakes winner Elmaamul. The second dam, Modena (by Roberto), is an unraced half-sister to the dam of Zafonic. (Khalid Abdulla). *"A smallish filly, I don't dislike her at all but the dam won over a trip so it's much more of a 3-y-o pedigree. For this season she's a seven furlong/mile prospect for August onwards".*

638. BIZZARRIA ★★★
ch.f. Lemon Drop Kid – Lynnwood Chase (Horse Chestnut). May 16. Sixth foal. 80,000Y. Tattersalls October Book 1. Not sold. Sister to the very smart Grade 1 12f Canadian International and Group 3 10f Tercentenary Stakes winner Cannock Chase, to the very

smart Group 2 10f Prix Eugene Adam and Group 3 10f Tercentenary Stakes winner Pisco Sour and the jumps winner Ultravox. The dam is a placed half-sister to 5 winners including the UAE Group 2 and Irish Group 3 Ballycorus Stakes winner Lord Admiral. The second dam, Lady Ilsley (by Trempolino), a winner in France and listed-placed twice, is a sister to the winner and Grade 2 second Najecam (herself dam of the Grade 1 Breeders' Cup Juvenile winner Action This Day) and a half-sister to 5 winners. *"She's very typical of the sire and be will wanting to run in a mile maiden for fillies in the autumn. She's a promising filly, medium–sized with a good attitude".*

639. CHIPPENHAM (IRE) ★★★
ch.c. Casamento – Ohiyesa (Noverre). January 30. Third foal. £140,000Y. Doncaster Premier. Blandford Bloodstock. Half-brother to the minor Italian 2-y-o winner Estate Fanese (by Blu Air Force). The dam, a fairly useful Irish 6f winner, was listed-placed twice and is a half-sister to 2 winners. The second dam, Crohal Di San Jore (by Saddlers' Hall), placed in France and Italy, is a half-sister to 5 winners. *"He's a nice type of horse with a good attitude and he moves well. Looks like a horse that'll want a mile in the autumn and I can see him running in September".*

640. CIRCLE D'OR ★★
b.f. Acclamation – Fleche D'Or (Dubai Destination). May 9. Fourth foal. Half-sister to the top-class Derby, Eclipse, Irish Champion Stakes and Prix de l'Arc de Triomphe winner Golden Horn (by Cape Cross) and to the listed 10f winner Eastern Belle (by Champs Elysees). The dam is an unraced half-sister to 10 winners including the Group 1 1m Coronation Stakes winner Rebecca Sharp, the Group 3 11.5f Lingfield Derby Trial winner Mystic Knight and the listed 11.4f Cheshire Oaks winner Hidden Hope. The second dam, Nuryana (by Nureyev), a useful winner of the listed 1m Grand Metropolitan Stakes, is a half-sister to 5 winners. *"She's just doing nice, normal canters at this stage. Her brother showed me a fair bit at two, but we're being patient with her and I'd expect to see her running in the autumn".*

641. CLEARLY ★★★
b.f. Invincible Spirit – Concordia (Pivotal). March 13. Third foal. Half-sister to the quite useful 6f (at 2 yrs) to 14f winner of 5 races Polarisation (by Echo Of Light) and to the quite useful 2-y-o 6f winner Ghazi (by Exceed And Excel). The dam is an unraced half-sister to numerous winners including the Derby, King George and Arc winner Lammtarra. The second dam, Snow Bride (by Blushing Groom), was awarded the Oaks on the disqualification of Aliysa and won the Group 3 Musidora Stakes and the Group 3 Princess Royal Stakes. *"She's fine, a nice type of filly but she's not going to be doing anything too early. One for the second half of the season, but she's done nothing wrong".*

642. CORONET ★★★★
gr.f. Dubawi – Approach (Darshaan). February 24. Eighth foal. Half-sister to the Group 2 Irish Derby Trial winner, Irish Derby second and St Leger second Midas Touch, to the quite useful 10f winner Murgan (both by Galileo) and the useful 10f winner and Group 3 third Streetcar To Stars (by Sea The Stars). The dam, a 7.5f (at 2 yrs) and listed 10f winner, was second in a US Grade 2 event and the Group 3 May Hill Stakes and is a full or half-sister 7 winners including the French 2,000 Guineas and US Grade 1 winner Aussie Rules. The second dam, Last Second (by Alzao), a dual Group 2 10f winner and second in the Group 1 Coronation Stakes, is a half-sister to the dams of the Group 1 winners Albanova, Alborada, Allegretto, Yesterday and Quarter Moon. *"A grey filly, she's a good type, has a good attitude and is a nice mover. A very promising filly for July/August over seven furlongs".*

643. CRACKSMAN ★★★
b.c. Frankel – Rhadegunda (Pivotal). April 9. Fourth living foal. Half-brother to the useful 2-y-o Group 3 7f Solario Stakes winner Fantastic Moon (by Dalakhani). The dam, a fairly useful dual 1m winner here, won a listed 9f event in France and is a half-sister to 5 winners. The second dam, St Radegund (by Green Desert), a fairly useful 7f winner, is a half-sister to 7 winners including the very useful listed 6f Sirenia Stakes winner Art of War. *"I trained the mother and she was a tough, staying type that won a listed in* France.

This colt is a lot like her and I see him as an autumn 2-y-o. He has good attitude and he moves well".

644. CUNCO (IRE) ★★★
b.c. Frankel – Chrysanthemum (Danehill Dancer). January 11. First foal. 280,000Y. Tattersalls October Book 1. Not sold. The dam, a winner of 5 races including the 2-y-o Group 3 7f C L Weld Park Stakes and the Group 3 Park Express Stakes, was third in the Group1 Pretty Polly Stakes and is a half-sister to 2 winners. The second dam, Well Spoken (by Sadler's Wells), a jumps winner in France, is a half-sister to 6 winners. *"From the Book One catalogue at Tattersalls where he didn't sell, he's a small, neat, strong colt and shows natural speed. He'll be quite early and I'll probably start him at five furlongs".*

645. CYRUS DALLIN (IRE) ★★★
b.c. Roderic O'Connor – Munaawashat (Marju). March 18. Fifth foal. €40,000Y. Tattersalls Ireland September. Blandford Bloodstock. Half-brother to Executive Bay (by Bushranger), placed fourth over 7f from 2 starts at 2 yrs in 2015. The dam, a fair 6f (at 2 yrs) to 8.5f winner of 5 races, is a half-sister to 9 winners including the Group 3 10f Mooresbridge Stakes winner Windsor Palace, the Irish listed winner Anna Karenina and the useful dual 7f winner and Group 3 Queen Mary Stakes second Al Ihsas. The second dam, Simaat (by Mr Prospector), a fair 1m winner, is a half-sister to 2 winners. *"A nice little colt owned by my wife. He goes alright and he's a nice type. 8He's named after a famous American sculptor".*

646. DAMOCLES (GER) ★★
b.c. Siyouni – Duty And Destiny (Montjeu). February 24. First foal. 130,000Y. Tattersalls October Book 2. Blandford Bloodstock. The dam, a fair 8.5f and 10f placed maiden, is a half-sister to one winner. The second dam, Swilly (by Irish River), is an unplaced half-sister to 7 winners including the Group 2 Premio Lydia Tesio winner Grey Way. *"He came out of the sales and he's a grand horse with plenty of scope and a good stride on him. He was bought very much to be an autumn 2-y-o and with his career as an older horse in mind, but he's pleasing us in simple canters at this time".*

647. DEFENCE COUNSEL (USA) ★★
ch.c. Afleet Alex – Faraway Flower (Distant View). February 23. Brother to the fair 2015 2-y-o 8.5f winner Sepal. The dam, a useful 2-y-o 6f winner, is a half-sister to 2 winners. The second dam, Silver Star (by Zafonic), won over 1m at 2 yrs in France, was listed-placed over 1m at 3 yrs and is a sister to the champion European 2-y-o Xaar (winner of the Group 1 Dewhurst Stakes and the Group 1 Prix de la Salamandre) and a half-sister to the Group 3 10.5f Prix Corrida winner Diese and the Group 3 1m Prix Quincey winner Masterclass. (Khalid Abdulla). *"He's a big, backward horse, very rangy and needs to furnish and strengthen. An autumn horse that doesn't look a 2-y-o type at all".*

648. DREAM FIELD ★★★★
b.c. Oasis Dream – Izzi Top (Pivotal). January 30. First foal. 1,100,000Y. Tattersalls October Book 1. John Ferguson. The dam, a winner of 6 races including the Group 1 Prix Jean Romanet and the Group 1 Pretty Polly Stakes, is a half-sister to 2 winners including the listed winner Jazzi Top. The second dam, Zee Zee Top (by Zafonic), won the Group 1 10f Prix de l'Opera and is a half-sister to the Group 1 winners Opera House and Kayf Tara and to the unraced dam of the Group 1 winner Necklace. *"He's a good mover, a cheeky fella and full of himself. Obviously I know his parents really well – they were both Group 1 winners for us. This colt goes absolutely fine and I think he could be out in June. He's a first foal so he's a neat colt and more like the sire than the dam".*

649. ELDRITCH (IRE) ★★★
gr.c. Dark Angel – Henties Bay (Cape Cross). May 2. Fourth foal. 75,000Y. Tattersalls December. Blandford Bloodstock. Half-brother to the fairly useful 10f to 12f winner of 4 races Sparring (by Teofilo) and to the fair 7f and 1m winner Wandsworth (by Authorized). The dam is an unraced half-sister to 11 winners including the Group 1 6f Middle Park Stakes winner Zieten, the Group 1 6f Cheveley Park Stakes winner Blue Duster and the French 1m listed winner Slow Jazz. The second dam, Blue Note (by Habitat), won 5 races from 5f to 7f in France including the Group 2 Prix Maurice de Gheest and the Group 3 Prix de le Porte Maillot and is a half-sister to 5 winners.

"He's an attractive, medium-sized colt that moves well. I'd hope to have him out in late June. Not an Ascot 2-y-o but he'll be appearing shortly afterwards".

650. ENABLE ★★★★
b.f. Nathaniel – Concentric (Sadler's Wells). February 12. Fourth foal. Half-sister to the dual 1m winner Tournament (by Oasis Dream) and to the French 1m 7f winner Contribution (by Champs Elysees). The dam, a useful French listed 10f winner, was second in the Group 3 10.5f Prix de Flore and is a sister to the Group 2 12.5f Prix de Royallieu winner Dance Routine and to the French 11f winner and Group 3 placed Light Ballet, closely related to the dual Group 3 1m winner Apsis and a half-sister to the listed 12f winner Space Quest. The second dam, Apogee (by Shirley Heights), won the Group 3 12f Prix de Royaumont and is a half-sister to the Group 2 12f Grand Prix de Chantilly winner Daring Miss. (Khalid Abdulla). *"A powerful filly, she's strong, moves well and does everything easily. I won't be tempted to go early with her, just because she could. I'll wait for the seven furlong maidens with her – she's got the strength to run over six but I wouldn't be in a hurry to do it right now. She's a very likeable filly".*

651. GLENCADAM GLORY ★★★
b.c. Nathaniel – Lady Grace (Orpen). February 4. Fifth foal. 90,000Y. Tattersalls October Book 1. Blandford Bloodstock. Half-brother to the German listed 6f winner Penmaen (by Pivotal), to the fair 6f winner Milady (by Shamardal) and the modest 1m winner Darling Grace (by Nayef). The dam, a useful 6f to 1m winner at 2 to 4 yrs and Group 3 placed twice, is a sister to the 2-y-o Group 3 7f Prestige Stakes winner Gracefully and to the useful 2-y-o 6f winner and Group 3 third Visionist and a half-sister to 3 winners. The second dam, Lady Taufan (by Taufan), placed 5 times in Ireland, is a sister to the listed winner and Group 2 Lowther Stakes third Princess Taufan. *"There's a bit of speed on the dam's side and he goes well. I see him as a mid-season type for seven furlongs, but he's a nice type of colt with a very positive attitude".*

652. GOOD CRAIC ★★★
b.c. Invincible Spirit – Riotous Applause (Royal Applause). March 28. Sixth foal. Brother to the useful 2-y-o listed 6f winner Invincible Warrior and half-brother to the quite useful 7f winner Riot Of Colour (by Excellent Art) and the quite useful 7f to 8.5f winner of 4 races Crowdmania (by Shamardal). The dam, a fairly useful dual 6f winner (including at 2 yrs), was listed-placed and is a sister to one winner and a half-sister to 6 winners including the high-class 2-y-o Group 1 1m Racing Post Trophy winner Crowded House and to the placed dam of the US dual Grade 1 winner Ticker Tape. The second dam, Wiener Wald (Woodman), is an unplaced half-sister to 6 minor winners abroad. *"He's a nice type of colt with a good action and a good attitude. Looks like the type that could be out in May".*

653. GREAT SOUND (IRE) ★★
b.c. Galileo – Wanna (Danehill Dancer). April 12. Fourth foal. 320,000Y. Tattersalls October Book 1. John & Jake Warren. Closely related to a winner in Australia by Montjeu and half-brother to the 2-y-o 7f winner and listed-placed Tannaaf (by High Chaparral). The dam, a quite useful 12f winner, is a full or half-sister to 6 winners including Wannabe Grand (Group 1 6f Cheveley Park Stakes), Wannabe Better (Group 3 Ballycorus Stakes) and Wannabe Posh (listed 12f Galtres Stakes). The second dam, Wannabe (by Shirley Heights), a quite useful 1m and 10f winner, is a half-sister to 3 winners including the Group 1 Cheveley Park Stakes second Tanami (dam of the Group 2 Rockfel Stakes winner Cairns). *"He moves fine and has a good attitude, but he'll be trained entirely with his middle-distance career as a 3-y-o in mind".*

654. GYMNASTE (IRE) ★★
b.f. Shamardal – Galipette (Green Desert). March 4. Fifth foal. €260,000Y. Arqana Deauville August. Equine Advisory Agency. Half-sister to the French 5-y-o 7f winner Omy (by Zamindar). The dam, a modest 5f and 6f placed maiden, is closely related to four winners by Oasis Dream including the Group 2 6f Gimcrack Stakes winner Showcasing and a half-sister to four winners including the very smart listed 6f winner Camacho. The second dam, Arabesque (by Zafonic), a useful listed 6f winner, is a sister to 2 winners including the useful 5f and 6f winner Threat and a half-sister to 4 winners including the Group 2 1m

Prix de Sandringham winner Modern Look. *"A big, rangy girl, she's well-grown but very much one for seven furlongs in the second half of the season. So she wants to be given plenty of time and I can see her appreciating some cut in the ground".*

655. HARTSWELL ★★★
b.c. Nathaniel – Bahama Spirit (Invincible Spirit). March 14. First foal. €190,000Y. Goffs Orby. John Ferguson. The dam, a quite useful 2-y-o 6f winner, is a full or half-sister to 7 winners including the 2-y-o Group 3 6f Swordlestown Stud Sprint Stakes winner Brazilian Bride and the very useful 2-y-o 7.5f winner and Group 3 7f second Brazilian Star. The second dam, Braziliz (by Kingmambo), is an unplaced half-sister to Or Vision (dam of the Group 1 winners Saffron Walden, Insight and Dolphin Street). *"Out of an Invincible Spirit mare, he's very 'together' and he's a neat colt that's already moving forward. I see no reason why he shouldn't be running in May over a stiff six furlongs".*

656. HAWANA (USA) ★★★
b.f. War Front – Tare Green (Giant's Causeway). March 24. Second foal. $350,000Y. Keeneland September. Rabbah Bloodstock. The dam is an unraced half-sister to the US, Canadian and Brazilian Grade 1 winner Leroidesanimaux (by Candy Stripes), the Brazilian Grade 1 winner Uapybo (by Blush Rambler) and the US Grade 3 winner Disport (by Blue Stag). The second dam, Dissemble (by Ahonoora), is an unraced half-sister to the outstanding broodmare Hasili and to the listed 15f winner Arrive (herself dam of the Group 1 Pretty Polly Stakes winner Promising Lead). *"A very neat filly that goes well, I hope she'll be out in June over six furlongs. A nice type of filly and very business-like".*

657. ILLAUNMORE (USA) ★★★★
br.f. Shamardal – Illaunglass (Red Clubs). March 30. First foal. The dam, a useful 2-y-o 6f winner, was third in the Group 3 Albany Stakes and is a half-sister to 4 winners including the listed 1m Heron Stakes winner and Group 1 1m Criterium International third Redolent. The second dam, Esterlina (by Highest Honor), won over 1m at 3 yrs in Ireland and is a half-sister to 3 minor winners in France. *"She's doing her canters at this stage, she's light on her feet, goes well and she's grown a bit so needs to fill out her frame again. To that extent she's not typical of the sire, but she's a nice type of filly that we hope to run around the end of May".*

658. JOSHUA REYNOLDS ★★★
b.c. Nathaniel – Dash To The Front (Diktat). March 12. Fifth foal. 115,000Y. Tattersalls October Book 1. Not sold. Half-brother to the 2015 2-y-o 1m winner, on his only start, Next Stage (by Dubawi), to the useful listed 10f winner Speedy Boarding (by Shamardal) and the quite useful 9f and 12f winner of 4 races Miss Dashwood (by Dylan Thomas). The dam, a listed 10.8f winner, is a half-sister to the 2-y-o listed 1m winner and Group 1 Fillies' Mile and Group 1 Yorkshire Oaks placed Dash To The Top. The second dam, Millennium Dash (by Nashwan), a fairly useful 10.2f winner, is a half-sister to 4 winners and to the dam of the Sun Chariot Stakes winner Kissogram. *"A rangy colt with a good attitude, he moves well and although he's very much an autumn 2-y-o he looks very promising at this stage".*

659. LADY HESTA ★★★
b.f. Bernardini – Questing (Hard Spun). March 19. First foal. The dam won over 7f at 2 yrs here and the Grade 1 9f CCA Oaks and Grade 1 10f Alabama Stakes in the USA and is a half-sister to several winners. The second dam, Chercheuse (by Seeking The Gold), won two listed events in France over 6f and 7f at 3 and 4 yrs and is a half-sister to several winners including the listed 10f winner Asawer. *"She has a lot of her mother's fire about her, full of assertiveness. She goes fine, looks a top of the ground type and would be a mid-season 2-y-o over seven furlongs like her mother".*

660. LAVASPIN ★★★
b.c. Hard Spun – Belenkaya (Giant's Causeway). February 17. First foal. The dam, unplaced in one start, is a half-sister to the US dual Grade 1 8.5f winner Country Star out of Rings A Chime (by Metfield). *"He's a promising, neat colt that goes well. He's forward and should be out in May".*

661. LIGHTNING MARK ★★★★
b.f. Invincible Spirit – Maakrah (Dubai Destination). March 18. Third foal. 130,000foal. Tattersalls December. Norris/Huntingdon. Closely related to the fair 7f and 1m winner Matravers (by Oasis Dream) and half-sister to Fiftyshadesofpink (by Pour Moi), unplaced in one start at 2 yrs in 2015. The dam is an unraced sister to 2 winners including the Group 3 Winter Derby winner and Grade 1 Breeders' Cup Juvenile third Farraaj and a half-sister to 9 winners including the triple Group 2 winner and sire Iffraaj and the useful 2-y-o Group 3 7f Prix du Calvados winner Kareymah. The second dam, Pastorale (by Nureyev), a fairly useful 3-y-o 7f winner, is a half-sister to 8 winners including the Group 1 Lockinge Stakes winner and high-class sire Cape Cross. *"A filly that's done quite a bit of growing through the spring, she's a good mover and I see her very much as one for July/August time. A quality filly".*

662. LOUJAIN (IRE) ★★★
ch.c. Dubawi – Eshaadeh (Storm Cat). March 9. Half-brother to the very useful 2-y-o Group 2 5f Queen Mary Stakes winner and Group 1 6f Cheveley Park Stakes third Maqaasid (by Green Desert). The dam, unplaced in 2 starts, is a half-sister to 7 winners including the 1,000 Guineas and Coronation Stakes winner Ghanaati and the Group 3 12f Cumberland Lodge Stakes winner Mawatheeq. The second dam, Sarayir (by Mr Prospector), a listed 1m winner, is closely related to the top-class Champion Stakes winner Nayef and a half-sister to the 2,000 Guineas, Eclipse, Derby and King George winner Nashwan. (Hamdan Al Maktoum). *"A nice colt, he's strong, goes well and has a good attitude. A very nice type of horse that's bred to be a 2-y-o and he'll be alright".*

663. LUQYAA ★★★
b.f. Smart Strike – Maqaasid Green Desert). January 23. Second foal. Half-brother to the unraced 2015 2-y-o Sarmady (by Street Cry). The dam, a very useful 2-y-o Group 2 5f Queen Mary Stakes winner, was third in the Group 1 6f Cheveley Park Stakes. The second dam, Eshaadeh (by Storm Cat), unplaced in 2 starts, is a half-sister to 7 winners including the 1,000 Guineas and Coronation Stakes winner Ghanaati and the Group 3 12f Cumberland Lodge Stakes winner Mawatheeq. (Hamdan Al Maktoum). *"She's a likeable filly, we know the family well and we're pleased with her. She won't be that early and although her dam won the Queen Mary she won't be ready in time Ascot. We haven't worked her yet either, so we don't know about her ability just yet".*

664. MADEENATY (IRE) ★★★
b.f. Dansili – Mooakada (Montjeu). April 26. Sister to the useful 1m and listed 10f winner of 4 races at 3 and 4 yrs Mahsoob. The dam, a useful 2-y-o 1m winner, was listed-placed over 10f and 12f. The second dam, Sulaalah (by Darshaan), unplaced in one start at 2 yrs, is a half-sister to 2 winners. The second dam, Bint Shadayid (by Nashwan), a very useful winner of the Group 3 7f Prestige Stakes, was placed in the 1,000 Guineas and the Fillies Mile. (Hamdan Al Maktoum). *"A likeable filly, rangy like her mother, she has a good action and is very much one for a mile maiden in September here in Newmarket – the one that Taghrooda won. She's very much that type of filly".*

665. MAGIC ★★
b.f. Galileo – Danehurst (Danehill). April 6. Ninth foal. Half-sister to the quite useful 2-y-o 6f winner Ski Slope (by Three Valleys), to the fair 2-y-o 5f winner Jamboree Girl (by Bahamian Bounty) and the modest 7f and 1m winner King Pin (by Pivotal). The dam, winner of the Cornwallis Stakes (at 2 yrs), the Curragh Flying Five, the Prix de Seine-et-Oise and the Premio Umbria, is a half-sister to 6 winners including Humouresque (Group 3 10.5f Prix Penelope) and the dual Group 2 third Mighty. The second dam, Miswaki Belle (by Miswaki), second over 7f on her only start, is a half-sister to 9 winners including the Dazzle (Group 3 6f Cherry Hinton Stakes). *"A nice type of filly, she looks like one for the autumn and will want ten furlongs next year. She's done nothing wrong but at this stage she just wants time, which is no surprise".*

666. MARK OF APPROVAL (USA) ★★★
ch.c. Lemon Drop Kid – Agreeable Miss (Speightstown). April 1. Fourth foal. $400,000Y. Keeneland September. John Ferguson. Half-brother to the useful 2-y-o 6f winner and listed-placed Faydhan (by War Front). The

dam is an unraced half-sister to 7 winners including the dual Grade 3 placed Sweet And Flawless. The second dam, Sweet And Ready (by El Prado), won the Grade 2 Princess Stakes and is a half-sister to 5 winners. *"A lovely-moving horse for the second half of the season. You should mention him – he's got quality".*

667. MASTER SINGER (USA) ★★★
c. Giant's Causeway – Ring Of Music (Sadler's Wells). Half-brother to the multiple German and Italian Group 1 12f winner Campanologist (by Kingmambo). The dam is an unplaced half-sister to Singspiel and Rahy. The second dam, Glorious Song (by Halo), won four Grade 1 events in the USA. *"A brother to Campanologist, he's a nice, rangy, very likeable colt for the second half of the year".*

668. MIDDLE KINGDOM (USA) ★★★★
b.c. War Front – River Belle (Lahib). March 4. Seventh foal. 775,000Y. Tattersalls October Book 1. China Horse Club. Half-brother to the useful 7f (at 2 yrs) and listed 1m UAE 1,000 Guineas winner Siyaadah (by Shamardal), to the 2-y-o 1m and subsequent US Grade 3 winner and Grade 1 second Strathnaver (by Oasis Dream) and the quite useful 7f (at 2 yrs) to 12f winner of 5 races Bridal Belle (by Dansili). The dam won the Group 3 6f Princess Margaret Stakes and the US Grade 2 8.5f Mrs Revere Stakes, was Grade 1 placed and is a half-sister to 5 winners including the Group 2 Italian 1,000 Guineas third Kiralik. The second dam, Dixie Favor (by Dixieland Band), was a quite useful Irish 6f (at 2 yrs) to 1m winner of 3 races. *"A rangy colt and a good mover, he's a nice type of horse and one for seven furlongs around July/August time. There's a lot to like about him".*

669. MONARCH'S GLEN ★★★★
b.c. Frankel – Mirabilis (Lear Fan). February 5. Half-brother to the quite useful 5f and 6f winner Cordial (by Oasis Dream) and to the fair 9f winner Ruffle (by Harlan's Holiday). The dam, a listed 7f winner in France, was third in the Group 1 7f Prix de la Foret and subsequently won a Grade 3 event in the USA over 1m at 4 yrs. She is a half-sister to the Group 1 1m Prix du Moulin and Group 1 10.5f Prix de Diane winner Nebraska Tornado and the Group 2 10f Prix Eugene Adam winner Burning Sun. The second dam, Media Nox (by Lycius), winner of the 2-y-o Group 3 5f Prix du Bois, is a half-sister to the Prix d'Aumale, Prix Vanteaux and Prix de Malleret winner Bonash. (Khalid Abdulla). *"A big, strapping colt that moves well, he goes nicely and I like him for seven furlongs in the middle of the season".*

670. MOOLTAZEM (IRE) ★★★
b.c. Elzaam – Whisper Dance (Stravinsky). April 7. Fourth foal. 90,000Y. Tattersalls October Book 2. Shadwell Estate Co. The dam, placed fourth once over 8.5f in Ireland, is a half-sister to 6 winners including a stakes winner in Japan. The second dam, My Cherie (by Woodman), a minor winner at 2 yrs in the USA, is a half-sister to 6 winners including the Group 3 Kiveton Park Stakes and Group 3 Duke Of York Stakes winner Green Line Express. *"He's a strong horse, he goes nicely and I hope to have him out in May over six furlongs".*

671. MURAAQEB ★★
b.c. Nathaniel – Tesary (Danehill). March 18. Sixth foal. £190,000Y. Doncaster Premier. Shadwell Estate Co. Half-brother to the fairly useful 5f (at 2 yrs) and 6f winner Englishman (by Royal Applause), to the quite useful 5f (at 2 yrs) and 6f winner Verbeeck (by Dutch Art) and the modest 1m winner Merton Lady (by Beat Hollow). The dam, a useful 5f (at 2 yrs) to 7f winner, is a half-sister to 4 winners including the fairly useful 7f and 1m winner Baldour. The second dam, Baldemara (by Sanglamore), is an unraced half-sister to 5 winners including the Group 1 5.5f Prix Robert Papin winner Balbonella (herself dam of the top-class sprinter Anabaa, the French 1,000 Guineas winner Always Loyal and the useful sire Key Of Luck). *"He's still at the stud because of a small setback, so when he arrives he'll need plenty of time. A nice horse, but he won't be racing until the autumn".*

672. NATURE'S ORDER (IRE) ★★★
b.c. Dansili – Nature Spirits (Beat Hollow). February 11. First foal. The dam, a 10f and listed 12f winner, is a half-sister to several winners including the Group 2 1m Beresford Stakes and Group 3 10f Mooresbridge Stakes winner Curtain Call. The second dam, Apsara

(by Darshaan), is an unplaced half-sister to numerous winners including the Group 1 10.5f Prix Lupin and US Grade 2 1m winner Johann Quatz and the Group 1 Prix du Jockey Club and Group 1 Prix Lupin winner Hernando. (Niarchos Family). *"A nice colt, he's grown, filled his frame out well, travels nicely and does everything fine. He's very much one for the mid-season, seven furlong maidens on the July course. You wouldn't want to be running him over six".*

673. NOBLY BORN ★★★
ch.c. Mayson – Noble One (Primo Dominie). April 15. Half-brother to six winners, four of them by Pivotal including the Group 1 1m Sun Chariot Stakes and Group 1 1m Lockinge Stakes winner Peeress and the quite useful 6f and 7f winner Entitled, the quite useful triple 6f winner Noble Deed (by Kyllachy) and the quite useful 2-y-o 5f winner Carte Royale (by Loup Sauvage). The dam, a useful dual 5f winner (including at 2 yrs), is a half-sister to 6 winners including the fairly useful 10f winner Maiden Castle. The second dam, Noble Destiny (by Dancing Brave), was a fairly useful 2-y-o 7f winner. (Cheveley Park Stud). *"The only Mayson we've got, he's a nice colt that moves well and he's got some scope about him. He doesn't look like he wants to be running over five furlongs next week, but he strikes me as a horse who could be running over six at the end of May or early June. He goes well".*

674. OUTRE MER (IRE) ★★★
b.c. Raven's Pass – Sea Chanter (War Chant). March 7. Half-brother to the US 9.5f winner Ocean Telegraph (by Street Cry). The dam was a US 2-y-o Group 3 1m and listed 1m winner out of the US Grade 1 second Smooth Charmer (by Easy Goer). *"I like him, he's a progressive horse that could be out in June over six furlongs".*

675. PEACEFUL PASSAGE (USA) ★★★
b.f. War Front – Flying Passage (A P Indy). March 31. Half-sister to the dual US Grade 2 winner (over 1m and 9f) Hungry Island (by More Than Ready), to the US Grade 3 1m winner and Grade 2 placed Soaring Empire (by Empire Maker) and the US Grade 3 placed Tokyo Time (by Medaglia D'Oro). The dam,

a minor US 3-y-o winner, is a half-sister to the US Grade 2 winners Waldoboro and Tara Roma. The second dam, Chic Shirine (by Mr Prospector), won the Grade 1 Ashland Stakes and is a sister to the US Grade 1 winner Queena. *"A big, rangy, powerful filly, she looks like a colt. Very strong, she does everything easily but I won't be tempted to push her too early, she wouldn't want that. We'll wait for mid-season, she looks a talented filly but it would be a big mistake to go too early with her".*

676. PEALER ★★
b.c. Campanologist – Praia (Big Shuffle). March 13. Fifth foal. 140,000Y. Tattersalls October Book 1. Blandford Bloodstock. Half-brother to 3 winners in Germany including the Group 3 10f winner Potemkin (by New Approach) and the listed 1m winner and Group 3 placed Paraisa (by Red Ransom). The dam, a listed-placed 3-y-o winner in Germany, is a half-sister to 4 winners including the Group 1 Criterium de Saint-Cloud winner Paita. The second dam, Prada (by Lagunas), a German 3-y-o listed winner, is a half-sister to 6 winners. *"An attractive horse, he was expensive and he's out of a good, tough, German family. He moves beautifully and was bought to be a back-end 2-y-o and for middle-distances at three. He looks the business for that".*

677. PETERPORT ★★★★ ♣
b.c. Nathaniel – Spinning Queen (Spinning World). March 2. Closely related to the useful listed 12f winner Gallipot (by Galileo) and half-brother to 4 winners including the useful dual 1m and 10f winner Trade Commissioner (by Montjeu), the quite useful 2-y-o 7f winner Peterhof (by Dansili) and the fair 7f (at 2 yrs) and 9.5f winner The Third Man (by Dalakhani). The dam, winner of the Group 1 1m Sun Chariot Stakes and the Group 3 7f Brownstown Stakes, is a half-sister to 5 winners. The second dam, Our Queen Of Kings (by Arazi), is an unraced half-sister to 7 winners including Labeeb (Grade 1 9f Hollywood Derby), Fanmore (Grade 2 Arlington Handicap) and Alrassaam (Group 2 9f Budweiser International). (Lady Rothschild). *"A good type of colt that moves well, he's one you shouldn't leave out".*

678. PRECIOUS RAMOTSWE ★★
b.f. Nathaniel – Miss Pinkerton (Danehill). February 17. Half-sister to the fairly useful listed-placed 8.5f winner Vanity Rules (by New Approach), to the fairly useful listed-placed dual 10f winner This Is The Day (by Footstepsinthesand), the modest 1m to 12f winner of 7 races General Tufto (by Fantastic Light), the modest 1m to 10f winner Smart Step (by Montjeu) and the moderate 7f winner Hard Ball (by Pivotal). The dam, a useful 6f (at 2 yrs) and listed 1m winner, is a half-sister to 4 winners including the smart 7f (at 2 yrs) and 10f winner Grand Central. The second dam, Rebecca Sharp (by Machiavellian), winner of the Group 1 1m Coronation Stakes, is a half-sister to 8 winners including the Group 3 11.5f Lingfield Derby Trial winner Mystic Knight. *"She's fine, but very much an autumn filly which is what you'd expect from a Nathaniel. A likeable filly from a nice family, but it's all about getting a run or two later in the year".*

679. PRESENT TENSE ★★★★
b.f. Bated Breath – Zenda (Zamindar). January 30. Seventh foal. Closely related to the smart Group 3 10f winner of 3 races Remote and to the quite useful 7f winner Panzanella (both by Dansili) and half-sister to the high-class Group 1 1m Irish 2,000 Guineas, St James's Palace Stakes, Sussex Stakes and Prix Jacques le Marois winner Kingman (by Invincible Spirit). The dam won the French 1,000 Guineas, was second in the Coronation Stakes and the Grade 1 Queen Elizabeth II Challenge Cup at Keeneland and is a half-sister to the July Cup and Nunthorpe Stakes winner Oasis Dream and the dual listed 1m winner Hopeful Light. The second dam, Hope (by Dancing Brave), is an unraced sister to the Group 1 Irish Oaks winner Wemyss Bight. (Khalid Abdulla). *"I like her a lot, she's very strong and does everything easily. She's a little bit immature right now and wouldn't want to be pressed but she's very likeable filly. I would see her running over six furlongs but not until July".*

680. PRIVATE ADVISOR ★★
b.f. Pivotal – Confidential Lady (Singspiel). April 2. Sixth foal. Half-sister to the French 10f winner and Group 2 10f Prix Greffulhe second Untold Secret (by Shamardal). The dam, winner of the Group 3 7f Prix du Calvados (at 2 yrs) and the Group 1 10.5f Prix de Diane, is a half-sister to 5 winners. The second dam, Confidante (by Dayjur), a fairly useful 3-y-o dual 7f winner, is a half-sister to 6 winners including the 2-y-o 6f winner Wind Cheetah, the Group 3 7f Solario Stakes winner White Crown and the 11.8f winner Zuboon — all useful. (Cheveley Park Stud). *"Mentally she wasn't in tune with us for some time but in fairness she's coming along now and has much improved over the last six weeks. Nevertheless she won't be out until the autumn".*

681. PROFILING ★★★
b.c. New Approach – Forensics (Flying Spur). April 12. Half-brother to the modest 2015 6f and 1m placed 2-y-o Criminalistic (by Dubawi) and to the fairly useful dual 7f winner Wordcraft (by Shamardal). The dam, winner of three Group 1 events in Australia over 6f (at 2 yrs) and 1m, is out of Prove It (by Dehere). *"An attractive, rangy colt, he's a nice sort and one for the second half of the season".*

682. REGAL SPLENDOUR ★★
b.f. Pivotal – Regal Realm (Medicean). February 7. First foal. The dam, a 2-y-o Group 3 7f Prestige Stakes and 3-y-o Group 3 7f Oak Tree Stakes winner, is a half-sister to 2 winners. The second dam, Regal Riband (by Fantastic Light), a modest 7f winner at 2 yrs from three starts, is a half-sister to 3 winners. (Cheveley Park Stud). *"Rather backward at the moment, she's very much an autumn type. She'll want some cut in the ground and seven furlongs. Pivotal doesn't usually get precocious types".*

683. SAMHARRY ★★★
b.c. Exceed And Excel – Ballymore Celebre March 4. Eighth foal. 600,000Y. Tattersalls October Book 1. Shadwell Estate Co. Half-brother to the smart 2-y-o Group 2 6f July Stakes winner Anjaal (by Bahamian Bounty), to the fair 2m winner No Time To Lose (by Authorized), the fair 10f and 12f winner Pintrada (by Tiger Hill) and the modest 10f winner Sweet Secret (by Singspiel). The dam won twice at 3 yrs in France and is a half-sister to 10 winners including the Irish multiple Group 3 winner Nysaean. The second dam, Irish Arms (by Irish River), won once in France and is a half-sister to 9 winners including the US Grade 2 winner Morold. *"A big boy, he has*

a nice attitude and goes well. I see him as a six/seven furlong horse and he should make a 2-y-o".

684. SEVEN HEAVENS ★★★
b.c. Frankel – Heaven Sent (Pivotal). May 21. Fourth foal. 620,000Y. Tattersalls October Book 1. Juddmonte Farms. Half-brother to the 2015 7f and 1m placed 2-y-o (on both his starts) You're Hired (by Dalakhani) and to the quite useful 2-y-o 1m winner Firmament (by Cape Cross). The dam, a winner of 6 races including the Group 3 Dahlia Stakes (twice), was Group 1 placed three times and is a sister to the US dual Grade 1 winner Megahertz and the fairly useful dual 1m winner and listed-placed Heavenly Dawn. The second dam, Heavenly Ray (by Rahy), a fairly useful 7f and 1m winner, is a half-sister to 3 winners. *"A nice type of colt with a quick action, business-like and with a good engine. He's likeable but has a late foaling date and I see him being on the racecourse around June/July".*

685. SILVERLIGHT ★★★★
b.c. Dubawi – Arizona Jewel (Dansili). April 1. First foal. The dam, a quite useful 10f winner, is a sister to the US dual Grade 2 winner Riposte, closely related to the listed 5f and listed 6f winner Kind (by Danehill and herself the dam of Frankel) and a half-sister to 5 winners including the high-class 7f (at 2 yrs) and Group 2 12f Great Voltigeur Stakes winner Powerscourt, the Group 3 winning stayer Last Train and the smart 14f winner of 3 races Brimming. The second dam, Rainbow Lake (by Rainbow Quest), a smart winner of 3 races including the Group 3 12f Lancashire Oaks and the listed 10f Ballymacoll Stud Stakes, is a half-sister to several winners. (Khalid Abdulla). *"A colt that moves well, he's very likeable and is probably a seven furlong type 2-y-o, but we might run him over six in mid-season. He's strong and has a good attitude".*

686. SPIRITOUS (USA) ★★★★
b.c. Invincible Spirit – Andina (Singspiel). March 14. First foal. $160,000Y. Keeneland September. John Ferguson. The dam, a stakes winner of 4 races in North America and Grade 2 placed twice, is a half-sister to 8 winners. The second dam, Fragrant Oasis (by Rahy), won the listed King Charles II Stakes and is a half-sister to the US stakes winner and Grade 3 second Mr Notebook. *"This is a neat, 'together' 2-y-o type and I'd hope to be running him in May. He has the speed for six furlongs and he's working particularly well".*

687. TINTED ★★★
b.f. Galileo – Regal Rose (Danehill). May 19. Seventh foal. Half-sister to the quite useful 2015 2-y-o 7f winner Bobby Wheeler (by Pivotal), to the fairly useful 6f (including at 2 yrs) and 5f winner of 7 races Regal Royale, the quite useful 2-y-o 6f winner and US Grade 3 1m placed Royal Banker, the fair 7f and 1m winner Merchant of Medici (all by Medicean) and the fair 6f (including at 2 yrs) and 5f winner of 7 races Regal Riband (by Fantastic Light and herself dam of the dual Group 3 winner Regal Realm). The dam won both her starts including the Group 1 6f Cheveley Park Stakes and is a full or half-sister to 9 winners. The second dam, Ruthless Rose (by Conquistador Cielo), ran twice unplaced and is a half-sister to 9 winners including the high-class miler Shaadi. (Cheveley Park Stud). *"A nice filly with a good attitude and a good action. She'll need time to strengthen and develop but she's got some quality about her. I still see her very much as one for September time".*

688. VALCARTIER ★★★
b.c. Redoute's Choice – Vadawina (Unfuwain). March 1. Seventh foal. €950,000Y. Arqana Deauville August. John Ferguson. The dam won the Group 1 Prix Saint-Alary and is a half-sister to 7 winners including the Prix Saint-Alary winner Vazira and the Group 3 Prix Cleopatra winner Vadapolina. The second dam, Vadaza (by Zafonic), a listed-placed 10f winner in France, is a half-sister to the Group 1 Queen Anne Stakes winner Valixir. *"A nice type of colt, he moves well, has a good action and a good attitude".*

689. VIA EGNATIA (USA) ★★★
b.c. Distorted Humor – Honest Lady (Seattle Slew). April 8. Half-brother to numerous winners including the US Grade 1 7f Forego Stakes winner First Defence (by Unbridled's Song), the useful 2-y-o listed 7f winner Honest Quality (by Elusive Quality) and the French listed 1m winner Phantom Rose (by Danzig).

The second dam, Honest Lady (by Seattle Slew), winner of the Grade 1 Santa Monica Handicap, is a half-sister to the US triple Grade 1 winner Empire Maker and the Grade 1 Arlington Million winner Chester House. (Khalid Abdulla). *"A big boy, he's just doing his canters but he's coming along OK and I'd be happy enough with everything he's doing. There's no reason why he shouldn't be out in late May and he's fine. A nice type of horse that goes well".* The Via Egnatia was a Roman road that connected ports on the Adriatic Sea with Byzantium.

690. VIVIAN WARD ★★★
b.f. Kyllachy – Al Joudha (Green Desert). March 14. Seventh foal. 24,000Y. Tattersalls October Book 2. Not sold. Half-sister to the fair 2-y- 7f winner Gilbey's Mate, to the modest 7f winner All Honesty (both by Medicean), the fair 6f winner Premier Lad (by Tobougg) and a minor winner at 2 and 3 yrs in Italy by Nayef. The dam is an unplaced half-sister to 5 winners including the Swedish Group 3 winner King Quantas and to the placed dam of the dual Group 1 winner and sire Dutch Art. The second dam, Palacegate Episode (by Drumalis), a useful sprint winner of 11 races including a Group 3 in Italy and numerous listed events, is a full or half-sister to 5 winners including the triple listed winning sprinter Palacegate Jack. *"She shows some promise and looks like she'll be a mid-season 2-y-o with speed".*

691. WHISPERING BELL (IRE) ★★★★
b.f. Galileo – Red Avis (Exceed And Excel). January 21. First foal. 200,000Y. Tattersalls October Book 1. Blandford Bloodstock. The dam, a fair Irish 2-y-o 7f placed maiden, is a half-sister to the 2-y-o Group 3 Albany Stakes winner Newfangled. The second dam, Scarlet Ibis (by Machiavellian), a quite useful French 1m winner, is a half-sister to 4 winners including the US 2-y-o 1m winner and Grade 3 placed Anasheed. *"A strong, attractive, filly, she's very 'together' and I like her. Should be one for seven furlongs on the July course and looks a very promising filly".*

692. UNNAMED ★★
b.c. Galileo – Adoration (Honor Grades). April 10. The dam, a US dual Grade 1 winner, is a half-sister to numerous other winners including the US Grade 3 placed winner Mo Mon. The second dam, Sewing Lady (Key To The Mint), is an unraced half-sister to 9 winners including the Irish listed winner Astraeus. *"He's a nice type of colt that moves well. He has grown and now needs to furnish and strengthen, so he'll be appearing in the mile maidens in the autumn. He'll be a mile and half colt next year".*

693. UNNAMED ★★★★
b.c. War Front – Bel Air Beauty (Smart Strike). January 31. Fifth foal. $525,000Y. Keeneland September. John Ferguson. Half-brother to 3 winners including the Canadian stakes winner and Grade 2 placed Stacked Deck (by First Samurai) and the Grade 2 placed winner Valentino Beauty (by Vindication). The dam, winner of the Grade 2 Alcibiades Stakes and the Grade 3 Pin Oak Valley View Stakes, is a half-sister to 4 winners. The second dam, Awe That (by Boundary), a US stakes-placed 2-y-o winner, is a half-sister to 5 winners including the US Grade 3 winner Anklet. *"A nice type of horse, I like him a lot. His knees are still immature so I'm just going quietly with him for now and he's one that's likely to appear around August/September time over seven furlongs. A very likeable colt".*

694. UNNAMED ★★★★ ♠
b.f. Dubawi – Brigitta (Sadler's Wells). March 8. Ninth foal. 425,000Y. Tattersalls October Book 1. Charlie Gordon-Watson / Al Shaqab. Half-sister to the listed 1m (at 2 yrs), German Group 2 1m and Group 3 9.5f Prix Daphnis winner Emerald Commander, to the fair 11f winner Past Forgetting (both by Pivotal), the quite useful 5f winner Gold Lace (by Invincible Spirit) and the fair 2-y-o 7f winner Albaraari (by Green Desert). The dam won over 1m and 10f and is a sister to the 2-y-o Group 1 1m Racing Post Trophy winner Commander Collins, closely related to the Grade 1 Breeders' Cup Sprint winner Lit de Justice and the 2,000 Guineas and Derby placed Colonel Collins and a half-sister to the Group 2 Royal Lodge Stakes winner City Leader. The second dam, Kanmary (by Kenmare), won the 2-y-o Group 3 5f Prix du Bois. *"A nice filly that goes well, has a good attitude and is likely to be out in mid-season. A nice type".*

695. UNNAMED ★★
ch.c. Choisir – Damhsa Le Cheile (Teofilo). January 30. First foal. 115,000Y. Tattersalls October Book 2. John & Jake Warren. The dam ran once unplaced and is a half-sister to 4 winners including the 6f (at 2 yrs) and Group 2 7f Challenge Stakes winner Stimulation. The second dam, Damiana (by Thatching), was placed 5 times in France at 2 and 3 yrs and is a half-sister to 4 winners including the listed Prix Coronation winner and US Grade 2 placed Dirca. *"A very tall, rangy colt, untypical of the sire. He's more likely to make a mid-season 2-y-o than for earlier on"*.

696. UNNAMED ★★★★★ ♠
b.c. Frankel – Dar Re Mi (Singspiel). March 19. Third foal. 750,000Y. Tattersalls October Book 1. Al Shaqab Racing. Half-brother to the 2015 2-y-o 1m winner, on her only start, So Mi Dar (by Dubawi) and to the 7f (at 2 yrs) and 10f winner and multiple Group 3 placed De Treville (by Oasis Dream). The dam won the Pretty Polly Stakes, Dubai Sheema Classic and Yorkshire Oaks (all Group 1 events) and is a half-sister to 9 winners including the Group 1 winners Rewilding, Diaghilev and Darazari. The second dam, Darara (by Top Ville), won the Group 1 Prix Vermeille and is a half-sister to 11 winners including the French Derby winner and high-class sire Darshaan. *"A lovely horse with scope, he has great presence about him and he moves well. A really nice type of horse for seven furlongs around July time. He looks good"*.

697. UNNAMED ★★
b.c. Holy Roman Emperor – Disco Volante (Sadler's Wells). March 31. Eighth foal. 120,000Y. Tattersalls October Book 1. Charlie Gordon-Watson / Al Shaqab Racing. Half-brother to 5 winners including the smart 7f (at 2 yrs), Group 3 12f and Group 3 2m winner Namibian (by Cape Cross), the fairly useful triple 7f winner Westwood Hoe, the fair 1m winner Flying Fantasy (both by Oasis Dream) and the quite useful 10f winner Mary Goodnight (by King's Best). The dam, a useful listed-placed 1m winner, is a half-sister to 3 winners including the Group 1 placed Valentino. The second dam, Divine Danse (by Kris), won the Group 2 Prix du Gros Chene and the Group 3 Prix du Ris-Orangis and is a half-sister to the Group 2 Prix Maurice de Gheest winner Pursuit of Love. *"A mid-season type 2-y-o for seven furlongs, he's just going through a growth spurt at the moment which buys him a bit of time"*.

698. UNNAMED ★★★
b.f. Raven's Pass – Elas Diamond (Danehill Dancer). January 27. First foal. 160,000Y. Tattersalls October Book 1. Not sold. The dam, a fairly useful 2-y-o 1m winner, was listed placed and is a half-sister to 2 winners including the listed winner and Group 2 third Pallasator. The second dam, Ela Athena (by Ezzoud), a winner of 3 races including the Group 3 Lancashire Oaks, was placed in seven Group/Grade 1 events and is a half-sister to 5 winners. *"A very 'together' filly, she looks precocious and I hope to have her out in early May. She has a nice attitude and looks to have some speed about her"*.

699. UNNAMED ★★★★
gr.f. Mastercraftsman – Flanders (Common Grounds). April 27. Twelfth foal. 300,000Y. Tattersalls October Book 1. Hugo Lascelles. Half-sister to 10 winners including the Group 1 Haydock Park Sprint winner G Force (by Tamayuz), the US Grade 3 Miesque Stakes winner Louvain (by Sinndar and herself dam of the dual Group 1 winner Flotilla), the listed 10f winner Laajooj (by Azamour), the fairly useful Irish 10f winner Lagoon (by Montjeu) and the quite useful 5f and 6f winner and Group 3 third Desert Poppy (by Oasis Dream). The dam, winner of the listed Scarbrough Stakes and second in the Group 2 King's Stand Stakes, is a half-sister to 8 winners. The second dam, Family at War (by Explodent), a fair 2-y-o 5f winner, is a half-sister to 4 minor winners. *"A grand filly with a good attitude, she moves well and looks very much the type for seven furlongs in September. Looks very promising"*.

700. UNNAMED ★★★
ch.f. Foxwedge – Generous Diana (Generous). April 1. Ninth foal. 65,000Y. Tattersalls October Book 2. Hugo Lascelles. Half-sister to the Group 2 Jockey Club Stakes and Group 3 September Stakes winner of 9 races Dandino (by Dansili) and to a hurdles winner by Doyen. The dam, a fair 9f to 10.5f winner, is a half-sister to 7 minor winners. The second dam,

Lypharitissima (by Lightning), is an unraced sister to the Group 1 Prix de Diane winner Lypharita. *"A nice, attractive filly that moves well, she doesn't look in any way precocious but that's no surprise. A filly for the autumn, but she's got a bit of quality about her".*

701. UNNAMED ★★★ ♠
b.c. Dansili – Giants Play (Giant's Causeway). January 27. Second foal. 260,000Y. Tattersalls October Book 1. Hugo Lascelles. The dam, a US Grade 2 10f winner, is a half-sister the US Grade 3 12f winner Anjaz and to the listed 1m winner Tearless. The second dam, Playful Act (by Sadler's Wells), a Group 1 Fillies' Mile, Group 2 Lancashire Oaks and Group 2 May Hill Stakes winner, is a sister to the Group 2 Yorkshire Cup winner Percussionist and the US dual Grade 3 winner Changing Skies and a half-sister to the dual Group 1 winner Nathaniel and the Group 1 Irish Oaks winner Great Heavens. *"A rangy colt with a good attitude, he moves well and I can see him starting in a seven furlong maiden in July/August. A nice type of colt with some quality, but he's not an early type that's all".*

702. UNNAMED ★★★★
b.c. Oasis Dream – Gull Wing (In The Wings). March 11. Fifth foal. Half-brother to the high-class Group 2 12f King Edward VII Stakes winner Eagle Top and to the very useful 1m (at 2 yrs) and Group 2 Park Hill Stakes winner The Lark (both by Pivotal). The dam, a 10f and listed 14f winner, is a half-sister to the 7f (at 2 yrs), Epsom Oaks and Irish Oaks winner Sariska. The second dam, Maycocks Bay (by Muhtarram), a useful 14f listed winner, is a half-sister to several winners including the useful 7f and 1m winner (at 2 yrs) and listed 10.3f placed 3-y-o Indian Light. *"A strong colt and a typical Oasis Dream, he's going to be a mid-season 2-y-o and he's coming along nicely. He'll probably end up a middle-distance horse because they all stay out of the mare".*

703. UNNAMED ★★★ ♠
b.f. Exceed And Excel – Lady Hawkfield (Hawk Wing). April 22. Third foal. 180,000Y. Tattersalls October Book 1. One Agency. Half-sister to the fair 2015 2-y-o 7f winner Royal Reserve (by Duke Of Marmalade) and to the useful 8.5f (at 2 yrs) and Group 3 Classic Trial winner Master Apprentice (by Mastercraftsman). The dam ran once unplaced and is a half-sister to the Group 1 1m Coronation Stakes and Group 1 1m Matron Stakes winner Lillie Langtry and to the listed 7f winner and Group 3 third Count Of Limonade (by Duke Of Marmalade). The second dam, Hoity Toity (by Darshaan), is an unraced half-sister to 5 winners. *"She's come along quite nicely and is doing her canters well. Pretty excitable when she came in, but she's settled down now and we're very happy with her. I wouldn't think she'd be ready to run until at least June and I think she'll be a sprinter – a lot by this sire want to be".*

704. UNNAMED ★★★★ ♠
b.c. Holy Roman Emperor – Larceny (Cape Cross). February 11. Third foal. €210,000Y. Arqana Deauville August. Charlie Liverton. Half-brother to The Black Princess (by Iffraaj), a promising 1m winner on her only start at 2 yrs in 2015 and to the minor French 12f winner Lucelle (by High Chaparral). The dam ran once unplaced and is a half-sister to 6 winners including Latice (Group 1 Prix de Diane), Lawman (Group 1 French Derby and Group 1 Prix Jean Prat) and Satri (Group 3 Prix du Palais-Royal). The second dam, Laramie (by Gulch), placed fourth once over 7f at 3 yrs in Ireland, is a half-sister to 2 minor winners. *"He's a good-going horse, quite long like his half-sister The Black Princess who we have here, and I like him but he's not one that needs to be got at yet. I see him as very much one for August time".*

705. UNNAMED ★★★★
b.f. Fastnet Rock – Lauren Louise (Tagula). March 26. Seventh foal. 320,000Y. Tattersalls October Book 1. Hugo Lascelles. Half-sister to the 2-y-o Group 2 6f Gimcrack Stakes winner Blaine (by Avonbridge), to the very useful 2-y-o listed 6f winner Bogart (by Bahamian Bounty) and the fair 2-y-o 7f winner Longton (by Myboycharlie). The dam, a moderate 6f winner at 4 yrs, is a half-sister to 5 winners. The second dam, Movie Star (by Barathea), ran once unplaced and is a full or half-sister to 3 winners including the French listed winner Kilometre Neuf. *"She's a very good-looking filly and a good mover with a nice mind on her. Not precocious, but a very nice type of filly with quality".*

706. UNNAMED ★★★
b.f. Redoute's Choice – My Branch (Distant Relative). April 26. Eleventh foal. 400,000Y. Tattersalls October Book 1. Charlie Gordon-Watson. Half-sister to 7 winners including the Group 1 6f Haydock Sprint Cup winner Tante Rose (by Barathea), the 2-y-o listed 7f winner Bay Tree (by Daylami), the useful 1m winner and listed-placed Melodramatic (by Sadler's Wells) and the 2-y-o winners Bold Lass (by Sea The Stars), Priceless Jewel (by Selkirk) and Rosie's Posy (by Suave Dancer) – all quite useful. The dam won the listed 6f Firth Of Clyde Stakes (at 2 yrs) and the listed 7f Sceptre Stakes, was third in the Irish 1,000 Guineas and is a full or half-sister to 7 winners. The second dam, Pay The Bank (by High Top), was a quite useful 2-y-o 1m winner. *"A nice type of filly that's done an awful lot of growing this spring and has really changed. Like a lot of them she's just filling back into her frame but she's very nice. I'll be patient with her, I like what I saw early on but I can see her being very much an August time 2-y-o, not before".*

707. UNNAMED ★★★
ch.c. Archipenko – Oshiponga (Barathea). January 25. Twelfth foal. 60,000Y. Tattersalls October Book 2. Charles Liverton. Half-brother to 7 winners including the 2-y-o Group 2 7f Superlative Stakes and US Grade 3 7f winner Hatta Fort (by Cape Cross), the 2-y-o Group 3 Sweet Solera Stakes winner Blue Bayou (by Bahamian Bounty), the fair dual 1m winner Ostentation (by Dubawi), the fair 6f and 7f winner Caramack (by Danehill Dancer) and the modest 9f winner Teide Lady (by Nashwan). The dam, a fair 9f winner, is a half-sister to 8 winners including the Grade 1 E P Taylor Stakes winner Miss Keller and the Group placed Sir George Turner and Kotsi. The second dam, Ingozi (by Warning), a fairly useful listed winner, is a half-sister to 7 winners. *"A strong colt that'll be a middle-distance type next year, so he's going to be very much an autumn 2-y-o".*

708. UNNAMED ★★★
b.c. Sepoy – Our Faye (College Chapel). May 2. Fourth foal. 55,000Y. Tattersalls October Book 2. John Ferguson. Half-brother to the quite useful 6f winner Effectual (by Exceed And Excel). The dam, a fairly useful winner of 7 races from 6f to 1m including the Group 3 Summer Stakes, is a half-sister to 3 winners. The second dam, Tamara (by Marju), a fairly useful 2-y-o 5f winner, is a half-sister to 2 winners. *"A character, he's got plenty to say for himself and he's a big boy, but to stay on top of him I'll probably get him out at the end of April. Otherwise he might decide that girls are more attractive than racing. He's got talent but he's just full of himself".*

709. UNNAMED ★★★
b.c. High Chaparral – Pearl City (Zamindar). January 29. Second foal. 50,000Y. Tattersalls October Book 2. Blandford Bloodstock. The dam is an unraced half-sister to 2 winners including the listed Dance Design Stakes winner and Group 1 Pretty Polly Stakes second Beach Bunny (herself the dam of two listed winners). The second dam, Miss Hawai (by Peintre Celebre), is an unraced half-sister to 5 winners including the 1,000 Guineas winner Miss France. *"A nice sort of horse that goes well, he's very much one for the second half of the season over seven furlongs. A likeable, solid, strong type of colt".*

710. UNNAMED ★★★
b.c. Lope De Vega – Promesse De L'Aube (Galileo). January 29. Third foal. €520,000Y. Arqana Deauville August. John Ferguson. The dam, a German listed 10f winner, is a half-sister to 4 winners. The second dam, White Rose (by Platini), won the 2-y-o Group 3 7f Prix Miesque, was placed in the German 1,000 Guineas and German Oaks and is a half-sister to 4 winners including the German Group 2 winners Wild Side and Win For Us. *"As they often do at this time of year he's just grown, changed and gone a bit weak behind, but that'll all come back together. He's a nice colt for seven furlongs and a mile from September onwards with a bit of cut in the ground".*

711. UNNAMED ★★★★
b.c. Invincible Spirit – Rakiza (Elnadim). March 6. Fifth foal. 150,000foal. Tattersalls December. John Ferguson. Brother to the quite useful 2-y-o 5f winner Suite and half-brother to the fairly useful 2-y-o 6f winner and triple listed placed Exactement (by Speightstown). The dam, a French 7f (at 2 yrs) and 6f winner, was listed-placed and is a half-sister to 4

winners including the Group 2 1m Prix de Sandringham winner Baqah. The second dam, Filfilah (by Cadeaux Genereux), a useful 6f and 7f winner, is a full or half-sister to 6 winners including the Canadian Grade 2 winner Muntej. *"He's showing promise, goes nicely and I see him racing in May over six furlongs"*.

712. UNNAMED ★★★ ♠
b.f. Fastnet Rock – Rose Blossom (Pastoral Pursuits). March 3. Second foal. 220,000Y. Tattersalls October Book 2. BBA (Ire). Half-sister to the fair 2015 5f and 6f placed 2-y-o Muatadel (by Exceed And Excel). The dam won 5 races including the Group 3 6f Summer Stakes and the listed Flying Five and is a half-sister to 3 winners. The second dam, Lamarita (by Emarati), a quite useful dual 5f winner, is a half-sister to 12 winners. *"She's still in pre-training with Malcolm Bastard but she's a nice filly and you should mention her. She goes well and she's got good length and quality. She's a nice filly but Fastnet Rock 2-y-o's are not precocious"*.

713. UNNAMED ★★★ ♠
b.f. Sea The Stars – Royale Danehill (Danehill). April 2. Fourth living foal. 200,000Y. Tattersalls October Book 1. Blandford Bloodstock. Half-sister to the quite useful triple 6f winner from 2 to 4 yrs Souville (by Dalakhani) and to the quite useful 2-y-o 6f winner Bircham (by Dubawi). The dam won 2 minor races at 4 yrs in France and is a half-sister to 6 winners. The second dam, Royal Ballerina (by Sadler's Wells), winner of the Group 2 12f Blandford Stakes and second in the Oaks, is a half-sister to 7 winners including the dual Group 2 10f Sun Chariot Stakes winner Free Guest (herself dam of the Group 1 Fillies Mile winner and Oaks second Shamshir). *"This a nice filly, she'll be one for seven furlong maidens in mid-season and she's got quality"*.

714. UNNAMED ★★★ ♠
b.f. Sepoy – Samdaniya (Machiavellian). February 14. Fifth foal. 100,000Y. Tattersalls October Book 2. Blandford Bloodstock. Half-sister to the fair 14f and hurdles winner Samtu (by Teofilo). The dam, a modest 9.7f winner, is a half-sister to 8 winners including Queen's Best (Group 3 10f Winter Hill Stakes) and the French listed 12f winner and dual Group 3 placed Reverie Solitaire. The second dam, Cloud Castle (by In The Wings), winner of the Group 3 Nell Gwyn Stakes, was placed in the Group 1 Yorkshire Oaks and the Group 1 Prix Vermeille and is a half-sister to 5 winners including the multiple Group 1 winners Warrsan and Luso. *"A good sort for June and six furlongs, she's got some speed about her and she's a good sort of filly"*.

715. UNNAMED ★★★
ch.c. Lope De Vega – Savignano (Polish Precedent). May 16. Twelfth foal. 225,000Y. Tattersalls October Book 1. John & Jake Warren. Half-brother to 4 winners including the Group 2 1m Premio Ribot winner Saint Bernard (by Three Valleys), the Italian listed winner Momix (by Selkirk), the fairly useful 7f (at 2 yrs) and Hong Kong winner Easy Ahead (by Hawk Wing) and the quite useful 12f, 14f and hurdles winner Who Dares Wins (by Jeremy). The dam, a French 3-y-o winner, is a half-sister to 7 winners including the Group 1 Prix de la Foret winner and smart broodmare Field Of Hope. The second dam, Fracci (by Raise A Cup), an Italian listed winner, was Group 3 placed twice. *"He's gone through a growing phase and he's 'up behind' at present and there's a lot of length about him. He was a late foal so he needs some time but he's a promising colt"*.

716. UNNAMED ★★★★
b.f. Galileo – Sundari (Danehill). March 15. Closely related to the very useful 11f and Group 3 13f winner Mr Singh (by High Chaparral). The dam, a useful 2-y-o 6f and 1m winner, was third in the Group 3 Cherry Hinton Stakes and is a half-sister to numerous winners including the US Grade 3 placed Twin Spires. The second dam, My Ballerina (by Sir Ivor), a fairly useful 10f and 12f winner, is a half-sister to 3 winners including the very useful dual 6f winner and Group 1 1m Coronation Stakes third Zarani Sidi Anna and to the dam of the US Grade 2 winner Striking Dancer. (Lady Bamford). *"An elegant filly and a good mover, she should be coming out in a seven furlong or mile maiden in August/September. She's a likeable filly and should be on your list"*.

717. UNNAMED ★★★★
b.f. Kodiac – Windy Lane (Dubai Destination). February 1. First foal. 125,000Y. Tattersalls October Book 1. Blandford Bloodstock. The dam is an unraced half-sister to 4 winners including the very smart Group 2 10f Prix Guillaume d'Ornano, Group 2 York Stakes and dual Group 3 winner Sri Putra. The second dam, Wendylina (by In The Wings), is an unraced half-sister to 9 winners including the Group 1 10.5f Prix de Diane winner Caerlina. *"A nice type of filly, she moves well, has a good attitude and a good action. We hope to have her out at the end of April/early May. A racy filly for five/six furlongs".*

RAE GUEST

718. CHAMPAGNE QUEEN ★★★
ch.f. Showcasing – Night Haven (Night Shift). April 2. Twelfth foal. 19,000Y. Tattersalls October Book 2. Rae Guest. Half-sister to 7 winners including the useful listed 10f winner and US dual Grade 2 placed Rosa Grace (by Lomitas), the fairly useful listed-placed 5f and 6f winner Secret Night (by Dansili), the fair 6f (at 2 yrs) and 10f winner Eastern Destiny (by Dubai Destination), the fair 7.5f and 1m winner Flycatcher (by Medicean) and the fair dual 7f winner Perfect Haven (by Singspiel). The dam, a fairly useful listed-placed 5f (at 2 yrs) and 6f winner, is a sister to 3 winners including the French 2-y-o listed 5f winner Shoalhaven. The second dam, Noble Haven (by Indian King), won once at 2 yrs and is a half-sister to 6 winners including the listed winner Shoalhaven. (The Reprobates). *"She's by the very popular sire Showcasing and we had her half-sister Rosa Grace who was a listed winner for us, so we're very happy to have her. She was small but she's grown now and should be alright. One to start her career over six furlongs or maybe seven in the second half of the season".*

719. CHICONOMIC (IRE) ★★★
b.f. Clodovil – Ashdali (Grand Lodge). April 30. Fifth foal. 5,000Y. Tattersalls October Book 3. Rae Guest. Half-sister to the unplaced 2015 2-y-o Lily Ash (by Lilbourne Lad) and to the moderate 1m winner Wot A Shot (by Refuse To Bend). The dam is an unraced half-sister to 9 winners including the listed winner Sinntara (the dam of Sinndar). The second dam, Sidama (by Top Ville), won 4 races in France at 3 yrs and is a half-sister to 5 winners including the dual Group 2 winner Sadjiyd. (The Reprobates). *"She's a very nice filly, she's done very well and we're pleased with her. She'll hopefully be one of our early ones, Clodovil's tend to like a bit of soft ground but at the moment she seems to be able to go on any ground".*

720. GIRLOFINKANDSTARS ★★
b.f. Power – Gasalee (Toccet). March 30. Second foal. 40,000Y. Arqana Deauville August. Not sold. The dam, a modest 9f and 2m winner, is a half-sister to 6 winners including Coconut Show (the dam of two listed winners). The second dam, Vingt Et Une (by Sadler's Wells), a minor French 3-y-o winner, is a sister to the Group 1 10.5f Prix Lupin and US Grade 2 1m winner Johann Quatz and to the 10.5f to 13.5f listed winner Walter Willy and a half-sister to the top-class middle-distance colt Hernando, winner of the Group 1 Prix du Jockey Club and the Group 1 Prix Lupin. (Paul Smith & Rae Guest). *"She's done very well and looks lovely. A good, strong filly, there's plenty of substance to her but she's probably one for the autumn. We trained her dam who won for us but wanted a trip. I like her".*

721. MISS OSIER ★★
ch.f. Mastercraftsman – Lacy Sunday (King's Best). April 5. Fourth foal. 5,000Y. Tattersalls October Book 2. Rae Guest. The dam, a German listed-placed 3-y-o winner, is a half-sister to one winner. The second dam, Lungta (by Storm Cat), is an unraced half-sister to 8 winners including the dams of the Group 1 winners Sequoyah, Listen, Dolphin Street, Insight and Saffron Walden. (Peter Saunders & Rae Guest). *"She's growing into a nice filly. She was cheap because she was a box walker but since we've had her here we put a friend alongside her to talk to and she's not doing it! An autumn filly for seven furlongs plus. I'm very pleased with her".*

722. NOSTALGIE ★★★
gr.f. Archipenko – Neige D'Antan (Aussie Rules). March 23. First foal. The dam, a modest 9.5f and 10f winner of 3 races, is a half-sister to 4 winners including the useful 2-y-o 6f

winner and 7f Group 3 placed Nataliya. The second dam, Ninotchka (by Nijinsky), a listed winner in Italy and third in the Group 3 12f Lancashire Oaks and the Group 3 12f Princess Royal Stakes, is a half-sister to 5 winners. (Miss K Rausing). *"She's going well and every Archipenko I've had has won, so I hope she can keep the record going. You'd say she'd want a bit of a trip, but she's not slow and she's showing plenty of speed at the moment. So I think she'll be alright as a 2-y-o, probably starting at seven furlongs".*

723. ODE TO GLORY ★★★★
b.f. Poet's Voice – Blue Lyric (Refuse To Bend). February 17. Third foal. 20,000Y. Tattersalls October Book 2. Rae Guest. Half-sister to the moderate 5f winner Fine Judgement (by Compton Place). The dam, a fair 2-y-o dual 7f winner, is a half-sister to one winner. The second dam, Powder Blue (by Daylami), placed twice over 7f (both her starts), is a half-sister to 3 minor winners including the dam of the Group 3 winners Fantasia and Pink Symphony. (The Reprobates). *"A lovely looking filly, she's strong, a bit feisty but goes very nicely and she's one we're looking forward to. There's speed on the dam's side and I guess this filly will want six furlongs to a mile. Not a big filly, but well-made and she looks the part".*

724. UNNAMED ★★★★
b.f. Dandy Man – Carrauntoohil (Marju). March 18. Third foal. 5,000Y. Tattersalls December. Rae Guest. Half-sister to Miletaketheball (by Vale Of York), placed fourth over 1m on his only start at 2 yrs in 2015. The dam is an unplaced half-sister to 3 minor winners. The second dam, Tashyra (by Tagula), is an unplaced half-sister to 4 winners including the German Group 2 winner Tagshira. (RGRL Syndicate 2). *"She was a really cheap buy but she's done very well and she's going very well. I think she'll be a 2-y-o, she has a nice big backside and five furlongs will suit her to start with because she looks sharp".*

725. UNNAMED ★★
b.f. Invincible Spirit – Lady Angola (Lord At War). March 16. Seventh foal. 80,000Y. Tattersalls October Book 1. Not sold. Half-sister to 5 winners including the Group 2 winner and 7f Group 3 placed Duke Of Cambridge Stakes winner and triple Group 1 placed Duntle (by Danehill Dancer), the quite useful 9f to 12f and hurdles winner Edmaaj (by Intikhab), the fair 2-y-o dual 6f and subsequent US winner Raiding Party (by Orpen) and the fair 6f and 7f winner of 4 races Tislaam (by With Approval). The dam, a quite useful 12f winner, is a half-sister to 6 winners including the dam of the US Grade 1 winner Honor In War. The second dam, Benguela (by Little Current), won twice at 4 yrs in the USA and is a half-sister to 12 winners including the US Grade 1 winners Al Mamoon and La Gueriere. *"She's not here yet, they're pleased with her at the stud and it's great to be getting an Invincible Spirit, but I don't know anything about her yet".*

726. UNNAMED ★★★
b.f. Acclamation – Midnight Shift (Night Shift). February 27. Half-sister to 7 winners including the smart 5f and 6f winner of 6 races (including the Portland Handicap) Out After Dark, to the useful 5f and 6f winner of 5 races Move It (both by Cadeaux Genereux), the Group 3 5f Ballyogan Stakes winner Miss Anabaa (by Anabaa), the fair triple 6f winner Midnight Fantasy (by Oasis Dream) and the fair 8.5f and 10f winner Memoria (by Teofilo). The dam, a fair dual 6f winner at 3 yrs, is a half-sister to 8 winners including the Group 1 6f July Cup winner Owington. The second dam, Old Domesday Book (by High Top), a fairly useful 10.4f winner, was third in the listed 10f Sir Charles Clore Memorial Stakes. (Chris Mills). *"She came in just after the New Year and she's in very good heart. We know the family very well and this filly looks a typical five/six furlong Acclamation 2-y-o type".*

727. UNNAMED ★★★
b.f. Canford Cliffs – Quiet Waters (Quiet American). April 19. Sixth foal. 10,000Y. Tattersalls December. Rae Guest. Half-sister to the fair 12f winner Rivers Run, to the Scandinavian 3-y-o winner Hi Finn (both by High Chaparral) and a hurdles winner by Montjeu. The dam ran once unplaced and is a half-sister to 7 winners including French Group 3 winner Summertime Legacy (herself dam of the French Group 1 winners Mandaean and Wavering). The second dam, Zawaahy (by El Gran Senor), a quite useful 1m winner, is a

half-sister to 4 winners including the Derby winner Golden Fleece. (RGRL Syndicate 2). *"She's a nice filly that's doing very well and she should be running by mid-summer the way she's going. She'll want six furlongs to start with and is the first one out of the dam that on pedigree was ever likely to make a 2-y-o. She certainly seems sharp enough. One of the syndicate members is the owner of California Chrome".*

728. UNNAMED ★★★
ch.f. Kyllachy – Solfilia (Teofilo). February 22. First foal. 10,000Y. Tattersalls December. Rae Guest. The dam, a quite useful 2-y-o 6f winner, is a half-sister to 2 winners. The second dam, Suntory (by Royal Applause), an Irish 6f and 7f winner, is a half-sister to 7 winners including the Group 2 Derrinstown Stud Derby Trial winner Fracas. (RGRL Syndicate 2). *"A nice type, she had a cough and a cold over Christmas but it probably did her a favour because she's matured as a result of being able to take things easy. She's cantering away now and for a Kyllachy I think she was a cheap horse. She's nice and sound, moving well and I'm hopeful she'll be a 2-y-o winner like her dam. She should be out by mid-summer".*
TRAINERS' BARGAIN BUY

729. UNNAMED ★★
b.f. Excelebration – Velvet Star (Galileo). February 4. First foal. 18,000Y. Tattersalls October Book 3. Rae Guest. The dam is an unplaced half-sister to 5 winners including the Group 2 10.5f Dante Stakes and Group 3 10f Select Stakes winner Moon Ballad and to the unraced dam of the dual Group 2 winner Telescope. The second dam, Velvet Moon (by Shaadi), a Group 2 6f Lowther Stakes and listed 10f winner, is a half-sister to 6 winners including the dual Group 1 winner Central Park. (Mr C J Murfitt). *"She's a nice, big filly from a staying family. Seven furlongs in the autumn should be her starting point I think".*

WILLIAM HAGGAS

730. ADDEYBB (IRE) ★★★
ch.c. Pivotal – Bush Cat (Kingmambo). February 9. Eighth foal. 200,000Y. Tattersalls October Book 2. Shadwell Estate Co. Half-brother to the quite useful 2-y-o 1m winner and subsequent US Grade 3 placed Meer Kat (by Red Ransom), to the quite useful 7f (at 2 yrs) and UAE 10f winner Blue Tiger's Eye (by Motivator) and the moderate dual 1m seller winner Ask Dan (by Refuse To Bend). The dam, a quite useful 2-y-o 7f winner, is a half-sister to 8 winners. The second dam, Arbusha (by Danzig), a listed 1m stakes winner in Germany, was third in the Group 3 Royal Whip Stakes and is a sister to the Group 2 6f Goldene Peitsche winner Nicholas and a half-sister to 11 winners including the dam of the dual Group 1 winner Strategic Choice. (Sheikh Ahmed Al Maktoum. *"An expensive yearling, he's a lovely mover and has a good attitude. He needs quite a bit of time and, although there's quite a bit of speed and precocity in the family, I can't see him being out until late-summer. He's got lots of scope and should make up into a nice three-year-old".*

731. AFDEEK ★★★
b.c. Bated Breath – Soviet Terms (Soviet Star). March 25. Fifth foal. 200,000Y. Tattersalls October Book 1. Shadwell Estate Co. Half-brother to the fair 2015 2-y-o 5f winner Summer Chorus (by Exceed And Excel), to the fair triple 6f and subsequent UAE winner Pirate's Song (by Bahamian Bounty) and the modest 7.5f winner It's My Time (by Green Desert). The dam ran twice unplaced and is a half-sister to 4 winners including Best Terms (2-y-o Group 2 Lowther Stakes). The second dam, Sharp Terms (by Kris), is an unraced half-sister to 9 winners including the Group 2 winners First Charter and Anton Chekhov and the Group 1 Italian Derby second Private Terms. (Hamdan Al Maktoum). *"I wasn't berserk about him at the sales but I loved him when he came in. He's a beautiful, big, strong, well-made horse. I don't know that he's that precocious but he cost a lot of money and he's got a bit of quality. One for the second half of the season I would think, hopefully starting off at six furlongs".*

732. ALROOM (IRE) ★★★★
b.c. Kodiac – Beverley Macca (Piccolo). February 27. Sixth foal. £92,000Y. Doncaster Premier. Shadwell Estate Co. Closely related to the fair 2-y-o dual 5f winner Little Big Boy (by Danetime) and half-brother to the quite useful 2-y-o 5f winner Captain Midnight (by Bushranger) and the fair 2-y-o 5f winner

Zipedeedodah (by Zebedee). The dam, a fair 5f winner of 4 races including at 2 yrs, is a half-sister to 6 winners including the 2-y-o Group 1 Cheveley Park Stakes winner Airwave and the Group 1 Nunthorpe Stakes winner Jwala. The second dam, Kangra Valley (by Indian Ridge), a moderate 2-y-o 5f winner, is a half-sister to 7 minor winners. (Hamdan Al Maktoum). *"I like him and he'll be one of the early ones. Very uncomplicated and solid, he'll run in mid-May and we'll try and turn him into an Ascot horse. He'll do well this year and he's a straightforward colt with a good mind"*.

733. ALWAHSH (IRE) ★★★

b.c. Dubawi – Gile Na Greine (Galileo). April 10. Second foal. Brother to the quite useful 9f winner Mawjood. The dam, an Irish 2-y-o 7f winner, was second in the Group 1 Coronation Stakes and third in the 1,000 Guineas and is a sister to the smart 2-y-o dual Group 3 6f winner and 1,000 Guineas second Cuis Ghaire, the Group 3 9f Meld Stakes winner Scintillula and the Irish 1m winner and dual Group 3 placed Claiomh Solais. The second dam, Scribonia (by Danehill), is an unraced half-sister to 6 winners including the very useful 2-y-o listed 6f winner and dual Group 1 placed Luminata and the very useful dual 6f winner (including at 2 yrs) and Group 3 placed Aretha. (Hamdan Al Maktoum). *"A much smaller version of his full-brother Mawjood, who wants at least two miles! This horse shouldn't want that far, he's a nice horse and a good moving colt for around September time. It's a very nice pedigree but he's not early"*.

734. AWAAFY ★★★

b.f. Street Cry – Ethaara (Green Desert). February 21. Sister to the useful listed 1m winner Etaab and half-sister to the fairly useful triple 1m winner Estiqaama (by Nayef) and the quite useful 6f winner, from two starts, Farsakh (by Smart Strike). The dam, a useful listed 6f winner, is closely related to the very useful 2-y-o listed 7f Star Stakes winner and Group 3 7f Prestige Stakes second Mudaaraah and a half-sister to the useful 2-y-o listed 7f winner Sudoor. The second dam, Wissal (by Woodman), is an unraced sister to the high-class 2-y-o Group 2 7f Laurent Perrier Champagne Stakes winner Bahhare and a half-sister to the Group 1 1m St James's Palace Stakes and Group 1 1m Queen Elizabeth II Stakes winner Bahri. (Hamdan Al Maktoum). *"She's a nice, big, scopey filly from a very good family with whom we've had a bit of success. The type for later in the year but if she's any good she'll start over six furlongs. She should get a mile at three"*.

735. BATTERED ★★★

b.c. Foxwedge – Swan Wings (Bahamian Bounty). February 26. Third foal. 45,000Y. Tattersalls October Book 2. Amanda Skiffington. Closely related to the fair 4-y-o 7f winner Dutch Garden (by Fastnet Rock) and half-brother to the 2015 2-y-o 6f winner, from two starts, Sunflower (by Dutch Art). The dam, a fairly useful 2-y-o 5f winner, is a half-sister to 7 winners. The second dam, Star Tulip (by Night Shift), a useful winner of 3 races over 6f including the listed Sandy Lane Stakes, is a half-sister to 4 minor winners. (Mr B Haggas). *"A nice, strong colt, I'm not sure how early he'll be because I have a couple of Foxwedge's and they don't look that early. But he's strong and well-made so he should be alright in time. He'll be a 2-y-o and he'll be fast, but I'm not sure how precocious"*.

736. BIOLOGIST (IRE) ★★★

b.f. Sir Prancealot – Miss Rosie (Librettist). March 25. First foal. 20,000Y. Tattersalls October Book 3. Amanda Skiffington. The dam was a modest 2-y-o 5f winner form three starts. The second dam, Hunter's Fortune (by Charismatic), was a stakes-placed winner at 2 and 3 yrs in the USA and is a half-sister to 6 winners. (Mr C Humber & Somerville Lodge Ltd). *"A sharp, racy filly and quite strong. She's not very big, but she's a dead-set 2-y-o. She should have a good season"*. **TRAINERS' BARGAIN BUY**

737. CALL TO MIND ★★★

b.c. Galileo – Memory (Danehill Dancer). February 5. Second foal. Brother to the smart 2015 2-y-o Group 3 7f Acomb Stakes winner Recorder. The dam won the Group 2 6f Cherry Hinton Stakes and is a sister to one winner and a half-sister to 4 winners including the 2-y-o Group 3 Tyros Stakes winner Remember Alexander. The second dam, Nausicaa (by Diesis), won 3 races at 2 and 3 yrs in France and the USA over 7f and 1m, was third in the

Grade 3 Miesque Stakes and is a half-sister to 3 winners. (The Queen). *"He's a full-brother to Recorder but he's nothing like him. He's a scopey horse that'll take a bit more time so he'll be a late maturer. I like him a lot but he's for a bit later on".*

738. CIRCULATE ★★★★ ♠
b.f. Dutch Art – Royal Whisper (Royal Applause). February 6. First foal. £68,000Y. Doncaster Premier. Cheveley Park Stud. The dam is an unraced sister to the useful 5f, 7f (both at 2 yrs) and listed 7f winner and Group 2 7f Rockfel Stakes third Royal Confidence and a half-sister to 3 winners. The second dam, Never A Doubt (by Night Shift), a very useful 2-y-o winner of the Group 2 5.5f Prix Robert Papin, is a half-sister to 3 winners. (Cheveley Park Stud). *"She was bought to be sharp and she is. She's a tough, quite genuine filly and she'll take her racing well. She'll start around June time".*

739. CONTENTMENT ★★★★ ♠
b.f. Cacique – Cartimandua (Medicean). April 10. Fifth foal. 160,000Y. Tattersalls October Book 1. John & Jake Warren. Half-sister to the useful 2015 2-y-o 6f winner and Group 2 July Stakes third Elronaq (by Invincible Spirit). The dam, a dual listed 6f winner and third in the Group 3 Ballyogan Stakes, is a half-sister to 3 winners. The second dam, Agrippina (by Timeless Times), a useful 2-y-o listed 7f winner, is a half-sister to 2 winners. (Highclere Thoroughbred Racing). *"I like her very much. The dam showed a bit of speed and it's quite a fast, tough, hard knocking family. She moves really well, has a nice temperament and a nice action, so she's got a chance".*

740. CRISTAL FIZZ (IRE) ★★★
ch.f. Power – Effervesce (Galileo). February 27. Second foal. 45,000Y. Tattersalls October Book 1. Jill Lamb. Half-sister to the fairly useful 2-y-o 6f winner Qeyaadah (by Acclamation). The dam, a fair 10f winner, is a half-sister to 4 winners including the dual Group 3 6f Greenlands Stakes and UAE Group 3 6f winner of 11 races (including at 2 yrs) Hitchens. The second dam, Royal Fizz (by Royal Academy), won once over 6.5f at 2 yrs in France and is a half-sister to 7 winners here and abroad including the £1.4m Hong Kong earner Floral Pegasus. (Roberts. Green, Savidge, Whittal-Williams). *"She was a bit small but she's grown and she's quite a strong filly. I always thought she'd be sharp but she's just growing a bit, so won't be quite as sharp as I thought. I think she will be fast though and as long as she doesn't continue growing I think she'll be out in June".*

741. DELEYLL ★★★
ch.c. Sepoy – Strings (Unfuwain). March 3. Eighth foal. 82,000Y. Tattersalls October Book 2. Shadwell Estate Co. Half-brother to the fairly useful 2-y-o 1m winner State Opera (by Shamardal), to the quite useful dual 7f (at 2 yrs) and dual 10f winner Bahamian Flight (by Bahamian Bounty), the quite useful 1m and 10f winner of 4 races Qanan (by Green Desert) and a minor winner at 2 and 3 yrs in Germany by Exceed And Excel. The dam is an unraced half-sister to 6 winners including the French 2,000 Guineas winner Victory Note. The second dam, Three Piece (by Jaazeiro), an Irish placed 2-y-o, is a half-sister to 8 winners including Orchestration (Group 2 Coronation Stakes) and Welsh Term (Group 2 Prix d'Harcourt). (Sheikh Ahmed Al Maktoum). *"I'm disappointed that the Sepoys I have aren't more precocious. They're nice looking horses but they're not hitting me and saying I need to work them. This colt is the same but he gets a bit above himself so we've done a bit with him. He'll be a July 2-y-o I should think".*

742. DIAGNOSTIC ★★★★★
gr.f. Dutch Art – Holistic (Pivotal). March 6. First foal. The dam is an unraced sister to 2 winners including the fairly useful listed 6f winner of 5 races Prescription and a half-sister to numerous winners including the smart Group 3 7f Horris Hill Stakes winner of 7 races Cupid's Glory, the listed 1m and 10f winner of 6 races Courting and very useful Group 3 9f and triple listed 1m winner Clinical. The second dam, Doctor's Glory (by Elmaamul), a fairly useful 5.2f (at 2 yrs) and 6f winner, is a half-sister to 6 winners. (Cheveley Park Stud). *"This is the one I've always liked the most. I adore her, she's a beautiful mover, she's strong and will be a summer 2-y-o. She's got real quality and she'll win a good race. Sir Mark Prescott trained the dam and he thought she was very good but she got an injury".*

743. DREAMING OF PARIS ★★★
b.f. Oasis Dream – Parisi (Rahy). February 7. First foal. 90,000Y. Tattersalls October Book 1. David Redvers. The dam is an unraced half-sister to 2 minor winners. The second dam, Her Own Kind (by Dubai Millennium), a fairly useful 2-y-o 1m winner from two starts, is a half-sister to 7 winners including the multiple Group 1 winner (including the St Leger and Coronation Cup) Mutafaweq and the dual US Grade 1 Flower Bowl Invitational winner Dimitrova. (Qatar Racing Ltd). *"I like her, I think she's a six/seven furlong 2-y-o, she moves well and just needs some sun on her back".*

744. ELYAASAAT ★★★
b.c. Frankel – Lahudood (Singspiel). March 12. Half-brother to the French listed 10f winner Aghareed (by Kingmambo) and to the US 7d and 1m winner Munasara (by Bernardini). The dam, a French listed 9f and subsequent US Grade 1 10f and Grade 1 11f winner, is a half-sister to 4 winners including the French listed 10f winner Kareemah. The second dam, Rahayeb (by Arazi), a fair 12.3f winner, is a full or half-sister to 4 winners. (Hamdan Al Maktoum). *"By a champion out of a Breeders' Cup winner. This horse has yet to arrive but I saw him out in Dubai in March and he's a beautiful colt with a great step to him and weighs around 560 kilos. He has every chance of being a star and whilst I can't envisage him being anything but a back-end two-year-old, he could be a very exciting three-year-old".*

745. FEINT ★★★
ch.f. Teofilo – Ruse (Diktat). April 15. Half-sister to the quite useful 2015 2-y-o 5f winner, from two starts, Alkhor (by Exceed And Excel), to the French 2-y-o winner and German 1m listed-placed Rowan Brae (by Haafhd), the quite useful 7f and 1m winner of 3 races Flying Hammer (by Acclamation) and the modest 1m winner Confusing (by Return To Bend). The dam is a placed half-sister to 9 winners including the very useful Group 3 7f Jersey Stakes winner Ardkinglass and the dam of the listed winners Succession and Succinct. The second dam, Reuval (by Sharpen Up), a useful winner of 2 races over 1m at 3 yrs, is a half-sister to 6 winners and to the dams of the Group 2 winners Ozone Friendly, Reprimand and Wiorno. (Hamer, Hawkes, Hellin & Player). *"Has recently arrived and she's a nice filly with a good action and a good mind. She won't be early but she's a half-sister to a colt I trained last year, Flying Hammer, who was unbeaten and was subsequently sold to Hong Kong. She'll be out later in the season but she moves well and I like her".*

746. GLITTER GIRL ★★★★
b.f. Invincible Spirit – Glitterball (Smart Strike). April 22. First foal. The dam is an unraced half-sister to 3 winners including the fairly useful 2-y-o winners and listed-placed Treasury Devil and Crystany. The second dam, Crystal Music (by Nureyev), won the Group 1 Fillies' Mile at 2 yrs and is closely related to the Group 3 12f John Porter Stakes winner Dubai Success and the smart 7f (at 2 yrs) and 10f winner Tchaikovsky and a half-sister to the Group 3 winners Solar Crystal and State Crystal. (Cheveley Park Stud). *"I like her, she's very racy and very active in her mind. Quite buzzy, I suspect she'll be early because of it and I won't be hanging around with her. She's quick and I hope she goes the right way for racing".*

747. GOOD OMEN ★★★
b.c. Holy Roman Emperor – Magic Nymph (Galileo). April 10. Second foal. 40,000Y. Tattersalls October Book 2. Not sold. Half-brother to the 2015 2-y-o 7f winner, from two starts, Folkswood (by Exceed And Excel). The dam is an unraced sister to the listed Godolphin Stakes winner and Group 2 placed Galactic Star and to the multiple Irish listed-placed winner El Salvador and a half-sister to 4 winners. The second dam, Balisada (by Kris), won the Group 1 1m Coronation Stakes and is a half-sister to 6 winners. (Anthony Oppenheimer). *"A nice colt belonging to Mr Oppenheimer. Despite being by a relatively fast stallion he looks as though he's going to stay well. He has a good attitude and should do well from the second half of the season".*

748. HAKEEM ★★★
b.c. Exceed And Excel – Khazeena (Oasis Dream). March 14. First foal. The dam, a fair 1m winner, is a half-sister to 4 winners including the listed 10f winner and Group 3 Gordon Richards Stakes third Shamali. The second dam, Shamaiel (by Lycius), a useful

listed 14f March Stakes winner, is a half-sister to the dual Group 2 7f winner Naayir and to the UAE Group 3 12f winner and Group 1 Coronation Cup second Highest. (Hamdan Al Maktoum). *"A lovely horse, he's backward and having a break at the moment because he's very tall and wasn't coping with what we were doing with him, but he's beautiful. The dam wasn't much but she's bred a lovely horse with this colt. When he comes back in I'm expecting to see a much stronger and much nicer individual"*.

749. LYNIQUE ★★★
ch.f. Dylan Thomas – Danse Grecque (Sadler's Wells). May 1. Eighth foal. €100,000Y. Goffs Orby. B Grassick Bloodstock. Sister to the Grade 1 E P Taylor Stakes winner Tannery and half-sister to the quite useful 7f and 10f winner General Brook (by Westerner) and two hurdles winners. The dam is an unraced half-sister to the Group 2 Geoffrey Freer Stakes winner Multicolored, the Group 1 12f Grand Prix de Saint-Cloud winner Gamut and the listed 10f winner Athens Belle. The second dam, Greektown (by Ela-Mana-Mou), a French 10f and 12f winner, is a half-sister to the high-class stayer Sought Out (dam of the Derby winner North Light) and to the dam of the Group 2 Great Voltigeur Stakes winner Bonny Scot. (Yvonne Jacques). *"This is a leggy filly but she has a beautiful stride and whilst she's a little bit light-mouthed at the moment, I think that will improve with time. She's a full-sister to a Group 1 winner and whilst her father is not the most fashionable, he's well capable of getting a good horse and I hope this is one. I hope she'll be strong enough to run in the autumn and develop from there"*.

750. MAJBOOR (IRE) ★★★
ch.c. Dragon Pulse – City Vaults Girl (Oratorio). March 12. Third foal. 72,000Y. Tattersalls October Book 2. William Haggas. Half-brother to the fair 2-y-o 7f winner City Of Stars (by Lilbourne Lad). The dam, a fair 10f winner, is a half-sister to 3 winners including the Canadian Grade 3 winner Uchenna and the Hong Kong stakes winner Uramazin. The second dam, Uriah (by Acatenango), won 5 races from 10f to 12f in Germany and the USA including the Grade 2 Long Island Handicap and is a full or half-sister to 10 winners. (Sheikh Ahmed Al Maktoum). *"He has a sore shin at the moment so I have to take my time a bit, but he's a sweet horse. Just a kind, professional horse that may lack a bit of quality but I think he'll be a 2-y-o for six furlongs. If you saw him you'd comment on how nice he looks, but he's not flash"*.

751. MEYRICK ★★★★ ♠
b.c. Helmet – Esteemed Lady (Mark Of Esteem). April 19. Eighth foal. 110,000Y. Tattersalls October Book 1. Gill Richardson. Closely related to the quite useful 6f winner Mutawathea (by Exceed And Excel) and half-brother to the quite useful dual 6f (at 2 yrs) and 1m winner Edgewater (by Bahamian Bounty), the fair 5f and 6f winner of 12 races Sleepy Blue Ocean (by Oasis Dream) and a winner abroad by Refuse To Bend. The dam, placed once over 6f at 2 yrs, is a half-sister to 6 winners including the 2-y-o Group 2 6f Richmond Stakes winner Revenue. The second dam, Bareilly (by Lyphard), is an unraced three-parts sister to the Group 3 1m Prix de la Grotte winner Baya and the Italian Group 2 winner Narrative. (John & Julia Aisbit). *"I like him, he's out with a pre-trainer at the moment but he's done really well. He's strong, well-made and a July type 2-y-o with the scope to be a 3-y-o as well"*.

752. MOJITO (IRE) ★★★★ ♠
b.c. Requinto – Narva (Grand Slam). February 2. Second foal. €320,000Y. Arqana Deauville August. Amanda Skiffington. The dam is an unraced half-sister to the useful 2-y-o 6f winner and Group 3 Musidora Stakes second Gold Bubbles. The second dam, Well Revered (by Red Ransom), is an unplaced half-sister to 5 winners including Fahal (Group 3 Rose Of Lancaster Stakes). (Fiona Carmichael & Ian Jennings). *"He cost a lot of money but he's a nice horse, very big but well-balanced and a nice mover. I don't think he's that early but he'll be a 2-y-o. A very nice-looking horse"*.

753. MUBTASIM (IRE) ★★★★
b.c. Arcano – Start The Music (King's Best). April 11. Fifth foal. 38,000Y. Tattersalls October Book 2. Rabbah Bloodstock. Half-brother to the quite useful 2-y-o 7f and 1m winner Stec (by Bushranger). The dam, a minor winner at 3 yrs in France, is a half-sister to 6 winners

including the 2-y-o Group 1 Phoenix Stakes second Big Time. The second dam, Beguine (by Green Dancer), is an unplaced half-sister to 8 winners including the champion two-year-old and smart sire Grand Lodge and the listed winners La Persiana and Papabile. (Sheikh Rashid Dalmook Al Maktoum). "I like him, he's strong and well-made. He shows a bit of speed already so I think he'll be a 2-y-o but he's a good size. If he stays the same he'll definitely be a 2-y-o and I see the Supersprint being his target".

754. NAAFER ★★★★
b.f. Oasis Dream – Shabiba (Seeking The Gold). April 8. Fifth foal. Sister to the useful 6f (at 2 yrs) and dual listed 7f winner Ertijaal and half-sister to the useful 2-y-o 6f winner and listed-placed Odooj (by Pivotal) and the fair 7.5f winner Sharqeyi (by Shamardal). The dam, a useful 6f (at 2 yrs) and listed 1m winner, was third in the Group 3 7f Oak Tree Stakes and is a half-sister to the useful 2-y-o 6f winner and Group 3 placed Darajaat. The second dam, Misterah (by Alhaarth), a very useful listed 6f (at 2 yrs) and Group 3 7f Nell Gwyn Stakes winner, is sister to one winner and a half-sister to the useful 2-y-o 6f winner Muqtarb. (Hamdan Al Maktoum). "I've had a few out of the dam and this is a very racy filly that'll be a 2-y-o. A nice filly, probably for six furlongs".

755. NADIA PROMISE ★★★
ch.f. Galileo – Majestic Sakeena (King's Best). February 26. Seventh foal. Half-sister to the very useful dual listed 10f winner Nouriya (by Danehill Dancer), to the smart 1m winner Yuften (by Invincible Spirit), the fairly useful 2-y-o 7f winner and triple listed 10f placed Lady Nouf (by Teofilo) and the quite useful 10f winners Bella Nouf (by Dansili) and Zanotti (by Authorized). The dam is an unraced half-sister to the German listed sprint winner Shy Lady (dam of the St James's Palace Stakes winner Zafeen) and to the French listed winner Sweet Story. The second dam, Shy Danceuse (by Groom Dancer), a minor French 1m winner, is a half-sister to the dual Group 3 winner Diffident. (Saleh Al Homaizi & Imad Al Sagar). "We've had a few out of this mare and they've all been bay, but suddenly out pops a chestnut. They've been talented, good horses, so this mare could easily throw a proper one because

she's hit the post a couple of times. I hope this is the one, she's a nice looking filly for next year but if she's got the speed she'll win at two".

756. NEW TALE ★★★★
b.c. Harbour Watch – Perfect Story (Desert Story). January 31. Fifth foal. 72,000Y. Tattersalls October Book 2. Shadwell Estate Co. Half-brother to the quite useful 2-y-o 6f winner Tanseeb (by Royal Applause), to the quite useful 7f to 10f winner of 8 races Perfect Cracker (by Dubai Destination) and the fair 6f winner Quite A Story (by Equiano). The dam, a quite useful 6f and 7f winner of four races at 3 and 4 yrs and listed-placed, is a half-sister to 3 winners. The second dam, Shore Lark (by Storm Bird), is an unraced half-sister to 11 winners including the smart Group 2 5f Temple Stakes winner Tipsy Creek, the Group 3 Ballycorus Stakes winner Abunawwas and the listed winners Wathik and Magic Cove. (Sheikh Ahmed Al Maktoum). "I had one or two to buy for Sheikh Ahmed and I bought this one because he was an absolute ringer for a useful horse we used to have here called Justineo who is very fast. So as soon as I saw him I thought we must buy him. He's had ringworm but he's fine now and he's a nice horse. He'll be fast, but not necessarily that precocious. I like him".

757. NOVOMAN ★★★
ch.c. Sir Prancealot – Rublevka Star (Elusive Quality). March 10. Third foal. 90,000Y. Tattersalls October Book 2. Shadwell Estate Co. Half-brother to a minor 3-y-o winner in Germany by Zebedee. The dam, a moderate 2-y-o 5f winner, is a half-sister to 3 winners including the South African listed stakes winner Distance Done. The second dam, Al Desima (by Emperor Jones), a fairly useful 2-y-o 7f winner, subsequently won in the USA, was third in the Grade 1 Yellow Ribbon Stakes and is a half-sister to 9 winners. (Sheikh Ahmed Al Maktoum). "A nice colt who looks as if he's going to be a two-year-old. He hasn't been very good in the stalls so far but is improving and I suspect he might well be out in May/June time. He should get better as the season goes on".

758. ON HER TOES (IRE) ★★★★
b.f. Kodiac – Dancing Jest (Averti). March 31. Third foal. €155,000Y. Goffs Orby. Cheveley Park Stud. Half-sister to the modest 2015 5f and 6f placed 2-y-o Komedy (by Kodiac) and to the French 2-y-o 5f winner and Group 3 Prix du Bois second Jane's Memory (by Captain Rio). The dam, a modest 1m and 10f winner of 3 races, is a half-sister to 5 winners including the Group 2 6f Duke Of York Stakes winner The Kiddykid. The second dam, Mezzanine (by Sadler's Wells), is an unraced half-sister to 3 winners here and abroad. (Cheveley Park Stud). *"Very well named, she's a quite active but racy filly that should make a 2-y-o in May or June".*

759. ORIGINAL CHOICE (IRE) ★★★★
ch.c. Dragon Pulse – Belle Watling (Street Cry). April 11. Second foal. 100,000Y. Tattersalls October Book 2. John & Jake Warren. Half-brother to the fair 2-y-o 5f winner Paddy Again (by Moss Vale). The dam is an unplaced half-sister to 6 winners including the listed winners Asawer and Chercheuse (herself dam of the US dual Grade 1 winner Questing). The second dam, Sassy Bird (by Storm Bird), is a placed sister to the Group 2 winner Mukaddamah and a half-sister to 8 winners including the Group 2 winner Tatami. (Mr Albert Goodman). *"He cost a lot of money and, like my other Dragon Pulse 2-y-o, he's a very good-looking horse. He was bought to be a 2-y-o with a bit of scope for next year and he's exactly that. A beautiful looking horse, he's big, strong and powerful. I'm slightly concerned because it's the sire's first season and we don't know how he'll go on, but he's bred me two particularly nice horses".*

760. PRAZERES ★★★★
b.c. Sepoy – Sewards Folly (Rudimentary). May 1. Half-brother to the Group 2 6f Diadem Stakes winner and Group 1 6f Middle Park Stakes second Sayif (by Kheleyf), to the useful Group 3 5f Cornwallis Stakes winner and Group 2 Flying Childers Stakes second Hunter Street (by Compton Place) and a hurdles winner by Tobougg. The dam was placed at 2 yrs and is a half-sister to 6 minor winners. The second dam, Anchorage (by Slip Anchor), won twice at 3 yrs and is a half-sister to 6 winners including the Group 3 Ormonde Stakes winner Brunico. (Saleh Al Homaizi & Imad Al Sagar). *"I like him, I think he's the sharpest Sepoy I've got and he's a half-brother to Sayif who is a stallion. There's quite a lot of speed in that family and they've found some precocity too so I think he'll be quite early. He doesn't act like a May foal".*

761. QUINQUEREME ★★★
b.f. Elusive Quality – Finding Neverland (Green Desert). January 24. First foal. The dam, a French 2-y-o dual 1m winner, was listed-placed three times and is a half-sister o one winner. The second dam, Francais (by Mark Of Esteem), ran once unplaced and is a half-sister to 8 winners including the Group 3 7f Tetrarch Stakes winner and Irish 2,000 Guineas second France and two listed winners. (The Queen). *"She's a good-looking filly, a little bit quirky but she moves nicely and there are no problems at all".*

762. RED GUNNER ★★★
b.c. Oasis Dream – Blue Maiden (Medicean). January 2. First foal. 115,000Y. Tattersalls October Book 1. Highflyer Bloodstock. The dam, a winner of four races here and in the USA including a listed stakes, was second in the Nell Gwyn Stakes and the Sweet Solera Stakes (both Group 3) and is a half-sister to 4 minor winners. The second dam, Bluebelle (by Generous), a quite useful 12.5f winner, is a half-sister to 6 winners including the German Group 2 winner Centaine. (Simon Munir & Isaac Souede). *"He was a very expensive foal bought by John Ferguson for Godolphin and he returned him because he had a problem. He's had an operation which was successful and now he's a strong, well-made 2-y-o".*

763. SECOND THOUGHT (IRE) ★★★
b.c. Kodiac – Bobby Jane (Diktat). May 10. Fourth foal. 70,000Y. Tattersalls October Book 2. Jill Lamb. Half-brother to the quite useful 5f and 6f winner of 3 races Ifittakesforever (by Kodiac). The dam, a fair 7f (at 2 yrs) and 6f placed maiden, is a half-sister to 3 minor winners. The second dam, Twilight Sonnet (by Exit To Nowhere), a quite useful 2-y-o dual 5f winner, is a half-sister to 9 winners including the 1,000 Guineas and Coronation Stakes winner Sky Lantern and the Group 3 winners Shanty Star and Arctic. (Mr L Sheridan). *"I like*

him, he had a few issues in the winter but he's fine now. He'll want cut in the ground and he was a late foal but he's very much a 2-y-o type".

764. SEED CORN ★★★★
b.f. Exceed And Excel – Scarlet Runner (Night Shift). January 15. The dam, a very useful Group 3 Princess Margaret Stakes (at 2 yrs) and Group 3 7f Nell Gwyn Stakes winner, is a half-sister to 2 winners. The second dam, Sweet Pea (by Persian Bold), a quite useful 1m winner of 4 races, is a half-sister to numerous winners including the listed 6f winner Star Tulip. (Mr N Jones). *"A 2-y-o type. The dam won two Group 3's, so she was smart and this is a strong, well-made filly. Should do well as a 2-y-o".*

765. SENIORITY ★★★
ch.c. Dubawi – Anna Palariva (Caerleon). March 15. Brother to the Group 3 1m Prix de la Grotte winner and Irish 1,000 Guineas second Anna Salai and the useful 7f (at 2 yrs) to 2m winner Anglophile and half-brother to 6 winners including the very useful listed 7f and UAE multiple 1m winner Iguazu Falls, the fairly useful 10f winner Anomaly (both by Pivotal), the very useful winner of four listed events from 1m to 10f Advice and the fairly useful 7.5f and 1m winner Anglo Saxon (both by Seeking The Gold). The dam won the 2-y-o Group 3 1m Prix d'Aumale and is a half-sister to three stakes-placed winners. The second dam, Anna Of Saxony (by Ela-Mana-Mou), won the Group 2 14.6f Park Hill Stakes and is a half-sister to the French dual Group 2 12f Annaba. (The Queen). *"A nice, bonny colt who has only recently arrived. He has good manners and lots of strength about him and I wouldn't be surprised if he was a late-summer two-year-old. He moves well".*

766. STUDY (IRE) ★★★
b.c. Holy Roman Emperor – Bayalika (Selkirk). April 11. Eighth living foal. 105,000Y. Tattersalls October Book 1. John & Jake Warren. Half-brother to the Group 2 7f Champagne Stakes winner and 2,000 Guineas second Vital Equine (by Danetime), to the quite useful 1m winner Bramaputra (by Choisir), the fair 7f winner Poltergeist (by Invincible Spirit) and the fair 10f winner Vita Lika (by Dansili). The dam is an unraced half-sister to 6 winners including an Italian listed winner. The second dam, Bayrika (by Selkirk), won the Group 3 Prix Berteux and is a half-sister to 8 winners including the Group 2 Prix Hubert de Chaudenay winner and smart broodmare Behkara. (Highclere Thoroughbred Racing). *"A strong, butty, well-made horse. I haven't seen the sire but I imagine he looks like that too because a lot of his offspring are the same. A little bit short of leg, but very well-made and with a great big backside on him. He won't be early but he'll be a 2-y-o for sure".*

767. TADKHIRAH ★★★★
b.f. Acclamation – Pin Cushion (Pivotal). April 15. Second foal. £50,000Y. Doncaster Premier. Shadwell Estate Co. Half-sister to the modest 2015 2-y-o 7f winner Pinch A Kiss (by Sakhee's Secret). The dam, a fair 6f winner, is a half-sister to 2 winners. The second dam, Frizzante (by Efisio), won 7 races including the Group 1 July Cup and is a half-sister to 4 winners including the Stewards Cup winner Zidane and the dual 6f listed winner Firenze. (Hamdan Al Maktoum). *"I like her, we bought her at Doncaster and since then she's grown a lot. She's out having a break at the moment but I liked everything about her, she's sharp in her a mind and she's a runner. Looks well-bought and very much a June 2-y-o".*

768. THE GRAND VISIR ★★★
b.c. Frankel – Piping (Montjeu). March 12. Third foal. €750,000Y. Arqana Deauville August. Tony Nerses. The dam is an unraced half-sister to 9 winners including the Prix de l'Arc de Triomphe winner Sagamix, the Group 1 Criterium de Saint-Cloud winner Sagacity and the Group 2 Prix de Malleret winner Sage Et Jolie (dam of the Group 1 Prix d'Ispahan winner Sageburg). The second dam, Saganeca (by Sagace), was a very smart winner of the Group 2 12.5f Prix de Royallieu. (Saleh Al Homaizi & Imad Al Sagar). *"A lovely mover and a nice, back-end of the season type horse. If he shows speed he'll start over seven furlongs. He could be a quality horse next year, he has a nice pedigree, was a bit weak behind but he's done well and he moves well".*

769. TIRANIA ★★★
b.f. Pivotal – Tiriana (Common Grounds). April

22. Eleventh foal. €37,000Y. Goffs Orby. Brian Grassick Bloodstock. Sister to the Group 3 7f Fred Darling Stakes winner and Irish 1,000 Guineas second Penkenna Princess and half-sister to 5 winners including the quite useful listed-placed 2-y-o 5f winner Mystery Ocean (by Dr Fong), the quite useful 6f and 7f winner Divine Power (by Kyllachy) and the fair winner of 3 races at around 1m Madamoiselle Jones (by Emperor Jones). The dam is a placed half-sister to 8 winners including the 2-y-o listed 5f winner Head Over Heels. The second dam, Proudfoot (by Shareef Dancer), won over 14f in Ireland and is a full or half-sister to 7 winners. (Yvonne Jacques). *"She'll need some time, she's out at the moment and she's grown which is a good thing because she was a bit small. She has a bit of a temperament but she's a nice filly that's got a chance. Very well bred, she has a lot of quality and I like her"*.

770. WUROOD ★★★★★
gr.f. Dark Angel – Key Rose (Key Of Luck). March 25. Third foal. £125,000Y. Doncaster Premier. Shadwell Estate Co. Half-sister to the fair 2015 2-y-o 6f winner Sir Theodore (by Arcano) and to the fair 2-y-o dual 5f winner M'selle (by Elnadim). The dam, a fairly useful Irish 2-y-o 6f and subsequent dual US winner, was listed-placed and is a full or half-sister to 5 winners including the useful Irish 6f and 7f winner of 6 races Empirical Power and the dam of the champion older sprinter Slade Power. The second dam, Rumuz (by Marju), was placed 4 times at up to 10f and is a half-sister to 7 winners. (Hamdan Al Maktoum). *"A Dark Angel filly that cost a bit of money, she's small and strong and she'll be a 2-y-o. She'll be out in May and I hope she'll develop into an Ascot filly. A filly with a very good head carriage, she's a worker and very willing. One to look out for I should think"*.

771. YARAKI ★★★★
b.f. Frankel – Superstar Leo (College Chapel). April 4. Half-sister to 7 winners including the very smart Group 3 5f Molecomb Stakes and Group 3 5f King George Stakes winner Enticing (by Pivotal), to the useful listed 1m winner and Group 3 7f Jersey Stakes second Sentaril, the fair 7f winner Cloud Line (both by Danehill Dancer), the quite useful 1m winner Auspicion (by Dansili) and the quite useful dual 5f winner at 2 and 3 yrs Speed Song (by Fasliyev). The dam won 5 races the Group 2 5f Flying Childers Stakes and the Weatherbys Super Sprint and is a full or half-sister to numerous winners. The second dam, Council Rock (by General Assembly), a fair 9f and 10f placed 3-y-o, is a half-sister to 6 winners including the Group 3 winner and high-class broodmare Glatisant. (Lael Stable). *"She's the closest one we've had to her mother and she's lovely. Very strong, very well-made, she should be a 2-y-o. We're a bit biased in favour of Superstar Leo because she's been such a star to us, but this is a strong, quality filly with a big backside and she should be a summer 2-y-o"*.

772. UNNAMED ★★★ ♣
ch.f. Pivotal – Best Terms (Exceed And Excel). January 24. First foal. 330,000Y. Tattersalls October Book 1. F Barberini. The dam, a champion 2-y-o filly in England, won four races at 2 yrs including the Group 2 6f Lowther Stakes and the Group 2 5f Queen Mary Stakes and is a half-sister to 3 winners. The second dam, Sharp Terms (by Kris), is an unraced half-sister to 9 winners including the Group 2 winners First Charter and Anton Chekhov. (Appletree Stud). *"Very racy, the owners are new to us and this was an expensive purchase, but I think she's going to change because she was a first foal and quite small. It would help if she did grow, even though it would mean she wouldn't be early like her dam was. Pivotal doesn't put that much precocity into his stock and I think it would be a danger to try and train this filly for Ascot. I'll let her develop the way she wants to. She's nice and a pretty filly"*.

773. UNNAMED ★★
b.f. Frankel – Beyond Desire (Invincible Spirit). March 14. First foal. The dam, winner of the Group 3 5f Prix de Saint-Georges and the listed 6f Cecil Frail Stakes, is a half-sister to the fair 6f (at 2 yrs) to 10f winner of 8 races Cherri Fosfate. The second dam, Compradore (by Mujtahid), a quite useful 5f to 7f winner of 4 races, is a half-sister to 6 winners including the Group 3 Princess Royal Stakes winner Mazuna. (Qatar Racing & Steve Parkin). *"A small filly, but maybe that's because she was a first foal. She hasn't come into training yet"*.

774. UNNAMED ★★★
ch.f. Dubawi – Check The Label (Stormin Fever). April 18. First foal. The dam won 6 races at 2 and 3 yrs in the USA including the Grade 1 9f Garden City Stakes and the Grade 2 Sands Point Stakes and is a half-sister to the US Grade 1 8.5f winner Include Me Out and the minor US stakes winner On The Menu. The second dam, Don't Trick Her (by Mazel Trick), is an unraced half-sister to a US stakes winner. (Lael Stable). *"I like her, the dam won a few stakes races and this filly will need some time but there's just something about her. I'm such a fan of Dubawi – they're so hard-knocking, they get any distance and they all want to race. I like the look of her and I think it was a nice mating. These days your mare has to be pretty good to get into Dubawi".*

775. UNNAMED ★★★★
ch.c. Exceed And Excel – Clinical (Motivator). January 24. First foal. 450,000Y. Tattersalls October Book 1. China Horse Club. The dam, a very useful Group 3 9f and triple listed 1m winner, is a half-sister to 9 winners including the smart Group 3 7f Horris Hill Stakes winner of 7 races Cupid's Glory, the listed 1m and 10f winner of races Courting and the fairly useful listed 6f winner of 5 races Prescription. The second dam, Doctor's Glory (by Elmaamul), a fairly useful 5.2f (at 2 yrs) and 6f winner, is a half-sister to 6 winners. (China Horse Club). *"This colt is from a really good family, I loved him as a yearling and when China Horse Club bought him I thought that would be the last I saw of him. But in December they offered him to us, which is great. He's a nice horse, a good mover and good natured. I like the look of him".*

776. UNNAMED ★★★
b.c. Sepoy – Electra Star (Shamardal). February 5. Second foal. 36,000Y. Tattersalls October Book 3. Not sold. Half-brother to the fair 2015 dual 7f winner Electra Voice (by Poet's Voice). The dam, a fairly useful triple 1m winner, is a half-sister to 6 winners including to the useful 2-y-o 5f and 7f winner Asia Winds and the useful 2-y-o dual 6f winner Fancy Lady. The second dam, Ascot Cyclone (by Rahy), a fairly useful 5.7f (at 2 yrs) and 7f winner, is a full or half-sister to 13 winners including the Group 1 7f Prix de la Salamandre second Bin Nashwan and the US Grade 2 winner Magellan. (Mohammed Obaida). *"I trained the mother and also her first foal Electra Voice who was only 15 hands at best but she won a couple of races and was as tough as anything. But this horse is enormous and he's got a head like a Grand National Horse! Saying that, he's a very good mover although I can't imagine he'll be early. He's not bad at all, but he's one for the autumn I would think".*

777. UNNAMED ★★
b.f. Fastnet Rock – Enticing (Pivotal). April 1. Fifth foal. Half-sister to the quite useful 6f and 7f winner of 5 races Triple Chocolate (by Danehill Dancer) and to the fair triple 6f winner Jacob's Pillow (by Oasis Dream). The dam, a very smart Group 3 5f Molecomb Stakes and Group 3 5f King George Stakes winner, is a sister to one winner and a half-sister to 5 winners including the useful listed 1m winner Sentaril. The second dam, Superstar Leo (by College Chapel), a very smart 2-y-o, won 5 races including the Group 2 5f Flying Childers Stakes and the Weatherbys Super Sprint and is a full or half-sister to numerous winners. (Lael Stable). *"These Fastnet Rock's need time and the suggestion is that it's because he's been bred to mares by Galileo with plenty of stamina. They seem to think he wants speedy mares, so here he's got speed. I don't know what to make of her yet, but she's a good-looking filly with a huge backside and she moves well".*

778. UNNAMED ★★★
b.f. Galileo – Family (Danzig). March 10. Eleventh foal. 200,000Y. Tattersalls October Book 1. Ballyhane Stud. Half-sister to the 2-y-o Group 3 7f Acomb Stakes winner and Group 2 7f Champagne Stakes second Dundonnell, to the fair 6f winner Amber Isle (both by First Defence) and the modest 1m winner Family Pride (by Proud Citizen). The dam is an unraced sister to the top-class sprinter and sire Danehill, the US Grade 2 9f winner Eagle Eyed, the Group 3 Criterion Stakes winner Shibboleth and the US Grade 3 winner Harpia. The second dam, Razyana (by His Majesty), was placed over 7f at 2 yrs and 10f at 3 yrs. (Clipper Logistics). *"A filly bought relatively cheaply. She's not a gangly, backward Galileo,*

she's quite strong and whilst she obviously won't be that early I could see her running in the autumn. She has a lovely pedigree and I hope that she'll develop into a nice 3-y-o".

779. UNNAMED ★★★ La Figlia
ch.f. Frankel – Finsceal Beo (Mr Greeley). March 25. Fifth foal. €1,800,000 foal. Goffs November foals. D Farrington. Closely related to the 2-y-o Group 2 1m Beresford Stakes winner Ol' Man River (by Montjeu) and to the fair 2-y-o 10f winner Too The Stars (by Sea The Stars). The dam, winner of the Prix Marcel Boussac, 1,000 Guineas and Irish 1,000 Guineas, is a half-sister to the German Group 2 1m winner Frozen Power. The second dam, Musical Treat (by Royal Academy), a useful 3-y-o 7f winner and listed-placed twice, subsequently won four races at 4 yrs in Canada and the USA and is a half-sister to 6 winners. (Paul Makin). "What a privilege it is to get a horse like this. She's obviously an attractive filly with a classy look to her, she's a nice mover and has a lovely attitude. Unfortunately she met with a setback in February so she's been out of training for a bit, but when she was here we liked everything about her, which I suppose is natural. She has a good attitude and a lovely action and could be anything. The dam has bred a stakes winner, so she can do it. If all goes well I'd say she's more likely to be a Guineas type than Oaks – I just hope she's good. She'll probably start her career at seven furlongs". The most expensive Frankel offspring to be sold at auction to date".

780. UNNAMED ★★★
ch.c. Teofilo – Juno Marlowe (Danehill). May 17. Ninth foal. 110,000Y. Tattersalls October Book 1. Al Shaqab/D Farrington. Half-brother to the 2015 2-y-o Group 2 Beresford Stakes fourth Stellar Moss (by Sea The Stars) and to 6 winners including the US stakes winner and Grade 1 second Marzelline (by Barathea), the German 2-y-o winner and Group 3 third Sun Of Jamaica (by Cape Cross), the very useful listed-placed 10f and 12f winner of 6 races Fairmile (by Spectrum) and the quite useful 1m winner Shooting Line (by Motivator). The dam, a fairly useful dual 7f winner, is a full or half-sister to 9 winners including the Group 3 Select Stakes winner Leporello. The

second dam, Why So Silent (by Mill Reef), is an unraced half-sister to 5 winners. (Al Shaqab Racing). "I quite like him, he's a late foal but a nice mover if a little bit flighty. He's quite tall, leggy and narrow, but I'm not sure he's that weak and I wouldn't be surprised if he won a maiden in September, that sort of thing. He's a nice horse".

781. UNNAMED ★★★
ch.f. Frankel – Kirinda (Tiger Hill). March 1. Second foal. 300,000Y. Tattersalls October Book 1. Al Shaqab Racing. Half-sister to the fair 2015 2-y-o Spiegel (by Oasis Dream), placed fourth once over 9.5f. The dam, a useful Irish 2-y-o 7f winner and second in the Group 3 9f Kilboy Estates Stakes, is a half-sister to 3 winners including the fairly useful 7f (at 2 yrs) and listed 12f winner Karasiyra. The second dam, Kerania (by Daylami), unplaced in one start, is a half-sister to 2 winners including the useful Irish 12f winner and dual Australian Group 2 placed Kerdem. (Al Shaqab Racing). "She's got a bit of ringworm at the moment which is unfortunate because I thought she'd be quite an early 2-y-o. Now I'd say she could be a late summer 2-y-o and I like the look of her, she doesn't look weak. Frankel got the best mares ever, so I don't think he can fail".

782. UNNAMED ★★★
gr.f. Sea The Stars – Lady Springbank (Choisir). February 22. Second foal. 160,000foal. Tattersalls December. BBA (Ire). Half-sister to the fair 2015 2-y-o 5f winner Alizoom (by Invincible Spirit). The dam won 3 races including the Group 3 7f C L Weld Park Stakes (at 2 yrs) and the Group 3 7f Irish 1,000 Guineas Trial and is a half-sister to 4 minor winners. The second dam, Severa (by Kendor), won twice at 3 yrs in Germany and is a half-sister to 10 winners. (David & Yvonne Blunt). "A lovely filly, she's been out for a break, she doesn't look backward she's a strong, attractive 2-y-o. She has a bit about her – a lot of the Sea the Stars need plenty of time but I can see her running in August or September".

783. UNNAMED ★★★
b.g. Dutch Art – Map Of Heaven (Pivotal). January 20. Second foal. Half-brother to the quite useful 2015 2-y-o 6f winner Field Of

Stars (by Acclamation). The dam, a fair 7f winner, is a sister to the very smart Group 3 5f Molecomb Stakes and Group 3 5f King George Stakes winner Enticing and a half-sister to several winners including the useful listed 1m winner and Group 3 7f Jersey Stakes second Sentaril. The second dam, Superstar Leo (by College Chapel), a very smart 2-y-o, won 5 races including the Group 2 5f Flying Childers Stakes and the Weatherbys Super Sprint and is a full or half-sister to numerous winners. (Lael Stable). *"This is a racy horse from a speedy family but he had a bad attitude and was cut in the spring. He's done well for that, should be out in mid-summer and I suspect he'll be a six furlong horse".*

784. UNNAMED ★★★★
b.f. Dansili – Politesse (Barathea). May 4. Half-sister to the very smart Group 1 6.5f Prix Maurice de Gheest and Group 2 6f Diadem Stakes winner of 7 races King's Apostle (by King's Best), to the fairly useful 6f and 7f winner of 4 races Cape Classic (by Cape Cross), the 7f to 10f winner of 7 races Kalk Bay (by Hawk Wing) and the 6f and 7f winner Floating Along (by Oasis Dream) – both quite useful. The dam is an unraced half-sister to 4 minor winners out of the Group 1 6f Cheveley Park Stakes winner Embassy (by Cadeaux Genereux), herself a half-sister to 6 winners including the Group 2 Pretty Polly Stakes winner Tarfshin. (Mr B Kantor). *"She's a lovely filly from a family we know well. This is the nicest the mare has ever had in my opinion, she has lots of quality and a good mind – and she's a nice mover too. None of the family have been very precocious, but plenty of them have been quite fast. I don't suppose this filly will be that early but I could see her running in August and suspect she will likely enjoy fast ground".*

785. UNNAMED ★★★
b.f. Acclamation – Roo (Rudimentary). April 14. Tenth living foal. €280,000Y. Goffs Orby. China Horse Club. Half-sister to 7 winners including the very smart 6f (at 2 yrs) and 7f winner and Group 2 Prix Morny second Gallagher (by Bahamian Bounty), the very useful 7f (including at 2 yrs) to 10f winner and listed-placed Quick Wit (by Oasis Dream), the useful 5f (at 2 yrs) and 7f winner and listed-placed Roodeye (by Inchinor) and the quite useful 2-y-o winners Cockney Dancer (by Cockney Rebel) and Roodolph (by Primo Valentino). The dam, a quite useful listed-placed 2-y-o 5f and 6f winner, is a half-sister to the Group 2 6f Gimcrack Stakes winner Bannister. The second dam, Shall We Run (by Hotfoot), a 5f placed 2-y-o, is a half-sister to the Group 1 6f Cheveley Park Stakes winner Dead Certain. (China Horse Club). *"She's a naughty girl, but she's strong and seems to have something about her. She's got an aversion to conforming, so she's gone off to Gary Witheford for a lesson in how to behave. I'm sure she'll come round, she's very strong, very racy and if she allows herself to behave I'm sure she'll be quite good and she really is a 2-y-o. But blimey, she's spicy!"*

786. UNNAMED ★★★
b.c. Lope De Vega – Sahara Sky (Danehill). March 25. Half-brother to the promising 2015 7f and 1m placed 2-y-o Carenot (by Iffraaj), to the 2-y-o Group 1 6f Phoenix Stakes winner Dick Whittington (by Rip Van Winkle), to the fairly useful 2-y-o 5f winner Sign From Heaven (by Raven's Pass) and the fair dual 6f winner Lisiere (by Excellent Art). The dam is an unraced half-sister to 9 winners including the Group 1 6f July Cup winner Owington. The second dam, Old Domesday Book (by High Top), a fairly useful 10.4f winner, was third in the listed 10f Sir Charles Clore Memorial Stakes. (Paul Makin). *"A homebred colt belonging to Mr Makin. We have his half-sister, Carenot, who was placed in both her starts as a two-year-old and should do well this year. This is a half-brother to Dick Whittington but he's much stronger than Carenot was at this stage and I can see him making an August 2-y-o. He has a bit of scope and a lot of power but he may well need cut in the ground as most Lope De Vegas do".*

787. UNNAMED ★★★★
b.f. Invincible Spirit – Salonblue (Bluebird). March 30. Ninth foal. 310,000Y. Tattersalls October Book 1. China Horse Club. Half-sister to 4 winners including the useful German 11f and Australian listed 9f winner Salon Soldier (by Soldier Hollow), the Italian listed 1m winner Monblue (by Monsun) and the German listed-placed 15f winner Sommernachtstraum

(by Shirocco). The dam, a German Group 3 10f winner, is a half-sister to 8 winners including the Group 3 Curragh Cup winner Peppertree Lane. The second dam, Salonrolle (by Tirol), a dual 2-y-o winner in Germany, was third in the Group 2 German 1,000 Guineas and is a half-sister to 6 winners. (China Horse Club). *"A lovely filly, she reminds me very much of Rosdhu Queen. Beautiful to look at, but maybe not as good a mover as you'd expect from looking at her. We've had a bit of luck with the sire".*

788. UNNAMED ★★★
b.c. Galileo – Sent From Heaven (Footstepsinthesand). May 20. Second foal. €1,200,000Y. Goffs Orby. David Redvers/ Steve Parkin. The dam, winner of the 2-y-o Group 3 7f Prestige Stakes and fourth in the 1,000 Guineas, is a half-sister to 5 winners including the Group 3 Classic Trial winner Above Average. The second dam, Crystal Valkyrie (by Danehill), a fair 10f winner, is a half-sister to 3 minor winners. (Steve Parkin & Qatar Racing). *"Quite a narrow horse at the moment but I think he'll develop well. Very expensive, he's a lovely horse and not weak but he'll be much better towards the back-end. If he's good he'll run and win this year. The dam was a good 2-y-o".*

789. UNNAMED ★★★
b.c. Elusive Quality – Sharnberry (Shamardal). February 2. The dam, a fairly useful 2-y-o 6f winner and second in the Group 3 Fred Darling Stakes second, is a sister to one winner and a half- sister to several winners. The second dam, Wimple (by Kingmambo), a useful 5f and 6f winner at 2 yrs, was listed-placed and is a half-sister to 3 winners. (St Albans Bloodstock). *"Big, strong and well-made but a little bit too active at the moment. He needs to relax but I think he has potential and he's a beautiful horse".*

790. UNNAMED ★★★
b.f. Dubawi – Wonder Why (Tiger Hill). February 26. Sixth foal. Sister to the fair 2015 dual 7.5f placed 2-y-o Jordan Sport and to the smart Irish 7f (at 2 yrs) and listed 1m winner and subsequent dual Hong Kong Group 1 10f winner Akeed Mofeed and half-sister to the fairly useful 11.5f and 12f winner Wonder Laish (by Halling) and the quite useful 1m winner Waahy (by Manduro). The dam is an unraced half-sister to 5 winners including two German listed winners. The second dam, Wells Whisper (by Sadler's Wells), placed over 1m and 10f, is a sister to the very useful Group 1 10.5f Prix Lupin and US Grade 2 1m winner Johann Quatz and a half-sister to the top-class middle-distance colt Hernando. (Jaber Abdullah). *"She's a lovely filly and I love her half-brother Wonder Laish, but she's all about next year. A lovely, scopey filly for the back-end and if she's any good she'll run and win, but I won't be training her early at all".*

MICHAEL HALFORD

791. ALLOGRAPHY (IRE) ★★★
ch.c. Iffraaj – Anamarka (Mark Of Esteem). April 27. Second foal. €130,000Y. Goffs Orby. John Ferguson. Half-sister to Hint Of Grey (by Mastercraftsman), unplaced in two starts at 2 yrs in 2015. The dam won twice at 3 yrs abroad and is a half-sister to 8 winners including Salzgitter (the dam of four stakes winners in Germany). The second dam, Anna Of Brunswick (by Rainbow Quest), won once at 3 yrs and is a half-sister to the dams of numerous stakes winners. (Godolphin). *"A nice colt with a good temperament and attitude. For what he's done we're pleased with him and he'll probably want seven furlongs".*

792. ARABIAN VERSE ★★★★
b.f. Exceed And Excel – Danse Arabe (Seeking The Gold). February 28. Half-sister to the 2-y-o 6f winner and Group 3 7f Prestige Stakes second Rakasa (by Redoute's Choice) and the modest 11.5f winner World Map (by Pivotal). The dam is an unraced half-sister to the French 1,000 Guineas winner Valentine Waltz and the US 2-y-o Grade 1 winner Sense Of Style. The second dam, Save Me The Waltz (by Kings Lake), won once in France over 6.5f at 2 yrs and is a half-sister to 10 winners including the Breeders' Cup Mile, King's Stand Stakes and William Hill Sprint Championship winner Last Tycoon and the Group winners Astronef and The Perfect Life. (Godolphin). *"A lovely, sharp filly with a great temperament, she's the most forward of our fillies and she'll be ready to start as soon as the ground improves. She'll be running in late April/early May. She goes well and she's been pleasing us in her work".*

793. HUNAINA (IRE) ★★★
b.f. Tamayuz – Hanakiyya (Danehill Dancer). January 29. Second foal. Half-sister to the quite useful 2015 triple 7f placed 2-y-o Haraz (by Acclamation). The dam, a fair 1m winner, is a half-sister to 5 winners including the Irish Group 3 7.5f Concorde Stakes winner Hamairi and the Irish 5f (at 2 yrs) and 3-y-o listed 6f winner Hanabad. The second dam, Handaza (by Be My Guest), a 1m winner at 3 yrs in Ireland, is out of Hazaradjat (by Darshaan), herself a half-sister to the Middle Park Stakes winner Hittite Glory. (H H Aga Khan). *"She's a lovely, sharp filly with a good action and a good attitude. She's quite forward for an Aga Khan bred filly and she could be running in May or June, probably over six furlongs".*

794. KHANISARI (IRE) ★★★
br.c. Dark Angel – Kadayna (Dalakhani). April 15. Half-brother to the quite useful Irish 2015 2-y-o 7f winner Kadra (by Holy Roman Emperor). The dam is an unraced half-sister to one winner. The second dam, Kadaka (by Sadler's Wells), a useful 11.5f and Italian listed 15f winner, is a half-sister to the Derby winner Kahyasi. (H H Aga Khan). *"He's a lovely horse with a great action and a good temperament. He's clean-winded, we like him, he has a nice bit of pace and probably wants seven furlongs. Everything he's done has been nice so far".*

795. LAURA'S OASIS ★★★
b.f. Oasis Dream – All For Laura (Cadeaux Genereux). April 5. Fifth foal. 120,000Y. Tattersalls October Book 1. Not sold. Sister to the Group 2 6f Cherry Hinton Stakes winner and Group 1 Cheveley Park Stakes second Misheer and to the fairly useful 2-y-o 7f winner Night Song and half-sister to the fair 6f winner of 4 races at 2 and 3 yrs Hartwright and the fair 5f winner of 5 races Storm Lightning. The dam, a fairly useful 2-y-o 5f winner, was listed-placed and is a full or half-sister to 5 minor winners. The second dam, Lighthouse (by Warning), a fairly useful 3-y-o 8.3f winner, is a half-sister to 4 winners including the Group 1 Middle Park Stakes winner First Trump. (Michael Enright). *"She's a lovely filly, a backward type but with a great attitude. She was weak but she's done particularly well recently. She'll take a bit of time but she could be one for June or July time".*

796. MORITZBURG ★★★★
ch.c. Dutch Art – Providencia (Oasis Dream). March 9. Second foal. 85,000foal. Tattersalls December. John Ferguson. The dam is an unraced half-sister to 2 minor winners. The second dam, Innocent Air (by Galileo), won the listed 7f Washington Singer Stakes (at 2 yrs) and the listed 10f Severals Stakes and is a half-sister to 6 winners including the dual listed winner and US Grade 1 third Skipping and the dams of the Group/Grade 1 winners Folk Opera and Proportional. (Godolphin). *"He's certainly one of the most forward colts we have, he's a beautiful horse with a good action and he goes well. A smart colt with a good temperament, he could start off at six furlongs because he has pace".*

797. PETTICOAT ★★★
b.f. Cape Cross – Minidress (Street Cry). February 9. First foal. The dam, a fairly useful 2-y-o 7f winner, was listed-placed at 3 yrs and is a half-sister to one winner. The second dam, Short Skirt (by Diktat), a very useful winner of 4 races including the Group 3 10.4f Musidora Stakes and the Group 3 12f St Simon Stakes, was third in the Oaks and is a full or half-sister to numerous winners including Little Rock (Group 2 Princess Of Wales's Stakes) and Whitewater Affair (Group 2 Prix de Pomone). (Godolphin). *"A lovely, big filly with plenty of size and scope. She has a good attitude, moves well and is one for the second half of the year over seven furlongs".*

798. REHANA (IRE) ★★★★
b.f. Dark Angel – Rayka (Selkirk). April 15. Second foal. Half-sister to the fairly useful 2015 2-y-o listed-placed 1m winner Rayisa (by Holy Roman Emperor). The dam, placed over 12f, is a half-sister to numerous winners including the Group 3 7f Killavullan Stakes winner and Irish 2,000 Guineas second Rayeni. The second dam, Rayyana (by Rainbow Quest), an Irish 10f winner, is a half-sister to 4 winners. (H H Aga Khan). *"She's a lovely mover, clean-winded and with a good attitude. It looks like she'll make a 2-y-o around June time over six furlongs because she's been showing pace in her work. We like her".*

799. ROSE OF CHINA ★★
ch.f. Pivotal – Antique (Dubai Millennium). March 27. Fifth foal. Sister to the quite useful 7f (at 2 yrs), 12f and hurdles winner Chesterfield. The dam, a French listed 1m winner, was third in the Group 3 Prix de Psyche and is a half-sister to several winners. The second dam, Truly Generous (by Generous), won the listed Prix Petite Etoile and is closely related to the Group 3 10.5f Prix de Royaumont winner Truly Special (herself dam of the E.P. Taylor Stakes winner Truly A Dream) and a half-sister to 7 winners including the Group 2 13.5f Grand Prix de Deauville winner Modhish and the Group 2 12.5f Prix de Royallieu winner Russian Snows. (Godolphin). *"She's a good-moving filly, pleasing us in her work and she'll be one for the middle part of the year onwards. She's a little bit backward at present and we haven't done much with her yet".*

800. SHIMMLL (IRE) ★★★
ch.c. Casamento – Tempete (Dubai Millennium). May 1. Half-brother to the quite useful triple 7f winner Khatiba and to the lightly-raced 10f winner Gusting (by Tobougg). The dam is an unraced half-sister to 5 winners including the Group 1 10f Nassau Stakes and Group 10.4f Musidora Stakes winner Zahrat Dubai. The second dam, Walesiana (by Star Appeal), won the German 1,000 Guineas and is a half-sister to 8 winners. (Godolphin). *"A beautiful, big horse just like his sire was, he has a great temperament and lots of scope. For what he's doing he's pleasing us and he'll be one for seven furlongs in the second half of the year. I like him".*

801. SPANISH DAWN (IRE) ★★★
ch.f. Helmet – Bright Morning (GB) (Dubai Millennium). March 14. Closely related to the quite useful 2015 2-y-o 6f winner Rosy Morning (by Exceed And Excel) and half-sister to the fairly useful 2-y-o 6f winner Risen Sun (by Shamardal) and the French dual 7.5f winner Incorruptible (by Cape Cross). The dam, a French 2-y-o 6.5f winner, is a half-sister to numerous winners including the top-class National Stakes, Irish 2,000 Guineas and Irish Derby winner Desert King and the useful 2-y-o 6f and 7f winner and Group 2 7f Champagne Stakes third Chianti. The second dam, Sabaah (by Nureyev), a modest 8.2f placed maiden, is a full or half-sister to 8 winners including the Group 1 1m Queen Elizabeth II Stakes winner Maroof and to the placed dam of the Canadian Grade 2 winner Callwood Dancer. (Godolphin). *"A lovely-moving filly, she's done particularly well and everything she's done has been done well. She has a great action and I like her a lot".*

802. VINCY (IRE) ★★★
b.c. Elzaam – Instant Memories (Ad Valorem). April 14. First foal. €20,000Y. Goffs Sportsmans. M Halford. The dam, placed over 8.5f at Galway at 3 yrs on her only start, is a half-sister to 4 winners including the useful Irish 2-y-o 6f winner and Group 2 Railway Stakes second In Some Respect. The second dam, Burnin' Memories (by Lit de Justice), won 5 races at 2 to 5 yrs in the USA including a minor stakes event and is a half-sister to 7 winners. (M Halford). *"He's a lovely colt, well-balanced and grown a lot lately so I just backed off him a little. He has a wonderful temperament and he goes well. He'll make a 2-y-o by June or so".* **TRAINERS' BARGAIN BUY**

803. UNNAMED ★★★★
b.c. Invincible Spirit – Alshahbaa (Alhaarth). February 23. Second foal. Half-brother to the 2015 2-y-o 1m winner, on his only start, Melfit (by Sea The Stars). The dam, a useful Irish 2-y-o 6f winner, was third in the Group 3 7f Silver Flash Stakes and is a half-sister to 4 winners including the useful 2-y-o 6f winner and Group 3 7f Killavullan Stakes third Aaraas. The second dam, Adaala (by Sahm), an Irish 7f (at 2 yrs) and listed 9f winner, is a half-sister to 2 winners. (Michael Enright). *"A lovely, big horse with a great action and great presence. There's lots of style about him and he's been pleasing us in his work. He looks like he'd have enough pace to start off around June time over six furlongs and he's a smart colt".*

804. UNNAMED ★★★
b.c. Invincible Spirit – Cabaret (Galileo). February 3. Third foal. €115,000Y. Goffs Orby. BBA (Ire). The dam, a very useful 2-y-o Group 3 7f Silver Flash Stakes winner, is a half-sister to 4 winners including the 2-y-o Group 3 7f Solario Stakes and subsequent dual 10f

winner Drumfire and the useful 2-y-o 6f winner, Group 2 6f Gimcrack Stakes second and subsequent Hong Kong stakes winner Ho Choi. The second dam, Witch Of Fife (by Lear Fan), a fairly useful 2-y-o 6f and 7f winner and third in the listed 7f Sweet Solera Stakes, is a half-sister to 6 winners. (Tay Hu Chor & E Koh). *"A very big horse and one for the second half of the year, he's a beautiful mover and for what he's done so far he's pleased us"*.

805. UNNAMED ★★★
ch.f. Distorted Humor – Crazy Party (A P Indy). January 29. First foal. $270,000Y. Keeneland September. John Ferguson. The dam, a minor US 2-y-o winner, is a half-sister to 5 winners including the Group 3 Prix Miesque winner and Group 1 French 1,000 Guineas second Quiet Royal and the French Group 3 winners Acago and Sandwaki. The second dam, Wakigoer (by Miswaki), a minor French 3-y-o winner, is a half-sister to the US Grade 1 winners Go Deputy and Dare And Go. (Godolphin). *"A very good-looking filly, she goes well and has a good action. She's ready to step it up now and looks like she'll make a 2-y-o"*.

806. UNNAMED ★★★
b.br.c. Congrats – Diva Delite (Repent). March 12. Second foal. $160,000Y. Saratoga August. John Ferguson. The dam won 8 races including the Grade 3 Florida Oaks and is a half-sister to 2 winners. The second dam, Tour Hostess (by Tour d'Or), a stakes-placed winner of 12 races, is a half-sister to 4 winners. (Godolphin). *"A great mover with loads of size and scope about him. He does everything nicely, he's certainly one for the second half of the year and he's got plenty of style about him. He covers a lot of ground"*.

807. UNNAMED ★★★
gr.c. Dark Angel – Heeby Jeeby (Lawman). January 24. First foal. £110,000Y. Doncaster Premier. John Ferguson. The dam is an unplaced half-sister to 5 winners including the smart 2-y-o 5f and 6f and subsequent US Grade 2 Oak Tree Derby winner Devious Boy. The second dam, Oh Hebe (by Night Shift), a fair 3-y-o 7f winner, is a half-sister to 9 winners including the Group 3 Select Stakes winner Leporello and the listed winners Calypso Grant and Poppy Carew. (Godolphin). *"A nice horse that's done everything right so far and he looks like the type to make a 2-y-o. He was a little bit keen to begin with but he's settling into his work right now and he's been pleasing us lately"*.

808. UNNAMED ★★★
b.c. Bernardini – Looking Glass (Seeking The Gold). April 9. Third foal. Half-brother to the modest 2015 7f placed 2-y-o Hyaline (by Shamardal). The dam is an unplaced half-sister to Fantastic Light and to the listed Pretty Polly Stakes winner Hi Dubai. The second dam, Jood (by Nijinsky), was placed on both her starts, over 7f (at 2 yrs) and 10f. She is a half-sister to the US Grade 1 winners Gorgeous and Seaside Attraction), the Canadian dual Grade 3 winner Key to the Moon and the Group 3 Princess Margaret Stakes winner Hiaam. (Godolphin). *"A lovely-moving, well-balanced horse, he's shown us a nice bit of pace considering he'll probably want seven furlongs in the second half of the year. He does everything well"*.

809. UNNAMED ★★★
b.c. Casamento – Marhaba (Nayef). March 2. Second foal. €40,000Y. Goffs Sportsmans. John Ferguson. Half-brother to the quite useful 2015 2-y-o 6f winner Taurean Star (by Elnadim). The dam, unplaced on her only start, is a half-sister to the US listed stakes winner Sol Mi Fa. The second dam, Sil Sila (by Marju), winner of the Group 1 10.5f Prix de Diane and placed in the Fred Darling Stakes and the Musidora Stakes, is a half-sister to the useful 2-y-o 5f and 6f winner and Group 1 placed Frequent Flyer. (Godolphin). *"He's a nice, good-actioned horse that's grown a lot recently so we haven't done as much with him as some of the others. He'll probably want seven furlongs, we like him and he has plenty of style about him"*.

810. UNNAMED ★★★
ch.f. Shamardal – Nadia (Nashwan). March 2. Sister to the fairly useful listed-placed 7.5f (at 2 yrs) and 1m winner Namecheck and half-sister to the fairly useful 2015 2-y-o triple 7f winner Race Day (by Dubawi), the quite useful French 10f winner Cartel (by Cape Cross), the quite useful 5f and 6f winner Shipyard (by Pivotal), the fair 6f and 7f winner of 9 races

Ace Of Spies (by Machiavellian) and the fair 9f winner Pastiches (by Street Cry). The dam, winner of the Group 1 10f Prix Saint-Alary and second in the Group 1 Prix de Diane, is a half-sister to 3 winners. The second dam, Nazoo (by Nijinsky), a very useful Irish 2-y-o winner of 4 races from 6f to 7f, is a full or half-sister to numerous winners including the Group 1 6f Prix Morny placed Heeremandi and the dam of the multiple US Grade 1 winner Flawlessly. (Godolphin). *"A filly that's grown a lot recently, she's a good mover and a tough filly that enjoys her work. We'll just have to give her a bit of time so she's one for the second half of the season. She'll probably get seven furlongs"*.

811. UNNAMED ★★★
b.f. Street Cry – Northern Melody (Singspiel). April 3. Fourth foal. Half-sister to the quite useful 2-y-o 1m winner Greatest Hits (by Cape Cross), to the quite useful 1m (at 2 yrs), 12f and 14f winner Rythmic (by Dubai Destination) and a hurdles winner by Nayef. The dam is an unraced sister to one winner and a half-sister to the Group 1 12f Prix du Jockey Club winner Anabaa Blue and the listed 10f winners Reunite and Measured Tempo. The second dam, Allez les Trois (by Riverman), winner of the Group 3 10.5f Prix de Flore, is a half-sister to 6 winners including the Prix de l'Arc de Triomphe winner and outstanding broodmare Urban Sea and the 2,000 Guineas winner King's Best. (Godolphin). *"A nice, clean-winded filly that moves well, we haven't done a lot with her but she does everything nicely. A filly for the second half of the year and she'll go seven furlongs"*.

812. UNNAMED ★★★
ch.c. Pure Prize – Perils Of Pauline (Stravinsky). April 15. Third foal. €36,000Y. Goffs Orby. BBA (Ire). Half-brother to a stakes winner in Panama by Macho Uno. The dam ran once unplaced in the USA and is a half-sister to 4 winners including the Group 3 Premio Dormello winner Ombrage. The second dam, Hideaway Heroine (by Hernando), a useful listed-placed 7f winner, is a half-sister to 3 minor winners. (Tay Hu Chor, E Koh & Dermot Cantillon). *"A well-balanced colt that goes well, he just needs to strengthen a bit but he'll be ready for June or July time"*.

813. UNNAMED ★★★★
b.c. Elusive Quality – Tactfully (Discreet Cat). April 28. First foal. The dam, a quite useful 2-y-o 1m winner, is a half-sister to 2 winners. The second dam, Kydd Gloves (by Dubai Millennium), a fairly useful 1m and 10f winner, is a half-sister to the US 2-y-o Grade 3 6.5f winner and Grade 1 second Untouched Talent out of Parade Queen (by A P Indy). (Godolphin). *"A lovely horse, he's very athletic and done really well of late. He'll probably start off over seven furlongs any time after June, he has a good attitude and we like him"*.

RICHARD HANNON

Many thanks to Richard and his assistants Tony Gorman, Steve Knight and Tom Ward. They were kind enough to go through the list of their lovely two-year-olds from the Herridge and Everleigh training yards with me.

814. ABOUT GLORY ★★★★
b.c. Nayef – Lemon Rock (Green Desert). February 17. Second foal. 55,000Y. Tattersalls October Book 2. Peter & Ross Doyle. Half-brother to the modest 2015 7f placed 2-y-o Aizu (by Sakhee's Secret). The dam, a fair 5f and 6f placed 2-y-o, is a half-sister to 3 winners including the useful listed 6f (at 2 yrs) and listed 7f winner Selinka. The second dam, Lady Links (Bahamian Bounty), a dual listed 6f winner (including at 2 yrs), is a half-sister to 5 winners. *"A lovely colt, he's very well-balanced and everything's in the right place. Very good-looking, he might even be a Chesham Stakes horse. We've had a good winter and the 2-y-o's seem to be further forward than at this point last year"*.

815. ACCLAIMED ★★
b.c. Pastoral Pursuits – Amalfi (Acclamation). March 7. First foal. £52,000Y. Doncaster Premier. Peter & Ross Doyle. The dam, a winner at 3 yrs in Belgium, is a half-sister to the German winner and Group 2 placed Artemesia. The second dam, Antique Rose (by Desert King), a listed-placed winner in Germany, is a half-sister to 7 winners including the triple Group 3 winner Amarillo. *"Quite leggy at the moment, but he's a nice horse and one for the middle of the season over five or six furlongs"*.

816. ALMOREB IRE) ★★★
b.c. Raven's Pass – Macadamia (Classic Cliché). March 9. Seventh foal. 180,000Y. Tattersalls October Book 2. Peter & Ross Doyle. Brother to the useful 2-y-o 6f and 1m winner, listed Chesham Stakes third and subsequent 3-y-o UAE listed 1m winner Lovely Pass and half-brother to the fairly useful triple 1m winner Spirit Raiser (by Invincible Spirit), the quite useful 2-y-o 7f winner Kona Coast and the fair dual 1m winner Roxelana (both by Oasis Dream). The dam won 5 races including the Group 2 1m Falmouth Stakes and is a half-sister to 9 winners including the listed winner Captivator Scandinavian Group 3 winner Pistachio. The second dam, Cashew (by Sharrood), a quite useful 1m winner, is a half-sister to 6 winners here and abroad. *"A lovely, big horse that's very correct and good-looking. One for the second half of the season and he has a super temperament".*

817. AT THE BEACH ★★★
ch.c. Harbour Watch – Almatinka (Indian Ridge). February 14. Fifth foal. 30,000Y. Tattersalls October Book 2. Peter & Ross Doyle. Half-brother to the 2015 1m placed 2-y-o Dwight D (by Duke Of Marmalade) and to a minor winner in the USA by Oasis Dream. The dam, a minor winner at 3 yrs in France, is a half-sister to 4 winners including the dual Group 3 winner Alanza and the listed winner Alonsoa. The second dam, Alasha (by Barathea), a 7f (at 2 yrs) and listed 1m winner, was second in the Grade 1 E P Taylor Stakes and third in the 1,000 Guineas and is a half-sister to 8 winners including the Irish listed 1m winner Alaiyma. *"A really nice horse and a six furlong type 2-y-o, he could be one for the middle of the season but he goes very well so he might be earlier".*

818. AURIC GOLDFINGER (IRE) ★★★
b.c. Kyllachy – Ghenwah (Selkirk). March 15. Sixth foal. 60,000Y. Tattersalls October Book 2. Peter & Ross Doyle. Half-brother to the fairly useful 1m winner of 5 races at 3 and 4 yrs Halation (by Azamour). The dam is an unraced half-sister to 3 winners. The second dam, Time Of Trouble (by Warning), a quite useful 2-y-o 6f winner here, subsequently won in France and the UAE and is a half-sister to 5 winners. *"A nice, big, strong sort that should be early.*

He's a five/six furlong type 2-y-o and one for the first half of the season, but he does have scope and shouldn't just be a 2-y-o".

819. BARNEY ROY ★★★★
b.c. Excelebration – Alina (Galileo). January 29. First foal. £70,000Y. Doncaster Premier. Peter & Ross Doyle. The dam, unplaced, is out of smart Irish Group 3 7f and Group 3 1m winner Cheyenne Star, herself a half-sister to 4 winners and to the unraced dam of the dual Group 1 sprint winner Gordon Lord Byron. *"A grand horse, had a bit of a sore shin so we laid off him for a bit. He ought to make a very nice horse for somewhere like the July meeting. A lovely, big horse with a lot of scope".*

820. BISMARCK THE FLYER (IRE) ★★★★ ♠
b.c. Requinto – Livia's Wake (Galileo). January 20. First foal. £36,000Y. Doncaster Premier. Peter & Ross Doyle. The dam, placed over 9.5f and 11f, is out of the French 3-y-o 9f winner and Group 3 placed Liska (by Bigstone), herself a half-sister to 8 winners. *"Very sharp, he'll be one of our first runners and he seems to have plenty of ability. He goes really well and he's a proper 2-y-o with the scope to continue throughout the season".*

821. BLACK BOLT (IRE) ★★
br.c. Cape Cross – Safiya Song (Intikhab). April 23. Third foal. 30,000Y. Tattersalls October Book 2. Peter & Ross Doyle. Half-brother to Malakky (by Tamayuz), unplaced in one start over 6.5f at 2 yrs in 2015 and to the fairly useful 2-y-o dual 6f winner Fuwairt (by Arcano). The dam is an unraced sister to the listed-placed winner In Safe Hands and a half-sister to 5 winners including the Group 2 Flying Childers Stakes winner Cayman Kai. The second dam, Safiya (by Riverman), is an unraced sister to the German Group 2 winner and Group 1 Premio Parioli third Sulaafah and a half-sister to 3 winners. *"A lovely Cape Cross colt, he's a lovely mover and covers plenty of ground. Probably the type to have just the odd run at the end of the year. He isn't doing much yet, but whatever he does he finds it nice and easy".*

822. BRAZTIME ★★★
b.f. Canford Cliffs – Briery (Salse). April 9. Tenth foal. £54,000Y. Doncaster Premier.

Peter & Ross Doyle. Half-sister to 7 winners including the quite useful 6f and 7f winner of 6 races Great Charm (by Orpen), the quite useful 7f to 15f winner of 5 races Fregate Island, the fair 10f, 11f and hurdles winner Pearl (both by Daylami) and the quite useful 10f winner Rosaceous (by Duke Of Marmalade). The dam, a modest 3-y-o 7f winner, is out of the unraced Wedgewood (by Woodman), herself a half-sister to 10 minor winners. *"A leggy filly, she's got plenty of ability and we really like her. She looks like a filly that needs time but she seems to be coping with everything and she won't be far off doing a bit of work in April or May. Probably a six furlong type to begin with".*

823. BRISTOL MISSILE (USA) ★★
b.c. Kitten's Joy – Dearest Girl (Galileo). March 27. First foal. €145,000Y. Goffs Orby. Peter & Ross Doyle. The dam, a fair Irish 12f winner, is a half-sister to 3 winners. The second dam, Shastri (by Alleged), a modest 14f and 2m winner, is a half-sister to 6 winners including the Group 2 Prix Dollar and dual Group 3 winner State Shinto. *"A real good-looking horse, but he's a bit backward and leggy at the moment. We won't see him until the seven furlong races".*

824. BUSKIN RIVER (IRE) ★★★
b.c. Kodiac – Miss Smilla (Red Ransom). April 13. Fourth foal. £72,000Y. Doncaster Premier. Peter & Ross Doyle. Half-brother to the modest 2-y-o 6f winner Smart Stepper (by Acclamation). The dam, a fair 2-y-o 6f winner, is a half-sister to 3 winners including the Group 2 and dual Group 3 sprint winner The Trader. The second dam, Snowing (by Tate Gallery), a quite useful dual 5f winner at 3 yrs, is a half-sister to 2 minor winners. *"A lovely colt, he's nice and compact and will probably start to do a bit of work in April and be racing not long after that. He should be sharp enough for five and six furlongs".*

825. CARAMURU (IRE) ★★★★
b.c. Casamento – Zaynaba (Traditionally). March 9. Third foal. £80,000Y. Doncaster Premier. Peter & Ross Doyle. Half-brother to a hurdles winner by Bushranger. The dam is an unraced half-sister to 6 winners including the listed winner and Group 3 placed Zanughan.

The second dam, Zanara (by Kahyasi), an Irish 12f winner, is a half-sister to 6 winners. *"A lovely horse that's doing everything right. He's a really nice mover that will probably take a bit longer than our other Casamento colt, but we like them both a lot. A six/seven furlong type that doesn't have to be pushed to do anything".*

826. CONTRAST ★★★ ♣
ch.c. Dutch Art – Israar (Machiavellian). March 10. Fifth foal. 100,000Y. Tattersalls October Book 1. John & Jake Warren. Half-brother to the quite useful triple 12f winner Soul Searcher (by Motivator), to the fair 2-y-o 7f winner and UAE Group 2 third Rutland Boy (by Bertolini), the moderate 5f and subsequent Greek winner Exceed Power (by Exceed And Excel) and a winner in Greece by Teofilo. The dam is an unraced half-sister to 5 minor winners. The second dam, El Opera (by Sadler's Wells), a useful dual 7f winner, is a half-sister to 8 winners including the very useful Group 1 6f Phoenix Stakes winner Pharaoh's Delight. *"A gorgeous looking colt, he's a strapping chestnut with a couple of white socks. A horse with a nice temperament, he ought to make a nice, mid-summer 2-y-o for six and seven furlongs".*

827. CONTROL CENTRE (IRE) ★★★
b.c. Dragon Pulse – Margaux Magique (Xaar). March 23. Third foal. £35,000Y. Doncaster Premier. Peter & Ross Doyle. The dam, a minor winner at 4 yrs in Germany, is a sister to the Group 2 German 2,000 Guineas winner Royal Power and a half-sister to 3 winners. The second dam, Magic Touch (by Fairy King), is an unraced half-sister to 5 winners including the German 2,000 Guineas winner Sharp Prod. *"Not as big as the other Dragon Pulse we have here at Herridge (Whip Nae Nae). He's a tidy colt for six/seven furlongs from the middle of the season onwards and he goes very well".*

828. CURRY (IRE) ★★★
b.f. Acclamation – Marvada (Elusive City). February 2. First foal. £58,000Y. Doncaster Premier. Peter & Ross Doyle. The dam, winner of the Group 3 Brownstown Stakes and second in the Group 3 Ballycorus Stakes, is a half-sister to 4 winners including the listed-placed Italian 1m (at 2 yrs) to 11f winner of 6 races

and useful broodmare Paint In Green. The second dam, Theory Of Law (by Generous), won 3 races at 3 yrs in France and is a half-sister to the 2-y-o Group 1 Prix Morny and triple US Grade 2 winner Charge D'Affaires. *"A nice, sharp filly, she hasn't done any work yet but looks like she'll be quite early. A sweet filly and the type for five/six furlongs"*.

829. DESERT WATER (IRE) ★★★
b.f. Sepoy – Desert Sunrise (Green Desert). March 18. First foal. 80,000Y. Tattersalls October Book 2. Peter & Ross Doyle. The dam, a fair 6f and 7f placed maiden, is a half-sister to 3 winners including the Group1 Middle Park Stakes winner Primo Valentino and the Group 2 Cherry Hinton Stakes winner Dora Carrington. The second dam, Dorothea Brooke (by Dancing Brave), a fair 9f winner, is a half-sister to 6 winners. *"I quite like these Sepoys and this appears to be a nice filly. We're in no rush with her but she's a nice filly for six or seven furlongs I would think"*.

830. DEVIL'S BRIDGE (IRE) ★★★★
b.c. Casamento – Cantaloupe (Priolo). February 16. Tenth foal. £58,000Y. Doncaster Premier. Peter & Ross Doyle. Half-brother to 7 winners including the modest 10f and hurdles winner Cantabilly (by Distant Music), the fair 12f and 2m winner Sky Pilot (by Dilshaan) and the fair 2-y-o 8.5f winner Pinarius (by Amadeus Wolf). The dam is an unraced half-sister to 9 winners including the French Group 3 12f Prix de Royaumont winner Cantilever. The second dam, Cantanta (by Top Ville), won over 2m at 3 yrs and is a sister to the Irish Oaks winner Princess Pati and a half-sister to the Group 2 Great Voltigeur Stakes winner Seymour Hicks. *"He does everything right, he's a lovely horse, a good mover and a six/seven furlong horse with a lot of ability. We're happy with where he's at and he's giving us the right signs"*.

831. DICK TRACY (IRE) ★★★
b.c. Lawman – Modeeroch (Mozart). February 2. Third foal. €115,000Y. Arqana Deauville August. Peter & Ross Doyle. Half-brother to the French 3-y-o 1m winner Damsah (by Mr Greeley). The dam, a triple listed 7f winner (including at 2 yrs), was placed in six Group races including the Group 2 7f Debutante Stakes and is a half-sister to 7 winners including the Group 1 Cheveley Park Stakes third Danaskaya (dam of the Dewhurst Stakes winner Belardo). The second dam, Majinskaya (by Marignan), winner of the listed 12f Prix des Tuileries, is a half-sister to 6 winners including the dam of the Group 1 5f Prix de l'Abbaye winner Kistena. *"A fine, big, strapping horse with a lot of scope. He ought to make a middle to back-end 2-y-o over seven furlongs or a mile. A lovely strong colt"*.

832. DOURADO (IRE) ★★★
b.c. Dark Angel – Skehana (Mukaddamah). March 24. Eighth foal. 130,000Y. Tattersalls October Book 2. Tony Nerses. Brother to the fair 2015 2-y-o 7f winner Ambriel and half-brother to the fairly useful 6f (at 2 yrs) and 1m winner Jake's Destiny (by Desert Style),, the fair dual 8.5f winner Molten Lave (by Rock Of Gibraltar), the modest 7f (at 2 yrs) to 9f winner San Silvestro (by Fayruz) and the moderate 2-y-o 6f winner Peppercorn Rent (by Fasliyev). The dam, a fair 2-y-o 7f winner, is a half-sister to the very smart sprinter and Group 1 Golden Jubilee Stakes winner Fayr Jag. The second dam, Lominda (by Lomitas), a quite useful 2-y-o 6f winner, is a half-sister to 8 winners. *"A sharp horse and a really good mover. Could be an early season type for five and six furlongs. A real nice horse"*.

833. EUGINIO (IRE) ★★★
b.c. Fastnet Rock – Starstone (Diktat). February 13. Sixth foal. 155,000Y. Tattersalls October Book 1. Tony Nerses. Half-brother to the useful 7f (at 2 yrs) and listed 1m winner Handassa (by Dubawi), to the fair 2-y-o 6f winner Emirates Hills and the fair 5f (at 2 yrs) and 6f winner Dutch Heritage (by Dutch Art). The dam is an unraced half-sister to the Group 1 July Cup winner Pastoral Pursuits and the Group 1 Haydock Park Sprint Cup winner Goodricke. The second dam, Star (by Most Welcome), a quite useful 5f winner, is a half-sister to 7 winners including the useful 2-y-o listed 5f winner Four-Legged-Friend and the US dual Grade 3 winner Superstrike. *"A lovely, big horse, he's very strong and there's an awful lot of power about him. If he has the speed to go with his backside I'd like to think he'd be a six furlong sprinter in mid-season"*.

834. FABRIC ★★★ ♠
b.f. Acclamation – Decorative (Danehill Dancer). February 4. Second foal. 80,000Y. Tattersalls October Book 2. John & Jake Warren. Half-sister to the fair 2015 2-y-o 7f winner Aneesah (by Canford Cliffs). The dam, a fairly useful 6f (at 2 yrs) and 1m winner, is a full or half-sister to 3 minor winners. The second dam, Source Of Life (by Fasliyev), is an unraced half-sister to 9 winners including the Group 3 winners Australie and Forgotten Voice. *"We'll be getting on with him because he's a sharp, early type for five and six furlongs. Very strong-looking, well-made and correct".*

835. FLEETING MOTION ★★
ch.f. Sepoy – Fleeting Image (Sir Percy). March 8. First foal. 125,000Y. Tattersalls October Book 2. Peter & Ross Doyle. The dam, a quite useful dual 12f winner, is a half-sister to 6 winners including the Group 1 Tattersalls Gold Cup winner Rebelline (dam of the Group 3 winner Recharge) and the Group 2 Blandford Stakes winner Quws. The second dam, Fleeting Rainbow (by Rainbow Quest), a modest 10f placed 3-y-o, is a half-sister to 3 winners. *"A nice filly that hasn't done anything yet, so we'll take another look at her in mid-season".*

836. GIOVANNI ACUTO ★★★★ ♠♠
gr.c. Redoute's Choice – Alla Speranza (Sir Percy). February 6. First foal. €140,000Y. Goffs Orby. Peter & Ross Doyle. The dam, a useful Irish 1m (at 2 yrs) and Group 3 10f Kilternan Stakes winner, is a half-sister to 3 winners. The second dam, Alvarita (by Selkirk), a French listed 10.5f winner, is a sister to one winner and a half-sister to the 10f winner and Group 2 10f Prix Greffulhe second Albion. *"A lovely colt, he was a bit of a monkey early on so we started to do a bit with him and he settled down. He's fine now and he'll be a very nice horse for seven furlongs in late summer. We really like him but he hasn't done any work yet".*

837. HAKEEM (FR) ★★★★
b.c. Wootton Bassett – Diamond Star (Daylami). April 3. Fifth foal. €80,000Y. Tattersalls Ireland September. BLM Bloodstock. Half-brother to the French 3-y-o 7.5f and 9f winner by Dylan Thomas. The dam, a moderate Irish 12f placed maiden, is a sister to the Group 1 Irish Derby and Tattersalls Gold Cup winner Grey Swallow and a half-sister to the Group 3 1m winner Moonlight Dance and the dam of the Group 1 Gran Criterium winner Night Style. The second dam, Style Of Life (by The Minstrel), won over 6f and 7f in Ireland. *"A lovely horse, he goes very well and if there were races for him now we'd probably be working him. We'll wait for the six furlong races, he's well-balanced and everything's good about him".*

838. HIMSELF ★★★★ ♠
b.c. High Chaparral – Self Centred (Medicean). January 31. First foal. The dam, a quite useful listed-placed 2-y-o 7f winner, is a half-sister to 6 winners including the useful 7f (at 2 yrs) and 1m winner and listed-placed Chef. The second dam, Ego (by Green Desert), a dual listed-placed 2-y-o dual 6f winner, is a half-sister to 3 winners. *"Quite smart, he's a lovely mover with a good attitude and hopefully we'll be able to get on with him earlier than most 2-y-o's by the sire. A really nice sort that finds everything easy, Tom Marquand's been riding him and he really likes him".*

839. HIPPOCAMPUS (IRE) ★★★
b.c. Born To Sea – Tolzey (Rahy). April 27. Seventh foal. £70,000Y. Doncaster Premier. Peter & Ross Doyle. Half-brother to 4 winners including the quite useful French 7f (at 2 yrs) and 1m winner and listed-placed Game Mascot (by Kheleyf), the quite useful 7f (at 2 yrs) and 10f winner Solicitor (by Halling) and the modest 1m winner Rosie Crowe (by Approve). The dam, a fairly useful 2-y-o 6f winner, was triple listed-placed and is a sister to the French 2-y-o listed 7f winner Inner Temple and a half-sister to 2 winners. The second dam, Legal Opinion (by Polish Precedent), placed at 2 yrs in France, is a half-sister to 7 winners. *"A lovely horse for six/seven furlongs. He has a lot of ability and he's a good mover, so we're happy with him. He's a bit leggy and backward, so he's one for the second half of the season".*

840. HUSHOOD (IRE) ★★★
b.c. Champs Elysees – Cochin (Swain). March 21. Ninth foal. 160,000Y. Tattersalls October Book 2. Peter & Ross Doyle. Brother to the minor French 11f and 12f winner and Group

3 third Seaport, closely related to the French 12f and 14f, and Australian dual Group 3 winner Permit (by Dansili) and half-brother to the fair 2-y-o 1m winner Ritchie McCaw (by Zamindar). The dam, a minor 3-y-o winner in France, stayed middle-distances and is a half-sister to 8 winners including the US dual Grade 1 winner Senure. The second dam, Diese (by Diesis), won 3 races in France including the Group 3 10.5f Prix Corrida and two listed events and is a half-sister to 13 winners including the champion European 2-y-o Xaar. *"A big horse and a bit leggy, we won't be in any hurry with him. A good-looking horse for seven furlongs".*

841. INFERAD ★★★★ ♠
b.f. Lonhro – Aquarius Star (Danehill Dancer). January 1. Second foal. €250,000Y. Goffs Orby. Peter & Ross Doyle. The dam, a fair 10f winner, is a half-sister to 2 winners including the 2-y-o 5f and 6f winner, Group 1 Middle Park Stakes third and subsequent US Grade 3 winner Doc Holiday. The second dam, Easter Heroine (by Exactly Sharp), was placed over 7f (at 2 yrs) and 10f in Ireland and is a half-sister to 4 winners. *"A beautiful filly and a standout at the sale, she's big, scopey and classy. Seven furlongs beckons for her and hopefully she'll appear in the Fillies' Mile you never know, she's a nice filly though".*

842. JERSEY HEARTBEAT ★★★
b.f. Bated Breath – Selkirk Sky (Selkirk). March 8. Sixth foal. 40,000Y. Tattersalls October Book 2. Amanda Skiffington. Half-brother to the quite useful 2015 2-y-o 6f winner Torment (by Dark Angel), to the fair dual 5f winner (including at 2 yrs) Flicka's Boy (by Paco Boy) and the Scandinavian winner Mr Fong (by Dr Fong). The dam, a moderate 7f winner, is a half-sister to 3 winners including the triple listed winner and Group 2 6f Gimcrack Stakes second Andronikos. The second dam, Arctic Air (by Polar Falcon), a quite useful 2-y-o 7f winner, is a sister to the useful listed 7f winner Arctic Char and a half-sister to 6 winners including the Group 2 winners Barrow Creek and Last Resort, and to the dam of the Group 2 winner Trans Island. *"A nice-enough filly, but she hasn't done a lot yet. She ought to be quite quick being by Bated Breath and she's a sweet little filly".*

843. JUAN HORSEPOWER ★★★
b.c. Foxwedge – Elysee (Fantastic Light). March 17. Second foal. £50,000Y. Doncaster Premier. Sackville/Donald. Half-brother to Super Sasha (by Modigliani), a winner of 16 races in Italy. The dam is an unraced half-sister to 7 winners including Dordogne (Group 3 Derby Trial). The second dam, Riberac (by Efisio), a smart winner of 10 races from 5f to 1m including three listed events, is a full or half-sister to 5 winners. *"By the Australian sprinting stallion Foxwedge, it'll be interesting to see what his progeny do up here. Looks more of a six furlong 2-y-o than five but he's all there for now, so we might get on with him in the next month or so. A nice horse".*

844. KEIR HARDIE (IRE) ★★★
gr.c. Dark Angel – Penicuik (Hernando). April 15. Fifth foal. 50,000Y. Tattersalls December. Peter & Ross Doyle. Half-brother to the useful listed 5f St Hugh's Stakes winner and dual Group 3 placed WhatdoIwantthatfor (by Kodiac). The dam ran once unplaced and is a half-sister to 7 winners including the US dual Grade 1 winner White Heart and the listed winner Kind Regards. The second dam, Barari (by Blushing Groom), is an unraced half-sister to 9 winners including the Group 2 Prix de l'Opera winner Colour Chart (herself dam of the Grade 1 Breeders' Cup Juvenile Fillies winner Tempera). *"A nice, big, tall colt with a lot of daylight beneath him so he's got a lot of scope. He should be a mid-season horse and he's filling out his frame nicely".*

845. KHAFOO SHEMIMI (IRE) ★★★
b.c. Dark Angel – Appleblossom Pearl (Peintre Celebre). April 20. Fifth foal. 80,000Y. Tattersalls October Book 2. Peter & Ross Doyle. Closely related to the moderate 6f winner John Coffey (by Acclamation) and half-brother to the fair 2-y-o 6f winner Silent Footsteps (by Footstepsinthesand). The dam, a minor 4-y-o Irish 7f winner, is a half-sister to 6 winners including the Group 3 placed Rabi and Kawagino. The second dam, Sharakawa (by Darshaan), is an unraced half-sister to 4 winners including the Irish Group 3 placed Mempari. *"He lost a bit of weight early in the year so we dropped him back and he's done well for it. He'll take a bit of time because we'll need to look after him for a bit, but he's fine now. Probably one for seven furlongs".*

846. KREB'S CYCLE (IRE) ★★★★
ch.c. Helmet – La Noe (Nayef). April 12. First foal. €85,000Y. Goffs Orby. Peter & Ross Doyle. The dam, a minor dual 3-y-o winner in France, is a half-sister to one winner abroad. The second dam, Snow Gretel (by Green Desert), a German listed 1m winner, is a half-sister to 6 winners including the 2-y-o Group 2 1m Royal Lodge Stakes winner and 2,000 Guineas second Snow Ridge. *"He worked the other day and we were really pleased with how he went – he seems to have plenty of ability. A lovely horse and five furlongs wouldn't be too sharp for him".*

847. LEGENDARY LUNCH (IRE) ★★★★
ch.c. Dragon Pulse – Taalluf (Hansel). March 20. Ninth foal. £78,000Y. Doncaster Premier. Peter & Ross Doyle. Half-brother to 6 winners including the useful listed-placed 2-y-o 5f winner Middleham (by Best Of The Bests), the fair 7f and 1m winner of 9 races Talent Scout (by Exceed And Excel), the fair 6f (including at 2 yrs) to 1m winner Sun Catcher (by Cape Cross) and the fair 2-y-o 6f winner Bathwick Gold (by Noverre). The dam, a quite useful 6f placed 2-y-o, is a half-sister to 3 minor winners. The second dam, Tatwij (by Topsider), a quite useful 2-y-o dual 5f winner, is a half-sister to the triple US Grade 1 winner Tejano. *"Probably one of the nicest colts we have at Everleigh. We're really happy with our Dragon Pulse's and this colt has a good engine and finds everything fairly easy at the moment. We're chuffed with him and hopefully he's one we can get on with a bit earlier than the rest of them. A very nice horse".*

848. LEXINGTON SKY (IRE) ★★★
b.f. Iffraaj – Hurricane Lily (Ali-Royal). April 16. Seventh foal. 55,000Y. Tattersalls October Book 2. Peter & Ross Doyle. Half-sister to 4 winners including the fair 2015 2-y-o 6f winner Mon Beau Visage (by Footstepsinthesand), the quite useful dual 5f winner Kool Henry (by One Cool Cat) and the 5f to 7f winner of 10 races Moscow Eight (by Elusive City). The dam, placed fourth twice over 6f at 2 yrs, is a half-sister to 7 winners including the Group 2 Sandown Mile and Group 3 Craven Stakes winner Hurricane Alan. The second dam, Bint Al Balad (by Ahonoora), a modest 7f placed 3-y-o, is a sister to the useful Group 3 7f Nell Gwyn Stakes winner A-To-Z. *"A lovely filly. She's an early type, definitely over six and maybe even five furlongs. She did her first bit of work really nicely. A very correct filly".*

849. LIMELITE (IRE) ★★★ ♠
b.f. Dark Angel – Light It Up (Elusive City). March 23. Fourth foal. 50,000Y. Tattersalls October Book 2. Will Edmeades. Closely related to the fairly useful 2-y-o dual 5f winner Dangerous Moonlite and to the minor winner of 10 races abroad Touch Paper (both by Acclamation). The dam, a fair 5f and 6f placed maiden, is a half-sister to the dual 2-y-o 7f and subsequent South African Group 2 winner Purple Orchid. The second dam, Fabuco (by Mujadil), a modest 2-y-o 5f winner, is a sister to 2 winners including the useful 2-y-o 5f winner and Group 3 placed Connemara and a half-sister to 3 winners. *"A nice filly that came in quite late, but she's settled in well and ought to make a six/seven furlong filly. Quite sweet".*

850. LOGI (IRE) ★★★
b.c. Kodiac – Feet Of Flame (Theatrical). April 17. Ninth foal. 75,000Y. Tattersalls October Book 2. Peter & Ross Doyle. Half-brother to the fair 2015 2-y-o 7f and 8.5f winner Threebagsue (by Lord Shanakill), to the fairly useful 7f to 10f winner and Group 3 third Kinky Afro (by Modigliani), the fairly useful 2-y-o 8.7f winner Fullback (by Redback) and the fair 2-y-o 7f winner Orpen Fire (by Orpen). The dam is a placed half-sister to one winner in the USA. The second dam, Red Hot Dancer (by Seattle Dancer), is a US placed half-sister to 5 winners including the Stewards Cup winner Green Ruby and the minor US stakes winner Madame Secretary (dam of the French 1,000 Guineas winner Ta Rib). *"A tidy horse that'll be racing in the early part of the season and he's ready to start work now".*

851. LUDUAMF (IRE) ★★★
ch.c. Tamayuz – Aphorism (Halling). February 16. Sixth foal. 18,000Y. Tattersalls October Book 3. Peter & Ross Doyle. Half-brother to the 2015 1m placed 2-y-o Golden Isles (by Mastercraftsman) and to the fair 2-y-o dual 5f winner Danz Choice (by Kheleyf). The dam, a fair 12f to 2m 2f winner, is a half-sister to 11 winners including the Group 2 12f Princess Of Wales's Stakes winner Craigsteel and the

Group 1 Prix du Cadran winner and Ascot Gold Cup second Invermark. The second dam, Applecross (by Glint Of Gold), a smart winner of 3 races from 10f to 13.3f and placed in the Park Hill Stakes and the Princess Royal Stakes, is a half-sister to 6 winners including Coigach (Group 3 Park Hill Stakes). *"He looks a nice, sharp colt and I thought all the way along he was cheap".* **TRAINERS' BARGAIN BUY**

852. MALCOLM THE PUG (IRE) ★★★
b.c. Acclamation – La Zona (Singspiel). March 24. First foal. 48,000Y. Tattersalls October Book 2. Peter & Ross Doyle. The dam won 11 races including four listed events in Scandinavia and is a half-sister to 4 winners. The second dam, Reine De Neige (by Kris), a fairly useful 8.5f winner, was listed-placed twice and is a half-sister to 3 winners. *"A nice horse, he ought to be sharp enough being by Acclamation and he goes well. Doing everything as he should and hopefully he'll waken up when we give him a bit of work".*

853. MAMDOOD (IRE) ★★★
gr.c. Clodovil – Fact (American Post). March 2. Third foal. 45,000Y. Tattersalls October Book 2. Peter & Ross Doyle. Half-brother to the minor French 2015 2-y-o 8.5f winner Bounty Boy (by Bushranger). The dam ran once unplaced and is a half-sister to 2 winners including the Group 3 Boland Stakes winner Polar Way. The second dam, Fetish (by Dancing Brave), won twice over 1m and is a half-sister to 8 winners including the Group 2 6f Lowther Stakes winner and Group 1 Cheveley Park Stakes second Kingscote (dam of the smart Group 3 1m winner and French 2,000 Guineas second Rainbow Corner). *"A strong-looking horse, he's going well and finds everything quite natural. One for six furlongs".*

854. METRONOMIC (IRE) ★★★
b.c. Roderic O'Connor – Meon Mix (Kayf Tara). February 17. Sixth foal. €75,000Y. Goffs Orby. Peter & Ross Doyle. Half-brother to the quite useful 1m and 10f winner Sublimation (by Manduro). The dam, a moderate fourth placed maiden, is a half-sister to the very useful 2-y-o listed 1m winner and Group 1 Fillies' Mile and Group 1 Yorkshire Oaks placed Dash To The Front and to the useful listed 10.8f winner Dash To The Top. The second dam, Millennium Dash (by Nashwan), a fairly useful 10.2f winner, is a half-sister to 4 winners and to the unplaced dam of the Sun Chariot Stakes winner Kissogram. *"Will take a bit longer than most of ours but he's worth keeping an eye on at the back-end".*

855. MONEY IN MY POCKET (IRE) ★★★
b.f. Acclamation – Azabara (Pivotal). April 4. Third foal. €90,000Y. Arqana Deauville August. Peter & Ross Doyle. Half-sister to a minor French winner of 3 races by Dansili. The dam, a listed 1m Prix des Lilas winner, is a half-sister to 2 winners. The second dam, Danella (by Highest Honor), a French listed 3-y-o 7f winner, is a half-sister to 5 minor winners in France and Italy. *"A lovely filly that came from France. She's quite long, has a nice pedigree and ought to make a six/seven furlong filly later in the year. Very sweet and with a good temperament".*

856. MONOSHKA (IRE) ★★★
b.c. Kodiac – Coastal Waters (Halling). January 27. Third foal. £75,000Y. Doncaster Premier. Peter & Ross Doyle. The dam, a fair 7f winner, is a half-sister to 7 winners. The second dam, Gretel (by Hansel), a useful 2-y-o 7f winner and third in the Group 3 1m May Hill Stakes and is a half-sister to 5 winners. *"Just like the other Kodiac we have here at Everleigh, Buskin River, he's finding things quite easy at the moment and he's fairly forward. He's a bit of a lad but he's a lovely colt and we're looking forward to getting on with him when he's ready".*

857. MOUILLE POINT ★★
b.f. Motivator – Turning Leaf (Last Tycoon). March 13. Twelfth foal. 300,000Y. Tattersalls October Book 1. Mayfair Speculators / Peter & Ross Doyle. Half-sister to 5 winners including the German 3-y-o Group 3 1m and listed 11f winner Turning Light (by Fantastic Light and herself dam of the US stakes winner Surrey Star), the fairly useful 2-y-o 7f winner Oxsana (by Dubawi) and the quite useful 2-y-o 6f winner Exceptionelle (by Exceed And Excel). The dam, a German 2-y-o winner and third in the Group 2 German 1,000 Guineas, is a half-sister to 6 winners. The second dam, Tamacana (by Windwurf), a German listed winner of 3 races at 2 and 3 yrs, is a half-sister to 4

winners. *"She's a nice filly and for a Motivator quite relaxed but it'll be a while before she does anything serious. One for the back-end of the year I should think".*

858. MR SCARAMANGA ★★★
b.c. Sir Percy – Lulla (Oasis Dream). March 16. First foal. €78,000Y. Tattersalls Ireland September. Peter & Ross Doyle. The dam, a quite useful 5f winner, is a half-sister to 3 winners. The second dam, Dominica (by Alhaarth), winner of the Group 2 5f King's Stand Stakes and the Group 3 Cornwallis Stakes, is a half-sister to 3 winners. *"A nice little colt that's well-balanced and looks like a 2-y-o type for six/seven furlongs".*

859. MR TYRRELL ★★★
b.c. Helmet – Rocking (Oasis Dream). March 19. Fifth foal. 62,000Y. Tattersalls October Book 2. Peter & Ross Doyle. Half-brother to the fairly useful 2-y-o 5f winner and 3-y-o Group 3 6f Ballyogan Stakes second Boston Rocker (by Acclamation), to the fair 2-y-o 5f winner Rocking The Boat (by Zebedee) and the modest 2-y-o 5f winner Sleepy Joe (by Jeremy). The dam, a quite useful 2-y-o 5f winner, is a half-sister to 10 winners including the very smart Group 2 5f Flying Childers Stakes winner Superstar Leo (herself the dam of two stakes winners). The second dam, Council Rock (by General Assembly), a fair 9f and 10f placed 3-y-o, is a half-sister to 9 winners including the dam of the Group 1 winners Footstepsinthesand and Pedro The Great. *"A nice, strong, quite tall horse with a bit of scope. We haven't worked him yet but we're pleased with him so far".*

860. MUMS THE WORD ★★★★♠
b.f. Mayson – Tell Mum (Marju). April 4. Third foal. 52,000Y. Tattersalls October Book 2. Peter & Ross Doyle. Half-sister to Malmostosa, unplaced in one start at 2 yrs in 2015 and to the fair 2-y-o 5f winner Granny Alice (both by Intikhab). The dam is an unraced half-sister to 4 winners including the 2-y-o Group 3 Horris Hill Stakes winner Tell Dad. The second dam, Don't Tell Mum (by Dansili), a useful 5f (at 2 yrs) and 6f winner and second in the Super Sprint, is a half-sister to 2 winners including the listed National Stakes winner and Group 3 third Icesolator. *"A beautiful filly, she's very sharp and racy. Could be a Queen Mary filly and I really like her".*

861. MUQAATIL (USA) ★★★★★
b.c. Lonhro – Lightning Lydia (Broad Brush). April 3. Eighth foal. 160,000Y. Tattersalls October Book 2. Peter & Ross Doyle. Half-brother to 4 winners in the USA including the listed winner and Grade 2 third Walkwithapurpose (by Candy Ride), the listed winner Charges Cotton (by Dehere) and the minor stakes-placed winner of 11 races Go Maire Tu (by Congrats). The dam, a minor US 3-y-o winner, is a sister to the US dual Grade 1 winner Schossberg and a half-sister to 7 winners. The second dam, a minor US winner of 3 races, is a half-sister to 8 winners. *"A lovely horse and I think Lonhro will make a good stallion. This colt moves very well and ought to make a seven furlong/miler. A very nice horse with a good attitude, he's a five star 2-y-o in my book".*

862. MUSCIKA ★★★
b.c. Kyllachy – Miss Villefranche (Danehill Dancer). April 13. Second foal. 75,000foal. Tattersalls December. Shadwell Estate Co. Half-brother to the modest 2016 1m placed 3-y-o Redmane (by Bahamian Bounty). The dam, a modest dual 9f winner, is a half-sister to 3 winners including the very useful 1m winner and listed-placed Moyenne Corniche. The second dam, Miss Corniche (Hernando), a 7f (at 2 yrs) and listed 10f winner, is a full or half-sister to 10 winners including the listed winner Miss Riviera Golf. *"A big, strong Kyllachy colt that's done very well. A six furlong type and a really nice horse".*

863. MUSTARRID (IRE) ★★★
b.c. Elzaam – Symbol Of Peace (Desert Sun). February 23. Fourth living foal. €140,000Y. Goffs Orby. Shadwell Estate Co. Half-brother to the 2-y-o Group 3 7f Acomb Stakes winner Treaty Of Paris (by Haatef) and to the fair 1m winner All Nighter (by Bertolini). The dam, a fair 9.5f winner, is a half-sister to 5 other minor winners. The second dam, Rosy Lydgate (by Last Tycoon), is a placed half-sister to 5 winners including the US Grade 3 winner Supreme Sound. *"A lovely horse, he has a nice attitude, he's well-balanced and should make a 2-y-o over seven furlongs".*

864. MUTAHAADY (IRE) ★★★
b.c. Elzaam – Midnight Oasis (Oasis Dream). February 17. Third foal. 120,000Y. Tattersalls October Book 2. Peter & Ross Doyle. Half-brother to the useful 6f winner of 5 races at 3 and 4 yrs Mr Win (by Intikhab) and to the fairly useful 6f winner of 4 races at 2 and 3 yrs George Bowen (by Dark Angel). The dam is an unplaced half-sister to 7 winners including Miss Anabaa (Group 3 Ballyogan Stakes). The second dam, Midnight Shift (by Night Shift), a fair dual 6f winner at 3 yrs, is a half-sister to 8 winners including the high-class Group 1 6f July Cup winner Owington. *"Very similar to the other Elzaam colt but maybe an inch bigger. A horse with a good temperament, he's nicely-balanced and probably one for seven furlongs".*

865. MUTAWATHEB (IRE) ★★★★
gr.c. Dark Angel – Queen Myrine (Oratorio). March 1. Second foal. 180,000Y. Tattersalls October Book 2. Shadwell Estate Co. Half-brother to the 2015 Irish 2-y-o 7f winner, from two starts, Roibeard (by Big Bad Bob). The dam ran twice unplaced and is a half-sister to 4 winners including the Grade 1 Hollywood Turf Cup winner Boboman. The second dam, Slewvera (by Seattle Slew), a winner and Group 3 second in France, subsequently won and was Grade 2 second in the USA. *"A lovely, easy-moving horse that could be early. A grey horse with a black mane, he's certainly a six furlong type and I like him a lot. Could be a very nice horse".*

866. NATIONS ALEXANDER (IRE) ★★★
gr.f. Dark Angel – Party Whip (Whipper). March 9. Second foal. 50,000Y. Tattersalls October Book 2. Peter & Ross Doyle. The dam ran once unplaced and is a half-sister to 6 winners including the 2-y-o Group 2 6f Richmond Stakes winner and dual Group 1 6f third Always Hopeful. The second dam, Expectation (by Night Shift), a modest 6f placed 2-y-o, is a half-sister to 5 minor winners here and abroad. *"She's a nice filly, gets loose the odd time because she has a bit of a temperament but she's quite sharp. She'll make a 2-y-o in the first half of the season, over six and seven furlongs I should imagine".*

867. NIBRAS BOUNTY (IRE) ★★★★ ♠
ch.c. Bahamian Bounty – Oh Sedulous (Lawman). March 28. First foal. 52,000Y. Tattersalls October Book 2. Peter & Ross Doyle. The dam is an unraced half-sister to 9 winners including the dam of the multiple Group 1 winner and sire Shirocco. The second dam, Sedulous (by Tap On Wood), a very useful winner from 5f to 1m at 2 yrs in Ireland including the Group 3 Killavullen Stakes, subsequently won in the USA and is a sister to the listed winner Tapolite and a half-sister to 3 winners. *"A really nice type, we could be getting on with him soon so he may be racing in the early part of the season and enter the picture for Royal Ascot".*

868. OPENING TIME ★★★
b.c. Harbour Watch – Dozy (Exceed And Excel). January 19. First foal. 52,000Y. Tattersalls October Book 2. Peter & Ross Doyle. The dam, a fairly useful 2-y-o dual 5f winner, is a half-sister to 7 winners including the 2-y-o listed winner and Group 3 Albany Stakes third Patience Alexander. The second dam, Star Profile (by Sadler's Wells), an Irish 2-y-o 6f winner, is closely related to the dual 2-y-o Group 3 winner Lady Alexander (dam of the dual Group 3 winner and sire Dandy Man). *"A lovely horse by the first season stallion Harbour Watch, he's fairly precocious and should be running in May. He finds it all very easy, he's a good mover and although we haven't done any work with him yet when we do I'm sure we'll find he has an engine".*

869. PACO PUNCH (IRE) ★★
b.c. Paco Boy – Trilemma (Slip Anchor). January 30. Fifth foal. €85,000Y. Goffs Orby. Peter & Ross Doyle. Half-brother to the useful listed 10f placed Mariner's Cross (by Dubawi), to the fair 5f (at 2 yrs) to 8.5f winner Hedge End (by Verglas) and a hurdles winner by Xaar. The dam, a quite useful dual 2m winner, is a half-sister to 5 winners. The second dam, Thracian (by Green Desert), a fairly useful 2-y-o 6f and 7f winner, is a half-sister to 12 winners including Third Watch (Group 2 12f Ribblesdale Stakes), Richard Of York (Group 3 Prix Foy), the Group 2 Premio Dormello winner Three Tails (dam of the high-class colts Tamure and Sea Wave), the Group 3 winner Maysoon and the dams of the Group winners

Lend A Hand and Talented. *"A big horse and one of the bigger Paco Boys, I wouldn't expect to see him in the first half of the season. More of a seven furlong horse".*

870. PEAK PRINCESS (IRE) ★★★
b.f. Foxwedge – Foot Of Pride (Footstepsinthesand). February 7. Second foal. 90,000Y. Tattersalls October Book 1. Sackville/Donald. The dam, unplaced in two starts, is a half-sister to 5 winners including the smart Irish Group 3 7f and Group 3 1m winner Cheyenne Star and to the unraced dam of Gordon Lord Byron (Group 1 Haydock Sprint Cup and Group 1 Prix de la Foret). The second dam, Charita (by Lycius), a listed 1m winner in Ireland, is a half-sister to 4 winners including the Italian Group 2 winner Stanott. *"A nice filly, good-sized and goes very well. We quite like the Foxwedges and this is a six/seven furlong 2-y-o. A good type".*

871. PERSOPHANIE ★★★
br.f. Sepoy – Wosaita (Generous). January 17. Fourteenth foal. 250,000Y. Tattersalls October Book 1. Tony Nerses. Half-brother to 7 winners including the useful 7f (at 2 yrs), listed 1m and Italian Group 3 1m winner Whazzis (by Desert Prince), the useful 2-y-o listed 7f Chesham Stakes winner Whazzat (by Daylami), the 2-y-o 8.6f winner Whatizzit (by Galileo), the 2-y-o 7f and 1m winner Special Envoy (by Barathea) and the 10f winner High Admiral (by New Approach) – all 3 quite useful. The dam, a fair 12.3f placed maiden, is a half-sister to 10 winners including the Group 1 10.5f Prix de Diane winner Rafha (the dam of Invincible Spirit). The second dam, Eljazzi (by Artaius), a fairly useful 2-y-o 7f winner, is a half-sister to 8 winners including the high-class miler Pitcairn. *"Our Sepoys are very similar and she's another for the middle of the season so we won't be in a hurry with her. Six or seven furlongs should suit and she's a good mover with a good temperament".*

872. PREROGATIVE (IRE) ★★★
b.c. Rock Of Gibraltar – Tedarshana (Darshaan). March 10. Eighth living foal. €155,000Y. Goffs Orby. John & Jake Warren. Half-brother to 3 winners including the Irish listed 12f winner Honoria (by Sadler's Wells) and the Canadian 3-y-o winner Seanachi (by El Prado). The dam won 3 races in France and the USA, was third in the Grade 2 La Prevoyante Handicap and is a half-sister to 6 winners including the US stakes winner and Grade 2 placed The Key Rainbow. The second dam, Te Kana (by Northern Dancer), a minor winner in France, is a half-sister to 7 winners including the US champion 2-y-o Ogygian. *"Even though he's a Rock Of Gibraltar he could be sharp and he should be ready for the first six furlong races. He did his first of work the other day and did it really well. He goes really well and is a horse you'd like a lot ".*

873. PRIMADONIA ★★★
b.f. Bated Breath – Pretty Primo (Kyllachy). February 3. First foal. 55,000Y. Tattersalls October Book 2. Peter & Ross Doyle. The dam, a quite useful 6f winner, is a half-sister to 7 winners including the very smart 2-y-o Group 1 7f Prix Jean-Luc Lagardere winner of 5 races Wootton Bassett. The second dam, Balladonia (by Primo Dominie), a useful 9f winner, was listed-placed twice over 10f and is a half-sister to 5 winners. *"A good type that should be early and be racing over five/six furlongs. A good strong filly, there's plenty to like about her".*

874. PROCURATOR (IRE) ★★★
b.c. Canford Cliffs – Lulawin (Kyllachy). March 18. Third foal. 120,000Y. Tattersalls October Book 1. Peter & Ross Doyle. Brother to the smart 2015 2-y-o Group 2 Railway Stakes winner Painted Cliffs and half-brother to the fair 7f (at 2 yrs) and 1m winner Rockaroundtheclock (by Starspangledbanner). The dam is an unraced half-sister to 6 winners including the Group 1 St James's Palace Stakes winner and Grade 1 Breeders' Cup Mile second Excellent Art and the smart 7f (at 2 yrs), to 2m 4f winner Double Obsession. The second dam, Obsessive (by Seeking The Gold), a useful 2-y-o 6f winner and third in the Group 3 Musidora Stakes, is a half-sister to 7 winners. *"A leggy colt that'll want six or seven furlongs in mid-season. He's a nice type that'll win this year but we won't be in a hurry with him".*

875. PROMISING (IRE) ★★★★
b.f. Invincible Spirit – Lethal Quality (Elusive Quality). March 16. Third foal. €350,000Y. Goffs Orby. Peter & Ross Doyle. The dam, a US stakes-placed winner of 3 races at 3 and

4 yrs, is a half-sister to 2 winners. The second dam, Lethal Temper (by Seattle Slew), a winner of 3 minor races at 3 and 4 yrs in the USA, is a half-sister to 8 winners including the very smart colt Diffident, winner of the Group 3 6f Diadem Stakes, the Group 3 6f Prix de Ris-Orangis and the listed 7f European Free Handicap. *"A lovely filly that's had a few niggling problems but she's back on the road now. We'd like to think she could be a Royal Ascot filly because she's a really sharp type, knows her job and is very professional".*

876. PUSSY GALORE (IRE) ★★★
b.f. Harbour Watch – Green Chorus (Oratorio). February 20. First foal. £46,000Y. Doncaster Premier. Peter & Ross Doyle. The dam, a moderate Irish middle-distance placed maiden, is a half-sister to 5 winners including the listed winner Ithoughtitwasover. The second dam, Green Castle (by Indian Ridge), was placed once over 1m at 4 yrs in Ireland from only 2 starts and is a half-sister to 12 winners including the dual Group 2 placed Luchiroverte. *"A sharp filly, hopefully she should run when the six furlong maiden fillies' races come. She'll be a nice type. We like Harbour Watch – we think he'll make a stallion. They're nice types with good bone and there's a lot to like about them".*

877. REPTON ★★★★
b.c. Zebedee – African Moonlight (Halling). February 7. Third foal. 80,000Y. Tattersalls October Book 2. Peter & Ross Doyle. Half-brother to the US Grade 3 9f winner Syntax (by Haatef) and to the Italian listed-placed 2-y-o winner Sir Gin (by Moss Vale). The dam ran twice unplaced and is a sister to the Irish dual Group 3 winner of 8 races Mkuzi and a half-sister to 8 winners. The second dam, African Peace (by Roberto), a French listed-placed winner, is s half-sister to 2 winners. *"A very nice colt with a bit of class about him. A six to seven furlong horse, he's very nice and very correct. We think Zebedee will have a good year because we've got a few nice ones".*

878. RESTORE (IRE) ★★★
b.c. Dark Angel – Attracted To You (Hurricane Run). April 22. Second foal. 55,000Y. Tattersalls October Book 3. Peter & Ross Doyle. Half-brother to the 2016 3-y-o 7f winner War Glory (by Canford Cliffs). The dam, a quite useful 2-y-o 6f winner, is a half-sister to 2 winners including the Italian dual listed 1m winner Super Motiva. The second dam, Haute Volta (by Grape Tree Road), is an unraced half-sister to 7 winners including the 2-y-o Group 1 National Stakes winner Heart Of Darkness. *"He'll be quite early and he's a nice horse. We've done one piece of work with him, he went nicely and he finds things quite easy. A five furlong type 2-y-o, despite being a late April foal".*

879. RITA'S MAN (IRE) ★★★
b.c. Lawman – French Fern (Royal Applause). February 27. Fifth foal. £62,000Y. Doncaster Premier. Peter & Ross Doyle. Brother to the useful 3-y-o 6f and 1m winner and 2-y-o Group 3 7f Acomb Stakes second Fort Bastion and half-brother to the moderate 2-y-o 6f winner Piping Dream (by Approve) and a minor winner abroad by Librettist. The dam, placed at 2 yrs in Ireland and a minor US dual 4-y-o winner, is a half-sister to 3 winners including the Group 2 Criterium de Maisons-Laffitte winner Captain Marvelous. The second dam, Shesasmartlady (by Dolphin Street), is an unplaced half-sister to 8 winners including the Irish listed winners Dashing Colours and Dash Of Red. *"A nice six/seven furlong horse. Lawmans tend to take a little time, so although physically he's there for us we're just taking our time with him".*

880. RUXLEY'S STAR (USA) ★★★
b.f. Artie Schiller – Ladue (Demons Begone). February 14. Ninth foal. 50,000Y. Tattersalls October Book 1. Peter & Ross Doyle. Half-sister to the Grade 1 Garden City Breeders' Cup Stakes winner Lucifer's Stone (by Horse Chestnut), to the minor US stakes winner Lilly Ladue (by Chief Three Sox) and a minor winner in the USA by Rubiano. The dam, a minor US winner of 3 races, is a half-sister to 6 winners. The second dam, Breathless Charm (by Miswaki), is an unraced half-sister to 3 winners including the triple US Grade 1 winner Left Bank. *"A lovely filly, there's plenty to like about her. She's big and we wouldn't be in a hurry with her as she's more of a seven furlong type. Very nice and very classy".*

881. SADHBH (IRE) ★★★
b.f. Lilbourne Lad – Stoney Cove (Needwood Blade). March 14. Fourth foal. €20,000Y. Tattersalls Ireland September. Peter & Ross Doyle. Half-sister to the quite useful 2015 6f and 7f placed 2-y-o Bernie's Boy (by Lilbourne Lad) and to the fair 5.5f and 6f winner Gentlemen (by Ad Valorem). The dam is an unraced half-sister to the Group 2 Italian 1,000 Guineas winner Golden Nepi and the useful 7f (at 2 yrs), 12f and 2m winner Juniper Girl. The second dam, Shajara (by Kendor), is a placed half-sister to 4 winners. *"She's not very big so we'll probably get on with her because hopefully she'll be sharp enough for five furlongs. She finds it all nice and easy so far"*.

882. SAWLAAT (IRE) ★★★★★
b.c. Clodovil – Jaywick (Jade Robbery). April 16. Fourth foal. £185,000Y. Doncaster Premier. Peter & Ross Doyle. Half-brother to the modest 6f to 1m winner of 3 races Blue Deer (by Bahamian Bounty). The dam is an unplaced half-sister to 5 winners including the listed winner Icklingham. The second dam, Braiswick (by King Of Spain), winner of the Group 1 E P Taylor Stakes and the Group 2 Sun Chariot Stakes, is a half-sister to 6 winners including the Group 3 11f September Stakes winner Percy's Lass (dam of the Derby winner Sir Percy). *"He was a standout at the sales. A lovely colt, he's very strong, very well-built and hopefully he'll be sharp enough for six and seven furlongs. Ascot is a possibility for him"*.

883. SECOND PAGE ★★
b.c. Harbour Watch – Almunia (Mujadil). March 12. Sixth foal. 60,000Y. Tattersalls October Book 2. Peter & Ross Doyle. Half-brother to the quite useful 2015 2-y-o 5f winner Ayresome Angel (by Captain Gerrard) and to the fairly useful 6f winner and Group 2 6f July Stakes second Lewisham (by Sleeping Indian). The dam is an unraced sister to the dual 5f winner and Group 3 Princess Margaret Stakes third Kachina Doll and a half-sister to 8 winners. The second dam, Betelgeuse (by Kalaglow), a quite useful 14f winner, is a half-sister to 5 winners. *"A big, strong colt, we wouldn't be in a hurry with him and he's one for the second half of the season"*.

884. SEE THE SEA (IRE) ★★
b.f. Born To Sea – Shahmina (Danehill). April 15. Sixth foal. £62,000Y. Doncaster Premier. Peter & Ross Doyle. Half-sister to the quite useful 1m (at 2 yrs) and 10f winner Swing Easy (by Zamindar). The dam, a fair 12f and 13f placed maiden, is a sister to the useful 2-y-o 6f and 1m winner and Group 3 Cherry Hinton Stakes third Sundari and a half-sister to 6 winners. The second dam, My Ballerina (by Sir Ivor), a fairly useful 10f and 12f winner, is a half-sister to 3 winners including the Group 1 1m Coronation Stakes third Zarani Sidi Anna and to the dam of the US Grade 2 winner Striking Dancer. *"She's still growing so she'll take time and may be a back-end type 2-y-o. Hopefully we'll get a couple of runs into her then. She'll get a trip, so we're holding her back until she's ready to do a bit of work"*.

885. SOCIAL SECRETARY (IRE) ★★★
b.f. Tamayuz – Society Gal (Galileo). January 28. Fourth foal. £32,000Y. Doncaster Premier. Kern/Lillingston. Half-sister to the modest 2015 7f fourth placed 2-y-o Goldenfield (by Footstepsinthesand), to the quite useful 2-y-o listed-placed 6f winner Red Icon (by Acclamation) and the fair Irish 2-y-o 1m winner Bleeding Hearts (by Peintre Celebre). The dam is an unraced half-sister to the US Grade 3 winner Good Mood. The second dam, Pillars Of Society (by Caerleon), a fairly useful Irish 10f winner, was Group 3 placed and is a half-sister to 5 winners. *"A sharp filly, she's done one bit of work and did it very nicely. When the 2-y-o maiden races for filly's start we'll be looking to run her. At the moment she's sharper than the Tamayuz colt we have"*.

886. SPONGIE CAKE (IRE) ★★
b.f. Lawman – Belgique (Compton Place). April 22. Third foal. €75,000Y. Goffs Orby. Peter & Ross Doyle. Half-brother to the fair 7f winner Zylan (by Kyllachy). The dam, the quite useful 7f and 1m winner, is a half-sister to 3 winners including the useful Irish 2-y-o 6f and listed 7f winner Bruges. The second dam, Liege (by Night Shift), is an unraced half-sister to 2 winners including the dam of the multiple Group 1 winner Moonlight Cloud. *"Not very big but she's a nice enough filly that does everything nice and easy. Five furlongs will probably be a bit sharp for her but we'll see when we work her"*.

887. STERLING SILVA (IRE) ★★★★
ch.c. Sakhee's Secret – Silicon Star (Starborough). March 25. Seventh foal. €70,000Y. Tattersalls Ireland September. Peter & Ross Doyle and MPR. Half-brother to the quite useful 2015 2-y-o 1m winner Pythius (by Lord Shanakill), to the fairly useful listed-placed 6f and 7f winner Sacha Park (by Iffraaj), the minor French winner of 4 races (including at 2 yrs) Silicone Tune (by Green Tune) and the minor French 2-y-o winner Lukes Well (by Shirocco). The dam is an unplaced half-sister to 10 winners including Latona (Group 3 Prix de Saint-Georges). The second dam, Silicon Lady (by Mille Balles), won the Group 3 Prix Thomas Bryon and is a half-sister to 14 winners including the dual Group 3 winner Silicon Bavaria. *"He's done a bit of work, he's a lovely horse and we've always touted him as quite a nice 2-y-o. Doing everything right, he's a classy horse that should be racing in April. He should be sharp enough for five furlongs although I think six would probably be his trip".* Won on his debut at Leicester in early April.

888. STORMY CLOUDS (IRE) ★★★
b.f. Sir Prancealot – Singingintherain (Kyllachy). February 2. Second foal. £24,000Y. Doncaster Premier. Peter & Ross Doyle. The dam, a modest 6f and 1m placed maiden, is a half-sister to 3 winners including useful dual 5f (at 2 yrs) and listed 6f winner and dual Group 3 placed Danehill Destiny. The second dam, Comeraincomeshine (by Night Shift), a modest 5.5f winner, is a half-sister to 5 winners including the high-class Group 1 1m Queen Elizabeth II Stakes winner Where Or When and the smart 10f and 12f winner and Group 1 St Leger fourth All The Way. *"She's been working really nicely and will have already started her career by the time your book is out. She finds it all very easy, we gave her a bit of work this morning and she did it really nicely. She's quite strong, so I'd say she's not just an early 2-y-o, she should train on".*

889. SUFFRAGETTE CITY (IRE) ★★★★
b.f. Dragon Pulse – Queen Of Stars (Green Desert). March 14. Seventh foal. £80,000Y. Doncaster Premier. Peter & Ross Doyle. Half-sister to the 2015 2-y-o Group 2 Duchess Of Cambridge Stakes and Group 3 Albany Stakes winner Illuminate (by Zoffany), to the fair 5f and 6f winner Rhal (by Rahy) and a winner in Japan by Singspiel. The dam is an unraced half-sister to the Group 3 1m Premio Dormello winner and Group 1 Italian Oaks third Lady Catherine. The second dam, Queen Catherine (by Machiavellian), a useful French 2-y-o and 3-y-o 1m winner, is a half-sister to 5 winners. *"A lovely filly, she'll take a bit of time but we really like her. We haven't really done a lot with her so far but she has a good action and a good head on her. I can see her being ready by late May or June".*

890. SUREYOUTOLDME (IRE) ★★★
ch.c. Tamayuz – Place De Moscou (Rock Of Gibraltar). January 11. Third foal. 35,000Y. Tattersalls October Book 2. Peter & Ross Doyle. Half-brother to the quite useful 2-y-o 6f winner Lady Moscou (by Sir Percy) and to the quite useful 10f and Australian 12f winner Soviet Courage (by Dutch Art). The dam, placed once at 3 yrs in France, is a half-sister to 9 winners including the French listed winners Pretty Tough and Parisienne. The second dam, Poughkeepsie (by Sadler's Wells), won once at 3 yrs in France and is a daughter of the King George and Oaks winner Pawneese. *"A strong, well-built colt, he's one we might start getting after because he could be running in the first half of the season".*

891. SWAG (IRE) ★★★★
b.c. Bahamian Bounty – Tahtheeb (Muhtarram). February 17. Fourth foal. £125,000Y. Doncaster Premier. Peter & Ross Doyle. Half-brother to a winner in Greece by Clodovil. The dam, a listed-placed 9f winner here at 2 yrs and subsequently a winner in the USA, is a half-sister to 5 winners including the South African Group 2 winner Mujarrib. The second dam, Mihnah (by Lahib), a quite useful 6f (at 2 yrs) and 1m winner, is a half-sister to 9 winners including the smart Group 2 14.6f Park Hill Stakes winner Ranin. *"A lovely, very well-built colt, he probably needs to lose a bit of weight at the moment but he'll be really sharp when we get stuck into him in the next couple of weeks. I like him a lot".*

892. TADWEEN (IRE) ★★★★
b.c. Tagula – Stained Glass (Dansili). February 13. Second foal. £90,000Y. Doncaster Premier.

Peter & Ross Doyle. Half-brother to the poor 2015 1m fourth placed 2-y-o Window Shopping (by Lilbourne Lad). The dam is an unraced half-sister to 4 winners including the dual listed winner and Group 3 10f Select Stakes second Mirror Lake. The second dam, Reflections (by Sadler's Wells), ran once unplaced and is a half-sister to 10 winners including the smart Group 3 12f Prix de Minerve and dual 10f listed winner Danefair, to the Group 3 9f Prix Chloe winner Prove, the smart multiple 7f to 8.5f winner Vortex and the listed 12f Prix Joubert winner Erudite. *"We haven't done a huge amount with him but he's a lovely horse and a good mover. A nice-looking horse but we haven't uncovered how much ability he's got yet"*.

893. TAFAAKHOR (IRE) ★★★
gr.c. Dark Angel – Tellelle (Trans Island). April 29. Second foal. 190,000Y. Tattersalls October Book 2. Peter & Ross Doyle. The dam, a quite useful 6f and 7f winner in Ireland at 3 and 4 yrs, is a half-sister to 5 winners here and abroad. The second dam, Lomond Heights (by Lomond), placed once over 1m at 2 yrs, is a half-sister to 8 winners. *"He seems to be a very nice horse and is one we're looking forward to doing faster work with"*.

894. TAI HANG DRAGON (IRE) ★★★★ ♠
b.f. Tamayuz – Give A Whistle (Mujadil). January 22. Tenth foal. €200,000Y. Goffs Orby. Sackville/Donald. Half-sister to 6 winners including the smart 2-y-o listed 5f winner Come To Heel, the Irish 2-y-o listed 5f and subsequent US Grade 3 6f winner Pasar Silbano (both by Elnadim), the useful 2-y-o listed 6f winner Gerfalcon (by Hawk Wing) and the fair 2-y-o 7f winner Give Way Nelson (by Mount Nelson). The dam, a dual 5f winner at 3 and 4 yrs, is a half-sister to one winner. The second dam, Repique (by Sharpen Up), a fair 6f and 7f winner, is a half-sister to 8 winners including the Group winners Indian Lodge, Sarhoob and Sifting Gold. *"A lovely filly, she's quite sharp and should make a 2-y-o over six or seven furlongs. Has a lovely attitude and should be one to watch out for"*.

895. TESKO FELLA (IRE) ★★★
b.c. Myboycharlie – Foundation Filly (Lando). February 28. Second foal. €100,000Y. Arqana Deauville August. Peter & Ross Doyle. The dam, a listed-placed winner of 3 races at 2 to 4 yrs in France, is a half-sister to the Group 1 Premio Lydia Tesio winner Floriot. The second dam, Fureau (by Ferdinand), won 3 minor races in Germany and is a half-sister to 5 winners. *"A nice colt, he wouldn't be early and is one for six and seven furlongs. A good-looking horse and quite muscular"*.

896. TIGGALISCIOUS (IRE) ★★★
b.f. Acclamation – Mea Parvitas (Oasis Dream). February 10. First foal. £50,000Y. Doncaster Premier. The dam, a moderate 6f to 1m placed maiden, is a half-sister to 5 winners including the dual listed 10f winner Foodbroker Fancy (the dam of two stakes winners) and the listed winner Femme Fatale. The second dam, Red Rita (by Kefaah), a fairly useful 4-y-o 6f winner and second in the Cherry Hinton Stakes and the Princess Margaret Stakes, is a half-sister to 3 minor winners. *"Not very big, she'll be racing early enough, probably over five furlongs and she finds it nice and easy"*.

897. TOMILY (IRE) ★★★★ ♠
b.c. Canford Cliffs – Cake (Acclamation). January 16. Third foal. Half-brother to the useful 2-y-o 5f and listed 6f winner Fig Roll (by Bahamian Bounty). The dam, a useful 2-y-o listed 5f winner of 4 races, is a full or half-sister to 6 winners. The second dam, Carpet Lady (by Night Shift), a fair dual 6f placed 2-y-o, is a half-sister to 5 winners including the Hong Kong stakes winner Classic Fountain. *"A smashing horse, he'll be an early 2-y-o and could be anything. I really like him and he may start off in early April. A lovely, strong colt with a bit of scope and he's out of a very good mare"*.

898. VENTURA BLUES (IRE) ★★★★
b.br.f. Bated Breath – Salmon Rose (Iffraaj). March 6. First foal. £68,000Y. Doncaster Premier. Peter & Ross Doyle. The dam is an unraced half-sister to 5 winners including the Group 1 Dubai World Cup winner Prince Bishop. The second dam, North East Bay (by Prospect Bay), is an unplaced half-sister to 8 winners including the US Grade 2 winner Blingo. *"Probably a six/seven furlong 2-y-o, she's quite nice, a good mover and we really like her. She covers the ground effortlessly and she's a really nice filly – a possible for Royal Ascot"*.

899. WARRIOR'S SPIRIT (IRE) ★★
b.c. Requinto – Sandbox Two (Foxhound). February 16. Fifth foal. 100,000Y. Tattersalls October Book 1. Peter & Ross Doyle. Half-brother to the smart Group 2 1m Topkapi Trophy and listed 7f winner and 2,000 Guineas second Glory Awaits (by Choisir) and to a minor winner of 3 races at 2 yrs in Italy by Spartacus. The dam is an unplaced half-sister to 4 minor winners. The second dam, Moorfield Daisy (by Waajib), is an unplaced half-sister to 7 winners. *"A nice horse but he's big and we won't see him for a while. One for seven furlongs from mid-summer onwards I should think. He's grown a lot and seems to have a nice attitude".*

900. WEFAIT (IRE) ★★★
b.c. Harbour Watch – Night Club (Mozart). May 9. Seventh foal. £32,000Y. Doncaster Premier. Peter & Ross Doyle. Half-brother to the quite useful 12f, 14f and hurdles winner Sebastian Beach (by Yeats), to the fair dual 1m winner Opening Nite (by Azamour) and the modest 2-y-o 5f and 6f winner Dunmore Boy (by Iffraaj). The dam is an unplaced half-sister to 12 winners including the French 1,000 Guineas and Group 1 7f Prix de la Foret winner Danseuse du Soir (herself dam of the Group 1 Gran Criterium winner Scintillo). The second dam, Dance By Night (by Northfields), a quite useful 2-y-o dual 7f winner, is a half-sister to 3 winners. *"This colt will take a bit of time because he's a bit tall and leggy but we really like him, he's a really nice horse. The Harbour Watch 2-y-o's seem to be nice horses and although it's early days they seem to go well. They have good attitudes like he did".*

901. WHIP NAE NAE (IRE) ★★★★
ch.c. Dragon Pulse – Love In May (City On A Hill). March 2. Fifth foal. 60,000Y. Tattersalls October Book 2. Sackville/Donald. Half-brother to the fairly useful 7f to 8.5f winner Gabrial's Kaka (by Jeremy). The dam, a fair 2-y-o 5f and 6f winner, is a half-sister to 3 winners. The second dam, May Hinton (by Main Reef), a listed-placed 2-y-o winner, is a half-sister to 4 winners. *"A smashing horse, he's doing very well and finds everything pretty easy. He looks a natural 2-y-o and I'd say six furlongs should suit him".*

902. WITH ONE ACCORD ★★
b.f. Acclamation – Raymi Coya (Van Nistelrooy). March 15. Fourth foal. Half-sister to the fairly useful 2015 2-y-o 6f winner and 7f listed-placed Make Fast (by Makfi). The dam, a useful 2-y-o Group 3 7f Oh So Sharp Stakes winner, is a half-sister to 5 winners including the US 2-y-o and 4-y-o winner and stakes-placed Olympia Fields. The second dam, Something Mon (by Maria's Mon), is an unraced half-sister to 5 winners including the champion German 2-y-o and Group 2 winner Somethingdifferent. (The Queen). *"She's small, fairly sharp and finds things quite easy but we haven't kicked on with her yet. Five or six furlongs will be her starting point".*

903. ZEBBY SIZZ (IRE) ★★★
gr.c. Zebedee – Derval (One Cool Cat). January 14. Third foal. £50,000Y. Doncaster Premier. Peter & Ross Doyle. Brother to the modest 2015 2-y-o 5f winner Zoraida. The dam is an unplaced half-sister to 6 winners including the French listed winner Arikaria and the Hong Kong stakes winner Sacred Nuts. The second dam, Sagrada (by Primo Dominie), a minor German 3-y-o winner, is a full or half-sister to 10 winners including two listed winners in Germany. *"A nice horse and he'll be early enough because he's done a bit of work already. A sharp, early 2-y-o that's not over-big but finds things quite easy".*

904. UNNAMED ★★★
b.c. Power – Al Ihtithar (Barathea). February 22. Ninth foal. 160,000Y. Tattersalls December Book 1. Al Shaqab Racing/Peter & Ross Doyle. Half-brother to 4 winners including the useful French listed 12f winner Mahaatheer (by Daylami), the fairly useful 2-y-o 1m winner and listed-placed Mustaqer and the fair 2-y-o 7f winner Amthal (both by Dalakhani). The dam, a very useful 10f and 10.3f listed winner, is a sister to the useful 7f to 11f winner Ihtiraz and a half-sister to 9 winners including the Group 3 Prix Berteux winner Samsaam. The second dam, Azyaa (by Kris), a useful 7.5f winner, is a half-sister to 5 winners. *"He's a nice colt, has a bit of an attitude and is probably a seven furlong horse for August/September. A nice, big horse that'll take a bit of time".*

905. UNNAMED ★★★
b.f. Kodiac – Alexander Wonder (Redback). April 7. Fifth foal. £60,000Y. Doncaster Premier. Amanda Skiffington. Half-brother to the modest 2-y-o 5f winner of 5 races Hardy Blue (by Red Clubs). The dam is an unraced half-sister to 6 winners including the dual Group 3 sprint winner Triple Aspect and the French 2-y-o listed winner Wonderfilly. The second dam, Wicken Wonder (by Distant Relative), a fair 2-y-o 6f winner, is a half-sister to 7 winners. *"A nice, sharp little filly, she's a little bit open of her knees so we've had to take it easy but she's probably going to make a sprinting 2-y-o".*

906. UNNAMED ★★★
b.f. Requinto – Amour Fou (Piccolo). March 5. First foal. £32,000Y. Doncaster Premier. Peter & Ross Doyle. The dam, a modest dual 5f winner, is out of the quite useful 2-y-o 7f winner Elm Dust (by Elmaamul). *"Quite precocious, she's really quite nice and we'll be getting on with her soon. A lovely filly".*

907. UNNAMED ★★★ ♠
b.c. Shamardal – Ballybacka Lady (Hurricane Lad). March 19. Second foal. 525,000Y. Tattersalls October Book 1. Peter & Ross Doyle / Mayfair Speculators / China Horse Club. The dam, a 6f (at 2 yrs) and Group 3 Irish 1,000 Guineas Trial winner, is a half-sister to 3 winners. The second dam, Southern Queen (by Anabaa), a French listed-placed 2-y-o 7f winner, is a half-sister to one winner. *"A nice colt that's settled in very well, he has a good attitude. A good mover that could be anything, he's probably one for the second half of the season".*

908. UNNAMED ★★★
gr.c. Clodovil – Boucheron (Galileo). April 11. Second foal. €60,000Y. Tattersalls Ireland September. Peter & Ross Doyle. The dam, a quite useful 12f winner, is a half-sister to another minor winner. The second dam, Rainbow Lyrics (by Rainbow Quest), is an unraced half-sister to 4 winners. *"A lovely horse, he's leggy and will take a bit of time but he's a good mover with a good attitude. One for six/seven furlongs a bit later in the season".*

909. UNNAMED ★★★
gr.f. Dark Angel – Bun Penny (Bertolini). March 21. Third foal. £180,000Y. Doncaster Premier. Peter & Ross Doyle. The dam is an unplaced half-sister to 4 winners. The second dam, Mint Royale (by Cadeaux Genereux), is an unplaced sister to the 2-y-o dual Group 1 winner and sire Bahamian Bounty. *"She's nice and ought to be sharp. She has quite a big head and is a bit heavy but she'll make a 2-y-o in the first half of the season over six furlongs".*

910. UNNAMED ★★★
b.f. Invincible Spirit – Countess Ferrama (Authorized). February 5. 260,000Y. Tattersalls October Book 1. Al Shaqab Racing/ Peter & Ross Doyle. The dam, a fair 12f winner, is a half-sister to 10 winners including Indian Haven (Irish 2,000 Guineas) and Count Dubois (Group 1 Gran Criterium). The second dam, Madame Dubois (by Legend Of France), won the Group 2 Park Hill Stakes and the Group 2 Prix de Royallieu and is a half-sister to 4 winners. *"A lovely, classy filly that ought to make a 2-y-o over six furlongs".*

911. UNNAMED ★★
gr.c. Dark Angel – Delira (Namid). March 21. Second foal. 150,000Y. Tattersalls October Book 1. Peter & Ross Doyle. The dam, a modest 5.5f winner, is a half-sister to 6 winners including Barrier Reef, a winner of 8 races and second in the Group 3 Beresford Stakes. The second dam, Singing Millie (by Millfontaine), won twice in Ireland at 3 yrs and is a half-sister to 7 winners. *"A nice big horse, but he's got a lot of scope and a lot of filling out to do. He's quite tall so he'll be given time and we'll see him from August onwards over seven furlongs".*

912. UNNAMED ★★
b.f. Canford Cliffs – Divine Grace (Definite Article). March 30. Ninth foal. 180,000Y. Tattersalls October Book 1. Al Shaqab Racing / Peter & Ross Doyle. Half-sister to 7 winners including the German Group 2 6f Goldene Peitsche winner of 5 races Electric Beat (by Shinko Forest), the useful 2-y-o 6f winner and Group 2 Rockfel Stakes third Gray Pearl (by Excellent Art), the fairly useful 2-y-o 7f winner and listed placed Blakey's Boy (by Hawk Wing) and the fair 8.5f winner Lamyaa

(by Arcano). The dam ran unplaced twice and is a half-sister to 2 minor winners. The second dam, Grey Patience (by Common Grounds), is an unraced half-sister to 8 winners including the listed winners Cape Town and Regiment. *"A nice filly that's starting to grow now so we'll have to lay off her for a bit. One for later in the season".*

913. UNNAMED ★★★
b.f. Invincible Spirit – Forgotten Me (Holy Roman Emperor). February 28. Second foal. 150,000Y. Tattersalls October Book 1. Peter & Ross Doyle. Half-sister to the fair 2015 6f placed 2-y-o Remember Me (by Acclamation). The dam is an unraced half-sister to 7 winners including the listed 6f winner and Irish 1,000 Guineas second Dimenticata and the useful listed 6f winner Master Fay. The second dam, Non Dimenticar Me (by Don't Forget Me), a modest 5f winner, is a half-sister to 7 winners. *"A very sharp filly, she'll hopefully be running in the first part of the season and we'd like to think she'd be going for some nice races".*

914. UNNAMED ★★★
gr.f. Dark Angel – Fruit O'The Forest (Shinko Forest). January 19. Second foal. 80,000Y. Tattersalls October Book 2. Peter & Ross Doyle. The dam is an unraced half-sister to 5 winners including the Irish and Singapore listed winner Immovable Option. The second dam, Perfect Welcome (by Taufan), an Irish 3-y-o 7f winner, is a half-sister to 7 winners including Chalon (Group 2 Coronation Stakes) and Executive Perk (Irish dual Group 3 winner). *"A lovely, big filly, she's a leggy type and we won't be in a hurry with her. I love her but she's one for a bit later on".*

915. UNNAMED ★★★
b.f. Dandy Man – Gala Style (Elnadim). April 15. Ninth foal. £85,000Y. Doncaster Premier. Tony Nerses. Sister to the smart 2-y-o 6f winner, Group 2 Coventry Stakes second and Group 2 Gimcrack Stakes third Parbold and half-sister to the very useful dual listed 7f winner and dual Group 3 placed Majestic Myles, the fairly useful 6f (at 2 yrs) and 7f winner of 7 races Majestic Moon (both by Majestic Missile) and the quite useful 7f winner Oonagh (by Arakan). The dam is an unraced half-sister to 2 minor winners. The second dam, Style N' Elegance (by Alysheba), is a placed half-sister to 11 winners including the Irish 1,000 Guineas winner Trusted Partner. *"A sharp type, good-looking and five or six furlongs should be right for her in the first half of the season. There's a lot to like about her".*

916. UNNAMED ★★
b.c. Frankel – Latin Love (Danehill Dancer). March 29. Third foal. 130,000Y. Tattersalls October Book 1. Rabbah Bloodstock. The dam, an Irish dual listed 1m and 9f winner and Grade 2 Canadian Stakes second, is a half-sister to two winners. The second dam, Ho Hi The Moon (by Be My Guest), a minor French 3-y-o 9f winner, is a sister to the French listed winner Diner De Lune and a half-sister to 8 winners including the Group 1 Irish Oaks winner Moonstone, the Group 1 10f Prix Saint-Alary winner Cerulean Sky and the Breeders' Cup second L'Ancresse. *"A nice horse as you'd expect being by Frankel, but we haven't done much with him yet so he'll take a bit of time. He's actually done well in the last few weeks, physically he's getting stronger but we'll just keep him ticking over until later in the year. I like him and he's a bit of a character but he's still a bit weak at the moment. Hopefully he'll find some speed once he matures".*

917. UNNAMED ★★★
b.c. Acclamation – Miss Hawai (Peintre Celebre). March 21. Ninth foal. 100,000Y. Tattersalls October Book 2. Hyphen Bloodstock. Half-brother to the Irish listed 9f winner, Group 1 Pretty Polly Stakes second and smart broodmare Beach Bunny (by High Chaparral) and to the quite useful 6f winner Robinson Cruso (by Footstepsinthesand). The dam is an unraced half-sister to 4 winners including the 1,000 Guineas winner Miss France and the French dual listed winner Mer de Corail. The second dam, Miss Tahiti (by Tirol), won the Group 1 Prix Marcel Boussac and is a half-sister to 3 winners. *"A correct, well-balanced horse, he could be a 2-y-o in the first part of the season".*

918. UNNAMED ★★
b.f. Nathaniel – Mosqueras Romance (Rock Of Gibraltar). March 23. Second foal. €170,000Y. Arqana Deauville August. Peter & Ross Doyle. The dam, a quite useful 1m winner, was

listed-placed six times and is a half-sister to 4 winners. The second dam, Mosquera (by Acatenango), won 5 races including two listed events in Germany, was third in the Group 3 Prix de Psyche and is a full or half-sister to 8 winners. *"A very nice filly that's just cantering away for now. One for the middle part of the season onwards, she has a good temperament".*

919. UNNAMED ★★★
b.c. Kodiac – Novel Fun (Noverre). April 2. Third foal. 360,000Y. Tattersalls October Book 1. Al Shaqab Racing / Peter & Ross Doyle. Half-brother to the unplaced 2015 2-y-o Fine Share (by Art Connoisseur) and to the minor Italian winner of 3 races at 2 and 3 yrs Bridge Artemide (by Majestic Missile). The dam is an unraced half-sister to 3 winners including Hunan (Group 3 Prix de Cabourg). The second dam, Foolish Fun (by Fools Holme) was placed fourth once over 1m at 2 yrs and is a half-sister to 5 winners. *"A nice horse with a good way of going and a good temperament, he's just starting to grow a bit now so we won't rush him. A six/seven furlong type".*

920. UNNAMED ★★★★
b.br.c. Elusive Pimpernel – Spiritville (Invincible Spirit). April 13. Fifth foal. €120,000Y. Tattersalls Ireland September. BLM Bloodstock. Brother to the useful 2015 2-y-o 7f winner and Group 2 Superlative Stakes fourth They Seek Him Here and half-brother to the fair 12f and hurdles winner Officer Drivel (by Captain Rio). The dam, a moderate 6f (at 2 yrs) and 6.5f placed maiden, is a half-sister to 5 minor winners. The second dam, Woodville (by Deploy), is an unraced half-sister to 9 winners. *"A lovely horse, everything's in the right place and he goes very well. Being by Elusive Pimpernel you'd think you shouldn't push on with him, but I'd say he could be going for some nice six furlong races".*

JESSIE HARRINGTON

921. AWARENESS (USA) ★★★
b.f. Distorted Humor – Visions Of Clarity (Sadler's Wells). April 23. Sister to the 2-y-o Group 1 7f National Stakes and Group 2 7f Futurity Stakes winner Pathfork and half-sister to the quite useful dual 12f winner Tacticus (by A P Indy) and a minor French 12f winner by Hernando. The dam, a French listed 1m winner, is a half-sister to the multiple Group 1 winner Spinning World. The second dam, Imperfect Circle (by Riverman), winner of the 2-y-o listed 6f Firth of Clyde Stakes and second in the Group 1 Cheveley Park Stakes, is a half-sister to the Group/Grade 1 winners Denon and Chimes of Freedom (herself the dam of 2 Grade 1 winners). (Flaxman Stables Ireland). *"She might not appear before mid-summer but she's well-grown and maybe even a bit taller than her full brother Pathfork was at this stage. She's going well and she's a nice filly with a bit of quality about her".*

922. BISOUS Y BESOS (IRE) ★★★
b.f. Big Bad Bob – Adoring (One Cool Cat). Fourth foal. €20,000Y. Tattersalls Ireland September. BBA(Ire). Sister to the quite useful Irish 8.5f and hurdles winner Buyer Beware and half-sister to the Italian winner of 3 minor races at 2 and 3 yrs Imperioso (by Mastercraftsman). The dam, a quite useful 7f winner, is a half-sister to 5 winners including the Group 2 6f Mill Reef Stakes winner and Group 1 placed Galeota, the 11f and listed 13f winner Loulwa and the fairly useful 2-y-o 5f Weatherbys Supersprint winner Lady Livius. The second dam, Refined (by Statoblest), a fairly useful dual 5f winner, is a half-sister to 6 winners including the very smart Group 3 7f Criterion Stakes winner Pipe Major. *"She's a fine, big filly, short-coupled and looks to go very nicely. She'll probably go six/seven furlongs this year".*

923. CLOISTERED ★★★
gr.f. Clodovil – Namibia (Galileo). January 30. Fourth foal. €65,000Y. Goffs Orby. BBA (Ire). Half-sister to a minor winner in Germany by Monsun. The dam, a German listed 1m winner, is a half-sister to 4 winners including the multiple listed winner Narrow Hill. The second dam, Narooma (by Silver Hawk), a German 2-y-o Group 3 1m winner, is a half-sister to 2 winners. (Russell Jones, Patrick Cooper & Ms Suzi Pritchard Jones). *"She's done very well since we bought her, she's well-grown, strong and I would hope she'd be running in May over six furlongs".*

924. GRANDEE (IRE) ★★★
b.c. Lope De Vega – Caravan Of Dreams (Anabaa). March 16. Fourth foal. 110,000Y. Tattersalls October Book 1. BBA (Ire). Brother to Sabre Squadron, unplaced in one start at 2 yrs in 2015 and half-brother to the fairly useful 12.5f and 14f winner Weather Watch (by Hurricane Run). The dam, a fair 2-y-o 1m placed maiden, is a half-sister to the dual Group 3 winner and multiple Group 2 placed Royal And Regal and to the listed winner and Group 2 Dante Stakes second Celtic Silence. The second dam, Smart 'n Noble (by Smarten), won the Group 2 Barbara Fritchie Handicap in the USA and is a half-sister to 7 winners. (Millhouse LLC). *"He's done a bit of work, he's nice and more forward than I thought he would be, but I trained his half-brother Weather Watch and he didn't even run at two".*

925. HEAD MONITOR ★★★★ ♠
b.c. Archipenko – Almiranta (Galileo). February 27. Third foal. 115,000Y. Tattersalls December. BBA (Ire). Half-brother to the promising 2015 dual 1m placed 2-y-o Alyssa (by Sir Percy) and to the 2-y-o Group 3 1m Prix Thomas Bryon winner Alea Iacta (by Invincible Spirit). The dam, placed third over 9f at 3 yrs on her only start, is a half-sister to 3 winners including the Irish Group 3 10f winner Alla Speranza. The second dam, Alvarita (by Selkirk), a French listed 10.5f winner, is a full or half-sister to 3 winners out of the dual Champion Stakes winner Alborada (by Alzao). *"A lovely, big Archipenko colt, he has a lot of quality about him, goes nicely and he was an early foal. So despite his size he could be out as early as May".*

926. JOHN HONEYMAN (IRE) ★★★★
gr.c. Dark Angel – Trinity Scholar (Invincible Spirit). April 14. Third foal. 120,000Y. Tattersalls October Book 1. BBA (Ire). Half-brother to the 2015 Italian 2-y-o winner Vernaccia (by Amadeus Wolf). The dam, a quite useful Irish 7f winner, is a half-sister to 7 winners including the Group 1 Prix de la Foret and Group 2 Celebration Mile winner Caradak. The second dam, Caraiyma (by Shahrastani), won over 9f in Ireland and is a sister to the Irish dual Group 3 winner Cajarian and a half-sister to 7 winners including the dam of the Group 1 Nunthorpe Stakes winner Margot Did. (Millhouse LLC). *"He's nice, he's forward and I would expect to see him out in May. He certainly looks like a 2-y-o, he's fairly well developed, a little bit on the leg but he looks the type".*

927. LADY BEWARE (IRE) ★★★
ch.f. Dragon Pulse – Dancing Duchess (Danehill Dancer). March 29. €22,000Y. Tattersalls Ireland September. BBA (Ire). Half-sister to the quite useful dual 2-y-o 6f winner Ailsa Carmel and to the fair 2-y-o 5f winner Roman Dancer (both by Antonius Pius). The dam was a quite useful Irish listed-placed 2-y-o 5f winner out of True Colour (by Known Fact). *"A very strong, well-grown, good-moving filly, she'll be running very shortly and she'll want six furlongs".* **TRAINERS' BARGAIN BUY**

928. ONE LINER ★★
b.c. Delegator – Quip (Green Desert). April 22. Fifth foal. €46,000Y. Tattersalls Ireland September. Amanda Skiffington. Half-brother to the modest 2-y-o dual 7f winner Mr Shekells (by Three Valleys) and to 2 winners in Poland by Refuse To Bend and With Approval. The dam ran once unplaced and is a sister to the listed winner Secret Charm and a half-sister to the listed winner Relish The Thought. The second dam, Viz (by Kris S), a winner at 2 yrs in the USA and third in the Grade 1 Starlet Stakes, is a sister to one listed stakes winner and a half-sister to another. (Carmichael Jennings). *"A big horse that moves beautifully, he's very nice but because of his size you wouldn't imagine he'd be out until August time, looking at him. A seven furlong type 2-y-o".*

929. TWO FOR TEA (IRE) ★★
b.f. Mount Nelson – Eccentricity (Kingmambo). May 11. Seventh foal. €35,000Y. Goffs Orby. BBA (Ire). Half-sister to 5 winners including the useful 2015 2-y-o 7.5f winner Radiantly (by Rock Of Gibraltar), the quite useful 12f winner Phosphorescence (by Sakhee) and two minor winners in France by Acclamation and Teofilo. The dam, placed once over 1m at 3 yrs from 2 starts, is a half-sister to 3 winners. The second dam, Shiva (by Hector Protector), winner of the Group 2 10.5f Tattersalls Gold Cup and the Group 3 10f Brigadier Gerard

Stakes, is a sister to the Group 2 12f Prix Jean de Chaudenay winner Limnos and a half-sister to 8 winners. (Russell Jones, Patrick Cooper, Ms Suzi Pritchard Jones & Partners). *"Very nice, but she's a bit backward, slightly tall and on the leg. She was a late foal and won't be ready until mid-season. By the look of her you'd say she'd be a seven furlong /mile 2-y-o".*

930. UNNAMED ★★★
b.c. Fastnet Rock – Arosa (Sadler's Wells). May 6. Sixth foal. €44,000Y. Goffs Orby. Not sold. Half-brother to the useful triple 1m winner at 2 and 3 yrs and Group 3 third Water Hole (by Oasis Dream). The dam, a fairly useful Irish 9f and subsequent US stakes winner, is a sister to the German Group 2 8.5f and Italian Group 2 1m winner Crimson Tide and to the Group 3 12f Give Thanks Stakes winner Tamarind and a half-sister to the US Grade 2 and Group 3 Prix de Sandringham winner Pharatta and the US stakes winner and Grade 2 placed La Vida Loca. The second dam, Sharata (by Darshaan), is an unraced half-sister to Shahrastani. *"A lovely colt, he's very nice although he's quite big and on the leg at the moment. He's done very well but he's started growing again, so I don't imagine we'll see him out until midsummer. He goes nicely and he's a nice colt".*

931. UNNAMED ★★
ch.c. Mastercraftsman – Dromod Mour (Azamour). April 26. Third foal. €22,000Y. Tattersalls Ireland September. BBA (Ire). The dam is an unraced half-sister to 3 winners including the useful 2-y-o listed 9f winner Tiz The Shot. The second dam, Green Lassy (by Green Tune), won over 13f and 14f at 4 yrs in Ireland and is a half-sister to 5 winners including the French dual Group 2 winner (over 15f and 2m) Cut Quartz. (Vimal Khosla). *"He's grown a lot and is slightly backward. He's almost certain to want seven furlongs to start with but I can see him being out in midsummer".*

932. UNNAMED ★★★
b.f. Arcano – Heart's Desire (Royal Applause). February 20. Eighth foal. €38,000Y. Tattersalls Ireland September. Hussey/Harrington. Sister to the fair 8.5f winner Faddwa and half-sister to the Irish 2-y-o listed 6f winner Heart Of Fire (by Mujadil), the fairly useful Irish 1m (at 2 yrs) and 14f winner Knight Eagle (by Night Shift), the fairly useful 6f (at 2 yrs) to 10f winner Unsinkable (by Verglas) and the modest 2-y-o 7f winner Hearts And Minds (by Clodovil). The dam, placed over 7f and 1m, is a half-sister to 6 winners. The second dam, Touch And Love (by Green Desert), a French 2-y-o winner and second in the Group 2 Prix du Gros-Chene, is a half-sister to 8 winners. (Mr John Hussey). *"She's a lovely, strong filly, hasn't done any work yet but she's a good mover. She was quite small at the sales but she's grown and she'll make a 2-y-o alright – she's certainly bred to".*

933. UNNAMED ★★★
b.f. Acclamation – Manieree (Medicean). January 24. First foal. 200,000Y. Tattersalls October Book 1. BBA (Ire). The dam won four races including the Group 2 10f Blandford Stakes and the Group 3 9f Kilboy Estate Stakes and is a half-sister to 5 winners. The second dam, Sheer Spirit (by Caerleon), won over 12f at 3 yrs and is a half-sister to 9 winners including the Derby winner Oath and the triple Group 1 winner Pelder. (Stonethorn Stud Farm). *"A beautiful looking filly, going nicely now and she's done well. She'll be one for July or August, because although she's by Acclamation the dam stayed a mile and a quarter. She was expensive, but she's a beauty".*

934. UNNAMED ★★
b.f. Excelebration – Scotch Bonnet (Montjeu). April 24. Sixth foal. 18,000Y. Tattersalls October Book 2. A C Elliott. Half-sister to the fair Irish 11.5f winner Mindy (by Zamindar). The dam won twice over 11f and 14f in France is a half-sister to 4 winners including the 10f winner and Group 1 Irish Oaks third Sister Bella and the dam of the US Grade 2 winner Beautyandthebeast. The second dam, Valley Of Hope (by Riverman), is an unraced half-sister to 5 winners including Vacarme (the Mill Reef Stakes and Richmond Stakes) and Vin de France (Prix Jacques le Marois). *"She's very well-grown, strong and well-forward. A nice filly, she'll probably be out before mid-season and you'd expect the sire to get them speedy".*

CHARLIE HILLS

It was another enjoyable and productive visit for me to the Hills' yard, discussing these two-year-olds at length with Assistant Trainer Kevin Mooney.

935. AFAAK ★★★
b.c. Oasis Dream – Ghanaati (Giant's Causeway). March 3. Third foal. Half-brother to the fair 1m winner Alnashama (by Dubawi). The dam, winner of the 1,000 Guineas and Coronation Stakes, is a half-sister to numerous winners including the Group 3 12f Cumberland Lodge Stakes winner and Group 1 Champion Stakes second Mawatheeq and the useful 1m (at 2 yrs) and listed 9f winner Rumoush. The second dam, Sarayir (by Mr Prospector), winner of a listed 1m event, is closely related to the Champion Stakes winner Nayef and a half-sister to Nashwan and Unfuwain. (Hamdan Al Maktoum). *"A big horse that's going to want a bit of time. He won't be a speed horse so he'll probably want to set off at seven furlongs from July onwards. He's a good mover and light on his feet"*.

936. ANGEL OF DARKNESS ★★
b.f. Dark Angel – Chelsea Morning (Giant's Causeway). April 6. Second foal. £52,000Y. Doncaster Premier. BBA (Ire). Half-sister to the fair 2015 2-y-o 7f winner Pickett's Charge (by Clodovil). The dam, a fair 12f winner, is a half-sister to 2 winners. The second dam, Binya (by Royal Solo), won the listed Prix de Saint-Cyr in France and the Grade 3 The Very One Handicap in the USA and is a half-sister to 8 winners including the US Grade 1 winner Sabin. *"A big, weak filly that'll need plenty of time"*.

937. ARWA (IRE) ★★★
b.f. Holy Roman Emperor – Another Storm (Gone West). May 5. Ninth foal. €360,000Y. Goffs Orby. Tony Nerses. Half-sister to 5 winners including the 1m (at 2 yrs) and Group 1 Irish St Leger winner Order Of St George (by Galileo), the 2-y-o 1m and subsequent French Group 3 1m winner Asperity (by War Chant), the US Grade 3 9f winner Angel Terrace (by Ghostzapper) and the Scandinavian listed 12f winner Sehoy (by Menifee). The dam, a minor US 2-y-o winner, is a half-sister to 3 winners. The second dam, Storm Song (by Summer Squall), was a dual Grade 1 winner and champion 2-y-o filly. *"She's going to be a seven furlong filly but she's done everything asked of her and she's cantering away. A good mover and a nice filly, I think we'll see her out in mid-summer"*.

938. BALESTRA ★★★★
b.c. Bated Breath – Nimble Thimble (Mizzen Mast). February 15. First foal. The dam, a fair 9.5f winner, is a sister to one winner and a half-sister to 6 winners including the 2-y-o Group 3 Coventry Stakes and subsequent US Grade 2 winner Three Valleys. The second dam, Skiable (by Niniski), won four times at up to 9f in France and the USA and is a half-sister to several winners including the listed winner Arrive and the outstanding broodmare Hasili (the dam of Dansili and of the Group 1 winners Heat Haze, Intercontinental, Banks Hill, Cacique and Champs Elysees). (Khalid Abdulla). *"He's just got a touch of sore shins at the minute but everyone likes him and he's a good-looking horse. A bit immature, but he's a real nice horse and the people at the stud keep asking about him so they must have thought a fair bit of him. He'll be a 2-y-o alright"*.

939. BARRINGTON (IRE) ★★★
b.c. Casamento – Mia Divina (Exceed And Excel). March 23. First foal. 60,000Y. Tattersalls October Book 2. Sackville/Donald. The dam is an unraced half-sister to 5 winners in Italy including a dual listed winner. The second dam, Maschera d'Oro (by Mtoto), a minor Italian winner of 5 races, is a half-sister to 2 winners. *"A nice horse, he's strong, compact and has a good action. He gets on with his work so he'll definitely be a 2-y-o"*.

940. BATTAASH ((IRE) ★★★
b.c. Dark Angel – Anna Law (Lawman). February 10. First foal. 200,000Y. Tattersalls October Book 2. Shadwell Estate Co. The dam is an unplaced half-sister to 8 winners including the 2-y-o Group 2 Champagne Stakes winner and Group 1 July Cup third Etaala. The second dam, Portelet (by Night Shift), a fairly useful 5f winner of 4 races, is a half-sister to 4 winners. *"He's not over-big and is probably one of those that hasn't grown much, but saying that he's quite set so he's probably not going to. He should make a 2-y-*

941. BORN LEGEND (IRE) ★★★
b.c. Born To Sea – Hallowed Park (Barathea). March 24. Fourth living foal. €115,000Y. Goffs Orby. Sackville/Donald. Half-brother to the quite useful 2015 2-y-o 1m winner Taqwaa (by Iffraaj), to the quite useful 9f and 10f winner Stetchworth (by New Approach) and the fair 7f winner (including at 2 yrs) and 6f winner Shamrocked (by Rock Of Gibraltar). The dam is an unraced half-sister to 5 winners including the Derby second Walk In The Park and the listed winner Soon. The second dam, Classic Park (by Robellino), won 3 races including the Irish 1,000 Guineas and is a half-sister to 10 winners including the US Grade 2 winner Rumpipumpy. *"A nice horse, everyone who rides him loves him. He won't be that early but he's a good mover and well put-together. Probably one to set off at seven furlongs because he's not precocious".*

942. BORTHWEN (IRE) ★★
b.f. Lawman – Apticanti (Aptitude). April 10. Second foal. €140,000Y. Goffs Orby. BBA (Ire). The dam ran twice unplaced and is a half-sister to 4 winners including the champion 2-y-o Distant Music, winner of the Group 1 7f Dewhurst Stakes, the Group 2 7f Champagne Stakes and the Group 2 9f Goffs International Stakes and the Group 3 Lancashire Oaks third New Orchid (dam of the Group 1 Haydock Sprint Cup winner African Rose). The second dam, Musicanti (by Nijinsky), a French 14.5f winner, is a half-sister to 9 winners including Vanlandingham, winner of the Washington D.C. International, the Jockey Club Gold Cup and the Suburban Handicap. *"She's out having a break but she's a nice filly and is one for later in the year".*

943. CAPTAIN HAWK ★★★
b.c. Acclamation – Vintage Gardenia (Selkirk). April 23. Second foal. €140,000Y. Goffs Orby. BBA (Ire). The dam, a minor French 10.5f winner at 3 yrs, is a sister to the smart Group 3 10f Winter Hill Stakes and subsequent US Grade 2 1m winner Tam Lin and a half-sister to 6 winners. The dam won over 7f at 2 yrs and was placed in both the French and Irish 1,000 Guineas and is a half-sister to 7 winners. The second dam, La Nuit Rose (by Rainbow Quest), a 2-y-o 7f winner, was third in the French and Irish 1,000 Guineas and is a half-sister to 7 winners. *"This horse should be earlyish. He does everything right and has done well in the last few weeks. He wasn't an early foal and he's out of a Selkirk mare, but the signs are that he's more forward than you'd think. We'll carry on with him until he tells us otherwise".*

944. CORAL SEA ★★★
gr.f. Excelebration – Tropical Paradise (Verglas). March 4. Second foal. 100,000Y. Tattersalls October Book 1. Sackville/Donald. Closely related to Al Zubarah (by Exceed And Excel), unplaced in two starts at 2 yrs in 2015. The dam won 6 races including the Group 3 7f Oak Tree and Group 3 7f Supreme Stakes and is a half-sister to 3 winners including the Italian Group 3 winner Harlem Shake. The second dam, Ladylishandra (by Mujadil), an Irish 2-y-o 6f winner, is a half-sister to 7 winners. *"Not overly-big but she looks like she could have speed. A nice filly, but if the Verglas influence comes through she may want some cut in the ground".*

945. COYA ★★★
b.f. Paco Boy – Toffee Vodka (Danehill Dancer). April 13. Sixth living foal. Half-sister to the fair 2016 3-y-o 10f winner Carry Me Home (by Dark Angel), to the fair 2-y-o 6f winner No One Knows (by Pastoral Pursuits), the fair 2-y-o 6f winner Toffee Tart (by Dutch Art) and 2 minor winners abroad by Dutch Art and Sleeping Indian. The dam, a fair 6f (at 2 yrs), to 1m winner, is a half-sister to 6 minor winners. The second dam, Vieux Carre (by Pas de Seul), is an unplaced half-sister to 6 winners. *"Could be another La Cucaracha, a lovely filly we had here a few years ago, but she's backward at the minute and I don't think we should be pushing ahead with her just yet. A nice-looking filly".*

946. DARK HERO (IRE) ★★★ ♠
b.c. Kodiac – Mistress Marina (Galileo). April 12. First foal. €125,000Y. Goffs Orby. Sackville/Donald. The dam is an unraced half-sister to 3 winners including a listed stakes winner in Singapore. The second dam, Millennium Miss (by Flying Spur), was placed in Australia and is a half-sister to 4 winners in Australia. *"He*

should be our first two-year-old runner. He's got plenty of boot and he's a hardy little colt".

947. DOCTOR BARTOLO (IRE) ★★★
gr.c. Sir Prancealot – Operissimo (Singspiel). March 29. Sixth foal. 40,000Y. Tattersalls October Book 1. C De Moubray. Half-brother to the fairly useful 2-y-o 6f winner and Group 3 1m Prix Thomas Bryon second Silver Grey (by Chineur), to the fairly useful 1m listed-placed maiden Kodiva (by Kodiac), the quite useful dual 10.5f winner The Character (by Bushranger) and the minor French 2-y-o winner Allegrissimo (by Redback). The dam is an unraced sister to the 2-y-o Group 3 1m Prix Thomas Bryon winner Songlark and a half-sister to 5 winners including the dam of the multiple Group 1 winner Sky Lantern. The second dam, Negligent (by Ahonoora), won the 2-y-o 7f Rockfel Stakes, was third in the 1,000 Guineas and is a half-sister to 5 winners. *"He's a big, strong 2-y-o. We gave him a fortnight off because he was a bit too keen but he's started back now. He's a nice horse and a good mover but as he's out of a Singspiel mare maybe he's more precocious than we would have ideally wanted. I can't dislike him, he's a nice horse".*

948. DR GOODHEAD (FR) ★★
b.f. Zoffany – Whoosh (Muhtathir). April 19. Fifth foal. £50,000Y. Doncaster Premier. BBA (Ire). The dam is an unraced sister to the US Grade 1 Beverly D Stakes, dual US Grade 2 and Group 3 Prix de Cabourg winner Mauralakana and a half-sister to 3 winners including the French listed dual winner Petit Calva. The second dam, Jimkana (by Double Bed), a minor 4-y-o winner, is a sister to 2 winners including the Grade 1 Hong Kong International Cup winner Jim And Tonic and a half-sister to 7 winners. *"A filly that's growing at the moment and unless she suddenly sparkles we won't see her out for a while. She's done well lately but we're not in a rush".*

949. DRUMOCHTER ★★★★
br.f. Bated Breath – Dixey (Diktat). February 12. Third foal. £70,000Y. Doncaster Premier. BBA (Ire). Half-sister to the quite useful 2-y-o 10f winner Dullingham (by Dubawi). The dam, a fairly useful dual 7f winner (including at 2 yrs), is a full or half-sister to 3 winners. The second dam, Hoh Dancer (by Indian Ridge), was placed over 5f and is a half-sister to 3 winners including the listed Doncaster Stakes winner Infanta Real. *"A nice filly that carries a lot of condition. Barry Hills likes her – he thinks she could be good. A good-looking filly, she goes well, has a bit of a knee action and if Barry likes her that's good enough for me".*

950. EXQUISITE RUBY ★★ ♠
b.f. Exceed And Excel – Ruby Rocket (Indian Rocket). February 27. Seventh foal. Sister to the quite useful 6f and 1m winner Mississippi and half-sister to the Group 1 Prix de l'Abbaye, Group 2 Duke Of York Stakes and Group 2 6f British Champions Sprint Stakes winner of 13 races Maarek (by Pivotal) and the modest 7f winner Ermine Ruby (by Cape Cross). The dam, a listed 5f and listed 6f winner, was Group 3 placed twice and is a half-sister to 8 winners including the Irish 2-y-o 6f listed winner Alexander Alliance and the German listed winner and Group 3 6.5f Prix Eclipse second Inzar's Best. The second dam, Geht Schnell (by Fairy King), is a placed half-sister to one winner abroad. *"She's had a few niggles and we won't see her out for some time yet. Probably one for the second half of the season".*

951. FAROOK (IRE) ★★★★
b.br.c. Raven's Pass – Wrong Answer (Verglas). February 26. Third foal. 420,000Y. Tattersalls October Book 1. Shadwell Estate Co. The dam, a useful 2-y-o listed 5f Marble Hill Stakes winner, is a half-sister to 3 winners including the useful dual 1m winner and UAE Group 2 second Albaasil. The second dam, Wrong Key (by Key Of Luck), an Irish 7f (at 2 yrs) and listed 1m winner, was placed in the Group 2 1m Goffs International Stakes and the Group 2 10f Pretty Polly Stakes and is a sister to the Group 3 10f and 12f winner Right Key and a half-sister to 4 winners. *"A real nice horse and a good-looker, he'll definitely be a 2-y-o but probably not a five furlong type".*

952. FOREVER EXCEL (IRE) ★★
b.f. Excelebration – Never A Doubt (Night Shift). May 1. Ninth foal. Half-sister to the quite useful 2015 2-y-o 6f winner Imperious One, to the useful 5f, 7f (both at 2 yrs) and listed 7f winner and Group 2 7f Rockfel Stakes third Royal Confidence (both by

Royal Applause), the quite useful 1m winner Rougette (by Red Ransom) and the quite useful 7f winner Doctor Sardonicus (by Medicean). The dam, a very useful 2-y-o winner of the Group 2 5.5f Prix Robert Papin, is a half-sister to 3 winners including the Group 3 5f third Jonny Mudball. The second dam, Waypoint (by Cadeaux Genereux), a fairly useful 6f and 7f winner of 4 races, is a half-sister to 5 winners including the Group 2 6f Diadem Stakes winner and sire Acclamation. *"A filly from a family we know well, I'd say she'll set off at seven furlongs because she has plenty of size. She actually looks like her mother who was a tough racemare".*

953. GLORIOUS ARTIST (IRE) ★★★
b.c. Zoffany – Queenie Keen (Refuse To Bend). February 2. Second foal. 60,000Y. Tattersalls October Book 2. Sackville/Donald. Half-brother to the unplaced 2015 2-y-o Alyaa (by Iffraaj). The dam, a quite useful Irish 6f and 6.5f winner, is a half-sister to 2 winners including the Group 3 Sirenia Stakes second Diosypros Blue. The second dam, Calamander (by Alzao), a minor Irish 1m winner, is a half-sister to 4 winners including the listed winning 2-y-o Duty Paid. *"He's precocious but we don't want him to be because he's a bit on edge and we have to take things steady with him. He's just a horse at the minute but if he fills his frame and we can keep the lid on he'll do well".*

954. GLORIOUS POWER (IRE) ★★★
ch.c. Power – Arpege (Sadler's Wells). March 30. Ninth foal. €105,000Y. Goffs Orby. Sackville/Donald. Half-brother to 7 winners including the French listed-placed middle-distance winner Beau Vengerov (by Danehill) and the fair 1m and 10f winner Destiny Blue (by Danehill Dancer). The dam is an unraced sister to the German Group 2 8.5f and Italian Group 2 1m winner Crimson Tide and to the Group 3 12f Give Thanks Stakes winner Tamarind and a half-sister to the US Grade 2 and French Group 3 winner Pharatta and the US stakes winner and Grade 2 placed La Vida Loca. The second dam, Sharata (by Darshaan), is an unraced half-sister to Shahrastani. *"We've just had to stop him recently because of a niggling problem. It won't stop him for long and he's a nice, strong-bodied colt that'll be*

alright. I think the sire's going to be successful because the word is that they're strong types. A nice colt that's done nothing wrong".

955. HIGH EXCITEMENT (USA) ★★★★
b.f. Blame – Excelente (Exceed And Excel). April 30. Third foal. Half-sister to the quite useful 2015 2-y-o 5f winner Little Voice (by Scat Daddy) and to the quite useful 10f and 11.5f winner Lemoncetta (by Lemon Drop Kid). The dam, a fairly useful listed-placed Irish 2-y-o 7f winner, subsequently won twice in the USA and is a half-sister to 3 winners including the useful 1m and listed 15f winner Anousa and the useful 7f (at 2 yrs) and 11f winner Prince Nureyev. The second dam, Annaletta (by Belmez), a minor French 12f winner and listed-placed in Germany, is a half-sister to 7 winners including the dam of the Grade 1 E P Taylor Stakes winner Fraulein. *"A real nice filly and maybe one for Royal Ascot. Very good-looking and well-made, she's done well lately and has a great temperament. Could be anything".*

956. HILARIO ★★★
b.c. Sepoy – Persario (Bishop Of Cashel). March 27. Seventh foal. £160,000Y. Doncaster Premier. Tony Nerses. Half-brother to the very smart Group 2 6f Qipco British Champions Sprint and triple Group 3 sprint winner Deacon Blues (by Compton Place), to the fair 6f winner of 4 races If So (by Iffraaj), the quite useful 5f winner of 4 races Holley Shiftwell (by Bahamian Bounty) and the quite useful dual 6f winner The Tin Man (by Equiano). The dam, a quite useful 6f and 7f winner, is a half-sister to 3 winners including the triple Group 3 winner and Group 1 Prix de la Foret third Warningford. The second dam, Barford Lady (by Stanford), a fairly useful 7f and 1m winner, is a half-sister to 5 winners. *"A nice colt, he could well be a 2-y-o. He's done nothing wrong and we've just given him a little break because he's never had a day off throughout the winter. He looks set now and doesn't look likely to grow much more".*

957. HURRICANE RUSH (IRE) ★★★ ♠
b.c. Helmet – Without Precedent (Polish Precedent). February 1. Third foal. 60,000Y. Tattersalls October Book 2. Sackville/Donald. Half-brother to the modest 11.5f winner

Mistamel (by Rip Van Winkle). The dam, a French listed-placed 2-y-o 6f winner, is a half-sister to 2 winners including the German dual listed winner Stark Danon. The second dam, Sue Generoos (by Spectrum), a listed-placed winner in France, is a half-sister to one winner abroad. *"We have two by the first-season sire Helmet and they're both big horses so I think they're going to need time but this is a well-made colt".*

958. IMPERIAL CITY (USA) ★★★★
ch.f. City Zip – Imperial Pippin (Empire Maker). January 23. First foal. The dam, a useful 10f winner, was listed placed three times and is a half-sister to several winners. The second dam, The second dam, Apple Of Kent (by Kris S), winner of the Grade 2 1m Shuvee Handicap, is a sister to one winner and a half-sister to 9 winners including the US dual Grade 2 winner True Flare (the dam of three graded stakes winners) and the Group/Grade 3 winners Set Alight, Capital Secret and War Zone. *"This filly could be early. She's showing all the right signs so I'd have to put her in the list of those we'll be seeing out sooner rather than later. A nice filly, she has a bit of an attitude but you need that, she's well-made, has a good action and definitely a five furlong type 2-y-o".*

959. IT'S HOW WE ROLL (IRE) ★★
b.c. Fastnet Rock – Clodora (Linamix). April 20. Half-brother to 6 winners including the French 2,000 Guineas winner and sire Clodovil (by Danehill), the Group 3 10f Gordon Richards Stakes winner Colombian (by Azamour), the French listed-placed winner Clodovina (by Rock Of Gibraltar), the four-time 10f winner Ouri (by Dansili) and the French 2-y-o 7.5f winner Cloword (by Spinning World). The dam won the Group 2 9.3f Prix de l'Opera and the listed Prix de la Calonne. The second dam, Cloche d'Or (by Good Times), won the Group 3 6f Princess Margaret Stakes and is a half-sister to 5 winners. *"We haven't had a lot of luck with Fastnet Rock's and you wouldn't know what trip they want, but of course he's done really well in Australia. This colt hasn't done any work yet, he's just cantering away and looks a likely seven furlong starter".*

960. MAGILLEN (IRE) ★★★
ch.c. Lope De Vega – Lady Natilda (First Trump). April 12. Eighth foal. €120,000Y. Goffs Orby. BBA (Ire). Half-brother to 5 winners including the fairly useful 2-y-o listed 5f winner Primo Lady, to the quite useful 2-y-o dual 5f winner Lucky Mellor (both by Lucky Story), the quite useful triple 6f winner Ziggy's Stardust (by Zafeen) and the modest 2-y-o 5f winner Modern Lady (by Bertolini). The dam, a modest 2-y-o 5f winner, is a half-sister to 3 winners. The second dam, Ramajana (by Shadeed), won 2 races at 2 and 4 yrs in Germany and is a half-sister to 6 winners here and abroad. *"This horse has done well and he's quite well-related. He has a long stride and a good action, so I don't think he'll be a five furlong 2-y-o. A nice horse for the middle of the season onwards. Could be alright".*

961. MALMAS (USA) ★★★★
gr.c. Street Cry – Wid (Elusive Quality). January 6. Fourth foal. Half-brother to the fair 7f winner Tawteen (by Street Sense). The dam, a useful 2-y-o dual 6f winner, was dual listed-placed and a half-sister to several winners including the useful 7f to 9f winner and listed-placed Haatheq. The second dam, Alshadiyah (by Danzig), a useful 2-y-o 6f winner, is a half-sister to 7 winners including the smart 7f (at 2 yrs) and 10f listed winner Imtiyaz and the very useful Bint Shadayid, winner of the Group 3 7f Prestige Stakes and placed in the 1,000 Guineas and the Fillies Mile. (Hamdan Al Maktoum). *"A very nice colt, he's not been here long because he's wintered in Dubai, but he looks a picture and we're looking forward to running him".*

962. MANAAHIL ★★★
b.f. Dubawi – Mudaaraah (Cape Cross). February 25. Third foal. The dam, a very useful 2-y-o listed 7f Star Stakes winner and second in the Group 3 7f Prestige Stakes, is closely related to the listed 6f winner Ethaara and a half-sister to 3 winners. The second dam, Wissal (by Woodman), is an unraced sister to the high-class 2-y-o Group 2 7f Laurent Perrier Champagne Stakes Bahhare and a half-sister to the Group 1 1m St James's Palace Stakes and Group 1 1m Queen Elizabeth II Stakes winner Bahri. (Hamdan Al Maktoum). *"Not over-big, but a strong, well-set little filly that's*

just ticking away gently. A nice filly, there's nothing wrong with her at all and she'll be one for the middle of the season".

963. MARETTIMO (IRE) ★★
b.c. Harbour Watch – Renowned (Darshaan). April 10. Eleventh foal. €80,000Y. Goffs Orby. BBA (Ire). Half-brother to 5 winners including the Italian listed 11f winner Renowing, the fair 12f and hurdles winner Legion D'Honneur (both by Halling) and the useful 10f to 12f winner of 4 races Varsity (by Lomitas). The dam is an unraced sister to the top-class colt Mark of Esteem, winner of the 2,000 Guineas, Queen Elizabeth II Stakes and Tripleprint Celebration Mile. The second dam, Homage (by Ajdal), is an unraced half-sister to 7 winners including Local Talent (Group 1 Prix Jean Prat). *"This colt has grown a lot and he's very tall and big now. He's had a bit of a stop/start campaign so far, so he'll be one to watch because I wouldn't know which way to go with him for now. We'll just have to see".*

964. MULHIMATTY ★★★
b.f. Invincible Spirit – Raasekha (Pivotal). February 6. First foal. The dam, a fairly useful listed-placed 1m winner, is a half-sister to 5 winners including the multiple Group 1 winning sprinter Muhaarar, the very useful 2-y-o 7f winner and subsequent UAE Group 3 1m second Tamaathul and the useful 2-y-o listed 6f winner Sajwah. The second dam, Tahrir (by Linamix), a useful dual 7f winner, is a sister to the listed winners Mister Charm and Green Channel and a half-sister to the Group 3 Prix de Guiche winner Mister Sacha. (Hamdan Al Maktoum). *"We had the mare who wasn't precocious. This is a nice-looking filly that should set off at six furlongs and end up as a miler".*

965. MUSAWAAT ★★★★★
b.c. Equiano – Starry Sky (Oasis Dream). March 15. Fifth foal. 95,000Y. Tattersalls October Book 2. Shadwell Estate Co. Half-brother to the unplaced 2015 2-y-o Dutch Dream (by Dutch Art), to the fairly useful Irish 2-y-o 6f winner Blackbriar (by Kyllachy) and the Irish 2-y-o 6f winner Tarn (by Royal Applause). The dam, a fair 2-y-o 7f winner, is a half-sister to 2 winners. The second dam, Succint (by Hector Protector), a useful listed 10f winner, is a half-sister to 4 winners including the German listed winner Succession. *"I love this horse. The sire's stock aren't generally precocious and they come through as 3-y-o's but I'm going to stand by this one. This could be a proper horse, I can see him starting off at six furlongs and he's a good-looker that's never had a problem – we've never had to go into his box from day one. So he's straightforward and done everything asked of him. A standout, you can spot him in the string straight away".*

966. NAFAAYES (IRE) ★★★★
ch.f. Sea The Stars – Shamtari (Alhaarth). April 19. Third foal. Half-sister to the fairly useful dual 6f winner Greeb (by Oasis Dream). The dam is an unraced sister to the 2,000 Guineas and Champion Stakes winner Haafhd and a half-sister to numerous winners including the Group 2 Challenge Stakes winner Munir and to the unraced dam of the dual Group 1 winner Gladiatorus. The second dam, Al Bahathri (by Blushing Groom), won the Irish 1,000 Guineas and the Coronation Stakes and is a half-sister to the US Grade 2 winner Geraldine's Store and to the dam of the US Grade 1 winner Spanish Fern. (Hamdan Al Maktoum). *"A particularly good-looking filly, she'll be worth watching out for. She only arrived from Dubai two weeks ago but she's already made an impression on us. Could be anything".*

967. NAYYAR ★★★★
ch.c. Exceed And Excel – Miss Queen (Miswaki). February 24. Tenth foal. Half-brother to 8 winners including the very useful 2-y-o Group 2 5f Flying Childers Stakes and subsequent Hong Kong winner Chateau Istana (by Grand Lodge), the very useful 2-y-o Group 3 6f Sirenia Stakes winner Prince Of Light (by Fantastic Light), the very useful 7f (at 2 yrs) and 1m Britannia Handicap winner and listed-placed Mandobi (by Mark Of Esteem) and the quite useful 7f winner Druids Ridge (by Paco Boy). The dam, a minor winner over 6f in the USA, is a half-sister to 8 winners including the useful 2-y-o Group 3 6f Princess Margaret Stakes winner Tajannub. The second dam, Empress Jackie (by Mount Hagen), won 8 races in the USA including two stakes and is a half-sister to the Derby and Irish Derby third Star Of Gdansk and the US Grade 3 winner

W D Jacks. *"A good-looking little colt, he's the right size for a 2-y-o and he's going to grow much more. I don't think he's a five furlong horse, but he's got a good skin on him at the minute and he looks a smart little horse. I like him a lot".*

968. NESHMEYA ★★★★
b.f. Lawman – High Heeled (High Chaparral). March 23. Second foal. 425,000foal. Tattersalls December. Shadwell Estate Co. The dam, a winner of four races including the Group 3 St Simon Stakes and Group 1 placed in the Oaks and Coronation Cup, is a half-sister to 2 winners and to the dam of the Irish 1,000 Guineas winner Just The Judge. The second dam, Uncharted Haven (by Turtle Island), won two Grade 2 events in the USA and is a half-sister to 6 winners. *"A big, strong-bodied filly, she had a few niggling problems so we've taken our time with her. She'll take a while and wants seven furlongs to start with, but she's a nice filly I'll tell you".*

969. NEVER SURRENDER (IRE) ★★
b.c. High Chaparral – Meiosis (Danzig). May 11. Eleventh foal. 50,000Y. Tattersalls October Book 1. BBA (Ire). Half-brother to the smart 2-y-o 6f winner and Group 1 French 1,000 Guineas third Rahiyah, to the useful 5f (at 2 yrs) and 6f winner League Champion (both by Rahy) and the quite useful triple 7f winner Little Shambles (by Shamardal). The dam, a useful 7f winner, is a half-sister to 6 winners. The second dam, Golden Opinion (by Slew O'Gold), won the Group 1 Coronation Stakes and the Group 3 Prix du Rond Point, was second in the July Cup and third in the French 1,000 Guineas and is a half-sister to 7 winners. *"He hasn't got the substance that a lot of High Chaparral's have and he's 'on the go' all the time too, so we gave him a break and then brought him back. I'd say he's too precocious for his own good, he needs to settle down".*

970. PARYS MOUNTAIN (IRE) ★★★
gr.c. Dark Angel – Muzdaan (Exceed And Excel). February 25. First foal. €100,000Y. Goffs Orby. BBA (Ire). The dam ran twice unplaced and is a half-sister to 7 winners including the dam of the Hong Kong triple Group 1 winner Lucky Nine. The second dam, Belle Genius (by Beau Genius), won the 2-y-o Group 1 7f Moyglare Stud Stakes and is a half-sister to 3 winners. *"He should be a 2-y-o and looks a typical Dark Angel. Not over-big, but he's got plenty of size and although we gave him a break because he looked too precocious if anything it hasn't changed him and he is what he is. Will be a 2-y-o".*

971. PINK BUBBLES (IRE) ★★
b.f. Dutch Art – Royal Fortune (Invincible Spirit). March 16. First foal. €210,000Y. Arqana Deauville August. BBA (Ire). The dam, a minor winner in France, is a sister to a listed winner in Italy. The second dam, Seerah (by Machiavellian), is an unplaced half-sister to one winner. *"On the back burner at the minute because she's a bit immature and needs a bit of time. A nice-looking filly, her action is good and she never does anything wrong".*

972. PRETTY PASSE ★★★
b.f. Exceed And Excel – Passe Passe (Lear Fan). March 17. Thirteenth foal. 75,000Y. Tattersalls October Book 1. Not sold. Half-sister to 8 winners including the fairly useful 10.2f and 12f winner and Australian Grade 2 placed Magic Instinct (by Entrepreneur), the fairly useful 7f (at 2 yrs) and 10f winner Cabinet (by Grand Lodge), the quite useful winner of 5 races (including over 5f at 2 yrs) Ryedale Ovation (by Royal Applause) and the fair 2-y-o 7f winner Pasticcio (by New Approach),. The dam, a fair 7f to 12f placed maiden, is a half-sister to the Irish listed winner and French Group 2 second Windermere. The second dam, Madame L'Enjoleur (by L'Enjoleur), a US 2-y-o stakes winner and Grade 1 placed twice, is a half-sister to the Grade 1 winner Labeeb. (Anthony Oppenheimer). *"She is a strong, well-made filly who shows a bit of speed and I could see her being out in July. She has the scope to do well at three as well".*

973. REBEL DE LOPE ★★★★
b.c. Lope De Vega – Rivabella (Iron Mask). February 20. First foal. 82,000Y. Tattersalls October Book 2. Not sold. The dam, an Italian listed 10f winner of 6 races at 2 and 3 yrs, is a half-sister to 3 minor winners. The second dam, Royale Highnest (by Highest Honor), a minor French 3-y-o winner, is a half-sister to 3 winners. *"A big, strong colt, he's a good-looker that does everything right and he goes well.*

I'd say he'll be one to start off at six furlongs before stepping him up in trip. He's light on his feet and will certainly make a 2-y-o".

974. REDGRAVE (IRE) ★★★
b.c. Lope De Vega – Olympic Medal (Nayef). February 2. Third foal. 100,000Y. Tattersalls October Book 1. John & Jake Warren. Half-brother to the fair 1m winner Wajeeh (by Raven's Pass). The dam ran twice unplaced and is a sister to one winner and a half-sister to 5 winners including the smart Group 2 12f Ribblesdale Stakes winner Phantom Gold (herself dam of the Oaks second Flight Of Fancy and the dual listed winner Golden Stream) and the useful 10f listed and US Grade 3 winner Fictitious. The second dam, Trying For Gold (by Northern Baby), a useful 12f and 12.5f winner at 3 yrs, is a half-sister to 4 winners. *"He's done well lately and is a good looking horse – if a bit upright. He's just ticking away at the minute so he won't be early and we'll take our time with him. One for the second half of the year".*

975. RISING EAGLE ★★★
b.c. Royal Applause – The Clan Macdonald (Intikhab). March 3. First foal. £16,000Y. Doncaster Premier. Not sold. The dam, a quite useful 2-y-o 6f winner from two starts, is a sister to the useful 7f to 10f winner of 4 races Crafty Choice. The second dam, Song Of Passion (by Orpen), a useful 6f to 7.6f winner of 5 races at 2 to 4 yrs, is a half-sister to 6 winners including the Group 2 Sandown Mile and Group 3 Craven Stakes winner Hurricane Alan and the fairly useful 2-y-o 8.6f winner and listed-placed winner of 6 races Aaim To Prosper. *"He was late coming in but he's a smart looking little colt. He should get a mention in the book because he's definitely a 2-y-o type".*

976. RUBENS DREAM ★★★
ch.c. Dutch Art – Apace (Oasis Dream). March 6. Second foal. £140,000Y. Doncaster Premier. Howson & Houldsworth. Half-brother to the fair 2015 2-y-o dual 5f winner Curtain Call (by Acclamation). The dam, a quite useful 7f (at 2 yrs) and 5f winner, is a sister to the useful listed 5f winner and Group 3 third Sugar Free and a half-sister to the useful 1m (at 2 yrs) and 9f winner High Twelve. The second dam, Much

Faster (Fasliyev), a winner of 4 races including the Group 2 6f Prix Robert Papin and second in the Group 1 Prix Morny, is a half-sister to 5 winners. *"A nice horse for early summer. The sire certainly gets 2-y-o's – such as Dutch Connection who we still train – so I think this could be another".*

977. SHANGHAI SILVER (IRE) ★★
ch.c. Kendargent – Ispanka (Invincible Spirit). March 25. First foal. 120,000Y. Tattersalls October Book 1. KIR / Sackville/Donald. The dam, a minor 3-y-o winner in France, is a half-sister to 3 other minor French winners. The second dam, Russian Love (by Machiavellian), is a placed half-sister to 10 winners including Esoterique (Group 1 Prix Rothschild) and the French Group 2 winners Russian Hope, Russian Cross and Archange d'Or. *"A nice colt with a lot of white about him, he's a good mover that definitely won't be early. One for later on and he'll train on to be a better 3-y-o".*

978. SPRING ETERNAL ★★
b.f. Oasis Dream – Short Dance (Hennessy). February 18. Seventh foal. Sister to the quite useful 7f winner Plover and half-sister to the quite useful 7f (at 2 yrs) and 1m winner Fray (by Champs Elysees). The dam, a very useful 6f, listed 7f (both at 2 yrs) and listed 1m winner, is a half-sister to the very useful 2-y-o 7f winner Yankadi. The second dam, Clog Dance (by Pursuit Of Love), a useful maiden, was second in the Group 3 7f Rockfel Stakes and the listed 10f Pretty Polly Stakes and is a half-sister to the smart 14f Ebor Handicap winner Tuning. (Khalid Abdulla). *"We trained the mare and this filly has a bit of a temperament like she had. She's not very big and in terms of her mind perhaps Oasis Dream mixed with Short Dance isn't the best combination".*

979. SUKIWARRIOR (IRE) ★★★
ch.f. Power – Umniya (Bluebird). February 3. Eighth foal. £46,000Y. Doncaster Premier. BBA (Ire). Half-sister to the modest 2-y-o 7f winner Pat Mustard (by Royal Applause). The dam, a quite useful 2-y-o 6f winner, was third in the Group 3 Premio Dormello and is a half-sister to 5 winners including the dual listed 6f winner Lady Links (herself dam of the dual listed winner Selinka). The second dam,

Sparky's Song (by Electric), a moderate 10.2f and 12f winner, is a half-sister to the Group 1 6.5f winner Bold Edge and the listed winner and Group 2 second Brave Edge. *"This filly looks like being early. She's built like a tank and hasn't done any work yet but we'll be hooking onto her soon. She won't need a lot of teaching because she looks like she'll come together quick and be a tough filly"*.

980. SUN BEAR ★★★
b.c. Dansili – Great Heavens (Galileo). March 8. First foal. The dam won the Group 1 Irish Oaks and the Group 2 Lancashire Oaks and is a sister to the King George VI and Queen Elizabeth Stakes and Eclipse winner Nathaniel and a half-sister to 8 winners including Playful Act (Group 1 Fillies' Mile), Percussionist (Group 3 11.5f Lingfield Derby Trial) and Echoes In Eternity (Group 2 1m Sun Chariot Stakes). The second dam, Magnificient Style (by Silver Hawk), won the Group 3 10.5f Musidora Stakes and is a half-sister to the US Grade 1 10f winner Siberian Summer. *"He hasn't been in long and when he came to us he'd had a bit of a problem – but he's a natural. Not very big, he does everything right, he's well-balanced and despite his middle-distance pedigree he actually looks like a typical 2-y-o type. His pedigree shows he won't be an early 2-y-o but I can see him being out by mid-season"*.

981. SWILLY BAY (IRE) ★★★
gr.c. Mastercraftsman – Eastern Appeal (Shinko Forest). March 17. Fourth foal. €100,000Y. Goffs Orby. BBA (Ire). Half-brother to the fair 2015 2-y-o 8.5f winner Lord Kelvin (by Iffraaj). The dam, a dual Group 3 7f winner in Ireland, is a half-sister to 4 winners. The second dam, Haut Volee (by Top Ville), a German 2-y-o 6f and 1m winner, is a half-sister to 9 winners. *"A weak-looking colt but that's because he's growing at the minute so we're just ticking away with him. He has a nice character, does nothing wrong and his movement is fine. One for later on"*.

982. TAI SING YEH (IRE) ★★★
b.c. Exceed And Excel – Cherry Orchard (King's Best). February 13. Third foal. 240,000Y. Tattersalls October Book 1.Sackville/Donald. The dam, a minor French 3-y-o 1m winner, is a half-sister to 3 winners including the smart 10f winner and Group 1 St Leger second The Last Drop. The second dam, Epping (by Charnwood Forest), a quite useful 3-y-o 7f winner, is a half-sister to 7 winners including the French listed winner and multiple Group-placed Self Defense. *"A big horse, he's grown and is tall now so he's going to be one for later on. He's nice, he's done everything asked of him and he's sound in wind and limb, so he'll be alright"*.

983. THAAQIB ★★★
gr.c. Invincible Spirit – Light Shine (Dansili). March 5. First foal. 450,000Y. Tattersalls October Book 1. Shadwell Estate Co. The dam, a fair 9f winner, is a half-sister to 3 other minor winners. The second dam, Light Of Morn (by Daylami), a useful 11.5f winner, was listed-placed and is a half-sister to 5 winners including the smart listed 14f winner Moments Of Joy. *"Only arrived a fortnight ago but he looks a picture and should make a nice 2-y-o once he's acclimatised"*.

984. THAFEERA (USA) ★★★
b.f. War Front – Aqsaam (Dynaformer). February 12. The dam was Grade 3 placed over 12f in the USA and is a half-sister to the US dual Grade 2 placed Lady Lumberjack. The second dam, Harbor Blues (by Petionville), is a half-sister to the US Grade 2 winner Night Patrol. (Hamdan Al Maktoum). *"Before she arrived from Dubai a couple of weeks ago we were told she had a bit of a temper but we've seen none of that. She's a cracker and should be worth looking out for"*.

985. THE BIG SHORT ★★★
ch.c. Bahamian Bounty – Royal Punch (Royal Applause). March 17. Seventh foal. £70,000Y. Doncaster Premier. Kern/Lillingston. Half-brother to the listed 6f Rockingham Stakes winner and Group 2 Lowther Stakes third Royal Rascal (by Lucky Story), to the quite useful 2-y-o 5f winner Cocktail Charlie (by Danbird), the modest 5f and dual 6f winner Another Royal (by Byron) and the modest 5f winner Penny Royale (by Monsieur Bond). The dam ran once unplaced and is a half-sister to 5 winners including the US Grade 3 winner Tigah. The second dam, Macina (by Platini), a winner in Germany and Group 3 third, is a half-sister to 4 winners. *"A nice stamp of a

horse, he's big and strong, we haven't done much with him yet but he's done nothing wrong. He should make a 2-y-o, looking at him".

986. TITANICUS ★★★
b.c. Myboycharlie – Royal Confidence (Royal Applause). February 20. The dam, a useful 5f (at 2 yrs) and listed 7f winner, was third in the Group 2 7f Rockfel Stakes and is a half-sister to the quite useful 1m winner Rougette. The second dam, Never A Doubt (by Night Shift), a very useful 2-y-o winner of the Group 2 5.5f Prix Robert Papin, is a half-sister to 3 winners. "He's changed since he came in this horse. He's out of a mare we trained and she was better over seven furlongs than shorter. He'll probably have a run at six furlongs but be better over seven, he's done nothing wrong to date, he's cantering upsides and you couldn't fault what he's done so far".

987. USTUDIO ★★★
ch.c. Dutch Art – Rotunda (Pivotal). March 15. Fifth foal. 100,000Y. Tattersalls October Book 2. Shadwell Estate Co. Brother to the quite useful 5f (at 2 yrs) and 6f winner Dutch Interior and to the fair 2-y-o 7f winner Finial. The dam is an unraced half-sister to 5 winners including the Group 2 1m May Hill Stakes (at 2 yrs) and Group 2 1m Windsor Forest Stakes winner and 1,000 Guineas second Spacious and the Canadian Grade 2 winner Dimension. The second dam, Palatial (by Green Desert), a useful winner of 4 races over 7f (including at 2 yrs), is a half-sister to 7 winners including the useful listed 10f winners Portal and Ice Palace. "A nice, big horse, very upright in front and a good-looker. He'll want plenty of time I think".

988. WAQAAS ★★★★
b.c. Showcasing – Red Mischief (Red Clubs). March 2. First foal. £170,000Y. Doncaster Premier. Shadwell Estate Co. The dam, a modest 2-y-o 6f winner, is a half-sister to 2 winners including the listed-placed Guto. The second dam, Mujadilly (by Mujadil), a poor maiden, is a half-sister to 4 minor winners. "He should certainly make a 2-y-o. He's a nice, good-looking horse that's never had a day off and is perfectly sound. Does everything right".

989. UNNAMED ★★★
ch.f. Sepoy – Ainia (Alhaarth). March 15. Fourth foal. €63,000Y. Osarus September. Sackville/ Donald. Half-sister to the fair 1m placed 2-y-o Deluxe (by Acclamation). The dam, a fair 4-y-o 9f winner, is a half-sister to 9 winners including the Group 3 1m Autumn Stakes second Taameer, the dual listed 1m winner Expensive and the US Grade 3 placed Sweet Prospect – all three useful. The second dam, Vayavaig (by Damister) a fair 2-y-o 6f winner, is a half-sister to 6 winners including the Group 3 Palace House Stakes winner Vaigly Great and the July Cup second and good broodmare Vaigly Star. "She was small when she came in but she's grown recently and got stronger. She looks a different filly now, she needed to change and she's done that and she's actually a nice little filly. She'll probably set off at six furlongs and get a trip later on".

990. UNNAMED ★★★
b.c. Bated Breath – Bimini (Sadler's Wells). January 30. Fifth foal. €65,000Y. Goffs Orby. BBA (Ire). Half-brother to the quite useful dual 12f winner Rocket Ship (by Sinndar). The dam is an unraced sister to the 1m (at 2 yrs) and Group 1 10f Grand Prix de Paris winner Beat Hollow and a half-sister to 3 winners including the US Grade 3 winner Yaralino. The second dam, Wemyss Bight (by Dancing Brave), a very smart filly, won 5 races including the Group 1 12f Irish Oaks and the Group 2 12f Prix de Malleret and is a half-sister to 6 winners. "He's had sore shins but I still think he'll be a 2-y-o. He's a big, strong horse with a bit of a knee action. A nice colt".

991. UNNAMED ★★
ch.f. Intikhab – Esloob (Diesis). February 23. Eighth foal. 30,000Y. Tattersalls October Book 3. Rabbah Bloodstock. Half-sister to the fair 2-y-o 7f winner Huroof and the minor French 3-y-o 1m winner Halaqa (both by Pivotal). The dam, a 7f (at 2 yrs) and listed Pretty Polly Stakes winner, was third in the Group 1 Fillies' Mile and is a half-sister to 4 winners including the Pretty Polly Stakes winner Siyadah. The second dam, Roseate Tern (by Blakeney), winner of the Group 1 12f Yorkshire Oaks and the Group 2 12f Jockey Club Stakes, was second in the Epsom Oaks and third in the St Leger and is a half-sister to the high-class

middle-distance stayer Ibn Bey. *"Not very big but strong, she's not going to be early and is one for later on. She'll be tough though".*

992. UNNAMED ★★★
b.c. Galileo – Half Queen (Deputy Minister). January 30. Half-brother to the US 2-y-o Grade 1 7f and Grade 1 8.5f winner Halfbridled (by Unbridled). The dam, a minor US winner, is a half-sister to the US dual Grade 2 winner Lu Ravi out of At The Half (by Seeking The Gold). *"A nice, big horse with plenty to like about him. He does nothing wrong but he's not going to be early. He'll want a bit of time".*

993. UNNAMED ★★★
b.c. Raven's Pass – Ripalong (Revoque). March 1. Eighth foal. 95,000Y. Tattersalls October Book 1. Hugo Merry. Half-brother to the very useful 6f (including at 2 yrs) and Irish Group 3 1m winner of 6 races Shamwari Lodge (by Hawk Wing), to the listed 7f winner of 7 races Imperial Rome (by Holy Roman Emperor), the quite useful 10f winner Royal Toast (by Duke Of Marmalade) and the modest 12f winner Shamardal Phantom (by Shamardal). The dam is an unplaced half-sister to 13 winners including Pipalong (Group 1 6f Haydock Park Sprint Cup). The second dam, Limpopo (by Green Desert), a poor 5f placed 2-y-o, is a half-sister to 8 winners. *"A big, strong horse that goes alright and he's a good looker. He's a 'goer' but probably not a five furlong 2-y-o. A real nice horse".*

994. UNNAMED ★★★
ch.f. Tamayuz – Solar Event (Galileo). March 28. Second foal. 40,000Y. Tattersalls October Book 1. Not sold. The dam, a modest 12f placed maiden, is a half-sister to 3 winners including the Group 2 Prix de Malleret and listed Cheshire Oaks winner Time On and the dam of the Group 1 Moyglare Stud Stakes winner Cursory Glance. The second dam, Time Away (by Darshaan), won the Group 3 10.4f Musidora Stakes, was third in the Group 1 Prix de Diane and the Group 1 Nassau Stakes and is a half-sister to 6 winners including the Prix de Diane second Time Ahead. *"A filly built like a colt, she has a big, strong neck and backside. A seven furlong filly and one that'll come alive from the mid-season onwards".*

995. UNNAMED ★★★
b.f. Dutch Art – Through The Forest (Forestry). February 6. Third foal. €140,000Y. Goffs Orby. BBA (Ire). Half-sister to the fair 2015 6f and 7f placed 2-y-o Dark Forest (by Iffraaj) and to the modest 2-y-o 5f winner Bountiful Forest (by Bahamian Bounty). The dam, a moderate 11f winner, is a half-sister to 3 winners including the minor US stakes winner Dattts Our Girl. The second dam, Lakefront (by Deputy Minister), is an unraced half-sister to 5 winners including the US listed winner Sluice (herself dam of the US Grade 1 winner Mushka). *"She's had a few niggling problems but she's just getting going now and she's a nice-looking filly that's worth mentioning in the book".*

RICHARD HUGHES

996. ALL INDIA ★★★
b.c. Sepoy – Zanzibar (In The Wings). March 8. Ninth foal. 100,000Y. Tattersalls October Book 2. Hillen & Hughes. Closely related to the fairly useful UAE dual 7f winner Zurbriggen (by Raven's Pass) and half-brother to 4 winners including the smart 10f and 12f and subsequent US Grade 2 8.5f and dual Grade 3 winner Spice Route (by King's Best), the fair 10f and 12f winner Halfway House (by Dubai Destination) and the fair 11f winner Celtic Dragon (by Fantastic Light). The dam, winner of the Group 1 11f Italian Oaks, is a half-sister to the listed winner New Guinea. The second dam, Isle Of Spice (by Diesis), a fair 3-y-o 9.7f winner, is a half-sister to 5 winners. *"He'll be an early type, he's a strong, precocious 2-y-o and I won't be hanging about with him, although I don't think the first crop of Sepoy's down under are faring that well so far".*

997. ANGEL OF ROME (IRE) ★★★
gr.f. Mastercraftsman – Bright Sapphire (Galileo). January 15. Second foal. 85,000Y. Tattersalls October Book 1. Richard Hughes / John Lund. Half-sister to the 2015 2-y-o 6f winner, from two starts, Wall Of Fire (by Canford Cliffs). The dam ran twice unplaced and is a half-sister to 3 minor winners. The second dam, Jewel In The Sand (by Bluebird), a winner of 4 races including the Group 2 6f Cherry Hinton Stakes and the listed Albany Stakes, is a half-sister to 4 winners including the German 3-y-o listed 6f winner Davignon. (Mr J E Lund). *"One of the reasons I bought*

this filly was because I rode her brother Wall Of Fire when he won first time out. A lovely filly, she's big and strong with a great mind and a masculine look to her. I can see her being one to start over seven furlongs but she'll be a better 3-y-o".

998. AVENTUS (IRE) ★★★
b.c. Zebedee – Irish Design (Alhaarth). March 20. Seventh foal. 72,000Y. Tattersalls October Book 2. Badgers Bloodstock / R Hughes. Closely related to the fair 2m and hurdles winner Mohanad (by Invincible Spirit) and half-brother to the modest 2-y-o 1m winner Rising Dawn (by Dark Angel). The dam ran once unplaced and is a half-sister to 4 winners including the multiple Irish Group 3 winner Idris and to the dams of three stakes winners. The second dam, Idara (by Top Ville), won twice in France at 3 yrs and was third in the Group 2 Prix de Pomone and is a half-sister to 2 winners. (Mr D S Waters). *"A very nice colt that's probably in my second batch of 2-y-o's. I'd like to think I'd get a run into him in May and then see if he's good enough for Royal Ascot. He cost as much as he did because he's a beautiful looking individual and when I saw him at Tattersalls he reminded me of Ivawood".*

999. CASPIAN GOLD (IRE) ★★★
ch.c. Born To Sea – Eminence Gift (Cadeaux Genereux). February 20. Fifth foal. 120,000Y. Tattersalls October Book 2. Sackville/Donald & R Hughes. Half-brother to the quite useful 2015 2-y-o 7f winner Spongy (by Zoffany), to the fair 6f (at 2 yrs), 1m and bumpers winner Saint Jerome (by Jeremy) and a minor 2-y-o winner abroad by Intense Focus. The dam, a moderate dual 10f winner, is a sister to the listed-placed dual 1m winner and smart broodmare Granted and a half-sister to 4 winners including the Italian listed winner Lucky Chappy. The second dam, Germane (by Distant Relative), a useful winner of the Group 3 7f Rockfel Stakes and placed in two listed events, is a half-sister to 9 winners including the very useful German 10f winner Fabriano. (M Hughes & M Kerr Dineen). *"As an individual I thought he was one of the best walkers at the sale. He's one for the middle to back-end of the season on pedigree, but he's coming to hand so quickly we're* having to slow him down. An exceptionally good mover and he might even be a Chesham Stakes type of horse – although personally I'm not mad about that race. His brother, Spongy, was a very strong horse and maybe I should have won more races with him but he kept getting left at the start".

1000. CHAPLIN (FR) ★★
b.c. Myboycharlie – Lady Oriande (Makbul). February 5. Sixth foal. €90,000Y. Arqana Deauville August. Badgers/R Hughes. Half-brother to the 2-y-o Group 3 7f Prix La Rochette and listed 6f winner My Name Is Bond (by Monsieur Bond), to the modest 2-y-o 5f winner Ruthie Babe (by Exceed And Excel) and two minor winners abroad by Multiplex. The dam is a placed sister to the Group 2 6f Goldene Peitsche and Group 3 6f Prix de Ris-Oranges winner Striking Ambition. The second dam, Lady Roxanne (by Cyrano de Bergerac), a moderate 5f seller and 6f winner, is a sister to the US Grade 3 Hollywood Turf Express Handicap winner Cyrano Storme and a half-sister to 6 minor winners. (Macdonald, Wright, Creed, Jiggins & Miller). *"The first horse I bought last year, he's done a lot of growing but he's come out the other side of that now. We've haven't been able to do anything with him because he's done so much growing, but he'll make a 2-y-o over seven furlongs and a mile".*

1001. CLEMENTO (IRE) ★★★★
b.c. Canford Cliffs – Street Style (Rock Of Gibraltar). April 4. Fourth foal. 240,000Y. Tattersalls October Book 1. Tony Nerses. Half-brother to the Irish Group 3 10.5f Diamond Stakes winner Panama Hat (by Medicean) and to a hurdles winner by Moss Vale. The dam, a fair 9f winner, is a half-sister to 5 winners including the US Grade 1 winner and Irish 1,000 Guineas third Luas Line and the Group 2 Bosphorus Cup winner Lost In The Moment. The second dam, Streetcar (by In The Wings), is a placed half-sister to 9 winners including Intimate Guest (Group 3 May Hill Stakes). (Saleh Al Homaizi & Imad Al Sagar). *"The apple of my eye at the moment, he seems to do everything very easily and is an exceptionally good mover. He takes everything in his stride but I wouldn't be in any rush with him because he's over 500kgs.*

I found out last year with a lot of the Canford Cliff 2-y-o's that although they looked precocious when you actually squeezed them they weren't. But they came good towards the back-end. I'll bear that in mind and look after him, so you won't see him until later in the season".

1002. CURVE BALL (IRE) ★★★ ♠
b.c. Requinto – Royal Esteem (Mark Of Esteem). March 15. Fifth foal. £65,000Y. Doncaster Premier. A Skiffington. Half-brother to the fair 1m winner of 4 races Hostile Fire (by Iffraaj) and to a 2-y-o winner in Russia by Ramonti. The dam, a dual winner at 3 yrs in the USA, is a half-sister to one winner abroad. The second dam, Inchacooley (by Rhoman Rule), an Irish and US listed winner of 6 races at 3 to 8 yrs, is a half-sister to one winner. (Carmichael Jennings). *"At the moment he looks in the early band of 2-y-o's, so he's probably one for the first six weeks of the season. He's easy to deal with, he's put on a lot of weight since he got here and he's much stronger now. A nice horse at the sale and even nicer now, he's probably a six furlong 2-y-o but I could start him off at five".*

1003. DELFIE LANE ★★★
b.c. Harbour Watch – Anneliina (Cadeaux Genereux). March 15. Ninth living foal. £35,000Y. Doncaster Premier. Hillen & Hughes. Half-brother to 5 winners including the quite useful 5f winner of 8 races Cadeaux Pearl, the fair 5f winner Bonheurs Art (both by Acclamation), the quite useful 5.8f (at 2 yrs) and 7f winner Rioliina (by Captain Rio) and the quite useful 2-y-o triple 6f winner Cheap Street (by Compton Place). The dam is a fair 6f placed half-sister to 5 minor winners. The second dam, Blasted Heath (by Thatching), a dual listed winner over 5f (at 2 yrs) and 1m, is a half-sister to Balla Cove (Group 1 Middle Park Stakes). *"This lad will be racing in the first six weeks of the season. He's done amazingly well since we bought him and he's after growing a little bit now. He has a beautiful head on him and he'll be versatile where I go because he has a solid mind on him. That's half the battle with these 2-y-o's".*

1004. FOOTMAN (GER) ★★
b.c. Cacique – Flames To Dust (Oasis Dream). March 29. Fourth foal. 75,000Y. Tattersalls October Book 2. John & Jake Warren. The dam is an unraced sister to one winner and a half-sister to 6 winners including the 2-y-o Group 2 Royal Lodge Stakes second and subsequent Hong Kong stakes winner Bahamian Dancer. The second dam, Fantastic Flame (by Generous), a fair 10f winner, is a sister to the Group 3 Gordon Richards Stakes winner Germano and a half-sister to 9 winners including the US Grade 2 winner Moon Solitaire. (Highclere Thoroughbred Racing – Oscar Wilde). *"I was delighted that Highclere didn't send me a precocious 2-y-o because I had my own list of early types I wanted to buy. This is a lovely, backward horse and definitely one for next year, but at the same time he's a very agile colt and we'll have no problem getting him out towards the end of the season. I rode the sire myself and also rode the last good one he had, Census, for Highclere and Richard Hannon. I'd like to repay Highclere with this colt".*

1005. GOODWOOD CRUSADER (IRE) ★★★
b.c. Sir Prancealot – Pale Orchid (Invincible Spirit). January 25. First foal. 44,000Y. Tattersalls October Book 2. R Frisby. The dam, a quite useful 5f and 6f winner of 5 races, is a half-sister to the smart Group 3 6f Prix de Ris-Orangis and listed 1m winner Thawaany. The second dam, Chelsea Rose (by Desert King), won the Group 1 7f Moyglare Stud Stakes and three listed events, was Group 1 placed twice and is a half-sister to 8 winners including the Irish listed 1m winner and subsequent US Grade 2 placed European. *"Should be in my first batch of runners, he's a compact little horse with a very good nature. He's easy to deal with and precocious".*

1006. HATHFA (FR) ★★★ ♠
gr.f. Dark Angel – Nepali Princess (Mr Greeley). January 24. First foal. €260,000Y. Arqana Deauville August. Al Shaqab Racing/Mandore Int. The dam is an unraced half-sister to the 2-y-o Group 1 Prix Morny, Group 1 Middle Park Stakes and dual Group 2 winner Shalaa. The second dam, Ghurra (by War Chant), a quite useful 2-y-o 6f winner, subsequently won in the USA and was third in the Grade

3 Wilshire Handicap. She is a sister to the winner and US Grade 2 third Zifzaf and a half-sister to 7 winners including the smart 2-y-o Group 1 6f Middle Park Stakes winner Hayil and the US Grade 2 second Tamhid. (Al Shaqab Racing). *"She looked expensive at the time but since Shalaa has done so well she's probably worth that all day long. She's precocious and should be racing plenty early enough. I've ridden her myself and she's a nice filly to sit on"*.

1007. JASHMA (IRE) ★★★
b.c. Power – Daganya (Danehill Dancer). May 23. Eighth foal. €110,000Y. Goffs Orby. Hillen & Hughes. Half-brother to the 7f to 10.5f winner of 8 races Akasaka (by King's Best), to the dual 12f winner Cape Of Good Grace (by Cape Cross), the 5f and 6f winner Kernoff (by Excellent Art) – all fairly useful, the fair 2015 2-y-o 6f winner Dancing Years (by Iffraaj) and the modest dual 6f winner Chasca (by Namid). The dam, a listed 6f event in Ireland, was second in the Group 2 5f Flying Five. She is a sister to the listed 5f winner Snaefell and a half-sister to 4 winners. The second dam, Sovereign Grace (by Standaan), won over 5f in Ireland and is a half-sister 9 winners. (M Clarke, S Geraghty, J Jeffries). *"He was a late foal but he certainly doesn't act that way. Very strong and very precocious, as a rule I like these Power's. I think they're big, strong and tough. This colt has a good mind on him, he goes as straight as an arrow – never deviates – and I'd be surprised if he wasn't my quickest 2-y-o but not necessarily the best"*.

1008. JUMPING JACK (IRE) ★★★
b.c. Sir Prancealot – She's A Character (Invincible Spirit). March 7. First foal. £35,000Y. Doncaster Premier. Hillen & Hughes. The dam, a fair 6f (at 2 yrs) to 9f winner, is a half-sister to 4 winners. The second dam, Cavernista (by Lion Cavern), is a placed half-sister to 11 winners including the Group 1 Prix du Cadran winner Give Notice and the triple Group 2 winning stayer Times Up. (Mr D S Waters). *"He'll be one of my first runners. At the sales I wasn't mad on him until he entered he ring and then he looked like he'd grown a leg! His name reflects how he prances around as if he owns the place. A brilliant mover for an early 2-y-o, I don't know how good he'll be but he's certainly going to be early. Hopefully I'll get him into the auction races"*.

1009. KING OF PARIS ★★
b.c. Exceed And Excel – Dubai Queen (Kingmambo). February 11. Second foal. Half-brother to the 2015 2-y-o 7.5f winner, from two starts, Sharja Queen (by Pivotal). The dam, a fairly useful listed-placed 1m winner, is a half-sister to 5 winners, notably Dubawi. The second dam, Zomaradah (by Deploy), a winner of 6 races including the Group 1 Italian Oaks, the Group 2 Royal Whip Stakes and the Group 2 Premio Lydia Tesio, is a half-sister to several winners. (Sheikh Mohammed Obaid Al Maktoum). *"A big, heavy horse, I won't be in any rush with him. He's an easy horse to deal with, has a good mind and is starting to look nicer now than he was. Seven furlongs should do for him to start with"*.

1010. LAWFILLY ★★★
b.f. Lawman – Red Boots (Verglas). February 28. Third foal. 40,000Y. Tattersalls October Book 2. Stephen Hillen. Half-sister to the quite useful dual 5f winner Stocking (by Acclamation). The dam, a modest 7f placed 2-y-o, is a half-sister to 2 winners including the Irish dual listed winner and dual Group 3 placed Rose Bonheur. The second dam, Red Feather (by Marju), a Group 3 1m winner in Ireland, was second in the Group 1 Moyglare Stud Stakes and is a half-sister to 3 winners. (The Saints). *"A nice filly with a very good, old fashioned pedigree. She was misbehaving at the sale and wouldn't go into the ring, so I bought her quite cheaply. After the first four weeks she hasn't put a foot wrong. A filly with a big, deep girth, she probably needs a bit of time and may be more of a 3-y-o"*.

1011. LUZIA ★★★
b.f. Cape Cross – Bint Almukhtar (Halling). February 17. First foal. The dam is an unraced half-sister to one winner. The second dam, Dabawiyah (by Intikhab), placed once over 10f from two starts, is a half-sister to 7 winners including the very smart 7f (at 2 yrs) and Group 3 12f Gordon Stakes winner Rabah and the useful 2-y-o 6f winner and Group 1 Cheveley Park Stakes third Najiya and to the placed dam of the Irish Oaks second

Ice Queen. (Sheikh Mohammed Obaid Al Maktoum). *"Probably one of my nicer fillies, she's a gorgeous specimen to look at and moves really well. I could run her tomorrow if I had to, despite the pedigree. I won't be rushing her but she's another that's coming to hand too easy and I have to slow her down".*

1012. METEORIC RISER (USA) ★★★
b.c. More Than Ready – Silimiss (Dansili). February 20. First foal. 60,000Y. Tattersalls October Book 2. Hillen & Hughes. The dam, a minor French 3-y-o winner, is a half-sister to 7 winners including the French listed winner Destruct and the Group 3 Musidora Stakes second Quickfire. The second dam, Daring Miss (by Sadler's Wells), won 4 races in France including the Group 2 12f Grand Prix de Chantilly and is a half-sister to 5 winners including the Group 3 12f Prix de Royaumont winner Apogee. (Mr D S Waters). *"A mid-season type 2-y-o and a very easy-moving horse. They tell me that More Than Ready crossed with a Danehill stallion is very good. At the sales he was grinding his teeth and I reckon that's why we got him without paying too much. When we got him home we could see the problem was ulcers and he's fine now. One for August-time I'd say and I'm very pleased with him".*

1013. NATHANIA ★★★★
ch.f. Nathaniel – Glen Rosie (Mujtahid). February 14. Ninth living foal. 105,000Y. Tattersalls October Book 2. Hillen & Hughes. Half-sister to the promising 2015 2-y-o 7f debut winner Vincent's Forever (by Pour Moi), to the useful 2-y-o listed 7f winner Kings Quay, the fairly useful triple 10f winner Milne Garden (both by Montjeu), the quite useful listed-placed 10f and 11f winner Fastback (by Singspiel) and the modest 10f and hurdles winner Calculated Risk (by Motivator). The dam, a 2-y-o 5f winner and second in the Group 3 Fred Darling Stakes, is a half-sister to 5 winners including the Group 3 Irish Derby Trial and triple US stakes winner Artema. The second dam, Silver Echo (by Caerleon), is an unraced sister to the listed 6f winner Dawn Success and a half-sister to the Group 3 7f Gladness Stakes winner Prince Echo. (Harvey Rosenblatt & Friends). *"She could be a filly for Ascot. You should be saying the Chesham Stakes but the way she's going at the moment maybe she'll make the Albany. I won't be rushing her, but she's works effortlessly, is a real good colour and has a good eye. I won on her half-brother Kings Quay and I'd say this filly has a lot of talent. Two of the part owners are me and Tony McCoy!"*

1014. OCEAN PROMISE (USA) ★★★
b.f. Quality Road – I'm From Dixie (Dixieland Band). April 9. Fourth foal. $110,000Y. Keeneland September. Private Sale. The dam, placed at 3 yrs in the USA, is a half-sister to four US stakes winners including the US Grade 2 Black Eyed Susan Stakes winner Sweet Vendetta. The second dam, Sand Pirate (by Desert Wine), won 7 minor races in the USA from 3 to 7 yrs. (Danny Waters & Adrian Regan). *"I bought her in Keeneland but the whole journey and the quarantine knocked a bit out of her for a while. She's an effortless mover and her half-sister has recently won in America. She's the tallest of her family so I'm told, but she's got to grow a bit before I start to be serious with her. She won't take long to get ready though".*

1015. PACO'S ANGEL ★★★
b.f. Paco Boy – Papabile (Chief's Crown). February 2. Ninth foal. Half-sister to the fair 10f winner Papality (by Giant's Causeway), to the French 1m winner Paperchain (by Dubawi) and the Italian listed-placed Neon Glitter (by Kyllachy). The dam, a useful winner of 3 races over 1m including two listed events, is a sister to the champion 2-y-o Grand Lodge and a half-sister to 6 winners including the dual listed winner La Persiana. The second dam, La Papagena (by Habitat), is an unraced half-sister to 7 winners including Eagling, Pamina and Lost Chord (all very useful). *"I'm trying to get her ready early because I think she's well up for it. We use a heart monitor and the results for her are staggering – they show how easy she finds everything".*

1016. PATCHWORK ★★★
ch.c. Paco Boy – Medley (Danehill Dancer). April 29. Half-brother to the useful 2015 2-y-o 7f winner Light Music and to the fairly useful winner of 5 races at around 1m Sea Shanty (both by Elusive Quality). The dam, a fairly useful 6f (at 2 yrs) and listed 7f winner, is a

half-sister to 8 winners. The second dam, Marl (by Lycius), a fairly useful 2-y-o 5.2f winner, is a half-sister to 4 winners including the very useful 2-y-o listed 5f National Stakes winner Rowaasi. (The Queen). *"Moves exceptionally well and should be early which is probably why he was sent to me. A good-natured horse that doesn't seem to have any quirks, I've ridden him myself and he's thriving now. I also rode the dam to be beaten a head at Windsor when she was drawn on the wrong side. She was quick".*

1017. ROCK N ROLL GLOBAL (IRE) ★★★★
ch.c. Power – Laughter (Sadler's Wells). February 27. Third foal. €62,000Y. Goffs Orby. Hillen & Hughes. The dam, a quite useful 2-y-o 7f winner, is a half-sister to 3 winners in Japan and the USA. The second dam, Smashing Review (by Pleasant Tap), a listed winner of 5 races in the USA, is a half-sister to 2 winners. (Jed Gaffney & Frank McGrath). *"This horse weighs 540kgs – he's just a big ball of strength. I don't think he's backward, he's just bigger, stronger and more mature than most of mine. He'll be out in April or May and he's quite unusual in that he's a chestnut with black spots on his coat. John Warren tells me that's going back three generations".*

1018. TWENTY TIMES (IRE) ★★★
b.f. Dream Ahead – Mad Existence (Val Royal). May 5. Third foal. €100,000Y. Goffs Orby. Badgers/Hughes. Half-sister to the 2015 French 1m listed-placed 2-y-o Secret Existence (by Sakhee's Secret) and to the French dual 10f winner Morigny (by Royal Applause). The dam, a modest dual 10f winner, is a half-sister to 7 winners. The second dam, Hanzala (by Akarad), won 3 listed events in France. (True Reds). *"A nice filly I bought at Goffs. I just love the way she moves effortlessly and I think she'll be like her 3-y-o half-sister and be a middle to back-end 2-y-o".*

1019. ZAVIKON ★★★
b.c. Compton Place – Hakuraa (Dixie Union). January 30. First foal. £75,000Y. Doncaster Premier. Amanda Skiffington. The dam is an unraced half-sister to one winner. The second dam, Miss Donovan (by Royal Applause), a quite useful Irish listed-placed 6f winner, is a half-sister to 8 winners including the Group 2 Coventry Stakes winner Hellvelyn. (Embleton, Galloway, Hanley & Lawrence). *"He was a ready-made horse when I bought him at Doncaster and then grew an awful lot so he's not as precocious as I thought he'd be. Nevertheless he'll be out in May over six furlongs. A very good-moving horse".*

1020. UNNAMED ★★★
b.c. Harbour Watch – Al Hawa (Gulch). January 28. Third living foal. 18,000Y. Tattersalls October Book 2. Hillen & Hughes. Half-brother to a minor 2-y-o winner in the Czech Republic by Mount Nelson. The dam is an unraced half-sister to 7 winners including the Group 3 Winter Derby and recent UAE Group 1 winner Tryster, the smart 10f, 12f and UAE listed winner Mutasallil and the useful 10f and 11f winner and Group 3 Cumberland Lodge Stakes third Ajhar. The second dam, Min Alhawa (by Riverman), a useful 7f (at 2 yrs) to 10f winner, was listed-placed and is a sister to the 1,000 Guineas winner Harayir and a half-sister to 3 winners. (The Heffer Syndicate). *"He looks like he's worth a lot more now than he cost at the sales. A big, strong horse, we haven't asked any questions yet because he's done a bit of coughing. Once he turns the corner I'd say he'll come quick, he's a nice sort and I believe Harbour Watch will do well".* **TRAINERS' BARGAIN BUY**

1021. UNNAMED ★★★
b.f. Exceed And Excel – Naruko (Street Cry). February 6. First foal. 100,000Y. Tattersalls December. Demi O'Byrne. The dam was a minor French 3-y-o 1m winner. The second dam, Lake Toya (by Darshaan), a useful dual listed 10f winner, is a half-sister to 8 winners including the listed winner Sixth Sense and the Group 3 Musidora Stakes second Glen Innes. (Coolmore). *"A nice filly bought at the December sale, she does things very easily. She'll be ready to go when I want her to and if she's good enough for Ascot that's where we'll go".*

WILLIAM JARVIS

1022. GIRL SQUAD ★★★
b.f. Intikhab – Foxtrot Alpha (Desert Prince). February 22. Second foal. 7,000Y. Tattersalls October Book 3. William Jarvis. The dam, a fair 6f (at 2 yrs) and 7f winner of 4 races, is a half-sister to 7 winners including the quite useful 2-y-o 6f winner and subsequent US Grade 3 placed winner Rapadash. The second dam, Imelda (by Manila), ran once unplaced at 2 yrs and is a half-sister to 6 winners including the high-class Group 2 Prix du Rond-Point and Group 2 Prix d'Astarte winner Shaanxi. (Raceology Partnership). *"A cheap buy, she's got a bit of spirit about her and took a bit of breaking-in. She goes perfectly well and there's no reason why she shouldn't win a little maiden auction before going on. We like her and she looks a 2-y-o"*. **TRAINERS' BARGAIN BUY**

1023. JUANITO CHICO (IRE) ★★★★
br.c. Pour Moi – Miss Kittyhawk (Hawk Wing). February 15. Third foal. €50,000Y. Goffs Orby. Ric Wylie. Half-brother to the 2-y-o listed 1m winner and Group 1 1m Racing Post Trophy third Celestial Path (by Footstepsinthesand). The dam, a modest 1m placed maiden, is a half-sister to 3 winners including the Group 1 1m Matron Stakes winner Chachamaidee. The second dam, Canterbury Lace (by Danehill), is an unraced sister to the Group 3 winner Alexander Of Hales and a half-sister to 4 winners including the 1,000 Guineas winner Virginia Waters. (A N Verrier). *"We like him a lot, he's a very nice horse. He's finding life very easy at the moment, he's by a Derby winner and his half-brother was held in high regard by Sir Mark Prescott. He would be as nice as we've got and may have enough toe to start over six furlongs before stepping up to seven. He's not over-big, just a well-proportioned horse and with scope".*

1024. OFF TO BOND STREET ★★
b.g. Paco Boy – Woodbeck (Terimon). March 24. Thirteenth foal. 22,000Y. Tattersalls October Book 2. M C Banks. Half-brother to 7 winners including the very smart 7f (at 2 yrs), Group 2 Yorkshire Cup and Group 3 11.8f Lingfield Derby Trial winner Franklins Gardens (by Halling), the very smart Group 3 7f and Group 3 1m winner Polar Ben (by Polar Falcon), the fairly useful 10f winner and listed placed Wood Chorus (by Singspiel), the quite useful 1m to 10f winner of 8 races Polar Forest (by Kyllachy) and the quite useful 7f to 10f winner of 4 races Willow Beck (by Shamardal). The dam, a fairly useful 3-y-o dual 7f winner, is a half-sister to 8 winners including the fairly useful 2-y-o winners Optimistic and Carburton. The second dam, Arminda (by Blakeney), is an unraced half-sister to the Group 1 Prix de Diane winner Madam Gay. (Mr R L Banks). *"He's a half-brother to two good horses although there are mixed messages in his pedigree as to what his best trip should be. His action suggests he'll need seven furlong to start off with. A tall horse, we needed to geld him but he's coming round to our way of thinking and he's a loose-actioned horse with a bit of size about him. He goes well".*

1025. RED GUANA (IRE) ★★★
ch.f. Famous Name – Guana (Dark Angel). March 29. First foal. Tattersalls October Book 3. W Jarvis. The dam is an unraced half-sister to 3 winners including the dam of the Group 2 Superlative Stakes winner Birchwood. The second dam, Guana Bay (by Cadeaux Genereux), is an unraced full or half-sister to 6 winners including the Group 2 winners Prince Sabo and Millyant, and the listed winner Bold Jessie (dam of the Group 2 Gimcrack Stakes winner Abou Zouz). (G.B. Turnbull Ltd). *"Her pedigree includes Birchwood who was placed in the Breeders' Cup Juvenile. I think the sire Famous Name was a very tough horse and Mr Turnbull was very keen on buying one of his yearlings. This a strong filly, she's doing everything we ask and I see her being out in the summer".*

1026. UNNAMED ★★
b.f. Pour Moi – Double Green (Green Tune). April 4. Seventh foal. €75,000Y. Goffs Orby. Ric Wylie. Half-sister to the minor French 11f and 12f winner Eurato (by Medicean). The dam, a French listed 15f winner and third in the Group 3 Prix de Lutece, is a half-sister to 4 winners. The second dam, Green Bend (by Riverman), is a placed half-sister to 9 winners including the French Group 3 winner and smart broodmare Brooklyn's Dance and to the unraced dam of the Derby winner Authorized. (Mr K J Hickman). *"I like her, although she's*

much more in the stamp of a backward, autumn filly. A good-size, she's a bit weak at the moment, but has a good-action. The owner won't be in any hurry with her".

1027. UNNAMED ★★★
ch.f. Bated Breath – Ocean View (Gone West). April 21. Thirteenth foal. €60,000Y. Goffs Orby. Ric Wylie. Half-sister to 7 winners including the moderate 2015 2-y-o 5f winner Lolamotion (by Equiano), the US Grade 3 winner Officer Rocket (by Officer), the quite useful 7f winner Paradise Watch (by Royal Applause) and the fair 2-y-o 8.3f winner and US stakes-placed Desert View (by Sadler's Wells. The dam won twice in the USA, was Grade 1 placed twice and is a sister to the Grade 2 winner Westerly Breeze and a half-sister to 9 winners including the US Grade 2 placed Jacksonport. The second dam, On The Brink (by Cox's Ridge), was a dual US 3-y-o winner. (Mr K J Hickman). *"We like her, she goes nicely, is still a bit backward in her coat as we speak but she's doing two nice canters. She'll be ready to step up in the next month with a view to her seeing a racecourse in May. I should imagine she'd need six furlongs but she's a likeable filly that goes well".*

1028. UNNAMED ★★★
ch.c. Sepoy – One Giant Leap (Pivotal). May 2. Fifth living foal. 20,000Y. Tattersalls October Book 2. William Jarvis. Half-brother to the quite useful dual 5f winner Morocco Moon (by Rock Of Gibraltar) and to the modest 5f and 6f winner Lunarian (by Bahamian Bounty). The dam, a modest 7f winner, is a half-sister to 9 winners including the useful 2-y-o Group 3 7f C L Weld Park Stakes winner Rag Top and the dam of the 2-y-o listed winner Elhamri. The second dam, Petite Epaulette (by Night Shift), a fair 5f winner at 2 yrs, is a full or half-sister to 3 winners. *"A bonny, tough, hardy horse. I haven't done a lot with him but I like him, he's straightforward and he'll certainly be a summer 2-y-o for five/six furlongs".*

1029. UNNAMED ★★★★
b.f. Lawman – Wizz Kid (Whipper). February 28. First foal. €160,000Y. Arqana Deauville August. Ric Wylie. The dam, winner of the Group 1 5f Prix de l'Abbaye and the Group 2 5f Prix du Gros-Chene (twice), is a half-sister to the listed 10f winner Mustaheel. The second dam, Lidanski (Soviet Star), a fairly useful Irish 7f winner, was listed-placed and is a half-sister to 5 winners including the listed winner Yaa Wayl. (Mr K J Hickman). *"Quite an expensive purchase, she's not over-big and may not have as much speed as her dam who was a Group One winner, but she'll be ready to hit the track in June. We hope she lives up to her pedigree, she has enough speed for six furlongs and the Cherry Hinton at Newmarket's July meeting would be nice".*

1030. UNNAMED ★★
b.c. Aqlaam – Shersha (Priolo). March 2. Seventh foal. 11,000Y. Tattersalls October Book 3. Blandford Bloodstock. Half-brother to the fair 7f winner Sherzam (by Exceed And Excel), to the fair 10f and 12f winner Royal Dutch (by Nayef), the modest 7f and 9f winner Sur Empire (by Equiano), the Qatar winner of 4 races Sherston (by Shamardal) and a minor winner abroad by Red Ransom. The dam, a useful Irish 6f (listed) and dual 1m winner at 3 and 6 yrs, is a half-sister to 2 winners. The second dam, Sheriya (by Green Dancer), is an unraced half-sister to the French listed winner Sherema. *"A tough, strong horse, he's got quite a lot of quality. The dam was a tough, hard knocking filly and she breeds winners, so I see no reason why he shouldn't be another".*

1031. UNNAMED ★★
ch.c. Casamento – Two Marks (Woodman). April 22. Eighth foal. 18,000Y. Tattersalls October Book 2. Not sold. Closely related to the quite useful 2015 2-y-o dual 6f winner Spennithorne (by Shamardal) and half-brother to the fair 2-y-o 10.5f winner Framley Garth (by Clodovil), to the quite useful 9f and subsequent Saudi Arabian 10f winner Stock Market (by Rahy), the minor US winner of 13 races from 3 to 6 yrs Cat In The Forest (by Forestry) and a winner in Macau by Holy Roman Emperor. The dam, a fair 8.5f and 12f winner, is a half-sister to 9 winners including the US Grade 1 Travers Stakes winner Alpha and the French listed winner and Group 3 second Mystic Melody. The second dam, Munnaya (by Nijinsky), won of the listed 11.5f Lingfield Oaks Trial is a half-sister to 8 winners. (Dr Jim Walker). *"A big, backward horse. We won't see him until the autumn but he has a*

lovely attitude. The sire has been well-received but this would be one of his cheaper horses. A big, tall, rangy horse for much later on".

EVE JOHNSON HOUGHTON

1032. ACCIDENTAL AGENT ★★★
b.c. Delegator – Roodle (Xaar). April 8. First foal. 8,000Y. Tattersalls October Book 3. Not sold. The dam, a quite useful 5f (at 2 yrs) and 7f winner, is a half-sister to 4 winners including the US Grade 2 and Grade 3 Prize Exhibit. The second dam, Roodeye (by Inchinor), a useful 5f (at 2 yrs) and 7f winner, was listed-placed and is a half-brother to 5 winners including the Group 1 Prix Morny second Gallagher. (Mrs F M Johnson Houghton). *"The first foal out of a good family, he's a bit backward but he's showing some promise and should be alright in time. You look at his pedigree and wonder why he didn't sell, but agents had decided that Delegators were no good at that point. There's nothing wrong with him and I imagine he'll start over six furlongs and go on from there".*

1033. BAHAMADAM ★★★
b.f. Bahamian Bounty – Pelagia (Lycius). May 4. Seventh foal. Half-sister to the useful 6f (at 2 yrs) and 1m winner and Group 2 6f Richmond Stakes second Upper Hand (by Mark Of Esteem), to the fair 7f (at 2 yrs) and dual 1m winner Dutiful (by Dubawi) and the modest 14f winner Musically (by Singspiel). The dam is a 7f fourth-placed half-sister to the Group 1 1m Prix Marcel Boussac winner Lady Of Chad and the Group 1 Prix Royal-Oak winner Alcazar. The second dam, Sahara Breeze (by Ela-Mana-Mou), a quite useful 7f and 1m placed maiden, is a half-sister to 5 winners including the Group 1 Fillies Mile winner Ivanka and the dam of the top-class stayer Yeats. (J P Repard). *"A nice filly that's done nothing but improve since she came in. She's still a bit unfurnished and she was a late foal but she goes very nicely and we like her a lot. The dam's bred three winners from five, so she's done well".*

1034. DESERT EXPLORER (IRE) ★★
b.c. Henrythenavigator – Bee Eater (Green Desert). March 28. Fifth foal. 25,000Y. Tattersalls October Book 2. Eve Johnson Houghton. Half-brother to the minor French winner of 7 races Picking Up Pieces (by Montjeu) and to the quite useful Irish 7f winner Leafcutter (by Shamardal). The dam, a listed-placed 6f winner of 4 races, is a half-sister to 6 winners. The second dam, Littlefeather (by Indian Ridge), a very useful 5f (at 2 yrs) and 6f winner of 4 races, was third in the Group 1 7f Moyglare Stakes and is a half-sister to 7 winners including the multiple Group 1 winner Marling and the Group 1 National Stakes winner Caerwent. (The Pantechnicons VI). *"The sire isn't everyone's cup of tea but this is a good-looking horse and he goes well. He won't be very early and I haven't done a lot with him, but he's a nice type".*

1035. DIABLE D'OR (IRE) ★★★★
b.c. Clodovil – Caherassdotcom (Compton Place). February 26. Third foal. €16,000Y. Tattersalls Ireland September. Eve Johnson Houghton. The dam, a fair 5f to 7f placed maiden, is a half-sister to 8 winners including the very useful 6f (at 2 yrs) and triple listed winner Dubai's Touch, the Group 3 Diomed Stakes third Wannabe Around, the useful triple 6f winner (including at 2 yrs) and subsequent Abu Dhabi listed winner Grantley Adams and the French Group 3 1m third Nobelist. The second dam, Noble Peregrine (by Lomond), an Italian 10f winner, is a half-sister to 7 winners. (Astor, Baring, Brown & Cochrane). *"One of my earlier types. He goes well, he's been doing a bit of faster work and he's sharp. I love the sire and I always win with them".* **TRAINERS' BARGAIN BUY**

1036. FAVOURITE ROYAL (IRE) ★★★
b.f. Acclamation – Affirmative (Pivotal). April 22. Third foal. 40,000Y. Goffs Orby. Eve Johnson Houghton (private sale). Sister to the quite useful 2015 2-y-o 7f winner John Splendid. The dam is an unraced half-sister to 3 minor winners. The second dam, Favourable Terms (by Selkirk), winner of the Group 1 Nassau Stakes, the Group 2 Windsor Forest Stakes and Group 2 1m Matron Stakes, is a half-sister to 4 winners. (J Cross, M Duckham, L Godfrey, P Wollaston). *"She's well-bred, still unfurnished and is one for the middle to back-end of the season. She goes nicely and could well be a seven furlong type like her year older brother, but we haven't pressed any buttons with her".*

1037. FIVE STAR FRANK ★★
b.c. Exceed And Excel – Anadolu (Statue Of Liberty). March 19. Second foal. 18,000Y. Tattersalls October Book 2. Eve Johnson Houghton. The dam, a fairly useful 2-y-o listed 5f winner, is a half-sister to 7 winners. The second dam, Afto (by Relaunch), won the Grade 2 Railbird Stakes in the USA and is a half-sister to 7 winners. (Mr R F Johnson Houghton). *"Known as "Fat Frank" to his friends because he doesn't miss a feed! He's a lovely horse and I like to think he'll be racing by June but at this stage I couldn't tell you much about him because he's been on the back burner".*

1038. FUNKY FOOTSTEPS ★★★
ch.f. Footstepsinthesand – Felin Gruvy (Tagula). April 10. Sixth foal. Goffs HIT November. Not sold. Half-sister to the fair 5.5f (at 2 yrs) and 12f winner Uncle Roger (by Camacho). The dam, placed once over 6f at 2 yrs, is a full or half-sister to 5 winners. The second dam, Felin Special (by Lyphard's Special), an Irish 2-y-o 6.5f winner, is a half-sister to 5 winners. (Mrs J E O'Halloran). *"She's the nicest the dam's had and although she won't be super smart she'll win races".*

1039. HEDGING (IRE) ★★★
gr.c. Mastercraftsman – Privet (Cape Cross). April 27. Fourth foal. 8,500Y. Tattersalls October Book 3. Eve Johnson Houghton. Half-brother to the modest 2015 2-y-o 7f winner Cryptic (by Lord Shanakill), to the fair UAE 6f and 7f winner Just A Penny (by Kodiac) and the minor French 7f winner Bilge Kagan (by Whipper). The dam, a fair 6f (at 2 yrs) to 1m placed maiden, is a sister to the German 2-y-o Group 2 winner Mokabra and a half-sister to 6 winners. The second dam, Pacific Grove (by Persian Bold), a fairly useful 2-y-o listed-placed winner of 3 races from 7f to 1m, is a half-sister to 5 winners including the listed winners Mauri Moon and Kimbridge Knight. (The Picnic Partnership). *"He's really nice actually. When I bought him the dam's record was one winner from three but now it's three from three, so that's always nice to see. I think he'll be sharper than his pedigree suggests, he's not very big but he goes nicely. I'll start him off at six furlongs".*

1040. JANNIA ★★★
b.f. Iffraaj – Fairy Moss (Amadeus Wolf). April 22. First foal. 10,000foal. Tattersalls December. Not sold. The dam, a moderate 5f placed 2-y-o, is a half-sister to numerous winners including the smart multiple listed winner (from 7f to 10f) Nashmiah, the useful 2-y-o 7f and listed 1m winner Streets Ahead, the useful French listed 9f winner Ighraa (by Tamayuz) and the fairly useful 2-y-o 6f winner and listed-placed Ridder. The second dam, Frond (by Alzao), a quite useful 2-y-o 7f winner, is a half-sister to 8 winners. (Overbury Racing Club). *"She's a small filly and although she was a fairly late foal I don't think she's going to develop much, so I'll try to get her out in April or May. She goes nice and is fairly straightforward, quite switched on and she'll be one of the earlier fillies".*

1041. NUPTIALS (USA) ★★★★
b.f. Broken Vow – European Union (Successful Appeal). February 16. Second foal. 30,000Y. Tattersalls October Book 1. Eve Johnson Houghton. The dam is an unraced half-sister to 3 winners including the US stakes-placed winner of 3 races Chatham (dam of the triple Group 1 winning 2-y-o Air Force Blue). The second dam, Circle Of Gold (by Seeking The Gold), is an unraced sister to the US champion 2-y-o filly and dual Grade 1 winner and good broodmare Flanders and a half-sister to 7 winners. (Mrs H B Raw). *"She's very nice and I can't believe we got her for that price. She's related to Air Force Blue and she's done really well. Not very big at the sales, she's grown and goes nicely. I think she'll be out at the end of April over six furlongs, she's done a bit of work and with a pedigree like hers if we can a win a race with her she'll be quite valuable".*

1042. ON TO VICTORY ★★
br.c. Rock Of Gibraltar – Clouds Of Magellan (Dynaformer). April 2. Fourth foal. 18,000Y. Tattersalls October Book 2. Highflyer Bloodstock/Shefford Bloodstock. Half-brother to 2 minor winners in Italy by Singspiel and Dylan Thomas. The dam, placed over 10f and 12f in France, is a half-sister to 6 winners including the French listed winner It's Midnight and the Group 1 Prix Jacques le Marois second Holocene. The second dam, Witching Hour (by Fairy King), a minor

winner at 3 yrs in France, is a half-sister to 10 winners including the triple listed winner Party Doll (dam of the dual Group 2 winner and sire Titus Livius). (W H Ponsonby). *"A big, leggy, unfurnished colt, he's nice and does everything easily but he won't be early. Looking at his pedigree it's hard to say what trip he'll want".*

1043. SUPER JULIUS ★★★★

ch.c. Bated Breath – Paradise Isle (Bahamian Bounty). April 27. Fifth foal. 35,000Y. Tattersalls October Book 2. Sackville/Donald & Eve Johnson Houghton. Half-brother to the listed-placed dual 7f winner at 2 and 3 yrs Meeting Waters (by Aqlaam), to the fair dual 5f winner (including at 2 yrs) Exotic Isle (by Exceed And Excel) and the modest 2-y-o 5f winner Princess Banu (by Oasis Dream). The dam, a useful 5f (at 2 yrs) and 6f winner of 8 races including two listed events, was third in the Group 3 6f Summer Stakes and is a full or half-sister to 9 winners including the useful broodmare Clincher Club. The second dam, Merry Rous (by Rousillon), a moderate 2-y-o 6f winner, is a half-sister to 5 winners including the dual Group 3 winning sprinter Tina's Pet. (Mr B Miller). *"He's very nice. A fairly late foal, he's from a small family so he's not big but he's got plenty about him and has plenty of pace. I like him very much and he might be racing in April".*

1044. WAVES (IRE) ★★★★

b.f. Born To Sea – Johannesburg Cat (Johannesburg). April 7. Third foal. €23,000Y. Goffs Orby. Eve Johnson Houghton. Half-sister to the moderate 12f winner Zambezi Tiger (by Tiger Hill) and to the minor German winner of 4 races The Danzig Factor (by Ad Valorem). The dam, a minor German 2-y-o 6f winner, is a half-sister to 3 winners including the dual Group 1 winning sprinter Society Rock. The second dam, High Society (by Key Of Luck), an Irish 2-y-o listed 6f and subsequent US stakes winner, was Grade 2 placed and is a half-sister to 4 winners. (Mr B McNamee & Mr R Maynard). *"I liked the Born To Sea's at the sales and this is a nice filly, she's well-related and I'll start her off over six or seven furlongs in mid-season".*

1045. UNNAMED ★★★

b.f. Lawman – Fontley (Sadler's Wells). February 28. First foal. The dam, a fairly useful listed-placed 7f (at 2 yrs) and 1m winner, is a half-sister to 4 winners including the Group 3 12f Pinnacle Stakes winner Moment In Time. The second dam, Horatia (Machiavellian), a 10f winner here, subsequently won a Grade 3 in the USA and is a half-sister to 7 winners including the triple Group 2 winner Opinion Poll. (Mrs V D Neale). *"She's very nice and a June type 2-y-o I should think. I trained the dam and this is a nice type from a good family".*

MARK JOHNSTON

1046. BOATER

b.f. Helmet – Cercle D'Amour (Storm Cat). January 29. Fifth foal. Half-sister to the fair 11f winner Dorfman (by Halling). The dam is an unraced sister to the listed Irish 1,000 Guineas Trial winner Royal Tigress and to the 2-y-o winner and Group 3 5.5f Prix d'Arenburg third Thunderous Mood and a half-sister to the Group 3 Norfolk Stakes winner Warm Heart and the 2-y-o listed 6f winner Miguel Cervantes. The second dam, Warm Mood (by Alydar), won 4 races at up to 9f in the USA and is a half-sister to a stakes winner in Japan. A winner at Kempton on her debut in late March.

1047. BOOK OF POETRY (IRE)

b.c. Poet's Voice – Duniatty (Green Desert). January 19. First foal. €160,000Y. Goffs Orby. John Ferguson. The dam, a minor French 2-y-o winner, is a half-sister to 3 winners including the Group 2 Lennox Stakes and Group 3 Jersey Stakes winner Tariq. The second dam, Tatora (by Selkirk), is an unraced half-sister to 3 winners and to the placed dam of the Group 2 Flying Childers Stakes winner Wi Dud. The second dam, Tatouma (by The Minstrel), won twice at 2 yrs and is a half-sister to 4 winners. (Hamdan bin Mohammed Al Maktoum).

1048. CAMARGUE

b.f. Invincible Spirit – Chaquiras (Seeking The Gold). April 22. Half-sister to the quite useful UAE triple 7f winner Beachy Head (by Shamardal) and to the French 1m winner Chequers (by Pivotal). The dam is an unraced sister to the outstanding Dubai Millennium, winner of the Dubai World Cup, the Prix Jacques le Marois, the Prince Of Wales's Stakes and the Queen Elizabeth II Stakes (all Group 1 events) and a half-sister to the Group 2 10.5f Prix Greffuhle second Denver County. The second dam, Colorado Dancer (by Shareef Dancer), won the Group 2 13.5f Prix de Pomone and the Group 3 12f Prix de Minerve, is closely related to the Group/Grade 1 winners Hamas, Fort Wood, Northern Aspen and a half-sister the champion US 2-y-o colt Timber Country. (Hamdan bin Mohammed Al Maktoum).

1049. CHUPALLA
b.f. Helmet – Dubai Sunrise (Seeking The Gold). April 7. Half-sister to the minor French 3-y-o dual winner Solar Moon (by Pivotal) and to the minor Italian 3-y-o dual winner Bewilder (by Invincible Spirit). The dam is an unraced sister to the outstanding colt Dubai Millennium (four Group 1 wins including the Dubai World Cup) and a half-sister to four stakes-placed winners. The second dam, Colorado Dancer (by Shareef Dancer), won the Group 2 13.5f Prix de Pomone and the Group 3 12f Prix de Minerve, is closely related to the Group/Grade 1 winners Hamas, Fort Wood, Northern Aspen and a half-sister the champion US 2-y-o colt Timber Country. (Hamdan bin Mohammed Al Maktoum). This filly won on her debut at Kempton in late March.

1050. CURLEW RIVER
b.f. Casamento – Dubai Opera (Dubai Millennium). March 5. Fifth foal. Closely related to the quite useful 2-y-o 7f and 1m winner Grigolo (by Shamardal) and half-sister to the fair dual 9.5f winner Rebel Song (by Refuse To Bend). The dam is an unraced half-sister to 4 winners including the listed 10f and listed 12f winner Nabucco. The second dam, Cape Verdi (by Caerleon), was a top-class winner of the 1,000 Guineas and the Lowther Stakes. (Hamdan bin Mohammed Al Maktoum).

1051. DAHL (IRE)
b.c. Shamardal – Illandrane (Cape Cross). January 17. First foal. 120,000foal. Tattersalls December. John Ferguson. The dam is an unraced half-sister to the US Grade 2 winner Arvada and the Group 3 Craven Stakes winner Adagio. The second dam, Lalindi (by Cadeaux Genereux), a fair middle-distance winner of 7 races, is a half-sister to 5 winners including the useful 2-y-o winner Sumoto (herself dam of the Group 1 winners Summoner and Compton Admiral). (Hamdan bin Mohammed Al Maktoum).

1052. DIZZY
ch.f. Dutch Art – Spiralling (Pivotal). February 12. Fifth foal. 40,000Y. Tattersalls October Book 2. Not sold. Half-sister to the quite useful 2-y-o triple 6f winner Felix Leiter (by Monsieur Bond). The dam is an unraced half-sister to 5 winners including the Group 2 Topkapi Trophy and dual Group 3 winner Producer. The second dam, River Saint (by Irish River), a fair 7f and 7.5f placed maiden, is a half-sister to 5 winners including the multiple US Grade 1 winner Serena's Song (herself the dam of four Group winners including Group 1 Coronation Stakes winner Sophisticat). (Trevor Stewart).

1053. DUALITY (IRE)
b.f. Shamardal – Double Vie (Tagula). April 29. Fifth foal. €40,000Y. Goffs Orby. Mark Johnston. Half-sister to the fairly useful 5f, 6f (both at 2 yrs) 7f and subsequent US winner Big Note (by Amadeus Wolf). The dam, a listed 1m winner at 3 yrs in France, is a half-sister to 4 minor winners. The second dam, The Good Life (by Rainbow Quest), won once at 3 yrs in France and is a half-sister to 3 minor winners. (Hamdan bin Mohammed Al Maktoum).

1054. FRANKUUS
gr.c. Frankel – Dookus (Linamix). April 18. Fifth foal. €130,000Y. Goffs Orby. Mark Johnston. Half-brother to the 2-y-o Group 3 Prix Thomas Bryon winner and Group 1 Criterium International third US Law (by Lawman). The dam ran once unplaced and is a half-sister to 7 winners including the Irish 2-y-o listed 6f winner Pharmacist (herself dam of the Breeders' Cup Turf winner Red Rocks). The second dam, Pharaoh's Delight (by Fairy King), won the Group 1 5f Phoenix Stakes, was Group 1 placed four times and is a half-sister to 8 winners. (Hussain Lootah).

1055. HOCHFELD (IRE)
b.br.c. Cape Cross – What A Charm (Key Of Luck). March 16. First foal. 50,000foal. Tattersalls December. John Ferguson. The dam, a useful Irish 7f (at 2 yrs) and listed 12f winner, is a half-sister to 4 winners including the Group 3 Park Express Stakes winner Marjalina. The second dam, Atalina (by Linamix), won once over 12.5f in France and is a half-sister to 4 winners including the French listed winner Paix Blanche (the dam of two stakes winners). (Hamdan bin Mohammed Al Maktoum).

1056. IL SICARIO (IRE)
b.c. Zebedee – Starring (Ashkalani). April 20. Ninth foal. €70,000Y. Goffs Orby. Mark Johnston. Brother to the fairly useful 2015 2-y-o 7f winner and Group 3 Solario Stakes second Manaafidh and half-brother to 6 winners including the 2-y-o listed 1m winner Letsgoroundagain (by Redback), the quite useful 7f to 9f winner of 11 races Spinning (by Pivotal), the quite useful 7f to 12f and hurdles winner Goodwood Starlight (by Mtoto) and the fair 2-y-o 5f winner Daisy Moses (by Mull Of Kintyre). The dam, placed once at 3 yrs, is a half-sister to 5 winners the dual listed 5f winner Watching. The second dam, Sweeping (by Indian King), a useful 2-y-o 6f winner, is a half-sister to 10 winners. (Mr Peter Savill).

1057. KAHRAB (IRE)
gr.c. Dark Angel – Dance Club (Fasliyev). March 13. Fourth foal. 110,000Y. Tattersalls October Book 2. Shadwell Estate Co. Closely related to the fairly useful listed-placed triple 5f winner at 2 and 3 yrs Online Alexander (by Acclamation) and half-brother to the quite useful 1m (at 2 yrs) and 10.5f winner Bnedel (by Teofilo). The dam, a modest 7f winner, is a half-sister to 3 winners including the Group 1 Haydock Park Sprint Cup, Group 2 6f Coventry Stakes and Group 2 Diadem Stakes winner Red Clubs. The second dam, Two Clubs (by First Trump), won 5 races over 6f including the listed Doncaster Stakes and the listed Prix Contessina and is a half-sister to 7 winners including the 5f Windsor Castle Stakes winner Gipsy Fiddler. (Hamdan Al Maktoum).

1058. KATEBIRD (IRE)
b.f. Dark Angel – She Basic (Desert Prince). March 12. Second foal. €35,000Y. Goffs Orby.

Mark Johnston. The dam, a winner in Italy at 3 yrs and third in the Group 2 Premio Regina Elena, is a half-sister to 6 winners including two listed winners in Italy and a minor US stakes winner. The second dam, She Bat (by Batshoof), won the Group 3 Premio Bagutta and is a half-sister to 5 winners. (J D Abell).

1059. KILMAH
b.f. Sepoy – Perfect Star (Act One). January 31. Third living foal. 32,000Y. Tattersalls October Book 1. Mark Johnston. Half-sister to the quite useful 1m (at 2 yrs) to 12f winner of 4 races Tears Of The Sun (by Mastercraftsman). The dam, a useful 7f (including at 2 yrs) and listed 1m winner of 5 races, is a half-sister to 4 winners including the listed winner Rewarded. The second dam, Granted (by Cadeaux Genereux), a useful 1m and 8.3f winner, was listed placed at up to 9f and is a half-sister to 5 winners. (Mr Abdullah Al Mansoori).

1060. LA VIE EN ROSE
b.f. Henrythenavigator – Lady Jane Digby (Oasis Dream). February 17. Third foal. Half-sister to the fair 10.5f winner Poniatowski (by Dubawi). The dam, a smart German Group 1 10f and Group 3 11f winner, is a half-sister to 9 winners including the very smart Group 3 7f and 9f winner and Group 1 placed Gateman and the smart 1m Royal Hunt Cup winner Surprise Encounter. The second dam, Scandalette (by Niniski), is an unraced half-sister to 9 winners including the Group 1 July Cup winner Polish Patriot and the Italian listed winner Grand Cayman. (Miss K Rausing).

1061. LOVE DREAMS (IRE)
b.c. Dream Ahead – Kimola (King's Theatre). January 22. Seventh foal. 42,000Y. Tattersalls October Book 2. Mark Johnston. Half-brother to the fairly useful Irish 6f (at 2 yrs) and 10f winner and Group 3 Irish 2,000 Guineas Trial third Whipless (by Whipper), to the fairly useful Irish 2-y-o dual 6f winner Tomas An Tsioada (by Bachelor Duke) and the moderate 14f winner Moving Waves (by Intense Focus). The dam won 9 races in Scandinavia including 2 listed events and is a half-sister to 4 winners. The second dam, La Mortola (by Bold Lad), is an unraced half-sister to 5 winners including the Irish 1,000 Guineas winner Katies. (Crone Stud Farms Ltd).

1062. LOVE OASIS
b.f. Oasis Dream – Pickle (Piccolo). March 31. Fifth foal. €45,000Y. Goffs Orby. Mark Johnston. Sister to Gusto, a smart winner of four listed races over 6f (including at 2 yrs) and 7f and half-sister to the fair 2-y-o 7f winner Pinter (by Exceed And Excel). The dam won 7 races here and in the USA including the Grade 3 Wilshire Handicap and the Grade 3 Yerba Buena Breeders' Cup Handicap and is a half-sister to 5 winners. The second dam, Crackle (by Anshan), a quite useful 5.7f (at 2 yrs) to 10f winner, is a half-sister to 5 winners including the listed winner Ronaldsay. (Crone Stud Farms Ltd).

1063. LOVE POWER (IRE)
b.c. Power – Royal Fizz (Royal Academy). April 25. Fourteenth foal. €50,000Y. Goffs Orby. Mark Johnston. Half-brother to 5 winners including the Group 3 6f Greenlands Stakes and UAE Group 3 6f winner of 11 races (including at 2 yrs) Hitchens (by Acclamation), the useful listed-placed 2-y-o dual 7f winner Grand Marque (by Grand Lodge) and the useful triple 6f winner Tanzeel (by Elusive City). The dam won once over 6.5f at 2 yrs in France and is a half-sister to 7 winners here and abroad including the £1.4m Hong Kong earner Floral Pegasus. The second dam, Crown Crest (by Mill Reef), won once at 3 yrs and is a sister to the high-class middle-distance horses Glint Of Gold and Diamond Shoal. (Crone Stud Farms Ltd).

1064. MAKKAAR (IRE)
b.c. Raven's Pass – Beneventa (Most Welcome). February 3. Sixth foal. 85,000Y. Tattersalls October Book 2. Shadwell Estate Co. Half-brother to the smart 7f (at 2 yrs), listed 1m and Irish Group 2 1m winner Bow Creek (by Shamardal), to the useful 1m and 10f winner and subsequent Australian Group 3 placed Dare To Dance (by Danehill Dancer) and the fair 12f winner Bint Nayef (by Nayef). The dam won 7 races including the Group 3 Dahlia Stakes and two listed events and is a half-sister to 4 minor winners. The second dam, Dara Dee (by Dara Monarch), a quite useful 7f and 1m winner, is a half-sister to 10 winners including Bay Empress (Group 3 Brownstown Stakes). (Hamdan Al Maktoum).

1065. MAMBO DANCER
b.c. So You Think – Mambo Halo (Southern Halo). April 8. Seventh foal. 42,000Y. Tattersalls October Book 2. Mark Johnston. Half-brother to the very useful 2-y-o listed 6f winner Earl Of Leitrim (by Johannesburg), to the quite useful 5f (at 2 yrs) to 7f winner Mambo Paradise (by Makfi) and the fair 10.5f and 12.5f winner Mambo Rhythm (by Authorized). The dam, a 2-y-o winner in Argentina, is a half-sister to the listed Lupe Stakes winner and Group 1 Yorkshire Oaks second Ocean Silk. The second dam, Mambo Jambo (by Kingmambo), a minor winner in France, is a full or half-sister to 10 winners including the multiple Group 1 winners Divine Proportions and Whipper. (J S Morrison & Around The World Partnership).

1066. MLLE GEORGES
ch.f. Archipenko – Mme De Stael (Selkirk). April 16. Second foal. The dam, a modest 12f winner, is a half-sister to numerous winners including the German Group 1 10f winner Lady Jane Digby, the very smart Group 3 7f and 9f winner and Group 1 placed Gateman and the smart 1m Royal Hunt Cup winner Surprise Encounter. The second dam, Scandalette (by Niniski), is an unraced half-sister to 9 winners including the Group 1 July Cup winner Polish Patriot and the Italian listed winner Grand Cayman. (Miss K Rausing).

1067. MONTATAIRE (IRE)
b.c. Cape Cross – Chantilly Pearl (Smart Strike). February 14. Second foal. €90,000Y. Goffs Sportsmans. John Ferguson. The dam, a fair 2-y-o 6f winner, is a sister to a US stakes-placed winner and a half-sister to 5 winners including the US listed winner and Grade 2 placed Lemon Chiffon. The second dam, Cataballerina (by Tabasco Cat), was placed in the USA and is a half-sister to 5 winners. (Hamdan bin Mohammed Al Maktoum).

1068. NEPETA (USA)
ch.f. Kitten's Joy – La Coruna (Thunder Gulch). March 6. Fifth foal. €50,000Y. Goffs Orby. Mark Johnston. Sister to the US winner and triple listed-placed Spooky Kitten and to the French 2-y-o winner Conquistadorkitten. The dam, a minor US 3-y-o winner, is a half-sister to the US dual Grade 3 winner Eye Of Taurus. The

second dam, Ocean Shore (by Silver Hawk), is an unraced sister to the listed winner and St Leger second Minds Music and a half-sister to 7 winners. (N Browne, M Bradford, S Frosell, S Richards).

1069. PEACH MELBA
b.f. Dream Ahead – Nellie Melba (Hurricane Sky). February 4. Half-sister to the fairly useful listed-placed dual 6f winner Major Crispies (by Pastoral Pursuits), to the fairly useful listed-placed dual 5f winner including at 2 yrs Dam Beautiful (by Sleeping Indian) and the quite useful 5f (including at 2 yrs) and 6f winner of 8 races Bosun Breese (by Bahamian Bounty). The dam, a fair 7f and 1m winner of 3 races, is a half-sister to 4 other minor winners. The second dam, Persuasion (by Batshoof), won 2 races over 10f and 12f and is a half-sister to 2 winners. (Countess Of Lonsdale).

1070. POET'S SOCIETY
ch.c. Poet's Voice – Rahiyah (Rahy). March 29. Fifth foal. Half-brother to the useful 2015 2-y-o dual 5f winner Rah Rah (by Lonhro), to the useful French 6f (at 2 yrs) and 1m winner and 2-y-o Group 3 7f second Decathlete (by Medaglia D'Oro) and the French 6.5f and 7f winner Rivalba (by Street Cry). The dam, a very useful 2-y-o 6f winner, was second in the Group 2 Rockfel Stakes and third in the Group 1 French 1,000 Guineas and is a sister to one winner and a half-sister to another. The second dam, Meiosis (by Danzig), a useful 3-y-o 7f winner, is a half-sister to 6 winners. (Hamdan bin Mohammed Al Maktoum).

1071. QUEEN IN WAITING (IRE)
gr.f. Exceed And Excel – Princess Taise (Cozzene). May 6. Fourth foal. Half-sister to the fair 2015 2-y-o 7f winner Simple Attack, to the modest 7f winner Highest Quality (both by Invincible Spirit) and the fairly useful 7f (at 2 yrs) and 1m winner Elkhart (by Refuse To Bend). The dam, a useful 2-y-o 7f winner, was second in the Group 3 Sweet Solera Stakes and is a half-sister to 3 winners including the French winner of 21 races Graphic Design. The second dam, Cumulate (Gone West), a fair 7f placed 2-y-o, is a half-sister to 6 winners including the US Grade 2 9f Jim Dandy Stakes winner Composer. (Hamdan bin Mohammed Al Maktoum).

1072. SUTTER COUNTY
b.c. Invincible Spirit – Rio Osa (Canny Lad). February 13. The dam is a half-sister to the Australian 2-y-o Group 1 7f winners Denman and Preserve out of Peach (by Vain). (Hamdan bin Mohammed Al Maktoum). This colt won this year's first two-year-old race of the season on the 25th March and then won again at Newmarket just over two weeks later, despite hating the ground and carrying a 6lb penalty. A big horse, he'll appreciate better ground next time.

1073. THE LAST LION (IRE)
b.c. Choisir – Mala Mala (Brief Truce). February 12. Ninth foal. €82,000Y. Goffs Orby. Mark Johnston. Closely related to two winners including the very useful dual listed 6f winner and French Group 3 Prix de Meautry second Contest (by Danehill Dancer) and half-brother to 5 winners including the useful UAE listed 5f winner of 11 races Russian Rock (by Rock Of Gibraltar) and the fairly useful 2-y-o 7f winner Horizon Sky (by Duke Of Marmalade). The dam, a very useful 3-y-o 5f winner, was third in the Group 1 Moyglare Stud Stakes and Group 1 Cheveley Park Stakes and is a half-sister to the Group 2 10f winner Mister Monet and the Irish 1,000 Guineas winner Tarascon. The second dam, Breyani (by Commanche Run) was a useful winner at up to 2m. (John Brown & Megan Dennis).

1074. TOWN CHARTER (USA)
gr.c. Lonhro – Summer Fete (Pivotal). February 22. Third foal. Half-brother to the fair 12f winner Good Judge (by Cape Cross). The dam won the listed 7f Radley Stakes (at 2 yrs) and the Group 3 7f Oak Tree Stakes and is a full or half-sister to 3 minor winners. The second dam, Tamarillo (by Daylami), a fairly useful 2-y-o 8.3f and UAE 3-y-o winner, is a half-sister to numerous winners. (Hamdan bin Mohammed Al Maktoum).

1075. YALTA (IRE)
b.c. Exceed And Excel – Lacily (Elusive Quality). March 19. First foal. The dam, a quite useful 2-y-o 1m winner, was listed-placed over 10f at 3 yrs and is a half-sister to the Group 3 Prix Gladiateur winner Ley Hunter and the US Grade 2 placed Gabriel's Hill. The second dam, Lailani (by Unfuwain), winner of the

Group 1 Irish Oaks, the Group 1 Nassau Stakes and two US Grade 1 events, is a half-sister to several winners including the listed 12f winner Copper Carnival. (Hamdan bin Mohammed Al Maktoum).

SYLVESTER KIRK

1076. ARBORIST (IRE)
gr.c. Dark Angel – Ride For Roses (Barathea). February 12. Second foal. 60,000Y. Tattersalls October Book 2. Malih Al Basti. Brother to the quite useful 2015 2-y-o 7f winner Dark Devil. The dam, a minor Swedish 3-y-o winner of 3 races, is a half-sister to 4 winners including the 2-y-o 5f and 5.7f winner, Group 3 Cornwallis Stakes third and subsequent US Grade 3 placed Shermeen (dam of the Group 1 Phoenix Stakes winner Sudirman) and the very useful listed 5f and listed 6f winner Mister Manannan. The second dam, Cover Girl (by Common Grounds), a fair 2-y-o 6f and 7f and subsequent Scandinavian listed winner, is a half-sister to 3 winners. (Malih L Al Basti).

1077. FALCON RISING
b.c. Kyllachy – Fly Free (Halling). April 23. Fifth foal. 30,000Y. Tattersalls October Book 3. S Kirk. Half-brother to the fairly useful 2015 2-y-o 6f and 7f winner Flying Empress (by Holy Roman Emperor). The dam, a quite useful 7f winner, is a half-sister to 5 winners including the Group 2 Goodwood Cup and dual Group 3 winner of 10 races Illustrious Blue and the useful listed 6f winner of 5 races Mullein. The second dam, Gipsy Moth (by Efisio), a quite useful dual 5f winner at 2 yrs, subsequently won a listed event in Germany and is a half-sister to 4 winners including the useful listed 1m winner and Group 2 Falmouth Stakes second Heavenly Whisper. (Malih L Al Basti).

1078. FAMILY FORTUNES
ch.c. Paco Boy – Barawin (Hawk Wing). April 22. Third foal. 18,000Y. Tattersalls December. S Kirk. Half-brother to the modest 2015 7f and 1m placed 2-y-o Kelvin Hall (by Halling) and to the useful 7f (at 2 yrs) and 12f winner Sir Jack Leyden (by Sir Percy). The dam, a quite useful 2-y-o 1m winner, is a half-sister to 3 winners. The second dam, Cosabawn (by Barathea), is an unplaced half-sister to 7 winners. (Mr Richard Hannon).

1079. LATEST QUEST
b.c. Zebedee – Fancy Theory (Quest For Fame). April 8. Eighth foal. 18,000Y. Tattersalls October Book 3. RA & ME Gander. Half-brother to the useful 2-y-o triple 6f winner Eureka (by Kheleyf) and to the modest 12f and jumps winner Mad Professor (by Mull Of Kintyre). The dam is an unraced half-sister to 3 winners. The second dam, Latest Creation (by Affirmed), an Irish 10f and 12f winner, is a half-sister to 5 winners. (Mr & Mrs R Gander).

1080. NEPTUNE'S SECRET
ch.c. Sakhee's Secret – Lochangel (Night Shift). April 11. Half-brother to the quite useful 7f winner Star Pupil (by Selkirk), to the quite useful 6f winner Strictly Dancing (by Danehill Dancer) and the fair 5f winner Celestial Dream (by Oasis Dream). The dam, a very smart winner of the Group 1 5f Nunthorpe Stakes, is a half-sister to the champion sprinter Lochsong. The second dam, Peckitts Well (by Lochnager), was a fairly useful winner of five races at 2 and 3 yrs from 5f to 6f. (Mr J C Smith).

1081. PRAIRIE LIGHT
b.f. High Chaparral – Dimelight (Fantastic Light). February 18. Half-sister to the quite useful 6f and 7f winner of 4 races (including at 2 yrs) Elusive Flame (by Elusive City), to the quite useful 7f to 14f and hurdles winner Odin, the fair 11.5f and hurdles winner (both by Norse Dancer) and the modest 7f (at 2 yrs) and 1m winner of 3 races Secret Lightning (by Sakhee's Secret). The dam, a fair 9f and 10f placed maiden, is a half-sister to numerous winners including the smart Group 3 Prix La Rochette winner Guys And Dolls, the smart 1m (including at 2 yrs) to 11f listed winner Pawn Broker and the useful dual 7f 2-y-o winner and Group 3 placed Blushing Bride. The second dam, Dime Bag (by High Line), a quite useful winner of 4 races at up to 2m, is a half-sister to 7 minor winners. (J C Smith).

1082. SALOUEN (IRE)
b.c. Canford Cliffs – Gali Gal (Galileo). April 27. Fourth foal. €85,000Y. Goffs Sportsmans. S Kirk. Half-brother to the French 10.5f and 12f winner Madernia (by Duke Of Marmalade). The dam, a fair Irish 10.5f winner, is a half-sister to 4 winners including the US dual

Grade 2 second Californian. The second dam, Asterita (by Rainbow Quest), won the listed Oaks Trial and is a half-sister to 7 winners. (Mr H Balasuriya).

1083. STAR MAKER
ch.c. Mastercraftsman – Snoqualmie Star (Galileo). March 7. Second foal. The dam, a quite useful 1m and 10f winner, is a half-sister to numerous winners including the smart listed 10f winner and Group 2 Dante Stakes third Snoqualmie Boy and to the very useful listed 1m (at 2 yrs) and listed 10f winner Snoqualmie Girl. The second dam, Seattle Ribbon (by Seattle Dancer), placed over 9f and 10f at 3 yrs, is a sister to the 2-y-o Group 1 1m winner Seattle Dancer. (J C Smith).

1084. SYNCOPATION (IRE)
br.c. Dark Angel – Cross Section (Cape Cross). March 5. Third foal. 40,000Y. Tattersalls October Book 2. Not sold. The dam, a modest 6f to 8.5f placed maiden from 2 to 4 yrs, is a half-sister to 6 winners including the listed winners Coy and Il Warrd. The second dam, Demure (by Machiavellian), is an unraced half-sister to 9 winners including the very smart colt Diffident, winner of the Group 3 6f Diadem Stakes, the Group 3 6f Prix de Ris-Orangis and the listed 7f European Free Handicap. (Malih L Al Basti).

1085. ZAMADANCE
ch.c. Zamindar – Opera Dancer (Norse Dancer). May 9. Second foal. Half-brother to the fair 2015 2-y-o 7f and 8.5f winner Opera Baron (by Equiano). The dam, a fair 2-y-o 7f winner, is a half-sister to numerous winners including the very smart 2-y-o Group 3 7f Solario Stakes winner and Group 1 Dewhurst Stakes third Opera Cape, the high-class stayer Grey Shot and the smart sprint winner of 4 races Night Shot. The second dam, Optaria (by Song), a quite useful 2-y-o 5f winner, is out of the unplaced Electo (by Julio Mariner). (J C Smith).

WILLIAM KNIGHT

1086. ANY QUESTIONS ★★
ch.c. Poet's Voice – Funday (Daylami). February 15. Third foal. 32,000Y. Tattersalls October Book 1. Rabbah Bloodstock. Half-brother to the fairly useful 10f to 12f placed maiden Miss Giler (by High Chaparral). The dam, a quite useful listed-placed 10f and 12f winner, is a half-sister to 8 winners including the very smart Group 2 1m Royal Lodge Stakes winner Mons and the smart 10f winner and Irish Oaks third Inforapenny. The second dam, Morina (by Lyphard), won over 11f in France and is a half-sister to 10 winners. (S Ali). *"A big colt and a nice-moving horse, I haven't done much with him other than cantering. I can see him coming out around August time in a seven furlong maiden, he's a nice, big, scopey horse and a good mover. He'll be a ten furlong horse next year".*

1087. CIRCUIT JUDGE ★★★★
b.c. Lawman – Gimasha (Cadeaux Generoux). April 8. Seventh foal. Half-brother to the fairly useful 2-y-o 6f winner and 3-y-o 6f listed-placed Samminder (by Red Ransom), the fairly useful triple 6f winner at 2 and 3 yrs Queen's Pearl (by Exceed And Excel) and to the 7f winner Platinum Pearl (by Shamardal). The dam, a useful 5f and 6f winner of 5 races, is a half-sister to 5 winners including the very useful triple 1m and hurdles winner Atlantic Rhapsody and the useful French winner of 3 races and Group 3 Prix Thomas Bryon third Gaitero. The second dam, First Waltz (by Green Dancer), winner of the Group 1 6f Prix Morny, was second in the Cheveley Park Stakes. (Peter Winkworth). *"A big, scopey individual, he has a big stride and he's a very mature-looking type. I don't think he'll have the speed for six furlongs, I would say he'll be a seven furlong 2-y-o and a miler next year".*

1088. DUTCHESS OF FIFE ★★
ch.f. Dutch Art – La Adelita (Anabaa). April 5. Third foal. Half-sister to the fair 2-y-o 6f winner L'Addition (by Exceed And Excel). The dam, a quite useful 2-y-o 7f winner, is a half-sister to 4 winners including the useful listed 10.5f winner Princess Loulou and the useful listed-placed Easy Target. The second dam, Aiming (by Highest Honor), was placed over 7f (at 2 yrs) and 1m and is a half-sister to 5 winners including the very smart dual listed 5f winner Watching. (Mrs M Bryce). *"She was weak when she came in and she's quite backward so she'll need time. A nice mover, but it's early days for her".*

1089. EOLIAN ★★★★
b.c. Poet's Voice – Charlecote (Caerleon). February 20. Eighth foal. 45,000Y. Tattersalls October Book 2. Richard Knight. Half-brother to the Irish 2-y-o 1m winner (from two starts) Dubaya (by Dubawi), to the fairly useful 7f (at 2 yrs) to 2m and hurdles winner and listed-placed Ghimaar (by Dubai Destination), the fairly useful 7f to 10f winner of 6 races King Charles (by King's Best), the fair 1m (at 2 yrs) to 14f winner Mykingdomforahorse (by Fantastic Light) and the fair 10f winner Man Look (Nayef). The dam is an unraced half-sister to 2 minor winners. The second dam, Foulard (by Sadler's Wells), is an unraced sister to Barathea and Gossamer. (Mr & Mrs Mark Tracey). *"A nicely-made colt, he's medium-sized, quite precocious, a good mover and quite sensible. He's coming along quite nicely and he'll be ready to go when the seven furlong maidens start. I quite like him".*

1090. ETERNAL DREAM ★★★
ch.c. Dream Ahead – Get Happy (Zamindar). February 6. First foal. £22,000Y. Doncaster Premier. Richard Knight. The dam won twice at in France and was listed-placed over 1m and is a half-sister to 2 winners. The second dam, Happy At Last (by In The Wings), a quite useful 2-y-o 1m winner, is a half-sister to 11 winners including Capal Garmon (Group 2 Jockey Club Cup). (Mrs Susie Hartley & Ms Elaine Chivers). *"He's growing on me and he's a nice mover that should be ready for June. I don't think he'll have the speed for six furlongs, so I think he'll be one for seven furlongs. Not over-big, but an athletic horse and relatively precocious".*

1091. JINKIE PINK (IRE) ★★
b.f. Teofilo – Hurricane Havoc (Hurricane Run). April 8. Second foal. 17,000Y. Tattersalls October Book 2. Richard Knight. Half-sister to the moderate 2016 5f and 6f placed 3-y-o Rojina (by Intense Focus). The dam, a useful 7f (at 2 yrs) and 10f winner, was third in a Group 3 9.5f event in Ireland and listed placed three times. The second dam, Cheeky Madam (by Night Shift), placed once at 3 yrs in France, is a half-sister to 6 winners including the Group 1 Criterium de Saint-Cloud winner Linda's Lad. (Elaine Chivers & Merlin Racing). *"A lovely mover, she's quite light-framed so I wouldn't want to rush her, but she finds it all quite easy for a filly that'll want middle-distances next year. I like her but she'll be a slow burner, potentially one for seven furlongs this year".*

1092. SEA SHACK ★★★
b.c. Equiano – Folly Bridge (Avonbridge). January 29. Second foal. 30,000Y. Tattersalls October Book 3. Richard Knight. The dam, a fairly useful 6f (including at 2 yrs) and 7f winner of 4 races, is a half-sister to 5 winners. The second dam, Jalissa (by Mister Baileys), a quite useful 6f winner, is a half-sister to 4 winners including the smart 7f (at 2 yrs) to 10f winner of 7 races Vintage Premium. (Seabrook Miller). *"A big, strong individual but like a lot by the sire I think he just needs a bit of time. He was a January foal but a recent x-ray of his knees shows them to be still slightly open, so we can't press on just yet. I don't think he'll see a racecourse before September time but he's a good-looking horse and he'll be a six furlong 2-y-o".*

1093. UNIT OF ASSESSMENT (IRE) ★★★★ ♠
b.c. Dragon Pulse – Before The Storm (Sadler's Wells). March 10. Seventh foal. £40,000Y. Doncaster Premier. Richard Knight. Half-brother to the fairly useful 2015 2-y-o dual 7f winner Storm Rising (by Canford Cliffs), to the fairly useful 2-y-o 5f and subsequent French 1m winner Mr Majieka (by Oasis Dream) and the fair 9f, 10f and hurdles winner Landau (by Aussie Rules). The dam, a modest 6f and 1m placed maiden, is a half-sister to 4 winners including the dual listed winner Valentine Girl. The second dam, Set Fair (by Alleged), a French 10f winner, is a sister to the Group 2 winner Non Partisan and to the Canadian Grade 3 winner Jalaajel and a half-sister to the dam of the Group/Grade 1 winners Raintrap and Sunshack. (Mr A Hetherton). *"I like him, he's a nice colt and probably wants a bit of cut in the ground looking at the pedigree. He'll have the speed for six furlongs and will probably end up a miler I would have thought. Coming along nicely, he's a really well-made, strong-looking colt. Should be ready around June time".*

1094. UNNAMED ★★★
b.c. Elnadim – Albeed (Tiger Hill). April 11. Second foal. €23,000Y. Tattersalls Ireland

September. Richard Knight. Half-brother to the quite useful 2015 2-y-o 5f winner Halsall (by Kodiac). The dam, a fair 14f winner, is a half-sister to 6 winners including the very useful Group 2 2m and Group 3 2m winner of 8 races Akmal. The second dam, Ayun (by Swain), a useful 1m and 10f winner, is a half-sister to 4 winners including the smart 7f (at 2 yrs) and Group 3 1m Desmond Stakes winner Haami. (Angmering Park Thoroughbreds V). *"I can't quite work out what trip he'll want yet. He's out of a staying Tiger Hill mare and I don't think he'll be a sprinting 2-y-o like the half-brother was last year. I'll probably set him off at seven furlongs around July time. A nice looking horse, with a bit of quality about him".*

1095. UNNAMED ★★★ ♠
b.c. Footstepsinthesand – All Night Dancer (Danehill Dancer). May 5. Second foal. €55,000Y. Goffs Sportsmans. Richard Knight. The dam, a fair Irish 2-y-o 5f winner, is a half-sister to 2 minor winners. The second dam, Nocturnal (by Night Shift), placed fourth twice over 5f in Ireland, is a half-sister to 4 minor winners. (Willis & Angmering Park Thoroughbreds V). *"He's got a lot of quality and finds it all very easy at the moment, but I'm keeping the handbrake on him. He was a May foal and I wouldn't want to get stuck into him too soon. A lovely mover, he may have the speed for six furlongs to start with despite the fact he won't be running until towards the back-end. I do like him – I think he's a nice horse".*

1096. UNNAMED ★★★
b.c. Paco Boy – Amanda Carter (Tobougg). April 26. Third foal. 25,000Y. Tattersalls October Book 2. (Sheikh Abdullah Almalek Alsabah). Half-brother to Ixchell (by Equiano), unplaced in two starts at 2 yrs in 2015 and to the useful triple 7f winner (including at 2 yrs) and Group 2 1m Royal Lodge Stakes third Salateen (by Dutch Art). The dam, a fair 9f to 13f winner of 6 races on the Flat and one over hurdles, is a half-sister to 7 winners here and abroad. The second dam, Al Guswa (by Shernazar), a dual 1m (at 2 yrs) and 10f winner in Ireland, is a half-sister to 5 winners. (Sheikh Abdullah Almalek Alsabah). *"Quite a nervy type, but he's done well. He has a fairly late foaling date and I think he's one for September time, but he has a good back-end on him and he'll probably have the speed for six furlongs".*

1097. UNNAMED ★★★
ch.c. Thewayyouare – Ask Annie (Danehill). May 15. Seventh foal. €24,000Y. Tattersalls Ireland September. Richard Knight. Half-brother to the quite useful 11f winner Askmour (by Azamour) and to the fair 10f winner King's Warrant (by King's Best). The dam is an unraced half-sister to 7 winners including the dams of the Group 1 winners Youmzain and Creachadoir. The second dam, Anima (by Ajdal), was placed once at 3 yrs and is a half-sister to 8 winners (including 6 stakes winners), notably the multiple Group 1 winner Pilsudski. (The Oil Men Partnership). *"I like him, he's a nice, big colt with plenty of scope about him. He was a May foal but despite that he finds it all quite easy, so I think he'll be a nice horse to start in a seven furlong maiden around July/August time.* **TRAINERS' BARGAIN BUY**

1098. UNNAMED ★★★
b.f. Royal Applause – Brazilian Style (Exit To Nowhere). February 15. Fifth foal. Half-sister to the fairly useful 2015 2-y-o listed-placed 6f winner Lady Macapa (by Equiano), to the fair dual 6f winner Smidgen (by Bahamian Bounty), the fair 2-y-o 5f winner Mrs Brown's Boys (by Verglas) and the modest 7f winner Loving Thought (by Oasis Dream). The dam was placed in all three of her starts over 5f at 2 yrs and is a half-sister to 2 minor winners. The second dam, Cosmic Star (by Siberian Express), is a placed full or half-sister to 8 winners including Jubilee Song (dam of the Group 2 winners Millyant and Prince Sabo). (Peter Winkworth). *"She's quite small but has a good back-end on her, slightly on the edge, temperamentally, but she's fine at the moment. I have the 3-y-o half-sister Lady Macapa who won over six last year this filly will also be a six furlong type I think. Probably a July type 2-y-o because she didn't come in until quite late".*

1099. UNNAMED ★★★
b.c. Sixties Icon – Cyclone Connie (Dr Devious). April 20. Eighth living foal. 24,000Y. Tattersalls October Book 3. Richard Knight. Half-brother to 5 winners including the Group 3 Flying

Five and Group 3 Sapphire Stakes winner of 12 races Judge 'n Jury (by Pivotal), the quite useful 7f winner Flight Plan (by Best Of The Bests) and the modest 2-y-o 7f winner Spithead (by Tiger Hill). The dam, a fairly useful 6f winner, is a half-sister to 6 winners including the smart listed winning sprinter Colonel Cotton. The second dam, Cutpurse Moll (Green Desert), a fair 7f winner at 3 yrs, is a half-sister to the dual listed winner Polka Dancer. *"A well-made horse, he's strong, scopey and a July type 2-y-o. He's doing everything I've asked of him at the moment and he's a likeable colt. Probably one for six/seven furlongs this year"*.

DANIEL KUBLER

1100. AV A WORD
b.c. Aussie Rules – Real Me (Mark Of Esteem). February 26. First foal. The dam is an unraced half-sister to 7 winners including the Group 3 Railway Stakes winner Camargo. The second dam, You Make Me Real (by Give Me Strength), was a minor winner in the USA. (Onslow & Nash). *"He would have been quite early but for a small setback but we're cracking on with him now. He's not far away from doing fast work and I can see him being out in June. A nice type"*.

1101. DIAMANTE ★★
b.f. Big Bad Bob – Miracle Steps (Theatrical). March 22. Second foal. €40,000Y. Tattersalls Ireland September. Kubler Racing. The dam, a modest 4-y-o 12f winner, is a half-sister to 6 winners including the Canadian stakes winner and Grade 2 placed Nymphenburg and the minor US stakes winner La Habitant Time. The second dam, Schonbrunn (by Val de l'Orne), a minor US 3-y-o winner, is a sister to the champion Canadian filly La Lorgnette (herself the dam of Hawk Wing). *"She's a lovely filly and very athletic, but much more of a 3-y-o type than for this year. One or two runs this year should be fine for her. A very nice filly though"*.

1102. DIXIE'S DOUBLE ★★
b.f. Multiplex – Dress Design (Brief Truce). March 7. Tenth foal. Half-sister to the modest 5f and 6f winner of 5 races, including at 2 yrs, Whisky Bravo (by Byron), to the modest 7f winner Whisky Jack (by Bahamian Bounty), the Italian winner of 4 races Green Target (by Catrail) and the moderate 1m to 12f winner of 5 races Dandarrell (by Makbul). The dam, a minor Irish 2-y-o 5f winner, is a half-sister to 4 winners. The second dam, Lady President (by Dominion), won 2 minor races in Ireland at 3 and 4 yrs and is a half-sister to 6 winners including the Group 3 winner and Group 1 placed Citidancer. (Onslow & Nash). *"She's a tough, hardy filly and I'm sure she'll be a lot of fun. Her dam won over five furlongs as a 2-y-o and she has the same sort of make and shape"*.

1103. FLOODED ★★★
ch.c. Archipenko – Spate Rise (Speightstown). February 7. Second foal. 4,000Y. Tattersalls October Book 3. Not sold. The dam is an unraced half-sister to two minor winners in the USA and to the modest 2-y-o 6f winner X Raise. The second dam, Raise (by Seattle Slew), a minor US winner at 4 yrs, is a half-sister to 7 winners including the Irish Group 2 Railway Stakes winner Lizard Island and to the dams of the US Grade 1 winner Corinthian and the Group 3 Ballycorus Stakes winner Six Of Hearts. (Onslow, Alan Bell & Gary Middlebrook). *"He's a very big horse and yet seems quite forward and is in the most advanced group of 2-y-o's. He's a good mover and I wouldn't be surprised if he starts off at six furlongs before running over seven when those races start"*. **TRAINERS' BARGAIN BUY**

1104. I WOULDN'T BOTHER ★★★
b.c. Captain Gerrard – Dalmunzie (Choisir). February 21. Fourth foal. Brother to He's My Cracker, unplaced in one start at 2 yrs in 2015 and to the fair 2-y-o 5f winner You're My Cracker. The dam ran twice unplaced and is a half-sister to 4 winners including the listed-placed Gaelic Princess and Berenica. The second dam, Berenice (by Marouble), was unraced. (Paul & Clare Rooney). *"A well put-together horse, he's quite good-looking and does nothing wrong. One for six furlongs and he'll be a tough, hard knocking 2-y-o"*.

1105. JACK BLANE ★★
b.c. Kheleyf – Blane Water (Lomond). April 16. Eighth foal. Half-brother to the fair 2-y-o 5f winner Trinity River (by Three Valleys), to the modest 9f and 10f winner Bracklinn (by

Deploy) and a winner in Hungary by Benny The Dip. The dam, a quite useful 2-y-o 6f winner, is a half-sister to 4 winners. The second dam, Triode (by Sharpen Up), a useful 1m winner, was third in the Group 3 Premio Bagutta and is a half-sister to 2 winners. (Mr P Whitten). *"We had the half-sister Trinity River who won at two. This colt looks just as his late foaling date would suggest, so we won't be seeing him out until mid-summer. A five/six furlong horse I should think".*

1106. MUTINEER ★★★★
ch.c. Sepoy – Violet (Mukaddamah). March 29. Thirteenth foal. 40,000Y. Tattersalls October Book 2. Kubler Racing. Half-brother to 6 winners including the dual 6f and subsequent US Grade 2 winner and Grade 1 second Starlarks (by Mujahid), the quite useful 1m to 9.3f winner of 5 races Boo (by Namaqualand) and the modest 7f and 1m winner Kannon (by Kyllachy). The dam, a fair 6f and 8.5f winner, is a full or half-sister to 8 winners including the 10.4f John Smiths Handicap and triple Hong Kong stakes winner and Group 2 third Sobriety. The second dam, Scanno's Choice (by Pennine Walk), a middle-distance placed maiden, is a half-sister to 6 winners including the US Grade 2 winner Dilmoun. (Ontoawinner & Capture the Moment IV).
"A nice horse for six/seven furlongs. He's just done his first piece of work and he did it well, we like him and he should be a six furlong 2-y-o. A straightforward type, he's strong and has done really well in the last month or so".

1107. SNIPER VIPER ★★
ch.f. Paco Boy – Brilliance (Cadeaux Genereux). April 8. Ninth foal. £600Y. Ascot February. Selwood Bloodstock. Half-sister to the useful 3-y-o listed 7f winner Tora Bora (by Grand Lodge), to the fairly useful dual 7f winner Chorus Of Angels (by Rock Of Gibraltar), the modest 12f and 14f winner Collette's Choice (by Royal Applause), the Hong Kong winner of 5 races Fat Choy Forever (by Desert Style) and a winner over hurdles by Robellino. The dam, a fair 8.2f winner, is a half-sister to 11 winners including the US Grade 2 winner Sign Of Hope and the Group 2 placed Carmot and Finian's Rainbow. The second dam, Rainbow's End (by My Swallow), was a quite useful 2-y-o 6f winner. *"She only has one eye so we paid almost nothing for her. You wouldn't know she had the problem though because she was born with it and it doesn't bother her. A good-looking, well-made horse that moves well, she's having a break now and is one for later in the season".*

1108. SOCRATES ★★
b.c. Dick Turpin – Lisathedaddy (Darnay). March 24. Third foal. Half-brother to the fair 10f and 12f winner Lisa's Legacy (by Kyllachy) and the modest dual 10f winner Who'sthedaddy (by Avonbridge). The dam, a quite useful 10f winner of 4 races, is a half-sister to a winner. The second dam, Erith's Chill Wind (by Be My Chief), was a poor 10f winner. (Wilbart Racing). *"Both his half-brothers improved from two to three and he's probably not dissimilar, but he's a better model. A good-looking horse – he's the best Dick Turpin I've seen. We'll take our time with him".*

1109. SOLENT MEADS (IRE) ★★
ch.g. Intense Focus – No Trimmings (Medicis). March 21. First foal. €26,000Y. Goffs Sportsmans. Kubler Racing Ltd. The dam, a fair winner of 5 races in Ireland over 1m from 3 to 6 yrs, is a half-sister to 3 other minor winners. The second dam, Cheviot Indian (by Indian Ridge), placed fourth once over 5f in Ireland, is a half-sister to 2 winners. (Mr P Britton). *"A very nice horse and a very good mover for the second half of the season. The dam was a hardy racehorse and he's got that real grit in him".*

1110. UNNAMED ★★★★
b.c. Invincible Spirit – Albertine Rose (Namid). March 28. Fourth foal. Half-brother to the fair 2015 2-y-o 5f winner Paytheprice (by Lawman) and to the modest 8.5f winner Mandria (by Duke Of Marmalade). The dam, a quite useful 2-y-o 6f winner, was listed placed over 6f and is a half-sister to 3 winners. The second dam, Barathiki (by Barathea), a quite useful 2-y-o dual 6f winner, is a half-sister to 3 winners including the useful Peacock Alley, a winner of 3 races at around 7f and listed-placed. (Mr & Mrs G Middlebrook). *"The mare throws good-looking horses and this colt should be a 2-y-o. The cross suggests five/six furlong speed and he's a better looking horse than his winning sibling Paytheprice. A nice, good-looking colt that moves well".*

1111. UNNAMED ★★★
b.f. Excelebration – Blue Azure (American Chance). February 5. Fifth foal. Half-brother to the 2-y-o Group 3 6f Firth Of Clyde Stakes winner and Group 3 Ballyogan Stakes third Distinctive (by Tobougg) and to the fairly useful triple 5f winner Blue Aegean (by Invincible Spirit). The dam, a modest 5f placed maiden, is half-sister to 2 minor winners in the USA. The second dam, Kibitzing (by Wild Again), a US stakes-placed winner at 3 yrs, is a half-sister to 6 winners. (Mr & Mrs G Middlebrook). *"A lovely filly. A light mover and very athletic, she's filling out and strengthening now and is certainly a 2-y-o type. I see her as a six/seven furlong 2-y-o".*

1112. UNNAMED ★★★★
b.c. Invincible Spirit – Love Everlasting (Pursuit Of Love). March 1. Ninth foal. 220,000Y. Tattersalls October Book 1. Not sold. Half-brother to the fairly useful 12f winner and listed Cheshire Oaks second Acquainted (by Shamardal), to the quite useful 2-y-o dual 7f winner Penny Rose (by Danehill Dancer), the fair 10f winner Covenant (by Raven's Pass) and the fair 2m winner Yours Ever (by Dansili). The dam, a 7.5f (at 2 yrs) and Group 3 12f Princess Royal Stakes winner of 6 races, is a half-sister to 6 winners including the smart Group 3 10f Scottish Classic winner Baron Ferdinand. The second dam, In Perpetuity (by Great Nephew), a fairly useful 10f winner, is a half-sister to 6 winners including the Derby winner Shirley Heights. (Mr & Mrs G Middlebrook). *"A very good-looking colt, he's well-bred and the pedigree suggests to me he'll be a seven furlong 2-y-o, but as he's quite forward we may start him off at six. A quality colt".*

DAVID LANIGAN

1113. CARTAVIO (IRE) ★★★
b.c. Cacique – Star Cluster (Observatory). March 29. Seventh foal. 50,000Y. Tattersalls October Book 2. J Brummitt / Kingsdown Racing. Brother to the fair 2015 1m winner Executor and half-brother to the modest 12f winner Asterism (by Motivator) and the moderate 5.5f and 6f winner Encapsulated (by Zamindar). The dam, a useful 7f (at 2 yrs) and listed 1m winner, is a half-sister to 7 winners including the 6f (at 2 yrs here) and US Grade 2 8.5f winner Didina (herself dam of the high-class broodmare Tantina) and the smart French listed 10f winner Espionage. The second dam, Didicoy (by Danzig), a listed-placed winner of 3 races over 6f, is closely related to the Group 3 1m Prix Quincey winner Masterclass and a half-sister to 12 winners including the champion 2-y-o Xaar. (Mick & Janice Mariscotti). *"A lovely horse, he's very well-made and strong. Doing very well but having a short break now because of sore shins".*

1114. EXPOSITION (IRE) ★★★
ch.f. Exceed And Excel – Paramita (Galileo). February 8. First foal. The dam is a half-sister to the Group 2 5f Prix du Gros-Chene winner of 3 races Planet Five. The second dam, Six Perfections (by Celtic Swing), won the Prix Marcel Boussac, the Prix Jacques le Marois and the Breeders' Cup Mile (all Group 1 1m events). (Niarchos Family). *"A nice filly, she's a bit light and not the strongest filly in the world but she's doing alright. She's having a break at the moment because her knees are immature, but she'll be fine and when she comes back in hopefully she'll have turned inside out. She looks like being a sprinter but is one for the back-end of the season".*

1115. GETGO ★★★
b.c. Excelebration – Hip (Pivotal). April 12. Fourth foal. 20,000Y. Tattersalls December. J Brummitt/Kingsdown Racing. Half-brother to the fair 2013 2-y-o 5f winner Vine De Nada (by Bahamian Bounty) and to the quite useful 6f, 7f (both at 2 yrs) and 1m winner Hipster (by Kingsalsa) and the moderate 8.5f winner Overlord (by Lawman). The dam, a quite useful 2-y-o 6f winner, is a half-sister to 4 winners including the 2-y-o Group 1 6f Cheveley Park Stakes winner Hooray and the 2-y-o listed winner Hypnotic. The second dam, Hypnotize (by Machiavellian), a useful 2-y-o dual 7f winner, is a half-sister to 8 winners including the Group 3 6f Cherry Hinton Stakes winner Dazzle and the listed winners Baschar and Fantasize. *"A lovely horse, he's a great walker and might take a bit of time but he's worth being patient with. He'll strengthen up all the time, he's very good looking and has a great action. If he does anything this year he might be very nice as a 3-y-o".* **TRAINERS' BARGAIN BUY**

1116. KUIPER BELT (USA) ★★★★★
b.c. Elusive Quality – Youre So Sweet (Storm Cat). February 14. Fourth foal. Half-brother to the modest 2016 1m placed 3-y-o Granita (by Blame). The dam is an unraced half-brother to numerous winners including the Derby winner Kris Kin and the French winner and Group 2 10f placed Bravodino. The second dam, Angel In My Heart (by Rainbow Quest), dam won the Group 3 10f Prix de Psyche and was second in the Matriarch Stakes, the Yellow Ribbon Stakes, the Santa Ana Handicap (all Grade 1 events) and the Group 2 Prix de l'Opera. She is a half-sister to the Group 1 Prix de la Salamandre winner and useful sire Common Grounds. (Flaxman Stables). *"A lovely colt, he's strong and very straightforward. I've ridden him myself and he's the nicest I've sat on for a long time. I think he'll make a 2-y-o by mid-season and he's a smashing horse".*

1117. NORTHDOWN ★★
b.c. Paco Boy – Hazita (Singspiel). March 29. Third foal. 22,000Y. Tattersalls December. J Brummitt/Kingsdown Racing. The dam ran once unplaced and is a half-sister to 7 winners including the Group 3 winners Hazariya and Hazarista. The second dam, Hazaradjat (by Darshaan), won over 7f (at 2 yrs) and 10f in Ireland and is a full or half-sister to 10 winners including Hittite Glory (Flying Childers and Middle Park Stakes). (Mr & Mrs Kevin Scott). *"A nice horse, he's strong and seems to have the right attitude – some of those Paco Boy's can be a bit hot. He does everything right and he's a straightforward colt that'll hopefully be a bit of fun for the owners. He'll make a 2-y-o over six/seven furlongs".*

1118. RETRIBUTION ★★★★
b.c. Iffraaj – The Giving Tree (Rock Of Gibraltar). February 24. First foal. 30,000Y. Tattersalls October Book 2. J Brummitt / Kingsdown Racing. The dam, a fair dual 8.5f winner including at 2 yrs, is a half-sister to 2 winners including the Group 3 Park Express Stakes third Starbright. The second dam, Starry Messenger (by Galileo), a fair 12f winner, is a half-sister to the US Grade 1 Gamely Handicap winner Tuscan Evening and the dual listed winner Barbican. (Paul Brosnan). *"A lovely horse and the nicest one I bought on spec last year. He's very well-made, has a great attitude and he's a big, strong colt. He'll make a 2-y-o, starting off at six furlongs".*

1119. UNNAMED ★★★
b.f. Bated Breath – Intermission (Royal Applause). April 18. Fifth foal. 22,000Y. Tattersalls October Book 3. Not sold. Half-brother to the fair 2015 dual 6f placed 2-y-o Cee Jay (by Kyllachy), to the quite useful 7.5f and 1m winner Between Wickets (by Compton Place) and the modest 2-y-o 7f winner Secret Symphony (by Sakhee's Secret). The dam is an unraced half-sister to 3 winners including the US Grade 1 Citation Handicap and dual Grade 2 winner Ashkal Way. The second dam, Golden Way (by Cadeaux Genereux), a fairly useful 10.5f winner, is a half-sister to 8 winners including the useful Polish Spring (a winner here and a dual US stakes winner) and the French listed 11f winner and Group 3 placed Go Boldly. (Jane Keir). *"A lovely filly, she was quite a late foal so I left her out at pre-training because of that. She's straightforward and I told her owner at the sales to keep her. She'll come in at the end of March and she's a nice, attractive filly".*

1120. UNNAMED ★★★
b.c. Kitten's Joy – Iteration (Wild Again). March 13. Eighth foal. 100,000Y. Tattersalls October Book 1. Not sold. Brother to 3 winners including the US stakes winner and Grade 1 third Charming Kitten and the stakes winner and multiple Grade 3 placed Queen'splatekitten. The dam, placed once at 3 yrs in the USA, is a half-sister to 6 minor winners. The second dam, Lady Madonna (by Chief's Crown), won two minor races at 3 yrs in Germany and is a half-sister to 5 winners. (Mr & Mrs Ken Ramsay). *"Probably the most forward of the Kitten's Joy 2-y-o's we have, he's having a little break but that won't do him any harm. He's a nice, strong horse".*

1121. UNNAMED ★★★
b.c. Archipenko – Jardin (Sinndar). March 31. Sixth living foal. 30,000Y. Tattersalls October Book 3. J Brummitt / Kingsdown Racing. Half-brother to the hurdles winner Dollar Bill

(by Medicean) and a minor winner abroad by Manduro. The dam is an unraced half-sister to 9 winners including Sleeping Indian (Group 2 7f Challenge Stakes) and Felicity (Group 3 10f Golden Daffodil Stakes). The second dam, Las Flores (by Sadler's Wells), a useful 10f winner, second in the Lingfield Oaks Trial and third in the Italian Oaks, is a full or half-sister to 5 winners including the Group 2 Royal Whip Stakes winner Bach. *"I wouldn't have been a fan of the sire but this colt is actually well-made and I think he was well-bought. Could make a 2-y-o around August time"*.

1122. UNNAMED ★★★
b.f. Kitten's Joy – Manda Bay (Empire Maker). February 10. First foal. 60,000Y. Tattersalls October Book 1. Not sold. The dam, a minor US 3-y-o winner, is a sister to the US winner and Grade 2 placed Bahama Bound and a half-sister to 2 winners. The second dam, Summer Wind Dancer (by Siberian Summer), won 5 races at 2 and 4 yrs in the USA including a Grade 2 and a Grade 3 stakes and is a half-sister to 4 winners. (Mr & Mrs Ken Ramsay). *"The dam isn't very big and this filly isn't either. She's a nice, sensible filly that does everything right. Quite a showy, feminine filly and if she has an engine she'll be alright. I haven't done enough with her to know but she's got a good mind on her and she looks like she'll make a 2-y-o"*.

1123. UNNAMED ★★★★
b.f. Exceed And Excel – Sunset Avenue (Street Cry). March 11. Second foal. 70,000Y. Tattersalls October Book 1. R Cowell. The dam, a fair 2-y-o 7f winner on her only start, is a half-sister to 6 winners including the listed winner subsequent US dual Grade 2 second True Cause. The second dam, Dearly (by Rahy), won the Group 3 Blandford Stakes and is a half-sister to 4 winners including Balletto (US Grade 1 Frizette Stakes). (Saif Ali). *"A lovely filly, she's well put-together, strong and forward-looking. It'll be interesting to see how she goes on, she wants to be a little bit edgy but she's settling down all the time. A well-made filly and a good size, she'll be a 2-y-o for July onwards, but you couldn't push buttons too early with her. As nice a filly as I've had from the owner out of his home-breds"*.

GER LYONS

1124. BRUTAL ★★★ ♠
b.c. Pivotal – Loreto (Holy Roman Emperor). January 21. First foal. £250,000Y. Doncaster Premier. David Redvers. The dam, a quite useful dual 1m winner, is a half-sister to 4 winners including the Group 3 winners Cabaret and Drumfire and, the Group 2 6f Gimcrack Stakes second and subsequent Hong Kong stakes winner Ho Choi. The second dam, Witch Of Fife (by Lear Fan), a fairly useful 2-y-o 6f and 7f winner, was listed-placed and is a half-sister to 6 winners. (Qatar Racing Ltd). *"A big, backward type, he's gorgeous and typical of Pivotal. He has a great temperament and he's as laid-back as they come but he's not one you'd rush. You'll see him from the middle of the year onwards with a bit of juice in the ground"*.

1125. BUDDHA BOY ★★★
b.c. Bated Breath – Midnight Fantasy (Oasis Dream). January 19. Third foal. 52,000Y. Tattersalls October Book 2. BBA (Ire). Half-brother to verysister to 6 winners including Miss Anabaa (Group 3 Ballyogan Stakes). The second dam, Midnight Shift (by Night Shift), a fair dual 6f winner at 3 yrs, is a half-sister to 8 winners including the Group 1 6f July Cup winner Owington. *"I'm keen on the first season sire Bated Breath. This is the only one of his I bought, he looks sharp and early but won't be out before May. Looks a sprinter type"*.

1126. BUFFALO BLUES ★★★
b.c. Harbour Watch – Artistic License (Chevalier). February 24. Fourth foal. £38,000Y. Doncaster Premier. BBA (Ire). Half-brother to the fair 2015 6f to 1m placed 2-y-o Phantom Flipper (by Bahamian Bounty) and to the modest 7f winner Monsieur Jimmy (by Monsieur Bond). The dam, a quite useful 5f (at 2 yrs) and 6f winner of 6 races, is a half-sister to 3 winners. The second dam, Alexander Eliott (by Night Shift), an Irish maiden, was placed at up to 10f and is a half-sister to one winner. *"A lovely colt, I have three by this sire and two of them are very backward. This one is more precocious and I can see him being out in May or June over six furlongs. I like him"*.

1127. DANCING WAVES (IRE) ★★★
b.f. Zoffany – Hearthstead Dancer (Royal Academy). March 31. Third foal. €30,000Y. Tattersalls Ireland September. Ger Lyons. The dam, a fair 2-y-o 7f winner, is a half-sister to 3 minor winners in France and the USA. The second dam, Amity (by Afleet), a stakes-placed winner of 6 races in the USA, is a half-sister to 8 winners. *"She grand but we haven't done much with her yet because she's a big, backward type. I don't imagine her running before the seven furlong races".*

1128. IMAGINE IF ★★★
br.c. Dream Ahead – Bogini (Holy Roman Emperor). March 30. Second foal. €70,000Y. Tattersalls Ireland September. Ger Lyons. Half-brother to the modest 2015 8.5f fourth placed 2-y-o Caribbean Spring (by Dark Angel). The dam, a quite useful 5f (including at 2 yrs) and 6f winner of 4 races, is a half-brother to 3 winners including the listed Tetrarch Stakes winner Alkasser. The second dam, Alexander Queen (by King's Best), a fairly useful 2-y-o 5f winner, is a half-sister to 5 winners including the Group 2 Queen Mary Stakes winner Anthem Alexander and the Group 3 Palace House Stakes winner and sire Dandy Man. *"A lovely horse, he works well and physically he's precocious but not mentally. I can see him being out during the second half of May and I like him".*

1129. JACK FLASH (IRE) ★★★★
gr.c. Dark Angel – Lexi The Princess (Holy Roman Emperor). February 16. First foal. €55,000Y. Arqana Deauville August. David Redvers. The dam, a fair 2-y-o 5f winner, is a half-sister to 7 winners including the listed 2-y-o winner Patience Alexander. The second dam, Star Profile (by Sadler's Wells), an Irish 2-y-o 6f winner, is closely related to the very useful Group 3 6.3f Anglesey Stakes and Group 3 5f Molecomb Stakes winner Lady Alexander. (Qatar Racing Ltd). *"He's our most precocious 2-y-o colt. He's ready to run, he's maturing all the time and you'll see him from May onwards. My type of horse".*

1130. KING ELECTRIC (IRE) ★★★
b.c. Elzaam – Kind Regards (Unfuwain). March 27. €25,000Y. Tattersalls Ireland. Church Farm. Half-brother to 4 winners including the fairly useful UAE 1m (at 2 yrs) to 12f winner Moonlight Dash (by Monsun), the quite useful 2-y-o 7f winner Sanjuro (by Manduro) and the fair 2-y-o 7f winner Daheeya (by Daylami). The dam, a very useful 9.2f to 12f winner of 5 races including a listed race, is a half-sister to 6 winners including the Group 3 1m Oettingen-Rennen and listed Doncaster Mile winner White Heart. The second dam, Barari (by Blushing Groom), is an unraced half-sister to 9 winners including the Canadian Grade 1 winner Rainbows For Life and the Group 2 Prix de l'Opera winner Colour Chart (dam of the Grade 1 winner Tempera). (Sean Jones). *"This colt could well be the bargain I think. He's a smart, precocious type that'll be running before your book's out".* **TRAINERS' BARGAIN BUY**

1131. KISS THE WIND IRE) ★★★
b.f. Casamento – Ava's World (Desert Prince). March 5. Third foal. €31,000Y. Tattersalls Ireland September. Ger Lyons. Half-sister to a minor Italian 4-y-o winner by Marju. The dam, a quite useful 2-y-o 6f winner, is a half-sister to 3 winners. The second dam, Taibhseach (by Secreto), winner of the listed 7f Blenheim Stakes in Ireland, is a half-sister to 5 winners including the US Grade 1 10f and 12f winner Mi Selecto and the US dual Grade 2 winner Bar Dexter. *"She's a cracking filly and I love the Casamento's that I have. Good, tough and hardy, I may wait until the seven furlong races with her but she could be earlier than that. I've been a bit easy on the fillies but I like what I'm seeing and you'll see them starting out from the end of May onwards. She's got a great temperament and a great attitude".*

1132. LIGHTENING FAST ★★★★
b.c. Frankel – Lightening Pearl (Marju). March 12. First foal. The dam, winner of the 2-y-o Group 1 6f Cheveley Park Stakes and the Group 3 6f Round Tower Stakes, is a sister to the 3-y-o 11f winner and 2-y-o Group 3 Tyros Stakes third Jolie Jioconde and to the Japanese dual Group 2 winner over 10f and 11f Satono Crown. The second dam, Jioconda (by Rossini), won the listed Silken Glider Stakes and was third in the Group 3 Killavullan Stakes. (Qatar Racing Ltd). *"He's the star of the show – our Group One horse. He's lovely and the image of his mother, she was introduced*

in June and he'll probably come out around the same time. Like the other Frankel I have he can't do enough for you – always trying to please and impress you. If he keeps progressing like that he'll be very nice".

1133. MEDICINE JACK (IRE) ★★★
ch.c. Equiano – Agony Aunt (Formidable). May 7. Twelfth foal. €28,000Y. Tattersalls Ireland September. Ger Lyons. Half-brother to 8 winners including the listed 1m winner Agony And Ecstasy, the fair 2-y-o winners Captain Revelation and Rio's Pearl (all by Captain Rio), the fairly useful 6f winner of 7 races Doctor Hilary (by Mujahid), the quite useful 6f winner Cool Tune and the modest 5f (at 2 yrs) to 7f winner Only If I Laugh (both by Piccolo). The dam, a quite useful 10f winner, is out of the unplaced Loch Clair (by Lomond), herself a half-sister to 6 winners including the German Group 1 winner Wind In Her Hair (dam of the champion Japanese horse Deep Impact). "A lovely colt, he's just back from sore shins and he's very precocious, so he's one of our earlier types and could be smart. I've been lucky with the sire and I think this colt was good value".

1134. MELISANDRE (IRE) ★★
ch.f. Intense Focus – I Hearyou Knocking (Danehill Dancer). April 3. Fifth living foal. £22,000Y. Doncaster Premier. BBA (Ire). Half-sister to the quite useful 2015 2-y-o 1m winner Restive (by Rip Van Winkle) and to the moderate 1m to 9f winner of 3 races Let Me In (by Pivotal). The dam is an unplaced half-sister to 5 winners and to the unraced dam of the Group/Grad 1 winner Landseer. The second dam, Flood (by Riverman), a 6f winner in the USA, is a half-sister to 3 winners including the US Grade 1 winner Sabona. "A lovely filly, we like her and for a chestnut her temperament is good. She's very straightforward and we think she's nice".

1135. MIAMI BLUE (IRE) ★★★
b.f. Kodiac – Hemaris (Sri Pekan). April 3. Second foal. €125,000Y. Goffs Orby. David Redvers. The dam, a quite useful dual 6f winner at 2 and 3 yrs, is a half-sister to 5 winners including the triple Group 3 winner Snaefell and the listed 6f winner and Group 2 5f Flying Five second Daganya. The second

dam, Sovereign Grace (by Standaan), won over 5f in Ireland and is a half-sister 9 winners. (Qatar Racing Ltd). "She going through a growth spurt at the minute but she's typical of the sire and she's precocious enough without doing too much. We'll see her out in April I should think".

1136. NOBLE INTENTION (IRE) ★★★
b.c. Zebedee – Lear's Crown (Lear Fan). March 30. Twelfth foal. 40,000Y. Tattersalls October Book 2. BBA (Ire). Half-brother to 7 winners including the useful 5f, 6f (both at 2 yrs) and listed 7f winner Howya Now Kid (by Daggers Drawn), the quite useful 2-y-o 6f winner Byronic (by Byron), the fair 6f to 9f winner of 12 races Violent Velocity (by Namid), the fair 7f (at 2 yrs) and subsequent US winner Temeritas (by Tamarisk) and the fair Irish 12f winner Security Breach (by Red Clubs). The dam, a fair 12f winner, is a half-sister to 5 winners here and in North America. The second dam, Crowning Ambition (by Chief's Crown), a fair 7f winner, is a half-sister to 6 winners including the Grade 1 Test Stakes winner Fabulously Fast. "I trained his half-brother Howya Now Kid and that's why I bought him. If he's as good as him he'll do and I like what I see at the minute. A big, heavy horse, as soon as I get the weight off him he'll be running – probably sometime in May".

1137. NOVEMBER TALE (IRE) ★★★
ch.f. Casamento – Skeleton (Tabougg). March 23. Third foal. 36,000Y. Tattersalls October Book 2. BBA (Ire). The dam, a modest 2-y-o 1m and 9f winner, is a half-sister to 5 winners including the Group 3 10.5f Rose Of Lancaster Stakes winner of 6 races Mulaqat. The second dam, Atamana (by Lahib), a quite useful 1m winner, is a half-sister to 7 winners including the Irish 2-y-o 6f winner and Group/US Grade 3 placed Dance Clear. "Another nice filly, very similar to the Casamento filly I have out of Ava's World. Once we get some kinder weather I'll start squeezing them a bit more but they're doing everything I'm asking at the minute".

1138. PSYCHEDELIC FUNK (IRE) ★★★★
ch.c. Choisir – Parabola (Galileo). April 28. Third foal. £30,000Y. Doncaster Premier. BBA (Ire). Half-brother to the quite useful

6f winner Gurkha Friend (by Showcasing) and to the modest 6f winner Munjally (by Acclamation). The dam, a fair Irish 7f to 11f placed maiden, is a half-sister to 3 minor winners. The second dam, Zietory (by Zieten), a 2-y-o 6f and 3-y-o dual 1m listed winner, is a half-sister to 4 winners. *"He already has a race entry and he's typical of what I would call smart – he could be anything. I love the fella and he's very precocious. He could win wherever he goes and he was a bargain for what he cost".*

1139. ROCK IN PEACE (IRE) ★★★
br.c. Kodiac – Felina (Lawman). February 6. First foal. £34,000Y. Doncaster Premier. BBA (Ire). The dam, a fair Irish 2-y-o 5f winner, is a half-sister to 2 winners. The second dam, Roshanak (by Spinning World), a quite useful 2-y-o 6f winner, is a half-sister to the Group 1 Melbourne Cup winner Fiorente. *"A typical Kodiac, he was probably a bit small early doors but he's grown into a bonny little horse. We'll be kicking on with him soon enough and he's a nice colt".*

1140. ROOM TO ROAM (IRE) ★★★
b.c. Fast Company – Lady's Locket (Fasliyev). April 26. First foal. 37,000Y. Tattersalls October Book 2. BBA (Ire). The dam is an unplaced half-sister to 5 winners including the Irish 2-y-o listed 6f winner Heart Of Fire. The second dam, Heart's Desire (by Royal Applause), a fair 7f and 1m placed maiden, is a half-sister to 6 winners including the French listed winner and Group 3 placed Bashful. *"A lovely Fast Company with a very good temperament, he's just started to grow a bit but I've liked what I've seen. He's a nice, good-natured horse that should win his Irish maiden".*

1141. SPECIAL OPS ★★★
b.c. Frankel – Diary (Green Desert). April 30. Eighth foal. Half-sister to the Group 1 5f Prix de l'Abbaye and dual listed 6f winner Total Gallery (by Namid), to the 5f winner (at 2 yrs) and Group 1 Fillies' Mile second Lady Darshaan, the useful listed 13f winner Tempest Fugit (both by High Chaparral) and a winner abroad by Lujain. The dam won 3 races in Greece over 7f at 3 yrs and is a half-sister to 4 winners including the Group 1 Gran Criterium third Al Waffi and the Triumph Hurdle winner Made In Japan. The second dam, Darrery (by Darshaan), won 3 races at 3 and 4 yrs, was listed-placed and is a half-sister to 3 winners. (Qatar Racing Ltd). *"A gorgeous colt, I have two Frankels and although they're completely different types they both have great attitudes to the job – they try to please you every time they go to the gallops. This colt is not as precocious as he thinks he is, but he'll still be out from June onwards over seven furlongs. He's starting to thrive and if he continues to improve the way he is doing he could be anything".*

1142. THUNDER CRASH (IRE) ★★
b.g. Footstepsinthesand – Llew Law (Verglas). January 29. First foal. €37,000Y. Goffs Sportsmans. Ger Lyons. The dam, a moderate Irish middle-distance placed maiden, is a half-sister to the listed Windsor Castle Stakes winner Hototo. The second dam, Harlem Dancer (by Dr Devious), a French listed-placed 10f and 11f winner, is a half-sister to 3 winners. *"A good, hardy horse and typical of the sire, he's the only one I've gelded to this point. We like what he's doing and we know he's got an engine but he's doing a bit of growing and we just have to cuddle him for a bit".*

1143. TYPHOON RISING (IRE) ★★
b.c. Thewayyouare – Exquisite Note (Hawk Wing). April 19. Third foal. €42,000Y. Tattersalls Ireland September. Ger Lyons. The dam is an unraced half-sister to 6 winners including the useful 14.7f winner and Group 2 Park Hill Stakes second Perihelion (herself dam of the Oaks winner Qualify). The second dam, Medicosma (by The Minstrel), a quite useful 12f and 2m winner, is a half-sister to 5 winners including the Park Hill Stakes winner Eva Luna (the dam of four stakes winners) and the dam of the US Grade 1 winner Flute. *"A big, backward colt that went feminine on me just after Christmas but he's starting to thrive now. He's a horse I liked at the sales, but then went off him when I got him home, now I'm beginning to like him again. He'll need a bit of time and at least seven furlongs".*

1144. VELVETEEN ★★★★ ♠
b.f. Exceed And Excel – Ermine And Velvet (Nayef). January 22. Third living foal. 50,000Y. Tattersalls October Book 1. David Redvers.

Half-sister to the quite useful 7f and 8.5f winner Sir Guy Porteous (by Shamardal). The dam, a quite useful 7f listed-placed maiden, is a sister to 4 winners including the Group 1 German Derby third Top Lock. The second dam, Ermine (by Cadeaux Genereux), a quite useful 7f placed 3-y-o here and a 1m winner abroad, is a half-sister to 7 winners including the Group 3 10f Brigadier Gerard Stakes winner and 2,000 Guineas and Derby third Border Arrow. (Qatar Racing Ltd). *"She's very smart and could be out early. We could run her now but we'll wait for the wet weather to end. She should be one to look out for".*

1145. WAYFLOWER ★★★★
b.f. Shamardal – Umseyat (Arch). February 18. Second foal. €110,000Y. Goffs Orby. David Redvers. Half-sister to Senses Of Dubai (by Royal Applause), placed second over 7f on his only start at 2 yrs in 2015. The dam, a quite useful 2-y-o 1m winner, is a half-sister to 4 winners the smart listed 11f winner and Group 2 12f Princess Of Wales's Stakes second Alwaary. The second dam, Tabrir (by Unfuwain), is an unraced full or half-sister to 6 winners including the 1,000 Guineas and Group 2 7f Rockfel Stakes winner Lahan. (Qatar Racing Ltd). *"A lovely filly, I like her a lot. Mentally she's immature just now, but physically she's ready. As long as I do everything right by her she'll be fine, she has an engine and I would hope she's smart".*

1146. UNNAMED ★★★
ch.c. Galileo – Jacqueline Quest (Rock Of Gibraltar). February 4. Second foal. 1,200,000Y. Tattersalls October Book 1. China Horse Club/David Redvers. The dam, a smart 2-y-o 7f winner, Group 1 1,000 Guineas second and Group 1 Coronation Stakes third, is a half-sister to 2 winners. The second dam, Coquette Rouge (by Croco Rouge), a quite useful Irish 12f and 17f winner, is a half-sister to 5 winners including the Group 3 Classic Trial winner Regime and the 2-y-o 5f listed winner and Group 2 Cherry Hinton second Salut d'Amour. *"There's quality all through him and he's typical of Galileo. He'll definitely run at two but we'll take our time with him. One for later in the year but we like the vibes he's giving us at the minute. I'm glad to have him".*

GEORGE MARGARSON

1147. CINDERELLA QUEEN (IRE) ★★
b.f. Makfi – Spring Star (Danehill). May 8. Eighth foal. 22,000Y. Tattersalls October Book 1. A C Elliott. The dam won the Group 2 Prix de Sandringham, the US Grade 2 Palomar Breeders' Cup Handicap and the Grade 3 Wilshire Handicap and is a half-sister to 11 winners including a French listed winner. The second dam, L'Irlandaise (by Irish River), won the listed Prix de Honfleur and is a half-sister to 2 winners. (J Abdullah). *"A very nice filly, she's well-made but won't be early. One for the mid-season onwards, she's a good-moving, big, strong 2-y-o. She's only cantering at the moment but she looks a nice type, so I'm hopeful".*

1148. DARING GUEST ★★★★
b.c. Fast Company – Balm (Oasis Dream). April 22. Second foal. 25,000Y. Tattersalls October Book 2. A & E Bloodstock. Half-brother to the 2015 Irish 5f placed 2-y-o Foxen (by Kodiac). The dam, a fair 2-y-o 5f winner, is a half-sister to 3 winners. The second dam, Alovera (by King's Best), a fairly useful 2-y-o 6f winner, is a sister to the smart 6f (at 2 yrs) and listed 8.3f winner Army Of Angels and a half-sister to 6 winners including the useful 2-y-o 6f winner and Group 2 Lowther Stakes second Seraphina. (John Guest Racing Ltd). *"He'll probably be racing as soon as he sees his second birthday. He wasn't an expensive yearling but he probably would have been if he hadn't got an injury on his way to the sales. He's fine now and he's a gorgeous horse. He'll be out by the end of April and I wouldn't be surprised if he was an Ascot 2-y-o. He could win over five furlongs, but he'll be better over six and he's a nice type".* **TRAINERS' BARGAIN BUY**

1149. FERREIRA ★★
b.f. Sayif – Manaaber (Medicean). May 2. Second foal. Half-sister to Omeed (by Equiano), unplaced in one start at 2 yrs in 2015. The dam, a fair 2-y-o 6f winner, is a half-sister to 3 winners including the fairly useful triple 1m winner Cornrow. The second dam, Needlecraft (by Mark Of Esteem), won 4 races including the Group 3 Prix Chloe and the Group 3 Premio Sergio Cumani

and is a half-sister to 7 winners including the Group 2 Prix Dollar and triple Group 3 winner Fractional. (Saleh Al Homaizi & Imad Al Sagar). *"A good, easy-moving filly, she was a late foal and probably wants a bit of time. I had the half-sister last year who was nuts, but this is a different type. A big, sprinting type that shows me ability but her coat hasn't come yet. She looks a 2-y-o but she came in late so she's been a bit behind, but she's cantering with the other 2-y-o's now".*

1150. GOLDEN GUEST ★★★
ch.c. Bated Breath – Si Belle (Dalakhani). February 23. Fourth foal. 28,000Y. Tattersalls October Book 2. A & E Bloodstock. Half-brother to the moderate 2016 1m placed 3-y-o Betsalottie (by Aqlaam). The dam, a fairly useful 12f and 14f winner here, was listed-placed in Germany and is a half-sister to 4 winners. The second dam, Stunning (by Nureyev), a listed Prix Imprudence winner, was second in the Group 2 Criterium de Maisons-Laffitte and is a half-sister to 6 winners out of the triple US Grade 1 winner Gorgeous (by Slew O'Gold). (John Guest Racing Ltd). *"He's real nice, he was bought cheaply as an early season runner and he's not letting me down in that regard. I think he'll be better over six furlongs, he's developed quite well and he's a strong, powerful horse. Mentally he was very keen early on but we started going steady with him and ever since then he's been more relaxed".*

1151. HAPPY QUEEN ★★★
ch.f. Mayson – Rhal (Rahy). January 31. Second foal. 18,000Y. Tattersalls October Book 3. Rabbah Bloodstock. Half-sister to the fair 2016 3-y-o 7f winner Rocket Power (by Kyllachy). The dam, a fair 5f and 6f winner, is a half-sister to 2 winners including the Group 2 Duchess Of Cambridge Stakes winner Illuminate. The second dam, Queen Of Stars (by Green Desert), is an unraced half-sister to the Group 3 1m Premio Dormello winner and Group 1 Italian Oaks third Lady Catherine. (Jaber Abdullah). *"She's from a decent family and yet we picked her up quite cheaply. She's done a bit of work and we marked down that we'd bring her on to run in late April/early May, but we wouldn't rush with her. She's still 'up behind' but she'll be a sprinter, has a good temperament and she's shown us enough to suggest she could win a maiden".*

1152. LADY KAVIAR (IRE) ★★★
b.f. Lope De Vega – Maoin Dor (Manduro). March 20. First foal. 40,000Y. Tattersalls December. A & E Bloodstock. The dam is an unraced half-sister to one winner. The second dam, Royal Alchemist (by Kingsinger), a winner over 6f (at 2 yrs) and two listed events over 1m and 9f, was placed in four Group events and is a half-sister to 3 winners. (Graham Lodge Partnership). *"A very nice filly, she's a sharp type that'll progress, so she won't just be a 2-y-o. I'm giving her a bit of time, she's still growing, works on the grass and she's very straightforward but I think she'll be better over six furlongs. I'd be surprised if she didn't win before mid-summer and I think she'll get seven as well".*

1153. POET'S WISH ★★
b.c. Poet's Voice – Winner's Wish (Clodovil). February 13. First foal. The dam, a quite useful 10f and 14f winner, is a half-sister to 4 winners including the German 2-y-o winner and listed-placed All Annalena. The second dam, Alla Prima (by In The Wings), is an unplaced half-sister to 6 winners including the 2-y-o Group 3 1m Prix d'Aumale winner and smart broodmare Anna Palariva and the dam of the US Grade 1 winner Ave. (Mr A Al Mansoori). *"A scopey horse with a decent pedigree, at the moment he's just cantering. One for the mid-summer onwards, he'll be seen at his best over seven furlongs later in the year. A good, easy-moving horse, he's sensible and, touch wood, I think he'll make a nice type".*

1154. SHYARCH ★★★
b.c. Archipenko – Coconut Shy (Bahamian Bounty). March 5. Third foal. Brother to the fair 2015 2-y-o 7f winner Shypen and half-brother to the quite useful 6f and 7f winner of 6 races from 2 to 4 yrs Shyron (by Byron). The dam, a fair 2-y-o 5.5f and 6f winner, is a sister to one winner and a half-sister to another. The second dam, Lets Be Fair (by Efisio), a useful 2-y-o 5f and 6f winner, is a half-sister to 6 winners including the listed winner Miss Mirasol. (F Butler). *"A lovely horse and the apple of my eye at the moment. He's out of*

a family I know well, he's the best-looking of them and they always say the third foal is the best! I've won 2-y-o races with both of the first two foals and this is a proper horse. He's big and powerful so I have to give him some time. I've got a lot of time for him and the way he's progressed he could be a Chesham Stakes horse, so I'm really looking forward to him. He'll want seven furlongs".

1155. UNNAMED ★★
b.f. Sayif – Delma (Authorized). February 8. First foal. The dam is an unraced half-sister to a hurdles winner by Dubawi. The second dam, Contradictive (by Kingmambo), is an unraced half-sister to 8 winners including the Group 1 Prix Lupin winner Gracioso, to the US Grade 2 winner Caesour and the listed Galtres Stakes winner Professional Girl. (Saleh Al Homaizi & Imad Al Sagar). *"She came in late but she's picked up quite quick, I haven't rushed her but although her damsire is Authorized if you told me to crack on with her I'd tell you she's a 2-y-o. Big and scopey, she has a lot about her and as soon she comes in her coat I'll be working her".*

ROD MILLMAN
1156. COMPTON LANE ★★★
b.c. Compton Place – Dubai Affair (Dubawi). January 13. First foal. £40,000Y. Doncaster Premier. Howson / Houldsworth / Millman. The dam, a modest 2-y-o 5f winner, is a half-sister to 3 winners including the useful 2-y-o listed 6f winner Queen's Grace. The second dam, Palace Affair (by Pursuit Of Love), a multiple listed winner from 5f to 7f, is a sister to one winner and a half-sister to 9 winners including Sakhee's Secret (Group 1 6f July Cup). (The Links Partnership). *"A very good-looking individual, he's sharp and he'll be out any time from mid to late April. He was very well-presented at the sales, in fact the vendor couldn't have had him looking better and I thought he might have made more than he did. He was easy to break and he's done everything right so far"*

1157. DRAVID ★★★
b.c. Famous Name – Sweet Power (Pivotal). January 20. Fifth foal. £30,000Y. Doncaster Premier. Howson & Houldsworth / Millman. Half-brother to the modest 6f winner Bread (by Alfred Nobel) and to the poor 7f winner Sweet Force (by Beat Hollow). The dam was unraced. The second dam, Sweet Ludy (by Be My Guest), won the Grade 2 Honeymoon Handicap and the Grade 2 San Clemente Stakes and is a half-sister to 4 winners. (The Links Partnership). *"Famous Name wouldn't shout at you as being a sire of early 2-y-o's but this is a very correct individual, he's strong and looks the part. I can see him staying further later on, but he's ready to run now over five furlongs and we'll look at six or seven later".*

1158. GLORY OF PARIS (IRE) ★★★★
b.c. Sir Prancealot – Paris Glory (Honour And Glory). February 20. Seventh foal. £22,000Y. Doncaster Premier. Howson & Houldsworth. Half-brother to the fair triple 5f winner Vale Of Paris (by Vale Of York) and to a minor winner abroad by Speightstown. The dam is an unraced half-sister to 4 winners including the Group 1 Prix Morny winner and sire Elusive City. The second dam, Star Of Paris (by Dayjur), is an unraced half-sister to 8 winners including Millions, winner of the Grade 3 Laurel Futurity. (The Links Partnership). *"He's a really good-looking, strong type but he met with a little setback and he won't run now until June. He's a very nice, good-topped horse and would have been my Brocklesby 2-y-o if he hadn't been injured. A big horse, I think he'll be a sprinter when his time comes and I like him. Sir Prancealot will sire a lot of winners this year in my opinion – we have two nice ones here".*

1159. HAWRIDGE GLORY ★★★
b.c. Royal Applause – Saint Lucia (Whipper). February 14. First foal. £20,000Y. Doncaster Premier. Howson & Houldsworth/Millman. The dam ran once unplaced and is a half-sister to 4 winners including the useful 2-y-o listed 6f winner and Group 2 6f Mill Reef Stakes second Sir Xaar and the fairly useful Irish 1m to 9.5f winner and listed-placed Fuerta Ventura. The second dam, Cradle Brief (by Brief Truce), ran once unplaced in a bumper and is a half-sister to the Group 3 6f Greenlands Stakes winner Tiger Royal. *"Not over-big but very well put-together, he looks a sprinter and he'll be racing in late April".*

1160. HELLOFAHASTE ★★
b.f. Hellvelyn – Hasten (Lear Fan). February 23. £3,000Y. Doncaster November. Not sold. Half-sister to the quite useful 2-y-o 7f winner Great Run (by Compton Place), to the fair 2-y-o 1m winner Clutchingatstraws (by Showcasing), the fair UAE 6f and 7f winner Myownway (by Dubawi), the fair 1m winner Hasty Lady (by Dubai Destination), the modest 2-y-o 7f winner Gassal and a minor winner abroad by Johannesburg. The dam was placed twice in the USA and is a half-sister to 6 winners including the 2-y-o Group 3 Autumn Stakes winner and Group 1 Racing Post Trophy second Fantastic View. The second dam, Promptly (by Lead On Time), a quite useful 6f winner here, subsequently won a minor stakes event over 1m in the USA and is a half-sister to 7 winners. *"A tall, lengthy filly that probably won't run until June, she's from quite a good family. I think the sire slips under the radar a bit because he can get a good one from limited books of mares. All this filly has ever done since she's been here is improve, she fills the eye. Probably one for six furlongs first time out".*

1161. HOLYROMAN PRINCESS ★★
b.f. Holy Roman Emperor – Princess Ellen (Tirol). May 4. Closely related to the useful listed 1m winner Prince Of Dance (by Danehill Dancer) and half-brother to 4 winners including the French and Belgian winner and 2-y-o listed 5f placed Candelabro (by Elusive Quality), the quite useful and very tough 9f to 2m and hurdles winner of 29 races La Estrella (by Theatrical) and the fair 1m winner Stravella (by Stravinsky). The dam, a smart listed 7f Sweet Solera Stakes winner at 2 yrs, was second in the 1,000 Guineas and the Coronation Stakes and third in the Nassau Stakes (all Group 1 events) and is a half-sister to one winner out of the unraced Celt Song (by Unfuwain), herself a half-sister to 4 minor winners. *"One for the second half of the season because she was broken-in late, but she's a nice filly. Her dam was second in the Guineas and it was very nice to receive this home-bred filly from her owner. She's strong, only cantering at the moment and she'll be one for six furlongs plus".*

1162. ICE PAC ★★
br.f. Paco Boy – Arctic Char (Polar Falcon). April 8. Seventh foal. Half-sister to the useful dual 1m winner and Group 3 1m Atalanta Stakes third Black Cherry (by Mount Nelson), to the useful 2-y-o 1m winner Alfathaa (by Nayef), the quite useful 7f and 1m winner of 6 races Boots And Spurs (by Oasis Dream) and the modest dual 5f winner Piste (by Falbrav). The dam, a useful listed 7f winner, is a half-sister to 7 winners including the Group 2 winners Barrow Creek and Last Resort and the dam of the Group 2 winner Trans Island. The second dam, Breadcrumb (by Final Straw), a very useful 6f and 7f winner, is a half-sister to 4 winners including the Group 2 Prix Maurice de Gheest winner College Chapel. (Miss G J Abbey). *"She's going to need a bit of time yet and won't run until the second half of the season. A bit backward at the moment, she'll probably want seven furlongs to begin with".*

1163. SIR PLATO ★★★
b.c. Sir Prancealot – Dessert Flower (Intikhab). May 10. Third foal. £6,000Y. Doncaster Silver. Howson, Houldsworth & Millman. Half-brother to a minor 3-y-o winner in Italy by Zebedee. The dam, a minor French placed 3-y-o, is a half-sister to 4 winners including the US Grade 2 placed Sharpbill. The second dam, Division Bell (by Warning), a minor French 3-y-o winner, is a half-sister to 4 winners. (B R Millman). *"He was bought very cheaply at the sales, partly because he was a May foal I think, but he doesn't look like a May foal. He'd have been ready to run now but he had juvenile warts that had to be burned off. He'll be OK, he's a bonny little chap and I really like him. He's one of only two 2-y-o's I've entered for the Super Sprint and he's turned into quite a nice horse, so I think he'll be OK".* **TRAINERS' BARGAIN BUY**

1164. SWEET PURSUIT ★★
b.f. Pastoral Pursuits – Sugar Beet (Beat Hollow). April 6. First foal. The dam, a quite useful 5f and 6f winner of 6 races (including at 2 yrs), was listed-placed and is a half-sister to 5 winners including the very useful 6f (at 2 yrs), 9f and subsequent Hong Kong winner Zabaglione and the fairly useful 5f to 7f winner Lutine Bell. The second dam, Satin Bell (by

Midyan), a useful 7f winner, is a half-sister to 4 winners including the useful listed 6f winner Star Tulip and the dam of the dual Group 3 winner Scarlet Runner. (Always Hopeful Partnership). *"One for the second half of the season because she's a bit backward, but the dam was quite good and I would think this filly will be a sprinter when her turn comes".*

STAN MOORE

1165. ANGIE BABY ★★★
b.f. Compton Place – Angie And Liz (Spectrum). February 12. Fifth foal. £1,000Y. Ascot December. Not sold. Half-sister to the fairly useful 2-y-o 6f winner and Group 3 Brownstown Stakes second Song Of Time, to the quite useful Irish 2-y-o 7f winner Caprella (both by Kheleyf) and the modest 6f winner Oliveraie (by Dutch Art). The dam, a moderate 6f (at 2 yrs) and 5f winner, is a half-sister to 2 winners. The second dam, Mary Magdalene (by Night Shift), a fair 5f winner, is a half-sister to 2 winners. (Tom & Evelyn Yates/J S Moore). *"A home-bred and a half-sister to a black type filly, she'll be tough and win her races. I expect six furlongs will be right for her, she's a good mover and will want firm ground".*

1166. CAUTIOUS CHOICE (IRE) ★★
b.f. Elzaam – On Thin Ice (Verglas). January 24. Third foal. €3,000Y. Tattersalls Ireland September. Stan Moore. The dam is an unraced half-sister to 5 winners including the Group 2 Railway Stakes second Tough As Nails and the smart dual 6f winner (including at 2 yrs) Strahan. The second dam, Soreze (Gallic League), a useful Irish 2-y-o listed 5f Marble Hill Stakes winner, is a half-sister to 6 winners. (Wendy Jarrett, Sara Moore & J S Moore). *"She'll be a tough filly, very willing and straightforward. I can see her being out in May over six furlongs. Probably a nursery type 2-y-o. An honest, game filly".*

1167. DAFFODIL MULLIGAN ★★★
b.f. Showcasing – Anapola (Polish Precedent). March 19. Tenth foal. 12,000Y. Tattersalls October Book 3. Stan Moore. Half-sister to 5 winners including the fair 7f (at 2 yrs), 2m and hurdles winner Blazing Buck (by Fraam), the modest 2-y-o 6f winners Announcement and La Salida (both by Proclamation) and the modest dual 6f winner Bathwick Xaara (by Xaar). The dam won twice at 3 yrs in Germany and is a half-sister to 8 winners. The second dam, Angelica (by Gay Mecene), a German listed winner, is half-sister to 6 winners including the German Group 1 winner Ataxerxes. (Mr Keiron Badger & J S Moore). *"She's sharp and is a half-sister to a few 2-y-o winners. She's qualified for French premiums so we could be heading there with her. A typical Showcasing, not over-big but well-made and wouldn't win a beauty contest. The name comes from an Irish folk song".*

1168. DOLOKHOV ★★
b.c. Harbour Watch – Forest Prize (Charnwood Forest). March 24. 8,000Y. Tattersalls October Book 2. Not sold. Half-brother to the quite useful dual 7f winner at 2 and 3 yrs Invincible Prince (by Invincible Spirit) and to the moderate 7f winner Polish Prize (by Polish Precedent). The dam, a quite useful 2-y-o dual 6f winner, is a half-sister to 6 winners including the high-class sprinter Somnus. The second dam, Midnight's Reward (by Night Shift), a quite useful 2-y-o 5f winner, is a half-sister to 11 winners. *"A good-sized 2-y-o, he'll have begun his career before the book is printed but he'll be better over six furlongs. A horse with a bit of class about him".* Pulled up on his debut in France in March.

1169. FOREST STEPS (IRE) ★★★★
b.f. Footstepsinthesand – Zeena (Unfuwain). March 29. Second foal. €4,500Y. Tattersalls Ireland September. G V March. Half-sister to the fair 2015 2-y-o dual 1m winner Premier Currency (by Elusive Pimpernel). The dam, a modest 10f placed maiden, is a half-sister to 4 winners including the Hong Kong Group 1 10f and UAE Group 1 9f winner Presvis. The second dam, Forest Fire (by Never So Bold), a quite useful 1m to 12f winner of 4 races, is a half-sister to 4 minor winners here and abroad. (G V March & J S Moore). *"She moves really well and does everything as well as you'd want her to. I really like her, she'll be a six/seven furlong 2-y-o and will get a mile later on. I don't know why she was so cheap at the sale but maybe it came too soon for her and she just looked immature. She could end up one of our nicer ones".*

1170. GOG ELLES (IRE) ★★
b.f. Helmet – Hear My Cry (Giant's Causeway). April 5. Third foal. 5,000Y. Tattersalls October Book 2. Stan Moore. Half-sister to the fair 2015 7f fourth placed 2-y-o Princesses Voice (by Poet's Voice) and to the minor Italian winner of 5 races at 2 and 3 yrs Magia Nera (by Bellamy Road). The dam was unplaced in the USA on her only start and is a half-sister to 8 winners including the US Grade 2 winner Blingo and the listed winner Hold To Ransom and to the dam of the UAE Grade 1 winner Prince Bishop. The second dam, Wassifa (by Sure Blade), a fairly useful 11f winner here, subsequently won 3 minor races in the USA and was stakes-placed. (Caroline Instone & J S Moore). *"I think Helmet will be a very good sire. This filly does everything really nice, she's done quite a bit of growing so she won't be early and has plenty of size and scope".*

1171. HOLD ME TIGHT (IRE) ★★
b.c. Zoffany – All Embracing (Night Shift). April 13. Ninth foal. €4,000Y. Tattersalls Ireland September. Stan Moore. Half-brother to the modest 2015 2-y-o 6f winner Burningfivers (by Paco Boy) and to the French 3-y-o 7f winner Cricqueboeuf (by Cape Cross). The dam, a quite useful 7f winner, is a half-sister to 5 winners including the very smart 6f and 7f (at 2 yrs) and Group 2 10f Prix Guillaume d'Ornano winner Highdown and the Group 2 12f King Edward VII Stakes second Elshadi. The second dam, Rispoto (by Mtoto), a modest 12f winner, is a half-sister to 7 winners including the Group 3 10f Royal Whip Stakes winner Jahafil. (Wendy Jarrett, Sara Moore & J S Moore). *"A big horse, he was slack of his pasterns so wasn't expensive but he's come up on them now. A mid-season type 2-y-o, he's big and scopey but could develop into anything. He's by the right sire anyway".*

1172. HOT N SASSY (IRE) ★★
ch.f. Arcano – Cheeky Weeky (Cadeaux Genereux). March 3. Twelfth foal. €4,000Y. Tattersalls Ireland September. Stan Moore. Half-sister to 7 winners including the quite useful 7f (at 2 yrs) and dual 6f winner Golden Shaheen, to the 2-y-o dual 6f winner Pretty Majestic (both by Invincible Spirit), the 2-y-o 6f winner and subsequent US stakes-placed winner Tent (by Distant Music), the 10f winner Cellarmaster (by Alhaarth) – all quite useful. The dam was placed five times in France at up to 1m and is a half-sister to 4 winners. The second dam, Fadaki Hawaki (by Vice Regent), is a placed half-sister to 5 winners including the Group 2 Princess Of Wales's Stakes winner Fruits Of Love and the Group 3 5f Cornwallis Stakes winner and useful sire Mujadil. (Wendy Jarrett, Sara Moore & J S Moore). *"She'll be a tough, hardy filly for six furlongs and one that'll run often. She'll win her races and is an auction/nursery type".*

1173. IF I SAY SO ★★
b.g. Sayif – Glen Molly (Danetime). March 29. Fourth foal. £3,000Y. Ascot December. Not sold. The dam, a fairly useful 6f (at 2 yrs) and 7f winner, is a half-sister to one winner. The second dam, Sonorous (by Ashkalani), an Irish 1m and 10f winner, was listed-placed and is a half-sister to 4 winners. (Douglas Pride). *"I've got two by this sire and there's a lot to like about them. He'll be a tough horse that'll win his races over six/seven furlongs. His owner would like him to be racing in France from August onwards".*

1174. LADY PARKER ★★
gr.f. Zebedee – Westering Home (Mull Of Kintyre). May 5. €2,500Y. Goffs HIT November. The dam, a fair 2-y-o 7f winner, is a half-sister to 2 winners. The second dam, Glympse (by Spectrum), placed fourth once over 9f in Ireland, is a half-sister to 4 winners and to the dams of six stakes winners. *"She goes well and could end up rated in the mid-seventies. The type to win her maiden and go on to nurseries".*

1175. RADAR LOVE (IRE) ★★
b.f. Sir Prancealot – Sonic Night (Night Shift). April 11. Sixth foal. £6,000Y. Doncaster Silver. Stan Moore. Half-sister to the modest 7f winner of 4 races at 2 and 3 yrs Mick Slates (by Moss Vale). The dam ran once unplaced and is a half-sister to a 2-y-o winner in Belgium. The second dam, Latin Crystal (by Kris), ran once unplaced and is a half-sister to 6 winners. (Mr David Klein & J S Moore). *"She'll be sharp and should win her maiden handily enough. Doing everything right, I think she'll be a six furlong 2-y-o".*

1176. SHEILA'S FANCY (IRE) ★★★★
ch.c. Casamento – Fancy Vivid (Galileo). March 18. Third foal. 10,000Y. Tattersalls October Book 3. Stan Moore. Half-brother to the modest 2015 7f placed 2-y-o Leia Organa (by Mastercraftsman) and to the moderate Irish 7f winner Double Fast (by Fast Company). The dam, a modest 8.5f placed maiden, is a half-sister 2 winners. The second dam, Starchy (by Cadeaux Genereux), a fair 2-y-o 6f winner, is a sister to the smart Group 2 5f Flying Childers Stakes and Group 3 5f King George V Stakes winner Land Of Dreams (dam of the multiple Group 1 winner Dream Ahead) and a half-sister to 5 winners. (Mr Ray Styles & J S Moore). *"I think he's very nice and should be a 2-y-o for seven furlongs or a mile. Out of a Galileo mare, he seems to have a lot of class about him and although he needs time I think he'll end up my nicest colt".*

1177. SHEILA'S LAD ★★★
b.g. Lilbourne Lad – Lady Dottie (Motivator). February 15. First foal. 4,000Y. Tattersalls October Book 3. Stan Moore. The dam was unraced. The second dam, Aunt Dottie (by Rahy), is an unraced half-sister to 4 winners including the dual Group 2 and triple Group 3 winner Banimpire. *"He didn't cost much and doesn't have the best pedigree in the world, but he goes very nicely. He could win over five or six furlongs and continue to progress as the year goes on. A possibility for the Brocklesby Stakes, he's one to follow in the first half of the season".* **TRAINERS' BARGAIN BUY**

1178. TO HAVE A DREAM (IRE) ★★★
b.f. Zoffany – Tessa Romana (Holy Roman Emperor). March 4. First foal. €7,000Y. Tattersalls Ireland September. Stan Moore. The dam is an unraced half-sister to 10 winners including the Italian listed-placed Persian Filly (herself the dam of two listed winners in Italy). The second dam, Kafayef (by Secreto), is an unplaced half-sister to 10 winners including 3 stakes winners. (Mr G V March & J S Moore). *"She's not very big but she's very sharp and is one to follow during the first half of the season. She'll definitely win her races and is as hard as nails, but whether she'll carry on to the end of the season I don't know".*

1179. UNNAMED ★★★
b.f. Excelebration – La Baracca (Hurricane Run). March 10. First foal. €90,000Y. Arqana Deauville August. Not sold. The dam is an unraced half-sister to the Group 1 1m Coronation Stakes and Group 1 1m Matron Stakes winner Lillie Langtry and to the listed 7f winner and Group 3 third Count Of Limonade (by Duke Of Marmalade). The second dam, Hoity Toity (by Darshaan), is an unraced half-sister to 5 winners. *"She has a fantastic pedigree and won't be over-raced at two. I'll be trying to get her to win her maiden first time out because she'll be worth a lot of money.*

1180. UNNAMED ★★★
b.f. Casamento – Reign Of Fire (Perugino). April 26. Seventh foal. €7,000Y. Goffs Sportsmans. Stan Moore. Half-sister to the quite useful 2-y-o 6f winner King Dragon (by Iffraaj), to the fair 2-y-o 7f winner Not Bad For A Boy (by Elusive City) and the multiple Italian winners Canarina (by Amadeus Wolf) and Very Glamour (by Pyrus). The dam was placed at 2 yrs and is a half-sister to 4 winners including the US Grade 3 winner and Group 3 July Stakes second Media Mogul. The second dam, White Heat (by Last Tycoon), was placed at 2 yrs and is a half-sister to 5 winners including the dual listed winner Watching. *"She'll win over six furlongs but will end up going seven. There's plenty to like about her and she's pretty tough so she'll come to hand in time for her to start in May. I think Casamento will end up one of the top first season sires.*

1181. UNNAMED ★★
b.c. Requinto – Silk Point (Barathea). April 14. Eleventh foal. 16,000Y. Tattersalls October Book 2. Stan Moore. Half-brother to the quite useful dual 7f winner (including at 2 yrs) All Of Me (by Xaar), to the fair dual 7f winner Ixelles Diamond (by Diamond Green), the modest triple 9f winner (including at 2 yrs) Empress Leizu (by Chineur) and a minor 3-y-o winner in Germany by Noverre. The dam is an unraced half-sister to 4 winners including the dam of the dual Group 3 winning sprinter Captain Gerrard. The second dam, Scimitarra (by Kris), a listed 10f Lupe Stakes winner, is a half-sister to 6 winners including the top class sprinter Double Form. *"A big horse, we haven't done much with him because of that but he*

moves very well. He won't run until July time over seven furlongs, but there's more to like about him than not".

DAVE MORRIS/RICHARD SPENCER

It was a pleasure to visit Dave's yard in Newmarket for the first time and to chat with him and his assistant Richard Spencer about the Rebel Racing two-year-olds. Shortly after my visit to the yard Richard was made trainer of these Rebel Racing two-year-olds.

1182. BAGGY TROUSERS ★★
b.c. Makfi – Fame Is The Spur (Motivator). January 31. Third foal. 40,000Y. Tattersalls October Book 2. Bobby O'Ryan/Rebel Racing. Half-brother to the modest 2-y-o 6f winner Lightning Stride (by Equiano). The dam, a fair 10f winner, is a half-sister to 11 winners including the US dual Grade 2 10f winner Battle Of Hastings and the listed 12f winner Villa Carlotta. The second dam, Subya (by Night Shift), was a very useful winner of 5 races from 5f (at 2 yrs) to 10f including the Lupe Stakes, the Masaka Stakes and the Star Stakes (all listed events). (Rebel Racing 2). "Well put-together, he's quite big and will probably want seven furlongs to start with, so there's no rush with him and he'll set off in mid-season all being well. He has a lovely attitude but being by Makfi and out of a Motivator mare he'll need some time and he'll get a trip".

1183. BERNARDO O'REILLY ★★★
b.c. Intikhab – Baldovina (Tale Of The Cat). February 25. Fifth foal. £10,000Y. Doncaster Premier. Phil Cunningham. Half-brother to the moderate 2015 7f placed 2-y-o Bulge Bracket (by Great Journey), to the Group 2 5f Queen Mary Stakes winner Ceiling Kitty (by Red Clubs) and the fair 2-y-o triple 5f winner Van Go Go (by Dutch Art). The dam is a placed half-sister to 4 winners including the Japanese dual Group 3 winner One Carat. The second dam, Baldwina (by Pistolet Bleu), won the Group 3 Prix Penelope and is a half-sister to 6 winners. (Rebel Racing 2). "He's a bit of a boy and he's best behaved when he's working but he's doing everything nicely and you can't fault his work. He's coming to hand now and we'll probably get him out in May over six furlongs to start with, although he travels well and he's probably going to want

further. Like most by this sire he has a bit of a knee action. For what he cost you can't go wrong, he's tough and not a bad model at all".
TRAINERS' BARGAIN BUY

1184. CARELESS WHISPER ★★★
b.f. Cockney Rebel – Vino Veritas (Chief's Crown). April 23. Twelfth foal. €60,000Y. Tattersalls Ireland September. Rebel Racing. Sister to the fair 2015 2-y-o 7f winner Nucky Thompson, to the fairly useful 1m (at 2 yrs) to 11f winner and Group 2 Park Hill Stakes second Groovejet, the quite useful 2-y-o 7f winner Na Zdorovie and the modest 14f and 2m winner Illya Kuryakin and half-sister to 4 winners including the useful 2-y-o 7f winner and US triple Grade 2 10f winner Slim Shadey (by Val Royal). The dam, placed fourth once over 7f at 2 yrs, is a half-sister to the multiple Hong Kong and Japanese Group 1 winner Bullish Luck. The second dam, Wild Vintage (by Alysheba), a minor French 10f winner, is a half-sister to 7 winners including the Group 1 Prix Marcel Boussac winner Juvenia. (Rebel Racing 2). "She was late coming in so we haven't done much with her yet. She's not a big filly, but nicely put together and I'd say she'll want seven furlongs as a 2-y-o".

1185. GUSTAVO FRING ★★
b.c. Kodiac – Maleha (Cape Cross). February 28. Third foal. 21,000Y. Tattersalls October Book 2. Bobby O'Ryan / Rebel Racing. Half-brother to the fairly useful 2-y-o 6f winner Malilla (by Red Clubs) and to the fair 7f and 1m winner Desert Ranger (by Bushranger). The dam is an unraced half-sister to the useful listed 1m winner of 7 races Yamal and to the quite useful 2-y-o 6f winner Trailblazing. The second dam Pioneer Bride (by Gone West), is an unplaced half-sister to 7 winners including Faithful Son (Group 2 10f Prince of Wales's Stakes) and Always Fair (Group 3 Coventry Stakes and Prix Quincey) and to the dam of the Irish Oaks winner Lailani. (Rebel Racing 2). "He's a giant and weighs 580kgs, but he's not fat – just tall. Everything's in proportion and for a big horse he's very light on his feet when cantering. He has a great attitude and it's difficult to know what sort of trip he'll want. Obviously Kodiac gets fast 2-y-o's but to look at him there's a lot of Cape Cross there, so he might want a bit further. We'll give him a bit of time but he's doing everything nicely".

1186. KEYSER SOZE ★★★★
ch.c. Arcano – Causeway Queen (Giant's Causeway). April 14. Third foal. 50,000Y. Tattersalls October Book 3. Bobby O'Ryan / Rebel Racing. Half-brother to the fairly useful 2015 2-y-o listed-placed 6f winner Surbett (by Rock Of Gibraltar). The dam is an unraced half-sister to 3 winners including the Group 3 Dee Stakes winner and Epsom Derby third Astrology. The second dam, Ask For The Moon (by Dr Fong), won 5 races including the Group 1 10f Prix Saint-Alary and is a half-sister to one winner. (Rebel Racing 2). *"A very good-looking model, he's quite flashy when he's out and is one that people would notice. He's doing everything we'd want at the moment and six furlongs is probably his starting point. A good-moving horse and we're pleased with him".*

1187. LA ISLA BONITA ★★★
b.f. Foxwedge – Excello (Exceed And Excel). April 9. Third foal. 21,000Y. Tattersalls October Book 3. Bobby O'Ryan/Rebel Racing. Half-sister to the 2015 6f placed 2-y-o, on his only start, Private Donald (by Sakhee's Secret) and to the modest 5f winner Ernest (by Showcasing). The dam, a fairly useful listed-placed 2-y-o 5f winner, is a half-sister to 5 winners including the fairly useful 2-y-o dual 5f and subsequent UAE listed 6f winner Rafeeej. The second dam, Muffled (by Mizaaya), a modest 7f winner, is a half-sister to 3 other minor winners. (Rebel Racing 2). *"She's a gorgeous filly, a good mover and probably a six furlong 2-y-o although there's plenty of five furlong speed in the pedigree".*

1188. OH GENO ★★★
b.c. Paco Boy – Key Light (Acclamation). March 25. Third foal. £32,000Y. Doncaster Premier. Phil Cunningham. Brother to the smart 2-y-o Group 2 5f Flying Childers Stakes winner of 4 races Beacon and half-brother to the unplaced 2015 2-y-o Cool Image (by Elnadim). The dam, a fair dual 6f winner including at 2 yrs, is a half-sister to 3 winners. The second dam, Eva Luna (by Double Schwartz), a very useful winner of 5 races at up to 6f at 2 yrs including the Group 1 Phoenix Stakes and the Group 3 6f Railway Stakes, is a sister to the Group 3 1m Futurity Stakes winner Cois Na Tine and a half-sister to 5 winners. (Rebel Racing 2). *"A full brother to Beacon, he's a strong, well put together colt so he looks a 2-y-o and we'll probably start him at five furlongs".*

1189. SIR HARRY COLLINS ★★★
b.c. Zebedee – Unreal (Dansili). March 22. Seventh foal. 45,000Y. Tattersalls October Book 3. Bobby O'Ryan / Rebel Racing. Half-brother to the modest 2-y-o 5f winner Britain (by Manduro). The dam, a fair 2-y-o 5f winner, is a half-sister to 7 winners including the Group 1 Racing Post Trophy third Illustrator. The second dam, Illusory (by Kings Lake), a quite useful 6f winner, is a sister to the Group 2 Lowther Stakes winner Kingscote (the dam of four stakes winners). (Rebel Racing 2). *"He looks a 2-y-o, he's a strong type and I'd say five furlongs at the end of May would suit him to begin with. He's doing everything we ask of him".*

1190. SOLITARY SISTER ★★★
b.f. Cockney Rebel – Sweet Afton (Mujadil). February 7. Fifth foal. €30,000Y. Tattersalls Ireland September. Phil Cunningham. Sister to the quite useful 2-y-o 6f and subsequent 8.5f winner Funk Soul Brother and to the fair 8.5f winner Rock 'n' Roll Star. The dam, a fairly useful 5f (at 2 yrs) and 6f winner, was listed-placed twice and is a half-sister to 5 winners. The second dam, Victory Peak (by Shirley Heights), is an unplaced half-sister to 6 winners out of the French Oaks winner Lypharita. (Rebel Racing 2). *"She's quite a tall filly but everything's in proportion and she's very much like her brother Funk Soul Brother, a typical Cockney Rebel. Six furlongs in May should be her starting point, although she's just holding on to her coat at the minute. A good-looking filly".*

1191. THISTIMENEXT YEAR ★★
b.c. New Approach – Scarlet Empire (Red Ransom). April 25. Fourth foal. 70,000Y. Tattersalls October Book 2. Bobby O'Ryan / Rebel Racing. Half-brother to the fairly useful 9f, 10f and subsequent Australian listed winner Danchai (by Authorized). The dam is an unraced half-sister to 10 winners including the multiple Group 1 winner Sky Lantern and the Group 3 winners Arctic and Shanty Star. The second dam, Shawanni (by Shareef Dancer), a useful 2-y-o 7f winner, is a half-sister to 5

winners including the UAE Group 3 winner Blatant and the Group 3 Prix Thomas Bryon winner Songlark. (Rebel Racing 2). *"Very much like his sire, he's well put together and there's plenty of size about him. He's probably going to be a better 3-y-o and he'll be one for the middle to back end. He's nice and I'm not saying he won't be doing anything at two, but he's well named!"*

1192. TWISTON SHOUT ★★★
b.c. Lawman – Minkova (Sadler's Wells). January 26. Sixth foal. 41,000Y. Tattersalls October Book 3. Bobby O'Ryan / Rebel Racing. Half-brother to the fairly useful Irish 2-y-o 7f winner and dual listed-placed East Meets West (by Dansili), to the quite useful 12f to 2m winner Magic Circle (by Makfi) and the fair 10f and hurdles winner Thorpe (by Danehill Dancer). The dam is an unraced half-sister to the Irish dual listed winner Chamonix. The second dam, L'Ancresse (by Darshaan), an Irish listed winner and second in the Irish Oaks and Breeders' Cup Filly & Mare Turf, is a sister to 2 winners including the Group 1 Prix Saint-Alary winner Cerulean Sky and a half-sister to 7 winners including the Irish Oaks winner Moonstone. (Rebel Racing 2). *"A good-sized horse, he's well put-together and one that'll be suited by seven furlongs in mid-season. The way he looks he should be a good 3-y-o prospect as well".*

HUGHIE MORRISON

1193. BAHAMIAN PARADISE ★★★
ch.f. Bahamian Bounty – Amanjena (Beat Hollow). February 10. Second foal. 16,000Y. Tattersalls October Book 3. Blandford Bloodstock. The dam, a quite useful dual 10f winner, is a half-sister to 4 winners including the useful 5f listed (at 2 yrs) and 7f listed winner Presto Vento. The second dam, Placement (by Kris), is an unraced half-sister to 4 winners including the Group 2 Sun Chariot Stakes winner Danceabout and the Group 3 6f Prix de Meautry winner Pole Position. (Mr M E Wates). *"She might be running by mid-summer, I like the look of her and she has a good attitude. Her dam was big and took time so she might start growing again. If not she'll be running by July or August and there's a bit of speed in the pedigree".*

1194. BEACONSFIELD ★★★
b.c. Foxwedge – Italian Connection (Cadeaux Genereux). February 20. Fourth foal. 35,000Y. Tattersalls October Book 1. H Morrison. Half-brother to the quite useful 1m and 9f winner Talyani (by Halling) and to the quite useful Irish 7f winner I'vegotafeeling (by Rock Of Gibraltar). The dam is an unraced sister to the listed placed 2-y-o 7f winner Pietra Dura (herself dam of the US Grade 3 winner and Grade 1 second Turning Top) and a half-sister to 4 winners including the dam of the Group 1 King George VI winner Postponed. The second dam, Bianca Nera (by Salse) won the Group 1 Moyglare Stud Stakes and is a half-sister to the Moyglare Stud Stakes second Hotelgenie Dot Com (dam of the dual Group 1 winner Simply Perfect). (Mr Simon Malcolm). *"A lovely, big Foxwedge colt. There's a lot of size to him, he has a nice attitude but is too big to gallop yet. He'll be alright later in the season so we'll look after him. He's a big, strong horse and a nice type".*

1195. CALEDONIAN KING (FR) ★★
b.c. Rip Van Winkle – Water Fountain (Mark Of Esteem). April 18. Fifth foal. 28,000Y. Tattersalls October Book 1. Stroud & Coleman/H Morrison. Closely related to the useful dual 1m winner, Group 3 Meld Stakes third and Irish Derby fourth Ponfeigh. The dam is an unraced sister to the Group 3 Prix Cleopatre winner Spring Oak and a half-sister to 8 winners including listed winner Fragrant Hill (the dam of five stakes winners including the French Group 1 winners Fragrant Mix and Alpine Rose). The second dam, English Spring (by Grey Dawn II), won the Group 2 Prince of Wales's Stakes and is a half-sister to 4 winners including Dance of Life (Grade 1 Man O'War Stakes). (The Caledonian Racing Society). *"Another well-bred but reasonably bought horse, his pedigree suggests he's one to come out in the autumn and show that he's alright. We had one by the same sire that won three races for us and this colt was bought as a two year project, so he'll be better as a 3-y-o".*

1196. CURTSY (IRE) ★★★
ch.f. Galileo – Acts Of Grace (Bahri). May 14. Sixth foal. €50,000Y. Goffs Orby. Dermot Farrington. Half-sister to the fair 10f winner Contradict (by Raven's Pass), to the fair 9f

winner Damascene (by Oasis Dream) and the minor 6f winner (from two starts) Blaugrana (by Exceed And Excel). The dam won the Group 3 12f Princess Royal Stakes and is a half-sister to 10 winners including the Group 1 Sprint Cup winner and good sire Invincible Spirit. The second dam, Rafha (by Kris), won the Group 1 10.5f Prix de Diane and is a half-sister to 9 winners including the Group 2 Blandford Stakes winner Chiang Mai (dam of the Group 1 winner Chinese White). (Mr M Kerr-Dineen & Mr M Hughes). *"A small, really tough little filly that you could probably run next week but she more than likely needs a mile. If she doesn't start growing we'll be running her in June or July over seven furlongs".*

1197. FORWARD CONTRACT ★★★

ch.c. Exchange Rate – Persistent Penny (A P Indy). February 10. Third foal. 45,000Y. Tattersalls October Book 2. H Morrison. Half-brother to a minor winner abroad by Arch. The dam, a minor US 3-y-o winner, is a half-sister to 3 minor winners. The second dam, Penny's Gold (by Kingmambo), a French Group 3 1m and US dual Grade 3 winner, is a half-sister to 3 winners and to the dam of the Japanese Group 1 winner Curren Black Hill. (Mr H Scott-Barrett & Mr S De Zoete). *"He's progressed well and strengthened up lately. He could be a horse we'll have to back-off but I like to think he'll be on the course by July. The sire injects speed, the family preferred a mile".*

1198. MELLOW ★★★

ch.f. Bahamian Bounty – Tarqua (King Charlemagne). March 18. Third foal. Closely related to the quite useful 2-y-o dual 5f winner Field Game (by Pastoral Pursuits) and half-sister to the unplaced 2015 2-y-o Ambuscade (by Dick Turpin. The dam is an unplaced half-sister to the 2-y-o Group 2 6f Mill Reef Stakes winner Cool Creek. The second dam, Shining Creek (by Bering), won twice at around 7f at 2 and 3 yrs in Italy and is a half-sister to 6 winners. (Lord Carnarvon). *"She was neat and small in the autumn but has grown more than any other 2-y-o in the yard. I shouldn't think she'll be racing before July but she's stopped growing now and looks less of a sprinter than her three-parts brother Field Game was".*

1199. MULSANNE CHASE ★★

b.c. Sixties Icon – Hot Pursuits (Pastoral Pursuits). April 8. Second foal. 7,000foal. Tattersalls December. Ballinvana House Stud. Half-brother to the 2015 2-y-o 6f winner, from two starts, Desirable (by Stimulation). The dam, a fair 5f (at 2 yrs) and 6f winner, is a half-sister to 3 minor winners. The second dam, Perfect Partner (by Be My Chief), is an unraced half-sister to 6 winners including the 6f Ayr Gold Cup and Washington Singer Stakes winner Funfair Wane and the Italian listed 7.5f winner Cabcharge Striker. (Mrs I Eavis). *"He's done a lot of growing and is a back-end of the season 2-y-o. I don't think he'll show us a lot this year and it's impossible to know what trip he'll want because he's by a St Leger horse out of a sprinter".*

1200. MUSIC LESSON ★★

ch.f. Dutch Art – Triple Sharp (Selkirk). April 11. Ninth foal. 25,000foal. Tattersalls December. Not sold. Half-sister to the useful 6f (including at 2 yrs) and 7f winner of 4 races and triple listed-placed Nasri (by Nayef), to the useful 6f (at 2 yrs) to 11f winner and 2-y-o Group 2 7f Superlative Stakes third Ellmau (by Dr Fong), the French 2-y-o 7f winner Royal Sharp, the moderate 9.5f winner Triple Star (both by Royal Applause), the listed-placed Laureldean Express (by Inchinor) and a winner in Spain by Vettori. The dam, a quite useful 10f and hurdles winner, is a half-sister to 5 winners including the US stakes winner and Grade 2 placed Pina Colada and to the unraced dam of the top-class miler Canford Cliffs. The second dam, Drei (by Lyphard), placed fourth over 1m at 3 yrs on her only outing, is a half-sister to 3 winners. (Lady Hardy). *"She's only just come in and is finding her feet, but she's progressing. Quite a nice filly, she's a bit leggy and I can't see her being ready before August over seven furlongs".*

1201. POET'S PRINCESS ★★★★

ch.f. Poet's Voice – Palace Affair (Pursuit Of Love). March 28. Ninth foal. 34,000Y. Tattersalls October Book 1. Sackville/Donald, H Morrison. Closely related to the modest 2-y-o 5f winner Dubai Affair (by Dubawi) and half-sister to the useful 2-y-o listed 6f winner Queen's Grace, to the modest 2-y-o 6f winner Black Rodded (both by Bahamian

Bounty) and the fair 7f to 9f winner of 15 races April Fool (by Pivotal). The dam, a multiple listed winner from 5f to 7f, is a sister to one winner and a half-sister to 9 winners including Sakhee's Secret (Group 1 6f July Cup). The second dam, Palace Street (by Secreto), a dual listed winner including the Cammidge Trophy, is a half-sister to 7 winners including the dual listed winner Indian Trail. (Mr Paul Brocklehurst). *"A sharp filly, I could run her now but she has a nice pedigree and I don't want to knock her about early on. If everything goes alright she'll be out in May. She looks well-bought and is quite neat at the moment but two of her siblings were just the same. One of them grew (Queens Grace) and the other (Black Rodded) didn't".*

1202. PRIVATE MISSION ★★
ch.c. Sepoy – Pivotal Drive (Pivotal). April 6. Fifth foal. 75,000Y. Tattersalls October Book 2. Stroud/Coleman & H Morrison. Half-brother to the fairly useful 1m to 14f winner of 6 races Swivel (by Shirocco) and to the quite useful 6f (including at 2 yrs) and 7f winner Meet Me Halfway (by Exceed And Excel). The dam is an unraced half-sister to 4 winners including the listed 1m and 10f winner Sublimity and the UAE Group 3 1m winner Marbush. The second dam, Fig Tree Drive (by Miswaki), a fairly useful 2-y-o 6f winner on her only start, is a half-sister to 4 winners. (Mr M Kerr-Dineen, Mr W Eason, Mr D Malpas & Mr G Rothwell). *"A similar type to the Exchange Rate colt. He's 'up behind' and I'm always nervous about training young horses like that because you can ruin them. He has a nice attitude and does everything we ask, lacks a bit of scope perhaps, but he's got a look about him which suggests he'll grow again".*

1203. RUMPOLE ★★★
b.c. Lawman – Complexion (Hurricane Run). February 19. Second foal. 130,000Y. Tattersalls October Book 2. Stroud/Coleman. Half-brother to the fair 2016 3-y-o 10f winner King Of Dreams (by Dream Ahead). The dam, a quite useful 1m winner, is a half-sister to 3 winners including the high-class 7f (at 2 yrs) and Group 2 Celebration Mile winner and Group 1 Queen Elizabeth II Stakes second Zacinto. The second dam, Ithaca (by Distant View), a useful 2-y-o 7f winner and second in the Group 3 7f Prestige Stakes, is a half-sister to 5 winners including the Canadian Grade 3 14f winner Eagle Poise. (Mr M Kerr-Dineen, Mr M Hughes & Mr W Eason). *"A charming horse. He's quite neat so he may be out before August over seven furlongs despite being out of a Hurricane Run mare. You'd like him to grow a bit, but he's round and robust with a good attitude".*

1204. SPECIAL RELATION (IRE) ★★
b.c. Casamento – Sindiyma (Kalanisi). May 5. Third foal. 30,000Y. Tattersalls October Book 2. H Morrison. Half-brother to the 2015 6f placed 2-y-o, from two starts, Sikandarabad (by Dr Fong). The dam, a quite useful Irish 12f winner, is a half-sister to 3 winners including the fairly useful 7f (at 2 yrs) and listed 11f winner Sindirana. The second dam, Sinndiya (by Pharly), a minor Irish 12f winner, is a half-sister to the top-class middle-distance colt Sinndar, winner of the Derby, the Irish Derby and the Prix de l'Arc de Triomphe. (Mr M Hankin, Mr C Fenwick & Mr C Noell). *"Casamento seems to have put a bit of maturity into the pedigree. It's a nice, staying pedigree and he was bought for that purpose – to train on and be a dual purpose horse. I can easily see him being out in August or September. A nice-looking horse but scopey and we haven't done anything with him yet".*

1205. TEMPLE CHURCH (IRE) ★★★
b.c. Lawman – All Hallows (Dalakhani). January 28. Second foal. 27,000Y. Tattersalls October Book 2. James Toller. Brother to the modest 2015 10f placed 2-y-o Argyle. The dam is an unraced half-sister to 6 winners including the Group 1 Prix Royal-Oak winner Allegretto. The second dam, Alleluia (by Caerleon), won the Group 3 Doncaster Cup and is a half-sister to 7 winners including the Nassau Stakes and Sun Chariot Stakes winner Last Second (dam of the French 2,000 Guineas winner Aussie Rules) and the dams of the Group 1 winners Alborada, Albanova, Yesterday and Quarter Moon. The second dam, Alruccaba (by Crystal Palace), was a quite useful 2-y-o 6f winner. (Mr P C J Dalby & R D Schuster). *"A lovely, big, scopey horse, he's very attractive and a good move. Could be anything. His pedigree suggests he should have made more at the sale and he could be*

a proper 3-y-o. He's a nice horse we'll hope to see out in early autumn". **TRAINERS' BARGAIN BUY**

1206. TOWIE (IRE) ★★★★
b.br.c. Sea The Stars – Epping (Charnwood Forest). February 10. Ninth foal. 90,000Y. Tattersalls October Book 1. Sackville/Donald. Half-brother to the smart 10f winner and Group 1 St Leger second The Last Drop, to the useful Irish 2-y-o 7f winner and listed-placed Nebula Storm, the quite useful 12f winner Ardlui (all by Galileo) and the minor French 3-y-o 1m winner Cherry Orchard (by King's Best). The dam, a quite useful 7f winner, is a half-sister to 7 winners including the French listed winner and multiple Group-placed Self Defense. The second dam, Dansara (by Dancing Brave), is an unraced half-sister to 10 winners including Princess Pati (Irish Oaks) and Seymour Hicks (Great Voltigeur Stakes). (Mr M Kerr-Dineen & Mr M Hughes). *"A very nice looking horse. Bred to need a trip, he's a quality horse we'll look to start off over seven furlongs in late summer. He wasn't cheap, but looking at him he could be a very nice horse".*

1207. UNNAMED ★★
b.c. Lawman – Convention (Encosta De Lago). March 25. Second foal. 20,000Y. Tattersalls October Book 2. H Morrison. The dam, a fair 9.5f winner, is a half-sister to 6 winners including the Group 1 6f Haydock Park Sprint Cup winner Regal Parade and the Group 3 Acomb Stakes winner Entifaadha. The second dam, Model Queen (by Kingmambo), a fair 3-y-o 7f winner, is a half-sister to 5 winners including the French listed 1m winner Arabride. (Mr Andrew Stone). *"He's quite backward but has coped well with everything we've done which is always a good sign. He won't be ready before the autumn though".*

WILLIE MUIR

1208. CUTTIN' EDGE (IRE) ★★★★
b.c. Rip Van Winkle – How's She Cuttin' (Shinko Forest). April 18. Third living foal. 50,000Y. Tattersalls October Book 1. William Muir. Half-brother to the 2015 2-y-o listed Windsor Castle Stakes winner Washington DC (by Zoffany). The dam, a quite useful 5f winner of 7 races, was listed-placed and is a half-sister to 3 winners. The second dam, Magic Annemarie (by Dancing Dissident), a fair 5f and 6f winner of 3 races, is a half-sister to 3 winners. *"If he was by a more successful sire he'd have cost three times his purchase price. I like him, he moves well and at this present time I couldn't say anything but nice things about him. He's developing, has a good page and will make a 2-y-o".*

1209. IRON LADY (IRE) ★★★★
b.f. Exceed And Excel – Kahlua Kiss (Mister Baileys). March 22. Fifth foal. 52,000Y. Tattersalls October Book 1. William Muir. Half-sister to the smart 6f (at 2 yrs) and dual listed 10f winner of 6 races and Group 2 York Stakes third Windhoek (by Cape Cross) and to the quite useful 12f winner Spiritoftheunion (by Authorized). The dam, a fairly useful 7f (at 2 yrs) and 10f winner of four races, was listed-placed twice and is a half-sister to the 2-y-o winner and dual Group 3 placed Mister Genepi. The second dam, Ring Queen (by Fairy King), is an unraced half-sister to 10 winners including the US dual Grade 1 winner Special Ring. *"A filly from a good black type family, if she didn't even see a racecourse she's worth good money, but she moves well and looks like she'll make a 2-y-o by the second half of the season. I like her and I like the family".*

1210. MASTER BILLIE (IRE) ★★★
ch.c. Mastercraftsman – Billie Jean (Bertolini). April 13. Fourth foal. 26,000Y. Tattersalls October Book 3. William Muir. Half-brother to the quite useful 2-y-o 6f winner Racquet (by Pastoral Pursuits), to the moderate dual 7f winner at 2 and 3 yrs Celestine Abbey (by Authorized) and a minor winner abroad by Footstepsinthesand. The dam, a modest 5f winner, is a half-sister to 8 winners including the 2,000 Guineas and Irish 2,000 Guineas winner Cockney Rebel. The second dam, Factice (by Known Fact), an Irish 2-y-o 5f winner, is a half-sister to 5 winners. *"He moves well, the mare's had three winners from three runners and one of them won as a 2-y-o, so this colt will have a chance of winning later on this season. I like everything he does, he has a good mind on him, a good way about him and I really like the sire. This colt does nothing wrong and looking at him you couldn't say he*

won't be a 2-y-o because he's quite short-coupled and solid. Probably one for seven furlongs in the second half of the season".

1211. MOONLIGHT SILVER ★★
gr.f. Makfi – Moon Empress (Rainbow Quest). March 18. Fifth foal. 20,000Y. Tattersalls October Book 3. William Muir. Half-sister to the moderate 2015 1m placed 2-y-o Lunar Son (by Medicean) and to the useful 2-y-o 1m winner and Group 3 Autumn Stakes second Restorer (by Mastercraftsman). The dam, a fair dual 12f winner, is a half-sister to one winner. The second dam, Diamoona (by Last Tycoon), a French listed-placed winner, is a half-sister to 8 winners including the French Group winners Diamond Mix, Diamond Dance and Diasilixa. *"A very nice-moving filly, the owner didn't get what he wanted for her at the sales so I was the lucky man to get to train her. She's a better mover than her brother Restorer, more athletic, I like the family and I like the sire. One for the middle to back-end of the season. A filly with a lot of character and she does everything right".* **TRAINERS' BARGAIN BUY**

1212. PHIJEE ★★★★
br.c. Sepoy – Likeable (Dalakhani). March 3. Fifth foal. 30,000Y. Tattersalls October Book 1. William Muir. Half-brother to the 2015 7f placed 2-y-o White Shaheen (by Makfi). The dam is an unraced half-sister to 4 winners including the UAE Grade 2 and Group 3 Select Stakes winner Alkaadhem. The second dam, Balalaika (by Sadler's Wells), a useful 4-y-o listed 9f winner, is a sister to the high-class Group 2 10f Prince of Wales's Stakes and dual US Grade 2 winner Stagecraft and a half-sister to 5 winners including the Group 3 Strensall Stakes winner Mullins Bay. *"I went to look for him at the sale because I think his half-brother White Shaheen is pretty useful. It's a nice family, I like him a lot and he shows he's got talent. He's out of a Dalakhani mare and I'll need to take my time with him but I really like what I see".*

1213. QUEEN BEATRICE ★★★
b.f. Iffraaj – Skirrid (Halling). January 23. Second foal. 20,000Y. Tattersalls October Book 2. Not sold. Half-sister to the quite useful 2015 2-y-o 6f winner Easy Code (by Bahamian Bounty). The dam is an unraced half-sister to 5 winners including the smart 10f and 12f and subsequent US Grade 2 8.5f and dual Grade 3 winner Spice Route. The second dam, Zanzibar (by In The Wings), winner of the Group 1 11f Italian Oaks, is a half-sister to 2 winners. *"A home-bred, she could be sharper than most and she's from a very good family. Not overly-big, we could crack on and start doing something with her now. She was only broken-in after Christmas but she's done really well".*

1214. QUEEN'S LIGHT ★★
b.f. Fastnet Rock – Quesada (Peintre Celebre). February 3. Second foal. €42,000Y. Arqana Deauville August. William Muir. The dam, a German listed 1m winner, is a half-sister to one winner. The second dam, Queen Of Fire (by Dr Fong), a fairly useful 2-y-o 6f winner, was listed-placed at 3 yrs and is a half-sister to 2 winners. *"The first filly I bought at the yearling sales, being by Fastnet Rock she'll take plenty of time but she moves well and does everything nicely. I like her a lot and she's owned by a lucky man".*

1215. TEXAS WEDGE ★★★★
b.c. Foxwedge – Sacre Coeur (Compton Place). May 15. Fourth foal. 32,000Y. Tattersalls October Book 2. William Muir. Half-brother to the Group 2 Sapphire Stakes and Group 3 Flying Five Stakes winner and Group 1 placed Stepper Point (by Kyllachy), to the fair 2-y-o 5f winner Cross My Heart (by Sakhee's Secret) and the modest 5f (at 2 yrs) to 7f winner Gulland Rock (by Exceed And Excel). The dam, a fair 2-y-o 6f winner, is a half-sister to 5 winners including the listed-placed dual 10f winner Lonely Heart (dam of the Group 3 Tetrarch Stakes winner Leitrim House). The second dam, Take Heart (by Electric), a quite useful 7f to 10f winner, is a half-sister to 3 winners. *"He's Stepper Point's half-brother so at the sale I probably found it hard to turn away from him, but saying that I don't think he was expensive. The family take time to come to themselves but we know they're good once they're there. I also had Gulland Rock out of the family and he won as a 2-y-o but this colt is more like Stepper Point in that he's quite short-coupled. I like him a lot but he was a late foal so I'll wait with him but he's making up into a strong little horse".*

1216. UNNAMED ★★★
b.c. Raven's Pass – Crystal Melody (Nureyev). February 20. Seventh foal. 33,000Y. Tattersalls October Book 2. William Muir. Half-brother to the US Grade 2 8.5f Dahlia Handicap and French listed winner Grande Melody, to the quite useful 10f winner Crystal Swan (by Dalakhani) and a minor winner in the USA by Grand Lodge. The dam is an unraced sister to the Group 1 Fillies' Mile winner Crystal Music and a half-sister to 6 winners including the Group 3 winners Solar Crystal, State Crystal and Dubai Success. The second dam, Crystal Spray (by Beldale Flutter), a minor Irish 4-y-o 14f winner, is a half-sister to 8 winners including the Group 3 Scottish Classic winner Crystal Hearted. *"A nice colt, the mare's had three winners from five runners including a Grade 2 and it's something of a staying family but this colt has definitely got something about him. He moves well, takes everything you can give him and I think he was cheap. He's a bit of a Jack the Lad so I have to do a bit of work with him and I'd say he'd be one for the second half of the season".*

1217. UNNAMED ★★
ch.f. Bahamian Bounty – Dame Shirley (Haafhd). May 5. First foal. The dam, unplaced in two starts, is a half-sister to 4 winners including the useful 7f winner (here) and UAE Group 3 5f winner Fityaan. The second dam, Welsh Diva (by Selkirk), an Italian Group 3 1m and Ascot listed 1m winner, is a sister to 2 winners including the Group 2 1m Prix du Rond-Point and Group 3 8.5f Diomed Stakes winner Trans Island and a half-sister to 6 winners. *"A big filly, she does things well and she's from a nice, speedy family. I like her although she was one of the last to be broken-in so I haven't done a lot with her yet".*

1218. UNNAMED ★★
b.c. Poet's Voice – Electric Feel (Firebreak). March 9. First foal. The dam, a useful listed 7f winner and second in the Group 3 Oh So Sharp Stakes, is a half-sister to 5 winners. The second dam, Night Gypsy (by Mind Games), a fair 2-y-o 5f winner, is a sister to 2 winners including the listed 2-y-o winner On The Brink and a half-sister to 3 winners including the listed winner and dual Group 3 placed Eastern Romance. *"He's quite a nice individual and although he was only broken-in late he's caught up well. I think the sire still has to prove himself though".*

1219. UNNAMED ★★
b.f. Royal Applause – Miss University (Beau Genius). March 5. Twelfth foal. Half-sister to the US Grade 2 winner and triple Grade 1 placed Three Degrees, the minor US winners Megaspiel (both by Singspiel) and Vapour Musing (by Manduro), the quite useful 7f (at 2 yrs) and 6f winner Mehronissa (by Iffraaj) and a winner over hurdles by Erhaab. The dam ran unplaced twice and is a half-sister to 9 winners. The second dam, Gorgeously Divine (by Al Hattab), is an unplaced half-sister to 3 winners. *"A home-bred, she has a nice page and is a sweet-natured filly that'll take a bit of time. A good mover, last year's 2-y-o out of the dam won but I can't press on with this filly yet. I like the way she moves and her attitude".*

1220. UNNAMED ★★★★
ch.c. Exceed And Excel – Putois Peace (Pivotal). February 13. Second living foal. 120,000Y. Tattersalls October Book 1. William Muir. Half-brother to Calvados Spirit (by Invincible Spirit), unplaced in two starts at 2 yrs in 2015. The dam is an unraced half-sister to 8 winners including the Group 2 12f Lancashire Oaks winner Pongee, the listed 12f and listed 14f winner Lion Sands and the dam of the French Group 3 winner Pacifique. The second dam, Puce (by Darshaan), a very useful listed 12f winner, is a half-sister to 10 winners including the dam of the dual Oaks winner Alexandrova and the Cheveley Park Stakes winner Magical Romance. *"A half-brother to Calvados Spirit who I love, he's a big horse, stronger than Calvados and I thought he'd cost more than he did. One for the middle to back-end of the season over seven furlongs. I like him a lot".*

1221. UNNAMED ★★★★
br.c. Shamardal – Saphira's Fire (Cape Cross). March 19. Third foal. Half-brother to the very useful 2015 2-y-o Group 3 6f Grangecon Stud Stakes winner Most Beautiful (by Canford Cliffs) and to the modest 1m winner Pick Your Battle (by Makfi). The dam, a listed 10f winner, was twice placed third in the Group 2 Pride Stakes and is a half-sister to 2 winners.

The second dam, All Our Hope (by Gulch), a winner at 3 yrs and third in the Sun Chariot Stakes, is a half-sister to 7 winners. *"He could be anything. A really nice individual by a good stallion, there's no reason why he couldn't be a very nice 2-y-o. The only reason he's not bashing on with the others is because of a small setback but that's settled down now. I like him a lot".*

1222. UNNAMED ★★★★
b.f. Kyllachy – Secret Era (Cape Cross). February 2. First foal. The dam, a modest 9f winner, is a half-sister to 2 winners including the useful 10f and 11f winner of 7 races Area Fifty One. The second dam, Secret History (by Bahri), won 4 races including the Group 3 Musidora Stakes and is a half-sister to 6 winners including the Group 3 7f Prix du Calvados second Laureldean Gale and the US stakes winner Costume Designer. *"She didn't go to the sales because the owners wanted to keep the first filly out of the mare. I love her, she's a big, strong filly that moves well and I trained both her dam and her half-brother Area Fifty One. She's got better conformation than either of them and I love the sire. I like her a lot and she could be a decent 2-y-o".*

1223. UNNAMED ★★
b.c. Cacique – Snow Crystal (Kingmambo). March 17. Sixth foal. 68,000Y. Tattersalls October Book 2. William Muir. Half-sister to the fair 12f winner Sky Crystal (by Galileo) and to a minor winner abroad by Monsun. The dam, a quite useful 2-y-o 7f winner, is a half-sister to 6 winners including the Group 1 Fillies' mile winner Crystal Music and the Group 3 winners Solar Crystal, Dubai Success and State Crystal and to the unraced dam of the US Grade 2 winner Grande Melody. The second dam, Crystal Spray (by Beldale Flutter), a minor Irish 4-y-o 14f winner, is a half-sister to 8 winners including the Group 2 winner Crystal Hearted. *"The mare's had two winners from four runners and I do like this little horse, I like the way he does everything. He's just growing and going through an ugly duckling stage at the moment but he does do everything well. Cacique's take a bit of time so I'll need to be patient with him".*

1224. UNNAMED ★★★★
ch.c. Dutch Art – Thrill (Pivotal). May 6. Third foal. 160,000Y. Tattersalls October Book 1. William Muir. Half-brother to the fair 5f (at 2 yrs) and 6f winner Effusive (by Starspangledbanner). The dam, a quite useful 2-y-o 7f winner, is a full or half-sister to 4 winners including the 7f (at 2 yrs) and Group 3 7f Nell Gwyn Stakes winner and Coronation Stakes and Falmouth Stakes second Infallible and to the unraced dam of the Group 1 Prix Maurice de Gheest winner Garswood. The second dam, Irresistible (by Cadeaux Genereux), a fairly useful 5f (at 2 yrs) and listed 6f winner, is a half-sister to 2 winners. *"I have a lot of time for him. He moves well and he's a bonny colt but a May foal so I'll take my time with him. I like the family, there's plenty of speed in there and he does everything right. A good-looker, he could be a very nice individual and I really like him".*

1225. UNNAMED ★★
b.c. Equiano – Varnish (Choisir). February 28. First foal. The dam, a quite useful 10f and 12f winner, is a half-sister to one winner. The second dam, Bronze Star (by Mark Of Esteem), a modest dual 10f winner, is a half-sister to 4 winners including the Group 2 12f Ribblesdale Stakes second Eldalil and the dam of the Group 3 winner Cappella Sansevero. *"A big, strong, sturdy colt that has a great temperament for an Equiano, he moves well and I think he could have a big future. He looks like some of the big, strong, powerful-to-the-eye Equiano's I've seen. I like him, he moves well but I wouldn't rush him".*

JEREMY NOSEDA

1226. EUQRANIAN (USA) ★★★
b.f. Galileo – Anne Of Kiev (Oasis Dream). January 16. Second foal. $320,000Y. Keeneland September. The dam, a useful listed 5f and listed 6f winner, is a half-sister to 5 winners. The second dam, Top Flight Queen (Mark Of Esteem), a quite useful 10f winner, is a half-sister to 6 winners including the Group 2 Great Voltigeur Stakes winner Sacrament and to the unraced dam of the Group 1 Pretty Polly Stakes winner Chorist. (Marc Keller). *"She's in America, cantering and in pre-training out there. She's done really well and she'll keep improving but she's a late summer type filly".*

1227. INTERLOPE (IRE) ★★★
b.f. Fastnet Rock – Kiyra Wells (Sadler's Wells). March 30. Fourth foal. €200,000Y. Goffs Orby. Fiona Shaw/Marc Keller. Closely related to the quite useful 6f winner Seas Of Wells (by Dansili) and half-sister to the quite useful 10f winner Lilian Bayliss (by Shamardal). The dam, a quite useful 7f winner, is closely related to the Group 1 Phoenix Stakes and Group 2 Queen Mary Stakes winner Damson (dam of the 2-y-o Group 2 winner Requinto) and the Group 3 7f Prestige Stakes winner and Group 3 Musidora Stakes second Geminiani. The second dam, Tadkiyra (by Darshaan), a French 10f winner, is a half-sister to the Group 3 winners Tashtiya, Tassmoun and Tashkourgan. (Marc Keller). *"A lovely filly with a great action and a good temperament. A late summer prospect, she's a lovely, well-balanced filly that moves well and I like her".*

1228. INTREPIDLY (USA) ★★★
b.c. Medaglia D'Oro – Trepidation (Seeking The Gold). March 18. Ninth foal. Half-brother to 3 winners including the Group 3 6f Round Tower Stakes (at 2 yrs) and the Group 3 7f Leopardstown 1,000 Guineas Trial winner Maoineach (by Congaree) and the US listed winner and Group 2 placed Tiz Now Tiz Then (by Tiznow). The dam is an unraced half-sister to 4 winners. The second dam, Troubling (by Storm Cat), is an unraced half-sister to 5 winners. (The Hon. Earl Mack & T Hind Racing). *"A good-moving horse, he's straightforward and with a good attitude. He looks to me like a mid-summer 2-y-o for fast ground and I'm delighted with him at this stage. I view him as a seven furlong horse".*

1229. JUS PIRES (USA) ★★★★
br.c. Scat Daddy – Liza Lu (Menifee). February 25. Fourth foal. Brother to the fair 2015 2-y-o 7f winner, on his only start, Good Intent. The dam won 3 minor races in the USA at 3 and 4 yrs and is a half-sister to 2 winners. The second dam, Chamrousse (by Peaks And Valleys), won 4 races including the Grade 2 Black-Eyed Susan Handicap and was second in the Grade 1 Mother Goose Stakes and is a half-sister to 7 winners including My Name's Jimmy (Group 2 American Derby). (Nigel O'Sullivan). *"A big, strong imposing horse, he's one for late summer/autumn over seven furlongs. I like what I see and he's got the size, strength and scope to be a good horse in time. He's a horse I really like and if I have a proper one amongst my 2-y-o's he could be the one".*

1230. LIGHT HUMOR (USA) ★★★
br.f. Distorted Humor – Aldebaran Light (Seattle Slew). May 2. Tenth foal. Half-sister to 3 winners including the 2-y-o Group 1 6f Middle Park Stakes and Group 2 6f Gimcrack Stakes winner Balmont (by Stravinsky) and the US Grade 1 Wood Memorial Stakes winner Eskendereya (by Giant's Causeway). The dam, a winner of 3 races at around 1m in the USA, is a half-sister to 3 winners including the 2-y-o 5.2f and subsequent US Grade 2 Blazonry. The second dam, Altair (by Alydar), is an unraced half-sister to one winner. (S Robertson). *"She's currently in America but I've seen her twice this winter and she's cantering each day. She's backward and I wouldn't expect to get her out before the autumn. A good mover and light on her feet. I'm happy enough with her".*

1231. UNNAMED ★★★
b.c. Dragon Pulse – Emsiyah (Bernardini). April 22. Second foal. €120,000Y. Goffs Orby. Jeremy Noseda. Half-brother to the fair 2015 dual 1m placed 2-y-o Absolute Zero (by Cape Cross). The dam ran twice unplaced and is a half-sister to one winner. The second dam, Menhoubah (by Dixieland Band), won the Group 1 Italian Oaks, was third in the 2-y-o Group 1 Moyglare Stud Stakes and is a half-sister to 2 winners. (Paul Roy). *"A lovely, good-moving horse with a lot of scope, he's going to take a lot of time and is an autumn type 2-y-o. He's a good individual and I was underbidder on Dragon Pulse as a yearling. I saw this colt out of the corner of my eye at Goffs and he was such a lovely individual I thought I had to give it a go".*

1232. UNNAMED ★★★★
b.f. Giant's Causeway – High On The Hill (Fusaichi Pegasus). February 28. Third foal. $360,000 2-y-o. Ocala Breeze Up Sale. The dam is an unraced half-sister to 5 winners including Lil's Lad (Grade 2 Fountain Of Youth Stakes), Cherokee (Group 3 Round Tower Stakes) and the Irish listed winner Art Museum. The second dam, Totemic (by Vanlandingham), won the Grade 3 Honeybee

Stakes in the USA. (Marc Keller). *"I did particularly well with my purchases at the Ocala breeze up sale last year, especially with Nemoralia who was Grade 1 placed for me twice in America and with Abe Lincoln who is rated 93. So I went back to Ocala recently and I bought three 2-y-o's from the breeze up including this one. I loved her when I saw her at her consignor's in February, went to the sale and was impressed with the way she breezed – she did two furlongs in twenty and four fifths. I really like her, she looks a great type to me and I'd say she's an August type filly with the scope to be a 3-y-o as well. I'd be very disappointed if she couldn't be making an impact this year. She's got size, scope and quality and I'm delighted with her".*

1233. UNNAMED ★★★
b.c. Choisir – Katherine Lee (Azamour). February 4. First foal. 60,000Y. Tattersalls October Book 2. J Noseda. The dam, a quite useful dual 1m winner, is a half-sister to 4 winners. The second dam, Lady Of Kildare (by Mujadil), a fairly useful 2-y-o listed 6f winner, is a half-sister to one winner. (Paul Roy). *"A good, solid individual that moves well, I'm pleased with him and he's a nice, straightforward horse. The sort that should be ready by mid to late summer and I'd be hopeful of him winning as a 2-y-o".*

1234. UNNAMED ★★★
br.f. Wildcat Heir – Love In Bloom (More Than Ready). January 19. Second foal. $165,000 2-y-o. Ocala Breeze Up Sale. Half-sister to a minor 3-y-o winner in the USA by Pomeroy. The dam, a minor US 4-y-o winner, is a half-sister to the minor US stakes winner Our Eleanor. The second dam, Pretty Jane (by Subordination), a US stakes winner of 5 races, was Grade 2 placed. *"Another one of my Ocala purchases, I'm not sure about the sire but to me this filly looks like the damsire More Than Ready and I've had a bit of luck with that stallion. She breezed very fast, I liked her as an individual and she looked sharp and early. A nice filly, she's just started back training in America and she'll be with here with me in mid-April. I hope to be running her in late May, she'll want fast ground and I bought her specifically to be an Ascot 2-y-o. She reminds me of the ones I've had a lot of luck with in the past".*

1235. UNNAMED ★★★
b.br.c. Stay Thirsty – Milliondollarbill (Speightstown). February 25. Third foal. $100,000 2-y-o. Ocala Breeze Up Sale. The dam, a minor US winner of 4 races at 3 yrs, is a half-sister to 3 winners including the US Grade 2 winner Brooke's Halo. The second dam, Salty lady (by Salt Lake), was 3 races at 3 yrs in the USA and was Grade 3 placed and is a half-sister to 6 winners. *"A neat, very racy horse, bought at the breeze up sale where he breezed quickly, he was bought to be a sharp, early 2-y-o and he looks that. The sire is a son of Bernardini who is more of a dirt stallion than turf, but the dam won on the grass as did her sire Speightstown who is a track record holder at Santa Anita over five furlongs. It's a fast pedigree and this horse looks that way as well, so he'll be a real, sharp 2-y-o".*

1236. UNNAMED ★★★
ch.f. Dutch Art – Parakopi (Green Desert). February 23. Fourth foal. €50,000Y. Goffs Orby. MPH Racing. Half-sister to the modest 7f to 8.5f winner Tanawar (by Elusive City). The dam, a minor winner at 3 yrs in Germany, is a half-sister to 2 winners abroad. The second dam, Siringas (by Barathea), won the Group 2 Nassau Stakes and the listed Brownstown Stakes and is a half-sister to 4 winners. *"A good mover, she's grown a lot but she's developed in the right way. I'm more than happy with her progress at this point and I view her as likely to be ready around July/August. Six/seven furlongs should be fine for her".*

1237. UNNAMED ★★★★
b.c. More Than Ready – Return The Jewel (Broken Vow). January 19. Second foal. $40,000Y. Keeneland January. Not sold. The dam was a stakes-placed winner of 3 races in the USA. The second dam, Appealing Jewel (by Saint Ballado), was placed in the USA and is a half-sister to 11 winners. (Paul Roy). *"My most precocious 2-y-o, he's already done a couple of half-speeds and I'm more than hopeful he'll be running at the end of April. He's definitely got the ability to win races and I'm hopeful he'll be even better than that. He looks like he's got the speed to run over five furlongs but he'll get six, maybe even seven later. A fast ground horse, he looks tough and sturdy".*

THE LIVING LEGEND RACING PARTNERSHIP

For an inexpensive way to enjoy the benefits of being a racehorse owner, join us in 2016.

Call Steve Taplin on 07754 094204
or e-mail stevetaplin@blueyonder.co.uk

At Park House Stables, Kingsclere. March 2016

HARBOUR WATCH

THERE'S A STORM BREWING

ACT OF VALOUR
HARBOUR WATCH x B BERRY BRANDY

Michael O'Callaghan
Trainer

" My Harbour Watch is a very nice colt with size and scope who is quite precocious and forward in his work now. He's a lovely moving horse with a lot of power and does everything so easily. He should be very nice. "

OPENING TIME
HARBOUR WATCH x DOZY

Richard Hannon
Trainer

" A lovely horse. He finds it all very easy, he's a good mover and although we haven't done any work with him yet when we do I'm sure we'll find he has an engine. "

DEE BLERE
HARBOUR WATCH x SISTER SWANK

François Rohaut
Trainer

" My Harbour Watch is an exciting filly who has a mature physique and a great temperament. She looks quite precocious. "

HARBOUR WATCH x JULES

Mick Channon
Trainer

" This filly is very nice, sharp and certainly a 2yo. She's well put together and one to look out for because she looks like an athlete and joined the top group quickly. "

QATAR BLOODSTOCK

+44 (0)1452 700177
www.tweenhills.com

TWEENHILLS

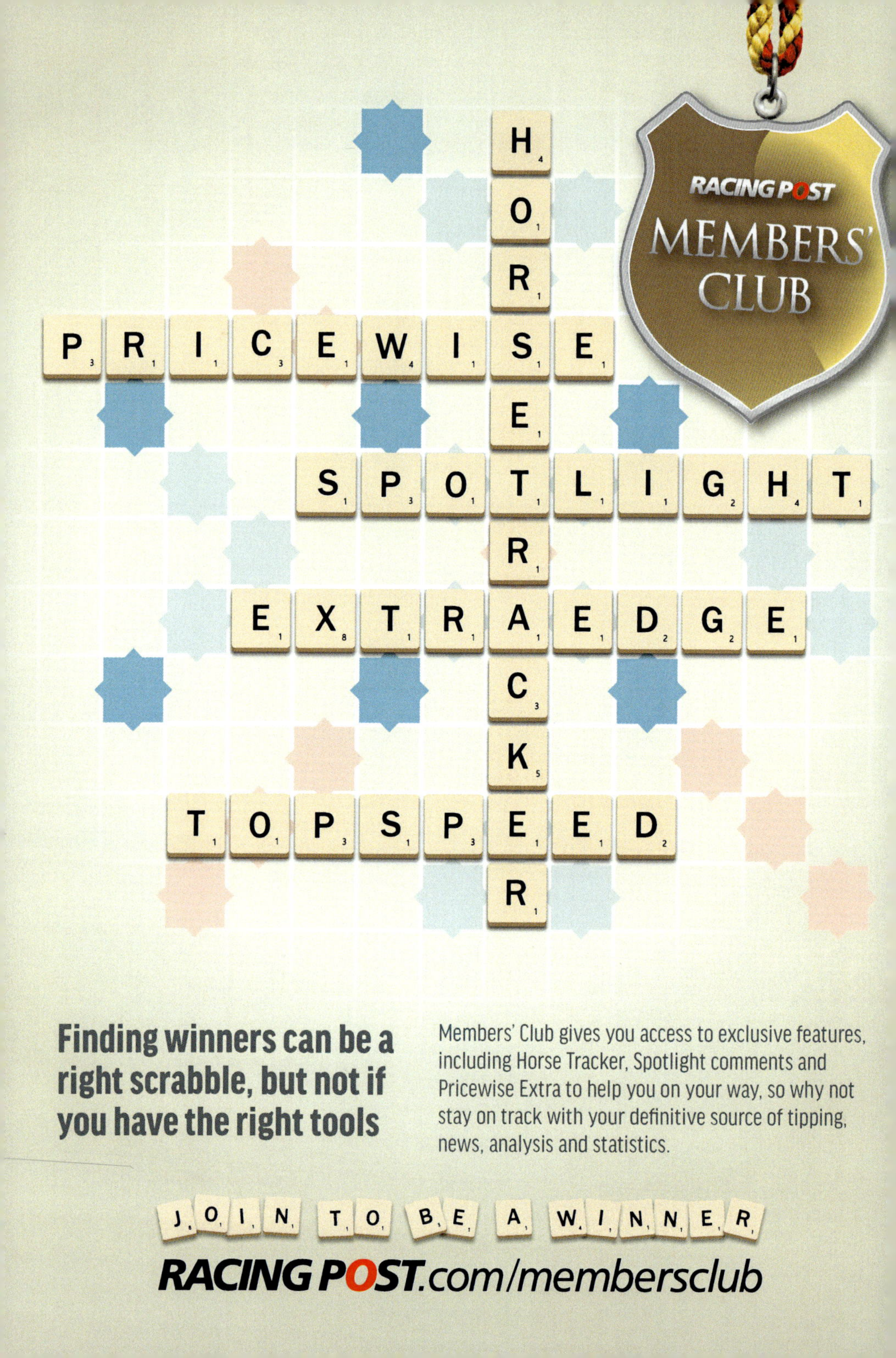

1238. UNNAMED ★★★
b.f. Sixties Icon – Spinning Lucy (Spinning World). February 12. Third foal. The dam, a 2-y-o listed 6f winner, is a half-sister to the 2-y-o listed 6f Bosra Sham Stakes winner Midris. The second dam, Dolara (by Dolphin Street), is an unraced half-sister to 4 winners including Idris, a winner of four Group 3 races in Ireland. (Paul Roy). *"A nice, solid, well-made filly, she needs time to mature and I don't envisage getting her out before the autumn. She's been with me for six weeks now and we're definitely seeing progress".*

1239. UNNAMED ★★
b.f. Lonhro – Wear Red (Henny Hughes). April 3. Third foal. The dam, a winner over 1m at 2 yrs in the USA, is a half-sister to the 2-y-o Group 1 6f Middle Park Stakes and Group 2 6f Gimcrack Stakes winner Balmont (by Stravinsky) and the US Grade 1 Wood Memorial Stakes winner Eskendereya (by Giant's Causeway). The second dam, Aldebaran Light (Seattle Slew), a winner of 3 races at around 1m in the USA, is a half-sister to 3 winners including the 2-y-o 5.2f and subsequent US Grade 2 Blazonry. (Sandy Robertson). *"She's in America and I haven't seen her for a little while, she needed a bit of time after the sale and she's in pre-training now. She'll appear here in mid-May and we won't see her on the track before the autumn".*

AIDAN O'BRIEN

Aidan's son and assistant trainer, Joseph, is in charge of some of these two-year-olds, including Hyzenthlay who won a fillies' maiden at Naas in mid-April.

1240. AMBIGUITY
b.c. Fastnet Rock – Descant (Nureyev). March 15. Brother to the Group 3 1m Desmond Stakes winner Cougar Mountain and half-brother to several winners including the useful 7f and 1m winner of 4 races Roaring Forte (by Cape Cross) and the fair 5f and 6f winner Far Note (by Distant View). The dam is an unraced half-sister to numerous winners including Zafonic and Zamindar. The second dam, Zaizafon (by The Minstrel), won twice over 7f at 2 yrs, was placed in the Group 1 1m Queen Elizabeth II Stakes and is a half-sister to the unraced Modena, herself dam of the Eclipse Stakes and Phoenix Champion Stakes winner Elmaamul.

1241. ARMY GENERAL (USA)
b.c. War Front – Charming (Seeking The Gold). May 28. $1,250,000Y. Saratoga August. Willis B Horton. Half-brother to the US 2-y-o dual Grade 1 8.5f winner Take Charge Brandi (by Giant's Causeway). The dam, a minor winner in the USA, is a half-sister to the US Grade 1 winners Take Charge Indy and Will Take Charge. The second dam, Take Charge Lady, won three US Grade 1 events.

1242. BRAVE ANNA
b.f. War Front – Liscanna (Sadler's Wells). May 12. Sixth foal. Sister to the 2015 2-y-o Grade 1 Breeders' Cup Juvenile Turf winner Hit It A Bomb. The dam, an Irish 2-y-o Group 3 6f Ballyogan Stakes winner, is a half-sister to the Irish 7.5f (at 2 yrs) and Group 3 10f Kilternan Stakes winner and dual Group 2 placed The Bogberry. The second dam, Lahinch (by Danehill Dancer), a useful listed 5f (at 2 yrs) and listed 6f winner, was second in the Group 2 Rockfel Stakes and is a half-sister to 7 winners including the smart 2-y-o 5f and subsequent US stakes winner Perugino Bay.

1243. CARAVAGGIO (USA)
gr.c. Scat Daddy – Mekko Hokte (Holy Bull). February 23. Sixth foal. Half-brother to the US Grade 2 8.5f winner My Jen (by Fusaichi Pegasus). The dam is out of Aerosilver (by Relaunch).

1244. CASTLE HOWARD
b.c. Excelebration – Four Eleven (Arch). March 6. First foal. €220,000foal. Goffs November foals. M V Magnier. The dam, a minor winner at 3 yrs in the USA, is a half-sister to 6 winners including the Group 3 Prix des Reservoirs winner Summertime Legacy (herself dam of the Group 1 winners Mandaean and Wavering). The second dam, Zawaahy (by El Gran Senor), a fairly useful 1m winner, was placed at up to 11.5f and is closely related to the Derby winner Golden Fleece.

1245. CLIFFS OF MOHER (IRE)
b.c. Galileo – Wave (Dansili). March 12. First foal. The dam, a quite useful 2-y-o 5f

winner, is closely related to the very useful 6f (at 2 yrs) and listed 7f winner Francis Of Assisi and to the listed 1m winner and Group 2 10f Blandford Stakes second Look At Me. The second dam, Queen Cleopatra (by Kingmambo), won the Group 3 Irish 1,000 Guineas Trial, was third in the Irish 1,000 Guineas and the Prix de Diane and is a sister to the multiple Group 1 1m winner Henrythenavigator.

1246. CUFF (IRE)
ch.f. Galileo – Massarra (Danehill). February 8. Sister to the 2-y-o Group 3 7f Silver Flash Stakes winner Wonderfully, to the Irish 2-y-o 7f winner and Group 1 St James's Palace Stakes third Mars and the fairly useful 2-y-o 7f winner Toscanelli and half-sister to 3 winners including the 2-y-o Group 1 1m Gran Criterium winner Nayarra (by Cape Cross). The dam, a useful listed 6f winner and second in the Group 2 Prix Robert Papin at 2 yrs, is a sister to one winner, closely related to the Group 1 6f Haydock Park Sprint Cup winner Invincible Spirit and a half-sister to the Group 3 winners Acts Of Grace and Sadian. The second dam, Rafha (by Kris), won the Group 1 10.5f Prix de Diane, the Group 3 Lingfield Oaks Trial and the Group 3 May Hill Stakes and is a half-sister to 9 winners.

1247. DIODORUS
b.c. Galileo – Divine Proportions (Kingmambo). May 9. Half-brother to the 2-y-o Group 3 6f Prix Eclipse and 5-y-o listed 1m winner Eightfold Path and to the French 9.5f winner Monoceros (both by Giant's Causeway). The dam, a champion 3-y-o filly and multiple Group 1 winner, is a full or half-sister to 11 winners including the triple Group 1 winner Whipper. The second dam, Myth To Reality (by Sadler's Wells), a triple listed winner of 4 races at 3 yrs in France, was second in the Group 3 Prix de Minerve and is a full or half-sister to 6 winners.

1248. ELIZABETH BROWNING (IRE)
b.f. Galileo – Inca Princess (Holy Roman Emperor). April 15. Second foal. Sister to the 2015 2-y-o Group 1 7f Criterium International winner and Group 1 Racing Post Trophy second Johannes Vermeer. The dam, a quite useful Irish 2-y-o 6f winner, is a half-sister to 2 winners including the smart Irish 10f and 13f winner Changingoftheguard. The second dam, Miletrian (by Marju), a smart Group 2 Ribblesdale Stakes and Group 3 Park Hill Stakes winner, is a sister to one winner and a half-sister to the Group 2 Geoffrey Freer Stakes winner Mr Combustible.

1249. ENSIGN ♠
b.c. Invincible Spirit – Alta Moda (Sadler's Wells). February 11. Fifth foal. 190,000Y. Tattersalls October Book 2. M V Magnier. Half-brother to the fairly useful 2-y-o 7.5f winner and dual listed-placed Groor (by Archipenko) and to the useful 2-y-o dual 7f and US dual 9f winner Ghurair (by Elusive Quality). The dam is an unraced half-sister to 4 winners including the listed Prix Petite Etoile winner Alvarita. The second dam, Alborada (by Alzao), winner of the Champion Stakes (twice), the Group 2 Nassau Stakes and the Group 2 Pretty Polly Stakes, is a sister to the triple German Group 1 winner Albanova and a half-sister to 7 winners.

1250. FALLING LEAVES (IRE)
b.f. Galileo – Again (Danehill Dancer). January 26. Second foal. Sister to the 2-y-o listed 7.5f winner Indian Maharaja. The dam won the 2-y-o Group 1 Moyglare Stud Stakes and the Irish 1,000 Guineas and is closely related to 2 winners including the fairly useful 9f winner and Group 3 12f third Arkadina. The second dam, Cumbres (by Kahyasi), is an unraced half-sister to Montjeu.

1251. GUSTAV KLIMT
b.c. Galileo – Miarixa (Linamix). April 5. Seventh foal. Brother to the fair 2016 3-y-o 7f winner Stars At Night and half-brother to the 1,000 Guineas, Irish Oaks and Yorkshire Oaks winner Blue Bunting (by Dynaformer) and the modest 2m and hurdles winner Descaro (by Dr Fong). The dam is an unraced sister to the French winner and Group 3 placed Mister Kick and a half-sister to 3 winners including the French listed winner Marque Royale (the dam of two listed winners). The second dam, Mrs Arkada (by Akarad), a listed winner and third in the Group 1 Prix Saint-Alary, is a half-sister to the Group 3 winners Mister Sicy, Manninamix and Mister Riv.

1252. HOW (IRE)
b.f. Galileo – Lillie Langtry (Danehill Dancer). May 17. Second foal. Sister to the 2015 2-y-o Group 1 Moyglare Stud Stakes and Group 1 Fillies' Mile winner Minding and to the Group 3 1m Irish 1,00 Guineas Trial winner Kissed By Angels. The dam, a very smart winner of 5 races including the Group 1 1m Coronation Stakes and Group 1 1m Matron Stakes, is a half-sister to 2 winners including the very useful 3-y-o listed 1m winner and 2-y-o Group 3 6f Anglesey Stakes third Count Of Limonade. The second dam, Hoity Toity (Darshaan), is an unraced half-sister to 5 winners.

1253. HYDRANGEA (IRE)
b.f. Galileo – Beauty Is Truth (Pivotal). April 1. Sister to the 7f (at 2 yrs), Group 3 10f and Australian Group 2 12.5f winner The United States and to the useful 2-y-o 9f winner Buonarotti and half-sister to the triple Group 3 6f winner and dual Group 1 placed Fire Lily (by Dansili). The dam, winner of the Group 2 5f Prix de Gros-Chene, is a half-sister to numerous winners including the French listed 9f winner Glorious Sight. The second dam, Zelda (by Caerleon), a French 6.5f winner, is closely related to the dam of the French 1,000 Guineas winner Valentine Waltz and a half-sister to the dual Group 1 winner Last Tycoon and the Group winners Astronef and The Perfect Life.

1254. HYZENTHLAY (IRE)
b.f. Henrythenavigator – Anka Britannia (Irish River). March 22. Half-sister to the French 12f and German 11f winner and Group 3 placed Britannic, to the French 10f and 11f winner Cool Britannia (both by Rainbow Quest), the fair 12f winner of 4 races Asia Minor (by Pivotal) and a minor winner in Italy by In The Wings. The dam, placed at 3 yrs in France, is a half-sister to 4 winners including the US Grade 1 10f winner Deputy Commander. The second dam, Anka Germania (by Malinowski), won 16 races in France and the USA including a US Grade 1 12f event and is a half-sister to 5 winners including the US Grade 1 winner Mourjane. This filly won a fillies' maiden at Naas over five furlongs in mid-April.

1255. ISTAN
b.c. Excelebration – Something Exciting (Halling). February 25. Sixth foal. €150,000Y. Goffs Orby. Amanda Skiffington. Half-brother to the fair triple 5f winner Fascinating (by Cape Cross) and to Somethingthrilling (by Makfi), a quite useful 7f winner on her only start. The dam won 4 races over 1m and 10f at 2 and 3 yrs including the listed Lupe Stakes and was second in the Epsom Oaks and is a half-sister to one winner. The second dam, Faraway Waters (by Pharly), a useful 6f winner (at 2 yrs) and listed 10f Pretty Polly Stakes second, is a half-sister to 7 winners including the UAE Group 3 winner Gower Song.

1256. JUSTICE FREDERICK
b.c. Lawman – Sheer Spirit (Caerleon). February 15. Half-brother to numerous winners including the Group 2 10f Blandford Stakes and Group 3 9f Kilboy Estate Stakes winner Manieree (by Medicean), the useful 6f (at 2 yrs) and 7f winner River Bravo (by Indian Ridge), the fairly useful 10f winner and listed-placed Bold Choice (by Dubai Destination) and the fairly useful listed-placed 2-y-o 6f to 1m winner Solid Rock (by Rock Of Gibraltar). The dam won over 12f and is a half-sister to 9 winners including the Derby winner Oath and the triple Group 1 winner Pelder. The second dam, Sheer Audacity (by Troy), placed twice in Italy, is closely related to the Ribblesdale Stakes winner and good broodmare Miss Petard.

1257. NORTH CAROLINA (IRE)
b.c. Galileo – Tarbela (Grand Lodge). May 9. Eighth foal. Half-brother to the smart 2-y-o listed 7f and listed 1m winner Big Audio (by Oratorio), to the modest 6f winner Spiritual Healing (by Invincible Spirit) and a minor winner abroad by Kheleyf. The dam, a moderate 7f placed 2-y-o in Ireland, is a half-sister to 3 winners and to the dams of the Group 1 winners Arcano and Gilt Edge Girl. The second dam, Tarwiya (by Dominion), won the Group 3 7f C L Weld Park Stakes, was third in the Irish 1,000 Guineas and is a half-sister to 5 winners including the Group 3 Norfolk Stakes winner Blue Dakota.

1258. PEACE ENVOY
b.c. Power – Hoh My Darling (Dansili). March 14. €125,000Y. Arqana Deauville August. Horse France. Half-sister to 5 winners including the 12f Czech Derby winner and French 2-y-o Group 3 1m Prix des Chenes third Kadyny (by Zamindar), the French 7.5f and 8.5f winner Halowin (by Beat Hollow) and the French 9.5f and 10.5f winner Pretty Darling (by Le Havre). The dam, a modest 10f winner, is a half-sister to the useful 2-y-o 7f winner and Group 3 May Hill Stakes third Everlasting Love. The second dam, Now And Forever (by Kris), is an unraced half-sister to 8 winners including the Group 3 Curragh Cup winner Witness Box. This colt won on his debut on the polytrack at Dundalk in early April.

1259. PRONOUNCED
b.c. Power – Le Montrachet (Nashwan). April 6. Ninth foal. €70,000Y. Goffs Orby. Peter & Ross Doyle. Half-brother to 6 winners including the quite useful 2-y-o 6f winner Barzan (by Danehill Dancer), the quite useful 12f winner Baba Ganouge (by Desert Prince), the quite useful 8.5f and 10f winner Daredevil Day (by Holy Roman Emperor) and the fair 2-y-o 1m winner Fly By White (by Hawk Wing). The dam is an unraced half-sister to the Group 1 Coronation Stakes and Group 1 Prix Marcel Boussac winner Gold Splash and to the top-class broodmare Born Gold (dam of the outstanding Goldikova and the Group 1 winner Galikova). The second dam, Riviere d'Or (by Lyphard), won the Group 1 10f Prix Saint-Alary.

1260. ROLY POLY
b.f. War Front – Misty For Me (Galileo). February 2. Second foal. The dam won the Moyglare Stud Stakes, Prix Marcel Boussac (both at 2 yrs), Irish 1,000 Guineas and Pretty Polly Stakes (all Group 1 events) and is a sister to the Group 1 Prix Marcel Boussac winner Ballydoyle and the useful 7f (at 2 yrs) and listed 9f winner and dual Group 3 placed Twirl. The second dam, Butterfly Cove (by Storm Cat), is an unraced sister to the Group 3 Irish 1,000 Guineas Trial winner Kamarinskaya and a half-sister to 5 winners including the champion 2-y-o colt Fasliyev.

1261. SAO PAULO (IRE)
b.c. Power – Amber Nectar (Barathea). March 27. Third foal. €150,000Y. Goffs Orby. M V Magnier. Half-brother to the fair Irish 1m winner Koybig (by Kodiac). The dam is an unraced sister to 2 winners including the Group 2 Pretty Polly Stakes second Molomo (herself dam of the Group 3 Jersey Stakes winner Rainfall) and a half-sister to 3 winners. The second dam, Nishan (by Nashwan), is a placed half-sister to 3 winners including the Group 3 Prix de Sandringham winner Orford Ness (herself the dam of 3 stakes winners).

1262. SINGER SARGENT (IRE)
ch.c. Galileo – Turbulent Descent (Congrats). February 16. First foal. The dam, a winner of four Grade 1 stakes in the USA from 2 to 4 yrs and from 7f to 8.5f, is out of Roger's Sue (by Forestry).

1263. SOMERSET MAUGHAM
b.c. Galileo – Meow (Storm Cat). January 31. Second foal. Brother to the Irish dual 7f placed 2-y-o Curlylocks. The dam, a useful listed 5f winner, was second in the Group 2 5f Queen Mary Stakes and is a half-sister to 2 winners including the Group 3 9f winner Aloof. The second dam, Airwave (by Air Express), a champion 2-y-o filly and winner of 6 races including the Group 1 6f Cheveley Park Stakes, is a half-sister to 6 winners.

1264. TAJ MAHAL
b.c. Galileo – You'resothrilling (Storm Cat). January 28. Brother to the 2015 2-y-o Group 3 7f CL & MF Weld Park Stakes winner Coolmore, to the National Stakes (at 2 yrs), 2,000 Guineas, Irish 2,000 Guineas and St James's Palace Stakes winner Gleneagles and the 1m (at 2 yrs) and Group 1 Irish 1,000 Guineas winner Marvellous. The dam, winner of the Group 2 Cherry Hinton Stakes, is a sister to several winners and a half-sister to the multiple Group 1 winner Giant's Causeway. The second dam, Mariah's Storm (by Rahy), won 10 races in the USA including six Graded stakes events from 1m to 9f and is closely related to the Group 2 winner Panoramic.

1265. THE ALBATROS (IRE)
b.c. Oasis Dream – Toi Et Moi (Galileo). March 5. Second foal. 350,000 foal. Tattersalls

December. Blandford Bloodstock. The dam, a French listed 10f and listed 12f winner, was Group 3 placed in Italy and is a half-sister to 5 winners including the Group 2 Italian Oaks second Moi Non Plus. The second dam, Di Moi Oui (by Warning), won the Group 3 Prix Chloe and the Group 3 Prix de la Nonette and is a half-sister to 5 winners. n.b. The Albatros, a former Dutch cargo ship built in 1899, is now moored on the quay of Wells-next-the-Sea in Norfolk.

1266. THE STATESMAN
b.c. Zoffany – Chelsey Jayne (Galileo). March 7. Fifth foal. £60,000Y. Doncaster Premier. M V Magnier. Half-brother to the fair 2-y-o 7f winner Chelsea Mick (by Hawk Wing). The dam, placed fourth once over 10f, is a sister to the fairly useful 2-y-o listed 1m winner Classic Legend, closely related to the useful 10f winner and listed-placed Popmurphy and a half-sister to 4 winners including the Group 3 July Stakes third Jallota. The second dam, Lady Lahar (by Fraam), a useful 2-y-o Group 3 7f Futurity Stakes and 3-y-o 8.3f winner, was third in the Group 2 Cherry Hinton Stakes and the Group 2 Falmouth Stakes and is a half-sister to 4 winners.

1267. VAN DONGEN (IRE)
b.c. Galileo – Alluring Park (Green Desert). January 27. Eighth foal. 1,250,000Y. Tattersalls October Book 1. M V Magnier. Brother to the Group 1 Oaks winner and triple Group 1 placed Was and to the useful French 2-y-o 7f winner and Group 3 placed Al Namaah and half-brother to the useful listed 7f winner Janood (by Medicean), to the fair Irish 7f winner Initiation (by Rock Of Gibraltar) and a winner in Japan by Daylami. The dam, a 2-y-o 6f winner and dual listed-placed, is a sister to the Japanese stakes winner Shinko Forest and a half-sister to 6 winners including the champion 2-y-o and Epsom Derby winner and sire New Approach. The second dam, Park Express (by Ahonoora), won the Group 1 10f Phoenix Champion Stakes and is a half-sister to 6 winners.

1268. WILD IRISH ROSE (IRE)
b.f. Galileo – Mariah's Storm (Rahy). June 1. Sister to the useful Irish Group 3 placed 1m winner Hanky Panky and half-sister to

Giant's Causeway (six Group 1's including the St James's Palace Stakes, Eclipse Stakes and Juddmonte International), to the Group 2 Cherry Hinton Stakes winner You'resothrilling, the smart 1m winner Freud and the useful 2-y-o winners Tiger Dance, Roar Of The Tiger and Tumblebrutus (all by Storm Cat). The dam, a winner of 10 races in the USA including six Graded stakes events from 1m to 9f, is closely related to the Group 2 Prix d'Harcourt winner Panoramic. The second dam, Immense (by Roberto), won the US Grade 3 8.5f Little Silver Handicap.

1269. UNNAMED ♠
b.f. Galileo – A Z Warrior (Bernardini). March 7. Second foal. 1,300,000Y. Tattersalls October Book 1. M V Magnier. Sister to the quite useful 2015 8.5f and 9f placed 2-y-o Cole Porter. The dam, winner of the US Grade 1 Frizette Stakes and third in the Grade 1 Santa Anita Oaks, is a half-sister to 6 winners including the US Graded stakes winners Jojo Warrior and E Z Warrior. The second dam, Carson Jen (by Carson City), a US listed-placed winner of 4 races, is a half-sister to 5 winners.

1270. UNNAMED
b.c. Galileo – Famous (Danehill Dancer). January 19. Third foal. The dam, a useful Irish 2-y-o 7f winner, was second in the Group 1 7f Moyglare Stud Stakes and is a sister to the Group 1 Phoenix Stakes, National Stakes and Irish 2,000 Guineas winner Mastercraftsman and closely related to the US Grade 3 winner Genuine Devotion. The second dam, Starlight Dreams (by Black Tie Affair), won twice at 3 yrs in the USA and is a half-sister to 5 winners including the listed Zetland Stakes winner Matahif and the dam of the dual Group 1 winner Pressing.

1271. UNNAMED
b.f. War Front – Imagine (Sadler's Wells). May 1. Sister to the fairly useful 2015 2-y-o 7f winner General Macarthur and half-sister to the 2-y-o Group 1 7f Prix Jean Luc Lagardere winner Horatio Nelson (by Danehill), to four winners by Giant's Causeway including the Irish listed 7f winner and Group 2 Champagne Stakes second Viscount Nelson, the 2-y-o Group 2 7f Rockfel Stakes winner Kitty Matcham and the Irish 10f winner and Group

1 placed Red Rock Canyon (both by Rock Of Gibraltar). The dam, winner of the Irish 1,000 Guineas and Epsom Oaks, is a half-sister to Generous, winner of the Derby, Irish Derby, King George VI and the Dewhurst Stakes. The second dam, Doff The Derby (by Master Derby), is an unraced half-sister to the Prix Ganay winner Trillion (herself dam of the outstanding racemare Triptych).

1272. UNNAMED
b.c. Galileo – Love Me True (Kingmambo). April 27. Brother to the Epsom Derby winner Ruler Of The World and to the 2-y-o 1m winner and Group 1 Irish Derby third Giovanni Canaletto, closely related to the quite useful 2-y-o 7f winner So In Love With You (by Sadler's Wells) and half-brother to 3 winners including the multiple Group 1 10f to 12f winner Duke Of Marmalade (by Danehill). The dam, an Irish 1m winner and third in the Group 3 Killavullan Stakes, is a half-sister to US Grade 2 winner Bite The Bullet and the listed 10f winner Shuailaan. The second dam, Lassie's Lady (by Alydar), a stakes-placed winner in the USA, is a half-sister to 10 winners including the high-class sprinter Wolfhound.

1273. UNNAMED
b.f. Deep Impact – Maybe (Galileo). February 8. First foal. The dam, a 2-y-o Group 1 7f Moyglare Stud Stakes winner and third in the 1,000 Guineas, is a sister to one winner. The second dam, Sumora (by Danehill), a 2-y-o listed 5f St Hugh's Stakes winner, is a sister to the useful Irish 7f winner Fleeting Shadow and a half-sister to the Oaks and German Oaks winner Dancing Rain.

1274. UNNAMED
b.c. Deep Impact – Peeping Fawn (Danehill). February 2. Third foal. Half-brother to the useful 2-y-o 6f winner and Group 2 Coventry Stakes third Sir John Hawkins (by Henrythenavigator). The dam won the Pretty Polly Stakes, Irish Oaks, Nassau Stakes and Yorkshire Oaks (all Group 1 events) and is a half-sister to the very smart 2-y-o Group 1 Criterium International winner Thewayyouare. The second dam, Maryinsky (by Sadler's Wells), a 2-y-o 7f winner, was second in the Group 1 Fillies Mile and is a half-sister to the Grade 2 9f Demoiselle Stakes winner Better Than Honour, the smart Group 2 1m Beresford Stakes winner Turnberry Isle and the Group 2 1m Prix d'Astarte winner Smolensk.

1275. UNNAMED
ch.f. Galileo – Remember When (Danehill Dancer). March 25. Third foal. Sister to the 2015 2-y-o 1m winner and Group 2 1m Beresford Stakes third Beacon Rock and to the smart Group 2 9f Kilboy Estate Stakes winner Wedding Vow. The dam was second in the Oaks and is closely related to the top-class middle-distance winner of six Group 1 events Dylan Thomas and a half-sister to the champion 2-y-o filly and Group 1 6f Cheveley Park Stakes winner Queen's Logic. The second dam, Lagrion (by Diesis), was placed 5 times in Ireland and stayed 12f and is a sister to the Group 1 Middle Park Stakes second Pure Genius.

1276. UNNAMED
b.c. Frankel – Rosie's Posy (Suave Dancer). April 16. Half-brother to the promising 2015 French 2-y-o 9f winner Estikmaal (by Oasis Dream, to the Group 1 French 2,000 Guineas and Group 1 7f Prix de la Foret winner Make Believe (by Makfi), the US Grade 1 9f and 10f winner Dubawi Heights (by Dubawi) and the useful 6f (at 2 yrs) and 1m winner Generous Thought (by Cadeaux Genereux). The dam, a quite useful 2-y-o 5.7f winner, is a half-sister to 6 winners including the Group 1 6f Haydock Sprint Cup winner Tante Rose. The second dam, My Branch (by Distant Relative), won the listed 6f Firth Of Clyde Stakes (at 2 yrs) and the listed 7f Sceptre Stakes, was placed in the Group 1 Cheveley Park Stakes and the Irish 1,000 Guineas and is a half-sister to 7 winners.

1277. UNNAMED
b.c. War Front – Sun Shower (Indian Ridge). March 14. Half-brother to the high-class triple Group 1 1m winner and sire Excelebration (by Exceed And Excel) and to the fairly useful 7f and 1m winner Mull Of Killough (by Mull Of Kintyre). The dam is a placed half-sister to 2 minor winners in France. The second dam, Miss Kemble (by Warning), ran once unplaced and is a full or half-sister to 10 winners including the high-class Irish Oaks winner Princess Pati and to the Great Voltigeur Stakes winner Seymour Hicks.

1278. UNNAMED
b.f. War Front – Together (Galileo). January 27. First foal. The dam, a 2-y-o Group 3 7f Silver Flash Stakes and subsequent US Grade 1 9f winner, was also Group 1 placed four times in Ireland and is a sister to the listed-placed winner Terrific and closely related to the 2-y-o Group 1 1m Criterium International winner and Irish Derby third Jan Vermeer. The second dam, Shadow Song (by Pennekamp), a French 3-y-o winner, is a half-sister to 7 winners including the Group 3 May Hill Stakes winner Midnight Air (dam of the Group 3 and subsequent US Grade 2 winner Midnight Line) and to the placed dam of the Group 1 Prix de l'Abbaye winner Imperial Beauty.

1279. UNNAMED
b.f. War Front – Wading (Montjeu). January 29. First foal. The dam won the 2-y-o Group 2 7f Rockfel Stakes and is a sister to the Group 1 Irish Oaks winner Bracelet. The second dam, Cherry Hinton (by Green Desert), a useful maiden, was second in the Group 3 10f Blue Wind Stakes and third in a listed event over 9f in Ireland. She is closely related to the outstanding colt Sea The Stars (winner of the 2,000 Guineas, Derby, Prix de l'Arc de Triomphe etc) and a half-sister to 6 winners including the top-class dual Derby and King George VI winner and sire Galileo, and the dual Group 1 winner Black Sam Bellamy.

JAMIE OSBORNE
1280. AURORA SPRING (IRE) ★★★
b.f. Power – Blue Iris (Petong). April 21. Thirteenth foal. Half-sister to the dual listed 5f winner (including at 2 yrs) Swiss Lake (by Indian Ridge and herself the dam of three stakes winners), to the fairly useful 5f (including at 2 yrs) and 6f winner and listed-placed Dubai Princess (by Dubai Destination), the fairly useful 6f and 7f winner of 6 races Hajoum (by Exceed And Excel), the fairly useful 2-y-o 1m winner Pupil (by Mastercraftsman) and the fair Irish 2-y-o 5f winner Nero Emperor (by Holy Roman Emperor). The dam, a useful winner of 5 races over 5f and 6f including the Weatherbys Super Sprint and the Redcar Two-Year-Old Trophy, is a half-sister to 10 winners. The second dam, Bo' Babbity (by Strong Gale), a fair 2-y-o 5f winner, is a half-sister to 6 winners including the Group 3 5f King George Stakes winner Anita's Prince. (Andy Smith & Friends). *"It's a decent pedigree and she didn't go through a ring but was sent to me. Obviously it's difficult to know what a "Power" is yet because he's a first season sire, but this filly is strong, she'll be one for mid-season, she moves well and with her pedigree you'd expect her to be quick. At the moment I haven't done a lot with her".*

1281. GENTLEMAN GILES (IRE) ★★★
b.c. Dutch Art – Sularina (Alhaarth). April 19. Fifth foal. €90,000Y. Goffs Orby. Simon Christian. Half-brother to Bergholt (by Sir Percy), placed fourth over 7f on all three of his starts at 2 yrs in 2015 and to the 1m, 10f and listed 12f winner Khione (by Dalakhani). The dam, placed fourth over 1m on her only start, is a half-sister to 4 winners including the Group 3 Park Hill Stakes winner Discreet Brief (dam of the Group 2 Royal Lodge Stakes winner Steeler). The second dam, Quiet Counsel (by Law Society), won once over 12f and is a half-sister to 7 winners including the Group 1 Yorkshire Oaks winner Key Change. (D Christian). *"A nice horse, he was quite expensive but he's strong. He's a very good model by a good stallion, he moves well and the early signs are good. I would hope he'd be out before Ascot".*

1282. HARBOUR MASTER ★★★★
b.c. Harbour Watch – Roodeye (Inchinor). April 30. Seventh foal. 50,000Y. Tattersalls October Book 2. Barberini Bloodstock. Half-brother to 5 winners including the US Grade 2 and Grade 3 winner Prize Exhibit (by Showcasing), the quite useful 5f (at 2 yrs) and 7f winner Roodle (by Xaar), the fair 2-y-o 6f winner Must Be Me (by Trade Fair) and the moderate dual 2m winner Hoonose (by Cadeaux Genereux). The dam, a useful 5f (at 2 yrs) and 7f winner, was listed-placed and is a half-sister to 5 winners including the Group 1 Prix Morny second Gallagher. The second dam, Roo (by Rudimentary), a quite useful 2-y-o 5f and 6f winner, is a half-sister to 6 winners including the Group 2 6f Gimcrack Stakes winner Bannister. (M Buckley & C Noell). *"I trained his half-sister Prize Exhibit who finished fourth in the Breeders' Cup Juvenile. It's hard to know what a Harbour Watch is yet but the early signs are very*

good for this horse. I like him, he's a beautiful mover, the family are all a bit quirky but this fellow is a bit more sane than Prize Exhibit! There are similarities in the way they go, she always looked smart and this horse is showing the signs of looking quite smart already. So we like him".

1283. LONG JOHN SILVER (IRE) ★★
b.c. Rip Van Winkle – Tropical Lady (Sri Pekan). March 22. Seventh foal. €160,000Y. Goffs Orby. F Barberini. Half-brother to the 2015 2-y-o 1m winner Von Blucher (by Zoffany) and to the Irish 7f winner Tropical Mist (by Marju) – both quite useful. The dam won 8 races including the Group 2 10f Royal Whip Stakes, the Group 3 10f Meld Stakes and the Group 3 7f Brownstown Stakes and is a half-sister to 5 winners. The second dam, Tropical Lake (by Lomond), won six races on the flat from 1m to 2m and four races over hurdles and is a half-sister to 7 winners. (M Buckley & T Hyde). *"He's going to be backward but he's a lovely horse with a bit of scope. Looks more of a 3-y-o, so he'll be a two-year project by the look of him, but he's a lovely horse".*

1284. UNNAMED ★★★
b.c. Casamento – Annouska (Ad Valorem). March 8. Second foal. 150,000Y. Tattersalls October Book 1. Al Shaqab Racing/ Peter & Ross Doyle. Half-brother to the modest 2015 6f and 7f placed 2-y-o Don't Tell Her (by Tagula). The dam is an unraced half-sister to 4 winners including the useful 1m and listed 15f winner Anousa. The second dam, Annaletta (by Belmez), a minor French 12f winner and listed-placed in Germany, is a half-sister to 7 winners including the dam of the Grade 1 E P Taylor Stakes winner Fraulein. *"A lovely horse, he failed his wind for Al Shaqab so we took him on a "sale or return" type scenario and I've loved him from the day he arrived. A beautiful mover, his wind is fine and he has a lot of quality. Casamento is a first season sire of course so we're guessing a bit, but I wouldn't imagine this is a 2-y-o for the first half of the season. He has a lot of quality and should be a lovely horse to have for a bit later on and for next year".*

1285. UNNAMED ★★★
b.c. Holy Roman Emperor – Challow Hills (Woodman). January 27. Fourth foal. €95,000Y. Goffs Orby. George Moore. The dam, a modest 1m winner, is a half-sister to 5 winners including the US stakes winner and dual Grade 3 placed Teide. The second dam, Cascassi (by Nijinsky), a fair 10f winner here, also won at 4 yrs in France and is a half-sister to 5 winners including Diminuendo (Epsom, Irish and Yorkshire Oaks winner) and the Oaks second Pricket. *"He's quite big, but not as backward as a lot of big horses. A nice mover, the early signs are good and he's done well since the sale in that he's grown, developed and got a lot stronger. He has the look of a nice horse and I see him probably needing six furlongs to begin with".*

1286. UNNAMED ★★★
b.f. Approve – Coin Box (Dubai Destination). March 14. Second foal. €28,000Y. Tattersalls Ireland September. F Barberini. Half-sister to the fair 2015 2-y-o 5f and 6f winner Rial (by Dark Angel). The dam is an unplaced half-sister to one minor winner. The second dam, Small Change (by Danzig), a fairly useful 2-y-o 7f winner, is a sister to the smart Group 1 6f Middle Park Stakes winner Zieten and to the Group 1 6f Cheveley Park Stakes winner Blue Duster and closely related to numerous winners including the French listed 1m winner Slow Jazz. *"She's sharp and could be one of the earliest ones. A good mover, I know the stallion's been sent abroad but she's a great model and she's got great strength. Showing all the right signs".*

1287. UNNAMED ★★★
ch.c. Sir Prancealot – Fey Rouge (Fayruz). April 29. Tenth foal. €26,000Y. Goffs Orby. F Barberini. Half-brother to 6 winners including the Irish 7f and 1m winners and Group placed Crystal View (by Imperial Ballet) and Miss Trish (by Danetime), the quite useful listed 6f winner Pride And Joy (by Dark Angel) and the Irish 5f winner Bye Bye Ben (by Beckett). The dam is an unplaced full or half-sister to 9 winners. The second dam, Isa (by Dance In Time), is an unraced half-sister to 4 winners. *"I trained a half-brother to this colt who was alright. He's good-looking but not over-big and I probably need to get him out in the*

first half of the year. It's a fast pedigree, he's showing all the right signs and the sire ought to get early types. So the throttle will be down on him and the early signs are OK".

1288. UNNAMED ★★★
b.c. Tagula – Lupine (Lake Coniston). April 1. Third living foal. 16,000Y. Tattersalls October Book 3. F Barberini. Half-brother to the quite useful Irish 2-y-o 6f winner Foot Perfect (by Footstepsinthesand). The dam, a quite useful 2-y-o 5f winner, is a half-sister to 7 winners including the Irish 2-y-o dual 5f winner and listed-placed Blue Crush and the fairly useful 2-y-o triple 5f winner Barringer. The second dam, Prosaic Star (by Common Grounds), a quite useful Irish 2-y-o 1m winner, is a half-sister to 4 winners. *"He looked like being quite early but then started to grow and went a bit weak-looking. A lovely mover, I've had a lot of luck with the stallion who I think is underrated because he can get a good horse. I've just got to leave him alone for a bit now to let him develop, but it looks like he could make sprint type 2-y-o in the first half of the season".*

1289. UNNAMED ★★★
b.c. Elnadim – Meanwhile (Haafhd). February 8. First foal. €48,000Y. Goffs Orby. F Barberini. The dam, a modest 2-y-o 7f winner, is a half-sister to 3 winners including the Italian 2-y-o winner and Group 2 German 1,000 Guineas third Temida. The second dam, Interim Payment (by Red Ransom), a quite useful dual 10f winner, is a half-sister to 6 winners including the US Grade 1 winner Midships, the multiple listed winner Principal Role and the US Grade 1 second Staging Post. (M Buckley & C Noell). *"A good-looking horse, I like the stallion and this is a colt with a lot of quality. He's a little bit lazy in his work but could well be alright".*

1290. UNNAMED ★★★
b.f. Poet's Voice – Nawaashi (Green Desert). February 19. Second foal. £32,000Y. Doncaster Premier. F Barberini. The dam, a fair 2-y-o 6f winner, is a half-sister to 3 minor winners. The second dam, Shatarah (by Gulch), placed four times over 7f, including at 2 yrs, is a half-sister to the Group 1 6f Golden Jubilee Stakes winner Malhub, to the US Grade 3 winner Dhaamer and to the unraced dams of the Group 3

winners Yellow Rosebud and Heeraat. *"She's a quality filly, the jury's out on the stallion but this is a good mover and we like her. She's strong enough to be running in the first part of the season but with the scope to go on".*

1291. UNNAMED ★★★
b.f. Elzaam – Noble View (Distant View). April 25. Ninth foal. €50,000Y. Goffs Sportsmans. F Barberini. Half-sister to 7 winners including the useful 2-y-o listed 6f winner of 9 races and Group 2 7f Vintage Stakes third Corporal Maddox, the quite useful 6f to 1m winner of 8 races Silver Hotspur (both by Royal Applause) and the fair 6f and 7f winner Aegean Shadow (by Sakhee). The dam, placed fourth over 5f and 6f at 2 yrs, is a half-sister to 5 winners including the French 1,000 Guineas winner Houseproud. The second dam, Proud Lou (by Proud Clarion), won the US Grade 1 Frizette Stakes and is a half-sister to 7 winners. (Ian Barrett, Stephen Short & Adam Signy). *"She's going OK and I hope she's going to be early but she's a bit laid-back in her work. She's getting there though and she's a good mover. Hopefully one for the first half of the season".*

1292. UNNAMED ★★★
ch.f. Dragon Pulse – Ra Hydee (Rahy). April 7. Eleventh foal. €25,000Y. Tattersalls Ireland September. F Barberini. Half-sister to the 1m winner and Group 2 UAE Derby second Jack Junior, to the fairly useful 2-y-o 5f winner and listed-placed Perfect Paula, the fair 2-y-o 7f winner Liturgical (all by Songandaprayer) and a minor US 4-y-o winner by Devil's Bag. The dam, a minor US 3-y-o winner, is a half-sister to 7 winners including the US stakes winners Jonowo and Stolie. The second dam, Youpickem (by Droll Role), a minor US 3-y-o winner, is a half-sister to 6 winners including the US Grade 2 winner Terra Incognita. *"She's got quite a nice pedigree and she's a nice filly that's strong enough and moves well. I haven't worked her yet and we don't know how Dragon Pulse will fare as a stallion, but she'll be worth putting in the book".*

1293. UNNAMED ★★★
ch.c. Power – Reveuse De Jour (Sadler's Wells). April 27. Fifteenth foal. €50,000Y. Goffs Orby. F Barberini. Half-brother to 7 winners including the Group 3 Premio Sergio Cumani winner

and Group 1 Coronation Stakes second Nova Hawk (by Hawk Wing), the quite useful 7f and 8.6f winner Grand Jour (by Grand Lodge), the minor French 2-y-o winner Dream Of Day (by Machiavellian) and the fair Irish 1m winner Day Ticket (by Mtoto). The dam, a fair 7f placed 3-y-o, is a half-sister to 9 winners including Enthused (Group 2 6f Lowther Stakes). The second dam, Magic Of Life (by Seattle Slew), won the Group 1 1m Coronation Stakes and is a half-sister to 4 winners. (Mr & Mrs I Barrett). *"He's quite a mixture, being by a sprinter and out of a Sadler's Wells mare. He's good-looking, has plenty of quality, not over-big and I'll be kicking on with him. Not really bred to be a five furlong horse"*.

1294. UNNAMED ★★★★
b.c. Kodiac – Roisin's Star (Accordion). February 1. Fourth foal. €75,000Y. Goffs Sportsmans. F Barberini. The dam, a quite useful Irish 2-y-o dual 6f winner, is out of the moderate 2-y-o 7f winner Lightning Bolt (by Magical Strike), herself a half-sister to 6 winners. (Ian Barrett, Stephen Short & Adam Signy). *"Out of a good racemare who lacked pedigree but was quick, this colt isn't very big so I'll probably have to get him out in the first half of the year, but the signs are looking alright. The sire can produce a good one and he's a good mover. I'm not quite as forward with him as I'd have liked to have been, but I think he's going to be OK"*.

1295. UNNAMED ★★★
b.c. Sixties Icon – Rose Cheval (Johannesburg). March 22. Fourth foal. 6,500Y. Tattersalls October Book 3. Brother to the quite useful 2015 2-y-o dual 6f winner Sixties Sue and to the fair 2-y-o dual 5f winner Scargill. The dam, a fair 7f (at 2 yrs) to 9f placed maiden, is a half-sister to 2 winners in North America. The second dam, La Samanna (by Trempolino), won 2 minor races at 3 and 4 yrs in the USA and is a half-sister to 5 winners. *"I haven't had any Sixties Icon's before but this year I have three. He gets hardy horses and mine are all tough – they're not shirkers. This is a nice horse and he won't take that long either. I haven't let the hand brake off yet but he's a horse that doesn't tire easily and I think he's a sneaky one that could be alright"*. **TRAINERS' BARGAIN BUY**

1296. UNNAMED ★★★★
b.f. Acclamation – Semaphore (Zamindar). April 4. Sixth foal. 80,000Y. Tattersalls October Book 2. Sackville/Donald. Half-sister to 5 winners including the quite useful 2015 2-y-o 6f winner Reputation (by Royal Applause), to the useful 2-y-o 7f winner and Group 3 7f Oh So Sharp Stakes third Annie's Fortune (by Montjeu), the quite useful triple 1m winner Semaral (by High Chaparral) and the fair 2-y-o 6f winner Deep Blue Sea (by Rip Van Winkle). The dam is an unraced half-sister to 3 winners including the dam of the Group 3 winners Fantasia and Pink Symphony. The second dam, Blue Duster (by Danzig), winner of the Group 1 6f Cheveley Park Stakes, is a sister to the smart Group 1 6f Middle Park Stakes winner Zieten and a half-sister to 9 winners. (Rebels With A Cause). *"She's grown and done really well. A big, strong filly with a lot of quality, we like her and she's one for the first half of the season for sure. We could well be starting her off at five furlongs and she may even get seven eventually"*.

1297. UNNAMED ★★★
b.c. Exceed And Excel – Sharp Terms (Kris). May 14. Ninth foal. 80,000Y. Tattersalls October Book 2. Barberini Bloodstock. Brother to the 2-y-o Group 2 6f Lowther Stakes and Group 2 Queen Mary Stakes winner Best Terms and to the fair 3-y-o 5f and 6f winner Miracle Garden and half-brother to the Group 3 placed Italian winner Sunsemperchi (by Montjeu and herself the dam of two stakes winners), the quite useful 10f and hurdles winner Helvelius (by Polish Precedent) and the fair 9f winner Miss Chicane (by Refuse To Bend). The dam is an unraced half-sister to 9 winners including the Group 2 winners First Charter and Anton Chekhov. The second dam, By Charter (by Shirley Heights), a 2-y-o winner and second in the listed Cheshire Oaks, is a sister to the smart Group 2 winner Zinaad. (M Buckley). *"A full-brother to a Queen Mary winner, he's not as forward as she was but he has a lot of quality and has a bit more scope. Physically he needs to develop a little bit yet so we're not going to be in a rush with him"*.

1298. UNNAMED ★★★
ch.c. Helmet – Smoken Rosa (Smoke Glacken). February 9. Fifth foal. 35,000Y. Tattersalls

October Book 2. Barberini Bloodstock. Half-brother to the modest 2015 2-y-o 6f winner Miss Phillyjinks (by Zoffany), to the fair Irish 7f winner Refusetolisten (by Clodovil) and the modest triple 1m winner Bosstime (by Clodovil). The dam, placed 3 times in the USA, is a half-sister to 4 winners including Snowdrops (three Graded 3stakes wins). The second dam, Roses In The Snow (by Be My Guest), a useful 1m winner and listed-placed here, subsequently won in the USA and is a half-sister to 6 winners. (Ian Barrett, Stephen Short & Adam Signy). *"A lovely horse but probably more of a 3-y-o type, he's big, strong and not early but a beautiful mover with a lot of quality. I like the look of this horse, he could be alright and he's got that stride to him that you really like".*

JOHN OXX

1299. BIRDS OF PREY (IRE) ★★★
b.g. Sir Prancealot – Cute (Diktat). April 7. Fourth foal. €100,000Y. Goffs Orby. Sackville/Donald. Half-brother to a minor winner in Russia by Kyllachy. The dam, a fairly useful 5f placed 2-y-o, is a half-sister to 8 winners including Arabian Gleam (Group 2 Challenge Stakes and Group 2 Park Stakes, twice) and the dams of the Group winners Lucky Kristale and Skia. The second dam, Gleam Of Light (by Danehill), won over 7f and is a full or half-sister to 4 winners. *"He's working away and I hope to run him in mid-May or so. A very good-looking horse and quite expensive for Sir Prancealot, he's coming along well".*

1300. BORN TO BE (IRE) ★★★★
b.c. Born To Sea – Duquesa (Intikhab). February 27. Second foal. 98,000Y. Tattersalls October Book 1. Not sold. Half-brother to the 2015 dual 6f placed 2-y-o Birkdale (by Elnadim). The dam, a modest 6f (at 2 yrs) and 11.5f winner, is a half-sister to 4 winners including the listed placed Silver Bracelet. The second dam, Love Of Silver (by Arctic Tern), won the 2-y-o Group 3 7f Prestige Stakes and is a half-sister to 6 winners. *"He's quite sharp, coming along well and he'll hopefully be running in the first half of May. He's always looked like a 2-y-o type, he's a quick learner and we're happy with him, so he should make a nice 2-y-o".*

1301. CHINESE ART (IRE) ★★
b.c. Dutch Art – Overturned (Cape Cross). February 28. Second foal. 85,000Y. Tattersalls October Book 2. Sunderland Holding Inc. The dam, a minor 9f winner in France, is a sister to the listed 1m winner and Group 1 Falmouth Stakes and Group 1 Sun Chariot Stakes third Musicanna and a half-sister to 8 winners. The second dam, Upend (by Main Reef), winner of the Group 3 St Simon Stakes and second in the Group 3 Princess Royal Stakes, is a half-sister to 6 winners including the dam of the high-class stayer and champion hurdler Royal Gait. *"He's a beautiful mover but he's out of a Cape Cross mare and he looks like he'll take a little bit of time. Just because he's by Dutch Art that doesn't necessarily mean he'll make an early 2-y-o. There are mixed messages in the pedigree as to what trip he'll want, but he has a lovely, big, long stride so I think he'll need a distance".*

1302. DECISIVE INTENT (IRE) ★★★
b.f. Lawman – Best Intent (King's Best). April 27. Second foal. €110,000Y. Arqana Deauville October. John Oxx. Half-sister to a minor 3-y-o winner in France by Dubawi. The dam, a fair 10f winner, is a half-sister to 7 winners including the French listed 7f winner Esperero and the Japanese stakes winner Shinko Calido. The second dam, Hydro Calido (by Nureyev), won the Group 2 1m Prix d'Astarte, was second in the French 1,000 Guineas and is a half-sister to the champion European 2-y-o Machiavellian, the Group 1 Prix Morny and Group 1 Prix de la Salamandre winner Coup de Genie and the Group 1 Prix Jacques le Marois winner Exit to Nowhere. *"A good-looking filly, she's a very fluent mover and we're just starting to go a bit faster. I'd say she'll come along quickly enough and she should be able to run in June. A nice filly for six or seven furlongs, I like her".*

1303. DRAKE PASSAGE (IRE) ★★★
ch.c. Dandy Man – Piece Unique (Barathea). April 2. Seventh foal. €75,000Y. Goffs Orby. Sackville/Donald. Half-brother to the quite useful dual 1m winner Ruban (by Dubawi), to the fair 2-y-o 5f winner Lady Lydia (by Kheleyf) and the modest 6f winner Hugie Boy (by Art Connoisseur). The dam was placed 3 times at 3 yrs in France and is a half-sister to 8

winners including the French Group 3 winner Donkey Engine and the US Grade 3 winner Petit Pouchet and to the unraced dam of the dual Group 3 winner and sire Arakan. The second dam, City Ex (by Ardross), won at 3 yrs in France and is a half-sister to 9 winners. *"A fine, very good-looking horse, he's big, rangy and a beautiful mover, so he's not a sharp-looking Dandy Man. I think it may be mid-season before he runs but we like him and he's starting some work now. We're happy with him".*

1304. DRAMATIC EXIT ★★★
b.c. Exceed And Excel – Starbound (Captain Rio). March 16. First foal. 150,000Y. Tattersalls October Book 1. Sunderland Holding Inc. The dam, a fair 1m winner, is a half-sister to 3 winners including the Group 1 Phoenix Stakes and Group 2 Railway Stakes winner Alfred Nobel. The second dam, Glinting Desert (by Desert Prince), a fair 2-y-o 7f winner, is a half-sister to 4 minor winners. *"A very nice colt, bigger than the other two I have by this sire, so he might need a little bit of time. He looks like he learns quickly but he's growing a bit at the moment so again that may mean he'll need more time but I do like him. He's big, strong and powerful with a good action".*

1305. MY TIMING ★★★
ch.f. Street Cry – Lay Time (Galileo). March 4. First foal. 520,000Y. Tattersalls October Book 1. Sunderland Holding Inc. The dam, a very useful Group 3 10f Winter Hill Stakes winner, was third in the Group 2 Windsor Forest Stakes and is a half-sister to 5 winners including the smart Group 2 12f King Edward VII Stakes winner Plea Bargain and the listed Empress Stakes winner Jira. The second dam, Time Saved (by Green Desert), a fairly useful 10f winner, is a sister to the useful 1m winner Illusion and a half-sister to 5 winners including Zinaad and Time Allowed (both winners of the Group 2 12f Jockey Club Stakes). *"A very nice-looking filly with a very good pedigree and she cost a lot of money at Tattersalls. A well-grown, rangy filly that'll take a bit of time and I'd say she'll be one for the autumn. She hasn't done anything serious yet, just cantering, but she's very nice".*

1306. NIGG BAY (IRE) ★★★
b.c. Exceed And Excel – Muaamara (Bahamian Bounty). March 27. First foal. 110,000Y. Tattersalls October Book 2. BBA (Ire). The dam, a quite useful dual 6f winner (including at 2 yrs), is a half-sister to 4 winners including the very useful 2012 2-y-o listed 6f winner and Group 2 Mill Reef Stakes second Master Of War. The second dam, Mamma Morton (by Elnadim), a fair 10f and 11f placed maiden, is a half-sister to 11 winners. *"A really nice colt, he's done some sharper canters lately and he's a beautiful mover and a nice type. He'll be one for July, he's a sharp sort and not bred to stay at all. A precocious colt and a quick learner".*

1307. OLLY'S FOLLY (IRE) ★★★
b.c. Poet's Voice – Pearl Diva (Acclamation). February 25. First foal. €75,000Y. Goffs Orby. John Oxx. The dam, a fairly useful 2-y-o 5f winner, was second in the listed Empress Stakes and is a half-sister to 2 minor winners. The second dam, Lassie's Gold (by Seeking The Gold), is an unraced half-sister to 6 winners including the US multiple Grade 1 winner and sire Lemon Drop Kid and the Group 2 Coventry Stakes winner Statue Of Liberty. *"A sharp 2-y-o type, he's had a couple of little setbacks that have held him up but he's a quick-learning, sharp sort of horse. If he stays out of trouble he should be running by June, something like that. A nice, tidy horse and if he's got ability he should show it at two".*

1308. RENAMED ME KING (IRE) ★★★★
b.c. Kodiac – Unicamp (Royal Academy). March 5. Eleventh foal. 85,000Y. Tattersalls October Book 1. Sunderland Holding Inc. Half-brother to 7 winners including the quite useful 2015 2-y-o 7f winner Forever A Lady (by Dark Angel), the quite useful Irish 2-y-o 7f, 1m and hurdles winner Kempes, the modest 7f (at 2 yrs) to 10f winner Singora Lady (both by Intikhab) and the quite useful 7f and 1m winner of 13 races (including at 2 yrs) Smarty Socks (by Elnadim). The dam, a quite useful 2-y-o 6f winner, is a half-sister to 5 winners. The second dam, Honeyspike (by Chief's Crown), placed over 1m, is a half-sister to 6 winners including the Irish listed 10f winner and US Grade 1 second Casey Tibbs. *"He's a sharp-looking colt who is showing a fair bit and he should be able to run in early*

May although he wants good, fast ground – not soft. He seems to know his job and he's going nicely at the moment. He'll run well when he runs".

1309. SANTA ANABAA (IRE) ★★★★ ♠
b.f. Exceed And Excel – Santa Agata (Anabaa). January 29. Second foal. 330,000Y. Tattersalls October Book 1. Sunderland Holding Inc. Half-sister to the modest 2015 1m placed 2-y-o Indulgent (by Makfi). The dam, a listed-placed 2-y-o 1m winner in France, is a half-sister to 6 winners including the Irish and German Group 3 winner Common World. The second dam, Spenderella (by Common Grounds), a minor winner at 3 yrs in France, is a sister to the listed winner Raissonable and a half-sister to 7 winners including the US Grade 1 winner Aube Indienne. *"A very good-looking filly and a quick learner. Exceed And Excels are sharp and want to get on with it. A lovely looking filly, she was an expensive yearling and I can see her being out in late May or early June".*

1310. SEA MY ANGEL (IRE) ★★★★
b.f. Dark Angel – Tarawa (Green Tune). February 18. Second foal. €75,000Y. Arqana Deauville August. Mandore International. The dam is an unraced half-sister to 3 winners and to the unraced dams of the Group 1 winner Arcano and Gilt Edge Girl. The second dam, Tarwiya (by Dominion), winner of the Group 3 C L Weld Park Stakes and third in the Group 1 Irish 1,000 Guineas, is a half-sister to 5 winners. *"She's a nice filly, very racy and a quick learner. She's starting to work now so she should be ready by June time. A filly with a good attitude and a good temperament and she's a quick learner. It's a family I've had a lot of luck with in the past, so she's promising".*

1311. SEA OF GRACE (IRE) ★★
ch.f. Born To Sea – Lady Dettoria (Vettori). January 22. Third foal. €260,000Y. Arqana Deauville August. Mandore International. Half-sister to the quite useful 7f (at 2 yrs) to 10.5f winner of 4 races Jumeirah Glory (by Fast Company) and to the Italian 2-y-o winner and listed-placed Pepparone (by Stormy River). The dam, a minor French 12f winner, is a half-sister to 3 winners including the Irish Group

3 placed and US Grade 2 placed Cougar Bay. The second dam, Delimara (by In The Wings), won a listed event in France and is a half-sister to 6 winners including the Group 3 1m Prix d'Aumale winner Mackla. *"Quite a big, good-looking filly, she made a big price at Deauville as a yearling. Because of her size she may not be as precocious as some of the others by the sire. She's just starting to do a bit of faster work now, but as the dam won at a mile and half I think that will be a big influence on the trip this filly will want. Probably one to start off at seven furlongs".*

1312. WHAT A HOME (IRE) ★★★
b.f. Lope De Vega – Inchmahome (Galileo). April 2. Sixth foal. 300,000Y. Tattersalls October Book 1. Sunderland Holding Inc. Half-sister to the Group 3 12f Give Thanks Stakes and Group 3 Noblesse Stakes winner and Group 1 Irish Oaks second Venus De Milo (by Duke Of Marmalade), to the quite useful 10f winner Earl Of Menteith (by Shamardal) and the fair 2m winner Wayne Manor (by Cape Cross). The dam, a modest 11f winner, is a half-sister to 7 winners including the triple Group 3 7f winner and sire Inchinor. The second dam, Inchmurrin (by Lomond), a Group 2 Child Stakes winner, was second in the Group 1 1m Coronation Stakes and is a half-sister to 7 winners including Welney (Mill Reef Stakes). *"Quite a nice filly, not as forward as some of the others because of a small setback since Christmas. But she's cantering away, she's a lovely mover and an elegant sort of filly. She cost a bit of money as a yearling and she'll be a nice filly from mid-season onwards".*

HUGO PALMER

1313. AFANDEM (IRE) ★★★
b.c. Vale Of York – Al Mahmeyah (Teofilo). February 12. First foal. The dam, a fair 2-y-o 6f winner, is a half-sister to numerous winners including the fairly useful Irish listed-placed 2-y-o 5f and 7f winner Spirit Of Pearl. The second dam, Aguilas Perla (by Indian Ridge), is an unraced sister to the Irish listed 7f winner Cool Clarity and a half-sister to the listed winners Artistic Blue and Queen Of Palms. *"He's worked already and he's a strong, forward going, five/six furlong horse that should be racing in early May. He looks a straightforward, muscular 2-y-o".*

TWO-YEAR-OLDS OF 2016

1314. ALOUJA (IRE) ★★★
ch.f. Raven's Pass – Artisti (Cape Cross). April 24. Fifth foal. 420,000Y. Tattersalls October Book 1. Tony Nerses. Half-sister to the Italian and German Group 3 10f winner Magic Artist (by Iffraaj) and to a winner in Austria by Nayef. The dam is an unraced half-sister to 5 winners including the Group 1 winner Gran Criterium winner Kirklees and the Group 1 St Leger and Hong Kong Vase winner Mastery and to the dam of the Group 1 Eclipse Stakes winner Mukhadram. The second dam, Moyesii (by Diesis), won once at 3 yrs in France and is a half-sister to 3 winners including the Group 3 Prix de Fontainebleau winner Bowman. (Saleh Al Homaizi & Imad Al Sagar). *"She's in pre-training after having had an injury, but she's absolutely fine now. A really strong filly, I'm looking forward to her coming back because I loved what I saw beforehand".*

1315. BEE CASE ★★★★
br.f. Showcasing – Binabee (Galileo). February 3. First foal. The dam is an unraced half-sister to several winners including the Australian Group 3 12.5f winner Excess Knowledge (by Monsun). The second dam, Quenched (by Dansili), a useful listed 12f winner, is a half-sister to the Group 2 Dante Stakes second Raincoat. (Khalid Abdulla). *"She's already done a bit of work, she's got lots of speed and I can see her starting in May over five furlongs. She looks really quick, will probably stay six furlongs in time and is still strengthening up. She could be a Royal Ascot type of filly when you consider that she's well-bred, by a good stallion, shows lots of speed and has a lovely attitude. In late April she'll be ready to rock n roll".*

1316. BUSH HOUSE (IRE) ★★★ ♠
b.c. Canford Cliffs – Magena (Kingmambo). May 6. Second foal. £150,000Y. Doncaster Premier. A C Elliott. Brother to the fair 2015 2-y-o 7f winner Poplar Close. The dam is an unraced half-sister to 8 minor winners here and abroad. The second dam, Vingt Et Une (by Sadler's Wells), a minor French 3-y-o winner, is a sister to the Group 1 10.5f Prix Lupin and US Grade 2 1m winner Johann Quatz and to the 10.5f to 13.5f listed winner Walter Willy and a half-sister to the top-class middle-distance colt Hernando, winner of the Group 1 Prix du Jockey Club and the Group 1 Prix Lupin. (W J & T C O Gredley). *"A lovely colt, he's not forward because he had a long break after the sales and considering he's a May foal by Canford Cliffs I think he'll be a lovely 2-y-o come August time. He's a good size and a good mover, we like him but he hasn't been here very long".*

1317. CHOUMICHA ★★★ ♠
b.f. Paco Boy – Galicuix (Galileo). February 25. £280,000Y. Doncaster Premier. Tony Nerses. Sister to the Group 2 7f Vintage Stakes winner Galileo Gold. The dam ran twice unplaced and is a half-sister to the Group 1 5f King's Stand Stakes and Group 1 Prix de l'Abbaye winner Goldream. The second dam, Clizia (by Machiavellian), is an unraced half-sister to 3 winners including the multiple listed winner and Group 2 placed Mont Rocher. (Saleh Al Homaizi & Imad Al Sagar). *"A full-sister to my 3-y-o colt Galileo Gold, she's quite different to him but changing and developing all the time. She's very straightforward whereas he's quite quirky and has his own ideas about things. She's good mover, I'm very happy with her and I'm thinking she'll be out in June or July".*

1318. CLOUD DRAGON (IRE) ★★★
br.c. Dark Angel – Karliysha (Kalanisi). April 17. Fifth foal. 115,000Y. Tattersalls October Book 2. Sun Bloodstock. Half-brother to the fair 7f to 10f winner of 5 races Maude Adams (by Rock Of Gibraltar). The dam, a minor French 3-y-o winner, is a half-sister to 7 winners including Karasta (2-y-o Group 3 1m May Hill Stakes), Kasthari (Group 2 2m 2f Doncaster Cup in a dead-heat) and Kargali (Group 3 Gladness Stakes). The second dam, Karliyka (by Last Tycoon), a French 3-y-o winner of 4 races, was listed placed over 1m and 10f and is a half-sister to 4 winners. (Sun Bloodstock Sarl). *"A big, strong horse, quite mature and I think he could easily run in June. I like what I've seen, he moves well and he's taken his work well so far".*

1319. COPPER KNIGHT (IRE) ★★★★
b.c. Sir Prancealot – Mystic Dream (Oasis Dream). January 15. Second foal. £30,000Y. Doncaster Premier. Anglia Bloodstock. The dam, a quite useful French 7f winner, is a half-sister to 2 winners. The second dam, Tarot

Card (by Fasliyev), a useful 2-y-o 6f winner, is a half-sister to 6 winners including the very useful listed 1m and subsequent US Grade 3 8.5f winner Out Of Reach and to the useful 2-y-o 6f winner and Cherry Hinton Stakes and Fred Darling Stakes placed Well Warned. (Anglia Bloodstock Syndicate VIII). *"He should be one of our first 2-y-o's to run. He's built like a tank, not a very tall tank but really strong and he's done a couple of bits of work. I don't think he'd want cut in the ground so we might run him on the polytrack or wait for the Conditions race at the Craven meeting that Gifted Master won last year. He goes well, the noises I hear about the sire are good and the jockeys who have ridden this colt say he's the sort that might have a bit of class, so not just an early type".* **TRAINERS' BARGAIN BUY**

1320. ESCOBAR (IRE) ★★★ ♠

b.c. Famous Name – Saying Grace (Brief Truce). April 7. Sixth foal. €105,000foal. Goffs November foals. Bobby O'Ryan. Half-brother to the fair 9f, 10f and Hong Kong winner Ghetto Gospel (by Celtic Swing) and to the minor Irish 2-y-o 6f winner Bobbi Grace (by Big Bad Bob). The dam, an Irish 6f and 6.5f winner, was third in the Group 2 Prix d'Astarte and is a half-sister to 5 winners. The second dam, Adamparis (by Robellino), a modest dual 7f winner, is a half-sister to 3 winners. (Carmichael Jennings). *"A beautiful, big, strong, really athletic colt. He's not a forward 2-y-o type but he finds it all easy and I'd say he'll be racing by late summer/early autumn".*

1321. EVERGATE ★★★★

b.c. Exceed And Excel – Lion Forest (Forestry). March 8. Fourth foal. Half-brother to the fair 2015 2-y-o 7f winner Gaspirali (by Oasis Dream). The dam is an unraced sister to the US Grade 1 Hollywood Starlet Stakes winner Diplomat Lady and a half-sister to 9 winners including the US Grade 2 Comely Stakes winner Dream Play. The second dam, Playcaller (by Saratoga Six), a winner of 3 stakes races at 2 and 3 yrs in the USA, is a half-sister to 8 winners. (Mr V I Araci). *"This is a difficult one because I adored his brother last year and although he did eventually win he ultimately let me down. As a result I'm trying not to get over-excited about this colt because he's a better individual. A really good mover with a good head on him, he's very good-looking and in isolation I'd be really excited about him".*

1322. EXPRESS LADY (IRE) ★★★ ♠

b.f. Helmet – Star Express (Sadler's Wells). April 11. Tenth foal. 40,000Y. Tattersalls October Book 2. Rob Speers. Half-sister to the quite useful 1m and 9f winner Dubai Sunshine (by Dubawi), to the fair 7f winner Desert Shine (by Green Desert), the modest 5f winner Star Twilight and the moderate 6f winner Haedi (both by King's Best). The dam, a minor 12f winner, is a sister to the Group 3 Greenham Stakes winner Yalaietanee and a half-sister to the Group 3 Molecomb Stakes winner Sahara Star (dam of the Group 2 winner Land Of Dreams). The second dam, Vaigly Star (by Star Appeal), a smart sprint winner of 3 races and second in the Group 1 July Cup, is a half-sister to the high-class sprinter Vaigly Great. (Dr A Ridha). *"I was glad to see Mark Johnston's pair of Helmet 2-y-o's win in late March because I love this filly and yet all my Australian contacts have been saying rude things about the sire. He hasn't had a winner down there yet. This filly is strong but not quite as forward as I first thought she'd be, but she is out of a Sadler's Wells mare. I like her a lot and I'd be disappointed if she weren't a smart filly this year".*

1323. FORTITUDE (IRE) ★★★★

b.f. Oasis Dream – Sweepstake (Acclamation). January 25. Fourth foal. 240,000Y. Tattersalls October Book 1. John & Jake Warren. The dam, a 2-y-o listed 5f winner, was third in the Group 3 6f Princess Margaret Stakes and second in a US Grade 3 stakes and is a full or half-sister to 5 winners. The second dam, Dust Flicker (by Suave Dancer), placed fourth once over 10f, is a half-sister to 6 winners including the Group 3 winners Dust Dancer (dam of the US Grade 2 winner Spotlight) and Bulaxie (dam of the Group 2 winner Claxon). (Mr I Al Khalifa). *"She's all about being a 2-y-o and looks like a very good cross of Oasis Dream and Acclamation. She was an early foal but she's still growing, has good closed growth plates in her knees and has done one piece of work which she did well. She has a lovely attitude and she looks every inch a 2-y-o type".*

1324. GLOBAL ALEXANDER (IRE) ★★★
br.f. Dark Angel – Taraeff (Cape Cross).
February 19. First foal. €160,000Y. Goffs Orby.
BBA (Ire). The dam is an unraced half-sister
to 2 minor winners. The second dam, Tarfshi
(by Mtoto), a winner of 5 races from 7f (at 2
yrs) to 10f including the Group 2 Pretty Polly
Stakes, is a full or half-sister to 6 winners
including the champion 2-y-o filly and
Cheveley Park Stakes winner Embassy. (Mr
Noel O'Callaghan). *"A lovely big, strong filly,
she's a bit more Cape Cross than Dark Angel
to look at. She's cantering now after a short
break, doing well, and I would guess she'll be
racing from July onwards. There's nothing to
dislike about her".*

1325. GULLIVER ★★★
b.c. Sayif – Sweet Coincidence (Mujahid).
April 8. Ninth foal. 50,000Y. Tattersalls October
Book 1. Tony Nerses. Half-brother to the
smart 2-y-o dual 6f winner and English and
Irish Group 1 1,000 Guineas second Lightning
Thunder (by Dutch Art), to the quite useful
11f to 14f winner of 6 races Lucky Punt, the
fair 14f and 17f winner May Contain Nuts,
the modest 2-y-o 9f winner Llandavery (all
by Auction House), the fair 2-y-o 6f winner
Rafale (by Sleeping Indian) and fair 10f winner
Sweet Selection (by Stimulation). The dam, a
fair 2-y-o 6f winner, is a half-sister to 3 other
minor winners. The second dam, Sibilant (by
Selkirk), placed at 3 yrs in France, is a half-
sister to 3 winners. (Saleh Al Homaizi & Imad
Al Sagar). *"He's a really good style of a horse.
Well-balanced, strong and forward-going, I'd
be disappointed if he's not a 2-y-o winner".*

1326. HYPERFOCUS (IRE) ★★★★ ♠
b.br.c. Intense Focus – Jouel (Machiavellian).
March 11. Fourth foal. €32,000Y. Tattersalls
Ireland September. Amanda Skiffington. Half-
brother to the quite useful 6f and 1m winner
King Bertie (by Clodovil) and to the modest 7f
winner Ingleby Spring (by Zebedee). The dam,
placed twice at 3 yrs in France, is a half-sister
to 2 minor winners. The second dam, Visions
On Space (by Lure), a minor French 3-y-o
winner, is a half-sister to 10 winners including
the Group 1 winners Dolphin Street, Insight
and Saffron Walden. (MPH Racing – II). *"He
looks like he's got an engine, he has a fantastic
attitude and looks like he wants to find the line
and win. I think he'll be a six furlong 2-y-o,
he's still growing and developing and I think
he'll continue to do that all year. He's looks
plenty speedy enough and does everything
right".*

1327. IBN ALEMARAT (IRE) ★★★
b.c. Zoffany – Trois Graces (Alysheba). April
29. Thirteenth foal. 42,000Y. Tattersalls
October Book 2. Stephen Hillen. Half-brother
to 5 winners including the 2-y-o listed 5f
Prix Yacowlef winner and Group 3 second
Abbeyside (by Danehill Dancer), the listed
1m winner Flat Spin (by Spinning World) and
the fairly useful 2-y-o 7f winner Goodness
Gracious (by Green Desert). The dam, a
French 1m winner, is a half-sister to the
Group 3 winners Rami and Crack Regiment
and to the Prix de l'Abbaye second La Grand
Epoque. The second dam, Ancient Regime (by
Olden Times), won the Group 1 Prix Morny
and is a sister to the Prix Maurice de Gheest
winner Cricket Ball. (A Al Shaikh). *"I have a
few Zoffany 2-y-o's and he may be the most
forward of them. He's getting better every
week, has a nice attitude and he's a nice
mover. Hard to fault at this stage".*

1328. INSPECTOR ★★★
b.c. Lawman – Helter Helter (Seeking The
Gold). February 7. Third foal. 95,000Y.
Tattersalls October Book 2. John Warren.
Half-brother to the fair 13f and 2m winner
Trafalgar Rock (by Mount Nelson). The dam, a
12f winner of 3 races in France, is a half-sister
to 6 winners including the US Grade 3 winner
Beauty Parlor and the French listed winner The
Brothers War. The second dam, Moon Queen
(by Sadler's Wells), won the Group 2 Prix de
Royallieu and a US Grade 3 stakes and is a
sister to the very useful dual 12f winner and
Group 2 placed Rostropovich, closely related
to the Group 3 Premio Dormello winner
Barafamy and a half-sister to the US Grade 2
winner Innuendo. (Highclere Thoroughbred
Racing – TS Eliot). *"A strong, well-made colt
and a great mover with a good attitude. He's
one of those horses that never really grew a
winter coat, which is what I always like to see. I
always think it's a sign that a horse is thriving.
He has a Derby entry so he's not doing serious
stuff now, but with everything he's doing he
looks nice".*

1329. KHATTAR ★★★
b.c. Frankel – Danceabout (Shareef Dancer).
April 10. Eleventh foal. €300,000Y. Arqana
Deauville August. Al Shaqab Racing. Half-
brother to the French listed 9f winner and
Group 3 placed Rainbow Dancing (by
Rainbow Quest), to the fairly useful 1m
(at 2 yrs) to 14f winner and listed-placed
Handsome Man (by Nayef), the fairly useful
2-y-o 6f winner Zaffaan (by Efisio) and the fair
10f winner Making Shapes. The dam won the
Group 2 Sun Chariot Stakes and is a half-sister
to the dual Group 3 winner Pole Position. The
second dam, Putupon (by Mummy's Pet), a
fairly useful 2-y-o 5f winner, is half-sister to
the good horses Jupiter Island, Pushy and
Precocious. (Al Shaqab Racing). *"He's got a
real air about him this lad. At the sale he really
filled the bridle and he's got a purposeful,
workmanlike attitude. He's getting stronger
and stronger, moves like Frankel when he
canters and gallops but physically he actually
looks like his damsire Shareef Dancer. A lovely
colt – I love all three of my Frankels. One for
seven furlongs and a mile later on, he doesn't
look like he wants rushing but he's doing it all
himself quite naturally".*

1330. KODIAC KHAN (IRE) ★★★
b.c. Kodiac – Mirwara (Darshaan). May
3. Ninth living foal. €65,000Y. Goffs Orby.
Howson & Houldsworth. Brother to the fair
11.5f winner Stolen Story and half-brother
to 6 winners including the useful 1m to 10.5f
winner of 16 races and listed-placed Dunaskin
(by Bahhare), the Irish 9f to 2m and hurdles
winner Piltown (by Namid) and the minor US
4-y-o winner Mirific (by Perugino). The dam is
an unraced half-sister to 7 winners including
the Group 3 Prix de Flore winner Miliana. The
second dam, Mirana (by Ela-Mana-Mou),
a useful Irish 12f winner, is a half-sister to 5
winners. (Mr H A Lootah). *"He was very small
when we bought him but he was a late foal.
He's always done everything with an air of
class and ability, he's grown, developed and
he isn't small anymore. I'll be pushing on with
him soon and I'm very happy with him".*

1331. LEWINSKY (IRE) ★★★ ♠
b.f. Famous Name – Happy Flight (Titus Livius).
April 30. Eighth foal. £38,000Y. Doncaster
Premier. Amanda Skiffington. Half-sister to
the Italian listed-placed winner of 8 races
Red Kimi (by Denon). The dam won 4 races
at 2 and 3 yrs in Italy and is a half-sister to 4
other minor winners abroad. The second dam,
Gezalle (by Shareef Dancer), won over 1m
and 9f in Ireland at 3 yrs and is a half-sister to
6 winners. (Anglia Bloodstock Syndicate IX).
*"Small samples are dangerous things but I'd
be tipping the first season sire Famous Name
to have a good start on the two that I've got.
Great movers with great attitudes and with
size and scope to them. This is a nice filly for
the second half of the season, she's lovely".*

1332. MAJORIS (IRE) ★★★
b.c. Frankel – Drops (Kingmambo). February
14. First foal. The dam, a modest 9f placed
maiden in Ireland, is a half-sister to the French
Group 2 1m 7f Prix Kergorlay winner Alex
My Boy. The second dam, Alexandrova (by
Sadler's Wells), won the Oaks, the Irish Oaks
and the Yorkshire Oaks and is a sister to the
Derby third Masterofthehorse and closely
related to the 2-y-o Group 1 6f Cheveley Park
Stakes winner Magical Romance. (Al Asayl
Bloodstock). *"I've got three Frankels and I
think this one is the most forward. He's the
smallest, the mare wasn't a great deal but it's
a lovely family and I imagine he'll be one of
Frankel's first runners. I'm hoping he'll start in
a Newbury maiden in June and then go for the
Chesham Stakes. I'm very happy with him, all
of my Frankels are beautiful movers and they
have active minds, but not silly or quirky".*

1333. MAZYOUN ★★★★ ♠
b.c. Mayson – Hypnotize (Machiavellian).
February 3. Tenth foal. 115,000Y. Tattersalls
October Book 1. Al Shaqab Racing. Closely
related 2-y-o Group 1 6f Cheveley Park
Stakes and Group 2 6f Lowther Stakes winner
Hooray (by Invincible Spirit) and half-sister
to the useful 2-y-o listed 8.3f winner of 7
races Hypnotic (by Lomitas), the fairly useful
2-y-o 1m winner Notorize (by Hernando), the
quite useful 2-y-o 6f winner Hip (by Pivotal)
and the quite useful dual 7f winner Macedon
(by Dansili). The dam, a useful 2-y-o dual 7f
winner, is a half-sister to 8 winners including
Dazzle (Group 3 6f Cherry Hinton Stakes).
The second dam, Belle et Deluree (by The
Minstrel), won over 1m (at 2 yrs) and 10f in
France and is a half-sister to 5 winners. (Al

Shaqab Racing). *"A three-parts brother to the champion 2-y-o filly Hooray. If I remember rightly the only fault she had was she was very small. This colt is not that way at all – he's a big colt, but he's mature, has a great mind and a great action. He hasn't worked yet but we'll probably have a look soon to see if he should run in May over six furlongs. It's a 2-y-o family, he doesn't move as though he necessarily wants soft ground and he's a proper looking horse. I'm hoping he's a bit like Ivawood – just bigger and more advanced than most of his generation. I'm looking forward to seeing what's under the bonnet".*

1334. MUNAWER ★★★
ch.c. Dutch Art – Cantal (Pivotal). February 12. First foal. 350,000Y. Tattersalls October Book 1. Al Shaqab Racing. The dam, a fair 2-y-o 7f winner, is a half-sister to 2 winners including the 2-y-o Group 3 7f winner Horris Hill Stakes winner Evasive (by Elusive Quality). The second dam, Canda (by Storm Cat), is an unraced half-sister to 3 winners including the 2-y-o Group 3 5.5f Prix d'Arenburg winner Moon Driver and the Grade 2 Californian Stakes second Mojave Moon. (Al Shaqab Racing). *"He looks like a solid, strong, Dutch Art type of 2-y-o sprinter. Everyone who rides him likes him, so I hope he's as nice as he looks because Cheveley Park didn't give him away. He canters like a horse that cost a lot of money and although it's early days for him yet he's doing well".*

1335. NADIA GLORY ★★★
b.f. Oasis Dream – Soon (Galileo). January 23. First foal. The dam, a fairly useful Irish 7f (at 2 yrs) and listed 8.5f winner, was Group 3 placed twice and is a half-sister to 5 winners including the Derby second Walk In The Park. The second dam, Classic Park (by Robellino), won 3 races including the Irish 1,000 Guineas and is a half-sister to 10 winners including the US Grade 2 winner Rumpipumpy. (Saleh Al Homaizi & Imad Al Sagar). *"Her dam was bought, with this filly inside her, for 800,000 Gns. She goes nicely, isn't as forward as some Oasis Dream's but I think that's the Galileo coming through. She has a really deep girth, there's nothing to dislike about her and I would have thought she'd be one to appear in late summer. Even though she may want sprint trips she doesn't look sharp".*

1336. NILE EMPRESS ★★★★
b.f. Holy Roman Emperor – Temple Of Thebes (Bahri). February 16. Fourth foal. 20,000Y. Tattersalls October Book 2. Hugo Palmer. Half-sister to the quite useful triple 6f winner Ex Ex (by Exceed And Excel), to the modest 1m to 10.5f winner Walk Like A Giant and the modest 10f to 13f winner Percella (both by Sir Percy). The dam, a quite useful dual 6f winner, is a half-sister to 2 winners including the 2-y-o listed 5f Windsor Castle Stakes winner and US Grade 3 placed Flashman's Papers. The second dam, Franglais (by Lion Cavern), won 3 races from 6f to 1m at 3 and 4 yrs in Germany and is a half-sister to 6 winners including the Grade 1 E P Taylor Stakes winner Fraulein. (Mr & Mrs A E Pakenham). *"She looks sharp and is virtually ready to run but I don't think she'll want soft ground. A dry spell now and we'll be running her, she's a beautifully balanced filly with a lovely stride and a great attitude. Probably the strongest and the sharpest of my fillies at this stage".*

1337. NURSE NIGHTINGALE ★★★
b.f. Nathaniel – Whazzat (Daylami). March 14. Sixth foal. 100,000Y. Tattersalls October Book 1. Not sold. Half-sister to the fairly useful 7.5f (at 2 yrs) and 1m winner and dual listed-placed The Shrew (by Dansili) and to the quite useful 6f (at 2 yrs) and 7f winner Theladyinquestion (by Dubawi). The dam, a useful 2-y-o listed 7f Chesham Stakes winner, is a half-sister to 6 winners including the listed 1m and Italian Group 3 1m winner Whazzis. The second dam, Wosaita (by Generous), a fair 12.3f placed maiden, is a half-sister to 10 winners including the Group 1 Prix de Diane winner Rafha (dam of the Group 1 Haydock Sprint Cup winner and sire Invincible Spirit). (W J & T C O Gredley). *"A big, scopey filly, very attractive and much like her sire. I would have thought she'd be an August/September type of filly. A nice mover, she's getting stronger all the time".*

1338. OMEROS ★★★★ ♣♣
ch.c. Poet's Voice – Caribbean Pearl (Silver Hawk). January 26. Sixth foal. 50,000Y. Tattersalls October Book 1. Amanda Skiffington. Half-brother to the fairly useful 10f winner Saab Almanal (by Dubawi). The dam, a fair 10f and 12f winner, is a half-

sister to 4 winners including the Group 3 7f Criterion Stakes winner Racer Forever. The second dam, Ras Shaikh (by Sheikh Albadou), a quite useful 2-y-o 6f winner, was listed-placed at 3 yrs and is a half-sister to the fairly useful dual 6f winner Epsom Cyclone. (Mr C Humber). *"This is a gorgeous horse with a Book One pedigree. He's really nice and we felt that last year was the time to buy a Poet's Voice because the year before they were too expensive. He's extremely nice and his name comes from a Caribbean epic poem".*

1339. STAR ARCHER ★★★★
b.c. Champs Elysees – Postale (Zamindar). January 25. First foal. The dam is an unplaced sister to the French listed placed Pure Joy and a half-sister to 5 winners including the Group 1 Prix Jean Prat winner Mutual Trust. The second dam, Posteritas (by Lear Fan), a fairly useful listed 10f winner, is a half-sister to 7 winners. (Khalid Abdulla). *"He is absolutely stunning. A colt with a great stride, he's obviously not going to be an early 2-y-o but if he were to win a race or two at the backend we could be talking about exciting races for him next year. It would be no surprise on what I've seen so far".*

1340. TZAVO ★★★★★
b.c. Frankel – Hazel Lavery (Excellent Art). April 10. First foal. The dam, a 7f (at 2 yrs) and Group 3 12f St Simon Stakes and listed 10f Aphrodite Stakes winner, is a half-sister to the useful 10f and 12f winner and Group 3 12f second Leo Gali. The second dam, Reprise (by Darshaan), placed fourth once over 10f, is a half-sister to 3 winners. (Al Asayl Bloodstock). *"Of the three Frankels I have this is the only one that looks like him and as such, he's very impressive to look at. He's very immature but furnishing and maturing all the time. He's been in, done well, had a break and he's back in pre-training now. He moves really well and his pedigree makes you dream he may be the heir to his Dad. He's hard to fault".*

1341. UNFORGETABLE FILLY ★★★
b.f. Sepoy – Beautiful Filly (Oasis Dream). March 1. Fourth foal. 50,000Y. Tattersalls October Book 2. Hugo Palmer. Half-sister to the quite useful 6f and 7f winner at 2 and 3 yrs Speedy Move (by Iffraaj) and to the fair 2-y-o 7f winner Wickhambrook (by Dubawi). The dam, a fair 6f and 7f winner at 3 yrs, is a half-sister to one minor winner in the USA. The second dam, Royal Alchemist (by Royal Academy), was placed in the USA and is a half-sister to 4 winners including the Group 1 Sprint Cup winner Dowsing and the US Grade 1 winner Fire The Groom (dam of the dual Group 1 winning sprinter Stravinsky). (Dr A Ridha). *"Sepoy isn't exactly storming away with honours Down Under but I like the ones I have. This filly is strong, well-made, she moves well and there's nothing wrong with her at all. Still quite immature, but she's ticked all the boxes so far. I would guess she'll make a mid-summer 2-y-o".*

1342. VOI ★★★
b.f. Holy Roman Emperor – Bride Unbridled (Hurricane Run). February 18. First foal. The dam is an unraced half-sister to the fairly useful 2-y-o dual 6f winner and Group 2 Railway Stakes third French Emperor. The second dam, Se La Vie (by Highest Honor), won 2 minor races at 2 and 3 yrs in France and is a half-sister to 4 winners including the Canadian stakes winner and Grade 2 placed Daylight Come. (Al Asayl Bloodstock). *"I like everything that I see. She's a good-mover with a good attitude and looks like a summer 2-y-o".*

1343. WEDDING BREAKFAST (IRE) ★★★ ♣
ch.f. Casamento – Fair Countenance (Almutawakel). February 21. Third foal. £26,000Y. Doncaster Premier. Sackville/Donald. The dam, a moderate 9f winner, is a half-sister to useful 5f (at 2 yrs) and 6f winner and second in the Super Sprint, is a half-sister to 2 winners including the listed National Stakes winner and Group 3 third Icesolator and the dam of the Group 3 Horris Hill Stakes winner Don't Tell Dad. The second dam, Zinnia (by Zilzal), ran once unplaced and is a half-sister to 4 winners including the dam of the Group 3 Cornwallis Stakes winner Mubhij. (De La Warr Racing). *"She has quite immature knees at the moment so we're going carefully with her, but she has quite a fast ground action and is a big, attractive filly. I think she was well-bought and I'm very sweet on her".*

1344. WHITE ROSA (IRE) ★★★
b.f. Galileo – Dhanyata (Danetime). April 11. Fourth foal. 150,000Y. Tattersalls October Book 1. Stephen Hillen. Half-sister to the fair 2015 6f placed 2-y-o Wernotfamusanymore (by Oasis Dream). The dam, a smart 2-y-o Group 3 6f Sirenia Stakes winner, was second in the Group 1 Cheveley Park Stakes and is a half-sister to 5 winners including the smart 6f Stewards Cup winner Guinea Hunter. The second dam, Preponderance (by Cyrano de Bergerac), a quite useful 2-y-o dual 5f winner, is a half-sister to 6 winners. (Highbank Stud). *"More forward than my other 2-y-o Galileo filly but maybe that's the Danetime coming through. She's just got a bit of class about her, she's not going to be that forward but looks strong enough to be a 2-y-o later on"*.

1345. ZAHIYA ★★★★ ♠
b.f. Invincible Spirit – Dalasyla (Marju). January 30. Fifth foal. 300,000Y. Tattersalls October Book 1. Al Shaqab Racing. Half-sister to the fairly useful listed 7f winner Dalkova (by Galileo) and to the minor French 3-y-o winner Diavola (by Duke Of Marmalade). The dam won once at 3 yrs in France and is a half-sister to the Group 1 Coronation Cup and Group 1 Hong Kong Vase winner Daliapour and to the smart 2m Queens Vase winner Dalampour. The second dam, Dalara (by Doyoun), winner of the Group 2 12.5f Prix de Royallieu, was third in the Group 1 Prix Royal-Oak and is a half-sister the French Derby winner and high-class sire Darshaan and the Prix Vermeille winner Darara (dam of the Group 1 winners Dar Re Mi, Rewilding, Diaghilev and Darazari). (Al Shaqab Racing). *"Absolutely beautiful. By an excellent stallion, she was the first of all the 2-y-o's to come in her coat and does everything with an air of class. It's not a sharp family and if I wasn't aware of it I'd be thinking this filly is a speedy, early 2-y-o. I hope her apparent precocity is ability that will serve her well over seven furlongs and a mile later on"*.

1346. ZUMRAN ★★★
b.f. Rock Of Gibraltar – Maid For Winning (Gone West). March 31. Fourth foal. 45,000Y. Tattersalls October Book 1. Rob Speers. Half-sister to the very useful 7f (at 2 yrs) and 1m winner and Group 2 Joel Stakes third Hors de Combat, to the useful 6f (at 2 yrs) and 6.5f winner and Group 3 third Stroll Patrol (both by Mount Nelson) and a minor 2-y-o winner in Germany by Forestry. The dam is an unplaced half-sister to 7 winners including the US Grade 1 9f winner Stroll and the US stakes winner and Grade 1 third Patrol. The second dam, Maid For Walking (by Prince Sabo), a 2-y-o 5f and 6f winner, was second in the Group 3 Princess Margaret Stakes and is a half-sister to 5 winners. (Mr V I Araci). *"She's not very big, keen to get on with things and looks like she goes well. She's sharp, didn't cost a lot by the owner's standards and she looks all there, so she'll be racing in April"*.

1347. UNNAMED ★★★
b.c. Exceed And Excel – Adonesque (Sadler's Wells). March 6. Ninth living foal. 110,000Y. Tattersalls October Book 1. Hugo Palmer. Half-brother to 6 winners including the fairly useful 7f to 10f winner Busker (by Street Cry), the French listed-placed winner Bergamask (by Kingmambo and herself dam of the Group 2 Coventry Stakes winner Buratino), the fairly useful 2-y-o 6f winner Alderney (by Elusive Quality) and the quite useful 2-y-o dual 1m winner Fareej (by Kingmambo). The dam, a listed 10f winner, is a half-sister to Danehill Dancer. The second dam, Mira Adonde (by Sharpen Up), ran once unplaced and is a half-sister to 4 winners. (Sheikh R D Al Maktoum). *"A gorgeous colt, he just had a tiny setback and he's still in pre-training. A big colt, he's all class"*.

1348. UNNAMED ★★★★
b.c. Excelebration – Blissful Beat (Beat Hollow). March 23. Third foal. €160,000Y. Arqana Deauville August. Rob Speers. Half-brother to the smart Group 3 7f Minstrel Stakes winner Home Of The Brave (by Starspangledbanner). The dam is an unraced half-sister to 8 winners including the Group 3 9f Prix de Conde winner Rashbag and the Group 3 7f Criterion Stakes winner Suggestive. The second dam, Pleasuring (by Good Times), is a sprint placed half-sister to 5 winners including Rose Of Montreaux (Group 3 1,000 Guineas Trial) and the Group 3 Princess Elizabeth Stakes winner Bay Street (herself the dam of 5 stakes winners). (Mr V I Araci). *"Whether he'll end up a better horse than his half-brother I don't*

know, but he's been a better model all along – a bit more masculine, bigger and stronger. Although he's very similar in many ways I'm not sure he'll have Home Of The Brave's raw speed, but he looks the part and it's hard not to fall in love with him. I think he'll be a seven furlong/mile type".

1349. UNNAMED ★★★
b.c. Zoffany – Corking (Montjeu). April 25. Third foal. €80,000Y. Goffs Orby. MPH Racing. The dam, a moderate 2m winner, is a full or half-sister to 8 winners including the smart 10.4f John Smiths Handicap and triple Hong Kong listed stakes winner Sobriety and the dam of the US Grade 2 winner Starlarks. The second dam, Scanno's Choice (by Pennine Walk), a modest middle-distance placed maiden in Ireland, is a half-sister to 6 winners including the US Grade 2 winner Dilmoun. (MPH Racing – II). *"He's done very well, he came in late due to a small injury but he's totally over that and he's been going well. A strong, well-made, good-moving type".*

1350. UNNAMED ★★★
b.c. Kodiac – Fee Eria (Always Fair). March 22. Tenth living foal. €130,000Y. Tattersalls Ireland September. Amanda Skiffington. Half-brother to the fair triple 6f winner Dametime (by Danetime), to the moderate dual 7f winner Mutassem (by Fasliyev), a minor 2-y-o French winner by Bushranger and a winner in Greece by Spinning World. The dam is an unplaced half-sister to 6 winners including the Grade 1 Hollywood Derby winner Super Quercus. The second dam, Ginger Candy (by Hilal), was a listed-placed winner of 3 races in France. (Woodhurst Construction Ltd). *"A beautiful horse, he's been away a bit because of a slight injury but he's fine now. He's strong and quite big for a Kodiac, but not ungainly at all. One for the second half of the season and I'm very happy with him. A nice, solid colt".*

1351. UNNAMED ★★★
b.c. Zoffany – Luminous Gold (Fantastic Light). March 15. Third foal. 42,000Y. Tattersalls October Book 2. Seventh Lap. Half-brother to the fairly useful 2-y-o 6f winner and Group 3 Prestige Stakes third Zifena (by Zamindar). The dam, a fair 5f and 6f winner of 3 races from 2 to 5 yrs, is a half-sister to 7 winners including the Group 2 5f Flying Childers Stakes third Kissing Lights. The second dam, Nasaieb (by Fairy King), a fairly useful 2-y-o 5f winner, was third in the listed 5f National Stakes and is a half-sister to 5 winners including the Group 3 7f Solario Stakes winner Raise A Grand. (Seventh Lap Racing). *"He'll definitely be a 2-y-o, he's a very good mover and possibly the earliest of my Zoffany 2-y-o's. Still growing and developing, he's going well but still a bit immature".*

1352. UNNAMED ★★★
b.f. Oasis Dream – Maskunah (Sadler's Wells). March 18. Twelfth foal. Sister to the fair 2015 2-y-o 1m winner Natural Beauty, closely related to the Group 3 Cumberland Lodge and Group 3 September Stakes winner Laaheb and to the useful dual 7f winner and Group 3 second Ruwaiyan (both by Cape Cross) and half-sister to 2 winners including the fairly useful listed-placed 7f winner Guarantia (by Selkirk). The dam is an unraced half-sister to 6 winners including the multiple Group 1 winners Warrsan and Luso, and the Group winners Cloud Castle and Needle Gun. The second dam, Lucayan Princess (by High Line), won the listed 6f Sweet Solera Stakes at 2 yrs and is a half-sister to 7 winners. (S Manana). *"She was quite a plain thing when she came in but she's getting better looking and stronger as every week goes by. She has a bit of class about her, isn't an early type, but I'm sure she'll be a 2-y-o from mid-summer onwards".*

1353. UNNAMED ★★★
b.c. High Chaparral – Missionary Hymn (Giant's Causeway). April 9. Third foal. 125,000Y. Tattersalls October Book 2. MPH Racing. Brother to the fair 10f winner High And Flighty and half-brother to Gaelic Angel (by Pour Moi), unplaced in two starts at 2 yrs in 2015. The dam is an unraced half-sister to 8 minor winners. The second dam, Minister's Song (by Deputy Minister), is an unraced half-sister to 9 winners including the US multiple Grade 1 winners Devils Bag and Glorious Song (the dam of Singspiel). (MPH Racing – II). *"A beautiful horse, he's having a break at the moment but he's got substance, style and scope. He's got a Derby entry, he's all class and hard to fault".*

1354. UNNAMED ★★★
b.f. Invincible Spirit – Queen Of Tara (Sadler's Wells). March 21. Fifth foal. €150,000Y. Goffs Orby. Amanda Skiffington. Sister to the fairly useful 2-y-o 6f winner and listed-placed Mar Mar and half-sister to the minor French 3-y-o winner Like Me (by Duke Of Marmalade). The dam is an unraced half-sister to 9 winners including the 2-y-o Group 1 1m Grand Criterium winner Second Empire, the Group 3 10f Ballysax Stakes winner Balestrini and the listed winners Ihtiram, Ajhiba and Hemingway. The second dam, Welsh Love (by Ela-Mana-Mou), a minor Irish 12f winner, is a half-sister to 8 winners including the Coronation Stakes winner Flame of Tara (dam of the Group 1 winners Salsabil and Marju) and to the dam of the Breeders' Cup Turf winner Northern Spur. (Carmichael Jennings). *"She's lovely, not a big 2-y-o but I don't think it's a big family. She has a great way of going and I would have thought she'd be a 2-y-o from July onwards".*

1355. UNNAMED ★★★
b.f. Showcasing – Small Fortune (Anabaa). February 12. Fourth foal. 70,000Y. Tattersalls October Book 1. Rabbah Bloodstock. Half-sister to the quite useful 13f and hurdles winner Bank Bonus (by Motivator). The dam, a fair 1m winner, is a half-sister to 5 winners including the useful dual 6f winner (including at 2 yrs) Instalment and the listed-placed Pack Together. The second dam, New Assembly (by Machiavellian), a useful 9f and 10f winner, was stakes-placed in the USA and is a sister to the 7f (at 2 yrs) and Group 1 9f Dubai Duty Free Stakes winner Right Approach and a half-sister to 7 winners. (Mr A Al Mansoori). *"A big, strong filly, not seemingly that early and more like a seven furlong type 2-y-o. A really nice filly with size and scope, I'm sure she'll have the opportunity to win this year and do well as a 3-y-o as well".*

1356. UNNAMED ★★★
ch.c. Sepoy – Sweet Folly (Singspiel). April 10. Ninth foal. 50,000Y. Tattersalls October Book 2. Not sold. Half-brother to the quite useful 7f winner Frivolous (by Green Desert), to the quite useful 10f winner Fort Belvedere (by King's Best) and the fair 12f and hurdles winner Gilded Age (by Cape Cross). The dam, winner of the Group 3 11f Prix Cleopatre, was third in the Group 2 12f Prix de Malleret and is a half-sister to 7 winners including the Coronation Stakes winner Kissing Cousin and the Group 3 Earl Of Sefton Stakes winner Apprehension. The second dam, First Kiss (by Kris), a quite useful 10f winner, is a half-sister to 2 winners. (Mr A Menahi). *"He was very light and ribby, but he's done well and furnished as every week goes by. A really good mover, I like what I see of my Sepoy 2-y-o's but I'd be more optimistic if Sepoy started to get winners in Australia".*

1357. UNNAMED ★★★
gr.f. Native Khan – Unity (Sadler's Wells). March 1. Second foal. The dam, a useful 12f winner and third in the Group 3 12f Noblesse Stakes, is closely related to 2 winners including the Group 3 Give Thanks Stakes third Eternal Beauty. The second dam, Moments Of Joy (by Darshaan), a smart 12f and listed 14f winner, is a half-sister to 5 winners. (Mr V I Araci). *"She's the only 2-y-o by her sire in training in Europe. Native Khan (a son of Azamour) stands in Turkey but he was a Group 3 winning 2-y-o and was third in the Guineas. This filly is lovely, she's developing all the time, has a real fast ground action and a good attitude. I'd be very disappointed if she wasn't able to be winning races from August onwards".*

1358. UNNAMED ★★★
b.f. Oasis Dream – Virginia Waters (Kingmambo). March 29. Seventh foal. €295,000Y. Arqana Deauville August. Rob Speers. Half-sister to the very useful 6f (at 2 yrs), 7f and listed 1m winner Emperor Claudius (by Giant's Causeway). The dam won the 1,000 Guineas and is a half-sister to the Group 3 Gallinule Stakes winner and Irish Derby second Alexander Of Hales and to the 2-y-o 1m winner and Group 1 1m Criterium International second Chevalier. The second dam, Legend Maker (by Sadler's Wells), won the Group 3 10.5f Prix de Royaumont and is a half-sister to 7 winners including Amfortas (Group 2 12f King Edward VII Stakes). (Mr V I Araci). *"A gorgeous filly, she'll hopefully be a seven furlong type 2-y-o around August time. She's got real class and is impossible to dislike. Because she's so well-bred and so nice we gave her a short break and she's just come back into work now".*

AMANDA PERRETT

1359. CHAPARRACHIK (IRE) ★★★ ♠
b.c. High Chaparral – Chocolat Chaud (Excellent Art). February 11. First foal. €170,000Y. Arqana Deauville August. P & R Doyle / A Perrett. The dam is an unplaced half-sister to 11 winners including the very useful dual 1m winner Kismah. The second dam, Thaidah (by Vice Regent), a 5f (at 2 yrs) and listed 7f winner, is a half-sister to the champion US 2-y-o Devil's Bag and to the top-class filly Glorious Song (the dam of Singspiel and Rahy). (John Connolly & Odile Griffith). *"He was bought at Deauville last year, he's a first foal but the second dam has produced 11 winners. A nice, colt and a February foal, I should think we'd be starting him over seven furlongs from June time onwards. He's got a good attitude, his knees are nice and mature and he's ready to be trained".*

1360. DASCHAS ★★★
b.c. Oasis Dream – Canada Water (Dansili). May 10. Second foal. Half-brother to the 2015 2-y-o Group 3 7f Prix La Rochette second Lawmaking (by Zamindar). The dam, a French 1m placed 3-y-o, is a half-sister to 8 winners including the Prix de l'Arc de Triomphe and Grand Prix de Paris winner Rail Link, the French Group 2 12f and dual Group 3 10f winner Crossharbour and the smart French 1m and 10f performer Chelsea Manor. The second dam, Docklands (by Theatrical), a French 1m and 10f performer, is a half-sister to the smart performer at up to 9f Wharf. (Khalid Abdulla). *"A lovely individual, he's a May foal so he's going to want a bit of time and he's got quite a bit of growing to do. He hasn't been with me very long and I should think he's one for the second half of the season, but he's a bonny colt with a beautiful pedigree. He has a nice, quick action so I should think he'll start over six furlongs. He's going well on the gallops".*

1361. GARNETTA ★★★
b.f. Poet's Voice – Petit A Petit (Holy Roman Emperor). January 18. First foal. 20,000Y. Tattersalls October Book 2. Amanda Perrett. The dam, a minor winner over 12f at 4 yrs in France, is a half-sister to 5 winners including the South African Group 3 winner Hawk's Eye. The second dam, Inchiri (by Sadler's Wells), a very useful listed 12f winner, is a half-sister to 4 winners. (The Garnetta Partnership). *"She's a nice filly, didn't cost a lot at the sales and it's a great filly family. We trained the second dam's half-sister Whirly Bird who has bred the smart dual Group 3 winner Malabar. She's a January foal and a strong type that's going nicely at the moment. Poet's Voice didn't seem to get precocious types in his first crop last year and the dam won over a mile and a half, so she'll a bit of time. Realistically I imagine she'll start at seven furlongs".* **TRAINERS' BARGAIN BUY**

1362. LIGHTENING DANCE ★★★★
b.f. Nathaniel – Dance Lively (Kingmambo). April 14. Half-sister to the Japanese Group 3 1m winner Live Concert (by Singspiel), to the fairly useful 1m (at 2 yrs) and listed 13f winner Charleston Lady (by Hurricane Run), the fair 1m winner Tap Dance Way (by Azamour) and a winner in Greece by High Chaparral. The dam is an unraced half-sister to 9 winners including 3 stakes winners in the USA. The second dam, Tivli (by Mt Livermore), a US stakes winner of 7 races, is a half-sister to a stakes winner. (Mrs A J Chandris). *"I have two Nathaniel's and I like both of them a lot. This filly is very athletic and the dam has bred two stakes winners. I really like her and she's one for seven furlongs in mid-season".*

1363. MILIUM (USA) ★★★
gr.f. First Defence – Magnifica (Mizzen Mast). February 18. First foal. The dam is an unraced sister to 3 winners including the Hong Kong Grade 1 1m winner Giant Treasure and the US Grade 3 7f and Grade 3 1m winner and Grade 1 Santa Monica Handicap second Jibboom and a half-sister to the useful 7f and 1m winner (including at 2 yrs) Self Evident. The second dam, Palisade (by Gone West), a quite useful 2-y-o 7f winner, is a half-sister to the useful 3-y-o 1m winner Emplane and to the useful 2-y-o 1m winner Boatman. (Khalid Abdulla). *"A neat filly, we're just starting to kick on with her a bit now, she's nice, sharp and ready to go. Should win at two".*

1364. MY LADY MARIE ★★
b.f. Bated Breath – Poppo's Song (Polish Navy). April 16. Seventh foal. 16,000Y. Tattersalls October Book 2. Amanda Perrett. Half-sister to the French 7.5f (at 2 yrs) to 9.5f winner

of 3 races and listed-placed Nabbaash (by Aqlaam), to the moderate 5f winner Talqaa (by Exceed And Excel), the fair 2m 1f winner Petaluma (by Teofilo) and the Italian winner of 5 races at 3 and 4 yrs Pretium Sceleris (by Johannesburg). The dam, a Canadian stakes winner of 2 races at 3 and 4 yrs, is a half-sister to 3 winners. The second dam, Bridled Song (by Seattle Slew), is a placed half-sister to 4 winners. (Ashley Lewer & Derek James Partnership). *"She's got a bit of size to her and she's a mid-April foal so a bit immature at the moment, but the dam won twice and she's bred four winners. So I don't see why she shouldn't win at some point, but I haven't done much with her so far. With Bated Breath as the sire we may get away with starting her at six furlongs, if not it'll be seven".*

1365. OPEN WIDE (USA) ★★★
b.br.c. Invincible Spirit – Nunavik (Indian Ridge). April 2. Fourth foal. 125,000Y. Tattersalls October Book 1. Amanda Perrett / Peter & Ross Doyle. Brother to the quite useful 7f and 1m winner Katimavik and the fair 11f winner Gelenschik (by Dalakhani). The dam is an unraced sister to the useful Irish 1m winner Legal Jousting and a half-sister to the Group 2 12f Ribblesdale Stakes winner and smart broodmare Irresistible Jewel and the listed 12f winner Diamond Trim. The second dam, In Anticipation (by Sadler's Wells), won over 12f and 14f in Ireland and is a half-sister to 6 winners. (George Materna & John McInerney). *"A lovely horse with plenty of class about him. A nice individual, he'll probably want a bit of cut in the ground, the dam was unraced but she's had two winners from two runners, so there's no reason why he shouldn't be another. We bought him from Corduff Stud who have been great producers for us over the years".*

1366. OPINIONATE ★★★
b.c. Cacique – Comment (Sadler's Wells). February 22. Fourth foal. The dam is an unraced sister to the 1m (at 2 yrs) and Group 1 10f Grand Prix de Paris winner Beat Hollow and a half-sister to 3 winners including the US Grade 3 winner Yaralino. The second dam, Wemyss Bight (by Dancing Brave), a very smart filly, won 5 races including the Group 1 12f Irish Oaks and the Group 2 12f Prix de Malleret. (Khalid Abdulla). *"A big colt – he's 16.1 hands and 1250lbs, but he's got nice mature knees. The dam was unraced but it's a very good family and this is a really nice, quality colt for later in the year".*

1367. RED EMPEROR (IRE) ★★★
b.c. Holy Roman Emperor – Rougette (Red Ransom). April 29. Second foal. Half-brother to the fair 2015 5f placed 2-y-o Equinette (by Equiano). The dam, a quite useful 1m winner, is a half-sister to 3 winners including the useful 5f ,7f (both at 2 yrs) and listed 7f winner and Group 2 7f Rockfel Stakes third Royal Confidence. The second dam, Never A Doubt (by Night Shift), a very useful 2-y-o winner of the Group 2 5.5f Prix Robert Papin, is a half-sister to 3 winners including the Group 3 5f third Jonny Mudball. (D M James). *"It's a good, sharp family and this little colt has plenty of speed. He's a late April foal and I should think you'll see him out over six furlongs in June".*

1368. SALUTI (IRE) ★★★
b.c. Acclamation – Greek Easter (Namid). March 29. Third living foal. 42,000Y. Tattersalls October Book 2. A Perrett / Peter & Ross Doyle. Brother to the quite useful 2016 3-y-o 7f winner Easter Mate. The dam, a 7f and 1m winner in Germany and subsequently a fair 10f winner here, is a half-sister to the 2-y-o 5f and 6f winner, Group 1 Middle Park Stakes third and subsequent US Grade 3 winner Doc Holiday. The second dam, Easter Heroine (by Exactly Sharp), was placed over 7f (at 2 yrs) and 10f in Ireland and is a half-sister to 4 winners. *"A really lovely individual and the full brother won first time out this year having been placed as a 2-y-o. He's a big colt and he'll want a bit of time, but he has a great attitude and I like him. I don't think we'll see him before June or July time – Goodwood maybe. He looks the type for five and six furlongs".*

1369. TAPDANCE ALLTHEWAY ★★★
b.f. Nathaniel – Tap Dance Way (Azamour). March 26. Second foal. Half-sister to the modest 2015 7f placed 2-y-o Lady Rocka (by Rock Of Gibraltar). The dam, a fair 1m winner, is a half-sister to the Japanese 1m stakes winner Live Concert and to the fairly useful 1m (at 2 yrs) and listed 13f winner Charleston Lady. The second dam, Dance

Lively (by Kingmambo), is an unraced half-sister to 9 winners including 3 stakes winners in the USA. (Mrs A J Chandris). *"From the same sort of family as my other Nathaniel 2-y-o Lightening Dance, this filly is slightly bigger – she's 16 hands already. Bred to be seen out in the second half of the year, I'm looking forward to running her and I should think a Salisbury seven furlong maiden in the first week of September will be perfect for her debut. She's totally different to her 3-y-o half-sister because she's got size, scope and a bit of class".*

1370. ZOFFANIST (IRE) ★★★★★
ch.c. Zoffany – Frynia (Cat Thief). March 8. Third foal. €60,000Y. Arqana Deauville August. P & R Doyle / A Perrett. Half-brother to the Group 3 Prix Penelope winner and Group 1 Prix Saint-Alary third Ferevia (by Motivator). The dam, a minor French winner of 2 races at 3 yrs, is a half-sister to 5 winners. The second dam, Wayward Bound (by Mr Prospector), won 2 minor races at 4 yrs in the USA and is a sister to the triple Group 1 winner Ravinella and the US Grade 3 winner Line In The Sand. (John Connolly & Odile Griffith). *"This is the Zhui Feng for this year I think. A lovely colt, he's 16.2 hands already and I can't believe we managed to buy him for what we did at the sale. The dam's already done it because she's bred a Group winner and this colt is just a natural athlete, he has lots of ability. He has the speed to start at six furlongs but he has a nice long stride on him, so he'll be better at seven".*

JONATHAN PORTMAN

1371. ASHAZURI ★★
b.f. Dick Turpin – Shesha Bear (Tobougg). May 3. Half-sister to the quite useful 6f (at 2 yrs) to 10f winner of 5 races and listed-placed Pasaka Boy (by Haafhd). The dam, a fair 10f to 12f winner of 5 races, is a half-sister to numerous winners including the useful 6f (at 2 yrs) to 1m (in Sweden) winner Warming Trends. The second dam, Sunny Davis (by Alydar), was a fair 2-y-o 7f winner. (RWH Partnership). *"She has a bit of spirit and a little bit of class about her. We know the family well, she was quite small when she came in but she's growing now and I see her as a late June type 2-y-o. A nice type".*

1372. BALGAIR ★★★★
ch.g. Foxwedge – Glencal (Compton Place). March 8. Fourth foal. 12,000Y. Tattersalls October Book 3. J Portman. Half-brother to the quite useful 2-y-o 6f winner Inniscastle Lad (by Kyllachy) and to the moderate 5f winner Sweet Angelica (by Pastoral Pursuits). The dam, a modest 6f and 7f winner of 3 races, is a half-sister to 2 winners including the useful listed 1m winner of 6 races Kasumi. The second dam, Raindrop (by Primo Dominie), placed fourth once over 7f, is a half-sister to 5 winners. (J T Habershon-Butcher). *"A very nice type who was a lovely yearling at the sales and now he's a good, strong, tough sort who knows his job. One to look forward to in the summer, he's probably a six/seven furlong 2-y-o and I think he should have cost more than he did".* **TRAINERS' BARGAIN BUY**

1373. BROAD APPEAL ★★
ch.c. Medicean – Shy Appeal (Barathea). March 11. Fourth foal. £18,000Y. Doncaster Premier. Jonathan Portman. Half-brother to the fair 8.5f (at 2 yrs) and 12f winner Bold Appeal (by Nayef). The dam, a modest 7f placed 2-y-o in Ireland, is a half-sister to the Group 3 Premio Tudini winner Victory Laurel. The second dam, Special Cause (by Fasliyev), won once over 7f at 3 yrs in France and is a half-sister to 6 winners including the dam of Zafeen (Group 1 St James's Palace Stakes). (Berkeley Racing). *"A seven furlong type 2-y-o. We bought him at the sales after already having seen him at the stud and liked what we saw. A nice, strong 2-y-o, we still like him and he should develop and make a nice 3-y-o as well".*

1374. FRESH FOX ★★★
ch.f. Sakhee's Secret – May Fox (Zilzal). March 3. Fourth living foal. 41,000Y. Tattersalls December. R Frisby. Half-sister to the very useful Group 3 7f Oak Tree Stakes and US Grade 3 1m winner of 6 races Annecdote (by Lucky Story), to the quite useful 6f (at 2 yrs) to 9f winner of 4 races Meglio Ancora (by Best Of The Bests) and the fair 8.5f winner Down To Earth (by Aussie Rules). The dam is an unraced half-sister to 5 winners here and in Turkey. The second dam, Folly Fox (by Alhijaz), is an unraced half-sister to 5 winners. (The Hon. Mrs R Pease). *"She's a half-sister to Annecdote*

who served us well. She's got a bit of growing to do being quite leggy and when she does come right I think she'll be nice, but she's just immature at the moment. The sire gets horses that tend to want to go a little bit further than you might expect, so she'll start off at seven furlongs in July".

1375. HARBOURING ★★★
ch.f. Harbour Watch – Juncea (Elnadim). February 17. Fifth foal. £5,500Y. Doncaster Premier. Jonathan Portman. Half-sister to the quite useful 2-y-o 5f and 6f winner Juncart (by Dutch Art). The dam, a fair 2-y-o 6f winner, is a half-sister to 2 winners. The second dam, Strelitzia (by Fort Wood), a listed winner in South Africa, is a sister to the South African Group 1 and dual Group 2 winner Fort Defiance. (Philip Afia). *"She's a lovely filly. Everyone thinks she's a 3-y-o when they see her because she's enormous. From day one she's always done everything very easily and was a cheap purchase because she's not 100% correct, but she moves very well. A nice type, on pedigree you'd have to think she'd have speed, but because of her size we can't get at her too early. Probably one to start over six furlongs".*

1376. INTISHA (IRE) ★★★
b.f. Intikhab – Shawaaty (Monsun). March 2. Second foal. 16,000Y. Tattersalls October Book 2. J Portman. The dam, placed once at 3 yrs in France, is a half-sister to 4 winners including the French listed winner Mahaatheer. The second dam, Al Ihtithar (by Barathea), a very useful 10f and 10.3f listed winner, is a full or half-sister to 10 winners including the Group 3 Prix Berteux winner and dual Group 2 second Samsaam. *"Another very tough, spirited individual. She's not very big but she is at least growing. She's always been on top of the lad's list at home, showing a very deliberate attitude and she just wants to get on with it. She's out of a Monsun mare so you could see her getting a trip in due course, but there's a lot to like about her".*

1377. MANCINI ★★★★
ch.c. Nathaniel – Muscovado (Mr Greeley). March 3. Fourth foal. 27,000Y. Tattersalls October Book 2. Sackville/Donald & J Portman. Half-brother to the quite useful triple 10f winner Maybelater (by Mount Nelson) and to the fair dual 1m winner Monsieur Rieussec (by Halling). The dam ran twice unplaced and is a half-sister to 4 minor winners here and abroad. The second dam, Only Royale (by Caerleon), won 9 races including the Group 1 Yorkshire Oaks (twice) and the Group 2 Jockey Club Stakes and is a half-sister to 5 winners. (Laurence Bellman). *"A big horse that does everything incredibly easily, he has a winning temperament and we like him very much. He's a handsome horse and he knows it, but he's big and with big horses you worry about doing too much with them too soon. Having said that, when they move so easily the temptation is to run them! Perhaps we'll start him off at the end of May and I thought he was well-bought".*

1378. ORIN SWIFT (IRE) ★★
b.g. Dragon Pulse – Hollow Green (Beat Hollow). April 26. Second foal. 28,000Y. Tattersalls October Book 3. J Portman. Half-brother to the modest 5f and 1m winner at 3 and 4 yrs Limerick Lord (by Lord Shanakill). The dam, a fair 7f (at 2 yrs) to 11.5f winner of 8 races, is a half-sister to 4 winners including the French listed winner Safe And Sound. The second dam, Three Greens (by Niniski), a winner and 12f listed-placed in France, is a half-sister to 9 winners including the US 2-y-o Grade 1 8.5f Starlet Stakes winner Creaking Board (herself dam of the US Grade 3 winner Crowd Pleaser) and the Group winners Dakhla Oasis and Dyhim Diamond. (J T Habershon-Butcher). *"He was a little bit weedy, narrow and nervous when we started on him. We gelded him and he's filled out very nicely, he concentrates on his work a lot more now and enjoys it. We like him, but he's a late foal and you could see him running over seven furlongs in July".*

1379. SWAN SERENADE ★★★
b.f. Paco Boy – Accede (Acclamation). April 5. Fourth foal. £12,000Y. Doncaster November. J Portman. Half-sister to the fair 2015 2-y-o 6f winner Poster Girl (by Excellent Art) and to the quite useful 7f (at 2 yrs) and 1m winner of 4 races Miss Van Gogh (by Dutch Art). The dam, a quite useful 2-y-o 6f winner, is a half-sister to one winner. The second dam, Here To Me (by Muhtarram), a fair 3-y-o 6f winner, is a

half-sister to 5 winners. (The Hon. Mrs D Joly). *"She's nice and sharp, not very big and with a hell of a backside on her. She has a lovely attitude, is a joy to train and has a bit of spirit which is nice. We know the family well and she looks a little bit sharper than the others. She could be our first 2-y-o runner and I love her".*

1380. TALLULAH ROCKS ★★
b.f. Tagula – Daunt Rock (Rock Of Gibraltar). February 1. First foal. The dam is an unraced half-sister to 3 winners including the French listed 10f and listed 11f winner and Group 2 Prix Hocquart third Shujoon. The second dam, Marie De Blois (by Barathea), won twice at 3 yrs in Germany and was listed-placed and is a half-sister to 2 winners. (Daunt Rock Partnership). *"She's doing well and strengthening up all the time. Very straightforward and amenable, I could see her running over six or seven furlongs in mid-summer. There's nothing flashy about her, but there's more to her than meets the eye".*

1381. UNNAMED ★★★
b.f. Sakhee's Secret – Dancing Nelly (Shareef Dancer). April 13. Ninth foal. Sister to the quite useful 6f (at 2 yrs) to 1m winner Mystical Man and half-sister to the fair 5f and 6f winner of 10 races (including at 2 yrs) here and in Germany Vanhillen (by Bertolini), to the modest 2-y-o 6f winner Some Show (by Showcasing), the modest dual 10f winner Ice Nelly (by Iceman) and the modest 7f winner Fly By Nelly (by Compton Place). The dam, a moderate 6f placed maiden, is out of the unraced Silent Witness by Inchinor), herself a half-sister to 9 winners including Busy Flight (Group 2 Doncaster Cup). (Lady Hardy). *"She's not a substantial filly to look at, but she's a wonderful mover, very athletic and forward going. You'd have to think she'd need a bit of time though".*

1382. UNNAMED ★★
b.f. Royal Applause – Tease (Green Desert). February 15. Sixth foal. 14,000Y. Tattersalls October Book 3. J Portman. Half-sister to the fairly useful 2-y-o 7f winner and listed-placed Jazz Police (by Beat Hollow), to the fair dual 10f winner Sit Tight (by Act One), the moderate 1m winner Double Star (by Elusive City) and a winner in Greece by Shamardal.

The dam, a fair 3-y-o 7f winner, is a half-sister to the Irish listed winner Galistic. The second dam, Mockery (by Nashwan), won 2 minor races in France over 10.5f and 15f and is a half-sister to 3 other minor winners. *"I bought her thinking she'd be sharp and early, but once we got her going we could see that she had immature knees and would want more time. She's grown a bit now and I could see her coming good. She looked beautiful at the sale but Royal Applause doesn't usually get early types and I see her as one for the second half of the season. She's still for sale".*

KEVIN PRENDERGAST

1383. ALTHIBA ★★★
b.f. Shamardal – Aaraas (Haafhd). March 15. First foal. The dam, a useful 2-y-o 6f winner and third in the Group 3 7f Killavullan Stakes, is a half-sister to the useful Irish 2-y-o 6f winner and Group 3 7f Silver Flash Stakes third Alshahbaa and the fairly useful listed-placed winners Daymooma and Asheerah (by Shamardal). The second dam, Adaala (by Sahm), an Irish 7f (at 2 yrs) and listed 9f winner, is a half-sister to 2 winners. (Hamdan Al Maktoum). *"A big filly, she goes nicely and she'll want six furlongs plus. We like her well and she'll be out in mid-season. Quite big and well-muscled".*

1384. ANNEEN (IRE) ★★★★
b.br.f. Lawman – Asheerah (Shamardal). March 3. Second foal. Half-sister to the fairly useful 2015 2-y-o dual 7f winner Awtaad (by Cape Cross). The dam, a fairly useful Irish listed-placed 7f winner, is a half-sister to useful 2-y-o 6f winner and Group 3 7f Killavullan Stakes third Aaraas, to the useful Irish 2-y-o 6f winner and Group 3 7f Silver Flash Stakes third Alshahbaa and the fairly useful listed-placed winner Daymooma. The second dam, Adaala (by Sahm), an Irish 7f (at 2 yrs) and listed 9f winner, is a half-sister to 2 winners. (Hamdan Al Maktoum). *"She'll take a bit of time but she's nice and one for six/seven furlongs in mid-season. I think she's one of the better ones and we like her".*

1385. BUTOOLAT ★★★
b.f. Oasis Dream – Handassa (Dubawi). March 19. First foal. The dam, a useful 7f (at 2 yrs) and listed 1m winner, is a half-sister

to two fair 2-y-o 6f winners. The second dam, Starstone (by Diktat), is an unraced half-sister to the Group 1 July Cup winner Pastoral Pursuits and the Group 1 Haydock Park Sprint Cup winner Goodricke. (Hamdan Al Maktoum). *"She'll be ready to run in May over six furlongs if the ground dries up. We like her, she goes nicely, not a big filly so she's a typical first foal, but she's very muscular. She's a lovely filly and the dam was a listed winner for us".*

1386. DIME A DANCE (IRE) ★★★
b.f. Art Connoisseur – Dance Hall Girl (Dansili). February 11. Third foal. Half-sister to the very useful 2015 2-y-o listed 7f winner Tashweeq (by Big Bad Bob) and to the fairly useful Irish 5f (including at 2 yrs) and 6f winner Kasbah (by Acclamation). The dam, a quite useful Irish 7f winner, is a half-sister to 3 winners including the listed winner Solar Deity. The second dam, Dawn Raid (by Docksider), a quite useful Irish 3-y-o 7f winner, is a half-sister to 8 winners including the French and Irish 2,000 Guineas and Richmond Stakes winner Bachir. (Lady O'Reilly). *"I thought she'd be one of our first runners until she met with a little setback. She's coming along nicely now but we'll have to wait for six weeks or so before we can get her out. When we had her going she seemed to move very well and she has a good attitude. One for six furlongs I should think, I trained the dam and her 2-y-o last year was useful for John Gosden".*

1387. DUCK EGG BLUE (IRE) ★★★
b.f. Haatef – Sapphire Spray (Viking Ruler). March 1. Fourth foal. €4,000Y. Tattersalls Ireland September. Mike Carty. Sister to the minor French 2-y-o 5f winner My Sapphire. The dam, a fair 1m winner, is a half-sister to 4 winners including the quite useful dual 7f winner (including at 2 yrs) and US Grade 3 placed Musical Rain. The second dam, Rainbow Melody (Rainbows For Life), a quite useful dual 7f winner (including at 2 yrs), is a half-sister to 6 winners including the listed 5f winner and Group 1 Nunthorpe Stakes third Indian Prince. (Mrs Prendergast). *"I bred her and she'll be running in mid-April. I think she wants goodish ground and as there's been so much rain lately we'll go to Dundalk on the*

all-weather. Not a big filly, but very muscular and typical of her sire. A nice filly, we'll start her at five furlongs and see where we go from there".

1388. MABAADY ★★★
b.c. Bated Breath – Fifty (Fasliyev). February 10. Fourth foal. £100,000Y. Doncaster Premier. Shadwell Estate Co. The dam, a fair 6f winner, is a half-sister to 5 winners. The second dam, Amethyst (by Sadler's Wells), winner of the Leopardstown 1,000 Guineas Trial and second in the Irish 1,000 Guineas, is a sister to the 2,000 Guineas and Group 1 National Stakes winner King Of Kings and to the Group 3 Athasi Stakes winner Lucky and a half-sister to 4 winners including the Group 2 5.5f Prix Robert Papin winner General Monash. (Hamdan Al Maktoum). *"A nice horse for six furlongs plus in mid-season. He seems to go well and has a nice temperament".*

1389. MARKUS TWAIN (IRE) ★★★
b.c. Dragon Pulse – Yara (Sri Pekan). March 22. Ninth living foal. €32,000Y. Goffs Orby. Kevin Prendergast. Half-brother to 6 winners including the UAE listed 1m winner Emirates Gold (by Royal Applause), the French listed 10f winner Yarastar (by Cape Cross), the Irish 2-y-o 7f and subsequent US stakes-placed winner Yario (by Danehill Dancer) and the Irish 6f (at 2 yrs) and 7f winner Yaria (by Danehill). The dam was placed second ten times including in the Group 1 5f Heinz 57 Phoenix Stakes. The second dam, Your Village (by Be My Guest), placed fourth once over 12f in Ireland, is a half-sister to 6 winners including Mister Majestic (Middle Park Stakes) and Homme de Loi (Grand Prix de Paris). (Mrs Prendergast). *"I bought him, haven't sold him so I'm the sole owner and I hope he's good! We like both our Dragon Pulses, this one is a nice, big horse, a good mover and one for the middle of the season".*

1390. MYSTICAL (IRE) ★★★
ch.f. Dragon Pulse – Brave Madam (Invincible Spirit). March 5. Sixth foal. €30,000Y. Goffs Sportsmans. Kevin Prendergast. Half-sister to the quite useful 6f (at 2 yrs) and 7f winner Azagal, to the quite useful Irish 10f winner Azamata (both by Azamour) and a winner

in Greece by Iffraaj. The dam is an unraced half-sister to 6 winners including the US listed stakes winner Insan Mala. The second dam, Madame Claude (by Paris House), a fair 2-y-o 6f winner, is a half-sister to 4 winners including the Irish dual listed winner Nashcash. (Mr J Vasicheck). *"A very nice filly owned by a very lucky man – he owned the Group 1 winners La Collina and Termagant. We like this filly a lot and she'll run in May when the six furlong races start. She's a nice, big filly".*

1391. PRESIDENTIAL (IRE) ★★★★
b.c. Invincible Spirit – Poetical (Croco Rouge). April 12. Fifth foal. 50,000Y. Tattersalls December. Not sold. Half-brother to the smart Dragon Pulse (by Kyllachy), winner of the 2-y-o Group 2 7f Futurity Stakes and the Group 3 Prix de Fontainebleau and second in the Group 1 7f National Stakes. The dam, a useful 1m winner in Ireland, was third in the Group 3 7f Concorde Stakes and is a half-sister to 3 winners. The second dam, Abyat (by Shadeed), is an unraced half-sister to 9 winners including Hayil (Group 1 Middle Park Stakes) and the dam of the dual Group 1 winning 2-y-o Shalaa. (John Tuthill). *"A half-brother to Dragon Pulse, he's a very nice horse, I like him and he'll be a 2-y-o over six/seven furlongs in mid-season. Not a big horse, but he has quality, so he's typical of the sire".*

1392. PURDEY ★★★
ch.f. Mastercraftsman – Corryvreckan (Night Shift). April 22. Ninth foal. £26,000Y. Doncaster Premier. Derek Veitch. Half-sister to the quite useful 2-y-o 5f winner Leftontheshelf (by Namid), to the fair 2-y-o 6f winner Entwined (by Elusive City), the fair 2-y-o 6f and 7f winner Mecado (by Compton Place), the modest Irish 2-y-o 7f winner Dearg (by Intikhab) and the moderate 2m winner Mollyow (by Iceman). The dam, a fair Irish 7f and 1m placed maiden, is a half-sister to 9 winners including the very useful listed sprint winners Bufalino and Maledetto. The second dam, Croglin Water (by Monsanto), is an unplaced half-sister to the smart sprinter Governor General. (D Veitch, K M Smyth, J Egan & K Prendergast). *"Goes well, she's a big, strong filly for mid-season over seven furlongs".*

1393. RISE AGAIN (IRE) ★★★
b.f. Arcano – Rise And Fall (Quiet American). February 10. €9,000Y. Goffs HIT November. Jeremy Harley. Half-sister to the fairly useful 2-y-o 6f winner and listed-placed Prime Delivery (by More Than Ready), to the quite useful dual 7f winner Desert Wings (by Raven's Pass), the modest triple 12f winner Quiet Appeal (by Cape Cross), the modest 7f to 8.5f winner Fluctuation (by Street Cry) and the minor US winner Elite Wildcat (by Forest Wildcat). The dam won once at 3 yrs in the USA and is a half-sister to 4 winners including the listed winner and multiple Group 3 placed Zaham. The second dam, Guerre Et Paix (by Soviet Star), a winner at 2 and 4 yrs in France, was listed-placed and is a half-sister to 6 winners. (Jeremy Harley & Kevin Prendergast). *"I had her ready to run but she got a little setback otherwise she'd have been running now. She'll go five, six or seven furlongs, we like her a lot and she goes well".* **TRAINERS' BARGAIN BUY**

1394. TAWALEEF (IRE) ★★★
b.c. Bahamian Bounty – Literacy (Diesis). March 4. Sixth foal. £105,000Y. Doncaster Premier. Shadwell Estate Co. Half-brother to the quite useful 2-y-o dual 7f winner Jubilance (by Oratorio) and to the fair 10f to 14f winner of 10 races Gabrial The Duke (by Duke Of Marmalade). The dam, a modest 10f and 11f winner here, subsequently won in the USA and was second in the Grade 2 Long Island Handicap and is a half-sister to 2 winners. The second dam, Tuviah (by Eastern Echo), is a placed half-sister to 6 winners including the Group 3 Park Stakes winner Duck Row. (Hamdan Al Maktoum). *"He had a run in bad ground and we were pleased enough with him but he didn't take the race too good because the ground was very heavy. We ran him because he was a bit colty, but we've eased him off and I'd say we won't be running him now until he gets six or seven furlongs, which is unusual for a Bahamian Bounty".*

1395. TREVANNA ★★★
b.f. Requinto – Flamelet (Theatrical). March 22. 10,500Y. Tattersalls December. K Prendergast. Half-sister to the fairly useful 2-y-o 6f and 7f winner Flash Fire (by Shamardal), to the

French listed-placed 10f winner Seeking Solace (by Exceed And Excel), the quite useful 1m winners Arc Lighter (by Street Cry) and Summerstrand (by Cape Cross), and a hurdles winner by Daylami. The dam, an Irish 7.5f winner, was Group 3 placed and is a half-sister to several winners including the French 7f listed winner Bezrin. The second dam, Darling Flame (by Capote), a useful 6f (at 2 yrs) and 7f winner, is a half-sister to several winners including the very smart Japanese Group 1 winning miler Heart Lake. (Ann & Trevor McCormack). *"We like her a lot and she belongs to my daughter. The sire was fast and the dam was rated 97 so she's got every chance and she'll run when we get some better weather, around mid to late May".*

1396. ZIHAAM ★★★
ch.c. Dutch Art – Hymnsheet (Pivotal). May 11. Third foal. 170,000Y. Tattersalls October Book 2. Shadwell Estate Co. Closely related to Rubensian (by Medicean), unplaced in two starts at 2 yrs in 2015 and to a minor 3-y-o winner in Italy by Rock Of Gibraltar. The dam, a quite useful 2-y-o 1m winner, is a sister to 2 winners including the Group 1 10f Curragh Pretty Polly Stakes and dual Group 3 winner Chorist and a half-sister to 7 winners. The second dam, Choir Mistress (by Chief Singer), is an unraced half-sister to 7 winners including the smart Group 2 11.9f Great Voltigeur Stakes winner Sacrament. (Hamdan Al Maktoum). *"I like him a lot but he was a late foal and he's going to take time. A nice colt, but backward".*

SIR MARK PRESCOTT

1397. ALABASTER ★★ ♠
gr.f. Archipenko – Alvarita (Selkirk). April 26. Eighth foal. 100,000Y. Tattersalls October Book 2. J Brummitt. Half-brother to the useful Irish 1m (at 2 yrs) and Group 3 10f Kilternan Stakes winner Alla Speranza (by Sir Percy), to the useful 11f winner and Group 3 second Altesse, the fairly useful 10f to 14f winner of 6 races Alcaeus and the quite useful 12f and 13f winner Albert Bridge (all by Hernando). The dam, a French listed 10.5f winner, is a full or half-sister 4 winners including the Group 2 10f Prix Greffulhe second Albion. The second dam, Alborada (by Alzao), won the Champion Stakes (twice), the Nassau Stakes and Pretty Polly Stakes and is a sister to the German triple Group 1 winner Albanova and a half-sister to 7 winners. (Charles C Walker – Osborne House & Miss K Rausing). *"This colt has a good pedigree and he should be seen out this season, but he'll be much more likely to win next year than this".*

1398. ALLEGIANCE ★★
gr.f. Archipenko – Alba Stella (Nashwan). April 14. Eighth foal. Sister to the fair 2015 2-y-o 1m winner Albe Back, closely related to the 10f to 12f winner Aleatricis (by Kingmambo) and half-sister to 5 winners including the 7f (at 2 yrs) and 12f winner Hernandoshideaway (by Hernando), the 14f and 2m winner All My Heart (by Sadler's Wells) and the 12f winner All That Rules (by Galileo) – all four quite useful. The dam, a fairly useful dual 12f winner, is a half-sister to the dual Champion Stakes winner Alborada and the triple German Group 1 winner Albanova. The second dam, Alouette (by Darshaan), a useful 1m (at 2 yrs) and listed 12f winner, is a half-sister to the dams of the Group 1 winners Quarter Moon, Yesterday, Aussie Rules and Allegretto. (Miss K Rausing). *"Another good type that will almost certainly be at her best next year. She's the sort to have the odd run or two at the back-end of this year".*

1399. ANNA MEDICI ★★★★
b.f. Sir Percy – Florentia (Medicean). April 13. Third foal. Sister to the fair 2-y-o 6f to 7.f winner of 3 races Flora Medici and half-sister to the modest 2015 2-y-o 7f winner Cote D'Azur (by Champs Elysees). The dam, a modest 1m and 10f winner, is a half-sister to 9 winners including the useful 6f and 7f winner of 4 races Flying Officer. The second dam, Area Girl (by Jareer), a fair 2-y-o 5f winner, is a half-sister to 3 minor winners. (Mr N Greig). *"A lot of the family win at two including the dam's first two foals. She threw a splint in the early spring and is only just resuming, but if the dam's record is anything to go by this filly should show something this year".*

1400. BOOST ★★★★
b.f. Pivotal – Hooray (Invincible Spirit). April 7. Second foal. Closely related to the 2015 5f placed 2-y-o, from two starts, First Rate (by Kyllachy). The dam, a smart winner of 5 races including the Group 1 6f Cheveley Park Stakes

and the Group 2 6f Lowther Stakes, is a half-sister to 4 winners including the useful 2-y-o listed 8.3f winner of 7 races Hypnotic. The second dam, Hypnotize (by Machiavellian), a useful 2-y-o dual 7f winner, is closely related to 2 winners including Dazzle (Group 3 6f Cherry Hinton Stakes) and a half-sister to 5 winners including the listed 1m winner Fantasize and to the placed dam of the Group 2 winning sprinter Danehurst. (Cheveley Park Stud). *"She's 'Heath House Stables' through and through because the sire and the dam were both trained here and indeed the dam was the world champion two-year-old filly. So this filly is bred to fly at some point but she does look more like Pivotal than her mother, so she could take more time than Hooray did"*.

1401. CLIFDEN ARTS ★★★
b.f. Acclamation – Aravonian (Night Shift). March 31. Eighth foal. Half-sister to the dual 5f (at 2 yrs) and Group 3 6f Ballyogan Stakes winner Age Of Chivalry, to the fair 2-y-o 5f winner The Cuckoo, the fair 2-y-o 5f winner Neighbother (all by Invincible Spirit) and the smart Irish 2-y-o 7f winner, Group 3 7f Somerville Tattersall Stakes second and subsequent US Grade 1 second Sebastian Flyte (by Observatory). The dam won once over 1m at 3 yrs. The second dam, Age Of Reality (by Alleged), is a placed full or half-sister to 8 winners including the Group 2 Royal Whip Stakes winner Chancellor. (Mrs P K O'Rourke). *"She comes from a precocious family although I haven't trained any of them. She'll start work in late April and the dam's record with producing 2-y-o winners is encouraging"*.

1402. DIPTYCH (USA) ★★★★
br.f. Hat Trick – Fork Lightning (Storm Cat). February 12. First foal. The dam, a fairly useful 9f winner, is a half-sister to numerous winners including the French 2,000 Guineas and US Grade 1 winner Aussie Rules, the useful 7.5f (at 2 yrs) and listed 10f winner and US Grade 2 second Approach and the very useful 2-y-o 8.5f winner and Group 1 Prix Marcel Boussac fourth Intrigued. The second dam, Last Second (by Alzao), winner of the Group 2 10f Nassau Stakes and the Group 2 10f Sun Chariot Stakes, is a half-sister to 7 winners including the Moyglare Stud Stakes third Alouette (dam of the Group 1 winners Albanova and Alborada) and the Group 2 Doncaster Cup winner Alleluia (dam of the Group 1 winner Allegretto) and to the placed dam of the Group 1 winners Yesterday and Quarter Moon. (Denford Stud). *"The mother didn't run until she was three and she was just short of black type. We've had all the family, this filly has done a lot of growing lately but she looks like a mid-season 2-y-o and she's always cantered well"*.

1403. ESPRESSO FREDDO (IRE) ★★★
b.c. Fast Company – Spring Bouquet (King's Best). April 19. Second foal. €36,000Y. Tattersalls Ireland September. J Brummitt. The dam, a modest 7f placed 2-y-o, is a half-sister to 5 winners including the fairly useful 2-y-o dual 5f winner Alutiq. The second dam, Marasem (by Cadeaux Genereux), a quite useful 3-y-o 7f winner, is a half-sister to 6 winners including the very useful Group 2 7f Rockfel Stakes winner Sayedah. (Middleham Park Racing). *"He's bred to be a 2-y-o at some point and he'll be starting work soon. He canters well but other than that I don't know"*.

1404. IMPASSIONED ★★★
ch.f. Bahamian Bounty – Ardent (Pivotal). April 29. Second foal. Half-sister to the 2015 2-y-o 7f winner, on her only start, Eternally (by Dutch Art). The dam, a quite useful 6f winner, is a half-sister to the fairly useful 5f (at 2 yrs) and listed 6f winner Irresistible. The second dam, Polish Romance (by Danzig), a minor 7f winner in the USA, is a sister to the US stakes winner Polish Love and a half-sister to 3 minor winners. (Cheveley Park Stud). *"She looks as if she's a 2-y-o filly to run in July. Probably a firm ground filly, she canters well"*.

1405. LAW POWER ★★★★
b.c. Lawman – Clarietta (Shamardal). March 16. Second foal. 150,000Y. Tattersalls October Book 2. Not sold. Half-brother to the quite useful listed-placed dual 1m winner Clarentine (by Dalakhani). The dam, a fairly useful 2-y-o dual 7f winner, was listed-placed twice and is a half-sister to 5 winners including the useful 7f (at 2 yrs), listed Lingfield Oaks Trial and subsequent US Grade 3 winner and Group 1 Nassau Stakes second Cassydora and the listed 10f winner Classic Remark. The second dam, Claxon (by Caerleon), a very useful 1m

(at 2 yrs) and Group 2 10f Premio Lydia Tesio winner, is a half-sister to 3 winners including the Group 2 placed Bulwark. (Bluehills Racing Ltd). *"He was a home-bred that wasn't sold as a yearling. He's small, solid, has always cantered quite strongly and looks a 2-y-o type. He had a setback in the early spring and he's just resuming now"*.

1406. MISS MIRABEAU ★★★
b.f. Oasis Dream – Miss Corniche (Hernando). March 13. Ninth foal. Half-sister to the very useful 1m winner and listed-placed Moyenne Corniche (by Selkirk), to the quite useful 14f to 2m winner Italian Riviera (by Galileo), the quite useful 6f (at 2 yrs) and dual 7f winner Miss Eze and the modest dual 9f winner Miss Villefranche (both by Danehill Dancer). The dam, a 7f (at 2 yrs) and listed 10f winner, is a sister to 2 winners and a half-sister to numerous winners including the listed 1m winner Miss Riviera Golf. The second dam, Miss Beaulieu (by Northfields), was a useful 6f and 10f winner. (J L C Pearce). *"Most of them out of the mare stay well, but this one is by a much quicker stallion. I shall certainly have a go with her and see how she works in a few weeks time"*.

1407. PENTITO RAP (USA) ★★★
b.c. Smart Strike – Sing Like A Bird (Lawyer Ron). January 26. First foal. $120,000Y. Keeneland September. Oliver St Lawrence. The dam, a minor US 3-y-o winner, is a half-sister to the US stakes winner Wiredfortwotwenty. The second dam, Birthday Wire (by Birdonthewire), is an unraced half-sister to 10 winners including two US stakes winners. (Mr & Mrs John Kelsey-Fry). *"He's a January foal so he'll be a 2-y-o at some point. Whether he'd have the speed for shorter than seven furlongs I wouldn't know until I work him in late April"*.

1408. PIEDITA (IRE) ★★
b.f. Authorized – Archina (Arch). February 27. First foal. 75,000Y. Tattersalls October Book 2. Blandford Bloodstock. The dam, a moderate 7f to 9.5f winner of 3 races, is a half-sister to one winner. The second dam, Cross Your Fingers (by Woodman), is an unraced sister to the Group 1 Cheveley Park Stakes winner Gay Gallanta (herself dam of the Group 2 winner and sire Byron) and a half-sister to 11 winners including the Group 2 Gallinule Stakes winner Sportsworld. (Mrs Carmen Fruhbeck & Denford Stud). *"She's tall, leggy, scopey and canters very well. Quite impetuous, you can imagine that she might show something in the autumn because she's a quick learner. So she'll show more this season than you would expect on pedigree because she's pretty switched on"*.

1409. REFRESHED (IRE) ★★★
b.f. Rip Van Winkle – Elegant Beauty (Olden Times). March 1. Sixth foal. 50,000Y. Tattersalls October Book 1. Sir Mark Prescott. Half-sister to the Group 3 1m Prix d'Aumale winner Shahah (by Motivator), to the quite useful dual 6f (at 2 yrs) and 8.5f winner Ligeia (by Rail Link) and the fair 5f and 6f winner Royal Guinevere (by Invincible Spirit). The dam is an unraced half-sister to 8 winners including the champion 2-y-o Grand Lodge and the listed winners La Persiana and Papabile. The second dam, La Papagena (by Habitat), is an unraced half-sister to 7 winners including the listed winners Lost Chord and Eagling. (Lady O'Reilly). *"She's gone out for a break but she'll probably run around August time over seven furlongs. The sire's not popular but the dam's done well"*.

1410. SINGLE ESTATE ★★★
b.c. Tamayuz – Duo De Choc (Manduro). February 11. First foal. 45,000Y. Tattersalls October Book 2. J Brummitt. The dam is an unraced half-sister to 4 winners including the Group 3 12f Godolphin Stakes winner Chock A Block, the listed Pomfret Stakes winner Khateeb and the listed winner Courcheval. The dam, winner of the Grade 1 E P Taylor Stakes and a listed event in France, is a half-sister to the Canadian Grade 2 winner Royal Oath and to the Irish listed winner Quinmaster. The second dam, Sherkaya (by Goldneyev), is an unraced half-sister to 3 winners including the very smart Group 2 10f Gallinule Stakes winner Shemaran. (Mr David Howard, Mr Colin Chisholm & Sir Mark Prescott). *"He'll be working in late April/early May to see whether he's got the pace for shorter distances. Despite being out of a Manduro mare he seems sensible!"*

1411. TORONTO SOUND ★★
b.c. Aussie Rules – Caribana (Hernando). April 3. Sixth foal. 58,000Y. Tattersalls October Book 2. J Brummitt. Half-brother to the Group 3 John Porter and Group 3 St Simon Stakes winner Cubanita (by Selkirk), to the 2015 7f placed 2-y-o (on his only start) Archimento and the quite useful 1m winner Camagueyana (both by Archipenko). The dam, a fair 9.5f winner, is a half-sister to 2 minor winners. The second dam, Carenage (by Alzao), a quite useful 12 winner, is a half-sister to 6 winners out of the Group 1 Yorkshire Oaks winner Key Change. (Mr William Rucker). *"The family tend to want soft ground, but I haven't had any of them. It's a good family and this colt looked a nice horse when I had him in, but he's gone out for a break and he'll be an autumn 2-y-o".*

1412. XENON ★★★★
b.f. Kyllachy – Cool Question (Polar Falcon). March 24. Sister to the very smart Group 1 6f Golden Shaheen winner of 9 races Krypton Factor and half-sister to 4 winners including the quite useful dual 5f winner (including at 2 yrs) Fairfield Princess (by Inchinor), the quite useful 2-y-o dual 6f winner Haven't A Clue (by Red Ransom) and the modest 1m winner North Pole (by Compton Place). The dam, a useful 2-y-o 5f and listed 6f winner, is a half-sister to 4 winners. The second dam, Quiz Time (Efisio), a fairly useful 2-y-o 5f winner, was second in the listed St Hugh's Stakes and is a half-sister to 6 winners including the Group 3 Premio Dormello winner Brockette. (The Lady Fairhaven & Hon James Broughton). *"She'll be a quick, short runner. Not over-big, she's a half-sister to Krypton Factor who won a Group 1 when he was five having previously won no less than six races for us as a 2-y-o. A five furlong 2-y-o".*

JOHN QUINN

1413. ACTUALISATION ★★★
b.c. Exceed And Excel – Eluding (Street Cry). February 25. First foal. 75,000Y. Tattersalls October Book 1. Richard Knight / Sean Quinn. The dam, a fair 7f (at 2 yrs) to 10f placed maiden, is a half-sister to one winner. The second dam, Without A Trace (by Darshaan), a useful 11f and 12f winner, was third in the Group 2 Prix Hubert de Chaudenay and is a half-sister to 7 winners including the listed winner Patience Alexander. (Racing Ventures). *"He's showing up nicely at home, moves nicely and we've done a couple of small bits of work with him. Probably one for six/seven furlongs in mid-season and he'll go forward, because he's a big, scopey horse. There's plenty about him".*

1414. BEST BID ★★★
ch.f. Mayson – High Reserve (Dr Fong). April 1. Seventh foal. £10,000Y. Doncaster Premier. Ed Walker. Half-sister to the quite useful dual 1m winner Critical Risk (by Pivotal) and to the modest 9f winner Pedantic (by Danehill Dancer). The dam, a fairly useful 1m and 10f winner, is a half-sister to 6 winners including the dual Group 3 winner Poet and to the dams of the Group 3 winners France and Alessandro Volta. The second dam, Hyabella (by Shirley Heights), won three races over 1m at 3 yrs including two listed events and is a half-sister to 6 winners including the Prince of Wales's Stakes winner Stagecraft. (Kaniz Bloodstock). *"She's quite forward, we like what we see and she'll be ready to run in early May. She's showing enough to say she'll be able to win over five furlongs because she's quick".*

1415. BREAKING FREE ★★★★ ♠
ch.c. Kyllachy – Hill Welcome (Most Welcome). April 24. Twelfth foal. £38,000Y. Doncaster Premier. Richard Knight. Brother to the fair 5f and 6f winner Jack Rackham and half-brother to 7 winners including the fairly useful 2015 2-y-o listed-placed 6f winner Above N Beyond, the fairly useful dual 5f winner (including at 2 yrs) Exceedance (both by Exceed And Excel), the useful 2-y-o dual 5f winner and Group 3 Molecomb Stakes second Mary Read (by Bahamian Bounty), the useful listed-placed 2-y-o 6f winner Tiana (by Diktat) and the fairly useful 6f (at 2 yrs) to 1m winner of 10 races Dubai Hills (by Dubai Destination). The dam, placed twice at 2 yrs, is a half-sister to 5 winners including the Group 1 6f Middle Park Stakes winner Stalker. The second dam, Tarvie (by Swing Easy), was a useful sprint winner of 3 races. (Adams, Blades, Bruton, Ellis). *"The dam is a very good broodmare, everything she has wins and you'd hope that this fella would follow suit. He's very sharp and he'll run before the end of April".*

1416. DOUBLE DUTCH ★★★★
ch.c. Dutch Art – Duchess Dora (Tagula). April 11. First foal. €42,000Y. Tattersalls Ireland September. Richard Knight / John Quinn. The dam, a useful listed-placed 5f winner of 7 races (including 3 times at 2 yrs), is a half-sister to 7 winners. The second dam, a fairly useful 2-y-o 6f winner, is a half-sister to 6 winners. (Maxilead Ltd). *"We trained his dam, she was very fast and as tough as old boots. She was good over five furlongs and it looks like he's inherited her speed because he'll be ready to start over five furlongs before the end of April. We like him, he'll soon be ready to rock n roll and I should imagine he'd be quick enough to win over five furlongs".*

1417. GEORGE REME (IRE) ★★★ ♣
ch.c. Power – My Sweet Georgia (Royal Applause). January 27. Third foal. £35,000Y. Doncaster Premier. Richard Knight. Half-brother to the fairly useful 6f (at 2 yrs) to 1m winner and listed-placed You're Fired (by Firebreak). The dam, a modest 6f and 7f winner, is a half-sister to 3 winners including the US listed winner Strike Rate. The second dam, Harda Arda (by Nureyev), a modest 9f winner, is a half-sister to 8 winners including the US triple Grade 2 and dual Grade 3 winner Phantom Breeze. (Mr R L Houlton). *"He's a very good mover so I would imagine he'd want decent ground. He has a brilliant attitude, is probably a six/seven furlong horse and he definitely has ability. He's the only horse we have by Power, but on the back of him I certainly wouldn't mind having another".*

1418. LONDON GRAMMAR (IRE) ★★★
b.f. Sir Prancealot – Emmas Princess (Bahhare). April 11. Fifth foal. €27,000Y. Tattersalls Ireland September. Kevin Prendergast. Half-sister to the fair 2-y-o 6f and 1m winner Lake Louise (by Haatef), to the fair dual 6f winner at 2 and 3 yrs Angel Flores (by Art Connoisseur) and the modest triple 1m winner Capitol Gain (by Bahamian Bounty). The dam, a fairly useful Irish dual 10f winner, is a half-sister to 4 winners including the Group 1 10f Premio Presidente della Repubblica and Group 3 8.5f Diomed Stakes winner Polar Prince. The second dam, Staff Approved (by Teenoso), a fairly useful 2-y-o 1m winner, is a half-sister to 11 winners including the US Grade 2 winner Irish Heart. *"Her dam was decent enough in Ireland and she stayed ten furlongs. This filly won't want that far, she's a nice type and probably a six/seven furlong filly. We feel she's showed enough to suggest she'll win this year".*

1419. OCEANIC (IRE) ★★★
b.c. Born To Sea – Shanghai Lily (King's Best). March 23. Eighth foal. 25,000Y. Tattersalls October Book 2. Richard Knight. Half-brother to the fairly useful 2-y-o 6f and 1m winner Cafe Elektric (by Pivotal) and to the fair dual 10f winner Morocco (by Rock Of Gibraltar). The dam, a very useful 2-y-o 6f and 7f winner, is a half-sister to 3 winners including the very useful listed-placed General Eliott. The second dam, Marlene-D (Selkirk), a minor Irish 3-y-o 9f winner, is a half-sister to 7 winners including the Queen's Vase winner Arden, the French listed winner Kerulen and the dam of the US Grade 1 winner Kiri's Clown. (Fletcher, Outhart, Maddison & Moran). *"This is a nice horse, he's thriving all the time and his dam was quite a good 2-y-o for Sir Michael Stoute but was tailed off in the 1,000 Guineas and never ran again. This fella is a really good mover, he was good from day one on the lunge and he's great on the gallops. He moves like a cat, I should imagine he'd want six/seven furlongs on decent ground. We haven't galloped him yet but I'd keep him on your list because he's a nice type".*

1420. PERFORMING (IRE) ★★★
ch.c. Showcasing – Mansiya (Vettori). April 27. Sixth foal. €75,000Y. Goffs Orby. Richard Knight/Quinn. Brother to the modest 2015 6f placed 2-y-o Tabikat Elle and half-brother to 3 winners including the quite useful 7f winner Hunt (by Dark Angel). The dam, a modest 7f (at 2 yrs) to 9f placed maiden, is a half-sister to 6 winners including the useful listed 11.4f Cheshire Oaks winner Abury and to the dam of the South African dual Group 1 winner Bad Girl Runs. The second dam, Bay Shade (by Sharpen Up), a fairly useful 7f (at 2 yrs) and Italian listed 1m winner, is a half-sister to 12 winners including the Group/Grade 3 winners Daarik and Bex (the dam of 5 stakes winners). (Racing Ventures). *"He hasn't done much at all yet, he was quite a late foal and he's just been cantering, so I couldn't tell you too much about him. He's a good mover, he'll want top*

of the ground and we'll probably start him over six furlongs in mid-summer. He smacks us a real 2-y-o type".

1421. SHE'S ZOFF (IRE) ★★★
b.f. Zoffany – Vindication People (Vindication). March 29. Third foal. 50,000Y. Tattersalls October Book 1. Richard Knight / Sean Quinn. Half-sister to the Italian listed 10f winner Freedom Holder (by Holy Roman Emperor). The dam, placed at 2 and 3 in Italy, is a half-sister to 5 winners including the US Grade 3 winner Midnight Hawk. The second dam, Miss Wineshine (by Wolf Power), a US listed stakes winner and Grade 1 placed, is a sister to the US listed stakes winner Delta Wolf and a half-sister to 8 winners. (Racing Ventures). *"Zoffany did particularly well with his first crop of two-year-olds last year. This filly is probably a six furlong horse, she's a really good mover so I would imagine she'd want decent ground, she has a brilliant attitude to her work and is very straightforward. I'd be surprised if she didn't have plenty of ability".*

1422. SUNSET SALLY (IRE) ★★★
b.f. Clodovil – Trentini (Singspiel). March 21. Third foal. 20,000Y. Tattersalls October Book 3. Sam Hoskins. Half-sister to the quite useful 2015 2-y-o 7f and 1m winner Speed Company (by Fast Company). The dam, a minor French 3-y-o 10f winner, is a sister to one winner. The second dam, Nawadi (by Machiavellian), a quite useful 10f winner, is a sister to the very smart Group 2 Celebration Mile and Group 2 Queen Anne Stakes winner No Excuse Needed and to the Group 3 Norfolk Stakes third Skywards and a half-sister to the UAE Group 1 winner Capponi. (Mr T Burns). *"We trained her half-brother Speed Company last year who won over 7f and a mile. I think this filly will want the same sort of trip, she's showing up nicely at home and her pedigree is decent enough to suggest she'll be OK. She's one for the second half of the season and we like her".*

1423. THE NAZCA LINES (IRE) ★★★★
ch.c. Fast Company – Princess Banu (Oasis Dream). February 3. First foal. £44,000Y. Doncaster Premier. John & Sean Quinn. The dam, a modest 2-y-o 5f winner, is a half-sister to 2 winners. The second dam, Paradise Isle (by Bahamian Bounty), a useful 5f (at 2 yrs) and 6f winner of 8 races including two listed

events, was third in the Group 3 6f Summer Stakes and is a full or half-sister to 9 winners including the useful broodmare Clincher Club. (Mr R Harmon). *"He shows us a lot of speed at home, he's a good mover and I should imagine he'll want good ground. He'll be out sooner rather than later and we like him quite a lot, the dam was as tough as nails and he looks very similar. He's very straightforward and just about ready to go".*

1424. UNNAMED ★★★
b.f. Requinto – A L'Aube (Selkirk). May 9. Eighth foal. €20,000Y. Tattersalls Ireland September. Half-sister to the 2-y-o 5f winner on his only start Racing Mate (by Art Connoisseur), to the quite useful 6f to 1m winner of 9 races from 2 to 7 yrs Amethyst Dawn (by Act One) and the fair Irish 1m and 9f winner Jpevie (by Amadeus Wolf). The dam is an unraced sister to the French listed-placed 3-y-o winner Aube d'Irlande and is a half-sister to 8 minor winners. The second dam, Adjala (by Northfields), won once at 2 yrs and is a half-sister to 5 winners. *"The dam must be a good broodmare because she's been to poor stallions but still bred winners with decent ratings. Requinto is a first season sire so you can't say for sure, but I think he's probably the best sire she's been to. This filly will be a six furlong 2-y-o, she's a May foal so we're giving her a bit of time, but she'll definitely win in the summer".*

1425. UNNAMED ★★★
b.f. Helmet – Dorothy Dene (Red Ransom). March 14. Third foal. £38,000Y. Doncaster Premier. Richard Knight. Half-sister to the fairly useful dual 6f winner at 2 and 3 yrs Navigate (by Iffraaj). The dam is an unraced half-sister to 3 winners including the Group 1 Middle Park Stakes winner Primo Valentino and the Group 2 6f Cherry Hinton Stakes winner Dora Carrington. The second dam, Dorothea Brooke (by Dancing Brave), won over 9f and is a half-sister to 6 winners including Conmaiche (Group 3 Prix Saint-Roman). (Richard Kent). *"Obviously Helmet has had a good start with his first two-year-olds this season. This filly comes from a fast family, she's not ready to go yet and we haven't galloped her but whatever she's done up to now has been fine. We do like her and it would be a surprise if there wasn't something under the bonnet".*

1426. UNNAMED ★★★

br.g. Zebedee – Journey's End (In The Wings). March 23. Sixth foal. 15,000Y. Tattersalls October Book 3. Richard Knight. Half-brother to fairly useful 7f (at 2 yrs) and 1m winner Pit Stop (by Iffraaj) and to 2 winners in Italy by Kheleyf and Noverre. The dam ran twice unplaced and is a half-sister to 8 winners including the Irish listed winners Dashing Colours and Dash Of Red and the dam of the 2-y-o Group 2 winner Captain Marvelous. The second dam, Near The End (by Shirley Heights), is an unraced half-sister to 2 winners. *"A nice horse, we gelded him a few weeks ago but he was showing up nicely beforehand. I think he's probably a six furlong 2-y-o, he's a very nice mover and I think he was value for money"*. **TRAINERS' BARGAIN BUY**

KEVIN RYAN

1427. ANGELS ACCLAIM (IRE)

b.f. Dark Angel – Miss Otis (Danetime). February 27. Fifth foal. £29,000Y. Doncaster Premier. Hillen & Ryan. Half-sister to the quite useful dual 5f winner Lady Kyllar (by Kyllachy), to the quite useful triple 7f winner Fanoos (by Dutch Art), the fair 2-y-o 6f winner Pyjama Day (by Royal Applause) and the minor Italian 3-y-o winner Danzig's Bone (by Bertolini). The dam, a fair 2-y-o 5f winner, is a half-sister to 2 winners including the Group 3 Palace House Stakes second Hoh Hoh Hoh. The second dam, Nesting (by Thatching), is an unplaced full or half-sister to 3 winners and to the dams of the Group 2 winners Tariq and Wi Dud. (Hambleton Racing Ltd XLV).

1428. BACKINANGER

b.g. Royal Applause – Giusina Mia (Diesis). April 15. Ninth foal. £30,000Y. Doncaster Silver. Hillen & Ryan. Half-brother to 5 winners including the modest 2-y-o 7f winner Dominic Cork (by Zebedee), the quite useful 7f winner and Hong Kong stakes placed Vaticano (by Medicean), the 2-y-o 5f winner and listed placed Tia Mia (by Dr Fong) and the fairly useful dual 5f winner Leiba Leiba (by Librettist). The dam won once over 10f in Italy and is a half-sister to 4 minor winners abroad. The second dam, Swiss Prospector (by Crafty Prospector), won once at 3 yrs in the USA and is a half-sister to 5 winners including the Group/Grade 1 winner Swink. (Ontoawinner 8).

1429. DREAM OF DREAMS (IRE)

ch.c. Dream Ahead – Vasilia (Dansili). February 7. Fifth foal. £44,000Y. Doncaster Premier. Not sold. Brother to the fairly useful 2015 2-y-o 6f winner Candelisa and half-brother to the useful 2-y-o 5f winner and Group 2 7f Superlative Stakes third Silverheels, to the quite useful 7f (at 2 yrs) to 9.5f winner Fiftyshadesfreed (both by Verglas) and the fairly useful 2-y-o 5f winner and listed-placed Lasilia (by Acclamation). The dam is an unraced half-sister to 7 winners including the Group 1 6f Cheveley Park Stakes and dual Group 2 winner Airwave. The second dam, Kangra Valley (by Indian Ridge), a moderate 2-y-o 5f winner, is a half-sister to 7 minor winners. (Prostock Ltd). This colt made an eye-catching debut when a fast finishing second on softish ground at Newmarket in mid-April.

1430. EVERYTHING FOR YOU (IRE)

b.c. Pivotal – Miss Delila (Malibu Moon). April 12. Sixth foal. 75,000Y. Tattersalls October Book 1. Stephen Hillen. Closely related to the useful 2015 2-y-o 6f winner and Group 3 Albany Stakes second Ashadihan (by Kyllachy) and half-brother to 4 winners including the quite useful 2-y-o 6f and 7f winner Lady Of The House (by Holy Roman Emperor), the quite useful dual 10f winner Mythical Madness (by Dubawi) and the fair German dual winner Marching On (by Rock Of Gibraltar). The dam is an unplaced half-sister to 5 winners including Sander Camillo (Group 2 Cherry Hinton Stakes and Group 3 Albany Stakes). The second dam, Staraway (by Star de Naskra), won 20 races in North America including three listed stakes and is a half-sister to 5 winners. (Mr T A Rahman).

1431. HEIR OF EXCITEMENT (IRE)

b.c. Tagula – Gimli's Treasure (King's Best). March 15. Third foal. £32,000Y. Doncaster Silver. Hillen & Ryan. The dam, a moderate Irish 9f winner, is a half-sister to 3 winners. The second dam, Alexandra S (by Sadler's Wells), is an unplaced sister to the Group 3 Gallinule Stakes winner Glyndebourne and a half-sister to 6 winners. (STS Racing Ltd).

1432. LUALIWA

b.c. Foxwedge – Sunpearl (Compton Place). March 9. First foal. £40,000Y. Doncaster

Premier. Hillen & Ryan. The dam is an unraced half-sister to 8 minor winners. The second dam, Star Tulip (by Night Shift), a useful winner of 3 races over 6f including the listed Sandy Lane Stakes, is a half-sister to 4 minor winners. (Mr & Mrs Julian & Rosie Richer).

1433. MAJOR JUMBO
gr.c. Zebedee – Gone Sailing (Mizzen Mast). March 8. Second foal. £37,000Y. Doncaster Silver. Hillen & Ryan. Half-brother to the moderate dual 6f winner Goadby (by Kodiac). The dam is an unraced half-sister to one minor winner. The second dam, Shoot (by Barathea), The second dam, Shoot (by Barathea), a fair 3-y-o 7f winner here, later won in the USA and is a half-sister to 6 winners including the Australian triple Group 1 winner Foreteller, the Group 2 winner Modern Look and the listed winner Arabesque (dam of the Group winners and sires Showcasing and Camacho). (Mr T A Rahman).

1434. NAUTICAL HAVEN
b.c. Harbour Watch – Mania (Danehill). February 2. Ninth foal. 45,000Y. Tattersalls October Book 2. S Hillen & K Ryan. Half-brother to 7 winners including the fairly useful 2-y-o 6f winner Fanatical (by Mind Games), the quite useful 2-y-o 6f winners Koptoon (by Rip Van Winkle) and Gower Valentine (by Primo Valentino), the German listed-placed 6f winner Domineer (by Shamardal) and the fair 2-y-o 6f winner (on her only start) Marrayah (by Fraam). The dam is an unraced half-sister to 7 winners including the dam of the Group 1 winners Youmzain and Creachadoir. The second dam, Anima (by Ajdal), was placed once at 3 yrs and is a half-sister to 8 winners (including 6 stakes winners), notably the multiple Group 1 winner Pilsudski. (Mr Hanson & Sir Alex Ferguson).

1435. PERFECT MADGE (IRE)
b.f. Acclamation – Soul Mountain (Rock Of Gibraltar). March 12. Sixth foal. £45,000Y. Doncaster Premier. Hillen & Ryan. Sister to the fair dual 6f winner Hills and Dales and half-sister to the modest 2015 6f to 1m placed 2-y-o Lady Canford (by Canford Cliffs) and 3 winners including the quite useful Irish 2-y-o 1m winner and 3-y-o Italian Group

3 10f second French Quebec (by Excellent Art). The dam, a quite useful 10.5f and 11f winner, is a sister to the listed-placed winner Londonintherain and a half-sister to the US Grade 2 winner Girl Warrior. The second dam, Qhazeenah (by Marju), a useful 6.5f (at 2 yrs) to 7f winner, is a half-sister to 9 winners including Ranin (Group 2 Park Hill Stakes). (Mr T A Rahman).

1436. TAGUR (IRE)
ch.c. Tagula – Westcote (Gone West). April 14. Second foal. £28,000Y. Doncaster Premier. Hillen & Ryan. Half-brother to the fair 1m winner Equitissa (by Chevalier). The dam, a fair 9f winner at 4 yrs, subsequently won in Germany and is a half-sister to 7 winners including 4 stakes winners, notably the dual Group 1 second Rainbow Corner. The second dam, Kingscote (by Kings Lake), won 3 races from 5f to 6f including the Lowther Stakes and is a full or half-sister to 8 winners. (Andy Turton & John Blackburn).

1437. TEOMARIA
b.f. Teofilo – Sylvestris (Arch). February 7. First foal. 60,000foal. Tattersalls December. BBA (Ire). The dam, a fairly useful listed-placed dual 7f winner (here and in the USA), is a half-sister to 2 winners including the fairly useful 2-y-o 5f winner and dual listed-placed Roof Fiddle. The second dam, Woodmaven (by Woodman), placed once at 3 yrs in the USA, is a half-sister to 3 winners including the dual Group 3 winner and 1,000 Guineas second Arch Swing. (Mr David Blunt).

1438. UNNAMED
ch.f. Dutch Art – Carraigoona (Rock Of Gibraltar). April 24. Fifth foal. £45,000Y. Doncaster Premier. Hillen & Ryan. Half-sister to the fair 2-y-o 5f winner Bheleyf (by Kheleyf) and to a minor French 3-y-o by Verglas. The dam, a modest 10f placed maiden, is a half-sister to 6 winners including the Group 2 10f Prix Guillaume d'Ornano winner Highdown and the Group 2 12f King Edward VII Stakes second Elshadi. The second dam, Rispoto (by Mtoto), a modest 12f winner, is a half-sister to 7 winners including the Group 3 10f Royal Whip Stakes winner Jahafil and the French listed 12f winner Mondschein.

1439. UNNAMED
b.f. Exceed And Excel – Chili Dip (Alhaarth). March 4. Sixth foal. 31,000Y. Tattersalls October Book 2. Hillen/Ryan. Half-sister to the quite useful 2015 2-y-o listed 6f placed White Bullet (by Exceed And Excel) and to the quite useful 2-y-o 7f and 1m winner Zakreet (by Cadeaux Genereux). The dam is an unraced sister to the listed Oaks Trial winner Birdie and a half-sister to 7 winners including the French middle-distance winner of 10 races (including 4 listed events) Faru and the listed winner Fickle (herself the grand dam of Camelot). The second dam, Fade (by Persepolis), is an unraced half-sister to Tom Seymour, a winner of five Group 3 events in Italy. (Guy Reed Racing).

1440. UNNAMED
b.c. Firebreak – Dayville (Dayjur). February 12. Sixteenth foal. £35,000Y. Doncaster Premier. Hillen/Ryan. Brother to the quite useful 5f and 6f winner Daylight and half-brother to 7 winners including useful Group 3 placed 7f and 1m winner Day Of Conquest (by Major Cadeaux), the listed-placed 5f and 6f winner Day By Day (by Kyllachy), the Irish 5f winner Alexander Ballet (by Mind Games and dam of the Group 1 Gran Criterium winner Hearts Of Fire) and the 2-y-o 1m winner Musical Day (by Singspiel) – all quite useful. The dam, a quite useful triple 6f winner, is a half-sister to the US Grade 1 winner Spanish Fern and to the dams of the Group/Grade 1 winners Lord Shanakill and Heatseeker. The second dam, Chain Fern (by Blushing Groom), is an unraced sister to the dual Group 1 winner Al Bahathri (the dam of Haafhd).

1441. UNNAMED
ch.c. Dragon Pulse – Degree Of Honor (Highest Honor). March 12. Seventh foal. £40,000Y. Doncaster Premier. Hillen/Ryan. Half-brother to 4 winners including the quite useful Irish 2-y-o 6f winner Beau Amadeus (by Amadeus Wolf), the minor French 2-y-o winner The Mole Catcher and the minor French 3-y-o winner Dock (both by Whipper). The dam, a moderate 10f to 12f placed maiden, is a half-sister to 6 winners in France including the listed winner Barings. The second dam, Sheba Dancer (by Fabulous Dancer), winner of the Group 3 Prix Vanteaux and second in the Group 1 Prix de Diane, is a half-sister to 4 winners.

1442. UNNAMED
b.c. Zoffany – Flying Flag (Entrepreneur). March 21. Ninth foal. 320,000 2-y-o. Tattersalls Craven Breeze Up. Hillen/Ryan. Half-brother to the quite useful 2015 2-y-o triple 7f winner Montsarrat (by Poet's Voice), to the Italian 2-y-o listed 7.5f and 3-y-o listed 9f winner Laguna Salada (by Invincible Spirit), the Italian listed-placed 10f winner Laguna Salada (by Celtic Swing) and four other minor winners abroad. The dam is an unplaced half-sister to the winner and US Grade 2 placed Azillion. The second dam, Olivia (by Ela-Mana-Mou), won once at 3 yrs and is a half-sister to 4 winners.

GEORGE SCOTT

1443. CHOTTO (IRE) ★★
b.f. Royal Applause – Alta Definizione (Hawk Wing). February 2. First foal. £10,000Y. Doncaster Premier. Elliott & Scott. The dam, a minor Italian winner of 6 races from 2 to 4 yrs, is a half-sister to the French winner of 8 races, including twice over 5.5f at 2 yrs, Wild Horse. The second am, Life Rely (by Maria's Mon), is an unraced half-sister to 3 winners including the Group 1 Italian Oaks winner and Group 1 Moyglare Stud Stakes third Menhoubah. (The Old Guard). *"She's bred to be pretty precocious and that's what she looks like. She's done really well recently and she'll be moving into faster work in early April, I imagine her being one for nurseries over five/six furlongs. When you're only paying that sort of money you have to be lucky and the owners are a small group of friends of mine who'll be happy if she wins a race".*

1444. ESSENTIAL ★★★★
b.c. Pivotal – Something Blue (Petong). April 10. Eleventh foal. 50,000Y. Tattersalls October Book 1. John & Jake Warren. Closely related to the useful Group 3 5f Prix de Saint-Georges winner of 9 races Mood Music, to the useful 2-y-o 6f winner The Long Game and the fairly useful 2-y-o 6f winner The Long Game (all by Kyllachy) and half-brother to 5 winners including the fairly useful 5f (including at 2 yrs) to 7f winner Steel Blue (by Atraf) and the quite useful 5f and 6f winners Reqaaba (by Exceed And Excel) and Memphis Man (by

Bertolini). The dam is an unplaced full or half-sister to 6 winners. The second dam, Blueit (by Bold Lad, Ire), a useful 2-y-o 5f winner, is a full or half-sister to 3 winners. (The Pivotal Club). *"He's a lovely horse and probably my nicest 2-y-o at this stage. He's got a solid pedigree, he's very correct and has a really good attitude. I'm going to give him an opportunity to be a Royal Ascot horse but he'll work properly around Guineas time. That'll tell us if he's able to run in a maiden in time for Ascot or not. We're pretty relaxed about it though and if he can't go, so be it. He's very nice and has a lot of quality".*

1445. GILGAMESH ★★
b.c. Foxwedge – Flaming Cliffs (Kingmambo). April 18. Sixth foal. Half-brother to the French dual 9.5f winner Maxxi (by Dansili). The dam is a placed half-sister to 4 winners including the 7f winner and Group 1 Prix Jean Prat third Ershaad. The second dam, Insight (by Sadler's Wells), won the Grade 1 E P Taylor Stakes and is a sister to the Irish 2,000 Guineas winner Saffron Walden and a half-sister to the Group 1 Prix de la Foret winner Dolphin Street. (Niarchos Family). *"A nice, big colt but he's huge. He weighs 530 kgs and keeps growing on me, but he's quite straightforward and despite his size he'll be a summer 2-y-o. A solid type, we're looking forward to seeing what the sire Foxhound does with his first crop and this is a very good-looking colt – almost my most attractive looking 2-y-o. He has an old fashioned look about him which some of my lads who worked for Henry Cecil say wouldn't have looked out of place with his horses".*

1446. JACK THE TRUTH ★★★
ch.g. Dandy Man – Friendly Heart (Lion Heart). April 2. Second foal. £40,000Y. Doncaster Premier. Elliott & Scott. Half-brother to My Cool Friend (by Acclamation), unplaced in one start at 2 yrs in Ireland in 2015. The dam is an unraced half-sister to 2 winners including the triple Canadian listed winner Edenworld. The dam, a minor winner at 3 yrs in the USA, is a half-sister to 5 winners including the US Grade 2 winner Vice N' Friendly. (Jack Stephenson). *"I love this horse, he's fast and is going to be working in early April. We had to geld him because he was a bit of a monkey and now he's taking a bit of time to fill his frame. He's all speed, wants top of the ground I think he's got quite a lot of ability. He cost quite a bit for a Dandy Man, but that sire's good sprinter Peniaphobia was a Group 1 winner in Dubai recently".*

1447. SAYIF MAGIC ★★★
br.c. Sayif – Pearl Magic (Speightstown). March 24. Second foal. £16,000Y. Doncaster Premier. George Scott. Half-brother to the modest 2015 5f and 7f placed 2-y-o Grizzly Bear (by Kodiac). The dam is an unraced half-sister to 10 winners including the very smart 7f (at 2 yrs) and Group 3 1m winner and Group 2 1m Queen Anne Stakes third Tough Speed. The second dam, Nature's Magic (by Nijinsky), is a placed half-sister to the US dual Grade 3 9f winner Stalwars and the French listed 7f winner and German Group 2 second Joy Of Glory. (Saleh Al Homaizi & Imad Al Sagar). *"He'll make his debut in early April, he's straightforward, has good constitution and although he's not a superstar he'll know his job and he'll give a good honest account of himself. Might be a six furlong horse in time and he should be doing his winning sooner rather than later. I'd love to have a winner by Sayif for these owners!"*

1448. STAY SHARP ★★
b.c. Intense Focus – Cuiseach (Bachelor Duke). March 31. Second foal. £20,000Y. Doncaster Premier. Elliot & Scott. Brother to the 2015 2-y-o Bonfire Bank, placed fourth over 1m on his only start. The dam is an unraced half-sister to 4 winners including the Irish 2-y-o listed winner Teolane. The second dam, Masnada (by Erins Isle), was a useful Irish 8.5f to 10f winner of 9 races. (Saffron Racing). *"A really honest, likeable horse that was well-bought. He does everything easily and although I can see him being better when he stretches out next year over a mile or so I'm thinking of starting him in May because he's so straightforward. He loves training, wants to please and I can see him running ten times this year if all goes well".*
TRAINERS' BARGAIN BUY

1449. UNNAMED ★★★
b.f. Kodiac – Baltic Belle (Redback). April 30. Sixth foal. 140,000Y. Tattersalls October Book 1. Tony Nerses. Sister to the listed Bosra Sham Stakes winner Terror and half-sister to the

quite useful 5f winner of 6 races (including at 2 yrs) Sonko (by Red Clubs) and the fair 7f and hurdles winner Rathealy (by Baltic King). The dam, a quite useful 7f and 1m winner, is a half-sister to 3 winners. The second dam, Skerries Belle (by Taufan), was placed in Ireland before winning 3 races in Belgium and is a half-sister to 7 winners including the Group 2 Mill Reef Stakes winner and Group 1 July Cup third Indian Rocket. (Saleh Al Homaizi & Imad Al Sagar). *"A very nice filly that matches her pedigree, she's pretty precocious and I can see her starting around Guineas time. She could be a Queen Mary filly. That's the plan and as she's doing everything right at the moment I think we've got to give it a shot. I'd be hopeful of her breaking her maiden before Ascot and then we'll see".*

1450. UNNAMED ★★★
ch.f. Dutch Art – Injaaz (Sheikh Albadou). March 20. Fifth foal. 50,000Y. Tattersalls October Book 2. Not sold. Half-sister to the fairly useful listed-placed triple 5f winner Top Boy, to the fair 2-y-o 6f winners Fardyieh (by King's Best) and Classic Fortune (by Royal Applause) and the modest 5f winner Shaft Of Light (Exceed And Excel). The dam, a quite useful listed-placed 6f winner, is a sister to the fairly useful 6f winner of 3 races Corndavon (dam of the smart 2-y-o Nevisian Lad) and a half-sister to the dam of the listed winners Pyman's Theory and Forthefirstime. The second dam, Ferber's Follies (by Saratoga Six), a 2-y-o sprint winner and Grade 2 6f Adirondack Stakes third, is a half-sister to 11 winners. (H Lascelles). *"A nice filly with a solid pedigree, being a short-coupled, athletic little filly she looks like a sprinter. She probably won't be ready until June/July because I'm not pushing her. She has an easy way of going but is behind my most forward bunch so I don't know that much about her yet. Looks like a filly that's going to win races".*

DAVID SIMCOCK

1451. AKRANTI ★★★
ch.f. Pivotal – Akdarena (Hernando). April 26. Third foal. The dam, a smart 9f (at 2 yrs), Group 3 10f Blue Wind Stakes and listed 10f winner, was third in and Group 1 10f Pretty Polly Stakes and is a half-sister to 3 winners. The second dam, Akdariya (by Shirley Heights), an Irish 12f winner, was second in the Group 2 12f Ribblesdale Stakes and is a half-sister to 6 winners including Akbar (Group 2 2m Henry II Stakes). *"Quite a natural filly, not over-big but big enough. She was a bit slow to come to hand but she's going well now. I'm quite pleased with her, she doesn't look backward at all and shows a bit of speed".*

1452. BAB EL MANDEB (IRE) ★★
b.c. Blame – April Pride (Falbrav). February 25. Second foal. $70,000Y. Keeneland September. Blandford Bloodstock. Half-brother to the quite useful 2-y-o 7f winner Henrytheaeroplane (by Henrythenavigator). The dam won the 2-y-o Group 3 7f Prestige Stakes here and a Grade 3 stakes in the USA. The second dam, Hasta (by Theatrical), a minor US 3-y-o winner, is a half-sister to 7 winners. *"Not as forward as the other Blame we have. He went very weak when he arrived from America and took time to come to hand but he's strengthened up now and does everything in a very nice way. He's one for the second half of the season".*

1453. CAPTOR ★★★★
b.c. Frankel – Hasten (IRE) (Montjeu). February 22. The dam is an unplaced sister to 2 winners including the 2-y-o Group 1 1m Criterium International winner and Irish Derby third Jan Vermeer and a three-parts sister to the 2-y-o Group 3 7f Silver Flash Stakes winner, multiple Group 1 placed and subsequent US Grade 1 9f winner Together and the fairly useful 2-y-o 7f and 1m winner and listed-placed Terrific. The second dam, Shadow Song (by Pennekamp) won race at 3 yrs in France and is a half-sister to the Group 3 May Hill Stakes winner Midnight Air (herself dam of the Group 3 and US Grade 2 winner Midnight Line) and to the placed dam of the Group 1 Prix de l'Abbaye winner Imperial Beauty. (Al Asayl Bloodstock). *"A lovely horse, he has a lot of size and scope and has done everything asked of him. Out of all the Frankel's I've got he's probably the nicest one and I think he could be a very progressive horse. It's a lovely family, he's slightly unfurnished and not the finished article yet, but he shows up nicely and does everything very naturally".*

1454. COOL BREEZE (IRE) ★★
b.f. Dream Ahead – Dead Cool (Kyllachy). March 10. 68,000Y. Tattersalls October Book 2. Not sold. The dam, a modest dual 6f winner, is a half-sister to 8 winners including the very useful 2-y-o 5f and 6f winner and Cornwallis Stakes second Deadly Nightshade. The second dam, Dead Certain (by Absalom), a very smart winner of the Group 1 6f Cheveley Park Stakes, the Queen Mary Stakes, the Lowther Stakes (all at 2 yrs) and the Group 2 6.5f Prix Maurice de Gheest, is a half-sister to 7 winners. *"A neat filly, not overly big and she had a couple of setbacks early in the year which has put us a bit behind. But she's done everything asked of her and I'd like to think she'd be a six furlong 2-y-o. Not the biggest, so I'd like to be getting on with her early".*

1455. CRIMSON LAKE ★★★
b.f. Makfi – Liberty Chery (Statue Of Liberty). April 26. Fourth foal. Sister to the quite useful 2-y-o 5f and 6f winner Taking Libertys. The dam, a French 1m winner, was listed-placed twice and is a half-sister to 2 winners including the 2-y-o 7f winner and Group 1 Criterium de Saint-Cloud second Fauvelia. The second dam, Marion (by Doyoun), a minor French dual winner at 3 yrs, is a half-sister to 5 winners. *"Neat, not overly-big, looks quite forward and I'm sure she'll appreciate a bit of give in the ground. She might have the speed to start at six is but more likely to start in one of the early seven furlong races".*

1456. DALAVIDA (FR) ★★★★
gr.f. Kendargent – Dalawysa (Dalakhani). February 4. Second foal. 68,000Y. Tattersalls October Book 2. Blandford Bloodstock. The dam, a minor French placed 3-y-o, is a half-sister to the French listed winner Valima - herself the dam of three Group winners including Valyra (Group 1 Prix de Diane). The second dam, Vadlawysa (by Always Fair), a minor French 3-y-o winner, is a sister to the Group 2 Prix Hocquart winner Vadlawys and a half-sister to the Grade 1 Breeders' Cup Mile winner Val Royal. *"Like a lot by the sire she's a little bit "busy" but she's very likeable, quite strong and mature. A good goer, I imagine she'll be starting at seven furlongs unless she shows a lot of speed. A mid-season 2-y-o".*

1457. FIBONACCI ★★★
ch.c. Galileo – Tereschenko (Giant's Causeway). February 16. First foal. The dam, unplaced on her only start, is a half-sister to the champion 2-y-o colt Fasliyev and to the Group 3 Irish 1,000 Guineas Trial winner Kamarinskaya. The second dam, Mr P's Princess (by Mr Prospector), is an unraced half-sister to the US Grade 1 winners Menifee and Desert Wine. *"A giant of a horse, but he's very natural and has a good action. He has an easy, almost languid style and he's very likeable to watch. The dam is closely related to Fasliyev and I think when you have a Galileo having speed on the dam's side is very important. For a big horse he has a very easy action".*

1458. HARBOUR ROCK ★★★
b.c. Harbour Watch – Rock Lily (Rock Of Gibraltar). April 27. Fifth foal. 110,000Y. Tattersalls October Book 1. David Redvers. Half-brother to the fairly useful 2-y-o 5f winner and dual listed-placed Botanic Garden (by Royal Applause) and to the modest 7f winner Rockme Cockney (by Cockney Rebel). The dam, a quite useful Irish 2-y-o 1m winner, is a half-sister to 8 winners including the Group 2 6f Cherry Hinton Stakes winner Please Sing and the very useful 7f (at 2 yrs) to 10f winner and Group 1 National Stakes third Mountain Song. The second dam, Persian Song (by Persian Bold), is an unplaced sister to the Solario Stakes winner Bold Arrangement (placed in seven Group/Grade 1 races including the Kentucky Derby). *"A nice horse, he came to us in November and he's a good-looking, attractive colt. He had a month off due to a little setback and during that period he grew and put weight on. I'm very pleased with him, he has a good action and is quite likeable".*

1459. ISLAND IN THE SKY (IRE) ★★★
b.f. Kodiac – When Not Iff (Iffraaj). March 14. First foal. £55,000Y. Doncaster Premier. David Redvers. The dam, a fairly useful Irish dual 7f winner (including at 2 yrs), is a full or half-sister to 4 winners. The second dam, Sheer Bliss (by Sadler's Wells), a fair 2-y-o 1m winner, is a half-sister to 9 winners including the Derby winner Oath and the triple Group 1 winner Pelder. *"She came in late so we're playing catch-up a little bit more than I'd have*

liked. Neat and strong, we'll push on with her now but ability-wise it's difficult to weigh up".

1460. MASHADIE BOY ★★★
b.c. Rip Van Winkle – Happy Holly (Holy Roman Emperor). January 21. First foal. 40,000Y. Tattersalls October Book 1. Blandford Bloodstock. The dam, a minor French 3-y-o winner, is a half-sister to 6 winners including the Group 1 Prix de l'Opera winner Lily Of The Valley and the Group 2 UAE Derby winner Mubtaahij. The second dam, Pennegale (by Pennekamp), is a French placed half-sister to 5 winners. *"I like this horse. The stallion's dead in the water so we bought a very good-looking horse for reasonable money. He's pleasing, hasn't let us down in any way and is far more forward than I thought he'd be. Goes nicely".*

1461. MISS SUGARS ★★★
ch.f. Harbour Watch – Three Sugars (AUS) (Starcraft). January 26. First foal. Tattersalls October Book 4. 10,000Y (private sale). The dam, a modest 6f winner from two starts at 2 yrs, is a half-sister to 5 winners including the French listed winner Kissing The Camera and the dam of the dual Grade 1 Northern Dancer Turf Handicap winner Wigmore Hall. The second dam, Hoh Dear (by Sri Pekan), won four races here and in North America including the 6f Empress Stakes (at 2 yrs) and the Grade 3 Natalma Stakes and was second in the Group 2 Cherry Hinton Stakes. *"A tough, hard-knocking filly, we've thrown plenty at her and she's taken it very well. She wants to please, has a great attitude and will be running in six furlong races from May onwards. She'll be fine, maybe not a superstar, but she'll be OK".* **TRAINERS' BARGAIN BUY**

1462. MYSTIC DAWN (IRE) ★★★★
b.f. Oasis Dream – Frivolity (Pivotal). March 30. Fourth foal. Half-sister to the fair 5.5f winner Ashkari (by Dutch Art). The dam is an unraced half-sister to numerous winners including the smart 2-y-o Group 2 6f Mill Reef Stakes winner Byron and the useful 1m and 10.3f winner Gallant Hero. The second dam, Gay Gallanta (by Woodman), a very smart winner of the Group 1 6f Cheveley Park Stakes and the Group 3 5f Queen Mary Stakes, was second in the 1m Falmouth Stakes and is a half-sister to the smart Group 2 10f Gallinule Stakes winner Sportsworld. *"A filly that shows a lot of speed, we don't deal with too many five furlong 2-y-o's but she looks like one. She'll be our first 2-y-o runner if everything goes to plan and I'm very pleased with her. The dam's been a bit disappointing but this filly looks all Oasis Dream, which is a positive".*

1463. SABADILLA ★★★
b.f. Archipenko – Songerie (Hernando). April 9. Sixth foal. Half-sister to the quite useful 2015 2-y-o 1m winner Valitop (by Pivotal) and to the fairly useful 12f and 13f winner Hardstone (by Birdstone). The dam won the Group 3 1m Prix des Reservoirs at 2 yrs, was third in the Group 2 Park Hill Stakes and is a sister to the fairly useful 2-y-o 7.2f and German listed winner and Group 1 Italian Oaks third Souvenance and a half-sister to 6 winners including the useful listed winners Soft Morning and Sourire. The second dam, Summer Night (by Nashwan), a fairly useful 3-y-o 6f winner, is a half-sister to 7 winners including the Group 3 Prix d'Arenburg winner Starlit Sands. (Miss K Rausing). *"I quite like her, shrew a splint in February having trained very naturally and well up to that point. A good goer and quite strong, we've had quite a few Archipenko's and this is probably the most forward we've ever had. I'm very pleased with her. She's quite natural, so that's a good sign and I see her as a seven furlong starter".*

1464. SEIRIOS (IRE) ★★★
b.c. Frankel – Drifting (Sadler's Wells). February 16. Fifth foal. €190,000Y. Goffs Orby. Not sold. Half-brother to the quite useful 2-y-o 1m winner Devdas (by Dylan Thomas) and to the quite useful 12f winner Allegria (by Dalakhani). The dam, a fair Irish 3-y-o 6f winner, is a half-sister to 4 winners including the fair 2-y-o 7f winner Glinting Desert (herself dam of the Group 1 Phoenix Stakes winner Alfred Nobel). The second dam, Dazzling Park (by Warning), a very smart winner of the Group 3 1m Matron Stakes and a listed 9f event, was placed in the Group 1 Irish Champion Stakes and the Irish 1,000 Guineas and is a half-sister to 7 winners including New Approach. *"We had his half-brother who was very backward. This fellow is a smarter type of horse, a little bit more natural and a bit more forward. He got a*

sore shin just as were about to step him up but he moves well. We don't know enough about him yet but he's certainly a second half of the season 2-y-o".

1465. SOUL SILVER (IRE) ★★★
ch.f. Dragon Pulse – Free Lance (Grand Lodge). February 19. Fifth foal. €75,000Y. Goffs Orby. David Redvers. Half-sister to the quite useful 6f and 7f winner Poole Harbour, to the Irish 2-y-o 5f and subsequent Hong Kong winner Machaputo and the modest 2-y-o 5f winner Sandsend (by Elusive City). The dam is an unplaced half-sister to 4 winners including the Irish listed winner Flash McGahon. The second dam, Astuti (by Waajib), a quite useful 2-y-o 6f winner, is a half-sister to 6 winners including the Group 2 King's Stand Stakes winner The Tatling. *"A really tough filly, everything we throw at her she seems to take and she's thrived on hard work. She's almost innocuous in the way she goes about things but when she gets competitive she does well. Not the biggest but she's hardy and tough, we quite like her and she'll be a six furlong filly"*.

1466. ZANOBIA ★★★
b.f. Invincible Spirit – Zallerina (Zamindar). February 21. First foal. The dam is an unraced half-sister to the Italian listed placed Sgarzulina. The second dam, Zakania (by Indian Ridge), is an unraced daughter of the Group 3 Prix de Sandringham winner Zarkiya. *"A little bit busy and scatty, but she has a big stride and when she's on the canter she's very professional. What she does in between home and the canter is a little bit lively, but she's a nice goer, has a long stride on her and I don't dislike her at all"*.

1467. UNNAMED ★★★
b.c. Lope De Vega – Black Dahlia (Dansili). February 19. Second foal. €75,000Y. Arqana Deauville August. Private Sale. The dam, a quite useful 7f to 10f winner, was listed-placed and is a half-sister to 4 winners. The second dam, South Rock (by Rock City), a useful winner of 4 races from 7f to 8.2f including the listed Prix de Saint-Cyr, is a half-sister to 5 minor winners. *"A lovely horse, he's good sized and has plenty of quality about him. I think he was probably quite well bought in Deauville and although he's a big horse he's not short of speed. I like this horse and I'd say he's one for the middle of the season"*.

1468. UNNAMED ★★★
ch.f. Arcano – Boo Boo Bear (Almutawakel). April 14. Third foal. 40,000Y. Tattersalls December. Rabbah Bloodstock. Half-sister to the useful listed 6f winner Letters Of Note (by Azamour). The dam, a fair Irish 1m winner, is a sister to the winner and dual listed placed Eddie Jock and a half-sister to 3 winners including the 2-y-o winner and Group 2 Beresford Stakes second Mawaakef. The second dam, Al Euro (by Mujtahid) a moderate 6f placed 2-y-o, is a half-sister to 5 winners including the Group 1 1m Queen Elizabeth II Stakes winner Air Express. *"Her sister was quite smart and she shows plenty of speed and plenty of zest. She was bought at the December sales so she was a bit behind when she came in but she's caught up very well. She's ready to work now"*.

1469. UNNAMED ★★★
b.c. Medicean – Despatch (Nayef). February 11. First foal. 105,000Y. Tattersalls October Book 2. Blandford Bloodstock. The dam is an unplaced half-sister to 6 winners including the smart 7f (at 2 yrs) and Group 2 12f King Edward VII Stakes winner Plea Bargain and the very useful Group 3 10f Winter Hill Stakes winner Lay Time. The second dam, Time Saved (by Green Desert), a fairly useful 10f winner, is a sister to the useful 1m winner Illusion and a half-sister to 5 winners including Zinaad and Time Allowed (both winners of the Group 2 12f Jockey Club Stakes). *"A lovely horse, very well put-together, quite strong and mature. It's a slightly late developing family but he's far more natural than that and I'd like to think he'll be a mid-season 2-y-o"*.

1470. UNNAMED ★★
b.f. Frankel – First (Highest Honor). February 9. Half-sister to 6 winners including the smart listed 1m and listed 10f winner and dual Group 3 third Perfect Stride, the fairly useful 2-y-o 6f winner Among Equals, the quite useful 1m winner of 4 races First Dream (all by Oasis Dream), the French dual listed 12f and Australian Group 2 12f winner Au Revoir (by Singspiel) and the French 2-y-o listed 6f winner Law Lord (by Diktat). The dam, a

French listed 1m winner, is a half-sister to 12 winners including the smart Group 3 winners Bluebook and Myself. The second dam, Pushy (by Sharpen Up), won the Group 2 Queen Mary Stakes and is a half-sister to the high-class 2-y-o Precocious and the Group 1 Japan Cup winner Jupiter Island. (Hesmonds Stud). *"She's on the small side and needs to develop plenty, so there's a long way to go with her".*

1471. UNNAMED ★★★
b.f. Canford Cliffs – Gilded Vanity (Indian Ridge). April 18. Ninth foal. 200,000Y. Tattersalls October Book 1. Demi O'Byrne. Half-sister to the useful 6f (at 2 yrs) to 1m winner of 8 races and Group 2 Superlative Stakes second Birdman, to the Irish 2-y-o Group 3 6f placed A Mind Of Her Own (both by Danehill Dancer), the fair 2-y-o 5f winner Roman Seal (by Holy Roman Emperor) and the fair 6f winner of 4 races Desert Icon (by Desert Style). The dam, an Irish 5f winner, is a sister to the Irish 2,000 Guineas second Fa-Eq and a half-sister to 5 winners. The second dam, Searching Star (by Rainbow Quest), was a modest 6f to 11.3f placed half-sister to 8 winners. *"A half-sister to Birdman who we trained, this is a much bigger and more classical type than him. She has a good attitude and a lovely action but will be one for later in the year"*,

1472. UNNAMED ★★★★
b.c. Holy Roman Emperor – Kentucky Warbler (Spinning World). February 16. Fifth foal. 180,000Y. Tattersalls October Book 1. Blandford Bloodstock. Half-brother to the useful Irish 7f (at 2 yrs) and 1m winner and dual Group 1 fourth Learn and to the quite useful dual 10f winner Ray Ward (both by Galileo). The dam, a modest 12f winner, is a half-sister to 3 winners including the listed-placed Higher Love. The second dam, Dollar Bird (by Kris), a useful 2-y-o 8.2f winner and second in the listed Oaks Trial, is a half-sister to 7 winners including the Group 2 King Edward VII Stakes winner Amfortas and the Group 3 winner Legend Maker (dam of the 1,000 Guineas winner Virginia Waters). *"A much stronger type than his half-brother Ray Ward who we trained, he's well put-together, he shows up well and I'm very pleased with his progress. He's not short of a bit of speed and I like him".*

1473. UNNAMED ★★★
b.c. Dream Ahead – Malladore (Lawman). February 18. First foal. 115,000Y. Tattersalls October Book 2. Mark Crossman. The dam is an unraced half-sister to 2 winners including the dual listed-placed Witches Brew. The second dam, Macheera (by Machiavellian), a quite useful 2-y-o 1m winner in France, is a half-sister to 7 winners including the 2-y-o 7f winner and French and Irish 1,000 Guineas third La Nuit Rose. *"A lovely big horse, he's very mature and is showing up well so far. Plenty of size and scope, he's a big-striding horse and I'd love to think he'll be starting in six furlong maidens in May or June time".*

1474. UNNAMED
b.c. Frankel – Marine Bleue (Desert Prince). March 13. Sixth foal. Half-brother to the French listed 12f winner Marina Piccola (by Halling), to the quite useful 2-y-o 6f winner and UAE Group 3 1m third Wednaan (by Dubawi) and two minor winners in France by Beat Hollow and Medicean. The dam, a German Group 3 and listed 1m winner at 3 yrs, is a half-sister to 3 winners including the French listed winner Mystic Spirit. The second dam, Mirina (by Pursuit Of Love), a minor French 3-y-o winner, is a half-sister to 6 winners including the dam of the Group 1 Grand Prix de Paris winner Mirio. *"I haven't seen him yet, but it's a later developing family and I should think he'll be the same. For example his year-older half-sister by Makfi will start her career shortly in a 3-y-o maiden. I have four Frankel's and they're all different shapes and sizes".*

1475. UNNAMED
b.c. Deep Impact – Musical Way (Gold Away). January 30. Fourth foal. Brother to the Japanese dual Group 1 winner over 10f and 12f Mikki Queen. The dam won 8 races including the Group 2 10f Prix Dollar and Group 3 10f La Coupe de Maisons-Laffitte. *"He hasn't arrived here yet but I'm looking forward to it. Deep Impact is the best stallion in the world in my opinion".*

1476. UNNAMED ★★★
b.c. Kheleyf – My Lucky Liz (Exceed And Excel). February 12. First foal. The dam, a quite useful 2-y-o dual 6f winner, is a half-sister to

3 winners including the useful 2-y-o 7f and listed 1m winner Go Angellica (by Kheleyf). The second dam, Areyaam (by Elusive Quality), a fair maiden, was placed three times over 1m and is a half-sister to 2 winners. *"I trained the dam who was a really tough, hard knocking filly that went wrong at three. This colt is a good size, he's well put-together and very strong. He's just picked up the bridle now and we're learning plenty about him, he carries plenty of condition and I don't dislike him".*

1477. UNNAMED ★★
b.c. Archipenko – Oval Office (Pursuit Of Love). February 26. Sixth foal. 25,000Y. Tattersalls October Book 2. Blandford Bloodstock. Half-brother to the smart 2-y-o Group 3 6f Sirenia Stakes winner Glass Office (by Verglas) and to the very useful 9.5f to 12.5f winner Captain Morley (by Hernando). The dam, a fairly useful 3-y-o dual 1m winner, is a half-sister to 12 winners including the smart 6f (at 2 yrs) and Nell Gwyn Stakes winner Myself and the smart 2-y-o 6f Princess Margaret Stakes and 3-y-o 6f Prix de Seine et Oise winner Bluebook. The second dam, Pushy (by Sharpen Up), a very useful 2-y-o winner of 4 races including the Queen Mary Stakes, is a half-sister to 10 winners including the good winners Precocious and Jupiter Island. *"If you compare him to his siblings he looks more like Captain Morley than Glass Office. He's a good-sized, long horse that looks like he'll want a trip, but he has a good action and I'm happy with him".*

1478. UNNAMED ★★
b.f. Dutch Art – Plethora (Sadler's Wells). May 1. Fifth foal. The dam is an unraced sister to the Group 1 Racing Post Trophy and Group 1 St Leger winner Brian Boru and to the listed winner Kitty O'Shea and a half-sister to the Group 2 winners Sea Moon and Moon Search and to the dam of the Derby winner Workforce. The second dam, Eva Luna (by Alleged), won the Group 3 Park Hill Stakes and the listed Galtres Stakes. *"A tall filly who was late coming in and was very sick. She looks a lot better now and she has a good action but she's very tall and needs to furnish."*

1479. UNNAMED ★★★★
b.f. Dutch Art – Rare Ransom (Oasis Dream).

February 5. Fourth foal. Half-sister to the fair 2015 8.5f placed 2-y-o Vizier (by Pivotal) and to the quite useful 1m (at 2 yrs) and 10f winner Alex Vino (by High Chaparral). The dam, a fairly useful Irish 7f (at 2 yrs) and 1m winner and third in the Group 3 7f Debutante Stakes, is a full or half-sister to 5 winners. The second dam, Rapid Ransom (by Red Ransom), a quite useful Irish 10f winner, was Grade 3 placed in the USA and is a half-sister to the Irish 2-y-o listed winner Warrior Queen (dam of the US Grade 2 winner and Grade 1 placed A P Warrior). *"She goes well, she's a good bodied filly, looks every inch a 2-y-o and is very natural. Taking her training very well, I'm pleased with her".*

1480. UNNAMED ★★★★
b.c. Pivotal – Shatter (Mr Greeley). March 17. First foal. 40,000Y. Tattersalls October Book 2. Blandford Bloodstock. The dam is an unplaced half-sister to 3 minor winners. The second dam, Watership Crystal (by Sadler's Wells), ran twice unplaced and is a sister to the Group 3 winner Dubai Success and to the Irish Derby third Tchaikovsky and a half-sister to 5 winners including Crystal Music (Group 1 Fillies' Mile). *"A lovely big horse with loads of size and scope. A very natural horse with a good action, I'm very happy with him".*

1481. UNNAMED ★★★★
b.c. Galileo – Simply Perfect (Danehill). February 5. Brother to the very useful listed 9f (at 2 yrs) and Group 3 10f Friarstown Stakes winner of 5 races Mekong River and to the fair 2-y-o 1m winner Really Lovely. The dam won the Group 1 Fillies' Mile and the Group 1 Falmouth Stakes and is a half-sister to 2 winners. The second dam, Hotelgenie Dot Com (by Selkirk), a 7f winner at 2 yrs, was second in the Group 1 7f Moyglare Stud Stakes and third in the Group 1 Fillies' Mile and is a half-sister to 4 winners including the Moyglare Stud Stakes and the Group 2 6f Lowther Stakes winner Bianca Nera. *"A strong, compact, deep-girthed horse – there's a lot of substance there. He's a big baby really but at the same time he takes everything you throw at him. The dam's been a little disappointing so far but this colt has every chance and we'll kick on with him".*

1482. UNNAMED ★★★★
b.c. Galileo – Walklikeanegyptian (Danehill).
April 27. Brother to the 2015 2-y-o Group 3 7f
Tyros Stakes winner and Group 2 Royal Lodge
Stakes second Deauville, to the smart Group
3 11f and listed 10f winner of 5 races The
Corsican and the quite useful 2-y-o 1m winner
Heatstroke. The dam, a fair 2-y-o 5f and
subsequent US winner, was Grade 3 placed
and is closely related to numerous winners
including the Canadian Grade 2 Nassau Stakes
winner Callwood Dancer and the Group 2
Italian Oaks winner Contredanse. The second
dam, Ahdaab (by Rahy), placed once over
10f, is a half-sister to 8 winners including the
Group 1 1m Queen Elizabeth II Stakes winner
Maroof and to the placed dam of the Irish
Derby winner Desert King. *"A real athlete,
it's a good family and one I know well. He's
a much better looking horse than his brother
The Corsican, he has a good attitude and
wants to please. I'm very pleased with him"*.

1483. UNNAMED ★★
b.c. Henrythenavigator – Zimira (Invincible
Spirit). February 7. First foal. The dam, a
quite useful 2-y-o 1m winner, is a half-sister
to numerous winners including the Group 2
placed Mathematician, the Irish 2,000 Guineas
third Oracle and the dam of the Group 2
Champagne Stakes winner Saamidd. The
second dam, Zibilene (by Rainbow Quest),
a useful 12f winner and listed-placed over
10f, is a half-sister to 7 winners including the
Breeders' Cup Mile, Irish 2,000 Guineas and
Queen Anne Stakes winner Barathea and the
Fillies Mile and Irish 1,000 Guineas winner
Gossamer. *"He came in late and he's not the
biggest horse but he's well put together, has
a good attitude and a good action. He's just
finding his feet at the moment"*.

TOMMY STACK

1484. AEGEAN GIRL (IRE) ★★★
b.f. Henrythenavigator – Catch The Moon
(Peintre Celebre). April 17. 70,000foal.
Tattersalls December. Justin Casse. Half-sister
to the Group 3 6f Bengough Stakes winner
Lightning Moon (by Shamardal), to the useful
Irish 2-y-o listed 6f winner Song Of My Heart
(by Footstepsinthesand), the Irish 2-y-o 6f
winner from two starts Gift From Heaven
(by Excellent Art), the quite useful 6f and 7f
winner Orbit The Moon (by Oratorio) and the
2-y-o 6f and subsequent Hong Kong winner
Catskill Mountain (by One Cool Cat). The
dam, a minor French 3-y-o 9f winner, is a half-
sister to one other minor winner in France.
The second dam, Sensitivity (by Blushing
John), a listed winner in France and second
in the Group 3 Prix Chloe, is a half-sister to
7 winners including the US Grade 3 winner
Luftikus and the dams of the US Grade 1
winner Love Theway Youare. *"She's quite a big
filly, a good mover and probably one for seven
furlongs in the second half of the year"*.

1485. CAPE SUNSHINE (IRE) ★★★
b.f. Cape Blanco – Shermeen (Desert Style).
January 25. Fourth foal. 140,000Y. Tattersalls
October Book 1. C McCormack. Half-sister
to the very smart 2-y-o Group 1 6f Phoenix
Stakes and Group 2 6f Railway Stakes winner
Sudirman and the French 1m winner Rayyan
(both by Henrythenavigator). The dam, a
useful 2-y-o 5f and 5.7f winner, was third in
the Group 3 Cornwallis Stakes and a Grade 3
stakes in the USA and is a sister to the very
useful dual listed 6f winner Mister Manannan
and a half-sister to 3 winners. The second
dam, Cover Girl (by Common Grounds), a fair
2-y-o 6f and 7f and subsequent Scandinavian
listed winner, is a half-sister to 3 winners.
*"A good-moving filly and a half-sister to a
Phoenix Stakes winner, she probably won't
take as long to come to hand as you might
expect for a Cape Blanco. She'll set off at six
furlongs I should think and end up a seven
furlongs/mile filly at the back-end of the
season"*.

1486. OLYMPIC LEGEND (IRE) ★★★
ch.c. Choisir – Margaret's Dream (Muhtarram).
March 10. Fourth foal. £55,000Y. Doncaster
Premier. Not sold. Half-brother to the
unplaced 2015 2-y-o Class Honours (by
Alfred Nobel), to the modest dual 1m winner
Balmont Blast (by Balmont) and the moderate
6f (at 2 yrs) and dual 7f winner Whats For
Pudding (by Kheleyf). The dam was placed 12
times from 6f to 1m and from 2 to 5 yrs and
is a half-sister to 4 winners including the triple
Group 1 winner Olympic Glory. The second
dam, Acidanthera (by Alzao), a quite useful
3-y-o 7.5f winner, is a half-sister to 2 winners.
*"He's a forward colt and he'll probably start

his career in April over five furlongs, but I think six is more likely to be his trip this year. A tough, strong, hardy 2-y-o".

1487. SON OF REST ★★★★
b.c. Pivotal – Hightime Heroine (Danetime). March 19. Fourth foal. €70,000Y. Goffs Orby. C McCormack. The dam, a fair 6f winner, is a half-sister to 5 winners including the listed 1m Heron Stakes winner and Group 1 1m Criterium International third Redolent. The second dam, Esterlina (by Highest Honor), won over 1m at 3 yrs in Ireland and is a half-sister to 3 minor winners in France. *"Quite a nice horse that's grown a lot since we bought him as a yearling. He seems to have plenty of pace, he goes nicely and he's probably going to be a six furlong 2-y-o from the end of May/ early June".*

1488. UNNAMED ★★★
b.f. Iffraaj – Desert Alchemy (Green Desert). March 27. Ninth foal. 32,000Y. Tattersalls October Book 3. De Burgh Equine. Half-sister to the quite useful dual 5f winner Present Alchemy (by Cadeaux Genereux), to the fair triple 6f winner (including at 2 yrs) Perfect Alchemy (by Clodovil), the fair 2-y-o 5f winner Strictly Ballroom (by Choisir) and the fair 7f winners Rosko (by Selkirk) and Easy Over (by Dr Fong). The dam, a useful listed 7f winner, is a half-sister to 5 winners including Express Wish (Group 3 Supreme Stakes). The second dam, Waffle On (by Chief Singer), a quite useful 6f winner, subsequently won in France and is a half-sister to 5 winners. *"A very good-looking filly, she's quite big and moves well but she's definitely one for the second half of the season".*

1489. UNNAMED ★★★
b.f. Fastnet Rock – Front House (Sadler's Wells). February 20. Fourth foal. The dam, a South African and UAE Grade 2 12f winner, is a half-sister to 5 winners including the listed Marble Hill Stakes and Group 1 Phoenix Stakes second Access All Areas. The second dam, Adjalisa (by Darshaan), was placed once over 7f at 5 yrs and is a half-sister to 5 winners including the listed Leopardstown 2,000 Guineas Trial winner and Group 1 placed Adjareli. *"We have her 3-y-o full sister Balcony who's only just made her debut over ten furlongs. This filly is totally different, she's smaller and stockier, so she won't take as long to come to hand. She seems to have a bit of toe and I can imagine her starting off towards the end of May over six furlongs".*

1490. UNNAMED ★★
b.c. Fastnet Rock – Green Castle (Indian Ridge). April 26. Ninth foal. 58,000Y. Tattersalls October Book 2. De Burgh Equine. Closely related to the fair 10f and 12.5f winner Love Marmalade (by Duke Of Marmalade) and half-brother to 4 winners including the quite useful 2-y-o 1m winner Raven Ridge (by High Chaparral), the useful listed 12f winner Ithoughtitwasover (by Hurricane Run) and the fairly useful 1m (at 2 yrs) and 7f winner and listed-placed Greenisland (by Fasliyev). The dam, placed once over 1m from two starts, is a half-sister to 12 winners including the dual Group 2 placed Luchiroverte. The second dam, Green Lucia (by Green Dancer), won over 6f and 10f, was placed in the Oaks and the Yorkshire Oaks and is a half-sister to Old Vic. *"A big, good-looking horse, with what we've done with him so far he's taken his work well but he's probably going to want seven furlongs. So we'll be looking to start him off in June or July".*

1491. UNNAMED ★★★
b.f. Fastnet Rock – Ittasal (Any Given Saturday). January 26. First foal. 50,000Y. Tattersalls October Book 1. C McCormack. The dam, a quite useful 2-y-o 7f winner, is a half-sister to 6 winners including the very useful 2-y-o 6f winner and Group 3 Firth Of Clyde Stakes third La Presse. The second dam, Journalist (by Night Shift), a useful 2-y-o 6f winner, was second in the Group 3 6f Princess Margaret Stakes and is a half-sister to the Group 2 Flying Childers Stakes winner Sheer Viking. *"A strong filly and a good mover that looks like a 2-y-o. I don't think she'll take too long to come to hand and I'd say she'd be happy with six furlongs to start with. It's quite a fast family".*

1492. UNNAMED ★★★★
b.f. Royal Applause – Nasij (Elusive Quality). February 18. Sixth foal. €67,000Y. Tattersalls Ireland September. Ashtown Bloodstock. Half-sister to 4 winners including the fairly

useful 10f to 12f winner of 3 races Tanfeeth (by Singspiel), the quite useful 8.5f winner Mugazala (by Sakhee) and the modest 1m to 11f winner from 2 to 8 yrs Rezwaan (by Alhaarth). The dam, a useful 6f (at 2 yrs) and listed 1m winner, was Group 3 placed twice and is a half-sister to 5 winners. The second dam, Hachiyah (by Generous), a fairly useful 10f winner, is a half-sister to 3 winners including the listed winner Hiwaya and the Italian Derby third Mutawwaj. *"A good-looking filly, she'll probably be ready to go in mid-May over six furlongs. A good mover and with a good temperament. She goes quite well".*

1493. UNNAMED ★★★
gr.f. The Factor – Sayedah (Darshaan). February 10. Tenth foal. $160,000Y. Saratoga August. Tommy Stack. Closely related to the Irish 2-y-o 6f winner and Group 2 Beresford Stakes third Battle Of Marathon (by War Front) and half-sister to one minor winner. The dam, winner of the Group 2 7f Rockfel Stakes, is a half-sister to 5 winners. The second dam, Balaabel (by Sadler's Wells), a quite useful 1m winner, is a half-sister to 6 winners including the US Grade 2 7f winner Kayrawan and the good broodmare Sayedat Alhadh (dam of the Group winners Haatef and Walayef). *"She's had one or two niggling problems but when we get a clear run with her she shouldn't take long. She's a good, strong filly, her sire wasn't a bad 2-y-o in America and her dam won the Rockfel. She's ready to kick on with now, but we don't know an awful lot about her yet".*

1494. UNNAMED ★★
b.br.f. Bated Breath – Time Ahead (Spectrum). March 23. Seventh foal. €65,000Y. Goffs Orby. Fozzy Stack. Half-sister to the fair 11.5f winner World Time (by Dalakhani). The dam, a 10f winner and second in the Group 1 French Oaks, is a half-sister to 6 winners including the Group 3 10.4f Musidora Stakes winner and Group 1 Prix de Diane third Time Away (dam of the Group 2 winner Time On). The second dam, Not Before Time (by Polish Precedent), is an unraced half-sister to 7 winners including the very useful Group 3 12f winners Zinaad and Time Allowed and the dams of the Group 2 winners Anton Chekhov,

First Charter and Plea Bargain. *"She's quite a nice mover but she'll probably take a bit of time. A nice filly that hasn't done anything in earnest yet".*

1495. UNNAMED ★★★
b.c. Power – Varmint Lady (Orpen). May 7. Third foal. £34,000Y. Doncaster Premier. C McCormack. Half-brother to the moderate 1m winner Better Value (by Ad Valorem). The dam, placed fourth over 5f once at 2 yrs, is a sister to the listed-placed winner Little White Lie. The second dam, Miss Informed (by Danehill), is an unraced half-sister to the Group 3 winning sprinter Exhibitionist. *"Even though he was a May foal he's a strong colt and he moves well. He doesn't look like he'll get too far, he probably wants good ground and I can see him being out around late May".*

SIR MICHAEL STOUTE

1496. BELIEVABLE
b.f. Acclamation – Irresistible (Cadeaux Genereux). April 6. Half-sister to the very smart 7f (at 2 yrs) and Group 3 7f Nell Gwyn Stakes winner and Coronation Stakes and Falmouth Stakes second Infallible, to the useful dual 6f winner Watchable, the quite useful dual 7f winner at 2 and 3 yrs Thrill, the fair 7f (at 2 yrs) and 6f winner of 4 races New Decade (all by Pivotal) and the fairly useful 7f and 1m winner Chilled (by Iceman). The dam, a fairly useful 5f (at 2 yrs) and listed 6f winner, is a half-sister to 2 winners. The second dam, Polish Romance (by Danzig), a minor 7f winner in the USA, is a sister to a US stakes winner and a half-sister to 5 minor winners. (Cheveley Park Stud).

1497. BLUSHING ROSE
ch.f. Dalakhani – Russelliana (Medicean). January 23. First foal. The dam, a useful 2-y-o 6f winner, was second in the Group 2 6f Cherry Hinton Stakes and is a half-sister to 2 winners. The second dam, Rosacara (by Green Desert), a modest 7f and 1m placed maiden, is a half-sister to the high-class triple Group 1 winner Notnowcato.

1498. CRYSTAL OCEAN
b.c. Sea The Stars – Crystal Star (Mark Of Esteem). February 8. Half-brother to the very smart dual Group 2 12f Pride Stakes, Group

2 12f Princess Of Wales's Stakes and Group 3 10.3f Middleton Stakes winner Crystal Capella (by Cape Cross), to the very smart Group 2 10f winner Hillstar (by Danehill Dancer), the listed 10f winner Crystal Zvezda (by Dubawi) and the fairly useful 1m and 10f winner Sandor (by Fantastic Light). The dam, winner of the listed Radley Stakes and second in the Group 3 Fred Darling Stakes, is a half-sister to 6 winners. The second dam, Crystal Cavern (by Be My Guest), a fairly useful 2-y-o 7f winner here and subsequently a dual winner in Canada, is a half-sister to 5 winners including the French 1,000 Guineas winner Rose Gypsy. (Evelyn de Rothschild).

1499. DESERT CAPELLA
b.c. Dubawi – Crystal Capella (Cape Cross). February 4. First foal. The dam, a very smart dual Group 2 12f Pride Stakes, Group 2 12f Princess Of Wales's Stakes and Group 3 10.3f Middleton Stakes winner, is a half-sister to the very smart Group 2 10f winner Hillstar (by Danehill Dancer) and the fairly useful 1m and 10f winner Sandor (by Fantastic Light). The second dam, Crystal Star (by Mark Of Esteem), winner of the listed Radley Stakes and second in the Group 3 Fred Darling Stakes, is a half-sister to 6 winners.

1500. FRONTISPIECE
b.c. Shamardal – Free Verse (Danehill Dancer). February 6. First foal. The dam, a fairly useful 2-y-o 6f and 7f winner, is a sister to the useful listed-placed winner Quadrille and a half-sister to 3 winners. The second dam, Fictitious (by Machiavellian), a useful 10f listed winner, is a sister to the smart Group 2 12f Ribblesdale Stakes and Group 2 13.3f Geoffrey Freer Stakes winner Phantom Gold (herself dam of the Oaks second Flight Of Fancy). (The Queen).

1501. INTERWEAVE
ch.f. Dutch Art – Interlace (Pivotal). March 13. Third foal. Sister to the minor winner of 5 races abroad Labjaar. The dam, a quite useful 2-y-o 6f winner, is a sister to two winners including the very smart 6f and 7f winner of 7 races Feet So Fast and a half-sister to 4 winners including the smart Group 2 6f Lowther Stakes and Group 3 Princess Margaret Stakes winner Soar. The second dam, Splice (by Sharpo), a smart winner of the listed 6f Abernant Stakes, is a full or half-sister to 7 winners. (Cheveley Park Stud).

1502. KARAWAAN (IRE)
b.c. Sea The Stars – Magic Sister (Cadeaux Genereux). February 12. Eighth foal. 250,000foal. Tattersalls December. Shadwell Estate Co. Half-brother to the very smart listed 1m (at 2 yrs) and Group 1 1m Falmouth Stakes winner Rajeem (by Diktat). The dam, a modest 3-y-o 7f placed maiden, is a sister to the very smart 2-y-o Group 1 6f Prix Morny and Group 3 5f Molecomb Stakes winner Hoh Magic and a half-sister to 5 winners. The second dam, Gunner's Belle (by Gunner B), a modest 7f and 10f winner, is a half-sister to 8 winners including the very smart Group 2 Prince Of Wales's Stakes winner Crimson Beau.

1503. MAWQED (IRE)
b.f. Invincible Spirit – Mumayeza (Indian Ridge). March 25. Half-sister to the quite useful 2-y-o 6f winner Mezel (by Tamayuz). The dam, a fair 10f winner, is a half-sister to numerous winners including the Group 2 12f Hardwicke Stakes winner Maraahel and the Britannia Handicap winner Mostashaar. The second dam, Nasanice (by Nashwan), a fairly useful Irish 3-y-o 9f winner, is a half-sister to the listed 12f winner Sahool. (Hamdan Al Maktoum).

1504. MELTING DEW
b.c. Cacique – Winter Sunrise (Pivotal). May 2. Fourth foal. Closely related to the 7f (at 2 yrs) and Group 1 10f Nassau Stakes winner Winsili (by Dansili). The dam, a useful dual 10f winner, is a half-sister to 5 winners including the Group 2 10f Prix Greffulhe winner Ice Blue. The second dam, Winter Solstice (by Unfuwain), a French 2-y-o 1m winner and second in the Group 3 1m Prix d'Aumale, is a half-sister to the Grade 1 Manhattan Handicap winner Meteor Storm, to the Group 2 12.5f Grand Prix de Deauville winner Polish Summer, the Group 3 2m winner Host Nation and the French 10f listed winner Morning Eclipse. (Khalid Abdulla).

1505. MIRAGE DANCER
b.c. Frankel – Heat Haze (Green Desert). April 18. Half-brother to Forge, unplaced in one start at 2 yrs in 2015 and to the useful

2-y-o 7f winner and listed-placed Radiator (both by Dubawi). The dam, winner of the Grade 1 Matriarch Stakes and the Grade 1 Beverly D Stakes, is closely related to the Coronation Stakes, Prix Jacques Le Marois and Breeders' Cup Filly & Mare Turf winner Banks Hill, to the Grade 1 Matriarch Stakes winner Intercontinental, the US dual Grade 1 winner Cacique, the North American triple Group 1 winner Champs Elysees and the Group 2 winner and high-class sire Dansili. The second dam, Hasili (by Kahyasi), won over 5f at 2 yrs and stayed a mile. (Khalid Abdulla).

1506. MORI
b.f. Frankel – Midday (Oasis Dream). February 1. Second foal. Closely related to the very promising 2015 2-y-o 1m debut winner Midterm (by Galileo). The dam was a high-class racemare and the winner of six Group 1 races – Breeders' Cup Filly & Mare Turf, Prix Vermeille, Yorkshire Oaks and Nassau Stakes (three times) and is a full or half-sister to several winners including the smart 1m (at 2 yrs) and Group 3 7f winner and Group 1 Nassau Stakes third Hot Snap. The second dam, Midsummer (by Kingmambo), a quite useful listed-placed 11f winner, is a half-sister to the Oaks and Fillies Mile winner Reams of Verse and the Eclipse Stakes and Phoenix Champion Stakes winner Elmaamul. (Khalid Abdulla).

1507. NOBLE MASTERPIECE
ch.c. Dutch Art – Elysian (Galileo). January 31. First foal. 170,000Y. Tattersalls October Book 1. Charlie Gordon-Watson. The dam, a modest 4-y-o 12f winner, is a half-sister to 3 winners including the Group 1 Falmouth Stakes and dual Group 2 winner Integral. The second dam, Echelon (by Danehill), won the Group 1 1m Matron Stakes, the Group 2 Celebration Mile and four Group 3 events and is a half-sister to the dual Group 2 1m Celebration Mile winner Chic.

1508. PANOVA ♠
b.f. Invincible Spirit – Safina (Pivotal). March 14. Third foal. Half-sister to the useful 2015 2-y-o 7f winner, Group 2 1m May Hill Stakes second and dual Group 3 placed Marenko (by Exceed And Excel) and to the quite useful 2-y-o 6f winner Vesnina (by Sea The Stars). The dam, a fairly useful 7f winner, was listed-placed over 1m and is a half-sister to 2 winners. The second dam, Russian Rhythm (by Kingmambo), won the 1,000 Guineas, Coronation Stakes, Nassau Stakes and Lockinge Stakes and is a half-sister to several winners including the 2-y-o Group 2 1m Royal Lodge Stakes winner Perfectperformance. (Cheveley Park Stud).

1509. PARLANCE (IRE)
b.f. Invincible Spirit – Pleasantry (Johannesburg). February 11. Second foal. 450,000Y. Tattersalls October Book 1. Cheveley Park Stud. The dam is an unraced half-sister to the top-class miler and multiple Group 1 winner Kingman and to the Group 3 Tercentenary Stakes winner Remote. The second dam, Zenda (by Zamindar), won the French 1,000 Guineas, was second in the Coronation Stakes and the Grade 1 Queen Elizabeth II Challenge Cup at Keeneland and is a half-sister to the Middle Park Stakes, July Cup and Nunthorpe Stakes winner Oasis Dream.

1510. PARTITIA
b.f. Bated Breath – Palmette (Oasis Dream). February 7. First foal. The dam, a fair 6f winner, is a sister to the Group 2 6f Gimcrack Stakes winner Showcasing and to the stakes-placed winners Tendu and Bouvardia and a half-sister to 3 winners including the very smart listed 6f winner Camacho. The second dam, Arabesque (by Zafonic), a useful listed 6f winner, is a sister to 2 winners including the useful 5f and 6f winner Threat and a half-sister to the Australian triple Group 1 winner Foreteller and the Group 2 1m Prix de Sandringham winner Modern Look. (Khalid Abdulla).

1511. PRECISION ♠
b.c. Galileo – Pearl Earrine (Kaldounevees). March 20. Fourth foal. €250,000Y. Arqana Deauville August. John Warren. Half-brother to the 2-y-o 7f and 1m winner, Group 1 Prix Marcel Boussac second and Group 2 Prix de Sandringham second Topaze Blanche (by Zamindar). The dam, a minor French winner, is a half-sister to 4 winners including Varxi (Group 3 Prix Thomas Bryon). The second dam, Girl Of France (by Legend Of France), a dual listed winner in France, was second in the Group 3 Prix Quincey.

1512. QUEEN'S CASTLE
b.f. Dansili – Queen's Best (King's Best). April 11. Fourth foal. Sister to the 2015 2-y-o 7f winner, from two starts, Queen's Trust and to the fairly useful dual 7f winner Royal Seal. The dam, a smart winner of the Group 3 10f Winter Hill Stakes and the listed 12f Chalice Stakes, was second in the Group 2 Blandford Stakes and is a half-sister to 4 winners including the Group 3 Prix de Royaumont third Reverie Solitaire. The second dam, Cloud Castle (by In The Wings), winner of the Group 3 Nell Gwyn Stakes and placed in the Group 1 Yorkshire Oaks and Group 1 Prix Vermeille, is a half-sister to the multiple Group 1 winners Warrsan and Luso, and the dam of the Group 3 winners Tastahil, Hattan, Blue Monday and Laaheb. (Cheveley Park Stud).

1513. RAINBOW LEGACY (IRE)
b.c. Frankel – Gift Range (Spectrum). March 4. Half-brother to the modest 12f winner Christmas Hamper (by Dubawi). The dam, a useful 1m winner, was third in the Group 3 10f Blue Wind Stakes and is a sister to the 2,000 Guineas and King George VI and Queen Elizabeth Stakes winner Golan and to the Group 2 10.5f Dante Stakes winner Tartan Bearer and a half-sister to 5 winners. The second dam, Highland Gift (by Generous), a fairly useful 10f winner, is a half-sister to the Group 2 12f Great Voltigeur Stakes winner Bonny Scot. (Ballymacoll Stud Farm).

1514. SPATIAL
b.f. Galileo – Spacious (Nayef). March 7. Third foal. The dam, a Group 2 1m May Hill Stakes (at 2 yrs) and Group 2 1m Windsor Forest Stakes winner, was placed in five Group 1 events including the 1,000 Guineas and is a full or half-sister to 5 winners. The second dam, Palatial (by Green Desert), a useful winner of 4 races over 7f (including at 2 yrs), is a half-sister to 6 winners including the useful listed 10f winners Portal and Ice Palace.

1515. SPLASH AROUND
ch.c. Nathaniel – Splashdown (Falbrav). April 10. Fourth foal. 160,000Y. Tattersalls October Book 1. Charlie Gordon-Watson. Half-brother to the quite useful 2015 2-y-o 1m winner Baydar (by Rock Of Gibraltar), to the 2-y-o Group 3 7f Solario Stakes winner and Group 2 Superlative Stakes second Aktabantay (by Oasis Dream) and the quite useful 7f winner Synergise (by Danehill Dancer). The dam, a listed 10f winner and listed-placed another four times, is a half-sister to 4 winners including listed 10f winner Cosmodrome. The second dam, Space Time (by Bering) was placed over 7f at 2 yrs in France and is a half-sister to 5 minor winners.

1516. TAAMOL (IRE)
b.c. Helmet – Supreme Seductress (Montjeu). January 11. Second foal. 140,000Y. Tattersalls October Book 2. Shadwell Estate Co. Half-brother to the unplaced 2015 2-y-o Prepotent (by Kodiac). The dam is an unplaced half-sister to 3 winners including the Group 1 Italian Oaks winner Menhoubah. The second dam, Private Seductress (by Private Account), a US stakes-placed winner of 3 races, is a half-sister to 4 winners.

1517. TEXTURED (IRE)
b.f. Dark Angel – Timbre (Dubai Destination). January 23. Second foal. €100,000Y. Goffs Orby. Cheveley Park Stud. Sister to the modest 2015 5f and 6f placed 2-y-o Stroke Of Midnight. The dam is an unraced half-sister to 5 winners including the 2-y-o listed Chesham Stakes winner Champlain. The second dam, Calando (by Storm Cat), won the Group 3 1m May Hill Stakes, was second in the Group 1 Fillies Mile and third in the French 1,000 Guineas and is a half-sister to 3 winners.

1518. UNNAMED
b.c. Nathaniel – Kinnaird (Dr Devious). February 24. Seventh foal. 525,000Y. Tattersalls October Book 1. Charlie Gordon-Watson/ Al Shaqab Racing. Half-brother to the Group 2 Royal Lodge Stakes and listed Chesham Stakes winner Berkshire (by Mount Nelson), to the quite useful dual 1m winner Keene Dancer (by Danehill Dancer) and the fair 10f and 12f winner Keenes Royale (by Red Ransom) and herself dam of the 2-y-o dual Group 2 winner Ivawood. The dam won the Group 1 Prix de l'Opera and the Group 3 May Hill Stakes and is a half-sister to the Group 3 Chester Vase winner Mickdaam. The second dam, Ribot's Guest (by Be My Guest), is an unplaced half-sister to 6 winners.

JAMES TATE

1519. CAPE FALCONE ★★
b.f. Camacho – Asinara (Big Shuffle). May 19. Fifth foal. 22,000Y. Tattersalls October Book 3. Rabbah Bloodstock. Half-sister to the quite useful 7f and 9.5f winner Affileo (by Teofilo) and to the fair 2-y-o 7f winner Complexity (by Multiplex). The dam, a German 2-y-o 7.5f winner, is a half-sister to 3 winners including the French 2-y-o winner and Group 3 Prix Thomas Bryon third Ameer. The second dam, Ailette (by Second Set), won once at 2 yrs in Germany and is a half-sister to 10 winners including the Group 2 German 2,000 Guineas winner Aviso and the dam of the Group 1 German Oaks winner Amarette. *"Despite being a late foal she'll be an early type. Not a star, but she'll be alright. She's shown speed and should be out in May when her second birthday arrives".*

1520. FIRST DANCE (IRE) ★★★★★
b.f. Cape Cross – Happy Wedding (Green Tune). February 17. First foal. 40,000Y. Tattersalls October Book 2. Rabbah Bloodstock. The dam, a French 9f to 10.5f winner, is a half-sister to the German listed winner Separate Opinion. The second dam, Diamond White (by Robellino), won 6 races including the Group 2 Prix de l'Opera and is a half-sister to 3 winners. (S Ali). *"She goes very well and will make her debut over six furlongs in a fillies' maiden in May, possibly at Newmarket. She's my five star pick for this year".*

1521. LIGHTNING NORTH ★★★
b.f. Mayson – Purple Tiger (Rainbow Quest). February 18. 10,000Y. Tattersalls October Book 3. James Tate. Half-sister to the very useful 6f (at 2 yrs) and 5f winner of 6 races and Group 2 6f Gimcrack Stakes second Taajub, to the quite useful 2-y-o 5f and 6f winner Excel Yourself (both by Exceed And Excel) and the quite useful 5f and 6f winner Polish Pride (Polish Precedent). The dam is an unraced half-sister to 6 winners including the German Group 2 winner and Italian Group 1 second Notability. The second dam, Noble Rose (by Caerleon), won the Group 3 Park Hill Stakes and the listed Galtres Stakes and is a half-sister to Simeon (Group 3 Sandown Classic Trial). (S Ali). *"The dam has produced plenty of useful five furlong 2-y-o's and this filly is very much in the same mould. So we'd expect her to win two-year-old races over five furlongs".*

1522. MYTHICAL SPIRIT ★★★
b.f. Dragon Pulse – Call This Cat (One Cool Cat). April 2. Second foal. 28,000Y. Tattersalls October Book 3. Rabbah Bloodstock. Half-sister to the fair 10f winner Cat Royale (by Lilbourne Lad). The dam is an unplaced half-sister to 6 winners including the 2-y-o listed sprint winners Come To Heel, Pasar Silbano and Gerfalcon. The second dam, Give A Whistle (by Mujadil), a dual 5f winner at 3 and 4 yrs, is a half-sister to one winner. (Saeed Manana). *"A 2-y-o type that shows speed and she'll be racing in May. One for five/six furlongs".*

1523. ROYAL REQUEST ★★★
b.f. Royal Applause – Garbah (Kodiac). April 16. First foal. The dam, a fairly useful UAE 4-y-o 6f and 7f winner of 4 races, is a sister to 2 winners. The second dam, Baraloti (by Barathea), a fair maiden, was placed twice over 1m and is a half-sister to 4 minor winners. (Saeed Manana). *"She's a small, home bred filly that shows plenty of speed. We like to think she'll pick up an early five furlong 2-y-o race".*

1524. SEAFRONT ★★★★ ♠
b.f. Foxwedge – Locharia (Wolfhound). April 7. Eleventh foal. 18,000Y. Tattersalls October Book 3. Rabbah Bloodstock. Half-sister to 7 winners including the quite useful 6f to 9f and hurdles winner of 7 races Credit Swap (by Diktat), the quite useful 7f and 1m winner of 9 races Lochantanks (by Compton Place), the fair 5f winner Yanza (by Bahamian Bounty), the fair 2-y-o 6f winner Woodland Girl (by Kyllachy) and the fair 7f and 10f winner Lady Loch (by Dutch Art). The dam was a fairly useful 2-y-o 5f winner. The second dam, Lochbelle (by Robellino), a fair 10.2f winner, is a half-sister to the champion sprinter Lochsong and the Nunthorpe Stakes winner Lochangel. (Saeed Manana). *"Shows loads of speed, as might be expected considering her relatives. All being well she should make her debut in the five furlong fillies' maiden at Newmarket's Craven meeting".* **TRAINERS' BARGAIN BUY**

1525. UNNAMED ★★★
b.c. Lawman – Catbells (Rakti). February 15. Second foal. 40,000Y. Tattersalls October Book 3. Rabbah Bloodstock. The dam, a fair 9f winner at 4 yrs, was placed over 6f at 2 yrs and is a half-sister to 3 winners including the useful 2-y-o 6f winner and Group 2 Richmond Stakes second Exhibition. The second dam, Moonbi Ridge (by Definite Article), a winner of 3 races from 10f to 12f in Ireland, was listed-placed twice and is a half-sister to 4 winners. (Saeed Manana). *"A nice colt, but he's a great, big strong colt and more of a 3-y-o miler type. This year we'll set him off over six/seven furlongs in mid-season. He goes nicely and we like him".*

1526. UNNAMED ★★★★
b.f. Fastnet Rock – Cochabamba (Hurricane Run). March 5. First foal. 55,000Y. Tattersalls October Book 2. James Tate. The dam, a fairly useful 6f (at 2 yrs) and 8.5f winner and second in the Group 2 Rockfel Stakes and the Group 3 Prestige Stakes, is a half-sister to one winner. The second dam, Bolivia (by Distant View), is an unraced half-sister to 11 winners including the 3 stakes winners. *"She's a big, strong filly and the first foal of a mare who was second in the Rockfel. She looks really nice and she'll probably start off at six furlongs in May".*

1527. UNNAMED ★★★
b.f. Foxwedge – Lomapamar (Nashwan). January 31. Seventh foal. 10,000Y. Tattersalls October Book 3. Rabbah Bloodstock. Half-sister to the fair 1m (at 2 yrs) to 14f winner Getaway Car (by Medicean), to the fair 2-y-o 6f winner Ghost Cat (by Equiano), the moderate 1m and hurdles winner Mister Fantastic (by Green Tune) and a hurdles winner by Beat Hollow. The dam, a fair 10f winner, is a half-sister to 8 winners including the 2-y-o Group 2 1m Royal Lodge Stakes winner Mons and the Irish Oaks third Inforapenny. The second dam, Morina (by Lyphard), won over 11f in France and is a half-sister to 10 winners. (Saeed Manana). *"She had a little setback in December so she hasn't really done much yet, but she's moves really well and she's a really attractive, well-muscled filly. I would think she'll be out in May or June and we like what we've seen so far".*

1528. UNNAMED ★★★
b.c. Sir Percy – Mexican Hawk (Silver Hawk). February 15. 9,000Y. Tattersalls October Book 3. Rabbah Bloodstock. Half-brother to the fairly useful 2-y-o listed 5f winner Accipiter (by Showcasing), to the quite useful 14f and 2m winner Bin Singspiel (by Singspiel), the quite useful 9f and 12f winner Elegant Hawk (by Generous), the modest 9f winner Nellie The Elegant (by Mount Nelson) and the winner of 13 races in Greece at 3 to 5 yrs Mountain Glow (by Araafa). The dam, a fairly useful 10f winner, is a half-sister to 8 winners – three of them listed-placed. The second dam, Viva Zapata (by Affirmed), won the Group 2 Prix du Gros Chene and is a half-sister to 7 winners. (Saeed Manana). *"He was a cheap purchase due to some x-ray abnormalities, but he's a really nice stamp of a horse and a half-brother to Accipiter and to the dam of Regal Hawk – a horse we had that was rated 100. He won't run at less than six furlongs but he's a nice horse, especially for what he cost".*

1529. UNNAMED ★★★★
b.c. Poet's Voice – Neshla (Singspiel). March 22. Fifth foal. 45,000Y. Tattersalls October Book 1. Jamie Lloyd. Half-brother to the fair 2015 2-y-o 9f winner Nessita, to the quite useful 2-y-o 6f winner Wahylah, the quite useful UAE dual 1m winner Muhtaram (all by Shamardal) and the fair 2-y-o dual 7f winner Faraajh (by Iffraaj). The dam, a poor 11f placed maiden, is a half-sister to 9 winners including the Group 3 Fred Darling Stakes winner and Group 2 Nassau Stakes third Sueboog (dam of the Group 1 winner Best Of The Bests) and the listed winners Sell Out and Marika. The dam, Nordica (by Northfields), a useful 6f and 1m winner, is a half-sister to 2 winners. *"A big, strong colt who goes well, he won't set off at less than six furlongs but we like him".*

1530. UNNAMED ★★★
b.f. Medicean – Plucky (Kyllachy). April 23. Sixth foal. 115,000Y. Tattersalls October Book 3. Rabbah Bloodstock. Half-sister to the quite useful 7f and 1m winner Plucky Dip (by Nayef) and to the quite useful 7f (including at 2 yrs) and 6f winner Delft (by Dutch Art). The dam, a quite useful 7f winner, is a half-sister to 7 winners including the 2-y-o Group 2 5f Flying Childers Stakes and Group 3 5f

Molecomb Stakes winner Wunders Dream and the Group 3 Ridgewood Pearl Stakes winner Grecian Dancer. The second dam, Pizzicato (by Statoblest), a modest dual 5f winner, is a half-sister to 5 winners including the high-class Hong Kong horses Mensa and Firebolt. (Saeed Manana). *"Despite the fact she isn't very big and looks very much like a sprinter she'll be one for the second half of the season. She's done nothing but grow all the through the spring and she's still 'up behind' with open knees. So we haven't really tried her yet but she'll hopefully make a sprinter because she looks the type".*

1531. UNNAMED ★★★
b.f. Clodovil – Shambodia (Petardia). March 16. Eighth foal. 30,000Y. Tattersalls October Book 3. Rabbah Bloodstock. Sister to the useful 6f (at 2 yrs) and 7f winner and Group 2 Hungerford Stakes third Brazos, to the fairly useful triple 7f winner (including at 2 yrs) Bettalatethannever (by Titus Livius) and the fair 6f (at 2 yrs) to 1m winner of 6 races Master Of Dance (by Noverre). The dam is an unraced half-sister to 7 winners. The second dam, Lucky Fountain (by Lafontaine), is an unraced sister to the Group 2 Geoffrey Freer Stakes winner Shambo and a half-sister to 4 winners. (Saeed Manana). *"A tall, rangy, full-sister to Brazos, but she doesn't resemble him physically. She's taller, lengthier, a different colour and has more of a fast ground action. She goes nicely and she'll make her debut over six or seven furlongs in the middle of the season".*

1532. UNNAMED ★★
b.c. Sea The Stars – Silent Serenade (Bertolini). March 26. Second foal. 70,000Y. Tattersalls December. Rabbah Bloodstock. Half-brother to the moderate 2015 7f placed 2-y-o Global Avenger (by Kodiac). The dam ran once unplaced and is a half-sister to 10 winners including the Group 3 Select Stakes winner Leporello and the listed winners Calypso Grant and Poppy Carew. The second dam, Why So Silent (by Mill Reef), is an unraced half-sister to 5 winners including the US Grade 3 winner Supreme Sound. (Saeed Manana). *"A lovely, tall, rangy colt. I can't see him running at anything less than seven furlongs and he's definitely one for the second half of the season, but he does have a bit of something about him".*

1533. UNNAMED ★★★ ♠
b.c. Rio De La Plata – Silver Miss (Numerous). April 29. Fourth foal. 26,000Y. Tattersalls December. Rabbah Bloodstock. Half-brother to the fair triple 6f winner Birdie Queen (by Pastoral Pursuits). The dam, a minor French 3-y-o winner, is a half-sister to 7 winners including the French dual listed winner Silva. The second dam, Silverqueen (by Alydar), won once at 3 yrs in France and is a half-sister to 10 winners including the Group 1 Prix Jean Prat winner and sire Sillery. (Saeed Manana). *"A good-moving, attractive colt, he's unlikely to set off at less than six furlongs but we like him and he moves well".*

MARK TOMPKINS

1534. ASTROSHADOW ★★
gr.f. Aussie Rules – Astrodiva (Where Or When). February 19. First foal. The dam, a fair maiden, was placed ten times from 1m to 2m and is a half-sister to one winner. The second dam, Astromancer (by Silver Hawk), a moderate 4-y-o 14f winner, is a half-sister to one winner. (Mystic Meg Ltd). *"A filly that moves well, she's been growing a little just lately but we're going to be stepping her up soon and I think she'll be out in May. The dam was placed loads of times and was unfortunate not to win. This filly is a grey like the sire and he gets 2-y-o winners, so she'll be alright".*

1535. ASTROSTORM ★★
b.c. Medicean – Astrolibra (Sakhee). February 7. First foal. The dam, a moderate dual 10f and hurdles winner, is a sister to one winner and a half-sister to 3 winners. The second dam, Optimistic (by Reprimand) a fairly useful 2-y-o dual 7f winner, is a half-sister to several winners including the fairly useful 3-y-o dual 7f winner Woodbeck (dam of the Group 2 Yorkshire Cup winner Franklins Gardens). (Mystic Meg Ltd). *"He's a lovely type – a big, strong, very attractive colt. He'll need some time, but we'll see him from mid-season onwards over seven furlongs plus".*

1536. DIXON ★★★
b.c. Lawman – Pure Song (Singspiel). April 11. Fifth foal. 45,000Y. Tattersalls October

Book 2. M Tompkins. Half-brother to the very smart 10f and 11f winner and Epsom Derby and King George VI third Romsdal (by Halling) and to the fair 2-y-o 9.5f winner Wolf Albarari (by Medicean). The dam, a fair 12f and 14f placed maiden, is a half-sister to 4 winners including the smart 7f (at 2 yrs) and Group 3 10.5f Prix Fille de l'Air winner Goncharova. The second dam, Pure Grain (by Polish Precedent), won the Group 1 12f Irish Oaks and the Group 1 12f Yorkshire Oaks and is a half-sister to 8 winners including the dam of the Japanese Group 1 winner Fine Grain. (Dahab Racing). *"A very athletic colt, he's not big but he's quite strong and he's doing swinging canters now. He'll want seven furlongs or a mile this year without any doubt and he should stay well. He's a half-brother to a Derby third and I like Lawman as a sire, so I'm very happy with him".*

1537. STELLEKAYA ★★★
b.f. Mastercraftsman – Delitme (Val Royal). April 24. Sixth foal. 32,000Y. Tattersalls October Book 1. Dahab Racing. Half-sister to the fair 2015 2-y-o 6f winner Irish Eclare (by Fquiano) and to the modest 6f and 7f winner Art Dzeko (by Acclamation). The dam, a winner of 4 races in Italy at 2 and 3 yrs, is a half-sister to 7 winners including the very useful 6f (at 2 yrs) and Group 3 7f Nell Gwyn Stakes winner Reunion. The second dam, Phylella (by Persian Bold), a winner in France (over 10f) and the USA, is a sister to the US stakes winner Karman Girl and a half-sister to 4 winners. (Dahab Racing). *"She's a strong, attractive filly that's been growing lately. Typical of the sire she'll be one from the middle of the season onwards. She could be alright and she'll get a trip next year".*

1538. SANDWOOD BAY ★★★
b.f. Footstepsinthesand – Diverting (Nayef). February 4. First foal. The dam, a quite useful 1m and 9f winner of 4 races, is a half-sister to one winner. The second dam, Tawny Way (by Polar Falcon), was a quite useful 9f to 12f winner of 4 races. (J A Reed). *"She's the first foal of Diverting who won a few races for Mr Reed. She goes well and she's one who's just suddenly shot up on me. I thought she was going to be early because she was showing me plenty of speed. She's coming back now and hopefully she'll be seeing a track from May onwards".*

1539. TIME DOWN UNDER ★★★
b.c. Aussie Rules – Nice Time (Tagula). May 5. Fourth foal. Half-brother to the modest 1m and 12f winner Prayer Time (by Pastoral Pursuits). The dam, a fair 2-y-o 1m winner, is a half-sister to 3 winners including the useful 2-y-o 7f winner Prose, subsequently a winner in the USA. The second dam, Nicea (by Dominion), a fairly useful Irish 2-y-o 7f winner from 2 starts, is a half-sister to 2 winners. (Sarabex). *"He's strong, not very big but a fairly late foal. A great walker and mover, he'll definitely be alright".*

1540. VELVET VOICE ★★
b.f. Azamour – Battery Power (Royal Applause). March 11. First foal. The dam, a fair 1m (at 2 yrs) and 12f winner, is a half-sister to 5 winners including the quite useful Irish 2-y-o 7f winner Captain Cullen. The second dam, Missouri (by Charnwood Forest), a quite useful 15f winner, is a half-sister to several winners. (Sarabex). *"The first foal of Battery Power who I held in high regard, she's a big, strong filly for a first foal. Very attractive, we like her a lot but she won't be running until much later on. She'll be a lovely horse in time".*

1541. UNNAMED ★★★
b.c. Sir Percy – Missouri (Charnwood Forest). March 19. Half-brother to 6 winners including the quite useful Irish 2-y-o 7f winner Captain Cullen (by Strategic Prince), the fair 1m (at 2 yrs) and 12f winner Battery Power (by Royal Applause), the fair 1m (at 2 yrs) and hurdles winner Crystal Pearl (by Beat Hollow), the modest 9f (at 2 yrs) to 12f and hurdles winner Dee Cee Elle (by Groom Dancer) and the modest 10f winner Bella Medici (by Medicean). The dam, a quite useful 15f winner, is a half-sister to several winners. The second dam, Medway (by Shernazar), a modest 12f winner at 3 yrs, is a half-sister to 8 winners including the high-class Hong Kong horse Indigenous. (Dullingham Park). *"He can't fail to be alright because he's a very nice, attractive colt. He's strong, well-grown and canters well, won't be early but he could be the nicest the dam's had. She breeds nothing but winners, including 2-y-o's".*

MARCUS TREGONING

1542. ARGENTERIE
ch.f. Archipenko – Sterling Sound (Street Cry). February 14. Third foal. The dam, a quite useful 1m winner, was listed-placed over 10f and is a sister to one winner and a half-sister to numerous winners including the US winner of 11 races Solid Silver Star (by Silver Deputy) and to the unraced dam of the US Grade 2 winner Quintons Gold Rush. The second dam, Lady In Silver (by Silver Hawk), winner of the Group 1 Prix de Diane and second in the Grade 1 Arlington Million, is a half-sister to 8 winners. (Miss K Rausing).

1543. DEAUVILLE DIVA (IRE)
b.f. Lawman – Sheila Toss (Galileo). March 18. Second foal. €95,000Y. Arqana Deauville August. M Tregoning. The dam, a fair 7f winner, is a half-sister to 4 winners including the very useful 1m and subsequent US Grade 3 9f winner Diamond Tycoon and the useful listed 11f winner Cassique Lady. The second dam, Palacoona (by Last Tycoon), a French listed 1m winner, was Group 3 placed and subsequently won in the USA and is a half-sister to 7 winners. (FTP Equine Holdings Ltd).

1544. DIVA POWER (IRE)
b.f. Power – Kotdiji (Mtoto). April 22. Ninth previous foal. €55,000Y. Goffs Sportsmans. M Tregoning. Half-sister to the useful dual listed 12f winner and Group 2 Lancashire Oaks second Polly's Mark (by Mark Of Esteem), to the quite useful 12f winner Instant Karma (by Peintre Celebre), the Irish 10f and hurdles winner Mister Carter (by One Cool Cat) and the modest 12f winner Yab Adee (by Mark Of Esteem). The dam is an unraced half-sister to 4 winners including the 1,000 Guineas winner Ameerat. The second dam, Walimu (by Top Ville), a quite useful winner of 3 races from 1m to 12f, is a half-sister to 6 winners. (FTP Equine Holdings Ltd).

1545. IMPHAL
b.h. Nathaniel – Navajo Rainbow (Rainbow Quest). March 27. Sixth foal. 75,000Y. Tattersalls October Book 2. M Tregoning. Half-brother to the quite useful 2015 1m placed 2-y-o Navajo War Chief (by Makfi), to the dual listed 1m winner Navajo Chief (by King's Best) and to a minor winner in Italy by Dr Fong. The dam, is an unraced half-sister to 8 winners including the 2-y-o Group 1 1m National Stakes winner Mus-If and the very smart 1m (at 2 yrs) and triple listed 10f winner Jammaal. The second dam, Navajo Love Song (by Dancing Brave), placed once at 4 yrs, is a half-sister to 5 minor winners in France and Italy. (Mrs H I Slade).

1546. KNIGHTHOOD
b.c. Delegator – Love Roi (Roi Danzig). April 14. Ninth foal. 55,000Y. Tattersalls October Book 2. Peter & Ross Doyle. Half-brother to 5 winners in Italy including the listed winners Mastroianni (by Selkirk), Walharer (by Cadeaux Genereux) and Verdetto Finale (by Nayef) and the listed-placed Leuci Lamps (by Hawk Wing). The dam, a listed winner of 7 races in Italy and second in the Group 2 Italian 1,000 Guineas, is a half-sister to 4 winners. The second dam, Law Tudor (by Law Society), a minor winner at 3 yrs in Italy, is a half-sister to 5 winners. (Lady Tennant).

1547. MOHSEN
b.c. Bated Breath – Harryana (Efisio). March 9. Eleventh foal. 80,000Y. Tattersalls October Book 2. Shadwell Estate Co. Half-brother to 7 winners including the fair 2015 2-y-o 6f winner Exist (by Exceed And Excel), the 2-y-o Group 2 6f Mill Reef Stakes winner Temple Meads (by Avonbridge), the useful 2-y-o 6f winner and Group 3 Firth of Clyde Stakes second Sneak Preview (by Monsieur Bond), the quite useful 5f (including at 2 yrs) and 6f winner Showstoppa (by Showcasing), the quite useful 2-y-o 5f winner O'Gorman (by Sleeping Indian) and the fair 2-y-o 5f winner Hot Secret (by Sakhee's Secret). The dam, a fair 2-y-o dual 5f winner, is out of the quite useful 3-y-o 5f winner Allyanna (by Thatching), herself a half-sister to 8 winners. (Hamdan Al Maktoum).

1548. MONAADHIL (IRE)
b.c. Dark Angel – Urban Daydream (Oasis Dream). February 16. First foal. 160,000Y. Tattersalls October Book 2. Shadwell Estate Co. The dam, a modest 9.5f placed maiden, is a half-sister to 5 winners including the very smart Group 1 12f Gran Premio del Jockey Club winner Rainbow Peak and the listed winner Celtic Heroine. The second dam, Celtic

Fling (by Lion Cavern), a fair 8.3f winner, is a half-sister to the champion 2-y-o Celtic Swing, winner of the French Derby and the Racing Post Trophy. (Hamdan Al Maktoum).

1549. NOBLE BEHEST
b.c. Sir Percy – Lady Hestia (Belong To Me). April 6. Third foal. 32,000Y. Tattersalls October Book 3. M Tregoning. Brother to the quite useful 12f and hurdles winner Perceus. The dam, a fair 12f to 2m 1f winner of 6 races, is a half-sister to 2 winners including the Group 3 Sagaro Stakes second Aajel. The second dam, Awtaan (by Arazi), a fair 14f winner, is a full or half-sister to 4 winners. (The FOPS).

1550. SILVER LINK (IRE)
b.f. Arcano – Miss Bellbird (Danehill). March 14. Half-sister to the quite useful 7f (at 2 yrs) and dual 1m winner Miss Buckshot (by Tamayuz), to the fair dual 10f winner Chatterer (by Alhaarth) and the fair 7f winner Dawn Calling (by Shamardal). The dam is an unraced half-sister to 8 winners including the Group 2 12f King Edward VII Stakes winner Amfortas and the Group 3 10.5f winner Legend Maker (dam of the 1,000 Guineas winner Virginia Water). The second dam, High Spirited (by Shirley Heights), a quite useful 14f and 2m winner, is a sister to the Premio Roma, Ribblesdale Stakes and Park Hill Stakes winner High Hawk (dam of the Breeders' Cup Turf winner In the Wings) and a half-sister to 8 winners. (Airlie Stud).

1551. STAR STREAM
b.c. Acclamation – Ellen (Machiavellian). May 17. Seventh foal. 62,000Y. Tattersalls October Book 2. M Tregoning. Half-brother to 5 winners including the French 4.5f and 5.5f 2-y-o winner and Group 3 Prix du Bois third Faslen (by Fasliyev), the fairly useful 2-y-o 6f winner Valais Girl (by Holy Roman Emperor), the quite useful dual 1m winner Mujrayaat (by Invincible Spirit) and the fair dual 1m winner Brasted (by Footstepsinthesand). The dam is an unraced half-sister to 3 winners including the Group 3 Winter Derby winner Gentleman's Deal. The second dam, Sleepytime (by Royal Academy), won the 1,000 Guineas and is a sister to the Group 1 Sussex Stakes winner Ali Royal and a half-sister to the German and Italian Group 1 winner Taipan. (R C C Villers).

1552. UNNAMED
b.f. Cape Cross – Estedaama (Marju). April 1. First foal. The dam, a quite useful 9.5f and 12f winner, is a sister to the French listed-placed winner Mutebah. The second dam, Mohafazaat (by Sadler's Wells), a modest 10f winner, is a half-sister to 5 winners including the US Grade 2 10f winner Makderah and the very useful 2-y-o 6f and 7f winner Oriental Fashion. (Hamdan Al Maktoum).

JOSEPH TUITE

1553. DARK DESTROYER (IRE) ★★★★
b.c. Helmet – Oeuvre D'Art (Marju). March 1. First foal. £32,000Y. Doncaster Premier. D Farrington. The dam won 3 races from 2 to 4 yrs in Italy, was third in the Group 2 Italian Oaks and is a half-sister to 3 winners. The second dam, Midefix (by Night Shift), a listed winner in Italy and Group 3 placed, is a half-sister to 6 winners. (Peter Gleason).
"He's absolutely gorgeous. A strong, very good-moving horse that'll want six furlongs. The damsire is Marju and he's a good sire of broodmares. We like this horse a lot.

1554. DONTFORGETTOCALL ★★★
ch.c. Foxwedge – Shaken And Stirred (Cadeaux Genereux). April 11. Seventh foal. €11,000Y. Tattersalls Ireland September. Hillen & Tuite. Half-brother to the fairly useful 5f and 6f winner and Group 3 Firth Of Clyde Stakes second Midnight Martini (by Night Shift). The dam is an unraced half-sister to 3 winners including the Group 3 Musidora Stakes third Sues Surprise. The second dam, My Micheline (by Lion Cavern), is an unraced half-sister to 4 winners including the listed winner Well Beyond (herself dam of the US Grade 3 winner Out Of Reach). (Mr A A Byrne).
"He'll be running in April, we like him and he goes about his work with a great attitude. We bought him cheaply because he had a dipped back – the same as Field Of Vision (a useful horse that won over five furlongs for us as a 2-y-o last year). This colt has a similar profile in that he was from the same sale and has a similar page with speed in there. He's a nice horse and we like the way he goes".
TRAINERS' BARGAIN BUY

1555. FALCON CLIFFS (IRE) ★★★★
b.f. Canford Cliffs – Circle (Galileo). February

18. First foal. €25,000Y. Tattersalls Ireland September. Hillen & Tuite. The dam, a quite useful Irish 3-y-o 7f winner, is a half-sister to a minor 3-y-o winner in France. The second dam, Winning Sequence (by Zafonic), a minor French 2-y-o winner, is a half-sister to 5 winners including Coquerelle (Group 1 Prix Saint-Alary). (Mr A A Byrne & Mr Mark Wellbelove). *"I think she's a very nice filly. One of the things that attracted us to her was the fact she's out of a Galileo mare. We thought we bought her well, she goes about her work in a very nice fashion and you'd like to see her on the track by late May or early June. Canford Cliffs 2-y-o's tend to come good in the second half of the season and this is a filly we have a lot of time for. She'll want six furlongs to start with".*

1556. FELSTEAD QUEEN ★★

ch.f. Bated Breath – Today's The Day (Alhaarth). February 12. Fifth foal. £18,000Y. Doncaster Premier. Hillen & Tuite. Half-sister to Renege (by Firebreak), unplaced in one start at 2 yrs in 2015 and to the fair 7f winner Rememberance Day (by Major Cadeaux). The dam, a fair 6f and 7f placed maiden, is a half-sister to 8 winners including the dam of the 2-y-o Group 1 Gran Criterium winner Hearts Of Fire. The second dam, Dayville (by Dayjur), a quite useful triple 6f winner, is a half-sister to 4 winners including the Grade 1 Yellow Ribbon Handicap winner Spanish Fern and to the unraced dams of the Grade 1 winners Lord Shanakill and Heatseeker. (Felstead Court Flyers). *"A nice filly that goes about her work in a nice fashion and she'll be running by the end of April. For what we've done with her so far we're happy. I'd say she'll start off at five furlongs but would want six to see her at her best".*

1557. HARBOUR FORCE (FR) ★★★

b.c. Harbour Watch – Dam Beautiful (Sleeping Indian). March 12. First foal. €120,000Y. Tattersalls Ireland September. Hillen & Tuite. The dam, a fairly useful listed-placed 5f winner at 2 and 3 yrs, is a half-sister to 2 winners. The second dam, Nellie Melba (by Hurricane Sky), a fair 7f and 1m winner of 3 races, is a half-sister to 4 other minor winners. (Mr A A Byrne). *"A real quality 2-y-o and the most expensive of ours. That sort of price tag comes with expectations, but we feel he's very nice and he goes about his work very nicely so we're more than happy with him at this stage. We're hoping to see him on the track in the second half of May over six furlongs and he's a big, strong, good-looking horse with a good attitude".*

1558. KADI ★★★

ch.f. Dandy Man – Roskeen (Grand Lodge). February 24. Seventh foal. €33,000Y. Tattersalls Ireland September. Sister to the useful 2015 2-y-o 5f and subsequent Turkish listed 6f winner Orvar and half-sister to the quite useful 2-y-o dual 7f winner Dark Kingdom (by Lord Shanakill) and the modest 7f winners Great Crested (by Clodovil) and Zahr Alyasmeen (by Iffraaj). The dam is an unraced half-sister to 5 winners including the dam of the Group 2 Gimcrack Stakes winner Shaweel and to the unraced dam of the dual Group 1 winner Samitar and the Group 3 Albany Stakes winner Nijoom Dubai. The second dam, Joyful (by Green Desert), a fair 7f winner at 3 yrs, is a half-sister to Golden Opinion (Group 1 1m Coronation Stakes). (Mr Abdulateef Al Zeer). *"She's only been with me a fortnight so I can't tell you much about her, but she's just a very nice filly. A good-moving 2-y-o with a good attitude, she's well-made and strong".*

1559. SHEIKSPEAR ★★★

b.c. Bahamian Bounty – Crinkle (Distant Relative). March 14. Ninth foal. £28,000Y. Doncaster Premier. Hillen & Tuite. Half-brother to the useful 2-y-o 1m winner and listed-placed Wave Aside (by Reset), to the fairly useful dual 6f winner Mr Sandicliffe, the quite useful 6f to 1m winner of 7 races Steed (both by Mujahid), the quite useful 7f and 1m winner Froissee (by Polish Precedent) and the fair 6f (at 2 yrs) and 7f winner Sardanapalus (by Byron). The dam is an unraced half-sister to 4 winners. The second dam, Crinolette (by Sadler's Wells), is an unplaced half-sister to the dual Group 3 winner Desert Style. (Spear Family). *"A bit backward at the moment, I see him wanting six/seven furlongs at the end of May/early June. He has a great attitude, I love the sire and this is a good walker and a strong colt".*

1560. SPIN TOP ★★★
b.c. Acclamation – Miss Work Of Art (Dutch Art). March 26. First foal. €42,000Y. Tattersalls Ireland September. Hillen & Tuite. The dam, a useful 2-y-o listed 5f winner of 3 races and second in the 3-y-o Group 3 6f Firth of Clyde Stakes, is a half-sister to 3 winners including the fairly useful 2-y-o 1m winner and Group 3 Musidora Stakes second Romantic Settings. The second dam, Lacework (by Pivotal), a fairly useful 7f (at 2 yrs) to 10f winner, is a sister to the Scandinavian Group 3 winner Entangle and a half-sister to 4 winners. (The Spin Top Partnership). *"He'll be my first 2-y-o runner, he's very early, very precocious and a professional. He knew his job in February really, he's got speed and I'd be disappointed if he couldn't win his maiden and progress from there. He's all about speed".*

ROGER VARIAN

1561. AJAMAN KING (IRE) ★★★
ch.c. Lope De Vega – Third Dimension (Suave Dancer). March 30. Ninth foal. €130,000Y. Goffs Orby. Roger Varian. Half-brother to 6 winners including the 14f winner and Group 2 Beresford Stakes second Orgilgo Bay (by Lawman), the quite useful winner of 4 races at around 2m Theola (by Kalanisi), the Italian winner of 6 races and listed placed My Pension (by Kendor) and the minor French winner of 6 races from 2 to 4 yrs Marie Octobre (by Daylami). The dam, a minor French 3-y-o winner, is a half-sister to 7 winners. The second dam, Fly Me (by Luthier), won the Group 3 10.5f Prix Corrida and is a half-sister to the Group 1 Grand Prix de Paris winner Galiani. (Sheikh Mohammed Obaid Al Maktoum). *"A lovely horse. He's medium-sized, well-developed, very athletic and he catches the eye. He'll be one for late summer or early autumn and he's a promising type. He looks to me like he'll be a miler in time".*

1562. AKDAAR ★★★
b.c. Dubawi – Min Banat Alreeh (Oasis Dream). March 15. First foal. The dam is an unraced sister to the Group 1 Prix Morny and Group 2 July Stakes winner and sire Arcano. The second dam, Tariysha (by Daylami), is an unraced half-sister to 2 winners and to the dam of the Group 1 Prix de l'Abbaye winner Gilt Edge Girl and the Group 2 Flying Childers Stakes winner Godfrey Street. (Hamdan Al Maktoum). *"A nice colt, in a way he's typical of Dubawi in that he's not flash at this early stage of the season but he has a nice way of going and a wonderful temperament. He'll be a horse for the second half of the season and he's a nice type. We had the dam in training here and she had injuries that kept her off the track but she was a nice filly, so it's nice to have a colt by Dubawi out of a full sister to the champion 2-y-o Arcano".*

1563. ALAMTHAL (IRE) ★★
b.f. Oasis Dream – Cuis Ghaire (Galileo). May 16. Fourth foal. The dam, a smart 2-y-o dual Group 3 6f winner and second in the 1,000 Guineas, is a sister to the Irish 2-y-o 7f winner and Coronation Stakes second Gile Na Greine, to the Group 3 9f winner Scintillula and the very useful Irish 1m winner and dual Group 3 placed Claiomh Solais. The second dam, Scribonia (by Danehill), is an unraced half-sister to 6 winners including the 2-y-o listed 6f winner and dual Group 1 placed Luminata. (Hamdan Al Maktoum). *"A lovely filly but she'll take time. There's nothing precocious about her and she'll be an autumn filly, but I like her a lot. I'd say she probably takes after her dam more than Oasis Dream".*

1564. ASAAS (USA) ★★★★
ch.c. Distorted Humor – Affectionately (Galileo). January 22. First foal. The dam is an unraced half-sister to 11 winners including the Group 1 Sprint Cup winner and good sire Invincible Spirit, the Group 3 12f winners Sadian and Acts O Grace, and the very smart sire Kodiac. The second dam, Rafha (by Kris), won the Group 1 10.5f Prix de Diane and is a half-sister to 9 winners including the Group 2 Blandford Stakes winner Chiang Mai (dam of the Group 1 winner Chinese White). *"From the family of Invincible Spirit and Kodiac, he's a precocious horse and I see him as a May/June starter. Very natural and very easy on the eye, I like him and you should definitely put him in the book".*

1565. CAPE BYRON ★★
ch.c. Shamardal – Reem Three (Mark Of Esteem). March 3. Fifth foal. Half-brother to the useful 7f (at 2 yrs) to 12f winner Naqshabban and to a hurdles winner (both

by Street Cry). The dam, a useful 8.5f to 10.5f winner of 3 races, was listed placed and is a half-sister to 3 winners including the very smart Group 2 Celebration Mile winner Afsare. The second dam, Jumaireyah (by Fairy King), a fairly useful 8.3f (at 2 yrs) and 10.3f winner, is a half-sister to numerous winners including the useful 10f to 14f winner Lost Soldier Three and the useful 10.5f and 12f winner Altaweelah. (Sheikh Mohammed Obaid Al Maktoum). *"A really nice horse but he's not precocious and we won't see him until late summer or early autumn. A lovely, strong, solid horse, he's straightforward and has a good mind".*

1566. COMMANDER ★★★
b.c. Frankel – Model Queen (Kingmambo). March 15. Eleventh foal. 670,000Y. Tattersalls October Book 1. China Horse Club. Half-brother to 7 winners including the Group 1 Haydock Sprint Cup and Group 1 Prix Maurice de Gheest winner Regal Parade (by Pivotal), the Group 3 7f Acomb Stakes winner and Group 2 7f Champagne Stakes third Entifaadha (by Dansili), the useful 1m (at 2 yrs) and 10f winner and triple Group 3 placed Hot Prospect (by Motivator) and the French listed placed 11f and 12f winner Mount Helicon. The dam, a fair 7f winner, is a half-sister to 5 winners. The second dam, Model Bride (by Blushing Groom), is an unraced half-sister to the dams of Elmaamul, Reams Of Verse, Zafonic and Zamindar. (China Horse Club). *"A lovely colt, he ticks all the boxes and is beautiful to look at – he cost a fair bit so he ought to be. He's a very good mover with a good mind, won't be early but he's a nice type of horse".*

1567. DAIRA BRIDGE (IRE) ★★★
b.c. Dream Ahead – Lady Livius (Titus Livius). March 5. Sixth foal. 110,000Y. Tattersalls October Book 1. Roger Varian. Half-brother to the smart 2-y-o Group 3 7f Sirenia Stakes winner Burnt Sugar (by Lope De Vega), to the 2-y-o Group 3 5f Molecomb Stakes and Group 3 Sirenia Stakes winner Brown Sugar (by Tamayuz), the quite useful 6f (at 2 yrs) and 7f winner Elle Woods and the minor French 4-y-o winner Widyaan (both by Lawman). The dam, a fairly useful 5f winner of 3 races from 2 to 4 yrs, is a half-sister to 5 winners including the Group 2 6f Mill Reef Stakes winner and

Group 1 placed Galeota. The second dam, Refined (by Statoblest), a fairly useful dual 5f winner, is a half-sister to 6 winners including Pipe Major (Group 3 7f Criterion Stakes). (Sheikh Mohammed Obaid Al Maktoum). *"He looks a fast horse but he's not early and is one for the second half of the season. He moves well, it's a very fast family and he'll be a six furlong horse when he gets going".*

1568. DAIRA PRINCE (IRE) ★★★
b.c. Dubawi – Chiang Mai (Sadler's Wells). May 12. Ninth foal. 110,000Y. Tattersalls October Book 1. A & E Bloodstock. Half-brother to four winners by Dalakhani including the Group 1 Pretty Polly Stakes and Group 2 Blandford Stakes winner Chinese White, the Irish listed-placed Highly Toxic and the quite useful 10f winner Raushan. The dam won the Group 3 12f Blandford Stakes and is a half-sister to 9 winners including the Group 1 10.5f Prix de Diane winner Rafha (the dam of four stakes winners including Invincible Spirit). The second dam, Eljazzi (by Artaius), a fairly useful 2-y-o 7f winner, is a half-sister to the high-class miler Pitcairn. (Sheikh Mohammed Obaid Al Maktoum). *"He was small as a yearling but he's grown and done well. A medium- sized colt now, he moves quite nicely but he was a late foal and he's not precocious, so I see him being one for the second half of the season. There's a lot to like about him".*

1569. DEALER'S CHOICE (IRE) ★★
gr.f. Exchange Rate – Micaela's Moon (Malibu Moon). March 14. Third foal. 33,000Y. Tattersalls October Book 2. Hetland Hill Farm. The dam, a minor US 3-y-o winner, is a half-sister to 8 winners including two US stakes winners and the dam of the Group 1 Prix Morny winner No Nay Never. The second dam, Comical Cat (by Exceller), a winner and Grade 3 placed in the USA, is a half-sister to 11 winners including the Group/Grade 2 winners Half A Year and Winning Pact. (J Shack). *"She had a setback early on so she's not with me yet, but she's a good-looking filly and she should make a 2-y-o"*

1570. DUBAWI PRINCE ★★★
b.c. Dubawi – Flawly (Old Vic). February 22. Eighth foal. 725,000Y. Tattersalls October Book 1. A & E Bloodstock. Half-brother to the

Group 3 10f Prix du Prince d'Orange winner and Group 1 French Derby second Best Name (by King's Best), to the German Group 3 11f winner February Sun (by Monsun) and the useful Irish listed 12f winner Heirloom (by Dansili). The dam, a French 12f winner and second in a Grade 1 9f event at Belmont Park, is a half-sister to 6 winners including the Group 3 Prix Penelope winner Ombre Legere. The second dam, Flawlessly (by Rainbow Quest), is a placed half-sister to 9 winners. (Sheikh Mohammed Obaid Al Maktoum). *"A lovely colt, very good-looking and a good mover with a good mind. He's not precocious and is one for later in the year over seven furlongs to a mile".*

1571. ELERFAAN (IRE) ★★★
b.c. Shamardal – Gorband (Woodman). April 27. Eighth foal. 100,000Y. Tattersalls December. Shadwell Estate Co. Half-brother to the 2-y-o Group 2 6f Richmond Stakes winner Harbour Watch (by Acclamation), to the South African Grade 1 10f winner Europe Point (by Rock Of Gibraltar), the quite useful triple 6f winner Ghalib (by Lope De Vega) and the quite useful UAE dual 7f winner Cross Grain (by Cape Cross). The dam, placed in the UAE, is a half-sister to 7 winners including the dual Group 2 winner Kabool and the listed 14f winner Sharaf Kabeer. The second dam, Sheroog (by Shareef Dancer), a fair 1m winner, is a sister to the dam of Dubai Millennium, closely related to the Group/Grade 1 winners Hamas, Northern Aspen and Fort Wood and a half-sister to the Grade 1 winner Timber Country. (Hamdan Al Maktoum). *"We bought him in December, he was broken late and he isn't with me yet. I liked him as a yearling though and he was my pick from that particular sale. I thought he was cheap really, being by Shamardal and having that good a page, but he's not precocious".*

1572. EMMAUS (IRE) ★★★★
b.c. Invincible Spirit – Prima Luce (Galileo). February 13. Fourth foal. €580,000Y. Goffs Orby. China Horse Club. Closely related to Fondie, unplaced in two starts at 2 yrs in 2015 and to the quite useful 1m winner Dawn Mirage (by Oasis Dream). The dam, winner of the Group 3 7f Athasi Stakes and second in the Group 3 Solonaway Stakes, is a half-sister to 5 minor winners. The second dam, Ramona (by Desert King), is an unraced half-sister to 9 winners including the Group 2 5f King's Stand Stakes winner Cassandra Go (herself dam of the triple Group 1 winner Halfway To Heaven) and the smart Group 3 6f Coventry Stakes winner and Irish 2,000 Guineas second Verglas. (China Horse Club). *"He's a cracking horse, very easy on the eye and a good mover. There's a lot to like about him. He'll make a 2-y-o by July I should think and he should be one to look out for".*

1573. EQUITATION ★★★
b.c. Equiano – Sakhee's Song (Sakhee). February 13. Fourth foal. 47,000Y. Tattersalls October Book 2. A & E Bloodstock. Half-brother to the very useful 2-y-o 6f winner and Group 2 6f Mill Reef Stakes third Taayel (by Tamayuz), to the quite useful listed-placed 2-y-o 7f winner Alfajer (by Mount Nelson) and the fair 6f winner Majestic Song (by Royal Applause). The dam, a useful Italian 5f and 6f winner, was Group 3 placed three times. The second dam, Show Me The Money (by Mujadil), won 5 races from 5f to 7f at 2 and 3 yrs including the Group 3 Cornwallis Stakes and three listed events in Ireland and was third in the Group 2 Diadem Stakes. She is a half-sister to 3 winners including the listed Doncaster Stakes winner Nero's Return. (The Equitation Partnership). *"A nice type of horse, he's a big colt so he'll take time. One for the second half of the season, he's got a fast pedigree and should be a strong, powerful horse one day".*

1574. FAIRY LIGHTS ★★
b.f. Shamardal – Suba (Seeking The Gold). March 29. Fourth foal. The dam, a quite useful 8.5f winner, is a half-sister to the high-class National Stakes (at 2 yrs), Irish 2,000 Guineas and Prix Jacques le Marois winner and sire Dubawi, to the listed 10f winner Princess Nada and the listed-placed winners Emirates Queen and Dubai Queen. The second dam, Zomaradah (by Deploy), a winner of 6 races including the Group 1 Italian Oaks, the Group 2 Royal Whip Stakes and the Group 2 Premio Lydia Tesio, is a half-sister to several winners. (Sheikh Mohammed Obaid Al Maktoum). *"She's not over-big but well-made and has a nice action. She doesn't stand out from the*

pack but there's nothing wrong with her and Shamardals can be rather plain. It's difficult to know what she's like yet".

1575. FUJAIRA BRIDGE (IRE) ★★★
b.c. Sea The Stars – Garanciere (Anabaa). March 14. Fifth living foal. 310,000Y. Tattersalls October Book 1. Roger Varian. Closely related to the very useful 2-y-o 7f winner and Group 2 7f Rockfel Stakes second I Love Me (by Cape Cross) and half-brother to the quite useful 1m (at 2 yrs) and 10f winner Ningara (by Singspiel). The dam, a minor 3-y-o winner in France, is a half-sister to 8 winners including the Group 1 Fillies' Mile winner Gloriosa. The second dam, Golden Sea (by Saint Cyrien), won 4 races at 2 and 4 yrs in France and is a half-sister to 8 winners including the French Group 2 winner Glity. (Sheikh Mohammed Obaid Al Maktoum). "A nice colt that moves well, there's a bit of quality about him and he's well-made. A horse with a good action, I like him and although he's by Sea The Stars he's out of Anabaa mare, so he might be a sharper Sea The Stars – if there is such a thing! One for later in the season".

1576. GOLDEN SLAM ★★★
ch.c. Pastoral Pursuits – Strawberry Leaf (Unfuwain). March 2. Sixth foal. £15,000Y. Doncaster Premier. Biddestone Racing. Half-brother to the quite useful 2-y-o dual 6f winner Bomber Jet (by Avonbridge). The dam, a quite useful 1m and 9f winner at 3 yrs, is a half-sister to 6 winners including the very useful 6f (at 2 yrs) and 9f winner Zabaglione. The second dam, Satin Bell (by Midyan), a useful 7f winner, is a half-sister to 4 winners including the useful listed 6f winner Star Tulip. "He was quite well-bought, he moves nicely and for what he cost I think he constitutes a bargain". **TRAINERS' BARGAIN BUY**

1577. HAMMERSTEIN ★★
b.c. Dansili – The Sound Of Music (Galileo). April 30. Half-brother to the 2015 7f placed 2-y-o My Favourite Thing (by Oasis Dream) and to the UAE dual listed placed Seema (by Dubawi). The dam is an unraced half-sister to 6 winners including the St Leger and Coronation Cup winner Scorpion, the US Grade 2 and Grade 3 winner Memories and the listed winners Danish Rhapsody and

Garuda. The second dam, Ardmelody (by Law Society), is an unraced half-sister to 8 winners. (Sheikh Mohammed Obaid Al Maktoum). "He could be a summer 2-y-o, he's a well-made horse, deep-girthed and a little feminine, but moves well".

1578. HORROOB ★★★★
b.c. Showcasing – Funny Enough (Dansili). February 1. Second foal. 85,000Y. Tattersalls October Book 2. R Varian. Half-brother to the fair 2015 2-y-o 7f winner Puzzled Look (by Sakhee's Secret). The dam is an unplaced half-sister to 5 winners including the Lingfield listed winner Oasis Dancer. The second dam, Good Enough (by Mukaddamah), a US 3-y-o winner, was third in the Group 1 Prix Saint-Alary and is a half-sister to the Group 3 Molecomb Stakes winner Classic Ruler. "I like him, he moves well and is one of our more forward types. A good, strong horse, he should be one for May or June over six furlongs".

1579. JUMIRA BRIDGE ★★★
b.c. Invincible Spirit – Zykina (Pivotal). March 24. Third foal. 85,000Y. Tattersalls October Book 1. Roger Varian. Half-brother to the fairly useful dual 7f winner Spangles (by Starspangledbanner). The dam is an unraced sister to the fairly useful 7f winner and listed-placed Safina and a half-sister to 2 winners. The second dam, Russian Rhythm (by Kingmambo), won the 1,000 Guineas, Coronation Stakes, Nassau Stakes and Lockinge Stakes and is a half-sister to 9 winners including the 2-y-o Group 2 1m Royal Lodge Stakes winner Perfectperformance. (Sheikh Mohammed Obaid Al Maktoum). "He's a nice horse that moves very well. Not an early 2-y-o, but he's an eye-catching horse and I like him".

1580. JUMIRA PRINCE (IRE) ★★★★
ch.c. Exceed And Excel – Aoife Alainn (Dr Fong). March 6. Second foal. €400,000Y. Goffs Orby. Roger Varian. Half-brother to the fair 2015 2-y-o 7f winner First To Post (by Acclamation). The dam, a winner of 5 races including the Group 1 Premio Lydia Tesio, is a half-sister to 5 winners including the Italian listed winner and Group 2 Italian 2,000 Guineas third Adorabile Fong. The second dam, Divine Secret (by Hernando),

is an unraced half-sister to 7 minor winners here and abroad. (Sheikh Mohammed Obaid Al Maktoum). *"He's one of my more forward 2-y-o's. Strong and with a good action, he looks the part and could be out in May".*

1581. MAAZEL (IRE) ★★★
b.c. Elzaam – Laylati (Green Desert). April 16. Fifth foal. 45,000Y. Tattersalls October Book 2. A & E Bloodstock. Half-brother to a winner in Denmark by Whipper. The dam, placed third over 5f and 6f at 2 yrs, is a half-sister to one winner. The second dam, Saeedah (by Bustino), was placed twice at 2 yrs and is a sister to the Group 3 Fred Darling Stakes winner Bulaxie (herself dam of the Group 2 winner Claxon) and a half-sister to 5 winners including the French Group 3 winner Dust Dancer (dam of the US Grade 2 winner Spotlight). (The Maazel Partnership). *"He'd be one of our more forward 2-y-o's, he skips along nicely and I quite like him. He could be a May runner and we trained the dam for Sheikh Ahmed. There's a bit of precocity in the pedigree and although she's been a bit disappointing I haven't given up on the mare just yet".*

1582. MARGHERITA ★★★
b.f. Mayson – Phillipina (Medicean). February 11. Third foal. 50,000foal. Tattersalls December. Mick Flanagan. The dam, a useful 10f winner, was listed-placed over 11f and is a half-sister to one winner. The second dam, Discerning (by Darshaan), a quite useful 11f winner, is a half-sister to 6 winners on the flat including the Group 2 Summer Mile winner Cesare and the Group 3 12f Prix la Force winner and French Derby second Nowhere To Exit and to the Grade 2 winning hurdler Trenchant. (Cheveley Park Stud). *"This filly moves well, there's a bit of strength to her and she's a nice type. She could be a summer 2-y-o starting at six furlongs and she's a good advert for the sire".*

1583. MATERIALIST ★★
b.c. Dansili – Mundana (King's Best). March 13. Second foal. The dam was a fairly useful 7f and 1m winner of 3 races. The second dam, Mail Express (by Cape Cross), a fair 6f winner at 3 yrs, is a half-sister to 5 winners including the Group 1 1m Premio Vittorio di Capua, Group 2 Challenge Stakes and Group 2 Italian 2,000 Guineas winner Le Vie Dei Colori. (Sheikh Mohammed Obaid Al Maktoum). *"A nice type of colt, he's well-balanced and moves well. He's not precocious but he has a good mind and is one for the second half of the season. More of a 3-y-o type really".*

1584. MESBAAR ★★★
b.c. Dalakhani – Wahylah (Shamardal). February 11. First foal. 105,000Y. Tattersalls October Book 2. Roger Varian. The dam, a quite useful 2-y-o 6f winner, is a half-sister to 2 winners. The second dam, Neshla (by Singspiel), a poor 11f placed maiden, is a half-sister to 9 winners including the Group 3 7.3f Fred Darling Stakes winner and Group 2 10f Nassau Stakes third Sueboog (herself dam of the Group 1 winner Best Of The Bests) and the listed winners Sell Out and Marika. (Sheikh Ahmed Al Maktoum). *"He's a nice colt, there's nothing wrong with him, he moves well and he's a solid horse for a Dalakhani. I quite like him, he's not going to be early but he's a nice type of horse".*

1585. MOUNTAIN ANGEL (IRE) ★★★
b.c. Dark Angel – Fanciful Dancer (Groom Dancer). April 22. Fourth foal. 100,000Y. Tattersalls October Book 2. Andrew Sime. Brother to the useful 6f (at 2 yrs) and listed 1m winner Fanciful Angel and half-brother to the minor French 2-y-o winner Naloudia (by Piccolo). The dam is an unraced half-sister to 3 winners including the dam of the dual listed winners Distinctly Dancer and Evening Time. The second dam, Fanciful (by Gay Mecene), a minor French 3-y-o winner, is a half-sister to 8 winners including the Group 2 6f Lowther Stakes winner and Group 1 second and smart broodmare Kingscote. (Z A Galadari). *"He's a nice colt that moves well. Not an early 2-y-o, he's going to be a July type horse and I quite like him. As a 2-y-o seven furlongs would probably be his trip".*

1586. NEWCOMER ★★★
ch.f. New Approach – Khor Sheed (Dubawi). January 10. Second foal. The dam, a Group 3 1m Premio Sergio Cumani, listed 6f (at 2 yrs) and listed 7f winner, is a half-sister to 4 winners including the Group 1 Prix d'Ispahan winner Prince Kirk. The second dam, Princess

Manila (by Manila), is an unplaced half-sister to 3 winners including the Group 1 Italian Derby winner Hailsham. (Sheikh Mohammed Obaid Al Maktoum). *"I like this filly. Not over-big, she looks to me to be a precocious New Approach and I see her running in June. She looks like a 2-y-o type and she moves well".*

1587. NOTHING BUT DREAMS ★★★
b.f. Frankel – Danedream (Lomitas). January 27. First foal. The dam, a top-class winner of 8 races from 6f (at 2 yrs) to 12f including the Group 1 King George VI and the Prix de l'Arc de Triomphe, is a half-sister to one winner. The second dam, Danedrop (by Danehill), is an unraced half-sister to 7 minor winners. (Teruya Yoshida). *"It's very nice for us to have a filly by Frankel and whose dam won the Arc. She's on the small side, but I believe the dam was the same and she was a cheap yearling so maybe she was an ugly duckling that turned into a swan. Physically this filly is improving all the time but she needs more time still. It's too early to judge her really and she's probably one for the back-end of the season".*

1588. ODEN ★★★
ch.c. Lope De Vega – Dashing (Sadler's Wells). March 26. Fifth foal. Half-brother to the fair 7f winner Azenzar (by Danehill Dancer). The dam is an unraced half-sister to 6 winners including the top-class multiple Group 1 winner Alexander Goldrun and the Group 3 Prix de la Jonchere winner and Group 1 placed Medicis. The second dam, Renashaan (by Darshaan), a listed winner in France, was third in the Group 3 9f Prix Vanteaux and is a half-sister to 4 minor winners. (Saleh Al Homaizi & Imad Al Sagar). *"A nice type, he's immature, still growing and a bit playful. He has a good action and is possibly the nicest the mare has thrown – I've trained a few of them and he could be the nicest of them in time".*

1589. PICHOLA DANCE (IRE) ★★★★
ch.f. Distorted Humor – Liffey Dancer (Sadler's Wells). February 16. Fourth foal. The dam is an unraced sister to 4 winners including the Group 1 7f Moyglare Stud Stakes winner Sequoyah (herself dam of the multiple Group 1 winner Henrythenavigator) and the 2-y-o Group 1 Fillies' Mile winner Listen and a half-sister to the listed 5.6f winner and Group 3 placed Oyster Catcher (by Bluebird). The second dam, Brigid (by Irish River), a minor French 1m winner, is a sister to the French listed 7f winner Or Vision (dam of the Group/Grade 1 winners Dolphin Street, Insight and Saffron Walden). (Merry Fox Stud Ltd). *"A nice filly, I've trained a few out of the dam and I think this is the nicest she's produced. She looks like being a summer 2-y-o and this is the same cross (Distorted Humor out of a Sadler's Wells mare) as the good filly we had, Cursory Glance. A small to medium-sized filly and well-made".*

1590. PLAYING TRIX ★★★★
b.f. War Front – Time Control (Sadler's Wells). February 27. Fourth foal. Half-sister to the 2-y-o Group 1 7f Moyglare Stud Stakes and Group 3 6f Albany Stakes winner Cursory Glance (by Distorted Humor). The dam, a quite useful 10f winner, is a sister to the Group 2 Prix de Malleret and listed Cheshire Oaks winner Time On. The second dam, Time Away (by Darshaan), won the Group 3 10.4f Musidora Stakes, was third in the Group 1 Prix de Diane and the Group 1 Nassau Stakes and is a half-sister to 6 winners including the 10f winner and Prix de Diane second Time Ahead. (Merry Fox Stud Ltd). *"She's a War Front half-sister to Cursory Glance, which makes her quite exciting for us. A real good model, she takes the eye and has the action to go with her looks. Maybe not quite as precocious as Cursory Glance was and I don't think she'll be running pre-Ascot, but I think she's quite nice and we'd be pretty hopeful for her".*

1591. PLEAD ★★
ch.f. Dutch Art – Entreat (Pivotal). April 13. Third foal. The dam, a fair 10f winner, is a half-sister to 4 winners including the Group 3 Supreme Stakes and Group 3 Criterion Stakes winner Producer (by Dutch Art). The second dam, River Saint (by Irish River), is a placed half-sister to 5 winners including the multiple US Grade 1 winner Serena's Song (herself the dam of four Group winners including Group 1 Coronation Stakes winner Sophisticat). (Cheveley Park Stud). *"She's not been with me long so can't tell you much about her, but she's a good-looking filly with a good action".*

1592. PROSPER ★★★
gr.f. Exceed And Excel – Ela Athena (Ezzoud). March 26. Tenth foal. €240,000Y. Arqana Deauville August. China Horse Club. Half-sister to 3 winners including the useful listed winner of 5 races from 10f to 2m Pallasator (by Motivator) and the fairly useful 2-y-o 1m winner and listed placed Elas Diamond (by Danehill Dancer). The dam, a winner of 3 races including the Group 3 Lancashire Oaks, was placed in seven Group/Grade 1 events and is a half-sister to 5 winners. The second dam, Crodelle (by Formidable), a French 3-y-o 9.5f winner, is a half-sister to 7 winners. (China Horse Club). *"A nice filly with a bit of scope for an Exceed And Excel, she's very balanced, has a good action and is likeable".*

1593. ROSENCRANZ ★★★
b.c. Dubawi – Rose Diamond (Daylami). April 7. Second foal. Half-brother to the quite useful dual 10f winner Real Smart (by Smart Strike). The dam, a fairly useful 2-y-o 6f winner, was second in the Group 3 7f Prestige Stakes. The second dam, Tante Rose (by Barathea), a winner of 5 races including the Group 1 Haydock Park Sprint Cup, the Group 4 7f Fred Darling Stakes and Group 3 6f Summer Stakes, is a half-sister to several winners including the Sweet Solera Stakes winner Bay Tree. (Sheikh Mohammed Obaid Al Maktoum). *"A lovely, good-looking horse with a good action and a good temperament. He won't be precocious but he could be a nice horse in time and I like him. One for late summer/early autumn, Dubawi's aren't usually as precocious as you might think".*

1594. SHARJA BRIDGE ★★★
br.c. Oasis Dream – Quetena (Acatenango). March 26. Seventh foal. 500,000Y. Tattersalls October Book 1. Roger Varian. Brother to the Group 1 10f Premio Presidente della Repubblica winner Querari and half-brother to 2 winners including the German Group 3 winner Quasillo. The dam, a German listed-placed winner, is a half-sister to 7 winners including the Group 3 Prix de Psyche winner Quilanga. The second dam, Quebrada (by Devil's Bag), won 7 races including the Group 2 German 1,000 Guineas and is a half-sister to 7 winners. (Sheikh Mohammed Obaid Al Maktoum). *"He's a lovely horse, a little bit feminine but well-proportioned and a real athlete. He's not a precocious horse, so I'd say he takes after the dam's side. He looks the type for ten furlongs next year, with a run or two this autumn. He's a nice horse and I like him".*

1595. SUBHAAN ★★★
ch.c. Dutch Art – Mamma Morton (Elnadim). March 22. Sixth foal. £205,000Y. Doncaster Premier. Shadwell Estate Co. Half-brother to 5 winners including the Irish 2015 2-y-o 6f winner on his only start Aca Awesome (by Makfi), the 2-y-o listed 6f winner and Group 2 Mill Reef Stakes and Group 2 Richmond Stakes second Master Of War (by Compton Place), the quite useful dual 7f winner Mr McLaren (by Royal Applause) and the quite useful dual 6f (including at 2 yrs) Muaamara (by Bahamian Bounty). The dam, a fair 10f and 11f placed maiden, is a half-sister to 10 winners. The second dam, Gharam (by Green Dancer), a very useful 2-y-o 6f winner, was third in the French 1,000 Guineas and is a half-sister to the US Grade 1 9f winner Talinum. (Hamdan Al Maktoum). *"He's a lovely mover, but he's had a little setback which means he won't be out early. A very athletic horse, he's a nice type".*

1596. TANBEEH ★★★
b.c. Approve – White Daffodil (Footstepsinthesand). March 26. Third foal. £72,000Y. Doncaster Premier. Shadwell Estate Co. Half-brother to the smart 2015 2-y-o 5f and listed 6f winner and triple Group 2 placed Log Out Island (by Dark Angel). The dam, a modest 5f (at 2 yrs) and 6f winner, is a half-sister to 5 winners including the dual listed 6f winner (including at 2 yrs) Lady Links (herself dam of the dual listed winner Selinka). The second dam, Sparky's Song (by Electric), a moderate 10.2f and 12f winner, is a half-sister to the very smart Group 1 6.5f winner Bold Edge and to the listed winner and Group 3 5f Temple Stakes second Brave Edge. (Hamdan Al Maktoum). *"He's a 2-y-o type, not as early as I thought he'd be, but he's one for June/July. He moves OK, he's speedily bred and hopefully he's got a bit of pace. We'll see how we go with him".*

1597. TRICK OF THE LIGHT (IRE) ★★★
ch.c. Dragon Pulse – Galistic (Galileo). March 25. Fifth foal. 48,000Y. Tattersalls October Book 2. A & E Bloodstock. Half-brother to the German listed 7f winner Guinnevre (by Duke Of Marmalade), to the quite useful 7f winner Aldayha (by Acclamation) and the fair 2-y-o 7f and 1m winner Hala Hala (by Invincible Spirit). The dam, a useful 10f, 12f and listed 14f winner in Ireland at 3 and 4 yrs, is a half-sister to one winner. The second dam, Mockery (by Nashwan), won 2 minor races at 3 yrs in France and is a half-sister to 3 other minor winners. (John Collins, Chris Fahy, Mrs H Varian). *"Quite a good-looking horse that moves nicely, I think he's got a future and he looks capable. Should make a 2-y-o by July over seven furlongs".*

1598. UAE KING (IRE) ★★★
b.c. Oasis Dream – Caphene (Sakhee). February 8. First foal. 750,000Y. Tattersalls October Book 1. Roger Varian. The dam is an unplaced half-sister to 6 winners including the useful 7f (at 2 yrs) and listed Lingfield Oaks Trial and subsequent US Grade 3 winner and Group 1 Nassau Stakes second Cassydora and the listed 10f winner Classic Remark. The second dam, Claxon (by Caerleon), a very useful 1m (at 2 yrs) and Group 2 10f Premio Lydia Tesio winner, is a half-sister to 3 winners including the dual Group 2 placed Bulwark. (Sheikh Mohammed Obaid Al Maktoum). *"A nice, well-made colt with a good action. He's very athletic and although he's not precocious he should be out in mid-summer".*

1599. UAE QUEEN ★★★
b.f. Oasis Dream – Pongee (Barathea). April 16. Seventh foal. 450,000Y. Tattersalls October Book 1. Roger Varian. Sister to the 2015 2-y-o 7f winner (on her only start) Materialistic and half-sister to 4 winners including the listed 10f winner Pinzolo (by Monsun), the quite useful listed-placed 2-y-o 1m winner Poplin (by Medicean) and the fair 10f winner Paisley (by Pivotal). The dam, a Group 2 12f Lancashire Oaks winner, is closely related to the listed 12f and listed 14f winner Lion Sands and to the listed-placed 11f winner Pukka and a half-sister to 5 winners. The second dam, Puce (by Darshaan), a listed 12f winner, is a half-sister to 10 winners including the dam of the dual Oaks winner Alexandrova and the Cheveley Park Stakes winner Magical Romance. (Sheikh Mohammed Obaid Al Maktoum). *"A very attractive filly, very athletic and with a good action. She's a likeable type".*

1600. VICTORY ANGEL (IRE) ★★★
b.c. Acclamation – Golden Shadow (Selkirk). March 9. Eighth foal. 140,000Y. Tattersalls October Book 2. Andrew Sime. Half-brother to 5 winners including the fairly useful 2-y-o 5f and 1m winner and listed-placed Lord ofthe Shadows (by Kyllachy), the French 2-y-o 6f winner You're Golden (by Lawman), the modest dual 1m winner Snappy Guest (by Kodiac) and the moderate 2m 1f winner Tigerino (by Tiger Hill). The dam, a fair 2-y-o dual 1m placed maiden, is a half-sister to 7 winners including the Group 1 1m Coronation Stakes winner Balisada. The second dam, Balnaha (by Lomond), a modest 1m winner, is a sister to the Child Stakes winner Inchmurrin (dam of the very smart and tough colt Inchinor) and a half-sister to the Mill Reef Stakes winner Welney. (Z A Galadari). *"I quite like him, he's one of the more forward 2-y-o's, he moves well and is very straightforward. He looks like he's ready to go on with now, so he could be a May runner and he's doing alright".*

1601. WATCHMAN ★★★★★
b.c. Frankel – Zomaradah (Deploy). March 10. Half-brother to 6 winners including the high-class National Stakes (at 2 yrs), Irish 2,000 Guineas and Prix Jacques le Marois winner and sire Dubawi (by Dubai Millennium), the Group 2 12f Lancashire Oaks winner Emirates Queen (by Street Cry), the listed 10f winner Princess Nada (by Barathea) and the fairly useful listed-placed 1m winner Dubai Queen (by Kingmambo). The dam won the Group 1 Italian Oaks, the Group 2 Royal Whip Stakes and the Group 2 Premio Lydia Tesio and is a half-sister to several winners. The second dam, Jawaher (by Dancing Brave), was placed over 1m and 9f and is a half-sister to the Derby winner High-Rise. (Sheikh Mohammed Obaid Al Maktoum). *"He's a lovely horse and he does look a bit like Frankel to me. He has a very impressive action, a good mind and he's just a nice horse. His starting point on the track would be in July at the earliest".*

1602. YABRAVE ★★★
b.c. Bahamian Bounty – Dare To Dream (Exceed And Excel). February 7. First foal. 130,000Y. Tattersalls October Book 2. Shadwell Estate Co. The dam, a fair 2-y-o 7f winner, is a half-sister to 2 minor winners. The second dam, Secret History (by Bahri), won 4 races including the Group 3 Musidora Stakes and is a half-sister to 6 winners. (Sheikh Ahmed Al Maktoum). *"He moves well and he's a forward type of horse that should be running in May or June. A straightforward, likeable horse with a good mind".*

1603. UNNAMED ★★★
b.br.c. Lonhro – Alzerra (Pivotal). March 17. Fifth foal. Half-brother to the 2015 2-y-o 7f winner, on his only start, Yattwee (by Hard Spun) and to the listed 7f (at 2 yrs) and listed 1m winner and Group 2 May Hill Stakes second Majeyda (by Street Cry). The dam won 3 races over 5f and 6f at 2 yrs including the Group 3 Cornwallis Stakes and is a full or half-sister to 4 winners. The second dam, Belle Argentine (by Fijar Tango), a listed winner in France and third in the French 1,000 Guineas, is a half-sister to one winner. (Sheikh Ahmed Al Maktoum). *"He's got a good action, he isn't precocious but he should make a 2-y-o later in the summer. He moves perfectly well and there's speed in the pedigree so hopefully he'll show us something".*

1604. UNNAMED ★★★
b.c. Zoffany – Dashing Beauty (Daggers Drawn). April 24. Fourth foal. 200,000Y. Tattersalls October Book 1. A & E Bloodstock. Half-brother to the quite useful 2015 2-y-o 5f and 6f winner Holy Grail (by Canford Cliffs) and the modest 4-y-o 14f winner Get Out Of Jail (by Authorized). The dam, a modest 4-y-o 6f winner, is a half-sister to 7 winners including the Irish listed winners Dashing Colours and Dash Of Red and the dam of the 2-y-o Group 2 winner Captain Marvelous. The second dam, Near The End (by Shirley Heights), is an unraced half-sister to 2 winners. (Mr M Almutairi). *"He's a likeable horse and could be one of our more forward types. One for May/June, he's a strong colt, moves well and has a good mind. Going the right way".*

1605. UNNAMED ★★★
b.c. Mastercraftsman – Endure (Green Desert). March 16. Seventh foal. 205,000Y. Tattersalls October Book 1. A & E Bloodstock. Half-brother to 5 winners including the very useful 2-y-o listed 7f winner Bunker (by Hurricane Run), the fairly useful dual 5f winner Imtiyaaz (by Starspangledbanner), the quite useful 2-y-o 6f winner Atacama Crossing and the fair 2-y-o 5f and 6f winner of 4 races at 2 and 3 yrs Beach Candy (both by Footstepsinthesand). The dam ran twice unplaced and is a half-sister to 7 winners including the Canadian Grade 3 winner Alexis and the Irish listed winners Miss Helga and Freshwater Pearl. The second dam, Sister Golden Hair (by Glint Of Gold), a listed-placed winner at 2 yrs in Germany, is a half-sister to 2 winners. (Mr M Almutairi). *"I quite like him, he moves nicely and looks a racehorse. One for July/August over seven furlongs and he's a nice type".*

1606. UNNAMED ★★
b.c. Dutch Art – Jamboretta (Danehill). February 20. Fourth foal. 150,000Y. Tattersalls October Book 2. Charlie Gordon-Watson / Paul Smith. Half-brother to the quite useful 7f winner Messila Star (by Pivotal) and to the quite useful 2-y-o 7f winner Music And Dance (by Galileo). The dam, a quite useful 9f winner, is a half-sister to the listed winner and Group 3 second Excusez Moi. The second dam, Jiving (by Generous), a fair 6f placed 2-y-o, is a half-sister to the outstanding broodmare Hasili (dam of the Group 1 winners Banks Hill, Cacique, Champs Elysees, Heat Haze and Intercontinental and the Group 2 winner and leading sire Dansili) and to the dams of the Grade/Group 1 winners Leroidesanimaux and Promising Lead. (Mr P D Smith). *"A big, tall horse with a good action, he's not going to be early but he could be a nice horse in time".*

1607. UNNAMED ★★★
b.c. Shamardal – Littlefeather (Indian Ridge). May 8. Tenth foal. 95,000Y. Tattersalls October Book 2. Magus Equine. Half-brother to 7 winners including the useful 2-y-o 6.5f winner and Group 3 third Expedition (by Oasis Dream), the listed-placed 6f winner of 4 races Bee Eater (by Green Desert), the quite useful

dual 9f winner Rare Tern (by Pivotal) and the fair 2-y-o 5f winner Rock Dove (by Danehill). The dam, a 5f (at 2 yrs) and 6f winner of 4 races and third in the Group 1 7f Moyglare Stakes, is a half-sister to the multiple Group 1 winner Marling and the multiple Group 1 placed Caerwent. The second dam, Marwell (by Habitat), a champion sprinter, won four Group 1 races. (Mr W Y C Leung). *"He's an athletic horse, not over-big by the sire's standards, but he looks a runner and has a good action. It's quite a fast family, so hopefully this horse will have a bit of speed"*.

1608. UNNAMED ★★★ ♠
gr.f. Dark Angel – Mahaazen (Cape Cross). March 28. First foal. £52,000Y. Doncaster Premier. A&E Bloodstock. The dam, a fair Irish 2-y-o 9f winner, is a half-sister to 3 minor winners. The second dam, Innclassic (by Stravinsky), a modest 6f winner, is a half-sister to 5 winners including the US dual Grade 1 winner Daytona. *"One of our more forward fillies, she moves nicely and she'll be out around May/June time. She's doing well"*.

1609. UNNAMED ★★
b.c. Holy Roman Emperor – Miss Rochester (Montjeu). April 28. Fifth foal. 120,000Y. Tattersalls October Book 2. Magus Equine. Half-brother to the moderate 2015 6f placed 2-y-o Texas Radio (by Kyllachy), to the fair 2-y-o 5f winner Exceedingly (by Exceed And Excel) and to a minor winner abroad by Azamour. The dam, a fair 10f winner, is a half-sister to 3 winners. The second dam, Pilgrim's Way (by Gone West), a quite useful 7f and 1m winner at 3 yrs, is a sister to the smart 6f and 1m winner Mugharreb and a half-sister to 4 winners. (Mr W Y C Leung). *"He's OK, he's got a good action, moves nicely but I don't think he's too precocious. He should be a nice horse in time"*.

1610. UNNAMED ★★★
b.c. Invincible Spirit – Rock Salt (Selkirk). May 28. Seventh foal. Half-brother to the Group 1 7f Moyglare Stud Stakes winner Termagant (by Powerscourt), to the fairly useful 1m (at 2 yrs) to 10f winner of 7 races and listed-placed Splinter Cell (by Johannesburg), the quite useful 7f and 1m winner of 4 races Kohlaan (by Elusive City), the fair 12f winner Swan Lakes (by Dalakhani) and the fair 2-y-o 6f winner Planet Waves (by Red Ransom). The dam, placed twice at 3 yrs in France, is a sister to the Group 2 10f Prix Eugene Adam and Group 3 9f Prix de Guiche winner Kirkwall and a half-sister to 4 winners. The second dam, Kamkova (by Northern Dancer), was a placed half-sister to the top-class US middle-distance colt Vanlandingham. (N Bizakov). *"An athletic, quite attractive horse, he's a bit playful but moves well and could be a summer 2-y-o"*.

1611. UNNAMED ★★
b.f. Azamour – Serres (Daylami). February 1. Fifth foal. Sister to the Group 3 10.5f Musidora Stakes winner Liber Nauticus (by Azamour) and half-sister to the useful 2015 2-y-o 7f winner and Group 2 Rockfel Stakes second Thetis, the fair 10f winner Indelible Ink (both by Invincible Spirit) and to a minor winner in Australia by Verglas. The dam is an unraced half-sister to 6 winners including the Breeders' Cup Turf, King George VI and St Leger winner Conduit and the Group 2 Great Voltigeur Stakes winner Hard Top. The second dam, Well Head (by Sadler's Wells), is an unraced half-sister to 6 winners including the dual Group 1 winner Spectrum and the dam of the champion filly Petrushka. *"This filly will take time, but I quite like her. She's got a bit of quality about her and a nice action, but there's nothing precocious about her so we'll wait and see how we go"*.

1612. UNNAMED ★★★
b.f. Invincible Spirit – Totally Devoted (Seeking The Gold). February 10. Third foal. Half-sister to the fair 2-y-o 7f winner Todegica (by Giant's Causeway). The dam, a useful listed-placed 1m winner, is a half-sister to 3 winners including the Group 1 St Leger and Group 2 Great Voltigeur Stakes winner Rule Of Law and the US winner and Grade 3 placed Dame Marie. The second dam, Crystal Crossing (by Royal Academy), a listed 6f winner, is a sister to the 2-y-o Group 3 7f Prestige Stakes winner and US Grade 2 placed Circle Of Gold and a half-sister to several winners. (N Bizakov). *"A nice filly that takes the eye, she's very attractive and has a good action. I like her"*.

ED VAUGHAN

1613. DANCESPORT ★★★
b.c. Kyllachy – Violet Ballerina (Namid). February 11. Fifth foal. 65,000Y. Tattersalls October Book 2. Paul Moroney. Half-brother to the fair 7f winner of 4 races Fab Lolly (by Rock Of Gibraltar), to the fair 7f and 8.5f winner Wolfie (by Rock Of Gibraltar) and two minor winners in Germany by Cape Cross and Cadeaux Genereux. The dam, a fair 7f (at 2 yrs) and 6f winner, is a half-sister to 3 winners including the very useful 2-y-o Group 2 6f Richmond Stakes winner Carizzo Creek. The second dam, Violet Spring (by Exactly Sharp), a 5-y-o 2m winner in Ireland, is a half-sister to 3 other minor winners. (Ballymore Down Under Syndicate). *"A lovely horse and there's plenty of speed in the family. I'd imagine he'd be a slow-maturing sprinter purely because he's a huge horse with a great hind end on him. He's very high behind, so he'll need time and I won't be pushing him".*

1614. GEORGE RAVENSCAR ★★★★
b.c. Pastoral Pursuits – Cosmic Destiny (Soviet Star). April 21. Fourth foal. Brother to the fairly useful 5f and 6f winner of 6 races at 2 and 3 yrs Primrose Valley and to the fair triple 6f winner Costa Filey. The dam, a modest but tough winner of 6 races over 5f and from 3 to 6yrs, is a half-sister to 3 winners. The second dam, Cruelle (by Irish River), was placed at up to 7.5f in France at 2 and 3 yrs and is a half-sister to 5 winners. (Alan Pickering). *"He looks very sharp and I like all the family, they can win at two and the only thing that stopped me going forward with him earlier is his foaling date. But he's very strong, has a lot of natural muscle and he's ready to start work. He won't take too long, he looks a natural and should be running at the end of April".*

1615. LITTLEBECK LADY ★★
b.f. Sir Percy – Mrs Snaffles (Indian Danehill). February 1. Sixth foal. 16,000Y. Tattersalls October Book 3. Ed Vaughan. Half-sister to the fair 2015 7.5f and 1m placed 2-y-o Catastrophe (by Intikhab) and to the fair 1m winner of 4 races at 2 and 3 yrs Karma Chameleon (by Haafhd). The dam, a fairly useful 2-y-o 6f winner, is a half-sister to 4 minor winners. The second dam, Lake Nyasa (by Lake Coniston), placed fourth once over 7f, is a half-sister to 6 winners including the Group 1 Ascot Gold Cup winner Mr Dinos. (Alan Pickering). *"She's grown quite a lot so I had to back-off her and now we're ready to step her up again. She probably needs fast ground or the polytrack".*

1616. TONAHUTU (IRE) ★★★★
b.f. Sir Prancealot – Really Polish (Polish Numbers). January 19. Ninth foal. £16,000Y. Doncaster Premier. Not sold. Half-sister to the quite useful Irish 2-y-o 7f and 1m winner Really Ransom (by Red Ransom), to the fair 2-y-o 7f winner Regal Kiss (by King's Best) and four minor winners in the USA, France, Italy and Greece by A P Indy, Highest Honor, Motivator and Maria's Mon. The dam won 9 races in the USA including the Grade 3 Dogwood Stakes and was third in the Grade 1 Kentucky Oaks. She is a half-sister to 3 winners including the US stakes winner Ragtime Hope (dam of the Grade 1 Breeders' Cup Sprint winner Secret Circle). The second dam, Good 'N Smart (by Smarten), a minor US winner, is a half-sister to 4 winners. (Ballymore Down Under Syndicate). *"A very nice filly, she's had a touch of sore shins so we've been taking our time with her and she's grown a bit, but I do like her a lot. I guess we'll start her at six furlongs, it looks like she'll go on pretty fast ground and she's a very forward-going filly. Mentally she's very switched on".* **TRAINERS' BARGAIN BUY**

1617. WHOSYOURHOUSEMATE ★★
ch.c. Bahamian Bounty – Starlit Sky (Galileo). April 1. Sixth living foal. 32,000Y. Tattersalls October Book 3. Paul Moroney. Half-brother to the quite useful 10f winner Sky Khan (by Cape Cross), to the fair 10f winner of 4 races Starlit Cantata (by Oratorio) and the modest 5f winner Green Warrior (by Green Desert). The dam is an unraced half-sister to 8 winners including the Group 2 13.5f Prix de Pomone winner Interlude and Success Story (the dam of three stakes winners). The second dam, Starlet (by Teenoso), won 7 races from 7f (at 2 yrs) to 12f including a Group 2 event in Germany and is a half-sister to the Grade 1 Arlington Handicap winner Unknown Quantity. (Ballymore Down Under Syndicate). *"A nice type of horse, but he's grown quite a lot and looks like he won't be ready until*

later in the season. He seems to take after the dam's side rather than Bahamian Bounty and he'll be a middle-distance horse next year".

1618. UNNAMED ★★
b.c. Jeremy – Ballygologue (Montjeu). April 25. First foal. €40,000Y. Tattersalls Ireland September. Paul Moroney. The dam, a fair 12f winner, is a half-sister to 2 minor winners. The second dam, Admiring (by Woodman), placed fourth once over 9f, is a half-sister to 4 winners. (Ballymore Down Under Syndicate). *"He's a great walker and at the sales he looked a very good specimen, so he wasn't cheap and quite a number of trainers and agents commented on what a nice type of yearling he was. He'll need time and seven furlongs to start with, covers the ground well and has a bit of a knee action, so he'll probably be better with a bit of juice in the ground".*

1619. UNNAMED ★★
b.c. Clodovil – Nordkappe (High Chaparral). February 8. Second foal. 26,000Y. Tattersalls October Book 2. Paul Moroney. Half-brother to the 2015 French 7f placed 2-y-o Narnia Dawn (by Roderic O'Connor). The dam is an unplaced half-sister to 3 winners – two of them listed-placed in Germany. The second dam, North Queen (by Desert King), a German Group 3 winner and third in the Group 1 German Oaks, is a half-sister to 8 winners. (MPH Racing). *"A nice colt with plenty of High Chaparral in him, he's a horse that's grown a lot. He might be quick enough for six, but I'd say he's more of a seven furlongs type to start off with. He's a bit unfurnished but has a nice way of going, he's done a couple of nice-paced canters and he goes quite well".*

1620. UNNAMED ★★★
b.c. Tin Horse – Plebeya (Dubawi). March 6. First foal. 48,000Y. Tattersalls October Book 2. Paul Moroney. The dam won twice at 3 yrs in France and is a half-sister to two other minor French winners. The second dam, Pygmalion (by Dr Devious), won 2 minor races at 3 yrs in France and is a half-sister to 4 winners. (Mike Hawkes & Anzac). *"A lovely horse, I fell in love with him at the sale. The sire won the French Guineas but this colt was bought purely because he looks like a clone of Dubawi. I imagine he'll be quick enough to start around* June time over six furlongs, but he'll be better suited by seven. He's really good-looking with good conformation and he's a good walker".

1621. UNNAMED ★★★
b.c. Arcano – Spa (Sadler's Wells). May 5. Half-brother to 5 winners including the smart 1m (at 2 yrs) and listed 10f winner and Group 2 Hardwicke Stakes third Persian Majesty, the quite useful Irish 7f and 9f winner Fitzroy (both by Grand Lodge) and the fairly useful 7f and 1m winner of 4 races Spa's Dancer (by Danehill Dancer). The dam is an unraced half-sister to the Group 2 Hardwicke Stakes winner Sandmason, the smart triple 12f winner Sebastian and the listed 10f winner Sardegna. The second dam, Sandy Island (by Mill Reef), won the Group 3 12f Lancashire Oaks and the 10f Pretty Polly Stakes and is closely related to Slip Anchor. *"A nice colt with plenty of Sadler's Wells in him. He's a late foal but I'd say we'll find ourselves going forward with him because he's a nice, active type of colt. I might give him a run over six furlongs to get him ready for seven. He looks pretty mature and he's a nice type of horse that looks like he'll go on pretty quick ground".*

ED WALKER

1622. ART'S DESIRE ★★
ch.f. Dutch Art – Zenella (Kyllachy). March 15. Second foal. 40,000Y. Tattersalls October Book 2. Sackville/Donald. Half-sister to the fair 2015 2-y-o 7f winner Dark Crescent (by Elnadim). The dam, a fairly useful 2-y-o listed 1m winner, is a half-sister to 2 minor winners. The second dam, West One (by Gone West), ran twice unplaced and is closely related to the US stakes-placed winner Go Baby Go and a half-sister to a winner in Italy. (Laurence Bellman & Billy Mills). *"A backward filly, she'll be one for August and September and next year. A nice filly, well-made and athletic, but still quite weak".*

1623. BLUE MEDICI ★★★
b.c. Medicean – Bluebelle (Generous). February 19. Tenth living foal. 42,000Y. Tattersalls October Book 2. Sackville/Donald. Brother to the 2-y-o 6f and subsequent US stakes winner and Group 3 Nell Gwyn Stakes second Blue Maiden and to the modest 9.5f winner Blue Oyster and half-brother

to 3 winners including the quite useful 10f and 14f winner Blue Destination (by Dubai Destination). The dam, a quite useful 12.5f winner, is a half-sister to 6 winners including the Group 2 German Oaks winner Centaine. The second dam, Hi Lass (by Shirley Heights), won the Group 3 Prix Gladiateur and is a half-sister to the Grade 1 Yellow Ribbon Invitational Handicap winner Bonne Ile and the Group 3 Cumberland Lodge Stakes winner Ile de Nisky. (Laurence Bellman & Billy Mills). *"A very nice, extremely athletic colt that will be a 2-y-o from seven furlongs to a mile and from the middle to back-end of the season. It's a decent pedigree, but he'll be better at three".*

1624. DARK PEARL ★★
b.c. Born To Sea – Luanas Pearl (Bahri). March 19. Fourth foal. 70,000Y. Tattersalls October Book 2. Sackville/Donald. Half-brother to the fair 11.5f winner Cosette (by Champs Elysees). The dam is an unraced half-sister to 8 winners including the Chester Vase, September Stakes and Winter Derby winner (all Group 3 events) Hattan and the Group 3 Jockey Club Cup winner Tastahil. The second dam, Luana (by Shaadi), a useful triple 6f winner (including at 2 yrs), was listed-placed and is a half-sister to 5 winners including the high-class middle-distance horses and Group 1 winners Warrsan and Luso and the Group winners Cloud Castle and Needle Gun. (Mr C U F Ma). *"I've got two Born To Sea 2-y-o's and I think they're both very nice. This colt won't be early, I think he'll be a 2-y-o but he's going to want a trip in time and he certainly won't be running any shorter than seven furlongs. Very athletic and scopey, he looks a racehorse".*

1625. ETTU ★★★
b.f. Excelebration – Tragic Moment (Pivotal). February 16. First foal. €100,000Y. Goffs Orby. Fiona Shaw. The dam is an unraced sister to the very useful dual listed winner Il Warrd and a half-sister to 5 winners including the listed winner Coy. The second dam, Demure (by Machiavellian), is an unraced half-sister to 9 winners including the very smart colt Diffident, winner of the Group 3 6f Diadem Stakes and the Group 3 6f Prix de Ris-Orangis. (Marc Keller). *"A sweet filly, she's racy and will be a 2-y-o. She was very small at the sales but she's grown, does everything nicely and goes well, I think she'll be a six furlong 2-y-o in mid-summer".*

1626. GLORIOUS FOREVER ★★★★ ♠♠
ch.c. Archipenko – Here To Eternity (Stormy Atlantic). February 24. Second foal. 110,000Y. Tattersalls October Book 2. KIR & Sackville/Donald. Brother to the useful 2015 2-y-o 7f and French listed 8.5f winner Time Warp. The dam, a modest 7f winner, is a half-sister to one winner. The second dam, Heat Of The Night (by Lear Fan), a dual 9f winner here, subsequently won a listed 1m event in Germany and is a half-sister to one winner. (Kangyu International HK). *"A very nice colt and a brother to Time Warp who did well for Sir Mark Prescott last year. He's probably a bit bigger and has a bit more scope than Time Warp and I think he's a 2-y-o for the second half of the season and be better next year. He's scopey, moves very well and does everything nicely".*

1627. HERNANDES (FR) ★★★
gr.c. Clodovil – Gontcharova (Zafonic). March 22. Twelfth foal. €45,000Y. Arqana Deauville October. Guy Petit. Half-brother to 5 winners including the French listed winner and dual Group 3 placed Mashoor (by Monsun), the French listed-placed Misk (by Linamix) and to the unraced dam of the French Group 3 winner Lixirova. The dam, a French listed-placed 1m winner, is a half-sister to 8 winners including the US Grade 1 winner Roi Normand and the US dual Grade 2 winner Trampoli. The second dam, Luth de Saron (by Luthier), won the Group 2 Prix de Mallerit. (John Moorhouse & John Nicholls). *"He's a 2-y-o type and a nice colt that goes well. He's made giant strides since the sales and will be earlier now than I first imagined. One for July time I should think".*

1628. INLAWED ★★★★
b.c. Bahamian Bounty – Regent's Park (Green Desert). March 17. Seventh foal. €55,000Y. Tattersalls Ireland September. Sackville/Donald. Half-brother to the quite useful Irish 2-y-o 1m winner Hassah (by Halling), to the quite useful dual 7f winner Outlawed (by Kyllachy) and a winner in Greece by Cockney Rebel. The dam, a quite useful 10f winner, is a

half-sister to 5 winners. The second dam, New Assembly (by Machiavellian), a useful 9f and 10f winner here, subsequently won and was listed-placed in the USA and is a sister to the 7f (at 2 yrs) and Group 1 9f Dubai Duty Free Stakes winner Right Approach and a half-sister to 7 winners. (L A Bellman). *"He wasn't a very nice yearling but we bought him because I trained his half-brother Outlawed who was decent and we sold him to Hong Kong. So although this colt walked very well I bought him on sentimental terms really, rather than loving him. But he's just absolutely blossomed and made up into a very good-looking 2-y-o type. He's sharper than Outlawed was and I think he'll start at six furlongs. He's got a bit of speed".*

1629. MADAME BOUNTY (IRE) ★★★★
b.f. Bahamian Bounty – Madame Boulangere (Royal Applause). April 29. Tenth foal. 54,000Y. Tattersalls October Book 1. Sackville/Donald. Sister to the useful 5f (including at 2 yrs) and 6f winner of 6 races Barracuda Boy and half-sister to the fairly useful 2-y-o dual 7f winner Lamh Albasser (by Mr Greeley) and the quite useful Irish 10f to 12f winner of 8 races Jazz Girl (by Johar). The dam, a useful dual 6f winner (including at 2 yrs), was listed-placed and is a half-sister to one winner. The second dam, Jazz (by Sharrood), a fair 7f (at 2 yrs) and 10f placed maiden, is a half-sister to 12 winners including the US Grade 2 winner Sign Of Hope and the Group 2 placed Finian's Rainbow and Carmot. (Paola Hewins, Olivia Hoare). *"She's sharp and a full sister to Barracuda Boy who was a good 2-y-o and improved. She'll probably be my first 2-y-o runner and I could see her being out in May over six furlongs. A strong filly, not overly-big and looks an out-and-out 2-y-o type to crack on with".*

1630. MASTERFILLY ★★★
gr.f. Mastercraftsman – Waldena (Storm Cat). February 24. Second foal. 70,000Y. Tattersalls October Book 2. Sackville/Donald. The dam is an unraced half-sister to 4 minor winners. The second dam, High Walden (by El Gran Senor), a smart 2-y-o 1m winner and third in the Group 3 Musidora Stakes, is closely related to the Oaks and Fillies Mile winner Reams of Verse and a half-sister to the Eclipse Stakes and Phoenix Champion Stakes winner Elmaamul. (Laurence Bellman & David Ward). *"A very nice filly, I thought she was going to be quite backward but I'm changing my mind. She's hugely athletic, has got a bit of speed and I think she'll be a 2-y-o from June onwards over seven furlongs".*

1631. NASTENKA ★★★
b.f. Aussie Rules – Nezhenka (With Approval). February 1. First foal. The dam, a quite useful 12f and 2m winner, is a half-sister to 4 winners including the useful 2-y-o 6f winner and 7f Group 3 placed Nataliya. The second dam, Ninotchka (by Nijinsky), a listed winner in Italy and third in the Group 3 12f Lancashire Oaks and the Group 3 12f Princess Royal Stakes, is a half-sister to 5 winners. (Miss K Rausing). *"A sweet filly, sadly her sire Aussie Rules has recently died. This is one for the second half of the season, she's strong and racy-looking, does everything well and should be racing from August onwards. There's plenty of stamina in the pedigree, but Aussie Rules does get his share of 2-y-o winners".*

1632. PEKING FLYER ★★★
b.c. Zoffany – Wing Diva (Hawk Wing). April 12. Third foal. 50,000Y. Tattersalls October Book 1. KIR & Sackville/Donald. The dam, a moderate 1m to 12f placed maiden, is a half-sister to 7 winners. The second dam, Sasimoto (by Saratoga Six), an Italian dual listed winner of 5 races, is a half-sister to 4 winners including the US Grade 2 and Grade 3 winner Notebook. (Kangyu International HK). *"He grew enormously after the sales and went through a big and weak stage. He's just starting to come back now and show the athleticism he showed early doors. He'll be a 2-y-o from the mid-to-late summer onwards, starting at seven furlongs. I like him a lot and he's a big, strong, athletic colt by a sire who did very well last year with his first crop".*

1633. POSEIDON ★★★
ch.c. Born To Sea – Maskaya (Machiavellian). February 23. Eighth foal. €320,000Y. Goffs Orby. Sackville/Donald. Half-brother to the Irish 2-y-o 7f winner and Group 1 Criterium de Saint-Cloud second Drumbeat (by Montjeu), to the fairly useful dual 10f winner California (by Azamour) and the

fair 7.6f winner Red Blooded Woman (by Red Ransom) and a winner in Japan by Giant's Causeway. The dam, an Irish 2-y-o 5f winner, is a half-sister to 7 winners including the Group 1 6f Cheveley Park Stakes third Danaskaya (dam of the Group 1 Dewhurst Stakes winner Belardo). The second dam, Majinskaya (by Marignan), a French listed 12f winner and Group 3 second, is a half-sister to 6 winners including the dam of the Group 1 5f Prix de l'Abbaye winner Kistena. (Mr P K Siu). *"Very similar to my other Born To Sea 2-y-o. He's very athletic, has grown and gone slightly weak and although I think he'll race this year we'll have our sights set on his 3-y-o career. I think he was the most expensive Born To Sea to be sold last year, he's a gorgeous horse, a good size, classy-looking and very exciting. One to look forward to".*

1634. ROMANOR ★★
b.g. Holy Roman Emperor – Salinia (Rainbow Quest). March 16. Third foal. €40,000Y. Goffs Orby. Not sold. The dam is an unplaced half-sister to 5 winners including the Group 1 French Derby and Australian Group 1 winner Reliable Man and the Australian Group 3 winner Imposing. The second dam, On Fair Stage (by Sadler's Wells), an Irish 4-y-o listed 1m winner, is a half-sister to 6 winners including Perfect Vintage (Group 3 1m Prix Quincey) and the listed 1m Sceptre Stakes winner Perfect Circle. (Mr P K Siu). *"A compact, slightly typical Holy Roman Emperor, he's just started back cantering after a gelding operation. He should be ready for the second half of the season but although the sire gets 2-y-o winners this family doesn't seem to, so we'll have to see".*

1635. ULTIMATE AVENUE ★★★★ ♠
b.c. Excelebration – Dance Avenue (Sadler's Wells). March 15. Third foal. €340,000Y. Goffs Orby. Sackville/Donald. The dam is an unraced half-sister to 6 winners including the Group-placed Middlemarch and Lady High Havens. The second dam, Blanche Dubois (by Nashwan), is an unraced half-sister to 10 winners including Indian Haven (Irish 2,000 Guineas) and Count Dubois (Group 1 Gran Criterium). (Mr P K Siu). *"He's one of our most exciting 2-y-o's. Big, but very athletic and light on his feet, he's done plenty and done it* all extremely well. He's just filling his frame now and should be a 2-y-o for mid-summer, probably starting in a seven furlong maiden".*

1636. VERMILION ★★★
ch.f. Dutch Art – Makara (Lion Cavern). May 3. Seventh foal. 58,000Y. Tattersalls October Book 2. Sackville/Donald. Sister to the fairly useful dual 5f winner and listed-placed Graphic Guest and half-sister to the Irish 5f (at 2 yrs) and dual listed winner (over 7f and 1m) Fourpenny Lane (by Efisio), the French dual 7f winner of 3 races at 2 and 3 yrs Asque and the fair 7f winner Copper Penny (both by Dansili). The dam is an unraced half-sister to 8 winners including the useful listed 7f winner Kalindi (the dam of 3 stakes winners). The second dam, Rohita (by Waajib), a fairly useful 2-y-o 5f and 6f winner, was third in the Group 3 6f Cherry Hinton Stakes and is a half-sister to 5 winners. (Laurence Bellman & David Ward). *"Her pedigree is all 2-y-o but to me she hasn't looked that way at all until just recently. She grew and went very leggy and weak, so we left her alone for a bit and now she's looking stronger and more up to it. So I'm hoping she'll live up to her pedigree and make a 2-y-o in the second half of the season. The mare's done well with her 2-y-o's and hopefully this will be another one to succeed".*

1637. UNNAMED ★★★
ch.c. Tagula – Fashion Guide (Bluebird). May 11. Eighth foal. €28,000Y. Tattersalls Ireland September. Charlie Gordon-Watson. Half-brother to the unplaced 2015 2-y-o Unfashionable (by Iffraaj), to the quite useful 7f (including at 2 yrs) and 6f winner Ortac Rock (by Aussie Rules) and to the fair 1m winner Spotty Muldoon (by Mull Of Kintyre). The dam, a 2-y-o 6f winner in Ireland, is a half-sister to 7 winners including the Group 3 1m Premio Dormello winner Foolish Heart. The second dam, Honorine (by Blushing Groom), placed once in France over 1m, is a half-sister to 6 winners including the Group 3 10.5f Prix Corrida winner Echoes. (S Al Ansari & E Walker). *"A relatively inexpensive purchase, he's very good-looking, lacks pedigree but was bought on looks. He does everything very well, was a late foal but will make a 2-y-o from around July onwards, starting off at six furlongs".* **TRAINERS' BARGAIN BUY**

1638. UNNAMED ★★★
b.c. Dutch Art – Loquacity (Diktat). February 13. Sixth foal. 77,000Y. Tattersalls October Book 2. Bobby O'Ryan. Brother to the useful 2-y-o 6f winner and dual Group 3 second Agent Allison and half-brother to the modest 1m and hurdles winner Masters Blazing (by Iceman). The dam is an unraced half-sister to 2 minor winners. The second dam, Cybinka (by Selkirk), a fairly useful listed 7f winner, is a half-sister to 2 minor winners. *"He's a 2-y-o type that could start in late May or June over six furlongs and will probably want a bit of cut in the ground. He's a full-brother to Agent Allison who was a decent 2-y-o and I think this guy's best days will be as a 2-y-o. He could be a really fun type for later in the year, but he'll start his career earlier".*

1639. UNNAMED ★★★
b.c. Frankel – Reaching (Dansili). February 16. First foal. 500,000Y. Tattersalls October Book 1. Not sold. The dam, a fair Irish 3-y-o 7f placed maiden, is a half-sister to the Group 1 Pretty Polly Stakes, Irish Oaks, Nassau Stakes and Yorkshire Oaks winner Peeping Fawn and to the 2-y-o Group 1 Criterium International winner Thewayyouare. The second dam, Maryinsky (by Sadler's Wells), a 2-y-o 7f winner, was second in the Group 1 Fillies Mile and is a half-sister to 8 winners including the Grade 2 9f Demoiselle Stakes winner Better Than Honour, the Group 2 1m Beresford Stakes winner Turnberry Isle and the Group 2 1m Prix d'Astarte winner Smolensk. (Reiko & Michael Baum). *"He's a stunning racehorse except for being on the small side – if he was two inches taller he'd almost be the perfect specimen. A really attractive colt that does everything nicely and moves very well, he's got a bit of character, was quite weak but is now strengthening up well and should be ready for when the seven furlong maidens start. It's a brilliant family, so he's bred to be very good but whether his size will let him down only time will tell".*

1640. UNNAMED ★★
b.c. Fastnet Rock – Wonder Of Wonders (Kingmambo). January 27. Second foal. $350,000Y. Keeneland September. The dam, a very smart listed 11f winner, was second in the Oaks and third in the Irish Oaks and is a half-sister to the dual listed winner Victory Song and to the winner and Group 3 placed Sparrow. The second dam, All Too Beautiful (by Sadler's Wells), a Group 3 10.5f Middleton Stakes and listed 10f winner, is a sister to the Derby, Irish Derby and King George VI and Queen Elizabeth Diamond Stakes winner Galileo and the dual Group 1 winner Black Sam Bellamy and a half-sister to four stakes winners notably the outstanding colt Sea The Stars. (Sheikh Mohammed bin Khalifa Al Thani). *"He's a big, striking colt and very good-looking which is quite unusual for a Fastnet Rock because they generally have plain, ugly heads. He's a proper horse, but big and immature, so we've still got half the handbrake on. Generally Fastnet Rock has been very disappointing in Europe despite the huge success he's had in Australia. Whatever this colt does this year will be a stepping stone to his 3-y-o career".*

CHRIS WALL

1641. ATLANTA BELLE (IRE) ★★
ch.f. Zebedee – Tara Too (Danetime). February 14. Fourth foal. 11,000Y. Tattersalls October Book 3. Chris Wall. Half-sister to the fair 1m winner Van Huysen (by Excellent Art) and to the moderate dual 10f winner Benhoordenhout (by Footstepsinthesand). The dam, a quite useful 5f (at 2 yrs) to 7f winner, is out of the unplaced Gone With The Wind (by Common Grounds), herself a sister to the very useful listed Scarborough Stakes winner and Group 2 King's Stand Stakes second Flanders (dam of the Group 1 Sprint Cup winner G Force) and a half-sister to 8 winners. (The Leap Year Partnership). *"A little Zebedee filly, she's one of our 'cheap and cheerfuls'. A strong type, she's done a bit of growing and she needs to finish that off before we can do anything with her. She seems to have a willing attitude and looks a summer 2-y-o for six furlongs".*

1642. CALM CHARM (IRE) ★★
ch.f. Teofilo – Mango Lady (Dalakhani). March 21. Fourth foal. 50,000Y. Tattersalls October Book 2. Not sold. Half-sister to the quite useful 2015 2-y-o 7f and 7.5f winner Mix And Mingle, to the minor German winner at 4 and 5 yrs Semai (both by Exceed And Excel) and the fair 9.5f and 10f winner of 4 races May

Queen (by Shamardal). The dam, a fair 12f winner, is a half-sister to 4 winners including the Group 2 12f King Edward VII Stakes and dual Group 3 winner High Accolade. The second dam, Generous Lady (by Generous), a listed-placed middle-distance winner of 4 races in Ireland, is a half-sister to 6 winners including the Italian Group 2 winner Jape. (Ms A Fustoq). *"A different type of filly altogether than her 3-y-o half-sister Mix And Mingle, she's much bigger and scopier, and more like the dam who won over 12f. Being by Teofilo I think she's going to need a trip, so I don't know how much we'll see of her this season. A big filly, but a nice type".*

1643. ENFORCING (IRE) ★★★
b.c. Canford Cliffs – Black Mascara (Authorized). January 19. First foal. 100,000Y. Tattersalls October Book 2. Suzanne Roberts. The dam, a fair 12f placed maiden, is a half-sister to 2 winners. The second dam, Pink Colada (by Sabrehill), a US stakes winner and Grade 2 placed, is a half-sister to 6 winners including the French and US Group 2 winner Triple Threat and to the unraced dam of the multiple Group 1 winner Canford Cliffs. (Mr Ben C M Wong). *"A nice, scopey colt but forward enough to make a summer 2-y-o over seven furlongs. He needs to mature a bit more at the moment but he's a colt with a pleasing attitude and a good stride. He should pay his way a bit through the summer".*

1644. ENTANGLING (IRE) ★★★★
b.c. Fastnet Rock – Question Times (Shamardal). January 17. Second foal. €380,000Y. Goffs Orby. S A Roberts. Brother to the quite useful Irish 2015 2-y-o 6f winner Diamond Fields. The dam, a fairly useful listed 6f placed 2-y-o and 6f 3-y-o winner, is a half-sister to the smart Group 3 Sceptre Stakes winner and Group 1 6f Cheveley Park Stakes second Sunday Times. The second dam, Forever Times (by So Factual), a fairly useful 5f (at 2 yrs) to 7f winner, is half-sister to 7 winners including Welsh Emperor (Group 2 7f Hungerford Stakes) and the listed 5f winner Majestic Times. (Mr Ben C M Wong). *"An expensive purchase, he's rather a plain colt which is typical of the sire but, that said, he belies his looks a bit and seems to do things OK. He'll be one for the mid-season onwards*

but I quite like him and he should do OK over seven furlongs and a mile. He creates a favourable expression".

1645. HEREITIZZ ★★
b.f. Henrythenavigator – Whatizzit (Galileo). February 19. Third foal. Half-sister to the fair 9f winner Dream Scape (by Oasis Dream). The dam, a fair 2-y-o 9f winner, is a half-sister to 6 winners including the useful 7f (at 2 yrs), listed 1m and Italian Group 3 1m winner Whazzis and the listed Chesham Stakes winner Whazzat. The second dam, Wosaita (by Generous), a fair 12.3f placed maiden, is a half-sister to 10 winners including the very smart Group 1 10.5f Prix de Diane winner Rafha (herself the dam of four stakes winners including the Haydock Sprint Cup winner Invincible Spirit) and the Group 3 12f Blandford Stakes winner Chiang Mai (dam of the Group 1 winner Chinese White). (Moyns Park Stud). *"A home-bred filly, she's the third one that's been out of sorts through the winter so although we got them broken-in we weren't able to do much with them. In her case it took ages for her to stop coughing. So I can't tell you much about her, but she ought to make a bit of a 2-y-o because she's the right physical model to do that".*

1646. MARILYN ★★
ch.f. Sixties Icon – Donatia (Shamardal). February 14. First foal. 4,000Y. Tattersalls October Book 4. The dam, a poor 9f fourth placed maiden, is a half-sister to 3 minor winners. The second dam, Dona Anna (By Be My Chief), is an unplaced sister to the US dual Grade 1 winner Donna Viola. (Tadgell, Swinburn & Wall). *"The mare was no good but this is quite a nice filly. She was always a good-looking filly and came recommended from Genesis Green Stud. We've bought horses from them for a long time. She has a bit of size and scope, the sire certainly gets 2-y-o winners despite the fact he won the St Leger and I can see this filly being a six furlong 2-y-o in mid-summer".*

1647. NARGIZA (USA) ★★★
ch.f. Elusive Quality – Any For Love (Southern Halo). March 20. Ninth foal. $100,000Y. Keeneland September. R O'Gorman. Half-sister to 5 winners including the US Grade 3 placed

Distorted Love (by Distorted Humor). The dam, a Grade 1 winner in Argentina, is a half-sister to a minor Argentine stakes winner. The second dam, Aludra (by Manguin), a Grade 3 winner in Argentina, is a half-sister to the Argentine dual Grade 1 winner Syzygy. (Ms A Fustoq). *"She could be one that's destined for Saudi Arabia but we'll have to see how she goes. Mr Fustoq bought two yearlings that may end up going to Saudi, but if they show anything above average they may stay here. She's quite nice, but she's a big filly and may be more of a 3-y-o, but you never know how they'll come together. She creates a favourable impression".*

1648. OH IT'S SAUCEPOT ★★★
b.f. Sir Percy – Oh So Saucy (Imperial Ballet). March 2. Second foal. Half-sister to the quite useful 2015 2-y-o dual 6f winner Dark Defender (by Pastoral Pursuits). The dam, a fair 7f and 1m winner of 5 races, is a half-sister to 2 minor winners. The second dam, Almasi by Petorius), a fair 7f winner of 8 races, is a half-sister to 2 winners. (The Eight Of Diamonds). *"The dam had a good start with her first foal who was a winning 2-y-o last year and I like this filly, she goes well. She's a bit leggy at the minute so she's not destined to run particularly early. We've had quite a few from the family and they aren't necessarily at their best as 2-y-o's, but I like her. She has a good attitude and a good action, so she should be able to give her owner a bit of fun".*

1649. SO CUTE (IRE) ★★★
ch.f. Lope De Vega – Lizzy's Township (Delaware Township). February 9. Fifth foal. 78,000Y. Tattersalls October Book 2. R O'Gorman. Half-sister to the minor French winner of 2 races at 3 and 4 yrs Kaniza (by Myboycharlie). The dam, a listed stakes winner of 3 races and 3 yrs in the USA, is a half-sister to 8 winners including two US stakes winners. The second dam, Tarahumara (by Black Tie Affair), is an unraced half-sister to 4 minor winners. (Ms A Fustoq). *"This is the other filly we bought with the idea she might end up in Saudi Arabia. She looks like a sharp 2-y-o, so we'll see what we can do and take it from there. A neat, compact filly that's well put together, she certainly seems to want to get on with things. She was a good-looking filly at the sale and the sire had a good year, so his yearlings were never going to be cheap".*

1650. TIP OF THE CITY ★★★
b.f. Oasis Dream – Always Remembered (Galileo). January 15. Second foal. Sister to the modest 2015 7f fourth placed 2-y-o Always A Dream. The unraced dam is closely related to the Derby, Racing Post Trophy and Dante Stakes winner Motivator and to the Group 2 12f Hardwicke Stakes winner Macarthur and a half-sister to the smart listed 10f winner Imperial Star. The second dam, Out West (by Gone West), a useful 7.5f (at 2 yrs) and listed 1m winner, is a half-sister to 3 winners including the US Grade 3 placed Auggies Here. (Ms A Fustoq). *"She's a different type of filly than her 3-y-o half-sister – she's bigger, scopier and stronger. I quite like her and although she's quite stoutly bred on the dam's side she shows enough to suggest we could be racing her around August time over seven furlongs".*

1651. UPENDED ★★★
b.g. Paco Boy – Upskittled (Diktat). March 24. Fifth living foal. 17,000Y. Tattersalls October Book 3. Chris Wall. Half-brother to the quite useful 2-y-o dual 6f winner Titled Gent (by Kheleyf), to the fair 7f winner Edge Of Love (by Kyllachy) and a winner abroad by Medicean. The dam, placed twice at 3 yrs in France, is a half-sister to 10 winners including the listed winner and dual Group 1 third Musicanna and to the dam of the champion sprinter Overdose. The second dam, Upend (by Main Reef), won the Group 3 St Simon Stakes and the listed Galtres Stakes and is a half-sister to 6 winners. (Mr Des Thurlby). *"He's done a lot of growing and he's a typical Paco Boy in that he has the odd day when he can be a bit silly, but on the whole he's fine. He's one for the mid-summer onwards and he could be running over seven furlongs I would have thought. We've had a bit of success with this family before".* **TRAINERS' BARGAIN BUY**

1652. UNNAMED ★★★
b.f. Bated Breath – Miss Meltemi (Miswaki Tern). March 24. Eleventh foal. 48,000Y. Tattersalls October Book 2. Rabbah Bloodstock. Sister to the very useful 7f (at 2

yrs) and listed 1m winner and Group 3 Dahlia Stakes third Don't Dili Dali, to the useful listed-placed 7f to 8.5f winner Balducci and the fairly useful listed-placed 1m winner Ada River and half-sister to 3 winners including the quite useful 2-y-o 5f winner Haigh Hall (by Kyllachy) and the quite useful 12f winner Zafarana (by Tiger Hill). The dam, a 2-y-o winner in Italy and third in the Group 1 Italian Oaks, is a half-sister to 3 winners. The second dam, Blu Meltemi (by Star Shareef), a winner of 5 races at 2 and 3 yrs in Italy and second in the Italian Oaks, is a half-sister to 3 winners. (Sheikh Juka Dalmook Al Maktoum). "She's a very good-looking filly and the right physical model to be a 2-y-o, but she threw a splint a couple of months ago and it kept her off work for quite a while. So we're only just finding our way with her. She looks the part though and is one for mid-season onwards over six/seven furlongs".

1653. UNNAMED ★★★
b.f. Iffraaj – Relinquished (Royal Applause). March 3. Third living foal. 20,000Y. Tattersalls October Book 2. Rabbah Bloodstock. Half-sister to the fair 6f winner Renounce (by Elnadim). The dam, a fair 2-y-o dual 7f winner, is a full or half-sister to 8 winners including the listed winner Medley and the dam of the Group 1 Australia Cup winner Spillway. The second dam, Marl (by Lycius), a fairly useful 2-y-o 5.2f winner, is a half-sister to 4 winners including the very useful 2-y-o listed 5f National Stakes winner Rowaasi. (Sheikh Rashid Dalmook Al Maktoum). "She was out of sorts over the winter and we're only just getting her going. She's not a big filly and she's by Iffraaj, so you'd expect her to be a mid-summer 2-y-o over six/seven furlongs".

1654. UNNAMED ★★★
ch.c. Raven's Pass – Sospira (Cape Cross). February 3. Second foal. 20,000Y. Tattersalls October Book 2. Richard Knight. Half-brother to the fair 1m winner Asima (by Halling). The dam is a 12f placed half-sister to 9 winners including the dual Group 2 7f winner Nayyir, the Group 2 and Group 3 winner Sky Hunter, the UAE Group 3 12f winner and Group 1 placed Highest and the listed 14f winner Shamaiel. The second dam, Pearl Kite (by Silver Kite), a useful 2-y-o 1m winner

and third in the Group 2 12f Ribblesdale Stakes, is a half-sister to 3 winners. (Sheikh Rashid Dalmook Al Maktoum). "A big, tall horse – he's well-grown for a 2-y-o. But he goes along quite nicely, carries himself well and looks quite promising at this stage. The question is when to kick off with him because with his size he's not one that you could start too early with. Hopefully he'll be a July/August type 2-y-o".

DERMOT WELD

1655. ALAHIDA (IRE) ★★★★
b.br.f. Redoute's Choice – Alanza (Dubai Destination). January 23. First foal. The dam, a smart dual Group 3 7f and dual listed winner, is a half-sister to the listed winner Alonsoa. The second dam, Alasha (Barathea), a useful 7f (at 2 yrs) and listed 1m winner, is a half-sister to 7 winners including the Irish listed winner Alaiyma. (H H Aga Khan). "A medium-sized, six/seven furlong filly, she'll make a nice 2-y-o. I like her and we should give her an extra star!"

1656. ALDHARA ★★★
b.f. Dubawi – Bethrah (Marju). January 5. Third foal. The dam won 3 races at 3 yrs including the Group 1 Irish 1,000 Guineas and the Group 3 1m Irish 1,000 Guineas Trial. The second dam, Reve d'Iman (by Highest Honor), a minor 3-y-o 9f winner in France, is a sister to the Group 1 Prix Saint-Alary winner Reve d'Oscar, the Group 2 Prix Hocquart winner Numide and the listed French 3-y-o winner Sir Eric. (Hamdan Al Maktoum). "A big, strong filly that wintered in Dubai, she's not been here long and I'd say she'll be one for the second half of the year over seven furlongs and a mile".

1657. ALJUNOOD (IRE) ★★★★
br.c. Bated Breath – Ataraxy (Zamindar). March 18. Third foal. 130,000foal. Tattersalls December. Shadwell Estate Co. The dam is an unraced half-sister to 7 winners including the Irish Oaks winner Wemyss Bight (dam of the Group 1 winner Beat Hollow) and the dams of three other Group 1 winners including Oasis Dream. The second dam, Bahamian (by Mill Reef), was a very useful winner of the Group 3 12f Lingfield Oaks Trial and was placed in the Prix de Pomone, Park Hill Stakes and Princess Royal Stakes. She is a half-sister to the very

useful winners Captivator, Eileen Jenny and Kasmayo. (Hamdan Al Maktoum). *"A very nice colt, he's one that I like a lot. He'll be a six/ seven furlong 2-y-o in the second part of the year. One to look out for".*

1658. ALL CRAZY NOW (IRE) ★★★
ch.c. Dutch Art – Supernovae (Dalakhani). March 25. First foal. The dam was a modest Irish 12f winner. The second dam, Dress To Thrill (by Danehill), won Grade 1 9f Matriarch Stakes and Group 2 1m Sun Chariot Stakes and is a sister to 2 winners and a half-sister to 7 winners. (Moyglare Stud Farms Ltd). *"Quite a nice colt, he'll make a 2-y-o over six/seven furlongs. The dam is by Dalakhani so she'll add plenty of stamina, but Dutch Art should put the pace in there".*

1659. ALL MINE (IRE) ★★★★
b.f. Pour Moi – Truly Mine (Rock Of Gibraltar). February 7. Sixth foal. Sister to the very useful 2015 2-y-o listed 6f winner and Group 3 6f second Only Mine and half-sister to the useful 1m, 10f (both at 2 yrs) and 12f winner Miner's Lamp (by Shamardal), the quite useful Irish 10f winner Truthwillsetyoufree (by Dalakhani) and the 2-y-o 7.5f winner Colour Rhapsody (by Rip Van Winkle). The dam, a useful listed 11f winner and third in the Group 3 1m Park Express Stakes, is a half-sister to 3 winners. The second dam, Truly Yours (by Barathea), a French 2-y-o 1m winner, is a half-sister to the French Group 2 winner Dream Peace and the French 2,000 Guineas second Catcher In The Rye. (Mr D K Weld). *"She's very nice, slightly different to her full sister who was a very good 2-y-o last year because she has more size and scope to her. I would say she'll be running in July/August over seven furlongs and she'll get a mile this year".*

1660. ASMAT (IRE) ★★★
b.f. Dansili – Askeria (Sadler's Wells). February 12. Third foal. Half-sister to the fairly useful Irish 1m winner Ashraf (by Cape Cross). The dam, a fair 12f placed maiden, is a half-sister to numerous winners including the Group 1 St James's Palace Stakes and Group 1 Irish Champion Stakes winner Azamour, the 2-y-o Group 2 7f Futurity Stakes winner and Group 1 National Stakes third Arazan and the useful 2-y-o 7f winner and Group 3 placed Surveyor.

The second dam, Asmara (by Lear Fan), a useful winner in Ireland at up to 10f, is a half-sister to the high-class Prix Ganay and Prix d'Harcourt winner Astarabad. (H H Aga Khan). *"She's nice, she goes well and I see her as a seven furlong 2-y-o a bit later on this season".*

1661. ASSAM ★★★★
b.f. Dansili – Sense Of Pride (Sadler's Wells). February 20. Second foal. Half-sister to Middleman (by Oasis Dream), unplaced in one start at 2 yrs in 2015. The dam, a fair 10.5f winner, is a sister to the multiple Group 3 middle-distance winner and French Derby fourth Day Flight and a half-sister to the very useful 2-y-o 7f winner Bionic, the Group 3 7f Prestige Stakes winner Sense Of Joy and the useful 2-y-o dual 7f winner Ashdan. The second dam, Bonash (by Rainbow Quest), a very useful filly, won 4 races in France from 1m to 12f including the Prix d'Aumale, the Prix Vanteaux and the Prix de Malleret and is a full or half-sister to 4 winners. (Khalid Abdulla). *"A nice filly that'll be running in July. She's very correct and you should watch out for her".*

1662. BEE QUEEN ★★★
b.f. Makfi – Trojan Queen (Empire Maker). March 29. Half-sister to the 2015 Irish 2-y-o 1m winner, on her only start, Emergent (by Oasis Dream). The dam was placed over 10f and 11f in France and is a half-sister to the Group 1 Prix Jean Romanet winner Romantica and to the dual listed winner Ideal World. The second dam, Banks Hill (by Danehill), won the Coronation Stakes, Prix Jacques Le Marois and Breeders' Cup Filly & Mare Turf and is a full or half-sister to the Group/Grade 1 winners Heat Haze, Intercontinental, Cacique and Champs Elysees and to the Group 2 winner and high-class sire Dansili. (Khalid Abdulla). *"A nice, quality filly for six/seven furlongs in July/August. Makfi's take a bit of time to come to hand and he's rather like his sire Dubawi in that respect".*

1663. BLUE BAHIA (IRE) ★★★
b.f. Big Bad Bob – Brazilian Bride (Pivotal). April 24. Fifth foal. Half-sister to the useful dual listed 6f winner Rivellino and to the fair Irish 5f winner Brazilian Breeze (both by Invincible Spirit). The dam won the Group 3

6f Swordlestown Stakes at 2 yrs and is a half-sister to 6 winners including the French listed winner Rio Tigre and the Group 3 7f second Brazilian Star. The second dam, Braziliz (by Kingmambo), placed fourth once over 5f at 2 yrs, is a half-sister to 8 winners including the dam of the Group 1 winners Saffron Walden, Insight and Dolphin Street. (Lady Chryss O'Reilly). *"She should be making her debut at Navan in mid-April. She's forward and she goes well".*

1664. CASCAVELLE (IRE) ★★★★
gr.c. Shamardal – Majestic Silver (Linamix). May 5. Fourth foal. Half-brother to the 2015 2-y-o 7f winner and Group 2 1m Beresford Stakes second True Solitaire (by Oasis Dream), to the dual Group 3 9f and dual listed winner Carla Bianca (by Dansili) and the minor 7f winner, from two starts, Joailliere (by Dubawi). The dam is an unraced half-sister to the Irish Group 3 12f and Group 3 14f winner Profound Beauty and to the useful 7f to 10f winner Rock Critic. The second dam, Diamond Trim (by Highest Honor), a winner of 5 races from 1m to 12f including a listed event, is a half-sister to 5 winners including the Group 2 12f Ribblesdale Stakes winner Irresistible Jewel. (Moyglare Stud Farm). *"He's very much a quality colt. Very likeable, we'll see him running in July/August and I like him. He's quite similar to his 3-y-o half-brother True Solitaire although he has more strength than him".*

1665. CRISTOFANO ALLORI (IRE) ★★★
b.c. Shamardal – Perfect Touch (Miswaki). April 24. Ninth foal. 200,000Y. Tattersalls October Book 2. C R Gonzales. Brother to the quite useful 1m and 10f winner Breden and half-brother to the useful 5f (at 2 yrs) and listed 6f winner and Group 3 Jersey Stakes third Rock Jock (by Rock Of Gibraltar) and the fairly useful 2-y-o 6f winner Shining Armour (by Green Desert). The dam won 3 races including the Group 3 Brownstown Stakes and is a half-sister to 7 winners including the Italian Group 2 and Irish Group 3 winner King Jock. The second dam, Glen Kate (by Glenstal), won three Grade 3 events in the USA and is a half-sister to 3 winners. (Mrs C C Regalado-Gonzalez). *"He's a horse that's done very well but he's not an early prospect. He'll take a little bit of time and I would see him starting over seven furlongs in September/October".*

1666. DELTA DREAMER ★★★★
b.f. Oasis Dream – Kilo Alpha (King's Best). March 12. Third foal. Sister to the French 2-y-o 1m winner and Group 3 1m Prix Thomas Bryon second Alpha Bravo and half-sister to the quite useful 2015 2-y-o 1m and 8.5f winner Cartago (by Dansili). The dam, a French listed 1m winner, is a sister to the very smart triple listed 10f winner Runaway. The second dam, Anasazi (Sadler's Wells), was placed over 9f and 10f in France and is a half-sister to the outstanding colt Dancing Brave and the Prix Vermeille and Prix de Diane winner Jolypha. (Mr K Abdulla). *"She has a lot of quality to her. I see her being a seven furlong 2-y-o that should debut in August/September".*

1667. EUROPIUM ★★★
b.f. Frankel – Revered (Oasis Dream). April 4. Third foal. Half-sister to the very useful 2-y-o Group 3 1m winner Commemorative (by Zamindar). The dam, a quite useful 2-y-o 7f winner, is a sister to the very smart Group 3 6f Princess Margaret Stakes and Group 3 7f Oak Tree Stakes winner Visit and a half-sister to the very smart Group 1 10f Pretty Polly Stakes winner Promising Lead. The second dam, Arrive (by Kahyasi), a very useful 10f (at 2 yrs) and listed 13.8f winner, is a half-sister to the outstanding broodmare Hasili (dam of the top-class performers Banks Hill, Heat Haze, Cacique, Intercontinental, Champs Elysees and Dansili). (Khalid Abdulla). *"A nice, strong filly but she's very much one for the second part of the year, probably September or October over seven furlongs. More of a 3-y-o type".*

1668. FIDAAHA (IRE) ★★★
ch.f. New Approach – Ceist Eile (Noverre). February 27. Fourth foal. €200,000Y. Goffs Orby. Shadwell Estate Co. Sister to the US Grade 3 winner Ceisteach and half-sister to the Group 3 Killavullan Stakes winner Steip Amach (by Vocalised). The dam, a fair Irish 9.5f placed maiden, is a half-sister to 2 minor winners. The second dam, Sharafanya (by Zafonic), is an unraced half-sister to 4 winners including the German Group 2 winner Giant Sandman. (Hamdan Al Maktoum). *"She's quite a nice filly for late summer over seven*

furlongs. A good-sized filly, Sheikh Hamdan liked her a lot when he saw her the other day".

1669. FIREY SPEECH (USA) ★★★
b.f. Street Cry – Firey Red (Pivotal). April 11. Third foal. The dam, a useful 6f (at 2 yrs) and 9f winner and third in the Group 3 1m Irish 1,000 Guineas Trial, is a half-sister to 3 winners. The second dam, Step With Style (Gulch), a quite useful Irish 1m winner at 3 yrs, is a half-sister to several winners including the Group 3 placed Absolute Glee. (Moyglare Stud Farm). *"This is a nice filly. She isn't precocious but she should be able to make it as a 2-y-o in the autumn".*

1670. FURUD (IRE) ★★★
b.c. Zebedee – Kahira (King's Best). March 24. Seventh foal. €200,000Y. Goffs Orby. Shadwell Estate Co. Half-brother to the listed 6f winner, Group 1 Prix Marcel Boussac third and Group 2 Lowther Stakes second Queen Catrine (by Acclamation) and to the quite useful Irish dual 7f winner Vastitas (by Green Desert). The dam, a fair 2-y-o 7f placed maiden, is a half-sister to the Group 1 6f Haydock Park Sprint Cup winner Tamarisk. The second dam, Sine Labe (by Vaguely Noble), is an unplaced half-sister to the Group 1 Prix Saint-Alary winner Treble. (Hamdan Al Maktoum). *"A very big colt, he's growing and developing. A quality colt, he's interesting and I see him as one for six/seven furlongs in September/October".*

1671. HONOUR AND GLORY (IRE) ★★★
ch.c. Famous Name – Let Your Love Flow (Iffraaj). March 6. First foal. €65,000Y. Goffs Sportsmans. Bobby O'Ryan. The dam, a modest 2-y-o 9f winner, is a half-sister to 4 winners. The second dam, Miss Odlum (by Mtoto), a fair 10f winner in Ireland, is a half-sister to one winner. (Dr Ronan Lambe). *"He's quite forward, precocious and I can see him racing by the end of May over six furlongs".*

1672. IMPART ★★★
b.f. Oasis Dream – Disclose (Dansili). February 8. Second foal. The dam, a French listed-placed 1m winner, is a sister to two winners including the useful French 7f (at 2 yrs) and 1m winner and listed placed World Ruler and closely related to the useful French 2-y-o dual 6f winner and Group 3 1m third Grand Vista.

The second dam, Revealing (by Halling), a very useful 2-y-o 1m winner, is a half-sister to the useful 12f winner and dual Group 3 placed Singleton and the useful 6f winner Brevity. (Khalid Abdulla). *"He's a nice colt and should be a six/seven furlong type in the late summer".*

1673. KARAGANDA (IRE) ★★★
b.f. Azamour – Karawana (King's Best). February 13. Sixth foal. Closely related to the fairly useful Irish 2-y-o 6f winner Karamaya (by Invincible Spirit) and half-sister to the French dual Group 3 10f winner Karaktar (by High Chaparral) and the fairly useful 10f winner Karatash (by Halling). The dam, a fairly useful Irish 1m and 10f winner, is a half-sister to 3 winners. The second dam, Karaliyfa (by Kahyasi), a quite useful 9f winner, is a half-sister to 6 winners including the 2-y-o Group 3 1m May Hill Stakes winner Karasta and to the Group 2 2m 2f Doncaster Cup dead-heat winner Kasthari. (H H Aga Khan). *"She's got a lot of quality to her and she'll make a seven furlong 2-y-o in July or August".*

1674. KNIGHT'S DREAM (IRE) ★★★
b.c. Sir Prancealot – Dream Date (Oasis Dream). March 4. Third foal. €62,000foal. Goffs November foals. Lynn Lodge Stud. Half-brother to the Group 3 5f winner and Group 1 Nunthorpe Stakes third Extortionist (by Dandy Man). The dam, a quite useful dual 7f winner, is a half-sister to 5 winners. The second dam, Femme Fatale (by Fairy King), a useful dual 6f winner of 2 races (including a listed event at 2 yrs), is a half-sister to 4 winners including the dual listed 10f winner and smart broodmare Foodbroker Fancy (herself dam of the Group 3 winner Dalvina). (Mr Kenneth Ramsay). *"A sharp colt that's coming along nicely, he'll be running over five furlongs in May".*

1675. LIGHT LAUGHTER (IRE) ★★★
ch.f. Distorted Humor – Sense Of Purpose (Galileo). March 19. First foal. The dam, a useful Group 3 12 Ballyroan Stakes and listed 14f winner, is a full or half-sister to 6 winners including the fairly useful 1m winner and listed-placed Dance Pass. The second dam, Super Gift (by Darshaan), a dual 2-y-o 1m winner and second in the Group 3 C L Weld Park Stakes, is a half-sister to 6 winners.

(Moyglare Stud Ltd). *"Not a big filly, but she won't be that early. She'll be a nice filly for around July over six furlongs and you should give her a mention".*

1676. MOGHRAMA (IRE) ★★★
ch.f. Harbour Watch – Mythie (Octagonal). January 27. Seventh living foal. 240,000foal. Tattersalls December. Shadwell Estate Co. Half-sister to 5 winners including the Group 3 Nell Gwyn Stakes winner and Group 3 Musidora Stakes third Esentepe (by Oratorio), the quite useful 7f to 9f winner of 8 races Yojimbo (by Aussie Rules), the fairly useful 2-y-o 6f winner Versaki (by Verglas) and the fair 1m winner My Strategy (by Strategic Prince). The dam, a minor French 1m winner, is a half-sister to 6 winners. The second dam, Mythologie (by Bering), won two races at 2 and 3 yrs in France and is a half-sister to 7 winners including Malaspina (Group 3 Prix Perth). (Hamdan Al Maktoum). *"A well-built, quality filly. She was an early foal but I still see her as one for August/September over six/seven furlongs".*

1677. MOTAHASSEN (IRE) ★★★
br.c. Lonhro – Journalist (Night Shift). May 13. Brother to the quite useful 2015 2-y-o listed-placed 5f winner Plagiarism and half-brother to the very useful 2-y-o 6f winner and Group 3 Firth Of Clyde Stakes third La Presse (by Gone West), the useful 7f and 1m winner of 4 races Paper Talk, the dual listed second Emirates Girl (both by Unbridled's Song) and the quite useful 2-y-o 7f winner Ittasal (by Any Given Saturday). The dam, a useful 2-y-o 6f winner, was second in the Group 3 6f Princess Margaret Stakes and is a half-sister to the useful sprinter Sheer Viking. The second dam, Schlefalora (by Mas Media), won at up to 1m in Sweden and is a half-sister to the 1,000 Guineas winner Las Meninas. (Hamdan Al Maktoum). *"Despite the precocity and speed on the dam's side this colt was a late foal and I see Lonhro's as normally being three and four year old types. So this year he'll be out from September onwards over seven furlongs".*

1678. MUQTANNY ★★★
b.c. Oasis Dream – Rifqah (Elusive Quality). April 9. Half-brother to the very smart Group 2 6f Greenlands Stakes and dual Group 3

winner Mustajeeb (by Nayef), to the useful 2-y-o 7f winner Muaanid (by Kheleyf) and the fair 7.5f winner Mulkeyya (by Mawatheeq). The dam is an unraced half-sister to 2 winners. The second dam, Anja (by Indian Ridge), a minor winner in the USA, is a half-sister to 4 winners including the Group 1 12f Prix du Jockey Club winner Anabaa Blue. (Hamdan Al Maktoum). *"He's a nice colt for August over six/seven furlongs".*

1679. MUZBID (IRE) ★★★
b.c. Lope De Vega – Kartiste (Kalanisi). April 22. Second foal. 70,000Y. Tattersalls October Book 2. Shadwell Estate Co. Half-brother to the quite useful 2015 2-y-o dual 5f winner Go Kart (by Intense Focus). The dam is an unraced half-sister to 2 minor winners. The second dam, Kart Star (by Soviet Star), won the listed Prix Coronation and is a half-sister to 5 winners including the listed winner and Group 1 French 1,000 Guineas second Karmifira. (Hamdan Al Maktoum). *"He's an active colt with a good action and a typical one for top of the ground. He should be out in mid-summer over six/seven furlongs".*

1680. NEOCLASSICAL (USA) ★★★
b.c. First Defence – Rio Carnival (Storm Cat). April 15. Third foal. Half-brother to the 2015 US 2-y-o Grade 3 1m placed Let's Meet In Rio (by Flatter). The dam, unplaced in two starts, is a half-sister to the top-class miler and multiple Group 1 winner Kingman and to the Group 3 Tercentenary Stakes winner Remote. The second dam, Zenda (by Zamindar), won the French 1,000 Guineas, was second in the Coronation Stakes and the Grade 1 Queen Elizabeth II Challenge Cup at Keeneland and is a half-sister to the Middle Park Stakes, July Cup and Nunthorpe Stakes winner Oasis Dream. (Khalid Abdulla). *"He came from America and he's quite a nice colt. I see him as being a horse for seven furlongs in July".*

1681. QUICK CHAT (USA) ★★★
b.br.f. First Defence – Discuss (Danzig). May 2. Half-sister to the French 2-y-o 1m winner and dual listed-placed Argumentative (by Observatory) and to the quite useful 6f (at 2 yrs) and 7f winner Idea (by Mizzen Mast). The dam, a useful 1m winner, was listed-placed and is a closely related to the French Group

3 10.5f winner Dance Dress (herself dam of the US dual Grade 2 winner Costume). The second dam, Private Line (by Private Account), a useful 7f (at 2 yrs) and listed 1m winner, is a half-sister to the listed winner and Group 1 placed Most Precious. (Khalid Abdulla). *"She's quite nice and I should be getting her out from August onwards. One for six/seven furlongs".*

1682. RICH HISTORY (IRE) ★★★
ch.c. Dubawi – Polished Gem (Danehill). February 6. Sixth foal. Half-brother to the Group 1 10f Prince Of Wales's Stakes winner Free Eagle (by High Chaparral), to the Group 2 12f British Champions Fillies' and Mares Stakes and dual Group 3 winner Sapphire (by Medicean) and the very smart triple Group 2 1m and triple Group 3 winner Custom Cut (by Notnowcato). The dam, an Irish 2-y-o 7f winner, is a sister to the Grade 1 9f Matriarch Stakes and Group 2 1m Sun Chariot Stakes winner Dress To Thrill and a half-sister to 7 winners. The second dam, Trusted Partner (by Affirmed), won the Irish 1,000 Guineas and is a sister to the useful winners Easy to Copy, Epicure's Garden and Low Key Affair. (Moyglare Stud Farm). *"He's a nice colt although he doesn't resemble his half-brother Free Eagle. He'll be one for August/September over seven furlongs".*

1683. RIGHT HONORABLE (IRE) ★★★
b.c. Famous Name – Agnetha (Big Shuffle). March 2. Tenth foal. 65,000Y. Tattersalls October Book 2. Bobby O'Ryan. Half-brother to 6 winners including the US dual Grade 3 winner Starstruck, the quite useful Irish 1m and 9f winner Anaverna (both by Galileo), the quite useful Irish 7f winner Scarlet O'Hara (by Sadler's Wells) and the quite useful 10f to 12f winner Der Meister (by Mastercraftsman). The dam won the listed Silver Flash Stakes (at 2 yrs) and the Group 3 5f King George Stakes and is a sister to the German Group 2 sprint winner Areion and to the Irish listed winner Anna Frid and a half-sister to 5 winners. The second dam, Aerleona (by Caerleon), a German 2-y-o 6f winner, is a half-sister to 5 winners including the Fillies' Mile winner Nepula. (Dr Ronan Lambe). *"He's a little bit more immature than my other 2-y-o by Famous Name, but I would still see him running from July onwards over six/seven furlongs".*

1684. ROYAL VIGIL (IRE) ★★★★
b.c. Shamardal – Spoil Yourself (Distorted Humor). March 31. Second foal. The dam is an unraced half-sister to the Group 2 12f Ribblesdale Stakes winner and Irish Oaks third Princess Highway, to the smart Irish Group 3 7f Gladness Stakes winner and multiple Group 1 placed Mad About You (by Indian Ridge) and the smart Group 1 Irish St Leger and dual Group 3 winner of 9 races Royal Diamond (by King's Best). The second dam, Irresistible Jewel (by Danehill), won the Group 2 12f Ribblesdale Stakes and the Group 3 10f Blandford Stakes and is a half-sister to 7 winners including the listed 12f winner Diamond Trim. (Moyglare Stud Farm). *"He's a nice colt and worth mentioning in the book. One for September onwards over seven furlongs".*

1685. SOLO SAXOPHONE (IRE) ★★★★
b.c. Frankel – Society Hostess (Seeking The Gold). April 18. Fourth foal. Half-brother to the useful listed-placed 6f winner Sailors Swan (by Henrythenavigator). The dam, a US Grade 3 7f and German listed winner, is a half-sister to several winners. The second dam, Touch Of Truth (by Storm Cat), a minor US winner of 2 races at 4 yrs, is a half-sister to 8 winners including the US Grade 1 winner Twilight Agenda and the dams of the Group/Grade 1 winners Refuse To Bend, Media Puzzle and Go And Go. (Moyglare Stud Farm). *"A late summer/autumn type 2-y-o, he's a nice medium-sized colt with good conformation. He's straightforward, immature at this time, but he'll make up into a nice horse".*

1686. SORELLE DELLE ROSE (IRE) ★★★★
gr.f. Dark Angel – Kelsey Rose (Most Welcome). March 16. Tenth foal. €350,000Y. Goffs Orby. Moyglare Stud Farm. Half-sister to 5 winners including the Group 1 Lockinge Stakes second Sovereign Debt and the Group 3 Fred Darling Stakes winner Puff (by Camacho), the quite useful 2-y-o dual 7f winner Marked Card (by Kheleyf) and the fair 2-y-o 6f winner Golden Rosie (by Exceed And Excel). The dam, a fairly useful 2-y-o 5f winner of 3 races, was listed-placed three times and is a half-sister to 3 winners. The second

dam, Duxyana (by Cyrano de Bergerac), is an unraced half-sister to 8 winners. (Moyglare Stud Farm). *"She's a quality-looking 2-y-o for May/June over five/six furlongs. A very correct filly"*.

1687. SWITCH IN TIME (IRE) ★★★★
b.f. Galileo – Switch (Quiet American). March 2. First foal. The dam won five races including the Grade 1 7f La Brea Stakes and the Grade 1 7f Santa Monica Stakes and is a half-sister to 4 winners including the minor US stakes winner Keystone Gulch. The second dam, Antoniette (by Nicholas), a Grade 3 and dual listed winner in the USA, is a half-sister to 8 winners including the US dual listed stakes winner French Charmer. (Moyglare Stud Farm). *"She's a quality, bay filly with a lovely white star and she'll be very nice in September and October over seven furlongs"*.

1688. TEMPERA ★★★★
b.f. Dansili – Portodora (Kingmambo). February 9. Fourth foal. Half-sister to the fairly useful 7f winner of 4 races Peril (by Pivotal) and to the quite useful 9f (at 2 yrs) and 10f winner Dissolution (by New Approach). The dam, a quite useful dual 7f winner, is a half-sister to 2 winners. The second dam, High Walden (by El Gran Senor), a smart 2-y-o 1m winner, was Group-placed and is closely related to the Oaks, Fillies Mile, Musidora Stakes and May Hill Stakes winner Reams of Verse and a half-sister to the Group 1 10f Coral Eclipse Stakes and Group 1 10f Phoenix Champion Stakes winner Elmaamul (by Diesis). (Khalid Abdulla). *"A very nice filly. She'll be lovely in the autumn going six/seven furlongs"*.

1689. TILLY TROTTER (IRE) ★★★★
b.f. Kodiac – Inourthoughts (Desert Style). March 10. Fourth foal. 90,000Y. Tattersalls October Book 2. D K Weld. Half-sister to the unplaced 2015 2-y-o Dreaming Of Rio (by Captain Rio) and to the fair 2-y-o dual 6f winner Focusofourthoughts (by Intense Focus). The dam, a quite useful Irish 2-y-o 5f winner, is a half-sister to 3 winners including the 2-y-o Group 2 Flying Childers Stakes winner Green Door. The second dam, Inourhearts (by Pips Pride), a useful listed 5f winner of 4 races, is a half-sister to 2 winners. (Mr Frank Gillespie). *"Already a winner at Dundalk over five*

furlongs, she's a sharp, very attractive filly. The plan now is to head for the listed six furlong race at Naas about three weeks before Royal Ascot. A very good-looking, precocious filly".

1690. TOCCO D'AMORE (IRE) ★★★★
b.f. Raven's Pass – Spirit Of Tara (Sadler's Wells). April 19. Twelfth foal. €2,000,000Y. Goffs Orby. Moyglare Stud Farm. Half-sister to the high-class Group 2 1m and Group 3 1m and 9f winner Echo Of Light (by Dubai Millennium), to the smart dual 12f listed winner Akarem, the Irish listed-placed 1m and 9f winner Multazem (both by Kingmambo), the useful 1m winner and Group 1 Coronation Stakes third Irish History (by Dubawi) and the useful listed-placed 10f winner Flame Of Gibraltar (by Rock Of Gibraltar). The dam, a 12f winner and second in the Group 2 Blandford Stakes, is a sister to Salsabil (1,000 Guineas, Oaks, Irish Derby and Prix Vermeille) and a half-sister to the Group 1 St James's Palace Stakes winner Marju. The second dam, Flame Of Tara (by Artaius), won the Coronation Stakes. (Moyglare Stud Farm). *"A quality filly, she has a nice bit of leg to her and she's doing everything right at the moment. One we'd aim to run over seven furlongs and a mile in September"*.

1691. UGNEYA (IRE) ★★★
br.f. Teofilo – Zahoo (Nayef). March 7. Third foal. Half-sister to the 2015 2-y-o 1m winner on her only start Zaakhir (by Raven's Pass) and to the very useful listed 7.5f (at 2 yrs) and Group 3 1m winner Convergence (by Cape Cross). The dam, a fairly useful 1m (at 2 yrs) and 10f winner and listed 10f second, is a half-sister to the smart Group 3 14f winner Tactic. The second dam, Tanaghum (by Darshaan), a useful listed-placed 10f winner, is a half-sister to 7 winners including the smart Group 2 10f Premio Lydia Tesio winner Najah. (Hamdan Al Maktoum). *"A very nice filly and one for August/September over seven furlongs, the dam's first two foals both won as 2-y-o's"*.

1692. ZIRCONIA ★★★★
b.c. Dansili – Zaminast (Zamindar). January 26. First foal. The dam, a useful listed 10f winner, is a sister the high-class Famous Name, a winner of 21 races including the Group 2 Royal Whip Stakes and twelve Group 3

events in Ireland from 1m to 10f and to the very useful Irish dual Group 3 7f winner Big Break and a half-sister to numerous winners. The second dam, Fame At Last (by Quest For Fame), a fairly useful 2-y-o 7f winner, is a half-sister to one winner. (Khalid Abdulla). *"A nice, big, very active colt. Surprisingly for a first foal he's big, lengthy and scopey. I see him running in September over seven furlongs to a mile".*

1693. UNNAMED ★★★★
ch.c. Galileo – Caumshinaun (Indian Ridge). February 28. Brother to the Group 1 Irish 1,000 Guineas winner Nightime, to the fairly useful 12f and 2m winner Olympiad and the quite useful 11f and 12f winner Phaenomena, closely related to the quite useful 11f winner Tajriba (by Teofilo) and half-brother to the fairly useful dual 7f winner Gunga Din (by Green Desert), the Irish 2-y-o 1m winner and listed-placed Mermaid Island (by Mujadil) and the UAE 7f and 1m winner Straight Talk (by Refuse To Bend). The dam won 5 races from 6f to 1m in Ireland at 3 and 4 yrs including a listed event, was Group 3 placed and is a half-sister to one winner. The second dam, Ridge Pool (by Bluebird), was an Irish 2-y-o 6f winner and a half-sister to one winner. (Noel Furlong). *"An especially nice colt. He's one to look forward to from September onwards over seven furlongs to a mile".*

1694. UNNAMED ★★★
b.f. Sepoy – Elbasana (Indian Ridge). March 31. Half-sister to the 2015 2-y-o 7f winner on her only start Embiyra (by Tamayuz), to the Group 3 12f winner Edelmira (by Peintre Celebre), the dual 11f winner and listed-placed Elishpour (by Oasis Dream) and the minor French 8.5f winner Edilisa (by Azamour). The dam, unplaced on her only start, is a half-sister to the Group 1 winners Ebadiyla (Irish Oaks), Edabiya (Moyglare Stud Stakes), Estimate and Enzeli (both Ascot Gold Cup). The second dam, Ebaziya (by Darshaan), won from 7f (at 2 yrs) to 12f including three listed races and was third in the Group 2 12f Blandford Stakes. (H H Aga Khan). *"She's a nice filly and relatively forward. One for June or July over six/seven furlongs".*

Sires Reference

This section deals with those sires represented by three or more two-year-olds in the book. All the top British and Irish sires are represented and you will also see some of the best sires standing in America such as Distorted Humor, Elusive Quality, Kitten's Joy, Medaglia D'Oro, Smart Strike, Street Cry and War Front.

There are plenty of first-season sires to look out for including Bated Breath, Born To Sea, Casamento, Dragon Pulse, Elzaam, Excelebration, Famous Name, Foxwedge, Harbour Watch, Helmet, Mayson, Nathaniel, Power, Requinto, Sepoy, Sir Prancealot and of course Frankel.

Please note that the reference numbers given with each sire correspond with their two-year-olds in the book.

ACCLAMATION (2000) Royal Applause – Princess Athena (Ahonoora). *Racing record:* Won 6 times, including Diadem Stakes. Also placed in King's Stand and Nunthorpe. *Stud record:* This is his Tenth crop and his Group winners to date are Dark Angel (G1 Middle Park Stakes), Equiano (G1 King's Stand Stakes), Harbour Watch, Saayerr (both winners of the G2 Richmond Stakes), Lidar (Group 2 in Australia), Lilbourne Lad (G2 Railway Stakes), Angels Will Fall (G3 Princess Margaret Stakes), Alsindi (G3 Oh So Sharp Stakes), Hitchens (G3 Greenlands Stakes), Ponty Acclaim (G3 Cornwallis Stakes), Talwar (G3 Solario Stakes) and Sparkling Power (G3 in Hong Kong). He also has numerous listed winners to his name. Standing at Rathbarry Stud, Ireland. *2016 fee:* €30,000.

APPROVE (2008) Oasis Dream – Wyola (Sadler's Wells). *Racing record:* Won three races at 2 yrs including the Group 2 5f Norfolk Stakes and the Group 2 6f Gimcrack Stakes and third in the Group 1 6f Middle Park Stakes. Unraced after his 2-y-o career. *Stud record:* With two crops to have raced so far his best are the smart Group 3 and listed sprint winner Waady and the Irish listed winner and Group 2 Flying Childers Stakes third Accepted. Now standing in Turkey. *2016 fee:* 9,000 Turkish Lira.

AQLAAM (2005) Oasis Dream – Bourbonella (Rainbow Quest). *Racing record:* Won the Group 1 Prix de Moulin and the Group 2 Jersey Stakes. *Stud record:* With three crops racing his best offspring include Moonee Valley (Group 3 Prix des Reservoirs), the useful miler Mitraad, the listed-placed winner Nabbaash and the listed Radley Stakes winner Aqlaam Vision. Standing at Nunnery Stud. Died in 2013.

ARAKAN (2000) Nureyev – Far Across (Common Grounds). *Racing record:* Won 6 races including the Group 3 Criterion Stakes, the Group 3 Supreme Stakes (both 7f), the listed Abernant Stakes and the City Of York Stakes (both 6f). *Stud record:* His best winners to date are the dual Group 1 and dual Group 2 winning miler Dick Turpin, the Group 1 National Stakes and triple Group 2 winner Toormore, the dual Group 2 and dual Group 3 winner Trumpet Major and the Irish dual Group 3 winner Sruthan. Standing at Ballyhane Stud. *2016 fee:* €3,500.

ARCANO (2007) Oasis Dream – Tariysha (Daylami). *Racing record:* Won three races at 2 yrs including the Group 1 6f Prix Morny and the Group 2 6f July Stakes. *Stud record:* This is his third crop racing. To date his highest rated offspring are the French winner and Group 2 placed King Genki, the Italian 2-y-o Group 3 winner Misterious Boy, the winner and Group 3 placed Mustadeem and the Irish listed-placed winner Tamadhor. Standing in Italy. *2016 fee:* €5,000.

ARCH (1995) Kris S – Aurora (Danzig). *Racing record:* 5 wins including the Super Derby and the Fayette Stakes. *Stud record:* Best winners so far include Arravale (Grade 1 Del Mar Oaks), Archarcharch (Grade 1 Arkansas Derby), Hymn Book (Grade 1 Donn Handicap), Blame (three US Grade 1 wins), Les Arcs (Golden Jubilee Stakes and July Cup), Love Theway Youare (Grade 1 Vanity Handicap), Overarching (South African dual Group 1 winner), Pine Island (dual US Grade 1 winner), Prince Arch (US Grade 1 winner), Montgomery's Arch (Group 2 Richmond Stakes), Pomology (Group 2 Lancashire Oaks), Waterway Run (Group 3 Oh So Sharp Stakes) and the Hong Kong Group 3 winner Art Trader. Standing at Claiborne Farm, Kentucky. *2016 fee:* $40,000.

ARCHIPENKO (2004) Kingmambo – Bound (Nijinsky). *Racing record:* Won the Group 1 10f Audemars Piguet Queen Elizabeth II Cup at Sha Tin and five other Group races including the Group 2 Summer Mile. *Stud record:* His third crop appeared in 2015 and his best winners to date are Madame Chiang (Group 1 British Champions Fillies/Mare Stakes), the South African Group 2 winner Kingston Mines and the listed winners Lady Penko (also Group 1 third), Algonquin, Medrano, Russian Punch and Time Warp. Standing at Lanwades Stud, Newmarket. *2016 fee:* £10,000.

AUSSIE RULES (2003) Danehill – Last Second (Alzao). *Racing record:* Won four races including the US Grade 1 Shadwell Turf Mile and the Group 1 French 2,000 Guineas. *Stud record:* His best winners to date are Fiesolana (Group 1 Matron Stakes), Djumama (two Group 3 wins in Germany), Duck Feet (Group 3 Premio Guido Berardelli), the Australian Group 3 winner Hard Ball Get and 14 listed winners including the Group placed Aussie Reigns, Bertinoro, Boomerang Bob, Cazals, Chinese Wall, Dinkum Diamond, Grand Treasure, Kramulkie and Private Jet. Standing at Lanwades Stud, Newmarket. *2016 fee:* £7,000.

AUTHORIZED (2004) Montjeu – Funsie (Saumarez). *Racing record:* Won four races including the Group 1 Racing Post Trophy, Epsom Derby, Juddmonte International (all Group 1 events). *Stud record:* The sire of four Group 1 winners to date – Ambivalent (Pretty Polly Stakes), Complacent, Hartnell (both in Australia) and Seal Of Approval (Qipco British Champions Fillies/Mare Stakes). His other stakes performers include the Australian Group 2 winner Maygrove and six Group 3 winners including Rehn's Nest (Park Express Stakes) and Sugar Boy (Sandown Classic Trial). Standing at Haras Du Logis. *2016 fee:* €10,000.

AZAMOUR (2001) Night Shift – Asmara (Lear Fan). *Racing record:* Won the St James's Palace Stakes, Irish Champion Stakes, Prince of Wales's Stakes and King George VI and Queen Elizabeth Diamond Stakes. *Stud record:* First runners appeared in 2009. Best winners to date include Covert Love (Group 1 Irish Oaks & Group 1 Prix de l'Opera), Valyra (Group 1 Prix de Diane), Dolniya (Group 1 Dubai Sheema Classic), the Group 2 winners Eleonora Duse, Shankardeh and Wade Giles and seven Group 3 winners including Azmeel, Colombian, Liber Nauticus and Native Khan. Died in 2014.

BAHAMIAN BOUNTY (1994) Cadeaux Genereux – Clarentia (Ballad Rock). *Racing record:* Winner of 3 races at 2 yrs, notably the Prix Morny and the Middle Park Stakes. *Stud record:* Sire of the Group 1 winners Pastoral Pursuits (July Cup) and Goodricke (Sprint Cup), the US Grade 2 winner Mister Napper Tandy, the Group 2 Hungerford Stakes winner Breton Rock, the 2-y-o Group 2 winners Anjaal and Sendmylovetorose and the Group 3 winners Cay Verde, Coral Mist, Donnerschlag, Life's A Bounty, Naahy, New Providence and Topatoo. Standing at the National Stud, Newmarket. *2016 fee:* £8,500.

BATED BREATH (2007) Dansili – Tantina (Distant View). *Racing record:* Winner of 6 races over 5f and 6f from 3 to 5yrs, notably the Group 2 Temple Stakes and placed in five Group 1 events. *Stud record:* First crop now two-year-olds. Standing at Banstead Manor Stud, Newmarket. *2016 fee:* £10,000.

BIG BAD BOB (2000) Bob Back – Fantasy Girl (Marju). *Racing record:* Won 8 races including a Group 3 10f event in Germany and listed races at Ascot (1m) and Deauville (10f). *Stud record:* His first crop appeared on the racecourse in 2010. To date he's had four Group 3 winners in Ireland (Berg Bahn, Bible Belt, Bocca Baciata and Brendan Brackan) and five listed winners (Backbench Blues, Bible Black and Bob Le Beau, Cherie Good and Tashweeq). Standing at the Irish National Stud. *2016 fee:* €9,000.

BLAME (2006) Arch – Liable (Seeking The Gold). *Racing record:* Won three Grade 1 events over 9f and 10f (Stephen Foster Handicap, Whitney Handicap and Breeders' Cup Classic) and three other Graded stakes. *Stud record:* His first crop of runners appeared in 2014 and his best to date include the US Grade 2 and Grade 3 winner March, the US

Grade 3 winner Far From Over, two listed winners and three Graded stakes placed horses. Standing at Claiborne Farm, Kentucky. *2016 fee:* $25,000.

BORN TO SEA (2009) Invincible Spirit – Urban Sea (Miswaki). *Racing record:* Won a listed 2-y-o event in Ireland and was second in the Group 1 Irish Derby, the Group 2 Royal Whip Stakes and the Group 3 Killavullen Stakes. *Stud record:* A half-brother to Galileo and Sea The Stars, his first two-year-olds appear this year. Standing at Gilltown Stud in Ireland. *2016 fee:* €10,000.

BULLET TRAIN (2007) Sadler's Wells – Kind (Danehill). *Racing record:* Won two races including the Group 3 Lingfield Derby Trial. *Stud record:* A three-parts brother to Frankel, his first crop are now two-year-olds. Standing at Crestwood Farm, Kentucky. *2016 fee:* $7,500.

BUSHRANGER (2006) Danetime – Danz Danz (Efisio). Race record: Won the Group 1 Prix Morny and the Group 1 Middle Park Stakes, both at 2 yrs. *Stud record:* From three crops racing he's had plenty of minor winners including a listed winner in Turkey, plus eight listed-placed horses here and abroad. Standing at Tally Ho Stud, Ireland. *2016 fee:* €2,500.

CACIQUE (2001) Danehill – Hasili (Kahyasi). *Race record:* Won 18 races from 3 to 5 yrs including the Grade 1 11f Man O'War Stakes, Grade 1 10f Manhattan Handicap and the Grade 2 1m Prix Daniel Wildenstein. *Stud record:* From limited books of mares he has the Group 1 winners Dominant (Hong Kong Vase), Mutual Trust (Prix Jean Prat) and Slumber (Manhattan Stakes), along with the Group 2 Prix de Chaudenay winner Canticum and the Group 3 Geoffrey Freer Stakes winner Census. Standing at Banstead Manor Stud, Newmarket. *2016 fee:* £12,500.

CANFORD CLIFFS (2007) Tagula – Mrs Marsh (Marju). *Racing record:* Won 7 races at 2 to 4 yrs and from 6f to 1m including the Irish 2,000 Guineas, St James's Palace Stakes, Sussex Stakes, Lockinge Stakes and Queen Anne Stakes (all Group 1 events). *Stud record:* His first crop of two-year-olds appeared in 2015 and he's had plenty of winners including the Group 2 Railway Stakes winner Painted Cliffs, the Group 3 Balanchine Stakes winner Most Beautiful and the French listed winner Aktoria. Standing at Coolmore Stud in Ireland. *2016 fee:* €17,500.

CAPE BLANCO (2007) Galileo – Laurel Delight (Presidium). *Racing record:* Won 9 races including the Irish Derby, Irish Champion Stakes, Man O'War Stakes, Arlington Million and Turf Classic (all Group/Grade 1 events). *Stud record:* His first crop were two-year-olds in 2015 but he's had limited success. Now standing in Japan.

CAPE CROSS (1994) Green Desert – Park Appeal (Ahonoora). *Racing record:* Won 4 races including the Lockinge Stakes, Queen Anne Stakes and Celebration Mile. *Stud record:* First runners in 2003. Sire of eleven Group 1 winners including two outstanding colt in Sea The Stars (2,000 Guineas, Derby, Prix de l'Arc de Triomphe, etc) and Golden Horn (Derby, Eclipse Stakes, Irish Champion Stakes and Prix de l'Arc de Triomphe), the top-class Ouija Board (7 Group 1 wins including the Oaks & the Breeders' Cup Filly and Mare Turf), Behkabad (Grand Prix de Paris), Nayarra (Group 1 Gran Criterium), the Hong Kong triple Group 1 winner Able One and the Australasian horses Gaze, I'm Your Man, Kindacross, Mikki Street and Seachange. His 20 Group 2 winners include Cape Dollar, Crystal Capella, Halicarnassus, Hatta Fort, Joviality, Moohaajim, Russian Cross, Sabana Perdida and Treat Gently. Standing at Kildangan Stud, Ireland. *2016 fee:* €20,000.

CAPTAIN RIO (2000) Pivotal – Beloved Visitor (Miswaki). *Racing record:* Won 4 times including the Criterium de Maisons-Laffitte at 2 yrs. *Stud record:* His best progeny to date include the Australian triple Group 1 winner Terravista, the New Zealand Group 1 winner Il Quello Veloce, the Australian Group 1 winner Brazilian Pulse, the New Zealand Group 2 winner Riomoral and the Group 3 winners Ainippe, Art Beat, Capt Chaos, Energised, Philario and Red Badge. Standing at Ballyhane Stud, Ireland. *2016 fee:* €3,500.

CASAMENTO (2008) Shamardal – Wedding Gift (Always Fair). *Racing record:* Won four races including the Group 1 Racing Post Trophy, the Group 2 Beresford Stakes (both at 2 yrs) and the Group 3 Prix du Prince d'Orange). *Stud record:* His first two-year-olds race this season. Standing at Dalham Hall Stud, Newmarket. *2016 fee:* £5,000.

CHAMPS ELYSEES (2003) Danehill – Hasili (Kahyasi). *Race record:* Won the Canadian International, the Hollywood Turf Cup and the Northern Dancer Turf Stakes (all Grade 1). *Stud record:* With three crops to have raced so far he's the sire of the winners of over 160 races including the Group 1 Ascot Gold Cup winner Trip To Paris, the Group 3 Silver Flash Stakes winner and Group 1 Irish Oaks second Jack Naylor, the Group 3 winner and French 1,000 Guineas third Xcellence and the listed winners and Group placed Avenue Gabriel, Eastern Belle, Lustrous and Regardez. Standing at Banstead Manor Stud, Newmarket. *2016 fee:* £8,000.

CLODOVIL 2001 Danehill – Clodora (Linamix). *Racing record:* Won 5 races including the French 2,000 Guineas. *Stud record:* His first crop were two-year-olds in 2007 and his best winners to date are Nahoodh (Group 1 Falmouth Stakes), Moriarty (Group 1 and three Group 2's in Australia), the Group 2 winners Es Que Love, Gregorian, Laugh Out Loud and Shining Emerald, the dual Group 3 winner Beacon Lodge and ten listed winners. Standing at Rathasker Stud, Ireland. *2016 fee:* €10,000.

COMPTON PLACE (1994) Indian Ridge – Nosey (Nebbiolo). *Racing record:* Won 3 races, notably the July Cup. *Stud record:* First runners in 2002. Sire of 11 Group winners and 13 listed winners, notably the dual Group 1 Nunthorpe Stakes winner Borderlescott, the Group 2 and multiple Group 3 winner Deacon Blues, the US Grade 2 winner Passified, the Group 2 winners Godfrey Street, Pearl Secret and Prolific, the Group 3 winners Easy Road, Hunter Street, Intrepid Jack, Minal, Pleasure Place, Champion Place and Shifting Place, and numerous useful performers including Angus News, Boogie Street, Compton's Eleven, If Paradise, Judd Street, Hunter Street, Master Of War, Pacific Pride and Pearl Secret. Died in 2015.

DALAKHANI (2001) Darshaan – Daltawa (Miswaki). *Racing record:* Won 8 of his 9 starts, including the Prix du Jockey Club and the Arc. *Stud record:* First crop were two-year-olds in 2007. *Stud record:* To date he's bred the Group 1 winners Conduit (St Leger, Breeders' Cup Turf (twice), King George VI & Queen Elizabeth Stakes), Integral (Sun Chariot and Falmouth Stakes), Moonstone (Irish Oaks), Chinese White (Pretty Polly Stakes), Reliable Man (Prix du Jockey Club), Duncan (Irish St Leger), Second Step (Grosser Preis von Berlin) and Seismos (Grosser Preis von Bayen). His nine Group 2 winners are Alex My Boy, Armure, Candarliya, Centennial, Democratie, Guardini, Silk Sari, Terrubi, Vadamar. There are a further ten Group 3 winners to his name. Standing at Haras de Bonneval, France. *2016 fee:* €15,000.

DANDY MAN (2003) Mozart – Lady Alexander (Night Shift). *Racing record:* Won 6 races including the Group 3 5f Palace House Stakes and two listed events. *Stud record:* Has sired the winners of over 135 races to date including plenty of 2-y-o's. His best runners to date are the Hong Kong Group 1 winner Peniaphobia, the Group 3 and listed winner Extortionist and the triple Group 2 placed Parbold. Standing at Ballyhane Stud. *2016 fee:* €8,000.

DANEHILL DANCER (1993) Danehill – Mira Adonde (Sharpen Up). *Racing record:* Winner of 4 races, including the Phoenix Stakes and National Stakes at 2 yrs and the Greenham at 3. *Stud record:* Sire of numerous Group 1 winners including Again, Alexander Tango, Atomic Force, Choisir, Dancing Rain, Lillie Langtry, Mastercraftsman, Planteur, Private Steer, Speciosa and Where Or When. Standing at Coolmore Stud, Ireland. Retired from stud.

DANSILI (1996) Danehill – Hasili (Kahyasi). *Racing record:* Won 5 races in France and placed in six Group/Grade 1 events including Sussex Stakes and Breeders' Cup Mile. *Stud record:* First runners in 2004. Sire of 19 Group/Grade 1 winners including Rail Link (Arc, Grand Prix de Paris), Harbinger (King George VI), Emulous (Matron Stakes), Fallen For You (Coronation Stakes), Flintshire (Grand Prix de Paris, etc), Foreteller (three in Australia), Giofra (Falmouth Stakes), Miss France (1,000 Guineas), Passage of Time (Criterium de Saint-Cloud), The Fugue (four Group 1's), We Are (Prix de l'Opera), Winsili (Nassau Stakes), Zoffany (Phoenix Stakes), Zambezi Sun (Grand Prix de Paris) and in the USA Dank, Laughing, Price Tag and Proviso. Standing at Banstead Manor Stud, Newmarket. *2016 fee:* £85,000.

DARK ANGEL (2005) Acclamation – Midnight Angel (Machiavellian). *Racing record:* Won four races at 2 yrs including the Group 1 Middle Park Stakes. *Stud record:* First runners 2011. Has built himself an excellent reputation. His best winners to date are Lethal Force (Group 1 July Cup & Group 1 Diamond Jubilee Stakes), Mecca's Angel (Group 1 Nunthorpe Stakes), Alhebayeb (Group 2 July Stakes), Birchwood (Group 2 Superlative Stakes), Estidhkaar (Group 2 Champagne Stakes & Group 2 Superlative Stakes), Gutaifan (Group 2 Flying Childers Stakes), the Group 3 winners Exogenesis, Heeraat, Lily's Angel, Markaz, Realtra, Sovereign Debt and Stormfly and eleven listed winners. Stands at Yeomanstown Stud, Ireland. *2016 fee:* €60,000.

DELEGATOR (2006) Dansili – Indian Love Bird (Efisio). *Racing record:* Won five races including the Group 2 Duke Of York Stakes and the Group 3 Craven Stakes. Second in the 2,000 Guineas and the St James's Palace Stakes. *Stud record:* His first runners appear this year. Standing at Overbury Stud. *2016 fee:* £4,000.

DICK TURPIN (2007) Arakan – Merrily (Sharrock). *Racing record:* Won 9 races from 6f to a mile and from 2 to 4 yrs including the Group 1 Prix Jean Prat and the Group 1 Premio Vittorio de Capua. *Stud record:* His first crop were two-year-olds in 2015 and he had four winners. Standing at the National Stud in Newmarket. 2015 stud fee: £3,000.

DISTORTED HUMOR (1993) Forty Niner – Danzig's Beauty (Danzig). *Racing record:* Won 11 races in the USA including the Champagne Stakes, Futurity Stakes, Haskell Invitational and Travers Stakes (all Grade 1). Champion 2-y-o. *Stud record:* Sire of fifteen Grade 1 winners – Aesop's Fables, Any Given Saturday, Awesome Humor, Bit Of Whimsy, Boisterous, Commentator, Cursory Glance, Drosselmeyer, Flower Alley, Fourty Niner's Son, Funny Cide, Hystericalady, Jimmy Creed, Pathfork and Rinky Dink. Standing at Win Star Farm, Kentucky. *2016 fee:* $100,000.

DRAGON PULSE (2009) Kyllachy – Poetical (Croco Rouge). *Racing record:* Won the Group 2 7f Futurity Stakes at the Curragh (at 2 yrs) and the Group 3 1m Prix de Fontainebleau. Second in the Group 1 National Stakes. *Stud record:* His first two-year-olds appear this year. Standing at the Irish National Stud. *2016 fee:* €5,000.

DREAM AHEAD (2008) Diktat – Land Of Dreams (Cadeaux Genereux). *Racing record:* Won five Group 1 races from 6f to 7f, at 2 and 3 yrs (Prix Morny, Middle Park Stakes, July Cup, Haydock Park Sprint Cup and Prix de la Foret). *Stud record:* His first crop were two-year-olds in 2015 and he had a good start to his stud career with the winners of 32 races, notably the Group 2 Criterium de Maisons-Laffitte winner Donjuan Triumphant and the Group 3 Anglesey Stakes winner Final Frontier. Standing at Ballylinch Stud in Ireland. 2015 stud fee: €17,500.

DUBAWI (2002) Dubai Millennium – Zomaradah (Deploy). *Racing record:* Won the National Stakes at 2 and the Irish 2,000 Guineas and Prix Jacques le Marois at 3. Third in the Derby. *Stud record:* An exceptional sire responsible for 65 Group winners including 23 Group 1 scorers. They include Al Kazeem (three Group 1's), Arabian Queen (Juddmonte International), Dubawi Heights (Gamely Stakes, Yellow Ribbon Stakes), Happy Archer (two Group 1's in Australia), Hunters Light (three Group 1's in Italy and Dubai), Lucky Nine (Hong Kong Sprint), Makfi (2,000 Guineas, Prix Jacques le Marois), Monterosso & Prince Bishop (both Dubai World Cup winners), , New Bay (French Derby), Night Of Thunder (2,000 Guineas and Lockinge Stakes), Poet's Voice (Queen Elizabeth II Stakes), Postponed (King George VI), Secret Admirer (two Group 1's in Australia), Sheikhzayedroad (Northern Dancer Turf Stakes), Waldpark (German Derby) and Willow Magic (in South Africa). Standing at Dalham Hall Stud, Newmarket. *2016 fee:* £225,000.

DUKE OF MARMALADE (2004) Danehill – Love Me True (Kingmambo). *Racing record:* Won 6 races including the Juddmonte International Stakes, King George VI and Queen Elizabeth Stakes, Prince of Wales's Stakes, Tattersalls Gold Cup and Prix Ganay. *Stud record:* His first two year olds appeared in 2012. His 14 Group winners to date include Nutan (Group 1 German Derby), Simple Verse (Group 1 St Leger), Star Of Seville (Group 1 Prix de Diane) and the Group 2 winners Big Orange (Princess Of Wales's Stakes and Goodwood Cup) and Big Memory (in Australia). Now standing in South Africa.

DUTCH ART (2004) Medicean – Halland Park Lass (Spectrum). *Race Record:* Won four races at 2 yrs including the Group 1 Prix Morny and the Group 1 Middle Park Stakes. *Stud record:* Leading first crop sire in 2011 and a consistently good sire ever since. His best winners to date include Slade Power (dual Group 1 6f winner), Garswood (Group 1 Prix Maurice de Gheest), Caspar Netscher (Group 2 Mill Reef Stakes and Group 2 Gimcrack Stakes), Producer (Group 2 in Turkey and the Group 3 Supreme Stakes), Dutch Connection (Group 3 Jersey Stakes and Group 3 Acomb Stakes), Dutch Masterpiece (Group 3 Flying Five), Lady's First (Group 3 Atalanta Stakes) and Lohit (Group 3 Premio Omenoni), along with eleven listed winners. Standing at Cheveley Park Stud. *2016 fee:* £40,000.

ELNADIM (1994) Danzig – Elle Seule (Exclusive Native). *Racing record:* Won 5 races, notably the July Cup and the Diadem Stakes. *Stud record:* Sire of the New Zealand Group 1 winner Culminate, the smart performers Al Qasi (Group 3 Phoenix Stakes), Caldra (Group 3 Autumn Stakes), Elletelle (Group 2 Queen Mary Stakes), Elnawin (Group 3 Sirenia Stakes), Wi Dud (Group 2 Flying Childers Stakes), Soraaya (Group 3 Princess Margaret Stakes), New Zealand Group 3 winners Accardo, Elblitzem and Pendragon, the US Grade 3 winner Pasar Silbano and the dual listed winner Almass. *2014 fee:* €4,000. Died January 2015.

ELUSIVE CITY (2000) Elusive Quality – Star Of Paris (Dayjur). *Racing record:* Won the 2-y-o Group 1 6f Prix Morny and third in the 2-y-o Group 1 6f Middle Park Stakes. *Stud record:* Sire of Elusive Wave (French 2,000 Guineas), three Group 1 winners in New Zealand, the 2-y-o Group 2 Criterium de Maisons Laffitte winner Kiram, three Group 2 winners in New Zealand and Australia, and seven Group 3 winners. Standing at Haras d'Etreham. *2016 fee:* €8,000.

ELUSIVE PIMPERNEL (2007) Elusive Quality – Cara Fantasy (Sadler's Wells). *Racing record:* Won the Group 3 7f Acomb Stakes (at 2 yrs) and the Group 3 1m Craven Stakes. Second in the Group 1 Racing Post Trophy. *Stud record:* His first crop were two-year-olds in 2015 and he has sired the winners of 9 races, plus two listed-placed. Standing at the Irish National Stud. *2015 stud fee:* €1,000.

ELUSIVE QUALITY (1993) Gone West – Touch of Greatness (Hero's Honor). *Racing record:* Won 9 races in USA including Grade 3 events at 7f/1m. *Stud record:* Sire of top-class Kentucky Derby/Preakness Stakes winner Smarty Jones, Breeders' Cup Classic and Queen Elizabeth II Stakes winner Raven's Pass, Prix Morny winner Elusive City, dual Group 1 winner Elusive Kate, Australian multiple Group 1 winner Sepoy, the US Grade 1 winners Quality Road and Maryfield, the Group winning two-year-olds Certify, Elusive Pimpernel and Evasive, numerous US graded stakes winners including Chimichurri, Elusive Diva, Girl Warrior, Omega Code, Royal Michele and True Quality, the Group 2 and triple Group 3 winner Shuruq and the smart dual listed winner Baharah. Standing at Jonabell Farm, Kentucky. *2016 fee:* $40,000.

ELZAAM (2008) Redoute's Choice – Mambo In Freeport (Kingmambo). *Racing record:* A listed 6f winner at 3 yrs. As a 2-y-o he won a 6f maiden at York and was placed in the Group 2 Coventry Stakes, the Group 2 July Stakes and the Group 3 Horris Hill Stakes. *Stud record:* His first two-year-olds appear in 2016. Standing at Ballyhane Stud, Ireland. *2016 fee:* €3,500.

EQUIANO (2005) Acclamation – Entente Cordiale (Ela-Mana-Mou). *Racing record:* Won 7 races starting with two wins as a 2-y-o over 7f in Spain, before maturing into a high-class sprinter and twice capturing the Group 1 5f King's Stand Stakes. *Stud record:* His first crop of 2-y-o's appeared in 2014. His best runners to date include the Group 3 winners Dark Reckoning, Fly On The Night and Strath Burn, listed winners Belvoir Bay (in the USA), Valliano (in Australia) and Waipu Cove (in Ireland) and the smart sprinter The Tin Man. Standing at Newsells Park Stud. *2016 fee:* £7,000.

EXCEED AND EXCEL (2000) Danehill – Patrona (Lomond). *Racing record:* Champion sprinter in Australia, won 7 races including the Grade 1 Newmarket H'cap, the Grade 1 Dubai Racing Club Cup and the Grade 2 Todman Stakes. *Stud record:* There are ten Group 1 winners to his name so far - Excelebration (Queen Elizabeth II Stakes, Prix du Moulin, Prix Jacques le Marois), Margot Did (Nunthorpe Stakes), Outstrip (Breeders' Cup Juvenile Turf), Amber Sky (Group 1 Al Quoz Sprint), Guelphe, Helmet, Earthquake, Flamberge, Overreach and Reward For Effort (all in Australia). His fourteen Group 2 winners include Buratino, Fulbright, Heavy Metal, Best Terms, Infamous Angel and Masamah. Standing at Kildangan Stud, Ireland. *2016 fee:* £40,000.

EXCELEBRATION (2008) Exceed And Excel – Sun Shower (Indian Ridge). *Racing record:* Won eight races from 6f (at 2 yrs) to 1m including three Group 1 stakes – the Prix du Moulin, Prix Jacques le Marois and Queen Elizabeth II Stakes. *Stud record:* His first two-year-olds appear on the track this season. Standing at Coolmore Stud, Ireland. *2016 fee:* €15,000.

FAMOUS NAME (2005) Dansili – Fame At Last (Quest For Fame). *Racing record:* Won 21 races in Ireland from 6f (at 2 yrs) to 10f including the Group 2 Royal Whip Stakes and twelve Group 3's. *Stud record:* His first two-year-olds appear this season. Standing at the Irish National Stud, Ireland. *2016 fee:* €4,000.

FAST COMPANY (2005) Danehill Dancer – Sheezalady (Zafonic). *Racing record:* Ran only three times, all at 2 yrs, winning the Group 3 7f Acomb Stakes and finishing second in the Group 1 7f Dewhurst Stakes. *Stud record:* Sired 26 individual winners from his first crop in 2014. His best winners to date include Baitha Alga (Group 2 Norfolk Stakes), the listed winner and Group 1 Irish 1,000 Guineas third Devonshire and the Group 3 placed Al Qahwa and Fast Act, and the useful triple winner Mutarakez. Standing at Overbury Stud. *2016 fee:* €4,000.

FASTNET ROCK (2001) Danehill – Piccadilly Circus (Royal Academy). *Racing record:* Raced in Australia and won two Grade 1's, two Grade 2's and two Grade 3 events over 5f and 6f. *Stud record:* A champion sire in Australia. He's produced over 50 stakes winners to date. His 22 Group 1 winners include Atlante, Atlantic Jewel, Diamondsandrubies, Fascinating Rock, Foxwedge, Irish Lights, Lone Rock, Mosheen, Nechita, Planet Rock, Qualify, Rock 'N' Pop, Rock Classic, Sea Siren, Super Cool, Wanted and Your Song. The vast majority of them have been in Australasia. Standing at Coolmore Stud, Ireland. *2016 fee:* Private.

FIREBREAK (1999) Charnwood Forest – Breakaway (Song). *Racing record:* Won the Godolphin Mile in Dubai (twice), Challenge Stakes and Hong Kong Mile. *Stud record:* From eight crops racing he has the winners of 128 races (to Feb 2016). His best winners to date are Hearts Of Fire (Group 1 Gran Criterium), Caledonia Lady (Group 3 Sandown Sprint Stakes), Fire Ship (Group 3 Prix Quincey), the listed Radley Stakes winner Electric Feel and the useful sprinter Ashpan Sam. Standing at Bearstone Stud. *2016 fee:* £4,500.

FIRST DEFENCE (2004) Unbridled's Song – Honest Lady (Seattle Slew). *Racing record:* Won the Grade 1 7f Forego Handicap and the Grade 3 6f Jaipur Stakes. *Stud record:* With three crops racing he is the sire of the winners of 228 races (to Feb 2016). His best runners have been the US multiple Grade 1 winner and $1.6m earner Close Hatches, Dundonnell (Group 3 Acomb Stakes), Antonoe (Group 3 Prix d'Aumale) and Irish Jasper (US Grade 3 Miss Preakness Stakes). Standing at Juddmonte Farms, Kentucky. *2016 fee:* $7,500.

FOOTSTEPSINTHESAND (2002) Giant's Causeway – Glatisant (Rainbow Quest). *Racing record:* Won all 3 of his starts, notably the 2,000 Guineas. *Stud record:* His best winners include the Chachamaidee (Group 1 Matron Stakes), the Italian and Argentine Group 1 winners Infiltrada, Sand Bijou and Shamalgan, Canadian Grade 1 winner Steinbeck, ten Group 2 winners including Barefoot Lady, Formosina, Giant Sandman, Living The Life, Minakshi and, in Argentina, King Kon, Sagitariana and Sand Puce, plus ten Group 3 winners and 21 Listed winners. Standing at Coolmore Stud, Ireland. *2016 fee:* €10,000.

FOXWEDGE (2008) Fastnet Rock – Forest Native (Forest Wildcat). *Racing record:* Won 3 races in Australia including Group 1 and Group 2 events over 6f. *Stud record:* His first Northern Hemisphere crop will be two-year-olds this year. Standing at Newgate Farm, Australia.

FRANKEL (2008) Galileo – Kind (Danehill). *Racing record:* A champion at two, three and four years of age, he won all 14 of his races, from 7f to 10.5f, including ten Group 1's. *Stud record:* His first crop will be two-year-olds in 2016. Standing at Banstead Manor Stud, Newmarket. *2016 fee:* 125,000 Guineas.

FROZEN POWER (2007) Oasis Dream – Musical Treat (Royal Academy). *Racing record:* Won five races from 6f to a mile including the Group 2 German 2,000 Guineas. *Stud record:* His first crop were two-year-olds in 2015 and he had 19 individual winners. Now standing in Italy.

GALILEO (1998) Sadler's Wells – Urban Sea (Miswaki). *Racing record:* Won 6 races including the Derby, Irish Derby and King George VI and Queen Elizabeth Stakes. *Stud record:* First runners in 2005. Sire of 54 Group 1 winners, notably the outstanding champion Frankel, champion 2-y-o's Teofilo and New Approach (subsequent Derby, Champion Stakes and Irish Champion Stakes winner), Derby, Irish Derby and Juddmonte International winner Australia, the triple Group 1 winner Rip Van Winkle, Sixties Icon (St Leger), triple Group 1 winner Noble Mission, Red Rocks (Breeders' Cup Turf), Allegretto (Prix Royal-Oak), Lush Lashes (three Group 1 wins), Soldier Of Fortune (Irish Derby & Coronation Cup), Nightime (Irish 1000 Guineas), Roderic O'Connor (Criterium International, Irish 2,000 Guineas), Cape Blanco (five Group 1 wins), Nathaniel (King George VI & Queen Elizabeth Stakes), Ruler Of The World (Epsom Derby), Treasure Beach (Irish Derby, Secretariat Stakes), dual Guineas and St James's Palace winner Gleneagles, Golden Lilac (French 1,000 Guineas, Prix d'Ispahan and Prix de Diane), dual Group 1 winning 2-y-o filly Minding, triple Group 1 winner Noble Mission, Was (Oaks), Misty For Me (four Group 1 wins), Maybe (Moyglare Stud Stakes) and Galikova (Prix Vermeille). Standing at Coolmore Stud, Ireland. *2016 fee: Private.*

GIANT'S CAUSEWAY (1997) Storm Cat – Mariah's Storm (Rahy). *Racing record:* Won 9 races, 6 of them Group 1 events, including the Prix de la Salamandre, Juddmonte International and Sussex Stakes. *Stud record:* First runners in 2004. The sire of 95 Group winners including 31 Group/Grade 1 winners including Shamardal (Dewhurst Stakes, St James's Palace Stakes and Prix du Jockey Club), Footstepsinthesand (2,000 Guineas), Ghanaati (1,000 Guineas and Coronation Stakes), Aragorn & Carpe Diem (dual US Grade 1 winners), Eishin Apollon (Group 1 miler in Japan), Heatseeker (Santa Anita Handicap), Maids Causeway (Coronation Stakes), Intense Focus (Dewhurst Stakes), Eskendereya, First Samurai, My Typhoon, Swift Temper (US Grade 1 winners), Dalkala (Prix de l'Opera) and Rite of Passage (Ascot Gold Cup). Standing at Ashford Stud, Kentucky. *2016 fee: $85,000.*

HARBOUR WATCH (2009) Acclamation – Gorband (Woodman). *Racing record:* Won three races at 2 yrs (all his starts) including the Group 2 6f Richmond Stakes. *Stud record:* His first two-year-olds appear on the racecourse this year. Standing at Tweenhills Farm & Stud. *2016 fee: £7,500.*

HARD SPUN (2004) Danzig – Turkish Tryst (Turkoman). *Racing record:* Won 4 races in the USA from 7f to 9f at 3 yrs including the Grade 1 King's Bishop Stakes, the Grade 2 Kentucky Classic and the Grade 2 Lane's End Stakes. *Stud record:* Sire of 36 stakes winners including the Grade 1 winners Hard Not To Like (turf), Wicked Strong (turf), Hard Aces, Hardest Core, Questing and Smooth Roller, the US Grade 2 winner Big John B and the Group 2 5f King George V winner Moviestar. Standing at Jonabell Farm, Kentucky. *2016 fee: $45,000.*

HELLVELYN (2004) Ishiguru – Cumbrian Melody (Petong). *Racing record:* Won five races over 5f and 6f including the Group 2 Coventry Stakes (at 2 yrs) and the listed Beverley Bullet Sprint and second in the Group 1 Phoenix Stakes. *Stud record:* His first crop appeared on the racecourse in 2014 and to date he has sired around 16 individual winners, notably the 2-y-o Group 3 6f winner La Rioja and the 2-y-o Group 3 Prestige Stakes second Bonny Grey. Standing at Bucklands Farm & Stud. *2016 fee: £3,000.*

HELMET (2008) Exceed And Excel – Accessories (Singspiel). *Racing record:* Won 6 races in Australia at 3 yrs from 6f to 1m including three Group 1's. *Stud record:* His first two-year-olds appear this season. Standing at Dalham Hall Stud, Newmarket. *2016 fee: £8,000.*

HENRYTHENAVIGATOR (2005) Kingmambo – Sequoyah (Sadler's Wells) *Racing record:* Won the Sussex Stakes, St James's Palace Stakes, 2000 Guineas and Irish 2,000 Guineas. *Stud record:* With four crops to have raced he's had 3 individual Group 1 winners – George Vancouver (Grade 1 Breeders' Cup Juvenile

Turf), Pedro The Great (Group 1 Phoenix Stakes) and Sudirman (Group 1 Phoenix Stakes). He also has one Group 3 winner in Australia (Lite'n My Veins), six listed winners and the Group 2 placed Cristoforo Colombo, Zhiyi, Amerigo Vespucci, Samuel Dechamplain and Sir John Hawkins. Standing at Coolmore Stud. *2016 fee:* €7,500.

HIGH CHAPARRAL (2000) Sadler's Wells – Kasora (Darshaan). *Racing record:* Won 10 races, including the Derby, Irish Champion Stakes and Breeders' Cup Turf (twice). *Stud record:* First crop were two-year-olds in 2007. His best performers include the multiple Group 1 winner So You Think, Group 1 Sussex Stakes and Queen Anne Stakes winner Toronado, Group 1 Prince Of Wales's Stakes winner Free Eagle, Australian Group 1 winners It's A Dundeel (six Group 1 wins), Descarado, Monaco Consul and Shoot Out, German Group 1 winner Lucky Lion, Grade 1 Northern Dancer Turf Stakes winners Redwood and Wigmore Hall, Grade 1 Breeders' Cup Turf winner Wrote and High Jinx (Group 1 Prix du Cadran). Died in 2014.

HOLY ROMAN EMPEROR (2004) Danehill – L'On Vite (Secretariat). *Racing record:* Won 4 races at 2 yrs including the Group 1 7f Prix Jean-Luc Lagardere, the Group 1 6f Waterford Phoenix Stakes and Group 2 6f Railway Stakes. *Stud record:* His best winners so far include Homecoming Queen (1,000 Guineas), Morandi (Group 1 Criterium de Saint Cloud), Hong Kong triple Group 1 winner Designs On Rome, New Zealand Group 1 winners Rollout The Carpet and Mongolian Khan, Grade 1 Santa Anita Sprint winner Rich Tapestry, 19 other Group winners including Angelic Light, Banimpire, Charles The Great, Mango Diva (all Group 2 winners) and the Group 1 placed Amarillo, Honorius, Ishvana, Leitir Mor, Princess Noor and Sunday Times. Standing at Coolmore Stud, Ireland. *2016 fee:* €17,500.

IFFRAAJ (2001) Zafonic – Pastorale (Nureyev). *Racing record:* Won 7 races including the Group 2 7f Park Stakes (twice), the Group 2 7f Betfair Cup (Lennox St) and the 6f Wokingham Stakes. *Stud record:* First runners came in 2010 when he had more winners (38) than any first-crop European sire ever. He now has 16 Group winners (to 1st March 2016) and amongst the best are Chriselliam (Group 1 Fillies' Mile and Grade 1 Breeders' Cup Juvenile Fillies), Wootton Bassett (Group 1 Prix Jean-Luc Lagardere), Rizeena (Group 1 Moyglare Stud Stakes), Benvenue (Gran Premio di Milano), the Australasian triple Group 1 winner Turn Me Loose, the New Zealand Group 2 winners Fix & Serena Miss, Hot Streak (Group 2 Temple Stakes) and Ribchester (Group 2 Mill Reef Stakes). Standing at Dalham Hall Stud, Newmarket. *2016 fee:* €22,500.

INTENSE FOCUS (2006) Giant's Causeway – Daneleta (Danehill). *Racing record:* Won the 2-y-o Group 1 7f Dewhurst Stakes. *Stud record:* From three crops racing he's the sire of the winners of 193 races (to 1st March 2016). Only one stakes winner to date, but that's the Group 1 Middle Park Stakes and Group 2 Gimcrack Stakes winner Astaire. He also has the Group 3 placed Heart Focus, Home School and Miss Elizabeth. Standing at Ballylinch Stud, Ireland. *2016 fee:* €5,000.

INTIKHAB (1994) Red Ransom – Crafty Example (Crafty Prospector). *Racing record:* 8 wins including the Diomed Stakes and the Queen Anne Stakes. *Stud record:* Sire of 10 Group winners and 14 listed winners (to 1stMarch 2016), including the outstanding racemare and multiple Group 1 winner Snow Fairy, the Group 1 Lockinge Stakes & Group 1 Matron Stakes winner Red Evie, the Group 1 Criterium de Saint-Cloud winner Paita, the Group 2 Yorkshire Cup winner Glen's Diamond and the Group 3 winners Ascertain, Circus Couture, Hoh Mike, Moon Unit, Tell Dad and Toupie. Standing at Derrinstown Stud, Ireland. *2016 fee:* €5,000.

INVINCIBLE SPIRIT (1997) Green Desert – Rafha (Kris). *Racing record:* 7 wins, notably the Group 1 Sprint Cup at 5 yrs. *Stud record:* First runners in 2006. High-class sire of twelve Group 1 winners – Charm Spirit (QE II Stakes, Prix Jean Prat & Prix du Moulin), Kingman – four Group 1's including the Sussex Stakes and St James's Palace Stakes), Lawman (French Derby & Prix Jean Prat), Fleeting Spirit (July Cup), Moonlight Cloud (six Group 1's in France), Mayson (July Cup), Hooray & Rosdhu Queen (both Cheveley Park Stakes), Shalaa (Middle Park and Prix Morny), Territories (Prix Jean Prat), Vale Of York (Breeders' Cup Juvenile) and Yosai (three Group 1 wins in Australia), plus 14 Group 2 winners – Ajaya,

Allied Powers, Cable Bay, Campfire Glow, Captain Marvelous, Conquest, Impassable, Madame Trop Vite, Muthmir, Our Jonathan, Speaking Of Which, Spirit Quartz, Spirit Song and Zebedee. Standing at the Irish National Stud. *2016 fee:* €120,000.

JEREMY (2003) Danehill Dancer – Glint in Her Eye (Arazi). *Racing record:* Won 4 races including the Group 2 Betfred Mile at Sandown and the Group 3 7f Jersey Stakes. *Stud record:* First runners 2011. His best runners to date are the dual Group 2 winning 2-y-o Kool Kompany, Baino Hope (Group 2 Prix de Pomone), Success Days (Group 3 Leopardstown Derby Trial), Yellow Rosebud (Group 3 Concorde Stakes and Group 3 1,000 Guineas Trial), the dual listed winner Pearl Of Africa and the Irish 1,000 Guineas third Princess Sinead. Died in 2014.

KHELEYF (2001) Green Desert – Society Lady (Mr Prospector). *Racing record:* Won 3 races including the Group 3 Jersey Stakes. *Stud record:* A good source of two-year-old winners, his best so far are Sayif (Group 2 Diadem Stakes), Penny's Picnic (Group 2 Criterium de Maisons Laffitte and Group 3 Prix Eclipse), Charlie Em (US Grade 3 Senorita Stakes), Percolator (Group 3 Prix du Bois), Group 1 Phoenix Stakes second Big Time, Group 3 Ballyogan Stakes winner Majestic Queen, the Italian Group 3 winner Plusquemavie and 14 listed winners including Captain Ramius, Playfellow (third in the Group 2 Champagne Stakes) and Vladimir (third in the Group 1 Prix Morny). Standing at Haras De Faunes. *2016 fee:* €3,000.

KITTEN'S JOY (2001) El Prado – Kitten's First (Lear Fan). *Racing record:* Won 9 races including the Grade 1 10f Secretariat Stakes and the Grade 1 12f Turf Classic. *Stud record:* A leading turf sire in the USA. Sire of 23 Graded and 40 Listed stakes winners. His best include the US Grade 1 winners Admiral's Kitten, Bobby's Kitten, Big Blue Kitten, Chiropractor, Kitten's Dumplings, Real Solution and Stephanie's Kitten, plus six Grade 2 winners (all in the USA). Standing at Ramsay Farm in the USA. *2016 fee:* $100,000.

KODIAC (2001) Danehill – Rafha (Kris). *Racing record:* Won 4 races here and in the UAE over 6f and 7f including the Datel Trophy and Group 3 placed. *Stud record:* His first runners appeared in 2010 and he's a reliable source of decent class winners with 10 Group winners and 13 Listed winners. They include the champion 2-y-o filly Tiggy Wiggy (Group 1 Cheveley Park Stakes), The Group 2 Sandy Lane and Group 2 Hungerford Stakes winner Adaay, the Group 2 Lowther Stakes winner Besharah, the Group 2 Celebration Mile winner Kodi Bear and six Group 3 winners – Bear Cheek, Coulsty, Gifted Master, Jamesie, Shaden and Spirit Of Xian. Standing at Tally Ho Stud, Ireland. *2016 fee:* €45,000.

KYLLACHY (1998) Pivotal – Pretty Poppy (Song). *Racing record:* Winner of 6 races including the Group 1 Nunthorpe Stakes at 4 yrs. *Stud record:* First runners in 2006. Sire of the dual Group 1 Nunthorpe Stakes and dual Group 1 King's Stand Stakes winner Sole Power, the Group 1 6f Golden Shaheen winner Krypton Factor, Group 1 Haydock Park Sprint Cup winner Twilight Son, Hong Kong Group 1 winner Dim Sum, the Group 2 winners Arabian Gleam, Dragon Pulse, Penitent, Stepper Point, Supplicant and Tariq and numerous smart performers including Awinnersgame, Befortyfour, Corrybrough, Kachy, Mood Music, Gracia Directa and Noble Hachy. Standing at Cheveley Park Stud, Newmarket. *2016 fee:* £15,000.

LAWMAN (2004) Invincible Spirit – Laramie (Gulch). *Racing record:* Won four races including the Group 1 Prix du Jockey Club and the Group Prix Jean Prat. *Stud record:* First runners 2011. To date he has four Group 1 winners – Just The Judge (Group 1 Irish 1,000 Guineas, E P Taylor Stakes), Most Improved (Group 1 St James's Palace Stakes), Marcel (Racing Post Trophy) and Law Enforcement (Group 1 Premio Gran Criterium) and the Group winners Agnes Stewart (Group 2 May Hill Stakes), Forces of Darkness (Group 3 Prix Minerve), Loi (Group 3 Prix de Conde), Lady Wingshot (Group 3 Fairy Bridge Stakes), Nargys (Group 3 Sceptre Stakes) and US Law (Group 3 Prix Thomas Bryon). Ballylinch Stud, Ireland. *2016 fee:* €25,000.

LE HAVRE (2006) Noverre – Marie Rheinberg (Surako). *Racing record:* Won 4 races including the Group 1 10.5f French Derby. *Stud record:* Sire of the winners of 100 races including the dual Group 1 and classic winner Avenir Certain

(French 1,000 Guineas and French Oaks), the Group 2 Prix Chaudenay winner Auvray, the 2-y-o Group 3 Prix du Calvados winner Queen Bee, Group 3 Prix de Meautry winner Suedois and nine listed winners including the Group 1 Prix Jean Prat third La Hoguette. Standing at Haras de la Cauviniere in France. *2016 fee:* €35,000.

LEMON DROP KID (1996) Kingmambo – Charming Lassie (Seattle Slew). *Racing record:* Won the Belmont Stakes, Whitney Handicap and Woodward Stakes (all Grade 1 events). *Stud record:* Best performers to date include the Grade 1 winners Cannock Chase, Richard's Kid, Santa Teresita, Christmas Kid, Cittronade, Somali Lemonade and Lemon's Forever, eleven Group/Grade 2 winners (Bronze Cannon, Balance The Books, Bear's Kid, Charitable Man, Dreamy Kid, Hangover Kid, It's A Knockout, Juniper Pass, Pisco Sour, Sparkling Review and Wilkinson) and 22 Group 3 scorers. Standing at Lane's End Farm, Kentucky. *2016 fee:* $40,000.

LILBOURNE LAD (2009) Acclamation – Sogno Verde (Green Desert). *Racing record:* Won 3 races including the Group 2 Railway Stakes. Raced only at 2 yrs. *Stud record:* His first crop were two-year-olds in 2015 and he did well in terms of numbers of individual winners with a total of 24. They include the Group placed Lil's Joy (in France) and Spinamiss (in the USA). Standing at Rathbarry Stud in Ireland. *2016 fee:* €5,000.

LOPE DE VEGA (2007) Shamardal – Lady Vettori (Vettori). *Racing record:* Won four races from 7f (at 2 yrs) to 11f including the Group 1 French Derby and the Group 1 French 2,000 Guineas. *Stud record:* His first crop were 2-y-o's in 2014 and he's had an excellent start at stud with 8 Group winners - the Group 1 Dewhurst Stakes winner Belardo, the Group 2 winners Hero Look (in Italy) and Very Special (UAE) and the Group/Grade 3 winners Blue De Vega, Burnt Sugar, Ride Like The Wind, Royal Razalma and Santa Ana Lane (in the USA). He also has five Listed winners. Standing at Ballylinch Stud, Ireland. *2016 fee:* €45,000.

MAKFI (2007) Dubawi – Dhelaal (Green Desert). *Racing record:* Won four races, notably the 2,000 Guineas and Prix Jacques le Marois. *Stud record:* His first runners appeared in 2014 and to date he's had the winners of 130 races

(to the 3rd March 2016) including the French 2,000 Guineas and Prix de la Foret winner Make Believe, the Australian Group 1 winner Marky Mark, New Zealand Group 2 winner Sofia Rosa, French Group 3 winner Miamara and three listed winners including Cornwallville in France. Standing at Haras de Bonneval. *2016 fee:* €20,000.

MANDURO (2002) Monsun – Mandellicht (Be My Guest). *Racing record:* Won the Group 1 1m Prix Jacques Le Marois, the Group 1 10f Prince of Wales's Stakes and Group 1 10f Prix d'Ispahan. *Stud record:* His first runners appeared in 2011. To date his best runners are the Group 1 winners Mandaean (Criterium de Saint Cloud), Charity Line (Premio Lydia Tesio), Braco Forte (in Brazil), Ribbons (Prix Jean Romanet), Ultra (Prix Jean-Luc Lagardere) and Vazirabad (Prix Royal-Oak), the Group 2 winners Bonfire (Dante Stakes) & Fractional (Prix Dollar) and the Group 3 winners Kolonel (Prix de Seine-et-Oise), Trois Lunes (Prix Vanteaux) and Meerjungfrau (in Germany). Standing at Haras du Logis, France. *2016 fee:* €7,000.

MASTERCRAFTSMAN (2006) Danehill Dancer – Starlight Dreams (Black Tie Affair). *Racing record:* Won 7 races, notably the Phoenix Stakes, National Stakes, St James's Palace Stakes and Irish 2,000 Guineas (all Group 1 races). *Stud record:* His first Two Year Olds appeared in 2013 and he was the leading European first-crop sire with 28 winners. The best of his winners to date are The Grey Gatsby (Group 1 French Derby and Group 1 Irish Champion Stakes), Amazing Maria (Group 1 Falmouth Stakes and Group 1 Prix Rothschild), Kingston Hill (Group 1 Racing Post Trophy and Group 1 St Leger), New Zealand Group 2 winners Mime, Sacred Master and Thunder Lady, nine Group 3 winners including Nakuti and Master Apprentice (both here), Craftsman and Iveagh Gardens (both in Ireland), and two Listed winners. Standing at Coolmore Stud, Ireland. *2016 fee:* €35,000.

MAYSON (2008) Invincible Spirit – Mayleaf (Pivotal). *Racing record:* Won five races over 5f and 6f, notably the Group 1 July Cup and the Group 3 Abernant Stakes. *Stud record:* His first runners appear on the racecourse this season. Standing at Cheveley Park Stud, Newmarket. *2016 fee:* €5,000.

MEDAGLIA D'ORO (1999) El Prado – Cappucino Bay (Bailjumper). *Racing record:* Won the Travers Stakes, Jim Dandy Stakes and San Felipe Stakes. *Stud record:* Best winners include the US champion Rachel Alexandra (five Grade 1 wins) and the Group/Grade 1 winners C. S. Silk, Champagne d'Oro, Coffee Clique, Gabby's Golden Gal, Passion For Gold, Marketing Mix, Mshawish, Plum Pretty, Songbird, Vancouver (in Australia), Violence and Warrior's Reward. Standing at Jonabell Farm, Kentucky. *2016 fee:* $150,000.

MEDICEAN (1997) Machiavellian – Mystic Goddess (Storm Bird). *Racing record:* 6 wins including the Lockinge Stakes and Eclipse. *Stud record:* First runners in 2005. Sire of 24 Group winners including the very smart Dutch Art (Prix Morny, Middle Park), the smart performer Nannina (Fillies' Mile, Coronation Stakes), Capponi and Al Shemali (both Dubai Group 1 winners), Siyouma (Group 1 Sun Chariot Stakes and Group 1 E P Taylor Stakes), Almerita & Neatico (both Group 1 German winners), Chevron (Group 1 Raffles International Cup), Bayrir (Grade 1 Secretariat Stakes), Hong Kong Group 1 winner Mr Medici, the Group 2 British Champions Fillies and Mares Stakes Sapphire, the very smart Dubai Group 2 and Group 3 winner Bankable, the Group 2 Blandford Stakes winner Manieree and the North American Grade 2 winners Dimension & Medici Code. Standing at Cheveley Park Stud. *2016 fee:* £7,000.

MORE THAN READY (1997) Southern Halo – Woodman's Girl (Woodman). *Racing record:* Won 7 races in the USA including the Grade 1 7f King's Bishop Stakes and the 2-y-o Grade 2 6f Sanford Stakes. *Stud record:* Sire of 66 Group/Graded stakes winners including 17 Group/Grade 1 winners – Benicio, Buster's Ready, Carry On Cutie, Daredevil, Regally Ready, Room Service, Verrazano (all in North America), Dreamaway, Entisaar, Gimmethegreenlight, More Joyous, More Than Sacred, Perfectly Ready, Perfect Reflection, Phelan Ready, Samaready and Sebring (all in Australia/New Zealand). Standing at WinStar Farm, Kentucky. *2016 fee:* $50,000.

MOUNT NELSON (2004) Rock of Gibraltar – Independence (Selkirk). *Racing record:* Won the Group 1 1m Criterium International at 2 yrs and the Group 1 10f Eclipse Stakes. *Stud record:* His first two-year-olds ran in 2012 and to date he's had the Group 2 Royal Lodge Stakes winner Berkshire, the Group 3 Prix du Calvados winner Purr Along, Group 3 Chartwell Stakes winner Emerald Star and the listed winners Holy Moly, Mohave Princess, Ninjago, Reine Magique, Special Meaning, Volume and Weltmacht to his name. Standing at Newsells Park Stud, Herts. *2016 fee:* £5,000.

MYBOYCHARLIE (2005) Danetime – Dulceata (Rousillon). *Racing record:* Won the Group 1 6f Prix Morny and the Group 3 6f Anglesey Stakes, both at 2 yrs. *Stud record:* The sire of three Group 1 winners – Jameka, Peggy Jean (both in Australia) and Euro Charlene (Beverly D Stakes), along with the Australian Group 2 6f winners Blueberry Hill and Charlie Boy. In Europe he has the French listed winners Art Of Raw and Salai. Standing at Haras du Mezeray. *2016 fee:* €5,000.

NATHANIEL (2008) Galileo – Magnificient Style (Silver Hawk). *Racing record:* Won four races notably the Group 1 12f King George VI and Queen Elizabeth Stakes and the Group 1 Eclipse Stakes. *Stud record:* His first two-year-olds appear on the track this year. Standing at Newsells Park Stud. *2016 fee:* £20,000.

NAYEF (1999) Gulch – Height of Fashion (Bustino). *Racing record:* Won 9 races including the Champion Stakes and the Juddmonte International Stakes. *Stud record:* His first crop were two-year-olds in 2007 and his best winners so far are Tamayuz (dual Group 1 winner in France), Lady Marian (Group 1 Prix de l'Opera), Forgotten Rules (Group 2 British Champions Long Distance Cup), Mustajeeb (Group 2 Greenlands Stakes), Snow Sky (Group 2 Yorkshire Cup and Hardwicke Stakes), Spacious (dual Group 2 winner and 1,000 Guineas second), Tasaday (Group 2 Prix de la Nonette), Valirann (Group 2 Prix Chaudenay) and the Group 3 winners Confront (Joel Stakes), Hawaafez (Cumberland Lodge Stakes), Sparkling Beam (Prix Chloe), Tabassum (Oh So Sharp Stakes). Standing at Nunnery Stud, Norfolk. *2016 fee:* £5,000.

NEW APPROACH (2005) Galileo – Park Express (Ahonoora). *Racing record:* Won five Group 1 events including the Derby, the Champion Stakes and the Irish Champion Stakes. *Stud record:* First two year olds appeared in 2012. Sire of the champion 2-y-o Dawn Approach (Dewhurst Stakes, National Stakes, 2,000 Guineas, St James's Palace Stakes), Talent (Group 1 Epsom Oaks), May's Dream (Group 1 Australasian Oaks), Sultanina (Group 1 Nassau Stakes), Libertarian (Group 2 Dante Stakes), Connecticut (Group 2 in Turkey), Herald The Dawn (Group 2 Futurity Stakes) and nine Group 3 winners including Cap O'Rushes (Gordon Stakes), Elliptique (Prix Chloe), Newfangled (Albany Stakes), Montsegure, Sword Of Light and Gamblin' Guru (all in Australia). Standing at Dalham Hall Stud, Newmarket. *2014 stud fee:* £60,000.

OASIS DREAM (2001) Green Desert – Hope (Dancing Brave). *Racing record:* Won 4 races, including the Middle Park Stakes, July Cup and Nunthorpe Stakes (all Group 1 events). *Stud record:* His first crop were two-year-olds in 2007 and he's built himself an outstanding reputation. His 14 Group 1 winners are Aqlaam (Prix du Moulin), Arcano (Prix Morny), Charming Thought (Middle Park Stakes), Goldream (King's Stand Stakes & Prix de l'Abbaye), Jwala (Nunthorpe Stakes), Lady Jane Digby (in Germany), Midday (six Group/ Grade One's including the Nassau Stakes, Prix Vermeille and Breeders' Cup Filly & Mare Turf), Muhaarar (July Cup, Commonwealth Cup and British Champions Sprint and Prix Maurice De Gheest), Naaqoos (Prix Jean-Luc Lagardere), Opinion (in Australia), Power (National Stakes & Irish 2,000 Guineas), Prohibit (King's Stand Stakes), Querari (in Italy) and Tuscan Evening (US Gamely Handicap). His 12 Group 2 scorers include Approve, Frozen Power, Misheer, Monitor Closely, Peace At Last, Quiet Oasis (in USA), Showcasing and Sri Putra. Standing at Banstead Manor Stud, Newmarket. *2016 fee:* £75,000.

PACO BOY (2005) Desert Style – Tappen Zee (Sandhurst Prince). *Racing record:* Won 10 races from 6f to 1m including the Group 1 Prix de la Foret, Queen Anne Stakes and Lockinge Stakes. *Stud record:* Had his first 2-y-o's in 2014 and to date he has the winners of 110 races (to 5th March 2016) including the Group 2 Flying Childers winner Beacon, the Group 2 Vintage Stakes winner Galileo Gold, the Group 3 Horris Hill winner Smaih and the listed winners Lexington Times, Making Trouble (in Germany), Peacock and Stella Di Paco (in New Zealand). Standing at Highclere Stud. *2016 fee:* £6,500.

PASTORAL PURSUITS (2001) Bahamian Bounty – Star (Most Welcome). *Racing record:* Won 6 races including the Group 1 6f July Cup, Group 2 7f Park Stakes and Group 3 6f Sirenia Stakes. *Stud record:* His first crop appeared as 2-y-o's in 2009 and his best winners to date are Pastoral Player (Group 3 John of Gaunt Stakes), Rose Blossom (Group 3 Summer Stakes), the listed winners Angel's Pursuit, Catalina Bay (in Italy), Lightscameraction, Marine Commando, Rooke (in France, Terra Di Tuffi (in Germany) and Ventura Mist, and the triple Group 3 placed Sagramor. Standing at the National Stud. *2016 fee:* £4,000.

PIVOTAL (1993) Polar Falcon – Fearless Revival (Cozzene). *Racing record:* 4 wins including the Nunthorpe Stakes and King's Stand Stakes. *Stud record:* First runners in 2000. An outstanding sire whose best winners include the Excellent Art (St James's Palace Stakes), Falco (French 2,000 Guineas), Farhh (Champion Stakes & Lockinge Stakes), Golden Apples (triple US Grade 1 winner), Halfway To Heaven (Irish 1,00 Guineas, Nassau Stakes and Sun Chariot Stakes), Immortal Verse (dual Group 1 winning miler), Kyllachy (Nunthorpe Stakes), Maarek (Prix de l'Abbaye), Regal Parade (Haydock Sprint Cup), Sariska (Oaks and Irish Oaks) and Somnus (Sprint Cup, Prix de la Foret, Prix Maurice de Gheest). Other top performers of his include Beauty Is Truth (Group 2 Prix du Gros-Chene), Captain Rio (Group 2 Criterium des Maisons-Laffitte), Chorist (Group 1 Pretty Polly Stakes), Izzi Top (Group 1 Prix Jean Romanet and Pretty Polly Stakes), Megahertz (two US Grade 1 events), Peeress (Lockinge Stakes, Sun Chariot Stakes), Pivotal Point (Group 2 Diadem Stakes), Saoire (Irish 1000 Guineas), Silvester Lady (German Oaks), Virtual (Lockinge Stakes) and Siyouni (2-y-o Group 1 Prix Jean-Luc Lagardere). Standing at Cheveley Park Stud, Newmarket. *2016 fee:* £45,000.

POET'S VOICE (2007) Dubawi – Bright Tiara (Chief's Crown). *Racing record:* Won 4 races over 7f and a mile, and at 2 and 3 yrs, notably the Group 1 Queen Elizabeth II Stakes, the Group 2 Champagne Stakes (at 2 yrs) and the Group 2 Celebration Mile. *Stud record:* His first crop were two-year-olds in 2015 and to date (6th March) he has the winners of 38 races including the Italian Group 3 winner Posta Diletto and the listed winners Voice Of Love (in Italy) and Whitman. Standing at Dalham Hall Stud in Newmarket. *2016 fee:* £12,000.

POUR MOI (2008) Montjeu – Gwynn (Darshaan). *Racing record:* Won 3 races, notably the Epsom Derby and the Group 2 10f Prix Greffulhe. *Stud record:* His first crop were two-year-olds in 2015 and to date his only stakes winner is the listed Bosra Sham Stakes winner and dual Group 3 second Only Mine. Standing at Coolmore Stud in Ireland. *2016 fee:* €10,000.

POWER (2009) Oasis Dream – Frappe (Inchinor). *Racing record:* Won 5 races from 5f to 1m including the Group 1 National Stakes, the Group 2 Coventry Stakes (both at 2 yrs) and the Group 1 Irish 2,000 Guineas. *Stud record:* His first crop are two-year-olds this season. Standing at Coolmore Stud in Ireland. *2016 fee:* €8,000.

RAIL LINK (2003) Dansili – Docklands (Theatrical). *Racing record:* Won seven races including the Prix de L'Arc de Triomphe, Prix Niel, Grand Prix de Paris and Prix du Lys. *Stud record:* His first runners appeared in 2011 and his best to date are Spillway (Group 1 10f in Australia), Epicuris (2-y-o Group 1 10f Criterium de Saint-Cloud), Bugie d'Amor (Group 3 Premio Dormello), Last Train (Group 3 Prix de Barbeville and second in the Group 1 Grand Prix de Paris), Sediciosa (Group 3 Prix de Royaumont), the listed winner and Group 1 Gran Premio di Milano second Wild Wolf and the listed winners Destruct and Trip To Rhodos. Standing at Haras National de Cercy La Tour. *2016 fee:* €2,800.

RAVEN'S PASS (2005) Elusive Quality – Ascutney (Lord At War). *Racing record:* Won 6 races, notably the Group 1 1m Queen Elizabeth II Stakes and the Grade 1 10f Breeders' Cup Classic. *Stud record:* His first crop of two-year-olds appeared in 2012 and his best winners to date are Steeler (Group 2 Royal Lodge Stakes winner and Group 1 Racing Post Trophy second), the Group 3 winners Malabar (Prestige Stakes), Secret Number (Cumberland Lodge Stakes), Kataniya (Prix de Royaumont), nine listed winners including Alonsoa, Alta Stima, Lovely Pass (Group 3 third in the UAE), Redbrook and Richard Pankhurst, Riflescope and the Group 2 placed winner Ibn Malik and Mutashaded. Standing at Kildangan Stud, Ireland. *2016 fee:* €15,000.

REQUINTO (2009) Dansili – Damson (Entrepreneur). *Racing record:* Only ran at 2 yrs and won four races including the Group 2 5f Flying Childers Stakes and the Group 3 5f Molecomb Stakes. *Stud record:* His first crop of two-year-olds appear this season. Standing at Coolmore Stud, Ireland. *2016 fee:* €5,000.

RIO DE LA PLATA (2005) Rahy – Express Way (ARG) (Ahmad). *Racing record:* Won eight races at 2 and 5 yrs and from 7f to 10f including the Prix Jean-Luc Lagardere, the Premio Vittorio Di Capua and the Premio Roma (all Group 1 events) and the Group 2 Vintage Stakes. *Stud record:* His first crop of two-year-olds appear this season. Standing at Haras Du Logis in France. *2016 fee:* €5,500.

RIP VAN WINKLE (2006) Galileo – Looking Back (Stravinsky). *Racing record:* Won five races from 7f (at 2 yrs) to 10f including the Group 1 Sussex Stakes, Queen Elizabeth II Stakes and Juddmonte International. *Stud record:* His first 2-y-o's ran in 2014 and to date his best have been the Group 1 Phoenix Stakes winner Dick Whittington, the New Zealand Group 2 winner Capella, the Group 3 winners I Am Beautiful and Magic Dancer (also in New Zealand) and three listed winners. Standing at Coolmore Stud, Ireland. *2016 fee:* €12,500.

ROCK OF GIBRALTAR (1999) Danehill – Offshore Boom (Be My Guest). *Racing record:* Won seven Group 1 races including the Dewhurst Stakes, 2,000 Guineas, St James's Palace Stakes and Sussex Stakes. *Stud record:* The sire of eleven Group 1 winners including the US dual Grade 1 winner Diamondrella, Eagle Mountain (in Hong Kong), Mount Nelson (Eclipse and Criterium International), Samitar (Irish 1,000 Guineas and Garden City Stakes), Prince Gibraltar (Criterium de Saint-Cloud), dual Group 1 winning sprinter Society Rock and Varenar (Prix de la Foret) as well as around 50 other Group winners. Standing at Coolmore Stud, Ireland. *2016 fee:* €10,000.

RODERIC O'CONNOR (2008) Galileo – Secret Garden (Danehill). *Racing record:* Won 3 races, notably the Group 1 1m Grand Criterium (at 2 yrs) and the Group 1 Irish 2,000 Guineas. *Stud record:* His first crop were two-year-olds in 2015 and to date (7th March 2016) he has the winners of 33 races to his name including Biz Heart (Italian Group 2 Premio Gran Criterium),

Great Page (Group 3 Prix du Calvados) and the Lingfield listed winner Haalick. Standing at the National Stud in Newmarket. *2016 fee:* £9,000.

ROYAL APPLAUSE (1993) Waajib – Flying Melody (Auction Ring). *Racing record:* Winner of 9 races, including Middle Park at 2 yrs and the Haydock Park Sprint Cup at 4 yrs (both Group 1). *Stud record:* First runners in 2001. Sire of the US dual Grade 1 winner Ticker Tape, the Group/Grade 2 winners Acclamation, Battle Of Hastings, Finjaan, Lovelace, Mister Cosmi, Nevisian Lad, Please Sing and Whatsthescript and numerous other very smart performers including Crime Scene, triple Group 3 winner Majestic Missile, Peak To Creek and Prince Siegfried. Standing at The Royal Studs, Norfolk. *2016 fee:* £9,000.

SAKHEE'S SECRET (2004) Sakhee – Palace Street (Secreto). *Racing record:* Won 5 races over 6f notably the Group 1 July Cup. *Stud record:* His first crop of 2-y-o's appeared in 2012. Sire of the New Zealand Group 1 10f winner Sakhee's Soldier, Italian Group 3 winner Salford Secret and the listed winners Thunder Strike, Fine Blend (in France) and Cryptic (in New Zealand). Standing in Italy. *2016 fee:* €5,000.

SAYIF (2006) Kheleyf – Seward's Folly (Rudimentary). *Racing record:* Won two races including the Group 2 6f Diadem Stakes. Also placed in Group 1 Middle Park Stakes (at 2 yrs) and five other Group/Graded stakes events here and in the USA. *Stud record:* This is his first crop of runners. Standing at Llety Farms. *2016 fee:* £3,000.

SCAT DADDY (2004) Johannesburg – Love Style (Mr Prospector). *Racing record:* Won four Graded Stakes from 6f to 9f and at 2 and 3 yrs notably the Grade 1 Champagne Stakes (at 2 yrs) and the Grade 1 Florida Derby. *Stud record:* His best winners to date include 13 Group 1 winners in South America, plus No Nay Never (Group 1 Morny and Group 2 Norfolk Stakes), Lady Of Shamrock (US dual Grade 1 winner) and Nickname (US Grade 1 Beldame Stakes), plus nine Group/Grade 2 winners including Acapulco (Queen Mary Stakes), Daddy Long Legs (Royal Lodge Stakes), Azar, Conquest Daddyo, Dice Flavor, Handsome Mike, El Kabeir, Frac Daddy and Pretty N Cool (all in the USA). Died in 2015 at Ashford Stud, Kentucky after his fee had been raised to $100,000 from $35,000.

SEA THE STARS (2006) Cape Cross – Urban Sea (Miswaki). *Racing record:* Outstanding winner of 9 races including the Derby, 2,000 Guineas, Prix de L'Arc de Triomphe, Irish Champion Stakes, Juddmonte International Stakes and Eclipse Stakes. *Stud record:* His first two-year-olds appeared in 2013 and he's already had three Group 1 winners to his name – Taghrooda (Oaks and King George VI), Sea The Moon (German Derby) and Vazira (Prix Saint-Alary), plus the Group 2 Great Voltigeur winner Storm The Stars and the Group 3 winners Afternoon Sunshine, Casual Smile (in the USA), Cloth Of Stars, My Titania, Quasillo (in Germany), Star Storm and Zarshana, twelve listed winners and the Group 1 French Derby second Shamkiyr. Standing at Gilltown Stud, Ireland. Stud fee: €125,000.

SEPOY (2008) Elusive Quality – Watchful (Danehill). *Racing record:* Champion 2-y-o and 3-y-o in Australia. Won four Group 1 sprints at 2 and 3 yrs. *Stud record:* His first northern hemisphere two-year-olds appear this season. Standing at Dalham Hall Stud, Ireland. Stud fee: €15,000.

SHAMARDAL (2002) Giant's Causeway – Helsinki (Machiavellian). *Racing record:* Won the Dewhurst Stakes, French 2,000 Guineas, French Derby and St James's Palace Stakes (all Group 1 events). *Stud record:* Has sired 16 Group 1 winners from his first six crops including Able Friend (four Group 1's in Hong Kong), Baltic Baroness (Prix Vermeille), Casamento (Racing Post Trophy), Lope De Vega (French 2,000 Guineas and French Derby), Lumiere (Cheveley Park Stakes), Mukhadram (Eclipse Stakes), Sagawara (Prix Saint-Alary) and Dunboyne Express (renamed 'Dan Excel' in Hong Kong). His 25 Group 2/Group 3 winners include the Group 1 placed Fintry, Ihtimal, Mukhadram, Elle Shadow (Germany), No Evidence Needed and Puissance de Lune (both in Australia). Standing at Kildangan Stud, Ireland. *2016 fee:* Private (was €70,000 in 2015).

SHOWCASING (2007) Oasis Dream – Arabesque (Zafonic). *Racing record:* Won 2 races at 2 yrs including the Group 2 6f Gimcrack Stakes. *Stud record:* Has had an excellent start, with 52 individual two-year-old winners from his first two European crops. They include Prize Exhibit (two Grade 2's and a Grade 3 in the USA), Toocoolforschool (Group 2 Mill Reef Stakes), Showbay (Group 2 in New Zealand), Cappella Sansevero (Group 3 Round Tower Stakes winner and Group 1 third), Quiet Reflection (Group 3 Cornwallis Stakes), Caorunn (2-y-o Group 3 in New Zealand) and five listed winners including Accipiter, Tasleet (also second in Group 2 Richmond Stakes) and Raghu (also Group 1 third in New Zealand). Standing at Whitsbury Manor Stud. *2016 fee: £25,000.*

SIR PERCY (2003) Mark of Esteem – Percy's Lass (Blakeney). *Racing record:* A champion 2-y-o, he won five races notably the Derby and the Dewhurst Stakes. *Stud record:* His first runners appeared in 2011. Sire of five Group winners – Lady Tiana (Group 2 Lancashire Oaks), Sir Andrew (Group 2 in New Zealand), Alla Speranza (Group 3 Kilternan Stakes), Lady Pimpernel (US Grade 3) and Wake Forest (German Group 3), along with eight listed winners including the Group 2 Royal Lodge Stakes second Nafaqa and the Group 2 Queen Mary Stakes third Newsletter. Standing at Lanwades Stud, Newmarket. *2016 fee: £7,000.*

SIR PRANCEALOT (2010) Tamayuz – Mona Em (Catrail). *Racing record:* Only ran at 2 yrs and won 3 of his 6 sprint races including the Group 2 Flying Childers Stakes and the listed National Stakes. Also second in the Group 2 Prix Robert Papin. *Stud record:* His first runners appear this season. Standing at Tally Ho Stud in Ireland. *2016 fee: €5,000.*

SIXTIES ICON (2003) Galileo – Love Divine (Diesis). *Racing record:* Won eight races including the Group 1 St Leger, the Group 2 Jockey Club Cup and four other Group events. *Stud record:* His first two year olds appeared in 2012 and his best winners to date include Chilworth Icon (Group 3 Premio Primi Passi & the listed Woodcote Stakes), the listed winners Audacia, Cruck Realta and Epsom Icon, along with the triple listed-placed Effie B. Sire of the winners of 97 races to March 2016. Standing at Norman Court Stud, Wiltshire. *2016 fee: £5,000.*

SMART STRIKE (1992) Mr Prospector – Classy 'n Smart (Smarten). *Racing record:* Won 8 races in the USA including the Grade 2 8.5f Philip H Iselin Handicap and the Grade 3 Salvator Mile. *Stud record:* Close on 60 Group winners including the top-class colt Curlin (Preakness Stakes, Dubai World Cup, Breeders' Cup Classic), the US Grade 1 winners Centre Court, English Channel, Fabulous Strike, Furthest Land, Lookin At Lucky, My Miss Aurelia, Never Retreat, Shadow Cast, Soaring Free, Square Eddie, Streaming and Swagger Jack and the Japan Cup winner Fleetstreet Dancer. Died in 2015.

STREET CRY (1998) Machiavellian – Helen Street (Troy). *Racing record:* 5 wins including the Group 1 10f Dubai World Cup and the US Grade 1 9f Stephen Foster Handicap. *Stud record:* First runners in 2006. Sire of the outstanding multiple Grade 1 winning racemare Zenyatta and the Group/Grade 1 winners Street Sense (Breeders' Cup Juvenile, Kentucky Derby, Travers Stakes), Cry And Catch Me (Oak Leaf Stakes), Majestic Roi (Sun Chariot Stakes), Street Boss (Triple Bend Invitational, Bing Crosby Handicap), Seventh Street (Go For Wand Handicap, Apple Blossom Handicap), Street Hero (Norfolk Stakes), Here Comes Ben (Forego Handicap), Victor's Cry (Shoemaker Mile Handicap), Street Hero (Norfolk Stakes), Zaidan (Hong Kong Classic Cup) and the Australian Group 1 winners Long John, Shocking (Melbourne Cup), Winx (four Group 1's) and Whobegotyou (Caulfield Guineas and Yalumba Stakes). Died in 2014.

TAGULA (1993) Taufan – Twin Island (Standaan). *Racing record:* Won 4 races including the Group 1 6f Prix Morny (at 2 yrs) and the Group 3 7f Supreme Stakes. *Stud record:* Sires plenty of winners, amongst the best being the high-class 2-y-o and miler Canford Cliffs, the Group 2 winners Tax Free (Prix du Gros-Chene), Atlantis Prince (Group 2 Royal Lodge Stakes) Tagshira (in Germany) and Limato (Park Stakes), plus seven listed winners – Bakewell Tart, Double Vie, Drawnfromthepast, King Orchisios, Macaroon, Pure Poetry and Red Millennium. Standing at Rathbarry Stud in Ireland. *2016 fee: €4,000.*

TAMAYUZ (2005) Nayef – Al Ishq (Nureyev). *Racing record:* Won the Group 1 1m Prix Jacques Le Marois and the Group 1 Prix Jean Prat. *Stud record:* His first two year olds appeared in 2012 and his best winners to date are G Force (Group 1 Haydock Park Sprint), Sir Prancealot (Group 2 Flying Childers Stakes), Group 3 Molecomb Stakes winner Brown Sugar, Japanese Group 3 winner Meiner Eternel, Group 3 Prix de Ris-Orangis winner Thawaany and the listed winners Best Regards, Blond Me (a US Grade 2 second), Fadhayyil (Group 2 Rockfel Stakes second), Ighraa, Royal Spring and Tupi (Group 2 Vintage Stakes second). Standing at Derrinstown Stud in Ireland. *2016 fee:* €12,500.

TEOFILO (2004) Galileo – Speirbhhean (Danehill). *Racing record:* Won 5 races at 2 yrs including the Group 1 Dewhurst Stakes and the Group 1 National Stakes. *Stud record:* His first runners appeared in 2011 and he has ten Group 1 winners so far – Parish Hall (Dewhurst Stakes), Havana Gold (Prix Jean Prat), Loch Garman (Criterium International), Pleascach (Irish 1,000 Guineas & Yorkshire Oaks), Trading Leather (Irish Derby), Kermadek, Palentino & Sonntag (all in Australia), Special Fighter (Al Maktoum Challenge) and Voleuse De Coeurs (Irish St Leger), plus another 7 Group/Grade 2 winners including the US Grade 1 placed Amira's Prince, the Group 1 Sussex Stakes second Arod, the Irish Derby third Light Heavy and Oaks second Tarfasha. Standing at Kildangan Stud, Ireland. *2016 fee:* €50,000.

THEWAYYOUARE (2005) Kingmambo – Maryinski (Sadler's Wells). *Racing record:* Won four races in France including the Group 1 1m Criterium International and the Group 3 1m Prix Thomas Bryon. *Stud record:* Sire of the high-class Group 2 UAE Derby winner and Grade 1 Breeders' Cup Classic second Toast Of New York, the Peruvian Grade 3 winner El Jader, the Group 3 placed Hug And A Kiss and Tommy Docc, and two listed winners in New Zealand. Standing in Germany (previously at Coolmore in Ireland). *2016 fee:* Private (previously €5,000).

VALE OF YORK (2007) Invincible Spirit – Red Vale (Halling). *Racing record:* Won 3 races including the Grade 1 9f Breeders' Cup Juvenile and the listed 7f Stardom Stakes and second in the Group 1 1m Gran Criterium (all at 2 yrs). *Stud record:* With two crops to have raced so far in 2014. To date (March 2016) he's the sire of the winners of nearly 80 races but not a lot in terms of quality. The best include the Italian dual Group 3 and dual listed winner Fontanelice and the French Group 3 placed 2-y-o Pleasemetoo. Standing at Haras Des Faunes. *2016 fee:* €3,000.

WAR FRONT (2003) Danzig – Starry Dreamer (Rubiano). *Race record:* Won four races at 3 and 4 yrs including the Grade 2 6f Alfred G Vanderbilt Breeders' Cup Handicap at Saratoga. *Stud record:* One of the world's top sires, in his first five crops he has sired ten Group 1/Grade 1 winners – Air Force Blue, War Command (both winners of the Group 1 Dewhurst Stakes), Declaration Of War (Juddmonte International, Queen Anne Stakes), Data Link, Hit It Like A Bomb, Jack Milton, Peace And War, Summer Soiree, The Factor (all in the USA) and Lines Of Battle (in Hong Kong). Also, he has seven Group/Grade 2 winners – Bashart, Departing, Pontchatrain, Soldat, State Of Play, Summer Front and War Dancer. Standing at Claiborne Farm, Kentucky. *2016 fee:* $200,000.

ZEBEDEE (2008) Invincible Spirit – Cozy Maria (Cozzene). *Racing record:* Won 6 races over 5f and 6f as a 2-y-o including the Group 2 Flying Childers Stakes, the Group 3 Molecomb Stakes and the listed Dragon Stakes. *Stud record:* First runners in 2014. He's had a good start, particularly with the dual Group 2 winner Ivawood, the Group 1 Sprint Cup third Magical Memory and the Group 3 placed Manaafidh and Parsley. Sire of the winners of 164 races to date (March 2016). Standing at Tally Ho Stud in Ireland. *2016 fee:* €8,000.

ZOFFANY (2008) Dansili – Tyranny (Machiavellian). *Racing record:* Won 5 races as a 2-y-o including the Group 1 6f Phoenix Stakes and the Group 3 7f Tyros Stakes. *Stud record:* His first crop were two-year-olds last year and he had an excellent start with the Group 2 winners Foundation, Illuminate and Waterloo Bridge, the listed winners Argentero and Washington DC, and the Group 3 placed Light Up Our World. Standing at Coolmore Stud in Ireland. *2016 fee:* €45,000.

Sires Index

SIRE	HORSE NO.
Acclamation	52, 163, 301, 629, 640, 726, 767, 785, 828, 834, 852, 855, 896, 902, 917, 933, 943, 1036, 1296, 1368, 1401, 1435, 1496, 1551, 1560, 1600
Afleet Alex	647
Approve	297, 500, 1286, 1596
Aqlaam	559, 1030
Arcano	152, 293, 440, 577, 630, 753, 932, 1172, 1186, 1393, 1468, 1550, 1621
Archipenko	80, 196, 318, 521, 707, 722, 925, 1066, 1103, 1121, 1154, 1397, 1398, 1463, 1477, 1542, 1626
Art Connoisseur	445, 1386
Artie Schiller	880
Aussie Rules	1100, 1411, 1534, 1539, 1631
Authorized	328, 349, 1408
Azamour	85, 1540, 1611, 1673
Bahamian Bounty	76, 237, 240, 438, 465, 554, 867, 891, 985, 1033, 1193, 1198, 1217, 1394, 1404, 1559, 1602, 1617, 1628, 1629
Bated Breath	53, 158, 329, 335, 347, 353, 361, 403, 493, 499, 570, 578, 634, 679, 731, 842, 873, 898, 938, 949, 990, 1027, 1043, 1119, 1125, 1150, 1364, 1388, 1494, 1510, 1547, 1556, 1652, 1657
Bernardini	659, 808
Big Bad Bob	69, 136, 509, 922, 1101, 1663
Blame	955, 1452
Born To Sea	54, 62, 215, 310, 463, 508, 839, 884, 941, 999, 1044, 1300, 1311, 1419, 1624, 1633
Broken Vow	1041
Bushranger	246, 302, 341, 431
Cacique	83, 101, 331, 739, 1004, 1113, 1223, 1366, 1504
Camacho	68, 473, 1519
Campanologist	676
Candy Ride	218
Canford Cliffs	226, 269, 273, 333, 398, 476, 478, 486, 522, 590, 601, 727, 822, 874, 897, 912, 1001, 1082, 1316, 1471, 1555, 1643
Cape Blanco	42, 551, 1485
Cape Cross	9, 38, 50, 193, 228, 261, 263, 357, 396, 401, 797, 821, 1011, 1055, 1067, 1520, 1552
Captain Gerrard	526, 1104
Caradak	479
Casamento	28, 63, 216, 221, 255, 326, 332, 639, 800, 809, 825, 830, 939, 1031, 1050, 1131, 1137, 1176, 1180, 1204, 1284, 1343
Champs Elysees	64, 81, 840, 1339

SIRES INDEX

Choisir	214, 633, 695, 1073, 1138, 1233, 1486
City Zip	958
Clodovil	309, 623, 719, 853, 882, 908, 923, 1035, 1422, 1531, 1619, 1627
Cockney Rebel	1184, 1190
Compton Place	75, 374, 529, 575, 1019, 1156, 1165
Congrats	806
Dalakhani	1497, 1584
Dandy Man	86, 324, 428, 430, 441, 444, 574, 603, 724, 915, 1303, 1446, 1558
Danehill Dancer	233
Dansili	91, 110, 264, 411, 496, 664, 672, 701, 784, 980, 1512, 1577, 1583, 1660, 1661, 1688, 1692
Dark Angel	15, 16, 58, 118, 166, 176, 258, 266, 267, 271, 286, 303, 330, 342, 382, 387, 495, 576, 587, 605, 613, 621, 649, 770, 794, 798, 807, 832, 844, 845, 849, 865, 866, 878, 893, 909, 911, 914, 926, 936, 940, 970, 1006, 1057, 1058, 1076, 1084, 1129, 1310, 1318, 1324, 1427, 1517, 1548, 1585, 1608, 1686
Deep Impact	39, 1273, 1274, 1475
Delegator	71, 555, 928, 1032, 1546
Diamond Green	520
Dick Turpin	87, 534, 536, 1108, 1371
Distorted Humor	173, 179, 186, 188, 244, 519, 689, 805, 921, 1230, 1564, 1589, 1675
Doncaster Rover	249
Dragon Pulse	141, 448, 449, 539, 584, 750, 759, 827, 847, 889, 901, 927, 1093, 1231, 1292, 1378, 1389, 1390, 1441, 1465, 1522, 1597
Dream Ahead	129, 185, 203, 372, 376, 417, 470, 530, 548, 1018, 1061, 1069, 1090, 1128, 1429, 1454, 1473, 1567
Dubawi	1, 2, 6, 7, 34, 144, 145, 169, 183, 184, 190, 195, 213, 220, 343, 358, 370, 402, 412, 596, 642, 662, 685, 694, 733, 765, 774, 790, 962, 1499, 1562, 1568, 1570, 1593, 1656, 1682
Duke Of Marmalade	281
Dutch Art	40, 147, 148, 219, 290, 294, 315, 386, 513, 569, 598, 620, 738, 742, 783, 796, 826, 971, 976, 987, 995, 1052, 1088, 1200, 1224, 1236, 1281, 1301, 1334, 1396, 1416, 1438, 1450, 1478, 1479, 1501, 1507, 1591, 1595, 1606, 1622, 1636, 1638, 1658
Dylan Thomas	749
Elnadim	625, 1094, 1289
Elusive City	366
Elusive Pimpernel	600, 920
Elusive Quality	20, 150, 435, 761, 789, 813, 1116, 1647
Elzaam	25, 247, 287, 426, 427, 483, 581, 670, 802, 863, 864, 1130, 1166, 1291, 1581
Equiano	33, 77, 102, 234, 238, 383, 395, 487, 490, 624, 965, 1092, 1133, 1225, 1573
Exceed And Excel	13, 32, 130, 159, 167, 170, 229, 257, 279, 285, 416, 467, 506, 514, 683, 703, 748, 764, 775, 792, 837, 950, 967, 972, 982, 1009, 1021, 1037, 1071, 1075, 1114, 1123, 1144, 1209, 1220, 1297, 1304, 1306, 1309, 1321, 1347, 1413, 1439, 1580, 1592

Excelebration	319, 443, 469, 501, 546, 556, 566, 595, 609, 729, 819, 934, 944, 952, 1111, 1115, 1179, 1244, 1255, 1348, 1625, 1635
Exchange Rate	390, 1197, 1569
Famous Name	1025, 1157, 1320, 1331, 1671, 1683
Fast Company	245, 305, 1140, 1148, 1403, 1423
Fastnet Rock	90, 108, 111, 117, 197, 368, 425, 550, 705, 712, 777, 833, 930, 959, 1214, 1227, 1240, 1489, 1490, 1491, 1526, 1640, 1644
Firebreak	131, 1440
First Defence	336, 340, 636, 1363, 1680, 1681
Footstepsinthesand	35, 352, 564, 1038, 1095, 1142, 1169, 1538
Foxwedge	232, 306, 371, 502, 700, 735, 843, 870, 1187, 1194, 1215, 1372, 1432, 1445, 1524, 1527, 1554
Frankel	29, 187, 191, 202, 225, 252, 253, 339, 350, 359, 362, 363, 422, 494, 547, 579, 588, 593, 637, 643, 644, 669, 684, 696, 744, 768, 771, 773, 779, 781, 916, 1054, 1132, 1141, 1276, 1329, 1332, 1340, 1453, 1464, 1470, 1474, 1505, 1506, 1513, 1566, 1587, 1601, 1639, 1667, 1685
Galileo	57, 92, 115, 223, 419, 421, 565, 653, 665, 687, 691, 692, 716, 737, 755, 778, 788, 992, 1146, 1196, 1226, 1245, 1246, 1247, 1248, 1250, 1251, 1252, 1253, 1257, 1262, 1263, 1264, 1267, 1268, 1269, 1270, 1272, 1275, 1344, 1457, 1481, 1482, 1511, 1514, 1687, 1693
Giant's Causeway	667, 1232
Haatef	1387
Halling	558
Harbour Watch	106, 239, 278, 292, 307, 439, 527, 567, 628, 756, 817, 868, 876, 883, 900, 963, 1003, 1020, 1126, 1168, 1282, 1375, 1434, 1458, 1461, 1557, 1676
Hard Spun	178, 259, 660
Hat Trick	380, 1402
Hellvelyn	1160
Helmet	177, 381, 751, 801, 846, 859, 957, 1046, 1049, 1170, 1298, 1322, 1425, 1516, 1553
Henrythenavigator	139, 284, 364, 485, 557, 1034, 1060, 1254, 1483, 1484, 1645
High Chaparral	121, 124, 133, 208, 230, 275, 561, 572, 709, 838, 969, 1081, 1353, 1359
Holy Roman Emperor	320, 481, 515, 618, 697, 704, 747, 766, 937, 1161, 1285, 1336, 1342, 1367, 1472, 1609, 1634
Iffraaj	243, 274, 497, 791, 848, 1040, 1118, 1213, 1488, 1653
Intense Focus	200, 207, 489, 1109, 1134, 1326, 1448
Intikhab	236, 365, 436, 459, 542, 991, 1022, 1183, 1376
Invincible Spirit	182, 254, 262, 378, 391, 392, 410, 415, 505, 563, 585, 615, 635, 641, 652, 661, 686, 711, 725, 746, 787, 803, 804, 875, 910, 913, 964, 983, 1048, 1072, 1110, 1112, 1249, 1345, 1354, 1365, 1391, 1466, 1503, 1508, 1509, 1572, 1579, 1610, 1612
Jeremy	1618
Kendargent	977, 1456
Kheleyf	43, 325, 377, 437, 627, 1105, 1476

SIRES INDEX

Kitten's Joy	455, 823, 1068, 1120, 1122
Kodiac	5, 11, 210, 241, 270, 299, 373, 379, 408, 429, 503, 571, 580, 717, 732, 758, 763, 824, 850, 856, 905, 919, 946, 1135, 1139, 1185, 1294, 1308, 1330, 1350, 1449, 1459, 1689
Kyllachy	19, 66, 78, 82, 95, 140, 268, 282, 312, 369, 397, 454, 533, 592, 602, 690, 728, 818, 862, 1077, 1222, 1412, 1415, 1613
Lawman	44, 55, 84, 119, 314, 317, 409, 414, 543, 607, 617, 831, 879, 886, 942, 968, 1010, 1029, 1045, 1087, 1192, 1203, 1205, 1207, 1256, 1302, 1328, 1384, 1405, 1525, 1536, 1543
Lemon Drop Kid	194, 638, 666
Lilbourne Lad	67, 484, 528, 881, 1177
Lonhro	3, 171, 172, 209, 841, 861, 1074, 1239, 1603, 1677
Lope De Vega	12, 60, 93, 114, 198, 222, 491, 518, 710, 715, 786, 924, 960, 973, 974, 1152, 1312, 1467, 1561, 1588, 1649, 1679
Majestic Missile	462
Makfi	88, 109, 507, 1147, 1182, 1211, 1455, 1662
Mastercraftsman	27, 30, 48, 79, 94, 164, 295, 400, 405, 549, 631, 699, 721, 931, 981, 997, 1039, 1083, 1210, 1392, 1537, 1605, 1630
Mawatheeq	619
Mayson	123, 384, 498, 583, 586, 591, 594, 614, 673, 860, 1151, 1333, 1414, 1521, 1582
Medaglia D'Oro	103, 132, 1228
Medicean	322, 1373, 1469, 1530, 1535, 1623
Miesque's Son	18
Mine	161
Mizzen Mast	610
More Than Ready	394, 1012, 1237
Motivator	544, 857
Mount Nelson	51, 65, 929
Multiplex	1102
Myboycharlie	316, 524, 895, 986, 1000
Nathaniel	56, 89, 128, 142, 338, 344, 348, 388, 404, 582, 650, 651, 655, 658, 671, 677, 678, 918, 1013, 1337, 1362, 1369, 1377, 1515, 1518, 1545
Native Khan	1357
Nayef	814
New Approach	22, 120, 199, 201, 204, 251, 313, 442, 681, 1191, 1586, 1668
Oasis Dream	107, 116, 137, 288, 354, 356, 407, 510, 511, 632, 648, 702, 743, 754, 762, 795, 935, 978, 1062, 1265, 1323, 1335, 1352, 1358, 1360, 1385, 1406, 1462, 1563, 1594, 1598, 1599, 1650, 1666, 1672, 1678
Paco Boy	45, 113, 535, 626, 869, 945, 1015, 1016, 1024, 1078, 1096, 1107, 1117, 1162, 1188, 1317, 1379, 1651
Passing Glance	37
Pastoral Pursuits	432, 471, 604, 815, 1164, 1576, 1614

Pivotal	127, 143, 446, 680, 682, 730, 769, 772, 799, 1124, 1400, 1430, 1444, 1451, 1480, 1487
Poet's Voice	59, 112, 155, 157, 168, 217, 360, 393, 474, 606, 723, 1047, 1070, 1086, 1089, 1153, 1201, 1218, 1290, 1307, 1338, 1361, 1529
Pour Moi	46, 552, 553, 1023, 1026, 1659
Power	70, 99, 100, 367, 456, 720, 740, 904, 954, 979, 1007, 1017, 1063, 1258, 1259, 1261, 1280, 1293, 1417, 1495, 1544
Pure Prize	812
Quality Road	17, 1014
Rajsaman	525
Raven's Pass	10, 47, 151, 156, 231, 298, 418, 674, 698, 816, 951, 993, 1064, 1216, 1314, 1654, 1690
Redoute's Choice	162, 321, 688, 706, 836, 1655
Requinto	452, 562, 597, 608, 752, 820, 899, 906, 1002, 1181, 1395, 1424
Rio De La Plata	23, 125, 1533
Rip Van Winkle	41, 149, 212, 389, 434, 464, 1195, 1208, 1283, 1409, 1460
Rock Of Gibraltar	424, 622, 872, 1042, 1346
Roderic O'Connor	645, 854
Royal Applause	96, 250, 346, 433, 531, 975, 1098, 1159, 1219, 1382, 1428, 1443, 1492, 1523
Sakhee's Secret	74, 375, 461, 523, 887, 1080, 1374, 1381
Sayif	138, 211, 227, 300, 323, 480, 1149, 1155, 1173, 1325, 1447
Scat Daddy	1229, 1243
Sea The Stars	192, 345, 355, 573, 713, 782, 966, 1206, 1498, 1502, 1532, 1575
Sepoy	8, 146, 256, 277, 337, 385, 458, 468, 492, 504, 611, 708, 714, 741, 760, 776, 829, 835, 871, 956, 989, 996, 1028, 1059, 1106, 1202, 1212, 1341, 1356, 1694
Shamardal	4, 21, 31, 174, 181, 189, 260, 351, 399, 406, 545, 612, 654, 657, 810, 907, 1051, 1053, 1145, 1221, 1383, 1500, 1565, 1571, 1574, 1607, 1664, 1665, 1684
Showcasing	72, 105, 160, 272, 450, 466, 532, 718, 988, 1167, 1315, 1355, 1420, 1578
Sir Percy	135, 858, 1399, 1528, 1541, 1549, 1615, 1648
Sir Prancealot	153, 280, 334, 453, 457, 475, 512, 736, 757, 888, 947, 1005, 1008, 1158, 1163, 1175, 1287, 1299, 1319, 1418, 1616, 1674
Sixties Icon	122, 289, 291, 296, 304, 308, 1099, 1199, 1238, 1295, 1646
Siyouni	646
Smart Strike	663, 1407
So You Think	560, 1065
Soldier Hollow	49
Stay Thirsty	126, 1235
Street Cry	24, 104, 165, 180, 734, 811, 961, 1305, 1669
Successful Appeal	98
Sunday Break	14
Tagula	311, 451, 568, 892, 1288, 1380, 1431, 1436, 1637

Tamayuz	224, 248, 447, 460, 477, 793, 851, 885, 890, 894, 994, 1410
Teofilo	36, 97, 205, 206, 235, 327, 413, 538, 745, 780, 1091, 1437, 1642, 1691
The Factor	517, 1493
Thewayyouare	61, 1097, 1143
Tin Horse	1620
Vale Of York	488, 616, 1313
War Front	175, 516, 656, 668, 675, 693, 984, 1241, 1242, 1260, 1271, 1277, 1278, 1279, 1590
Wildcat Heir	1234
Winker Watson	283
Zamindar	1085
Zebedee	154, 242, 265, 276, 472, 482, 540, 541, 599, 877, 903, 998, 1056, 1079, 1136, 1174, 1189, 1426, 1433, 1641, 1670
Zoffany	26, 73, 134, 420, 423, 537, 589, 948, 953, 1127, 1171, 1178, 1266, 1327, 1349, 1351, 1370, 1421, 1442, 1604, 1632

Racing Trends

The following tables focus on those two-year-old races that seem to produce winners that improve the following year as three-year-olds. This type of analysis can enable us to select some of the best of this year's classic generation.

In the tables, the figure in the third column indicates the number of wins recorded as a three-year-old, with GW signifying a Group race winner at that age and NR a non-runner.

The horses listed below are the winners of the featured races in 2015. Anyone looking for horses to follow in the listed and Group race events this season might well want to bear them in mind. I feel that those in bold text are particularly worthy of close scrutiny.

Air Force Blue	Manaafidh
Besharah	**Marcel**
Birchwood	Port Douglas
Epsom Icon	Promising Run
Folkswood	Qeyaadah
Galileo Gold	**Recorder**
Glamorous Approach	Sanus Per Aquam
Lumiere	**Stormy Antarctic**

Lowther Stakes York, 6 furlongs, August.		
2001	Queen's Logic	1 GW
2002	Russian Rhythm	3 GW
2003	Carry On Katie	0
2004	Soar	0
2005	Flashy Wings	0
2006	Silk Blossom	0
2007	Nahoodh	1 GW
2008	Infamous Angel	0
2009	Lady Of The Desert	1 GW
2010	Hooray	1
2011	Best Terms	0
2012	Rosdhu Queen	0
2013	Lucky Kristale	0
2014	Tiggy Wiggy	0
2015	Besharah	

This race is not the force it was of old and you have to go back to Nahoodh's Falmouth Stakes win in 2008 for the last Group 1 success. Besharah ran seven times last year and as well as winning this race she took the Princess Margaret Stakes. A tough, genuine Kodiac filly, she may not be as good this year as last, but another nice race can come her way.

Dewhurst Stakes Newmarket, 7 furlongs, October.		
2001	Rock Of Gibraltar	5 GW
2002	Tout Seul	0
2003	Milk It Mick	0
2004	Shamardal	3 GW
2005	Sir Percy	1 GW
2006	Teofilo	NR
2007	New Approach	3 GW
2008	Intense Focus	0
2009	Beethoven	1 GW
2010	Frankel	5 GW
2011	Parish Hall	0
2012	Dawn Approach	1 GW
2013	War Command	0
2014	Belardo	0
2015	Air Force Blue	

The Dewhurst Stakes remains our premier race for two-year-old colts. Frankel proved himself an outstanding champion of course and Rock of Gibraltar was a real star too. Other outstanding colts to win this in the last twenty years are Shamardal, Zafonic, Dr Devious, Grand Lodge, Sir Percy and New Approach. Last year Air Force Blue won the National Stakes as well as the Dewhurst. In the last 15 years only Teofilo, New Approach and Dawn Approach have done that. Further Group 1 glory beckons for Air Force Blue.

Zetland Stakes Newmarket, 10 furlongs, October/November.		
2000	Worthily	0
2001	Alexander Three D	2 GW
2002	Forest Magic	NR
2003	Fun And Games	NR

2004	Ayam Zaman	0
2005	Under The Rainbow	0
2006	Empire Day	NR
2007	Twice Over	2 GW
2008	Heliodor	1
2009	Take It To The Max	0
2010	Indigo Way	NR
2011	Mojave	0
2012	Restraint of Trade	NR
2013	Hartnell	2 GW
2014	Crafty Choice	NR
2015	Glamorous Approach	

Previous winners include the St Leger and Coronation Cup winner Silver Patriarch, the good four-year-olds Double Eclipse and Rock Hopper, Bob's Return (also a St Leger hero), the Ascot Gold Cup winner Double Trigger and of course Twice Over who won four Group 1's during his career with Henry Cecil including as a 6-y-o in 2011. Hartnell went on to win a Group 1 in Australia as a 4-y-o. So there's clearly an emphasis on winners of the Zetland improving with age. The Jim Bolger trained filly Glamorous Approach can improve further this year and will presumably step up to Group level now.

Cheveley Park Stakes
Newmarket, 6 furlongs, October.

2001	Queen's Logic	1 GW
2002	Airwave	1 GW
2003	Carry On Katie	0
2004	Magical Romance	0
2005	Donna Blini	1
2006	Indian Ink	1 GW
2007	Natagora	2 GW
2008	Serious Attitude	1 GW
2009	Special Duty	2 GW
2010	Hooray	1
2011	Lightening Pearl	0
2012	Rosdhu Queen	0
2013	Vorda	0
2014	Tiggy Wiggy	0
2015	Lumiere	

A number of these fillies have gone on to further Group race success. Indian Ink saved her best day for Royal Ascot, Natagora and Special Duty both went on to win the 1,000 Guineas and Serious Attitude returned to sprinting for another Group race success and the following year she won a Grade 1 sprint in Canada. Surprisingly though, no winner since 2010 has won again the following year. Lumiere will presumably take her chance in the Guineas and if she doesn't stay we can expect her to revert to sprinting. She has the speed and class to win another Group race or two.

Denford Stud Stakes (registered as Washington Singer Stakes) Newbury, 7 furlongs, August.

2001	Funfair Wane	1
2002	Muqbil	1 GW
2003	Haafhd	3 GW
2004	Kings Quay	0
2005	Innocent Air	1
2006	Dubai's Touch	2
2007	Sharp Nephew	1
2008	Cry of Freedom	0
2009	Azmeel	2 GW
2010	Janood	0
2011	Fencing	0
2012	Just The Judge	1 GW
2013	Somewhat	0
2014	Belardo	0
2015	Epsom Icon	

This race can often provide us with Group race or Classic pointers and in that regard the 90's winners Lammtarra and Rodrigo de Triano were outstanding and Haafhd won the 2,000 Guineas and the Champion Stakes. Azmeel trained on to win the Sandown Classic Trial and the Dee Stakes, but the race needed a pick-me-up and Just The Judge did that when winning the Irish 1,000 Guineas. Epsom Icon ran quite well on her 3-y-o debut in the Group 3 Nell Gwyn Stakes. She can get further black type and win another listed race this year.

Veuve Clicquot Vintage Stakes
Goodwood, 7 furlongs, July.

2001	Naheef	1 GW
2002	Dublin	1
2003	Lucky Story	0
2004	Shamardal	3 GW
2005	Sir Percy	1 GW
2006	Strategic Prince	0
2007	Rio De La Plata	0
2008	Orizaba	0
2009	Xtension	0
2010	King Torus	2
2011	Chandlery	0

2012	Olympic Glory	2 GW
2013	Toormore	1 GW
2014	Highland Reel	3 GW
2015	Galileo Gold	

All in all this race is very informative in terms of sorting out future stars, with the classic winners Sir Percy, Shamardal, Don't Forget Me, Dr Devious and Mister Baileys, plus the King George hero Petoski being the standouts of the past twenty odd years. Olympic Glory won two more Group 1's as a 4-y-o, so he can certainly be added to that list. Highland Reel won Grade 1's in the USA and Hong Kong last year. Galileo Gold acts on any ground and certainly has the ability to win more races.

National Stakes, Curragh, 7f, September.		
2001	Hawk Wing	1 GW
2002	Refuse To Bend	3 GW
2003	One Cool Cat	1 GW
2004	Dubawi	2 GW
2005	George Washington	2 GW
2006	Teofilo	NR
2007	New Approach	3 GW
2008	Mastercraftsman	3 GW
2009	Kingsfort	1
2010	Pathfork	0
2011	Power	1 GW
2012	Dawn Approach	1 GW
2013	Toormore	1 GW
2014	Gleneagles	2 GW
2015	Air Force Blue	

As one can see by the list of recent winners, this race is as important as any for figuring out the following year's top performers. For instance New Approach was outstanding when winning the Derby, the Champion Stakes and the Irish Champion, Mastercraftsman and Gleneagles both managed a couple of Group One wins at 3 yrs, and both Power and Dawn Approach notched up Group 1 successes as well. Air Force Blue was last year's champion two-year-old and he can surely win further Group 1's this year.

Racing Post Trophy *Doncaster, 8 furlongs, October.*		
2001	High Chaparral	5 GW
2002	Brian Boru	1 GW
2003	American Post	3 GW
2004	Motivator	2 GW
2005	Palace Episode	0
2006	Authorized	3 GW
2007	Ibn Khaldun	0
2008	Crowded House	0
2009	St Nicholas Abbey	0
2010	Casamento	1 GW
2011	Camelot	3 GW
2012	Kingsbarns	0
2013	Kingston Hill	1 GW
2014	Elm Park	1
2015	Marcel	

Some notable performers have won this race, including the outstanding colt High Chaparral, the Derby heroes Motivator and Authorized (both by Montjeu – also the sire of St Nicholas Abbey) and of course the 2,000 Guineas and Derby hero Camelot. Elm Park's sole success last year was in a listed event. Marcel may well find himself contesting the French 2,000 Guineas and French Derby, as opposed to the English equivalents. York's Dante Stakes could also be on the agenda. The Racing Post Trophy form was upheld when the second went on to win a Group 1 in France. I can see Marcel attaining further Group race glory this year.

Haynes, Hanson and Clark Stakes *Newbury, 8 furlongs, September.*		
2001	Fight Your Corner	1 GW
2002	Saturn	0
2003	Elshadi	0
2004	Merchant	NR
2005	Winged Cupid	NR
2006	Teslin	2
2007	Centennial	2 GW
2008	Taameer	0
2009	Ameer	0
2010	Moriarty	0
2011	Cavaleiro	0
2012	Wentworth	1
2013	Pinzolo	1
2014	Snoano	0
2015	Stormy Antarctic	

The high-class horses Rainbow Quest, Unfuwain, King's Theatre and Nayef have all won this race and indeed Shergar won it in 1980, but it's been a while since those glory days although Centennial did manage two Group race wins in 2008. Stormy Antarctic ran a remarkable race on his 3-y-o debut to win the Craven Stakes in impressive fashion. Whether or not that was due to the soft ground remains to be seen, but on that evidence he'll be a force to be reckoned with this year.

Somerville Tattersall Stakes Newmarket, 7 furlongs, September/October.

2001	Where Or When	2 GW
2002	Governor Brown	NR
2003	Milk It Mick	0
2004	Diktatorial	0
2005	Aussie Rules	2 GW
2006	Thousand Words	0
2007	River Proud	1
2008	Ashram	2
2009	Sir Parky	0
2010	Rerouted	0
2011	Crius	0
2012	Havana Gold	1 GW
2013	Miracle Of Medinah	0
2014	Maftool	1 GW
2015	Sanus Per Aquam	

The Group winners speak for themselves but Milk It Mick also went on to win a Grade 1 in America as a five-year-old. Aussie Rules took the French 2,000 Guineas and also won a Grade 1 event in America. Both River Proud and Ashram won listed races in their 3-y-o season and Havana Gold took the Prix Jean Prat over a mile. Maftool's sole success last year was in a Group 3 event in Dubai. The Jim Bolger trained Sanus Per Aquam is a son of Teofilo out of a half-sister to Dawn Approach, so the family has his fingerprints all over it. This colt will win again, possibly when stepped back up to a mile or further.

Rockfel Stakes, 7 furlongs, Newmarket.

2001	Distant Valley	0
2002	Luvah Girl	1 in USA
2003	Cairns	0
2004	Maids Causeway	1 GW
2005	Speciosa	1 GW
2006	Finsceal Beo	2 GW
2007	Kitty Matcham	0
2008	Lahaleeb	2 GW
2009	Music Show	2 GW
2010	Cape Dollar	0
2011	Wading	0
2012	Just The Judge	1 GW
2013	Al Thakhira	1
2014	Lucida	0
2015	Promising Run	

Three Newmarket 1,000 Guineas winners have hailed from the winners of this race since 1999 – Lahan, Speciosa and Finsceal Beo. For good measure Maids Causeway won the Coronation Stakes and Hula Angel won the Irish 1,000 Guineas (a race Finsceal Beo also added to her tally). Lahaleeb, Music Show and Just The Judge all went on to record Group 1 success at 3yrs. Al Thakhira's 3-y-o win came at listed level whilst Lucida was Group 1 placed twice but didn't notch up a win. Promising Run disappointed in the Fillies' Mile and yet she should get that trip. Worth another chance to win another nice race.

Beresford Stakes, Curragh, 1m.

2001	Castle Gandolfo	1
2002	Alamshar	3 GW
2003	Azamour	2 GW
2004	Albert Hall	0
2005	Septimus	1 GW
2006	Eagle Mountain	1 GW
2007	Curtain Call	1
2008	Sea The Stars	6 GW
2009	St Nicholas Abbey	0
2010	Casamento	1 GW
2011	David Livingston	0
2012	Battle of Marengo	2 GW
2013	Geoffrey Chaucer	0
2014	Ol' Man River	0
2015	Port Douglas	

Aidan O'Brien has taken over from John Oxx (Sea The Stars, Alamshar and Azamour) as the trainer who dominates this race, but his Ol' Man River was disappointing last year. After winning this race last year Port Douglas seemed to have his limitations exposed next time when fourth in the Racing Post Trophy, but as a son of Galileo and from a German middle-distance family he's likely to improve this season for a step up in trip.

Acomb Stakes, York, 7 furlongs, August.

2001	Comfy	NR
2002	Bourbonnais	0
2003	Rule Of Law	2 GW
2004	Elliots World	1
2005	Palace Episode	0
2006	Big Timer	0
2007	Fast Company	0
2008	ABANDONED	
2009	Elusive Pimpernel	1 GW

2010	Waiter's Dream	NR
2011	Entifaadha	0
2012	Dundonnell	1
2013	Treaty Of Paris	NR
2014	Dutch Connection	1 GW
2015	Recorder	

There have been a few disappointing seasons since the victories in the 90's of King's Best (2,000 Guineas) and Bijou d'Inde (St James's Palace Stakes), but Rule Of Law turned things around in 2004 with his St Leger victory and Elusive Pimpernel was successful in the Group 3 Craven Stakes. Dutch Connection won the Group 3 Jersey Stakes and was second in the Group 1 Prix Jean Prat. Owned by The Queen, the filly Recorder is by Galileo out of the smart but enigmatic racemare Memory. She should stay a mile this season and one would expect further improvement and another Group race victory.

Two-Year-Old Maiden for Colts Newbury Lockinge Meeting, 6 furlongs, May.

2001	Amour Sans Fin	0
2002	Cap Ferrat	2
2003	Grand Reward	1
2004	Iceman	0
2005	Championship Point (Div I)	1
	To Sender (Div II)	0
2006	Major Cadeaux	1 GW
2007	Coasting	NR
2008	Instalment (Div I)	1
	Orizaba (Div II)	0
2009	Canford Cliffs (Div I)	3 GW
	Meglio Ancora (Div II)	0
2010	Memen (Div I)	0
	Strong Suit (Div II)	3 GW
2011	Wise Venture	0
2012	Sir Patrick Moore	0
2013	Championship	1
2014	Adaay	3 GW
2015	Qeyaadah	

One of the season's first six furlong 2-y-o maidens, it regularly attracts a high quality field with plenty of winners going on to future success. Richard Hannon trained winners have regularly gone on to Group success and Canford Cliffs in particular is a standout here. Adaay did well last year, picking up a couple of Group 2's at Haydock Park and Newbury. Now a gelding, Qeyaadah is unlikely to be one of the better winners of this race in recent times.

7 furlong 2-y-o maiden at Newmarket's July Meeting (formerly the Strutt & Parker Maiden).

2001	Dubai Destination	0
2002	Tycoon Hall	0
2003	Josephus	0
2004	Belenus	2 GW
2005	Gin Jockey	0
2006	Kalgoorlie	0
2007	Rio De La Plata	0
2008	Soul City	0
2009	Elusive Pimpernel	1 GW
2010	Native Khan	1 GW
2011	Rougemont	0
2012	Ghurair	0
2013	True Story	1
2014	Lexington Times	1
2015	Manaafidh	

Although the statistics don't look that encouraging it should be noted that six out of the last ten winners went on to group success as older horses. Most notably, Dubai Destination took the Group 1 Queen Anne as a 4-y-o and Rio De La Plata was five before he won a pair of Group One's in Italy. Lexington Times won a listed event last year. A useful colt, Manaafidh may get a mile this year and he can win at listed level.

7 Furlong 2-y-o maiden (formerly the Trundle Maiden, Glorious Goodwood.

2001	Sweet Band	0
2002	Wahsheeq	0
2003	Psychiatrist	0
2004	Jonquil	0
2005	Opera Cape	0
2006	Kilburn	0
2007	Latin Lad	0
2008	Jukebox Jury	3 GW
2009	Stags Leap	1
2010	Pausanias	1 Listed
2011	Nawwaar	0
2012	Steeler	NR
2013	Snow Trouble	0
2014	Dutch Connection	1 GW
2015	Folkswood	

This was once a reliable maiden where numerous quality horses made their debuts in the 70's, 80's and early 90's. The quality of winners declined markedly but there have been signs of an upturn recently. Dutch Connection won the Group 3 Jersey Stakes as well as finishing runner-up in the Group 1 Prix Jean Prat. The lightly raced Folkswood should stay a mile and maybe ten furlongs this year. He should win another race or two at around listed level.

Superlative Stakes		
Newmarket, 7 furlongs, July.		
2001	Redback	1 GW
2002	Surbiton	NR
2003	Kings Point	0
2004	Dubawi	2 GW
2005	Horatio Nelson	0
2006	Halicarnassus	3 GW
2007	Hatta Fort	2 GW (in USA)
2008	Ole Ole	NR
2009	Silver Grecian	0
2010	King Torus	2
2011	Red Duke	0
2012	Olympic Glory	2 GW
2013	Good Old Boy Lukey	NR
2014	Estidhkaar	0
2015	Birchwood	

This race was raised to Group 2 from Group 3 in 2006. There are some very decent winners in this list, notably Dubawi and the more recent Olympic Glory who added two more Group 1's as a 4-y-o. Estidhkaar was Group 3 placed last year but didn't manage to win a race. Birchwood won three of his seven races last term and was third in both the Group 1 National Stakes and the Grade 1 Breeders' Cup Juvenile Turf. He should continue to give a good account of himself in races at around a mile.

Horse Index

HORSE	HORSE NO.
Abacus	122
Abatement	329
Abbu Rahy	123
Abiento	562
About Glory	814
Abouttimeyoutoldme	79
Above Normal	165
Accidental Agent	1032
Acclaimed	815
Actualisation	1413
Addeybb	730
Aegean Girl	1484
Afaak	935
Afandem	1313
Afdeek	731
Air Ministry	124
Ajaman King	1561
Akdaar	1562
Akhlaaq	251
Akranti	1451
Al Emaratalyoum	491
Al Hamdany	210
Al Nafoorah	493
Alabaster	1397
Alahida	1655
Alamthal	1563
Albizzia	80
Aldhara	1656
Alfawaris	252
Alfonso Manana	620
Aljunood	1657
All Crazy Now	1658
All India	996
All Mine	1659
Allegiance	1398
Alligator	492
Allography	791
Almoreb	816
Almukala	635
Alouja	1314
Alroom	732
Althiba	1383
Altiko Tommy	11
Alwaatheq	253
Alwafaah	254
Alwahsh	733
Always Amazing	369
Amabilis	81
Ambiguity	1240
Amelia Drean	282
American Patrol	125
Amna	211
Ancient Foe	21
Angel Down	268
Angel Of Darkness	936
Angel Of Rome	997
Angels Acclaim	1427
Angie Baby	1165
Anna Medici	1399
Anneen	1384
Any Questions	1086
Appreciating	22
Arabian Verse	792
Arborist	1076
Arc Royal	440
Argenterie	1542
Army General	1241
Art's Desire	1622
Arwa	937
Arzaak	255
Asaas	1564
Ashazuri	1371
Asking Price	636
Asmat	1660
Assam	1661
Assanilka	520
Astroshadow	1534
Astrostorm	1535
At The Beach	817
Atkinson Grimshaw	23
Atlanta Belle	1641
Atlantic Beauty	521
Atteq	563
Aureana	82
Auric Goldfinger	818
Aurora Gold	637
Aurora Spring	1280
Av A Word	1100
Aventus	998
Awaafy	734
Aware	24
Aware	314
Awareness	921
Azaly	256
Bab El Mandeb	1452
Backinanger	1428

Baggy Trousers	1182	Breakwater Bay		528
Bahamadam	1033	Bristol Missile		823
Bahamas	212	Broad Appeal		1373
Bahamian Paradise	1193	Brutal		1124
Bajan Spice	471	Buccaneer's Cove		564
Balestra	938	Buckeye		399
Balgair	1372	Buddha Boy		1125
Barney Roy	819	Buffalo Blues		1126
Barrington	939	Bush House		1316
Basheer	213	Buskin River		824
Battaash	940	Butoolat		1385
Battered	735	Butterfly Lily		84
Beach Break	83			
Beaconsfield	1194	Calamero		473
Bean Feasa	195	Caledonian King		1195
Beauchamp Opal	604	Call To Mind		737
Bee Case	1315	Calm Charm		1642
Bee Queen	1662	Camargue		1048
Believable	1496	Canaletto		565
Bella Alissa	315	Canford Tor		269
Benidiction	472	Cape Byron		1565
Bentayga Girl	370	Cape Falcone		1519
Berkshire Boy	25	Cape Sunshine		1485
Bernardo O'Reilly	1183	Captain Hawk		943
Best Bid	1414	Captor		1453
Big Time Baby	441	Caracas		331
Billy's Boots	283	Caramuru		825
Bing Bang Bank	69	Caravaggio		1243
Bint Batal	494	Caravela		284
Biologist	736	Careless Whisper		1184
Birds Of Prey	1299	Carson City		566
Bismarck The Flyer	820	Cartavio		1113
Bisous Y Besos	922	Cascavelle		1664
Bizzarria	638	Casimiro		332
Black Bolt	821	Caspian Gold		999
Blackbelle	442	Cassina Di Notte		216
Blazed	330	Castle Howard		1244
Blue Bahia	1663	Cautious Choice		1166
Blue Medici	1623	Champagne Queen		718
Blushing Rose	1497	Champion Harbour		567
Boater	1046	Chaparrachik		1359
Bobbio	214	Chaplin		1000
Bohemian Flame	26	Charity		85
Book Of Poetry	1047	Charlie Rascal		316
Booshbash	495	Chartbuster		27
Boost	1400	Cheerfilly		443
Born Legend	941	Cheerful Character		568
Born To Be	1300	Cheval Blanche		126
Borntosin	215	Chicago Star		285
Borthwen	942	Chiconomic		719
Brave Anna	1242	Chief Craftsman		400
Braztime	822	Chinese Art		1301
Breaking Free	1415	Chippenham		639

Chotto	1443	Cullingworth	571
Choumicha	1317	Cunco	644
Chupalla	1049	Curlew River	1050
Cinderella Queen	1147	Curry	828
Circle D'Or	640	Curtsy	1196
Circuit Judge	1087	Curve Ball	1002
Circulate	738	Cuttin' Edge	1208
Classical Times	317	Cyrus Dallin	645
Clearly	641		
Clef	569	Daffodil Mulligan	1167
Clem Fandango	426	Dagonet	334
Clemento	1001	Dahl	1051
Clenmistra	217	Daira Bridge	1567
Clifden Arts	1401	Daira Prince	1568
Cliff Bay	427	Dalavida	1456
Cliffs Of Moher	1245	Damocles	646
Cloistered	923	Dancesport	1613
Cloud Dragon	1318	Dancing Elegance	128
Coastal Cyclone	522	Dancing Waves	1127
Cobalty Isle	270	Dandy Roll	86
Comedienne	196	Daring Guest	1148
Commander	1566	Dark Destroyer	1553
Comprise	127	Dark Hero	946
Compton Lane	1156	Dark Pearl	1624
Computable	529	Daschas	1360
Comrade Conrad	333	Dash Of Spice	538
Condensed	496	Davinci Dawn	474
Conistone	157	Dawn Of A New Era	199
Conqueress	444	Dealer's Choice	1569
Constant Comment	197	Deauville Diva	1543
Contango	28	Decadent Times	445
Contentment	739	Decisive Intent	1302
Contessa Confessa	198	Decruz	271
Contrast	826	Defence Counsel	647
Control Centre	827	Deleyll	741
Cool Breeze	1454	Delfie Lane	1003
Cool Climate	570	Delta Dreamer	1666
Coping Stone	237	Desert Capella	1499
Copper Knight	1319	Desert Explorer	1034
Coral Sea	944	Desert Water	829
Coronet	642	Devillish Guest	286
Count Octave	29	Devil's Bridge	830
Coverham	158	Dewan	287
Coya	945	Diable D'Or	1035
Cracksman	643	Diagnostic	742
Crimson Lake	1455	Diamante	1101
Cristal Fizz	740	Dick Tracy	831
Cristofano Allori	1665	Dime A Dance	1386
Crossing Paths	401	Diodorus	1247
Cryptonite	605	Diptych	1402
Crystal Ocean	1498	Dirchill	70
Crystal Stanza	606	Discovered	335
Cuff	1246	Distant	336

Diva Power	1544	Eolian	1089		
Dixie's Double	1102	Equitation	1573		
Dixon	1536	Equity	238		
Dizzy	1052	Escobar	1320		
Doctor Bartolo	947	Espresso Freddo	1403		
Dolokhov	1168	Esprit De Corps	337		
Dontforgettocall	1554	Essential	1444		
Double Dutch	1416	Estrellada	288		
Dourado	832	Eternal Dream	1090		
Dr Goodhead	948	Etikaal	385		
Dr Julius No	87	Ettu	1625		
Dragstone Rock	539	Euginio	833		
Drake Passage	1303	Eula Varner	272		
Dramatic Exit	1304	Euqranian	1226		
Dravid	1157	Europium	1667		
Dream Field	648	Evergate	1321		
Dream Machine	129	Everything For You	1430		
Dream Of Dreams	1429	Exciting Times	447		
Dreaming Of Paris	743	Exposition	1114		
Dreamorchid	530	Express Lady	1322		
Driver's Girl	218	Exquisite Ruby	950		
Drochaid	30	Eynhallow	338		
Drumochter	949				
Duality	1053	Fabric	834		
Dubai Hero	166	Fair Cop	32		
Dubai Knights	475	Fair Eva	339		
Dubai One	167	Fair Head	497		
Dubara	402	Fairy Lights	1574		
Dubawi Prince	1570	Falcon Cliffs	1555		
Duck Egg Blue	1387	Falcon Rising	1077		
Dusky Maid	621	Falcon's View	169		
Dutch Quality	219	Falling Leaves	1250		
Dutchess Of Fife	1088	Family Fortunes	1078		
		Farleigh Mac	33		
Eartha Kitt	446	Farook	951		
Eastern	31	Father McKenzie	289		
Eiramach Na Casca	200	Favourite Royal	1036		
El Nino Sea	573	Fearsome	88		
Eldorado Creek	572	Feint	745		
Eldritch	649	Felstead Queen	1556		
Elementary	130	Ferreira	1149		
Elerfaan	1571	Fibonacci	1457		
Elizabeth Browning	1248	Fidaaha	1668		
Elliptical	371	Fiery Character	448		
Elyaasaat	744	Fiery Spice	372		
Emmaus	1572	Fire Brigade	131		
Enable	650	Firegate	340		
Endless Charm	1	Firey Speech	1669		
Enforcing	1643	First Dance	1520		
Ennjaaz	168	First Nation	2		
Ensign	1249	Five Star Frank	1037		
Entangling	1644	Flame Out	556		
Envoy	555	Flawlessly	159		

374 TWO-YEAR-OLDS OF 2016

Fleeting Motion	835	Great Court	405
Flooded	1103	Great Sound	653
Footman	1004	Grey Thou Art	273
For The Roses	89	Guiding Star	274
Forest Steps	1169	Gulliver	1325
Forever Excel	952	Gustav Klimt	1251
Forster Square	574	Gustavo Fring	1185
Fortitude	1323	Gymnaste	654
Forward Contract	1197		
Four Dragons	449	Hakeem	748
Frankuus	1054	Hakeem (FR)	837
Fresh Fox	1374	Hamelin Pool	275
Frontispiece	1500	Hammerstein	1577
Fujaira Bridge	1575	Handful	342
Full Intention	450	Happy Queen	1151
Funky Footsteps	1038	Haraka	90
Furud	1670	Harbour Force	1557
		Harbour Master	1282
Galactic Prince	34	Harbour Rock	1458
Garnetta	1361	Harbour Siren	239
Geego	575	Harbouring	1375
Gentle Whisper	607	Harlequin Rose	290
Gentleman Giles	1281	Hartswell	655
George Ravenscar	1614	Hathfa	1006
George Reme	1417	Hathiq	257
Getgo	1115	Hawana	656
Gilgamesh	1445	Haworth	160
Giovanni Acuto	836	Hawridge Glory	1159
Girl Squad	1022	Hazy Manor	451
Girlofinkandstars	720	Head Monitor	925
Glassalt	132	Heaven's Rock	452
Glencadam Glory	651	Hedging	1039
Glitter Girl	746	Heir Of Excitement	1431
Global Alexander	1324	Hellofahaste	1160
Global Applause	498	Henriqua	364
Glorious Artist	953	Here And Now	91
Glorious Forever	1626	Hereitizz	1645
Glorious Politics	71	Hernandes	1627
Glorious Power	954	Hidden Steps	35
Glorious Rocket	403	High Commander	36
Glory Of Paris	1158	High Excitement	955
God Given	404	High On Love	608
Gog Elles	1170	Highland Pass	37
Golconda King	576	Hilario	956
Golconda Prince	577	Himself	838
Golden Guest	1150	Hippocampus	839
Golden Handcuffs	201	Hochfeld	1055
Golden Slam	1576	Hold Me Tight	1171
Goldrush	202	Hollywood Harry	428
Good Craic	652	Holyroman Princess	1161
Good Omen	747	Honour And Glory	1671
Goodwood Crusader	1005	Horroob	1578
Grandee	924	Horseplay	38

Hot N Sassy	1172	Jack The Truth	1446
Hot Natured	476	Jakastar	276
Hotcake	318	Jannia	1040
Hotfill	72	Jashma	1007
How	1252	Jazaalah	259
Hugging The Rails	531	Je Suis Charlie	133
Hunaina	793	Jersey Heartbeat	842
Hurricane Rush	957	Jessinamillion	161
Hushood	840	Jinkie Pink	1091
Hydrangea	1253	Jive Talking	134
Hyperfocus	1326	John Honeyman	926
Hyzenthlay	1254	Joshua Reynolds	658
		Juan Horsepower	843
I Wouldn't Bother	1104	Juanito Chico	1023
Ibn Alemarat	1327	Julie In The Crown	292
Ice Pac	1162	Jumira Bridge	1579
If I Say So	1173	Jumira Prince	1580
Il Sicario	1056	Jumping Jack	1008
Illaunmore	657	Jupiter Ascending	609
Imagine If	1128	Jurassic	622
Imdancinwithurwife	453	Jus Pires	1229
Impact Point	39	Justice Frederick	1256
Impart	1672		
Impassioned	1404	Kachess	454
Imperial City	958	Kadi	1558
Imphal	1545	Kahrab	1057
In First Place	578	Kananee	170
In Somno	203	Karaganda	1673
Inconceivable	92	Karawaan	1502
Indigo Beat	477	Katebird	1058
Infanta Isabella	12	Katmandoo	455
Inferad	841	Kazawi	343
Ingleby Mackenzie	291	Keeper's Choice	365
Inlawed	1628	Keir Hardie	844
Inspector	1328	Keyser Soze	1186
Instigation	499	Khafoo Shemimi	845
Interlope	1227	Khanisari	794
Interweave	1501	Khattar	1329
Intimate Art	40	Khitaamy	500
Intisha	1376	Kick King Katie	532
Intrepidly	1228	Kilmah	1059
Investigation	41	King Electric	1130
Iron Lady	1209	King Of Nepal	277
Island In The Sky	1459	King Of Paris	1009
Isomer	42	King's Advice	579
Istan	1255	Kingston Tasmania	43
It's How We Roll	959	Kiruna Peak	293
Ivor's Fancy	540	Kiss The Wind	1131
Ivor's Magic	541	Knighthood	1546
		Knight's Dream	1674
Jaazem	258	Know The Truth	44
Jack Blane	1105	Kocollada	580
Jack Flash	1129	Kodi Da Capo	429

Name	No.	Name	No.
Kodiac Khan	1330	Lualiwa	1432
Kodiac Pearl	373	Lucata	457
Koeman	294	Luduamf	851
Kohinoor Diamond	501	Luqyaa	663
Kreb's Cycle	846	Luzia	1011
Kschessinska	135	Lynique	749
Kuiper Belt	1116		
		Maazel	1581
La Isla Bonita	1187	Mabaady	1388
La Vie En Rose	1060	Mabrook	220
Ladofash	478	Madame Bounty	1629
Lady Beware	927	Madeenaty	664
Lady Hesta	659	Mafaaheem	260
Lady In Question	581	Magdalene Fox	502
Lady Kaviar	1152	Magellan	345
Lady Louise	542	Maggi May	241
Lady Parker	1174	Magic	665
Last Paradise	479	Magic Pass	47
Latest Quest	1079	Magical Forest	221
Laura's Oasis	795	Magillen	960
Lavaspin	660	Majboor	750
Law Power	1405	Major Jumbo	1433
Lawfilly	1010	Majoris	1332
Leapt	344	Makkaar	1064
Legato	456	Makkadanddang	48
Legendary Lunch	847	Makman	503
Leontes	45	Malcolm The Pug	852
Lewinsky	1331	Malmas	961
Lexington Sky	848	Mambo Dancer	1065
Light Humor	1230	Mamdood	853
Light Laughter	1675	Manaahil	962
Lightable	406	Mancini	1377
Lightening Dance	1362	Mandarin	222
Lightening Fast	1132	Manners Maketh Man	93
Lightning Mark	661	Manolito De Madrid	49
Lightning North	1521	Maori Bob	136
Limelight Lady	523	Marettimo	963
Limelite	849	Margherita	1582
Liquid	73	Marilyn	1646
Liquid Gold	582	Mark Of Approval	666
Little Miss Lucky	623	Marketeer	407
Littlebeck Lady	1615	Markus Twain	1389
Logi	850	Mashadie Boy	1460
Lomu	430	Master Billie	1210
London Grammar	1418	Master Singer	667
Long John Silver	1283	Masterfilly	1630
Look My Way	46	Materialist	1583
Looting	240	Maths Prize	346
Loujain	662	Mawqed	1503
Love Dreams	1061	Max Zorin	50
Love Oasis	1062	Mazyoun	1333
Love Power	1063	Medicine Jack	1133
Loving Clarets	583	Megan Lily	584

HORSE INDEX

Name	No.	Name	No.
Melisandre	1134	Mulsanne Chase	1199
Mellow	1198	Mulzim	506
Melting Dew	1504	Mums The Word	860
Merlin	137	Munawer	1334
Mesbaar	1584	Munro	95
Meteoric Riser	1012	Muqaatil	861
Metronomic	854	Muqtanny	1678
Meyandi	51	Muraaqeb	671
Meyrick	751	Musawaat	965
Mia Tia	624	Muscika	862
Miami Blue	1135	Mushaireb	585
Middle Kingdom	668	Mushareefa	507
Mightaswellsmile	625	Music Lesson	1200
Migyaas	171	Music Seeker	557
Milium	1363	Mustarrid	863
Mimic's Memory	480	Mutahaady	864
Mirage Dancer	1505	Mutawatheb	865
Miss Anticipation	347	Mutineer	1106
Miss Bates	481	Muzbid	1679
Miss Fay	138	My Cherry Blossom	533
Miss Mirabeau	1406	My Lady Marie	1364
Miss Nouriya	223	My Timing	1305
Miss Osier	721	Myladyjane	295
Miss Patience	319	Mystic Dawn	1462
Miss Sugars	1461	Mystical	1390
Mistress Quickly	94	Mythical Spirit	1522
Mitigate	543		
Mlle Georges	1066	Naaeebb	172
Moamar	504	Naafer	754
Modern Approach	204	Nadia Glory	1335
Moghrama	1676	Nadia Promise	755
Mohsen	1547	Nafaayes	966
Mojito	752	Najashee	262
Monaadhil	1548	Nancy Hart	458
Monarch's Glen	669	Nargiza	1647
Money In My Pocket	855	Nastenka	1631
Monoshka	856	Natavia	348
Montataire	1067	Nathania	1013
Moolazim	224	Nations Alexander	866
Mooltazem	670	Native Prospect	53
Moonlight Silver	1211	Nature's Order	672
Mori	1506	Nautical Haven	1434
Moritzburg	796	Naval Warfare	54
Motahassen	1677	Nayyar	967
Mouille Point	857	Neoclassical	1680
Mountain Angel	1585	Nepeta	1068
Mr Scaramanga	858	Neptune's Secret	1080
Mr Tyrrell	859	Neshmeya	968
Mubtasim	753	Netley Abbey	524
Mucho Applause	52	Never A Word	3
Mudallel	505	Never Surrender	969
Muhajjal	261	New Tale	756
Mulhimatty	964	Newcomer	1586

Nibras Bounty	867	Paquita Bailarina	626
Nigg Bay	1306	Parisian Chic	408
Night Law	55	Parlance	1509
Nile Empress	1336	Partitia	1510
Noble Ballad	96	Party Nights	409
Noble Behest	1549	Parys Mountain	970
Noble Intention	1136	Patching	232
Noble Masterpiece	1507	Patchwork	1016
Nobly Born	673	Pattie	296
North Carolina	1257	Pavela	297
Northdown	1117	Peace Envoy	1258
Nostalgie	722	Peace Telegram	139
Nothing But Dreams	1587	Peace Terms	97
November Tale	1137	Peaceful Passage	675
Novoman	757	Peach Melba	1069
Nuncio	349	Peach Pavlova	483
Nuptials	1041	Peak Princess	870
Nurse Nightingale	1337	Pealer	676
		Peking Flyer	1632
Occurrence	350	Penny Green	558
Ocean Promise	1014	Pentito Rap	1407
Oceanic	1419	Perfect Angel	58
Oceanus	508	Perfect In Pink	298
Ode To Glory	723	Perfect Madge	1435
Oden	1588	Performing	1420
Off To Bond Street	1024	Persophanie	871
Oh Geno	1188	Peter Stuyvesant	366
Oh It's Saucepot	1648	Peterport	677
Okool	263	Petticoat	797
Olly's Folly	1307	Phijee	1212
Olympic Legend	1486	Piaffe	98
Omeros	1338	Pichola Dance	1589
Omneeya	225	Piedita	1408
On Her Toes	758	Pincheck	410
On Show	243	Pink Bubbles	971
On To Victory	1042	Pirate Look	226
One Liner	928	Plage Depampelonne	162
One Too Many	242	Playful Trickster	459
Open Wide	1365	Playing Trix	1590
Opening Time	868	Plead	1591
Opera Queen	56	Pleaseletmewin	99
Opinionate	1366	Poet's Princess	1201
Orange Gin	341	Poet's Society	1070
Original Choice	759	Poet's Vanity	59
Orin Swift	1378	Poet's Wish	1153
Orsino	57	Poker Alice	320
Our Lois	431	Portledge	163
Outre Mer	674	Poseidon	1633
		Power Home	367
Paco Punch	869	Power Surge	100
Paco's Angel	1015	Prairie Light	1081
Panova	1508	Prazeres	760
Panther In Pink	482	Precious Ramotswe	678

Precision	1511	Red Gunner	762
Prerogative	872	Red Label	412
Presence Process	411	Red Shanghai	460
Present Tense	679	Redgrave	974
Presidential	1391	Redicean	322
Pretty Passe	972	Refreshed	1409
Primadonna	873	Regal Splendour	682
Prince Monolulu	140	Rehana	798
Princess De Lune	351	Reign On	102
Princess Holly	374	Reinstorm	590
Private Advisor	680	Renamed Me King	1308
Private Matter	586	Repton	877
Private Mission	1202	Restore	878
Prize Diva	544	Retribution	1118
Procurator	874	Rich History	1682
Profiling	681	Rickrack	413
Promising	875	Right Honorable	1683
Pronounced	1259	Ringside Support	206
Prosper	1592	Ripper Street	509
Psychedelic Funk	1138	Rise Again	1393
Punte Linke	587	Rising Eagle	975
Purdey	1392	Ristretto	103
Pussy Galore	876	Rita's Man	879
		Rock In Peace	1139
Quantum Field	244	Rock N Roll Global	1017
Queen Beatrice	1213	Rock On Dandy	525
Queen In Waiting	1071	Roly Poly	1260
Queen Kindly	588	Romanor	1634
Queen Of The Ring	205	Romantic View	4
Queen Of Time	278	Ronald R	142
Queen's Castle	1512	Room To Roam	1140
Queen's Light	1214	Rose Of China	799
Quick Chat	1681	Rosebride	591
Quinquereme	761	Rosencranz	1593
		Royal Blue Caravel	485
Raawy	386	Royal Request	1523
Radar Love	1175	Royal Vigil	1684
Raffle King	299	Rubens Dream	976
Rainbow Legacy	1513	Rubiesnpearls	592
Rainbow Mist	484	Rumpole	1203
Rapid Rise	245	Ruxley's Star	880
Rashford's Double	589		
Ray's The Money	141	Sabadilla	1463
Reach High	173	Sadhbh	881
Reader's Choice	321	Salouen	1082
Really Special	174	Saluti	1368
Really Super	101	Samharry	683
Rebecca Rocks	279	Sanam	510
Rebel De Lope	973	Sand Shoe	352
Record Number	175	Sandwood Bay	1538
Red Emperor	1367	Santa Anabaa	1309
Red Ensign	387	Sao Paulo	1261
Red Guana	1025	Satin Ribbon	545

Savannah Slew	627	Six Strings	597
Sawlaat	882	Sniper Viper	1107
Sayesse	300	Snow Squaw	546
Sayif Dancing	323	So Cute	1649
Sayif El Barri	227	So Sleek	414
Sayif Magic	1447	Sobriety	598
Scarpach	432	Social Secretary	885
Scudding	610	Socrates	1108
Sea My Angel	1310	Solar Cross	355
Sea Of Grace	1311	Solar Shower	356
Sea Shack	1092	Solent Meads	1109
Seafront	1524	Solitary Sister	1190
Seaside Dreamer	143	Solo Saxophone	1685
Second Page	883	Somerset Maugham	1263
Second Thought	763	Somewhere Secret	375
Secret Soul	104	Somnambulist	434
Secret Strategy	5	Son Of Rest	1487
See The Sea	884	Sorelle Delle Rose	1686
Seed Corn	764	Soul Silver	1465
Seirios	1464	Sound Bar	107
Senator	593	Sounds Of April	229
Seniority	765	South Seas	60
Sentinel	611	Spanish Dawn	801
Seven Heavens	684	Sparkle	511
Sfumato	353	Spatial	1514
Shadow Wing	461	Special Ops	1141
Shanghai Silver	977	Special Relation	1204
Sharja Bridge	1594	Speciale Di Giorno	230
Shawami	301	Speed Freak	108
She	144	Spin Doctor	594
Sheikspear	1559	Spin Top	1560
Sheila's Fancy	1176	Spinnaka	415
Sheila's Lad	1177	Spirit Of Rome	164
Sheila's Rock	368	Spiritous	686
Sheppard's Gift	534	Splash Around	1515
She's Zoff	1421	Spongie Cake	886
Shift Cross	228	Spring Eternal	978
Shimmering Light	145	Springwood	599
Shimmll	800	Spun Gold	416
Show Me The Music	596	Stag Party	61
Shozita	105	Star Archer	1339
Shyarch	1154	Star Maker	1083
Sidewinder	462	Star Of Rory	463
Silent Echo	354	Star Stream	1551
Silver Line	176	Starboard Watch	628
Silver Link	1550	Starlight Romance	595
Silverlight	685	Starlite Sienna	600
Simmy's Temple	433	Stay Sharp	1448
Singer Sargent	1262	Stellekaya	1537
Singing Sands	106	Sterling Silva	887
Single Estate	1410	Stevie Brown	246
Sir Harry Collins	1189	Sticks McKenzie	146
Sir Plato	1163	Stone The Crows	357

HORSE INDEX

Stormy Clouds	888	Thafeera	984
Street Jazz	629	Thammin	267
Stringybark Creek	302	The Albatros	1265
Study	766	The Big Short	985
Subatomic	109	The Grand Visir	768
Subhaan	1595	The Lacemaker	513
Suffragette City	889	The Last Lion	1073
Sugar Beach	486	The Nazca Lines	1423
Suited	535	The Statesman	1266
Sukiwarrior	979	Thistimenext Year	1191
Sukoot	512	Three Duchesses	147
Sun Angel	280	Thunder Crash	1142
Sun Bear	980	Tiggaliscious	896
Sunset Sally	1422	Tilly Trotter	1689
Super Julius	1043	Time Chaser	358
Super Talent	177	Time Down Under	1539
Sureyoutoldme	890	Tinted	687
Sutter County	1072	Tip Of The City	1650
Swag	891	Tirania	769
Swan Serenade	1379	Tisbutadream	548
Sweet Pursuit	1164	Titanicus	986
Sweet Sue	388	To Have A Dream	1178
Swilly Bay	981	Tocco D'Amore	1690
Swiss Storm	547	Tomily	897
Switch In Time	1687	Tonahutu	1616
Syncopation	1084	Top Score	178
Syndicate	110	Torcello	62
		Toronto Sound	1411
Taamol	1516	Towie	1206
Tadkhirah	767	Town Charter	1074
Tadween	892	Trade Route	549
Tafaakhor	893	Tradfest	208
Tagur	1436	Trading Punches	247
Tai Hang Dragon	894	Trevanna	1395
Tai Sing Yeh	982	Trick Of The Light	1597
Taj Mahal	1264	Tropical Rock	111
Talaayeb	264	True Romance	631
Tallulah Rocks	1380	Turpin's Treasure	536
Tallulah Rose	13	Twenty Times	1018
Tanbeeh	1596	Twiston Shout	1192
Tapdance Alltheway	1369	Twizzel	487
Tawaafeej	265	Two For Tea	929
Tawaleef	1394	Typhoon Rising	1143
Tawny Port	630	Tzavo	1340
Tempera	1688		
Temple Church	1205	UAE King	1598
Teomaria	1437	UAE Queen	1599
Teo's Music	207	Ugneya	1691
Teqany	266	Ultimate Avenue	1635
Tesko Fella	895	Uncle Charlie	488
Texas Wedge	1215	Unforgettable Filly	1341
Textured	1517	Unit Of Assessment	1093
Thaaqib	983	Upended	1651

Ustudio	987	Wine List	64
		Winning Bid	526
Valcartier	688	Winston C	149
Van Dongen	1267	With One Accord	902
Vatican Hill	601	Wurood	770
Vaulted	602		
Velvet Voice	1540	Xenon	1412
Velveteen	1144		
Ventura Blues	898	Yabrave	1602
Ventura Jazz	603	Yalta	1075
Vermilion	1636	Yamarhaba Malayeen	389
Via Egnatia	689	Yaraki	771
Victory Angel	1600	Yes You	633
Vincy	802	Yorkshire Rover	249
Visionary	376		
Vivian Ward	690	Zahiya	1345
Voi	1342	Zain Star	612
Vote	559	Zamadance	1085
		Zamjar	514
Waishbooshbash	377	Zanobia	1466
Wakened	464	Zavikon	1019
Waqaas	988	Zebby Sizz	903
War Of Succession	63	Zefferino	359
War Office	148	Zig Zag Girl	304
Wardy	324	Zihaam	1396
Warm Oasis	632	Zirconia	1692
Warm Words	112	Zoffanist	1370
Warrior's Spirit	899	Zumran	1346
Watchman	1601		
Waves	1044	Unnamed	
Wayflower	1145	6-10, 15-20, 65-68, 75-78, 114-121, 150-156,	
Wedding Breakfast	1343	179-194, 209, 231, 233-236, 250, 305-313,	
Wedding Dress	248	325-328, 360-363, 378-384, 390-398, 417-	
Wefait	900	425, 435-439, 465-470, 489-490, 515-519,	
What A Boy	113	527, 537, 550-554, 561, 613-619, 634, 692-	
What A Home	1312	717, 724-729, 772-790, 803-813, 904-920,	
Whip Nae Nae	901	930-934, 989-995, 1020-1021, 1026-1031,	
Whispering Bell	691	1045, 1094-1099, 1110-1112, 1119-1123,	
White Rosa	1344	1146, 1155, 1179-1181, 1207, 1216-1225,	
Whiteley	303	1231-1239, 1269-1279, 1284-1298, 1347-	
Whosyourhousemate	1617	1358, 1381-1382, 1424-1426, 1438-1442,	
Wick Powell	74	1449-1450, 1467-1483, 1488-1495, 1518,	
Wild Irish Rose	1268	1525-1533, 1541, 1552, 1603-1612, 1618-	
Wild Shot	560	1621, 1637-1640, 1652-1654, 1693-1694	
Willwams	281		
Wind In The Trees	14		

Dams Index

DAM	HORSE NO.
A L'Aube	1424
A Z Warrior	1269
Aaraas	1383
Abandon	123
Abergeldie	132
Absolutely Cool	265
Accede	1379
Achieving	179
Acquifer	360
Acts Of Grace	1196
Admire The View	176
Adonesque	1347
Adoration	692
Adoring	922
Affectionately	1564
Affirmative	1036
African Moonlight	877
African Rose	339
Again	1250
Age Of Chivalry	386
Agnetha	1683
Agony Aunt	1133
Agreeable Miss	666
Ainia	989
Aiseiri	205
Akdarena	1451
Aktia	486
Al Hawa	1020
Al Ihtithar	904
Al Joudha	690
Al Mahmeyah	1313
Alanza	1655
Alba Stella	1398
Albeed	1094
Albertine Rose	1110
Aldebaran Light	1230
Alexander Goldrun	202
Alexander Wonder	905
Aliante	465
Alice Alleyne	240
Alifandango	428
Alina	819
Aljafliyah	603
Alkhawarah	508
All Embracing	1171
All For Laura	795
All Hallows	1205
All Night Dancer	1095
Alla Speranza	836
Alluring Park	1267
Almatinka	817
Almiranta	925
Almunia	883
Alshahbaa	803
Alta Definizione	1443
Alta Moda	1249
Altishaan	11
Altitude	80
Alvarita	1397
Always Remembered	1650
Alzerra	1603
Amalfi	815
Amanda Carter	1096
Amanee	225
Amanjena	1193
Amazed	369
Amazing Win	305
Amazon Beauty	142
Amber Nectar	1261
America Nova	417
Amorama	314
Amour Fou	906
Ana Style	524
Anadolu	1037
Anamarka	791
Anapola	1167
And Again	613
And I	306
Andina	686
Aneedah	418
Angelic Note	294
Angie And Liz	1165
Anka Britannia	1254
Anna Law	940
Anna Palariva	765
Annalina	515
Anne Of Kiev	1226
Anneliina	1003
Annouska	1284
Annus Iucundus	482
Another Storm	937
Antique	799
Any For Love	1647
Anyaas	459
Aoife Alainn	1580
Apace	976
Aphorism	851

Appleblossom Pearl	845	Balm	1148
Approach	642	Baltic Belle	1449
April	307	Baralinka	611
April Pride	1452	Barawin	1078
Apticanti	942	Barter	407
Aqraan	531	Battery Power	1540
Aqsaam	984	Bauble Queen	175
Aqualina	528	Bawaakeer	70
Aquarius Star	841	Bayalika	766
Arabescatta	162	Be Special	445
Aravonian	1401	Beautiful Filly	1341
Arazena	413	Beautiful Lady	75
Archina	1408	Beauty Is Truth	1253
Arctic Char	1162	Bee Eater	1034
Ardbrae Lady	550	Before The Storm	1093
Ardent	1404	Bel Air Beauty	693
Ardent Lady	589	Belenkaya	660
Areyaam	378	Belgique	886
Arizona Jewel	685	Belle Watling	759
Arosa	930	Bended Knee	146
Arpege	954	Beneventa	1064
Arrive	350	Best Bidder	526
Artisti	1314	Best Intent	1302
Artistic License	1126	Best Terms	772
Arty Crafty	410	Bethrah	1656
Aryaamm	180	Betrothed	61
Ascendancy	367	Beverley Macca	732
Ashdali	719	Bewitched	419
Asheerah	1384	Beyond Desire	773
Asinara	1519	Bidding Time	559
Ask Annie	1097	Bijan	432
Askeria	1660	Billie Jean	1210
Astrodiva	1534	Bimini	990
Astrolibra	1535	Binabee	1315
Astrologie	612	Bint Almukhtar	1011
Ataraxy	1657	Birmanie	57
Atishoo	431	Birthday Suit	535
Attracted To You	878	Bishop's Lake	453
Ava's World	1131	Black Belt Shopper	278
Avodale	376	Black Dahlia	1467
Avon Lady	30	Black Mascara	1643
Aweebounce	281	Black Meyeden	581
Azabara	855	Blanche Dubawi	233
Azita	105	Blane Water	1105
Azzoom	256	Blessings Count	390
		Blinking	13
Badalona	150	Blissful Beat	1348
Bahama Spirit	655	Blue Azure	1111
Baldovina	1183	Blue Crest	480
Balladiene	214	Blue Iris	1280
Ballybacka Lady	907	Blue Lyric	723
Ballygologue	1618	Blue Maiden	762
Ballymore Celebre	683	Bluebelle	1623

Name	Page	Name	Page
Bobby Jane	763	Catbells	1525
Bogini	1128	Catch The Moon	1484
Bonnie Brae	474	Catchline	181
Boo Boo Bear	1468	Catwalk	447
Bootery	244	Caumshinaun	1693
Born Something	412	Causeway Charm	69
Boucheron	908	Causeway Queen	1186
Bourbonella	331	Ceiling Kitty	446
Bowness	605	Ceist Eile	1668
Brave Madam	1390	Centenerola	471
Brazilian Bride	1663	Cercle D'Amour	1046
Brazilian Style	1098	Cesseras	634
Breedj	489	Challow Hills	1285
Brick Tops	237	Chance For Romance	620
Bride Unbridled	1342	Chantilly Pearl	1067
Bridle Belle	590	Chaquiras	1048
Briery	822	Charlecote	1089
Bright Morning	801	Charming	1241
Bright Sapphire	997	Chatline	552
Brigitta	694	Check The Label	774
Brilliance	1107	Cheeky Weeky	1172
Bruxcalina	84	Chelsea Morning	936
Bryanstown	391	Chelsey Jayne	1266
Bugie D'Amore	166	Cherry Orchard	982
Bun Penny	909	Chiang Mai	1568
Bush Cat	730	Child Bride	364
		Chili Dip	1439
Cabaret	804	Chocolat Chaud	1359
Caherassdotcom	1035	Chocolate Mauk	420
Cake	897	Choose Me	548
Cakestown Lady	379	Chrysanthemum	644
Call Later	28	Circle	1555
Call This Cat	1522	Circuit City	25
Canada Water	1360	City Vaults Girl	750
Candlehill Girl	295	Claba Di San Jore	6
Cant Hurry Love	608	Claiomh Solais	196
Cantal	1334	Clarietta	1405
Cantaloupe	830	Classic Remark	443
Caphene	1598	Clear Impression	606
Capulet Monteque	266	Clinical	775
Carallia	303	Clodora	959
Caravan Of Dreams	924	Cloud's End	514
Caribana	1411	Clouds Of Magellan	1042
Caribbean Pearl	1338	Coastal Waters	856
Carini	551	Cochabamba	1526
Carraigoona	1438	Cochin	840
Carrauntoohil	724	Coconut Shy	1154
Carsulae	65	Coin Box	1286
Cartimandua	739	Collada	580
Carved Emerald	578	Comment	1366
Caster Sugar	509	Complexion	1203
Casual Glance	46	Concentric	650
Cat O' Nine Tails	493	Concordia	641

Name	Number	Name	Number
Condition	361	Danedream	1587
Confidential Lady	680	Danehill Music	557
Confusion	622	Danehurst	665
Connote	319	Danelagh	209
Constitute	127	Daneleta	421
Convention	1207	Danse Arabe	792
Cool Question	1412	Danse Grecque	749
Corking	1349	Dar Re Mi	696
Corps De Ballet	337	Dare To Dream	1602
Corrine	140	Dark Orchid	530
Corryvreckan	1392	Dash To The Front	658
Cosabawn	23	Dashiba	538
Cosmic Destiny	1614	Dashing	1588
Counterclaim	392	Dashing Beauty	1604
Countess Ferrama	910	Daunt Rock	1380
Coyote	370	Dawaama	497
Crazy Party	805	Dayville	1440
Crazy Too	315	Dead Cool	1454
Crinkle	1559	Dearest Girl	823
Crinolette	232	Decorative	834
Cross Section	1084	Dee Dee Girl	239
Crossing	365	Degree Of Honor	1441
Crown	498	Delia Eria	342
Crystal Capella	1499	Delira	911
Crystal Curling	368	Delitme	1537
Crystal Melody	1216	Delma	1155
Crystal Moments	377	Derartu	43
Crystal Star	1498	Derval	903
Cuis Ghaire	1563	Descant	1240
Cuiseach	1448	Desert Alchemy	1488
Curras Spirit	478	Desert Sky	380
Cut Short	496	Desert Sunrise	829
Cute	1299	Despatch	1469
Cyclone Connie	1099	Dessert Flower	1163
Dabawiyah	93	Devious Diva	600
Daganya	1007	Dhanyata	1344
Dalasyla	1345	Diary	1141
Dalawysa	1456	Dimelight	1081
Dalmunzie	1104	Disclose	1672
Dam Beautiful	1557	Disco Volante	697
Dame Alicia	463	Discuss	1681
Dame Shirley	1217	Diva Delite	806
Damhsa Le Cheile	695	Diverting	1538
Dance Avenue	1635	Divine Design	408
Dance Club	1057	Divine Grace	912
Dance Hall Girl	1386	Divine Proportions	1247
Dance Lively	1362	Dixey	949
Danceabout	1329	Dixieland Kiss	255
Danceatdusk	614	Doctor's Glory	594
Dancing Abbie	151	Dolma	352
Dancing Duchess	927	Donatia	1646
Dancing Jest	758	Dookus	1054
Dancing Nelly	1381	Dorcas Lane	362

Dorothy Dene	1425	Elysee	843
Double Green	1026	Elysian	1507
Double Vie	1053	Eminence Gift	999
Doula	615	Emmas Princess	1418
Douro	466	Empire Rose	224
Dozy	868	Empress Anna	277
Drastic Measure	567	Empress Ella	601
Dream Date	1674	Emsiyah	1231
Dream Day	248	Endure	1605
Dream For Life	366	Enticing	777
Dream Scape	621	Entreat	1591
Dresden Doll	167	Epping	1206
Dress Code	527	Ermine And Velvet	1144
Dress Design	1102	Eroica	587
Drifting	1464	Eshaadeh	662
Dromod Mour	931	Esloob	991
Drops	1332	Estedaama	1552
Dubai Affair	1156	Esteemed Lady	751
Dubai Bounty	250	Ethaara	734
Dubai Diamond	334	Eucharist	568
Dubai Opera	1050	Eurolink Raindance	400
Dubai Pearl	616	European Union	1041
Dubai Princess	475	Ever Rigg	404
Dubai Queen	1009	Excelente	955
Dubai Smile	182	Excellent Day	296
Dubai Sunrise	1049	Excello	1187
Duchess Dora	1416	Exotic Beauty	479
Duniatty	1047	Expedience	217
Duo De Choc	1410	Express Way	183
Duquesa	1300	Exquisite Note	1143
Dusting	347		
Duty And Destiny	646	Fact	853
Dynaforce	422	Fair Countenance	1343
		Fairnilee	114
Eastern Appeal	981	Fairy Moss	1040
Eastern Joy	177	Falling Angel	268
Easy Times	210	Fame Is The Spur	1182
Ebony Street	435	Family	778
Eccentricity	929	Famous	1270
Echo River	533	Fanciful Dancer	1585
Effervesce	740	Fancy Theory	1079
Effige	243	Fancy Vivid	1176
Ela Athena	1592	Fantastic Opinion	436
Elas Diamond	698	Fantasy Princess	540
Elbasana	1694	Faraway Flower	647
Electra Star	776	Fashion Guide	1637
Electric Feel	1218	Fashion Rocks	298
Elegant Beauty	1409	Fee Eria	1350
Elektra Marino	106	Feet Of Flame	850
Elizabelle	472	Feis Ceoil	85
Ellbeedee	617	Felin Gruvy	1038
Ellen	1551	Felina	1139
Eluding	1413	Fey Rouge	1287

Fibou	454	Gala Style	915
Fifty	1388	Gali Gal	1082
Fin	133	Galicuix	1317
Finding Neverland	761	Galipette	654
Finsceal Beo	779	Galistic	1597
Firey Red	1669	Gallic Star	288
First	1470	Garanciere	1575
First City	144	Garbah	1523
First Lady	15	Gasalee	720
Five Bells	308	Gems Of Araby	501
Flambeau	618	Gemstone	511
Flamelet	1395	Generous Diana	700
Flames To Dust	1004	Gerika	226
Flaming Cliffs	1445	Get Happy	1090
Flanders	699	Ghanaati	935
Flawly	1570	Ghandoorah	254
Fleche D'Or	640	Ghenwah	818
Fleeting Image	835	Giants Play	701
Fleur De Lis	388	Gift Dancer	27
Florentia	1399	Gift Range	1513
Fly Free	1077	Gilded Vanity	1471
Flying Clarets	583	Gile Na Greine	733
Flying Flag	1442	Gilt	516
Flying Passage	675	Gimasha	1087
Folle Blanche	152	Gimli's Treasure	1431
Folly Bridge	1092	Gimme Some Lovin	267
Fontley	1045	Gin Twist	341
Foot Of Pride	870	Giusina Mia	1428
Forensics	681	Give A Whistle	894
Forest Prize	1168	Gleaming Silver	537
Forever Times	321	Glen Molly	1173
Forgotten Me	913	Glen Rosie	1013
Fork Lightning	1402	Glencal	1372
Foundation Filly	895	Glitterball	746
Four Eleven	1244	Glory Power	467
Foxtrot Alpha	1022	Glympse	423
Francesca D'Gorgio	565	Glyndebourne	332
Free Lance	1465	Go Maggie Go	461
Free Verse	1500	Goathemala	7
French Doll	245	Going For Gold	82
French Fern	879	Goldamour	464
Friendlier	122	Golden Shadow	1600
Friendly Heart	1446	Gonbarda	184
Frivolity	1462	Gone Sailing	1433
Front House	1489	Gontcharova	1627
Fruit O'The Forest	914	Gorband	1571
Frynia	1370	Grain Only	320
Fuerta Ventura	280	Granny Franny	455
Full Of Love	631	Great Heavens	980
Funday	1086	Greek Easter	1368
Funny Enough	1578	Green Castle	1490
Funseeker	409	Green Chorus	876
		Green Room	523

Greensand	487	Highland Shot	560
Guana	1025	Hightime Heroine	1487
Gull Wing	702	Hill Welcome	1415
Gutter Press	125	Hip	1115
Gwyllion	212	Hoh My Darling	1258
Gyroscope	371	Holistic	742
		Hollow Green	1378
Habita	609	Holly Blue	485
Hadarama	124	Honest Lady	689
Haiti Dancer	234	Honorine	29
Hakuraa	1019	Hooray	1400
Half Queen	992	Hot Pursuits	1199
Hall Hee	168	How's She Cuttin'	1208
Halla Siamsa	206	Hulcote Rose	76
Halliwell House	500	Humdrum	130
Hallowed Park	941	Humhum	566
Hammiya	260	Humouresque	569
Hanakiyya	793	Hurricane Havoc	1091
Handassa	1385	Hurricane Lily	848
Hapipi	153	Hurry Home Hydee	221
Happy Flight	1331	Hymn Of The Dawn	199
Happy Holly	1460	Hymnsheet	1396
Happy Wedding	1520	Hypnotize	1333
Haretha	553	Hypoteneuse	346
Harryana	1547		
Hasten	1160	I Hearyou Knocking	1134
Hasten	1453	Icon Project	363
Hawattef	154	Igreja	269
Hazarama	451	Illandrane	1051
Hazel Lavery	1340	Illaunglass	657
Hazita	1117	I'm From Dixie	1014
Hear My Cry	1170	Imagine	1271
Heart Of Ice	491	Imperial Pippin	958
Hearthstead Dancer	1127	Impulsive Decision	437
Heart's Desire	932	In My Life	94
Heat Haze	1505	Inca Princess	1248
Heat Of The Night	318	Inchmahome	1312
Heaven Sent	684	Indian Love Bird	393
Hector's Girl	345	Indication	110
Heeby Jeeby	807	Inis Boffin	134
Hel's Angel	473	Injaaz	1450
Helter Helter	1328	Inourthoughts	1689
Hemaris	1135	Instant Memories	802
Henties Bay	649	Intapeace	97
Here To Eternity	1626	Interlace	1501
Hezmah	385	Intermission	1119
Hidden Brief	585	Intimacy	40
Hidden Fire	556	Intishaar	625
Hidden Valley	35	Intricate Dance	448
High Heeled	968	Irish Design	998
High On The Hill	1232	Irresistible	1496
High Reserve	1414	Island Dreams	211
High Spice	372	Island Music	597

Island Rhapsody	131	Kind Regards	1130
Islandagore	62	Kinda Wonderful	17
Ispanka	977	Kinnaird	1518
Israar	826	Kiralik	247
Italian Connection	1194	Kirinda	781
Iteration	1120	Kirunavaara	293
Ittasal	1491	Kiyra Wells	1227
Ivory Rose	89	Kotdiji	1544
Iwunder	329	Kummel Excess	529
Izzi Top	648	Kurtanella	113
Jacaranda Ridge	99	La Adelita	1088
Jacqueline Quest	1146	La Baracca	1179
Jakarta Jade	53	La Coruna	1068
Jamboretta	1606	La Gessa	555
Jane Austen	481	La Noe	846
Janetstickettocats	3	La Zona	852
Janey Muddles	204	Lacily	1075
Jardin	1121	Lacy Sunday	721
Jasmine Flower	16	Ladue	880
Jaywick	882	Lady Angola	725
Jive Talk	517	Lady Brora	37
Johannesburg Cat	1044	Lady Caprice	326
Jouel	1326	Lady Dettoria	1311
Journalist	1677	Lady Dottie	1177
Journey's End	1426	Lady Gabrielle	542
Jules	292	Lady Gorgeous	381
Juncea	1375	Lady Grace	651
Juniper Girl	155	Lady Hawkfield	703
Juno Marlowe	780	Lady Hestia	1549
		Lady Jane Digby	1060
Kadayna	794	Lady Livius	1567
Kahira	1670	Lady Natilda	960
Kahlua Kiss	1209	Lady Of The Desert	588
Kalinova	325	Lady Oriande	1000
Karawana	1673	Lady Scarlett	282
Kareemah	252	Lady Springbank	782
Karliysha	1318	Lady's Locket	1140
Kartiste	1679	Lahudood	744
Katherine Lee	1233	Lake Moon	185
Kazeem	343	Larceny	704
Keep Dancing	323	Lark In The Park	375
Kelsey Rose	1686	Last Cry	129
Kentucky Warbler	1472	Latin Love	916
Key Light	1188	Laughter	1017
Key Rose	770	Lauren Louise	705
Khazeena	748	Lay Time	1305
Khazeena	837	Laylati	1581
Khor Sheed	1586	Le Badie	33
Khyber Knight	374	Le Montrachet	1259
Kibara	402	Lear's Crown	1136
Kilo Alpha	1666	Leceile	286
Kimola	1061	Lemon Rock	814

Les Hurlants	135	Lulawin	874
Let It Be Me	60	Lulla	858
Let Your Love Flow	1671	Luminance	406
Lethal Quality	875	Luminous Gold	1351
Lexi The Princess	1129	Luna Wells	90
Liberty Chery	1455	Lupine	1288
Librettista	285	Lynnwood Chase	638
Liel	344		
Life Rely	66	Maakrah	661
Liffey Dancer	1589	Macadamia	816
Light It Up	849	Mad Existence	1018
Light Shine	983	Madame Boulangere	1629
Lightening Pearl	1132	Madany	257
Lightning Lydia	861	Magena	1316
Likeable	1212	Magic America	47
Lillie Langtry	1252	Magic Nymph	747
Limber Up	112	Magic Sister	1502
Limonar	394	Magic Tree	116
Lion Forest	1321	Magnifica	1363
Lisa Gherardini	456	Mahaazen	1608
Lisathedaddy	1108	Mahbooba	220
Liscanna	1242	Maid For Winning	1346
Lisselan Firefly	18	Majestic Sakeena	755
Literacy	1394	Majestic Silver	1664
Littlefeather	1607	Majoune	395
Livia Galilei	197	Makara	1636
Livia's Wake	820	Make Amends	67
Lixian	88	Makhsusah	628
Lixirova	505	Mala Mala	1073
Liza Lu	1229	Maleha	1185
Lizzy's Township	1649	Malelane	502
Llew Law	1142	Malladore	1473
Lochangel	1080	Mambo Halo	1065
Locharia	1524	Mamma Morton	1595
Lomapamar	1527	Manaaber	1149
London Welsh	74	Manda Bay	1122
Look Here	91	Mango Lady	1642
Looking Glass	808	Mania	1434
Loquacity	1638	Manieree	933
Loreto	1124	Mansiya	1420
Lost Highway	427	Maoin Dor	1152
Lough Mewin	138	Maoineach	203
Loulwa	411	Map Of Heaven	783
Louvain	115	Maqaasid	663
Love Everlasting	1112	Margaret's Dream	1486
Love In Bloom	1234	Margarita	222
Love In May	901	Margaux Magique	827
Love Me True	1272	Marhaba	809
Love Roi	1546	Mariah's Storm	1268
Love Theway Youare	186	Marie De Medici	187
Luanas Pearl	1624	Marika	543
Lucky Leigh	623	Marine Bleue	1474
Lucky Token	458	Marine Girl	77

Mark Too	158	Miss Corniche	1406
Marvada	828	Miss Delila	1430
Mary Boleyn	79	Miss Hawai	917
Maryinsky	117	Miss Indigo	258
Masandra	64	Miss Kittyhawk	1023
Maskaya	1633	Miss Me	430
Maskunah	1352	Miss Meltemi	1652
Massarra	1246	Miss Otis	1427
Massuci	574	Miss Pinkerton	678
Max One Two Three	468	Miss Quality	219
May Fox	1374	Miss Queen	967
Mayano Sophia	573	Miss Rochester	1609
Maybe	1273	Miss Rosie	736
Mea Parvitas	896	Miss Smilla	824
Meanwhile	1289	Miss Universe	109
Medaille D'Or	521	Miss University	1219
Meddle	95	Miss Villefranche	862
Media Fire	340	Miss Work Of Art	1560
Medley	1016	Missionary Hymn	1353
Meiosis	969	Missouri	1541
Mekko Hokte	1243	Missy O'Gwaun	227
Melody Maker	96	Mistic Magic	304
Memory	737	Mistress Marina	946
Meon Mix	854	Misty For Me	1260
Meow	1263	Misty Night	484
Mexican Hawk	1528	Mme De Stael	1066
Mexican Milly	633	Modeeroch	831
Mia Divina	939	Model Queen	1566
Miarixa	1251	Modern Look	353
Micaela's Moon	1569	Mohican Princess	92
Michita	188	Molly Maxima	49
Mickleberry	382	Momentary	137
Midday	1506	Mondalay	4
Middle Persia	396	Money Note	302
Midnight Fantasy	1125	Mookada	664
Midnight Oasis	864	Moon Empress	1211
Midnight Shift	726	Morning After	383
Midsummer	637	Mosqueras Romance	918
Milford Sound	107	Mother Jones	249
Milliondollarbill	1235	Moyesii	2
Min Manat Alreeh	1562	Moynsha Lady	438
Minidress	797	Mrs Beeton	215
Minkova	1192	Mrs Snaffles	1615
Minnie's Mystery	525	Muaamara	1306
Mirabilis	669	Mudaaraah	962
Miracle Steps	1101	Mujarah	577
Mirwara	1330	Muluk	424
Mischief Making	38	Mumayeza	1503
Misheer	251	Munaawashat	645
Miss Apricot	161	Mundana	1583
Miss Bellbird	1550	Muqantara	261
Miss Brown To You	8	Muscovado	1377
Miss Chaussini	290	Music Show	596

Musical Bar	235	Novel Fun	919
Musical Way	1475	Nunavik	1365
Muzdaan	970	Nyarhini	327
My	50		
My Branch	706	Obama Rule	389
My Delirium	450	Ocean View	1027
My Dubai	172	Oeuvre D'Art	1553
My Lucky Liz	1476	Off Chance	163
My Sweet Georgia	1417	Oh Sedulous	867
Mysterious Girl	449	Oh So Saucy	1648
Mystic Dream	1319	Ohiyesa	639
Mythie	1676	Olympic Medal	974
		On Thin Ice	1166
Nadia	810	One Giant Leap	1028
Nadinska	309	Opera Dancer	1085
Namibia	923	Opera Gal	34
Nantyglo	355	Opera Glass	56
Naruko	1021	Operissimo	947
Narva	752	Orange Sunset	604
Nasharaat	599	Oriental Romance	246
Nasij	1492	Oshiponga	707
Nasmatt	171	Our Faye	708
Natalie Jay	291	Our Queen Of Kings	348
Nature Spirits	672	Oval Office	1477
Navajo Rainbow	1545	Overturned	1301
Nawaashi	1290		
Neat Shilling	405	Palace Affair	1201
Nebraas	584	Palatial	602
Neige D'Antan	722	Pale Orchid	1005
Nellie Melba	1069	Palisade	98
Nepali Princess	1006	Palitana	504
Neshla	1529	Palmette	1510
Never A Doubt	952	Papabile	1015
New Morning	169	Parabola	1138
Next Holy	189	Paradise Isle	1043
Nezhenka	1631	Paradise Place	554
Nice Time	1539	Parakopi	1236
Nigh	469	Paramita	1114
Night Carnation	55	Pardoven	198
Night Club	900	Paris Glory	1158
Night Haven	718	Parisi	743
Night Visit	200	Parisian Elegance	128
Nightswimmer	216	Party Whip	866
Nimble Thimble	938	Passage Of Time	358
Nimue	42	Passage To India	297
No Trimmings	1109	Passata	68
Noble One	673	Passe Passe	972
Noble View	1291	Pearl City	709
Nordkappe	1619	Pearl Dance	21
Northern Melody	811	Pearl Diva	1307
Northern Mischief	582	Pearl Earrine	1511
Nose One's Way	562	Pearl In The Sand	610
Nouriya	223	Pearl Magic	1447

Pediment	52	Princess Ellen	1161
Peeping Fawn	1274	Princess Serena	351
Pelagia	1033	Princess Taise	1071
Pelican Key	71	Privacy Order	586
Pellinore	36	Privalova	159
Penelewey	558	Privet	1039
Penicuik	844	Promesse De L'Aube	710
Penny Cross	48	Protectress	157
Perfect Star	1059	Provence	532
Perfect Story	756	Providencia	796
Perfect Touch	1665	Puerto Oro	310
Perils Of Pauline	812	Pure Joy	81
Persario	956	Pure Song	1536
Persistent Penny	1197	Purity	598
Pesse	300	Purple Tiger	1521
Petit A Petit	1361	Putois Peace	1220
Phillipina	1582		
Pickle	1062	Queen Myrine	865
Piece Of Cake	592	Queen Of Narnia	289
Piece Unique	1303	Queen Of Stars	889
Pietra Dura	518	Queen Of Tara	1354
Pin Cushion	767	Queenie Keen	953
Piping	768	Queen's Best	1512
Pitrizza	149	Queens Jubilee	102
Pivotal Drive	1202	Queen's Logic	579
Pivotal Lady	231	Quesada	1214
Place De Moscou	890	Questing	659
Platonic	494	Question	426
Playful Promises	73	Question Times	1644
Pleasantry	1509	Quetena	1594
Plebeya	1620	Quiet	354
Plethora	1478	Quiet Waters	727
Plucky	1530	Quip	928
Poetical	1391	Quixada	490
Polished Gem	1682		
Politesse	784	Ra Hydee	1292
Pongee	1599	Raasekha	964
Poppo's Song	1364	Ragazza Mio	19
Portmanteau	190	Rahiyah	1070
Portodora	1688	Rainbow Desert	156
Postale	1339	Rainbow Queen	561
Poyle Caitlin	536	Rainbow's Edge	499
Praia	676	Rakiza	711
Premier Prize	544	Rare Ransom	1479
Presbyterian Nun	275	Rascafria	316
Pretty Primo	873	Rayka	798
Price Tag	636	Raymi Coya	902
Prima Ballerina	626	Rayon Rouge	387
Prima Luce	1572	Reaching	1639
Primissima	564	Real Me	1100
Primrose Hill	126	Really Polish	1616
Princess Banu	1423	Rebecca Rolfe	279
Princess Danah	139	Rebelline	401

Name	Page	Name	Page
Red Avis	691	Rose Cheval	1295
Red Bloom	593	Rose Diamond	1593
Red Boots	1010	Rose Shift	228
Red Halo	322	Rosie's Posy	1276
Red Intrigue	118	Roskeen	1558
Red Japonica	26	Rotunda	987
Red Mischief	988	Rouge Noir	460
Red Trance	429	Rougette	1367
Reel Cool	72	Royal Assent	87
Reem	213	Royal Blush	440
Reem Three	1565	Royal Confidence	986
Regal Realm	682	Royal Esteem	1002
Regal Rose	687	Royal Fizz	1063
Regal Step	520	Royal Fortune	971
Regent's Park	1628	Royal Majestic	441
Reign Of Fire	1180	Royal Punch	985
Relinquished	1653	Royal Whisper	738
Remember When	1275	Royale Danehill	713
Renowned	963	Roystonea	273
Represent	397	Rublevka Star	757
Resistance Heroine	384	Ruby Rocket	950
Responsive	78	Rumba Boogie	39
Return The Jewel	1237	Rumh	174
Revered	1667	Rumoush	264
Reveuse De Jour	1293	Ruse	745
Rhadegunda	643	Russelliana	1497
Rhal	1151		
Ride For Roses	1076	Sacre Coeur	1215
Rifqah	1678	Safina	1508
Ring Of Music	667	Safiya Song	821
Rinneen	541	Sagina	328
Rio Carnival	1680	Sahara Sky	786
Rio Osa	1072	Sahraah	9
Riotous Applause	652	Saint Lucia	1159
Ripalong	993	Sakhee's Song	1573
Rise And Fall	1393	Salinia	1634
Rivabella	973	Salmon Rose	898
River Belle	668	Salonblue	787
Riymaisa	141	Samaah	506
Robema	45	Samasana	433
Rock Exhibition	539	Samdaniya	714
Rock Lily	1458	Sand Vixen	191
Rock Salt	1610	Sandbox Two	899
Rockfleet Castle	452	Sandglass	335
Rocking	859	Santa Agata	1309
Rohlindi	63	Saoirse Abu	165
Roisin's Star	1294	Saphira's Fire	1221
Ronaldsay	338	Sapphire Spray	1387
Ron's Secret	462	Saratoga Slew	627
Roo	785	Satulagi	24
Roodeye	1282	Savignano	715
Roodle	1032	Sayedah	1493
Rose Blossom	712	Saying Grace	1320

Name	Number	Name	Number
Sayyedati Storm	10	Silicon Star	887
Scarlet Empire	1191	Silimiss	1012
Scarlet Runner	764	Silk Point	1181
Scotch Bonnet	934	Silver Kestrel	477
Sea Chanter	674	Silver Miss	1533
Seasonal Cross	522	Silver Skates	100
Seattle Ribbon	545	Simply Perfect	1481
Secret Era	1222	Sindiyma	1204
See You Later	492	Sing Like A Bird	1407
Self Centred	838	Singingintherain	888
Selkirk Sky	842	Sister Moonshine	434
Semaphore	1296	Skehana	832
Sensationally	101	Skeleton	1137
Sense Of Pride	1661	Skirrid	1213
Sense Of Purpose	1675	Slieve Mish	148
Sent From Heaven	788	Small Fortune	1355
Serres	1611	Smart Step	119
Seschat	263	Smoken Rosa	1298
Sesmen	444	Snoqualmie Girl	546
Seta	510	Snoqualmie Star	1083
Sewards Folly	760	Snow Crystal	1223
Shabiba	754	Snow Key	44
Shahmina	884	So Blissful	287
Shaken And Stirred	1554	So Silk	414
Shall We Tell	5	Society Gal	885
Shamarlane	270	Society Hostess	1685
Shambodia	1531	Solace	236
Shamtari	966	Solar Event	994
Shanghai Lily	1419	Solar Pursuit	356
Shanghai Visit	549	Solfilia	728
Shannon Spree	398	Solmorin	283
Sharadja	311	Some Diva	160
Sharbat	218	Something Blue	1444
Sharnberry	789	Something Exciting	1255
Sharp Terms	1297	Something Mon	192
Shastye	104	Songerie	1463
Shatter	1480	Sonic Night	1175
Shawaaty	1376	Sonny Sunshine	312
She Basic	1058	Soon	1335
Sheer Spirit	1256	Soranna	86
Sheila Blige	503	Sospel	513
Sheila Toss	1543	Sospira	1654
Shemissa	12	Soul Mountain	1435
Sheppard's Watch	534	Sovereign Crisis	20
Shermeen	1485	Soviet Terms	731
Shersha	1030	Spa	1621
She's A Character	1008	Spacious	1514
Shesha Bear	1371	Spanish Sun	570
Short Dance	978	Spare Change	519
Shy Appeal	1373	Spate Rise	1103
Si Belle	1150	Speak Softly To Me	607
Silent Moment	173	Special Assignment	230
Silent Serenade	1532	Speckled Hen	242

Speed Cop	32	Sweet Folly	1356
Speirbhean	195	Sweet Lilly	313
Spinning Lucy	1238	Sweet Pilgrim	349
Spinning Queen	677	Sweet Power	1157
Spinning Well	415	Swift Winged	14
Spiralling	1052	Swiss Lake	547
Spirit Of Tara	1690	Switch	1687
Spiritville	920	Syann	41
Splashdown	1515	Sylvestris	1437
Spoil Yourself	1684	Symbol Of Peace	863
Sportsticketing	276		
Spring Bouquet	1403	Taalluf	847
Spring Fashion	439	Tactfully	813
Spring Star	1147	Tahtheeb	891
Stained Glass	892	Take Flight	208
Star Cluster	1113	Takizada	595
Star Express	1322	Tap Dance Way	1369
Star Value	22	Tap The Dot	299
Starbound	1304	Tara Too	1641
Starlit Sky	1617	Taraeff	1324
Starring	1056	Tarawa	1310
Starry Sky	965	Tarbela	1257
Stars In Your Eyes	357	Tare Green	656
Starstone	833	Tariysha	253
Start The Music	753	Tarqua	1198
Stella Point	284	Tasheyaat	619
Sterling Sound	1542	Tawaasul	630
Still I'm A Star	274	Tease	1382
Stoney Cove	881	Tedarshana	872
Strawberry Leaf	1576	Teddy Bears Picnic	476
Street Style	1001	Teeba	259
Strings	741	Tekhania	136
Striving	143	Tell Mum	860
Suba	1574	Tellelle	893
Sudden Blaze	330	Tempete	800
Sugar Beet	1164	Temple Of Thebes	1336
Sularina	1281	Tenderly	399
Summer Fete	1074	Teo's Sister	207
Summertime Legacy	145	Tereschenko	1457
Sun Shower	1277	Tesary	671
Sundari	716	Tessa Romana	1178
Sunday Times	317	The Clan Macdonald	975
Sunpearl	1432	The Giving Tree	1118
Sunset Avenue	1123	The Hermitage	58
Supernovae	1658	The Sound Of Music	1577
Superstar Leo	771	The Thrill Is Gone	108
Supreme Seductress	1516	Think	571
Surrey Storm	495	Third Dimension	1561
Susi Wong	51	Thought Is Free	31
Swan Wings	735	Three Days In May	54
Sweepstake	1323	Three Ducks	147
Sweet Afton	1190	Three Sugars	1461
Sweet Coincidence	1325	Thrill	1224

Through The Forest	995	Vasilia	1429
Tia Mia	624	Vedela	635
Tiffilia	201	Velvet Kiss	488
Timbre	1517	Velvet Star	729
Time Ahead	1494	Ventoux	336
Time Control	1590	Victoire Celebre	416
Tiriana	769	Victoire Finale	425
Today's The Day	1556	View	333
Toffee Vodka	945	Vindication People	1421
Together	1278	Vino Veritas	1184
Toi Et Moi	1265	Vintage Gardenia	943
Tolzey	839	Violet	1106
Tonnara	262	Violet Ballerina	1613
Totally Devoted	1612	Virevolle	241
Toy Show	457	Virginia Waters	1358
Tragic Moment	1625	Visions Of Clarity	921
Trail Of Tears	572	Visit	103
Tremelo Pointe	272		
Trentini	1422	Wadaat	442
Trepidation	1228	Wading	1279
Trilemma	869	Wahylah	1584
Trinity Scholar	926	Waitress	193
Trinny	238	Wake Me Up	120
Triple Sharp	1200	Wake Up Call	629
Trois Graces	1327	Waldena	1630
Trojan Queen	1662	Walklikeanegyptian	1482
Tropical Lady	1283	Wallis	563
Tropical Paradise	944	Wanna	653
Tropical Treat	111	Warling	632
Truly Mine	1659	Water Fountain	1195
Turama	359	Wave	1245
Turbulent Descent	1262	Wear Red	1239
Turning Leaf	857	Wedding Party	591
Two Marks	1031	Wemyss Bay	83
		Westcote	1436
Umniya	979	Westering Home	1174
Umseyat	1145	What A Charm	1055
Unicamp	1308	Whatizzit	1645
Unity	1357	Whazzat	1337
Unreal	1189	Whazzis	1
Up And About	403	When Not Iff	1459
Upskittled	1651	Whisper Dance	670
Urban Daydream	1548	White Daffodil	1596
		Whoosh	948
Vadawina	688	Why Now	324
Valandraud	470	Wickwing	229
Valediction	575	Wid	961
Valeur	301	Windsor County	178
Valmirez	373	Windy Lane	717
Vanity	59	Winesong	507
Vanity's Girl	576	Wing Diva	1632
Varmint Lady	1495	Winner	194
Varnish	1225	Winner's Wish	1153

Winter Sunrise	1504
Witch Of Fife	121
Without Precedent	957
Wizz Kid	1029
Wonder Of Wonders	1640
Wonder Why	790
Woodbeck	1024
Wosaita	871
Wrong Answer	951
Yandina	512
Yara	1389
Yazmin	271
Youre So Sweet	1116
You'resothrilling	1264
Zagreb Flyer	164
Zahoo	1691
Zallerina	1466
Zaminast	1692
Zanzibar	996
Zaynaba	825
Zeena	1169
Zenda	679
Zenella	1622
Zimira	1483
Zomaradah	1601
Zoowraa	170
Zvezda	483
Zykina	1579